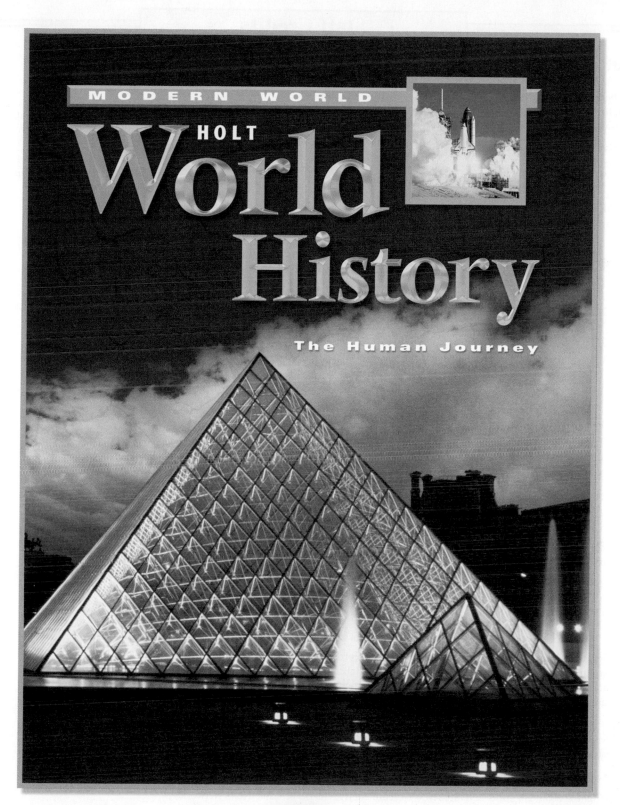

MODERN WORLD

HOLT

World History

The Human Journey

HOLT, RINEHART AND WINSTON

A Harcourt Education Company

Austin • Orlando • Chicago • New York • Toronto • London • San Diego

Staff Credits

Editorial

Sue Miller, *Director*
Robert Wehnke, *Managing Editor*
Dr. Melissa Langley-Biegert, *Project Editor*
Sue Minkler, *Assistant Editorial Coordinator*

Technology Resources

Annette Saunders, *Editor*

Art, Design & Photo

Book Design
Diane Motz, *Senior Design Director*
Lori Male, *Senior Designer*

Image Acquisitions
Joe London, *Director*

Tim Taylor, *Photo Research Supervisor*
Elaine Tate, *Art Buyer Supervisor*

Design New Media
Susan Michael, *Design Director*
Kimberly Cammerata, *Design Manager*
Michael Rinella, *Senior Designer*
Grant Davidson, *Designer*

Media Design
Curtis Riker, *Design Director*

Cover Design
Pronk & Associates

Design and Page Production
The Quarasan Group, Inc.

Pre-Press and Manufacturing

Production
Gene Rumann, *Production Manager*
Antonella Posterino, *Coordinator*
Jevara Jackson, *Manufacturing Coordinator, Book*
Rhonda Fariss, *Inventory Planning Analyst*
Kim Harrison, *Manufacturing Coordinator, Media*

COVER: *Louvre pyramid, Paris, France; space shuttle launch, Kennedy Space "Center"*

Printed in the United States of America

ISBN 0-03-038141-X

5 6 7 8 9   048   09 08 07

Editorial Review Board

Content Reviewers

Dr. Jack Balcer
Ohio State University
Ancient Greece

Dr. Lenard Berlanstein
University of Virginia
European social, modern France

Dr. Pierre Cagniart
Southwest Texas State U.
Ancient

Dr. Elton Daniel
University of Hawaii at Manoa
Islamic, West Asia, Iran

Dr. Toyin Falala
University of Texas at Austin
West Africa

Dr. Michael Hall
University of Texas at Austin
Colonial America

Dr. Arnold Krammer
Texas A&M University
Modern Europe, Germany

Dr. Julian Martin
University of Alberta
Science and medicine, early modern Britain

Dr. Alida Metcalf
Trinity University
Latin America, Brazil

Dr. Mark Parillo
Kansas State University
United States military, diplomatic, Japan

Dr. E. Bruce Reynolds
San Jose State University
Japan, China, Southeast Asia

Dr. Richard Saller
University of Chicago
Ancient, Roman

Dr. Lynn Struve
Indiana University
Premodern China, Chinese political and intellectual

Dr. Gerhard L. Weinberg
Emeritus, University of North Carolina—Chapel Hill
Modern Germany, WW I and WW II

Educational Reviewers

Peggy Altoff, Supervisor
Carroll County Public Schools
Westminster, Maryland

Laura L. Boelter
Shepherd Junior High School
Mesa, Arizona

Margaret Elaine Cox
Retired, Manatee High School
Bradenton, Florida

Alfred J. Hamel
South High Community School
Worcester, Massachusetts

Jay Harmon
Catholic High School
Baton Rouge, Louisiana

Paul Horne
Education Oversight Committee
Columbia, South Carolina

David Olson
Angola High School
Angola, Indiana

Madeleine Schmitt
St. Louis Public Schools
St. Louis, Missouri

Deanna Spring
Cincinnati Public Schools
Cincinnati, Ohio

Andy Turay
Bronx High School
Bronx, New York

Scott Whitlow
Round Rock High School
Round Rock, Texas

Laura Watkins
Acton Boxborough Regional High School
Acton, Massachusetts

Contents

Early Arab navigational instrument

The throne of Charlemagne

Copernican model showing planetary revolutions

The papal palace at Avignon

UNIT 3 From Absolutism to Revolution 256

CHAPTER 10

Monarchs of Europe
(1500 – 1800) 260

CHAPTER 11

Enlightenment and Revolution in England and America
(1550 – 1789) 284

CHAPTER 12

The French Revolution and Napoléon
(1789 – 1815) 314

UNIT 4 Industrialization and Nationalism 346

CHAPTER 13

The Industrial Revolution
(1600 – 1901) 350

The Great Wall of China

Glazeware from Safavid Persia

The golden fountain at Versailles

Sheffield, England, in the Industrial Revolution

Sculpture by Edgar Degas

*Irish immigrants
bound for North
America*

Hungarian independence fighters

Charles Lindbergh's Spirit of St. Louis

Notes and coins of the European Union

View of Torres del Paine National Park in Chile

Flag of the People's Republic of China

Primary Sources

History Makers Speak

Primary Source

History and Your World

Young drummer of the American Revolution

History and Your World *continued*

Cross–Cultural Connections

Islamic calligraphy and box of calligrapher's tools

CROSS-CULTURAL CONNECTIONS *Literature*

Giuseppe Garibaldi, Italy

Illustration from Chaucer's The Canterbury Tales

Interdisciplinary Activities

Historical Highlights

Early American stone-tipped spears

Historical Highlights *continued*

Empress Wu

Technology Activities

Holt Researcher go hrw com

Technology Activities *continued*

Skill-Building Activities

SKILL-BUILDING STRATEGIES

TIME LINES

Skill-Building Activities *continued*

Charts and Graphs

Maps

Skill-Building Activities *continued*

Renaissance Italy, c. 1500

Interpreting Maps During the Renaissance, Italy was a patchwork of states.

■ **Skills Assessment: Human Systems** What commercial cities became the centers of city-states?

How to Use Your Textbook

Use the chapter opener to get an overview of the time period.

The Chapter Time Line shows you selected events in world history within the timeframe of the chapter.

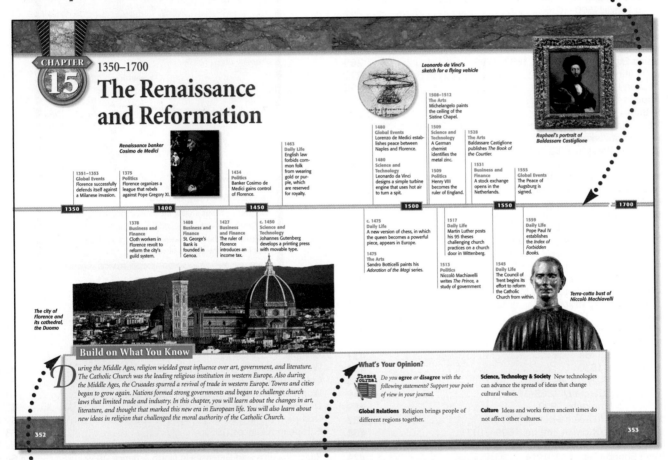

CHAPTER 15 1350–1700

The Renaissance and Reformation

Renaissance banker Cosimo de Medici

1351–1353
Global Events
Florence successfully defends itself against a Milanese invasion.

1375
Politics
Florence organizes a league that rebels against Pope Gregory XI.

1434
Politics
Banker Cosimo de Medici gains control of Florence.

1463
Daily Life
English law forbids common folk from wearing gold or purple, which are reserved for royalty.

Leonardo da Vinci's sketch for a flying vehicle

1480
Global Events
Lorenzo de Medici establishes peace between Naples and Florence.

1480
Science and Technology
Leonardo da Vinci designs a simple turbine engine that uses hot air to turn a spit.

1508–1512
The Arts
Michelangelo paints the ceiling of the Sistine Chapel.

1509
Science and Technology
A German chemist identifies the metal zinc.

1509
Politics
Henry VIII becomes the ruler of England.

1528
The Arts
Baldassare Castiglione publishes *The Book of the Courtier*.

1531
Business and Finance
A stock exchange opens in the Netherlands.

Raphael's portrait of Baldassare Castiglione

1555
Global Events
The Peace of Augsburg is signed.

| 1350 | 1400 | 1450 | 1500 | 1550 | 1700 |

1378
Business and Finance
Cloth workers in Florence revolt to reform the city's guild system.

1408
Business and Finance
St. George's Bank is founded in Genoa.

1427
Business and Finance
The ruler of Florence introduces an income tax.

c. 1450
Science and Technology
Johannes Gutenberg develops a printing press with movable type.

c. 1475
Daily Life
A new version of chess, in which the queen becomes a powerful piece, appears in Europe.

1475
The Arts
Sandro Botticelli paints his *Adoration of the Magi* series.

1517
Daily Life
Martin Luther posts his 95 theses challenging church practices on a church door in Wittenberg.

1513
Politics
Niccolò Machiavelli writes *The Prince*, a study of government

1559
Daily Life
Pope Paul IV establishes the *Index of Forbidden Books*.

1545
Daily Life
The Council of Trent begins its effort to reform the Catholic Church from within.

Terra-cotta bust of Niccolò Machiavelli

The city of Florence and its cathedral, the Duomo

Build on What You Know

During the Middle Ages, religion wielded great influence over art, government, and literature. The Catholic Church was the leading religious institution in western Europe. Also during the Middle Ages, the Crusades spurred a revival of trade in western Europe. Towns and cities began to grow again. Nations formed strong governments and began to challenge church laws that limited trade and industry. In this chapter, you will learn about the changes in art, literature, and thought that marked this new era in European life. You will also learn about new ideas in religion that challenged the moral authority of the Catholic Church.

What's Your Opinion?

Themes Journal Do you agree or disagree with the following statements? Support your point of view in your journal.

Global Relations Religion brings people of different regions together.

Science, Technology & Society New technologies can advance the spread of ideas that change cultural values.

Culture Ideas and works from ancient times do not affect other cultures.

352   353

Build on What You Know bridges the material you have studied in previous chapters with the material you are about to begin. As you read the Build on What You Know feature, take a few minutes to think about the topics that might apply to the chapter you are starting.

What's Your Opinion puts you in the place of the historian looking at the past. In this section, you will be asked to respond to three general statements about the chapter. Each statement is tied to one of the key themes of the program. You should respond based on your own knowledge, and record your responses in your journal. There are no right or wrong answers, just your informed opinion.

Use these built-in tools to read for understanding.

Read to Discover questions begin each section of *The Human Journey*. These questions serve as your guide as you read through the section. Keep them in mind as you explore the section content.

Define and Identify terms are introduced at the beginning of each section. The terms will be defined in context throughout the section.

Why It Matters Today is an exciting way for you to make connections between what you are reading and the world around you. In each section, you will be invited to explore a topic that is relevant to our lives today by using **CNNStudentNews.com** connections.

Interpreting the Visual Record features accompany many of the book's rich images. Pictures are one of the most important primary sources historians can use to help analyze the past. These features invite you to examine the images and make predictions about their content.

Reading Check questions appear throughout the book to allow you to check your comprehension while you are reading. As you read each section, pause for a moment to consider each Reading Check. If you have trouble answering the question, go back and examine the material you just read.

The Story Continues features an interesting episode from world history that shows you that history is not just a collection of facts, but a blend of many individual stories and adventures.

History Makers Speak quotations appear frequently throughout the book. These exciting primary source quotations give you a glimpse into the lives of the actual people who made history. Many of these quotations are accompanied by an **Analyzing Primary Sources** question to help you better interpret the sources and draw inferences about their importance.

Use these built-in tools to read for understanding.

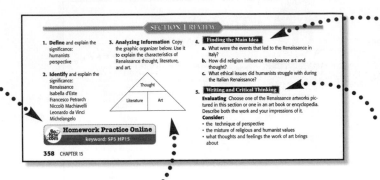

Homework Practice Online lets you log on to the **GO.hrw.com** Web site to complete an interactive self-check.

Finding the Main Idea questions help review the main points you have studied in the section.

Writing and Critical Thinking activities allow you to explore a section topic in greater depth and build your skills.

Graphic Organizers will help you pull together important information from the section. You can complete the graphic organizer as a study tool to prepare for a test or writing assignment.

Creating a Time Line and **Writing a Summary** activities help you to organize, sequence, and synthesize the chapter discussion and place major events and individuals into the historical chronology.

Reviewing Themes, Thinking Critically, and **Writing About History** activities help you to focus on key chapter ideas and enhance critical thinking and writing skills as you explore major chapter topics.

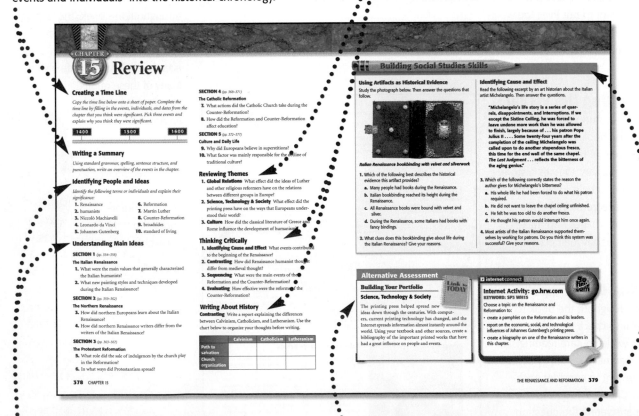

Identifying People and Ideas and **Understanding Main Ideas** reinforce learning by extending your understanding and comprehension of history-shaping people and concepts.

Building Social Studies Skills and **Building Your Portfolio** activities create exciting opportunities to practice social studies skills, to use interesting primary and secondary source materials, and to develop understanding of the connections between past and present.

Use these review tools to pull together all the information you have learned.

Homework Practice Online
keyword: SP3 HP13

Homework Practice Online lets you log on for review anytime. You'll find interactive activities for each section of the text.

internet connect

Internet Activity: go.hrw.com
KEYWORD: SP3 WH13

Choose a topic on the Rise of the Middle Ages to:
- evaluate primary and secondary sources about Charlemagne.
- create a poster on medieval art and architecture.
- write a report on daily life in the Middle Ages.

Internet Connect

activities are just one part of the world of online learning experiences that awaits you on the GO.hrw.com Web site. By exploring these online activities, you will take a journey through some of the richest world history materials available on the World Wide Web. You can then use these resources to create real-world projects, such as newspapers, brochures, reports, and even your own Web site!

Why History Matters Today

"History and destiny have made America the leader of the world that would be free. And the world that would be free is looking to us for inspiration."

Colin Powell

Right now, at this very second, somewhere in the world, someone is making history. It is impossible to know who, or in what way, but the actions of people today may become the history of tomorrow.

History and Your World

All you need to do is watch or read the news to see history unfolding. How many news stories do you see or hear about ordinary people doing extraordinary things? The Why It Matters Today feature beginning every section of *The Human Journey* invites you to use the vast resources of **CNNStudentNews.com** or other current event sources to examine the links between past and present. Through this feature you will be able to draw connections between what you are studying and the events that are taking place in our world today.

Anyone Can Be a History Maker

When you think of the word history, what comes to mind? Do you picture politicians sitting around a table deciding the future of the world? Or do you see a long list of dates and boring facts to be memorized? Of course, politicians, dates, and facts are part of history, but there is actually much more to understanding and exploring our past. Our world has developed through the efforts of many different people, from all backgrounds and walks of life. Many of them were teenagers like you. Did you know that teenagers have helped to shape the course of world history? It's true. For example, Joan of Arc was only about 17 when she led the French army that defeated the English at Orléans in 1429. Joan's victory was a turning point in the Hundred Years' War between France and England, a conflict that helped to build the French nation. Anne Frank, whose haunting account of Nazi persecution during World War II is an eloquent and timeless attack on all forms of political repression, was 16 years old when she died at Belsen concentration camp in 1945. Her tragic yet triumphant story has inspired people around the world. You might also be interested to know that young people in their teens helped to open and settle our own nation's frontiers long before there was a United States of America. These are just a few of the many examples of how people in their teens—people your age—have helped to shape our world's past. What contributions do you think your generation will make to world history?

History Makes Us Who We Are

There is no one single "story" in history. Instead, the combined experiences of millions of people across time have come together to form the societies and cultures of today's world.

Although the World War II Memorial was under construction when we visited, it was an awesome and inspiring sight.

*S*o when someone asks you, "Why does history matter today?," you might answer, "Because in our past, we see a reflection of ourselves."

Students of today dressed in Renaissance-era garb

Themes in World History

A Hindu religious sculpture from early India

The Human Journey begins every chapter with a set of theme statements under the heading "What's Your Opinion?" These statements are drawn from several broad themes central to world history: Geography, Economics, Government, Citizenship, Culture, Science, Technology & Society, Constitutional Heritage, and Global Relations. As you begin each chapter of *The Human Journey*, you will be asked to respond to the theme statements in a general way on the basis of your own knowledge. At the end of the chapter, you will be asked to respond to more specific questions about the themes, based on the chapter content.

Geography

The Geography theme explores ways in which our world's vast and diverse geography has played an important role in world history. The theme examines how the development of the world's resources has

The Astronomer, by Jan Vermeer

helped shape world economies, societies, and political structures. In addition, the Geography theme traces how public and government attitudes about resources and the environment have changed over time.

Economics

The Economics theme asks you to explore the relationship between history and economics over the course of human development. The theme examines how various, often very different economic systems have developed to address changing human needs and how they have influenced the world's political and social growth.

Gold Byzantine goblet

Government

The Government theme asks you to explore the workings of different systems of government—from the earliest forms of community organization to the complex structures of the present. This theme also examines the various aspects of different types of governments utilized by various societies throughout history and how different governmental systems affect societies in different ways.

Scene of Japanese Kabuki theater

Citizenship

Throughout history, people have struggled to define the rights and responsibilities of citizenship in their societies. The Citizenship theme explores how changing social, economic, and political conditions have influenced different societies and how those societies have perceived and addressed the ideas of citizenship.

Culture

The rich, unique, and diverse cultures that have developed over the course of history have emerged from our world's many ethnic, racial, and religious groups. The Culture theme examines how people have built their diverse cultures from earliest times to the present. It also investigates how various aspects of culture, including religion, rituals and shared traditions, art, music, and literature, have influenced social and political events throughout history.

Science, Technology & Society

From the building of the Egyptian pyramids and the irrigation systems of the earliest farming peoples to the development of advanced computers and the advent of the information age, science and technology have influenced every aspect of our world's cultures and societies. The Science, Technology & Society theme explores scientific and technological developments and their impacts on economic, political, and social developments around the world.

Constitutional Heritage

No study of world history would be complete without examining how the idea of constitutionalism developed over time. This includes influences on the United States Constitution, as well as comparisons of different constitutional systems as they developed over time.

Global Relations

The Global Relations theme invites you to trace ways in which different nations, cultures, and peoples around the world and throughout history have interacted with one another. It also explores issues and events that affect large segments of the world, not just one particular country.

Essential Elements of Geography

History and geography share many elements. History describes important events that have taken place from ancient times until the present day. Geography describes how physical environments affect human events. It also examines how people's actions influence the environment around them. One way to look at geography is to identify essential elements of its study. The following six essential elements, developed as part of the **National Geography Standards,** *will be used throughout* **The Human Journey:**

▶ **The World in Spatial Terms** This essential element refers to the way geographers view the world. They look at where things are and how they are arranged on Earth's surface. For example, geographers might be interested to learn why certain cities developed where they did.

▶ **Places and Regions** Geographers often focus on the physical and human characteristics that make particular parts of Earth special. A region is an area with common characteristics that make it different from surrounding areas. People create regions as a convenient way to study the world. Regions can be large like Asia, or small like a neighborhood.

Early Egyptian pyramids at Giza

▶ **Physical Systems** Geographers study the physical processes and interactions among four physical systems—Earth's atmosphere, land, water, and life. Physical processes shape and change Earth's physical features and environments.

▶ **Human Systems** As with physical systems, studying human systems can tell geographers much about the world around us. For example, studying population growth, distribution, and movement helps in understanding human events and their effect on the environment.

▶ **Environment and Society** One of the most important topics in geography is how people interact with the environment. Human activities can have both positive and negative effects on Earth's environment. However, people depend on the environment's natural resources for survival.

▶ **The Uses of Geography** Historians use geography to understand the past. They look not only at when things happened but at where and why they happened. But geography is also important to the present as well as the past. People use geography every day to determine how to use Earth's limited resources, such as water and minerals, more effectively and in ways that ensure the success of future generations.

Skills Handbook

Critical Thinking and the Study of History

Throughout *The Human Journey*, you are asked to think critically about the events and issues that have shaped world history. Critical thinking is the reasoned judgment of information and ideas. The development of critical thinking skills is essential to effective citizenship. Such skills empower you to exercise your civic rights and responsibilities. Helping you develop critical thinking skills is an important goal of *The Human Journey*. The following critical thinking skills appear in the section reviews and chapter reviews of the book.

 Analyzing Information is the process of breaking something down into its parts and examining the relationships between them. Analyzing enables you to better understand the whole. For example, to analyze the outcome of the Norman invasion of England in 1066, you might study the basis for Duke William of Normandy's claims to the English throne, why Harold Godwinson opposed those claims, and how the English people viewed the issues.

Emperor Maximilian I

Sequencing is the process of placing events in correct chronological order to better understand the historical relationships among these events. You can sequence events in two basic ways: according to *absolute* or *relative* chronology. Absolute chronology means that you pay close attention to the actual dates events took place.

Placing events on a time line would be an example of absolute chronology. Relative chronology refers to the way events relate to one another. To put events in relative order, you need to know which one happened, which came next, and so forth.

A sailor's astrolabe, an early navigational instrument

Categorizing is the process by which you group things together by the characteristics they have in common. By putting things or events into categories, it is easier to make comparisons and see differences among them.

Identifying Cause and Effect is a part of interpreting the relationships between historical events. A *cause* is an action that leads to an event. The outcome of the action is an *effect*. To explain historical events, historians often point out multiple causes and effects. For example, economic and political differences between the United States and the

Soviet Union led to the "cold war" that characterized the post–World War II era. These differences also resulted in an arms race that posed serious threats to world peace and development.

◆ Comparing and Contrasting

is the process of examining events, situations, or points of view for their similarities and differences. *Comparing* focuses on both similarities and the differences. *Contrasting* focuses only on differences. For example, a comparison of the development of civilization in the Indus River valley or northern India and the Hwang River valley of east-central China shows that certain factors were shared by each group of early people, while other factors were unique to one emerging civilization or the other.

Stone relief from early India

◆ Finding the Main Idea

is combining and sifting through information to determine what is most important. Historical writing often uses many examples and details to support the author's main ideas. Throughout *The Human Journey,* you will find numerous Reading Checks and questions in section reviews to help you focus on the main ideas in the text.

◆ Summarizing

is the process of taking a large amount of information and boiling it down into a short and clear statement. Summarizing is particularly useful when you need to give a brief account of a longer story or event. For example, Alexander the Great's conquest of the Persian Empire is an exciting but detailed story consisting of a complex chain of conditions, actions, and situations. Many different events came together to make up this story. You could summarize these events by saying something like, "Between 334 B.C. and 333 B.C., Alexander won major victories against the Persians at Granicus and then at Issus, where he defeated the Persian emperor, Darius III. Alexander then conquered the Persian-held lands of Syria, Egypt, and Mesopotamia. He met Darius again in 331 B.C., defeated him in the Battle of Gaugamela, and won control of the once-mighty Persian Empire."

◆ Making Generalizations and Predictions

is the process of interpreting information to form more general statements and guess about what will happen next. A *generalization* is a broad statement that holds true for a variety of historical events or situations. Making generalizations can help you see the "big picture" of historical events, rather than just focusing on details. It is very important, however, that when making generalizations you try not to include situations that do not fit the statement. When this occurs, you run the risk of creating a stereotype, or overgeneralization. A *prediction* is an educated guess about an outcome. When you read history, you should always be asking yourself questions like, "What will happen next? If this person does this, what will that mean for . . . ?", and so on. These types of questions help you draw on information you already know to see patterns throughout history

◆ Drawing Inferences and Conclusions

is forming possible explanations for an event, a situation, or a problem. When you make an *inference,* you take the information you know to be true and come up with an educated guess about what else you think is true about that situation. A *conclusion* is a prediction about the outcome of a situation based on what you already know. Often, you must be prepared to test your inferences and conclusions against new evidence or arguments. For example, a historian might conclude that women's leadership roles in the abolition movement led to the development of the early women's movement. The historian would then organize the evidence needed to support this conclusion and challenge other arguments.

Cover from Upton Sinclair's The Jungle

◆ Identifying Points of View

is the process of identifying factors that influence the outlook of an individual or group. A person's point of view includes beliefs and attitudes that are shaped by factors such as age, gender, religion, race, and economic status. This critical thinking skill helps you examine why people see things as they do and reinforce the realization that people's views may change over time or with a change in circumstances.

◆ Supporting a Point of View

involves choosing a viewpoint on a particular event or issue and arguing persuasively for that position. Your argument should be well organized and based on specific evidence that supports the point of view you have chosen. Supporting a point of view often involves working with controversial or emotional issues. For example, you might consider the points of view involved in the struggles between labor unions and business owners in Great Britain and the United States during the late 1800s. Whether you choose a position in favor of labor unions or in favor of business owners, you should state your opinion clearly and give reasons to support it.

◆ Identifying Bias

is the process of evaluating the opinions of others about events or situations. *Bias* is an opinion based on prejudice or strong emotions, rather that fact. It is important to identify bias when looking at historical sources because biased sources often give you a false sense of what really happened. When looking at both primary and secondary sources, it is always important to keep the author's or speaker's point of view in mind and to adjust your interpretation of the source based on any bias you might detect.

Soap advertisement reflecting a widespread bias of the late 1800s

◆ Evaluating

is assessing the significance or overall importance of something, such as the success of a reform movement, the actions of a president, or the results of a major conflict. You should base your judgment on standards that others will understand and are likely to share. For example, you might consider the outcomes of the Spanish conquests of the Aztec and Inca empires and evaluate their importance

Aztec dishware

relative to the development of Spain as a major European power. You could also evaluate the effect of the conquests on Native American peoples and civilizations.

◆ Problem Solving

is the process by which you pose workable solutions to difficult situations. The first step in the process is to identify a problem. Next you will need to gather information about the problem, such as its history and the various factors that contribute to the problem. Once you have gathered information, you should list and consider the options for solving the problem. For each of the possible solutions, weigh their advantages and disadvantages and, based on your evaluation, choose and implement a solution. Once the solution is in place, go back and evaluate the effectiveness of the solution you selected.

◆ Decision Making

is the process of reviewing a situation and then making decisions or recommendations for the best possible outcome. To complete the process, first identify a situation that requires a solution. Next, gather information that will help you reach a decision. You may need to do some background research to study the history of the situation, or carefully consider the points of view of the individuals involved. Once you have done your research, identify options that might resolve the situation. For each option, predict what the possible consequences might be if that option were followed. Once you have identified the best option, take action by making a recommendation and following through on any tasks that option requires.

Becoming a Strategic Reader

by Dr. Judith Irvin

Everywhere you look, print is all around us. In fact, you would have a hard time stopping yourself from reading. In a normal day, you might read cereal boxes, movie posters, notes from friends, T-shirts, instructions for video games, song lyrics, catalogs, billboards, information on the Internet, magazines, the newspaper, and much, much more. Each form of print is read differently depending on your purpose for reading. You read a menu differently from poetry, and a motorcycle magazine is read differently than a letter from a friend. Good readers switch easily from one type of text to another. In fact, they probably do not even think about it, they just do it.

When you read, it is helpful to use a strategy to remember the most important ideas. You can use a strategy before you read to help connect information you already know to the new information you will encounter. Before you read, you can also predict what a text will be about by using a previewing strategy. During the reading you can use a strategy to help you focus on main ideas, and after reading you can use a strategy to help you organize what you learned so that you can remember it later. *The Human Journey* was designed to help you more easily understand the ideas you read. Important reading strategies employed in *The Human Journey* include:

1. Methods to help you **anticipate** what is to come

2. Tools to help you **preview and predict** what the text will be about

3. Ways to help you **use and analyze visual information**

4. Ideas to help you **organize the information** you have learned

1. Anticipating Information

How can I use information I already know to help me understand what a new chapter will be about?

Anticipating what a new chapter will be about helps you connect the upcoming information to what you already know. By drawing on your background knowledge, you can build a bridge to the new material.

1 Each chapter of *The Human Journey* asks you to explore the main themes of the chapter before you start reading by forming opinions based on your current knowledge.

> **What's Your Opinion?**
>
> *Do you* **agree** *or* **disagree** *with the following statements? Support your point of view in your journal.*
>
> **Government** A strong army and government are necessary to maintain an empire.
>
> **Culture** Great civilizations build on the discoveries, developments, and contributions of earlier cultures.
>
> **Global Relations** An empire that enslaves conquered peoples is destined to fall.

Create a chart like this one to help you analyze the statements.

A **Before Reading** Agree/Disagree		B **After Reading** Agree/Disagree
2	Government—A strong army and government are necessary to maintain an empire.	**4**
	Culture—Great civilizations build on the discoveries, developments, and contributions of earlier cultures.	
	Global Relations—An empire that enslaves conquered peoples is destined to fall.	

3 Read the text and discuss with classmates.

5 You can also refine your knowledge by answering the Reviewing Themes questions in the chapter review.

Anticipating Information

Step ❶ Identify the major concepts of the chapter. In *The Human Journey*, these are presented in the What's Your Opinion? box at the beginning of each chapter.

▼

Step ❷ Agree or disagree with each of the statements and record your answers in your journal.

▼

Step ❸ Read the text and discuss your answers with your classmates.

▼

Step ❹ After reading the chapter, revisit the statements and answer them again based on what you have learned.

Reviewing Themes

1. **Government** What two major factors helped Rome unify its empire and maintain peace?
2. **Culture** What ideas and inventions did the Romans borrow and adapt from the Greeks?
3. **Global Relations** How did Rome's relationship with the people it conquered change over time?

2. Previewing and Predicting

How can I figure out what the text is about before I even start reading a section?

Previewing and Predicting

Step ❶ Identify your purpose for reading. Ask yourself what you will do with this information after you have finished reading.

▼

Step ❷ Determine the main idea of the text and the key vocabulary words you need to know.

▼

Step ❸ Use signal words to help identify the structure of the text.

▼

Step ❹ Connect the information to what you already know.

Previewing and **predicting** are good methods to help you understand the text. If you take the time to preview and predict before you read, the text will make more sense to you during your reading.

❶ Usually, your teacher will set the purpose for reading. After reading some new information, you may be asked to write a summary, take a test, or complete some other type of activity.

"After reading about the English Civil War, you will work with a partner to create a historical museum exhibit describing . . .".

❷ As you preview the text, use graphic signals such as headings, subheadings, and boldface type to help you determine what is important in the text. Each section of *The Human Journey* opens by giving you important clues to help you preview the material.

Read to Discover questions give you clues as to the section's main ideas.

Define and Identify terms let you know the key vocabulary you will encounter in the section.

Looking at the section's **main heading** and **subheadings** can give you an idea of what is to come.

3 Other tools that can help you in previewing are **signal words**. These words prepare you to think in a certain way. For example, when you see words such as *similar to*, *same as*, or *different from*, you know that the text will probably compare and contrast two or more ideas. Signal words indicate how the ideas in the text relate to each other. Look at the list below of some of the most common signal words grouped by the type of text structures they include.

Cause and Effect	Compare and Contrast	Description	Problem and Solution	Sequence or Chronological Order
because	different from	for instance	problem	not long after
since	same as	for example	the question is	next
consequently	similar to	such as	a solution	then
this led to . . . so	as opposed to	to illustrate	one answer is	initially
if . . . then	instead of	in addition		before
nevertheless	although	most		after
accordingly	however	importantly		finally
because of	compared with	another		preceding
as a result of	as well as	furthermore		following
in order to	either . . . or	first, second . . .		on (date)
may be due to	but			over the years
for this reason	on the other hand			today
not only . . . but	unless			when

4 Learning something new requires that you connect it in some way with something you already know. This means you have to think before you read and while you read. You may want to use a chart like this one to remind yourself of the information already familiar to you and to come up with questions you want answered in your reading. The chart will also help you organize your ideas after you have finished reading.

What I know	*What I want to know*	*What I learned*

3. Use and Analyze Visual Information

How can all the pictures, maps, graphs, and time lines with the text help me be a stronger reader?

Analyzing Information

Step 1 As you preview the text, ask yourself how the visual information relates to the text.

▼

Step 2 Generate questions based on the visual information.

▼

Step 3 After reading the text, go back and review the visual information again.

Using visual information can help you understand and remember the information presented in *The Human Journey*. Good readers make a picture in their mind when they read. The pictures, charts, graphs, cartoons, time lines, and diagrams included throughout *The Human Journey* are placed strategically to increase your understanding.

1 You might ask yourself questions like:

"Why did the author include this image with the text?"

"What details about this visual are mentioned in the text?"

After you have read the text, see if you can answer your own questions.

2

"What seems to be happening in this illustration?"

"Why are the people, their styles of dress, and their surroundings important?"

"How does this illustration reflect the social and political conditions of the era it portrays?"

Scene from the court of King Philip IV of France

3 After reading, take another look at the visual information.

4 Try to make connections to what you already know.

To help you remember what you have read, you need to find a way of **organizing information**. Two good ways of doing this are by using graphic organizers and concept maps. **Graphic organizers** help you understand important relationships—such as cause-and-effect, compare/contrast, sequence or events, and problem/solution—within the test. **Concept maps** provide a useful tool to help you focus on the text's main ideas and organize supporting details.

Identifying Relationships

Using graphic organizers will help you recall important ideas from the section and give you a study tool you can use to prepare for a quiz or test or to help with a writing assignment. Some of the most common types of graphic organizers are shown below.

Cause and Effect Events in history cause people to react in a certain way. Cause-and-effect patterns show the relationship between results and the ideas or events that made the results occur. You may want to represent cause-and-effect relationships as one cause leading to multiple effects, or as a chain of cause-and-effect relationships.

> **Constructing Graphic Organizers**
>
> **Step ①** Preview the text, looking for signal words and the main idea.
>
> ▼
>
> **Step ②** Form a hypothesis as to which type of graphic organizer would work best to display the information presented.
>
> ▼
>
> **Step ③** Work individually or with your classmates to create a visual representation of what you read.

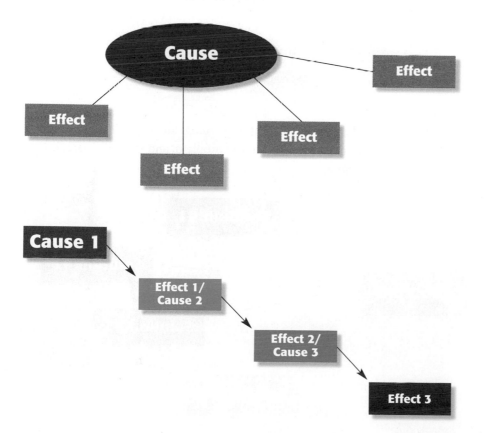

Comparing and Contrasting Graphic Organizers are often useful when you are comparing or contrasting information. Compare-and-contrast diagrams point out similarities and differences between two concepts or ideas.

Sequencing Keeping track of dates and the order in which events took place is essential to understanding history. Sequence or chronological-order diagrams show events or ideas in the order in which they happened.

Problem and Solution Problem-solution patterns identify at least one problem, offer one or more solutions to the problem, and explain or predict outcomes of the solutions.

Identifying Main Ideas and Supporting Details

One special type of graphic organizer is the concept map. A concept map, sometimes called a semantic map, allows you to zero in on the most important points of the text. The map is made up of lines, boxes, circles, and/or arrows. It can be as simple or as complex as you need it to be to accurately represent the text.

Here are a few examples of concept maps you might use.

Constructing Concept Maps

Step 1 Preview the text looking at what type of structure might be appropriate to display a concept map.

▼

Step 2 Taking note of the headings, bold-faced type, and text structure, sketch a concept map you think could best illustrate the text.

▼

Step 3 Using boxes, lines, arrows, circles, or any shapes you like, display the ideas of the text in the concept map.

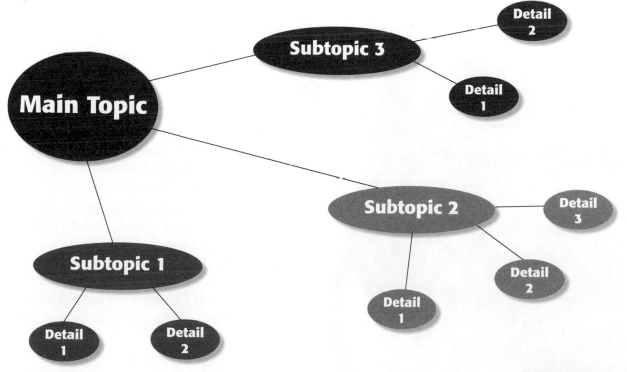

Standardized Test-Taking Strategies

A number of times throughout your school career, you may be asked to take standardized tests. These tests are designed to demonstrate the content and skills you have learned. It is important to keep in mind that in most cases the best way to prepare for these tests is to pay close attention in class and take every opportunity to improve you general social studies, reading, writing, and mathematical skills.

Tips for Taking the Test

1. Be sure that you are well rested.
2. Be on time, and be sure that you have the necessary materials.
3. Listen to the instructions of the teacher.
4. Read directions and questions carefully.
5. **DON'T STRESS!** Just remember what you have learned in class, and you should do well.

Practice the Strategies at go.hrw.com

Tackling Social Studies

The social studies portions of many standardized tests are designed to test your knowledge of the content and skills that you have been studying in one or more of your social studies classes. Specific objectives for the test vary, but some of the most common include:

1. Demonstrate an understanding of issues and events in history.
2. Demonstrate an understanding of geographic influences on historical issues and events.
3. Demonstrate an understanding of economic and social influences on historical issues and events.
4. Demonstrate an understanding of political influences on historical issues and events.
5. Use critical thinking skills to analyze social studies information.

Standardized tests usually contain multiple-choice and, sometimes, open-ended questions. The multiple-choice items will often be based on maps, tables, charts, graphs, pictures, cartoons, and/or reading passages and documents.

Tips for Answering Multiple-Choice Questions

1. If there is a written or visual piece accompanying the multiple-choice question, pay careful attention to the title, author, and date.
2. Then, read through or glance over the content of the written or visual piece accompanying the question to familiarize yourself with it.
3. Next, read the multiple-choice question first for its general intent and then reread it carefully, looking for words that give clues or can limit possible answers to the question. For example, words such as *most* or *best* tell you that there may be several correct answers to a question, but you will look for the one that is the most important or had the most effect.

4 Read through the answer choices. Always read all of the possible answer choices even if the first one seems like the correct answer. There may be a better choice farther down in the list.

5 Reread the accompanying information (if any is included) carefully to determine the answer to the question. Again, note the title, author, and date of primary-source selections. The answer will rarely be stated exactly as it appears in the primary source, so you will need to use your critical thinking skills to read between the lines.

6 Think of what you already know about the time in history or person involved and use that to help limit the answer choices.

7 Finally, reread the question and selected answer to be sure that you made the best choice and that you marked it correctly on the answer sheet.

Strategies for Success

There are a variety of strategies you can prepare ahead of time to help you feel more confident about answering questions on social studies standardized tests. Here are a few suggestions:

1 Adopt an acronym—a word formed from the first letters of other words—that you will use for analyzing a document or visual that accompanies a question.

Helpful Acronyms			
For a document, use SOAPS which stands for:		**For a picture, cartoon, map, or other visual piece of information, use OPTIC, which stands for:**	
S	**S**ubject	**O**	**O**verview
O	**O**ccasion (or time)	**P**	**P**arts (labels or details of the visual)
A	**A**udience	**T**	**T**itle
P	**P**urpose	**I**	**I**nterrelations (how the different parts of the visual work together)
S	**S**peaker/author	**C**	**C**onclusion (what the visual means)

2 Form visual images of maps and try to draw them from memory. The standardized test will most likely include important maps from the time period and subjects you have been studying. For example, in early Chinese history, be able to see in your mind's eye such things as the location and geographic outline of China Proper, the area's major land forms, rivers, and sea coasts, and the general geography of surrounding lands. Understand patterns of population distribution and ways in which humans interacted with the environment. Know major physical features, such as river and mountain systems, other topographic characteristics of the region, and the locations of important human systems, such as transportation routes and areas of major settlement.

3 When you have finished studying any historical era, try to think of who or what might be important enough for the test. You may want to keep your ideas in a notebook to refer to when it is almost time for the test.

4 Pay particular attention to the concept of constitutionalism. Many standardized tests contain questions dealing with this all-important idea and its historical development. Questions may test your understanding of Magna Carta, the English Bill of Rights, the American Declaration of Independence, the United States Constitution, as well as many other important historical documents. Questions may also cover the roles of various political thinkers and philosophers, such as the French *philosophes*.

5 For the skills area of the tests, practice putting major events and personalities in order in your mind. Sequencing people and events by dates can become a game you play with a friend who also has to take the test. Always ask yourself why this event is important.

6 Follow the tips under "Ready for Reading" on the next page when you encounter a reading passage in social studies, but remember that what you have learned about history can help you in answering reading comprehension questions.

Ready for Reading

The main goal of the Reading sections of most standardized tests is to determine your understanding of different aspects of a reading passage. Basically, if you can grasp the main idea and the author's purpose, and then pay attention to the details and vocabulary so that you are able to draw inferences and conclusions, you will do well on the test.

Tips for Answering Multiple-Choice Questions

1 Read the passage as if you were not taking a test.

2 Look at the big picture. Ask yourself questions like, "What is the title? What do the illustrations or pictures tell me?" and "What is the author's purpose?"

3 Read the questions. This will help you know what information to look for.

4 Reread the passage, underlining information related to the questions.

5 Go back to the questions and try to answer each one in your mind before looking at the answers.

6 Read all the answer choices and eliminate the ones that are obviously incorrect.

Types of Multiple-Choice Questions	
Main Idea	This is the most important point of the passage. After reading the passage, locate and underline the main idea.
Significant Details	You will often be asked to recall details from the passage. Read the question, and underline the details as you read, but remember that the correct answers do not always match the wording of the passage precisely.
Vocabulary	You will often need to define a word within the context of the passage. Read the answer choices and plug them into the sentence to see what fits best.
Conclusion and Inference	There are often important ideas in the passage that the author does not state directly. Sometimes you must consider multiple parts of the passage to answer the question. If answers refer to only one or two sentences or details in the passage, they are probably incorrect.

Tips for Answering Short-Answer Questions

1 Read the passage in its entirety, paying close attention to the main events and characters. Jot down information you think is important.

2 If you can't answer a question, skip it and come back later.

3 Words such as compare, contrast, interpret, discuss, and summarize appear often in short answer questions. Be sure you have a complete understanding of each of these words.

4 To help support your answer, return to the passage and skim the parts you underlined.

5 Organize your thoughts on a separate sheet of paper. Write a general statement with which to begin. This will be your topic statement.

6 When writing your answer, be precise but brief. Be sure to refer to details in the passage in your answer.

Targeting Writing

On many standardized tests, you will occasionally be asked to write an essay. In order to write a concise essay, you must learn to organize you thoughts before you begin writing the actual composition. This keeps you from straying too far from the essay's topic.

Tips for Answering Composition Questions

1 Read the question carefully.

2 Decide what kind of essay you are being asked to write. Essays usually fall into one of the following types: persuasive, classificatory, compare/contrast, or "how to." To determine the type of essay, ask yourself questions like, "Am I trying to persuade my audience? Am I comparing or contrasting ideas?," or "Am I trying to show the reader how to do something?"

3 Pay attention to keywords, such as compare, contrast, describe, advantages, disadvantages, classify, or speculate. They will give you clues as to the structure that your essay should follow.

4 Organize your thoughts on a separate sheet of paper. You will want to come up with a general topic sentence that expresses your main idea. Make sure this sentence addresses the question. You should then create an outline or some type of graphic organizer to help you organize the points that support your topic sentence.

5 Write your composition using complete sentences. Also be sure to use correct grammar, spelling, punctuation, and sentence structure.

6 Be sure to proofread your essay once you have finished writing.

Gearing Up for Math

On most standardized tests you will be asked to solve a variety of mathematical problems that draw on the skills and information you have learned in class. If math problems sometimes give you difficulty, have a look at the tips below to help you work through the problems.

Tips for Solving Math Problems

1 Determine the goal of the question. Read or study the problem carefully and determine what information must be found.

2 Locate the factual information. Decide what information represents key facts—the ones you must have to solve the problem. You may also find facts you do not need to reach your solution. In some cases, you may determine that more information is needed to solve the problem. If so, ask yourself, "What assumptions can I make about this problem?" or "Do I need a formula to help solve this problem?"

3 Decide what strategies you might use to solve the problem, how you might use them, and what form your solution will be in. For example, will you need to create a graph or chart? Will you need to solve an equation? Will your answer be in words or numbers? By knowing what type of solution you should reach, you may be able to eliminate some of the choices.

4 Apply your strategy to solve the problem and compare your answer to the choices.

5 If the answer is still not clear, read the problem again. If you had to make calculations to reach your answer, use estimation to see if your answer makes sense.

The Geographer's Tool Kit

A map is an illustration drawn to scale of all or part of Earth's surface. Knowing how to read and interpret maps is one of the most valuable tools you can use to study history.

Types of Maps

Types of maps include physical maps, political maps, and thematic (special-purpose) maps.

Physical maps illustrate the natural landscape of an area—the landforms that mark Earth's surface. Physical maps often use shading to show relief—the existence of mountains, hills, and valleys—and colors to show elevation, or the height above sea level. The map of the World on pages A2–A3 is strictly a physical map.

Political maps illustrate political units, such as states and nations, and use color variations and lines to mark boundaries, dots for major cities, and stars or stars within circles for capitals. Political maps show information such as territorial changes or military alliances. The map of the United States on page A4 is a political map.

Thematic (special-purpose) maps present specific information, such as the route of an explorer or the outcome of an election. The maps shown on page 12 ("Trade in the Ancient World") and page 15 ("The Spread of Christianity") of *The Human Journey,* for example, are thematic maps.

Map Features

Most maps have a number of features in common. Familiarity with these elements makes reading maps easier.

Titles, legends, and labels

A map's title tells you what the map is about, what areas are shown, and usually what time period is being represented. The legend, or key, explains any special symbols, colors, or shadings used on the map. Labels designate political and geographic

place-names, and physical features like mountain ranges, oceans, and rivers.

The global grid The absolute location of any place on Earth is given in terms of latitude (degrees north or south of the equator) and longitude (degrees east or west of the prime meridian). The symbol for a degree is °. Degrees are divided into 60 equal parts called minutes, which are represented by the symbol ´. The global grid is created by the intersecting lines of latitude (parallels) and lines of longitude (meridians). Lines of latitude and longitude may sometimes be indicated by tick marks near the edge of the map, or by lines across an entire map. Many maps also have locator maps, which place the area of focus in a larger context, showing it in relation to a continent or to the entire world.

Directions and distance Most maps in this textbook have a compass rose, or directional indicator. The compass rose indicates the four cardinal points—*N* for north, *S* for south, *E* for east, and *W* for west. You can also find intermediate directions—northeast, southeast, southwest, and northwest—using the compass rose. This helps in

The Unification of Spain, 1479–1515

Interpreting Maps
Four kingdoms on the Iberian Peninsula were united to form Spain.

■ **Skills Assessment:**
1. The World in Spatial Terms Which kingdom was largest? Which was second largest?
2. Sequencing By 1515, what two nations were on the Iberian Peninsula?

United by Ferdinand and Isabella, 1479

Conquered by Spain, 1492

Acquired by Spain, 1515

describing the relative location of a place. (If a map has no compass rose, assume that north is at the top, east is to the right, and so on.) Many maps in this textbook include a scale, showing both miles and kilometers, to help you relate distances on the map to actual distances on Earth's surface.

Map projections Because Earth is a sphere, it is best represented by a three-dimensional globe. Although a flat map is an imperfect representation of Earth's surface, mapmakers have devised various ways of showing Earth two dimensionally. These different flat views of Earth's surface are called projections.

Every map projection, and therefore every map, distorts to some extent at least one of the following aspects: (1) the shape of land areas, (2) their relative sizes, (3) directions, or (4) distances. Mapmakers choose the projection that least distorts what they wish to show. For example, an equal-area projection shows the relative sizes of different countries or continents quite accurately but distorts shapes somewhat.

How to Read a Map

1 Determine the focus of the map. Read the map's title and labels to determine the map's focus—its subject and the geographic area it covers.

2 Study the map legend. Read the legend and become familiar with any special symbols, lines, colors, and shadings used in the map.

3 Check directions and distance. Use the directional indicator and scale as needed to determine direction, location, and distance between various points on the map.

4 Check the grid lines. Refer to lines of longitude and latitude, or to a locator map, to place the area on the map in a larger context.

5 Study the map. Study the map's basic features and details, keeping its purpose in mind. If it is a special-purpose map, study the specific information being presented.

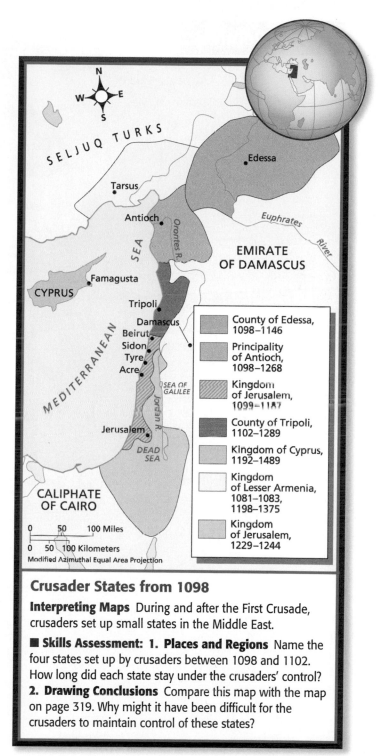

	County of Edessa, 1098–1146
	Principality of Antioch, 1098–1268
	Kingdom of Jerusalem, 1099–1187
	County of Tripoli, 1102–1289
	Kingdom of Cyprus, 1192–1489
	Kingdom of Lesser Armenia, 1081–1083, 1198–1375
	Kingdom of Jerusalem, 1229–1244

Modified Azimuthal Equal Area Projection

Crusader States from 1098

Interpreting Maps During and after the First Crusade, crusaders set up small states in the Middle East.

■ **Skills Assessment: 1. Places and Regions** Name the four states set up by crusaders between 1098 and 1102. How long did each state stay under the crusaders' control?
2. Drawing Conclusions Compare this map with the map on page 319. Why might it have been difficult for the crusaders to maintain control of these states?

ATLAS

World: Political

ARCTIC OCEAN

GREENLAND (Denmark)

Arctic

Nuuk

ICELAND

ALASKA (US)

60°N

CANADA

Aleutian Islands

Vancouver

Winnipeg

Ottawa

Montreal

ATLANTIC

NORTH AMERICA

Chicago

Toronto

New York City

40°N

UNITED STATES

Washington D.C.

OCEAN

Los Angeles

BERMUDA (UK)

Rabat

Casablanca

Houston

MOROCCO

MEXICO

THE BAHAMAS

WESTERN SAHARA (Sovereignty Disputed)

Tropic of Cancer

Havana

DOMINICAN REPUBLIC

CUBA

PUERTO RICO (US)

MAURITANIA

MAL

20°N

HAWAII (US)

Mexico City

JAMAICA

HAITI

Nouakchott

GUATEMALA

BELIZE

VIRGIN ISLANDS (US, UK)

ST. KITTS AND NEVIS

ANTIGUA AND BARBUDA

CAPE VERDE

SENEGAL

Dakar

Bamako

BURKIN

FAS

Guatemala City

HONDURAS

DOMINICA

GAMBIA

EL SALVADOR

NICARAGUA

ST. LUCIA

BARBADOS

GUINEA-BISSAU

GUINEA

Managua

GRENADA

ST. VINCENT AND THE GRENADINES

SIERRA LEONE

CÔTE D'IVOIRE

GHA

COSTA RICA

PANAMA

TRINIDAD AND TOBAGO

LIBERIA

Caracas

VENEZUELA

GUYANA

PACIFIC

Bogotá

Georgetown

Paramaribo

SURINAME

FRENCH GUIANA (France)

N

COLOMBIA

W

E

0°

Equator

Quito

S

KIRIBATI

Galápagos Islands (Ecuador)

ECUADOR

PERU

SOUTH AMERICA

OCEAN

BRAZIL

SAMOA

AMERICAN SAMOA

Lima

BOLIVIA

Brasília

La Paz

Sucre

20°S

TONGA

PARAGUAY

Río de Janeiro

Tropic of Capricorn

Asunción

São Paulo

CHILE

ATLANTIC

ARGENTINA

URUGUAY

OCEAN

Santiago

Buenos Aires

Montevideo

40°S

FALKLAND ISLANDS (UK)

SOUTH GEORGIA (UK)

SOUTH SANDWICH ISLANDS (UK)

60°S

160°W

140°W

120°W

100°W

80°W

60°W

40°W

20°W

Antarctic Circle

⊛ National capitals

• Other cities

SCALE: at Equator

0   500   1,000   1,500   2,000 Miles

0   1,000   2,000 Kilometers

Mollweide Projection

ATLAS   A1

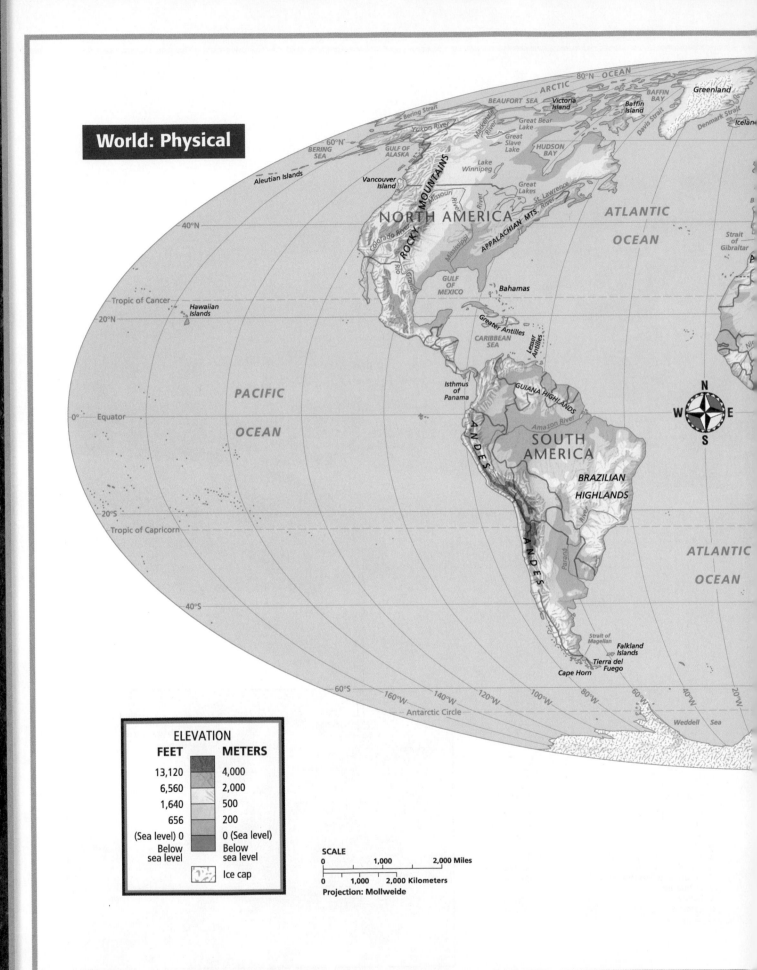

World: Physical

ARCTIC OCEAN
80°N
BEAUFORT SEA
BERING SEA
60°N
Bering Strait
Yukon River
GULF OF ALASKA
Aleutian Islands
Victoria Island
Great Bear Lake
Mackenzie River
Great Slave Lake
HUDSON BAY
BAFFIN BAY
Baffin Island
Davis Strait
Greenland
Iceland
Denmark Strait

Vancouver Island
NORTH AMERICA
ROCKY MOUNTAINS
Missouri River
Lake Winnipeg
Great Lakes
St. Lawrence River
APPALACHIAN MTS.
ATLANTIC OCEAN

40°N
Colorado River
Mississippi
Strait of Gibraltar

Rio Grande
GULF OF MEXICO
Bahamas

Tropic of Cancer
Hawaiian Islands
20°N
Greater Antilles
CARIBBEAN SEA
Lesser Antilles

PACIFIC OCEAN
Isthmus of Panama
GUIANA HIGHLANDS
Amazon River

0° Equator
ANDES
SOUTH AMERICA

BRAZILIAN HIGHLANDS

20°S
Tropic of Capricorn
ANDES
Paraná River
ATLANTIC OCEAN

40°S
Strait of Magellan
Falkland Islands
Tierra del Fuego
Cape Horn

60°S
160°W   140°W   120°W   100°W   80°W
Antarctic Circle
Weddell Sea

ELEVATION

FEET		METERS
13,120		4,000
6,560		2,000
1,640		500
656		200
(Sea level) 0		0 (Sea level)
Below sea level		Below sea level
	Ice cap	

SCALE
0   1,000   2,000 Miles
0   1,000   2,000 Kilometers
Projection: Mollweide

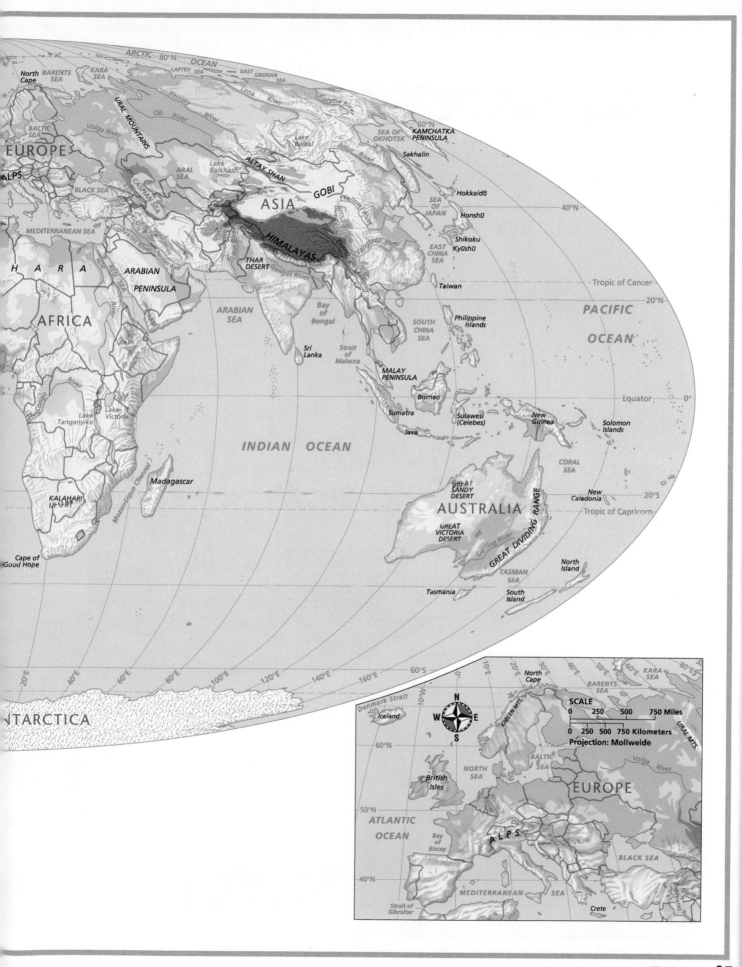

ARCTIC 80°N OCEAN

North Cape
BARENTS SEA
KARA SEA
LAPTEV SEA
EAST SIBERIAN SEA

BALTIC SEA
Volga River
Ob River
Yenisey River
Lena River
Kolyma River

URAL MOUNTAINS
60°N
SEA OF OKHOTSK
KAMCHATKA PENINSULA

EUROPE

ALPS

BLACK SEA
CASPIAN SEA
ARAL SEA
Lake Balkhash
ALTAY SHAN
Lake Baikal
Amur River
Sakhalin

MEDITERRANEAN SEA
Tigris River
Euphrates River
Persian Gulf
Indus River
ASIA
GOBI
Yellow River
40°N
SEA OF JAPAN
Hokkaidō
Honshū

S A H A R A

RED SEA

ARABIAN PENINSULA

THAR DESERT
HIMALAYAS
Ganges River
Yangtze River
Mekong River

Shikoku
Kyūshū
EAST CHINA SEA

Nile River

AFRICA

ARABIAN SEA

Bay of Bengal

Tropic of Cancer
20°N

Taiwan

PACIFIC

Congo River

Lake Tanganyika
Lake Victoria

Sri Lanka
Strait of Malacca

SOUTH CHINA SEA
Philippine Islands

OCEAN

MALAY PENINSULA
Borneo

Sumatra
Java

Sulawesi (Celebes)
New Guinea
Equator 0°
Solomon Islands

INDIAN OCEAN

Madagascar

Mozambique Channel

CORAL SEA

KALAHARI DESERT

GREAT SANDY DESERT

New Caledonia
20°S

AUSTRALIA

GREAT VICTORIA DESERT

Darling River
GREAT DIVIDING RANGE
Tropic of Capricorn

North Island

Cape of Good Hope

TASMAN SEA

Tasmania
South Island

20°E 40°E 60°E 80°E 100°E 120°E 140°E 160°E 60°S

ANTARCTICA

INSET MAP:

Denmark Strait
Iceland
North Cape
KJØLEN MTS.
BARENTS SEA
KARA SEA
URAL MTS.
10°E 20°E 30°E 40°E 50°E 60°E 80°E

N
W E
S

SCALE
0   250   500   750 Miles
0 250 500 750 Kilometers
Projection: Mollweide

60°N

NORTH SEA

BALTIC SEA

Volga River

EUROPE

ATLANTIC

British Isles

OCEAN

50°N
Rhine River

40°N

Bay of Biscay

Danube River
ALPS

BLACK SEA

MEDITERRANEAN SEA

Strait of Gibraltar

Crete

Tigris
Euphrates

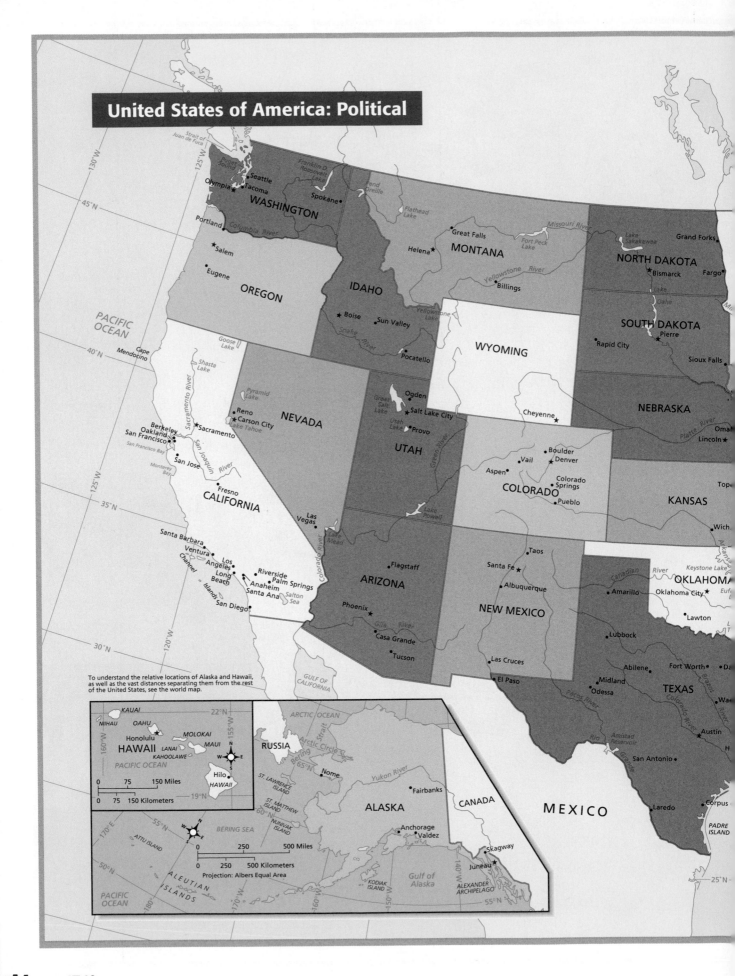

United States of America: Political

To understand the relative locations of Alaska and Hawaii, as well as the vast distances separating them from the rest of the United States, see the world map.

CANADA

NNESOTA
Duluth
Superior
Marquette
Sault Ste. Marie
Lake Superior

Minneapolis
St. Paul
Green Bay
WISCONSIN
Madison
Milwaukee
Lake Michigan
MICHIGAN
Grand Rapids
Saginaw
Lansing
Lake Huron

OWA
Cedar Rapids
Davenport
Des Moines
Rockford
Chicago
Gary
South Bend
Fort Wayne
Peoria
Ann Arbor
Detroit
Toledo
Cleveland
Akron
Youngstown
Lake Erie

INDIANA
Springfield
Indianapolis
Dayton
Cincinnati
OHIO
Columbus

ILLINOIS
St. Louis
East St. Louis
Louisville
Frankfort
Lexington
Evansville

MISSOURI
Springfield
Jefferson City
Lake Barkley
KENTUCKY
Ohio River

ARKANSAS
ayetteville
Little Rock
Pine Bluff
Memphis
Kentucky Lake
Nashville
Knoxville
Asheville
TENNESSEE
Chattanooga

MISSISSIPPI
Shreveport
Vicksburg
Meridian
Jackson
Huntsville
Birmingham
ALABAMA
Montgomery
Columbus
Macon
GEORGIA
Atlanta

LOUISIANA
Baton Rouge
eaumont
New Orleans
Biloxi
CHANDELEUR ISLANDS
Mobile
Pensacola
Tallahassee
Jacksonville
Gainesville
FLORIDA

GULF OF MEXICO

Orlando
Cape Canaveral
Tampa
St. Petersburg
Lake Okeechobee
Fort Myers
Fort Lauderdale
Miami
Cape Sable
FLORIDA KEYS
Straits of Florida

NORTH CAROLINA
Winston-Salem
Greensboro
Durham
Raleigh
Charlotte
Greenville
Cape Hatteras

SOUTH CAROLINA
Columbia
Charleston
Savannah
SEA ISLANDS

MAINE
Augusta
Burlington
Montpelier
Portland
VT
NH
Concord
Manchester
Lake Champlain

NEW YORK
Rochester
Syracuse
Buffalo
Albany
Springfield
Hartford
MA
Boston
Worcester
Providence
Cape Cod
CT RI
Bridgeport
New Haven
Long Island Sound
LONG ISLAND
Newark
Yonkers
New York City
Jersey City

PENNSYLVANIA
Allentown
Harrisburg
Pittsburgh
Philadelphia
Trenton
Camden
NJ
Atlantic City

Baltimore
MD
DE
Dover
Annapolis
Washington, D.C.
DELAWARE BAY

WEST VIRGINIA
Charleston
VIRGINIA
Richmond
Norfolk
Newport News
Virginia Beach

ATLANTIC OCEAN

National capital
State capitals
Other cities

THE BAHAMAS

CUBA

0   250   500 Miles
0   250   500 Kilometers
Projection: Albers Equal Area

ARCTIC OCEAN
NORTH AMERICA
EUROPE
ASIA
ATLANTIC OCEAN
AFRICA
Equator
PACIFIC OCEAN
SOUTH AMERICA
INDIAN OCEAN
AUSTRALIA
ANTARCTICA
Robinson Projection

50°N
60°W
45°N
40°N
35°W
35°N
30°N
25°N
70°W
75°W
85°W
80°W
90°W
65°W

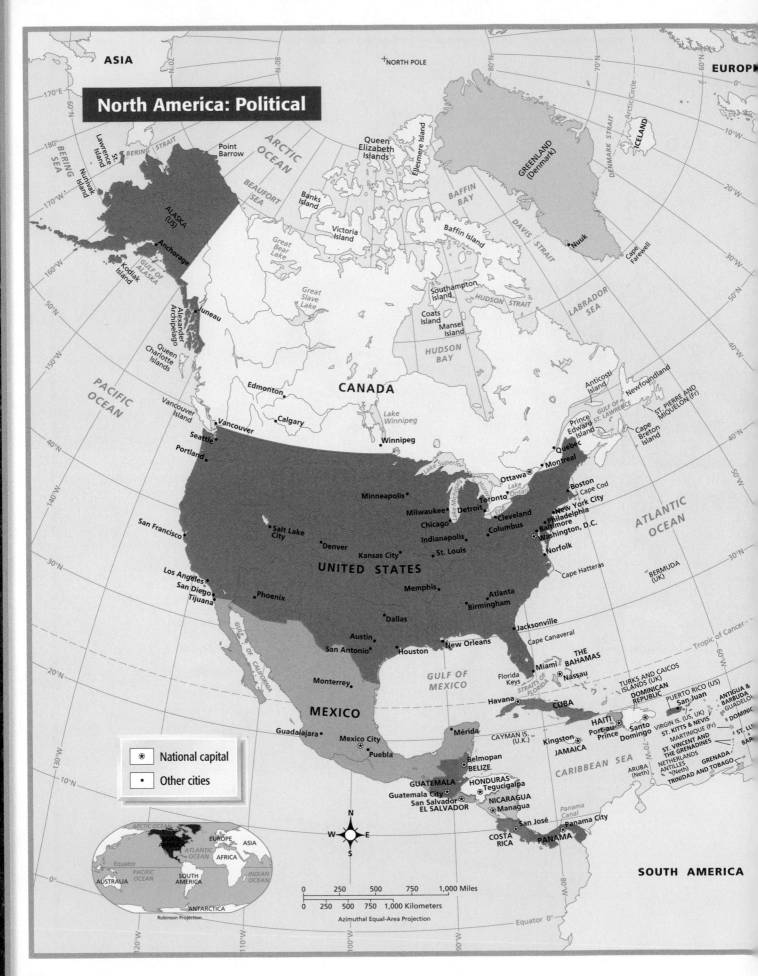

North America: Political

ASIA   +NORTH POLE   EUROPE

BERING SEA
St. Lawrence Island
Nunivak Island
BERING STRAIT
Point Barrow
ARCTIC OCEAN
BEAUFORT SEA
Queen Elizabeth Islands
Ellesmere Island
Banks Island
GREENLAND (Denmark)
Nuuk
ICELAND
DENMARK STRAIT

ALASKA (US)
Anchorage
Kodiak Island
GULF OF ALASKA
BAFFIN BAY
DAVIS STRAIT
Cape Farewell
Baffin Island

Alexander Archipelago
Juneau
Queen Charlotte Islands
Victoria Island
Great Bear Lake
Southampton Island
HUDSON STRAIT
LABRADOR SEA

PACIFIC OCEAN
Great Slave Lake
Coats Island
Mansel Island
HUDSON BAY

Vancouver Island
Edmonton
CANADA
Anticosti Island
Newfoundland
ST. PIERRE AND MIQUELON (Fr)

Vancouver
Calgary
Lake Winnipeg
Prince Edward Island
GULF OF ST. LAWRENCE
Cape Breton Island

Seattle
Portland
Winnipeg
Lake Superior
Quebec
Montreal
Ottawa

San Francisco
Minneapolis
Milwaukee
Lake Michigan
Detroit
Lake Huron
Lake Ontario
Toronto
Lake Erie
Cleveland
Boston
Cape Cod
New York City
Philadelphia
Baltimore
Washington, D.C.
ATLANTIC OCEAN

Salt Lake City
Denver
Chicago
Indianapolis
Columbus
UNITED STATES
Kansas City
St. Louis
Norfolk

Los Angeles
San Diego
Tijuana
Phoenix
Memphis
Atlanta
Birmingham
Cape Hatteras
BERMUDA (UK)

Dallas
Austin
San Antonio
Houston
New Orleans
Jacksonville
Cape Canaveral
Tropic of Cancer

GULF OF CALIFORNIA
Monterrey
GULF OF MEXICO
Miami
Florida Keys
THE BAHAMAS
Nassau
STRAITS OF FLORIDA
TURKS AND CAICOS ISLANDS (UK)
PUERTO RICO (US)
San Juan
ANTIGUA & BARBUDA
GUADELOU

MEXICO
Guadalajara
Mexico City
Puebla
Mérida
Havana
CUBA
CAYMAN IS. (U.K.)
Kingston
JAMAICA
HAITI
Port-au-Prince
Santo Domingo
DOMINICAN REPUBLIC
VIRGIN IS. (US, UK)
ST. KITTS & NEVIS
MARTINIQUE (Fr)
ST. VINCENT AND THE GRENADINES
NETHERLANDS ANTILLES (Neth)
ST. LU
DOMINIC
BAR

Belmopan
BELIZE
GUATEMALA
Guatemala City
San Salvador
EL SALVADOR
HONDURAS
Tegucigalpa
NICARAGUA
Managua
CARIBBEAN SEA
ARUBA (Neth)
GRENADA
TRINIDAD AND TOBAGO

Panama Canal
San José
COSTA RICA
Panama City
PANAMA

SOUTH AMERICA

⊛ National capital
• Other cities

ARCTIC OCEAN
NORTH AMERICA
EUROPE
ASIA
ATLANTIC OCEAN
AFRICA
Equator
PACIFIC OCEAN
SOUTH AMERICA
INDIAN OCEAN
AUSTRALIA
ANTARCTICA
Robinson Projection

N W E S

0 250 500 750 1,000 Miles
0 250 500 750 1,000 Kilometers
Azimuthal Equal-Area Projection

Equator 0°

South America: Political

CENTRAL AMERICA

CARIBBEAN SEA

Barranquilla
Cartagena

Caracas

VENEZUELA

Lake Maracaibo

Orinoco River

Medellín

Bogotá

COLOMBIA

Georgetown
Paramaribo

GUYANA

Cayenne

SURINAME

FRENCH GUIANA (Fr)

Cali

Malpelo Island (Colombia)

Quito

ECUADOR

Equator

Guayaquil

Galápagos Islands (Ecuador)

Río Negro

Amazon River

Amazon River

Belém

BRAZIL

PERU

Marañón River

Ucayali River

Trujillo

Recife

Callao
Lima

PACIFIC OCEAN

Arequipa

Lake Titicaca

La Paz

BOLIVIA

Lake Poopó

Sucre

Salvador

Brasilia

São Francisco River

Belo Horizonte

PARAGUAY

Campinas

São Paulo

Río de Janeiro

Tropic of Capricorn

Asunción

Curitiba

Tropic of Capricorn

San Ambrosio Island (Chile)

San Félix Island (Chile)

CHILE

Paraná River

Pôrto Alegre

ATLANTIC OCEAN

Juan Fernández Islands (Chile)

Córdoba

URUGUAY

Valparaíso
Santiago

Rosario

Buenos Aires
Morón
San Justo
Lomas de Zamora

Paraguay River

Uruguay River

Montevideo

RÍO DE LA PLATA

ARGENTINA

N
W   E
S

National capital

Other cities

STRAIT OF MAGELLAN

FALKLAND ISLANDS (UK)

Tierra del Fuego

SOUTH GEORGIA ISLAND (UK)

0   250   500   750   1,000 Miles
0   250   500   750   1,000 Kilometers
Azimuthal Equal-Area Projection

ARCTIC OCEAN

NORTH AMERICA   EUROPE   ASIA

ATLANTIC OCEAN   AFRICA

Equator

PACIFIC OCEAN   SOUTH AMERICA   INDIAN OCEAN

AUSTRALIA

ANTARCTICA

Robinson Projection

Europe: Political

National capital ⊛
Other cities •

500 Miles
500 Kilometers
250
250

ATLAS

A8

Africa: Political

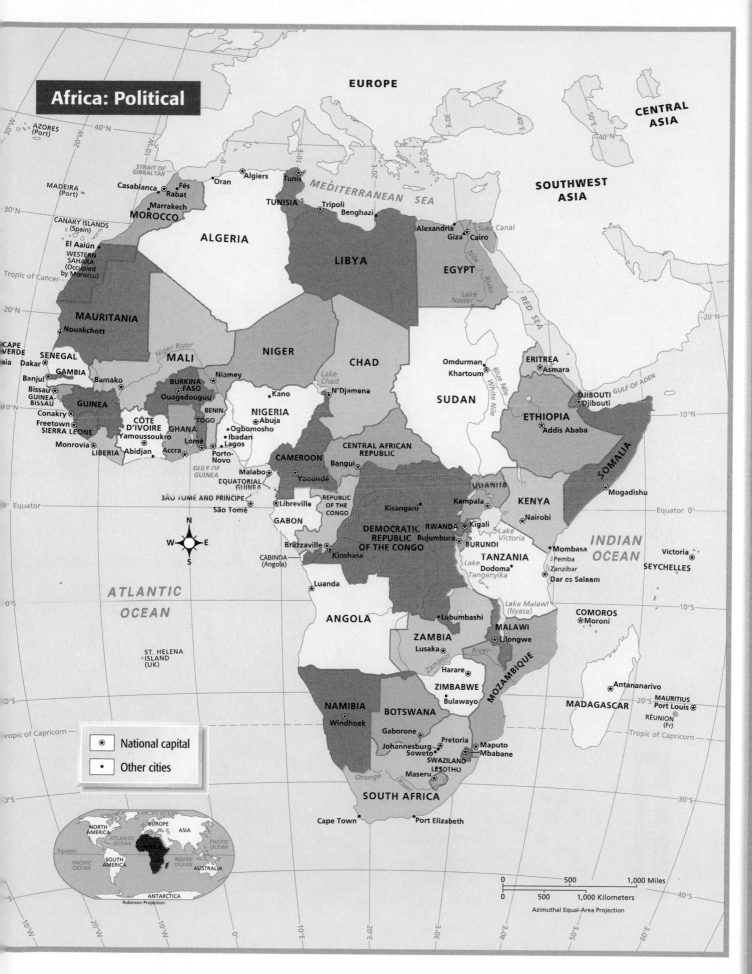

EUROPE

CENTRAL ASIA

SOUTHWEST ASIA

MEDITERRANEAN SEA

AZORES (Port)

MADEIRA (Port)

STRAIT OF GIBRALTAR

Casablanca • Fés Rabat
• Oran • Algiers • Tunis
Marrakech TUNISIA • Tripoli • Benghazi

MOROCCO

CANARY ISLANDS (Spain)

El Aaiún

WESTERN SAHARA (Occupied by Morocco)

Tropic of Cancer

ALGERIA

LIBYA

Alexandria • Suez Canal
Giza • Cairo

EGYPT

Lake Nasser

Nile River

RED SEA

MAURITANIA
• Nouakchott

CAPE VERDE

SENEGAL
Dakar ⊛
GAMBIA
Banjul ⊛
Bissau
GUINEA-BISSAU
GUINEA
Conakry
Freetown ⊛
SIERRA LEONE
Monrovia
LIBERIA

Niger River

MALI
Bamako ⊛

BURKINA FASO
Ouagadougou ⊛

Niamey

NIGER

Kano •

Lake Chad

N'Djamena •

CHAD

Omdurman •
Khartoum ⊛

Blue Nile
White Nile

SUDAN

ERITREA
Asmara ⊛

DJIBOUTI
Djibouti

GULF OF ADEN

CÔTE D'IVOIRE
Yamoussoukro ⊛
Abidjan •
GHANA
Accra ⊛
TOGO
BENIN
Lomé
Porto-Novo

NIGERIA
Abuja ⊛
• Ogbomosho
• Ibadan
• Lagos

CAMEROON
Yaoundé ⊛

Bangui •

CENTRAL AFRICAN REPUBLIC

ETHIOPIA
Addis Ababa ⊛

SOMALIA
• Mogadishu

GULF OF GUINEA

Malabo ⊛
EQUATORIAL GUINEA

SÃO TOMÉ AND PRÍNCIPE
São Tomé

GABON
Libreville ⊛

REPUBLIC OF THE CONGO

Congo River

Kisangani •

UGANDA
Kampala ⊛

RWANDA
Kigali ⊛
Bujumbura •
BURUNDI

KENYA
Nairobi ⊛

Lake Victoria

INDIAN OCEAN

Equator

Equator

Brazzaville ⊛
CABINDA (Angola)
Kinshasa ⊛

DEMOCRATIC REPUBLIC OF THE CONGO

TANZANIA
Dodoma ⊛
• Mombasa
Pemba
Zanzibar
Dar es Salaam

Victoria ⊛
SEYCHELLES

ATLANTIC OCEAN

Luanda ⊛

Lake Tanganyika

ANGOLA

• Lubumbashi

Lake Malawi (Nyasa)

COMOROS
Moroni •

ST. HELENA ISLAND (UK)

ZAMBIA
Lusaka ⊛

MALAWI
Lilongwe ⊛

Zambezi River

Harare ⊛

MOZAMBIQUE

Antananarivo ⊛

MAURITIUS
Port Louis ⊛

NAMIBIA
Windhoek ⊛

BOTSWANA

ZIMBABWE
• Bulawayo

MADAGASCAR

RÉUNION (Fr)

Tropic of Capricorn

Gaborone ⊛

Tropic of Capricorn

Johannesburg •
Soweto •
Pretoria ⊛
Maputo ⊛
Mbabane ⊛
SWAZILAND
LESOTHO
Maseru ⊛

Orange River

SOUTH AFRICA

Cape Town • Port Elizabeth

Legend
⊛ National capital
• Other cities

N W E S

Robinson Projection

ARCTIC OCEAN
NORTH AMERICA
EUROPE ASIA
ATLANTIC OCEAN
PACIFIC OCEAN
Equator
SOUTH AMERICA
INDIAN OCEAN
AUSTRALIA
PACIFIC OCEAN
ANTARCTICA

0   500   1,000 Miles
0   500   1,000 Kilometers
Azimuthal Equal-Area Projection

Asia: Political

National capital ✴
Other cities •

NORTH AMERICA

PACIFIC OCEAN

EUROPE

RUSSIA

RUSSIA

MONGOLIA

CHINA

KAZAKHSTAN

JAPAN

NORTH KOREA

SOUTH KOREA

Tokyo

Beijing

Shanghai

TAIWAN

Hong Kong

MYANMAR (BURMA)

THAILAND

VIETNAM

LAOS

CAMBODIA

PHILIPPINES

MALAYSIA

BRUNEI

SINGAPORE

INDONESIA

AUSTRALIA

IRIAN JAYA

INDIA

New Delhi

SRI LANKA

MALDIVES

NEPAL

BHUTAN

BANGLADESH

PAKISTAN

AFGHANISTAN

TURKMENISTAN

UZBEKISTAN

TAJIKISTAN

KYRGYZSTAN

IRAN

IRAQ

SAUDI ARABIA

YEMEN

OMAN

UNITED ARAB EMIRATES

QATAR

BAHRAIN

KUWAIT

JORDAN

ISRAEL

LEBANON

SYRIA

CYPRUS

TURKEY

GEORGIA

ARMENIA

AZERBAIJAN

INDIAN OCEAN

ARABIAN SEA

BAY OF BENGAL

MEDITERRANEAN SEA

RED SEA

BLACK SEA

CASPIAN SEA

AFRICA

1,000 Miles

1,000 Kilometers

Modified Oblique Conic Projection

500

500

0

0

Australia, New Zealand, and the Pacific Islands: Political

National capital
Other cities

Scale: At Equator
Miller Cylindrical Projection

1,000 Miles
1,000 Kilometers

Robinson Projection

NORTH AMERICA

ASIA

SOUTH CHINA SEA

PHILIPPINE SEA

BONIN ISLANDS (Japan)

VOLCANO ISLANDS (Japan)

NORTHERN MARIANAS (US)

GUAM (US) · Agña

Koror PALAU

MICRONESIA

Chuuk Islands

FEDERATED STATES OF MICRONESIA

Palikir

MARSHALL ISLANDS

Eniwetok I.

Kwajalein Island

Majuro

WAKE ISLAND (US)

MIDWAY ISLAND (US)

JOHNSTON ISLAND (US)

Hawaiian Islands

HAWAII (US)

International Date

NAURU

Yaren

Gilbert Islands

Tarawa

KINGMAN REEF (US)

PALMYRA ISLAND (US)

Teraina

Tabuaeran

HOWLAND ISLAND (US)

BAKER ISLAND (US)

McKean I.

Gardner

Phoenix Islands

KIRIBATI

JARVIS I. (US)

Starbuck Island

POLYNESIA

Marquesas Islands (Fr)

Tuamotu Archipelago (Fr)

FRENCH POLYNESIA

Papeete
Tahiti (Fr)

Society Islands (Fr)

Manihiki Island

COOK ISLANDS (NZ)

Rarotonga Island

Austral Islands (Fr)

Rapa Island (Fr)

Easter Island (Chile)

PITCAIRN (UK)
Pitcairn Island
Ducie Island

TUVALU
Funafuti

TOKELAU (NZ)

SAMOA
Apia

AMERICAN SAMOA
Pago Pago

NIUE (NZ)

TONGA
Nuku'alofa

WALLIS & FUTUNA (Fr)

FIJI
Suva

MELANESIA

SOLOMON ISLANDS
Honiara

Guadalcanal Island

New Guinea

PAPUA NEW GUINEA
Port Moresby

Bismarck Archipelago

CORAL SEA

VANUATU
Port-Vila (Fr)

Espíritu Santo I.

Malekula I.

NEW CALEDONIA (Fr)
Nouméa

Loyalty Islands (Fr)

NORFOLK ISLAND (Aust)

Kermadec Islands (NZ)

SOUTH PACIFIC OCEAN

NEW ZEALAND
Wellington

Chatham Islands (NZ)

Bounty Islands (NZ)

Auckland Islands (NZ)

TASMAN SEA

INDONESIA

ARAFURA SEA

TIMOR SEA

AUSTRALIA

Perth

Brisbane

Sydney
Canberra

Melbourne

INDIAN OCEAN

ATLAS **A11**

3,700,000 B.C.–A.D. 1500

The Ancient World

Neolithic stone axe and carved ivory tool

Mosaic depicting Plato's Academy

2,500,000 B.C.
Science and Technology
The first stone tools appear.

c. 600 B.C.
Business and Finance
The Lydians invent coined money.

2,500,000 B.C.	3000 B.C.	1000 B.C.	500 B.C.

c. 3200 B.C.
Global Events
Upper and Lower Egypt are unified.

c. 2500 B.C.
Politics
The Harappan civilization appears in the Indus River valley.

c. 1000s B.C.
Politics
The Zhou dynasty begins in China.

c. 1000 B.C.–700 B.C.
The Arts
Phoenicia improves metalworking and glassblowing.

c. 800s B.C.–700s B.C.
Politics
Sparta and Athens develop into powerful city-states.

c. 387 B.C.
The Arts
Plato founds the Academy in Athens.

Harappan animal sculptures, c. 2000 B.C.

Build on What You Know

You are a member of a civilized society. You are a part of history, part of the modern world. In this chapter, you will review what you have learned about prehistory—the period of time before people began keeping written records. You will also learn about the thousands of years during which people lived in what we call the ancient world. In the ancient world, civilizations emerged in different regions of the earth. Many of these civilizations flourished and made important advances. By reviewing the achievements and ways of life of these early peoples, you will be better able to understand how the modern world that we live in developed.

The Roman poet Ovid

This brass sculpture of a hunting scene, made by the Akan people of West Africa, was used as an instrument for weighing gold dust in trade.

A.D. 162
Science and Technology
The Greek doctor Galen begins a medical practice in Rome.

A.D. 476
Global Events
The last Roman emperor in the West is overthrown.

A.D. 1100s–A.D. 1400s
Business and Finance
Gold mining and trade thrive in Great Zimbabwe.

C. A.D. 220
Politics
The Han dynasty ends in China.

C. A.D. 700–A.D. 1300
Business and Finance
East Africa has a golden age of trade.

C. A.D. 1150
Politics
The rulers of Cahokia lose control of the central Mississippi Valley.

| 1 B.C. | A.D. 500 | A.D. 1000 | A.D. 1500 |

C. A.D. 500s
Daily Life
The Maya establish the city of Chichén Itzá.

C. A.D. 900s
Daily Life
Bantu-speaking societies are established across southern Africa.

C. A.D. 1400
Daily Life
Drought strikes the Great Plains, destroying many farming communities.

A.D. 8
The Arts
The Roman poet Ovid writes the *Metamorphoses*.

A.D. 320–C. A.D. 550
The Arts
The golden age of India occurs under the Gupta dynasty.

27 B.C.
Global Events
The Roman Republic becomes the Roman Empire.

The Mississippians of Cahokia built earthen mounds in the shapes of animals, similar to this one made by the Adena or Hopewell people, in what is now Ohio.

What's Your Opinion?

Themes Journal *Do you **agree** or **disagree** with the following statements? Support your point of view in your journal.*

Government Civilizations must have some form of government.

Global Relations Societies gain knowledge of other societies, cultures, and lifestyles through trade.

Culture A stable government promotes cultural growth.

The First Civilizations

READ TO DISCOVER

❶ What are the characteristics of a civilization and where did the first civilizations develop?

❷ What were the achievements of the kingdoms of the Nile?

❸ What were the achievements of the kingdoms of the Tigris-Euphrates Valley?

❹ What were the achievements of the Phoenicians, Lydians, and Hebrews?

DEFINE

civilization
division of labor
cultural diffusion
cuneiform
ethical monotheism

IDENTIFY

Menes
Amenhotep IV
Hammurabi

WHY IT MATTERS TODAY

Researchers continue to discover new facts about prehistoric human life. Use 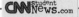 or other **current event** sources to learn about recent archaeological discoveries. Record your findings in your journal.

CNN Student News.com

The Main Idea
Scholars have determined that prehistoric people first developed organized societies in four river valleys.

The Story Begins *In 1978 in Tanzania scientist Mary Leakey discovered a series of footprints made millions of years ago. She described the simple action shown by the prints. "The traveler stops, pauses, turns to the left to glance at some possible threat or irregularity, then continues to the north." Leakey believed the prints were made by a hominid, one of the humanlike creatures who came before us on Earth.*

The Emergence of Civilizations

Archaeologists are the scientists who study ancient fossils, settlements, and artifacts. They have limited evidence about humans who lived before the development of writing. Even so, researchers have been able to find a great deal of information about the development of early civilization. This period before the invention of writing is called prehistory.

Prehistoric peoples. Archaeologists know that humanlike creatures first appeared on earth millions of years ago. Probably between 100,000 and 400,000 years ago, the species known as *Homo sapiens* may have appeared in Africa. At first, early humans were nomads, moving from place to place in search of food. During the Ice Age the sea level dropped because so much water was frozen in the icecaps. As the sea level fell, land bridges emerged between the continents. People and animals crossed the land bridges into new areas. In this way, humans spread into all parts of the world.

During the Middle Stone Age—which in different parts of the world lasted from about 10,000 to 5,500 years ago—people tamed the dog. They also invented the bow and arrow, fishhooks, fish spears, and harpoons made from bones and antlers.

The New Stone Age lasted until about 4,000 years ago. During this period, some peoples began settling in permanent villages and learned to grow their own plants for food. This led to the development of agriculture and the domestication, or taming, of herd animals such as cattle and sheep.

INTERPRETING THE VISUAL RECORD

Reconstructing the past
Archaeologists have discovered the remains of mud-brick houses and shrines at Çatalhüyük in present-day Turkey. *What might archaeologists learn from these ruins?*

The History of Communication

The invention of writing was just one step in a long history of changes in the way people communicate. Reading a time line of events in communications history helps us to understand the absolute and relative chronology of when events happened.

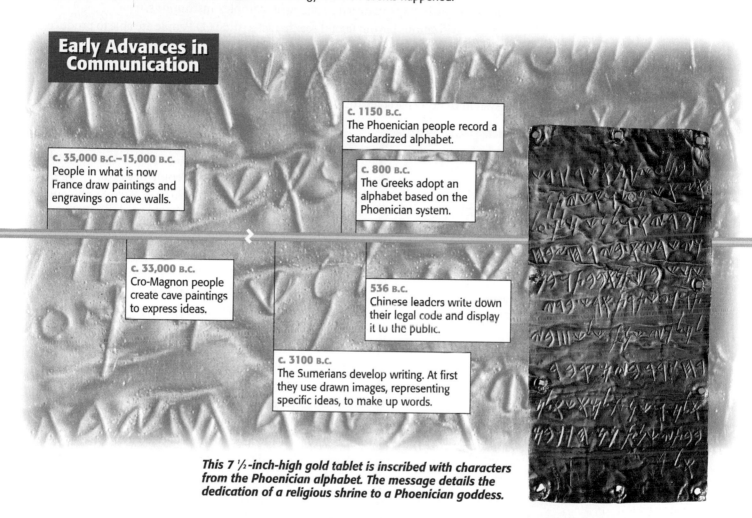

Early Advances in Communication

C. 1150 B.C.
The Phoenician people record a standardized alphabet.

C. 35,000 B.C.–15,000 B.C.
People in what is now France draw paintings and engravings on cave walls.

C. 800 B.C.
The Greeks adopt an alphabet based on the Phoenician system.

C. 33,000 B.C.
Cro-Magnon people create cave paintings to express ideas.

536 B.C.
Chinese leaders write down their legal code and display it to the public.

C. 3100 B.C.
The Sumerians develop writing. At first they use drawn images, representing specific ideas, to make up words.

This 7 ½-inch-high gold tablet is inscribed with characters from the Phoenician alphabet. The message details the dedication of a religious shrine to a Phoenician goddess.

Skills Reminder

A time line shows the dates events happened, or their absolute chronology, as well as when events happened relative to each other, or their relative chronology. This book follows a system of dating years based on the traditional date of birth of Jesus Christ. We use this system because it is the one you will most often encounter in encyclopedias and other reference materials. Years following Jesus's birth are numbered in order. They start with A.D., which stands for the Latin phrase *Anno Domini* ("in the year of the Lord" or "since the birth of Christ"). Years before Jesus's birth are numbered in reverse order. They are followed by B.C. ("**B**efore **C**hrist"). The initial *c.* (for "circa," meaning "approximately") indicates that the exact date is unknown and that the one given is a good estimate.

Skills Practice

❶ Read the time line of major events in the history of communication. Approximately how many years passed between the invention of writing by the Sumerians and the Greek adoption of an alphabet?

❷ What does the passage of time between these two events imply about the development of communication? Based on the other information given, what else does the time line imply about the development of communication?

❸ Using information in your textbook and from other sources, create your own time line of events reflecting a characteristic other than writing that was crucial to the development of early civilizations.

The development of agriculture and the domestication of animals—the Neolithic agricultural revolution—changed the way people lived. Some people became farmers and settled in one area. Others survived by herding animals and continuously moving in search of grazing land.

The foundations of civilization. As people learned to farm and began to settle down, they also began to establish towns. Over time, people created civilizations. A **civilization** is a highly organized society with complex institutions.

Most civilizations have at least three characteristics: (1) People are able to produce extra food, (2) People have built large towns or cities with some form of government, and (3) A **division of labor** exists, in which different people perform different jobs, instead of each person doing all kinds of work. Some historians also consider a writing system to be a characteristic of civilization.

Improvements in agriculture helped civilizations develop. Irrigation and better tools created a surplus of higher quality food. As a result, populations increased, and villages grew into cities. People began working in different jobs; skilled craft workers, merchants, and traders appeared. Traders not only moved goods for sale, but also passed along ideas. We call the spread of aspects of culture from one geographic area to another **cultural diffusion.** Writing developed as trade grew and civilizations discovered the need to keep records. People also developed calendars because they needed to know when to plant and harvest their crops.

The first civilizations that we know of developed in or around four great river valleys: the Nile valley in Africa, the Tigris-Euphrates valley in Southwest Asia, the Indus valley in South Asia, and the Huang valley in East Asia. Farming in these river valleys depended on irrigation. Farmers needed water during the dry season. They also needed to control floods during rainy periods. Historians believe governments may have developed as a way to direct and plan large irrigation and flood control projects.

✔ **READING CHECK: Finding the Main Idea** What main characteristics do civilizations share, and where did the first civilizations develop?

Egypt: The New Kingdom, c. 1450 B.C.

Interpreting Maps The New Kingdom extended Egypt's borders.

■ **Skills Assessment: 1. The World in Spatial Terms** Approximately how many miles is it from the northernmost point to the southernmost point of the New Kingdom?

2. Drawing Inferences Why did the New Kingdom not expand further to the east or west?

Kingdoms of the Nile

Yearly floods of the Nile River in North Africa left rich soil in its valley. The river water also provided irrigation for farmers. Strong leaders brought together farming settlements into two kingdoms, Lower Egypt in the north and Upper Egypt in the south. Sometime after 3200 B.C., a king of Upper Egypt known as **Menes** (MEE·neez) united the two kingdoms. In later years

Egyptian rulers took the title of pharaoh. They crushed rebellions, gained new lands, controlled irrigation, and encouraged trade. These policies increased peoples' well-being in Egypt.

From the time of Menes to almost 300 B.C., about 30 Egyptian dynasties, or families of rulers, rose and fell. Egyptian civilization was very stable during its long history. The Egyptians developed a remarkably accurate calendar to keep track of the Nile floods. They used geometry to calculate how to redraw the boundaries of fields after floods and to build the pyramids. Egyptian architects and engineers were among the best in the ancient world.

Religion was at the center of Egyptian civilization. Egyptians believed in many gods, a practice known as polytheism. In the 1300s B.C. the pharaoh **Amenhotep IV** tried to make his people adopt monotheism, the belief in only one god. After Amenhotep's death, the priests brought back the traditional polytheistic religion. Egyptians believed immortality was possible if a dead body was preserved. They developed a process called mummification that preserved bodies for centuries. A belief in an afterlife also led Egyptians to build elaborate tombs like the pyramids. Typically these tombs were built for members of the Egyptian royalty and upper classes.

✔ **READING CHECK: Categorizing** In what areas did ancient Egyptians make major accomplishments?

Kingdoms of the Tigris-Euphrates

Civilization developed in a different way in the Tigris-Euphrates Valley in Southwest Asia. This area is sometimes called Mesopotamia, or the Fertile Crescent. Many historians believe that the Fertile Crescent may be the area where agriculture first developed.

Sumerian civilization. Over time, humans developed a number of city-states in Sumer, in southern Mesopotamia. A city-state included not only the city itself but also the lands, fields, and villages around it. Sumerian temples, known as ziggurats, were the central features of the city-states. Sometime after 3000 B.C. the Sumerians developed a new form of wedge-shaped writing known as **cuneiform,** from the Latin word for "wedge." Some scholars think Sumerians were also the first to develop and use the wheel.

Empires of the Fertile Crescent. In about 2330 B.C. the Akkadians conquered the Sumerians. They created a great empire that extended as far west as the Mediterranean Sea. The Akkadian Empire lasted about 150 years and was just the first of many to take control of the area. In about 1792 B.C. a powerful ruler named **Hammurabi** (ham·uh·RAHB·ee) came to power in the city of Babylon and conquered most of the upper Tigris-Euphrates Valley. He is best known for the Code of Hammurabi, a collection of laws put together under his direction. Part of the code appears below.

History Makers Speak **"If a builder build[s] a house for a man and [does] not make its construction firm, and the house which he has built collapse[s] and cause[s] the death of the owner of the house, that builder shall be put to death. If it cause[s] the death of a son of the owner of the house, they shall put to death a son of that builder."**

Code of Hammurabi

Analyzing Primary Sources

Identifying a Point of View
Why do you think the Code of Hammurabi called for such harsh punishments?

In the 1600s B.C. a period of invasions by migrating peoples began in the Tigris-Euphrates Valley. The Hittites, who came from Asia Minor, were the first to smelt iron. In about 900 B.C. the Assyrians began creating a large empire throughout the Fertile Crescent. Eventually it stretched from Egypt to the Iranian Plateau. In the 600s B.C. the Chaldeans conquered most of the Fertile Crescent. In 539 B.C. the Persians took control of the region and created the largest empire yet seen.

✔ **READING CHECK: Supporting a Point of View** What evidence supports the view that the Sumerians and Babylonians contributed greatly to civilization?

The Torah consists of the Hebrews' most sacred writings, including their code of laws. The Torah also describes traditions surrounding the creation of the universe and contains a narrative history of the Hebrews up to the death of Moses.

The Phoenicians, Lydians, and Hebrews

The people who lived in the western end of the Fertile Crescent and in western Asia Minor did not create large empires. However, they had great influence on the modern world. Phoenicia was a loose union of city-states. Each was governed by a different king. The Phoenicians became the greatest traders in the ancient world. Perhaps most important, the Phoenicians developed the alphabet on which our own alphabet is patterned. The Lydians of Asia Minor are remembered as the first people in history to use coined money, beginning in about 600 B.C.

A series of people lived in Canaan, which lay south of Phoenicia along the land bridge between Asia and Africa. One such group, the Semitic-speaking Hebrews, had a great influence on this region and on all of history. The Hebrews worshiped one god, Yahweh, as the creator of the universe. Part of the Hebrew scriptures, the Torah, outlined the Hebrew code of laws. This code set a higher value on human life than had earlier law codes. Judaism is the Hebrew form of monotheism. Because of its focus on ethics, or proper conduct, Judaism is often called **ethical monotheism.** This is one of the Hebrews' most important contributions to Western civilization.

✔ **READING CHECK: Summarizing** What were some of the achievements of the first civilizations of the western Fertile Crescent and western Asia Minor?

SECTION 1 REVIEW

1. Define and explain the significance:
civilization
division of labor
cultural diffusion
cuneiform
ethical monotheism

2. Identify and explain the significance:
Menes
Amenhotep IV
Hammurabi

Homework Practice Online
keyword: SH3 HPP

3. Summarizing Copy the graphic organizer below. Use it to show the major accomplishments of the first civilizations.

Western Fertile Crescent accomplishments

Asia Minor

Nile accomplishments

Tigris-Euphrates accomplishments

4. **Finding the Main Idea**
a. What are the characteristics of a civilization?
b. Where did the first civilizations develop, and why did they develop in these areas?

5. **Writing and Critical Thinking**
Evaluating In your opinion, what are the three most important contributions from the early civilizations?
Consider:
• the different accomplishments of each early civilization
• what effect these accomplishments had on early people
• what other achievements these accomplishments might have led to

READ TO DISCOVER

❶ What were the characteristics of early Indian civilizations?

❷ What were the major accomplishments of the Qin and Han dynasties in China?

DEFINE

caste system

IDENTIFY

Siddhartha Gautama
Shang
Zhou
Qin
Han
Confucius
Daoism
Legalism

WHY IT MATTERS TODAY

Hinduism and Buddhism are still important world religions. Use CNN News.com or other **current event** sources to find out where Hinduism and Buddhism are practiced today and how they influence politics in those areas. Record your findings in your journal.

CNN student News.com

Ancient India and China

The Main Idea
People living in river valleys in ancient India and China developed some of the earliest civilizations.

The Story Continues *"One man on the battlefield conquers an army of a thousand men. Another conquers himself—and he is greater." These words from Siddhartha Gautama reflect a belief of Buddhism, a religion that arose in ancient India and spread to China. Like the civilizations along the Nile and the Tigris-Euphrates, early civilizations developed in Indian and Chinese river valleys.*

Ancient Indian Civilization

The first civilization in India developed about 4,500 years ago, in the valley of the Indus River. This new society—the Harappan civilization—began several hundred years after civilizations developed in Egypt and Sumer.

Ruins from two early Indian cities—Harappa and Mohenjo Daro—show very advanced city planning and design. Both cities had wide streets laid out on a grid pattern. They also had public baths and a covered brick sewer system. The early Indus River valley people also developed their own written language.

Harappan Civilization, c. 1700 B.C.

Interpreting Maps Rivers formed natural highways that encouraged exchange as well as unity in the Harappan civilization.

■ **Skills Assessment:**
1. **Locate** Identify the major waterways in the Indus River valley.
2. **Drawing Conclusions** How might the location of Harappa and Mohenjo Daro have affected their relationship? Why?

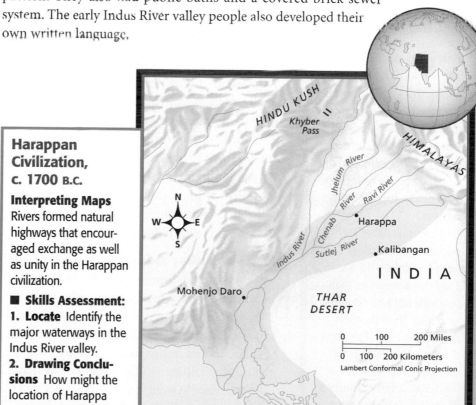

In about 1750 B.C. new groups of Indo-European-speaking peoples began to move south through mountain passes into northern India. The Indo-Aryan settlers developed a complex social system in northern India. Warriors and later priests were at the top, followed by merchants, traders, farmers, and servants.

Hinduism and Buddhism. Two of the world's great religions developed in ancient India—Hinduism and Buddhism. According to Hinduism, the soul does not die with the body. It is reincarnated, or reborn, in the body of another being, either human or animal. For Hindus, dharma is reaching one's moral duty in this life so that the soul can make progress in the next life. Karma is the positive or negative force created by a person's actions. It determines the person's status in the next life. People who fulfill their dharma are rewarded with good karma and are reborn into a higher social group. People who do not fulfill their dharma are reborn into a lower social group, or as animals or insects.

The Bhagavad Gita, "Song of the Lord," is a sacred text in the Hindu religion. In this excerpt, the Hindu god Krishna describes the practice of yoga.

History Makers Speak

❝Holding the spine, the neck and the head steadily in a line and gazing at the tip of the nose without looking in any direction and without movement, the yogi of peaceful mind, fearless . . . should sit absorbed in me by controlling his mind.❞

from the Bhagavad Gita

Another great religion in India, Buddhism, was founded by **Siddhartha Gautama.** He became known as the Buddha, or "the Enlightened One." The Buddha accepted the Hindu belief that the progress of the soul depends on how one leads one's life. He taught that enlightenment comes from knowing the Four Noble Truths. The Four Noble Truths are that (1) human life involves suffering and sorrow, (2) the desire for pleasure and material gain causes suffering and sorrow, (3) renouncing desire frees people from suffering and helps them reach nirvana, the perfect peace, which releases the soul from the endless cycle of reincarnation, and (4) desire can be renounced by following the Eightfold Path.

The Eightfold Path consists of (1) right views, or seeing life as it truly is, (2) right intentions, (3) right speech, (4) right action, (5) right livelihood, (6) right effort, (7) right mindfulness, or constant awareness of one's self, and (8) right concentration to direct the mind in meditation. The Buddha did not accept the Hindu gods, and powerful Hindu priests opposed Buddhism, causing it to decline in India. However, Buddhism greatly influenced other parts of Asia.

Indian dynasties and culture. The first empire to successfully unify much of India was the Mauryan Empire. After the Mauryans fell in about 185 B.C., parts of northern India came under foreign rulers or splintered back into local kingdoms. In the A.D. 300s the Gupta dynasty reunited most of northern India. The Guptas' rule has been called a golden age of Indian history, when society and the arts prospered.

The ancient Indian societies created the basic social and cultural patterns of Indian civilization. Distinct social classes emerged and developed into a division of society called the **caste system.** These societies also left the world a rich legacy in art, literature, mathematics, and science. Indian mathematicians understood abstract numbers and negative numbers. Indian astronomers understood the rotation of the earth on its axis. Indian physicians invented the technique called inoculation—infecting people with a mild form of a disease so they would not get sick with the more serious form.

✔ **READING CHECK: Summarizing** What characterized ancient Indian civilization?

Analyzing Primary Sources

Drawing Inferences Why do you think followers of Hindu practiced yoga?

Fairy Tales

"Once upon a time . . ." is a phrase that we all recognize from the fairy tales that we read as children. The stories that we call fairy tales occur in many cultures around the world. Often the same basic tales can be found in several cultures.

The Jataka Tales are popular Indian stories taken from Buddhist writings. They use animals as characters to teach lessons about kindness. Their theme is good versus evil. The same theme underlies the story of Cinderella. There are at least 500 different versions of the tale from various cultures. **Why do you think similar themes are found in fairy tales from different cultures?**

Ancient Chinese Civilizations

China was cut off from other civilizations by geographical features such as the Gobi and the towering mountains of central Asia. So unlike civilizations farther west, Chinese civilization developed without outside influences. Like those other early civilizations, however, it began in a river valley. The valley of the Huang River is in the heartland of China. China's first dynasty, the **Shang,** began along the Huang River sometime between 1750 B.C. and 1500 B.C. The Shang developed a writing system. They also created a religious tradition that combined animism—a belief that spirits live in everything—and ancestor worship.

The Zhou, Qin, and Han dynasties. In about 1050 B.C. the Shang were conquered by the **Zhou** (JOU), who claimed the right to rule was divinely granted. They argued that this right, which they called the "Mandate of Heaven," had passed to them. Future Chinese leaders would also argue that they ruled because they had this mandate.

After about 800 years of Zhou rule, the **Qin** (CHIN) founded a new dynasty in 221 B.C. The Qin dynasty united China under a strong, central government for the first time in history. During their short rule, the Qin standardized weights, measures, and coinage.

Han Dynasty, 206 B.C.–A.D. 220

Interpreting Maps Trade and commerce helped the Han to extend their control far to the west of earlier Chinese dynasties.

■ **Skills Assessment: Human Systems** Name two cities through which a merchant would have to pass while traveling along the Silk Road.

Cheng More than 6,000 life-size terracotta figures of soldiers and horses were buried with the Qin emperor Cheng. *What does the placement of these figures in the emperor's tomb suggest about this civilization?*

They also created a uniform system of writing and put in place a single system of taxation. However, Qin rule was harsh. In 206 B.C. Liu Bang, a commoner who had become a general, overthrew the Qin and established a new dynasty, the **Han.**

The Han kept a strong centralized government, but ruled less harshly and more wisely. They increased trade and expanded the frontiers. China prospered under Han rule. Many new tools and luxury goods became available—including paper, a Chinese invention that later spread to the West. After the Han dynasty fell in A.D. 220, nomadic tribes roamed China for hundreds of years. In A.D. 581 a Chinese general once again unified China and brought back imperial rule.

Chinese life and culture. In the late Zhou period, Chinese philosophers developed ideas that would influence not only their culture but later Chinese history as well. One of their basic ideas was the dualism, or two-sidedness, of nature. They taught that through the balancing of two forces called yin and yang, people could achieve harmony. Perhaps the most influential teacher of this philosophy was K'ung Ch'iu, known in the West as **Confucius.** Confucian philosophy has three basic concepts—the importance of family, respect for one's elders, and respect for the past.

Another Chinese philosophy called **Daoism** complemented Confucianism. Daoists believed that people should withdraw and think about the natural harmony of the world. In this way they could learn Dao, or "The Way," and allow it to govern human behavior. In contrast, the philosophy of **Legalism** held very different beliefs. It taught that people were basically selfish and untrustworthy and had to be controlled with harsh measures. The Qin dynasty held Legalist views, while the Han rulers blended both Legalist and Confucian ideas.

The Chinese developed remarkable skills in the arts and sciences. Among the most important works of Chinese literature were the Five Classics: the *Book of History,* the *Book of Poems,* the *Book of Changes,* the *Spring and Autumn Annals,* and the *Book of Rites.* The Five Classics became the basis on which all Chinese scholars were educated. In science, early Chinese astronomers computed the year to be 365 ¼ days long. They also built special instruments to observe the movement of planets.

✔ **READING CHECK: Analyzing Information** What contributions did the Qin and Han dynasties make to Chinese civilization?

SECTION 2 REVIEW

1. **Define** and explain the significance:
   caste system

2. **Identify** and explain the significance:
   Siddhartha Gautama   Han
   Shang   Confucius
   Zhou   Daoism
   Qin   Legalism

3. **Summarizing** Copy the graphic organizer below. Use it to describe how Indo-Aryan society was structured.

Indo-Aryan society

4. **Finding the Main Idea**
   a. Sequence the dynasties in ancient China and summarize the major accomplishments of each.
   b. How did Confucianism and Daoism influence Chinese culture?

5. **Writing and Critical Thinking**
   Comparing and Contrasting Write a paragraph in which you analyze the similarities and differences between Hinduism and Buddhism.
   Consider:
   • the beliefs of Hinduism
   • the beliefs of Buddhism
   • the Buddha's acceptance or rejection of certain Hindu beliefs

Civilizations of the Mediterranean World

READ TO DISCOVER

❶ How and why did the government of the Greek city-states change over time?

❷ What were the major achievements of Greek civilization, and how did Hellenistic culture spread?

❸ How was the Roman Empire established and why did it end?

DEFINE

direct democracy
republic
pope

IDENTIFY

Homer
Socrates
Alexander the Great
Julius Caesar
Augustus (Octavian)
Jesus

▶ WHY IT MATTERS TODAY

The Olympic Games are still popular today. Use CNN Student News.com or other **current event** sources to find out how the modern Olympics compare to the ancient games in Greece. Record your findings in your journal.

CNN Student News.com

The Main Idea
Great civilizations developed in Greece and later in Rome, which built a vast empire.

The Story Continues *Drawing on earlier societies, new civilizations began to develop around the Mediterranean Sea. Their influence continues today. Historian Lionel Casson described one scene in ancient Greece. "One midsummer day in the year we calculate to have been 776 B.C., a 200-meter dash was run in a rural backwater in southwestern Greece, and a young local named Coroebus won it. It was an obscure event in an obscure spot but it earned him immortality: he is the first Olympic victor on record."*

The Greek City-States

By about 2000 B.C. Indo-European people had settled in the region of the Balkan Peninsula and the Aegean Sea. In time these people, known as Greeks, created a brilliant civilization. It became one of the foundations of modern Western civilization.

Various Greek-speaking peoples formed city-states in the 800s and 700s B.C. The most important of these were Athens and Sparta. Most Greek city-states were organized around a hilltop, known as an acropolis. Each had a marketplace, which was also the public meeting place. Surrounding lands were used for agriculture and herding.

Two great epic poems, the *Iliad* and the *Odyssey,* give us a glimpse of early Greek society. Scholars often call the era of these poems the Homeric Age, after the poems' author, **Homer.** During the Homeric Age the Greeks developed a religion that focused on explaining the natural world and human actions rather than on moral issues and life after death. The Greeks believed their gods enjoyed shows of strength and courage. Thus they held athletic contests in honor of the gods. The most famous of these contests were held every four years at Olympia in honor of Zeus, the king of the gods.

By 600 B.C. struggles for control of the city-states began between landowners on one side and soldiers and other nonaristocrats on the other. Some leaders became tyrants—people who took power unlawfully. Over time the tyrants became harsh and unjust, and the city-states removed them from power. Many city-states adopted the idea that people could and should rule themselves. In about 507 B.C. Cleisthenes overthrew the aristocrats who ruled Athens and created a **direct democracy.** This is a form of government in which all citizens participate directly in making decisions for the states.

✔ **READING CHECK: Sequencing** How did Greek city-states change over time?

Greek vase showing potters at work, c. 450 B.C.

Trade in the Ancient World, c. 750 B.C.–450 B.C.

Interpreting Maps The Greeks set up colonies along the Aegean, Black, and Mediterranean Seas.

■ **Skills Assessment: Places and Regions** What Black Sea colony exported grain and timber to other places in the Mediterranean region?

Greece's Golden and Hellenistic Ages

In the 400s B.C. the Persian king Darius I and his son Xerxes tried to conquer mainland Greece. In 480 B.C. Athens and Sparta combined to defeat the Persians in a battle that affected the course of world history.

During the 400s B.C. attempts to unify the Greek city-states failed. In fact, in 431 B.C. Sparta led other city-states in battle against Athens in the devastating Peloponnesian War. After a generation of fighting, Athens surrendered in 404 B.C. At the same time, however, Greek culture reached new heights. It was a period so magnificent that it is often called Greece's golden age. During these years Greek culture spread through trade and colonization.

The golden age. Greek art of the golden age reflected the way in which Greeks viewed themselves and the world. Their pride is shown in impressive buildings such as the Parthenon. Some of history's best sculptors lived during Greece's golden age. These include Myron, who created the famous *The Discus Thrower*. Greek vase paintings illustrated everyday life as well as myths.

Even before the golden age, Greek thinkers tried to find logical explanations for natural events. In the 500s B.C. the philosopher Pythagoras wrote that everything could be explained through numbers and the relationships between them. Hippocrates taught that disease

Construction of the Parthenon began in 447 B.C. and was completed about 15 years later.

comes from natural causes, not as punishment from the gods. Today medical doctors still take the Hippocratic oath, part of which follows.

 History Makers Speak **❝I swear . . . I will use treatment to help the sick according to my ability and judgment, but never with a view to injury and wrongdoing. . . . And whatsoever I shall see or hear in the course of my profession . . . I will never divulge [reveal], holding such things to be holy secrets. . . .❞**

from the Hippocratic oath

Analyzing Primary Sources

Evaluating Do you think the Hippocratic oath should still apply today?

During the golden age, Greek philosophers focused on the human mind. **Socrates** established a way of learning through questioning that we now call the Socratic method. Plato and Aristotle, philosophers who followed Socrates, expanded on his method of logical reasoning.

Alexander the Great. In the 300s the unification of the Greek city-states was finally completed. Following this, a Greek empire was established by one of the greatest military leaders in world history, **Alexander the Great.** By 331 B.C. Alexander had conquered Asia Minor, Syria, Egypt, Mesopotamia, and the rest of the Persian Empire. Under his leadership Macedonians, Greeks, and Persians often worked together to govern the empire. This enabled Alexander to rule more efficiently. It also helped to blend together the different cultures and peoples of the sprawling empire.

Alexander died at the age of 32. However, the empire he had founded would spread Greek ideas to many parts of the world. A new civilization, often called Hellenistic (meaning "Greek-like"), developed in those areas ruled by Alexander and the rulers after him.

After Alexander's death, his generals murdered his family and divided his empire among themselves. Even so, Hellenistic culture continued to spread through trade. Greek-speaking scholars in many lands continued to exchange ideas. New ideas developed in religion, philosophy, medicine, mathematics, and science.

This gold crown in the form of a wreath was discovered in Macedon and may have been worn by Alexander the Great.

✔ **READING CHECK: Summarizing** What were the major achievements of Greek civilization, and how did Hellenistic culture spread?

The Roman World

Hellenistic culture also spread in the western Mediterranean. Here it greatly influenced a new power on the Italian peninsula, the city of Rome.

The Roman Republic and Empire. In ancient times Latin villages along the Tiber River eventually united to form the city-state of Rome. In 509 B.C. the Roman aristocracy set up a **republic,** a form of government in which voters elect their leaders. By about 265 B.C. the Roman Republic controlled all of southern Italy.

Rome established colonies around the Mediterranean world. However, this expansion—and a growing number of poor city people—weakened Roman government and society. By 133 B.C. the Roman Republic faced serious problems. In 44 B.C. **Julius Caesar** became dictator for life, but his enemies stabbed him to death.

Julius Caesar is shown here with the laurel wreath traditionally awarded to triumphant Roman leaders.

After Caesar's death the Roman world divided into west and east. In 31 B.C. the western ruler, Octavian, defeated the eastern ruler, Marc Antony. In 27 B.C. Octavian became known as **Augustus,** or "the revered one." Historians mark Augustus's rule as the end of the republic and the beginning of the Roman Empire.

Augustus and his successors established Roman power throughout the Mediterranean world. Imperial rule extended from Spain in the west to Syria in the east, and from Egypt and the Sahara in the south to the Rhine and Danube Rivers in the north. Even the remote island of Britain was part of the empire. This period became known as the Pax Romana, or Roman Peace. Peace and economic prosperity lasted for more than 200 years. The Pax Romana came at a price, however. The political system that Augustus and his successors created greatly reduced the traditional powers of the Roman Senate, the assemblies, and the magistrates. Political power was centralized in the hands of the emperor. As a result, there was always the danger that an emperor would abuse his vast powers.

A great difference in wealth existed between the rich and the poor in Rome. However, the government did give poor residents free grain and entertainment. Romans greatly enjoyed theater and sports such as chariot racing. Gladiator combats between humans and beasts were popular in the Colosseum, Rome's great amphitheater. Roman engineers surpassed all others. They constructed magnificent roads, bridges, aqueducts, amphitheaters, and public buildings.

CONNECTING TO
Science and Technology

The Roman Aqueducts

The Roman aqueduct system carried water from the mountains to the city, often by aboveground channels. These channels occasionally ran over valleys on stone arches. Other parts of the aqueduct system were made of underground stone or terra-cotta pipes. Waterproof cement lined the pipes to stop leaks. The Romans carefully sloped the aqueduct system to allow gravity to move water along its path. An aqueduct not only carried water, it also purified it. Reservoirs were constructed along the aqueduct course. Sediment carried in the water was deposited in these reservoirs.

Understanding Science and Technology

How does the structure of the aqueduct system enable gravity to cause water to flow?

Many Roman aqueducts contained filtering systems. Water flowed through the filter's upper chambers. Dirt and sediment dropped into lower chambers, which were periodically cleaned.

The rise of Christianity. One of the world's major religions, Christianity, originated during the empire. The followers of a Jewish teacher, **Jesus** of Nazareth, founded Christianity. Jesus taught that people must love God above all else, and that they must love others as they love themselves. Jewish religious leaders opposed Jesus, and the Romans put him to death by crucifixion. Jesus' followers believed he rose from the dead and ascended into heaven. They believed his resurrection proved he was the Messiah, the savior of mankind sent by God.

Within 400 years Christianity spread throughout the vast Roman Empire. The religion's appeal was strengthened, in part, by the increasing violence and unrest that threatened the empire in the years following the Pax Romana. Many people turned to Christianity for hope in the face of growing instability. By the A.D. 300s the Christian church had become a powerful spiritual force within the empire, and in A.D. 391 it was named as Rome's official religion. Gradually Christianity developed a church organization. A bishop headed the church in each city. Over time, the bishop of Rome took the title **pope,** Latin for "father." The pope became head of the entire church.

The Spread of Christianity, A.D. 300–A.D. 600

Interpreting Maps Christianity spread throughout the Roman Empire.

■ **Skills Assessment: 1. Places and Regions** Around which physical features did the church establish the five Christian cities of Rome, Constantinople, Alexandria, Antioch, and Jerusalem? **2. Evaluating** Why might this have been so?

Shown here are the ruins of the Forum, which served as the center of government business and civic life in Rome.

The fall of the Western Roman Empire. During most of the A.D. 200s, the empire struggled with civil wars and barbarian invasions. Between A.D. 235 and A.D. 284, no less than 18 men claimed the title of emperor. It cost a lot of money to defend the frontiers. With the end of expansion, wealth coming into the empire began to decline, leading to a shortage of money. Economic problems coupled with invasions from outsiders made daily life in the empire very difficult.

Reforms by the emperors Diocletian and Constantine postponed the final fall of the empire for another 200 years. After Constantine's death, however, it permanently divided into eastern and western empires. The eastern empire emerged much stronger than the western empire.

Invaders, especially the German tribes including the Goths, Vandals, and Franks, took advantage of the weaknesses in the west to conquer Roman lands. The western empire finally fell apart in A.D. 476. In that year, the last Roman emperor was defeated and killed by invading Germans. The eastern empire, usually called the Byzantine Empire, continued to exist for nearly another thousand years.

✔ **READING CHECK: Identifying Cause and Effect** How was the Roman Empire established, and why did it end?

SECTION 3 REVIEW

1. **Define** and explain the significance:
   direct democracy
   republic
   pope

2. **Identify** and explain the significance:
   Homer
   Socrates
   Alexander the Great
   Julius Caesar
   Augustus (Octavian)
   Jesus

3. **Identifying Cause and Effect** Copy the graphic organizer below. Use it to show how the government of Rome changed.

   Government of Rome, republic to empire

4. **Finding the Main Idea**
   a. How did the government of Greece change over time?
   b. In what ways did the rise and fall of Julius Caesar represent a turning point in the history of Rome?
   c. What were Jesus's teachings and how did they affect the Roman Empire?

5. **Writing and Critical Thinking**
   Summarizing What were the achievements of Greek civilization?
   Consider:
   • Greek government
   • the arts
   • science
   • medicine
   • architecture

Homework Practice Online

keyword: SH3 HPP

READ TO DISCOVER
1 What factors affected the development of kingdoms in sub-Saharan Africa, and where did civilizations develop?
2 What were the most important civilizations to the Americas, and what were some of their achievements?

DEFINE
adobe

IDENTIFY
King 'Ēzānā
Swahili
Mansa Mūsā
Hopewell
Maya
Aztec
Inca

WHY IT MATTERS TODAY

Sites of ancient American civilizations are popular destinations for many tourists today. Use CNN Student News.com or other **current event** sources to find out which Maya and Inca ruins are the most popular tourist destinations. Record your findings in your journal.

Africa and the Americas

The Main Idea
Complex civilizations flourished in Africa and the Americas between the A.D. 500s and 1500s.

The Story Continues *African American poet Countee Cullen once asked, "What is Africa to me?" He was writing about his lost African heritage, but the question could be asked by almost anyone in the world today. Most scientists believe human life began in Africa. Some even call it the Mother of Civilization. Within Africa's history is the story of a great continent that housed a wealth of cultures.*

Africa

In early sub-Saharan Africa, people had very little contact with other regions of the world. Scholars believe that most Africans lived in small, independent villages. They worked as farmers, herders, or fishers. Family relationships formed the ties that held societies together. Religion was an important part of life in many African societies, and elders usually had authority over the village. Life in African villages was closely tied to the agricultural cycles of planting and harvesting. During the rise and fall of many kingdoms, the village survived as the basic unit of society and the economy.

African city-states. Some African peoples came together to create small city-states, kingdoms, and even empires. Along the Nile River, south of the major centers of ancient Egypt, arose a powerful kingdom known as Kush. At first Kush maintained close cultural contact and economic ties with Egypt. Between about 1100 B.C. and about 1000 B.C., however, Kush started to become more independent.

When the Assyrians invaded in 671 B.C., the kingdom of Aksum arose in the Ethiopian Highlands. For many years it competed with Kush for control of trade in the area. Finally in about A.D. 330, **King 'Ēzānā** of Aksum conquered Kush. During his reign 'Ēzānā converted to Christianity. As a result, Christianity became very influential in the region.

The Lion Temple of ancient Kush reflects the once powerful kingdom's high level of cultural development.

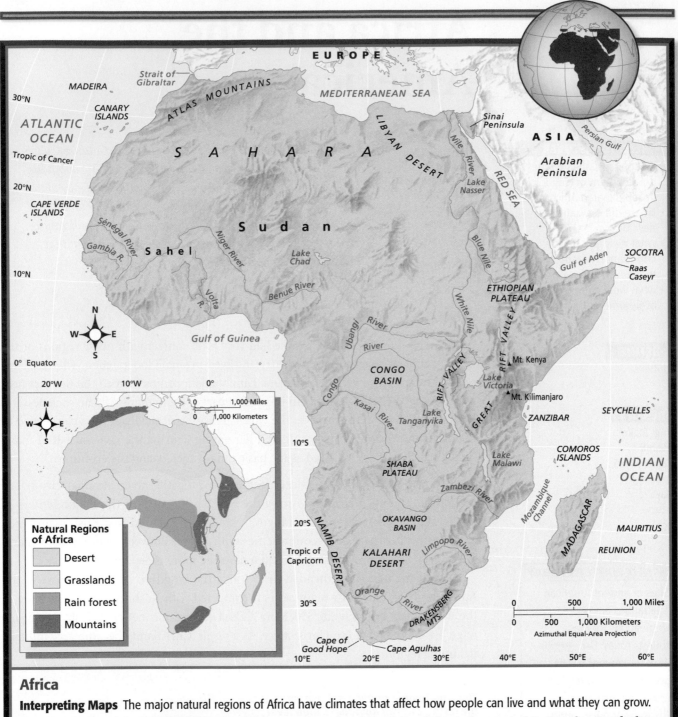

Africa

Interpreting Maps The major natural regions of Africa have climates that affect how people can live and what they can grow.

■ **Skills Assessment: 1. The World in Spatial Terms** Where does Africa lie in relation to the equator? **2. Drawing Conclusions** How might its position relative to the equator affect Africa's climate?

No large kingdoms emerged on the coast of East Africa. Instead a series of city-states arose along the African coasts of the Red Sea and the Indian Ocean. These city-states depended on coastal trade for their economic development. The spread of Islam during the A.D. 700s and after helped to promote the city-states' development by creating good conditions for trade. Commercial opportunities attracted Muslim merchants from Arabia and Persia to the East African coast. A new society that merged African, Arabic, and Persian elements began to appear. The language it produced, **Swahili,** shows the influence of these cultural groups.

Empires in West Africa. In West Africa, between Lake Chad and the Atlantic Ocean, the empires of Ghana, Mali, and Songhai flourished. Mali reached its peak in the early 1300s under the ruler **Mansa Mūsā**. A famous Muslim traveler of the 1300s, Ibn Battūtah, described the kingdom of Mali.

History Makers Speak

❝They [the people of Mali] are seldom unjust and have a greater abhorrence [dislike] of injustice than any other people. . . . There is complete security in their country. Neither traveler nor inhabitant in it has anything to fear from robbers or men of violence.❞

Ibn Battūtah, quoted in *The Horizon History of Africa,* edited by Alvin Josephy, Jr.

Analyzing Primary Sources

Identifying a Point of View
What opinion did Ibn Battūtah have of Mali society?

The wealth and strength of these West African kingdoms depended on control of the trade routes across the Sahara desert. At the desert's edge, traders exchanged gold from mines south of the desert region for salt, which was mined in the Sahara itself.

✔ **READING CHECK: Analyzing Information** What role did trade play in sub-Saharan Africa?

The Americas

Scientists believe the first Americans were nomadic hunters from Asia who crossed a land bridge over what is now the Bering Strait. The first people in the Americas lived by hunting and gathering. Gradually a new way of life came about as these groups began to farm.

The earliest Americans. In what is now the United States and Canada, many different cultures thrived. Each depended on the geography of the region in which the people lived. In the dry, desert-like conditions of the Southwest, farmers lived in permanent settlements. They built their houses out of **adobe,** a sun-dried brick. On the northwest coast of North America, on the other hand, people lived by fishing. They carved great totem poles with their family histories out of the enormous trees that forested the region. On the Great Plains, tribal people survived by hunting buffalo. More complex cultures developed in the Eastern Woodlands. The **Hopewell** culture, for example, left many mounds that scholars believe are burial sites and the foundations of buildings.

The empires of Mexico and Peru. Other early cultures in America included the Olmec in Mexico and the **Maya** in the Yucatan Peninsula. The Maya were farmers who were also skilled architects and engineers. They built steep, pyramid-shaped temples to their gods and invented the only writing system in the Americas. For reasons still unknown, the Maya suddenly left their ceremonial centers in A.D. 900.

Meanwhile, farther north, other civilizations had developed in central Mexico. In about A.D. 800 a people called the Toltec invaded central Mexico from the north. Ruled by a military class, the Toltec soon spread their culture as far south as the Yucatan. The **Aztec,** also invaders from the north, took control of the region around A.D. 1200. They developed a calendar and used mathematics. To sustain their gods, the Aztec practiced human sacrifice.

The ancient Maya became very advanced in the science of astronomy. This Maya observatory is located in Chichén Itzá on the Yucatán Peninsula.

Culture areas:
- Arctic
- Subarctic
- Pacific Coast
- Plateau
- Great Plains
- Eastern Woodlands
- Great Basin
- California
- Southwest
- Southeast

0 500 1,000 Miles
0 500 1,000 Kilometers
Azimuthal Equal-Area Projection

Peoples of North America, 2500 B.C.–A.D. 1500

Interpreting Maps Various groups of people settled across the North American continent, adapting to geographic conditions from the Arctic to the Southwest.

■ **Skills Assessment: Places and Regions** Which native North American cultural groups are enclosed on all sides by land?

About the same time that Aztec civilization was at its height, another civilization was expanding in the Andes Mountains of South America. These people—the **Inca**—based their religion on worship of the sun and moon. By the late 1400s the Inca Empire covered the present-day nations of Peru, Ecuador, Bolivia, and Chile. The Inca built fortresses and irrigation systems. They also laid roads, many of them paved. The rulers of the empire prevented starvation by keeping storehouses and giving out food when crops failed. After conquering their neighbors, the Inca tried to wipe out cultural differences in their empire. They created an educational system that taught the imperial language, Inca religion, and history. The Inca did not have a writing system, but they kept records using a quipu, a knotted string that aids memory. The Inca were also advanced in the practice of medicine, using anesthetic and even performing operations on the brain.

✔ **READING CHECK: Supporting a Point of View** List some evidence that could be used to support the idea that cultures in the Americas developed civilizations.

INTERPRETING THE VISUAL RECORD

Ancient apartments This group of dwellings is only one of the many prehistoric ruins found at Mesa Verde National Park in southwestern Colorado. *Why do you think people might have built their houses under a cliff such as this one?*

SECTION 4 REVIEW

1. **Define** and explain the significance:
   adobe

2. **Identify** and explain the significance:
   King 'Ēzānā
   Swahili
   Mansa Mūsā
   Hopewell
   Maya
   Aztec
   Inca

Homework Practice Online
keyword: SH3 HPP

3. **Categorizing** Copy the chart below. Use it to identify some achievements of early cultures in the Americas.

   Economy

   Early American cultures

   Engineering/construction   Science/mathematics

4. **Finding the Main Idea**

   a. What was daily life like in sub-Saharan Africa?

   b. How did geography influence the development of cultures in Africa and the Americas?

5. **Writing and Critical Thinking**

   Comparing and Contrasting Write an essay explaining how sub-Saharan African civilizations were both similar to and different from one another.
   Consider:
   • Nile—Kush, Aksum
   • east coast—city-states
   • West Africa—Ghana, Mali, Songhai

Review

Creating a Time Line

Copy the time line below onto a sheet of paper. Complete the time line by filling in the events, individuals, and dates from the chapter that you think were significant. Pick three events and explain why you think they were significant.

| 4500 B.C. | 1500 B.C. |
| 3000 B.C. | A.D. 1500 |

Writing a Summary

Using standard grammar, spelling, sentence structure, and punctuation, write an overview of the chapter.

Identifying People and Ideas

Identify the following terms or individuals and explain their significance:

1. Hammurabi
2. ethical monotheism
3. Confucius
4. direct democracy
5. Alexander the Great
6. republic
7. Julius Caesar
8. Swahili
9. adobe
10. Maya

Understanding Main Ideas

Section 1 *(pp. 2–6)*
The First Civilizations

1. What are the characteristics of a civilization?
2. Where did the first civilizations occur?

Section 2 *(pp. 7–10)*
Ancient India and China

3. What major religions developed in ancient India, and what are their beliefs?
4. What are some of the accomplishments of the Qin and Han dynasties?

Section 3 *(pp. 11–16)*
Civilizations of the Mediterranean World

5. How did Greek civilization spread to other regions?
6. How did the Roman Republic become the Roman Empire?

Section 4 *(pp. 17–21)*
Africa and the Americas

7. How did kingdoms in sub-Saharan Africa develop?
8. What were some of the achievements of early American cultures?

Reviewing Themes

1. **Government** Why is government important for the development of civilization?
2. **Global Relations** How does trade affect global relations?
3. **Culture** Give three examples showing how a stable government produces cultural growth.

Thinking Critically

1. **Evaluating** What major advances were made by the people of the earliest civilizations?
2. **Sequencing** Describe the development of democracy in ancient Greece.
3. **Drawing Conclusions** What effect did trade have on early cultures?
4. **Categorizing** How did different types of cultures develop in different parts of Africa?

Writing About History

Analyzing Information Choose one of the civilizations discussed in this chapter. Then write a brief paper that discusses the nature of the civilization and its contributions to world culture. Use the following diagram to organize your thoughts before you begin writing.

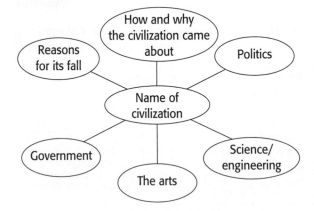

Interpreting a Graph

Study the graph below. Then use the information on the graph to help you answer the questions that follow.

Average Maximum Temperatures in African Cities (in Fahrenheit)

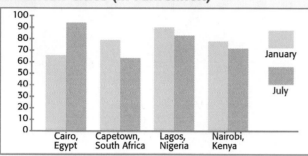

1. Which of the following is a correct general statement about temperatures in African cities?

   a. Lagos has a greater year-round temperature change than Cairo does.

   b. There is less than a 4°F difference between July temperatures in Capetown and Lagos.

   c. The average maximum temperature in Cairo is 93.9°F.

   d. The temperature in Nigeria and Kenya does not change significantly during the year.

2. Why are the temperatures in Capetown higher in January, while in Cairo they are lower in January?

Identifying Values and Opinions

Read the following excerpt from the Greek historian Herodotus, who wrote during the 400s B.C. Then answer the questions.

"As for Libya [Africa], we know that it is washed on all sides by the sea except where it joins Asia, as was first demonstrated, so far as our knowledge goes . . . by a Phoenician crew with orders to sail west-about and return to Egypt and the Mediterranean by way of the Straits of Gibraltar. These men made a statement which I do not myself believe . . . to the effect that as they sailed on a westerly course round the southern end of Libya, they had the [morning] sun on their right . . . ."

3. Which of the following from the excerpt expresses values or opinions held by the author?

   a. "so far as our knowledge goes" and "which I do not myself believe"

   b. "we know that it is washed on all sides by the sea"

   c. "These men made a statement"

   d. "to the effect that as they sailed on a westerly course"

4. Which of the statements in the excerpt are factual? Give reasons for your choices.

Alternative Assessment

Building Your Portfolio

Government

Link to TODAY

One characteristic of civilization is government. From the earliest civilizations, the concept of government has evolved. Compile descriptions of the various types of government throughout the ancient world and research whether these types can still be found today, and if so, where. Make a chart showing your findings.

internet connect

Internet Activity: go.hrw.com
KEYWORD: SH3 WHP

Choose a topic on the Ancient World to:

• explore Egyptian pyramids and create a brochure.

• create a model or structure that employs Roman architectural, artistic, or decorative styles.

• learn Maya number glyphs and calculate your birthday.

The World in Transition

395–1589

Main Events

- The rise of the Byzantine Empire
- The development of Islamic religion and culture
- The development of Asian civilizations
- The beginning of the Middle Ages
- The cultural conflict of the Crusades

Main Ideas

- What was the Byzantine Empire?
- What were some of the characteristics of the Islamic world?
- What effect did the Mongol Empire have on the civilizations of Eastern Asia?
- What was life like in the Middle Ages? How did the Crusades change medieval culture?

Islamic engraved globe, c. 1067

This painting from the period of China's Sung dynasty (c. 1000) shows scholars organizing literature.

25

CROSS-CULTURAL CONNECTIONS

Focus On: Culture

Main Idea **What is culture?** Many different elements make up a society's culture including art, music, literature, religious beliefs, and institutions of government and education. No two cultures are exactly alike—each develops unique traditions and beliefs. The societies in this unit all developed unique cultural traits that still define many groups descended from them today.

Japan

Byzantine Empire and Russia

Islamic Empire

Medieval Europe

395   432   552   570   1250   1573   1500   1589

Byzantine Empire and Russia, 395–1589

Icons Beginning in the 500s, icons, or holy images, played an important role in public and private religious life in the Byzantine Empire. Enemies saw icons as a form of idol worship. For believers, however, these images were a way to get close to God. Most icons were painted on wood, but some were also made of gold or ivory. Icons came in all sizes, from large screens that decorated churches to small images that could be carried in a pocket. Most homes had at least one icon, and they were displayed during important public ceremonies. In 726 Emperor Leo III outlawed the use of icons. However, they remained an important part of Byzantine culture. This icon showing Jesus gazing at the viewer reflects the typical Byzantine style of iconographic religious art.

Calligraphy In Islamic culture, calligraphy is considered a great art form. This style of fine handwriting first developed in Arabic culture in the 500s, before the rise of Islam. Later, Islamic scribes, or writers, made copies of the Qur'an with calligraphy. Scribes also used calligraphy in government documents, books, and inscriptions for buildings, palaces, and tombs. Calligraphers studied with a master for many years to learn their skill, usually specializing in two or three of the six classic styles. One style included beautiful floral designs and geometric patterns. In another technique, scribes worked words into the shapes of animals or objects. Whatever the form, calligraphy was the most highly valued art form in the Islamic world. The document pictured here is a copy of the Qur'an created in the 1300s.

Calligraphers often kept their valuable pens and inks in special boxes. In some instances, scribes even had their pens and inks buried with them.

Islamic Empire, 570–1250

Tea Ceremonies Tea began its important role in Japanese culture in the 1100s, when Buddhist priests brought back tea leaves from China. During the Kamakura period (1192–1600), monks first practiced tea drinking as a way to stay awake during long meditations. Later, other members of society, such as shoguns, samurai, and merchants, began drinking tea. In the late 1500s a formal tea tradition developed in Japan. During these tea ceremonies, people gathered in a special room isolated from the rest of the house. Sometimes while drinking their tea, they would listen to poetry or quietly think about a piece of art. Tea ceremonies offered the Japanese a means of spiritual reflection and a way to leave behind the world's worries.

Japan, 552–1573

Medieval Europe, 432–1500

Cathedrals During the Middle Ages cathedrals were the ultimate architectural expression of Christian faith in Europe. Between the 1100s and 1500s, this new church architecture created high ceilings and beautiful stained glass windows that provided more space and light than older churches. Intricate carvings inside and outside the cathedrals completed these inspiring works of art. Building cathedrals required the help of the entire community. Wealthy community members donated money. Artisans created intricate carvings and sculpture, and peasants and laborers provided the backbreaking work to build the structure. Cathedrals often took more than a century to complete. Inside the great cathedrals, such as the one shown here, the faithful could not help but feel they were closer to heaven.

Sculptors often carved horrible-looking creatures known as gargoyles on cathedrals with the belief that they would help scare away demons.

Why It Matters Today

Cultural differences often led to conflict during the Middle Ages. Yet contact between cultures also increased knowledge and led to new developments. Cultural exchange continues to take place today. **What examples of beneficial cultural exchanges do you see in the world today? What are some examples of cultural conflict?**

CHAPTER
1

A.D. 395–A.D. 1589

The Byzantine Empire and Russia

A.D. 395
Global Events
The Roman Empire splits into the Eastern Roman Empire and the Western Roman Empire.

A.D. 535
Politics
Belisarius occupies the Ostrogoth kingdom in Italy.

A.D. 600
The Arts
Coptic art—a combination of Byzantine, Egyptian, Arab, and Greek styles—has developed.

A.D. 900
Science and Technology
Vikings have highly developed shipbuilding.

C. A.D. 900s
Business and Finance
The Italian cities of Venice and Genoa begin to develop as maritime trading powers.

A.D. 300   **A.D. 550**   **A.D. 800**

A.D. 425
Politics
Germanic tribes settle in western Roman provinces.

A.D. 553 Business and Finance
The Byzantine Empire attempts to monopolize the silk industry.

A.D. 542
Daily Life
Rats from Egypt bring the plague to Constantinople.

Early Christian/Byzantine wall mosaic

Constantinople, C. A.D. 950

Build on What You Know

Native peoples in the Americas lived successfully off the land by hunting, gathering, and farming. Their cultures thrived for hundreds of years. Eventually some of these cultures became civilizations, some of which made great advances. Some civilizations acquired more land and wealth, often by invading neighboring peoples. In Europe the Roman Empire had suffered from invasions by Germanic peoples. Part of the empire remained intact, however, and began to grow again. In this chapter, you will learn about Byzantine and Russian civilizations and how they gained their power.

Mongol warriors in battle

Cross belonging to Emperor Justinian, c. A.D. 550

A.D. 911
Business and Finance
Kiev and Constantinople agree to commercial treaties.

C. A.D. 988
Daily Life
Vladimir of Kiev marries the sister of Byzantine Emperor Basil II.

A.D. 1054
Daily Life
The Christian church splits into two parts.

A.D. 1206
Global Events
Genghis Khan becomes chief prince of the Mongols.

A.D. 1390
Global Events
The Turks conquer all of Asia Minor except Constantinople.

A.D. 1453
Global Events
Constantinople falls to the Ottomans.

A.D. 1472
Global Events
Ivan III of Moscow marries Sophia, niece of the last Byzantine emperor.

A.D. 1050 | **A.D. 1300** | **A.D. 1550**

A.D. 1020
Politics
Yaroslav the Wise builds churches.

A.D. 941
Science and Technology
The Byzantines use "Greek fire" against a Rus fleet in the Black Sea.

C. A.D. 1242
Global Events
Batu Khan and the Mongol "Golden Horde" occupy the lower Volga River.

A.D. 1230
Daily Life
Crusaders bring leprosy to Europe.

A.D. 1204
Politics
Crusaders capture Constantinople.

A.D. 1509
Daily Life
An earthquake nearly destroys Constantinople.

A.D. 1494
Business and Finance
Grand Prince Ivan III of Moscow closes the Hanseatic League's trading office in Novgorod.

Byzantine containers for "Greek fire," c. A.D. 1450

What's Your Opinion?

Themes Journal *Do you **agree** or **disagree** with the following statements? Support your point of view in your journal.*

Government Governments are most successful when they have a powerful leader.

Geography Civilizations develop successfully only if the patterns of their historic settlement follow bodies of water.

Global Relations Rulers expect the people they govern to always think and act as they do.

SECTION 1

READ TO DISCOVER

❶ What factors contributed to the growth and strength of the Byzantine Empire?

❷ How did the Christian church come to be divided?

❸ What cultural contributions did the Byzantines make?

❹ What factors contributed to the downfall of the Byzantine Empire?

DEFINE

dowry
icon
iconoclasts
heresy
excommunication
mosaic

IDENTIFY

Justinian
Justinian Code
Theodora
Belisarius
"Greek fire"
Iconoclastic Controversy
Cyril and Methodius
Hagia Sophia
Ottoman Turks

▶ WHY IT MATTERS TODAY

The city of Istanbul in Turkey was once the ancient city of Constantinople. Use or other **current event** sources to explore what life today is like in Istanbul. Record your findings in your journal.

CNN Student News.com

The Byzantine Empire

The Main Idea
The Eastern Roman Empire lived on in the Byzantine Empire, which was centered around Constantinople.

The Story Continues *The "fall" of the Roman Empire was really only half a fall. Although Germanic tribes defeated the Western Roman Empire in the A.D. 400s and 500s, the Eastern Roman Empire successfully fought off the invaders. Also called the Byzantine Empire, it included Greece, Asia Minor, Syria, Egypt, and other areas. Through the Byzantines the glory of the Roman Empire lived on.*

The Growth of the Byzantine Empire

Many leaders of the Byzantine Empire hoped to revive the glory and power of the Roman Empire. The emperor **Justinian,** who ruled from A.D. 527 to A.D. 565, led the Byzantines in this revival. Justinian's accomplishments made this one of the greatest periods in Byzantine history.

The Justinian Code. One of the Byzantines' greatest contributions to civilization was the preservation of Roman law. In about A.D. 528 Justinian ordered his scholars to collect the laws of the Roman Empire. This collection, known as the **Justinian Code,** was organized into four parts. The first part, the *Code,* contained useful Roman laws. The second part, the *Digest,* summarized Roman legal opinions. The *Institutes* was a guide for law students. The last part was the *Novellae,* which contained laws passed after A.D. 534.

The Justinian Code formed the basis of Byzantine law. It covered such areas as crime, marriage, property, and slavery. By the A.D. 1100s, the Justinian Code was also being used in western Europe. It provided a framework for many European legal systems. The Code preserved the Roman idea that people should be ruled by laws rather than by the whims of leaders. This is the basis of English civil law, one of the major legal systems in the world today.

Able advisers. Justinian chose the people around him wisely. One of his advisers was his wife, **Theodora.** With Theodora's urging, Justinian changed Byzantine law to affect the status of women. He altered divorce laws to give greater benefit to women. He also allowed Christian women to own property equal to the value of their dowry. A **dowry** meant the money or goods a wife brought to a husband at marriage.

INTERPRETING THE VISUAL RECORD

Byzantine goldwork This golden Byzantine goblet from the A.D. 700s is decorated with Roman figures. *What do the relief figures that adorn this goblet suggest about the strength of the Roman tradition in the Byzantine Empire?*

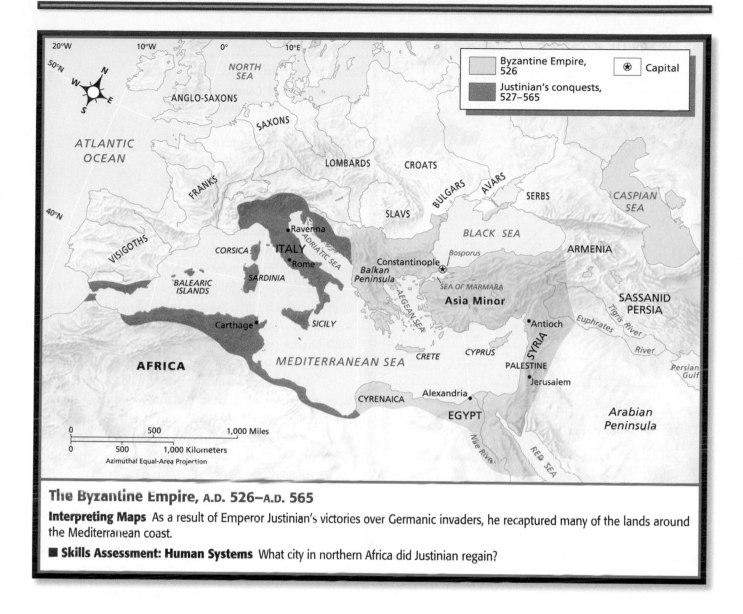

The Byzantine Empire, A.D. 526–A.D. 565

Interpreting Maps As a result of Emperor Justinian's victories over Germanic invaders, he recaptured many of the lands around the Mediterranean coast.

■ **Skills Assessment: Human Systems** What city in northern Africa did Justinian regain?

In A.D. 532 a rebellion called the Nika Revolt threatened to overthrow Justinian. During the attack Justinian wanted to flee Constantinople. Theodora talked him into staying and fighting. In a fierce battle Justinian's troops defeated the rebels.

Justinian wisely made **Belisarius** (bel·uh·SAR·ee·uhs) general of the army. An experienced commander, Belisarius also led the troops that crushed the Nika Revolt. He won former Roman lands back from the Germanic tribes. Thus during Justinian's reign the Byzantine Empire reached its greatest size.

✔ **READING CHECK: Identifying Cause and Effect** What effects did the political and legal ideas in Justinian's Code have on Byzantine and other societies?

Strengths of the Empire

An all-powerful emperor and a strong central government ruled the empire. Government officials made sure the empire ran smoothly. These officials were skilled, efficient, and well paid. The Byzantines were clever diplomats. For example, emperors created alliances through marriage with foreign powers.

Holt Researcher

go.hrw.com
KEYWORD: Holt Researcher
FreeFind: Justinian
          Theodora
After reading more about Justinian and Theodora on the Holt Researcher, create a chart listing the ways in which they affected future generations of people.

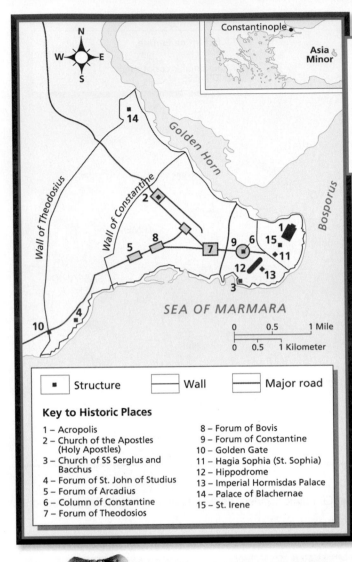

Constantinople, c. A.D. 600

Interpreting Maps Constantinople's location on vital trade routes made it a great commercial center.

■ **Skills Assessment: Human Systems** What types of public buildings flourished in Constantinople?

Structure · | Wall | Major road

Key to Historic Places

1 – Acropolis
2 – Church of the Apostles (Holy Apostles)
3 – Church of SS Serglus and Bacchus
4 – Forum of St. John of Studius
5 – Forum of Arcadius
6 – Column of Constantine
7 – Forum of Theodosios
8 – Forum of Bovis
9 – Forum of Constantine
10 – Golden Gate
11 – Hagia Sophia (St. Sophia)
12 – Hippodrome
13 – Imperial Hormisdas Palace
14 – Palace of Blachernae
15 – St. Irene

The Byzantine Empire had effective forces to protect its frontiers. Military forces were well trained, and weapons and armor were well designed.

During the A.D. 500s the Byzantines built a strong navy, in which ships were equipped with a chemical weapon known as **"Greek fire."** When sprayed or thrown onto enemy ships, the liquid burst into flames, setting them on fire.

The East had always been the richest part of the Roman Empire. At the heart of this wealth lay Constantinople. This grand city was strategically located where Europe meets Asia. Constantinople looked over the Bosporus Strait. This allowed the Byzantines to control the sea trade routes between Asia and Europe.

Goods from as far away as Scandinavia and China came into Constantinople. Imperial tax policies raised huge government revenues. The government used this income to pay soldiers and government officials. The emperor also paid for large, magnificent public buildings with these taxes.

✔ **READING CHECK: Making Generalizations** What kind of government did the Byzantine Empire have?

The Christian Church

The Christian church was an important part of life in the Byzantine Empire. However, church leaders in the West and East had different ideas about church practices. These differences led to a final division in the Christian church.

The pope was the most powerful leader of the Christian church in the West. The Byzantines, however, did not recognize the pope's authority. In the East the patriarch of Constantinople was the most powerful church leader.

Byzantines differed from the Western church on many issues. They also disagreed among themselves on issues of religious practice and belief within the Byzantine Church. One important debate concerned the role of icons. An **icon** is a holy picture of Jesus, the Virgin Mary, or the saints. Many Byzantines kept icons in their homes and venerated, or honored, them in churches. However, some Byzantines were iconoclasts. **Iconoclasts** believed that having icons in church was the same as worshipping idols. They felt this was wrong.

HISTORY MAKER

Empress Theodora
(c. A.D. 500–A.D. 548)

Theodora influenced Justinian to improve the status of women in society. She worked to change many laws so as to protect women. She donated money to churches and orphanages. **How did Theodora try to improve the lives of women?**

Views of Justinian and Theodora

Justinian and Theodora did many great things for the Byzantine Empire. Yet at times they could be harsh with their enemies. Their supporters viewed them as wise rulers protecting the empire. Their enemies viewed them as tyrants who forced their beliefs on others. Interpreting different aspects of rulers can be difficult for historians. In judging the usefulness of sources, historians must recognize the biases held by the author of the source. In the simplest sense, bias means the prejudice, or slanted viewpoint, a speaker or writer holds. Pre-existing biases often shape the ways observers describe historical events, causing them to leave out important facts or make statements without much supporting evidence. Historians themselves can even present a biased view of events.

Justinian (fifth from right) and his attendants

A Historian's View:

Procopius (pruh·кон·pee·uhs) was a Byzantine historian who lived during the reign of Justinian. In *The Secret History* he described the rule of Justinian and Theodora.

"... they were a pair of blood-thirsty demons.... For they plotted together to find the easiest and swiftest means of destroying all races of men and all their works ... [Justinian] would order tens of thousands of quite innocent persons to be put to death, cities to be razed to the ground, and all their possessions to be confiscated for the Treasury.... His ambition being to force everybody into one form of Christian belief he wantonly destroyed everyone who would not conform, and that while keeping up a pretense of piety. For he did not regard it as murder, so long as those who died did not happen to share his beliefs."

Theodora (third from right) and her attendants

Skills Reminder

Bias in historical sources may be either positive or negative. In either case, bias results in distortions that may mislead observers who do not carefully evaluate the source. Bias may cause observers to draw inaccurate conclusions or to misunderstand descriptions and outcomes of historical events. To identify bias, look for clues. What words or phrases convey a positive or negative meaning? Look at the evidence. Decide whether you agree or disagree with the attitude, based on the evidence presented. Analyze what information has been left out by the author. Assess how this changes the conclusions that may be drawn based on the source's description or analysis.

Skills Practice

1 How did Procopius feel about the rule of Justinian and Theodora? What words and phrases indicate this?

2 How does Procopius's description of Justinian's behavior support the same outlook?

3 What information about Justinian and Theodora does Procopius leave out? How might this change the conclusions the reader draws about their reign?

4 Read an article from a newspaper, magazine, or the Internet about a recent event and try to identify the author's bias. If possible, read another source's coverage of the same event. Do both authors have a similar or different bias?

Major Disagreements Between the Roman Catholic and Eastern Orthodox Churches		
	Roman Catholic	**Eastern Orthodox**
Clergy	No married priests allowed	Married priests allowed
Icons	Veneration accepted	Veneration initially rejected, later accepted
Leadership	Roman pope was supreme church authority	Rejected supremacy of Roman pope over local leaders
Trinity	Accepted the view that the Holy Spirit combines both Father and Son	Maintained supremacy of the Father in the Trinity

This debate between the opponents and defenders of icons is called the **Iconoclastic Controversy.** In A.D. 726 Emperor Leo III, an iconoclast, ordered the destruction of icons. However, many people refused to give up their icons. In the West, church leaders also condemned the use of icons. Many people in western Europe, however, could not read or write. Icons portrayed images and symbols that helped them to learn about Christianity.

In A.D. 787 the pope in Rome called bishops together to discuss the Iconoclastic Controversy. This council decided that it was a heresy *not* to allow the veneration of icons. A **heresy** is an opinion that conflicts with official church beliefs. The council threatened iconoclasts with **excommunication.** An excommunicated person cannot be a member of the church anymore.

The council's decision caused friction between the pope in Rome and the patriarch in Constantinople. Finally the Christian church split into two churches in 1054. The church in the West became the Roman Catholic Church, with the pope at its head. In the East it became the Eastern Orthodox Church, with the patriarch of Constantinople as leader. The two churches are still separate today. Ironically, the Eastern Church eventually came to accept icons, and they are now recognized as an important part of Eastern Orthodox tradition.

✔ **READING CHECK: Drawing Inferences** How did the council of bishops in Rome feel about Byzantine views of Christianity?

Byzantine Culture

While western Europe struggled to find a new way of life, Constantinople was the center of a great civilization. The Byzantine Empire provided a great service for cultures that followed it. Byzantine scholars produced many original works. In addition, they passed on to future generations the learnings of ancient Greece, Rome, and the East.

The Byzantine Empire also brought Mediterranean culture to lands beyond its borders. For example, the brothers **Cyril** (SIR·uhl) **and Methodius** (muh·THOH·dee·uhs) were Christian missionaries. They tried to teach the Bible to Slavs in central and eastern Europe. The Slavs had no written language, so Cyril and Methodius created an alphabet for them. This alphabet came to be known as Cyrillic (suh·RIL·ik). Many Slavic peoples today use Cyrillic or an alphabet derived from it.

The missionary brothers Cyril and Methodius present a scroll showing the Cyrillic alphabet.

Link to Today Although the Hagia Sophia was built in the A.D. 500s as a Christian church, it was used after 1453 as an Islamic mosque. How does the Hagia Sophia today reflect the history of the Byzantine Empire?

The interior of the Hagia Sophia was dramatically illuminated with natural lighting.

Art. Religion was the main subject of Byzantine art. Murals and icons covered the walls, floors, and ceilings of churches. Floors, walls, and arches glowed with mosaics. A **mosaic** is a picture or design made from small pieces of enamel, glass, or stone. The location of an image indicated its importance. For example, an image of the Father was always found in the dome of the church. To modern eyes Byzantine art may appear stiff or artificial. Byzantine artists did not try to imitate reality. They tried to inspire adoration of the religious figures and help people look toward an afterlife.

Architecture. The Byzantines created great religious architecture. One of the world's great buildings is the church of **Hagia Sophia** (meaning "holy wisdom") in Constantinople. Justinian ordered the building of the Hagia Sophia in A.D. 532. The Hagia Sophia is a huge building, considered by many to be an architectural and engineering wonder. Justinian devoted a great deal of money and energy to its completion, one reason that it was completed in the amazingly short time of about six years.

A huge dome sits on top of the church. The dome is 180 feet high and 108 feet wide. Romans and other peoples had built domes before. However, Byzantine architects were the first to solve the problem of placing a round dome over a rectangular building. The Hagia Sophia was completed in A.D. 537. The Byzantine historian Procopius described what he saw when entering the church:

History Makers Speak **❝The entire ceiling is covered with pure gold, which adds to its beauty. . . . who could tell of the beauty of the columns and marbles with which the church is adorned? One would think that one had come upon a meadow full of flowers in bloom. Whoever enters there to worship perceives at once that it is not by any human strength or skill, but by the favour of God that this work has been perfected; his mind rises sublime to commune with God, feeling that He cannot be far off. . . . ❞**

Procopius, *The Secret History*, translated by G. A. Williamson

Analyzing Primary Sources

Identifying a Point of View
According to Procopius, how would citizens feel upon entering the Hagia Sophia?

✔ **READING CHECK: Supporting a Point of View** What evidence would you give to show that the Byzantines built upon previous cultures and contributed to future cultures?

The Decline of the Empire

After Justinian died in A.D. 565, the Byzantine Empire suffered from many wars and conflicts with outside powers. To the east there was war with the Persians. The Lombards, a Germanic tribe, settled in Italy. The Avars and Slavs invaded the Balkan Peninsula. The Muslim Empire conquered Syria, Palestine, and much of North Africa. By A.D. 650 the Byzantines had lost many lands.

During the A.D. 1000s the Seljuq Turks, a nomadic people from central Asia, captured much of Asia Minor. This region was an important source of food and soldiers for the empire. Next the Turks prepared to attack Constantinople. The Byzantine emperor asked the West to help defend Constantinople. From A.D. 1096 to A.D. 1099 a western European army seized and eventually returned western Asia Minor to the Byzantines. In A.D. 1204, however, Western forces turned against the Byzantine Empire and captured Constantinople.

In A.D. 1261 the Byzantines recaptured Constantinople. The Byzantine Empire lasted for almost 200 more years. However, it never regained its former strength. In the A.D. 1300s a rising Asian power, the **Ottoman Turks,** began to threaten Byzantine territory. By the mid-1300s the Ottomans had begun to move into the Balkans. In A.D. 1361 they took Adrianople, one of the empire's leading cities. With the Ottoman capture of Constantinople in A.D. 1453, the Byzantine Empire finally came to an end.

This painting by an Italian artist dramatizes the Ottoman Turks' conquest of Constantinople in 1453.

✔ **READING CHECK: Identifying Cause and Effect** Why was the Seljuq Turks' invasion of Asia Minor so harmful to the Byzantine Empire?

SECTION 1 REVIEW

1. **Define** and explain the significance:
   dowry
   icon
   iconoclasts
   heresy
   excommunication
   mosaic

2. **Identify** and explain the significance:
   Justinian
   Justinian Code
   Theodora
   Belisarius
   "Greek fire"
   Iconoclastic Controversy
   Cyril and Methodius
   Hagia Sophia
   Ottoman Turks

3. **Comparing and Contrasting** Copy the Venn diagram below. Use it to organize the similarities and differences between the Eastern and Western Christian churches.

Eastern Christian church   Western Christian church

4. **Finding the Main Idea**
   a. What might have happened if Justinian had not survived the Nika Revolt?
   b. How might the Byzantine military have been affected by a bad economy?
   c. What factors contributed to the division of the Christian church?
   d. How did Justinian's interest in Roman law affect European legal systems for years to come?
   e. What events and developments led to the gradual decline of the Byzantine Empire?

5. **Writing and Critical Thinking**
   Categorizing Develop a table in which you classify the advantages and disadvantages of having an all-powerful emperor and a strong, centralized government in the Byzantine Empire.
   Consider:
   • how the Byzantine Empire grew
   • the results of collecting large tax revenues
   • the role of the emperor and the government in the development of the empire's code of law
   • the actions of the emperor and the government to manage the empire and to ensure its security from outside attack

Homework Practice Online
keyword: SH3 HP1

The Rise of Russia

READ TO DISCOVER

1 Why did different peoples settle in eastern Europe?

2 How did Kievan Russia differ from the Byzantine Empire?

DEFINE

steppe
boyars
taiga

IDENTIFY

Rurik
Rus
Yaroslav the Wise
Pravda Russkia
Vladimir I

WHY IT MATTERS TODAY

The economy in Kievan Russia depended largely on agriculture. Use CNNstudentnews.com or other **current event** sources to explore the Russian economy today. Record your findings in your journal.

CNNstudentnews.com

The Main Idea
Kievan Russia established many practices and traditions that defined Russian culture.

The Story Continues *The people who came to rule Russia were first mentioned in historical records in A.D. 860. In that year they launched a fierce surprise attack against the city of Constantinople. "The unexpectedness of the incursion [attack] and its extraordinary speed . . . ," recalled one Byzantine leader, "prove that this blow has been sent from heaven like a thunderbolt." Although the attack was unsuccessful, the Byzantines would not soon forget this fighting force.*

The Setting and People

A large plain stretches across eastern Europe and central Asia. It extends eastward from the Carpathian (kahr•PAY•thee•uhn) Mountains in Europe to the Ural (YOOR•uhl) Mountains at the western edge of Asia. In the south this plain is grassy and mostly treeless and is called the **steppe.** The steppe has black, fertile soil that is ideal for agriculture, particularly in the area that is now Ukraine.

The Ural Mountains run north and south at the eastern edge of the plain. These mountains are often considered the boundary between the continents of Europe and Asia. Europe and Asia actually form a huge landmass that is called Eurasia. Many rivers crisscross the plain and provide a network of transportation within the region. The Dniester, Dnieper, and Don Rivers are ideal for trade because they flow into the Black Sea and give access to the Mediterranean. Other major rivers, such as the Vistula, Neman, and Dvina, do not flow into the Black Sea and thus have somewhat less impact on trade. They provide important regional transportation links, however.

The southern part of eastern Europe has been inhabited since Neolithic times. Probably beginning during the very late 1500s B.C., several groups from this region invaded southwest Asia. These invasions took place over the course of centuries. After about the A.D. 400s, Slavs settled in much of eastern Europe. Other peoples, including the Avars, Huns, and Magyars, invaded the region at different times. These invaders frequently made the Slavs their subjects. From their servitude comes the word "slave."

During the A.D. 800s Vikings from Scandinavia drove into eastern Europe. Trade was the primary interest of the Vikings as they moved into the area.

INTERPRETING THE VISUAL RECORD

Viking ships Vikings from Scandinavia used longboats to conduct trade. *What design characteristics of this Viking longboat made it an excellent craft for navigating the shallow waters of coastal and inland rivers, as well as the open sea?*

The numerous large and small rivers of eastern Europe enabled them to build far-flung water-going trade routes.

✔ **READING CHECK: Categorizing** What groups of people lived in eastern and south-eastern Europe between the late 1500s B.C. and the A.D. 800s?

Kievan Russia

Cities such as Novgorod and Kiev lay along the Viking trade routes. **Rurik,** the leader of a people called the **Rus,** took control of Novgorod in A.D. 862. Rurik and his successors soon came to rule over Kiev as well as over Slavic tribes along the Dnieper River. The region under their control came to be called the Rus. The word *Russia* probably comes from this name. Kiev prospered because of its location along the rich trade route between Constantinople and the Baltic Sea. Kiev became the most important principality in Kievan Russia and served as the capital for nearly 300 years after about A.D. 879. As early as A.D. 911, Kiev was powerful enough to win a favorable trade treaty with the Byzantine Empire. Other principalities paid tribute to Kiev. Some towns, however, remained more independent.

Kievan Russia, A.D. 879–A.D. 1240

Interpreting Maps A network of rivers crosses the plain between the Carpathian and Ural Mountains.

■ **Skills Assessment: Environment and Society** What common geographic feature did the Kievan trade routes follow?

Government. Many areas in Kievan Russia were led by princes who governed with the advice of councils made up of **boyars,** or nobles. Another institution in Kievan Russia was the *veche,* or town meeting. When the prince requested it, all heads of households would meet in the public marketplace. They discussed important matters like wars, disputes between princes, or emergencies.

Yaroslav I ruled from A.D. 1019 to A.D. 1054, a great period in Russian history. He came to be known as **Yaroslav the Wise.** He built many churches and introduced Russia's first law code, the **Pravda Russkia** (the "Russian Justice"). Yaroslav's code seems to have combined elements of tribal customs and older laws and traditions. It outlined lawful responses in cases of violence and other harmful activity.

> *History Makers Speak*
>
> **❝**If a man kills a man: the brother is to avenge his brother; the son, his father; or the father, his son. . . . If there is no avenger, [the murderer pays compensation of] 40 *grivna.* . . . If a slave runs away . . . and [if a freeman who conceals that slave] does not declare him for three days, and [the owner of the slave] discovers him on the third day, he [the owner] receives his slave back and 3 *grivna* for the offense . . . if a slave strikes a freeman and hides in [his master's] house, and his master is not willing to give him up, the master has to pay 12 *grivna,* and the offended freeman beats the slave whenever he finds him. . . .**❞**

"The Pravda Russkia," from *Medieval Russian Laws,* translated by George Vernadsky

Religion. Traders and Greek missionaries brought Christianity to Kievan Russia in the A.D. 800s. However, little Christian activity took place until the mid-900s. In the A.D. 980s the ruler **Vladimir I** sent observers to Christian church services in several places. His officials were impressed with what they saw at the Hagia Sophia in Constantinople. They admired the services and rituals of Orthodox Christianity. Moreover, Vladimir wanted to marry Anna, the sister of the Byzantine emperor. In A.D. 988 he converted to Christianity. After converting he ordered all Kievans to become Christians. He also had all pagan statues destroyed.

Many Kievans still worshiped the spirits of their ancestors or gods of nature. However, the Byzantine church became a more and more important force in Kievan Russia. The patriarch in Constantinople chose the bishop of the Kievan church. Monasteries became centers of religious thought, social service, and the arts. This further strengthened the church. When the Christian church split in A.D. 1054, the Kievans followed the Eastern Orthodox Church.

Religious themes dominated Kievan culture during this period. Most writing focused on religion, in the form of hymns and sermons. Icon painting became the most distinctive Kievan art form. Artists also created mosaics and frescoes. Much of the decorative painting created by Kievan artists was designed to illustrate religious ideas and figures. The visual quality of these works was often powerful and stylized. Many Kievan mosaics, frescoes, and icons portrayed a deep and thoughtful spirituality. These art forms helped viewers to reflect on the meaning of religious ideas and values.

Economy. Kievan Russia included two major agricultural regions. North of the steppe lies the **taiga** (TY·guh). The taiga has great forests and receives much rainfall. However, winters are long and cold, and the growing season on the taiga is short. Therefore, everyone in a farm family worked long hours to grow and harvest crops. The steppe gets less rain than the taiga. However, the steppe has a milder climate and a longer growing season. People there had more time to plant and harvest crops.

HISTORY MAKER

Yaroslav the Wise
(A.D. 980–A.D. 1054)

Yaroslav's Pravda Russkia was in use until the A.D. 1550s in some parts of Russia. Before his death he divided his kingdom among his sons with instructions on how to rule. They ignored these instructions and civil war soon broke out. **How did Yaroslav continue to affect Russia after his death?**

Then & Now

Town Meetings

All free men in Kievan Russia had the right to speak at the *veche*—a village or town meeting. Town meetings like these continue today. They have become popular in the United States, where they are used to address many issues. Citizens sometimes discuss safety concerns or hear ideas for improving neighborhoods. The U.S. government has organized town meetings to share information with communities. Presidential candidates often hold town meetings to allow voters to ask questions and state their opinions. **What situations might make a town decide to hold a meeting?**

Kievan trade This modern painting shows one Russian artist's idea of what trade on the rivers of Kievan Russia may have looked like. *Based on this image, what was the impact of geography on economic activity in Kievan Russia?*

Kievan Russia traded agricultural goods and other products with the Byzantines. These products included wood, iron, salt, furs, and honey. Kievan Russia also provided slaves for the Byzantines. In return, the Kievans received goods such as wine, silk, spices, and fruit. From western Europe they received jewelry, silver, and textiles. By the early A.D. 1000s, trade had helped Kievan Russia become a strong, wealthy power.

Several social classes emerged in Kievan Russia. At the top were the local princes and their families, followed by the boyars. Next were the town artisans and merchants, who devoted themselves to trade. The largest and lowest class, however, were the peasants. Peasants lived in small villages in the country and produced the crops that fed Kievan Russia. The clergy formed another important group. They were not directly involved in the government or economic activities. Some clergy, however, enjoyed considerable influence over daily life in Kievan Russia. Clergy performed religious ceremonies and ran hospitals and charities.

✔ **READING CHECK: Contrasting** How did Kievan Russia's government and religion differ from the Byzantine Empire's?

SECTION 2 REVIEW

1. **Define** and explain the significance:
   steppe
   boyars
   taiga

2. **Identify** and explain the significance:
   Rurik
   Rus
   Yaroslav the Wise
   Pravda Russkia
   Vladimir I

3. **Summarizing** Copy the charts below. Use them to show the organization of the Kievan political system and the Kievan social classes.

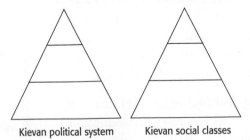

Kievan political system   Kievan social classes

4. **Finding the Main Idea**
   a. What geographic features characterize the plain of eastern Europe and central Asia, and why did these features attract human settlement?
   b. What importance did geography have in the development of Kiev as a powerful city?
   c. How did Kievan Russia and the Byzantine Empire similarly increase their wealth?

5. **Writing and Critical Thinking**
   Identifying Cause and Effect Write a paragraph explaining how Vladimir I's conversion to Christianity affected Russia.
   Consider:
   • how his religion affected Vladimir's policies
   • how the people reacted to these changes

Homework Practice Online
go.hrw.com
keyword: SH3 HP1

Russia and the Mongols

The Main Idea
Under Mongol rule the power of Kiev weakened while Moscow became stronger.

The Story Continues *When Yaroslav the Wise's rule ended in A.D. 1054, Kiev declined in power. During the first quarter of the A.D. 1100s, however, the city enjoyed a brief revival under the leadership of* **Vladimir Monomakh,** *who ruled from A.D. 1113 to A.D. 1125. In protecting the Kievan state, Vladimir was merciless against his enemies. As a result, Kiev was often at war during his reign.*

Attacks on Kiev

Kiev had declined because Kievan rulers gave the outlying towns to their sons to rule independently. Eventually these princes fought among themselves—and with Kiev itself—to expand their territory. At the same time the **Polovtsy** interfered with Kiev's trade. The Polovtsy were a Turkish people who after A.D. 1055 controlled the area south of Kiev. Vladimir Monomakh made his reputation by leading military campaigns against the Polovtsy. At one point he ordered the deaths of some 200 of their princes. Kievan trade may also have suffered from competition with Italian city-states that had developed new trade routes.

In A.D. 1169 and A.D. 1203, groups of princes sacked Kiev, ruining the city's prosperity. New invaders, the Mongols, took advantage of Kiev's weakness. The Mongols came from the Asian steppe east of the Ural Mountains. By A.D. 1240 they had conquered or destroyed almost every city in Kievan Russia. The Mongols continued across the Carpathian Mountains into Hungary and Poland. In A.D. 1242 they defeated the Hungarian and Polish armies. However, the Mongol leader Batu called off his attack to return to Russia. He wanted to influence the choice of the next Mongol leader. Thus Hungary and Poland escaped long-term Mongol rule.

Kievan Russia under the Mongols. Mongols controlled Kievan Russia until the late A.D. 1400s. This long Mongol presence had a strong influence on the Slavic way of life.

The Mongols sought to gain wealth from the region. They taxed the people heavily. As long as the Slavs paid, they could keep their own government and customs. Russian peasants in the conquered lands probably paid taxes in several ways. They may have paid in money or in goods, or they may have paid their Mongol overlords with labor.

Although the Mongols formed only a small ruling class, they influenced Slavic society in several ways. They built important roads and improved methods of taxation and communication. Some Mongol words entered the language that came to be called Russian, as did some Mongol customs, traditions, and patterns of behavior.

Skilled cavalry archers like the warrior pictured here helped the Mongols seize Kievan Russia.

Kievan Russia and its neighbors. During Mongol rule the Slavs of eastern Europe had some contact with central and western Europe. In the A.D. 1300s Lithuania and Poland took territory away from Kievan Russia. They formed a kingdom that was hostile to the eastern Slavs. There were also religious conflicts. The Poles had been converted to western Christianity, while the Slavs kept their Eastern Orthodox faith. This set the Slavs apart from both the Poles and the Mongols. To some degree, moreover, the Slavs became suspicious of western Europeans and their influence. Even today, this suspicion has not completely disappeared.

✔ **READING CHECK: Summarizing** How did society in Kievan Russia change under Mongol rule?

The Rise of Moscow

In time Mongol rule grew weaker. The princes of the region became more independent. During the early A.D. 1300s Moscow, or Muscovy, became a major Russian principality. Moscow's leader, Prince Ivan I, achieved this by cooperating with the Mongols. In return the Mongols awarded him with the title of Great Prince in A.D. 1328. Around the same time, the leader of the Orthodox Church moved to Moscow. This increased the city's power even more.

From A.D. 1462 to A.D. 1505 **Ivan III,** also called Ivan the Great, ruled as Great Prince. By this time Moscow had begun to assert its independence from the Mongols. By A.D. 1480 Ivan III no longer acknowledged the Mongol khan as Moscow's supreme ruler. He united many principalities. Ivan III became the first ruler of the independent state called Russia. He gained more territory through military conquest. His rule began a long tradition of absolute monarchy in Russia.

Ivan the Terrible. In A.D. 1533 the three-year-old Ivan IV became ruler of Russia. Because of his youth, for many years the boyars were actually in control. In A.D. 1547 Ivan IV finally took power for himself. He considered himself to be the true heir of the Roman and Byzantine Empires. Thus he took the title of **czar,** or caesar. Ivan was an able administrator who sponsored the development of a modernized legal code. He renewed trade with western Europe and opened the vast territory of Siberia to Russian settlement. During his reign, Ivan built the power and authority of the Russian monarchy.

Ivan formed a personal group of civil servants called the *oprichniki* (aw·PREECH·nee·kee). The *oprichniki* arrested boyars and gave their land to Ivan's supporters. He also led his army in an attack on Novgorod, destroying the city. Sometimes Ivan's actions were puzzling and cruel. In A.D. 1581 he even murdered his oldest son. These acts earned him the nickname **Ivan the Terrible.** However, Ivan did lay the foundations for a new Russian state. This state included old Kievan Russia and stretched from Siberia to the Caspian Sea. The czar had absolute power.

The growth of the church. The Orthodox Church in Russia grew more powerful by acquiring land. Much land was acquired by the church through donations from the faithful. By about A.D. 1500 the church was a major Russian landowner.

During Mongol rule, the Russian Orthodox Church had become more and more independent of Constantinople. In A.D. 1448 Russian bishops chose their own leader for the Orthodox Church in Moscow. In A.D. 1589 Moscow's church leader was named patriarch. This helped to make Moscow the center of the Russian church.

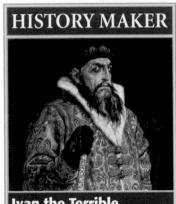

HISTORY MAKER

Ivan the Terrible
(A.D. 1530–A.D. 1584)

Ivan IV had a violent and unpredictable temper. Some people trace his violent nature to tragedies in his life. When he was very young, for example, Ivan's mother was murdered by nobles. As a ruler, he gained a reputation for cruelty toward his enemies.

Following the death of his wife in A.D. 1560, Ivan felt deep despair and became more ruthless than ever. Accusing the boyars of murdering his wife, Ivan ordered the execution of many nobles. Despite his violent behavior, Russia prospered under Ivan. In Russian, his nickname means "awe-inspiring." **How can Ivan IV's nickname be interpreted in different ways?**

A turning point in the development of the Russian church took place in A.D. 1453 with the fall of Constantinople to the powerful army of the Ottoman sultan, Mehmed II. The Turks' victory over the proud and ancient city of the Byzantine emperors removed a major source of competition for church leadership in the Orthodox Christian world.

With the fall of once-mighty Constantinople, Russians proclaimed Moscow to be the **"third Rome."** A Russian churchman explained this phrase by stating that the first Rome had fallen because of heresy. The second Rome, Constantinople, had been conquered by non-Christians. The churchman then claimed that Moscow—the third Rome—would bring the spiritual light of Christian orthodoxy to the whole world.

The new sense of Russian confidence reflected in the churchman's statements is seen in the art and architecture of this period. Domed churches were built and filled with beautiful artwork. Sparkling chandeliers and candles lit every space. These churches were meant to inspire awe, religious wonder, and a mystical feeling of spirituality among the people who worshiped there.

✔ **READING CHECK: Analyzing Information** In what ways did the Russian Orthodox Church gain from Moscow's growing power?

INTERPRETING THE VISUAL RECORD

St. Basil In keeping with the Russian Orthodox Church's growth in power, magnificent new churches were built. This photo shows the Cathedral of St. Basil the Blessed, built in Moscow between A.D. 1554 and A.D. 1560. *How does this church reflect a new Russian sense of power and confidence?*

SECTION 3 REVIEW

1. **Define** and explain the significance:
   czar
   "third Rome"

2. **Identify** and explain the significance:
   Vladimir Monomakh
   Polovtsy
   Ivan III
   Ivan the Terrible

3. **Identifying Cause and Effect** Copy the chart below. Use it to organize the forces acting between A.D. 1054 and A.D. 1203 that caused the downfall of Kievan Russia.

Kiev's power declines

4. **Finding the Main Idea**
   a. How did the distribution of land among Kievan princes help the Mongols to invade?
   b. How was Ivan IV's use of absolute rule different than Ivan III's?

5. **Writing and Critical Thinking**
   Contrasting Create a dialogue between a peasant and a prince discussing the differences in their lives and their ancestors' lives under the Mongols and Kievan Russia.
   Consider:
   • what life may have been like for a peasant during both eras
   • what life may have been like for landowners during both eras

Homework Practice Online
keyword: SH3 HP1

Creating a Time Line

Copy the time line below onto a sheet of paper. Complete the time line by filling in the events, individuals, and dates from the chapter that you think were significant. Pick three events and explain why you think they were significant.

 A.D. 527   **1019**   **1480**

Writing a Summary

Using standard grammar, spelling, sentence structure, and punctuation, write an overview of the events in the chapter.

Identifying People and Ideas

Identify the following terms or individuals and explain their significance:

1. Justinian
2. Iconoclastic Controversy
3. excommunication
4. Hagia Sophia
5. Rurik
6. Pravda Russkia
7. Polovtsy
8. Ivan the Terrible
9. czar
10. "third Rome"

Understanding Main Ideas

Section 1 *(pp. 30–36)*

The Byzantine Empire

1. Why was Justinian's Code important?
2. How was the Byzantine Empire able to last for 1,000 years?
3. What was the result of the Iconoclastic Controversy?
4. What are some cultural highlights of the Byzantine Empire?
5. What led to the decline of the Byzantine Empire?

Section 2 *(pp. 37–40)*

The Rise of Russia

6. How did Slavs benefit from the Vikings' travels in the southern part of eastern Europe?
7. Who had the least and most power in Kievan Russia?

Section 3 *(pp. 40–43)*

Russia and the Mongols

8. What demands did the Mongols make on the Kievan Russians?
9. Which rulers helped the rise of Moscow?
10. Why did the Russian Orthodox Church call Moscow the "third Rome"?

Reviewing Themes

1. **Government** Did Kievan Russia have a form of government in which citizens had a voice? Explain.
2. **Geography** What effects did access to bodies of water have on the Byzantine Empire and Kievan Russia?
3. **Global Relations** Which lasted longer, Mongol rule in Russia or the Byzantine Empire? How did the way in which these two powers ruled make a difference?

Thinking Critically

1. **Comparing** What similar factors contributed to the wealth of the Byzantine Empire and Kievan Russia?
2. **Analyzing Information** The Mongols in Russia were concerned with increasing their wealth through collecting taxes. Why did they bother improving the roads?
3. **Making Predictions** What might have happened to Kievan Russia if the Mongols had not invaded?

Writing About History

Making Predictions Write a newspaper editorial about the struggle for power following Yaroslav's death. Using the chart below, make a list of what might happen if the land is divided among the princes. Incorporate the list into an editorial. Discuss what might happen to the council of boyars, *veches*, and Russia's trade business.

If the land is divided up . . .
1.
2.
3.
4.

Building and Using Chronology

Order the statements below in their correct chronological sequence. Then use the information to answer the questions that follow.

Selected Events in the History of Kievan Russia, c. A.D. 500–A.D. 1300

1. Kiev becomes the capital of Kievan Russia, **c. A.D. 882.**
2. Beginning of Kievan economic and political decline, **c. A.D. 1170.**
3. Kiev is destroyed by Mongols under Batu Khan, **A.D. 1240.**
4. Christianity is introduced to Kiev, **c. A.D. 988.**
5. Kiev is incorporated into the Kingdom of Poland, **A.D. 1569.**
6. Kiev is founded, **c. A.D. 550.**

1. Which of the following best represents the actual chronological order of events shown above?
   a. 1, 6, 4, 5, 2, 3
   b. 6, 1, 4, 2, 3, 5
   c. 5, 6, 1, 3, 4, 2
   d. 6, 1, 4, 2, 5, 3

2. According to the chronology you have constructed, why might the Mongols have found Kiev a relatively easy target for destruction?

Identifying a Point of View

Read the following quote. It is from the preface to the book of laws compiled by the Byzantine emperor Justinian. Then answer the questions.

> **"The maintenance of . . . government depends upon two things, namely, the force of arms and the observance of the laws: and, for this reason, the fortunate race of the Romans obtained power and precedence over all other nations in former times, and will do so forever, if God should be propitious [kind] . . ."**

3. Which of the following statements best describes Justinian's point of view?
   a. The Romans will continue to have power over other nations for all time.
   b. A government succeeds only if it has a strong military to maintain order.
   c. The Romans succeeded because they enforced their laws and had a strong military.
   d. Laws must be obeyed for a government to gain power.

4. An individual's background and experience often influence that person's point of view. What personal experiences might have influenced Justinian's point of view? Give specific examples.

Alternative Assessment

Building Your Portfolio

Link to TODAY

Geography

Trace a physical map of Eurasia. Locate and highlight the rivers, straits, seas, and oceans that contributed to the growth of the Byzantine Empire and Kievan Russia. You may also want to include what goods were being traded and where. Identify cities, such as Constantinople and Kiev, as well as dates when trade was occurring in these cities. Create a key to help others interpret your map.

⚡ internet connect

Internet Activity: go.hrw.com
KEYWORD: SH3 WH1

Choose a topic on the Byzantine Empire and Russia to:

- summarize the global influence of the Roman ideas in the Justinian Code upon contemporary political issues such as individual rights and responsibilities.
- research Ivan IV and find out why he was called "Ivan the Terrible."
- create a piece of art or design a building or church in the Byzantine style.

CHAPTER 2

A.D. 570–A.D. 1250

The Islamic World

A page from the Qur'an

A.D. 622
Daily Life
The hijrah occurs.

A.D. 632
Politics
Abū Bakr becomes the first Muslim caliph.

C. A.D. 661
Politics
The Islamic split between the Sunni and the Shi'ah doctrines occurs.

A.D. 711
Business and Finance
The Moors bring rice, saffron, and sugar to Spain.

A.D. 732
Global Events
The Franks defeat the Moors at the Battle of Tours.

A.D. 785
The Arts
The Moors begin to build the Mosque of Córdoba.

A.D. 810
Science and Technology
Al-Khwārizmī first uses the term *al-jabr*, which we call algebra.

Bowl of saffron spice

A.D. 550

A.D. 650

A.D. 750

A.D. 850

C. A.D. 570
Daily Life
Muhammad is born.

C. A.D. 642
The Arts
Muslims begin to build the Amr Mosque in Cairo.

C. A.D. 635
Business and Finance
Arabs establish the major trading center of Basra on the Persian Gulf.

A.D. 711
Politics
Tāriq leads an expedition to Spain.

C. A.D. 691
The Arts
Muslims complete the Dome of the Rock in Jerusalem.

C. A.D. 793
Business and Finance
The city of Baghdad establishes a paper mill.

The Dome of the Rock mosque in Jerusalem

Build on What You Know

By the end of the A.D. 400s, the Western Roman Empire had collapsed. In the eastern part of the empire, however, the Byzantine culture kept Roman government and traditions alive. The Byzantines also passed on for future generations much learning and scholarship from Greek and Roman antiquity. However, during this time another vast empire with its own thriving economy based on trade was developing to the south and east of the Byzantines. In this chapter, you will learn about a new religion that inspired this empire and encouraged its growth, leading to new advances in the arts and sciences.

Book cover of
The Thousand
and One Nights

Manuscript page
from Ibn Sīnā's Canon
of Medicine

C. A.D. 942
The Arts
Arabs bring kettledrums
and trumpets to Europe.

C. A.D. 950
Daily Life
Córdoba becomes
the center of Arab
learning and com-
merce in Spain.

C. A.D. 1030
Science and Technology
Ibn Sīnā publishes
The Canon of Medicine.

A.D. 1206
Politics
Temüjin is
proclaimed
Genghis Khan.

A.D. 1215
Global Events
The Magna Carta
is signed.

A.D. 950　　　　**A.D. 1050**　　　　**A.D. 1150**

C. A.D. 900
The Arts
Writers start
collecting the
tales for *The*
Thousand and
One Nights.

C. A.D. 1000
Global Events
Leif Ericsson
explores the
North American
coast.

A.D. 1071
Global Events
The Turks
defeat the
Byzantines at
the Battle of
Manzikert.

A.D. 1154
Science and
Technology
Al-Idrīsī publishes
his book of maps.

C. A.D. 970
Science and
Technology
A public hospital
is founded in
Baghdad.

Celestial sphere, or globe
of the universe, used by
Muslim astronomers

What's Your Opinion?

Themes
Journal

Do you **agree** *or* **disagree** *with the*
following statements? Support your point
of view in your journal.

Science, Technology & Society Science flourishes
in societies open to other cultures' ideas.

Global Relations The peoples of conquering
and conquered nations can learn from each
other.

Culture Religion and culture have very little to
do with each other.

The Rise of Islam

The Main Idea
The founding of the Islamic religion in the Arabian Peninsula changed and unified the Arab world.

The Story Continues *As the Byzantines were struggling to carry on the traditions of the Roman Empire, another empire was developing on the Arabian Peninsula based on a new religion. This faith would affect cultures and civilizations in a large part of the world. It is still one of the strongest spiritual movements in the world of today.*

Arabia: Its Geography and People

The Arabian Peninsula is bordered on the south by the Arabian Sea, on the east by the Persian Gulf, on the west by the Red Sea, and to the north by the Syrian Desert. Except for narrow strips along the coasts, most of the Arabian Peninsula is desert. Because the desert dwellers could not grow crops, many herded sheep and camels. These Arab herders, called **bedouins** (BEH·duh·wuhnz), were nomads. Whole bedouin families moved with their flocks from one grazing area to another. The bedouins were organized into tribes. The leader of a tribe was called a sheikh (SHAYK). This title was a sign of respect that was given to a man because of his knowledge or position.

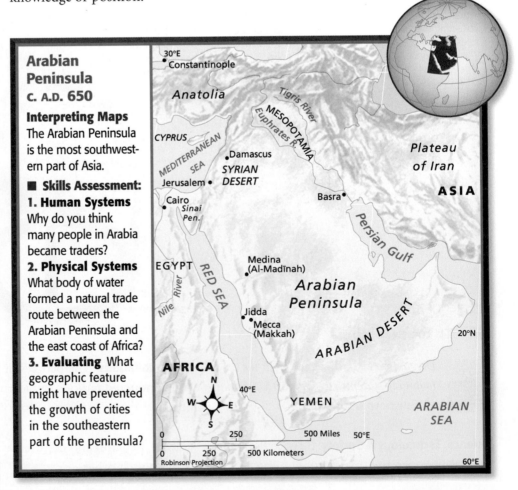

Arabian Peninsula
C. A.D. 650

Interpreting Maps
The Arabian Peninsula is the most southwestern part of Asia.

■ **Skills Assessment:**
1. Human Systems Why do you think many people in Arabia became traders?
2. Physical Systems What body of water formed a natural trade route between the Arabian Peninsula and the east coast of Africa?
3. Evaluating What geographic feature might have prevented the growth of cities in the southeastern part of the peninsula?

The areas along the coasts generally had milder climates that could support greater numbers of people. Towns grew up in these areas, and the townspeople became traders. For example, goods from Asia and Africa entered the port of Jidda on the Red Sea. From there they were transported inland to the city of Mecca (Makkah). Mecca was on a caravan route running north across the desert to Syria. Through trade, Arabs in the towns met and were influenced by people from many different cultures.

✔ **READING CHECK: Contrasting** How did the lifestyle of the desert Arabs differ from the lifestyle of the Arabs who lived along the coasts?

The Prophet Muhammad

In Mecca in about A.D. 570, a man named **Muhammad** was born into a poor clan of Mecca's ruling tribe. Like many Arabs in Mecca, Muhammad made a living as a caravan trader. As a trader, he came in contact with a variety of people. Some, such as Christians and Jews, were monotheists. They believed in a single god. Many of them, particularly the Arabs, were polytheists who worshiped many gods.

When he was about 40 years old, Muhammad reported that the angel Jibreel (Gabriel, in English) told him that he was called to be a prophet of God (in Arabic, Allah) and revealed verses that Muhammad was to recite. A little later, he was instructed to teach others. Over the next several years Muhammad reported receiving many more revelations.

The merchant rulers at Mecca were very much against Muhammad's teaching. They thought his ideas criticized their conduct and attitudes and threatened their authority. Every year Arab pilgrims came to Mecca to worship at the Kaaba (KAH·buh). The Kaaba was a stone building filled with idols that some people worshiped. The merchant rulers may have feared that Muhammad's teachings about one god might stop such pilgrimages. Before long, they began to harass Muhammad and his followers. Eventually Muhammad looked for a more accepting place.

In A.D. 622 Muhammad and his followers settled in the town of Yathrib. This journey from Mecca to Yathrib is known as the **hijrah** (hi·JY·ruh). Hijrah means "flight" or "migration." Later, Yathrib became known as Medina, or Al-Madinah, the "City of the Prophet." Eventually the year of the hijrah became the first year of the Muslim calendar.

After the move to Yathrib, Muhammad gained followers in greater numbers. Desert tribes began to accept his ideas, increasing tensions between Mecca and Medina. Several years of war followed. Finally, Mecca submitted. Muhammad went back to Mecca in A.D. 630. The idols in the Kaaba were destroyed, and it then became a holy place for Muhammad's followers. Muhammad rededicated the Kaaba to the worship of the One God, Allah.

Soon Arabs everywhere began to accept Muhammad's ideas. Through a combination of wise policies, tolerance, and force, Muhammad converted many of the bedouin tribes to his new religion, called **Islam.** By A.D. 632, when he died, many Arab tribes had become followers of Muhammad. Within a very few years, Islam had spread across Arabia and the Middle East and into North Africa.

✔ **READING CHECK: Sequencing** What were the important events in the development of Islam?

Today the Kaaba in the Great Mosque at Mecca serves as a spiritual sanctuary for Muslims.

Link to Today Why might modern followers of Islam consider the Kaaba a special place?

Holt Researcher go.hrw.com
go.hrw.com
KEYWORD: Holt Researcher
FreeFind: Muhammad
After reading more about Muhammad on the Holt Researcher, write a short essay explaining how he changed life on the Arabian Peninsula and beyond.

THE FIVE PILLARS OF ISLAM

1. **The profession of faith.**
   This includes acknowledging that there is no god but God (Allah) and that Muhammad is the messenger of God. It implies belief in earlier messengers.

2. **The five daily prayers.**
   This includes following a ritual of washing and prescribed movements and facing the direction of Mecca.

3. **Paying zakat.**
   This is an annual tax used to help the poor and others in need.

4. **Fasting during the holy month of Ramadan.** (RAH·muh·dahn)
   Muslims eat and drink nothing from dawn to sunset. This reminds them of the importance of self-discipline, dependence on the Creator, and the feelings of the poor.

5. **Making a pilgrimage to Mecca at least once, if possible.**
   During the pilgrimage, which takes place during a certain time of the year, Muslims meet to pray and perform rituals to remind them of the faith of Abraham, and the unity and equality of Muslims all over the world.

The Faith of Islam

Islam is based on the central beliefs that there is only one God, and that each believer must obey God's will. In fact, in Arabic the word *Islam* means "submission to [the will of] God." Followers of Islam are called **Muslims.** Today millions of people throughout the world are Muslims. The largest Muslim communities are in Asia, North Africa, and parts of eastern Europe.

The holy book of Islam is the **Qur'an** (kuh·RAN). According to Muslims, the Qur'an is the word of God as revealed to Muhammad. This includes rules and instructions for right living. There are five basic acts of worship, called the Five Pillars of Islam, required of all Muslims. There are other rules for Muslims to follow as well, such as living humble lives, being tolerant and generous, and not eating pork or drinking alcoholic beverages. Islam also emphasizes the importance of the **jihad** (ji·HAHD), which means "the struggle to defend the faith." Some Muslims believed that anyone who died in this struggle would be rewarded in heaven.

Muhammad taught that God had revealed the Qur'an as a sacred guide for all people. First written in Arabic, the Qur'an was not rapidly translated into other languages because Muslims believed that God's revelations might be lost or changed. As a result, Arabic became the common language of Muslims in religion, law, and literature. Muslims memorize and recite the Qur'an in Arabic.

Muslims worship in **mosques.** Mosques have no furnishings, only mats or rugs on which to kneel, and they never contain images of people or even animals. There is no official clergy in Islam. Men who are trained in the Qur'an and Islamic law guide the people in worship. On Friday at noon, Muslims gather together for congregational prayer and sermons. In most Islamic cultures, women say the same prayers at home or in a section of the mosque set aside for them.

✔ **READING CHECK: Finding the Main Idea** What are the central beliefs of Islam?

SECTION 1 REVIEW

1. **Define** and explain the significance:
   bedouins
   hijrah
   jihad
   mosques

2. **Identify** and explain the significance:
   Muhammad
   Islam
   Muslims
   Qur'an

3. **Sequencing** Copy the time line below. Use it to organize and identify events in the rise of Islam.

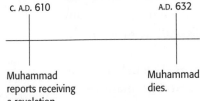

C. A.D. 610 — Muhammad reports receiving a revelation from God.

A.D. 632 — Muhammad dies.

4. **Finding the Main Idea**
   a. In what way did the geographic location of Mecca help its early merchant rulers establish their base of power there?
   b. How did belief in Muhammad's prophethood lead to the religion of Islam?
   c. What role did settled and nomadic Arabs play in the spread of Islam throughout the Arabian Peninsula?

5. **Writing and Critical Thinking**
   Comparing Imagine a meeting between a polytheist of Mecca and a convert to Islam. Write a dialogue between them comparing their faiths.
   Consider:
   • the beliefs of the polytheists
   • the beliefs of Muslims

 Homework Practice Online
keyword: SH3 HP2

SECTION 2

READ TO DISCOVER
❶ How did the Muslims expand their empire?
❷ Why did the Islamic community divide?

DEFINE
caliph
imams
sultan

IDENTIFY
Abū Bakr
'Umar
Sunni
Shi'ah
Sufi
Rābi'ah al-'Adawīyah
Tāriq
Moors

WHY IT MATTERS TODAY

Several million Muslims live in North America. Use or other **current event** sources to find out where the largest Islamic communities in North America are located. Record your findings in your journal.

CNN student News.com

The Spread of Islam

The Main Idea
After the death of Muhammad, the Islamic world greatly expanded, but soon split into two factions.

The Story Continues *According to the Qur'an and the Hadith, or sayings of the prophet, during a journey to Jerusalem, Muhammad traveled through seven heavens to visit the throne of God. Although some followers refused to believe the story at first, one faithful convert named Abū Bakr accepted it immediately. For his faithfulness he was called "The Upright."*

Expansion Under Abū Bakr and 'Umar

When Muhammad died in A.D. 632, his followers chose **Abū Bakr** (uh·BOO BAK·uhr) as his successor. Abū Bakr was Muhammad's oldest friend and one of his early converts. He was given the title **caliph** (KAY·luhf), meaning "successor to the Prophet." During his rule, Abū Bakr helped to bring the Arabic tribes together. He also began to expand Islam's influence northward.

In A.D. 634 **'Umar** (OO·mahr) succeeded Abū Bakr as caliph. 'Umar was a strong leader with a well-run government. Under 'Umar, Muslim expansion continued and people began to share in the empire's wealth. He continued conquering neighboring territories of non-Muslims. In about A.D. 640, for example, the growing armies of Islam under 'Umar's leadership won much of the once-mighty Persian Empire and took control of Iraq. Every victory further encouraged people from across the region to accept Islam. Within 25 years of Muhammad's death, the Muslim Empire included parts of Syria, Persia, and North Africa.

The Arab policy toward conquered people made expansion easier. Fierce and fearless in war, Arabs also entered into many treaties without battle. They were often more tolerant than other conquerors. They did not demand that all conquered people convert to Islam. In the early years, Arabs were particularly tolerant of Christians and Jews.

Muslims called Christians and Jews "People of the Book." Muhammad had accepted the Torah and the Christian Bible as part of God's teachings. Christians, Jews, and some other groups could choose to accept Islam or to pay extra taxes. Some people who refused both options were killed. Many conquered people, however, either paid or converted to Islam.

The caliphs who came after 'Umar expanded Muslim influence even more as the power of other empires, such as the Byzantines, was weakening. Within about 100 years after Muhammad's death, Muslims had swept eastward through part of India and moved westward to conquer much of North Africa. During this time of expansion, the Muslims also conquered islands in the Mediterranean Sea. These gave them control of important trade routes. In A.D. 711 a powerful Muslim force invaded Spain and thus brought Islam to Europe. Muslim troops also tried to conquer Constantinople, but their attempt failed when Byzantine armies successfully defended the city.

✔ **READING CHECK: Sequencing** What steps did Abū Bakr and 'Umar take to spread Islam?

THE ISLAMIC WORLD **51**

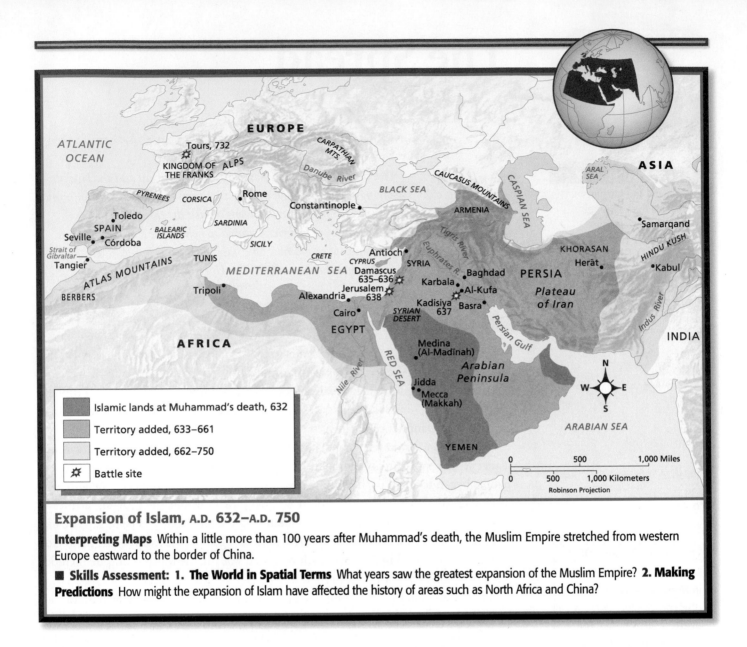

Expansion of Islam, A.D. 632–A.D. 750

Interpreting Maps Within a little more than 100 years after Muhammad's death, the Muslim Empire stretched from western Europe eastward to the border of China.

■ **Skills Assessment: 1. The World in Spatial Terms** What years saw the greatest expansion of the Muslim Empire? **2. Making Predictions** How might the expansion of Islam have affected the history of areas such as North Africa and China?

The Islamic Community Divides

The system of Islamic government allowed the caliphs to exercise great authority. From the beginning, however, people could not agree about who should be caliph. Eventually these disagreements split the Muslim community. The split began when 'Umar's successor, 'Uthmān (ooth·MAHN), was murdered. 'Uthmān was killed because rebels believed he favored his own clan. 'Alī was chosen to succeed 'Uthmān as caliph. 'Uthmān's relative Mu'awiyah (mooh·AH·wee·ya) protested. He accused 'Alī of helping the killers. War broke out between the two sides. In A.D. 661 'Alī was assassinated, and Mu'awiyah became caliph.

Most Muslims agreed to accept Mu'awiyah as caliph. These Muslims eventually became known as the **Sunni** (SOOH·nee). They were followers of the Sunna, meaning "way of the Prophet" or "habitual practice." The Sunni believed that agreement among the Muslim people should settle religious matters.

'Alī's followers insisted that only his descendants should be caliphs. This group later became known as the **Shi'ah** (SHEE·ah). The Shi'ah believed that 'Alī's descendants, called **imams** (i·MAHMZ), should decide religious and worldly matters.

The split between the two groups continued. The rift deepened when Mu'awiyah's descendants killed 'Ali's son Husayn. According to the Shi'ah, on a day of reckoning, Husayn's mother, Fatimah, will take her son's blood-stained shirt to God and say:

Primary Source **❝Oh God, you have given me and my son a promise. For the sake of his sacrifice, have mercy upon the people of the Last Prophet!❞**

Fatimah, from *Islam in Practice: Religious Beliefs in a Persian Village,* by Reinhold Loeffler

Then, in memory of Husayn's death, God will forgive the sins of the Shi'ah and there will be peace. Today the division between the Shi'ah and the Sunni still exists. Less than 10 percent of the world's Muslims are Shi'ah.

Later another group within Islam developed. Muslim mystics known as **Sufi,** such as **Rabi'ah al-'Adawiyah,** tried to live simple lives centered on God. They turned away from worldly possessions and success. The Sufi believed that faith in God was the only mark of a person's worth.

✔ **READING CHECK: Comparing and Contrasting** What are the similarities and differences between the Sunni and the Shi'ah?

The Empire Continues to Spread

Despite this split, the Muslim Empire continued to spread. Soon a North African people called the Berbers converted to Islam. In A.D. 711 a Berber general named **Tariq** led a Muslim army to Spain. They crossed the Mediterranean at the great rock that guards the strait between Africa and Europe. The rock became known as *Jabal Tariq,* or "Mount Tariq." In English it is called the Rock of Gibraltar.

The Moors. Tariq's Muslim army conquered Spain quickly. Those Muslims who made Spain their home were called **Moors.** Within a few years, the Moors crossed over the Pyrenees to raid central France. In A.D. 732 the Franks defeated the Moors at the Battle of Tours and the Moors eventually withdrew from France. They continued to rule parts of Spain, however, for more than 700 years.

Suleymaniye Mosque in Istanbul, Turkey

Analyzing Primary Sources

Identifying a Point of View Why might the Shi'ah consider Husayn's death a special sacrifice?

HISTORY MAKER

Rabi'ah al-'Adawiyah (C. A.D. 717–A.D. 801)

Rabi'ah al-'Adawiyah was one of the greatest Sufi mystics. Abandoned at a young age, she was later sold into slavery. While she filled her days with hard work, Rabi'ah spent her nights praying to Allah for help, guidance, and deliverance.

One night, a great light appeared above her head. Her master, recognizing her devotion to Allah, set her free. Rabi'ah went on to become one of the first female Sufi mystics. Her religious poetry and other writings still inspire Muslims today.

Because no known images of Rabi'ah al-'Adawiyah exist, the calligraphy above is used to symbolize her. It translates as: "In the name of Allah Most Gracious, Most Merciful." **How is Rabi'ah al-'Adawiyah important to Islam?**

The Expansion of Islam

Certain events happened in a certain way to help Islam succeed. Understanding the sequence in which events happened can help us understand why some events occurred as they did.

Abū Bakr followed Muhammad as the leader of Islam and became the faith's first caliph in A.D. 632.

In A.D. 711, less than a century after Muhammad's death, a Muslim army led by the Berber general Tāriq invaded Spain.

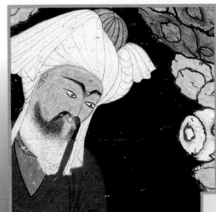

This Persian image shows Muhammad, his face covered, entering a town (possibly Medina or Mecca), probably at some point between A.D. 622 and A.D. 632.

A troop of Muslim Turkish cavalry is shown in battle formation in this image, c. A.D. 1050–c. A.D. 1100.

Skills Reminder

A sequence is an arrangement of things or events in a logical order. Creating a sequence helps you understand information. From the pattern you create, you can decide how events or things are related to each other. To help sequence information, look for calendar references; time periods; and clue words, such as *first, second, after, before, meanwhile,* or *later.* If there are no calendar references or clue words, look for an implied sequence. For example, could one event have happened without another taking place first?

Skills Practice

❶ Study the images and captions above. They show and describe historical events that occurred during the early history of Islam. These events helped lead to the rise and spread of Islam. The events described have been placed in random order. Reorganize the events to place them in their proper sequence.

❷ How does understanding the sequence in which these historical events occurred help to explain how Islam succeeded?

The great era of Arab Muslim expansion lasted until the 1100s. After that, the Turks became the ruling force in Islam. The Islamic empire, though, continued to expand under the Turks.

The Turks and Islam. Turkish-speaking groups from the steppes of central Asia began to move west and south. These tough, nomadic people lived as much by fighting and raiding as by herding. They developed a warlike culture that encouraged expansion and conquest. The conquests brought these Turkish peoples into contact with Arab and Persian Muslims of the Middle East. By the late A.D. 900s, large numbers of Turks had converted to Islam. Many of these people settled around the great Muslim city of Baghdad, in what is now Iraq, where they served the caliph as troops. The Turks supported Islamic law, but their growing power caused political authority to gradually shift away from the caliph. A **sultan** ruled the Turks and claimed to serve the caliph, who still played an important symbolic role. By the mid-1000s the Turks had won control of Baghdad. During the next century, they became the dominant ruling force throughout much of the Islamic world.

During the A.D. 1000s, Turkish Muslims seized Syria, Mesopotamia, and much of Asia Minor. The Turks were skillful warriors. They won a major victory against the Byzantines at the Battle of Manzikert in A.D. 1071. Meanwhile, Turkish Muslims began raiding northern India. The Indians fought fiercely. The Turks, however, fought on horseback. They used their horses cleverly and succeeded. By the early A.D. 1200s they controlled most of northern India.

In the A.D. 1250s outside forces slowed Turkish Muslim expansion. Christians from the West captured cities in a series of wars. Meanwhile, Mongols from the East destroyed Baghdad.

INTERPRETING THE VISUAL RECORD

Flag bearers This artwork from A.D. 1237 shows the flag bearers of an Islamic caliph. *How do the flag bearers indicate the importance of the caliph, even during the reign of the Turks?*

✔ **READING CHECK: Supporting a Point of View** What evidence would you give that the Muslims had a large and well-trained army?

SECTION 2 REVIEW

1. **Define** and explain the significance:
   caliph
   imams
   sultan

2. **Identify** and explain the significance:
   Abū Bakr   Sufi
   'Umar   Rābi'ah al-'Adawīyah
   Sunni   Tāriq
   Shi'ah   Moors

3. **Categorizing** Copy the chart below. Use it to organize the areas that the Muslims conquered during the expansion of the Muslim Empire.

	Arabs	Turks
Years		
Areas		

4. **Finding the Main Idea**

   a. In what ways did the geography of the Arabian Peninsula contribute to the spread of Islam?

   b. What effect might the split in the Islamic community have had on the expansion of the Muslim Empire?

5. **Writing and Critical Thinking**

   Evaluating Explain why the Muslims were able to expand their empire so rapidly.
   Consider:
   • how the Muslim government and military were organized
   • what the Muslim policies were toward conquered people
   • how conquered people reacted to Islam

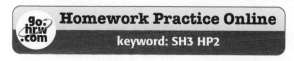

Homework Practice Online

keyword: SH3 HP2

SECTION 3

READ TO DISCOVER

❶ How did the location of Arabia affect trade in the Muslim Empire?

❷ What were Muslim society and family life like?

❸ What Muslim achievements were made in science?

❹ How did Islam influence Arab art and literature?

DEFINE

astrolabe
minaret

IDENTIFY

al-Rāzī
Ibn Sīnā
al-Idrīsī
The Thousand and One Nights

▶ **WHY IT MATTERS TODAY**

The role of women in Muslim society has changed throughout the years. Use or other **current event** sources to explore the role of women in Muslim societies today. Record your findings in your journal.

CNN student News.com

Islamic Civilization

The Main Idea
Muslims made many advances in economics, government, education, science, and the arts.

The Story Continues *Islam became more than just a religion. It was also a great cultural movement that affected virtually every aspect of life within the Islamic Empire. As one Muslim saying expressed: "Islam, the government, and the people are like the tent, the pole, the ropes, and the pegs. The tent is Islam; the pole is the government; the ropes and pegs are the people. None will do without the others."*

A Culture of Traders

The Arabs had been traders for centuries before their empire developed. Muhammad himself had been a trader. It is not surprising, then, that trade was important to Muslim culture. The empire was at the center of a world trade network that linked Europe, Asia, and Africa. India and China sent goods to ports in Syria and Egypt.

As trade grew, other cultures increasingly demanded the quality goods that Muslims produced, such as textiles manufactured from silk, cotton, and wool, as well as beautiful woven tapestries and carpets. Muslims also made metal products from gold and silver. Steel swords from Damascus and from the Spanish city of Toledo became world famous. Luxuries such as jewelry, perfumes, and spices were in great demand. Muslim artisans produced pottery and glassware. Artisans in North Africa and Spain made fine leather goods. All this trade made the Islamic Empire wealthy.

Muslims exchanged ideas with other cultures as well. Both Córdoba and Toledo in Spain were famous centers of learning. Christian and Jewish scholars carried Muslim ideas from Spain into western Europe. Sicily under the Muslims was known for its astronomers and geographers. They, too, influenced Europeans. Many Europeans, in fact, viewed the Muslim world as a source of advanced knowledge in many scientific areas and in banking and commerce.

✔ **READING CHECK:**
Evaluating How important was the location of the Arabian Peninsula to trade in the Muslim Empire?

Muslim merchants carried goods across a far-flung network of trade routes.

Government and Society

Under Arab rule, the Muslim Empire was organized into provinces. At first one caliph headed the government. Disagreement over succession to the position developed, however. In time, these disputes led to the breakup of the empire into three areas, or caliphates. The caliphates were ruled by caliphs in Baghdad, Cairo, and Córdoba.

Muslims throughout the Islamic Empire lived according to the Qur'an. It guided both their religious life and daily life—there was no separation. The Qur'an gave detailed instructions about how society should be organized and how people should live. All Muslims were expected to follow the Islamic laws in public and private life.

Slavery was common in Arabia. The Qur'an urged Muslims to free their slaves. Those who chose to keep slaves were required to treat them humanely. No free Muslim could be enslaved, and the children of a female slave and her master were free.

This illustration from an Arabic book shows the great detail used in Islamic art.

The family was the core of Muslim daily life. Muslims showed concern for all members of their family—parents, children, grandparents, aunts, uncles, and cousins. They particularly respected the elderly. In Islamic families everyone had specific roles and duties. Men were responsible for the family's needs. Women had the right to just treatment, and they could control property, but they were not required to contribute to the family's needs. As the Qur'an stated:

 ❝Women have such [as many] honourable rights as obligations, but their men have a degree [of rights and obligations] above them.❞

The Qur'an

Analyzing Primary Sources

Drawing Inferences How does this passage show that the Qur'an guided more than just religious beliefs?

Parents usually arranged marriages for their children. However, the Qur'an gave a woman the right to refuse the arrangement. The groom was required to give his bride a marriage gift of property or money.

It was common in Arabia for a man to have several wives. The Qur'an restricted a Muslim man to four wives, and he had to treat them equally. In fact, the Qur'an gave women more rights than they had received under traditional Arab law. For example, if a woman got divorced, she kept her own money and was free to remarry. She could also inherit money and own property. Muslim women enjoyed more freedom than most women at the time. Later, however, women began to be secluded and lost some rights.

The government supported schools and libraries. The family and the mosque also took responsibility for education. A person who could speak and write well was thought to be educated. Students attended religious study groups at the mosque. Advanced students could attend schools established for the study of science, mathematics, or law.

✔ **READING CHECK: Identifying Bias** How did old Arab customs and Islamic law affect Muslim family life?

Arab physicians This medieval artwork shows Arab doctors treating a patient. ***What do you think the doctor is doing?***

Link to Today How does this technique compare with that used by doctors today?

CONNECTING TO

Science and Technology

Muslim Medicine

The Arab surgeon Abū al-Qāsim (A.D. 936–1013) developed surgical techniques in Córdoba. He wrote the first illustrated surgical textbook.

Other Arab scientists were interested in chemistry. They learned to distill substances and make medicines. Many drugs used today are of Arab origin.

Understanding Science and Technology

How did Arabs of the Muslim Empire contribute to medical science?

The Sciences

Though divided politically, the Muslim world remained united in one great civilization. As Muslims expanded their empire, they learned from the people they conquered. They also learned from the merchants with whom they traded. The Arabs adopted the best ideas, customs, and institutions they found. They combined ideas of Greece, Rome, and Asia in their culture. From India the Muslims got new ideas about astronomy and mathematics. From China they learned about papermaking. They particularly learned from the writings of the Greek philosophers and scientists.

Medicine. Some of the most important contributions that Muslims made were to medical science. They studied the work of the famous Greek physicians Hippocrates and Galen. Then they added to what the Greeks had done.

Scientific advances in the use of herbs, foods, and prepared drugs added to the Islamic world's vast store of medical knowledge. Some of this early Muslim work in the development and preparation of pharmaceutical drugs is still in use today. In some cases, techniques such as distillation that were first used by Muslim scientists to prepare medical drugs are also followed by today's manufacturers.

Muslim doctors achieved great progress in the techniques of dissection to study anatomy. They also developed improved surgical instruments and processes. The Muslim surgeon Abū al-Qāsim, for example, practiced in Islamic Spain, in the city of Córdoba. His work did much to raise the surgical standards of the time, and his illustrated book of surgical techniques, the first of its kind, was widely used in Europe for centuries.

Muslim physicians learned to correctly diagnose certain diseases. They also pioneered in the development of new ideas concerning hygiene.

Muslim doctors in Baghdad were required to pass difficult examinations in order to practice medicine. They also established the world's first school of pharmacy and created the first encyclopedia of known drugs, the preparation of drugs, and their medical effects. A great public hospital was founded in Baghdad. Physicians at this hospital learned to diagnose and treat deadly smallpox and other diseases.

One of the greatest doctors of the Islamic world was **al-Rāzī**. He was chief physician at the hospital in Baghdad in the early A.D. 900s. Al-Rāzī was best known for a paper he wrote about smallpox and measles. He was the first to clearly describe these diseases so that doctors could tell them apart. Al-Rāzī also compiled a huge medical encyclopedia. It was translated into Latin and used in Europe for centuries.

Some of the greatest Islamic thinkers and scholars were also doctors. **Ibn Sīnā** (also called Avicenna) was among the best known. One of his textbooks was the encyclopedic *Canon of Medicine*.

A page from a text on Islamic medicine illustrates the anatomy of the human eye.

He wrote it in the early 1000s. This medical book was used in Europe until at least 1650. Ibn Sīnā's thoughts about his own training give a good picture of this extraordinary man.

 History Makers Speak ❝I busied myself with the study of . . . [a treatise by al-Farabi] and other commentaries on physics and metaphysics, and the doors of knowledge opened before me. Then I took up medicine . . . Medicine is not one of the difficult sciences, and in a very short time I undoubtedly excelled in it, so that physicians of merit studied under me. I also attended the sick, and the doors of medical treatments based on experience opened before me to an extent that can not be described. At the same time I carried on debates and controversies in jurisprudence [law]. At this point I was sixteen years old.❞

Ibn Sīnā, from his autobiography

The Muslim conquest of Spain contributed to an expansion of learning in that country. Córdoba became the medical equal of Baghdad. From Spain, Muslim medical science spread to other European centers of learning. Christians had preserved the old medical knowledge. Now it was combined with Muslim learning. Universities throughout Europe began to teach medicine based on Arab Muslim medical advances.

Geography. Because the Muslims were traders, they traveled and explored distant places. It is not surprising that they were interested in astronomy, navigation, and maps.

At first the Muslims studied the maps the Greeks made. Then they added their own improvements. In Baghdad astronomers developed a more accurate way to measure distances on earth. Geographers used their measurements to make better maps. One Muslim geographer, **al-Idrīsī**, sent people to other countries. He asked them to draw the geographic features they saw. Al-Idrīsī then combined what they found with existing maps to make new, more accurate maps.

Muslims adopted another Greek invention. This was the small instrument called the **astrolabe,** which allowed observers to chart the positions of the stars and thus calculate their own position on Earth. Muslim astronomers improved the astrolabe several centuries later. By the 1100s, mariners throughout Europe and the Muslim Empire were using astrolabes.

Analyzing Primary Sources

Drawing Conclusions Ibn Sīnā said that medicine is "not one of the difficult sciences." Why did he say that?

The astrolabe allowed Arab sailors to calculate latitude, longitude, and the time of day.

The maps that al-Idrīsī created in the 1100s were an important advance in geography.

Mathematics. In about the A.D. 800s Muslims learned a new number system from India. This system expressed any number using only 10 figures. It included a figure for zero to mean an empty place. Muslim scholars introduced the Indian number system into the Greek science of mathematics. When Europeans learned about this number system, they called the figures "Arabic". These are the same Arabic numerals in use today.

Muslims also got the idea of decimals from India. Al-Khwārizmī used them in an Arab arithmetic book. He also wrote about what he called *al-jabr,* or "restoring," which became *algebra* in English. During the A.D. 1000s scholars from Europe visited Muslim schools in Spain to learn about Muslim arithmetic and algebra. Soon the Muslim mathematical ideas spread to Europe.

✔ **READING CHECK: Supporting a Point of View** What evidence would you give that the Muslims were outstanding scientists?

The Arts

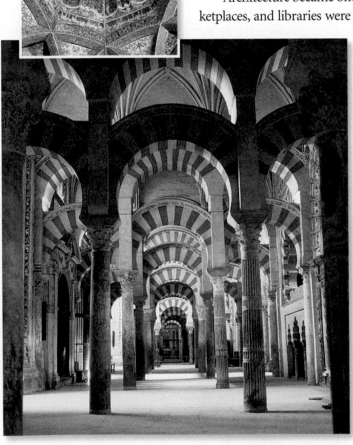

Islamic teaching forbids the use of images to show God. In fact, Islamic religious art avoided showing human or animal forms. Instead artists created beautiful geometric and floral designs. Calligraphy, the art of fine handwriting, was the highest art form. In their nonreligious art Muslims sometimes showed people in daily life, famous battles, or other similar scenes.

Architecture became one of the greatest forms of Islamic art. Mosques, palaces, marketplaces, and libraries were designed to show the glory of Islam. They also showed the power of the ruler who sponsored their construction.

The first Islamic mosques were modeled after Muhammad's private courtyard at Medina, where he had led the community in prayer. These earliest mosques were, in many cases, simple plots of ground marked as sacred. As the Islamic Empire expanded, Muslims built mosques in the territories they conquered. During the earliest years of growth and conquest, mosques that were constructed in conquered lands beyond the Arabian Peninsula were apparently not used solely as religious centers. Rather, they often served as community centers where many kinds of group activities, in addition to prayer and religious ceremonies, were conducted. The community's treasury might have been kept at the site of the mosque, and community social, political, and educational activities and events might also have been held there.

Over time the design of many mosques became more elaborate. In the western part of the Muslim world, the beautiful mosque at Córdoba, in Spain, was a fine example of this increasingly sophisticated architectural style. Built in stages between about A.D. 785 and about A.D. 988, this mosque remains as a magnificent monument to Islam.

The Great Mosque of Córdoba took more than 200 years to complete. It is a masterpiece of Islamic architecture. The inset shows a part of the ceiling.

Mosques were designed to house the thousands of followers who gathered to worship. The main part of the mosque was a vast area for prayer. A semicircular niche faced in the direction of Mecca. There also was a pulpit for the prayer leader. Often there was a **minaret,** or tower, attached to the outside of the mosque. Five times a day, a crier in the minaret would call Muslims to worship.

The Islamic Empire also produced outstanding poetry and literature. The caliphs were great patrons of the arts. Some writers lived at the caliph's court and wrote about what they saw.

One story in Muslim literature tells of a ruler who married a new bride each night. The next morning he would order her execution because he thought no wife would remain loyal. To save herself, one wife, Scheherazade (shuh·HEHR·uh·zahd), began to tell a story one night. She promised to finish it the next night. Interested and eager for the ending, her husband delayed her execution. Night after night she charmed him with stories. Each night she left the story unfinished. After a thousand and one nights, the king was convinced she would remain faithful and he abandoned his plans to execute her.

The story of Scheherazade is the tale around which a body of Muslim folktales was organized. Today we know the collection as *The Thousand and One Nights.* It includes the familiar tales of "Sinbad the Sailor," "Aladdin," and "Ali Baba and the Forty Thieves." They are among the most widely read stories in history.

✔ **READING CHECK: Identifying Cause and Effect** How did Islamic teachings influence Muslim art and architecture?

CONNECTING TO

Art

Weaving: Carpets of the Muslim World

For centuries Muslims who could afford them have knelt and prayed on beautiful rugs. A prayer rug must be placed on the floor so that the arch in the design points toward Mecca. The prayer rug shown here was woven in Turkey during the late 1600s or early 1700s. It has a border of wide and narrow stripes and various geometric designs. The parts of the carpet have specific meanings. Different colors, for example, may symbolize various attitudes or values.

Understanding the Arts

Which side of the rug pictured would be laid closest to Mecca? Why?

SECTION 3 REVIEW

1. Define and explain the significance:
astrolabe
minaret

2. Identify and explain the significance:
al-Rāzī
Ibn Sīnā
al-Idrīsī
The Thousand and One Nights

Homework Practice Online
keyword: SH3 HP2

3. Identifying Cause and Effect Copy the chart below. Use it to show how Muslim culture was influenced by other cultures and how it influenced other cultures.

| Muslim Culture | ↔ | Other Cultures |

4. **Finding the Main Idea**

a. What role did trade play in the Muslim Empire?
b. How did the Qur'an influence Muslim culture?
c. What were the main scientific and mathematic achievements of the Muslim Empire?

5. **Writing and Critical Thinking**

Summarizing Write an outline for a short story or folktale that takes place in the Muslim Empire.
Consider:
• the daily lives and occupations of men and women in various regions of the empire
• the importance of religion in the culture
• the themes of the folktales in *The Thousand and One Nights*

Review

Creating a Time Line

Copy the time line below onto a sheet of paper. Complete the time line by filling in the events, individuals, and dates from the chapter that you think were significant. Pick three events and explain why you think they were significant.

| A.D. 500 | A.D. 700 | A.D. 1000 | A.D. 1200 |

Writing a Summary

Using standard grammar, spelling, sentence structure, and punctuation, write an overview of the events in the chapter.

Identifying People and Ideas

Identify the following terms or individuals and explain their significance:

1. Muhammad
2. hijrah
3. Muslims
4. Qur'an
5. mosque
6. caliph
7. Tāriq
8. Moors
9. al-Rāzī
10. minaret

Understanding Main Ideas

Section 1 *(pp. 48–50)*
The Rise of Islam

1. Why did some Arab traders and others who lived in the Arabian Peninsula follow the lifestyles of nomadic herders?
2. Why do Muslims call Muhammad "the prophet of Islam"?
3. What role does the Qur'an play in the lives of faithful Muslims?

Section 2 *(pp. 51–55)*
The Spread of Islam

4. Which areas were included in the Muslim Empire by A.D. 750?
5. What was the result when the Berbers crossed into Spain?
6. What factors caused Islam to divide into two main branches?

Section 3 *(pp. 56–61)*
Islamic Civilization

7. What role did trade play in Muslim culture?
8. What navigational aids did the Muslims develop?
9. Why did Muslims produce the type of art they did?

Reviewing Themes

1. **Science, Technology & Society** Why was there a development and flow of scientific information in the Muslim Empire?
2. **Global Relations** How did conquest contribute to the spread of Muslim culture?
3. **Culture** In what ways did the Islamic religion shape how the Muslim culture developed?

Thinking Critically

1. **Summarizing** How did the rise of Islam change the course of Arab history?
2. **Drawing Conclusions** How was Islam linked to other faiths?
3. **Evaluating** How did *The Thousand and One Nights* reflect both the history of the culture in which it was created and universal themes?
4. **Supporting a Point of View** What do you think was the most important contribution of the Muslim Empire to the world? Why?

Writing About History

Summarizing Write a report describing how Islamic rules affected Muslim family life in the Islamic Empire. Use the chart below to organize your thoughts before you write.

	Islamic Rules	Effect
Men		
Women		
Marriage		
Slavery		

Using Art to Understand History

Study the illustration below. Then answer the questions that follow.

Islamic illustration of weighing goods, c. A.D. 900s–A.D. 1000s

1. Which statement best describes what you can conclude about daily life during the period illustrated?

   a. The people of this time invented the scales pictured.

   b. Merchants sold goods by weight, and wore clothing similar to that shown.

   c. Merchants only sold goods in bundles like those shown in the drawing.

   d. Only men could be merchants.

2. The subject of the drawing above is taken from Islamic daily life. What other subjects were used in Islamic art? Give specific examples.

Analyzing Historical Context

Read the following excerpt from a modern historian's description of the life of Muhammad. Then answer the questions below.

> "But at this point a group of pilgrims from Yathrib [the city of Medina] . . . met him [Muhammad] . . . and some time later a deputation [group of representatives] set out to invite the Prophet to make Yathrib his home and base. This was the first big breakthrough. Muhammad eagerly accepted the offer and . . . arrived safely in Yathrib in September, 622."

3. According to the excerpt above, which of the following statements best describes the reason that Muhammad settled in Yathrib?

   a. Muhammad was invited to settle in Yathrib by representatives of the city.

   b. Muhammad settled in Yathrib because it was a major commercial and trading center in the Arabian Peninsula.

   c. Muhammad refused to accept the Yathrib deputation's offer and thus had to be forced to settle in the city.

   d. Muhammad and his followers settled in Yathrib after city officials offered to build a great mosque there.

4. Why did the author of the excerpt above describe the events surrounding Muhammad's move to Yathrib as "the first big breakthrough"? Give specific reasons for your answer.

Alternative Assessment

Building Your Portfolio

Link to TODAY

Science, Technology & Society

The contributions to science, mathematics, and technology made by early Islamic societies had a far-ranging impact on the world. Identify a scientific, mathematical, or technological discovery of Islamic societies. Then trace the spread of these ideas to other civilizations and describe the changes they produced.

internet connect

Internet Activity: go.hrw.com
KEYWORD: SH3 WH2

Choose a topic on the Islamic World to:

- research Muslim contributions to medicine and science.
- research and report on Islamic culture.
- create a chart of Islamic calligraphy designs.

World Religions

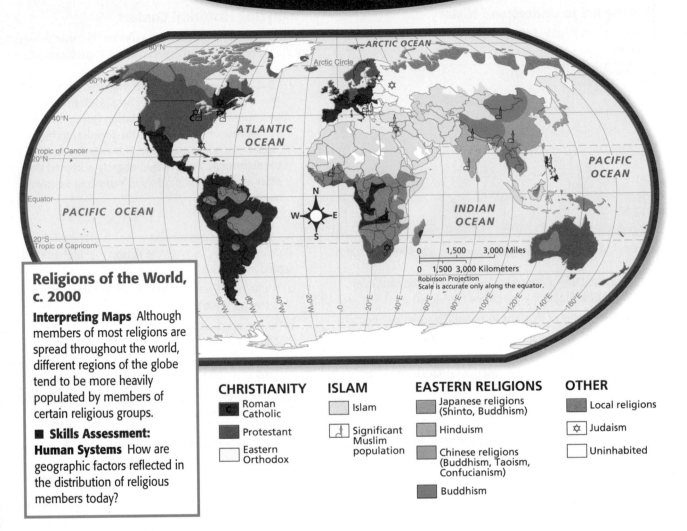

Religions of the World, c. 2000

Interpreting Maps Although members of most religions are spread throughout the world, different regions of the globe tend to be more heavily populated by members of certain religious groups.

■ **Skills Assessment: Human Systems** How are geographic factors reflected in the distribution of religious members today?

CHRISTIANITY
- **C** Roman Catholic
- Protestant
- Eastern Orthodox

ISLAM
- Islam
- Significant Muslim population

EASTERN RELIGIONS
- Japanese religions (Shinto, Buddhism)
- Hinduism
- Chinese religions (Buddhism, Taoism, Confucianism)
- Buddhism

OTHER
- Local religions
- Judaism
- Uninhabited

MEMBERSHIP IN WORLD RELIGIONS, c. 2000

Percentage of World Population

- Christianity 33%
- Islam 19.3%
- No Religion 15.3%
- Hinduism 13.4%
- Other 12.7%
- Buddhism 6%
- Judaism .2%
- Confucianism .1%

Number of Followers

Religion	Followers
Christianity	1,974,181,000
Islam	1,155,109,000
Hinduism	799,028,000
Buddhism	356,270,000
Judaism	14,313,000
Confucianism	6,253,000
All Other Religions	760,884,000

Source: *World Almanac and Book of Facts, 2001*

Interpreting the Graphs
The six major religions in this feature still have large followings throughout the world. *What religion has the most followers throughout the world? The second most? What percentage of the global population do they represent?*

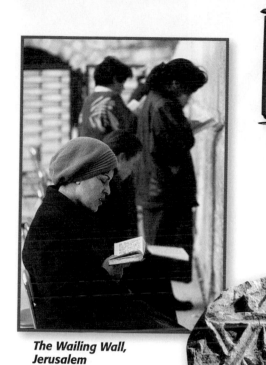

The Wailing Wall, Jerusalem

Sacred Text:
The Torah

◄ **Sacred Symbol:**
Star of David

▼ **Sacred Site:**
Jerusalem

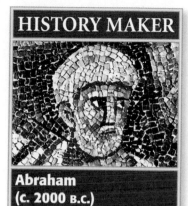

HISTORY MAKER

Abraham (c. 2000 B.C.)

According to biblical sources, Abraham was originally an inhabitant of Ur, where he was known as Abram. After establishing a covenant with God, he changed his name to Abraham, meaning "father of many." This reflected a promise that Abraham would be the leader of many peoples.

Abraham is a sacred figure to three religions: Judaism, Christianity, and Islam. All three faiths trace their heritage to Abraham through the line of prophets descended from his sons. Some people consider Abraham the first historical figure to follow a faith with one supreme deity. **How does Abraham's connection to modern religions reflect his name "father of many"?**

SPECIAL DAYS

Passover, in spring; Rosh Ha-Shanah and Yom Kippur, in autumn; and Hanukkah, in late autumn or winter

HINDUISM

HISTORY MAKER

Mahavira
(c. 599 B.C.–527 B.C.)

Over the years many religious leaders added to and expanded Hindu thought. One such person was Mahavira, also known as Vardhamana. He was born into a warrior clan in northeastern India. At the age of 30 he left his home and entered the forest to find spiritual fulfillment. He got rid of all his personal possessions, then spent more than 12 years wandering the countryside with nothing to his name and little contact with other people.

After he felt he had gained the answers to his questions about life, Mahavira began teaching others. He believed the key to enlightenment was to live apart from the material world as much as possible. Many early Hindus were influenced by his ideas. Eventually his beliefs became the basis of Jainism, a new religion. **How did Mahavira influence Hindus?**

▲ **Sacred Texts:**
The Vedas, Bhagavad Gita

Festival of Holi

Hindus consider it a sacred duty to bathe in the holy waters of the Ganges River. This ritual cleanses the bather's mind and spirit.

▲
Sacred Sites:
Ganges River, city of Varanas

Sacred Creature:
The cow

The cow is a particularly sacred animal in the Hindu faith in part because of the important role it has played in sustaining life.

SPECIAL DAYS

Festival of Holi, in spring; Diwali, or Deepavali (Festival of Lights) in autumn

Buddha Day festival

Bodhi tree

▲ **Sacred Site:**
Bodhgaya

◀ **Sacred Text:**
The Pali Canon

Sacred Objects:
Statues of the Buddha

HISTORY MAKER

Siddhartha Gautama
(c. 563 B.C.–483 B.C.)

Siddhartha Gautama was born the son of an Indian prince. At the age of 29, he left his palace and was shocked by the suffering he saw. As a result, he wondered about the great problems of life.

Gautama decided to spend the rest of his life seeking answers to his questions. In what is now called the Great Renunciation, he put aside all his possessions, left his family, and set out to search for truth. One day, while meditating under a bodhi tree near the town of Bodhgaya, Gautama realized the key to ending suffering. This led to the development of the Four Noble Truths and the Eightfold Path, which all Buddhists follow. After his experience under the bodhi tree, Gautama became known as the Buddha, or "enlightened one." **How did Siddhartha Gautama reject his old life?**

SPECIAL DAY   Buddha Day, celebrated at the full moon in May

CONFUCIANISM

Confucius
(551 B.C.–479 B.C.)

Westerners know K'ung Ch'iu as Confucius. He was born in the Chinese province of Lu. He spent much of his life tutoring and working in low-level government positions.

Confucius grew frustrated by other officials around him. In mid-life he left his government position and traveled the countryside promoting reform. After 13 years he returned to Lu to teach about the ideas he had formed during his travels.

Confucius had little to say about gods, the meaning of death, or the idea of life after death. For this reason some people do not consider Confucianism a religion, although the goal of Confucianism is to be in "good accord with the ways of heaven." Many followers of Confucianism practice his ideas as religion. **Why do some people not consider Confucianism a religion?**

▲ **Sacred Text:**
The Analects

Because Confucius emphasized the importance of education and learning, his followers celebrate his birthday as Teacher's Day.

◄ **Sacred Symbol:**
Yin-yang

▼ **Sacred Site:**
Confucian temple

SPECIAL DAY

Teacher's Day, in August or September

▲ **Sacred Text:**
The Bible

HISTORY MAKER

Jesus
(C. 6 B.C.–C. A.D. 30)

▲ **Sacred Sites:**
Bethlehem,
Jerusalem

*A Christmas
candlelight service*

◄ **Sacred Symbol:**
Cross

According to the Gospels, Jesus was born in Bethlehem, near Jerusalem, but grew up in Nazareth. He was a Jewish carpenter. In time he began preaching. As he traveled through the villages of Judaea, he assembled 12 disciples to help him preach. Jesus often taught using parables, or stories intended to teach a moral lesson. His followers believe that Jesus was the Son of God and that he was resurrected after his death. **Why do you think Jesus taught using parables?**

SPECIAL DAYS

Christmas, on December 25th (early January for some Orthodox churches); Easter, in the spring

ISLAM

HISTORY MAKER

Muhammad
(C. A.D. 570—A.D. 632)

In Islam, Muhammad is a messenger or prophet of God. Muhammad was born in Mecca (Makkah) and orphaned at an early age. He was from a respected but poor family. They belonged to a leading tribe of caravan merchants and keepers of Abraham's shrine and pilgrimage site, the Kaaba.

Islam prohibits the use of images for Muhammad. The symbol above, which means "Muhammad is the Prophet of God," is often used in place of his picture. **Why is a symbol used in place of Muhammad's image?**

▲ **Sacred Text:**
Qur'an

▲ **Special Objects:**
Prayer rugs

Muslim woman praying during Ramadan

Thousands of Muslim pilgrims gather around the Kaaba in Mecca.

Sacred Sites:
Mecca (Makkah), Al-Madīnah, Jerusalem

SPECIAL DAYS

Fast of Ramadan, during the entire ninth month of the Islamic year; 'Īd al-Fitr, at the end of Ramadan; and 'Īd al-Adha, at the end of the hajj in the twelfth lunar month

World Religions Review

Culture

The major religions of the world share many common ideas and histories. Using what you have read in this feature and in previous chapters, create a chart comparing the historical origins, central ideas, and spread of Judaism, Hinduism, Buddhism, Confucianism, Christianity, and Islam.

Global Relations

Religion has played an important role in many historical events and continues to shape events even today. Using what you have read in this book, as well as other sources, pick one of the religions covered in this feature and create a booklet identifying examples of its influence on both historic and modern world events.

A Roman Catholic cardinal and a Jewish rabbi shake hands. Christianity and Judaism share some traditions and beliefs.

Further Reading

Breuilly, Elizabeth, et al. *Religions of the World: The Illustrated Guide to Origins, Beliefs, Traditions, and Festivals.* Checkmark Books, 1997.

Crim, Keith, general editor. *The Perennial Dictionary of World Religions.* Harper San Francisco, 1989.

Smith, Huston. *The Illustrated World's Religions: A Guide to Our Wisdom Traditions.* Harper San Francisco, 1995.

Sullivan, Lawrence E. *Enchanting Powers: Music in the World's Religions.* Harvard University Press, 1997.

Wilson, Andrew, editor. *World Scripture: A Comparative Anthology of Sacred Texts.* Paragon House, 1995.

🖵 internet connect

Internet Activity: go.hrw.com
KEYWORD: SH3 Religions
KEYWORD: Holt Researcher

In assigned groups, develop a multimedia presentation about one of the world religions in this feature. Choose information from the HRW Go site and from the Holt Researcher that best reflects the major historical events, ideas, and traditions of that religion.

A.D. 552–A.D. 1573
The Civilizations of East Asia

C. A.D. 584
Science and Technology
Work begins on the Grand Canal.

A.D. 589
Politics
The Sui dynasty reunites China.

A.D. 618
Politics
The Tang dynasty begins in China.

A ceramic Chinese vase, from between A.D. 960 and A.D. 1127

C. A.D. 750
Daily Life
About 70 million people live in China.

C. A.D. 950
Science and Technology
The Chinese first use gunpowder in warfare.

C. A.D. 960
Business and Finance
Foreign trade begins to expand in China.

C. A.D. 960
The Arts
Chinese artisans perfect the craft of porcelain making.

A.D. 550	A.D. 750	A.D. 950

C. A.D. 700
Global Events
Buddhism is flourishing in Korea.

A.D. 700s
Daily Life
Zen Buddhism becomes the dominant form of Buddhism in Korea.

C. A.D. 670
Politics
The Kingdom of Silla unifies Korea.

A.D. 868
The Arts
The Chinese produce the world's first known printed book, the *Diamond Sutra*.

A.D. 960–A.D. 1279
Politics
The Sung dynasty exists in China.

A figure of a Bactrian camel from the Tang dynasty

*An illustration of the Buddha preaching, from the **Diamond Sutra***

Build on What You Know

*T*he people of the Islamic world fashioned a unique society based on a powerful religious ideal. Their culture lay at the crossroads of many civilizations and spread with the movement of people and with trade. In little more than a century after the death of Muhammad in A.D. 632, Islamic culture and beliefs had been carried throughout much of the Middle East, through large parts of Africa, Asia, and the Mediterranean, and even into Europe. In this chapter, you will learn about the unique cultures of East Asia that, like Islamic civilization, reflected a strong spiritual influence.

A.D. 1192
Politics
Minamoto Yoritomo gains
the title of shogun in Japan.

A Noh mask

C. A.D. 1240
Global Events
Mongols invade Europe.

C. A.D. 1260
Business and Finance
Kublai Khan issues
paper currency.

A.D. 1271
Politics
Kublai Khan founds the
Yuan dynasty in China.

C. A.D. 1040
Science and Technology
The Chinese develop
movable type for printing.

A.D. 1300s
The Arts
The first Noh plays
are performed in
Japan.

A.D. 1392
Politics
Koreans expel the
Mongols and found
the Yi dynasty.

A.D. 1150

A.D. 1350

A.D. 1550

C. A.D. 1000
The Arts
Lady Murasaki
Shikibu writes *The
Tale of Genji.*

A.D. 1300s
**Business
and Finance**
State-controlled
foreign trade
flourishes in China.

C. A.D. 1450
Daily Life
Emperor Sejong directs
the development of the
Korean alphabet.

A.D. 1281
Global Events
The "Divine Wind"
turns back a Mongol
invasion of Japan.

C. A.D. 1400
Daily Life
The tea ceremony
develops in Japan.

**Lady Murasaki
Shikibu**

C. A.D. 1275
Business and Finance
European trader Marco
Polo visits the court of
Kublai Khan.

A Japanese tea caddy

What's Your Opinion?

Do you **agree** *or* **disagree** *with the
following statements? Support your point
of view in your journal.*

Government It is difficult for even the strongest
rulers to continuously maintain their political
power for long periods of time.

Global Relations A powerful nation affects
the societies and cultures of its neighbors.

Culture Religious ideas can be reflected in
societies in a variety of ways.

1 How did Chinese civilization advance during the Sui and Tang dynasties?

2 What was daily life like for the Chinese people during the Sung dynasty?

IDENTIFY

Grand Canal
Li Bo
Du Fu
Empress Wu
Zen
Diamond Sutra

▶ WHY IT MATTERS TODAY

The differences between city and rural life are as real today in China as they were over 1000 years ago. Use CNN^{student}News.com or other **current event** sources to explore differences in the daily lives of people your age living in the cities or in the country. Record your findings in your journal.

China under the Sui, Tang, and Sung Dynasties

The Main Idea
The Sui, Tang, and Sung dynasties shaped China but could not maintain control over it.

The Story Continues *The fall of the Han dynasty in the 200s led to a long era of instability and decline in China. Hordes of invaders swept in and destroyed Han cities. An observer described visiting one such city in the 300s. "At this time in the city . . . there were not more than 100 families," he wrote. "Weeds and thorns grew thickly as if in a forest."*

The Sui and Tang Dynasties

The collapse of the Han dynasty in 220 signaled a long era of social and political disruption in China. Wave after wave of invaders swept into China from beyond its borders. Over time, these peoples settled in China, set up kingdoms, and adopted Chinese customs. In the late 500s one of these groups succeeded in reuniting China under its rule. The new dynasty, known as the Sui, came into power in 589. During their brief rule, the Sui emperors began construction of the **Grand Canal.** They connected existing and newly dug waterways, linking northern and southern China for the first time. The canal was one of the engineering marvels of the ancient world.

Despite their accomplishments, however, the Sui dynasty did not last. The rulers tried to do too much at once. They tried unsuccessfully to conquer southern Manchuria and northern Korea. In 615 invading Turks defeated them. An uprising in 618 ended the Sui dynasty and brought the Tang dynasty to power.

Expansion under the Tang. The early Tang rulers defeated the invading Turks to the north and west. They extended China's frontiers farther west than ever before. The Tang rulers made contact with India and with the Muslim Empire to the south and the west. To the east, Chinese ideas greatly influenced the people of Korea and Japan. This contact with other peoples also contributed to Chinese culture.

INTERPRETING THE VISUAL RECORD

Tang sculpture This ceramic figure of a girl was discovered in a Tang dynasty tomb. The Chinese also buried figures of servants, animals, and guards. *What might have been the purpose of these figures buried alongside wealthy Chinese people?*

The Tang made Xi'an their capital. During the 700s and 800s, about 2 million people lived there. This made Xi'an the largest city in the world at that time. Xi'an was both the center of government and a center of culture. People from many parts of the world settled there. Arabs, Persians, Jews, Greeks, and native Chinese lived side by side.

China flourished under the Tang dynasty. The Tang only ruled until 907, but they began what would be another golden age in China. For many years China was the most powerful and wealthy country in the world.

Literature under the Tang. The Tang dynasty marked a high point in the development of Chinese literature. Some 2,300 known poets lived and worked during the era of the Tang dynasty. Together, these poets wrote nearly 49,000 known works. Among the best of these poets were **Li Bo** (Li Po) and **Du Fu.** They both wrote during the 700s.

Li Bo, a Daoist, spent much of his life seeking pleasure. His poems describe life's delights in light, happy, elegant terms. His love of life, however, may have caused his death. According to legend, Li Bo became tipsy after drinking too much and drowned while reaching from a boat for the moon's reflection in the water.

Du Fu, on the other hand, wrote about serious subjects. He was a devout follower of the teachings of Confucius. Du Fu's carefully written verses showed his deep concern for the suffering and tragedy of human life. Du Fu used his poet's gift to

CONNECTING TO
Science and Technology

The Grand Canal

The Grand Canal is the world's oldest and longest canal system. It connects the Chinese cities of Hangzhou and Beijing, and is almost 1,000 miles long. Before the development of railroads, the canal was a convenient way to travel and transport goods between the northern and southern parts of China.

The canal was created over many hundreds of years. It was made by digging trenches to link lakes, rivers, and other canals. Dams were built to equalize water levels.

As railroads developed, the Grand Canal's importance faded, and it fell into a state of disrepair. By 1949 only small boats were able to use it. China repaired and modernized the canal system between 1958 and 1964. Today the Grand Canal again serves as a way for boats to transport goods and passengers.

Understanding Science and Technology

Why would floods be harmful to the Grand Canal?

The Grand Canal is still an important waterway today, as this photo indicates.

call for an end to the frontier wars and destructive uprisings that tore at Tang China. One of Du Fu's greatest works was entitled "A Song of War Chariots." This poem, a classic example of descriptive poetry, creates a mood of great sadness. It tells of the sorrow of parting as a young soldier goes off to fight. The poem also suggests that the life of a Tang soldier could be brutal and harsh.

Analyzing Primary Sources

Drawing Inferences How does Du Fu's poem reflect Chinese history?

Primary Source

>**The war-chariots rattle,**
>**The war-horses whinny,**
>**Each man of you has a bow and a quiver at his belt.**
>**Father, mother, son, wife, stare at you going,**
>**Till dust shall have buried the bridge beyond Xi'an,**
>**They run with you, crying, they tug at your sleeves,**
>**And the sound of their sorrow goes up to the clouds . . .**
>**Men of China are able to face the stiffest battle,**
>**But their officers drive them like chickens and dogs.**
>**Whatever is asked of them,**
>**Dare they complain?**

Du Fu, from Cyril Birch, ed., *Anthology of Chinese Literature*

Tang Dynasty, A.D. 814

Interpreting Maps The Tang rulers extended their empire westward into Central Asia and southward into Indochina.

■ **Skills Assessment: Physical Systems** Along what waterway could Tang people travel between the cities of Tianjin and Hangzhou?

Religion in Tang China. Missionaries from India brought Buddhism to China during the Han dynasty. Buddhism reached its peak under the Tang. **Empress Wu,** who ruled from 690 to 705, was an outspoken supporter of Buddhism. She was a strong leader and an able administrator. Empress Wu was also the only woman to hold the Chinese throne in her own name.

Wealthy Buddhists donated land for monasteries. Many different forms, or sects, of Buddhism appeared. The most famous sect is best known by its later Japanese name, **Zen.** Zen Buddhism stressed meditation as a means to enlightenment. It was similar in many ways to Daoism. Following the Buddhists' example, Daoists formed sects that appealed to the masses of peasants. In later years many Chinese adopted a mix of Buddhist and Daoist teachings.

In time the growing wealth of the Buddhist monasteries alarmed government officials. They seized the monasteries' lands and took art objects for the emperor's treasury. In the last century of the Tang dynasty, government officials persecuted Buddhists. They destroyed thousands of shrines and monasteries. They forced more than 250,000 monks and nuns to give up their duties and return to ordinary life. Buddhism continued to exist in China. However, it was never again so important a force in Chinese life.

The Tang rulers brought back Confucianism, especially its emphasis on ethics. This movement, called Neo-Confucianism, or "new Confucianism," remained the main religion of China's ruling classes until the early 1900s. Tang rulers built temples to Confucius and required government officials to study Confucian classics.

The decline of the Tang dynasty. The Tang dynasty reached its height in about 750. It then gradually declined under the rule of weak emperors. By 900 nomads had begun to invade China. In 907 a warlord who had murdered the emperor years earlier seized the throne for himself. The Tang dynasty ended.

✔ **READING CHECK: Finding the Main Idea** What were the main accomplishments in Chinese culture during the Sui and Tang dynasties?

Wu Hou first entered royal life at a young age as a member of the Tang emperor's household. She eliminated her female rivals within the palace and in A.D. 655 was made empress.

Wu Hou had her political opponents exiled or even executed. The emperor was often ill and relied on Wu Hou to manage state affairs. In 690 Wu Hou took power in her own name. Although ruthless against her opponents, Empress Wu ruled with great efficiency and she brought about needed social changes. **What did Empress Wu do once she gained power?**

China under the Sung Dynasty

In 960 Zhao Kuangyin (JOW KWAHNG·yin) established the Sung dynasty. China continued to flourish under Sung leadership. The emperors, however, never succeeded in winning control of all China. Rulers from Tibet held a kingdom in the northwest. A powerful Mongol tribe that held Manchuria increasingly threatened northeastern China. Like the Tang rulers before them, moreover, the Sung emperors faced constant pressure from foreign invasions and civil wars. Nevertheless, China under the Sung was a land of cultural and artistic progress.

By the mid-900s the main foreign danger to China came from the north. Mongols called the Qidan (CHI·DAHN) had taken Chinese territory in southern Manchuria. In time they invaded as far south as the Huang River. Finally the Sung agreed to a treaty with the Qidan. The Sung emperors had to pay a huge tribute to the Mongol invaders to avoid war. By 1042 the Sung were paying more than 200,000 ounces of silver to the Qidan every year. This was a great economic hardship.

Another Central Asian people, the Juchen, also moved into Manchuria. They took over northern China in 1126. The Juchen established the Jin dynasty in the north. Their capital was located at what is now Beijing. Hangzhou (HANG·CHOW) in the south became the new capital of the Sung dynasty.

Holt Researcher

go.hrw.com
KEYWORD: Holt Researcher
FreeFind: Empress Wu
After reading more about Empress Wu on the Holt Researcher, write a newspaper article describing her political, economic, and social influence on China.

The Sung and Jin Empires, A.D. 1141

Interpreting Maps After capturing the Sung capital city, the Jin's Juchen warriors expanded southward beyond the Huang River.

■ **Skills Assessment: Using Geography** About how far apart were the Sung and Jin capitals?

Trade and arts. Despite their troubles, the Sung emperors kept Chinese civilization at a high level. Foreign trade expanded. Hangzhou and Guangzhou became key port cities. Caravans brought in goods from Central Asia and India.

Exports included gold, silver, and copper. One of China's most valuable exports was porcelain, a fine, translucent pottery. Sung artisans perfected the art of making porcelain. They created delicate vases with colorful and complex designs. Sung artists also produced beautiful landscape paintings, inspired by the Daoist love of nature.

The civil service system. The Chinese further improved their civil service system during the Sung dynasty. Examinations took place in the capital every three years. To qualify, an individual first had to pass an examination at the local level. The Sung ended the need for sponsorship. This practice had allowed only those from important families to take the examinations.

Because some people tried cheating to pass the civil service exams, a system was developed to stop corruption. Applicants were assigned numbers and did not use their names on the exams. Guards probably watched over them as they took the exams. Clerks copied their answers so that their handwriting could not be recognized. Finally, three judges read each paper.

Great inventions. The Chinese invented gunpowder during the Han dynasty. At that time it was used only for fireworks and signals. Gunpowder was first used for warfare during the 900s. Printing was another important Chinese invention. The Chinese had learned very early how to make ink and paper. By 500 artisans were making seals of metal or wood that had inscriptions carved in reverse. The images they created resembled today's block prints. The world's first known printed book was the *Diamond Sutra,* a Buddhist religious text produced in China in 868. Movable type was developed in the 1040s. However, it was not as practical to use as carved blocks.

Peasant life. By about 1050 China's population was about 100 million people. Most were peasants who lived and worked in the countryside. Two important changes took place in peasant life during the Tang and Sung dynasties.

One change was an improvement in farming methods. Water-control projects allowed farmers to irrigate more fields so that they could grow more rice. A new type of quick-ripening rice from Southeast Asia let farmers grow two crops each year instead of one. Peasants could sell surplus food in the many small market towns. Another important crop during those years was tea, which was made into a drink that was popular throughout China.

The second major change made life harder for the peasants. New taxes levied by the Tang rulers fell particularly hard on them. Peasants who could not pay their taxes had to sell their farms. They became tenant farmers, paying high rents to landlords.

This image is taken from a Chinese scroll of the 1100s. Entitled "Spring Festival on the River," the image portrays a prosperous and orderly society.

City life. During the Sung dynasty, more Chinese than ever before lived in cities and towns. Hangzhou was said to have had a population of about 2 million, with perhaps as many as 2 million more living near the city. The cities of Sung China bustled with activity. Shipments of farm produce arrived daily in the marketplaces. Shopkeepers sold embroidered silks, printed books, and handicrafts. Shoppers watched puppet shows, plays, dancers, and acrobats in the streets.

Wealthy Chinese probably lived in fine homes surrounded by gardens and artificial lakes. Ordinary people, on the other hand, probably lived in crowded apartments, often in extended families of several generations. Some people had no homes at all and had to beg for food. The Sung government set up hospitals and orphanages to help the poor, but poverty and overcrowding remained a serious problem.

During this period the status of women in Chinese society began to change. There was less work for them to do in the cities than on the farms. The custom of footbinding spread among the wealthy classes. Girls' feet would be tied tightly with strips of linen, with their toes tucked underneath. Their feet would not be allowed to grow. The result was crippling. The custom was meant to show that a man was successful. His wife did not have to do housework because he could afford servants. Eventually, small feet became viewed as a sign of feminine beauty.

✔ **READING CHECK: Categorizing** What developments during the Sung dynasty improved life for the Chinese people? Which made life worse?

The custom of footbinding survived in China for centuries, as this photograph of a Chinese woman from the 1900s reveals.

SECTION 1 REVIEW

1. **Identify** and explain the significance:
   Grand Canal
   Li Bo
   Du Fu
   Empress Wu
   Zen
   Diamond Sutra

2. **Categorizing** Copy the chart below. Use it to identify the principal accomplishments of the Sui, the Tang, and the Sung dynasties.

3. **Finding the Main Idea**
   a. What were the most noteworthy advances in Chinese culture during the Sui, Tang, and Sung dynasties?
   b. How did life improve for ordinary people during the Sung dynasty?

4. **Writing and Critical Thinking**
   Evaluating Imagine yourself visiting Hangzhou. Write a poem or a song lyric about your impressions of the Sung capital.
   Consider:
   • what daily life was like for individuals living in the city
   • what items you might want to trade for to take back home with you

The Mongol Empire

READ TO DISCOVER

❶ How were the Mongol invaders able to conquer and rule so much of Asia?

❷ What effect did Mongol rule have on China?

IDENTIFY

Genghis Khan
Kublai Khan
Batu
Golden Horde
Marco Polo

▶ WHY IT MATTERS TODAY

Changing political boundaries can have important consequences for people. Use **CNN** Student News.com or other **current event** sources to locate a place in the world where changing boundaries have changed peoples' lives. Record your findings in your journal.

CNN Student News.com

The Main Idea
The powerful Mongol people established a large and strong empire in China and other areas.

The Story Continues *"The Tartars—that is, the Mongols—are the most obedient people in the world in regard to their leaders,"* noted a European traveler in the 1240s. *"They hold them [their leaders] in the greatest reverence and never tell them a lie."* The Chinese learned about Mongol leaders firsthand, as the invaders came to control the entire land.

Genghis Khan and the Mongols

The Mongols lived north of China in the rugged steppe region now called Mongolia. Although they were never a numerous people, the Mongols' culture encouraged the skills of battle. Mongol leaders could mobilize much of the population to engage in conquest. At its height, the Mongol army had about 100,000 cavalry. Mounted warriors enjoyed a great advantage over foot soldiers. Mongol cavalry could cover up to 100 miles in a day. Special saddles and iron stirrups allowed them to fire arrows accurately while riding at top speed. They made good use of their speed and mobility on horseback. In battle Mongol riders would surround their enemy like hunters surrounding wild game.

The Mongol armies were highly skilled in the use of massed firepower, rapid movement, and maneuvers. They would wear down an enemy through constant attack or threat of attack. They also used powerful weapons, possibly including catapults and

INTERPRETING THE VISUAL RECORD

Mongols This manuscript from the 1200s illustrates a battle between Mongol tribes. *What does this picture tell us about Mongol armor and weapons?*

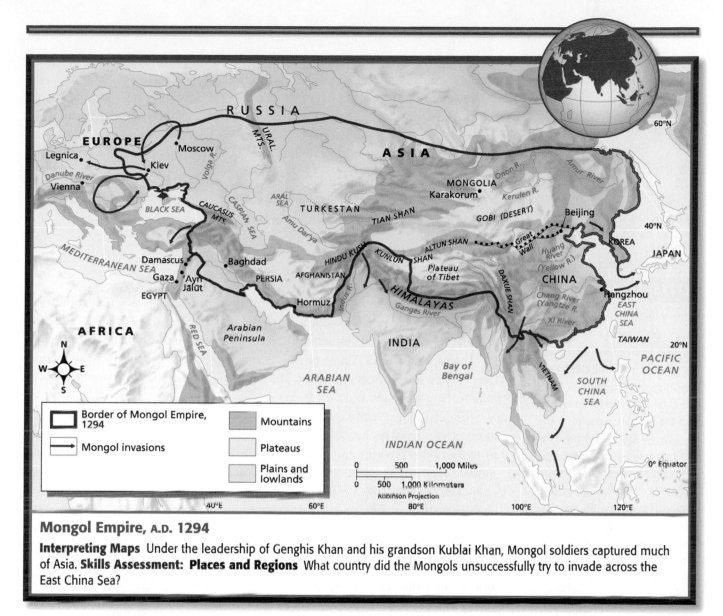

Mongol Empire, A.D. 1294

Interpreting Maps Under the leadership of Genghis Khan and his grandson Kublai Khan, Mongol soldiers captured much of Asia. **Skills Assessment: Places and Regions** What country did the Mongols unsuccessfully try to invade across the East China Sea?

giant crossbows mounted on stands. Battle provided a way for individual soldiers to acquire riches, honor, and personal power. The evidence suggests, too, that many of the Mongol generals were extremely capable.

The fiercest Mongol leader of all time was **Genghis Khan,** who lived from about 1162 to 1227. Originally named Temujin, he took the title Genghis Khan, meaning "Universal Ruler," in 1206. He went on to create an immense empire.

Mongol conquests. In the early 1200s, Mongols under Genghis Khan swept down from Karakorum, their capital. They captured the city now called Beijing and named it Khanbalik (kahn·buh·LEEK). They then turned westward, conquering Central Asia and most of Persia. Led by **Kublai** (KOO·bluh) **Khan,** a grandson of Genghis Khan, they conquered the rest of China. They also conquered the area now called Tibet and part of Southeast Asia. They tried but failed to capture Japan.

Another grandson of Genghis Khan, **Batu,** invaded Europe around 1240. His troops swept across Russia, Poland, and Hungary to the outskirts of Vienna. They plundered city after city, either killing the inhabitants or taking them as slaves. Frightened Europeans called the Mongolian invaders the **Golden Horde.** This name referred to the gold color of the Mongol tents in the sun. The Mongols soon left Poland and Hungary. They controlled Russia, however, for almost 200 years.

Holt Researcher
go.hrw.com
KEYWORD: Holt Researcher
FreeFind: Genghis Khan
After reading more about Genghis Khan on the Holt Researcher, create a collage that shows the changes his invasions brought to other parts of the world.

**Kublai Khan
(1215–1294)**

The grandson of the great Mongol warrior Genghis Khan, Kublai Khan also proved to be a great general and ruler. He would go on to conquer China and become the first emperor of the Mongol dynasty.

Kublai Khan was known for his capable governing and his mercy toward conquered peoples. He stressed religious toleration. He was also the first ruler to use only paper money. **What were some of Kublai Khan's achievements?**

Mongol rule. The Mongol Empire was divided into four parts. These four parts remained united until the 1300s, then slowly began to drift apart.

In 1260 Kublai Khan was given the title of Great Khan. He was recognized as the head of the whole Mongol Empire. He adopted many Chinese ways and introduced Chinese ceremonies to his court. He also relied on Chinese officials in the lower and middle ranks of the government. Kublai Khan built two palaces, one in Mongolia and one near Beijing.

✔ **READING CHECK: Identifying Cause and Effect** How were the Mongol nomads able to conquer so much of Asia?

China under the Mongols

In 1271 Kublai Khan announced the beginning of his own dynasty. Called the Yuan dynasty, it covered northern China, with its capital at Beijing. In 1279 Yuan forces defeated the Sung dynasty in southern China. The Yuan ruled China until 1368.

Under Mongol rule, China prospered in many ways. Once the Mongols secured their empire, a century of war ended. The population, which had dropped to about 60 million, began to grow again.

Kublai Khan extended the length of the Grand Canal by hundreds of miles in order to supply his new capital with food from the southern farmlands. He also fostered routes linking China with India and Persia. This greatly improved trade. Probably as many as 10,000 courier stations, each stabling hundreds of horses used by relay riders, dotted Yuan China. These stations, set about 25 miles from one another, enabled mounted couriers to carry news and imperial messages throughout the empire. The efficient Yuan system of communications connected to virtually every corner of the empire and helped to maintain unity and order. Improved trade and communication encouraged China's economic growth. At the same time, however, heavy taxes enforced by the Yuan emperors may have weakened the economy and created many hardships for farmers and merchants. Over time, the emperors' harsh taxes and frequent demands for tribute helped to undermine Yuan authority and to promote growing resentment toward Mongol rule.

Contact with Europeans. During Mongol rule, contact between China and the rest of the world increased. King Louis IX of France and the pope in Rome both sent ambassadors to China. Christian missionaries also traveled there, as did travelers from other non-European nations.

It was during the reign of Kublai Khan that the Italian **Marco Polo** traveled to China. Marco Polo was a famous merchant and explorer. At about the age of seventeen

Marco Polo, pictured here in Mongol dress, brought news of Kublai Khan's empire back to Europeans.

he left Venice with his father and uncle. After three years of difficult travel they arrived in China. Kublai Khan was impressed with the young Marco Polo. He employed Polo as his special representative. Polo traveled around China for 17 years and became famous. In his book *The Travels of Marco Polo,* he described Kublai Khan's court to his fellow Europeans:

❝When the Great Khan is holding court, the seating at banquets is arranged as follows. He himself sits at a much higher table than the rest . . . His principal wife sits next to him on the left. On the right, at a somewhat lower level, sit his sons in order of age . . . . They are placed so that their heads are on a level with the Great Khan's feet. Next to them are seated the other noblemen at other tables lower down again. . . . All the wives of the Khan's sons and grandsons and kinsmen are seated on his left at a lower level, and next to them the wives of his nobles and knights lower down still.❞

Marco Polo, *The Travels of Marco Polo,* trans. by R.E. Latham

Analyzing Primary Sources

Drawing Inferences What can you infer about the society of the Yuan dynasty from the way that people were seated at Kublai Khan's banquet?

Chinese-Mongol relations. The Yuan dynasty did much that was good for China. However, there were still tensions between the Mongols and the Chinese. For one thing, they spoke different languages. More importantly, the Mongols did not treat the Chinese as equals. Only Mongols or other non-Chinese people could hold important positions in the government. Mongol law punished Chinese criminals more harshly than non-Chinese ones. Moreover, the Mongols did not allow marriage between different groups of people.

Kublai Khan died in 1294, leaving China to weak successors. During the period after his death, the country experienced many problems. The Huang River flooded, destroying crops and causing famine. Rebellions sprang up. Finally, in 1368, the Yuan dynasty was overthrown.

The Mongols influenced China in several ways. They brought greater contact with Europe. They made local governments more responsible to the central government in Beijing. Later Chinese dynasties built on these political reforms by giving more powers to the emperor.

Paper money, as well as coins like those shown here, served as currency during the reign of Kublai Khan. Eventually only paper money was used.

✔ **READING CHECK: Making Generalizations** What were the good and bad effects of Mongol rule in China?

SECTION 2 REVIEW

1. Identify and explain the significance:
Genghis Khan
Kublai Khan
Batu
Golden Horde
Marco Polo

2. Sequencing Copy the graphic organizer below. Use it to illustrate the events that led the Mongol nomads from the plains of Central Asia to become rulers of China.

3. **Finding the Main Idea**

a. Why did the Mongol invaders want to conquer so much land in Asia?

b. Overall, was Mongol rule good or bad for the average Chinese person? Explain your answer.

4. **Writing and Critical Thinking**

Supporting a Point of View Write a letter to Kublai Khan requesting that he change some policy of his government with which you disagree.

Consider:
• the impact of Mongol rule on the Chinese people
• the way you think the Great Khan might expect to be addressed

Homework Practice Online
keyword: SH3 HP3

THE CIVILIZATIONS OF EAST ASIA **83**

❶ How did the geography of Japan influence its development?

❷ How did China influence the early development of Japan?

❸ How did changes in government influence society in feudal Japan?

❹ How was Southeast Asia influenced by China and India?

DEFINE

kami
shogun
samurai
seppuku
daimyo

IDENTIFY

Shinto
The Tale of Genji
Fujiwara
Minamoto
Ashikaga
Bushido
Yi
Sejong

▶ **WHY IT MATTERS TODAY**

Powerful nations can have enormous influence on their smaller neighbors. Use CNN student News.com or other **current event** sources to locate a place in the world where a large nation is changing the lives of people in a smaller nation. Record your findings in your journal.

CNN student News.com

Japan, Korea, and Southeast Asia

The Main Idea
China's culture strongly influenced other countries in eastern and southeastern Asia.

The Story Continues *Japan is a chain of islands in the western Pacific Ocean off the east coast of Asia. A Chinese observer once wrote about Japan, "The land of [Japan] is warm and mild. In winter as in summer, the people live on raw vegetables and go about barefoot." Although Japan is a country of great scenic beauty, its environment has often turned against its people.*

The Physical Setting

The modern nation of Japan consists of a string of thousands of islands in the western Pacific Ocean off the east coast of Asia. This island chain stretches over a distance of nearly 1,400 miles. The great majority of present-day Japan's large population lives on the country's four largest islands. These include Honshu (HAWN·shoo), Hokkaido (hoh·KY·doh), Kyushu (KYOO·shoo), and Shikoku (shee·KOH·koo). No place in Japan is more than about 100 miles from the ocean.

Japan is very mountainous. As a result, only a relatively small part of its land can be used for farming. Hard-working Japanese farmers still are able to produce a great deal of food. They are aided by plentiful rainfall, sunny days, and long growing seasons in some areas. Many rivers provide easy irrigation. Nature is not always kind to Japan, however. Earthquakes, tidal waves, and typhoons often strike the islands.

Until modern times, the seas surrounding Japan protected the islands from foreign influences. The Japanese people could choose whether or not they wanted to have contact with other peoples. At times in their history, they have showed interest in the outside world. At other times they have preferred to live in isolation.

The Mongols under Kublai Khan tried twice to conquer Japan without success. In 1281, a Mongol fleet carrying more than about 140,000 soldiers assembled to invade Japan. A powerful typhoon wrecked the fleet. The grateful Japanese called the storm *kamikaze*, or "Divine Wind."

✔ **READING CHECK: Finding the Main Idea** How did the geography of Japan affect Japanese contact with other peoples?

This detail from a Japanese painting is meant to depict the "Divine Wind."

Japan's Beginnings

In prehistoric times migrants from the Asian mainland settled the Japanese islands. By the first centuries A.D. these migrants had organized themselves into clans.

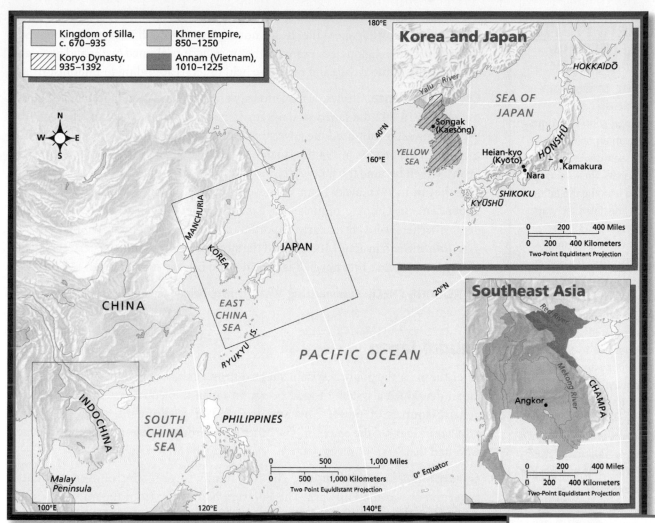

Map legend:
- Kingdom of Silla, c. 670–935
- Koryo Dynasty, 935–1392
- Khmer Empire, 850–1250
- Annam (Vietnam), 1010–1225

Korea and Japan

HOKKAIDŌ
Yalu River
SEA OF JAPAN
Songak (Kaesŏng)
YELLOW SEA
HONSHŪ
Heian-kyo (Kyōto)
Nara
Kamakura
SHIKOKU
KYŪSHŪ
0 200 400 Miles
0 200 400 Kilometers
Two-Point Equidistant Projection

MANCHURIA
KOREA
JAPAN
CHINA
EAST CHINA SEA
RYUKYU IS.
PACIFIC OCEAN
INDOCHINA
SOUTH CHINA SEA
PHILIPPINES
Malay Peninsula
0 500 1,000 Miles
0 500 1,000 Kilometers
Two-Point Equidistant Projection

Southeast Asia

Red River
Mekong River
CHAMPA
Angkor
0 200 400 Miles
0 200 400 Kilometers
Two-Point Equidistant Projection

The most powerful clans lived on the island of Honshu. Since then the Japanese people have come together to form a strong, unified society.

Early history. Religion played an important role in helping Japanese culture form. From earliest times, the Japanese believed in gods or nature spirits called **kami.** They believed that these spirits lived in natural objects. For example, kami could be in sand, waterfalls, or trees. Many Japanese clans trace their origins to a particular kami. This religion is now called **Shinto,** meaning "way of the kami." Shinto has no established scripture or doctrine. Shinto worship involves prayers and rituals to please the kami. People might ask for many children or bountiful crops. Shinto is also concerned with ritual cleanliness.

Shinto helped unify Japan under imperial rule. Early emperors seem to have acted as Shinto priests. For all of Japan's history, probably only one imperial family has reigned—the Yamato clan. The first Yamato emperor probably came to power during the early 300s.

Few records of early Japanese history exist. The Chinese, however, knew about Japan before 100. The Japanese adapted Chinese writing by at least the early 700s, and possibly much earlier. Another Chinese influence was Buddhism, introduced in 552. At first the emperor's advisers disliked the new religion. Eventually, the rulers allowed Buddhist temples to be built. Many people in the Japanese court became Buddhists.

Japan, Korea, and Southeast Asia,
c. A.D. 670–1392

Interpreting Maps Japan is a long, narrow country made up of four main islands. The Korean peninsula gave birth to the country of Korea.

■ **Skills Assessment:**
1. **Using Geography** At the narrowest point, approximately how much distance separates Korea from Japan?
2. **Drawing Inferences** How might this affect the relationship between the two countries?

In later centuries, Buddhism spread among the common people and became an important part of Japanese life. It did not replace Shinto, however. Most Japanese believed in both religions. For example, they may have celebrated births and marriages according to Shinto rituals and may have held funerals according to Buddhist rituals.

Chinese influence. Chinese art, science, government, and fashion influenced Japanese society. In 702 the Japanese emperor issued a new law code modeled on Tang dynasty laws. It centralized the government and gave the emperor more power over the lives of his people. In 794 the Japanese built a capital named Heian-kyo (HAY·ahn kyoh), which became the modern city of Kyoto (KYOH·toh). At the capital, the ruling class began to turn away from Chinese influence. Japanese culture became less dependent on Chinese models. For example, poets began to write in Japanese. Female writers were particularly important at Heian. Lady Murasaki Shikibu wrote *The Tale of Genji* in about 1000. It told the story of Prince Genji, the perfect courtier, and was the world's first novel. It is considered a literary masterpiece.

✔ **READING CHECK: Summarizing** What changes helped Japan develop its own culture?

Feudal Japan

After the 800s, the political system adapted from China began to decline. In its place, Japan developed a system of local power. In Japan the feudal system contained two general sources of power. One was the central government, where important families influenced the emperor. The other was a group of powerful local landowners who had their own warriors.

Government in feudal Japan. The first family to gain control over the central government was the **Fujiwara.** The Fujiwara had power from the mid-800s to the mid-1100s. In 1185 the **Minamoto** clan gained power. The reign of this clan marked a change in the way the government was run. In 1192 the emperor granted Minamoto Yoritomo the title of **shogun,** or general. The emperor kept his throne, but the shogun had control of the military, finances, and laws. In 1331, the Emperor Go-Daigo tried to regain power but failed. One of his generals, Ashikaga Takauji (ah·shee·KAH·gah tah·KOW·jee) claimed the shogunate for his own clan. The **Ashikaga** shoguns ruled for nearly 250 years.

At the local level, however, wealthy landlords held power. They hired warriors called **samurai** for protection. In some ways, the samurai were similar to European knights. A samurai was fiercely loyal to his lord and clan. His power rested on his skill with the sword. The samurai followed a code of behavior called **Bushido.** This means the "way of the warrior." Bushido stressed bravery, loyalty, and honor. Samurai would accept physical hardship without complaint and did not fear death. As one samurai scholar wrote,

 ❝The business of the samurai consists in reflecting on his own station in life, in discharging loyal service to his master . . . and with due consideration of his own position, in devoting himself to duty above all.❞

Yamaga Soko, quoted in Conrad Totman, *A History of Japan*

If samurai displeased their masters or were defeated in battle, they might practice seppuku. **Seppuku** was ceremonial suicide, also known in the West as hara-kiri. It was a way to avoid the dishonor that accompanied defeat or disobedience.

Japan's Feudal System

In Japan's feudal system some groups at lower levels of power actually had more influence than those at higher levels. For example, although the emperor and the shoguns held the top positions, they were often just figureheads. The daimyo had the most real power and were the most responsible for running the business of daily life for most of Japanese society. Reading an organization chart can help to show relationships within this system, using connecting lines to show who has authority over whom.

Emperor

Shogun

Daimyo

Samurai

Samurai

Peasant

Peasant

Skills Reminder

Charts are an effective way of visually organizing and communicating information to show relationships, comparisons, and contrasts. To read a chart, identify the type of chart and its purpose. Then identify the details given by the chart, such as labels and leader lines. Assess how the details relate to each other and what information this provides about a subject.

Skills Practice

❶ What can you determine about Japan's feudal system from the chart above?

❷ Using what you know about charts, draw an organization chart like the one above that shows the structure of the United States government. You may need to use an American government textbook to find the information necessary to practice this skill.

Zen garden Shown above is a Zen garden in contemporary Japan. The sand has been raked into spare, clean lines to represent the Zen Buddhist values of simplicity and appreciation of nature. ***What mood is suggested by the design of the landscape?***

The daimyo. In time local lords known as **daimyo** (DY·mee·oh), or "great names," gained great power. These lords and their samurai became the most powerful people in Japan during the Ashikaga shogunate. For a century, Japan had no effective central government and warfare was common. Despite this situation, Japan continued to grow economically and socially. Peasants produced greater crop yields, which meant more tax money for the daimyo. The daimyo promoted trade, which they also taxed. The taxes were very likely used to pay for the wars. Wars could offer people of lower status a chance to rise in society. Any man who could use a sword or lance could possibly join a daimyo's army. Those who fought well could be promoted to a higher rank.

Zen Buddhism. A religious awakening occurred in feudal Japan as Buddhists established new sects. Some taught that salvation could come through faith alone. Older sects asked people to give money to monasteries or study Buddhist scriptures. Therefore, the new sects appealed to ordinary people.

Zen Buddhism was introduced from China in the 1100s. It particularly interested warriors. Zen taught salvation through enlightenment, not faith. This perspective was very similar to the views embodied in Daoism. Zen Buddhism also taught that the life of the body was not important. Zen Buddhists developed self-discipline through long hours of meditation. These skills helped warriors in battle.

The Ashikaga shoguns supported Zen Buddhism. They encouraged the artistic efforts of Zen monks. New art forms inspired by Zen appeared in the late 1300s and early 1400s. One was landscape architecture, or the art of gardens. By arranging rocks, trees, and water, Zen artists tried to represent the beauty of nature. A related art form was the tea ceremony, designed to produce spiritual calm. People would gather in a simple room by a garden to quietly drink tea and admire the beauty of nature. Another important Zen art form was the Noh play. First performed in the 1300s, these were highly stylized dance dramas. Noh plays drew on religious, historical, or romantic themes. Male actors wearing masks would perform on a bare stage while a chorus chanted the story.

✔ **READING CHECK: Identifying Cause and Effect** How did the confusion in government offer new opportunities for people in Japanese society?

Korea

Korea is a rugged, mountainous peninsula that juts south from Manchuria into the sea between China and Japan. As is true of Japan, Korea's political and cultural development was strongly shaped by China.

Korea's history. Because of its location, Korea has long served as a bridge that has allowed the passage of people and ideas from the mainland of eastern Asia to neighboring island chains. The Korean Peninsula was first settled in prehistoric times by nomadic peoples from northeastern Asia. These people enjoyed abundant sources of food, including wild deer, fish and other seafoods, and certain plant foods. Agriculture—especially rice farming—reached Korea from China, perhaps as early as about 1500 B.C. Metalworking techniques also spread from China to early Korea.

As early as 300 B.C., migrants from China began to arrive in Korea, bringing with them knowledge of metalworking and agriculture. Not long afterward, the first strong Korean kingdom, Chosŏn, emerged in the northern part of the peninsula. By the early 100s B.C. Chosŏn was strong enough to hold some control over much of the Korean Peninsula.

In about 108 B.C. troops from Han China invaded Korea, conquered the kingdom of Chosŏn, and turned it into a Han colony. For the next 400 years the Chinese maintained tight control over northwestern Korea, allowing native Koreans little or no voice in their government. Elsewhere on the peninsula, however, three Korean kingdoms—Koguryo, Paekche, and Silla—arose in opposition to Chinese rule. Because these native kingdoms also fought amongst themselves, they were unable to challenge China's dominance in Korea. With the fall of the Han dynasty, Koguryo invaded the north and took over the one-time Chinese colony.

Unification under the Silla. Korea's three kingdoms continued to fight one another for the next several centuries. During the early A.D. 600s China's Sui dynasty attempted to conquer Korea but failed. Later, however, the rulers of Silla formed a strategic alliance with the Tang emperor of China. Working together, the armies of Silla and China conquered Paekche and Koguryo. Silla then turned on the Tang forces and drove them from Korea. By about 670 the kingdom of Silla had united Korea for the first time. Over time, Silla was weakened by internal rebellions and the loss of leadership. During the early 900s a new kingdom, Koryo (from which comes the name Korea), grew to challenge Silla's rule. By 935 Koryo had overthrown Silla and had taken control of the peninsula.

Korea remained independent throughout the era of the Tang dynasty. But in the mid-1200s the peninsula once again fell under the control of its powerful neighbor to the west, and Korea became part of the Mongol Empire. It was not until 1392 that Koreans regained their independence by driving out the Mongols. The **Yi** dynasty arose to rule the peninsula, lasting for centuries until Japan annexed Korea in 1910.

The growth of Korean culture. The culture and civilization of China has had a strong and lasting influence on Korea. Chosŏn, the first true kingdom in Korea, was founded in part by immigrants from China and clearly reflected many elements of Chinese culture. Korean rulers adopted Chinese as their written language, and they embraced China's Confucian traditions and ideas. They also followed the Chinese model of government. Korean rulers built dynasties controlled by hereditary kings. The rulers of Koryo used an examination process to select and train their government administrators. This process was based in large part on China's Confucian civil service system. The kings of Koryo, moreover, built Kaesong, a great capital city much like Xi'an, the imperial city of China's Tang dynasty.

During the 300s the ideals of Chinese Buddhism were brought to Korea. Many Koreans accepted the Buddhist philosophy and built magnificent temples that became major centers of learning. Buddhist teachings became part of Korean culture, philosophy, and morality. During the period of the three kingdoms, Buddhism became Korea's state religion. In the 700s Zen was introduced. It became the dominant form of Buddhism throughout the peninsula. Later, Korean scholars also studied the philosophy of Confucius and the Korean government adopted the Chinese civil service system.

INTERPRETING THE VISUAL RECORD

Dragon's head This gold and bronze dragon's head was fashioned in Korea to decorate the top of a flagstaff. *What does this metalwork suggest about Korean artistic and technological skills during the Silla and Koryo periods?*

Holt Researcher

go.hrw.com
KEYWORD: Holt Researcher
FreeFind: Sejong

After reading more about Sejong on the Holt Researcher, use a problem-solving process to evaluate how his administration improved upon Chinese traditions.

Koreans learned to use movable type from the Chinese. They advanced this technology by casting type blocks in metal.

Despite the strength of China's influence, however, Korea did not become an identical copy of its huge neighbor to the west. Instead, Koreans worked to maintain the strength and identity of their culture and traditions. As one ruler of Koryo insisted in 982, "Let us follow China in poetry, history, music, ceremony, and the [principles of Confucius], but in riding and dressing let us be Koreans." Thus, the people of ancient Korea built a civilization that was, in many important ways, unique and distinct from that of China. Korean Buddhism, for example, included many elements of traditional Korean beliefs.

Another important difference between Korean and Chinese cultures was the presence of a powerful nobility in Korea. Korean aristocrats, unlike Chinese nobles, had great influence on the country's political development. As a result, the power of Korea's Confucian-style government administration was limited. Korean society differed from that of China, too, because it never developed a large, well-educated social class of merchants, government administrators, and scholars. In China, this group formed a kind of middle class between the traditional nobles and the peasant farmers. Korean society, however, was more sharply divided between its small upper class and its very large lower class.

During the 1400s the emperor **Sejong** ordered the development of a Korean alphabet. The Koreans borrowed the Chinese invention of movable wood type and then improved upon it. They designed movable type blocks made of metal, which was far more durable and produced sharper images.

✔ **READING CHECK: Contrasting** How did Korean aristocrats differ from Chinese nobles?

Civilization in Southeast Asia

The mainland of Southeast Asia (also known as Indochina) is made up of the modern nations of Cambodia, Laos, Malaysia, Myanmar, Thailand (formerly Siam), and Vietnam. Like Japan and Korea, the kingdoms and peoples of ancient Southeast Asia were strongly and continuously influenced by China, which borders Southeast Asia to the north. The civilization of India, which lies to the region's northwest, also helped to shape Southeast Asian lifestyles, traditions, and beliefs. In a broader sense, however, the cultures that developed in Southeast Asia have their own distinct identities.

Northern Vietnam—known as Annam—was controlled by China throughout much of its history. By the 900s the Vietnamese had made several attempts to throw off Chinese dominance. It was not until 939, however, that the people of northern Vietnam won their independence from China. Soon after, Vietnam fell into widespread disorder and political violence. Finally, the emergence of several dynasties led to growing stability and the first steps toward the unification of the country.

The Vietnamese civilization that developed during these years was heavily influenced by contact with China. For example, Vietnam adopted Mahayana Buddhism from the Chinese. Over time, this form of Buddhism became the guiding philosophy of the Vietnamese culture. Daoism and Confucianism also contributed to the development of Vietnam's culture and society. In addition, Vietnam used the writing system and political organization of the Chinese.

Much of the rest of mainland Southeast Asia was shaped by Indian culture and tradition. Early in the history of Southeast Asia, people from India began to settle in the region, many of them perhaps Hindu and Buddhist missionaries.

The Sanskrit language came into use, helping to spread Indian literature and thought. In present-day Cambodia, ruins of the city of Angkor Thom and the huge temple of Angkor Wat offer reminders of Indian influence. Reliefs with scenes from the Hindu epics adorn Angkor Wat, one of the architectural wonders of the Far East.

Centered in modern-day Cambodia, the Khmer Empire grew to control much of Southeast Asia in the years between about 850 and about 1250. Khmer rulers, strongly influenced by Indian culture, adopted many Hindu and Buddhist beliefs. For many years, Khmer society embraced the Indian principle of a god-king. The rulers probably used forced labor and income from taxes to build elaborate cities, government centers, and magnificent temple complexes. At the same time, Khmer leaders undertook major construction projects for the public good. These included hospitals, travelers' rest-houses, and canal and water-control systems designed to encourage rice farming throughout the region.

The Khmer kings' abuse of their royal powers eventually led to social discontent and rebellion. The ideas of Theravada Buddhism became increasingly widespread throughout much of Southeast Asia. This Buddhist philosophy had no place for splendid ceremonies, elaborate temples such as Angkor Wat, or the concept of a god-king. Over time, the all-powerful Khmer kings were overthrown and Theravada Buddhism became the predominant form of Buddhism in Southeast Asia.

✔ **READING CHECK: Categorizing** In what ways did Korea and Southeast Asia develop their own cultures despite the influences of China and India?

INTERPRETING THE VISUAL RECORD

Angkor Wat The temple of Angkor Wat in Cambodia is one of the architectural wonders of the Far East. It is decorated with scenes from Hindu epics.

Link to Today How does this temple show evidence of Indian influence on Southeast Asian art and beliefs?

SECTION 3 REVIEW

1. **Define** and explain the significance:
   kami   seppuku
   shogun   daimyo
   samurai

2. **Identify** and explain the significance:
   Shinto   Ashikaga
   The Tale of Genji   Bushido
   Fujiwara   Yi
   Minamoto   Sejong

3. **Summarizing** Copy the graphic organizer below. Label the largest oval China and the others Japan, Korea, and Southeast Asia. Use it to identify the institutions and customs that the latter three adopted from China.

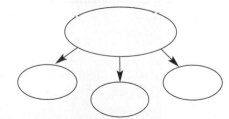

4. **Finding the Main Idea**

   a. How did the breakup of the central government in Japan lead to changes in feudal Japanese society?

   b. How did China influence the societies of Japan, Korea, and Southeast Asia?

5. **Writing and Critical Thinking**

   Supporting a Point of View What are the advantages and disadvantages of Bushido—the "way of the warrior"—as a code of behavior in feudal Japan?

   Consider:
   • the nature of society in feudal Japan and the values that it emphasized
   • the skills and behaviors that could help a person to advance in feudal Japan
   • the ways a person could express bravery, loyalty, and honor in daily life

go.hrw.com **Homework Practice Online**

keyword: SH3 HP3

3 Review

Creating a Time Line

Copy the time line below onto a sheet of paper. Complete the time line by filling in the events, individuals, and dates from the chapter that you think were significant. Pick three events and explain why you think they were significant.

| A.D. 552 | A.D. 1000 | A.D. 1573 |

Writing a Summary

Using standard grammar, spelling, sentence structure, and punctuation, write an overview of the events in the chapter.

Identifying People and Ideas

Identify the following terms or individuals and explain their significance:

1. Grand Canal
2. Empress Wu
3. Zen
4. *Diamond Sutra*
5. Genghis Khan
6. Kublai Khan
7. Golden Horde
8. Shinto
9. shogun
10. samurai

Understanding Main Ideas

Section 1 *(pp. 74–79)*

China under the Sui, Tang, and Sung Dynasties

1. What were the most important developments in Chinese culture during the Sui, Tang, and Sung dynasties?
2. Did life improve for ordinary people during the Sung dynasty? Explain.

Section 2 *(pp. 80–83)*

The Mongol Empire

3. How were the Mongol nomads able to gain power in China?
4. How did China change under Mongol rule?

Section 3 *(pp. 84–91)*

Japan, Korea, and Southeast Asia

5. How did Japan's geography affect its relations with its neighbors?
6. How did China influence Japanese society and culture?

7. What unique features of society in feudal Japan were the result of political confusion?
8. What were the influences of China and India on societies in Korea and Southeast Asia?

Reviewing Themes

1. **Global Relations** How did proximity to China affect the rest of Asian civilization?
2. **Government** Why were the rulers of the several Chinese dynasties unable to retain their hold on power?
3. **Culture** How were the various forms of Buddhism reflected in east Asian cultures?

Thinking Critically

1. **Drawing Inferences** How did the Sung and Yuan dynasties change China?
2. **Identifying Bias** Would Marco Polo have said that Kublai Khan's rule was good for China? Why or why not?
3. **Contrasting** How did the culture of feudal Japan differ from earlier Japanese culture?

Writing About History

Categorizing Write a report explaining the impact of Chinese culture on life in Mongol society and on Japan. Use the chart below to organize your thoughts before writing.

	Mongol society	Japanese society
Government		
Religion		
Art & literature		
Daily life		

Drawing Inferences

Study the chart below. Then use the information from the chart to answer the questions that follow.

The Sui Dynasty—Successes versus Problems	
Some Sui Successes	**Some Sui Problems**
• Reunited China	• Suffered defeats in Korea
• Rebuilt the Great Wall	• Constant demands for labor
• Constructed canals	• Heavy spending
• Built strong central government	• Excesses at court

1. Which statement below most accurately describes an inference that may be drawn from the chart?

   a. The Sui rulers were generally popular among the people they ruled.

   b. Military defeats in Korea probably had little effect on Sui rule at home.

   c. The people were probably willing to support heavy imperial spending, since it benefited them.

   d. Military defeats in foreign lands may have caused the Sui rulers to lose prestige among their people.

2. The Sui dynasty ruled for a relatively brief period of time. Write a short paragraph in which you analyze some of the factors in the dynasty's history that might explain why it could not maintain its rule.

Analyzing a Primary Source

Read the following quote from Ibn Battūtah, a Moroccan Muslim who traveled in China during the 1300s. Then answer the questions.

"In regard to portraiture there is none . . . who can match . . . [the Chinese] in precision, for in this art they show a marvellous talent. This is a custom of theirs, making portraits of all who pass through their country. In fact they have brought this to such perfection that if a stranger commits any offence that obliges him to flee from China, they send his portrait far and wide. A search is then made for him and wherever the person bearing a resemblance to that portrait is found, he is arrested."

3. Which statement best describes what you can infer about the Chinese attitude toward foreigners?

   a. They wanted to impress them with their artistic ability.

   b. They respected their privacy.

   c. They disliked them.

   d. They did not completely trust them.

4. What is your opinion of how the Chinese kept track of strangers? Give reasons for your point of view.

Alternative Assessment

Building Your Portfolio

Link to TODAY

Culture

Historical China had a powerful influence on the cultures of other nations. Using your textbook and other sources, make a list of ideas, institutions, and advances in mathematics, science, and technology that originated in China. Use a poster board to prepare a map of the world or a collage to trace the spread of these ideas to other civilizations.

internet connect

Internet Activity: go.hrw.com
KEYWORD: SH3 WH3

Choose a topic on the Civilizations of East Asia to:

• understand similarities and differences of Chinese, Japanese, and Korean art.

• research the early development of Korea, Vietnam, and the Khmer Empire of Southeast Asia.

• learn more about Genghis Khan.

A.D. 432–A.D. 1328

The Rise of the Middle Ages

A medieval crossbow

A.D. 782
Politics
Charlemagne executes Saxon hostages.

C. A.D. 542
Daily Life
A devastating plague begins to move across Europe, resulting in a decades-long population decline.

C. A.D. 476
Global Events
The last Western Roman emperor is deposed.

C. A.D. 797
Daily Life
French kings establish a royal messenger service.

| A.D. 425 | A.D. 525 | A.D. 725 | A.D. 825 |

A.D. 455
Global Events
Vandals attack Rome.

C. A.D. 500
Science and Technology
Architects develop the first plans for the Vatican in Rome.

C. A.D. 750
Daily Life
Beds become popular in France and Germany.

C. A.D. 787
Global Events
The first Viking raids into Britain occur.

Illustration of the invasion of England by Danish Vikings

Viking carving of a lion's head, A.D. 800s

Build on What You Know

G reat civilizations flourished in East and Southeast Asia in the thousand years after about the A.D. 500s. The cultures that emerged in China, Korea, Japan, and Southeast Asia reached new heights of achievement. Change and growth also characterized the civilizations that emerged in Europe during these same years. The barbarian peoples who overran much of the Roman Empire brought with them behaviors and traditions that gradually developed into a new and distinct European civilization. In this chapter, you will learn how new European societies and cultures arose from the ashes of Rome's collapse.

Detail from the Bayeux Tapestry depicting a battle scene between the English and the Normans

C. A.D. 1110
The Arts
The earliest recorded miracle play is performed in England.

C. A.D. 1253
Business and Finance
Linen is made in England.

C. A.D. 1314
Politics
Scotland becomes independent under Robert I, the Bruce.

C. A.D. 1125
The Arts
The "troubadour" tradition of wandering musicians begins in France.

C. A.D. 1190s
Science and Technology
The magnetic compass is used by mariners in Western Europe.

C. A.D. 1269
Business and Finance
The first English toll roads are built.

C. A.D. 1317
Politics
French law excludes women from inheriting the throne.

C. A.D. 900
Daily Life
European nobles begin to build fortified castles.

A.D. 925   **A.D. 1125**   **A.D. 1225**   **A.D. 1325**

C. A.D. 900s
Science and Technology
The crossbow is used in Europe.

C. A.D. 1124
Business and Finance
Coins are first minted in Scotland.

C. A.D. 1170
The Arts
Chrétien de Troyes writes the courtly love story "Lancelot."

A.D. 1215
Politics
King John I signs Magna Carta.

C. A.D. 1305
Business and Finance
Edward I standardizes measures, including the yard and the acre.

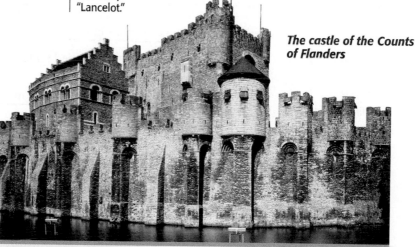

The castle of the Counts of Flanders

An idealized illustration of medieval knights

What's Your Opinion?

*Do you **agree** or **disagree** with the following statements? Support your point of view in your journal.*

Government Successful governments should establish a firm separation between the powers of church and state.

Constitutional Heritage Individual rights do not need to be included and defined in a constitution.

Economics Farming societies promote more secure and peaceful lifestyles than do societies that are centered upon industrial growth.

95

READ TO DISCOVER

❶ How did Frankish rulers gain control of Europe?

❷ What caused the decline of Charlemagne's empire?

DEFINE

medieval

IDENTIFY

Middle Ages
Clovis
Merovingians
Charles Martel
Carolingians
Charlemagne
Louis the Pious
Magyars
Vikings

▶ **WHY IT MATTERS TODAY**

The Vikings were known for their shipbuilding ability. Use 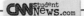 or other **current event** sources to discover how ships are part of peoples' lives in Scandinavia today. Record your findings in your journal.

CNN student News.com

The Rise of the Franks

The Main Idea
A new European civilization arose based on Roman and Germanic values and traditions.

The Story Continues *"Charles was large and strong, and of lofty stature. . . . his appearance was always stately and dignified . . . His gait [stride] was firm, his whole carriage manly, and his voice clear."* This is how one observer described Charlemagne, one of the strong rulers who helped bring order to Europe in the Middle Ages.

The Frankish Rulers

For hundreds of years following the breakup of the Western Roman Empire, Europe was the scene of widespread disorder and change. Waves of barbarian invasion and settlement brought new customs and lifestyles to many parts of western Europe. Over time the social and political patterns typical of life in the empire merged with new patterns brought by barbarian peoples who settled in the West.

An age of transition. Gradually Europeans began to restore order in their lives. Many historians see the years between the 400s and about 1500 as a transition in the development of Western culture. Thus this period is generally known as the **Middle Ages**, or the **medieval** period of European development. It is the time in history between the end of the classical age and the beginnings of the modern world.

Many Germanic tribes plundered Europe and established small kingdoms. One tribe proved to have a lasting impact on European history. This group of loosely organized Germanic peoples, known as the Franks, did much to shape the new culture of post-Roman Europe.

Clovis and the Merovingians. The Franks first came into contact with the Roman Empire during the 200s, when they began moving into the lower Rhine River valley. In 481 a ruler named **Clovis** became king of one of the Frankish tribes. Clovis and his successors were called **Merovingians** because Clovis traced his family back to an ancestor named Merovech. Clovis was an able military leader. He and his troops conquered and absorbed other Frankish tribes. Soon they controlled all of northern Gaul.

Because Clovis had by this time become a Christian, the Franks received the support of the Christian church. The Franks soon seized and began to rule southwestern Gaul. This is the area that today is occupied by France, which is named for the Franks. When Clovis died, his sons divided the kingdom, as was often the Frankish custom.

INTERPRETING THE VISUAL RECORD

Frankish warrior This medallion depicts a mounted Frankish warrior with his lance at the ready. Note the lack of a stirrup, which was a later development. *Why did the Frankish artist who crafted this object show the warrior on horseback?*

The Merovingian kings who ruled after Clovis were generally weak. Eventually the chief of the royal household, known as the "mayor of the palace," became the real ruler of each kingdom. One of these mayors was Pépin II, who ruled from 687 to 714. Pépin and his successors united the Frankish kingdoms.

Charles Martel and Pépin the Short. After Pépin II died, his son, **Charles Martel,** known as Charles the Hammer, became mayor of the palace. Charles Martel's cavalry defeated the Spanish Moors in 732 when they invaded France. This halted the Muslim advance in western Europe, although Muslim raids continued.

Charles Martel died in 741. His son, Pépin III, called "the Short," became the Merovingian kingdom's joint mayor of the palace with his brother, Carloman. Pépin, already king in all but name, overthrew Childeric III, the last Merovingian ruler, and claimed the Frankish throne for his own. In 751 Pépin was anointed king of the Franks. Pépin III's coronation established the **Carolingians,** a new line of Frankish rulers. The pope's confirmation of Pépin's rule, moreover, strengthened the legitimacy of the new Carolingian dynasty. This was because European Christians believed that the pope's blessing came directly from God. Over time monarchs throughout western Europe sought the church's blessing in order to support their rule.

The pope sought Pépin's help against the Lombards, a Germanic tribe that was attacking central Italy and threatening Rome. Pépin led a Frankish army into Italy and defeated the Lombards. The Franks won control of the territory around Rome and gave it to the pope. This gift of land is called the Donation of Pépin. It created the Papal States, which for centuries remained the stronghold of the church. The alliance that grew between the Franks and the church as a result of these actions made each side stronger. It also paved the way for the rise of **Charlemagne,** Pépin's son and the greatest of all Frankish kings.

Charlemagne's empire. Charlemagne inherited the Frankish throne in 768 and ruled until 814. During the 46 years of his reign, Charlemagne worked to build a "new Rome" centered in what is now France and Germany. As a devout Christian he helped to spread church teachings and Christian beliefs. His rule did much to bring civilization, order, and learning to barbarian Europe during the 800s.

Charlemagne spent much of his life at war. He defeated the Lombards in Italy, the Saxons in northern Germany, and the Avars in central Europe. He tried to conquer all of Muslim Spain, but failed. He was able, however, to drive the Moors back across the Pyrenees, a mountain range that separates Spain and France. Charlemagne's victory over the Moors added a small strip of Spanish land, called the "Spanish March," to his large empire. It also created a "buffer zone"—a kind of frontier—between Christian and Muslim Europe.

On Christmas Day of the year 800, Charlemagne was in Rome to worship at Saint Peter's Basilica. As Charlemagne knelt in prayer, Pope Leo III placed a crown on his head and declared him "Emperor of the Romans." Although the Roman Empire was long gone, the title indicates Charlemagne's importance to western Europe. He had united much of western Europe for the first time in

The simple, unadorned throne of Charlemagne, or "Charles the Great," did not reveal his power and importance.

HISTORY MAKER

Charlemagne (c. 742–814)

As emperor, Charlemagne united most of the Christian lands in western Europe. During his reign, Charlemagne strengthened the political power of the Franks. He also set into motion a cultural rebirth throughout Europe by supporting education, creating libraries, and sponsoring the collection and copying of ancient Roman manuscripts. Charlemagne's rule became a model for later kings in medieval Europe. **What were some of Charlemagne's accomplishments as a ruler?**

INTERPRETING THE VISUAL RECORD

The crowning of Charlemagne Pope Leo III crowns Charlemagne Emperor of the Romans. *Which figure—Charlemagne or Pope Leo—is depicted as more powerful in this French illustration from the 1300s? Why might that be so?*

400 years. Because of this, Europe regarded Charlemagne as the successor to the Roman emperors. The pope's coronation of Charlemagne was also significant because it showed the close ties that existed between the Franks and the Christian church.

Charlemagne was very conscious of his unique position as leader of a new western order. He saw himself, moreover, as the inheritor of Roman authority. He aimed to live up to the image of a Roman emperor in his actions, his policies, and the glory of his empire. He was greatly admired for his skills as a warrior as well as for his devotion to Christianity.

Government. Charlemagne's empire was divided into regions, each governed on the emperor's behalf by an official known as a count. Charlemagne established his capital at the northern Frankish city of Aix-la-Chapelle (EKS·LAH·shah·PEL), today the bustling German city of Aachen (AH·kuhn). The emperor used oaths of fidelity to ensure that the counts and other Carolingian officials ruled effectively under his command. Appointed officials helped Charlemagne run his empire. These officials were called *missi dominici* or "the lord's messengers." They would travel through the empire to hear complaints, investigate official misconduct, and determine the effectiveness of laws. The *missi dominici* ensured that the counts were serving the emperor and not themselves. Charlemagne viewed the *missi dominici* as his direct representatives and gave them a great deal of authority to make decisions in his name.

History Makers Speak

❝Let the *missi* themselves make a diligent investigation whenever any man claims that an injustice has been done to him by any one . . . and they shall administer the law fully and justly in the case of the holy churches of God and of the poor, of wards [orphans] and widows, and of the whole people.❞

Charlemagne, quoted in D.C. Munro, ed., *Translations and Reprints from the Original Sources of European History*, Vol. IV, *Laws of Charles the Great*

Education and learning. Although Charlemagne himself was not formally educated, he placed great value on education. He started schools at his palace for his own children and other young nobles. Scholars—usually monks—were invited from all over western Europe to teach at the school. Charlemagne appointed one of Europe's most respected thinkers, Alcuin (AL·kwihn) of York, to head the school and establish its course of learning. Alcuin developed a curriculum based on the Roman model, emphasizing grammar, rhetoric, logic, mathematics, music, and astronomy. Charlemagne also brought together scholars to produce a readable Bible. They used a new script called Caroline minuscule. The new Bible was used throughout Charlemagne's empire. Charlemagne also ordered the empire's bishops to create libraries.

Although some scholars claim Charlemagne never learned to write, he could read. Saint Augustine's *City of God* was one of his favorite books. Throughout his rule Charlemagne encouraged—sometimes forced—the empire's people to convert to Christianity.

✔ **READING CHECK: Summarizing** What steps did Charlemagne take to help assure that his officials ruled effectively and honestly?

The Decline of the Frankish Empire

The proud empire that Charlemagne had built and governed so well did not long survive his death in 814. His descendants did not inherit Charlemagne's energy, his ability, or his long-range point of view. As a result, the empire's strength declined rapidly. By the mid-800s the once mighty Carolingian state had begun to divide and collapse.

The empire after Charlemagne's death. Charlemagne's only surviving son, **Louis the Pious,** proved to be a well-educated and religious king but a weak and shortsighted ruler. When Louis died in 840, his sons Lothair, Charles the Bald, and Louis the German agreed to divide the empire among themselves after much dispute. This agreement, signed in 843, became known as the Treaty of Verdun.

Instead of uniting to overcome enemies from within and beyond the splintered empire, Charlemagne's grandsons and their successors fought among themselves. By

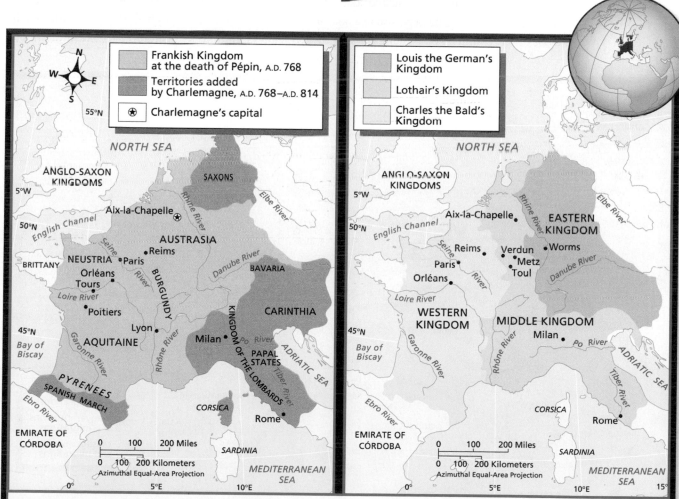

Charlemagne's Empire, 768–814 (left) and The Frankish Kingdoms After the Treaty of Verdun, 843 (right)

Interpreting Maps The Carolingian Empire, begun under Pépin III and expanded by Charlemagne, brought much of western Europe under Frankish rule. Charlemagne's grandsons divided the empire into three separate kingdoms.

■ **Skills Assessment: 1. Human Systems** Identify the Germanic tribes that Charlemagne incorporated into his empire.
2. Analyzing Information Whose kingdom after 843 claimed the most major cities?

870 the middle kingdom had been divided between the rulers of the eastern and western kingdoms. To make matters worse, powerful lords in these two kingdoms became increasingly independent of the Carolingian monarchs. These lords thought they could best serve their own interests by defying the weakening rule of the central monarchs.

Charlemagne's empire was further undermined by invasions of different peoples from beyond the empire's frontiers. Muslims from Africa invaded the Mediterranean coast. Slavs from the east raided central Europe. Another group from the east, the nomadic **Magyars** who settled in what is now Hungary, terrorized Europe for about 50 years before they were finally defeated.

The Vikings. The most feared invaders of western Europe during the 800s and the 900s were the Vikings from Scandinavia in the north. Vikings, or "Norsemen," were Germanic peoples from what are now the countries of Norway, Sweden, and Denmark. The Vikings' customs and myths centered on pagan gods. Archaeologists have excavated Viking burial mounds that include boats and tools for use in the afterlife. The Vikings would sometimes place a dead person in a boat and burn it. In about 930 an Arab, Ibn Fadlan, witnessed the funeral of a Viking chieftain. The chieftain's ship was hauled onto the land, and his body

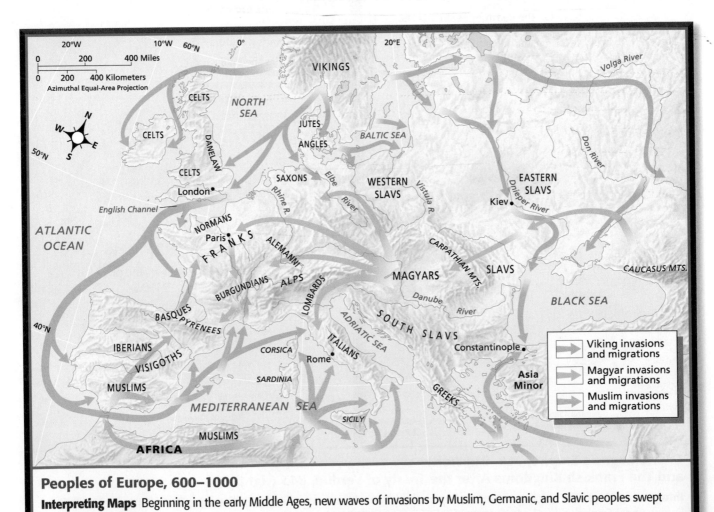

Peoples of Europe, 600–1000

Interpreting Maps Beginning in the early Middle Ages, new waves of invasions by Muslim, Germanic, and Slavic peoples swept across western Europe.

■ **Skills Assessment: 1. Human Systems** What major group of invaders was most concentrated in the Mediterranean Basin?

2. Drawing Inferences Why might both the Vikings and the Muslims have been drawn to Constantinople?

was placed on the ship along with rich grave goods. A historian, using Ibn Fadlan's account, described the Arab observer's experience:

Primary Source **"On the day of the burial, . . . the slave girl said, 'Lo, I see my lord and master he calls to me. Let me go to him.' Aboard the ship waited the old woman called the Angel of Death, who would kill her. The girl drank from a cup . . . and sang a long song. She grew fearful and hesitant. At once the old woman grasped her head and led her into the tent.**

Inside the tent the girl died beside her master by stabbing and strangling. Then the ship was fired."

Ibn Fadlan, quoted in Robert Paul Jordan, "Viking Trail East," *National Geographic Magazine,* March 1985

Although the Vikings were ruled by kings and nobles, their government was surprisingly democratic for its time. Assemblies of landowners made the laws. The Vikings were primarily farmers but also gathered, fished, and hunted. In the spring and summer the Vikings would travel south and west along the coasts of mainland Europe and the British Isles. They sailed rivers into Germany, France, and the Baltic area. The Vikings would raid and loot settlements and bring captives back to work as slaves on their farms in Scandinavia. Their way of capturing towns was often savage and cruel. Their use of axes and large dogs struck terror into people. The Vikings were also skilled in siege operations and could capture even strongly fortified towns.

Their sturdy ships carried the Vikings across the Atlantic Ocean to what is now Iceland, Greenland, and North America. In time they settled in England, Ireland, and parts of continental Europe. A large Viking settlement in northwestern France gave that region its name—Normandy, from the French word for "Northmen."

✔ **READING CHECK: Finding the Main Idea** Why were groups such as the Magyars and Vikings able to invade the Frankish Empire successfully?

Figure of the head of a Viking from about 850

SECTION 1 REVIEW

1. **Define** and explain the significance: medieval

2. **Identify** and explain the significance:
   Middle Ages
   Clovis
   Merovingians
   Charles Martel
   Carolingians
   Charlemagne
   Louis the Pious
   Magyars
   Vikings

3. **Categorizing** Copy the diagram and use it to show how Charlemagne organized his government and what responsibilities were held by the various officials.

4. **Finding the Main Idea**
   a. What actions helped Charlemagne to unify his empire?
   b. In what ways did the actions of Charlemagne's grandsons cause the Carolingian Empire to become vulnerable to invaders from the north, south, and east?

5. **Writing and Critical Thinking**
   Comparing and Contrasting Imagine that you are living in Paris at the end of the 800s. Write a journal entry in which you compare daily life in the western kingdom to stories that you have heard of life in the Carolingian Empire during Charlemagne's reign.
   Consider:
   • the actions that Charlemagne took to centralize and expand the empire
   • the effects of the Treaty of Verdun on the unity and security of the empire

Homework Practice Online
keyword: SH3 HP4

Feudalism and the Manorial System

The Main Idea
Feudalism and manorialism structured and organized European society in the Middle Ages.

The Story Continues *Society in the Middle Ages was strongly shaped by relationships of loyalty and service between higher and lower nobles. "I urge you . . . to maintain towards [your overlord] . . . a devoted and certain fealty [loyalty] both of body and soul," one mother advised her son. For centuries the nature of this binding relationship organized medieval society on the basis of military service and land ownership.*

Feudalism

Within 100 years of Charlemagne's death, organized, large-scale government in Europe all but disappeared. By the 900s most Europeans were governed by small, local, independent leaders, most often by local lords. The political organization these leaders represented is known as feudalism. ✳

The system. Within the feudal system a powerful noble granted land to a lesser noble. Actual ownership of the land remained with the noble who made the grant. The noble who received the grant was entitled to use of the land and its products, but could not "own" the land. This grant of land allowed the lesser noble to "maintain" himself and his household. In return for maintenance, the lesser noble promised loyalty, military assistance, and other services to the lord who granted the land. The person who granted land was a lord and the grant of land was called a fief. The person who received the fief was a vassal. The transaction of a noble granting land and a vassal receiving land created a contract between the two. A vassal could further divide the land he had been granted and grant it to others, such as knights. Thus, a vassal could also be a lord.

Eventually the fief became hereditary, as legal possession of the land passed from a vassal to his son. By about 1100 it had become customary for the eldest son of a lord or vassal to inherit ownership or possession of the land. This system of inheritance from father to eldest son is called primogeniture (pry·moh·JE·nuh·choohr). Women's rights regarding legal property were limited. A woman might have had fiefs in her dowry. However, when she married, her husband gained control over her dowry. In most cases a woman regained control of the property in her dowry if her husband died.

INTERPRETING THE VISUAL RECORD

Lord and vassal This stained-glass window depicts the relationship between a lord and his vassals. *How can you tell that the lord is more powerful than the vassals in this picture?*

Throughout the Middle Ages local lords held many of the powers associated with government. Kings were also bound by the customs and obligations of feudalism. In theory every landholder was a vassal to the king. In practice, however, the king controlled only those who lived on his feudal lands. Even the church was part of the feudal system. The medieval church owned vast amounts of land and had many vassals who were granted fiefs in return for military protection and service.

Warfare. Wars were common during the Middle Ages. Many wars grew out of private fights between feudal lords, or lords and vassals, and were local conflicts that involved only a handful of nobles and their knights. In other cases, wars could be large-scale events that involved whole regions and that could be immensely destructive.

Knights in the Middle Ages wore armor in battle and were heavily armed. In the early Middle Ages, armor was made of chain mail—small, interlocking metal links stitched to a knee-length leather shirt. The knight would also wear an iron helmet and carry a sword, a large shield, and a lance. With the introduction of gunpowder during the late Middle Ages, overlapping metal plates replaced chain mail. Often, plate armor was so heavy that knights had to be hauled onto their horses with cranes. Battle horses were much larger than today's saddle horses. The warhorses of the Middle Ages probably resembled today's Clydesdales and Percherons in size, weight, and power.

In medieval times wars had different effects on society. For nobles, wars were an opportunity for glory and wealth. For most people of the Middle Ages, however, war was a major cause of suffering and hardship. The church tried to limit the general suffering caused by war by issuing several decrees that prohibited acts of violence and private warfare near churches and other holy buildings. If the decrees were not obeyed, the church threatened punishment. The church also forbade violence against cattle and agricultural equipment as well as certain types of persons, including clergy, women, merchants, and pilgrims. The church tried to get all lords to accept another decree that forbade fighting on certain days, such as weekends and holy days. However, restrictions on fighting could almost never be enforced strictly. Private wars continued until kings became strong enough to stop them.

Feudal justice. Feudal justice differed greatly from Roman justice. A feudal trial was decided in one of three ways: trial by battle; compurgation, or oath taking; and trial by ordeal. A trial could be a duel between accuser and accused—or their representatives—in which the outcome determined innocence or guilt.

The knight Technical improvements, such as the development of the stirrup and better armor, added greatly to mounted knights' effectiveness in battle. ***How would stirrups help a knight's effectiveness in battle?***

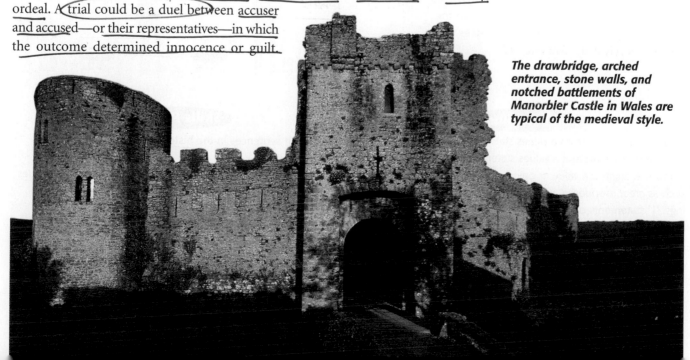

The drawbridge, arched entrance, stone walls, and notched battlements of Manorbier Castle in Wales are typical of the medieval style.

The Rise of Feudalism

When reading sources on the rise of feudalism, readers should be careful to distinguish between facts and values statements. A fact can be proven true or false. A values statement is an opinion that represents a particular point of view. For example, a writer can state that Charlemagne was a successful ruler. That is a values statement because it is based on the writer's idea of success. Sometimes a fact and a values statement can be included in the same sentence. For example, a writer may state that Charlemagne spoke Greek and Latin so beautifully he could have taught both languages. Charlemagne's ability to speak the languages can be proven true or false. However, whether he spoke them beautifully is a matter of opinion.

The Structure of Feudalism

King and Queen

Church Officials and Nobles

Knights

Peasants

A Historian's View

The statement below discusses one historian's view of the best way to define feudalism.

"The simplest way will be to begin by saying what feudal society was not. Although obligations arising from blood-relationship played a very active part in it, it did not rely on kinship alone...feudal ties...developed when those of kinship proved inadequate...

European feudalism should therefore be seen as the outcome of the violent disso-lution of older societies. It would in fact be unintelligible without the great upheaval of the Germanic invasions which, by forcibly uniting the two societies originally at very different stages of development, disrupted both of them and brought to the surface a great many...social practices of an extremely primitive nature."

Skills Reminder

To distinguish a fact from a values statement, review the differ-ence between a fact and a values statement. Then identify words that suggest a value or opinion. For example, adjectives such as *great, wonderful, horrible* are words that express feel-ings. "I" statements can also help determine whether a state-ment is a point of view. *In my opinion* or *I think* express a point of view. Finally, ask questions about the sentence. Can "That meal I had was really awful" mean more than one thing? What is the fact in the statement and what is the opinion?

Skills Practice

❶ Which sentences in the historian's statement contain facts?

❷ Which sentences in the historian's statement contain values statements?

❸ While listening to a radio or TV news report, identify the factual information provided by the report. Then identify statements of opinion and values statements, and analyze how those statements are used to influence the listener's/viewer's conclusions.

In compurgation, the accuser and the accused were supported by people who swore that the person they represented was telling the truth. The oath takers were probably similar to character witnesses in today's trials. The outcome of a trial by ordeal was determined by how the accused survived a particular ordeal. The accused had to carry a piece of hot iron, plunge his hand in a pot of boiling water, or survive extended immersion in cold water. If the accused person's wounds healed quickly and well, he was innocent; if not, he was guilty.

✔ **READING CHECK: Analyzing Information** What were some aspects of feudalism?

The Manorial System

Feudalism provided social and political structure to the culture of the Middle Ages. Similarly, manorialism shaped the economy of much of Europe during these years. The system took its name from the manors of the Middle Ages. Manors were large farming estates that included manor houses, cultivated lands, woodlands, pastures, fields, and villages.

Central authority and organized trade—key parts of most modern economies—were almost nonexistent during the Middle Ages. Thus people who lived on manors needed to be self-sufficient. They sought to produce everything they needed, including food, clothing, and shelter. Some items, however, such as iron, salt, wool, wine, and certain manufactured goods, were purchased.

A lord and several peasant families shared the land of the manor. Generally the lord kept about one third of the manor's lands, called the domain, for himself. The manor's peasants farmed the remaining two-thirds of the land for themselves. In return for being able to work the land, the peasants gave the lord some of their crops and helped to farm his land. The peasants also provided other services on the manor and paid many kinds of taxes.

Ideally a manor village was located along a stream or river, which provided waterpower for the village mill. For safety a small group of houses were clustered near the manor house or castle. The land surrounding the manor house included the village, vegetable plots, cultivated fields, pastures, and forests. Cultivated land was often divided into three large fields for growing grain. Only two of the three fields were planted at one time. The third field could lie fallow, or unplanted, for a season to regain its fertility. The three fields were divided into small strips distributed among the peasants. If the lord's domain was divided, he too had strips of land in each field.

Peasant life. Peasants' lives were difficult in medieval times because they spent long hours at backbreaking work in the fields. A text written during the Middle Ages described a typical workday from a peasant's point of view.

Peasant farmers This stylized image from the 1400s illustrates the work of medieval peasants during harvest time. *What evidence does this illustration provide of tools and techniques used by farm workers during the Middle Ages?*

Primary Source **"**. . . I work very hard. I go out at dawn, driving the oxen to the field, and I yoke them to the plough; however hard the winter I dare not stay at home for fear of my master; but, having yoked the oxen and made the plough-share . . . fast to the plough, every day I have to plough a whole acre or more. . . . It is hard work, because I am not a free man.**"**

Aelfric, *Colloquy*, translated by G.G. Coulton in *The Medieval Village*

Analyzing Primary Sources

Summarizing According to this account, why did the peasant find his work to be especially hard?

Young girls from the families of lesser nobles often went to live in the households of higher-ranking noblewomen. There they would be trained in the skills and responsibilities that were expected of women in their rank.

Generally the young noblewoman was taught to sew, to weave, to cook, to play musical instruments, and to sing. She learned, as well, the social conduct that was proper for women of the nobility. In some cases girls and young women were also instructed in the skills of household supervision. **Why might noble parents send their daughters to train in the households of higher-ranking nobles?**

Young women of the nobility serve a noblewoman.

Most peasants—called **serfs**—could not leave the land without the lord's permission. Their meals consisted mainly of black bread, lentils, some vegetables, and ale. Because livestock helped work the fields, and because peasants were generally forbidden to hunt on the lord's land, they could rarely afford to eat meat. Compared to life expectancies today, average life spans in the Middle Ages were very short. Among the factors that severely limited the life expectancies of most Europeans were disease, starvation, and frequent warfare. Very likely, peasants lived, worked, and died in the village in which they had been born.

Nobles' lifestyles. Frequently people think of the Middle Ages as a time when lords and knights lived in elegant castles. The upper classes of the Middle Ages, however, generally did not live in luxury or even in comfort by today's standards.

A castle was a fortified base from which the lord enforced his authority and protected the surrounding countryside. In the early Middle Ages, castles were simple structures made from earth and wood. Later they were made from stone.

Castles were usually built on hills or other landforms that would prevent easy attack. If a castle was on flat land that was difficult to defend, a ditch called a moat was built around it and sometimes flooded with water. A drawbridge extended across the moat to allow entry to the castle's courtyard. If the castle was attacked, the drawbridge could be raised.

A building called the "keep" was the main part of the castle. The keep was a strong tower that usually contained storerooms, workshops, and perhaps barracks and the lord's living quarters. In the great hall the lord received visitors. The castle's rooms had thick walls and small windows with no glass. As a result the rooms were usually dark and chilly. The lord spent most of his day looking after his land and dispensing justice among his vassals and serfs.

A lord or the head of a peasant family depended on his wife and children for help. Marriage was viewed as a way to advance one's fortune. Through marriage a man might acquire land. While marriage might bring a man land, it usually produced children who had to be cared for. A lord would often provide dowries for any daughters. Among peasants, children were often welcomed as a source of farm labor.

Chivalry. By the late 1100s a code of conduct known as **chivalry** had begun to bring major changes to feudal society. Chivalry was a system of rules that dictated knights' behavior towards others. The word chivalry comes from the French word *cheval*, meaning "horse," and refers to the fact that knights were mounted soldiers.

To become a knight, a boy had to belong to the noble class and had to pass through two stages of training. The first stage began at about the age of seven, when a boy would serve as a knight's page, or attendant. The page would learn knightly manners and begin to learn how to use and care for weapons. As a teenager the page would become a knight's assistant, called a squire. The squire would take care of the knight's horse, armor, and weapons. Then, probably when the knight thought that the squire was ready, the squire would accompany the knight into battle. If the squire proved himself to be a skilled and courageous fighter, he would be knighted in an elaborate religious ceremony.

A knight in full armor, wearing a closed helmet, often could be distinguished from other knights only by his coat of arms. The knight's coat of arms was a graphic symbol that identified him and that represented his personal characteristics. The coat of arms was painted or stitched onto the knight's shield or outer coat, his flag, or possibly his horse's trappings. Generally the coat of arms was passed along from one generation to the next.

According to the code of chivalry, knights were expected to be courageous in battle and to fight fairly. If a knight used tricks and strategy to overcome an opponent, he was considered a coward. A knight was expected to be loyal to his friends and to keep his word. He was required to treat his conquered foes gallantly. A knight was also expected to be courteous to women and the less powerful.

Chivalry did much to improve the rough and crude manners of early feudal lords. Behavior, however, did not become perfect by any modern standard. A knight was required to extend courtesy only to people of his own class. Toward others his attitude and actions could be coarse, bullying, and arrogant.

INTERPRETING THE VISUAL RECORD

Coats of arms The knights shown battling in this image bear coats of arms on their clothing and shields. A knight's coat of arms helped to identify him when he was fully armored. *What might the characters and symbols shown on each coat of arms represent?*

✔ **READING CHECK: Drawing Inferences** How did manorialism complement feudalism?

SECTION 2 REVIEW

1. **Define** and explain the significance:
   feudalism
   fief
   vassal
   primogeniture
   manorialism
   serfs
   chivalry

2. **Making Generalizations** Copy the graphic organizer below to demonstrate the responsibilities of lords and peasants on a manor.

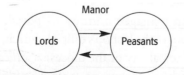

   Manor

   Lords → Peasants

3. **Finding the Main Idea**

   a. How was medieval Europe different from previous civilizations?

   b. What were the chief political and economic characteristics of feudalism and manorialism?

4. **Writing and Critical Thinking**

   Summarizing Imagine that you are a squire in service to a knight, or a young noblewoman in service to a lady. Compose a journal entry that describes your duties and goals.
   Consider:
   • the relationship between the squire and knight or the young noblewoman and the lady
   • the responsibilities of the servant

go.hrw.com **Homework Practice Online**
keyword: SH3 HP4

The Church

DEFINE

sacraments
curia
cardinals
monasticism
abbot
abbess
canon law
interdict
heretics
tithe
simony

IDENTIFY

Saint Benedict
Hildegard of Bingen
Saint Patrick
Saint Augustine
Inquisition

▶ **WHY IT MATTERS TODAY**

Papal powers and influence today differ greatly from the powers of the medieval popes. Use CNNstudentNews.com or other **current event** sources to find examples of papal authority in today's world. Record your findings in your journal.

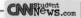

The Main Idea
The Roman Catholic Church was a central part of daily life in Europe during the Middle Ages.

The Story Continues *Throughout the Middle Ages the church was one of the few sources of leadership and stability that people could rely upon. One historian has noted that "The continuity and the authority of the Church of Rome stood out in marked contrast against . . . the short-lived kingdoms which rose and fell in [the early Middle Ages]." As a result, the Catholic church became one of medieval Europe's most powerful and enduring institutions.*

The Church Hierarchy

The medieval church had broad political powers, probably because Europe's central governments were weak if they existed at all. The church filled the need for leadership by performing many of the functions that modern governments provide today. Throughout most of the Middle Ages, the church was one of the only institutions whose presence was felt throughout Europe. Its powers extended across kingdoms and through every social and political level. The church was also a great economic force during the Middle Ages. By the 1100s the medieval church was one of Europe's leading landowners, and many of its leaders were powerful feudal overlords.

The parish priest. Within the church, members of the clergy were organized according to a strict hierarchy of rank. Each rank within the clergy had different responsibilities and powers. The parish priest held the lowest rank in the church hierarchy. The parish itself was the smallest division in the church, and the priest directly served the people in his parish. He was responsible for their religious instruction and for the moral and spiritual life of the community as a whole. In some remote parishes, however, people might still have mixed pagan beliefs and superstitions with elements of Christianity.

Although he held the lowest rank in the church, the parish priest was one of its most important officers. He could administer five of the seven **sacraments.** The sacraments were ceremonies at which participants received God's direct favor, or grace, to help ward off the consequences of sin. By the 1100s the church recognized seven sacraments that are still practiced today. Parish priests could perform baptism, Holy Communion, penance, matrimony, and the anointing of the sick and dying. Bishops performed the sacraments of confirmation and the taking of holy orders.

The bishop. The bishop managed a group of parishes called a diocese. The cathedral, the bishop's official church, was usually located in the principal city of the diocese. *Cathedra* is the Latin word for the bishop's throne, or chair. The king or powerful nobles usually controlled the selection of bishops on

This jeweled silver cup was made in Germany in the 1200s for use during the sacrament of Holy Communion.

the basis of family connections and political power. Many bishops were feudal lords or vassals in their own right and had vassals themselves.

Church leadership. A group of several dioceses, called an archdiocese, was managed by an archbishop. An archbishop had all the powers and responsibilities of a bishop and also had authority over the bishops of the archdiocese.

The pope held supreme authority in the church. The pope was advised by the **curia,** a group of counselors drawn from the highest ranks of the clergy. The curia's most important and powerful members were **cardinals,** the "princes of the church," who advised the pope on legal and spiritual matters. From the late 1100s on, only cardinals could elect the pope. With very few exceptions, a commoner could move up in the medieval world only by being a member of the church hierarchy. A man of great ability, regardless of birth, could rise to great heights within the church, although this did not happen often.

✔ **READING CHECK: Drawing Inferences** Why was the role of the parish priest among the most important within the hierarchy of the church?

Monasticism

The medieval church was made up of two types of clergy. Priests, bishops, and the pope were secular clergy. The word *secular* comes from the Latin word *saeculum,* which means "the present world." Secular clergy gave sacraments and preached the gospel among people in the everyday world. The second group of clergy was called regular clergy. The word *regular* comes from the Latin word *regula,* which means "rule." Male monks made up the regular clergy because they had to live in accordance with strict rules. Female nuns also lived in accordance with strict rules, but they were not considered clergy because only men could fulfill that role in the church.

Monastic lifestyles. Monks and nuns believed that they had to withdraw from the world and its temptations to live a Christian life. They chose to serve God through fasting, prayer, and self-denial. During the early centuries of Christianity, monks lived alone and practiced their devotion to God in many ways. They sometimes inflicted extreme physical suffering on themselves to prove their dedication. Eventually most monks and nuns gave up the hermit's lifestyle and formed religious communities. Monks lived in communities called monasteries, while nuns lived in convents. **Monasticism** refers to the way of life in convents and monasteries.

The Benedictine Rule. In some places efforts were made to organize the monastic communities before the 500s. Around that time a young Roman named Benedict became disgusted with the worldly corruption he witnessed. He left Rome to worship God as a hermit. Benedict's reputation for holiness spread and he attracted many followers. To accommodate his growing following, Benedict established a monastery at Monte Cassino, in the mountains of central Italy. Benedict—later **Saint Benedict**—created rules to govern monks' lives. Monasteries and convents all over Europe adopted these standards, called the Benedictine Rule.

The Benedictine Rule was fairly strict. Everything a monk or nun used or wore belonged to their community. Even the monk's time and labor belonged to his monastery. An **abbot** was the elected head of the community and controlled and distributed all property. An **abbess** served a similar role for women in convents. Monks and nuns spent many hours of each day in prayer. The rest of their days were taken up with tasks that the abbot or abbess assigned them.

The spread of monastic influence. Monks and nuns often took care of the needy in medieval society. In time many monasteries became rich as pious nobles gave money or land to monasteries in return for spiritual favor. Convents also received some gifts, but they generally did not become as wealthy as many monasteries.

Some monks left their monasteries to become missionaries. For example, **Saint Patrick** is credited with bringing Christianity to Ireland in 432. Monastic schools in Ireland were the basis of an advanced culture that lasted from about 500 to about 800. **Saint Augustine** led a group of monks to England. Eventually all of England accepted Christianity. Augustine became the Archbishop of Canterbury, and Canterbury became the center of the Christian church in England.

✔ **READING CHECK: Identifying Cause and Effect** How did Saint Benedict change monasticism?

The Church and Medieval Life

The Christian clergy—secular and regular alike—played a major role in medieval institutions and everyday life. Throughout the Middle Ages the church enjoyed great political, economic, and social influence across most of Europe.

Political role. In the Papal States the pope was both political and religious leader. Many popes claimed that the church held political as well as spiritual power over all monarchs. Church leaders also held positions of power as feudal lords and as advisors to kings and nobles.

The church had its own code of law, called **canon law,** and its own courts. Members of the clergy could be tried in this court and the court would rule accordingly, perhaps excommunicating them. An excommunicated person was cut off from the church and could not receive the sacraments or be buried in sacred ground. Excommunication was greatly feared by Christians because it effectively removed an individual from society.

The court could also issue an **interdict** against an entire region. All churches in that region would be closed, and clergy would be forbidden to perform marriages, burials, or other sacraments. People in an interdicted area could be at risk of eternal punishment. In many cases the church used its power of interdiction to turn a region's people against rulers who opposed church powers and policies. The church did not allow anyone to question the basic principles of the Christian religion. People who denied the truth of the church's principles or who preached beliefs not approved by the church were considered **heretics.** They were viewed as unbelievers whose sinful beliefs attacked the church and who thus deserved eternal damnation. In a sense, heresy was a threat to the church in the way that treason is a threat to a government.

The medieval church also had the power to tax. The parish priest collected a **tithe,** or one-tenth of a Christian person's income. The church also received a large income from its own lands. By the early 1200s, when the church was at the height of its power, it was perhaps the wealthiest single institution in Europe.

Economic and social role. The spiritual teachings of the church did much to shape the European economy of the Middle Ages. For example, the church generally did not approve of people gaining wealth at the expense of others. Instead it taught that people who labored should be regarded with the dignity of free people. Monks participated in agriculture and some monasteries were involved in large-scale trade.

The church considered the family a sacred institution. It did not allow divorce and said special prayers for family members. The clergy was involved with social work and took care of the poor and needy. Some religious orders even established hospitals.

Problems of the church. The church's great wealth and influence led to many problems. One major problem concerned lay investiture—the practice of a noble, such as a king, appointing a friend or relative to be a bishop or abbot. Church leaders held that only a member of the clergy could grant spiritual authority to another member. During the Middle Ages, moreover, people could buy high positions within the church hierarchy. This practice was called **simony.** The purchaser might have expected to gain wealth through his position, either from church income or by charging high fees for performing religious services. As time went on the practice of simony came under growing criticism from inside and outside the church.

Many church leaders and lay rulers attempted to bring about church reform. Two religious groups dedicated themselves to this goal. Saint Francis of Assisi founded the order of Franciscans in 1209. Saint Dominic founded the order of the Dominicans in 1216. Members of these orders, called friars, lived and preached among the people.

In the mid-1200s the church attempted to reform itself with the help of the Dominicans. The church ordered the Dominicans to seek out heretics and to stamp out teachings that opposed church doctrines. This search for heretics is known as the **Inquisition.** Heretics who confessed to sinful teachings or practices were forced to perform penance, a ritual designed to bring forgiveness. Those who did not confess were turned over to the government for punishment or execution, which sometimes involved burning at the stake. The church believed that these severe actions were needed to stop the spread of heresy in the Christian world.

✔ **READING CHECK: Summarizing** How was the church involved in the political and economic life of the Middle Ages?

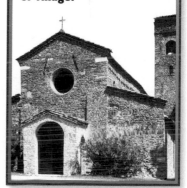

SECTION 3 REVIEW

1. **Define** and explain the significance:
   - sacraments
   - curia
   - cardinals
   - monasticism
   - abbot
   - abbess
   - canon law
   - interdict
   - heretics
   - tithe
   - simony

2. **Identify** and explain the significance:
   - Saint Benedict
   - Hildegard of Bingen
   - Saint Patrick
   - Saint Augustine
   - Inquisition

3. **Categorizing** Construct a chart like the one below to show the organization of church hierarchy during the Middle Ages.

   Church Hierarchy

4. **Finding the Main Idea**
   a. Why was the role of the parish priest important to the church?
   b. Describe how monasticism developed during the Middle Ages.
   c. How did the church attempt to reform itself?

5. **Writing and Critical Thinking**
   Supporting Points of View Write a dialogue between two peasants who are debating whether or not to join a monastic order or convent.
   Consider:
   • the lifestyles of monks, nuns, and peasants
   • the advantages and disadvantages of monasticism
   • the purpose of monasticism

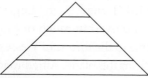

Homework Practice Online
keyword: SH3 HP4

DEFINE

shires
common law

IDENTIFY

Alfred the Great
Edward the Confessor
William the Conqueror
Henry II
Thomas Becket
Eleanor of Aquitaine
Magna Carta
Simon de Montfort

WHY IT MATTERS TODAY

Some challenges facing governments today are very similar to those that confronted the monarchies of the Middle Ages. Use CNN studentNEWS.com or other **current event** sources to find examples of issues that representative governments, such as the U.S. Congress or the British Parliament, are currently discussing. Record your findings in your journal.

CNN studentNews.com

The Struggle for Power in England and France

The Main Idea
Royal power gained supremacy over the power of the nobles in England and France during the Middle Ages.

The Story Continues *Kings, nobles, and church leaders sought to gain power over one another throughout the Middle Ages. King Philip II of France, for example, sought to control the election of bishops in the French church. "We warn the canons and monks," Philip ordered, "to elect someone who will be pleasing to God and useful to the realm." The struggle for power among these groups was a continuing theme in the development of medieval Europe.*

Anglo-Saxon and Norman England

In Europe before the 1000s, kings and lords often struggled for power. Some lords were as powerful as kings and served the kings when they wished. Some kings, however, tried to control the nobles. From this continual struggle for power the kingdoms of England and France emerged. Over time the power of the monarchs in these kingdoms became supreme.

Anglo-Saxon England. By about 450 Roman rule in Britain ended. Following the legions' withdrawal, Germanic tribes moved into the island, first as raiders, then as settlers. The culture that emerged from this Germanic settlement was named "Anglo-Saxon" after two of these tribes, the Angles and the Saxons. England, the "land of the Angles," refers to the eastern island of the British Isles, except for Scotland in the north and Wales in the west.

Over time the Anglo-Saxons formed several independent kingdoms in England. These kingdoms became known as Northumbria, in northern England and what is now southern Scotland; Mercia, in central England; and Wessex, in southern England. Eventually the Anglo-Saxons divided these kingdoms into governmental districts called **shires.** A shire was governed by a shire-reeve, which became the word *sheriff.*

Alfred the Great. By the early 800s the kings of Wessex controlled almost all of England. Viking raiders from the north, however (called "Danes" by the English), challenged the rule of Wessex and overran much of England. In 871 **Alfred the Great** came to the throne of Wessex determined to drive the Danes from the island. Alfred made a temporary peace after being defeated by the Danes. He spent the next five years building a powerful army and a fleet of fighting ships. In 876 Alfred attacked the Danes. By 886 the exhausted and weakened Danes had sued for peace.

Statue of Alfred the Great

The treaty that resulted allowed the Danes to live in parts of Mercia and Northumbria, where they were allowed to govern themselves.

Danish rule. During the 900s Alfred's successors were able to win more land back from the Danes. At the same time they unified the country, strengthened its government, and spread Christianity throughout the land. However, the Danes began to attack again at the end of the century. By 1013 the Danes once again controlled the entire country.

In 1016 King Canute of Denmark took the throne of England and most of Scandinavia in a combined kingdom. Canute was a wise ruler and spent much of his time in England. His sons, however, were weak rulers. By 1042 the Danish line had died out and the Anglo-Saxon nobles chose **Edward the Confessor** as their new king.

The Norman Conquest. Edward the Confessor was part Anglo-Saxon and part Norman. The powerful Duchy of Normandy was located in northwestern France. When Edward died without leaving an heir in 1066, a distant relative—Duke William of Normandy—claimed the English throne. The Anglo-Saxons refused to recognize his claim. Instead they selected Edward's brother-in-law, Harold of Wessex, to be king. William, determined to win the throne of England, crossed the English Channel with a powerful force of Norman knights. In a decisive battle William defeated Harold's Anglo-Saxon army at Hastings in October 1066. In December of that year, he was crowned King William I of England.

William, known today as **William the Conqueror,** soon overcame armed Anglo-Saxon resistance to his rule. In the years after the conquest, the Normans' laws, customs, and language were introduced in England. However, the Anglo-Saxons did not quickly accept them. Anglo-Saxon was a Germanic language. Norman French, in contrast, was based on Latin. As a result, the language of the Norman-English nobility continued to be French, while the language of most people in England continued to be Anglo-Saxon. Slowly, however, the lifestyles, laws, and customs of England grew to combine elements of both Anglo-Saxon and Norman cultures.

✔ **READING CHECK: Summarizing** Why is the year 1066 significant in English history?

The Conqueror and His Successors

William ruled England from 1066 to 1087. He brought feudalism from France to the newly conquered England. William shaped England's new feudal system, however, so that the king, not the nobles, held supreme authority. He required each feudal lord to swear personal loyalty directly to him. This meant that all English lords were vassals of the king. William also stopped the lords from uniting against him by scattering their fiefs throughout England. The new king's actions laid a strong foundation for centralized government and a strong monarchy in England.

The king also worked to determine the population, wealth, and ways that land was divided and used in his new kingdom. William sent royal commissioners to every English shire. Their task was to count each shire's people, assess landholdings, and measure type and value of property. The results of this great survey helped the king to set up an accurate, central tax system. The records that were gathered became known as the Domesday, or Doomsday, Book.

Holt Researcher go hrw com

go.hrw.com
KEYWORD: Holt Researcher
FreeFind:
William the Conqueror
After reading more about William the Conqueror on the Holt Researcher, evaluate his decision to take the throne by force, taking into account historical context. Then analyze how such a tactic would be viewed in the world today.

INTERPRETING THE VISUAL RECORD

Domesday Book This page from the Domesday Book is a record of property holdings in Bedfordshire and of boundary settlements among small tenants. *In what way was the Domesday Book evidence of the strength of William the Conqueror's monarchy?*

HISTORY MAKER

Eleanor of Aquitaine (c. 1122–1204)

Eleanor of Aquitaine was wife to two kings: first to Louis VII of France, and later to Henry II of England. She was also one of the most powerful women in medieval Europe.

As queen, Eleanor played an active role in the leadership of both France and England. In France, she created a center of medieval culture at the court of Poitiers. And although Eleanor's marriage to Henry II of England was often troubled, she and the king built a strong partnership and a strong kingdom.

How did Eleanor of Aquitaine use her position as queen?

Reforms under William's successors. Henry I, one of William the Conqueror's sons, ruled from 1100 to 1135. Henry was an able ruler and administrator who set up a new department, the exchequer, to handle the kingdom's finances. This made the central government more efficient. He also made an important contribution to England's legal system. Henry sent traveling judges throughout the country to try cases. This action weakened the feudal lords because the king's royal court, not the lords' feudal courts, dispensed justice.

Henry II, who ruled from 1154 to 1189, also made decisions that increased royal authority. Instead of performing feudal military service for the king, his vassals—the nobles—could pay him a fee. He would use the money to hire mercenaries, or soldiers from different places. In this way Henry II would have an army made up of soldiers who were loyal to him because he was paying them. An army made up of nobles might not have been as loyal.

England's legal system grew under Henry II's direction. Traveling judges established routes, or circuits, and further strengthened royal law throughout England. During the late 1100s the 12-member jury developed in the court system. Juries decided civil as well as criminal cases. Trial by jury to determine guilt or innocence replaced the feudal trial by ordeal and combat.

Henry aimed to increase the authority of his royal courts at the expense of the church. Thus he sought to try certain members of the clergy who had already been judged in church courts. **Thomas Becket,** the Archbishop of Canterbury, refused to allow his clergy to be tried in royal courts. Becket and Henry, who had once been good friends, became bitter enemies over the issue. Four of the king's knights, believing that they were helping Henry, murdered the archbishop in his cathedral.

Even though Henry II denied any part in the murder, he did penance to appease the church. Henry had to abandon his attempts to reduce the power of the English church. Becket was named a saint, and his shrine in Canterbury became a popular destination for pilgrims.

The last years of Henry II's reign were troubled. His sons plotted against him and his marriage to **Eleanor of Aquitaine** was stormy. The French lands that Eleanor had brought to Henry when they married, moreover, involved England in new conflicts with the French. Nevertheless, the years of Henry's rule had strengthened the English monarchy at the feudal lords' expense. Later kings were able to build upon Henry's work.

King John and Magna Carta. One of Henry II's sons, King John, is known for his actions that led to a revolt among England's nobles. John demanded that the nobles pay more taxes to support his wars in France. In 1215 a powerful group of high nobles—barons of the kingdom—joined together against the king and his demands. Their threats of an armed uprising against the throne forced John to accept a document known as **Magna Carta** (Latin for "Great Charter"). One eyewitness described the confrontation between John and the nobles who opposed his harsh and high-handed rule:

 ❝[The] nobles came to [King John] in gay military array, and demanded the confirmation of the liberties and laws of King Edward, with other liberties granted to them and to the kingdom and Church of England . . . The King, hearing the bold tones of the barons in making this demand, much feared an attack from them . . .**❞**

Roger of Wendover, "An Account of Magna Carta," quoted in *Problems in Western Civilization: The Challenge of History,* Vol. I, L. F. Schaefer, D. H. Fowler, and J. E. Cooke, eds.

Magna Carta protected the liberties of the nobles. It also provided a limited outline of rights for England's ordinary people. King John agreed not to collect any new or special taxes without the consent of the Great Council, a body of important nobles and church leaders who advised the king. John also promised not to take property without paying for it. He promised not to sell, refuse, or delay justice. The king also agreed to let any accused person be judged by a jury of his or her peers. John's acceptance of Magna Carta meant that the king—like his subjects—had to obey the law or face revolt and overthrow. Magna Carta made the law the supreme power in England.

✔ **READING CHECK: Summarizing** What contributions did William the Conqueror and his successors make to England?

Parliament and Common Law

Two other major developments took place in England in the years following Magna Carta. The first was the growth of Parliament and the beginnings of representative government. The second was the growth of **common law**—law based upon customs and judges' decisions, rather than upon written codes.

Parliament. A widespread revolt of nobles against King Henry III in the 1260s rocked England and again threatened the monarchy. **Simon de Montfort,** a powerful lord who led the revolt, aimed to build middle-class support for the nobles' cause. In this way, de Montfort reasoned, both the middle class and the nobility could combine forces against the king. In 1265 de Montfort asked representatives of the middle class to meet with the nobles and clergy who made up the Great Council. The middle-class representatives included four knights from each shire and two burgesses—leading citizens—from each of several major towns.

The practice of having members of the middle class meet with the clergy and the nobles in the Great Council remained. This representative body eventually became the English Parliament. Over time Parliament was divided into two parts, called "houses." Nobles and the clergy made up the House of Lords, and knights and burgesses made up the House of Commons.

The early Parliament mainly served to advise the king, but it also had the right to refuse new taxes sought by the king. As England's centralized government grew, taxes were needed to help meet its ever-increasing costs. Parliament's power to accept or reject new taxes became more and more important.

Common law. Edward I ruled England from 1272 to 1307. Edward, one of England's greatest monarchs, divided the king's court into three branches. The Court of the Exchequer kept track of the kingdom's financial accounts and tried tax cases. The Court of Common Pleas heard cases between ordinary citizens. The Court of the King's Bench conducted trials that concerned the king or the government.

The decisions made by the new royal courts were collected and used as the basis for future court verdicts. This collection of decisions became known as common law because it was applied equally and in common to all English people. Common law differed greatly from law that was based on statutes, such as Roman law. It was a "living law" in the sense that it changed to meet changing conditions.

✔ **READING CHECK: Comparing** How are the parliamentary system and common law similar to the government and laws practiced in the United States?

Rise of the Capetian Kings in France

The last Carolingian king died in 987. In the same year a group of nobles chose Hugh Capet to be King of France. Capet and his descendants, a line known as the Capetians, ruled for more than 300 years.

Hugh Capet ruled only a small area called the Île-de-France (eel·duh·FRAHNS). Feudal lords ruled the rest of France, holding areas known as duchies. The Capetians aimed to develop a strong central government and to unite the duchies of France under the rule of the monarchy.

The growth of royal territory. The Capetians sought to increase the lands under their control in several ways. For example, some Capetian kings married noblewomen whose dowries included great fiefs. They also took control of the lands of noble families that had died out. The Capetians looked, as well, to conquer French lands held by the English kings since the days of William the Conqueror. Philip II, known as Philip Augustus, particularly favored this policy of taking English holdings in France. King Philip, who ruled from 1180 to 1223, greatly increased royal landholdings by taking large provinces, such as Normandy and Maine, from the English.

Strengthening the central government. The Capetian kings appointed well-trained officials to run the government. They also extended the jurisdiction of the royal courts. The Parliament of Paris, the highest of the royal courts, eventually became a kind of supreme court, hearing appeals from all parts of the kingdom.

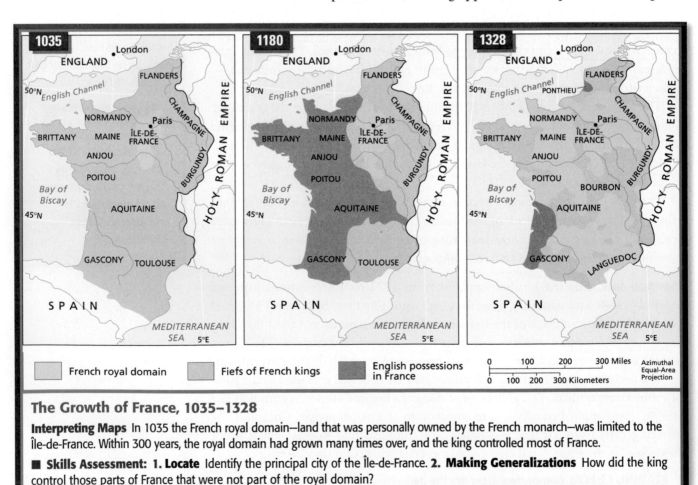

French royal domain | Fiefs of French kings | English possessions in France

The Growth of France, 1035–1328

Interpreting Maps In 1035 the French royal domain—land that was personally owned by the French monarch—was limited to the Île-de-France. Within 300 years, the royal domain had grown many times over, and the king controlled most of France.

■ **Skills Assessment: 1. Locate** Identify the principal city of the Île-de-France. **2. Making Generalizations** How did the king control those parts of France that were not part of the royal domain?

The Capetians' struggle for power continued under Philip IV (Philip the Fair), who ruled France from 1285 to 1314. Philip was able to increase royal power over the French church by taxing the clergy. When Pope Boniface VII opposed Philip, the king had him arrested. Following Boniface's death in 1303, Philip influenced the election of the next pope, Clement V. The shrewd king also moved to build his popularity among the French people. Philip convened the Estates General, a representative body made up of the three major social classes in France. The Estates General included commoners as well as nobles and members of the clergy. By involving the Estates General in his government, Philip secured widespread support in his struggle against the church.

Philip IV was one of France's mightiest rulers during the Middle Ages. In this 15th-century illustration, Philip is shown giving an audience to a French noble.

Royal power in France was greatly strengthened under Philip IV and the earlier Capetian rulers. Despite the centralizing reforms they achieved, however, France remained largely feudal in its political organization. The Capetian kings had a vision of France as a united country, but the idea of unification under the monarchy had little appeal at the local level. Thus the Capetians failed to achieve their great aim. By the 1300s, moreover, the dynasty itself had reached an end, for although Philip IV had three sons, none produced an heir to the throne. In 1328 the last of the Capetian rulers, Charles IV, died. A new line of French kings—the Valois—came into power.

✔ **READING CHECK: Comparing** How was the Estates General of France similar to England's Parliament?

SECTION 4 REVIEW

1. **Define** and explain the significance:
   shires
   common law

2. **Identify** and explain the significance:
   Alfred the Great
   Edward the Confessor
   William the Conqueror
   Henry II
   Thomas Becket
   Eleanor of Aquitaine
   Magna Carta
   Simon de Montfort

3. **Sequencing** Create a time line like the one below. Complete it to show the major events in the early development of representative government in medieval England.

   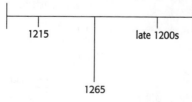

4. **Finding the Main Idea**

   a. How did William the Conqueror's actions in 1066 change England?
   b. In what ways did Magna Carta support the rise of representative government in England?
   c. What role did Simon de Montfort play in the development of Parliament?
   d. Why did the kings of France seek to weaken church power in their lands?

5. **Writing and Critical Thinking**

   Supporting a Point of View Write a paragraph that supports the following statement: "Americans today are governed by a constitution that traces its origins back to events in England in the 1200s."
   Consider:
   • the struggle for power between England's kings and nobles during the Middle Ages
   • the rights and freedoms that are guaranteed by our Constitution and Bill of Rights

Homework Practice Online
keyword: SH3 HP4

READ TO DISCOVER

❶ How did the Holy Roman emperors use their power?

❷ How did the struggle between the popes and emperors develop?

IDENTIFY

Otto I
Henry III
Henry IV
Pope Gregory VII
Frederick Barbarossa
Innocent III

WHY IT MATTERS TODAY

The Italian cities of Milan, Bologna, and Padua were great commercial centers during the Middle Ages. Use 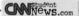 or other **current event** sources to investigate the role of these cities in Italian and world commerce today. Record your findings in your journal.

CNN student NEWS.com

The Clash over Germany and Italy

The Main Idea
Political conflict between the medieval popes and the German emperors weakened both sides.

The Story Continues *The struggle between church and state was particularly bitter in the Holy Roman Empire. Both the emperor and the pope held that their authority came from God. Pope Innocent III, who led the medieval church to its greatest power, claimed divine supremacy over all worldly rulers. According to Innocent, ". . . our power is not from man but from God." Ultimately the conflict between church and state weakened both.*

The Holy Roman Empire

While Charlemagne was still alive, Italy was part of his empire. However, his death in 814 caused Italy to fall into a state of disorder. Several of Charlemagne's descendants inherited the title of Holy Roman Emperor. However, they did not really rule Italy. In the years around 900, the Byzantine Empire held parts of Italy. The pope ruled the Papal States, while Arab Muslims ruled Sicily and frequently attacked the Italian mainland.

In Germany the great feudal lords elected **Otto I** their king in 936. Otto, a powerful and forceful ruler, became known as Otto the Great. Otto worked to develop a strong kingdom in Germany like that of the Capetians in France. However, the German king was also interested in Italy. In 951 Otto moved to seize territory in northern Italy. When Pope John XII struggled with Roman nobles, he begged Otto for help. The pope rewarded Otto's support by crowning him Emperor of the Romans in 962.

Otto's title was the same as that granted to Charlemagne 162 years earlier. Otto ruled Germany and northern Italy, however—a much smaller area than Charlemagne had held. Nevertheless, the empire stood as a major power in Europe for hundreds of years after Otto's crowning. It endured—in name, at least—until the early 1800s. Over time, however, the Holy Roman Empire was weakened by internal divisions, the rise of other European powers, and the ambitions of local nobles who sought to break from imperial control. Imperial power gradually declined until the emperor became little more than a figurehead. But the once mighty empire did leave an enduring legacy: a close and lasting tie between Germany and Italy.

INTERPRETING THE VISUAL RECORD

The coronation of Otto I Pope John XII placed this crown on the head of Otto I in 962, naming Otto "Emperor of the Romans." *In what way does the emperor's crown symbolize the relationship between church and state in the Holy Roman Empire of the Middle Ages?*

The reign of Emperor **Henry III** between 1046 and 1056 represented the height of imperial power. Henry, like Charlemagne, viewed the church as a branch of the imperial government. He expected the church to actively support the empire and its ruler. During Henry's reign, three different men claimed the papacy. Henry removed these men from office and elected a German as pope. He also chose the next three popes.

✔ **READING CHECK: Comparing** In what major way was Henry III's view of the church similar to the view of Charlemagne?

Struggles between the Papacy and European Rulers

Henry III's death in 1056 brought his five-year-old son, **Henry IV,** to the imperial throne. Powerful German nobles saw Henry's youth as an opportunity to regain their independence and feudal powers. The church, too, moved to restore the power it had lost during Henry III's reign. At the age of about 15, Henry moved to strengthen his imperial rule. Eventually Henry's actions brought him into conflict with one of the great leaders of the medieval church, **Pope Gregory VII.** The struggle between Henry and Gregory reflected the clash between church and state that was a continuing issue in the Middle Ages.

Meeting at Canossa In 1077 Pope Gregory VII (left) and Emperor Henry IV (center) settled some of their differences at Canossa. Countess Matilda of Tuscany (right) helped arrange the meeting. *What visual clues does the artist provide to indicate the dominant figure in this painting?*

Gregory and Henry IV. Pope Gregory was both devout and able. He worked to bring spiritual reform to the church by increasing the power and authority of the papacy. Gregory believed that the church was the supreme spiritual and temporal power on the earth. He felt that rulers and ordinary people alike were subject to the will of the church and its pope. Gregory did not hesitate to use the terrible punishment of excommunication as a way to resolve conflicts of church and state.

The conflict between Henry IV and Gregory VII concerned the old issue of lay investiture—the appointment of bishops by temporal rulers. Henry believed that he had the right to appoint bishops of the German church. Gregory angrily opposed lay investiture and responded to the emperor's attempt to name bishops by excommunicating Henry. In addition, Gregory released the emperor's subjects from their vows of loyalty to their ruler and urged the nobles to elect another emperor.

Imperial submission. Fearing rebellion, Henry sought the pope's mercy. During the harsh winter of 1077, Henry traveled to meet the pope. They met at Canossa, in the mountains of northern Italy. Henry and his attendants had to make their way through treacherous, ice-covered peaks. When he finally reached Canossa, the humiliated Henry waited in the bitter cold for three days to be admitted to the pope's presence. When they finally met, Henry pleaded for the pope's mercy. As a result, the pope revoked Henry's excommunication.

The struggle over lay investiture continued, however. Finally, in 1122, representatives of both sides met in the German city of Worms to settle the conflict. The agreement they reached, known as the Concordat of Worms, limited imperial power over the German church. The emperor could appoint bishops to fiefs. Only the pope, however, had the power to name bishops, whose spiritual authority came directly from the church.

The popes of the Middle Ages had great political power. In 1075 Pope Gregory VII said that the pope had power over all Christians and could get rid of church and political leaders. Pope Innocent III was involved in many of Europe's political affairs. He even overthrew two of Germany's kings.

Over time the papacy turned its attention to making the pope the spiritual leader of all Roman Catholics. Today the pope works to create and uphold the laws, traditions, and spiritual beliefs of the church. Officially the pope has less political power, although recent popes like John Paul II have tried to influence nations and their leaders through the power of persuasion. **How did Pope Innocent III's involvement in world political affairs differ from the approach of John Paul II?**

Holt Researcher
go.hrw.com
KEYWORD: Holt Researcher
FreeFind: Innocent III
John Paul II
After reading more about Innocent III and John Paul II on the Holt Researcher, analyze how they each influenced the eras in which they lived.

The Concordat of Worms recognized the spiritual leadership of the popes. Conflict between popes and emperors did not end in 1122, however. The German emperors continued to interfere in Italian politics and to threaten the popes' rule in the Papal States. The popes, in turn, opposed all attempts by the emperors to gain control in Italy.

Frederick Barbarossa. Frederick I, also known as **Frederick Barbarossa** (Frederick of the Red Beard), ruled Germany from 1152 to 1190. Frederick, like other emperors before him, sought to gain control of Italy.

In the northern Italian region known as Lombardy, the great trading centers of Bologna, Padua, Verona, and Milan had grown increasingly independent of imperial control. Each of these city-states had a wealthy merchant class. Frederick, seeking to strengthen his rule by gaining wealth, set out to capture the Lombard cities. Frederick sent imperial representatives to take control of the cities' governments. When Milan resisted, Frederick captured and destroyed the city and drove out the people.

The other city-states refused Frederick's demands. With the help of the pope, they united to form the Lombard League. They raised a powerful army that defeated Frederick in 1176. In the peace settlement that followed, the cities of the League recognized Frederick as overlord. In return, Frederick let the cities govern themselves. The Lombard League's success showed the growing political power of cities in medieval Europe.

Innocent III. Between 1198 and 1216, the strongest of the medieval popes—**Innocent III**—greatly strengthened the church and increased its worldly power. Innocent was a skillful political leader who, like Gregory VII before him, believed in the supreme earthly power of the papacy. To Innocent, emperors and kings were no more than servants of the church. Because of this belief Innocent felt that he had the authority to settle all political, as well as spiritual, problems. Temporal rulers and nobles could advise the pope, but they could not control him.

> **History Makers Speak**
>
> ❝Just as the founder of the universe [God] established two great lights in the firmament of heaven, a greater one to preside over the day and a lesser to preside over the night, so too . . . he instituted two great dignities [pope and monarch], a greater one [the pope] to preside over souls . . . and a lesser one [the monarch] to preside over bodies . . . These are the pontifical authority and the royal power.❞
>
> Innocent III, quoted in *The Crisis of Church & State: 1050–1300,* by Brian Tierney

Fresco portrait of Pope Innocent III

Innocent III involved himself in disputes all over Europe. He freely used his powers of excommunication and interdiction to settle conflicts. When he quarreled with King John of England, Innocent placed the entire realm under interdict. To have the interdict lifted, John was forced to become the pope's vassal and to pay an annual tithe to Rome. Innocent also used the interdict against the king of France, Philip Augustus, after Philip tried to have his marriage annulled. Innocent forced Philip to take his wife back and to restore her to her place as queen of France. Innocent also dominated nearly all of Italy. In Germany he overthrew two kings and put rulers of his choice on the throne.

Innocent was able to greatly increase papal authority and prestige in medieval Europe. Conditions in Europe, as well as Innocent's personal skill, helped him to build church power. Later popes, however, lacked both Innocent's abilities and the favorable conditions that had helped him to become supreme. As a result, papal power slowly declined after Innocent's death in 1216.

The great goal of uniting Germany and Italy was never achieved. During the early 1200s Emperor Frederick II tried to bring the two regions together under imperial rule. Like earlier emperors, however, Frederick failed.

Not only did imperial attempts to unify Italy and Germany fail, but each country also remained divided into small, independent cities and feudal states. The emperor had little real control over the fragmented kingdom. Italy remained divided into three regions. Northern Italy was controlled by the Lombard cities. The Papal States held power in Italy's center, and the kingdom of Sicily controlled the south. Neither Italy nor Germany were unified until the 1800s.

✔ **READING CHECK: Comparing** How were the aims of Gregory VII and Innocent III similar?

A bitter quarrel between Pope Innocent III and King John of England, shown hunting in this image, caused England to be placed under the Church's dreaded interdict.

SECTION 5 REVIEW

1. **Identify** and explain the significance:
   Otto I
   Henry III
   Henry IV
   Pope Gregory VII
   Frederick Barbarossa
   Pope Innocent III

2. **Summarizing** Copy the graphic organizer shown below. Use it to summarize the actions and events that led to Frederick Barbarossa's defeat by the Lombard League.

3. **Finding the Main Idea**

   a. Why was the issue of lay investiture considered so important by both German emperors and popes?

   b. Why do you think emperors and popes were unable to cooperate or to build alliances that would have strengthened both?

4. **Writing and Critical Thinking**

   Supporting a Point of View Imagine yourself as a literate citizen of the Holy Roman Empire during the late 1100s. Write a letter to Frederick Barbarossa with the aim of convincing him that the powers of church and state should be separate.

   Consider:
   • the extensive powers of the Holy Roman emperors
   • how Otto's empire might have benefited from a separation of church and state
   • why both the pope and the emperor might have gained by resolving their conflict for power

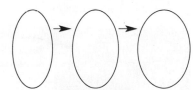

Homework Practice Online
keyword: SH3 HP4

CHAPTER 4 Review

Creating a Time Line

Copy the time line below onto a sheet of paper. Complete the time line by filling in the events, individuals, and dates from the chapter you think were significant. Pick three events and explain why you think they were significant.

| 455 | 768 | 1066 | 1215 |

Writing a Summary

Using standard grammar, spelling, sentence structure, and punctuation, write an overview of the events in the chapter.

Identifying People and Ideas

Identify the following terms or individuals and explain their significance:

1. Middle Ages
2. Charlemagne
3. feudalism
4. primogeniture
5. manorialism
6. Saint Benedict
7. Inquisition
8. Thomas Becket
9. Magna Carta
10. Eleanor of Aquitaine

Understanding Main Ideas

SECTION 1 *(pp. 96–101)*
The Rise of the Franks

1. Why would the pope's blessing strengthen a king's rule?
2. How did Magna Carta and the type of government that it fostered affect events in Europe?

SECTION 2 *(pp. 102–107)*
Feudalism and the Manorial System

3. How did the practice of primogeniture exclude women or peasants from controlling land?
4. How were feudal lords and peasants affected by the principles of chivalry?

SECTION 3 *(pp. 108–111)*
The Church

5. How was the church's organization similar to that of a centralized government?
6. What overall effect did Benedict have on the development of monasticism?
7. What were some of the problems the church faced in the Middle Ages?

SECTION 4 *(pp. 112–117)*
The Struggle for Power in England and France

8. Why are the years 1066 and 1215 significant to English history?
9. Describe how common law developed in England.
10. How did royal power in France and England differ?

SECTION 5 *(pp. 118–121)*
The Clash over Germany and Italy

11. Why was Otto's rule different than the Capetians' in France?
12. Contrast the conflicts between Henry II and Thomas Becket and Henry IV and Pope Gregory VII.

Reviewing Themes

1. **Government** How could religious leaders and kings have avoided many wars in the Middle Ages?
2. **Constitutional Heritage** How did Magna Carta and the type of government it fostered affect events in Europe?
3. **Economics** When would working the land for the lord of a manor not have provided a living for a peasant?

Thinking Critically

1. **Drawing Inferences** Why was it so important for kings, emperors, the church, and nobles to possess land?
2. **Analyzing Information** Why did the Concordat of Worms not end the struggles between popes and emperors?
3. **Identifying Cause and Effect** How did church officials, such as bishops, become involved in feudalism?

Writing About History

Comparing Write a report comparing the life of a present-day teenager to that of a squire or a young noblewoman in service to a higher-ranking noblewoman. Use the chart below to help you organize your thoughts.

	Squire or young noblewoman	Present-day teenager
Food		
Clothes		
Education		
Duties		
Chances for movement in society		

Interpreting Maps

Study the map below. Then use the information on the map to answer the questions that follow.

The Vikings in Britain, 700s–1100s

1. Based on the map, which of the following statements best describes how geographic factors influenced Viking settlement in England and Ireland?
   a. Britain is an island.
   b. The Vikings were in search of croplands.
   c. The Vikings settled along rivers and coastal areas.
   d. Open land for settlement was plentiful in Britain.

2. How successful do you think the Vikings were at expanding their settlements in England and Ireland? Explain your answer.

Decision Making

Read the quote below about London in the 1200s. Then answer the questions that follow.

> "In the thirteenth century, London succeeded in piping water from springs at Tyburn to a fountain in West Cheap, but there was neither pressure nor abundant quantity of water. The authorities intended the fountain to provide drinking water for the poor, and household water for the neighborhood. . . . but the chief sources of water . . . remained the wells, streams, . . . and the River Thames—the ultimate destination of most of London's garbage and sewage."

3. Which of the following statements best expresses what you think about an issue described in the quote?
   a. Piping water to a fountain was not a good idea because people would have fought over the water.
   b. The poor people in London did not have enough water and the authorities should have drilled wells for them.
   c. Dumping garbage and sewage into the Thames polluted it and the water would have been harmful to drink.
   d. The authorities should not have piped water from Tyburn because that left the people of Tyburn without water.

4. Why did you choose the statement you did in question 3? Use a decision-making process to explain your answer.

Alternative Assessment

Building Your Portfolio

Link to TODAY

Economics

The economies of modern, industrialized nations differ greatly from those of medieval societies. Research ways in which the high-technology economy of the United States functions differently than the agricultural economies of medieval Europe. Use a decision-making process to decide if you would rather live in the United States today or in medieval Europe. Write a summary of the steps you took to reach your decision.

☑ internet connect

Internet Activity: go.hrw.com
KEYWORD: SH3 WH4

Choose a topic on the Rise of the Middle Ages to:
- evaluate primary and secondary sources about Charlemagne.
- create a poster on medieval art and architecture.
- write a report on daily life in the Middle Ages.

1000–1500
The High Middle Ages

Crusaders at the gates of Jerusalem

1225
The Arts
Guillaume de Lorris writes "Roman de la Rose," a story of courtly wooing.

c. 1050
The Arts
English monks excel at embroidery.

1096–1291
Global Events
The Crusades are fought.

1174
Daily Life
The earliest known horse races occur in England.

c. 1241
Business and Finance
The Hanseatic League is formed.

c. 1000
Politics
European feudalism begins.

1000

1100

1200

c. 1000
Science and Technology
Arabs and Jews become court physicians in Germany.

c. 1054
Daily LIfe
The Christian church splits.

c. 1150
The Arts
Gothic architecture begins to develop.

c. 1202
Daily Life
The first court jesters appear at European courts.

1193
Business and Finance
The first known merchant guild is formed in London.

Figure of the head of a crusader

A medieval knight with a female admirer

Build on What You Know

During the early Middle Ages, the people of western Europe gradually developed new institutions based upon a combination of Roman and Germanic traditions, values, and lifestyles. Feudalism became the primary political system, while manorialism became the primary economic system. These structures helped shape the new civilization that grew across much of Europe. The Christian church, too, played a strong role in the political and economic growth of the time. In this chapter, you will learn how changes occurred in government, economics, culture, and religion during the later Middle Ages.

The Black Death

Joan of Arc

1347
Global Events
The Black Death sweeps through Europe.

1375
Business and Finance
The Hanseatic League establishes common weights, measures, and coinage.

1309–1377
Politics
The Babylonian Captivity takes place.

1382
Daily Life
The Bible is translated into English.

1431
Politics
Joan of Arc is burned at the stake.

1469
Politics
Ferdinand of Aragon and Isabella of Castile are married.

1300   **1400**   **1500**

c. 1345
The Arts
Notre Dame Cathedral in Paris is completed.

1378–1417
Daily Life
The Great Schism divides the church.

1415
Science and Technology
The English use the long-bow to defeat the French at the Battle of Agincourt.

1485
Politics
Henry VII founds the Tudor dynasty in England.

1337–1453
Global Events
The Hundred Years' War is fought.

1328
Science and Technology
The sawmill is invented.

Notre Dame Cathedral

What's Your Opinion?

Themes Journal *Do you* **agree** *or* **disagree** *with the following statements? Support your point of view in your journal.*

Economics The growth of trade and the growth of towns are related and dependent upon one another.

Global Relations Two groups of people cannot learn from each other when they are at war because of religion.

Government Shifts in the balance of political power almost always take place as new nations develop.

The Crusades

READ TO DISCOVER

❶ What were the main causes of the Crusades?

❷ What was the outcome of the First Crusade?

❸ What were the outcomes of the other major crusades?

❹ How did the Crusades affect Europe?

IDENTIFY

Seljuq Turks
Urban II
Crusades
Saladin
Children's Crusade

▶ **WHY IT MATTERS TODAY**

Conflicts continue today in the Holy Land. Use CNNstudentNEWS.com or other **current event** sources to find information on recent conflicts between the Israelis and the Palestinians. Record your findings in your journal.

CNNstudentNEWS.com

The Main Idea
European Christians tried to end Islamic rule of Palestine in a series of wars called the Crusades.

The Story Continues *To Christians, as well as to Jews and Muslims, Palestine was a holy land. Jerusalem, said one pope, was "the land which the Redeemer of mankind illuminated by his coming," the land where Jesus had lived, preached, and died. In the 600s Muslim Arabs took control of Palestine. They generally let Christians and Jews there practice their religions, travel freely, and trade. During the Middle Ages, however, this situation changed.*

Causes of the Crusades

During the late 1000s, the **Seljuq Turks,** a Muslim people from Central Asia, gained control of Palestine—known among Christians as "the Holy Land." The Turks went on to attack Asia Minor, part of the Byzantine Empire. When they threatened the capital city of Constantinople, the Byzantine emperor called on Pope **Urban II** in Rome for help. Because Christian pilgrims to Palestine reported that they had been persecuted by the Turks, the Byzantine emperor's appeal met with a warm reception.

Urban was eager to regain the Holy Land from the Turks. In 1095 he called a meeting of church leaders and feudal lords. They met in Clermont, France. Urban asked the lords to stop fighting among themselves and join in a great war to win back the Holy Land. They would "wear the cross of Christ on their right shoulder or back, and with one voice . . . cry out: 'God wills it, God wills it, God wills it!'"

Thus began the **Crusades,** a series of military expeditions to regain the Holy Land. At least 10,000 Europeans took up the cause. They sewed a cross of cloth on their clothes and were called crusaders. (The Latin word *cruciata* means "marked with a cross.")

Crusaders joined the cause for different reasons. Some went to save their souls. They believed that if they died on crusade they would go straight to heaven. Some knights hoped to gain land and wealth in Palestine and southwest Asia. Some merchants saw a chance to make money. Thus the Crusades appealed to a love of adventure and the promise of rewards, both spiritual and material.

✔ **READING CHECK: Identifying Cause and Effect** Why did Pope Urban II call for a crusade?

Pope Urban II called upon the nobles of western Europe to free the Holy Land from Seljuq rule.

The First Crusade

The First Crusade lasted from 1096 to 1099. French and Italian lords led several armies of crusaders from Europe to Constantinople. The Byzantine emperor, glad for help from the West against the Turks, was nonetheless suspicious of the crusaders. Seeing the crusader armies approach his city, the emperor feared they might capture and plunder the capital. After much discussion the emperor allowed the crusaders to pass through Constantinople.

Across Asia Minor the crusaders continued their long, hot march toward Palestine. In their wool and leather garments and heavy armor, the armies suffered severely from the heat. They lacked enough food and water because they had few pack animals to carry supplies. Despite such difficulties, the crusaders forged on to capture the city of Antioch.

The crusaders then marched down the coast toward Palestine and their main target—the holy city of Jerusalem. Fleets of ships from Italy brought supplies. The Turks, quarreling among themselves, were disunited and therefore unable to prevent the crusaders from surrounding the city. After a series of vicious battles, the crusaders captured Jerusalem. In a terrible massacre, they slaughtered its Muslim and Jewish inhabitants.

What If? The Byzantine emperor called for help from the pope in Rome to control the Turks in the Holy Land. **How might the history of European trade have been different if the Byzantine Christians had gained control of the Holy Land from the Turks and had not needed western Europeans' help?**

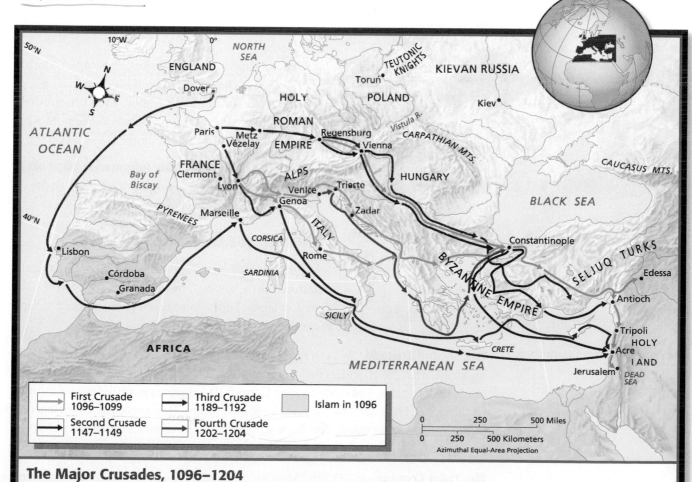

First Crusade 1096–1099
Second Crusade 1147–1149
Third Crusade 1189–1192
Fourth Crusade 1202–1204
Islam in 1096

0   250   500 Miles
0   250   500 Kilometers
Azimuthal Equal-Area Projection

The Major Crusades, 1096–1204

Interpreting Maps The crusaders set out from many European cities to free the Holy Land from the Turks.

■ **Skills Assessment: 1. Places and Regions** Near what city did the routes of the four crusades cross? **2. Comparing** Which crusade brought armies from the farthest distance to the Holy Land?

The Arab historians Ibn al-Athīr and Ibn al-Qalanisi described the crusaders' actions after their conquest of Jerusalem. According to them,

❝The population was put to the sword by the Franks [crusaders], who pillaged for a week. . . . the Franks slaughtered more than 70,000 people, among them a large number of Imams and Muslim scholars who had left their homelands to live in the pious seclusion of the Holy Place.❞

Ibn al-Athīr, quoted in Michael Foss, *People of the First Crusade*

❝The Jews [who lived in Jerusalem and who had been trapped by the crusaders' siege of the city] had gathered in their synagogue and the Franks burnt them alive. They also destroyed monuments of saints and the tomb of Abraham, may peace be upon him.❞

Ibn al-Qalanisi, quoted in Michael Foss, *People of the First Crusade*

The crusaders' capture of Jerusalem brought much of the Holy Land under European control. As a result, European customs and institutions were put into place in parts of southwest Asia and the Holy Land. The crusaders set up four small states. They introduced the idea of European feudalism and subdivided the land into fiefs, with lords and vassals. Trade between Europe and the Holy Land sprang up. Italian ships carried most of the trade goods.

Changes happened to the European occupiers during this time as well. The Christians and Muslims lived alongside each other and grew to respect each other. Many Europeans adopted Eastern customs and began to wear Eastern clothes and eat Eastern foods.

✔ **READING CHECK: Analyzing Information** What did the crusaders achieve as a result of the First Crusade?

The crusaders attack Jerusalem.

Other Major Crusades

For almost 100 years, European Christians held onto Palestine. Little by little, however, the Turks won back their lost lands. Popes and European rulers tried to stop them during three more major crusades.

The Second Crusade. By 1146 the Turks had united their forces. They started taking back cities that the crusaders had captured. In 1147 the Second Crusade began. King Louis VII of France and German king Conrad III led separate armies across Europe. At the city of Damascus, the two armies joined forces. The combined forces failed to recapture the city, however. The Turks held. In 1149 the crusaders returned to Europe in disgrace.

The Third Crusade. In 1187 the Muslim leader **Saladin** gained control of Jerusalem. Three European rulers—Holy Roman Emperor Frederick Barbarossa, King Philip II of France, and King Richard I of England—then led separate armies in the Third Crusade. The crusade lasted from 1189 to 1192. It, too, failed. When Barbarossa drowned on the way to the Holy Land, his army turned back. Philip and Richard quarreled, and Philip took his army back home to seize English lands in France. Richard and the forces under his command remained in the Holy Land, but they could not recapture Jerusalem. Richard settled for a truce with Saladin. Through the truce, the crusaders received control of some towns along the Palestinian coast. The truce also allowed Christians to enter Jerusalem freely.

The Fourth Crusade. Pope Innocent III gathered a group of French knights for the Fourth Crusade. In 1202 they left on ships provided by the Italian city-state of Venice. The Venetians persuaded the crusaders to attack Zadar—a trade rival to Venice—as they moved down the Adriatic coast. Because Zadar was a Christian city, however, the crusaders who attacked it were later excommunicated by Innocent III.

Then in 1204, the crusaders attacked and looted Constantinople, another Christian city. They stole many things that were holy to the Byzantine Christians. The Venetians gained control of Byzantine trade. Constantinople remained under western European control for about 60 years. The Byzantines eventually regained the city, but they never regained their strength. The once-mighty empire collapsed when the Turks seized Constantinople in 1453.

Other crusades. In 1212 the short-lived and unfortunate **Children's Crusade** took place. Young people from across Europe decided to march to the Holy Land and regain it for Christian Europe. The young crusaders lacked adequate training, equipment, and supplies. By the time they reached the Mediterranean coast, the army of children was little more than a hungry and disorganized mob. The pope sent some of them back home. Others reached southern France, where they were tricked into boarding ships that carried them off into slavery instead of to the Holy Land. Several thousand children, most from Germany and France, were lost in the course of this tragedy.

For many years, European crusaders tried to recapture the Holy Land. The Crusades continued until 1291, when the Muslims captured the city of Acre (AH·kruh). Acre was the last Christian stronghold in the Holy Land and, with its fall, the Crusades ended.

✔ **READING CHECK: Supporting a Point of View** What evidence would you give to show that from 1147 the Crusades were a failure?

Results of the Crusades

The goal of the Crusades was to take the Holy Land from the Turks. All the Crusades except the first failed to reach that goal. By the end of the Crusades, the Muslims again controlled Palestine. In Europe, however, the Crusades helped bring about many changes.

Crusader States from 1098

Interpreting Maps During and after the First Crusade, crusaders set up small states in the Middle East.

■ **Skills Assessment: 1. Places and Regions** Name the four states set up by crusaders between 1098 and 1102. How long did each state stay under the crusaders' control?

2. Drawing Conclusions Compare this map with the map on page 319. Why might it have been difficult for the crusaders to maintain control of these states?

The World of Arab Geographers

In Chapter 11 you read how Europeans learned about the geographical achievements of the Muslims. Arab geographers had published the world's first climatic atlas in the 900s. One Arab geographer, al-Muqaddasī, wrote a geographic encyclopedia in which he discussed not only physical systems such as climate and land but also human systems such as religion, society, commerce, and agriculture.

During the 1100s the great geographer al-Idrīsī completed his *Amusement for Him Who Desires to Travel Around the World.* He is also credited with creating the world's first globe.

Understanding Geography

What effect might such new geographical knowledge have had on Europeans?

Weapons and warfare. During the Crusades, the weapon of choice for many European soldiers was the crossbow. This weapon was a powerful bow that was held horizontally. It fired a short, heavy arrow called a bolt with the pull of a trigger. The crossbow required far less skill to use than did the traditional bow. Yet it was a deadly weapon that was capable of penetrating chain mail and plate armor. From the Byzantines and Muslims, Europeans also discovered new ways to wage war. For example, they learned how to undermine walls and use catapults to throw rocks. From the Muslims, they may have learned about gunpowder.

Political changes. To raise money to go on crusade, some lords had sold their land. Without land, they had no power in the feudal system. Many nobles also died fighting in the Crusades. With fewer lords, the power of European kings grew stronger. The kings placed new taxes and led armies drawn from their entire country. All these changes helped bring an end to feudalism.

During the Crusades, the Christian church became more powerful also. As organizers of crusades, the popes took on more importance. This was particularly true after the First Crusade.

Ideas and trade. Between 1096 and 1291, thousands of crusaders traveled through the Holy Land. They exchanged ideas with crusaders from other parts of Europe. They also gained knowledge from the Byzantines and Muslims whom they met. When the crusaders returned home, these new ideas helped to enrich European culture.

Changes in trade also took place. Italian cities became major trading centers. Ships from Italian cities carried crusaders to the Holy Land. The ships came back loaded with foods from southwest Asia. Europeans began buying such goods as apricots, lemons, melons, rice, and sugar.

✔ **READING CHECK: Summarizing** In what ways did the Crusades change Europe?

Map drawn by Arab geographer al-Idrīsī

SECTION 1 REVIEW

1. **Identify** and explain the significance:
   Seljuq Turks
   Urban II
   Crusades
   Saladin
   Children's Crusade

2. **Comparing and Contrasting** Copy the web diagram below. Use it to compare and contrast the outcomes of the first four Crusades.

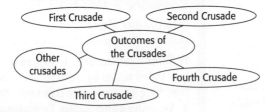

3. **Finding the Main Idea**
   a. What issues led to the Crusades?
   b. What long-term importance did the Crusades have for Europe?

4. **Writing and Critical Thinking**
   Identifying Cause and Effect Imagine you are a soldier during the Crusades. Write a field report identifying how new technology is changing the way you fight.
   Consider:
   • new forms of technology used by Muslims and Europeans during the Crusades
   • how this technology affected warfare

 Homework Practice Online
keyword: SH3 HP5

The Revival of Trade

READ TO DISCOVER

❶ What factors led to the revival of trade in Europe?

❷ What kinds of goods were traded, and why did fairs begin?

❸ What important business developments resulted from the growth of trade?

DEFINE

barter economy
domestic system
usury
capital
market economy

▶WHY IT MATTERS TODAY

Many nations have entered trade agreements with rules about prices and taxes, somewhat like the Hanseatic League. Use CNN Student News.com or other **current event** sources to find examples of trade agreements among nations today. Record your findings in your journal.

CNN Student News.com

The Main Idea
The Crusades spurred a revival of trade and led to economic growth throughout western Europe.

The Story Continues *It is fair day in a medieval town. Merchants from throughout Europe and even Asia and Africa hoist colorful tents and stalls and display their wares: spices from the East, silk from China, woolens from Flanders, cheese, leather goods, jewelry. Entertainers arrive as well—jugglers, acrobats, and musicians. Such a fair would not have been found 200 years earlier. After the Crusades, however, a fair was held somewhere on almost any given day of the year.*

Trade Routes

After the collapse of the Roman Empire in the 400s, trade almost died out in western Europe. With the rise of the Middle Ages, manors grew or made nearly everything they needed. Towns and cities, which depended on trade and manufacturing, shrank in population.

Because of the Crusades, trade began to grow again in Europe. Italy was the earliest site of this trade revival. Towns and trade had declined less there. Lying between northern Europe and southwest Asia, Italy's location also favored trade.

Trade in Italy. Northern Europeans wanted Asian goods, and those goods could be bought in southwest Asia. The Italian city-states of Genoa, Pisa, and Venice became important trading centers, acting as go-betweens for traders from Asia and northern Europe. The Crusades increased this trade. Ships from Italian city-states carried crusaders to Palestine. On their return trips, they brought back goods from Asia. These goods then traveled overland from Italy into central and northern Europe. This overland trade route led to the growth and increasing wealth of cities along its path.

Trade in northern Europe. Trade also began to grow again in northern Europe. Kiev, in what is now Ukraine, became a trading center. Before the year 1000, Viking traders from Kiev traveled to Constantinople. There they collected goods from Asia to bring back to cities in northern Europe.

Flanders became another important northern trading center. Now a part of Belgium, France, and the Netherlands, Flanders in the 1100s was the meeting point of several trade routes. Many traders came to Flanders from England, France, Germany, or countries along the Baltic Sea. They were eager to buy the fine woolen cloth made there. Flemish cities such as Bruges and Ghent grew in population and wealth.

The Hanseatic League. German cities on the Baltic and North Seas also became important trading centers. The most important were Bremen, Hamburg, and Lübeck. Germany's weak central government could not control trade. For that reason, the German trading cities joined together to form the Hanseatic League. In time, about 100 cities were members of the league. They set up trading posts in England, Flanders, Russia, and Scandinavia. During the 1300s and 1400s, the Hanseatic League increased trade in northwestern Europe.

Trade Routes of the Middle Ages

Interpreting Maps Medieval overland trade routes linked eastern and western Europe.

■ **Skills Assessment: 1. Human Systems** Who controlled most of the trade routes in Europe?

2. Evaluating Why did they not control trade in the North Sea and Baltic Sea?

The rules of the Hanseatic League were strict. Any member city that did not follow the league's rules lost its trading rights. Sometimes a country's ruler took away the rights of a Hanseatic trader. When that happened, the league stopped shipping goods to that country. This placed great pressure on the ruler to restore the trader's rights. League members also waged wars to win back trading rights.

✔ **READING CHECK: Making Generalizations** How did the geographic locations of Italy, Kiev, and Flanders and the power of the Hanseatic League revive trade in Europe?

Trade Goods and Markets

The Crusades had increased Europeans' demand for goods from Asia, especially those goods considered "exotic" or new. European merchants in the Middle Ages made their highest profits trading in luxury goods, including dyes, medicines, silks, and spices. Europeans also wanted manufactured goods such as cotton cloth, linen, and art objects. Moreover, Asia supplied Europe with fruit, grain, and rugs. In exchange Europe offered its own goods and products. Baltic countries traded fish, fur, and timber. Leather, oil, and soap came from Spain, and France produced wine. Venice exported glassware, and England and Flanders traded fine woolen cloth.

As trade grew, merchants needed places where they could exchange goods. Many villages held weekly market days. These local markets, however, did not attract large crowds. Then some merchants started selling goods during church festivals. Some local rulers also allowed fairs for the sale of imported goods. They placed a tax on each item that was sold. In return for the taxes, local rulers arranged special services for merchants. Armed guards protected merchants from robbery. They also kept the fairgrounds safe for everyone.

The most important and best-known fairs were held in Champagne. This section of northeastern France was on the trade route from Italy. At different times each year, four towns in Champagne held six fairs. Each fair lasted 49 days.

At first, business at fairs was done through a simple **barter economy.** Goods and services were exchanged for other goods and services without using money. As the fairs grew larger, a fixed value was placed on goods. This value could be in terms of goods, services, or money. However, local rulers each issued their own coins. Money changers placed a value on currencies from one region in relation to currencies from another region. Based on their value, money changers then exchanged coins from one region for coins of another. Little money ever changed hands at fairs. Buyers and sellers, however, started thinking of the value of a good in terms of money.

Although the major purpose of fairs was the buying and selling of goods, they became important social events as well. Fairs provided entertainment with clowns, jugglers, and musicians. People traveled from great distances to attend the large fairs. They met other travelers and shared news and ideas. In that way, fairs helped people broaden their outlook on the world.

✔ **READING CHECK: Finding the Main Idea** Why were fairs important during the Middle Ages?

Manufacturing, Banking, and Investment

The revival of trade in Europe during the Middle Ages led to three important business developments, each of which greatly affected economic life and progress down to the present day. During these years a new system of manufacturing began, a banking system developed, and the practice of investing wealth started.

Manufacturing. The system of manufacturing that developed during the Middle Ages was called the **domestic system.** Manufacturing took place in workers' homes rather than in a shop or factory. A good example of the domestic system was the woolen industry. An individual would buy wool and then hand it out to several workers. Each worker completed a different task, such as spinning, weaving, or dyeing. Then the owner of the wool collected the spun wool or finished cloth and sold it at the highest possible price. The domestic system began in towns but gradually spread to the countryside.

The annual fair at Lendit, France

CONNECTING TO
Economics

Trade Fairs of the Middle Ages

Fairs in the Middle Ages were colorful events. They were also the main method of carrying out trade. Because of the fairs, easier ways to trade developed.

For example, some goods were sold by length or weight. Because people came from all over Europe to trade fairs, a standard system of weights and measures was needed. The troy weight was set to weigh gold and silver. This weight, named for the town of Troyes, France, is still used today.

Trade fairs also helped develop the bill of exchange. This note was a written promise to pay a sum of money at a later time.

Understanding Economics

Why did new ways of carrying on trade develop from fairs?

Banking. Another new business system of the later Middle Ages was banking. The word *bank* comes from the old Italian word *banca*, meaning "money changer's bench." Money changers were the first bankers. Besides exchanging currencies at fairs, money changers began to provide other services. Lending money was the most important service early bankers offered. Rulers, nobles, and merchants often borrowed money to pay for their activities. During the early Middle Ages, Jews, who were not allowed to own land or join most groups for skilled workers, became the main moneylenders. The Christian church did not allow **usury** (YOO·zhuh·ree), or charging interest on loans. By the late Middle Ages, however, some Christians had also become moneylenders. Most law codes by then allowed the collection of interest on loans for business matters.

Bankers also made it easier to move money from one place to another. They developed special notes called bills of exchange. These notes were used in place of money. For example, a merchant might deposit money with a banker in Ghent in return for a bill of exchange in the amount of the deposit. The merchant could then cash the bill of exchange with a banker in Venice. This system was somewhat like present-day checking accounts.

Investing. In the later Middle Ages, Europeans began investing capital. **Capital** is wealth that is earned, saved, and invested to make profits. Sometimes, several people called investors formed a partnership. They put together their capital to pay for a new business. In that way, each partner shared in the cost. If the business made money, each partner would receive part of the profits.

Manufacturing, banking, and investing capital were the first steps toward the creation of a **market economy.** In a market economy, land, labor, and capital are controlled by individual persons. The medieval market economy formed the basis for our modern capitalist system.

This medieval illustration portrays aspects of banking and finance.

✔ **READING CHECK: Summarizing** What new business systems developed because of the revival of trade in Europe?

SECTION 2 REVIEW

1. **Define** and explain the significance:
   barter economy
   domestic system
   usury
   capital
   market economy

2. **Identifying Cause and Effect** Copy the chart below. Use it to show which cities in Italy, northern Europe, and the Hanseatic League became important trading centers and explain why each did.

Italy	Northern Europe	Hanseatic League

3. **Finding the Main Idea**
   a. What economic and social changes did fairs bring about in the Middle Ages?
   b. How did the revival of trade lead to the domestic system, a banking system, and the investing of capital?

4. **Writing and Critical Thinking**
   Analyzing Information Choose a town in Europe during the Middle Ages, and write an advertisement to attract people to its fair.
   Consider:
   • the location of the town
   • goods that will be for sale and where they are from
   • entertainment that will be provided

Homework Practice Online
go.hrw.com
keyword: SH3 HP5

The Growth of Towns

READ TO DISCOVER

❶ What rights did townspeople gain during the later Middle Ages?

❷ How did merchant and craft guilds contribute to their communities?

❸ How did the growth of cities help lead to the decline of serfdom?

DEFINE

merchant guild
craft guilds
apprentice
journeyman
middle class

IDENTIFY

Black Death

WHY IT MATTERS TODAY

Today different groups of workers organize into unions for many of the same reasons that medieval workers formed craft guilds. Use CNN Student News.com or other **current event** sources to find information about current union activities. Record your findings in your journal.

CNN Student News.com

The Main Idea
The growth of European towns accompanied the revival of trade during the Middle Ages.

The Story Continues *As trade increased in the late 900s, European towns grew larger and new towns sprang up. In the 1300s, however, the populations of both town and countryside throughout Europe would be devastated by, as the Welsh called it, "death coming into our midst like black smoke."*

The Rights of Townspeople

Trade and cities generally grow together. As towns grew in the Middle Ages, townspeople saw that they did not fit into the manorial system. They played little part in the farming economy of villages. Instead, townspeople made their living by making and trading goods.

Manor lords, however, still controlled the towns. They would give up control only if given something in return. In some towns the people won self-government by peaceful means. In others, they resorted to violence. Some lords granted their towns charters of liberties. A charter was a written statement of the town's rights. In time, townspeople throughout Europe gained four basic rights.

1. **Freedom.** Anyone who lived in a town for a year and a day became free. This included serfs who escaped from a manor to a town.

2. **Exemption.** Townspeople won the right of being exempt, or free, from ever having to work on the manor.

3. **Town justice.** Towns had their own courts. Leading citizens tried cases that involved townspeople.

4. **Commercial privileges.** Townspeople could sell goods freely in the town market. They could also charge tolls to outsiders who wanted to trade there.

✔ **READING CHECK: Summarizing** What rights did townspeople gain?

Guilds

As trade increased, towns grew larger and richer. Merchants and workers began to unite in associations called guilds.

Merchants. In each town, a merchant guild had the sole right to trade there. Merchants from other towns or nations could trade there only if they paid a fee. Merchant guilds also helped their members and members' families. For example, guilds looked after members who were in trouble and made loans to members. When guild members died, the guild aided the widow and children.

This illustration from about 1480 depicts medieval craft workers at their trades: an apprentice grinding colors (bottom left), a fresco painter (top), and a chest painter (bottom right).

Workers. In time, skilled workers came together in **craft guilds**. Each guild had members from a single craft, such as shoemaking or weaving. The craft guilds set rules for wages, hours, and working conditions. They also set standards for the quality of work. The guilds looked after ill members and those who could no longer work. Perhaps most important, the craft guilds controlled the training of skilled workers.

The master workers of each guild trained boys and men who wanted to join their guild. First, a boy served as an **apprentice**. His parents paid a master worker to house, feed, clothe, and train the boy. Apprentice training could take five to nine years. Next, the young man became a **journeyman**, a skilled worker who was paid wages by a master. After some time, a journeyman could become a master himself by making a masterpiece—a piece of work worthy of a master. If masters of the journeyman's guild approved his masterpiece, the journeyman could open his own shop. He was then a guild member. Some girls also served as apprentices.

The rise of the middle class. In time, towns' guild members—merchants and master workers—became the **middle class**. They were between the class of nobles and that of peasants and unskilled workers. The middle class favored kings over nobles because kings could provide stable governments that would protect trade, business, and property. In turn, kings looked to the middle class for advice. They also gave members of the middle class jobs in government. In these ways, during the later Middle Ages the middle class started to gain power.

✔ **READING CHECK: Problem Solving** If you were a young person in the Middle Ages who wanted work, how might a guild help you?

Medieval Towns

In the Middle Ages, most northern and western European cities had fewer than 2,000 people. A few cities were larger. By the 1200s, for example, about 150,000 people lived in Paris. Growing commercial cities like London, Ghent, and Bruges had about 40,000 residents each.

Town life. Towns offered serfs a chance to improve their lives. Some serfs escaped to towns to gain freedom. Others were pushed off the land as farming methods changed. They moved to cities to find jobs. Serfs who stayed on the manors sold their crops in town markets. They paid the manor lord with money rather than with their labor.

In the Middle Ages, cities often stood on hilltops or lay along river bends. Such locations made cities easier to defend. Most cities had little land, so houses were built several stories high. Each story extended a little beyond the one below it. At their tops, the houses almost touched over the middle of the street, darkening the narrow roadway below. Cities also had large public buildings, including churches or cathedrals, town halls, and guild halls.

The Spread of the Black Death

Between 1347 and 1351, Europe and the Mediterranean world were devastated by the "Black Death"—a deadly plague. Carried from China along sea and overland trade routes, the Black Death quickly swept through Europe's population. By studying a map that illustrates the spread of the plague, we can develop conclusions regarding its effect on the civilization of the late Middle Ages.

Trade route

Areas affected:

1347	After 1350
1348	Unaffected areas
1349	
1350	

Spread of the Black Death, 1347–1351

Skills Reminder

To use a map to analyze historical patterns, define the map's overall topic. Then identify the historical context of the map and the events or changes it is designed to illustrate. Connect the information on the map to the historical context of the subject. Analyze the change, trend, or pattern that is illustrated by the map and build a hypothesis to explain why it took place. Finally, determine how the map helps to show the change, pattern, or trend that came to represent a new historical reality.

Skills Practice

Study the map above and answer the following questions:

❶ How was the plague carried from Marseille to North Africa? From Marseille to Paris?

❷ Why might Paris have been stricken by the plague earlier than London but later than Constantinople?

❸ Why might the plague have been slower to reach eastern Europe than it was to reach western and northern Europe?

The devastating plague of 1347 through 1351 was carried by flea-infested rats.

The Black Death. The growing cities of the Middle Ages could be exciting places. However, many were also dark, unsafe, dirty, and unhealthy. There were no streetlights or police. People did not go out alone at night for fear of robbers. Waste was dumped into open gutters. For that reason, diseases spread quickly through the crowded cities.

Beginning in 1347, one such disease, a terrible plague called the **Black Death,** swept through Europe. The plague began in Asia and spread along busy trade routes. It entered ports by way of trading ships. Black rats on the ships carried the disease. The plague was spread to people by bites from fleas on the rats.

No one knows the exact number of plague deaths in Europe. They happened so rapidly and in such great numbers that often survivors could not keep up with burying the dead.

Analyzing Primary Sources

Drawing Conclusions What effect would such circumstances have on people's beliefs and morale?

History Makers Speak ❝They died by the hundreds, both day and night, and all were thrown in . . . ditches and covered with earth. And as soon as those ditches were filled, more were dug. And I buried my five children with my own hands.❞

Angolo di Tura, quoted in *The Black Death,* by Robert S. Gottfried

Some entire villages and towns were wiped out. By some estimates, about 25 million people died in Europe from 1347 to 1351—about one-third of the entire population.

The Black Death caused many changes in Europe. People's faith in God was shaken. The church lost some of its power and importance. Relations between the upper classes and lower classes changed. Workers, now in short supply, demanded higher wages. In several European countries, peasants staged uprisings.

✔ **READING CHECK: Analyzing Information** What role did towns and cities begin to play in the lives of serfs?

SECTION 3 REVIEW

1. **Define** and explain the significance:
   merchant guild
   craft guilds
   apprentice
   journeyman
   middle class

2. **Identify** and explain the significance:
   Black Death

3. **Sequencing** Copy the flowchart below. Use it to show the sequence of steps required to become a guild member.

   | Apprentice | → | Journeyman | → | Master Worker |

4. **Finding the Main Idea**
   a. How would the rights won by townspeople help break down manorialism?
   b. How did merchant and craft guilds help their members?
   c. How did the growth of towns and the Black Death lead to the decline of serfdom?

5. **Writing and Critical Thinking**
   Categorizing Write a short report that gives the advantages and disadvantages of living in a medieval city.
   Consider:
   • the rights of townspeople
   • health and safety factors
   • opportunities for work

Homework Practice Online

keyword: SH3 HP5

Life and Culture in the Middle Ages

READ TO DISCOVER

❶ How did languages and literature change during the Middle Ages?

❷ In what ways did education change?

❸ What developments were made in philosophy and science?

❹ What kind of architecture characterized the later Middle Ages?

DEFINE

vernacular languages
troubadours
scholasticism

IDENTIFY

Dante Alighieri
Geoffrey Chaucer
Peter Abelard
Thomas Aquinas
Gothic

WHY IT MATTERS TODAY

Styles of architecture continue to change today, just as they did during the Middle Ages. Use CNN Student News.com or other **current event** sources to find examples of recent buildings designed in new styles. Record your findings in your journal.

CNN Student News.com

The Main Idea
Much of medieval European life and culture centered on the Christian church and faith.

The Story Continues *"There was a knight, a most distinguished man, / Who from the day on which he first began / To ride abroad had followed chivalry, / Truth, honour, generousnous, and courtesy." Early civilizations arose only after humans had settled in towns and cities. In much the same way, medieval culture—as shown in the lines of poetry above—could flourish once city life regained importance.*

Language and Literature

Throughout the Middle Ages, European culture underwent many changes. Some of these changes took place in language and literature. Since the collapse of the Roman Empire, Latin had remained the written and spoken language of educated people in western Europe. However, people with little education spoke **vernacular languages.** These languages were everyday speech that varied from place to place. Present-day French, Italian, and Spanish came from early vernacular languages that were related to Latin. Present-day English and German came from other vernacular languages.

This manuscript from the 1200s shows a traveling singer performing.

Holt Researcher

go.hrw.com

KEYWORD: Holt Researcher

FreeFind: Geoffrey Chaucer

After reading more about Geoffrey Chaucer on the Holt Researcher, identify some of the universal themes in his works that still make them relevant today.

Analyzing Primary Sources

Identifying a Point of View How does the author of the epic poem portray Roland?

Dante's **The Divine Comedy** *masterpiece describes an imaginary journey in which he is guided through heaven by Beatrice, a woman he loves in a spiritual way.*

Early vernacular literature. During the Middle Ages writers began to use vernacular languages in their works. Troubadours' songs were one of the first forms of vernacular literature. **Troubadours** were traveling singers who wrote poems about love and chivalry. They sang their love poems in castles and in towns.

Romances, or fictional stories, written in vernacular were popular with medieval audiences. The best-known English romances were the adventures of King Arthur and his Knights of the Round Table.

Also popular were the French *fabliaux* (FA·blee·oh). These were short comic stories written in rhymed verse. The *fabliaux* laughed at the high ideals of chivalry, human foolishness, and the clergy. Animal stories, or fables, such as "Reynard the Fox," delighted medieval audiences too.

Another kind of vernacular literature was the national epic—a long poem about a hero. France's national epic was *The Song of Roland,* written in about 1100. The poem is set during the period of Charlemagne's wars with the Moors. It describes the death of Roland, one of Charlemagne's brave, loyal knights.

 History Makers Speak

❝Roland with pain and anguish winds
His Olifant [horn], and blows with all his might.
Blood from his mouth comes spurting scarlet-bright.
He's burst the veins of his temples outright.
From hand and horn the call goes shrilling high:
King Carlon [Charlemagne] hears it who through
the passes rides . . .
Quoth Charles: 'I hear the horn of Roland cry!
He'd never sound it but in the thick of fight.'❞

From *The Song of Roland*

Drama written in vernacular languages also developed during the Middle Ages. Miracle plays, morality plays, and mystery plays were short dramas with religious or biblical themes. At Christmas and Easter, the plays were sometimes part of church services. Later, as towns grew, they were also presented in town marketplaces. A favorite play was *Noye's Fludde,* "Noah's Flood."

The flowering of vernacular literature. During the Middle Ages vernacular literature reached its height in the works of two great medieval writers, **Dante Alighieri** and **Geoffrey Chaucer.** Dante Alighieri, commonly known simply as Dante, was born in the region of Tuscany, Italy, in 1265. He wrote his poems using the Tuscan form of Italian. People throughout Italy read Dante's works. In that way, the Tuscan dialect became Italy's written language. Today Dante is thought of by many historians and other scholars as the father of the Italian language.

Many readers consider *The Divine Comedy* to be Dante's greatest work of literature. In the course of this remarkable creative piece, Dante takes an imaginary journey through the three realms where a Christian soul might go after death. The three scenes of Dante's narrative include hell, purgatory, and heaven. The author placed his friends and supporters in heaven and his political enemies in hell. Dante used his descriptive narrative to point out the faults that he saw in Italian society.

Geoffrey Chaucer's writing and imagination had a great influence on literary styles and approaches. Chaucer was born in England about 1340 and spent much of his life in service to the English crown. He fought in France and, for about 10 years, served as a diplomat throughout western Europe. He was elected to the English Parliament in 1386.

Chaucer's most famous work is *The Canterbury Tales*, a group of stories told from the point of view of about 30 pilgrims traveling to the shrine of Saint Thomas à Becket at Canterbury. Chaucer's pilgrims poke fun at English society, especially at the clergy. Many church people, Chaucer believed, had made service to the church a profitable occupation rather than a spiritual calling.

Chaucer wrote numerous works in addition to *The Canterbury Tales.* Like Dante before him, Chaucer wrote in the vernacular, in the dialect known as Middle English, a forerunner to the modern English of today. Chaucer's use of the dialect and the popularity of his works gave Middle English great literary prestige. Later writers and poets followed his example by crafting their works in the vernacular.

Pilgrims in a scene from **The Canterbury Tales**

✔ **READING CHECK: Summarizing** What important changes took place in language and literature in the Middle Ages? Why?

Education

During the early Middle Ages, few people received an education. Those who did were mainly nobles and the clergy. Schooling was carried out at monasteries and in churches. As towns grew larger, however, other schools opened. These schools were somewhat like the schools in Athens under Plato and Aristotle. A teacher would set up a school and try to attract students. He admitted any males who wanted to study and could pay a fee.

In time, teachers and students united to form guilds to protect and gain rights for themselves. Such a guild was called a *universitas*, Latin for "association of people." Later, the word *university* came into use.

A lecturer teaches at a medieval university.

Between the late 1000s and the late 1200s, four great universities developed. The universities in Paris and at Oxford in England were best known for teaching theology, the study of religious beliefs, as well as the liberal arts—Latin, logic, rhetoric, mathematics, astronomy, and music. Students at the University of Bologna in Italy studied civil law and church law. The University at Salerno taught medicine.

By the end of the 1400s, many more universities had opened throughout Europe. By that time, all universities had the same programs. Students had to pass certain stages of study before receiving their degrees. The first degree was the bachelor of arts, which was similar to finishing an apprenticeship in a craft guild. After more studying and tests, students could receive the master of arts degree. At that point, students were admitted to the guild of teaching. Some students then went on to study law, medicine, or theology.

✔ **READING CHECK: Comparing** How were medieval universities like guilds?

Philosophy and Science

Muslim scholars had kept the works of Greek and Roman philosophers and scientists alive. During the Middle Ages, this knowledge was passed on to Europeans.

Philosophy. Medieval European philosophers tried to make Aristotle's ideas work with those of early church writers. Aristotle placed the most importance on human reason. For the church writers, however, faith was most important. This attempt to bring together faith and reason is called **scholasticism.**

Peter Abelard, an important philosopher of scholasticism, taught in Paris in the 1100s. Abelard wrote a book called *Sic et Non* ("Yes and No"), which raised many questions about the church's teachings. In it he included quotations from the Bible, statements from popes, and writings of church philosophers. Abelard showed that many of them conflicted with one another.

Probably the greatest medieval philosopher was **Thomas Aquinas,** a monk of the Dominican order. His principal work, *Summa Theologiae,* summarized medieval Christian thought.

Science. Few advances were made in science during the Middle Ages. The Bible and the church were the main sources for information about the world. Only two subjects received serious attention: mathematics and optics, the study of light. Europeans did make some technical advances that helped with everyday life, however. They designed better winches and pulleys to make lifting and pulling heavy objects easier. They made iron plows and better oxen yokes to make farming easier. Europeans also began to use windmills and waterwheels, inventions for drawing water that had been invented in Asia.

✔ **READING CHECK: Making Generalizations** How did religion affect philosophy and science during the Middle Ages?

Architecture

During the Middle Ages, church architecture was the main art form. Between about 1000 and about 1150, most architects followed the Romanesque style of architecture. They used arches, domes, vaults, and low horizontal lines in their churches. This style was like that used in the Roman Empire. A Romanesque church had a heavy domed stone roof. To support the roof, the walls were low with few windows. As a result, these churches were very dark inside.

During the mid-1100s, master builders developed a different style of church architecture. Many people did not like the new style and called it **Gothic** after the barbarian Goths. Gothic churches had tall spires. On the outside walls, builders placed rows of supporting structures called flying buttresses. The flying buttresses were connected to the church's walls with arches and carried part of the roof's weight. The church's walls could therefore be high and thin. Everything in Gothic churches—pointed arches, tall spires, and high walls—reached toward heaven.

Large stained-glass windows were set in the high walls. They filled the inside of the churches with light. Statues of the holy family, saints, and rulers lined the inside of Gothic churches, and relief sculptures adorned the walls.

The Gothic church was an example of how life had changed in the later Middle Ages. This tall building towered above the growing town around it. Traders did business in the marketplace near its walls. Religious plays were presented within and

Cathedral of Notre Dame in Paris The Cathedral of Notre Dame is a good example of Gothic architecture. Its high walls hold large stained-glass windows. Flying buttresses support the walls. *When looking at this cathedral, in what direction are the viewer's eyes pulled—up, down, or sideways? Why is this so?*

outside it. The highest artistic skills of the medieval world went into the building of this monument to God.

Gothic cathedrals were constructed in many parts of Europe, including France, England, and Germany. One of the earliest of these magnificent structures, begun in about 1140, was the abbey of Saint-Denis in Paris. Construction of the towering cathedral of Notre Dame, also in Paris, began in the early 1160s and continued in stages for about a century thereafter.

✔ **READING CHECK: Contrasting** How did the Romanesque and Gothic styles of church architecture differ from each other?

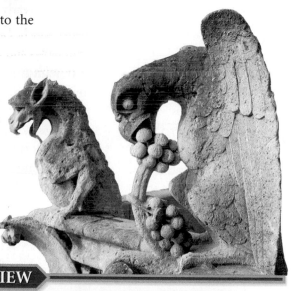

These gargoyles are found on the exterior of the Cathedral of Notre Dame.

SECTION 4 REVIEW

1. **Define** and explain the significance:
   vernacular languages
   troubadours
   scholasticism

2. **Identify** and explain the significance:
   Dante Alighieri
   Geoffrey Chaucer
   Peter Abelard
   Thomas Aquinas
   Gothic

3. **Summarizing** Copy the web diagram below. Use it to list ways in which language and literature, education, and architecture changed during the Middle Ages.

   Language and Literature
   Changes in Late Middle Ages
   Architecture   Education

4. **Finding the Main Idea**
   a. How did the writings of Dante and Chaucer reflect the history of the cultures in which they were produced?
   b. How did the church and religion influence medieval philosophy, science, and architecture?

5. **Writing and Critical Thinking**
   Making Generalizations Write an outline for a drama that might have been performed during the Middle Ages.
   Consider:
   • how medieval dramas reflected the culture of the times
   • how vernacular language influenced them

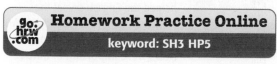

Homework Practice Online
keyword: SH3 HP5

Wars and the Growth of Nations

The Main Idea
The late Middle Ages saw the development of individual nations united under strong monarchs.

The Story Continues *Americans today fly the American flag and sing the national anthem to show their patriotism, or feeling of loyalty to their country. Under feudalism in the early Middle Ages, people of a country did not feel any such loyalty. This would change during the later Middle Ages, however, as states began to form and kings began to build their kingdoms as organized nations.*

England

By the late Middle Ages, England's feudal lords had lost much of their power to its king. The new class of townspeople supported a strong king. A single system of law and courts and a larger army of soldiers helped strengthen the king. In addition, as the country prospered, more taxes were paid to the king.

In the early 1300s the English king Edward III also held land in France. This made him a vassal of the French king. This fact helped lead to a series of conflicts between England and France called the **Hundred Years' War** (1337–1453).

The Hundred Years' War. In 1328 the last male member of France's Capetian dynasty died. Edward III claimed the French throne. The French assembly chose Philip VI, the Count of Flanders, as king instead. In 1337 Edward brought an army to Flanders, hoping to gain control of this rich trading area.

Thus the Hundred Years' War began. It continued for 116 years as a series of raids and battles. Sometimes there were long periods of uneasy peace. England won many battles but lost the war. By 1453 France controlled all of England's French lands except Calais.

The Hundred Years' War saw the use of new weapons in Europe. At the Battle of Agincourt (AJ·uhn·kohrt) in 1415, English foot soldiers used longbows. With these bows they could fire arrows quickly, hitting targets up to 200 yards away. French knights on horseback were no match for the English and their

INTERPRETING THE VISUAL RECORD

The longbow The six-foot longbow and its three-foot arrows, accurate over a range of 200 yards, helped the English defeat the French at Agincourt. *How does this illustration suggest that longbows were important in battle?*

longbows. Both the English and the French used gunpowder and cannons in battle. Castles no longer provided protection for a feudal lord because one powerful cannon blast could break through a castle's wall. Longbows, gunpowder, and cannons further weakened knightly warfare.

Besides loss of life and land, the Hundred Years' War had another important effect on England. Parliament, particularly the House of Commons, gained more power over the king. Members of the House of Commons were angry about the way the war was going. They won the right of a special council to advise the king and the right to consider new taxes before they were discussed by the House of Lords. By the late 1300s, the king needed Parliament's consent on all special taxes.

The War of the Roses. Shortly after the Hundred Years' War ended, a war for England's throne began. In 1455 the York and Lancaster families started the **War of the Roses.** The white rose was the badge of the House of York. The red rose was used by the House of Lancaster. In 1485 **Henry Tudor** of the House of Lancaster won the war. He defeated King Richard III of York. However, Henry married a daughter from the House of York. As King Henry VII, he set up a strong monarchy in England once again.

✔ **READING CHECK: Identifying Cause and Effect** Why did the Hundred Years' War begin and what were its results?

Territory held in 1430 by:

France	☼ French victory
England	☼ English victory
Burgundy	

France

During the Hundred Years' War, France suffered more than England because the war took place on French soil. Bands of English soldiers robbed the people and destroyed their property. Even during times of peace, the French people starved.

History Makers Speak

❝And in truth when good weather came, in April, those who in the winter had made their beverages from apples and sloe plums emptied the residue of their apples and their plums into the street with the intention that the pigs of St. Antoine would eat them. But the pigs did not get to them in time, for as soon as they were thrown out, they were seized by poor folk, women and children, who ate them with great relish, . . . for they ate what the pigs scorned to eat, they ate the cores of cabbages without bread or without cooking, grasses of the fields without bread or salt.❞

Quoted in J.B. Ross and M.M. McLaughlin, eds., *The Portable Medieval Reader*

A fight for the throne. During the Hundred Years' War, a fight for power broke out within the royal family. The House of Burgundy sided with the English against the House of Orléans, preventing France from uniting against the English. Finally in 1429, with the help of a young girl named **Joan of Arc,** Charles VII of Orléans was crowned king of France. The French backed their king and drove the English out.

Interpreting Maps Until 1429 the English had won the major battles of the Hundred Years' War.

■ **Skills Assessment:**
1. Places and Regions Which of the three powers represented by the map held the least amount of physical territory?
2. Finding the Main Idea What battle marked the end of the Hundred Years' War, and who was the victor?

**Joan of Arc
(c. 1412–1431)**

Joan of Arc, the "Maid of Orléans," is a revered figure in French history. Believing that God spoke to her through visions, Joan left home to aid the French king, Charles VII, in his struggle against the English. Her strong faith persuaded thousands to follow her into battle. Her most crucial test came when the teenage Joan led French troops to victory against the English at Orléans.

A short time later, Joan was captured by English troops. She was accused of heresy, tortured, and burned at the stake. Today Joan of Arc is a Catholic saint and a symbol of French patriotism. **What was Joan of Arc's role in building the nation of France?**

Holt Researcher

go.hrw.com
KEYWORD: Holt Researcher
FreeFind: Joan of Arc
After reading more about Joan of Arc on the Holt Researcher, create a cause-and-effect chart showing how her religious faith influenced her actions, which ultimately affected political events in France.

A return of strong kings. During the Hundred Years' War, the French Estates General controlled finances and passed laws. This representative assembly was similar to the English Parliament. It took its name from the groups that assembled for its meetings: clergy (First Estate), nobles (Second Estate), and common people (Third Estate). After the war, however, the Estates General lost some of its power.

In 1461 **Louis XI** followed Charles VII as king of France. Louis made the French monarchy even stronger. He set up a harsh but efficient government with high taxes. Through diplomacy and scheming, he seized the lands of the House of Burgundy. Under Louis, France became a united country. As in England, French feudal lords lost much power to their king. They kept many rights, however, and remained wealthy and important until the mid-1700s. French peasants, unlike those in England, gained little freedom. They still owed services to the manor and its lord.

✔ **READING CHECK: Supporting a Point of View** How would you support the view that France grew as a nation after the Hundred Years' War?

Spain

Spain became a united nation in 1479 under **Ferdinand** of Aragon and **Isabella** of Castile. In 1492 the Spanish army captured Granada, the last stronghold of the Moors, or Muslims, in Spain. In 1515 Ferdinand and Isabella added the kingdom of Navarre to their territory. Ferdinand and Isabella took powers away from church courts and from the nobles. Fervent Catholics, they did not look kindly on non-Christians in Spain. In 1492 they ordered all Jews to become Christians or leave Spain. Later, they gave the Moors the same choice. Most Jews and Moors did leave the country. As a result, Spain was robbed of many of its leaders in industry and trade.

The Unification of Spain, 1479–1515

Interpreting Maps
Four kingdoms on the Iberian Peninsula were united to form Spain.

■ **Skills Assessment:**
1. The World in Spatial Terms Which kingdom was largest? Which was second largest?
2. Sequencing By 1515, what two nations were on the Iberian Peninsula?

10°W 5°W

45°N ATLANTIC OCEAN
N W E S

FRANCE
5°E
PYRENEES
NAVARRE
Ebro River
CASTILE ARAGON
• Barcelona
PORTUGAL
40°N
Madrid •
Tagus River
• Toledo
BALEARIC ISLANDS
Lisbon •
0°
Córdoba •
• Granada
Guadalquivir R.
GRANADA
Cádiz •
MEDITERRANEAN SEA
0 100 200 Miles
0 100 200 Kilometers
35°N
AFRICA
Azimuthal Equal Area Projection

☐ United by Ferdinand and Isabella, 1479
☐ Acquired by Spain, 1515
☐ Conquered by Spain, 1492

Map of Europe, c. 1500

Interpreting Maps In 1500 the Holy Roman Empire reached from the North and Baltic Seas to the Mediterranean Sea.

■ **Skills Assessment: 1. Places and Regions** What countries bordered the Holy Roman Empire? **2. Analyzing Information** Which area was made up of small independent states?

✔ **READING CHECK: Comparing and Contrasting** How did Ferdinand and Isabella's policies both help and hurt Spain?

The Holy Roman Empire

By the 1500s England, France, and Spain had each formed powerful nations. Germany and Italy, which made up the Holy Roman Empire, remained divided into states and regions ruled by princes and knights. Over time, the Holy Roman emperors had given up much of their power to these nobles in return for military support. Therefore the emperors lacked the power needed to exercise complete control.

In the early days the rulers of many German states, along with the pope, elected the Holy Roman emperor. Gradually the number who could vote for emperor decreased. Finally, by a decree issued in 1356, Emperor Charles IV ruled that only

This portrait by an unknown artist depicts the Habsburg ruler Maximilian I, who became Holy Roman emperor in 1493.

seven electors—three archbishops and four German princes—would choose the emperor. By thus removing the pope from the process of electing emperors, Charles IV hoped to rebuild his own authority. However, the new system had the effect of making the seven electors almost completely independent rulers in their own territories. The emperor still had little real power, but the title did carry prestige. For this reason, the election became an occasion for bribery and political favors.

In 1273 a member of the **Habsburg** family became emperor. The Habsburgs ruled a small state in what is now Switzerland. They were weak, with little land. The Habsburgs did, however, use the title of emperor to arrange marriages with powerful families. They also followed careful strategies of armed conquest to gradually win land and power. In this way, the Habsburgs gained control of the duchy of Austria and surrounding lands in central Europe. By the 1400s the Habsburg family was clearly one of Europe's rising stars.

The Habsburg emperor Maximilian I followed his family's strategy of marriage and conquest to add to its power and wealth. Maximilian's marriage brought The Netherlands, Luxembourg, and Burgundy under Habsburg control. His son, Philip, followed by marrying into the Spanish royal family, thus gaining large Spanish and Italian holdings for the Habsburgs.

Over time, the Habsburgs became the most powerful family in Europe. They strengthened their position by ensuring that the imperial throne was held almost continuously by Habsburgs. They could not, however, unite the Holy Roman Empire or even regions within it. For example, the German states were still ruled by independent princes. These princes refused to surrender power to the emperor. Nor could Italy be united. The Papal States, ruled by the pope, stretched across the middle of the Italian Peninsula. The geographic location of the Papal States effectively blocked efforts to bring all of Italy under centralized imperial control.

✔ **READING CHECK: Drawing Inferences** Why were emperors unable to unite the Holy Roman Empire?

◣ SECTION 5 REVIEW ◢

1. **Identify** and explain the significance:
   Hundred Years' War
   War of the Roses
   Henry Tudor
   Joan of Arc
   Louis XI
   Ferdinand
   Isabella
   Habsburg

2. **Summarizing** Copy the chart below. Use it to name important rulers in England, France, and Spain and to show how they united their nations.

👑	👑	👑
England	France	Spain

Ways Ruler United the Country

3. **Finding the Main Idea**
   a. In what ways did the Hundred Years' War affect England and France differently?
   b. What happened in Spain in 1492 that changed the country's population?

4. **Writing and Critical Thinking**

   Analyzing Information Write a script for a newscast that describes the Battle of Agincourt and analyzes its importance.
   Consider:
   • the English use of the longbow
   • the French use of horses
   • the outcome of the battle

Homework Practice Online

keyword: SH3 HP5

READ TO DISCOVER
❶ What factors led to the decline of Catholic Church power during the late Middle Ages?
❷ How did the Babylonian Captivity and the Great Schism affect the church?
❸ Why did growing numbers of teachers and priests challenge the church during the later Middle Ages?

IDENTIFY
Babylonian Captivity
Great Schism
John Wycliffe
Jan Hus

WHY IT MATTERS TODAY

Today the pope often tries to work with government leaders to improve the lives of their people. Use **CNN** or other **current event** sources to find information about recent visits of the pope with world leaders. Record your findings in your journal.

CNN student **News**.com

Challenges to Church Power

The Main Idea
During the late Middle Ages the Catholic Church lost some of its political power in many parts of Europe.

The Story Continues *A papal palace in France? Three men claiming to be pope? Europe was indeed changing. Kings were developing strong national governments with rich treasuries. Townspeople were increasing in number and importance. Such changes had to affect the one power that had unified medieval Europe—the church.*

Church Power Weakens

Innocent III was pope from 1198 to 1216. Under him the medieval papacy reached the height of its power. After Innocent, however, the worldly power of the church began to weaken. This happened for several reasons.

First, power was shifting. The kings of England, France, and Spain were forming strong governments. The increased number of townspeople gave them added importance too. Many felt that church laws limited their trade and industry. Also, people began to question some church practices. For example, they found fault with its great wealth, its method of raising money, and the worldly lives of some clergy members.

In 1294 a conflict arose between the pope and a monarch. After this conflict, King Philip IV of France ordered the clergy in France to pay taxes. This angered Pope Boniface VIII. In 1302 Boniface decreed that popes had power over worldly rulers.

Philip responded by calling the first-ever meeting of the Estates General. He wanted support against Boniface. Philip charged the pope with heresy and of selling jobs in the church. He also wanted a church council to put Boniface on trial. Philip then had his envoys in Rome take the pope prisoner. Although Boniface was quickly let go, he died soon after. For the next 100 years, the church continued to lose power.

✔ **READING CHECK: Analyzing Information** How did changes that were taking place in Europe help lead to the struggle between Philip IV and Boniface VIII?

This portrait shows Philip IV, sometimes called "Philip the Fair," and his family.

The Babylonian Captivity and the Great Schism

After Boniface died, Philip had a French bishop elected pope. The new pope took the name Clement V. In 1309 Clement moved the headquarters of the church to Avignon, France. Until then, Rome had been the center of the church for 1,000 years. After Clement, the next six popes were French and lived in Avignon also.

The years that the popes lived in Avignon are called the **Babylonian Captivity** (1309–1377). The period was named for the time the ancient Hebrews were forced to live in Babylon, more than 1,800 years earlier. During the Babylonian Captivity, people in other countries lost respect for the church. They felt that the popes were being controlled by French kings.

In 1377 the French pope Gregory XI returned to Rome. A year later he died. Meeting in Rome, the cardinals elected an Italian pope to please local mobs, but later elected a French pope, who took up residence at Avignon. Until 1417 the church had two and sometimes three popes. This period of church history is called the **Great Schism** (SI·zuhm). The church was divided into opposing groups. For political reasons, each pope had the support of certain national rulers and their people and clergy.

Finally a church council met in Constance in 1414. Three years later, the Council of Constance ended the Great Schism. It removed the Italian and French popes; a third pope resigned. The council then elected a new Italian pope. It also suggested that other councils be held to correct church problems.

✔ **READING CHECK: Drawing Conclusions** How did the church become weaker during the Babylonian Captivity and the Great Schism?

INTERPRETING THE VISUAL RECORD

The Babylonian Captivity The popes had many enemies during the era known as the "Babylonian Captivity." The papal palace in Avignon was, in reality, a highly defensible fortress. It was built on land 190 feet above the town and surrounded by three miles of high, thick walls.

Link to Today Judging from this modern-day photograph, why might popes in Avignon have felt safe?

More Problems for the Church

The Babylonian Captivity and Great Schism not only weakened the authority of the pope but they also increased criticism of the church. Some of this criticism came from within the church itself.

In 1324 two teachers at the University of Paris wrote *Defender of the Faith*. It claimed that the pope was the elected head of the church alone. He had no power over worldly rulers. It also stated that the church's power belonged with a council of clergy and lay people. *Defender of the Faith* directly opposed the ideas in Pope Boniface's *Unam Sanctum.*

In the late 1300s **John Wycliffe** was a priest and teacher at Oxford University. Wycliffe attacked the wealth of the church and the immorality of some of its clergy. He also did not believe in the absolute power of the pope. Wycliffe wanted to replace the authority of the church, which he believed had been undermined, with that of the Bible. He held that individuals should be allowed to read and interpret scripture for themselves, without church intervention. This idea had great appeal among many Europeans who felt that the church and its clergy had surrendered spiritual authority. Wycliffe promoted the first translation of the Bible into English from Latin. English people could then read the Bible and decide for themselves what it meant. The church accused Wycliffe of being a heretic. The English royal court defended him. Because of this political support, unlike some other prominent heretics, Wycliffe was not executed. Instead he was banned from teaching and forced to retire. Wycliffe wrote to one duke: "I believe that in the end the truth will conquer."

On July 6, 1415, Jan Hus was led to his death. He was burned alive at the stake for heresy.

Like many others in England and the rest of Europe, **Jan Hus** read Wycliffe's works. Hus was a religious reformer and teacher at the University of Prague. He also criticized abuses in the church. His attacks angered the clergy. Hus was excommunicated. In 1414 the Council of Constance declared him a heretic and ordered his death. He was burned at the stake the following year.

Despite the church's reaction to their ideas, Wycliffe and Hus would have a profound impact on many people. Their questioning of church authority set the stage for later reformers who would radically alter the history of the Christian church.

✔ **READING CHECK: Summarizing** Who was finding fault with the church in the 1300s and 1400s, and what changes did they suggest?

SECTION 6 REVIEW

1. Identify and explain the significance:
Babylonian Captivity
Great Schism
John Wycliffe
Jan Hus

2. Sequencing Copy the time line below. Use it to organize the events that weakened the power of the church from 1294 to 1417.

```
|-------|-------|-------|
1300    1350    1400    1450
```

3. **Finding the Main Idea**

a. Why was the conflict between Philip IV and Boniface VIII the beginning of the weakening of church power in the late Middle Ages?

b. According to the church's critics, where did the real power of the church come from?

4. **Writing and Critical Thinking**

Analyzing Information Write the minutes of the meetings at the Council of Constance, which will be read at all Christian churches in Europe.

Consider:
• how the council ended the Great Schism
• suggestions it made for the future of the church
• how it dealt with Jan Hus

Homework Practice Online

keyword: SH3 HP5

Creating a Time Line

Copy the time line below onto a sheet of paper. Complete the time line by filling in the events, individuals, and dates from the chapter that you think were significant. Pick three events and explain why you think they were significant.

1100   **1200**   **1300**   **1400**   **1500**

Writing a Summary

Using standard grammar, spelling, sentence structure, and punctuation, write an overview of the events in the chapter.

Identifying People and Ideas

Identify the following terms or individuals and explain their significance:

1. Urban II
2. Crusades
3. domestic system
4. craft guilds
5. vernacular languages
6. Dante Alighieri
7. scholasticism
8. Joan of Arc
9. Great Schism
10. John Wycliffe

Understanding Main Ideas

SECTION 1 *(pp. 126–130)*

The Crusades

1. Why did Europeans fight in the Crusades?
2. How did the Crusades affect the government, economy, and culture of Europe?

SECTION 2 *(pp. 131–134)*

The Revival of Trade

3. Why did trade begin again in Europe during the late Middle Ages?
4. How did the revival of trade help in the development of manufacturing, banking, and investing?

SECTION 3 *(pp. 135–138)*

The Growth of Towns

5. How did life for people in towns change in the late Middle Ages?

SECTION 4 *(pp. 139–143)*

Life and Culture in the Middle Ages

6. How did education, philosophy, and architecture change in the later Middle Ages?

SECTION 5 *(pp. 144–148)*

Wars and the Growth of Nations

7. How did the Hundred Years' War affect the governments of England and France?
8. Why did Spain become a strong nation and the Holy Roman Empire become weaker?

SECTION 6 *(pp. 149–151)*

Challenges to Church Power

9. What events led to the weakening of the church during the later Middle Ages?

Reviewing Themes

1. **Global Relations** How did the Crusades promote an exchange of ideas and goods?
2. **Economics** How did the growth of trade and towns bring changes to the feudal and manorial systems?
3. **Government** What groups lost power as Europe's kings established strong nations?

Thinking Critically

1. **Making Generalizations** How did the church influence life during the Middle Ages?
2. **Analyzing Information** How did trade, universities, and large churches help medieval towns grow?
3. **Comparing and Contrasting** In what ways were the development of strong central governments in England, France, and Spain alike and different?
4. **Summarizing** What were the main advances in literature during the later Middle Ages?

Writing About History

Comparing and Contrasting Medieval Europe evolved over centuries from the ruins of the Roman Empire. Compare and contrast the institutions of medieval Europe with the Roman Empire at its height. Use the compare-contrast diagram below to organize your thoughts before writing.

Roman Empire		Medieval Europe
	Government	
	Economy	
	Religion	
	Culture	
	Thought	

Building Social Studies Skills

Reading a Chart

Study the chart below. Then answer the questions that follow.

The Hundred Years' War in France

Date	BattleSite	What Happened
1346	Crécy	English king claimed French throne. English army invaded France and defeated French army.
1356	Poitiers	English won great victory over French. French king captured.
1415	Agincourt	After intervals of peace, English renewed claim to French throne. English army defeated French army.
1429	Orléans	Joan of Arc led French army. French defeated English.
1453	Castillon	French defeated English. Only Calais on English Channel remained in English hands.

1. Which statement correctly describes what you can infer from the chart?

   a. The year 1429 was a turning point in the Hundred Years' War.

   b. The Battle of Poitiers lasted for many days.

   c. In 1346 the French army was massed along the English Channel.

   d. The city of Calais is an English colony.

2. What effect did Joan of Arc have on the Hundred Years' War? Give specific examples.

Understanding Frames of Reference

Read this quote from *Sir Gawain and the Green Knight*, a romance from the 1300s about King Arthur's court. Then answer the questions.

> "'Good sir,' said Gawain, 'Will you give my message to the high lord of this house, that I ask for lodging?' . . . 'Yes, by Saint Peter,' replied the porter, 'and I think you may lodge here as long as you like, sir knight.' . . . Then the prince . . . appeared from his chamber to meet in mannerly style the man in his hall. 'You are welcome to dwell here as you wish,' he said, 'treat everything as your own, and have what you please in this place.'"

3. Which of the statements below best describes how the author of *Sir Gawain and the Green Knight* might react to a short story that displayed a mocking attitude toward the manners of chivalry?

   a. He would not understand it.

   b. He would probably find it amusing.

   c. He would probably be offended by it.

   d. He would think that the story was similar to what he wrote.

4. How did the Crusades contribute to the decline of the lifestyle of chivalry portrayed in the quote? Give specific examples.

Alternative Assessment

Building Your Portfolio

Economics

Before and since the Middle Ages and even today, the shift of people from the country to towns affects not only the economy but also the government and culture of a region. Using your textbook and other sources, compile a list of previous and modern-day areas of the world where such a population shift has occurred or is occurring. Use the list to create a cause-effect chart of this shift from country to town.

Link to TODAY

✓ **internet** connect

Internet Activity: go.hrw.com
KEYWORD: SH3 WH5

Choose a topic on the High Middle Ages to:

• create a propaganda poster about the Crusades.

• learn more about the monarchies of Henry VII, Louis XI, and Ferdinand and Isabella of Spain.

• explore the effects of the Black Death on Europe in the 1300s.

Epic Poetry

Epics are dramatic poems that often glorify a nation's history and its heroes. Literary epics can express and even define a nation's sense of its history and destiny. The German national epic, the Nibelungenlied *(nee·buh·LOONG·uhn·LEET), was first written down in the 1100s. It was one of the first European epics to be written in the language that ordinary people spoke. In the following excerpt from the* Nibelungenlied, *the hero Siegfried (ZEEG·freed) is killed by his brother-in-law King Gunther (GOON·tuhr). Geoffrey Chaucer wrote* The Canterbury Tales *during the 1300s, when an English national identity was first forming. Chaucer's tales are told by a group of pilgrims on their way to a holy shrine at Canterbury. The following passage from the Knight's tale in* The Canterbury Tales *reflects the English ideal of chivalry. Arcita has been fatally wounded in a battle with Palamon over Emily, whom they both love. Here he bids both his foe and his lover goodbye.*

The Nibelungenlied

When lord Siegfried felt the great wound, maddened with rage he bounded back from the stream with the long shaft jutting from his heart.

The hero's face had lost its color and he was no longer able to stand. His strength had ebbed away, for in the field of his bright countenance he now displayed Death's token. Soon many fair ladies would be weeping for him. . . . "You vile cowards," he said as he lay dying. ". . . I was always loyal to you, but now I have paid for it. Alas, you have wronged your kinsmen so that all who are born in days to come will be dishonored by your deed. . . . You will be held in contempt and stand apart from all good warriors." The knights all ran to where he lay wounded to death. It was a sad day for many of them. Those who were at all loyal-hearted mourned for him, and this, as a gay and valiant knight, he had well deserved.

The Canterbury Tales *by Geoffrey Chaucer*

Farewell my sweet foe! O my Emily!
Oh take me in your gentle arms I pray,
For love of God, and hear what I will say.
"I have here with my cousin Palamon,
Had strife [conflict] and rancour [ill will] many a day that's gone,
For love of you and for my jealousy.
May Jove [the Roman god Jupiter] so surely guide my soul for me,
To speak about a lover properly,
With all the circumstances, faithfully—
That is to say, truth, honour, and knighthood,
Wisdom, humility and kinship good,
And generous soul and all the lover's art—
So now may Jove have in my soul his part
As in this world, right now, I know of none
So worthy to be loved as Palamon,
Who serves you and will do so all his life.
And if you ever should become a wife,
Forget not Palamon, the noble man."

Understanding Literature	What similarities exist in these German and English epics? How do they differ? What attitudes are expressed in the dying words of the two soldiers?

BUILDING YOUR **Portfolio**

Bronze and enamel dish crafted by an Islamic artist in the 1100s

Culture

Architecture is an important expression of culture in all societies. Imagine you are an art historian preparing a lecture on church architecture during the Middle Ages in Europe. Write an outline for a lecture describing the importance of church architecture during this period and the building techniques and materials used. Explain what the churches and cathedrals of the Middle Ages reveal about religious life in medieval society. Use the bibliography below to help you in your research. When your outline is done, prepare a bibliography of the sources you used.

Further Reading

Browning, Robert. *The Byzantine Empire.* Washington, D.C.: Catholic University of America, 1992. A general overview of the Byzantine Empire.

Cantor, Norman F., ed. *The Encyclopedia of the Middle Ages.* New York: Viking, 1999. A reference work covering politics, culture, daily life, religion, and important figures of the Middle Ages.

Dersin, Denise, ed. *What Life Was Like: In the Lands of the Prophet, Islamic World A.D. 570–1405.* Alexandria, Virginia: Time-Life Books, 1999. An overview of the history and culture of the Islamic world.

Hanawalt, Barbara. *The Middle Ages: An Illustrated History.* New York: Oxford University Press, 1999. A sweeping survey of the Middle Ages from 400–1500.

Ross, Frank and Michael Goodman. *Oracle Bones, Stars, and Wheelbarrows: Ancient Chinese Science and Technology.* New York: Houghton-Mifflin, 1990. An overview of early Chinese contributions to science and technology.

Geography

Geography significantly influences historical development. Imagine you are an Arab trader living in Morocco during the mid-1100s. You have just returned from a profitable trip to Constantinople. Your task is to create a map showing your journey and a chart of the types of goods you took with you and the types of goods you brought back. Be specific about the geographic obstacles you encountered, the places you stopped, and how the items you bought and sold reflected people's needs during this time.

Examples of medieval architecture: Chartres Cathedral in France (right) and the Monastery of St. Mary the Victorious in Portugal (below).

internet connect

Internet Activity
KEYWORD: SH3 U1

In assigned groups, develop a multimedia presentation about early East Asia, the Byzantine Empire, the Islamic Empire, or medieval Europe. Choose information from the chapter Internet Connect activities and the Holt Researcher that best reflects the major topics of the period. Write an outline and a script for your presentation, which may be shown to the class.

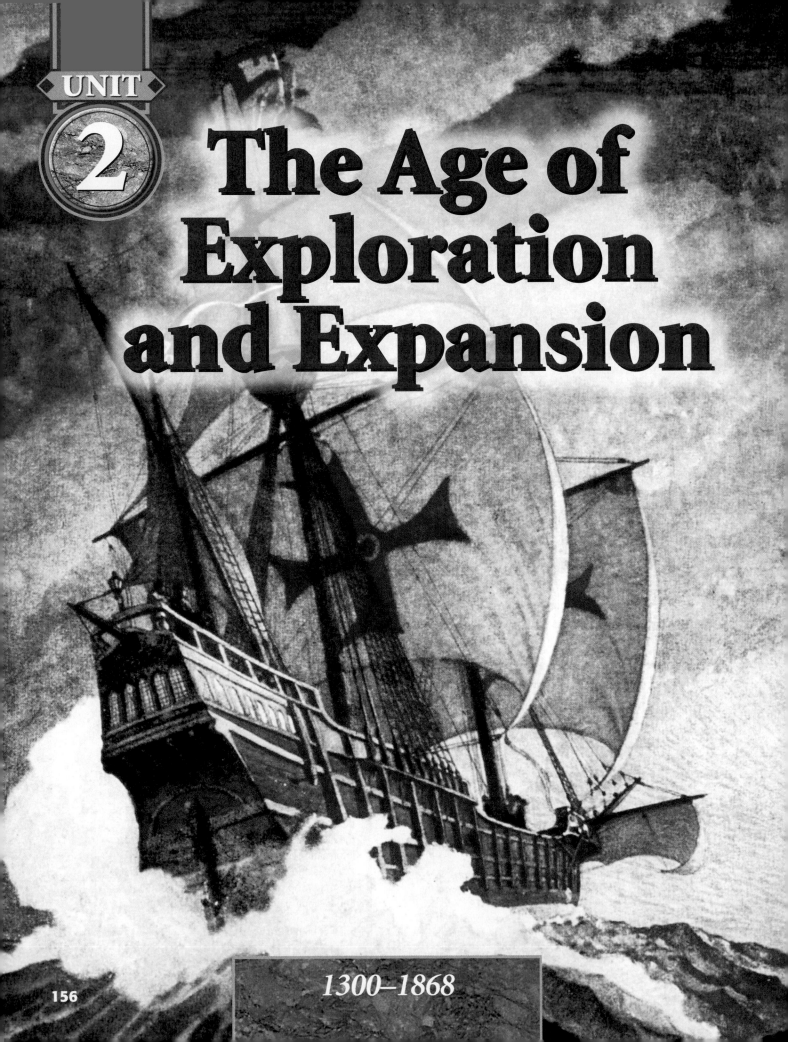

The Age of Exploration and Expansion

1300–1868

Main Events
- The significance of the Renaissance and the Reformation
- The impact of European exploration, expansion, and colonization
- The effects of the West on China and Japan
- The growth of Islamic empires

Main Ideas
- What was the Renaissance?
- Why did the Reformation happen and what effect did it have on Europe?
- What accounted for the interest in exploration? Why was it important?
- How did China and Japan deal with the increased interest of the West?
- Where were the Ottoman, Safavid, and Mughal Empires?

Sextant used by sailors in the 1700s to navigate

This painting shows one artist's conception of Columbus crossing the Atlantic.

CROSS-CULTURAL CONNECTIONS

Focus on: Economics

Main Idea **What events changed the economies of nations throughout the world?** A changing economy set in motion a number of dramatic events during the Renaissance. Cities became vital centers of economic activity. Rich merchants and bankers used their wealth to support the arts. Hoping to gain access to the treasures of the East, European monarchs became interested in overseas exploration. Exploration brought Europeans into contact with other peoples, which at times led to conflict.

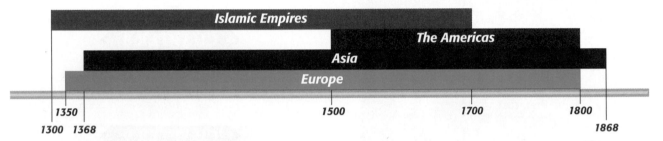

Islamic Empires

The Americas

Asia

Europe

1300   1350   1368   1500   1700   1800   1868

Europe, 1350–1800

During the Renaissance, monarchs and other wealthy Europeans began acquiring Eastern luxury items, such as this beautiful Persian carpet woven by highly skilled craftspeople in the late 1500s.

◄ **The European Marketplace** The Renaissance was not simply a period of artistic rebirth, it was also a time of significant economic growth. Between the 1300s and 1600s, several factors changed the European economy. New and more efficient methods of bookkeeping improved business practices. An increase in population, the rise of cities, a greater supply of money, and advances in transportation and communication meant that more people could buy a wider variety of goods. The center of business activity was the local marketplace, such as the Naples market pictured here. People came to markets to buy and sell food, household items, livestock, and tools. Merchants offered goods made by local artisans alongside exotic items from faraway lands.

The Slave Trade in the Americas Overseas exploration led to increased trade between European and African countries. The Portuguese, British, and French were among the first to participate in the Atlantic slave trade. In this exchange, Europeans captured or bought enslaved Africans in West Africa and transported them to the New World. Here they were sold to planters in North and South America or the Caribbean to fill a growing need for plantation labor. As European demand for plantation products such as sugar, tobacco, and cotton increased, the demand for slaves also rose. During the 1500s and 1600s, the Atlantic slave trade became centrally important to the economies of the colonial powers. This illustration shows slaves working on a Brazilian plantation in 1662.

The Americas, 1500–1800

Economic Growth Under the Ming China's economy grew strong during the Ming dynasty (1368-1644). Despite an official effort to discourage foreign trade, the European and Japanese demand for Chinese goods flourished. Europeans particularly prized the fine pottery Marco Polo had described as *porcellana* during his visit to China in the late 1200s. During the Ming period, Chinese artists created porcelain masterpieces with government support. Bright patterns—such as the one on this porcelain jar—became the dominant style in the late Ming period.

Asia, 1368–1868

Islamic Empires, 1300–1700

Safavid Prosperity Under the rule of Shah 'Abbās the Great in the late 1500s and early 1600s, the Safavid Empire in Persia reached new economic and cultural heights. 'Abbās encouraged manufacturing and trade, and Persian artisans produced carpets, fabrics, and ceramics that were prized around the world. This prosperity also helped Safavid arts and culture flourish, especially in the capital city of Eşfahān. Carefully planned and filled with major works of art and architecture, Eşfahān became known as one of the most beautiful cities of its day. In Eşfahān Shah 'Abbās built the Palace of Chihil Soutoun, which is where the fresco at left can be seen. In the fresco, a Persian princess writes a letter in a park while a kneeling attendant offers her a drink.

This handle in the form of a horse's head was made in the Mughal Empire sometime between about 1658 and 1710.

Why It Matters Today

Economic growth and foreign trade between the 1400s and 1800s led to a level of cultural contact most of the world had never before experienced. Today, economic factors such as trade, marketing, and advertising lead to cultural contact and cultural change. **What examples of economic influence on culture can you find today?**

1350–1700

The Renaissance and Reformation

*Renaissance banker
Cosimo de Medici*

**1351–1353
Global Events**
Florence successfully defends itself against a Milanese invasion.

**1375
Politics**
Florence organizes a league that rebels against Pope Gregory XI.

**1434
Politics**
Banker Cosimo de Medici gains control of Florence.

**1463
Daily Life**
English law forbids common folk from wearing gold or purple, which are reserved for royalty.

1350

1400

1450

**1378
Business and Finance**
Cloth workers in Florence revolt to reform the city's guild system.

**1408
Business and Finance**
St. George's Bank is founded in Genoa.

**1427
Business and Finance**
The ruler of Florence introduces an income tax.

**c. 1450
Science and Technology**
Johannes Gutenberg develops a printing press with movable type.

The city of Florence and its cathedral, the Duomo

Build on What You Know

During the Middle Ages, religion wielded great influence over art, government, and literature. The Catholic Church was the leading religious institution in western Europe. Also during the Middle Ages, the Crusades spurred a revival of trade in western Europe. Towns and cities began to grow again. Nations formed strong governments and began to challenge church laws that limited trade and industry. In this chapter, you will learn about the changes in art, literature, and thought that marked this new era in European life. You will also learn about new ideas in religion that challenged the moral authority of the Catholic Church.

Leonardo da Vinci's sketch for a flying vehicle

1508–1512
The Arts
Michelangelo paints the ceiling of the Sistine Chapel.

Raphael's portrait of Baldassare Castiglione

1480
Global Events
Lorenzo de Medici establishes peace between Naples and Florence.

1480
Science and Technology
Leonardo da Vinci designs a simple turbine engine that uses hot air to turn a spit.

1509
Science and Technology
A German chemist identifies the metal zinc.

1509
Politics
Henry VIII becomes the ruler of England.

1528
The Arts
Baldassare Castiglione publishes *The Book of the Courtier.*

1531
Business and Finance
A stock exchange opens in the Netherlands.

1555
Global Events
The Peace of Augsburg is signed.

1500　　　　　　**1550**　　　　　　**1700**

c. 1475
Daily Life
A new version of chess, in which the queen becomes a powerful piece, appears in Europe.

1475
The Arts
Sandro Botticelli paints his *Adoration of the Magi* series.

1517
Daily Life
Martin Luther posts his 95 theses challenging church practices on a church door in Wittenberg.

1513
Politics
Niccolò Machiavelli writes *The Prince,* a study of government

1545
Daily Life
The Council of Trent begins its effort to reform the Catholic Church from within.

1559
Daily Life
Pope Paul IV establishes the *Index of Forbidden Books.*

Terra-cotta bust of Niccolò Machiavelli

What's Your Opinion?

Themes Journal *Do you* **agree** *or* **disagree** *with the following statements? Support your point of view in your journal.*

Global Relations Religion brings people of different regions together.

Science, Technology & Society New technologies can advance the spread of ideas that change cultural values.

Culture Ideas and works from ancient times do not affect other cultures.

The Italian Renaissance

READ TO DISCOVER

❶ How did the Renaissance begin, and what characterized the thought of this era?

❷ How were Renaissance writers able to bring classical teachings and Christian doctrine together?

❸ How did Renaissance art differ from art of the Middle Ages?

DEFINE

humanists
perspective

IDENTIFY

Renaissance
Isabella d'Este
Francesco Petrarch
Niccolò Machiavelli
Leonardo da Vinci
Michelangelo

The Main Idea
The Renaissance brought a renewed interest in Greek and Roman culture and a new way of thinking.

The Story Continues *On November 4, 1966, the Arno River in northern Italy flooded its banks and sent a torrent of water into the museums, cathedrals, and libraries of the city of Florence. News of the flood damage alarmed the world. Why? Because Florence contained the world's greatest store of Renaissance art and literature. This outpouring of creativity that began in the 1300s changed the course of Western civilization.*

An Era of Awakening

In the early 1300s, a movement began in Italy that would alter how Europeans viewed themselves and their world. The **Renaissance**—or "rebirth"—was both a philosophical and artistic movement and the era when that movement flourished. It was marked by a renewed interest in ancient Greek and Roman literature and life. Medieval scholars had studied ancient history and tried to bring everything they learned into harmony with Christian teachings.

By contrast, Italian Renaissance scholars studied the ancient world to explore its great achievements. A new emphasis on the power of human reason developed, and many advances were made in the arts and sciences.

WHY IT MATTERS TODAY

Works of Renaissance art remain popular throughout the world today. Use CNN Student News.com or other **current event** sources to learn more about Renaissance art on display in museums. Record your findings in your journal.

CNN Student News.com

Renaissance Italy, c. 1500

Interpreting Maps
During the Renaissance, Italy was a patchwork of states.

■ **Skills Assessment: Human Systems**
What commercial cities became the centers of city-states?

Causes. In many ways it was natural that the Renaissance would begin in Italy. Ruins of the Roman Empire reminded Italians of Roman glory. The Crusades and trade had brought them into contact with the Byzantine civilization, whose scholars had preserved Greek and Roman learning. In addition, trade with southwestern Asia and Africa helped Italians learn of Arab and African achievements in science and medicine. Over time, these and other factors helped to encourage curiosity and the search for new knowledge among some Italian thinkers.

Italian cities such as Florence, Milan, Naples, Rome, and Venice had grown rich through trade and industry. Their citizens included educated, wealthy merchants and bankers. In Florence, for example, the Medici (MED·ee·chee) family grew rich, first as bankers and then as rulers of that city-state. As leader of Florence, Lorenzo de Medici used his wealth to become a great patron of the arts. In Mantua, **Isabella d'Este** filled her palace with paintings and sculptures by the finest Renaissance artists.

The humanities. In the early Renaissance of the 1300s, Italian scholars turned to classical Greek and Roman literature to study grammar, history, poetry, and rhetoric. These studies are called the humanities, and people who specialized in them were humanists. Renaissance humanists searched out manuscripts written in Greek and Latin. Often, they found more than one copy of a work. If the copies differed, the humanists compared them to determine which was the most authentic. In doing so, they displayed a critical approach to learning and scholarship. That is, they sought to verify through investigation. Some Christian scholars also turned to Jewish teachers to learn Hebrew, a language of the Bible. While there were still laws that restricted Jewish life, many Jewish humanists continued to strive for knowledge and to develop new ideas.

As humanists studied classical manuscripts, they came to believe that it was important to understand how things worked. This belief led humanists to emphasize education. They also maintained that a person should lead a meaningful life. People should also become actively involved in practical affairs, such as supporting the arts.

Although fascinated by the classics, most humanists were Catholics who remained committed to Christian teachings. For that reason, they sometimes felt a tension between their studies and their religion. Humanists viewed life not only as preparation for the afterlife, but also as a joy in itself. Along with a belief in human dignity came an admiration for individual achievement. Many individuals of this period displayed a variety of talents by being, for example, both poets and scientists.

✔ **READING CHECK: Summarizing** What were the main features of Renaissance humanist thought?

Italian Renaissance Writers

One of the first humanists was **Francesco Petrarch** (PEE·trahrk), who lived from 1304 to 1374. Like many humanists, Petrarch became famous as a scholar and a teacher. He also wrote poetry. His sonnets to Laura, an imaginary ideal woman, are considered some of the greatest love poems in literature.

Petrarch's main influence grew out of his desire to continue the work of the classical writers. Petrarch believed that the classical writers were committed to virtue in public and private life. He thought these writers could best be imitated by studying their writings. The study of ancient Greek and Roman literature came to be called classical education. Knowledge of classical Greek and Latin became the mark of an educated person. Petrarch thought it important to lead a full and active life here on earth. He also worried that his desire for fame, a relatively common ambition, might hurt his chances for salvation.

Other writers displayed less tension between spiritual and earthly quests. **Niccolò Machiavelli** (mahk·yah·VEL·lee), a Florentine diplomat and historian, lived from 1469 to 1527. In 1513 he wrote the essay *The Prince*. Machiavelli sought to describe government not in terms of lofty ideals but in the way it actually worked. He argued that a ruler should be concerned only with power and political success. Today some people refer to ruthless behavior to get ahead as "Machiavellian."

❝A controversy has arisen about this: whether it is better to be loved than feared, or vice versa. My view is that it is desirable to be both loved and feared; but it is difficult to achieve both and, if one of them has to be lacking, it is much safer to be feared than loved. . . . Men are less hesitant about offending or harming a ruler who makes himself less loved than one who inspires fear. For love is sustained by a bond of gratitude, which because men are excessively self-interested, is broken whenever they see a chance to benefit themselves. But fear is sustained by a dread of punishment that is always effective.❞

Niccolò Machiavelli, *The Prince*

Machiavelli can be considered a humanist because he looked to the ancient Romans as models. The lack of concern for conventional morality in *The Prince*, however, sets him apart from other humanists of the time.

Baldassare Castiglione (kahs·teel·YOH·nay), an Italian diplomat, lived from 1478 to 1529. In 1528 he published what was probably the most famous book of the Renaissance, *The Book of the Courtier*. The setting for the book is the court at Urbino, an Italian city-state where Castiglione lived for many years. In his book, Castiglione used real people engaged in fictional conversations to explain how gentlemen and gentlewomen should act in polite society.

✔ **READING CHECK: Contrasting** In what way does Machiavelli's work differ from that of other humanists?

Italian Renaissance Artists

Like literature, art flourished during the Italian Renaissance. During this era Italian artists produced some of the world's greatest masterpieces.

Medieval paintings had stressed the world beyond everyday life. They used formal figures to express religious concerns. Renaissance artists, in contrast, created realistic scenes and images. They depicted lifelike human figures in their paintings. Even the backgrounds of Renaissance paintings differed from those of medieval paintings. Earlier artists had often portrayed the Holy Land. Renaissance painters showed the rugged Italian countryside they knew so well.

Renaissance painters used a technique called **perspective** to make their paintings more lifelike. They made distant objects smaller than those in the foreground of the painting. This technique created the illusion of depth on the flat canvas.

Renaissance Art

Studying works of art produced during a specific period in history can teach us a great deal about the values of the people who created the art. For example, much of the art of the Middle Ages reflects religious values. In general, medieval art developed themes of faith and religious spirituality, rather than of human individuality. In contrast, Renaissance art combined such religious themes with the humanistic values of the era. As humanity became the center of life on earth, artists placed realistic human beings at the center of their works.

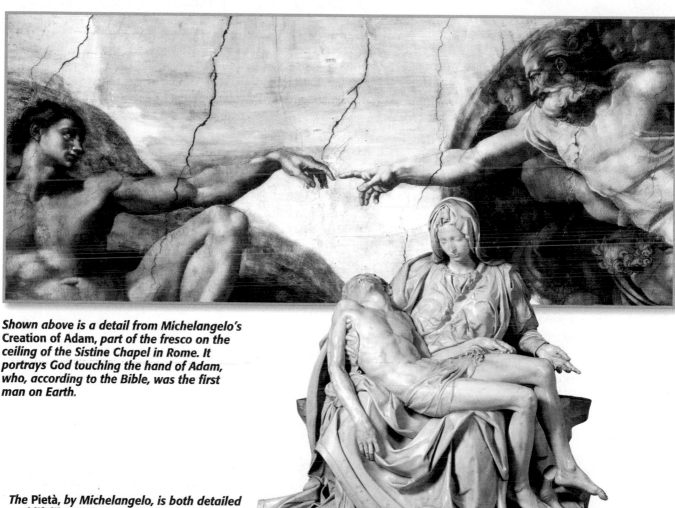

*Shown above is a detail from Michelangelo's **Creation of Adam**, part of the fresco on the ceiling of the Sistine Chapel in Rome. It portrays God touching the hand of Adam, who, according to the Bible, was the first man on Earth.*

*The **Pietà**, by Michelangelo, is both detailed and lifelike. It shows the Virgin Mary mourning over the body of her son, Jesus, after his crucifixion.*

Skills Reminder

To understand the values reflected by a piece of art, identify when the artwork was produced and what historical period it represents. Identify the theme—is it taken from religion, mythology, or daily life? Note the subject of the work of art and the details. Then use the theme and its treatment to infer the values of the historical period in which the artist created the work.

Skills Practice

1. What artistic ideals and visual principles are reflected in Michelangelo's works?
2. What Renaissance values are reflected in Michelangelo's fresco and in his *Pietà*?
3. Find and study a modern work of art. Explain how this artwork reflects the values of modern society.

The works of Rafael, like *Joan of Aragon, Queen of Naples* shown here, are masterworks of Renaissance art.

Giotto (JAWT·oh), who lived from about 1276 to 1337, was a magnificent early realist painter. According to legend, a fly in one of Giotto's works looked so real that an observer tried to brush it off the painting. Another important early realist was Masaccio (mah·ZAHT·choh), who lived from 1401 to 1428. Masaccio used light and shadows to create a powerful sense of depth in his paintings.

Scholars often call the late 1400s and early 1500s the High Renaissance. There were many great painters during this period. Four made particularly outstanding contributions to the arts.

Leonardo da Vinci (dah·VEEN·chee), who lived from 1452 to 1519, was a man of many talents. He was an architect, engineer, painter, sculptor, and scientist. He made sketches of plants and animals, as well as detailed drawings of a flying machine and a submarine. Da Vinci's science improved the quality of his paintings. His studies in anatomy helped him draw realistic human figures. He used mathematics to organize the space in his paintings. People throughout the world still marvel at his mural *The Last Supper*. Perhaps his most famous painting is the portrait called the *Mona Lisa*.

Another master of Renaissance art, **Michelangelo** (mee·kay·LAHN·jay·loh), lived from 1475 to 1564. Michelangelo was a brilliant painter. Millions of people have visited the Sistine Chapel of the Vatican, the residence of the pope in Rome, to view the frescoes Michelangelo painted on the chapel ceiling. His sculptures of biblical figures such as David also continue to be admired. In addition to his art, Michelangelo wrote poetry and helped to design St. Peter's Basilica in Rome.

Rafael (RAF·ee·el), who lived from 1483 to 1520, became so popular in Florence that the pope hired him to help beautify the Vatican. Rafael painted frescoes in the papal chambers. He is also known for his madonnas, paintings of the Virgin Mary.

Titian (TISH·uhn), who lived from about 1488 to 1576, spent most of his life in Venice. His works, such as *The Assumption of the Virgin*, are known for their sense of drama and rich colors. The Holy Roman emperor was a patron of Titian. In fact, Titian was one of the first painters to become wealthy from his work.

✔ **READING CHECK: Contrasting** How did Renaissance and medieval art differ from each other?

Holt Researcher

go.hrw.com
KEYWORD: Holt Researcher
FreeFind: Leonardo da Vinci
Michelangelo

After reading more about Leonardo da Vinci and Michelangelo on the Holt Researcher, draw a sketch or write a description of an art piece that reflects their style.

SECTION 1 REVIEW

1. **Define** and explain the significance:
   humanists
   perspective

2. **Identify** and explain the significance:
   Renaissance
   Isabella d'Este
   Francesco Petrarch
   Niccolò Machiavelli
   Leonardo da Vinci
   Michelangelo

3. **Analyzing Information** Copy the graphic organizer below. Use it to explain the characteristics of Renaissance thought, literature, and art.

4. **Finding the Main Idea**
   a. What were the events that led to the Renaissance in Italy?
   b. How did religion influence Renaissance art and thought?
   c. What ethical issues did humanists struggle with during the Italian Renaissance?

5. **Writing and Critical Thinking**
   Evaluating Choose one of the Renaissance artworks pictured in this section or one in an art book or encyclopedia. Describe both the work and your impressions of it.
   Consider:
   • the technique of perspective
   • the mixture of religious and humanist values
   • what thoughts and feelings the work of art brings about

Homework Practice Online
keyword: SH3 HP6

The Northern Renaissance

READ TO DISCOVER

1 How were the ideas of the Italian Renaissance spread to other parts of Europe?
2 In what ways did northern Renaissance writers differ from Italian humanists?
3 What were the principal characteristics of northern Renaissance art?

IDENTIFY

Johannes Gutenberg
Desiderius Erasmus
Thomas More
William Shakespeare
Flemish school

WHY IT MATTERS TODAY

William Shakespeare remains perhaps the most popular playwright in the world. Use CNNstudentNews.com or other **current event** sources to learn about modern plays or movies based on Shakespeare's work. Record your findings in your journal.

CNN student News.com

The Main Idea Art and literature in northern Europe also began to reflect Renaissance thought, styles, and values.

The Story Continues *"What a piece of work is a man! How noble in reason! How infinite in faculty!"* Those powerful lines from Shakespeare's Hamlet *celebrate the human potential and reflect how Renaissance humanist thought spread from Italy into northern Europe.*

The Spread of Ideas

Numerous mountain passes pierced the rugged Alps in northern Italy. These passageways allowed people and ideas to pass from Italy to northern Europe. The Danube, Rhine, and Rhone Rivers provided even easier routes. Renaissance ideas, often carried by northern European students who had studied in Italy, soon traveled to Germany, the Netherlands, France, and England. As increased commerce created new wealth and more people could afford higher education, many new universities were established in these countries.

A remarkable new process—printing—also helped spread Renaissance ideas. Hundreds of years earlier, the Chinese had learned how to etch writing or pictures onto wooden blocks. Printers put ink on the blocks and then pressed them onto paper. More ink was placed on the block, and the process was repeated. In this way writing or pictures could be reproduced many times. The Chinese also had learned how to assemble blocks from many separate pieces, or type, that could be used repeatedly. This was the beginning of movable type.

The European invention of printing appears to have been independent of the Chinese process. Scholars believe that in about 1450, **Johannes Gutenberg** of Mainz, Germany, became the first European to use movable type to print books. Gutenberg used his printing press to print copies of the Bible.

Not all Europeans were enthusiastic about Gutenberg's invention. Some complained that books printed on paper would not last long. Others noted that hand-copied manuscripts were far more beautiful than printed books. Scribes, who made a living by hand-copying manuscripts, realized that the printing press threatened their profession. The impact of Gutenberg's work was economic as well as social and technological.

This Latin version of the Gutenberg Bible was printed in Mainz in 1456.

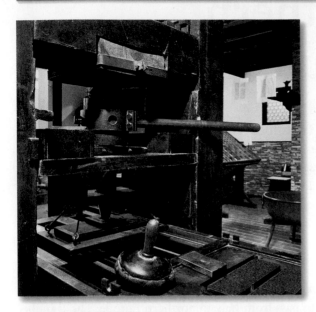

Such obstacles did not slow the spread of the printing press. Other European publishers quickly adopted the new technology. By 1475 printing presses operated in England, France, Germany, Italy, and several other European nations. The books that these printing presses produced helped spread new humanist ideas to a large audience.

✔ **READING CHECK: Identifying Cause and Effect** How did the printing press affect life in Europe?

Gutenberg's printing press with movable metal type allowed books to be printed quickly and economically.

Northern Renaissance Writers

The most influential humanist of northern Europe was **Desiderius Erasmus** (i·RAZ·muhs), a Dutch scholar who lived from about 1466 to 1536. As a young man, Erasmus entered a monastery. He later left the monastery so he could pursue his studies of the classics. Erasmus learned about the ideas of the Italian humanists from printed books.

Unlike the Italian humanists, Erasmus and other northern humanists were interested in the early Christian period as well as early Greek and Roman culture. Erasmus believed that the ideas of Christianity and of classical civilization could be harmonized. He used the critical method of the Italian humanists to study the Bible. Erasmus and other northern humanists criticized the church's lack of spirituality. They believed that medieval scholars had made Christian faith less spiritual and more complicated and ceremonial. Erasmus argued for a return to the original, simple message of Jesus.

Erasmus's most famous book was entitled *The Praise of Folly*. In this book he ridiculed ignorance, superstition, and vice among Christians. He criticized fasting, pilgrimages to religious shrines, and even the church's interpretation of the Bible.

Thomas More, an English humanist and friend of Erasmus, took a similar view. Early in life More showed an interest in the classics, and in 1516 he published *Utopia*. In this work, More condemned governments as corrupt and argued that private ownership of property causes unnecessary conflicts between people. He contrasted life in Europe with his description of an imaginary, ideal society. The word *utopia* has come to mean "an ideal place or society." In More's imaginary world, all male citizens were equal. Everyone worked to support the society.

History Makers Speak

❝ . . . wherever you are, you always have to work. There's never any excuse for idleness. . . . Everyone has his eye on you, so you're practically forced to get on with your job, and make some proper use of your spare time. Under such a system, there's bound to be plenty of everything, and, as everything is divided equally among the entire population, there obviously can't be any poor people or beggars. ❞

Thomas More, *Utopia*

More's *Utopia* became popular in Europe, where it was translated into German, Italian, French, English, Dutch, and Spanish. Thomas More wrote widely in both prose and verse. His work was read and generally acclaimed by humanist thinkers throughout much of Europe. Later in life More served King Henry VIII of England. Because More refused to agree that the king was the supreme head of the church in England, Henry had him executed. Some 400 years later, the Catholic Church made More a saint for his faith and service to the church.

English literature during the Renaissance reached its peak in the late 1500s and early 1600s. In classical dramas, angry gods punished humans. In English Renaissance drama, playwrights such as Christopher Marlowe wrote plays that tended to focus on human, rather than godly, actions. Marlowe used powerful language and imagery to convey his thoughts. Some of his work was composed in verse form.

William Shakespeare stands out as the leading literary figure of the time. Shakespeare built on the traditions established by Marlowe and other playwrights. Shakespeare's great strength lay in his ability to transform well-known stories into dramatic masterpieces. He portrayed personality and human emotions with a skill that few writers have matched. The moody *Hamlet*, the young lovers *Romeo and Juliet*, and the tragic *Macbeth* seem as real today as when Shakespeare created them.

✔ **READING CHECK: Contrasting** How did Erasmus and More differ from Italian humanists in their outlooks on life?

William Shakespeare is probably the most widely known author in all of English literature. His insight into human nature and use of the English language mark his many plays and his poetry.

Northern Renaissance Artists

Northern European merchants carried Italian paintings home. Painters from northern Europe studied with Italian masters. In these ways, the dynamic new painting techniques of Italian artists inspired other artists.

In Flanders a group of painters developed their own distinct style. Known among some historians and critics as the **Flemish school,** these painters are credited with perfecting certain techniques of painting in oil on canvas.

The Flemish brothers Jan and Hubert van Eyck paid great attention to detail. Their work reveals a strong interest in facial expressions. In their masterpiece, the altar-piece they painted for a church in the city of Ghent, the faces of Adam and Eve look realistic. They are markedly different from the symbolic depictions of the Middle Ages.

This detail from the center panel of the Ghent Altar-piece, called the Adoration of the Lamb, reveals the van Eycks' attention to detail. The face of Eve (above) is from one of the wings of the altar-piece.

INTERPRETING THE VISUAL RECORD

Northern Renaissance art This painting by Holbein, *The French Ambassadors,* is an example of the artist's style of total control of surface and design. *In what way is this painting more realistic than an Italian Renaissance painting?*

One of the most famous Flemish artists, Pieter Brueghel (BROO·guhl) the Elder, painted in the mid-1500s. Brueghel loved the countryside and the peasants of his native Flanders. He painted lively scenes of village festivals and dances. On the other hand, Brueghel also used his paintings to criticize the intolerance and cruelty he saw around him.

The German artist Albrecht Dürer (DYUR·uhr), who lived from 1471 to 1528, was famous for his copper engravings and woodcuts. Dürer studied in Germany and Venice. He also studied the classics and humanism. Dürer became one of the first artists to see the possibilities of printed illustrations in books.

Another German artist, Hans Holbein the Younger, who lived in the early 1500s, was influenced by Italian and Flemish styles of painting. Holbein traveled through Europe painting portraits of famous people. His work includes portraits of Erasmus, Thomas More, and King Henry VIII of England. This emphasis on portrait painting reflected the Renaissance interest in the individual.

Northern European artists of the Renaissance were certainly inspired by the techniques of Italian artists, such as the use of perspective. Thus, some of the characteristics of Renaissance painting in northern Europe resemble elements of Italian painting. However, the two styles also illustrate the differences between northern and southern European artists and their societies. Many Italian paintings by artists such as Michelangelo depict human figures based on the models of Greek and Roman art. Athletic figures with rippling muscles demonstrate the artist's admiration of the human form. In the work of many northern artists, however, the figures seem more like Europeans of the 1500s—bald, frail, and imperfect—than like Greek gods. However, some northern artists did often depict the early fathers of the Christian church, emphasizing the importance of the Bible as the basis for Christianity. In this way the work of the northern European artists continued to reflect the ideas of Christian humanism.

✔ **READING CHECK: Supporting a Point of View** What evidence would you give that realism was important in northern Renaissance art?

SECTION 2 REVIEW

1. **Identify** and explain the significance:
   Johannes Gutenberg
   Desiderius Erasmus
   Thomas More
   William Shakespeare
   Flemish school

2. **Comparing and Contrasting** Copy the Venn diagram below. Use it to show which characteristics the Italian Renaissance and the northern Renaissance shared and which were unique to each.

   Italian   Northern

3. **Finding the Main Idea**
   a. Why did the printing press spread so quickly throughout Europe?
   b. What were the main ideas and values of the northern Renaissance?

4. **Writing and Critical Thinking**
   Analyzing Information Write a short story about a utopian society.
   Consider:
   • the elements of utopian literature, including its imaginary nature
   • the use of utopias to analyze governmental and social systems

Homework Practice Online
keyword: SH3 HP6

READ TO DISCOVER
1 What developments led to the Reformation?
2 How did Martin Luther protest against the Roman Catholic Church and begin a new church?
3 What factors caused the spread of Protestantism?
4 What role did Calvinism play in the Reformation?

DEFINE
indulgences
sects
predestination
theocracy

IDENTIFY
Reformation
Martin Luther
Henry VIII
John Calvin
Huguenots

WHY IT MATTERS TODAY
Different Christian denominations continue today in the United States and throughout the world. Use or other **current event** sources to determine the doctrines and beliefs of some of the main denominations. Record your findings in your journal.

CNN Student News.com

The Protestant Reformation

The Main Idea
The Protestant Reformation split the Catholic Church and created several new churches.

The Story Continues *In the early 1500s a young German law student was returning to school from a visit home when he got caught in a violent thunderstorm. A blinding bolt of lightning struck nearby. The young man shouted, "Saint Anne, help! I will become a monk!" Not only did he enter a monastery, but the young Martin Luther also went on to create a religious revolution.*

An Era of Reform

The humanist Erasmus was not alone in his criticism of the church and some Christian practices. In about 1500 several northern humanists argued that the Roman Catholic Church had lost sight of its spiritual mission. Their claims would lead to a reform movement that would split the church in western Europe. This religious revolution is called the **Reformation.**

Causes. Some northern humanists maintained that the church seemed more interested in its income than in saving souls. They claimed that the popes acted as political leaders and warriors instead of setting an example of moral leadership. Some priests engaged in vice and misconduct instead of encouraging spiritual and moral behavior. These northern humanists sought a new emphasis on personal faith and spirituality.

The Catholic Church, however, ignored their concerns. The humanists then urged believers who were unhappy with traditional religion to withdraw from the church and meet with like-minded people.

The beginning. The first break with the Roman Catholic Church took place in what is now Germany. The political situation there helped lay the foundation for the Reformation. Unlike some countries during the 1500s, "Germany" was not a unified nation. Although it formed the core of the Holy Roman Empire, "Germany" was made up of about 300 independent states. Weak rulers could not control independent ideas about religion, nor could they prevent abuses of power by the pope.

In Rome, as Pope Leo X was continuing the rebuilding of St. Peter's Basilica, the Vatican sent a monk named Johann Tetzel to raise funds in the northern German states. Tetzel asked people to buy **indulgences,** or pardons from punishment for sin.

This German woodcut criticizes the pope himself, showing him as a moneychanger at the sale of indulgences.

**Martin Luther
(1483–1546)**

Martin Luther never wanted to leave the Roman Catholic Church. As a priest and teacher, he was strongly committed to his religious beliefs. He felt it necessary, however, to challenge certain church practices that he believed were unnecessary or wrong.

The church responded by throwing Luther out. As a result, Luther founded the Lutheran Church. **Why did Luther challenge the Catholic Church?**

Analyzing Primary Sources

Making Generalizations What behavior did Luther hope that Christians would engage in?

Indulgences had originally been a reward for pious deeds, such as helping a poor person go on a crusade. Renaissance popes, in contrast, sold indulgences simply to raise money. This misuse of indulgences outraged northern humanists, who wanted the church to become more spiritual. The concern became particularly widespread in the German states, where rulers allowed sellers of indulgences to move freely about.

✔ **READING CHECK: Drawing Inferences** How did the sale of indulgences play a role in the beginning of the Reformation?

Martin Luther

One critic of Tetzel's behavior was a monk named **Martin Luther.** Luther had quit law school and entered a monastery to spend his life in search of salvation. But Luther found that the church's methods for overcoming sin gave him no comfort. He did all the things required of him. Nothing, however, relieved his feeling of inadequacy.

Through his biblical studies, Luther received a revelation. On the basis of this new insight, Luther developed beliefs that later became known as Lutheranism. Luther taught that ceremonies and good deeds made no difference in saving a sinner. The only thing that counted, Luther decided, was an inner faith in God. People could receive salvation only through the grace of God, not through their own actions. According to Luther, simple faith could lead everyone to salvation. This idea was called "justification by grace through faith."

Luther's protest. Luther claimed that Tetzel committed a grave error by asking people to give up money for false promises of forgiveness. In 1517 Luther challenged Tetzel. He posted his 95 theses, or statements, about indulgences on a church door.

History Makers Speak (32) **"Those who believe that they can be certain of their salvation because they have indulgence letters will be eternally [cursed], together with their teachers."** (43) "Christians are to be taught that he who gives to the poor or lends to the needy does a better deed than he who buys indulgences."

Martin Luther, *Luther's Works*

News rapidly spread across Europe that a monk had publicly challenged the selling of indulgences. Luther clearly considered himself a reformer who was working from within the main tradition of the church. Initially, he probably did not intend to break with Rome and the Catholic Church. Because he challenged church practices, however, church leaders denounced him.

Break with the church. By 1520 Luther openly disagreed with many church doctrines. He claimed that the Bible was the sole religious authority. Popes and bishops could not tell a person what to believe. Luther argued that ceremonies could not make up for sins and that priests had no special role in helping people to salvation. He believed that God viewed all people of faith equally. Luther considered his church "a priesthood of all believers."

Luther took advantage of the printing press to spread his ideas. In his writings, Luther continued to attack certain church practices and approaches. In 1521 Pope Leo X declared Luther a heretic. He excommunicated, or expelled, Luther from the Roman Catholic Church.

Holy Roman Emperor Charles V then summoned Luther to appear before the Imperial Diet, a special meeting of the empire's rulers, at the city of Worms (VOHRMZ). There Luther was commanded to abandon his ideas. He refused. After the Diet of Worms the emperor declared Luther an outlaw and banned the printing and sale of his works. However, he lacked the power to enforce this ruling. Frederick the Wise, the Elector of Saxony (Luther's home state), whisked Luther away to hide until the uproar over the confrontation at the Diet of Worms died down. While under the protection of Frederick, Luther translated the Bible into German. Now all literate Christians in the German states could read the Bible themselves.

Protestantism. Emperor Charles V continued to oppose Luther's teachings. He did what he could to keep Lutheranism from spreading. The princes who supported Luther protested the emperor's treatment of Lutheranism. Because of the protest, Luther's followers and later reformers came to be called "Protestants."

Luther's works and ideas continued to spread. In time he established a new church, the Lutheran Church. He kept the organization of the new church very simple. Based on Luther's belief in the "priesthood of all believers," Lutheran ministers were less important than Catholic priests were. According to Luther, Christians were fully capable of interpreting and understanding scripture for themselves.

✔ **READING CHECK: Sequencing** What events led to the development of Protestantism?

The Spread of Protestantism

Luther had touched a very deep desire among many people in Europe for a simpler, more direct religious faith. Within a short time, many German rulers established the Lutheran Church within their states. In addition, dozens of reformers appeared who criticized both the Roman Catholic Church and the Lutheran Church.

Charles V tried to stop the spread of Protestantism. At first his attention was focused on fighting the Ottoman Turks and the French. Finally, in 1546, he sent his armies against the Protestant princes in Germany. Although his armies won most of the battles, the emperor could not defeat the princes or the Lutheran Church. Charles finally reached a compromise with the princes in 1555. The Peace of Augsburg stated that each German ruler had the right to choose the religion for his state. His subjects had to either accept the ruler's decision or move away. Almost all the princes of the northern German states chose Luther's faith in opposition to Rome.

This portrait depicts Emperor Charles V on horseback at the Battle of Muhlberg in 1546.

The rise of sects. During the 1520s and 1530s, hundreds of new religious groups appeared in Germany and Switzerland. These groups, known as **sects,** did not form organized churches. Many did not have clear-cut authority, discipline, membership, or rules. The sects were societies of a few people gathered together, usually with a preacher as their leader. Most of the sects later died out.

The Anglican Church. In England the Protestant Reformation came about in an entirely different way than in Germany. It was the king, **Henry VIII,** who caused the break between England and the Roman Catholic Church. The break was a political move that had

This famous portrait of Henry VIII was painted by Hans Holbein the Younger.

little to do with religious beliefs. In fact, before 1529, Henry VIII had defended the church against Luther's teachings. The pope had even granted Henry the title "Defender of the Faith."

England's break with Rome took place because Henry VIII wanted to divorce his wife, Catherine of Aragon. Henry was unhappy because Catherine had not had a son who could succeed him. The royal couple did have a daughter, Mary. However, England had no tradition of a ruling queen. Henry also wanted a divorce because he hoped to marry Anne Boleyn, a lady-in-waiting at the court.

The Catholic Church did not usually permit divorces. Although the pope was allowed to make exceptions to this general rule, Pope Clement VII refused to meet Henry's demand. This angered Henry. The king withdrew England from the Catholic Church and began a new church. Parliament passed a series of laws that created the Church of England, with the king as its head. Also known as the Anglican Church, the Church of England kept the organization and ceremonies of the Catholic Church. Over time, it also adopted some Protestant doctrines.

The Anglican Church granted Henry VIII a divorce. The king eventually married six times in all. He finally fathered a son, the future Edward VI. Of greater importance, Henry VIII's creation of the Anglican Church paved the way for the Protestant Reformation in England.

✔ **READING CHECK: Contrasting** How did the spread of Protestantism in England differ from that in the rest of Europe?

Calvinism

Huldrych Zwingli (TSVING·lee) was the vicar at the cathedral in Zürich, Switzerland, in the early 1500s. He was greatly influenced by the humanist writings of Erasmus. In fact, Zwingli was already calling for religious reform in Switzerland when he heard about Luther's 95 theses. Zwingli and Luther met and discovered they shared many ideas about church doctrine. They disagreed, however, about forms of worship and the use of religious images. For example, Zwingli's followers covered up wall decorations in churches. In 1531 Zwingli died in a battle between Catholics and Protestants. His work was carried on by a French Protestant named **John Calvin.**

Calvin's church. In Switzerland John Calvin founded a Protestant church that had a strong following. Then in 1536 he formulated and published a complete and clear set of religious beliefs, *The Institutes of the Christian Religion*. This work explained exactly what the faithful should believe on every major religious question. Calvin's followers—called Calvinists—now had a code that united and strengthened them against opposition and persecution.

Like Luther, Calvin relied on faith and on the Bible. Calvin also emphasized **predestination,** the idea that at the beginning of time God had decided who would be saved. Predestination was a common belief among Protestant thinkers in the 1500s. Calvin explained the logic of predestination. Those who were predestined—or chosen beforehand—for salvation were called "the elect." They formed a special community of people who were expected to follow the highest moral standards. These standards placed great emphasis on self-discipline. The individual was expected to be completely dedicated to God's wishes.

Holt Researcher

go.hrw.com

KEYWORD: Holt Researcher

FreeFind: John Calvin

After reading more about John Calvin on the Holt Researcher, write an outline for a sermon he might have given explaining his views.

In 1536 Calvin moved to the city of Geneva, where his doctrine of Calvinism became the official religion. In fact, Geneva became a **theocracy**, a government ruled by religious leaders who claimed God's authority. Calvinists attached great importance to righteous living. Thus citizens' lives were strongly regulated. Laws prohibited card playing, dancing, profane language, and showy dress. Breaking these laws resulted in severe punishment. Rather than being seen as a burden, however, this strictness was the heart of Calvinism's appeal. It gave its followers a sense of mission and discipline. Calvinists felt that they were setting an example and making the world fit for "the elect."

Calvinism spreads. In France many people, including high-ranking nobles, converted to Calvinism. These people were called **Huguenots** (HYOO·guh·nahts). Although France remained primarily Catholic, at one point about one third of the French nobility had become Calvinists. The Catholic French monarchs considered the Huguenots a threat to national unity. Beginning in 1562, the Huguenots defended themselves in a series of bloody civil wars with the Catholics. In 1598 King Henry IV issued the Edict of Nantes (NANTS). This proclamation gave the Huguenots freedom of worship and some political rights.

Calvinist minorities also existed in Poland and Hungary in eastern Europe. Large Calvinist populations were found in Scotland, in the northern Netherlands, and in some parts of the German states. In these areas the strength of the Calvinists among the nobility persuaded the rulers to change their views. In a form called Puritanism, Calvinism would play a vital role in England and in its North American colonies. By 1600 Calvinist churches were well established in parts of Europe.

✔ **READING CHECK: Finding the Main Idea** What role did John Calvin and Calvinism play in the Reformation?

This German woodcut depicts the Saint Bartholomew's Day Massacre in 1572. Pro-Catholic forces in France murdered thousands of Huguenots in the massacre.

SECTION 3 REVIEW

1. **Define** and explain the significance:
   indulgences
   sects
   predestination
   theocracy

2. **Identify** and explain the significance:
   Reformation
   Martin Luther
   Henry VIII
   John Calvin
   Huguenots

3. **Sequencing** Copy the flow chart below. Use it to illustrate the chain of events that led up to and occurred during the Reformation.

4. **Finding the Main Idea**
   a. What did Luther hope to achieve by posting the 95 theses?
   b. Would life in England have been different if the pope had granted Henry VIII a divorce?
   c. How did the views of John Calvin differ from those of the Catholic Church?

5. **Writing and Critical Thinking**
   Supporting a Point of View Imagine that you are calling for reform of the Catholic Church during the 1500s. Write several theses to persuade people that the sale of indulgences is wrong.
   Consider:
   • what indulgences were and why they were sold
   • Luther's objections to indulgences

Homework Practice Online
keyword: SH3 HP6

READ TO DISCOVER

❶ How did the Catholic Church respond to the Reformation?

❷ What were the results of the Reformation and the Counter-Reformation?

IDENTIFY

Counter-Reformation
Council of Trent
Jesuits
Ignatius de Loyola

▶ **WHY IT MATTERS TODAY**

Catholic and Protestant churches have made great strides toward acceptance and toleration of each other. Yet in some places, conflict still exists. Use CNN or other **current event** sources to learn more about theological conflicts that continue today between Christian groups. Record your findings in your journal.

The Catholic Reformation

The Main Idea
The Catholic Church countered the Protestant Reformation by making its own reforms.

The Story Continues *Ignatius de Loyola was a Spanish soldier whose leg had been shattered fighting for Charles V. Loyola's long period of recovery gave him time to reflect. Like Martin Luther, Loyola wondered how he could attain salvation for his sins. Unlike Luther, Loyola came to believe that one could be saved by doing good deeds. He put this belief to work in one of the many steps the Catholic Church took to combat the Reformation.*

The Counter-Reformation

It took some time for the Catholic Church to recognize that Protestantism posed a serious threat. At first the pope dismissed Luther's criticisms. A number of people within the Catholic Church, including Erasmus, had called for reform even before Luther appeared. They too had been ignored. As the Protestants gained ground, reformers finally convinced the pope of the drastic need for change.

In the 1530s the Catholic Church started a major reform effort known as the **Counter-Reformation.** It is sometimes called the Catholic Reformation. The Counter-Reformation began as an attempt to return the church to an emphasis on spiritual matters. It also allowed the church to make its doctrines more clear. In addition, it was a campaign to stop the spread of Protestantism.

Counter-Reformation tactics. Pope Paul III, who reigned as pope from 1534 to 1549, worked to revive a spiritual outlook in the Catholic Church. He appointed devout and learned men as bishops and cardinals.

Pope Paul III also brought the Inquisition to Rome. Since 1478 Spanish authorities had been putting accused heretics on trial. Punishments included extreme cruelties such as burning at the stake. In the past, governments had sometimes used extreme punishments against criminals and traitors. Now the church also used them. The leaders of the Inquisition did not focus on punishing Protestants. Instead, they regarded it as their responsibility to keep Catholics within the church.

In 1559 another method of combating heresy was introduced by Pope Paul IV. He established the *Index of Forbidden Books.* Catholics were banned from reading the listed books, which were considered harmful

Pope Paul III worked to reform the Catholic Church against the threat of the Protestant Reformation.

to faith or morals. The index revealed the role of the printing press in spreading the Reformation. Before printed books, the church could easily find and burn manuscripts it regarded as dangerous. Once books could be printed, it was easier simply to forbid people to read them.

The Council of Trent. Pope Paul III knew that attacks on Protestantism would fail unless Catholic doctrines were clearly defined. However, church authorities often disagreed about complicated matters. In 1545 Paul summoned church leaders to the Italian city of Trent. The **Council of Trent** met during three different periods between 1545 and 1563. It defined the official church position on matters of doctrine.

The Council of Trent acted to end the abuses that surrounded the sale of indulgences and to tighten discipline within the clergy. In most cases the council supported the Catholic beliefs that Protestants had rejected. It emphasized the need for ceremonies, arguing that God should be worshiped with splendor. It noted that people must depend on priests because God granted forgiveness only through the church. Unlike Luther, the council claimed that salvation came from ceremonial church actions as well as from individual faith. The council also stressed that every person had free will.

The decisions made at the Council of Trent were effective for many within the Catholic Church. While some people found the simplicity of Protestantism appealing, others found the Catholic ceremonies comforting. They were moved by the beautiful churches, respected the authority of the priests, and wanted to believe that a person could gain salvation through good works.

Soldiers of the Counter-Reformation. To further strengthen support for the church, existing Catholic religious orders reformed their rules, and new religious orders formed. One such order was the Society of Jesus, known as the **Jesuits.**

Ignatius de Loyola founded the Jesuits in 1534. In 1540 Pope Paul III recognized the Jesuits as an official order of the Catholic Church. Loyola believed that salvation could be achieved, in part, by doing good deeds. His followers took vows of chastity, poverty, and obedience to the pope.

History Makers Speak

"Putting aside all private judgement, we should keep our minds prepared and ready to obey promptly and in all things the true spouse of Christ our Lord, our Holy Mother, the hierarchical church [represented by the pope]."

Ignatius de Loyola, *The Spiritual Exercises of St. Ignatius,* translated by Anthony Mottola

Analyzing Primary Sources

Identifying Bias What in Loyola's statement would particularly please the pope?

INTERPRETING THE VISUAL RECORD

Council of Trent Pope Paul III commissioned the Venetian painter Titian to record the Council of Trent in session. *How does this picture reflect the Catholic Church at this time?*

Loyola organized the Jesuits like a military body, with discipline and strict obedience. The Jesuits quickly became the most effective agents in spreading Catholicism. By 1556 the order had about 1,000 members. Their missions took them as far away as China and Japan. In Europe their preaching slowed the spread of Protestantism in France, Germany, and Poland. The Jesuits stressed education, and founded some of the best colleges in Europe. They combined humanist values with Catholic doctrine to produce educated, dedicated supporters of the church.

✔ **READING CHECK: Summarizing** What reforms did the Catholic Church institute during the Counter-Reformation?

European Religions, 1600

Interpreting Maps The Reformation gained many converts in northern Europe, but southern Europe remained largely Catholic.

■ **Skills Assessment: 1. Places and Regions** What religion was dominant in England? Ireland? Spain? Sweden? **2. Making Predictions** What might result when such various religious groups come into contact?

Results of the Religious Upheaval

Some people hoped that the era of religious reformation would bring about tolerance. It did not. The period from the 1530s through the mid-1600s was a time of devastating religious wars in France, Germany, the Netherlands, and Switzerland. Not until the mid-1600s, when the wars ended, could the results of the Reformation and Counter-Reformation be seen.

Many schools, including the Dutch University of Leiden shown here, were established during the Reformation.

The most striking result of the religious struggle was the appearance of many different churches in Europe. In Italy, where Protestantism was never a powerful force, interest in Catholic Church reform remained strong. In fact, most people in southern and eastern Europe and the native population of Ireland remained Catholic. However, France and the Netherlands had large numbers of Protestants. In England and northern Europe, including Scandinavia, various Protestant faiths became established with the backing of the central government.

Another far-reaching result of the Reformation and the Counter-Reformation was a strong interest in education. During the 1400s and 1500s, many new universities had appeared because of humanist interest in learning. After the 1500s, enrollment in these universities grew dramatically. Religious reformers supported education. Jesuits and other religious orders worked to strengthen the faith of Catholics in their schools. Protestants believed that people could find their way to Christian faith by studying the Bible. As a result, reading became increasingly important. But education did not bring greater tolerance for new ideas. Both Catholic and Protestant authorities opposed views that differed from their own.

Finally, the Reformation led to an increase in the power of national governments and a decrease in the power of the pope. In Protestant regions such as England, each government took responsibility for the leadership of the official church. In some Catholic areas such as France, rulers loyal to the pope managed to gain some degree of control over their churches.

✔ **READING CHECK: Identifying Cause and Effect** How did the religious conflicts of the 1500s change life in Europe?

SECTION 4 REVIEW

1. Identify and explain the significance:
Counter-Reformation
Council of Trent
Jesuits
Ignatius de Loyola

2. Summarizing Copy the graphic organizer below. Use it to record ways in which the Catholic Church made reforms in response to the Protestant Reformation.

3. **Finding the Main Idea**

a. Why did Catholic leaders feel the need to launch the Counter-Reformation?

b. Were the results of the Counter-Reformation era largely positive or negative? Support your view.

4. **Writing and Critical Thinking**

Identifying Cause and Effect Imagine that you have lived through the religious turmoil of the 1500s. Write a journal entry about the changes you have seen in Europe.

Consider:
• the spread of Protestantism
• the growth of universities
• the growing power of national governments

Homework Practice Online

keyword: SH3 HP6

SECTION 5

READ TO DISCOVER

1 Why did Europeans believe in superstitions?
2 What characteristics were typical of daily life in Europe during the Reformation?
3 How did knowledge spread to European villages?
4 What factors caused changes in the daily lives of Europeans?

DEFINE

broadsides
almanacs
standard of living

▶ WHY IT MATTERS TODAY

Almanacs were a popular source of information in Europe during the 1500s. Today people still use almanacs. Use **CNN** or other **current event** sources to find and scan different almanacs to see the kinds of information they contain. Record your findings in your journal.

Culture and Daily Life

The Main Idea
As the ideas of the Reformation took hold, daily life throughout Europe began to change.

The Story Continues *The ideas that marked European lifestyles during the Renaissance, the Reformation, and the Counter-Reformation involved relatively few, and mostly upper-class, people. Ordinary people had their own views about themselves and the world around them—ideas that included witches flying at night and other superstitions, and village processions that mocked the powerful and the foolish.*

Superstitions

Although towns had grown in number and population, most Europeans still lived in or near small villages. They spent their entire lives struggling with nature in order to raise food. People close to the land never knew what life might bring next. A cow might fall ill, or lightning might burn down a cottage. Moreover, during the 1500s the population of Europe was increasing at a time of social and political upheaval. War, famine, and plague continued to affect people. At any time, life could take an unexpected turn for the worse. Many people looked to superstitions to explain and control their lives.

The world of spirits. Although most Europeans were Christians, they considered God to be a distant, unknowable force. They explained many of the events that took place around them as the doings of spirits. Because of this belief in spirits, most Europeans believed that nothing was an accident. Bad spirits—demons—made life difficult. If lightning struck a house, a demon had caused it. If a pitcher of milk spilled, a demon was the reason. In fact, many superstitions that may seem strange or difficult to explain today began during this period.

Village priests usually accepted these beliefs, or they ignored them. The ordinary villager was not very satisfied with the priests' explanation that misfortune was God's will, or perhaps God's punishment for sin. Villagers still, however, believed

that a priest's actions could have positive effects. For example, every spring a priest would go out into the fields, bless the earth, and pray for good crops. His blessing of a husband and wife at a wedding supposedly gave the new couple a good start in life. Baptism was thought to protect a newborn child.

Belief in fortune telling was common during the 1400s and the 1500s.

The priest was not the only person to whom the villagers turned in times of trouble. They also looked to a man or woman who was considered "wise" or "cunning." This person, usually an older village member, was thought to have a special understanding of how the world worked.

Ordinary people would explain their problem—a lost ring, a cruel husband, a sick pig—to the "wise" folk. People would also report anything unusual, even something simple like a frog jumping into a boat. Such events were taken as a warning. The wise man or woman would explain what the warning meant. Sometimes wise folk recommended a remedy for warding off evil. Remedies included chanting a spell, drinking a special potion, or wearing a good-luck charm.

Belief in witchcraft. Wise people were part of a traditional belief in witchcraft. Wise people were often called "good witches." If their relationship with their neighbors turned sour, or if misfortunes began to occur, they might be accused of being "bad witches." It was believed that bad witches had made a pact with the devil. In many cases, a person accused of witchcraft was an elderly widow. Without a husband or family, she would be the most defenseless person in the community. Such a woman was an easy target to attack.

Stories about witches became more sensational as they spread through the countryside. Outrageous accusations were made. A person might be accused of flying on a broomstick, sticking pins into dolls, or dancing with the devil in the woods at night. In some of these cases, a priest might be asked to hold a ceremony to exorcise, or drive out, a demon that was thought to have taken over the witch's body. In other cases, the accused person might be dragged to a bonfire, tied to a stake, and burned, perhaps with the approval of the local lord.

An enormous outburst of "witch hunting" occurred in Europe in the mid-1500s and lasted for more than one hundred years. Those accused of being witches were put on trial. The punishment was death. Both religious and secular leaders accepted witches as an explanation for problems in the world around them. The example of Jean Bodin, a French scholar, shows that even learned people believed in witches.

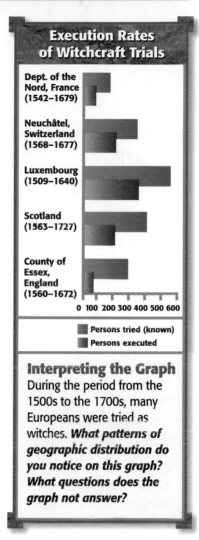

Execution Rates of Witchcraft Trials

Dept. of the Nord, France (1542–1679)

Neuchâtel, Switzerland (1568–1677)

Luxembourg (1509–1640)

Scotland (1563–1727)

County of Essex, England (1560–1672)

0 100 200 300 400 500 600

■ Persons tried (known)
■ Persons executed

Interpreting the Graph
During the period from the 1500s to the 1700s, many Europeans were tried as witches. *What patterns of geographic distribution do you notice on this graph? What questions does the graph not answer?*

History Makers Speak **"Now, if there is any means to appease the wrath of God, to gain his blessing, to strike awe into some by the punishment of others, to preserve some from being infected by others, to diminish the number of evil-doers . . . and to punish the most detestable crimes of which the human mind can conceive, it is to punish with the utmost rigor the witches. . . . Now it is not in the power of princes to pardon a crime which the law of God punishes with the penalty of death—such are the crimes of witches."**

Jean Bodin, *Witchcraft in Europe*

Analyzing Primary Sources

Identifying a Point of View
What is Bodin's opinion of the belief in witches?

Eventually fewer cases of witchcraft were reported. As the religious wars came to an end, people experienced greater security in their lives. They were less likely to worry about the influence of witches in everyday life.

✔ **READING CHECK: Identifying Cause and Effect** How did concerns about events in daily life lead to a belief in superstitions?

This English engraving shows a suspected witch being "swum" at a 1612 witchcraft trial.

Daily Life

For most Europeans in the 1500s and 1600s, daylight meant work and night meant sleep. Because farming was so time-consuming, people needed all the daylight hours to raise food. By evening most farmers were exhausted from working all day. Few could afford the candles needed for light. Still, people did find time for relaxation.

Forms of recreation. Every village had a gathering place where people came together to drink, sew, do simple chores, or tell stories. Some played games such as skittles, a form of bowling. Occasionally traveling companies of actors passed through and put on shows. The people also enjoyed special holidays during the year. Some were church holidays, while others honored a local saint or tradition. During some holidays, the villagers donned costumes and would often put on their own ceremonies.

One favorite holiday ceremony poked fun at village life. This ceremony went by different names in different parts of Europe. Whether it was called "rough music," "charivari," or "abbeys of misrule," the basic ceremony was much the same. The young men of the village formed a procession. They made fun of people who had behaved in unusual ways or had violated local custom.

Sometimes the marchers had more serious targets. They might want to show how things would be if the poor or the weak had power. They would dress someone like a bishop or put the poorest man in the village on a throne. At this point the jokes were no longer lighthearted. They revealed the resentment villagers felt about the privileges their rulers possessed.

Violence and protest in the village. People of this time identified closely with those of their own kind. In large towns, members of the same profession joined together in guilds and other groups. In small villages, which contained perhaps a few dozen families, whole communities tended to work and make decisions together.

Because villagers lived in close-knit communities, anyone who upset village traditions or behaved oddly was treated harshly. Quarrels between neighbors were common, and the bonds of mutual reliance that held the community together could loosen in times of stress. The strain of hardship or famine could cause villagers to respond violently. For example, if a local baker was suspected of hoarding bread or sending it elsewhere to make higher profits, villagers might band together to ransack the baker's shop.

✔ **READING CHECK: Making Generalizations** What were the main features of daily life in Europe during this period?

Games

People throughout the ages have played games for fun. In some cultures, games are a way for children to learn useful skills. Games provide relaxation and recreation.

Dice have been found in Egyptian tombs. The earliest form of the modern game of backgammon may date from about 3000 B.C. In recent years, people of all ages have been fascinated by the new games and twists on old games made possible by electronics and the computer. **Can you identify some games in the painting by Pieter Brueghel that people still play today?**

Children's games in the 1500s

The Spread of Knowledge

In the 1500s the world beyond the village began to affect village life. Printed works, and in some areas traveling preachers, inspired these changes.

Books for the masses. Few ordinary villagers could read. In some cases even the village priest could not read. Nevertheless, soon after the invention of movable type, publishers started selling popular works. Single printed sheets known as **broadsides** began to appear. A broadside might include a royal decree or news of some sensational crime or other event. Books and broadsides arrived in the village, carried by peddlers who brought goods from the outside world. When the villagers gathered together, they might enjoy listening to someone read the latest broadside.

Romances and epics of the classical era appealed to nobility. Publishers also found subjects that appealed to country folk and produced cheap books for this new market. The most common books were **almanacs,** which published predictions about the weather and prospects for growing crops. Almanacs also contained calendars, maps, and medical advice. The books were best-sellers because they spoke to the beliefs and concerns of ordinary people.

Religious ideas and education. Soon after Luther's break with the church in 1521, new religious ideas began to spread beyond urban areas. Sometimes preachers came to visit. Peddlers might sell books on religious themes. Perhaps people heard stories that attacked the church. The messages of Luther and Calvin traveled in this manner, as did translations of the Bible.

As Protestants and Catholics battled for the loyalties of ordinary people, leaders of both sides encouraged the founding of primary schools in the villages and towns. Both Protestant and Catholic leaders believed that knowledge would lead a person to support the faith. In spite of this common

CONNECTING TO
Science and Technology

The Printing Press

screw

type form

bed

platen
(flat plate)

During the Middle Ages books were written and copied by hand. The work was usually done by Christian monks, and it took a long time to produce a book. A German, Johannes Gutenberg, developed a faster way to print things by inventing the printing press in about 1450. Gutenberg developed the use of movable type. He then modified a wine press to push the paper onto the inked type, which made an impression on the paper. With the new press he could print ten sheets of paper per hour. The printing press allowed ideas and knowledge to be spread faster and farther than ever before. Many of today's presses are computerized and can print pages at high speeds. Daily life today is filled with printed materials, from books and magazines to posters and leaflets.

Understanding Science and Technology

How was the Gutenberg printing technique an improvement over older techniques?

concern for education, the followers of the differing religions struggled to coexist peacefully. However, because education became part of the struggle for followers, neither side included tolerance in its teachings.

✔ **READING CHECK: Summarizing** In what ways did knowledge spread to European villages?

Changes in Daily Life

In addition to undergoing religious and political change during the Renaissance and Reformation eras, Europeans experienced other changes.

The economy. The measure of the quality of life—the **standard of living**—is affected by many factors, including environment, health, home life, income, and working conditions. During the Renaissance peasants made up as much as 85 to 90 percent of the total European population, except in the highly urbanized areas of northern Italy and Flanders. As the manorial system continued to decline, so too did medieval concepts and practices of serfdom. Increasingly, the labor dues owed by a peasant to his lord were converted into rents paid in money. By the end of the 1400s, especially in western Europe, more and more peasants were becoming legally free. Furthermore, the Black Death of the 1300s had reduced the population by at least one third. This meant that there were now fewer people to work the land. Some peasants prospered, therefore, because their labor was in demand, which often resulted in higher wages.

By 1550, when the religious wars were ravaging Europe, conditions changed again. The population was growing rapidly. With population growth came inflation, a rise in prices for goods. After 1550 wages could not keep up with the rise in prices, especially of farm goods.

The image above shows some of the foods typical of European diets in the 1500s and 1600s. In the painting below, by Pieter Brueghel the Younger, peasants of the era share a meal as they rest from their work.

Diet. During this period, white bread made from wheat was rare. Meat was scarce and expensive, and fish only a little less so. Salt had long been an important trade item because it was needed to preserve foods, but it, too, was expensive. Cheese and eggs—cheap sources of protein—were an important part of the diet everywhere in Europe. Butter was not widely used outside northern Europe until the 1700s.

Most spices introduced into Europe from the East had been considered luxury items. By the 1500s and 1600s, the importation of spices had become very competitive. Increased competition often meant a drop in prices.

In the 1500s traders introduced new vegetables to Europe. Europeans had the opportunity to try asparagus, green beans, lettuce, melons, spinach, and tomatoes. Traders also brought new luxury items such as coffee and tea. Not everyone had access to the new and varied diets, however. Wealthy people still lived better than most people did. Peasants and the urban poor usually ate the same simple meals they had eaten for centuries.

Customs and table settings that we know today were not common in the early Renaissance period. People usually ate with their fingers. They picked what they wanted to eat from a common dish. In some areas people ate from wooden plates. Guests brought their own knives. Forks did not come into use until the 1500s, and spoons were not common until the 1600s.

Housing. After the 1500s brick and stone became more common construction materials in the growing cities of Europe. In the countryside housing remained much as it had during the Middle Ages. Peasants lived in small, thatch-roofed houses. Glass was expensive and often difficult to obtain, even for the wealthy. The scarcity of glass meant that most houses had shutters instead of glass windows. Peasant houses usually contained only the necessities of rural life—a large cooking pot, a bench, a table, and some tools. The lucky few had a bed. Most people slept on sacks filled with straw.

Decline of traditional culture. Many peasants were trapped in poverty. Hoping to escape their fate, some migrated to the cities. The movement of people from countryside to city during the Renaissance and Reformation eras further changed traditional popular culture. In the city, food came from a shop rather than directly from the fields. Local governments helped out when disasters occurred. If famine struck, authorities passed out bread. If plagues broke out, the government set up hospitals and quarantined sick people.

Gradually, the residents of cities and towns became more sophisticated in their attitudes. In particular, people's understanding of how things happen in the world began to change. Superstition no longer played an important role in people's views of daily life. Instead, people sought rational explanations for day-to-day events. They had less need for magic and "wise" folk. Some scholars have called this very important development the "disenchantment" of the world—the removal of "enchantment," or magic, from nature.

Daily work This sophisticated urban couple of the 1500s are working together in their banking business. *Compare this picture with the picture of peasants on the previous page. What role did women play in the world of work?*

✔ **READING CHECK: Contrasting** In what ways did life in Europe change during the early Renaissance?

SECTION 5 REVIEW

1. **Define** and explain the significance:
   broadsides
   almanacs
   standard of living

2. **Summarizing** Copy the concept map below. Use it to explain features of daily life in Europe during the 1500s.

Daily Life—1500s

3. **Finding the Main Idea**
   a. What evidence would you give that the printing press had significant influence during the Renaissance?
   b. Why did urban life lead to the growing "disenchantment" of the world?
   c. Did life improve for most Europeans during the 1500s?

4. **Writing and Critical Thinking**
   Analyzing Information Imagine that you are a European villager. Prepare a broadside that explains why people believe in superstitions.
   Consider:
   • attitudes toward God and nature
   • the role of "wise" folk in village life

go. hrw .com **Homework Practice Online**
keyword: SH3 HP6

THE RENAISSANCE AND REFORMATION **185**

CHAPTER 6 Review

Creating a Time Line

Copy the time line below onto a sheet of paper. Complete the time line by filling in the events, individuals, and dates from the chapter that you think were significant. Pick three events and explain why you think they were significant.

| 1400 | 1500 | 1600 |

Writing a Summary

Using standard grammar, spelling, sentence structure, and punctuation, write an overview of the events in the chapter.

Identifying People and Ideas

Identify the following terms or individuals and explain their significance:

1. Renaissance
2. humanists
3. Niccolò Machiavelli
4. Leonardo da Vinci
5. Johannes Gutenberg
6. Reformation
7. Martin Luther
8. Counter-Reformation
9. broadsides
10. standard of living

Understanding Main Ideas

SECTION 1 *(pp. 162–166)*

The Italian Renaissance

1. What were the main values that generally characterized the Italian humanists?
2. What new painting styles and techniques developed during the Italian Renaissance?

SECTION 2 *(pp. 167–170)*

The Northern Renaissance

3. How did northern Europeans learn about the Italian Renaissance?
4. How did northern Renaissance writers differ from the writers of the Italian Renaissance?

SECTION 3 *(pp. 171–175)*

The Protestant Reformation

5. What role did the sale of indulgences by the church play in the Reformation?
6. In what ways did Protestantism spread?

SECTION 4 *(pp. 176–179)*

The Catholic Reformation

7. What actions did the Catholic Church take during the Counter-Reformation?
8. How did the Reformation and Counter-Reformation affect education?

SECTION 5 *(pp. 180–185)*

Culture and Daily Life

9. Why did Europeans believe in superstitions?
10. What factor was mainly responsible for the decline of traditional culture?

Reviewing Themes

1. **Global Relations** What effect did the ideas of Luther and other religious reformers have on the relations between different groups in Europe?
2. **Science, Technology & Society** What effect did the printing press have on the ways that Europeans understood their world?
3. **Culture** How did the classical literature of Greece and Rome influence the development of humanism?

Thinking Critically

1. **Identifying Cause and Effect** What events contributed to the beginning of the Renaissance?
2. **Contrasting** How did Renaissance humanist thought differ from medieval thought?
3. **Sequencing** What were the main events of the Reformation and the Counter-Reformation?
4. **Evaluating** How effective were the reforms of the Counter-Reformation?

Writing About History

Contrasting Write a report explaining the differences between Calvinism, Catholicism, and Lutheranism. Use the chart below to organize your thoughts before writing.

	Calvinism	Catholicism	Lutheranism
Path to salvation			
Church organization			

Using Artifacts as Historical Evidence

Study the photograph below. Then answer the questions that follow.

Italian Renaissance bookbinding with velvet and silverwork

1. Which of the following best describes the historical evidence this artifact provides?

   a. Many people had books during the Renaissance.

   b. Italian bookbinding reached its height during the Renaissance.

   c. All Renaissance books were bound with velvet and silver.

   d. During the Renaissance, some Italians had books with fancy bindings.

2. What clues does this bookbinding give about life during the Italian Renaissance? Give your reasons.

Identifying Cause and Effect

Read the following excerpt by an art historian about the Italian artist Michelangelo. Then answer the questions.

> "Michelangelo's life story is a series of quarrels, disappointments, and interruptions. If we except the Sistine Ceiling, he was forced to leave undone more work than he was allowed to finish, largely because of . . . his patron Pope Julius II . . . . Some twenty-four years after the completion of the ceiling Michelangelo was called upon to do another stupendous fresco, this time for the end wall of the same chapel. *The Last Judgment* . . . reflects the bitterness of the aging genius."

3. Which of the following correctly states the reason the author gives for Michelangelo's bitterness?

   a. His whole life he had been forced to do what his patron required.

   b. He did not want to leave the chapel ceiling unfinished.

   c. He felt he was too old to do another fresco.

   d. He thought his patron would interrupt him once again.

4. Most artists of the Italian Renaissance supported themselves by working for patrons. Do you think this system was successful? Give your reasons.

Alternative Assessment

Building Your Portfolio

Link to TODAY

Science, Technology & Society

The printing press helped spread new ideas down through the centuries. With computers, current printing technology has changed, and the Internet spreads information almost instantly around the world. Using your textbook and other sources, create a bibliography of the important printed works that have had a great influence on people and events.

internet connect

Internet Activity: go.hrw.com
KEYWORD: SH3 WH6

Choose a topic on the Renaissance and Reformation to:

• create a pamphlet on the Reformation and its leaders.

• report on the economic, social, and technological influences of Johannes Gutenberg's printing press.

• create a biography on one of the Renaissance writers in this chapter.

1400–1800

Exploration and Expansion

Coin minted during the reign of Charles V

Woodcut from the 1500s showing Hispaniola

1492
Global Events
Columbus makes his first voyage to the Americas.

c. 1503–1506
The Arts
Leonardo da Vinci paints the *Mona Lisa.*

1532
Global Events
Francisco Pizarro invades the Inca Empire.

1556
Politics
Charles V divides his lands between members of his family.

1569
Science and Technology
The first Mercator projection map makes navigation much easier.

1400

1500

1600

1431
Daily Life
Joan of Arc is burned at the stake.

1519
Global Events
The Magellan-Elcano expedition begins its voyage around the world.

1543
Science and Technology
Copernicus publishes his heliocentric theory.

1588
Politics
The Spanish Armada sets sail against England.

1513
Global Events
Ponce de León explores and names Florida.

Galileo's telescope

Build on What You Know

*T*he Italian Renaissance of the 1300s marked a time of great change in Europe. Renaissance thinking and styles spread throughout western and northern Europe. The Protestant Reformation of the 1500s led to new social, political, and economic patterns across Europe. The Reformation challenged traditional approaches to religious thought and the individual's role in society. During this same era, new ways of studying and understanding the natural world brought about a scientific revolution. In this chapter, you will learn about the causes and effects of this revolution in thought.

A maritime trading company's crest

Dutch ship landing slaves in colonial Jamestown

1610
Business and Finance
The Dutch East India Company introduces the term "shares" of stock.

1619
Politics
Colonists of Jamestown, Virginia, form the first representative colonial assembly in America.

1619
Global Events
A Dutch ship brings the first cargo of African slaves to Jamestown.

c. 1674
Science and Technology
Antoni van Leeuwenhoek first observes bacteria through a microscope.

1750
Daily Life
The world's population reaches approximately 750 million.

1756
The Arts
Composer Wolfgang Amadeus Mozart is born.

1776
Business and Finance
Scottish economist Adam Smith writes about mercantilism in *Wealth of Nations*.

1700   **1800**

1628
Science and Technology
William Harvey accurately describes the human circulatory system.

1626
Business and Finance
The Dutch purchase Manhattan Island from American Indians.

1609
The Arts
William Shakespeare publishes a book of sonnets.

1708
Business and Finance
British traders dominate trade on the coasts of India.

The Leeuwenhoek microscope, shown here, was about 3 to 4 inches high. On the back of the instrument, a screw with a needle provided a place to hold the object being viewed. The microscope was then held up to the viewer's eye.

The Dutch purchased Manhattan Island for trade goods.

What's Your Opinion?

Do you **agree** *or* **disagree** *with the following statements? Support your point of view in your journal.*

Science, Technology & Society A society's approach to scientific study has little impact upon daily lifestyles and standards of living.

Economics A nation's need for natural resources encourages national commitment to exploration and discovery.

Global Relations Exploration can lead to confrontations and mistreatment of conquered peoples.

The Scientific Revolution

READ TO DISCOVER

❶ What factors contributed to the Scientific Revolution?

❷ How did Copernicus, Kepler, and Galileo challenge traditional thought?

❸ What were some of the important scientific discoveries of this period?

DEFINE

scientific method
geocentric theory
heliocentric theory

IDENTIFY

Roger Bacon
Scientific Revolution
Nicolaus Copernicus
Johannes Kepler
Galileo Galilei
Isaac Newton
Andreas Vesalius
René Descartes
Francis Bacon
Robert Boyle

▶ WHY IT MATTERS TODAY

Scientific discoveries can have both positive and negative effects on society. Use CNN or other **current event** sources to find several social issues that involve science or technology. Record your findings in your journal.

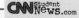

The Main Idea
The Scientific Revolution challenged and changed the way people thought about the world.

The Story Continues *In the early 1600s Spanish writer Miguel de Cervantes published a novel called* Don Quixote de la Mancha. *It told the story of an aging man stuck in the myths of the past. Cervantes's humorous tale reflected a new world that was rejecting the legends of old for a reality based on science.*

From Magic to Science

Until well into the 1500s, most Europeans saw little difference between science and magic. Alchemists used spells and magic formulas to try to change one substance to another—for example, lead into gold. Astrologers believed that the position of the stars in the sky influenced human life. People still believed many explanations of natural events proposed by Aristotle almost 2,000 years earlier. These people were called natural philosophers. They relied on religious teachings and the works of classical Greek and Roman thinkers to explain the mysteries of nature. Many scientists before the Renaissance were like **Roger Bacon,** an English philosopher and scientist of the 1200s. Bacon, a Franciscan monk who had studied at Oxford and Paris, was viewed as a leading scholar of his time. He was one of the earliest to favor a system of scientific experimentation, rather than faithful acceptance of religious ideas and ancient beliefs, as a means of finding truth. Nevertheless, he was shaped by the thinking of the time and mainly practiced alchemy. Famed for his teaching, Bacon became known as Doctor Mirabilis—wonderful teacher.

The spirit of the Renaissance encouraged curiosity, investigation, discovery, and the practical application of the knowledge of nature to everyday life. Some people felt freer to question old ideas and beliefs. They were more willing to use new approaches to answering questions about the natural world. During the era of the **Scientific Revolution,** people began using experiments and mathematics to understand these mysteries. The study of nature became more organized. They were no longer content to explain the world in terms of religious thought, magic, or the ideas of ancient writers.

INTERPRETING THE VISUAL RECORD

Alchemy Alchemists sought to understand and control the natural world through the use of magic. Some of their procedures and tools, however, were similar to those of early and later scientists. *Based on the picture, how might alchemists have contributed to the development of early scientific procedures?*

This new approach produced answers to many questions in physics, astronomy, and anatomy. It formed the basis for what we know today as science. Before the 1600s the word science meant "to know." After the 1600s the sense of the word changed into the narrower meaning it has today.

✔ **READING CHECK: Drawing Inferences** What role did the Renaissance play in the development of science?

The New Study of Nature

As scientists spent more time examining the world around them, they observed things that did not agree with traditional explanations. For this reason, early scientists of the 1500s began to question ancient beliefs. They learned to form conclusions based on what they could observe with their own senses. They also used three new tools— scientific instruments, mathematics, and experiments. This new approach to study and knowledge marked the beginnings of the Scientific Revolution. It was a turning point in thinking that led to a rapid increase in people's understanding of the world.

The ability to conduct experiments was key to this new approach to learning. Scientists used newly invented instruments such as the barometer, the microscope, the telescope, the air pump, and the thermometer. These tools greatly improved their ability to observe and measure. Scientists used mathematics to check and apply those measurements. Also, they repeated their experiments to make sure they got the same results. Then they drew conclusions about what they observed. This manner of study is called the **scientific method.**

✔ **READING CHECK: Drawing Conclusions** Why did the study of nature change during the 1500s and the 1600s?

Astronomy, Physics, and Anatomy

Three areas of study were especially interesting to some of the strongest thinkers of the times. Astronomy was the study of stars, planets, and other bodies in the sky. Another area, physics, focused on changes and properties of matter and energy. Scientists in the field of anatomy studied the structure of the human body, mainly by examining dead bodies. Several European scientists helped to shape the modern study of these important sciences.

Copernicus. In the A.D. 100s, the astronomer Ptolemy stated that Earth was the center of the universe. The sun and the planets, according to Ptolemy, moved around Earth. Ptolemy's theory is called the **geocentric,** or "Earth-centered," **theory.** The Greek word for Earth is *geo.* People believed this theory for many centuries.

During the early 1500s, Polish scientist **Nicolaus Copernicus** began to abandon Ptolemy's geocentric theory. Instead, he argued that the sun was the center of the universe. Copernicus developed the **heliocentric,** or "sun-centered," **theory.** *Helio* is the Greek word meaning "sun." Copernicus realized that his theory explained many of the then-known facts about astronomy.

When Copernicus's theory was published in 1543, people paid little attention. The theory seemed to deny what people's senses told them. Anyone could "see" that the sun and planets moved around Earth. Anyone could "feel" that solid Earth did not move.

HISTORY MAKER

Nicolaus Copernicus (1473–1543)

Nicolaus Copernicus, the great Polish scientist, is viewed today as the founder of modern astronomy. His heliocentric theory demonstrated that the earth is a moving planet and that it revolves around the sun. Copernicus became a symbol of the new ideas and approaches that brought about the Scientific Revolution. **How did Copernicus change our understanding of the universe?**

Model of Copernicus's theory of planetary revolutions

CONNECTING TO
Math

Kepler's Laws of Planetary Motion

Johannes Kepler tried to use mathematics to prove that the planets orbit around the sun. Kepler discovered three "laws" about how planets move in space. These laws are referred to as Kepler's laws of planetary motion.

Using the observations made by his employer, Tycho Brahe, Kepler found that planets travel around the sun in oval-shaped orbits called ellipses. Kepler's second discovery was that planets move faster when they are closer to the sun. Kepler's third law relates to the time it takes for a planet to complete an orbit around the sun.

Understanding Math

How would math help Kepler prove that his discoveries were true?

Kepler and Galileo. Copernicus had neither the instruments nor the mathematics to prove his theory. Proof came later with the work of two other scientists. **Johannes Kepler,** a German astronomer, and **Galileo Galilei,** an Italian scientist, each helped to confirm Copernicus's new understanding of the universe.

Johannes Kepler was a brilliant mathematician who used models, observation, and mathematics to test Copernicus's heliocentric theory. Some of the ideas on which Copernicus had based his theory were wrong. That slowed Kepler down, but he eventually proved the heliocentric theory correct. He published his laws of planetary motion in 1609. It took the work of an Italian scientist, however, to produce clear evidence that the earth moves around the sun.

Galileo Galilei had read of a Dutch device that made distant objects appear larger. Galileo built his own device—a telescope—and began studying the heavens. His telescope was very simple compared to those made today. However, Galileo was able to see things that no one had ever seen. He saw the mountains and valleys of the moon. He observed the rings around Saturn and spots on the sun. Galileo also observed the moons circling Jupiter. He used these observations to argue that not every heavenly body revolves around Earth. Galileo drew sketches of the things he observed through his telescope.

When Galileo published his findings in 1632, the work caused an uproar. Many scholars who still believed in Ptolemy's old geocentric theory refused to accept Galileo's findings. Church scholars disapproved because Galileo's theory seemed to contradict the Bible. Some said that the telescope was an invention of the devil.

In the central panel of this ceiling fresco, Galileo Galilei is shown demonstrating the use of his telescope. Later, Galileo was called before the Inquisition and forced to renounce his discoveries. He spent the rest of his life under house arrest.

Traditional scholars in physics were also displeased with Galileo. They believed, as Aristotle had said, that heavier objects fell faster than lighter ones. Using experiments and mathematics, Galileo proved this false. If there is no friction from air, all objects fall at the same rate. Galileo's discoveries formed the basis for the modern science of mechanics—the study of objects in motion.

Newton. In 1687 English scientist **Isaac Newton** published a book building on the work of Copernicus, Kepler, and Galileo. They had shown that the planets, including Earth, revolve around the sun. They had not, however, been able to explain why these bodies moved as they did.

After many experiments and measurements, Newton realized that the force that holds the planets in their orbits and the force that causes objects to fall to Earth are one and the same. He proposed the law of universal gravitation, which states that all bodies attract each other. Moreover, the force of this attraction can be measured. Both Kepler's Proof and Galileo's discoveries about falling objects were really examples of the law of universal gravitation. Newton also explained the laws of motion and developed the mathematical means of measuring motion. In one sweeping system, Newton tied together the movement of all things in the heavens and on Earth.

Newton's work had a huge impact on the science of his time. Even today, his laws of motion and gravitation are applied in the development of everything from automobile seatbelts to space travel. Furthermore, Newton's work changed the way people viewed the world. No longer would most well-educated Europeans see the universe as a place in which everything moved according to the constant attention of God and His angels. Most Europeans still accepted God as creator of the universe. However, they now began to think of that creation as a kind of giant mechanical clock. Once wound up by the divine clockmaker, it moved according to natural and universal laws of motion. So great was Newton's influence that the English poet Alexander Pope wrote:

> **"Nature and nature's laws lay hid in night;
> God said, 'Let Newton be!' and all was light."**
>
> Alexander Pope, epitaph intended for Sir Isaac Newton

Vesalius and Harvey. The great Renaissance artist Leonardo da Vinci was a student of the human body. To those who tried to describe the body, he once said, "I advise you not to trouble with words unless you are speaking to blind men." **Andreas Vesalius,** a Flemish scientist, heeded da Vinci's words and pioneered the study of anatomy. Vesalius refused to accept descriptions of human muscles and tissues written by Galen 1,400 years earlier. He did his own studies to see how the human body was constructed. In 1543, Vesalius published a seven-volume book called *On the Fabric of the Human Body.* The illustrations of the human body that Vesalius included in his work were amazingly detailed for the time. They helped readers to gain a visual understanding of the many complicated components of the body and of how they work together.

English physician William Harvey made equally important contributions. Using laboratory experiments, Harvey studied the circulation of blood. He described how blood moved through the veins and arteries. He also observed the working of the body's most important muscle—the heart.

✔ **READING CHECK: Making Generalizations** How did the work of early scientists during the Scientific Revolution lay the foundation for modern science?

HISTORY MAKER

**Galileo Galilei
(1564–1642)**

Galileo believed that scientific study would change the way people understood themselves and their world. Science, he felt, would lead to higher standards of living at every level of society. He believed, too, that science would weaken the social and economic barriers that separated people.

Because Galileo's findings challenged the traditional beliefs of the Catholic Church, church leaders kept him from teaching or writing about his ideas. **According to Galileo, in what ways would scientific progress affect society as a whole?**

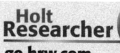

**Holt
Researcher**

go.hrw.com
KEYWORD: Holt Researcher
FreeFind:
   **Nicolaus Copernicus
   Galileo Galilei**
After reading more about Copernicus and Galileo on the Holt Researcher, write an imaginary dialogue between the two discussing their ideas about the universe.

René Descartes explained that the universe operates in a machine-like way according to the basic laws of physics. His philosophy became the basis of our modern Western view of the universe and its physical properties. **How did Descartes's view of the universe influence today's science?**

Analyzing Primary Sources

Identifying a Point of View How would Descartes view information that was assumed to be true or that was accepted as true on the basis of faith or tradition?

The Triumph of the New Science

The effects of discoveries made during the Scientific Revolution were felt throughout Europe. So much had been learned that scientists believed that the scientific method offered a map that could easily be followed in the search for knowledge.

During the Counter-Reformation, religious orders had helped to revive faith in church teachings. New scientific "orders" spread knowledge of the developments of the Scientific Revolution. Schools and societies devoted to science appeared in Rome, England, and France. The printing press helped scientists as it had helped religious reformers. Most of the new scientific societies published journals. Scientists everywhere could now read about scientific studies being done in Europe.

Descartes. French philosopher and mathematician **René Descartes** (day·KAHRT) was a leader of the Scientific Revolution. His ideas led to great advances in mathematics, the sciences, and philosophy.

Descartes felt that no assumptions should be accepted without question. He developed a philosophy based on his own reason. In *Discourse on Method* (1637), Descartes stated that all assumptions had to be proven on the basis of known facts. Only ideas that were true beyond all doubt could be accepted without risk. He believed, for example, that his own existence was proven by the fact that he could think. Descartes wrote, "I think, therefore I am." From this basic truth, he built a method of questioning that followed a clear, orderly progression of logical reasoning.

> **❝[I] was never to accept anything as true that I did not know to be evidently so: that is to say carefully to avoid precipitancy [hasty conclusions based upon assumptions, rather than observed facts] and prejudice, and to include in my judgements nothing more than what presented itself so clearly and so distinctly to my mind that I might have no occasion to place it in doubt.❞**
>
> René Descartes, *Discourse on Method*

In Descartes's view, all fields of scientific knowledge were connected, thus they should be studied together. Descartes's interests ranged across many fields. His work included studies in geometry and algebra, the scientific method, astronomy, and the physical sciences. He created a mathematical description of the way that light reflects from a smooth surface. This explanation led to the law of refraction, a basic principle in the study of optics. Much of Descartes's work challenged traditional church teachings. He was forced to live in the Protestant kingdom of Sweden, where he died in 1650.

Francis Bacon. English philosopher and scientist **Francis Bacon** lived around the same time as Descartes. Bacon believed that scientific theories could be developed only through observation. He said that no assumption could be trusted unless it could be proven by repeatable experiments. Bacon relied on truths that could be demonstrated physically, rather than through deductive thinking or reasoning. In 1620 he published *Novum Organum*, a book that outlined this new system of knowledge.

Other scientific discoveries. During the 1500s and the 1600s, scientific discoveries were made throughout Europe. German Gottfried Liebnitz (LIP·nits) and the English thinker Isaac Newton developed calculus, a new branch of mathematics. The two did not work together. They developed their mathematical ideas independent of one another.

Dutch scientist Antoni van Leeuwenhoek (LAY·ven·hook) used the microscope, invented in the late 1500s, to discover bacteria. He called them animalcules. He studied and wrote about a whole range of tiny life forms never before seen by the human eye.

An English-Irish scientist, **Robert Boyle,** helped to pioneer the modern science of chemistry. Chemistry studies the composition of matter and how it changes. In 1662, Boyle showed that temperature and pressure affect the space that a gas occupies. An English chemist, Joseph Priestley, discovered the element oxygen in 1774. Antoine Lavoisier (luhv·WAHZ·ee·ay), a French scientist, later named it.

Before Lavoisier, people believed that fire was an element. He showed that fire resulted when a substance rapidly combined with oxygen. Lavoisier also showed that steam mixes with the air and becomes invisible. In this way, Lavoisier proved that matter can change form, but that it can neither be destroyed nor created. This idea is known as the law of conservation of matter. It is one of the most important principles in the study of chemistry.

Priestley and Lavoisier made their discoveries in the late 1700s. By this time, the scientific approach had spread across Europe. The store of human knowledge and understanding had increased beyond measure and in a very brief span of time. In fact, speed of discovery and rapid spread and exchange of knowledge were important characteristics of the Scientific Revolution. These resulted, in part, from the printing press, the rise of scientific societies, and other communications improvements.

✔ **READING CHECK: Drawing Inferences** Why did so many important scientific advances take place in so brief a period of time?

The French Academy of Sciences was founded in 1666.

SECTION 1 REVIEW

1. **Define** and explain the significance:
   scientific method
   geocentric theory
   heliocentric theory

2. **Identify** and explain the significance:
   Roger Bacon
   Scientific Revolution
   Nicolaus Copernicus
   Johannes Kepler
   Galileo Galilei
   Isaac Newton
   Andreas Vesalius
   René Descartes
   Francis Bacon
   Robert Boyle

3. **Identifying Cause and Effect** Copy the web diagram below. Use it to show what factors led to the Scientific Revolution and what contribution each of the major scientists made.

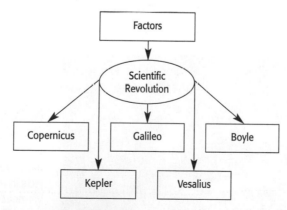

4. **Finding the Main Idea**
   a. Why were the scientific developments of the 1500s and the 1600s later called the Scientific Revolution?
   b. What did the work of Galileo, Newton, Vesalius, van Leeuwenhoek, and Lavoisier have in common?
   c. How did communications advances contribute to learning, discovery, and new scientific methods in Europe?

5. **Writing and Critical Thinking**
   Evaluating Write a short article for a science magazine describing the importance of the 1500s and the 1600s in the history of science.
   Consider:
   • how the study of science changed during this period
   • what discoveries were made that led to today's scientific and technical knowledge

READ TO DISCOVER

❶ What technological advances made European exploration possible?

❷ What effect did the Commercial Revolution have?

❸ What role did mercantilism play in the colonies?

DEFINE

compass
joint-stock company
mercantilism
favorable balance of trade
tariffs
subsidies

IDENTIFY

Commercial Revolution

WHY IT MATTERS TODAY

Social changes in one region of the world often cause people to move to other countries. Use or other **current event** sources to find out what recent social changes have caused people to leave their native countries. Record your findings in your journal.

CNN Student News.com

The Foundations of European Exploration

The Main Idea
Technological improvements led to exploration and fostered the growth of a new economy.

The Story Continues *Scientific advances would soon affect trade and the balance of political power in Europe. Rewards were offered to anyone who could invent a device for measuring longitude, since that would help ships sail more accurately and help nations compete for supremacy. It took over 100 years for someone to succeed. During that time, however, many other devices were invented that changed the global economy forever.*

Improvements in Technology

Since the time of the Crusades, Europeans had known about the riches of the East. Spices, silks, and jewels were prized as objects of trade because of their value. They came from the distant lands of India, China, and the islands of Southeast Asia. Traveling to and from these distant lands safely was essential if Europeans wished to compete with other traders. They began to focus on finding new sea routes to the East. To do this, Europeans needed better maps, navigation instruments, and ships. In short, they needed more advanced technology.

Mapmaking. Mapmaking improved during the Renaissance because of Europeans' growing interest in ancient geographers. Most scholars knew—as Ptolemy's maps had shown—that the world was round. During the Renaissance, information about Africa and Asia, unknown by Ptolemy, was added to his maps. The Americas, of course, were not yet known. Explorers believed that they could reach Asia more easily by sailing west across the Atlantic Ocean. Daring sea captains soon set out to find new trade routes to the East. Their discoveries opened whole new worlds to trade and settlement.

Navigation. Improved navigation instruments were just as important during this Age of Exploration as were more accurate maps. New navigation technology enabled ships to sail beyond sight of land without getting lost. One of the most important instruments to be developed during this time was the **compass.** In the 1100s, European navigators had learned that they could magnetize an iron needle. They rubbed the needle on a piece of lodestone—a kind of magnetic rock. When they floated the needle on water, it would point

INTERPRETING THE VISUAL RECORD

The Astronomer The Dutch artist Jan Vermeer, who worked during the 1600s, often showed his subjects in the midst of work activities. Vermeer's *The Astronomer* shows research and work connected to mapmaking. **What tools are being used by the astronomer to study the earth's surface?**

to the north. At some point during the 1200s or the 1300s, navigators created a true compass by fixing a magnetized needle to a card marked with directions.

New ships. If Europeans were to safely sail to the East, they needed better ships. Until well into the 1400s, long ships sometimes known as galleys were used by European sailors. These clumsy ships could sail using wind power only in the direction in which the wind blew. They sailed mostly along the coastlines. Sailors had to use long, heavy wooden oars to drive a galley against the prevailing winds.

In the late 1400s Spanish and Portuguese designers made important advances in ship-building technology. They built ships that were longer and larger than galleys. They also changed the size and shape of the sails. They moved the rudder—a steering device—from the side of the ship to its rear. These changes allowed ships to sail against the wind. Ships traveled more quickly and could be steered more easily. They could make way more reliably in different types of weather conditions, as well.

✔ **READING CHECK: Analyzing Information** Why did technological advances make sailors more able to explore distant lands?

Economic Changes

Improved ways of doing business also played an important part in new exploration. In some cases, banks added services to meet the needs of exploration. In other cases, Europeans changed basic economic practices. The changes were so great that many historians refer to the period between the late 1400s and the 1700s as the **Commercial Revolution.**

In many places in Europe before the 1300s and the 1400s, the value of coins could change depending on the amount of precious metal they contained. This changing value restricted European trade. Merchants and tradespeople needed a standard system of money.

As early as the mid to late 1200s, Italian cities were producing coins with fixed values. The gold florin of Florence and the ducat (DUHK·uht) of Venice were very dependable. This encouraged international trade and banking. In turn, banks could store large sums of money that they could lend governments or businesses wanting to explore overseas.

During the Commercial Revolution, individual merchants joined together into a new kind of business organization called a joint-stock company. Owners raised money by selling shares, or stock, in the company. Investors who bought the stock became co-owners and shared in the profits. The more shares they owned, the more of the profits they would receive. Joint-stock companies raised large sums of money from investors to finance exploration.

During the 1400s and 1500s, European monarchs supported exploration and colonization. Gaining riches through conquest and discovery would make them more powerful than rival countries. Although Italy had led the way in the Commercial Revolution, the Italians did not colonize. Instead, Portugal, Spain, and France built overseas empires. Trade shifted to these Atlantic nations.

✔ **READING CHECK: Identifying Cause and Effect** What effect did the standardization of money have on the ability of countries to trade?

The Astrolabe— An Early Guidance System

Sailors of the 1500s had only a few simple tools—such as the astrolabe—to guide them. Using the position of the sun and stars, these explorers sailed the oceans of the world. They could plot and hold a course and measure their progress. Of equal importance, they could estimate where they were with respect to land.

Astrolabes were usually made of brass or iron. A sailor would sight a star along the bar shown in the picture. By lining up the bar with markings on the disk, he could figure out the latitude of his ship's position. Astrolabes were used until the invention of more accurate instruments in the 1500s and 1600s.

Understanding Science and Technology

In addition to knowing distance north or south of the equator, what other information would a sailor need to know his exact position?

Lisbon Lisbon, capital of Portugal, was one of Europe's busiest seaports during the Age of Exploration. *How does this picture reflect Lisbon's role as a leading European trade center and sea power?*

Mercantilism

Economic and political changes linked to overseas expansion contributed to a new economic theory. **Mercantilism** stated that a country's government should do all it could to increase the country's wealth, which was measured by the amount of gold and silver the country possessed. According to this belief, the world contained a fixed amount of wealth. To increase its own wealth, one country had to take wealth from another country.

Balance of trade. According to mercantilists, a country could build wealth in two ways. It could mine gold and silver either at home or in its colonies. Or it could sell more goods than it bought from foreign countries, thus creating a favorable balance of trade. With a **favorable balance of trade,** a country received more gold and silver from other nations than it paid to them. This situation both strengthened the country and weakened its foreign rivals.

A favorable balance of trade was, therefore, the aim of many mercantilist countries. To achieve a favorable balance of trade, a country could do several things. First, it could reduce the amount of goods coming into it from other countries by placing **tariffs,** or import taxes, on these goods. The importer of a particular good paid the tariff and added that cost to the price of the good. The higher price discouraged people from buying it.

Second, a country could encourage exports. Manufactured goods, such as woolen cloth, were more valuable than raw materials, such as wool. Countries therefore encouraged manufacturing and the export of manufactured goods. They provided government **subsidies,** or grants of money, to help businesspeople start new industries and build ships.

Third, a country could work to gain and control overseas sources of raw materials and precious metals. A nation that controlled overseas sources of these goods would not need to import them from competing nations. Foreign countries were always considered rivals and might at any time become active enemies. The goal of winning overseas sources of materials helped fuel the race to gain colonies.

The role of colonies. Colonies played a major role in mercantilism. During the 1500s and after, European powers aimed to colonize overseas lands that were rich in gold, silver, and raw materials that could not be produced at home. A powerful nation sought to buy raw materials from its own colonies. That way, the country's wealth would remain with its own people. Most European colonial powers, moreover, forbid their colonies to sell raw materials to other countries. According to mercantilism, control of colonial markets and raw materials was key to a nation's success.

People in the home country's colonies provided strong markets for its manufactured goods. Governments passed strict laws that forbade colonies from buying foreign goods. In many cases, moreover, colonies were not allowed to manufacture goods. This forced colonies to buy manufactured goods only from their home country. Mercantilists argued that such laws were justified because colonies existed to benefit the home country.

✔ **READING CHECK: Finding the Main Idea** What was the overall aim of mercantilism?

Social Change

Advances in navigation and government economic policies by themselves did not lead to European exploration and overseas colonization. Certain social changes also helped create in people the desire to explore and resettle.

For one thing, the Renaissance and the Scientific Revolution had created a desire among many Europeans to learn more about the world and had added to the general store of geographic knowledge. Thus, simple curiosity and a spirit of discovery moved many people to explore the world outside Europe.

After the year 1500, moreover, the population of Europe increased. Some urban areas became very crowded. Adventurous people knew that overseas colonies might offer harsh living conditions. Some people were willing to accept these hardships, however, in return for the opportunity to gain land and possible wealth by settling in overseas colonies.

Other people went overseas hoping to reap quick profits. Tales of gold and silver and precious jewels—as well as fertile soil—persuaded thousands that easy wealth lay overseas. A few even went in search of fabulous cities with enormous riches, such as the legendary El Dorado (which means "the gilded one" in Spanish) in South America.

Finally, the Reformation and Counter-Reformation had led to the religious and political persecution of many. French Huguenots and others went overseas to seek religious freedom for themselves and to escape persecution at home. Some Christians went to spread their religion to non-Europeans.

In many cases, there was no single reason that motivated a person or group of people to explore or colonize. Rather, a combination of these hopes and aims led Europeans to leave their old lives for new and, to them, unknown lands.

✔ **READING CHECK: Summarizing** Why were some Europeans willing to explore and colonize distant lands?

Gold and cinnamon were highly sought-after trade goods.

DAILY LIFE

The New Commercial Economy

World exploration led to a new kind of economy in Europe. Goods brought from Africa, Asia, and the New World made many countries in Europe rich. Spices, silks, gold, silver, and precious stones were some of the most sought-after items.

The Portuguese, Spanish, and Dutch were the first European powers to build trading empires. Trade and commerce eventually replaced farming as the leading economic activity in Europe. Over time, the new commercial economy generally helped to spread wealth and improve living standards.

How did European countries benefit from the changes of the Commercial Revolution?

SECTION 2 REVIEW

1. Define and explain the significance:
compass
joint-stock company
mercantilism
favorable balance of trade
tariffs
subsidies

2. Identify and explain the significance:
Commercial Revolution

3. Summarizing Copy the table below. Fill in the ways in which each factor influenced exploration and colonization.

Factors	Influence on Exploration and Colonization
Technological Advances	
Economic Changes	
Mercantilism	
Social Changes	

4. **Finding the Main Idea**

a. Why were technological developments necessary before nations could begin exploration and colonization?

b. How did trade laws that limited colonies' economic freedom support the idea of mercantilism?

5. **Writing and Critical Thinking**

Supporting a Point of View Imagine you are living in the 1500s. Write a letter to a relative explaining why you will or will not leave Europe to settle in a colony.

Consider:
• what conditions are like in your home country
• what you might gain or lose by traveling to a distant land

Homework Practice Online
keyword: SH3 HP7

Voyages of Portugal and Spain

READ TO DISCOVER

1 What did early Portuguese explorers accomplish?
2 How did the voyages of Christopher Columbus influence the world?
3 Why did the Atlantic slave trade prosper?

DEFINE

triangular trade

IDENTIFY

Prince Henry
Bartolomeu Dias
Vasco da Gama
Christopher Columbus
Columbian Exchange
Treaty of Tordesillas
Amerigo Vespucci
Ferdinand Magellan
Middle Passage

▶ WHY IT MATTERS TODAY

People have always been interested in exploring what is beyond their present environment. Use CNN News.com or other **current event** sources to discover what kind of exploration is going on today. Record your findings in your journal.

CNNstudentNews.com

The Main Idea
Voyages sponsored by the Portuguese and Spanish led to new colonies and to the Atlantic slave trade.

The Story Continues *Life aboard a trading ship could be very difficult. "[Four galleys] were away three years, but only one galley returned and even on that galley most of the crew had died," one eyewitness recalled. "And those which survived could hardly be recognized as human." Despite such experiences, numerous sailors made voyages in search of riches for themselves and their countries.*

Portugal's First Explorers

Portuguese and Spanish explorers made the first European voyages into unknown waters. Curiosity, religion, and economic goals drove these courageous men forward. Their voyages resulted in great advances for the sponsoring governments and served as the foundation for future empires.

One man largely responsible for Portugal's interest in exploration was **Prince Henry** of the Portuguese royal family. Also known as "The Navigator," Prince Henry's first goal was to find gold for Portugal. The Portuguese also hoped to find a way to the rich spice trade of the Indies and to spread the Christian faith.

Henry gathered many of Europe's best geographers and navigators to plan expeditions. By about 1420 or earlier his navigators were exploring westward into the Atlantic, and by the 1430s they were moving southward along the west coast of Africa. These explorations taught navigators about currents, wind patterns, and climates, knowledge they needed as they ventured farther from home. Henry's explorers claimed the Azores for Portugal. In Africa, they began to trade for slaves, gold, and ivory.

The success of these early voyages of discovery and exploration created great excitement throughout Europe. Success encouraged more voyages. In 1488 **Bartolomeu Dias** sailed around the Cape of Good Hope at the southern tip of Africa. Although Dias had to turn back, he had found the route to the Indian Ocean.

Using this knowledge, **Vasco da Gama** sailed eastward across the Indian Ocean. He landed in India in 1498. Several years later, da Gama made a second voyage to India. He returned to Portugal, his ships full of valuable goods.

Thanks to Dias and da Gama, an overseas trade route from Europe to India and the East Indies was now available. Rich cargoes of spices and jewels arrived in Portugal. This direct ocean route saved the Portuguese from having to deal with middlemen traders. Now, the Portuguese could journey directly to the sources of the trade goods they sought. In many cases, too, ships could carry goods more cheaply than could overland caravans. Nor could Portuguese merchants be blocked or charged high tolls by competing powers that controlled overland routes. Overseas trade promised wealth for merchants and sailors and goods for Europe's markets.

READING CHECK: Summarizing What did the Portuguese gain from the voyages of their early explorers?

Christopher Columbus

Spain, too, became interested in the search for new trade routes. A Genoan navigator named **Christopher Columbus** had studied the writings of Marco Polo and Ptolemy's description of a round Earth. Columbus believed that a shorter route to Asia could be found by sailing westward instead of sailing around the tip of Africa. King Ferdinand and Queen Isabella of Spain agreed to finance Columbus's voyage of exploration.

In August 1492, Columbus set sail from Palos, Spain. His three small ships—the *Niña*, the *Pinta*, and the *Santa María*—sailed westward across the Atlantic. On October 12, 1492, the small fleet landed at a tiny island that Columbus named San Salvador. It was a historic moment when Columbus and his captains planted the Spanish flag. Columbus claimed the land that he had reached for Spain. Later, in reporting his discovery, Columbus wrote:

❝It appears to me that the people [the Native Americans who met Columbus] are ingenious [clever], and would be good servants and I am of the opinion that they would very readily become Christians, as they appear to have no religion. They very quickly learn such words as are spoken to them.❞

Christopher Columbus, extracts from journal, quoted in *Internet Medieval Source Book,* by Paul Halsall

After exploring other islands in the area Columbus returned triumphantly to Spain in 1493. Columbus believed the islands he had found lay off the east coast of India. Thus, he called them the Indies and their inhabitants Indians. However, Columbus had actually discovered islands in the Americas. They later became known as the West Indies. Between 1493 and 1504, Columbus made three more voyages to the "Indies." For the rest of his life, he believed that he had landed off the coast of Asia.

There was a major difference between the Portuguese explorers and Columbus. The Portuguese already knew that the lands they sailed to existed. Earlier people had written of their journeys between Europe and Asia and Europe and Africa. Columbus believed he was traveling to one of these lands by a different route. Earlier Viking voyages to the Americas were unknown. When Columbus stepped ashore in what is now the Bahamas, he stepped on land that was altogether new and unknown to Europeans.

✔ **READING CHECK: Finding the Main Idea** What significant event happened in 1492?

HISTORY MAKER

Queen Isabella (1451–1504)

Queen Isabella was one of Spain's greatest rulers. Her court was a center of learning and culture. With her husband, Ferdinand, she also helped to unify Spain.

Isabella approved the voyage of Christopher Columbus to India. Columbus found the New World and the great Spanish empire in the Americas was born. **What important events took place during Isabella's rule?**

Holt Researcher

go.hrw.com
KEYWORD: Holt Researcher
FreeFind:
    Isabella
    Christopher Columbus
After reading more about Isabella and Columbus on the Holt Researcher, create a Venn diagram that shows the similarities and differences in their beliefs about the lands and people Columbus encountered.

The effects of the Columbian Exchange are still felt today. For example, diet on both sides of the Atlantic changed. Potatoes from the Andes now feed millions of people in Europe. Corn, first grown by Native Americans, is a staple around the world today. Wheat was not grown in the Americas until it was brought there by Europeans. The tomato first grew not in Italy, but in the Americas.

Horses, cattle, goats, sheep, and other animals crossed the Atlantic with Europeans. North America, in exchange, gave Europe and Asia the turkey, the gray squirrel, and the muskrat.

Understanding Geography

What elements of the Columbian Exchange can you identify in your area?

The Impact of Columbus's Voyages

In the years following Columbus's voyages, a massive exchange took place between the so-called New World and the Old World of Europe. This interaction is often called the **Columbian Exchange.** Products, plants, animals, and even diseases traveled between the Western and Eastern Hemispheres. For example, gold and silver mined in South America were shipped eastward to Spain. This helped Spain become a major world power.

The exchange affected the way people in both worlds lived. American foods such as potatoes, tomatoes, beans, and corn were introduced in Europe. The Spanish brought horses to the Americas, thus changing the lifestyles of many Native American groups forever. This was especially true in areas such as the Great Plains.

Not everything the Columbian Exchange brought to the New World was helpful. European sailors carried smallpox and other diseases westward. The native population of Spanish America had no immunity to these diseases and millions died.

✔ **READING CHECK: Drawing Conclusions** Who benefited most—Europeans or Native Americans—from the Columbian Exchange? Why?

Dividing the New Lands

During the late 1400s Spain and Portugal—Europe's most active seagoing explorers—often claimed the same newly discovered lands. To settle these conflicts, Pope Alexander VI issued an edict in 1493. The Pope's edict drew an imaginary line from north to south through the middle of the Atlantic Ocean. Alexander gave Spain the rights to all newly discovered lands west of the line. Portugal could claim discoveries east of the line. Neither country, however, could take lands already held or claimed by another Christian ruler.

A year later, the **Treaty of Tordesillas** between Spain and Portugal moved the line farther west. This soon had an important impact. In 1500 the Portuguese navigator Pedro Cabral set sail westward for India. Cabral's tiny fleet of 13 ships was blown off course, and the Portuguese made landfall on the coast of what is now Brazil. Under the Treaty of Tordesillas, Cabral was able to claim this incredibly rich land for Portugal.

Over time, Spain took control of most of Central and South America. The Spanish also claimed the Philippines. In addition to the Brazilian coast, Portugal claimed lands on the eastern and western coasts of Africa. The Portuguese also claimed lands in Asia and the East Indies.

✔ **READING CHECK: Identifying a Point of View** How might the right of Spain and Portugal to claim lands not already occupied by Christians have been viewed by the people of those lands?

Vespucci, Balboa, and Magellan

Other European explorers followed Columbus westward. **Amerigo Vespucci** was an Italian navigator. Between 1497 and 1504, he crossed the Atlantic several times as part of Spanish and Portuguese expeditions. Unlike others, Vespucci did not think the land he saw was part of Asia. He called it a New World. A German mapmaker, impressed with Amerigo's argument, called the land America after Vespucci.

In 1513 Vasco Núñez de Balboa of Spain made an overland crossing of the Isthmus of Panama. Reaching a vast ocean, he named it the South Sea and claimed it for Spain. Balboa's discovery made it clear that the New World was not part of Asia.

Ferdinand Magellan, a Portuguese navigator sailing for Spain, proved Balboa was correct. In 1519 he set out from Spain with five ships to cross the Atlantic to South America. The ships sailed along its eastern shore until they reached the southernmost tip. After passing through the strait now named for him, Magellan found himself in a great ocean. He named it the Pacific Ocean because it was so calm. In Latin the word *pacificus* means "peaceful." This was Balboa's "South Sea."

Magellan sailed westward across the Pacific. He reached the Philippine Islands and died there in 1521 in a fight with the islanders. His crew, led by one of his officers, sailed on. In 1522 one ship and 18 crew members returned to Spain. They had made the first round-the-world voyage.

✔ **READING CHECK: Making Generalizations** What did Vespucci, Balboa, and Magellan contribute to Europeans' knowledge of the world?

HISTORY MAKER

**Ferdinand Magellan
(c. 1480–1521)**

Ferdinand Magellan became a page in the Portuguese court at a youthful age. Over time, he grew to become an experienced navigator and sailor.

Magellan became convinced that he could reach the Spice Islands in East Asia by sailing west. The circumnavigation of the globe by his fleet was not only a great achievement of navigation and courage; it also proved to the people of Europe that the world was round. **What was the outcome of Magellan's voyage?**

Portuguese Expansion

After the voyages of Dias and da Gama, the Portuguese dreamed of controlling trade with Asia. In about 1510 they conquered part of the southwest coast of India. The port of Goa (GOH·uh) became their administrative center. From India they moved on to the East Indies. They conquered Malacca (muh·LAK·uh) on the southwest coast of the Malay Peninsula and the Moluccas (muh·LUKH·uhz), a group of islands. Europeans called them the Spice Islands because of their large crops of valuable spices.

Next, the Portuguese added the island of Ceylon—now Sri Lanka—to their chain of trading bases. Ceylon was in a key location between Goa and Malacca. With its tea and spices, Ceylon helped the Portuguese control trade with the East Indies. The Portuguese also gained footholds in China and Japan. Finally, they established several armed trading posts on the East African coast. The Portuguese also established a colony in Brazil where they built huge agriculture estates.

✔ **READING CHECK: Drawing Inferences** Why did the trading posts set up by the Portuguese allow them to control trade with the East?

The Slave Trade

As they did in Asia, the Portuguese went to Africa to trade. At first, they maintained friendly relations with the Africans. Christian missionaries wanted to convert the continent's residents. Friendly relations soon collapsed, however, as the economic interests of the Portuguese—in gold and, over time, in slaves—became obvious.

Despite the fact that Europeans themselves had been slaves in the Byzantine, Arab, and Turkish empires, during the 1500s they began to use slave labor in their own overseas empires. Europeans tried enslaving Native Americans, but the system did not work well due to the devastation of the Native American population caused by disease and the difficulties of enslaving people in their own land. Instead, the Europeans began to rely more heavily on enslaved Africans.

The slave trade grew quickly when the Portuguese set up sugar plantations on islands off the coast of Africa. To make a profit, large numbers of slaves were required. Plantation owners got these slaves from the African mainland. Later, the Dutch, English, and French also became active in the slave trade. By the early 1600s the slave trade was the chief focus of European relations with Africa.

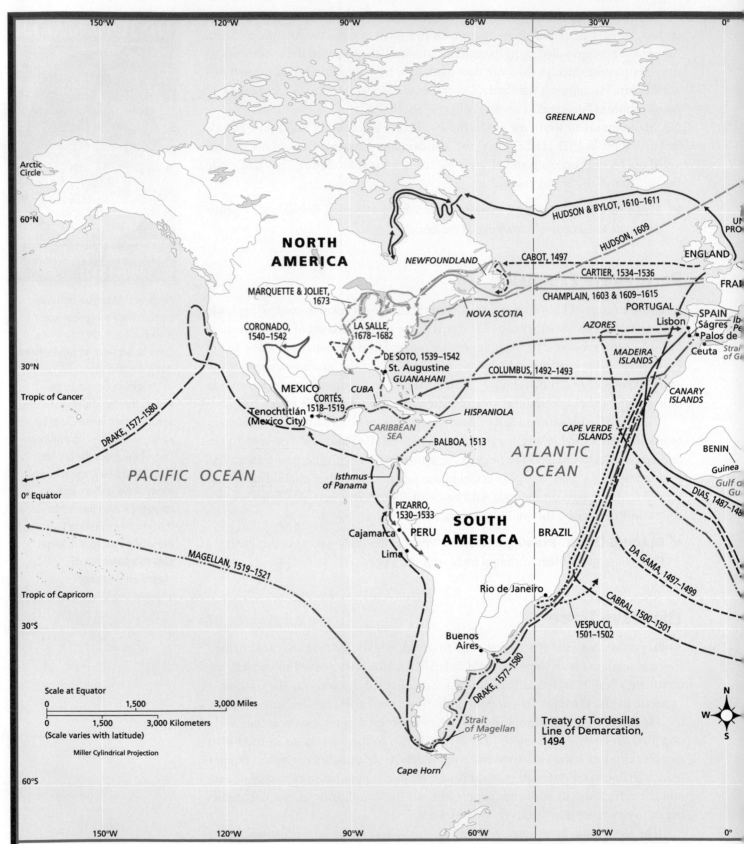

Map labels:

GREENLAND

Arctic Circle

60°N

NORTH AMERICA

HUDSON & BYLOT, 1610–1611
HUDSON, 1609
NEWFOUNDLAND
CABOT, 1497
CARTIER, 1534–1536
CHAMPLAIN, 1603 & 1609–1615
NOVA SCOTIA
ENGLAND
UN PRO
FRA

MARQUETTE & JOLIET, 1673
LA SALLE, 1678–1682
CORONADO, 1540–1542
DE SOTO, 1539–1542
St. Augustine
GUANAHANI
MEXICO
CORTÉS, 1518–1519
Tenochtitlán (Mexico City)
CUBA
HISPANIOLA
CARIBBEAN SEA
BALBOA, 1513
COLUMBUS, 1492–1493
PORTUGAL
SPAIN
Lisbon
Ságres
Palos de
Ceuta
AZORES
MADEIRA ISLANDS
CANARY ISLANDS
Ib Pe
Stra of G

30°N
Tropic of Cancer

DRAKE, 1577–1580

PACIFIC OCEAN

0° Equator

Isthmus of Panama

CAPE VERDE ISLANDS
ATLANTIC OCEAN
BENIN
Guinea
Gulf o Gu
DIAS, 1487–148

PIZARRO, 1530–1533
Cajamarca
PERU
Lima
SOUTH AMERICA
BRAZIL
DA GAMA, 1497–1499

MAGELLAN, 1519–1521

Tropic of Capricorn

30°S

Rio de Janeiro
CABRAL, 1500–1501
VESPUCCI, 1501–1502

Buenos Aires

DRAKE, 1577–1580

Scale at Equator
0   1,500   3,000 Miles
0   1,500   3,000 Kilometers
(Scale varies with latitude)
Miller Cylindrical Projection

Strait of Magellan

Treaty of Tordesillas Line of Demarcation, 1494

N
W   E
S

60°S

Cape Horn

150°W   120°W   90°W   60°W   30°W   0°

European Explorations, 1487–1682

Interpreting Maps The map shows the routes taken by Portuguese, Spanish, French, English, and Dutch explorers. They sailed both east and west to discover new lands.

Map Legend

- → Portuguese exploration
- → Spanish exploration
- → French exploration
- → English exploration
- → Dutch exploration

30°E 60°E 90°E 120°E 150°E 180°

EUROPE

ASIA

Arctic Circle

60°N

CHINA

JAPAN

30°N

Hormuz

Arabian Peninsula

INDIA

Diu

Tropic of Cancer

PACIFIC OCEAN

Calicut
Cochin

DA GAMA, 1497–1499

Strait of Malacca

PHILIPPINES

CEYLON

Malacca

MOLUCCAS (SPICE ISLANDS)

DRAKE, 1577–1580

ICA

CABRAL, 1500–1501

BORNEO

EAST INDIES

0° Equator

MAGELLAN, 1519–1521

Malindi
Mombasa

SUMATRA

INDIAN OCEAN

JAVA

Batavia

TASMAN, 1642–1643

TASMAN, 1642–1643

Tropic of Capricorn

DRAKE, 1577–1580

TASMAN, 1644

AUSTRALIA

e of
d Hope

1497–1499

ELCANO, 1521–1522

30°S

DA GAMA,

TASMAN, 1642–1643

Treaty of Tordesillas
Line of Demarcation,
1494

60°S

30°E 60°E 90°E 120°E 150°E 180°

■ **Skills Assessment: Human Systems** According to the map, what explorer duplicated Magellan's circumnavigation of the globe, and what nation did he represent?

Slave ships This sketch shows a diagram of slaves in the hold of a ship. Slaves were positioned below decks in such a way as to fit as many as possible on the ship. This helped to ensure a profitable voyage. *What does this diagram indicate about conditions on board a typical slave ship?*

Triangular trade. Slave trade in the Atlantic was part of a system known as the **triangular trade.** First, merchants shipped cotton goods, weapons, and liquor to Africa in exchange for slaves or gold. The second stage—called the **Middle Passage**—was the shipment of slaves across the Atlantic to the Americas. There, slaves were sold for goods produced on the plantations. To complete the triangle, merchants sent the plantations' products to Europe. They were used to buy manufactured products to be sold in the Americas.

The Middle Passage was brutal and degrading. Traders chained the slaves in the crowded hold of the ship. This stopped slaves from jumping overboard or causing trouble aboard ship. Slaves had little food or water and no sanitary facilities. Many died before reaching their destination.

At the height of the trade in the years between the mid-1700s and the early 1800s, European slave ships carried thousands of slaves each year. It has been estimated that some 10 million Africans survived the horrible journey to slavery in the Americas. Many perished during the horrible journey of the Middle Passage. Others died even earlier, on the hard trip from the African interior to slave ships on the coast.

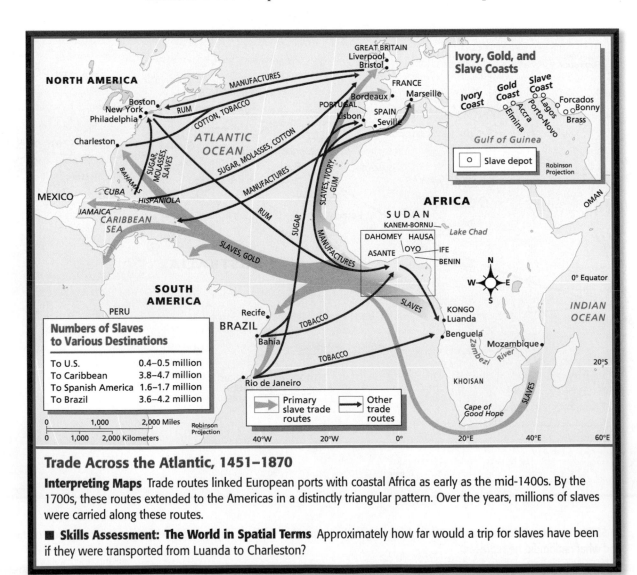

Trade Across the Atlantic, 1451–1870

Interpreting Maps Trade routes linked European ports with coastal Africa as early as the mid-1400s. By the 1700s, these routes extended to the Americas in a distinctly triangular pattern. Over the years, millions of slaves were carried along these routes.

■ **Skills Assessment: The World in Spatial Terms** Approximately how far would a trip for slaves have been if they were transported from Luanda to Charleston?

African kingdoms and slavery. During the 1400s and the 1500s, strong states began to rise in West Africa. Some of these kingdoms profited from the slave trade. Not all African states participated in the slave trade with Europeans. Many African societies, however, had practiced slavery well before the Europeans' arrival. Slaves were sometimes taken in war or during raids on neighboring groups. In some traditional African societies, slaves might be allowed to gain their freedom. Generally, they played a distinct role in society. Europeans, on the other hand, considered slaves as property to be bought and sold for profit.

Some Africans who lived in the interior helped the Europeans capture and move slaves. In return they received European-made arms and other goods. Neighboring groups either had to participate or be taken as slaves. During the years of the slave trade, native populations in some parts of Africa were greatly reduced. As demands for slaves increased, population losses had disastrous effects on Africa's development and progress.

✔ **READING CHECK: Supporting a Point of View** In what ways can you support the view that the slave trade slowed the development of the African continent?

The Portuguese Empire Weakens

The great Portuguese empire declined almost as rapidly as it had grown. The Portuguese government did not have the financial wealth to support so large an empire. Thousands of soldiers and sailors were needed to maintain and expand the empire, but many never returned from overseas. Shipwrecks and battles with enemies cost both money and lives. With its small population, Portugal could not replace the losses it suffered as a result of exploration and colonization.

Finally in 1580 Spain annexed Portugal. Portugal did not regain its independence until 1640. Under Spanish control, Portugal's trade was greatly restricted and its overseas colonies were neglected. Only Brazil and Angola survived as major Portuguese colonies.

✔ **READING CHECK: Drawing Conclusions** How did the relative size of Portugal and Spain influence their success in expansion and colonization?

SECTION 3 REVIEW

1. **Define** and explain the significance: triangular trade

2. **Identify** and explain the significance:
   Prince Henry
   Bartolomeu Dias
   Vasco da Gama
   Christopher Columbus
   Columbian Exchange
   Treaty of Tordesillas
   Amerigo Vespucci
   Ferdinand Magellan
   Middle Passage

3. **Analyzing Information** Copy the diagram below. Between each of the boxes, show the direction of trade in the triangular exchange and what type of cargo the ships carried.

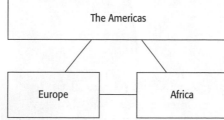

4. **Finding the Main Idea**
   a. Sequence the important discoveries of the explorers listed in question 2.
   b. What do you think might have happened on the African continent if the European slave trade had not taken place?

5. **Writing and Critical Thinking**
   Comparing and Contrasting Write a paragraph pointing out the positive and negative effects of the explorations of the Spanish and Portuguese.
   Consider:
   • the economic benefits to both countries
   • the effects on human life and populations

Homework Practice Online
keyword: SH3 HP7
go.
hrw
.com

DEFINE

viceroys
guerrilla warfare

IDENTIFY

Ponce de León
Hernán Cortés
Moctezuma II
Francisco Pizarro
Charles V
Philip II
William of Orange

WHY IT MATTERS TODAY

Two ways that nations increase their land are conquest and colonization. Use 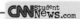 or other **current event** sources to find examples of both processes going on today. Record your findings in your journal.

CNN student News.com

The Spanish and Dutch Empires

The Main Idea
Spain created an empire in the Americas, while the Dutch set up trading colonies in Asia and the Americas.

The Story Continues *As Spanish explorers spread into the Americas, they came ready to conquer. "Some of them were dressed in glistening iron from head to foot," wrote one observer. "They terrified everyone who saw them." Their tactics established a powerful empire for Spain.*

Spain's Colonial Empire

Throughout the 1500s Spain was the most powerful nation in Europe, with the largest overseas empire. While Portugal focused mainly on Africa and Asia, Spain turned to the Americas. Beginning with Columbus, Spaniards explored the West Indies, Central America, and parts of North and South America. At first, they believed these lands were in the East Indies. However, the natural resources of the Americas provided riches other than spices and jewels.

Spanish explorers sailed outward from the Caribbean to the North American mainland. In 1513 **Ponce de León** sailed northward to what is now Florida. A later voyage to Florida in 1528, led by Pánfilo de Narváez, ended in disaster and shipwreck. A handful of survivors from this tragic voyage traveled overland across what is now the southwestern United States and Mexico. Their travels opened even more land to Spanish claims and settlement.

Conquests. Other Spanish explorers went to the Yucatán in Mexico. There they learned of the great Maya and Aztec civilizations. In 1519, with 11 ships and about 600 men, **Hernán Cortés** invaded Mexico. He seized the Aztec ruler **Moctezuma II,** also known as Montezuma. Cortés captured and destroyed the great Aztec city of Tenochtitlán. The Spanish later built Mexico City on its ruins. Spanish horses and guns, unknown in the Americas, helped the Spanish defeat the great Aztec armies, as did a smallpox epidemic that swept through the Aztecs.

INTERPRETING THE VISUAL RECORD

Cortés Hernán Cortés, at the head of about 600 Spanish soldiers, carved out a huge empire in Mexico and plundered the mighty Aztec civilization. Cortés is pictured here capturing the Aztec ruler Moctezuma II. *According to this picture, what advantages did the Spanish have over the Aztec?*

The Spanish also found rich civilizations in South America. In 1530 **Francisco Pizarro** led 180 men and 37 horses on an expedition. They traveled from the Isthmus of Panama to the capital of the Inca Empire in what is now Peru. In 1533 Pizarro claimed the land from present-day Ecuador to Chile for Spain.

Cortés and Pizarro destroyed many Aztec and Inca statues and temples. The gold and silver from these religious objects and buildings made the explorers and the Spanish treasury wealthy.

In time Spain controlled the West Indies, southern and western North America, Central America, and much of South America. Unlike Europeans in Africa and Asia, the Spanish established settlements throughout their vast empire.

Colonial government and society. Spain directed the colonial government. Officials called **viceroys** represented the monarchy in the colonies and reported to the Council of the Indies in Spain. The council planned and directed the empire's growth on behalf of the Spanish crown.

For a time, the colonies produced enormous wealth for Spain. There were rich silver mines in the regions that are now Peru and northern Mexico. Agriculture and trade remained important, but mineral resources were the main assets of Spain's colonies.

European diseases such as smallpox, typhus, and measles weakened the Native American societies conquered by Cortés and Pizarro. From what is now the southwestern United States through Mexico and much of Central America, millions of Native Americans died. Whole cultures that had lived and thrived for centuries were wiped out or broken up in a matter of a relatively few years. Exact losses cannot be accurately determined, but many historians believe that the numbers were enormous. This tragic outcome of expansion and colonization also promoted the growth of slavery. The Spaniards needed workers for mines and farms in the New World. To make up for the loss of native labor, they imported slaves from Africa.

✔ **READING CHECK: Analyzing Information** What were some of the factors that allowed so few Europeans to conquer large numbers of peoples in the Americas?

INTERPRETING THE VISUAL RECORD

Pizarro Francisco Pizarro and a handful of Spanish conquistadores overthrew the mighty Inca Empire of Peru. Here, Pizarro is shown refusing mercy to Atahualpa, the last emperor of the Inca. *What visual technique has the artist used to depict Pizarro's dominance in this scene?*

Spain's Colonial Rivals

The Spanish government wanted to keep the wealth of the Americas to themselves. They made laws keeping foreigners out of the Spanish colonies. Only Spanish ships could carry gold and silver out of the Americas.

Making laws, however, was easier than enforcing them. The French, Dutch, and English envied Spain's American wealth. They tried various methods to capture a share of it. They traded in Spanish American ports, their monarchs encouraged pirates to attack Spanish ships, and pirates raided Spanish towns.

Spain's rivals also tried to establish colonies in the Americas, ignoring Pope Alexander's line down the middle of the ocean. Despite their efforts, these rival countries had only limited success before 1600.

✔ **READING CHECK: Making Predictions** What did Spain's rivals hope to gain by having pirates attack Spanish ships and colonial towns?

Charles V

While their explorers were expanding the empire abroad, Spanish kings expanded their authority in Spain itself. One of the greatest of these kings was **Charles V.** Charles was a member of the Habsburgs, an old German family. Charles took the Spanish throne in 1516. Three years later he was elected Holy Roman Emperor.

With Charles's titles and power, he was torn between conflicting demands. As king of Spain, he had to adopt a Spanish viewpoint. As Holy Roman Emperor, he was expected to support German aims. Finally, as the political leader of Christian Europe, Charles had to defend Europe against the Ottoman Turks.

The nearly continuous religious wars during Charles's reign drained Spain's human resources and treasury. Spain lacked industries and the government did little to promote them. So much of Spain's land was devoted to raising sheep for wool that the country could not produce enough food to feed its people. Food prices increased many times over between 1500 and 1650.

Charles realized that the Spanish and Holy Roman empires had become too large for one man to rule. In 1556 he gave up his throne and divided the vast lands among members of his family. Charles's son **Philip II** received Spain and its possessions. His branch of the family became known as the Spanish Habsburgs. Charles's brother Ferdinand I was already king of Hungary and Bohemia. Now he became Holy Roman Emperor and head of the Austrian Habsburgs.

King Philip II of Spain personally managed the daily operations of the royal government.

✔**READING CHECK: Finding the Main Idea** What were some of the factors that led Charles to split up his lands?

Philip II

Unlike his father, Philip II was born and educated in Spain. He ruled from 1556 until his death in 1598. Philip was a dedicated monarch who worked long hours at being king. His goal was to strengthen Spain's hold as Europe's leading power. Philip built a new royal residence, El Escorial, 25 miles from Madrid. From there he took control of every facet of government. This nearly paralyzed his administration. Philip also saw himself as the leader of the Counter-Reformation. A very devout Catholic, he ordered the Spanish Inquisition to stamp out heresy at home. Abroad, Philip involved Spain in wars to defend Catholicism and bring glory to Spain. These efforts were so costly that taxes could never keep up with expenses. As bankers charged more and more interest on loans to Spain, the country's financial woes increased.

Although Philip was unable to defeat all the enemies of Spain and Catholicism, he did manage to defeat the Ottoman Empire in the Mediterranean. His attempted invasion of Protestant England by the huge Spanish Armada in 1588, however, ended in disaster. An attempt to invade France to prevent a Protestant from becoming king was also an expensive failure. Yet these setbacks were not the costliest errors in Philip's policy making.

✔ **READING CHECK: Drawing Inferences** Why might the kind of control that Philip exerted over his government paralyze his administration?

The Rise of the Dutch

Philip II's most costly policies were those toward the Netherlands, one of Europe's great trading centers since the Middle Ages. Philip had inherited the Netherlands. Because Calvinism was becoming popular in the area, Philip treated his Dutch subjects harshly. First, he ignored the Netherlands' long tradition of self-rule. He insisted that he, rather than the local nobles, held all authority. Second, he taxed Dutch trade heavily to pay for Spanish wars. Third, he persecuted the Calvinists. These actions turned the people's distrust of Philip to outright rebellion.

The Netherlands break from Spain. In 1568 **William of Orange** led a revolt against Philip. The people of the Calvinist northern provinces lived on land below sea level. Large dikes protected the land. The people opened the dikes, flooding the countryside and leaving Philip's army helpless. William sent small bands of soldiers on quick raids to keep the Spanish army confused. Today this military technique is called **guerrilla warfare.**

In 1579 under William's leadership, the northern provinces declared their independence from Spain. William was killed in 1584, but his descendants continued the war with Spain on and off until 1648. The southern provinces were heavily Catholic and remained under Spanish control as the Spanish Netherlands.

Dutch society. Because the Netherlands lay on the North Sea, the Dutch were a seafaring people. They built very efficient ships and were expert sailors. For these reasons, they ruled European commerce throughout the 1600s. Their ships carried most of Europe's trade and the city of Amsterdam became a world financial center. All segments of Dutch business stood as models of efficiency.

Calvinists became the dominant religious group in the Netherlands. Generally, however, the Dutch followed policies of religious tolerance. Amsterdam became a lively cultural center. Scholars such as René Descartes and artists such as Rembrandt and Vermeer thrived in this comfortable setting.

The Dutch colonial empire. In 1602 the Dutch East India Company was founded. It had total control over trading between the Netherlands and the East Indies. The first Dutch overseas colony was founded on the island of Java in 1619. The Dutch took over the entire island, with its valuable crops of sugar, tea, coffee, and spices. From Java, they expanded westward to Sumatra and eastward to the Spice Islands. Their colony at the Cape of Good Hope allowed them to supply and protect their trade routes to Asia.

The Dutch also gained a foothold in Japan. Because the Dutch did not come as missionaries, the Japanese allowed them to open a trading center in Nagasaki. In the Western Hemisphere the Dutch established colonies in the West Indies, South America, and North America. In 1626 they purchased Manhattan Island from the Native Americans and built the city of New Amsterdam there.

The Dutch colonial empire was much different from that of the Spanish. The Dutch never tried to convert conquered peoples to Christianity. They did not force them to speak Dutch or live under the laws of the Netherlands. The Dutch came as traders, with the sole intention of making money. This goal reflected their businesslike society.

✔ **READING CHECK: Drawing Inferences** In what ways did the Dutch gain access to trading opportunities that other countries had missed?

CONNECTING TO
Art

Painting:
Young Woman with Water Jug

In the 1600s the economy of the Netherlands prospered. Dutch merchants grew rich enough to buy handsome silks and linens for their wives. Some commissioned artists to paint for them. Dutch artists such as Rembrandt and Vermeer flourished. This painting, one of Vermeer's finest works, gives us a close look at Dutch daily life.

Understanding the Arts

What does this painting tell us about life in the Netherlands in the 1600s?

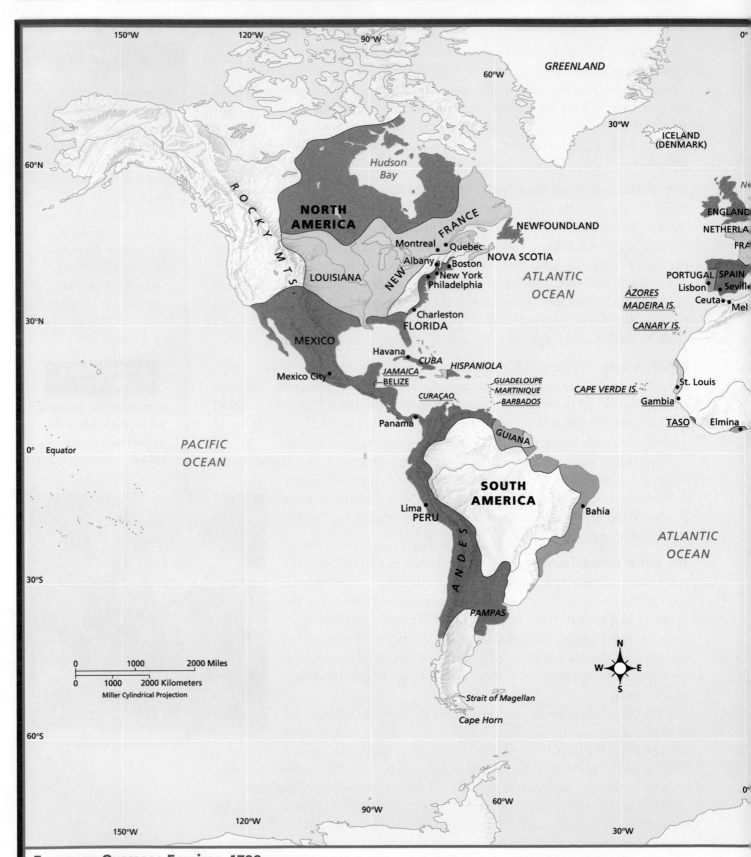

European Overseas Empires, 1700

Interpreting Maps The map shows the territories around the globe that were held by European countries in 1700.

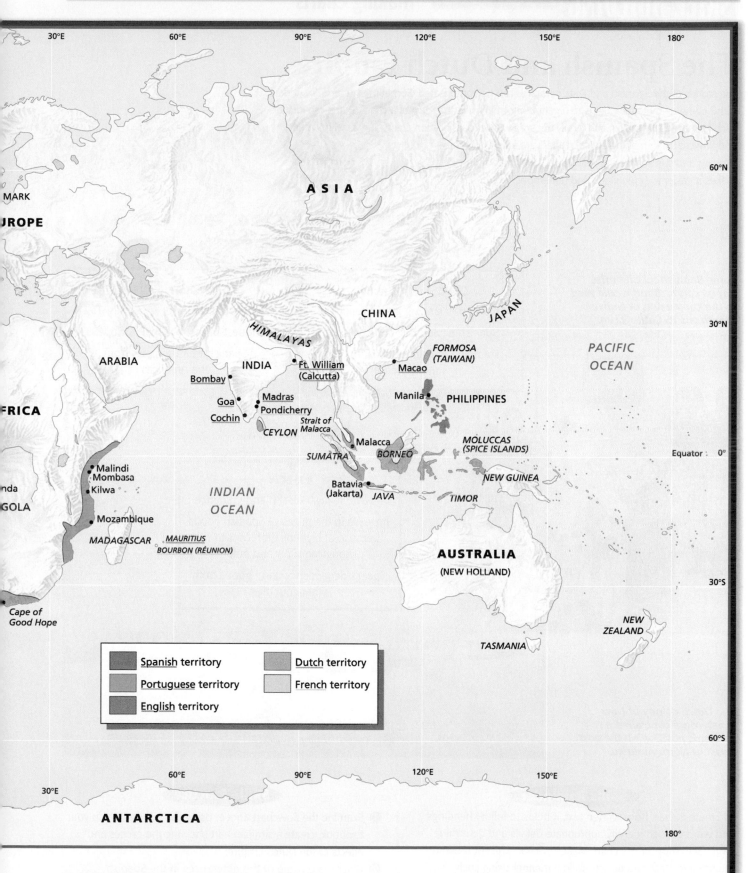

| 30°E | 60°E | 90°E | 120°E | 150°E | 180° |

60°N

ASIA

MARK

UROPE

30°N

ARABIA

INDIA

CHINA

HIMALAYAS

JAPAN

FORMOSA (TAIWAN)

PACIFIC OCEAN

Ft. William (Calcutta)

Bombay

Macao

Goa

Madras

Pondicherry

Cochin

Manila

PHILIPPINES

CEYLON

Strait of Malacca

Malacca

MOLUCCAS (SPICE ISLANDS)

Equator 0°

AFRICA

SUMATRA

BORNEO

nda

Malindi

Mombasa

Kilwa

NEW GUINEA

GOLA

INDIAN OCEAN

Batavia (Jakarta)

JAVA

TIMOR

Mozambique

MADAGASCAR

MAURITIUS

BOURBON (RÉUNION)

AUSTRALIA (NEW HOLLAND)

30°S

Cape of Good Hope

NEW ZEALAND

TASMANIA

60°S

	Spanish territory		Dutch territory
	Portuguese territory		French territory
	English territory		

| 60°E | 90°E | 120°E | 150°E |

30°E

ANTARCTICA

180°

■ **Skills Assessment: The World in Spatial Terms** What patterns can you identify regarding the distribution of European colonies in 1700?

The Spanish and Dutch Empires

The stories of the Spanish and Dutch empires can be complicated. Sometimes in order to understand complex material it helps to organize information in the form of a chart. Charts can include such formats as time lines and family trees, as well as classification charts, organization charts, and flowcharts. In making charts, readers are able to organize, simplify, and summarize information in a way that often makes it easier to understand and remember.

Causes and Effects of Spain's Age of Empire

Some Spanish missionaries hoped colonization would lead to the conversion of Native Americans to Catholicism.

LONG-TERM CAUSES

Columbus's landing in the Caribbean

Spanish exploration and conquest

Founding of colonies in North and South America

IMMEDIATE CAUSES

Conquest of the Aztec by Cortés, 1521

Conquest of the Inca by Pizarro, 1533

Spanish treasure fleets from the Americas

Spain's Golden Age 1492 to mid-1600s

EFFECTS

Rise in Spanish wealth and influence

Increase in the prices of Spanish goods because of high inflation caused by American silver and gold

Spain's dependency upon goods from other countries

The Dutch colony of New Amsterdam controlled a strategic position on the east coast of North America.

Skills Reminder

To create a chart from written text, it helps to follow headings and word cues to identify appropriate details and determine what facts support the chart. Make sure you present the information in a clear and easy-to-follow manner using such visual aids as heading, lines, or arrows. The final product should help to visually summarize and order information.

Skills Practice

❶ Examine the flowchart above. Using the information in your textbook, create a similar chart showing the causes and effects of the Dutch Empire.

❷ What were some of the differences in the Spanish and Dutch empires? What other questions do the charts raise?

The Spanish Empire Declines

Many factors played a part in the decline of the Spanish Empire. A growing population meant that more people needed to be fed, clothed, and housed. At the same time, gold and silver flowed into Spain from the colonies. Shortages and this increase in the amount of money drove prices up in Spain. Because it cost more to produce goods in Spain than in any other country, demand for Spanish-made products declined. This loss of markets, in turn, led to a general decline in Spain's industry and commercial activity.

A capable middle class might have helped Spanish industries to develop. Many Spanish nobles, however, preferred military service. Others chose careers in the church rather than in secular life. In addition, the Spanish crown expelled first the Jews and then the Moriscos—Moorish converts to Christianity—from Spain. Unfortunately for the Spanish economy, many of those expelled were skilled bankers, businesspeople and commercial leaders, and artisans. The persecution of the Jews and the Moriscos conducted by the Spanish crown and the church further weakened Spain's economy and drained talent and capability from the country.

Moorish rulers of Granada pay tribute to the Spanish royal couple.

Much of the empire's wealth simply passed through Spain and was used to buy goods from other countries. With the gold and silver they received for goods sold in Spain, countries such as France, England, and the Netherlands grew strong. They developed their own industries at Spain's expense.

At home, people became discontented with high taxes and inflation. Along with agricultural failures, this discontent drove many people from their homes. Eventually, many people emigrated from Spain.

✔ **READING CHECK: Categorizing** What were the major problems that led to the decline of the Spanish Empire?

SECTION 4 REVIEW

1. **Define** and explain the significance:
   viceroys
   guerrilla warfare

2. **Identify** and explain the significance:
   Ponce de León
   Hernán Cortés
   Moctezuma II
   Francisco Pizarro
   Charles V
   Philip II
   William of Orange

3. **Identifying Cause and Effect**
   Copy the web diagram below. Fill in each box to show how it contributed to the decline of the Spanish Empire.

4. **Finding the Main Idea**
   a. How did the Spanish expand their colonial empire?
   b. How did the Dutch colonial empire differ from the Spanish colonial empire?
   c. What developments limited the ability of the Spanish to fully benefit from their vast and rich overseas empire?

5. **Writing and Critical Thinking**
   Making Generalizations In a diary entry, describe a day in the life of a Spanish colonist in the Americas.
   Consider:
   • ways in which things would have been better or worse than in Spain
   • what was involved in meeting and dealing with native peoples

go. hrw .com **Homework Practice Online**
keyword: SH3 HP7

Creating a Time Line

Copy the time line below onto a sheet of paper. Complete the time line by filling in the events, individuals, and dates from the chapter that you think were significant. Pick three events and explain why you think they were significant.

1400	**1600**	**1800**

Writing a Summary

Using standard grammar, spelling, sentence structure, and punctuation, write an overview of the events in the chapter.

Identifying People and Ideas

Identify the following terms or individuals and explain their significance:

1. heliocentric theory
2. Galileo Galilei
3. mercantilism
4. Vasco da Gama
5. tariffs
6. Christopher Columbus
7. triangular trade
8. Middle Passage
9. Hernán Cortés
10. Philip II

Understanding Main Ideas

SECTION 1 (pp. 190–195)
The Scientific Revolution

1. How did the study of nature change during the Scientific Revolution?
2. What were some of the important scientific discoveries made during this period?

SECTION 2 (pp. 196–199)
The Foundations of European Exploration

3. What kinds of changes in science and economics made European exploration possible?
4. What role did mercantilism play in the way European countries dealt with their colonies?

SECTION 3 (pp. 200–207)
Voyages of Portugal and Spain

5. What new knowledge did early Portuguese explorers provide that increased successful exploration?
6. How did the voyages of Christopher Columbus influence the world?
7. What were some of the factors leading to the Atlantic slave trade?

SECTION 4 (pp. 208–215)
The Spanish and Dutch Empires

8. What led to the successful rise of Dutch exploration in the 1600s?
9. What factors led to the decline of the Spanish Empire?

Reviewing Themes

1. **Science, Technology & Society** How did the era known as the Scientific Revolution lead to developments in other areas of society?
2. **Economics** How did the theory of mercantilism influence nations' decisions to explore and colonize?
3. **Global Relations** What determined the kinds of relationships that European explorers formed with conquered peoples?

Thinking Critically

1. **Comparing and Contrasting** Compare and contrast the ways in which the Portuguese, Spanish, and Dutch went about exploration and colonization.
2. **Supporting a Point of View** Which European nation engaged in exploration, trade, and colonization during the age of exploration had the greatest effect on other peoples? Explain your answer.
3. **Sequencing** Trace the events leading to the rise and decline of the Spanish Empire.

Writing About History

Categorizing Many factors influenced European exploration. In turn, exploration had many effects on both Europeans and non-Europeans. Fill in the following chart, listing the political, economic, cultural, and technological influences of European expansion on both Europeans and non-Europeans.

Effects of European Conquest		
	Europeans	**Non-Europeans**
Political		
Economic		
Cultural		
Technological		

Interpreting Maps

Study the map below. Then use the information to answer the questions that follow.

Cabral's Route, April 1500

1. Which of the following correctly describes Cabral's course from Lisbon to the Cape of Good Hope?

    a. First south, then west

    b. First southwest, then southeast

    c. First northwest, then northeast

    d. First southeast, then southwest

2. Cabral did not intend to follow the course he did. He was blown off course. Why was this course change significant? Give specific reasons.

Problem Solving

Read the following quote written in 1517 by a Spanish priest in Mexico. Then answer the questions.

> "As the Indians saw that the Spaniards did not attack them . . . they came . . . unarmed with kindly faces. . . . They asked the captain by signs what he wanted to which he replied 'water to drink.' The Indians showed him a round walled-up well of good water . . . where [the Spaniards] took all the water needful for the ships. . . . When day broke, all the Indians came out of their town armed with bows and arrows, shields and lances . . . to tell [the Spaniards] to go to their ships. The Spaniards obeyed their order. . . ."

3. Which of the following is the best explanation of why the Indians changed their behavior toward the Spanish?

    a. The Indians thought the Spanish had stayed too long.

    b. The Indians had only pretended to be kind.

    c. Water was scarce and the Spanish had taken too much.

    d. The Indians realized the Spanish were after their gold.

4. Why did you choose the statement you did in question 3? Explain your reasoning, using a problem-solving process.

Alternative Assessment

Building Your Portfolio

Economics

The idea of a favorable balance of trade developed during the 1500s and the 1600s. Today, most nations still take steps to keep their imports and exports balanced. Using your textbook and other sources, find statistics and other information about economic processes that countries such as the United States, Great Britain, and Japan use to maintain favorable trade balances. Summarize your findings in a poster.

Link to TODAY

⬛ internet connect

Internet Activity: go.hrw.com
KEYWORD: SH3 WH7

Choose a topic on Exploration and Expansion to:

- research the Scientific Revolution and create a database of scientists, dates, and contributions.
- learn more about an explorer described in this chapter.
- explain the political, economic, and cultural impact of Spanish expansion in Mesoamerica and Andean South America.

1368–1868

Asia in Transition

Statue of King Sejong of Korea

c. 1350s–1370s
Business and Finance
In response to Japanese piracy, the Chinese ban all trade with Japan.

c. 1407
Science and Technology
The Chinese complete the "Yung Lo Ta Tien" encyclopedia.

c. 1430s
Business and Finance
Japan and China begin trading again.

c. 1514
Global Events
Portuguese ships reach the southeastern coast of China for the first time.

| **1350** | **1400** | **1450** | **1500** | **1600** |

1368
Politics
The Ming dynasty is established in China.

1420
The Arts
The Chinese build the Great Temple of the Dragon in Peking.

1446
Daily Life
King Sejong of Korea introduces a phonetic alphabet to Koreans.

1598
Science and Technology
The Korean navy develops an iron-clad warship.

1415
Global Events
A Chinese fleet arrives at Aden, on the southern coast of the Arabian Peninsula.

Great Wall of China

Build on What You Know

*E*ast Asia was one of the great cradles of early civilization. Over many centuries and through the course of many dynasties, China had expanded and its distinct culture had spread throughout much of Asia. Then China was conquered by the Mongols, who established the Yuan dynasty. Meanwhile, the people of Japan had developed a feudal society of their own, with a rich culture and a heritage of unique traditions and values. In this chapter, you will learn how both Chinese and Japanese rulers became increasingly concerned and threatened by the growing activity of foreigners, especially Europeans, in and around their lands.

Tea leaves from China

Chinese porcelain cups from the 1800s

c. 1610
Daily Life
A Dutch trader arriving from China intro-duces tea to Europeans.

1644
Politics
The Qing dynasty comes to power in China.

c. 1699
Business and Finance
The British establish a trading post at Guangzhou.

1796
Politics
The White Lotus Rebellion begins in China.

c. 1833
Business and Finance
Great Britain abolishes the British East India Company's trade monopoly.

1833
Global Events
Slavery is abolished in the British dominions.

| 1650 | 1700 | 1800 | 1850 |

c. 1635
Global Events
Japanese leaders close their country to all Europeans except Dutch merchants.

1629
The Arts
The Tokugawa shogunate bans women from performing in Japanese theater.

1703
Daily Life
An earthquake kills 200,000 Japanese in the city of Edo.

1867–1868
Politics
The Tokugawa shogunate falls from power in Japan and direct rule by the emperor is restored.

1854
Global Events
American naval officer Matthew Perry forces Japan to open two ports to American trade.

Japanese city of Edo (present-day Tokyo)

What's Your Opinion?

Themes Journal *Do you* **agree** *or* **disagree** *with the following statements? Support your point of view in your journal.*

Global Relations Nations can protect themselves by isolating their people and cultures from other nations.

Economics Cultural attitudes toward trade, commerce, and interaction with other peoples do not affect a country's economic growth.

Government A country requires a strong central government to provide certain services for its citizens and to protect its culture.

The Ming and Qing Dynasties

The Main Idea
Two powerful dynasties, the Ming and the Qing, ruled China as a self-sufficient state for more than 500 years.

The Story Continues *The Mongol Yuan dynasty borrowed many ideas from the Chinese in order to establish an effective imperial government. They wisely followed the advice of a Chinese-trained official who said: "The [Mongol] empire was created on horseback, but it cannot be governed on horseback." In 1368, however, a former Buddhist monk named Zhu Yuanzhang* (JOO YOO·en·JAHNG) *overthrew the Yuan and established the Ming, or "Brilliant," dynasty. The Ming would remain in power in China for almost 300 years.*

Ming Foreign Policy

During the early period of the Ming dynasty—the late 1300s and early 1400s—the Chinese were probably the most skilled sailors in the world. For example, they built large, sturdy ships that Europeans called **junks.** Some junks were more than 400 feet long. The Chinese had been navigating their ships with the compass, which they probably invented, since the early 1100s. In 1405 the Ming emperor financed a fleet that sailed around Southeast Asia to India. Another Chinese fleet sailed across the Indian Ocean. This fleet reached the southern coast of the Arabian Peninsula in 1415.

These and other voyages of trade and discovery took place almost 100 years

The Ming Empire, 1424

Interpreting Maps During the Ming dynasty, the imperial capital was moved back from Nanjing to Beijing.

■ **Skills Assessment:**
1. Environment and Society What Chinese feat of engineering shown on the map would block movement from one place to another? **2. Drawing Conclusions** What feat of engineering would help movement?

before Vasco da Gama sailed from Portugal to India by going around the tip of Africa. The Chinese clearly had the ability to become a great seafaring power. However, the naval expeditions of the early Ming period did not continue for very long. Later Ming emperors had little interest in sea power or in foreign trade. They stopped financing naval expeditions. For a time they even outlawed overseas trade.

Attitudes toward trade. After defeating the Mongols in 1368, the Ming emperors tried to rid China of all Mongol influences. They wanted China to be as great as it had been during the Han, Tang, and Sung dynasties. As part of that effort, the Ming emperors restored Confucianism as the official philosophy of the government. Confucian philosophy divided society into four classes.

The Four Classes under Confucianism			
Scholar-gentry	**Farmers**	**Artisans**	**Merchants**
This landed, highly literate class helped staff the royal bureaucracy.	They produced food and paid the taxes that supported the empire.	They made beautiful and useful objects.	At the bottom of the social order, they made their living by selling objects that peasants and artisans had produced.

The Ming emperors wanted China to be self-sufficient. They refused to rely upon foreign trade as a source of government revenue. In the minds of the emperors, foreign trade did not bring enough benefits to China to make it a worthwhile endeavor. This view differed from that of European monarchs, who were strongly influenced by the ideas of mercantilism.

The northern frontier. The Ming emperors also wanted to make sure that no Central Asian people ever conquered China again. They focused their efforts on the long northern land frontier. To protect that frontier, the Ming strengthened the Great Wall of China. They encouraged soldiers to move with their families into the frontier zone by offering them free land. The Ming also encouraged peasants and city dwellers to move there. When the Ming emperors first came to power, Nanjing, in central China, was their capital. In 1421, however, the imperial capital was relocated to Beijing in the north.

The Ming emperors also tried to prevent nomadic tribes in the north from uniting into a powerful fighting force. Tribes that submitted to the Ming sent tribute to Beijing. In return, the Ming gave nomadic leaders honors, gifts, and titles.

Defending the frontier required constant attention and a great deal of money. The overseas expeditions were also extremely expensive. The Ming did not have enough revenue to do both. They chose frontier defense over trade and sea travel.

✔ **READING CHECK: Identifying Cause and Effect**
Why did the Ming emperors abandon overseas expeditions?

What If? The Chinese had the means to become a great sea power. **What might have happened if they had used this ability as the Spanish and English did later?**

This busy festival scene provides a view of life in China during the Ming dynasty.

Founding the Qing Dynasty

In the early 1600s a new and serious threat to the Ming dynasty emerged. In Manchuria, to the northeast of China, a chieftain named Nurhachi unified many tribes into a single people, the Manchu. Nurhachi's son captured eastern Mongolia and Korea. He then declared the beginning of a new dynasty, the Qing.

In 1644 the Manchu captured Beijing with the help of a Chinese general. The Qing dynasty ruled China from this time until 1912. Once again, despite the efforts of the Ming, outsiders had conquered China and established their own dynasty.

The Qing emperors were not Chinese, but they adopted Chinese culture and ruled the country with traditional Chinese techniques. One such Qing ruler was the emperor **Hsüan-yeh** (shoo·AHN·yeh).

At the same time, Qing emperors tried to keep the Manchu people, a minority in the empire, separate and distinct from the far more numerous Chinese. All Manchu had to study the Manchu language and cultural traditions. The Qing emperors could marry only Manchu women. They banned further emigration of Chinese to Manchuria, which was set apart as a tribal homeland for the Manchu. Finally, the Qing required all Chinese men to wear their hair tied in a **queue** (tail), a style that was common among the Manchu. The queue symbolized Chinese submission to Manchu rule.

✔ **READING CHECK: Drawing Inferences** Why did Qing rulers strive to keep the Chinese and Manchu people separate?

Economy, Culture, and Society

Generally life under the Ming and Qing dynasties was similar. Both Ming and Qing emperors kept traditional political institutions. Both supported traditional ideas and values. However, changes soon occurred to alter some of their traditions.

Economy. China's economy continued to grow during the Qing dynasty. Some regions of Qing China began to specialize in the manufacture or production of certain goods. The Lower Yangtze region, inland from present-day Shanghai, for example, became a center for the weaving of cotton cloth. Traders transported such goods along canals, coastal waterways, and rivers. Father Matteo Ricci, an Italian missionary to China in the late 1500s and early 1600s, described this canal traffic.

 History Makers Speak ❝So great is the number of boats that frequently many days are lost in transit by crowding each other, particularly when water is low in the canals. To prevent this, the water is held back at stated places by wooden locks, which also serve as bridges. . . . At times . . . the rush of water is so high and strong, at the exit from one lock or the entrance to another, that the boats are capsized and the whole crew is drowned.❞

Matteo Ricci, from *China in the Sixteenth Century*

The Chinese also sent goods such as tea and silk by caravan to Central Asia and Russia. Despite government disapproval, some ships continued to sail to Southeast Asia and India to trade.

As they had during the Sung dynasty, Chinese cities continued to grow. Peace and urban growth contributed to the increase of trade within China's borders. In theory, the Chinese and their Qing rulers still looked down on merchants.

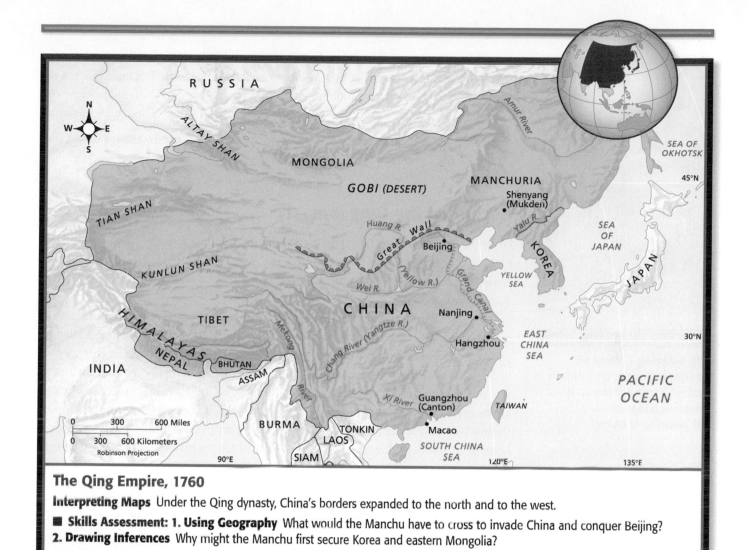

The Qing Empire, 1760

Interpreting Maps Under the Qing dynasty, China's borders expanded to the north and to the west.

■ **Skills Assessment: 1. Using Geography** What would the Manchu have to cross to invade China and conquer Beijing?

2. Drawing Inferences Why might the Manchu first secure Korea and eastern Mongolia?

In reality, however, they needed merchants to supply city-dwellers with clothing, food, and other essential goods.

Although cities grew, most of China's people still lived in the countryside. They increased the amount of land used for farming. In addition to rice, wheat, and tea, the rural Chinese planted new crops such as peanuts, sweet potatoes, and tobacco, which had been introduced from the Americas. The sweet potato became known as "the poor man's food" in southern China because it grew well in soil unsuited for the growing of rice. It also had more nutritional value than most other food crops.

Popular culture and society. As in Europe, the growth of cities and the increasing wealth of urban people led to the growth of popular culture in China. As early as the 1300s city people read novels and plays in the common everyday language. During the Ming and Qing dynasties, these popular novels and plays increased in number. Old tales about bandits and corrupt officials, once recited by street storytellers, now appeared in novels by professional authors. The writings of this period realistically portrayed Chinese society and family life.

Scholarship also flourished under both the Ming and the Qing. Scholars wrote detailed histories of earlier dynasties and essays on Confucian ethics. They studied ancient writings, much like the Renaissance humanists in Europe had. Qing scholars studied **philology,** the history of literature and language. In the 1700s Chinese scholars began to organize a manuscript library of rare works from the past.

Ivory figurine depicting a Daoist, c. 1500s–1600s

Silk weaving Chinese silk weavers during the Qing dynasty worked on manual looms. *What does this image reveal about silk weaving in China?*

China's society continued to be based on the family. The family, like the state, reflected the Confucian belief that each person had a role in life. The male head of the family directed the activities of family members for the good of the family as a whole. When a daughter married, she went to live with the family of her new husband.

✔ **READING CHECK: Summarizing** How did the Chinese economy change during the eras of Ming and Qing rule?

Decline of the Qing Dynasty

Under Qing rule China's population grew rapidly. Chinese farmers raised more crops, making it possible to feed more people. Peace also contributed to China's population growth. From about 1750 to the mid-1800s, China's population grew to more than 400 million people.

Qing China's rapidly growing population placed increasing pressure on the government. The Qing, however, found it increasingly difficult to meet the challenges posed by change and growth. Corruption at court and government inefficiency became more widespread. Growing numbers of bureaucrats demanded bribes in return for government services. During these years, China's enormous class of peasant farmers found it more and more difficult to hold their small farms and to support themselves and their families. Unrest spread throughout many parts of China. Disastrous floods and famine in various parts of China made the situation worse, as did growing pressure by the Western powers to gain economic control in China.

In 1796 discontent over increased taxes and growing government inefficiency led to a peasant rebellion. Members of a Buddhist cult called the White Lotus Society led the revolt, which was called the **White Lotus Rebellion.** After a difficult struggle, the government restored order in the early 1800s. Although it survived the rebellion, the Qing dynasty was seriously weakened. In addition, the basic causes of civil discontent remained. Rebellions occurred frequently after about 1850. The Qing dynasty was clearly in decline.

✔ **READING CHECK: Problem Solving** How might the Qing dynasty have brought peace to China?

SECTION 1 REVIEW

1. **Define** and explain the significance:
   junks
   queue
   philology

2. **Identify** and explain the significance:
   Hsüan-yeh
   White Lotus Rebellion

3. **Comparing and Contrasting** Copy the graphic organizer below. Use it to describe what remained stable and what changed during the Ming and Qing dynasties.

   Ming and Qing Dynasties

   Stable   Changed

4. **Finding the Main Idea**
   a. What changes did the growth of cities bring to China?
   b. What attitudes might Chinese rulers have had toward foreigners during the period of the Ming and Qing dynasties?

5. **Writing and Critical Thinking**
   Supporting a Point of View Imagine that you are involved in a rebellion against the Qing dynasty. Write a pamphlet that explains why you oppose Qing rule.
   Consider:
   • the spread of government inefficiency
   • the growth of corruption among officials

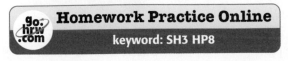

Homework Practice Online
keyword: SH3 HP8

China and Europeans

READ TO DISCOVER

1 What characterized early contact between Portugal and China?

2 Why did China and Great Britain go to war in the mid-1800s?

3 How did internal rebellions contribute to the Qing dynasty's decline?

DEFINE

free trade
extraterritoriality
"unequal" treaties

IDENTIFY

Opium War
Treaty of Nanjing
Taiping Rebellion

WHY IT MATTERS TODAY

Free trade remains an important economic concept and practice in the world today. Use CNNstudentNews.com or other **current event** sources to learn more about free trade in the modern world economy. Record your findings in your journal.

CNNstudentNews.com

The Main Idea
Growing contact with Europeans weakened the Qing dynasty and gradually undermined China's sovereignty.

The Story Continues *For more than 300 years after the first European trading stations were opened in China, European merchants and diplomats confronted a culture that viewed outsiders as inferior barbarians. In the early 1790s, for example, a British ambassador to the imperial Qing court offered gifts to the emperor. In turn, the emperor stated to the ambassador that ". . . we possess all things. I set no value on [foreign-made] objects strange or ingenious, and have no use for your country's manufactures."*

The Portuguese

In about 1514 Portuguese ships reached the southeastern coast of China. Over time the Portuguese were able to build trade ties with China. Finally, in 1557, the Chinese allowed the Portuguese to establish a trading station at Macao.

Portugal's influence, however, was not limited to trade. Jesuit missionaries also arrived on Portuguese ships. They used their knowledge of astronomy to gain admission to the emperor's inner circle. The emperor, who oversaw the prediction of eclipses and the timing of the seasons, appreciated the Jesuits' help in revising the Chinese calendar. He appointed Jesuit missionaries to official positions in his palace. He also gave them the opportunity to convert a number of high-ranking Chinese officials to Christianity. Gradually the Jesuits gained great power—economic and political, as well as spiritual—within the imperial court. Some even served as trusted advisers to the throne, quietly helping to shape imperial policies.

The Jesuits' power aroused jealousy and concern among some Chinese leaders. As a result, Qing rulers became suspicious of Christians and began to turn against them. The emperors realized that Chinese Catholics were expected to promise faith and allegiance to the pope. The Qing rulers feared that this would undermine the people's loyalty to the imperial throne and might bring about rebellion and overthrow. The emperors denounced Christianity as anti-Confucian, and the number of converts dwindled. China also deported European missionaries to Macao for a time.

✔ **READING CHECK: Summarizing** What was the initial Chinese attitude toward the Jesuits, and why did it change over time?

INTERPRETING THE VISUAL RECORD

Jesuits in China This early map of Nanjing, China, indicates the location of the Jesuit missions there. *Who do you think produced this map—European or Chinese mapmakers? Why?*

The British

During the late 1600s the British established a trading post at Guangzhou. By the early 1700s British ships regularly visited the port. The British came to China to buy silk and tea, which the Dutch had introduced to Europe in the 1600s. Great Britain had become a land of tea drinkers who regarded Chinese tea as the best in the world.

The British East India Company monopolized the new trade in Chinese teas. To get adequate supplies of tea, the company agreed to Chinese restrictions. Company ships could dock only at Guangzhou, and company representatives were required to stay in Guangzhou, where they lived in a special foreign settlement outside the city walls. Chinese regulations, moreover, demanded that the British trade only with a small number of officially approved Chinese merchants.

For a time, the Chinese policy worked. Contact between the British and Chinese people was kept to a minimum. In the late 1700s, however, two new developments—new ideas about trade and the sale of opium—damaged relations between the two nations.

Free trade ideas. The concept of **free trade** had developed in the West as a reaction to mercantilism. Supporters of free trade argued that governments should not restrict or interfere with international trade. British traders who did not work for the British East India Company resented the company's monopoly on the tea trade.

The British government became involved in the free trade debate. In part it did so because it hoped to gain additional overseas markets for British goods. In 1793 and again in 1816, British officials asked the Chinese government to open several more ports to British ships. Their efforts failed. In 1833 Great Britain abolished the British East India Company's monopoly on trade with China. Within a year the once-powerful company was little more than a managing agency for the British government in India.

The opium trade. The second development that came between the two countries involved the expansion of the tea trade. The British East India Company had paid for its tea purchases with cotton from India. There was a limit to Chinese demand for cotton, yet the British demand for tea kept growing. The company had to find a new product to exchange for tea. The product it chose was an addictive drug, opium.

From the late 1700s onward, British India produced opium and exported it to China. Opium addiction spread among the Chinese people. The Chinese government became alarmed, especially since China's silver supply was being used to pay for the opium. During these years, a huge trade imbalance grew, with far more silver flowing out of China than was being brought in. Chinese officials, fearing that China's economy was being undermined by the British, demanded that opium sales stop and that all opium cargoes be turned over to them. One Chinese official even pleaded with Queen Victoria of England to stop the opium trade.

The British were not the only admirers of Chinese tea, as the German advertisement at the top shows. Another Chinese product prized by Europeans was porcelain, like the decorative plate below it.

History Makers Speak **"Let us suppose that foreigners came from another country, and brought opium into England, and seduced the people of your country to smoke it. Would not you . . . look upon such a procedure with anger . . . ? Now we have always heard that your Highness possesses a most kind and benevolent [good] heart. Surely then you are incapable of doing or causing to be done unto another that which you would not wish another to do to you."**

Lin Tse-hsü, from *Commissioner Lin and the Opium War*

The Opium War. The British government did not respond to China's demands. When the Chinese tried to forcibly stop the opium trade, war broke out. The conflict between China and Britain, known as the **Opium War,** lasted from 1839 to 1842. Chinese army and naval forces were no match for the better-armed and better-trained British. A small British naval force that included iron-hulled steamships easily defeated Chinese forces as it sailed up the coast from Guangzhou. In 1842 the British gained control of the region near Nanjing. At that point, Qing officials agreed to negotiate on British terms.

Under the terms of the 1842 **Treaty of Nanjing,** China gave the island of Hong Kong to the British. It also opened five ports to British trade. British goods entering China through these ports were subject to a fixed, low tariff. In addition, British subjects in the ports would be governed by British, not Chinese, laws and would be tried in British courts. This requirement that foreigners must follow the laws of their home country instead of the laws of the country in which they live is called **extraterritoriality.**

More concessions. Great Britain did not keep its trade monopoly in China for long. Other Western powers, including France and the United States, also demanded trade treaties with China. Because the Chinese signed the treaties under the pressure of defeat and fear of further invasion, they called them **"unequal" treaties.** Most of the benefits of these treaties went to foreign powers. The Chinese gained little from them.

In 1856 China again went to war with Great Britain over a trade dispute. British forces, with French aid, again defeated the Chinese. The Chinese were forced to sign another "unequal" treaty. This treaty opened additional ports on the coast and along the Yangtze River. The Chinese had to allow the British to open an embassy in Beijing. Great Britain also took out a long-term lease on a small section of the Chinese mainland located opposite of Hong Kong. Finally the Chinese government had to agree to protect Christian missionaries and their converts in China.

Other foreign powers followed Britain and opened their own embassies in Beijing. In separate treaties, Russia also gained trade privileges and extraterritoriality. It received land bordering the Sea of Japan, or East Sea. The Russians established the port of Vladivostok in the southern part of this territory.

✔ **READING CHECK: Drawing Inferences** What was the British attitude toward the Chinese people and Chinese values?

The Opium War This painting from Britain's National Maritime Museum illustrates the British merchant steamer *Nemesis* attacking and destroying Chinese junks at Chuenpez, Canton. *What do you think viewers in the 1800s were supposed to learn from examining this image?*

The History of China

There are a wealth of sources that can be used to learn about the history of China. Thanks to computers, that information is easier than ever to find. While the computer has revolutionized many aspects of society, it also has made a significant contribution to the field of historical research. The Internet, for example, contains numerous databases, or information organized in a way that allows you to retrieve it quickly and easily with a few strokes of the keyboard. While it is an extremely valuable research tool, not all of the information on the Internet is accurate. In using the Internet for historical research, it is important that you evaluate the quality of its content.

The home page of a Web site may contain useful navigational links that describe other pages within the site and that will take you to selected pages. Click on these links to move forward or backward through the site, to learn more about its content, and to evaluate the scope of its coverage. The page may also contain links to other related Web sites that may provide valuable information.

Navigate to a Web page that contains information that is relevant to your research topic or that can help you to find such information. Type the address of the Web page—its URL—here and press ENTER or RETURN to reach the page of your choice.

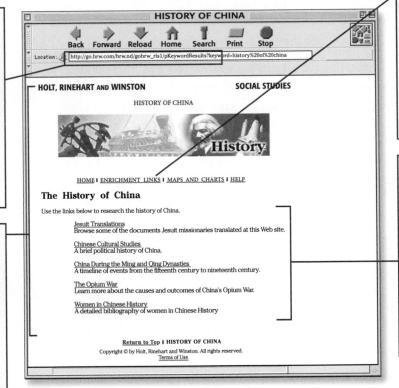

HISTORY OF CHINA

Back Forward Reload Home Search Print Stop

Location: http://go.hrw.com/hrw.nd/gohrw_rls1/pKeywordResults?keyword=history%20of%20china

HOLT, RINEHART AND WINSTON   SOCIAL STUDIES

HISTORY OF CHINA

History

HOME ▪ ENRICHMENT LINKS ▪ MAPS AND CHARTS ▪ HELP

The History of China

Use the links below to research the history of China.

Jesuit Translations
Browse some of the documents Jesuit missionaries translated at this Web site.

Chinese Cultural Studies
A brief political history of China.

China During the Ming and Qing Dynasties
A timeline of events from the fifteenth century to nineteenth century.

The Opium War
Learn more about the causes and outcomes of China's Opium War.

Women in Chinese History
A detailed bibliography of women in Chinese History

Return to Top ▪ HISTORY OF CHINA
Copyright © by Holt, Rinehart and Winston. All rights reserved.
Terms of Use

This Web page contains links and shortcuts to a broad number of other pages and activities on the Web. Explore these to determine if they will be useful as you conduct your research project. Such shortcuts may help you to sharpen the focus of your search.

Carefully review the Web page to determine its content or whether it can direct you via links to other relevant pages. Click on links that may be of interest or that may help you to extend your research.

Skills Reminder

To evaluate historical information on the Internet, determine if the site is published by a reputable authority or agency. In the case of individual Web publishers, try to find out if the author has credentials in the field or has a list of printed publications to his or her credit. Determine the objectivity of the site. Many Web sites are designed to sell products or to promote causes. The site's facts may be correct, but you should assess the author's point of view before deciding whether to use the information. Then evaluate the accuracy of the information. On the Internet, where anyone can be a publisher, there is a great deal of inaccurate information. Avoid sites with spelling or grammatical errors. Sites that attempt to dazzle the reader with eye-catching graphics and dramatic colors at the expense of content and substance should not be used. Also avoid sites filled with unsupported claims and undocumented arguments. Remember: a Web site's information should be as well documented as a printed page in a bound book.

Skills Practice

❶ Use the computer system at your school or library to locate one or more Web sites on one of the following:
 • the history of the Jesuits in China.
 • the geographic patterns and distribution of goods between the West and China during the 1700s and 1800s.
 • the Opium War.
Use information from the Web sites to write a one-page report on the topic you chose. Include a bibliography of the Web sites you used and who produced them. Include also a brief explanation of why you chose these sites, including questions you asked and your research outline.

❷ Working with a partner, research the Internet and create a database in the form of a chart or table about a topic in this chapter. If you have it available, use a database management system (DBMS) to add, delete, change, or update information on the chart or table.

Rebellions

An event that occurred within China made the intrusion of the Western powers even easier. In the mid-1800s southern and central China were torn by a great rebellion. The leader of this revolt was Hong Xiuquan (hoohng shee·oo·choo·ahn), who had been influenced by Christian teachings. Saying that he was the younger brother of Jesus, Hong declared that his mission was to establish a new dynasty. It was to be called Taiping, meaning "Heavenly Kingdom of Great Peace." Hong's ideas attracted many followers.

The **Taiping Rebellion** lasted from 1850 to 1864. It caused terrible destruction in southern China and the Yangtze valley. Millions of people were killed. Cities and farmlands were destroyed. To make matters more difficult for Qing rulers, Muslims in central and western China launched their own rebellions at the same time. After a long struggle, the Qing finally put down these rebellions in the late 1870s.

In this painting, soldiers in the Taiping Rebellion attack a Chinese town.

The Taiping Rebellion and the other revolts seriously weakened both the Qing dynasty and the nation as a whole. At the same time, foreign powers in China, seeking to take advantage of the nation's internal turmoil, demanded further concessions and the opening of more treaty ports. Continuing foreign interference in China's political and economic affairs was a serious problem for the nation and its Qing rulers. It weakened China's sovereignty and undermined the emperor's prestige. It also reduced the country's control over its own economy. Increasingly, the independence of China and its rulers was viewed by the Western powers as a sham.

✔ **READING CHECK: Analyzing Information** What role did religion play in rebellions against the Qing?

SECTION 2 REVIEW

1. **Define** and explain the significance:
   free trade
   extraterritoriality
   "unequal" treaties

2. **Identify** and explain the significance:
   Opium War
   Treaty of Nanjing
   Taiping Rebellion

3. **Sequencing** Copy the flowchart below. Use it to sequence the events that occurred between China and Britain between the 1600s and late 1800s. You may want to add more boxes.

No contact
   ↓
   ↓
   ↓
   | Trade with British in control |

4. **Finding the Main Idea**
   a. In what two ways did the Portuguese influence the Chinese?
   b. In what ways did unsuccessful rebellions succeed in weakening China?
   c. Why was the collection of China's customs duties by foreigners seen as a blow to Chinese sovereignty?

5. **Writing and Critical Thinking**
   Identifying Cause and Effect Imagine that you are a Chinese person who has witnessed the Opium War. Write a letter to a friend that explains the causes of the war and its effect on the Chinese.
   Consider:
   • the conflicts over free trade and the importation of opium
   • the terms of the "unequal" treaty

go. hrw .com Homework Practice Online
keyword: SH3 HP8

The Tokugawa Shoguns in Japan

READ TO DISCOVER

❶ How did the Tokugawa shogunate come to power?

❷ Why did Japan's rulers seek to isolate their nation from foreign influence?

❸ What were society and culture like under the Tokugawa shogunate?

❹ How was Japanese isolation brought to an end?

DEFINE

consulates

IDENTIFY

Oda Nobunaga
Toyotomi Hideyoshi
Tokugawa Ieyasu
Matthew Perry
Treaty of Kanagawa

WHY IT MATTERS TODAY

Japan has one of the world's leading economies today. Use **CNN** or other **current event** sources to learn about the Japanese economy and international trade. Record your findings in your journal.

The Main Idea
Despite their desire for isolation, Japan's rulers were unable to prevent foreign contact and trade.

The Story Continues *China's culture influenced that of early Japan. Over time the Japanese became increasingly isolated, especially from the rising nations of the West. By the 1850s, however, many Japanese were calling for an end to isolationism. For example, philosopher Yoshida Shoin believed that Japan would advance only if it blended Eastern thought with Western technology. Shoin urged the Japanese people to take action if their leaders failed to, arguing that "if it is true loyalty and service you seek, then you must abandon this fief and plan a grassroots uprising."*

Founding the Tokugawa Shogunate

In 1467 rival branches of the Ashikaga family in Japan became involved in a dispute over the selection of the next shogun. This conflict marked the beginning of 100 years of bitter, widespread, and almost constant warfare in Japan. Sensing the weakness and deep divisions within the Ashikaga family, local daimyo fought for control of the country. In the late 1500s a series of three daimyo emerged victorious from this long and destructive struggle. These powerful daimyo established themselves as overlords of the other daimyo and built a centralized feudal system in Japan.

Japan under the Tokugawa Shogunate, 1603–1867

Interpreting Maps Edo was the capital of the Tokugawa shogunate.

■ **Skills Assessment: Using Geography** Why might Edo have been a good location for the capital?

Oda Nobunaga. The first of these overlords, **Oda Nobunaga** (ohd·ah noh·boo·NAH·gah), began his rise to power as a minor daimyo. Through conquests and alliances, Nobunaga captured the city of Kyoto in 1568. He ended the Ashikaga shogunate in 1573 and then started to strengthen his power in central Japan. Before Nobunaga could defeat his rivals, however, one of his own vassals attacked him in 1582. Wounded, Nobunaga committed suicide.

Toyotomi Hideyoshi. The second of the overlords, **Toyotomi Hideyoshi** (toh·yoh·TOH·mee HEE·day·yoh·shee), had led Nobunaga's army. After Nobunaga's death, Hideyoshi succeeded him. During the 1580s Hideyoshi defeated several powerful daimyo in battle. He forced other daimyo to pledge their loyalty to him. Hideyoshi did not totally defeat other daimyo. Instead he weakened them by reducing the size of their territories so that they could not threaten him again. He also carried out a "sword hunt" to disarm the peasants. Thereafter peasants could no longer become warriors. Only men born into warrior families could become warriors.

In 1592 and again in 1597, Hideyoshi sent his army to invade Korea. He wanted to build an empire and give Japanese warriors the chance to fight. At first the Japanese invasion of Korea succeeded. As the battles continued, however, a Chinese army that was aiding the Koreans pushed Hideyoshi's warriors back to the coast. When Hideyoshi died in 1598, the Japanese left Korea and returned home.

Tokugawa Ieyasu. Hideyoshi's most powerful vassal, **Tokugawa Ieyasu** (toh·kuh·GAH·wah ee·YAH·soo) succeeded him as overlord. Ieyasu established his capital at Edo (AY·doh), the city that is now Tokyo. Other daimyo resisted Ieyasu, but he defeated them in 1600. In 1603 Ieyasu became shogun.

Tokugawa Ieyasu crushed his defeated rivals. He did allow some 250 to 260 daimyo to keep possession of their private lands. However, Ieyasu's actions clearly demonstrated that he was prepared to expand or reduce the size of their territories in the future. The Tokugawa family would keep the title of shogun for more than 250 years. They established a government known as the Tokugawa shogunate.

Tokugawa rule. The political system established by the Tokugawa shogunate was a cross between feudalism and a central monarchy. Within his domain, each daimyo governed as an almost absolute ruler. Local peasants paid taxes to support the daimyo and those who

HISTORY MAKER

Toyotomi Hideyoshi (1536–1598)

Born to a peasant family and poorly educated, Toyotomi Hideyoshi worked hard to make up for his humble beginnings. He rose from warrior to one of the greatest generals in Oda Nobunaga's army. When he succeeded Nobunaga, Hideyoshi continued the unification of Japan. **How did Hideyoshi make up for his humble beginnings?**

Holt Researcher

go.hrw.com
KEYWORD: Holt Researcher
FreeFind: Oda Nobunaga
            Toyotomi Hideyoshi
            Tokugawa Ieyasu
After reading more about the overlords on the Holt Researcher, create a time line of the major events during their reigns.

INTERPRETING THE VISUAL RECORD

Preparing for war Japanese warriors regularly exercised and meditated to keep fit for battle. *What evidence suggests that at least one man who is meditating is a warrior?*

This mounted Japanese warrior and his horse display traditional weapons and military dress.

served him, such as the samurai. The Tokugawa family had its own private domain, which included roughly one fourth of the nation's resources. Thus the Tokugawa did not rule the entire country directly. Nor did they personally tax the entire population. In this way Japan remained politically and economically decentralized to some degree.

Because of their wealth and military power, however, the Tokugawa had considerable influence over the daimyo. Some historians believe that the Tokugawa shoguns prohibited the daimyo from making alliances with one another. Most daimyo had to spend every other year in Edo, the shogun's capital. When they returned to their own domains, the daimyo left their families in Edo as hostages. Maintaining two residences—one in Edo and one in the provinces—proved very expensive for the daimyo. Traveling to and from Edo in a grand procession also drained their financial resources. In addition, living in Edo transformed many daimyo from warriors to courtiers. In this manner the Tokugawa shoguns maintained control over the daimyo.

The Tokugawa shogunate shaped Japanese life in several ways. Its strong central government brought more than two centuries of stability to Japan. Tokugawa control of the daimyo helped to keep peace in the countryside. In addition, the Tokugawa set trade restrictions and limited contact with foreigners. By doing so, they achieved almost complete isolation from Europe by 1650. Their desire for isolation was in response to contact with foreigners that had occurred beginning in the 1500s.

✔ **READING CHECK: Sequencing** What events led to the establishment of the Tokugawa shogunate?

Foreign Contact

Japanese soldiers and sailors had traveled overseas since the 1000s. In the early 1400s, during the Ashikaga shogunate, Japan's ships had sailed to China and Korea seeking trade. At times the Japanese acted as pirates, taking whatever they could from local peoples.

The Portuguese in Japan. In the mid-1500s the daimyo began to trade with the Portuguese, whose ships appeared in Japanese waters. Portuguese traders brought two items new to the Japanese: muskets and Christianity.

Apparently Oda Nobunaga had used troops armed with muskets in his battles against rival daimyo. However, some samurai did not approve of the musket. It violated the traditional samurai fighting ethic, which was based on skill. Anyone armed with a musket could overcome years of samurai training with a single shot.

In the wake of the Portuguese traders came Christian missionaries. Among the missionaries were the Jesuits, who achieved notable success during the Counter-Reformation in Europe. The Jesuits concentrated on converting the daimyo to Christianity. After a daimyo converted to Christianity, the Jesuits would seek converts in the daimyo's domain. It has been estimated that by the early 1600s the missionaries had converted as many as 300,000 Japanese to Christianity.

Closing the country. The Tokugawa shoguns concluded that Christianity was an undesirable threat to their rule. The shoguns saw Christianity as a force that might weaken their authority because it taught loyalty to a power other than the Tokugawa shogun. The shoguns also feared that Christianity would be a divisive belief in their tradition-based society. Early in the 1600s the shoguns acted on their concerns by forcing Portuguese traders and missionaries to leave the country.

By this time the Portuguese faced stiff competition in East Asia from Dutch traders. The Dutch had accepted a strictly controlled trading relationship with the Tokugawa shogunate. The shoguns themselves controlled the small amount of trade Japan conducted with the Dutch. In addition, a few Dutch merchants were allowed to live near Nagasaki. These Dutch merchants were the only Europeans allowed to trade in Japan after the 1630s.

The Tokugawa enforced other strict rules in order to keep Japan isolated from foreign influences. They banned most overseas trade. The Japanese people were prohibited from traveling abroad. Like China, Japan concentrated on domestic affairs and tried to ignore the outside world. Because Japan is an island nation, and because its leaders could take active steps to secure its coasts, the country was able to achieve a high degree of isolation.

✔ **READING CHECK: Decision Making** Why did the Tokugawa shogunate want to keep Japan isolated?

Life in Tokugawa Japan

The Tokugawa shoguns, like most emperors in neighboring China, did not promote change. The concept of stability was more important to the Japanese. The Confucian ideas, which the Japanese borrowed from the Chinese, supported this ideal.

Social classes. The Tokugawa shoguns adopted—with some changes—the Confucian ideal of social classes. The warrior class in Japan filled roughly the same role as the scholar-gentry in China. Therefore the samurai stood at the top of the Japanese social order. Peasants, artisans, and merchants followed in descending order of importance.

A person's social class was determined by birth. Sons followed the occupations of their fathers. For example, a person born into an artisan family in Osaka remained a member of the artisan class in Osaka for life.

The Tokugawa shoguns encouraged members of the samurai to study the Confucian classics. The shoguns established schools in the various domains to prepare young samurai for their peacetime roles as government officials. The shoguns, however, did not adopt the Chinese civil service examination system. In Japan, samurai became officials by heredity alone. Males born into low-ranking samurai families worked as low-ranking officials in their domain. Those born into high-ranking families served as high-ranking officials.

Kabuki theater is a purely Japanese art form. Often much interaction between actors and spectators takes place.

CONNECTING TO
Art

Theater: Kabuki
Kabuki, the most popular form of Japanese theater, began during the Tokugawa period. Based on street dances, Kabuki grew into a colorful art form with detailed costumes and makeup. The makeup is designed to show a character's emotions, such as anger or bravery. A Kabuki play includes song and dance. Older Kabuki plays had little speaking, but more modern ones have more. Actors use dramatic gestures to tell the story.

In 1629 women were banned from performing Kabuki. Since then, men and boys have played both male and female roles. Kabuki actors usually spend years learning the Kabuki style before being allowed to perform.

Understanding the Arts

Why do you think the Tokugawa might have banned women from Kabuki?

The shoguns usually required a samurai to live in the castle town of his daimyo. Instead of living on income from country estates, samurai now received salaries. This policy gave the shoguns greater control over the samurai, who could not develop wealth independently. It also eliminated any opportunity for the samurai to revolt against their lords.

Change and culture. As in China, the rulers of Japan could not prevent economic, political, and social change within their country. Much of the change that took place in Japan resembled that which occurred in China. Internal trade expanded. Various regions of the country began to specialize in certain crops and handicrafts. Cities grew in size. Many artisans and merchants became well-off.

These changes did not please everyone. One writer claimed that corruption had taken root in the government and that the common people were not prospering.

Analyzing Primary Sources

Identifying a Point of View Why did Yamagata Daini criticize merchants and trading?

> *History Makers Speak*
>
> **❝After wrenching a crop from the thin soil, they [farmers] must battle tax officers who demand sixty to seventy percent of the harvest . . . Whether soils are rich or poor, whether harvests are good or bad, farmers shiver and starve; and, ultimately, they give up farming. . . . Tillers become scarce and fields turn to wasteland . . . Those good at selling grow rich; those good at farming go hungry.❞**
>
> Yamagata Daini, from *A History of Japan*

There were some positive changes in Japanese life, however. As in both Europe and China, urban growth and increased wealth led to the rise of a popular culture. By the early 1700s new forms of art, literature, and theater had taken root. Many of these new forms appealed to the tastes of ordinary city residents.

✔ **READING CHECK: Categorizing** How would you classify the view of the Tokugawa shoguns and the Chinese emperors toward change—as supportive of or as resistant to change?

INTERPRETING THE VISUAL RECORD

Popular music This musical trio from the Tokugawa period includes a singer, a lute player, and a flutist. *What information can be gathered about the music and musicians in this image?*

The End of Japan's Isolation

As part of the Tokugawa plan to keep Japan isolated, the government refused to give shelter to ships from other nations during storms. This policy angered many Westerners. Western nations that sought commercial expansion wanted Japan to follow China's lead and end its isolation.

In 1853 President Millard Fillmore of the United States sent Commodore **Matthew Perry** and a powerful naval force to Japan. Perry had orders to negotiate a treaty that would guarantee the safety of U.S. sailors and open Japanese ports to American trade. Perry's squadron of heavily armed, steam-powered warships sailed into Tokyo Bay on July 8, 1853. In a show of force and dignity, Perry ceremoniously presented a letter from President Fillmore that urged the Japanese to accept the American treaty. Perry promised to return for an answer the following year.

The American visit sparked controversy within Japan. Some powerful leaders favored military resistance and continued isolation. Others, however, believed that Japan could not hold out against the United States. The shogun, worried about the threat of a naval attack by the Americans, reluctantly agreed to negotiate when Perry returned in 1854.

The negotiations between the shogun and Perry led to the **Treaty of Kanagawa** (kah·NAH·gah·wah) in 1854. Under the treaty the Japanese opened two ports to let Americans obtain fuel, shelter, and supplies. The opening of the ports permitted trade to begin between the two nations. Within two years, Japan signed similar treaties with Great Britain, the Netherlands, and Russia. As part of the agreements, foreign nations were allowed to establish **consulates**—diplomatic offices headed by consuls.

In this woodblock print, a Japanese artist recorded Commodore Perry's arrival in Edo Bay in 1853.

In 1858 the governments of Japan and the United States signed a new treaty. The two countries agreed to exchange ministers. In addition, the treaty allowed foreign residence in Edo and Osaka, extraterritorial privileges, and international trade. The Japanese also opened more treaty ports to the United States. Similar agreements between Japan and other nations soon followed.

Japanese opponents of the Tokugawa shogunate criticized the government for signing treaties with foreign powers. To many samurai, the government's inability to resist Western demands cast doubt on its right to rule Japan. Many Japanese began to complain about the weakness of the government abroad and its strict rule at home. In the 1860s civil war broke out in Japan. Supporters of the Tokugawa shogunate battled its opponents. Calling for major reforms, the anti-Tokugawa forces overthrew the shogunate in 1867. They restored the power of the emperor, moving Japan toward a more centralized government. The new emperor, a teenager, named his reign Meiji, meaning "Enlightened Rule."

✔ **READING CHECK: Problem Solving** Could the Tokugawa have resisted Western demands and retained control of Japan?

SECTION 3 REVIEW

1. **Define** and explain the significance:
   consulates

2. **Identify** and explain the significance:
   Oda Nobunaga
   Toyotomi Hideyoshi
   Tokugawa Ieyasu
   Matthew Perry
   Treaty of Kanagawa

3. **Categorizing** Copy the diagram. Use it to show the levels of government and classes in Japan during the era of Tokugawa rule.

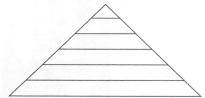

4. **Finding the Main Idea**
   a. Was the policy of isolation good for Japan and the Japanese people? Why or why not?
   b. What changes in Japanese society occurred under the Tokugawa shogunate?

5. **Writing and Critical Thinking**
   Decision Making Imagine that you are the shogun considering Matthew Perry's request for a treaty. Should you support such a treaty?
   Consider:
   • why the Americans wanted a treaty
   • how a treaty might benefit Japan
   • how a treaty might harm Japan
   • what actions a refusal might bring

Homework Practice Online
keyword: SH3 HP8

Creating a Time Line

Copy the time line below on a sheet of paper. Complete the time line by filling in the events, individuals, and dates from the chapter that you think were significant. Pick three events and explain why you think they were significant.

| 1400 | 1500 | 1600 |

Writing a Summary

Using standard grammar, spelling, sentence structure, and punctuation, write an overview of the events in the chapter.

Identifying People and Ideas

Identify the following terms or individuals and explain their significance:

1. Hsüan-yeh
2. free trade
3. Treaty of Nanjing
4. extraterritoriality
5. "unequal" treaties
6. Taiping Rebellion
7. Tokugawa Ieyasu
8. Matthew Perry
9. Treaty of Kanagawa
10. consulates

Understanding Main Ideas

Section 1 *(pp. 220–224)*
The Ming and Qing Dynasties

1. Why did the Chinese abandon overseas exploration?
2. How did the Chinese economy change under the Ming and Qing emperors?
3. How did government corruption affect the Qing dynasty?

Section 2 *(pp. 225–229)*
China and Europeans

4. Why did the Chinese resist free trade with Great Britain?
5. What were the effects of the Opium War on China?
6. What generally were the terms of the "unequal" treaties?

Section 3 *(pp. 230–235)*
The Tokugawa Shoguns in Japan

7. How did the Tokugawa shogunate weaken daimyo power?
8. Why did the Japanese rulers see the Jesuits as a threat?
9. Why did Japan open ports to American ships?

Reviewing Themes

1. **Global Relations** Why did Chinese and Japanese efforts to maintain isolation fail in the 1800s?
2. **Economics** How did attitudes about foreigners affect trade in China?
3. **Government** What was the result of the Qing dynasty's inability to provide services and loss of control over bureaucratic corruption?

Thinking Critically

1. **Identifying Cause and Effect** How did urban growth promote economic change in Asia?
2. **Comparing** Why did the Qing dynasty and the Tokugawa shogunate both collapse?
3. **Identifying Bias** Did British treatment of the Chinese reflect a concern for foreign peoples? Explain.
4. **Evaluating** What were the main difficulties that Asian societies faced during this period in history?
5. **Making Predictions** What might have happened if the Qing dynasty had improved tax reform and increased government services?

Writing About History

Comparing Write a report comparing China under the Qing dynasty with Japan under the Tokugawa shogunate. Use the chart below to organize your thoughts before writing.

Factors	China	Japan
Economy		
Government rule		
Popular culture		
Relations with foreign powers		

Interpreting a Time Line

Study the time line below. Then answer the questions that follow.

1557
Macao becomes a Portuguese trading station.

1842
The Treaty of Nanjing gives Hong Kong to the British.

1500   **1700**   **1900**

c. 1699
The British establish a trading post at Guangzhou.

1842
China is forced to open five ports to the British.

1. Which of the following correctly states the theme of this time line?

    a. The British and Portuguese traded with China for hundreds of years.

    b. European pressure slowly changed China's trade policies.

    c. Chinese ports were closed to the British until 1842.

    d. European pressure quickly changed China's trade policies.

2. What was the reason for the Treaty of Nanjing and what effect did it have on China? Support your answer with specific examples.

Identifying Bias

Read the following quote by Francis Xavier, a Jesuit missionary who went to Japan in 1549. Then answer the questions.

> "The people whom we have met so far are the best who have as yet been discovered, and it seems to me that we shall never find among heathens another race to equal the Japanese. They are a people of very good manners, good in general, and not malicious [mean]; they are men of honor to a marvel, and prize honor above all else in the world. . . . They have one quality which I cannot recall in any people of Christendom; this is that [they] . . . render as much honor to a poor gentleman as if he were passing rich."

3. Which of the following best describes how the author's experience influenced his viewpoint?

    a. Based on his experience, he was amazed the Japanese were so honorable.

    b. His experiences led him to believe manners were important.

    c. Since he was a poor missionary, he was surprised to be treated as if he were rich.

    d. He was surprised the Japanese were good people, because he had heard they were warriors.

4. How did the Tokugawa shoguns react to the Jesuit missionaries? Give specific examples.

Alternative Assessment

Building Your Portfolio

Link to TODAY

Economics

Opening new trade markets among nations is as topical an issue today as it was during the Qing dynasty and the Tokugawa shogunate. Using your textbook and other sources, compile a list of important trade treaties, both historical and modern day. Use the list to write a short summary of world trade.

🔲 **internet** connect

Internet Activity: go.hrw.com
KEYWORD: SH3 WH8

Choose a topic on Asia in Transition to:

• analyze art of the Ming and Qing dynasties.

• learn more about Kabuki theater and *Bunraku*, Japanese puppet theater.

• examine an issue from the point of view of a Japanese samurai warrior.

CHAPTER 9

1300–1700

Islamic Empires in Asia

1453
Science and Technology
The Ottomans use artillery cannons to capture Constantinople.

1453
Daily Life
The Ottomans convert the Hagia Sophia church in Constantinople into a mosque.

Ottoman cavalry sword

1326
Business and Finance
The Ottomans begin to mint coins.

1398
Politics
Timur destroys Delhi.

1458
Global Events
The Ottomans occupy the Acropolis in Athens, Greece.

1300	1375	1450

1337
Global Events
The Hundred Years' War begins.

Mongol forces invade India

1475
Daily Life
The world's first coffeehouse opens in Istanbul.

Turkish coffee urn

Build on What You Know

From the 1400s through the 1700s, rulers of China and Japan wanted to make their countries stable. They tried to prevent change by limiting contact with the outside world—particularly with the trading countries of the West. They also sought to maintain the traditions and values that had characterized their cultures for centuries. At the same time, Islamic rulers in Asia were trying to expand their empires through conquest. In this chapter, you will learn how Islamic empires grew and were organized. You will learn, too, how Islamic teachings were carried to many parts of Asia and how they influenced many traditional Asian cultures.

1501
Politics
The Safavid dynasty begins rule in Persia.

1526
Politics
Bābur founds the Mughal Empire in India.

1529
Daily Life
Turkish farmers grow vast fields of American maize.

c. 1529
The Arts
Bābur finishes writing his memoirs.

1558
Global Events
Elizabeth I becomes queen of England.

1599
Daily Life
Eşfahān becomes the capital of Safavid Persia.

1600
Daily Life
Thieves smuggle coffee beans from Arabia to India.

c. 1649
The Arts
Shah Jahān completes construction of the Taj Mahal in Agra.

Safavid glazeware

1525

1600

1675

1504
Science and Technology
Venice proposes construction of a Suez Canal to the Ottomans.

1536
Science and Technology
India rubber is mentioned for the first time.

1579
Science and Technology
The Ottomans build an astronomical observatory in Constantinople.

1617
The Arts
'Abbās's Royal Mosque at Eşfahān is completed.

1611
Business and Finance
The British East India Co. establishes its first factory in India.

1658
Politics
Aurangzeb seizes power in Mughal India.

Dome and minarets of a Safavid mosque

Mughal emperor Aurangzeb at prayer

What's Your Opinion?

Themes Journal *Do you* **agree** *or* **disagree** *with the following statements? Support your point of view in your journal.*

Global Relations A civilization that expands by conquest must support a large, strong military.

Culture The religious policies followed by a culture's leadership can help to unify or divide that culture.

Government The character of its rulers determines the effectiveness of a government.

SECTION 1

READ TO DISCOVER

1 How did the Ottomans build and expand their empire?

2 How did the Ottomans organize their government and society?

DEFINE

ghazis
reaya
millets

IDENTIFY

Osman
Janissaries
Timur
Mehmed II
Süleyman

WHY IT MATTERS TODAY

The present-day country of Turkey was once the center of the Ottoman Empire. Use or other **current event** sources to find out what kind of government Turkey has today. Record your findings in your journal.

CNN student News.com

The Ottoman Empire

The Main Idea
With their tough, disciplined army and strong rulers, the Ottomans built a powerful empire.

The Story Continues *During the 1300s and 1400s the Ottoman Empire built and expanded its power. Ottoman leaders such as Mehmed the Conqueror sought to capture the city of Constantinople. An observer described Mehmed's goals: "The empire of the world . . . must be one, one faith and one kingdom. To make this unity there is no place in the world more worthy than Constantinople."*

The Rise of the Ottomans

The first Ottomans were Turkish soldiers known as **ghazis,** or warriors for Islam. They had come to Anatolia (formerly called Asia Minor) with other Turks to escape the Mongols. In the late 1200s a ghazi leader named **Osman** had great success fighting the Byzantines. His tribe members became known as Ottomans.

During the 1300s the Ottomans took over a large part of Anatolia. Eventually Ottoman forces went to Europe. They tried to capture Constantinople but failed. In 1361 the Ottomans captured Adrianopolis, the second most important Byzantine city. They made the city their capital and renamed it Edirne. By 1396 the first Ottoman sultan had been appointed.

The elite Ottoman army. The Ottoman sultans created a highly trained troop of slave soldiers called **Janissaries.** Janissaries were young war captives and Christian slaves from Europe. First they were schooled in Islamic laws and converted to Islam, then trained as special soldiers. Janissaries belonged to the sultan, serving him for life. Eventually the Janissaries gained power and influence. They became an important political group in the Ottoman Empire.

Timur challenges the Ottomans. The Turko-Mongol leader **Timur** interrupted the Ottoman expansion. Timur was born in 1336 in what is now Uzbekistan. He claimed he was descended from the great Mongol leader Genghis Khan. Timur created an army and built his power in central Asia. Then he began a career of conquest.

By the end of the 1300s, Timur's forces were close to Ottoman territory. Several ghazi rulers fled to his court when the Ottomans conquered their states. They asked Timur to help them get their land back. In 1402 Timur invaded Anatolia. His forces defeated the Ottomans at the Battle of Ankara and captured the sultan. Timur made the Ottomans return the territory they had taken from the other ghazi rulers.

This richly decorated illustration from about 1500 shows an Ottoman sultan dining.

Recovery and expansion. Timur's victory over the Ottomans caused a crisis in the Ottoman Empire. A civil war broke out over who should be the next sultan. Finally Murad II took power and began a new period of expansion. In 1444 Murad's army defeated the last European crusaders at the Battle of Varna. After Murad's rule, **Mehmed II** became sultan. Mehmed conquered Constantinople in 1453, renamed the city Istanbul, and made it the Ottoman capital.

The greatest Ottoman sultan was **Süleyman,** who ruled from 1520 to 1566. He brought the Ottoman Empire to its height. Known as "the Magnificent" in Europe, Süleyman was called "the Lawgiver" by his own people.

Süleyman expanded the Ottoman Empire, conquering Hungary in 1526. Three years later the Ottomans nearly captured the city of Vienna. Vienna marked the limit of Ottoman expansion in Europe. By this time, however, the Ottomans ruled most of eastern Europe, western Asia, and northern Africa.

✔ **READING CHECK: Summarizing** What important military conquests led to the expansion of the Ottoman Empire?

The Ottoman Empire, 1453–1683

Interpreting Maps At its height under Süleyman, the Ottoman Empire included parts of eastern Europe, western Asia, and northern Africa.

■ **Skills Assessment: The World in Spatial Terms** Which two battle sites are found at about the 40° N parallel?

Ottoman Government and Society

The sultans were the supreme rulers of Ottoman society. Those second in command to the sultan were called grand viziers (vuh·ZIRZ). Ottoman society was divided into two major groups. One group was the small ruling class of Ottomans. The other included the masses of ordinary subjects, called **reaya** or the "protected flock." People did not have to remain in one of these groups for life. Reaya with ability could become part of the ruling class. Ottomans who lacked ability became reaya.

Europeans who observed Turkish society were impressed. One observer was Ogier Ghiselin de Busbecq, the Holy Roman Emperor's ambassador to Süleyman's court. He described his view of how the system worked.

History Makers Speak

❝No distinction is attached to birth among the Turks; the deference to be paid to a man is measured by the position he holds in the public service. . . . it is by merit that men rise in the service, a system which ensures that posts should only be assigned to the competent. Each man in Turkey carries in his own hand his ancestry and his position in life, which he may make or mar as he will.❞

Ogier Ghiselin de Busbecq, *The Life and Letters of Ogier Ghiselin de Busbecq*

The millet system. Different groups of people made up the reaya. Muslim Turks lived in the heart of the empire in Anatolia. Christians and Jews of various ethnic groups lived in the Balkans. Muslim Arabs lived in the Fertile Crescent and along the shore of northern Africa. Religious differences caused tension among these groups.

The sultans allowed the different groups to practice their own religions. They were organized into separate religious communities called **millets.** The millets were under the general control of the sultan, but they governed themselves. Each millet operated under its own laws and customs. It had its own courts and collected taxes. It also was responsible for the education, health, and safety of its members.

Slow decline begins. Süleyman the Magnificent died in 1566. His death marked the start of a slow decline of Ottoman power and influence as European states such as France, Spain, and Poland became stronger. Although the Ottoman army and navy

Analyzing Primary Sources

Drawing Inferences What does it mean to say, "Each man in Turkey carries in his own hand his ancestry and his position in life"?

HISTORY MAKER

Süleyman the Magnificent (c. 1495–1566)

As sultan of the Ottoman Empire, Süleyman was a brave and daring warrior. He is most remembered, however, for his accomplishments at home.

Süleyman surrounded himself with a group of able advisers. He built strong fortresses for defense as well as numerous roads, bridges, and mosques. He supported the arts and helped to make Constantinople the cultural and commercial center of his empire. **How did Süleyman improve the Ottoman Empire?**

This Ottoman image of the 1500s shows the Turks blockading the French port of Marseille.

were generally strong, they suffered some defeats. In 1571, for example, Philip II of Spain led a European navy against the Ottomans. The Europeans defeated the Turks at the Battle of Lepanto, near Greece. In 1683 troops led by the Polish king John III Sobieski again stopped the Turks outside Vienna.

By the 1600s the Ottoman government and economy faced real problems as well. During these years, the empire lost control of the highly profitable silk and spice trades between Europe and Asia. European naval powers opened new sea routes to Asia that bypassed the Turks and destroyed their trade monopoly. At the same time, the power and prestige of the Ottoman sultans weakened. The government became increasingly corrupt due to internal power struggles within its growing bureaucracy. Rebellions among the Janissaries, the Ottomans' elite slave troops, added to the empire's troubles. During the late 1700s the Ottomans lost the Crimean Peninsula and lands around the Black Sea and the Sea of Azov to the Russians. The French invaded Egypt, an Ottoman possession, in 1798. Ottoman lands in the Balkans were also lost. Some sultans attempted to reform Ottoman government and military structures but had limited success. The Ottoman Empire struggled to survive, finally ending in 1923 when Turkey established itself as a republic.

✔ **READING CHECK: Analyzing Information** What problems did the Ottoman Empire face?

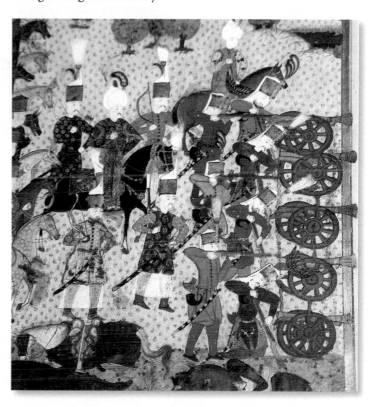

Ottomans in battle This painting shows Süleyman the Magnificent at the Battle of Mohács in Hungary. *What does this picture tell us about Ottoman military technology?*

SECTION 1 REVIEW

1. **Define** and explain the significance:
   ghazis
   reaya
   millets

2. **Identify** and explain the significance:
   Osman
   Janissaries
   Timur
   Mehmed II
   Süleyman

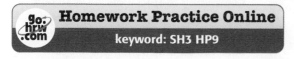

Homework Practice Online
keyword: SH3 HP9

3. **Sequencing** Copy the chart below. Use it to organize the major conquests and defeats that the Ottomans experienced between 1300 and 1700.

Conquests

Defeats

4. **Finding the Main Idea**
   a. What role did the Janissaries play in the success of the Ottoman Empire?
   b. How important do you think the Ottoman social system was to the success of the empire?

5. **Writing and Critical Thinking**
   Evaluating Explain your view of the Ottoman Empire's focus on military conquest.
   Consider:
   • how the people conquered were affected
   • how the Ottoman people were affected
   • the cost in both money and lives

The Safavid Empire

READ TO DISCOVER

❶ How was religion responsible for the development of the Safavid Empire?

❷ How did 'Abbās the Great bring the Safavid Empire to its height?

DEFINE

kizilbash

IDENTIFY

Safī od-Dīn
Esmā'īl
Tahmāsp
'Abbās

WHY IT MATTERS TODAY

The Iranian (Persian) government has kept Shi'ah Islam as the state religion from the time of the Safavids up to the present day. Use or other **current event** sources to explore how religious differences affect Iran's relationship with other countries. Record your findings in your journal.

The Main Idea
The Safavid rulers created a powerful Shi'ah Muslim empire with a prospering economy and culture.

The Story Continues *While the Ottomans were building their empire, the Safavid dynasty was gaining power in Persia. Shah Esmā'īl, the founder of this new empire, was driven by religious zeal. "I am committed to this action," he said. "God and the Immaculate [pure] Imams are with me, and I fear no one."*

The Rise of the Safavids

The Safavid (sah·FAH·vid) Empire was bounded on the west by the Ottoman Empire and on the east by the Mughal Empire of India. Today, much of what was the Safavid Empire is the country of Iran.

The Safavids were descended from **Safī od-Dīn,** head of the family in the 1200s. Like most Persians, the Safavids were Muslims. They belonged to the Sunni branch of Islam. In about 1399, however, the Safavids shifted from Sunni to the Shi'ah sect. As Shi'ah, they were persecuted by the Sunni.

Toward the end of the 1400s, the Safavids developed a military group to fight for political power. This army was called the **kizilbash,** meaning "Red Heads," for the red hats they wore. Other Persians killed or imprisoned many Safavids, but one of the youngest, **Esmā'īl** (is·mah·EEL), escaped into hiding. In about 1500 Esmā'īl became head of the kizilbash. In a series of victories, he brought all of modern Iran and part of present-day Iraq under his rule. In 1501 he captured the city of Tabrīz and made it the Safavid capital. Esmā'īl took the ancient Persian title of shah, or "king of kings," and reigned until 1524.

✔ **READING CHECK: Summarizing** What problems did the Safavids face during the 1400s?

Esmā'īl's religious policy. As soon as Esmā'īl became shah, he proclaimed that Shi'ah would be the religion of the Safavid Empire. Most Persians were Sunni, but Esmā'īl forced them to convert. Many people considered Esmā'īl a Muslim saint as well as shah, which helped in the process of conversion. Shi'ah gave the Persians an identity distinct from the great number of Sunni—Turks and Arabs—

INTERPRETING THE VISUAL RECORD

Continuing conflict Until the late 1580s the Safavids were often outmatched by the stronger Ottoman army. *What generalizations can be drawn from this image?*

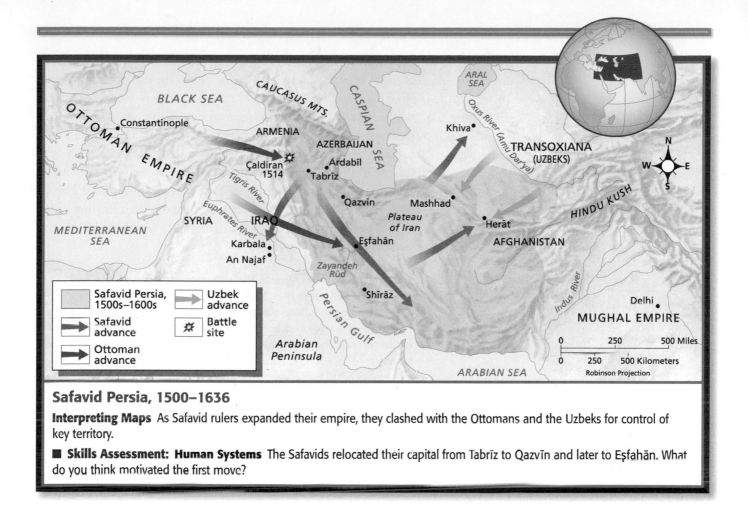

Safavid Persia, 1500–1636

Interpreting Maps As Safavid rulers expanded their empire, they clashed with the Ottomans and the Uzbeks for control of key territory.

■ **Skills Assessment: Human Systems** The Safavids relocated their capital from Tabrīz to Qazvīn and later to Eşfahān. What do you think motivated the first move?

who lived around them. The Persian language and history also contributed to a strong sense of identity, which continues in modern Iran.

Esmā'īl's support of Shi'ah threatened Persia's neighbors—the Sunni Ottomans and Uzbek tribes to the northeast. In 1514 the Ottomans invaded northwestern Persia. They defeated the Safavids at the Battle of Çaldiran. The struggle continued through the mid-1500s. After Esmā'īl died, his son **Tahmāsp** tried to carry on the fight. However, by the 1570s the Safavids had lost territory to both the Ottomans and the Uzbeks.

✔**READING CHECK: Finding the Main Idea** Why did Esmā'īl make Shi'ah the religion of the empire?

Shah 'Abbās the Great

When Tahmāsp died in 1576, the Safavid Empire was unstable. The kizilbash were no longer loyal to the shah. The struggles against the Ottomans and Uzbeks were going badly. Then in 1587 **'Abbās,** called "the Great," became shah.

Military reforms. 'Abbās realized he needed troops that would be loyal to him. He reformed the military, using the Ottoman army as a model. He created troops of foreign slaves who had been prisoners of war. After they were converted to Islam, they were trained for army service. These slave-soldiers belonged to the shah and were loyal only to him.

Eventually 'Abbās was ready to take on the Ottomans and Uzbeks. In 1598 his improved army defeated the Uzbeks and regained control of northeastern Persia. In a few years 'Abbās recovered all the territory the Safavids had lost.

Holt Researcher

go.hrw.com
KEYWORD: Holt Researcher
FreeFind: Abbas
After reading more about 'Abbās on the Holt Researcher, write a list of questions you would ask him if you had a chance to interview him. Then write his possible responses.

The height of the empire. In about 1599 'Abbās moved the Safavid capital to Eşfahān on the Plateau of Iran. Eşfahān soon became one of the most beautiful cities in the world. 'Abbās planned his new capital city carefully. It had wide streets and a huge central square. It had splendid mosques and monuments, as well as public baths and open markets. The center of Eşfahān was an enormous rectangular park that was large enough for polo games and that was surrounded by an arcade of shops. Large inns scattered throughout the city had central courtyards where camel caravans could be housed and rested. Eşfahān became known throughout Europe and the Middle East as a political, spiritual, and commercial center of the first order.

Even 'Abbās liked to walk around his city. Christian monks who had a mission in Eşfahān kept a record of what they observed.

Analyzing Primary Sources

Drawing Inferences How do you think the shopkeepers probably reacted to 'Abbās's behavior?

Primary Source

❝He ['Abbās] will come to the greengrocers, fruiterers, and those who sell preserves and sweetmeats. Here he will take a mouthful of this, there another of that . . . . Or he will enter the shop of a shoemaker, pick up a pair of shoes that takes his fancy, put them on at the door and then continue on his way.❞

From Clive Irving, *Crossroads of Civilization: 3000 Years of Persian History*

'Abbās's reign was also a time of economic development. The shah encouraged manufacturing and foreign trade. Carpet weaving became a major industry. Fine Persian rugs began to appear in the homes of wealthy Europeans. Persian merchants exported rich fabrics such as brocade, damask, and silk. The Safavids produced beautiful tiles and ceramics for their own use as well as for trade.

'Abbās died in 1629. For a while after his death, the Safavids continued to rule. However, rulers after 'Abbās proved increasingly inept. The empire began to decline and had ended by 1736. Eventually Persia split into a number of small states.

This glazeware from about 1625 shows typical Safavid artistry.

✔ **READING CHECK: Supporting a Point of View** What evidence would you give that 'Abbās was an especially capable ruler?

SECTION 2 REVIEW

1. **Define** and explain the significance:
   kizilbash

2. **Identify** and explain the significance:
   Safī od-Dīn
   Esmā'īl
   Tahmāsp
   'Abbās

3. **Identifying Cause and Effect** Copy the model below. Give the reasons why each event happened.

4. **Finding the Main Idea**
   a. What effect did the Safavid religious policy have on Persia?
   b. What were the results of the military reforms carried out under 'Abbās?
   c. What might a visitor to Eşfahān in the early 1600s conclude about the Safavid Empire?

5. **Writing and Critical Thinking**
   Summarizing Imagine you are a visitor to Eşfahān during Abbās's time. Write a description of your experience.
   Consider:
   • what the city looks like
   • what the people are doing in their everyday lives
   • what products and industries you see
   • in what ways the city of Eşfahān symbolizes Safavid strength and prosperity

Homework Practice Online
go.hrw.com
keyword: SH3 HP9

The Mughal Empire in India

READ TO DISCOVER

❶ How did the Mughal Empire begin?

❷ How did the Mughal Empire expand?

❸ What was the Mughal Empire like at its height?

IDENTIFY

Rajputs
Bābur
Akbar
Shah Jahān
Taj Mahal
Sikh
Aurangzeb

WHY IT MATTERS TODAY

The Taj Mahal in Agra, India, was built by a Mughal emperor. Thousands of tourists visit it each year. Use **CNN**student news.com or other **current event** sources to find out more about this architectural masterpiece. Record your findings in your journal.

CNNstudent news.com

The Main Idea
The Mughal rulers of India worked to unify and improve their vast, diverse Muslim empire.

The Story Continues *In 1605 the Mughal Empire was at the height of its glory. When Jahāngīr, son of Akbar, inherited his father's empire, his coronation ceremony reflected this splendor: "For forty days and forty nights I caused the . . . great imperial state drum, to strike up, without ceasing, the strains of joy and triumph;" he wrote, ". . . around my throne, the ground was spread by my directions with the most costly brocades [silks] and embroidered carpets. . . . Emirs of the empire, covered from head to foot in gold and jewels . . . stood round in brilliant array."*

The Origin of the Mughal Empire

During the 1300s Turkish Muslims controlled India, with Delhi as the capital of their sultanate. By the 1500s the power of the Delhi sultans had been greatly weakened. Indian warrior princes called **Rajputs** (RAHJ·poots) began to challenge them. The internal weakness of the sultanate drew the attention of India's powerful neighbors, as it had during Timur's time, and left India open to Mongol attack.

The attack came from a young leader known as "Bābur the Tiger." **Bābur** (also, Zahīr-ud-Dīn Muhammad) was a descendant of the Mongol leader Timur. He had tried to build an empire in central Asia, but the Uzbek people had driven him out. Bābur then focused on India. In 1526 he attacked the Sultanate of Delhi. A major battle took place at Panipat, a town north of Delhi. Bābur was greatly outnumbered, but he won the battle, as he described in his autobiography.

History Makers Speak

❝The kingdom of Hindustan [India] . . . was under the control of . . . [the sultan at Delhi] . . . His standing army was estimated at one hundred thousand. He and his commanders were said to have one thousand elephants. In such a state of affairs and with such strength, we put our trust in God . . . and faced a ruler with a huge army and vast realm. . . . God did not let our pains and difficulties go for naught and defeated such a powerful opponent and conquered a vast kingdom like Hindustan.❞

from The Baburnama: Memoirs of Babur, Prince and Emperor

This painting from about 1590 shows the richness and ease of life at the Mughal court.

Mughal Empire, 1526–1707

Interpreting Maps Many generations of Mughal emperors supported the arts and united most of India.

■ **Skills Assessment: Human Systems** What two cities on the west coast of the Indian subcontinent remained independent during Mughal rule?

After the victory at Panipat, Bābur occupied Delhi and the surrounding region. This territory became the core of the Mughal Empire.

✔ **READING CHECK: Summarizing** What role did Bābur play in establishing the Mughal Empire?

The Growth of Mughal Power

Bābur's grandson, **Akbar,** was the greatest Mughal emperor. He took the throne at the age of 13 and reigned from 1556 to 1605. Akbar gained support for his government in various ways. He married a Rajput princess and gave other Rajputs government positions. At times he used force to maintain power. By 1605 Akbar controlled all of northern and much of central India.

Akbar introduced an improved tax system that helped him control his empire. Taxes were based on an average of what a village might produce over a 10-year period. When the harvest was poor, the tax did not have to be paid. In a good harvest, the villagers could keep anything above the tax level.

Akbar was a great supporter of the arts. He encouraged Hindu as well as Muslim artists. Mughal artists, influenced by the Persian style, created delicate, colorful miniature paintings. Akbar also encouraged the development of literature in the Hindi and Urdu languages. The Mughals made great achievements in architecture, blending Persian, Islamic, and Hindu styles.

Religious policy. Perhaps most importantly, Akbar was tolerant of all religions. He repealed the special tax that non-Muslims had been forced to pay. Over time, however, he began to think of himself as a divine ruler. In the late 1500s he established a creed called the Divine Faith. The motto for the creed was *Allahu Akbar,* meaning either "God is great" or "Akbar is God." The creed blended elements of Islam, Hinduism, Jainism, Christianity, and other religions. It attracted few followers beyond Akbar's court because Muslims strongly opposed it.

Economy and trade. During Akbar's reign the economy improved. The empire's wealth and resources, and its location along the sea routes to Asia, attracted European traders. India had impressive quantities of jewels and gold. The climate allowed the peasants to grow a variety of crops and allowed more than one harvest a year. European travelers thought India's rulers lived in greater luxury than their European kings. India's cities, such as Agra and Delhi, were filled with beautiful buildings and monuments. The Mughal cities seemed much larger than any in Europe.

✔ **READING CHECK: Making Generalizations** What role did Akbar play in the growth of the Mughal Empire?

The Height of the Mughal Empire

The Mughal Empire was at its height during the reign of **Shah Jahān.** He ruled from 1628 to 1658. By this time the empire had expanded to reach its greatest extent of territory, including both northern and southern India.

Shah Jahān is best known for the two famous buildings that were constructed during his reign. The magnificent **Taj Mahal** at Agra remains one of the architectural wonders of the world. Shah Jahān had the Taj Mahal built as a tomb for his beloved wife, Mumtāz Mahal. It is made of marble inlaid with semiprecious gems. The other building, the Hall of Private Audience, is in the Red Fort at Delhi. This was Shah Jahān's palace. In the Hall of Private Audience are carved these famous lines: "If there be Paradise on Earth, It is Here, It is Here, It is Here!" These great buildings were enormously expensive to build.

At the same time, the Mughals were engaged in military campaigns against Persia. Their huge armies were very expensive to maintain. They believed these armies were necessary to hold their empire together. To meet his expenses, Shah Jahān increased taxes. His subjects had to pay him half of the crops they raised. Many people suffered under this terrible burden.

A new religion. Under the Mughals, a blending of Hindu and Muslim cultures occurred. In the 1500s an Indian mystic named Nānak tried to unite the Hindu and Muslim religions. Out of Nānak's teaching arose a new religion—the **Sikh** (SEEK) faith. This faith called for devotion to one God, a lack of idols, and a less rigid social system. These ideas conflicted with Hindu beliefs. Nānak became the first guru (leader or teacher) of the Sikhs. By the late 1600s the Sikhs had become militant. They became fierce enemies of the Mughal Empire and the Muslims.

The Taj Mahal Shah Jahān brought workers and materials from all over India and central Asia to build the Taj Mahal. It took more than 20,000 workers and over 20 years to finish the job. *What statement does this building make about the power of the Mughals?*

The Reign of Aurangzeb

A frame of reference is a set of ideas, conditions, or beliefs. Historians use different frames of reference to analyze a person, an event, or an era. For example, a historian may examine a subject from a social, economic, legal, or political frame of reference. As a result, different scholars may tell a very different story about the same historical subject. They can come to different conclusions based on their frame of reference. Knowing a historian's frame of reference helps you to understand what you read. Understanding different interpretations about Aurangzeb's rule requires analysis of the frames of reference used by the historians.

Historians' Views

"The predominant trait of the Mughal rulers of India was their political instinct. . . . Aurangzeb displayed this character to an eminent [outstanding] degree."

Mughal Empire in India

"[The] intolerance of Aurangzeb . . . hastened the ruin of the dynasty . . . his bigotry and persecutions rendered him hateful to his Hindu subjects."

A History of the Sikhs

"Aurangzeb's government made itself ridiculous by violently enforcing for a time, then relaxing, and finally abandoning a code of puritanical morals opposed to the feelings of the entire population . . ."

The Cambridge History of India

Skills Reminder

To understand frames of reference, first identify what factors the author emphasizes, such as economics, politics, or social outcomes. Also, identify the context in which the information is given. For example, is an analysis of a leader's rule being offered in the history of a people whom he conquered? Assess how this frame of reference might influence the information. Finally, compare how authors using different frames of reference might come to different conclusions about an event.

Skills Practice

❶ Study the passages above about the reign of the Mughal ruler Aurangzeb. What frame of reference is each historian using?

❷ What conclusions can you draw about Aurangzeb's rule from these passages?

❸ Write a brief summary of the rise and fall of either the Ottoman or Safavid empires using a particular frame of reference.

Despite his abuses Shah Jahān was an extremely vigorous ruler. During the 30 years of his rule, he put down several rebellions, built a magnificent new capital at Delhi, and conquered new territories in the Deccan. He also launched an unsuccessful attempt to recapture the old Mughal homeland in central Asia. The shah's Peacock Throne, designed to inspire awe, was the greatest symbol of Mughal splendor. The throne was encrusted with gold and the largest diamonds, emeralds, and other precious gems. Shah Jahān also sought to make Delhi the world's most beautiful capital as a means of reflecting his power.

Aurangzeb. In 1657 Shah Jahān became ill. His son Muhī-ud-Dīn Muhammad, known by his princely title of **Aurangzeb** (AWR·uhng·zeb), killed his older brother, imprisoned Shah Jahān, and declared himself emperor.

A devout Sunni Muslim, Aurangzeb followed strict Islamic law in his personal life. He dressed simply and expected his courtiers to follow his example. He ended government spending on buildings and monuments. He banned most celebrations, particularly those that included wine and music.

Aurangzeb persecuted all other faiths in the Mughal Empire. He insisted on strict observance of Islamic holy laws. He restored the hated tax on Hindus and destroyed thousands of Hindu temples. He also oppressed the Shi'ah and Sufi Muslims. When crowds gathered outside the Red Fort to protest, Aurangzeb used elephants to crush them. Religious groups rioted throughout the empire.

Under Aurangzeb the Mughal Empire was the largest it would ever be. Unfortunately, the widespread revolts and economic problems weakened the empire. Aurangzeb may have regretted the bloodshed of his reign. When he died in 1707, he wondered aloud whether his actions would please his God.

This image dating from the mid-1600s portrays Shah Jahān at the height of his power.

✔ **READING CHECK: Contrasting** How was the reign of Aurangzeb different from the reign of Shah Jahān?

SECTION 3 REVIEW

1. **Identify** and explain the significance:
   Rajputs
   Bābur
   Akbar
   Shah Jahān
   Taj Mahal
   Sikh
   Aurangzeb

2. **Sequencing** Copy the chart below. Use it to organize important events in the history of the Mughal Empire.

   1. Bābur wins battle at Paniput.
   2.
   3.
   4.
   5.
   6. Aurangzeb dies.

3. **Finding the Main Idea**
   a. What evidence shows that Akbar tried to unify his empire?
   b. How did Shah Jahān improve the empire?
   c. How did Shah Jahān raise funds for his ambitious building programs and his military policies?
   d. In what ways did the strict policies of Aurangzeb represent a return to intolerance in Mughal India?

4. **Writing and Critical Thinking**
   Drawing Conclusions Explain how Aurangzeb harmed the Mughal Empire.
   Consider:
   • his policies toward other religions
   • his response to protests
   • his strict observance of Islamic laws

Homework Practice Online
keyword: SH3 HP9

Review

Creating a Time Line

Copy the time line below onto a sheet of paper. Complete the time line by filling in the events, individuals, and dates from the chapter that you think were significant. Pick three events and explain why you think they were significant.

1300	1400	1500	1600	1700

Writing a Summary

Using standard grammar, spelling, sentence structure, and punctuation, write an overview of the events in the chapter.

Identifying People and Ideas

Identify the following terms or individuals and explain their significance:

1. millets
2. Janissaries
3. Süleyman
4. kizilbash
5. Esmāʿīl
6. ʿAbbās
7. Bābur
8. Akbar
9. Shah Jahān
10. Aurangzeb

Understanding Main Ideas

Section 1 *(pp. 240–243)*

The Ottoman Empire

1. What territory was included in the Ottoman Empire at its height?
2. Why were the Janissaries important to the Ottoman sultans?
3. How did the Ottoman Turks maintain peace among the various ethnic groups within their widespread empire?

Section 2 *(pp. 244–246)*

The Safavid Empire

4. What role did the Shiʿah religion play in the strengthening of the Safavid Empire and in the empire's relations with its neighbors?
5. How did Shiʿah affect the Persians' ideas about themselves?
6. Why did the Persians of the Safavid Empire call ʿAbbās "the Great"?

Section 3 *(pp. 247–251)*

The Mughal Empire in India

7. What event marks the beginning of the Mughal Empire?
8. What were Akbar's most important accomplishments?
9. How did Aurangzeb's approach to government spending differ from Shah Jahān's?

Reviewing Themes

1. **Global Relations** What evidence is there that the Islamic empires supported large, strong militaries?
2. **Culture** How did religious policies affect the Islamic empires?
3. **Government** What effect did the character of individual rulers have on the Islamic empires?

Thinking Critically

1. **Drawing Inferences** In what way did the building of the Taj Mahal contribute to the decline of the Mughal Empire?
2. **Comparing** Compare the policy toward Sunni Muslims in the Ottoman Empire to the policy in the Safavid Empire.
3. **Supporting a Point of View** What evidence would you give that in the Ottoman Empire ordinary people had an equal chance for success?

Writing About History

Comparing and Contrasting Write a report describing the similarities and differences among the Ottoman, Safavid, and Mughal empires. Use the chart below to organize your thoughts before you write.

	Ottoman	Safavid	Mughal
Title used by ruler			
Most successful ruler			
Official branch of Islam			
Policy toward other religions			
Present name of country			

Interpreting Maps

Study the map below. Then answer the questions that follow.

The Ottomans in Hungary, c. 1520–c. 1565

1. Which of the following statements best describes the Ottoman expansion into Hungary during the 1500s?

   a. The Ottomans' victory at Mohács had little impact on their movement into Hungary.

   b. The Ottomans' victory at Mohács allowed them to expand north, east, and west.

   c. Within ten years of their victory at Mohács, the Ottomans had taken control of all Hungary.

   d. Their victory at Mohács enabled the Ottomans to win control of the entire Mediterranean basin.

2. Why do you think the location of Mohács was important to Ottoman plans to conquer Hungary?

Sequencing

Read the sentences below about the Mughal rulers. Then answer the question that follows.

   A. Shah Jahān (ruled 1628–1658) built the Taj Mahal.

   B. The greatest Mughal emperor was Akbar. By the end of his reign in the early 1600s, Akbar controlled much of northern and central India.

   C. Bābur occupied Delhi in 1526 and founded the Mughal Empire.

   D. Economic problems had weakened the government by the time Aurangzeb died in 1707.

   E. By the early years of the 1500s, the Muslim Sultanate of Delhi was suffering from internal weakness and was being increasingly challenged by the Rajput princes and their armies.

3. Which of the following shows the events listed in the order in which they occurred?

   a. B, C, A, D, E

   b. C, A, D, E, B

   c. D, E, A, B, C

   d. E, C, B, A, D

4. What were the main differences between the way Akbar and Aurangzeb ruled the Mughal Empire? Give specific examples.

Alternative Assessment

Building Your Portfolio

Link to TODAY

Culture

In the world today, religious policies still unify or divide cultures. Use your textbook and other sources to find examples of cultures that have been either unified or divided by the religious policies of governments. Then prepare a script about your findings that a television reporter could read on the evening news.

✓ internet connect

Internet Activity: go.hrw.com
KEYWORD: SH3 WH9

Choose a topic on Islamic Empires in Asia to:

• create an illustrated time line of the major events in the history of the Ottoman Empire.

• research life and society in the Safavid Empire.

• create a newspaper article on the impact of the siege of Vienna in 1683.

Styles of Verse

Throughout the world's diverse societies, many forms of poetry have developed. Each culture's poetry has distinctive sounds and styles. The Persian poet Firdawsi (c. 935–1020) told the story of his nation's kings in an epic named Shah-nameh. This massive work contains 60,000 rhyming couplets. In the excerpt below the hero Sekander promises to care for King Dara as the king dies. William Shakespeare (1564–1616), an English writer, also wrote about death, but in a very different style. His sonnets are 14-line poems with a strict pattern of rhythm and rhyme. Japanese poet Banzan's haiku poem—written on his deathbed in 1730—follows the typical haiku form. In the original Japanese it contains five syllables in the first line, seven in the second, and five in the third.

Shah-nameh *by Firdawsi*

"I will have physicians brought for you from India and Rum [Rome] and I will cause tears of blood to flow for the pain you have suffered. . . . My heart bled and a cry issued from my lips when yesterday I heard from my elders that we two are of one stock and share a single shirt. Why should we extirpate [wipe out] our seed in rivalry?"

On hearing this, Dara said in a strong voice, ". . . Marry my pure-bodied daughter and maintain her in security in your palace. . . . It may be that by her you will have a noble son who will restore the name of Esfandiyar [an ancestor] to glory."

Shown here is the manuscript of a poem by the Japanese haiku master Bashō.

Haiku *by Banzan*

Mame de iyo
mi wa narawashi no
kusa no tsuyu.

(Translation:)
Farewell
I pass as all things do
dew on the grass.

"Sonnet 19" by *William Shakespeare*

Devouring time,
    blunt thou the lion's
    paws,
And make the earth
    devour her own
    sweet brood;
Pluck the keen teeth
    from the fierce
    tiger's jaws,
And burn the long-lived
    phoenix in her blood.
Make glad and sorry seasons as
    thou fleet'st,
And do whate'er thou wilt, swift-footed time,
To the wide world and all her fading sweets.
But I forbid thee one most heinous crime:
O, carve not with thy hours my love's fair brow,
Nor draw no lines there with thine antique pen.
Him in thy course untainted do allow
For beauty's pattern to succeeding men.
Yet do thy worst, old time; despite thy wrong
My love shall in my verse ever live young.

Understanding Literature

What similarities and differences do you find among these poems in their purpose, style, and tone?

Economics

A search for wealth motivated European exploration of the New World. Imagine that you are an English adventurer who wishes to undertake a voyage to America in the 1500s. You will need the financial support of the Queen to make the journey. Your task is to write a proposal showing why your trip to the New World would be economically beneficial to England. What types of evidence would you use to show the importance of exploration for the economic welfare of the kingdom?

Ferdinand Magellan and his fleet setting sail from Spain in 1519

Global Relations

During the 1400s and 1500s, the Ottoman Turks expanded the boundaries of their empire, conquering much of eastern Europe. Imagine that you are a soldier advancing with the Ottoman armies through eastern Europe in the 1520s. Create a diary in which you recount your experiences, including your impressions of European society, government, and religion. Based on your observations, discuss your view of the relations between the Ottoman Empire and the various kingdoms of eastern Europe.

Ottoman ceramic pitcher and plate

Further Reading

Dersin, Denise, ed. *What Life Was Like: At The Rebirth Of Genius, Renaissance Italy 1400-1550.* Alexandria, Virginia: Time-Life Books, 1999. A survey of daily life and culture in Renaissance Italy.

Goodwin, Jason. *Lords of the Horizons: A History of the Ottoman Empire.* New York: Owl Books, 2000. A thorough survey of the Ottoman Empire from its beginnings to its collapse.

Hale, J. R., ed. *The Thames and Hudson Encyclopedia of the Italian Renaissance.* London: Thames and Hudson, 1988. A reference work on the history, politics, culture, and society of the Italian Renaissance.

Meltzer, Milton. *Columbus and the World Around Him.* New York: Watts Franklin, 1990. A history of Christopher Columbus and his four voyages.

Pilbeam, Mavis. *Japan Under The Shoguns, 1185-1868.* New York: Raintree/Steck-Vaughn, 1999. A history of the shogunates, and a look at everyday life in Japan and the role of the samurai.

🔲 **internet** connect

Internet Activity
KEYWORD: SH3 U2

In assigned groups, develop a multimedia presentation about the Age of Exploration and Expansion. Choose information from the chapter Internet Connect activities and the Holt Researcher that best reflects the major topics of the period. Write an outline and a script for your presentation, which may be shown to the class.

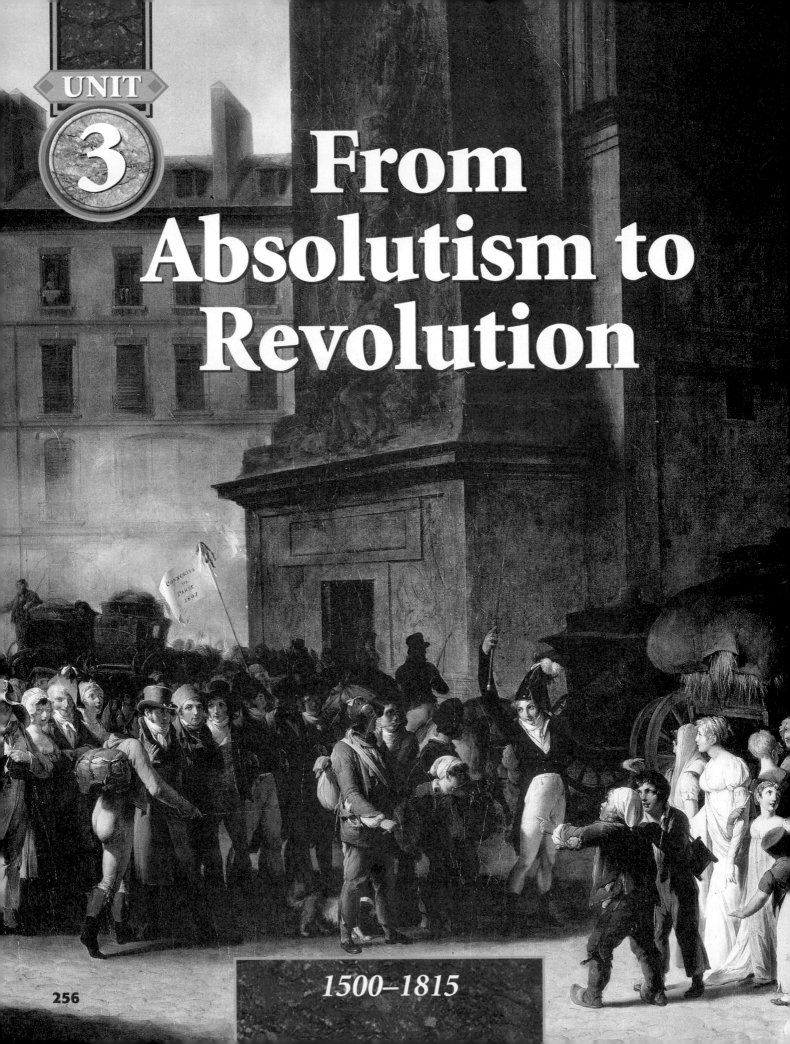

From Absolutism to Revolution

1500–1815

Main Events

- The Age of Absolutism occurs in France, Russia, and Central Europe
- The English Revolution challenges the monarchy
- The Age of Enlightenment and the American Revolution usher in new ideas about government
- The French Revolution fails, leading to the rise of Napoléon

Main Ideas

- What was the Age of Absolutism?
- What were the main ideas of the Enlightenment? How did they influence the American Revolution?
- What caused the French Revolution?
- How did Napoléon come to power?
- How was England's monarchy affected by the ideas of absolutism?

An artillery piece from the American Revolution

This painting by Louis-Léopold Boilly shows French recruits assembling for military service in 1807.

257

Focus On: Constitutional Heritage

Main Idea **What laws should rule?** During the 1500s European political and social thinkers began a debate about the proper nature of government. Some thought the best form of government was a single ruler, such as a king, who had absolute authority. Others believed a government should represent the people, who had the right to change the government if it ruled unjustly. Increasingly, constitutional forms of government, based on the authority of law, came into being. This type of government placed even rulers under the absolute power of the constitution.

America
France
England

1500   1620   1789   1800
1815

The Power of Parliament Monarchs in France and Russia governed with complete authority. Government worked differently in England, however, where even the monarch was subject to the law. The English designed Parliament to act as a check on the monarch's power. In this painting England's Queen Elizabeth I is shown presiding over an opening session of Parliament. Elizabeth could not impose new taxes or pass new laws without Parliament's approval. However, she skillfully used the group to her political advantage. Later monarchs did not work as well with Parliament, however, leading to a series of upheavals that came to be known as the English Revolution. By the time the revolution had ended, the power of parliamentary law was firmly established.

England, 1500–1800

This cartoon from the period of the English Civil War shows a London woman sending her husband off to fight for the forces of Parliament.

Thomas Jefferson's Vision American leaders of the late 1700s—such as Benjamin Franklin and Thomas Jefferson—were inspired by the ideas of the European Enlightenment. Enlightenment philosophy influenced the writing of both the Declaration of Independence and the U.S. Constitution. Thomas Jefferson also used Enlightenment principles to design the University of Virginia—the University's rotunda is shown at right—and his home at Monticello. Enlightenment faith in the powers of the mind and the concepts of reason, balance, and order were the focus of Jefferson's designs. Precise geometric forms, such as the dome, embodied the principle of reason. Jefferson's architectural designs reflected classical styles from Greece and Rome, as did many of Jefferson's beliefs about government.

America, 1620–1789

The French Republic The idea of a constitutional republic did not appeal just to French men alone. French women also supported the Revolution, which took place between 1789 and 1793. Some women attended meetings of revolutionary groups and voiced their opinions about affairs of state. Two women in Paris started their own group in 1793, called The Society for Revolutionary Republican Women. Members of this revolutionary club thought of themselves as a family of sisters ready to rush to the defense of their country. Women in patriotic clubs, such as the one pictured here, gathered to discuss the political issues of the day. At one point during the French Revolution, men in Paris outlawed women's political clubs.

France, 1500–1815

In this portrait a French woman is wearing the "bonnet rouge" (red cap) that became a symbol of the French Revolution and of the republic it produced.

This sketch shows the planned front elevation of Jefferson's estate at Monticello, c. 1790s. The finished construction, which differs somewhat from the original design, is shown at right.

Why It Matters Today

The principles of constitutional government and the rule of law developed over centuries. The basic ideals of constitutionalism—personal liberty, representative government, and political checks and balances—continue to affect today's nations.
How does constitutionalism shape the United States today?

CHAPTER 10

1500–1800
Monarchs of Europe

Sir Thomas More, Chancellor of England from 1529 to 1532

1556–1598
Politics
Philip II rules Spain.

1535
Politics
Sir Thomas More is executed for not recognizing Henry VIII as the head of the church in England.

1558–1603
Politics
Elizabeth I reigns in England.

1564
Politics
Russians force Ivan IV to leave Moscow.

A locket commemorating England's victory over the Spanish Armada

1588
Global Events
The English navy defeats the Spanish Armada.

1630
Business and Finance
Public advertising begins in Paris.

1632
Business and Finance
Russia begins a fur trade in Siberia.

1500

1600

1501
Daily Life
Card games increase in popularity all over Europe.

1530s
Daily Life
Henry VIII founds the Anglican Church in England.

1563
The Arts
Pieter Brueghel paints *The Tower of Babel.*

c. 1560s
Science and Technology
The first printing presses appear in Russia.

1606
The Arts
William Shakespeare writes *King Lear* and *Macbeth.*

1603
Politics
King James I founds the Stuart dynasty in England.

An oil-on-panel painting of the Tudor family

Build on What You Know

In the late 1400s, European society began to change dramatically. Technological advances in mapmaking, navigation instruments, and shipbuilding, and new knowledge of Earth's geography provided Europeans with the means to explore the world beyond Europe. New methods of organizing and conducting business led to widespread economic change as well. Nations began overseas exploration and colonization, and economic and political conditions in Europe led many people to move to the newly founded overseas colonies. In this chapter, you will learn how monarchs rose to power in Europe.

Desk of King Louis XIV

Catherine the Great, empress of Russia

1677
Daily Life
Ice cream becomes a popular dessert in Paris.

1707
Global Events
England and Scotland unite as Great Britain.

1740–1780
Politics
Maria Theresa rules Austria.

1742
The Arts
The first public performance of George Frideric Handel's *Messiah* takes place.

1762–1796
Politics
Catherine the Great rules Russia.

c. 1765
Daily Life
The potato becomes a popular food in Europe.

1700

1800

1686
Politics
Russia declares war on the Ottoman Empire.

1683
Politics
The Ottoman Turks besiege Vienna.

c. 1729–1732
Science and Technology
English scientist Stephen Gray discovers how electricity is conducted.

1756
Global Events
Britain declares war on France.

1756
The Arts
Austrian composer Wolfgang Amadeus Mozart is born.

1796
Science and Technology
English physicians introduce a vaccine against smallpox.

Section of the Catherine Palace, Russia

What's Your Opinion?

Themes Journal *Do you* **agree** *or* **disagree** *with the following statements? Support your point of view in your journal.*

Government A nation cannot survive without a strong central government.

Culture Religious beliefs have little, if any, effect on the degree of unity or disunity that characterizes a particular society.

Economics All citizens of a society should have the same amount of wealth.

France in the Age of Absolutism

READ TO DISCOVER

❶ How did Henry IV and Cardinal Richelieu strengthen France?

❷ How did Louis XIV strengthen the central government?

❸ Why did Louis XIV go to war, and what were the results?

DEFINE

intendants
divine right of kings
balance of power

IDENTIFY

Henry IV
Cardinal Richelieu
Thirty Years' War
Louis XIV
Jean-Baptiste Colbert
War of the Spanish Succession

▶ WHY IT MATTERS TODAY

Some nations today are still governed by a single ruler. Use CNN student News.com or other **current event** sources to find which nations are controlled by dictators or rulers with absolute power. Record your findings in your journal.

CNN student News.com

The Main Idea
Under the Bourbon kings, France became an absolute monarchy and Europe's leading power.

The Story Continues *Kings became stronger in Europe in the 1500s as the power of the church weakened. A French bishop explained just how strong monarchs were in the eyes of some: "Princes, thus, act as ministers of God, and as His lieutenants on earth. It is through them that He acts on His empire."*

Strengthening the Monarchy

From Navarre, a tiny kingdom in the Pyrenees Mountains between Spain and France, **Henry IV** came to the French throne in 1589. He was the first monarch of a new royal house—the Bourbons. Henry had been a Huguenot, a member of a Protestant minority group. However, he converted to Catholicism to help bring peace and unity to France. "Paris is well worth a mass!" he reportedly remarked. To protect the Huguenots, Henry issued the Edict of Nantes (NANTS). This order guaranteed freedom of worship and political rights and ended the religious wars.

Henry also tried to solve some of France's other major problems. Powerful nobles had weakened the central government of France in the 1500s. Henry worked to control the nobility and regain power.

However, one problem Henry could not fully solve was taxation. The burden of the French tax system was unfairly distributed, and many, including nobles and members of the clergy, were exempt from taxes altogether. People in large cities such as Paris were also exempt from the royal tax. The tax fell most heavily on members of the middle and lower classes. To improve the system, Henry placed the able Duke of Sully in charge of finances. Sully could not fix all the problems with the system, but he did end some of the abuses. More tax money thus went to the French treasury, and it was used to improve industry and trade.

Cardinal Richelieu. Henry IV was murdered in 1610. His son, Louis XIII, was just eight years old at the time. Louis's mother, Marie de Médicis, ruled as regent until Louis came to power in 1617. Louis was sickly and had trouble concentrating. To rule effectively, he chose wise advisers who provided strong leadership. Louis chose **Cardinal Richelieu** (RISH·uhl·oo) to be his chief minister.

Cardinal Richelieu ran the government of France from 1624 until 1642.

Richelieu was a political genius who wanted to make the king supreme in France and France supreme in Europe. To strengthen the monarchy, Richelieu worked to take power away from the nobles and political rights away from the Huguenots. To strengthen France, he encouraged trade and industry.

Richelieu believed that the freedom given to the Huguenots by the Edict of Nantes was dangerous. The Huguenots lived in fortified cities that were like states within a state. They made a strong central government in France impossible. In 1627 Richelieu led military attacks on Huguenot towns. After a year the Huguenots asked for peace. Richelieu still allowed them to practice their religion and hold public office, but he took away their special rights in fortified cities.

INTERPRETING THE VISUAL RECORD

The Thirty Years' War This painting from the 1600s depicts the Battle of Diedenhofen, in which French troops were defeated. Eventually, however, France emerged from the war as a strong nation while much of Germany was devastated by fighting. *What modern weapons of warfare are the soldiers in the center of the picture using?*

Richelieu took further steps to centralize power under the crown. He strengthened the authority of regional representatives of the king. These officials, known as **intendants,** were the monarchy's representatives in the provinces that made up France. Over time, they took administrative and financial power away from regional governors and military leaders and concentrated it in the hands of the king.

The Thirty Years' War. In 1618 the **Thirty Years' War** began in Prague as a Protestant rebellion against the Holy Roman Empire. France, Denmark, and Sweden were all looking for ways to weaken the empire and its ruling family, the Habsburgs. Richelieu saw the war as a great opportunity to strengthen France.

Richelieu worked to keep the war going, but for the most part he kept France out of it directly. Thus, other European countries became weak from fighting while France stayed strong. Most of the war took place in Germany, ruining much of that country. France eventually joined in the fighting. By 1648 the French and their allies had accomplished most of their goals.

The war ended when the countries involved signed the Treaty of Westphalia in 1648. France was strengthened by receiving Alsace, a valuable territory along the Rhine River. The treaty also gave independence to the Netherlands and Switzerland. It made the German princes more or less independent of the Holy Roman Emperor. All these changes weakened the Holy Roman Empire and the Habsburg family.

✔ **READING CHECK: Comparing and Contrasting** How did the methods of Henry IV and Richelieu for strengthening France and the French monarchy compare?

The Sun King

In 1643 **Louis XIV** became the king of France. He ruled for 72 years, the longest reign in French history. As a boy, Louis XIV lived through the Fronde rebellions, when French nobles and peasants had attacked the central royal government. Perhaps because of this experience, Louis worked to make the king's power absolute.

Versailles. Louis built a huge palace at Versailles (ver·SY), a few miles outside of Paris, and moved the French government there. The beautiful and elaborate palace was so expensive to build that it strained the French economy. Versailles represented the grandeur and power of the monarchy and of France. This was important to Louis because he believed in the **divine right of kings**—that God had chosen him to rule the nation. "*L'état, c'est moi*" ("I am the state"), he proclaimed.

Louis used the palace to control the nobles. He insisted that the most important nobles live at Versailles. In this way, Louis could always keep his eye on them. The nobles could advance only by gaining Louis's favor.

Louis XIV's court at Versailles became the ideal for European royalty. Other monarchs soon took on the language and customs of France. Louis himself adopted the sun as his personal symbol. The sun's rays reached far and wide, just like his power. For this reason, Louis was nicknamed the Sun King.

Domestic and economic policies. For Louis, absolute power meant making most of the important decisions himself. As he once told his officials,

History Makers Speak

❝You will assist me with your counsels when I ask for them. I request and order you to seal no orders except by my command. I order you not to sign anything, not even a passport without my command; to render account to me personally each day and to favor no one.❞

Louis XIV, from *Louis XIV* by John B. Wolf

Throughout his long reign, Louis XIV was directly involved in the day-to-day operations of the French government. He also chose able advisers who, for the most part, worked under his direct supervision. One of the best of these was **Jean-Baptiste Colbert** (kawl·BAIR), an expert in finance. Colbert, a well-educated member of the middle class, followed strong policies to promote economic development in France. He aimed to increase French industry at home and to build French trade abroad. Colbert granted government subsidies to private companies to build new industries or to strengthen existing ones. He placed high tariffs on foreign imports in an effort to protect French businesses, and worked to improve transportation. Colbert also encouraged French companies to establish colonies and to carry on trade with Canada, the West Indies, and East Asia. In addition, he took strong steps to eliminate corruption and waste in the French tax-collection system.

Colbert's efforts on behalf of the crown met with varying degrees of success. He worked to reform the nation's tax system by making it more evenly distributed across the population. Colbert's aim was to make the system more fair by eliminating some of the exemptions granted to the privileged. Under his administration trade and commerce grew, and France became a leading economic power in Europe. Colbert was able to raise government income to pay for economic improvements, the large and powerful French army, and overseas exploration. At the same time France became a leading naval power and a strong force in overseas trade and colonization.

Louis XIV was concerned with religious unity. He believed that the Huguenots disturbed the unity of France and weakened the authority of the central government. Thus, in 1685 he did away with the Edict of Nantes, ending France's policy of tolerance for Protestants. More than 200,000 Huguenots fled France rather than become Catholics. Because the Huguenots had been productive citizens, their loss weakened France in the long run.

✔ **READING CHECK: Identifying Cause and Effect** How did the behavior and policies of Louis XIV strengthen the monarchy but hurt France in some ways?

Analyzing Primary Sources

Identifying a Point of View
According to this quote, what role did Louis XIV see for his advisers and ministers?

YOUNG PEOPLE IN HISTORY

The Boy King

Louis XIV became the king of France at the age of four. Although he was surrounded by the luxury of the French court, the first years of his reign were not easy. When he was just nine, Louis had to flee Paris when the Fronde rebellions broke out between the French nobility and the crown. From 1648 to 1652, Louis kept moving through France, suffering from hunger, cold, and fear. The memory of that hardship stayed with Louis forever. He never again trusted the people of Paris or the nobility. **How did Louis XIV's childhood affect his rule?**

The Wars of Louis XIV

Louis reorganized and increased the size of France's military. Soldiers were well trained and discipline was strict. By the early 1700s the French had a force of about 400,000 soldiers—the most powerful army in Europe.

Fighting for new territory. Louis believed France's security depended on the country having natural frontiers. Much of France already had such borders. The Atlantic Ocean, the Pyrenees Mountains, the Alps, and the Mediterranean Sea surrounded much of France. Louis wanted to extend France's territory east to the Rhine River to form another natural border. To accomplish this, he fought four wars between 1667 and 1713.

Louis's goals alarmed other European nations, leading many to ally with one another against France. During the 1660s and the 1670s, the Netherlands, England, and Sweden formed alliances against France, as did Austria, Brandenburg, and Spain. These countries worked to achieve a **balance of power,** in which countries have equal strength in order to prevent any one country from dominating the others.

The wars took a toll on France's resources. After Louis's third war ended in 1679, France was under great financial strain.

War of the Spanish Succession. Louis XIV's last war was the **War of the Spanish Succession.** It was fought over who would become the next king of Spain. The last Spanish Habsburg king died in 1700, leaving the throne to Philip V, Louis's grandson. The other European nations did not like the idea of both France and Spain being

The golden fountain at Louis XIV's palace of Versailles symbolizes the French monarchy at its height.

The Growth of France under Louis XIV, 1643–1715

Interpreting Maps Louis XIV made France a large and powerful nation and added to its territory.

■ **Skills Assessment: 1. Physical Systems** What natural boundaries surrounded much of France? **2. Drawing Inferences** What city in southeastern France remained outside of Louis's control? Why might that be so?

Louis XIV encouraged improvements in much of French society, from art and literature to transportation.

under Bourbon rulers. They battled Louis's forces in Europe, in North America, and at sea. The French met defeat after defeat. Finally Louis agreed to a settlement in 1713.

The war ended with the Treaty of Utrecht, an important document for both Europe and America. The treaty recognized Louis's grandson as king of Spain, but it provided that the French and Spanish monarchies could never be united. The treaty also gave French lands in North America to Great Britain.

Louis XIV's legacy. With the Treaty of Utrecht, France began to lose some of the empire it had built up in the 1500s. Before Louis's reign, French explorers such as Jacques Cartier had already made several voyages to North America. Samuel de Champlain had founded the city of Quebec, and several other settlements were established in the St. Lawrence Valley and the Great Lakes region. The French ran a profitable fur trade and fishing industry in North America.

Under Louis XIV, the French explorer René-Robert Cavelier de La Salle sailed down the Mississippi River to the Gulf of Mexico, claiming the inland region of North America for France. He named this area Louisiana in honor of Louis XIV. The French also occupied Haiti and other West Indian islands. They set up colonies in Asia and controlled part of India.

Louis XIV's wars, however, took a toll. The continuing military effort cost many lives and placed a heavy strain on the French treasury. Yet despite his setbacks, Louis made France a very powerful nation. During these years Great Britain became a major colonial power. Within Europe, however, France was viewed by many as the leading continental power.

After Louis died in 1715, the nobles won back many of the powers he had taken from them. Louis's great-grandson, Louis XV, became king and ruled from 1715 to 1774. Louis XV and his successor, Louis XVI, were comparatively weak rulers. The French government appeared stable, but in fact the royal authority was in decline.

✔ **READING CHECK: Evaluating** In what ways did France both benefit and suffer as a result of the wars Louis XIV started?

SECTION 1 REVIEW

1. **Define** and explain the significance:
   intendants
   divine right of kings
   balance of power

2. **Identify** and explain the significance:
   Henry IV
   Cardinal Richelieu
   Thirty Years' War
   Louis XIV
   Jean-Baptiste Colbert
   War of the Spanish Succession

3. **Analyzing Information** Copy the model below. Use it to list steps that Louis XIV took both within and outside of France to strengthen the country.

In France

Outside France

4. **Finding the Main Idea**

   a. In what ways did Louis XIV's approach to controlling the French nobility differ from that taken by Cardinal Richelieu?

   b. What role did the balance of power play in Europe when Louis XIV reigned?

   c. Were the wars that France fought under Louis XIV good for the country? Explain your answer.

5. **Writing and Critical Thinking**

   Problem Solving Write a dialogue between Cardinal Richelieu and Marie de Medici about how much power Richelieu should have as Louis XIII's chief minister.
   Consider:
   • how old Louis XIII was at that time
   • what Marie de Medici may have wanted
   • what France needed at that time
   • Richelieu's aims

Homework Practice Online

keyword: SH3 HP10

Russia in the Age of Absolutism

READ TO DISCOVER

❶ In what ways was Russia isolated from western Europe?

❷ How did Peter the Great use his power to change Russia?

❸ How did Catherine the Great expand Russia's territory?

IDENTIFY

Michael Romanov
Peter the Great
Catherine the Great

WHY IT MATTERS TODAY

Peter and Catherine the Great were strong, absolutist rulers. Today Russia does not have such a strong ruler. Use CNN student News.com or other **current event** sources to learn about how Russia is currently ruled. Record your findings in your journal.

CNN student News.com

The Main Idea
Under two great rulers, Peter and Catherine, Russia became a westernized and powerful nation.

The Story Continues *Louis XIV had his Versailles, but in 1703 the Russian czar Peter the Great had an entire city. St. Petersburg, Russia's "window to the West," was built to show how Peter modeled his government, as well as much of Russian society, after the western European monarchies. The wide boulevards, magnificent palaces, and outstanding examples of architecture and engineering characteristic of St. Petersburg make for a beautiful city even today.*

Isolation and a New Dynasty

Several factors, both cultural and geographic, separated Russia from western Europe. For one, before 1480 much of Russia had been under Mongol rule for about 200 years, and thus had an Asian influence. For another, Western civilization had reached Russia through Constantinople and the Byzantine Empire, not from western Europe itself. Thus Russia's religion was Eastern Orthodox rather than Roman Catholic or Protestant. In addition, Russia used the Cyrillic alphabet. This made it hard to communicate with the rest of Europe, which used the Roman alphabet.

Most importantly, Russia's geography separated it from the rest of Europe. The country was almost entirely landlocked. The stronger kingdoms of Sweden and Poland blocked Russia off from the Baltic Sea. To the south, the Ottoman Turks controlled the coast of the Black Sea. To the west, the vast plains of Poland and eastern Europe hurt trade and commercial contact with Europeans. None of Russia's rivers flowed into the seas where trade took place.

Like some monarchs in western Europe, however, Ivan the Terrible had centered absolute power and authority on himself—the czar. After Ivan died in 1584, Russia went through a period of unrest. Nobles fought for power, and neighboring countries invaded. Then in 1613, the Russian national assembly elected **Michael Romanov** to be czar. Romanov was the grandnephew of Ivan IV. The Romanov family was large, powerful, and wealthy. It traced its origins to a nobleman who had lived in Moscow during the 1300s. Romanov czars ruled Russia for the next 300 years, during which the country became a leading European power.

The Romanovs sought to build the power of the czar. They suppressed protests by a religious group called the Old Believers, who opposed recent church reforms. The Romanovs established relations with groups of Cossack peoples who lived in southern Russia and the Ukraine. Over time, these people came under Moscow's rule.

The Cap of Monomach, pictured here, was used to crown czars from 1498 to 1682. It is studded with gems and trimmed with sable.

Thus the Romanovs continued and strengthened absolutism in Russia. In 1682 Peter I became czar at the age of 10. At first he shared power with his half brother and half sister. Then in 1689 Peter became the sole leader of Russia.

✔ **READING CHECK: Summarizing** What factors kept Russia isolated from the rest of Europe in the 1500s and 1600s?

Peter the Great

Czar Peter I, or **Peter the Great,** ruled Russia until 1725. Like Ivan, he could be ruthless. Yet Peter was also a leader of great vision. Above all, he believed that Russia had to become more like the rest of Europe.

Peter's foreign mission. One of Peter's major goals was to end Russia's landlocked situation. He wanted to acquire warm-water ports on the Sea of Azov and the Black Sea. However, these areas were controlled by the Ottoman Empire. To defeat the Turks, Peter needed a stronger Russia. He also knew that he would need help from western Europe.

In 1697 Peter, disguised as a private citizen, visited several western European countries. Peter's goal was to negotiate an alliance against the Ottoman Turks. He failed in this goal, but he learned many things about the West. He met with leading scientists and artisans. He even worked as a carpenter in a Dutch shipyard to learn about shipbuilding.

Westernizing Russia. Peter reorganized Russia along western European lines. Influenced by France, Peter improved his army's training and weaponry. In 1700 he started a long war with Sweden. When Russia finally won in 1721, it gained territory on the east coast of the Gulf of Finland. Now Russia had access to the Baltic Sea. In this new territory Peter built a completely new city, St. Petersburg. He moved the capital from Moscow to St. Petersburg, closer to the nations of western Europe. St. Petersburg represented the new, westernized Russia. Peter undertook a major building program to construct the city along Western architectural styles. He wanted St. Petersburg to be viewed as the capital of a progressive nation.

Westernization included social changes. Women became less socially isolated and took a greater part in the community. Peter forced the nobles to shave off their long beards and dress in European styles. Also important were the changes Peter made to Russia's government and economy. He modernized the army and reformed the government's administration. He also encouraged manufacturing and foreign trade.

Russian Expansion in Europe, 1682–1796

Interpreting Maps Peter the Great extended Russia's territory and increased trade by obtaining seaports.

■ **Skills Assessment: Human Systems** On what bodies of water were ports established?

Understanding Peter the Great

When you study history, you read primary and secondary sources to understand the facts of an event or the actions of a historical person. Behind those facts or those actions, however, is even more information. By reading "between the lines," you can find information that is only implied. Reading between the lines involves using reasoning ability to identify something that the writer does not actually state. This identification is an inference. Such a process is often very useful in understanding a historical person's personality. You can often infer things about the person from his or her actions.

Portrait of Peter the Great dressed as a shipwright

Primary and Secondary Sources

The passage below includes both primary and secondary information about Peter the Great.

Believing that the best way to learn was by doing, Peter traveled to the West, where, for example, he worked in a Dutch shipyard to learn shipbuilding. Likewise, in England he impressed his hosts with his willingness to work with his hands. As one bishop recorded:

"He is mechanically turned, and seems designed by nature rather to be a ship carpenter than a great prince; this was his chief study and exercise while he stayed here; he wrought much with his own hands, and made all about him work at the models of ships."

This image depicts Peter the Great (front) studying the elements of shipbuilding.

Skills Reminder

To draw inferences, determine the main idea or literal interpretation of the writing. Then look for clues that suggest additional meaning. Such clues might take the form of key phrases, emotional words, or active and colorful descriptions. These may signal that additional meaning is buried "between the lines" of the document. Add these clues to your original understanding of the document to create a revised interpretation based on both the stated ideas and the implied ideas. Finally, analyze the document to develop conclusions.

Skills Practice

❶ Read the primary and secondary sources above. You might also use the images of Peter to infer additional meaning. Then write two or three descriptions about Peter the Great that are not directly stated. What type of man was he? What type of monarch was he?

❷ Read a political article in the newspaper or listen to a televised news program that focuses on a political issue. Then list several facts and any inferences you can draw from the article or program.

HISTORY MAKER

Peter the Great (1672–1725)

Peter the Great used his absolute authority to change his country. Under his rule Russia became a major European power, able to compete with most western European nations. **How did Peter change Russia's standing with the rest of the world?**

Analyzing Primary Sources

Identifying Bias Do you think the archbishop could be trusted to speak for all Russians? Why might some people who lived under Peter's rule disagree with the archbishop?

Peter followed the absolutist ideas of Louis XIV of France, but because Russia was different from France, he was able to take them even further. He had complete control of a highly centralized government. Peter took measures to control the nobility, so that ultimately the nobles acted only as his agents. Even the Orthodox Church came under Peter's control.

Peter created a new system of nobility—a "service nobility"—in which the individual noble's rank depended on the performance of government service. In exchange for this service, the czar granted individual nobles large estates with thousands of serfs. He thereby increased the number of serfs in Russia and worsened their condition. Now the serfs were bound not only to the land but also to their lords. The nobles who received these grants, in turn, were bound to the czar with ties of personal dependence and loyalty. Their aristocratic lifestyles hinged entirely upon Peter's good will and appreciation, and they were much more likely to support the czar and his absolute power over the state.

Peter's reforms and his actions to achieve absolute power caused strong resentment among many Russians. The Russian Orthodox Church, for example, objected to his interference in traditional church practices and to his drive to control the clergy at every level. Many Russian nobles, moreover, were angered by Peter's moves to restructure the government and to centralize power in his own hands. During the course of his reign, Peter elevated the army, making it one of the government's most powerful institutions. Like Louis XIV in France, he sought to increase control over the nobles by restricting their freedom of movement and by isolating them from others. Peter required many of his most powerful nobles to build homes in St. Petersburg. There they were obliged to spend a great deal of time at court, where they could be kept under Peter's watchful eye. Despite the opposition of powerful Russian groups, however, the czar pushed ahead with his reforms.

Peter failed to westernize Russian society completely. However, under his leadership Russia became a great power. At Peter's funeral, the Archbishop of Novgorod—a loyal adviser to the czar—praised him in Biblical terms:

History Makers Speak

❝We are burying Peter the Great! Contrary to everybody's wishes and hopes he has come to his life's end, he who has been the cause of our innumerable good fortunes and joys; who has raised Russia as if from among the dead and elevated her to such heights of power and glory; . . . He was your Samson, Russia . . . He was your Moses . . . O Russia, he was your Solomon, who received from the Lord reason and wisdom in great plenty. . . . Most distinguished man! Can a short oration encompass his immeasurable glory?❞

Feofan Prokopovich, from *Peter the Great Changes Russia,* edited by Marc Raeff

✔ **READING CHECK: Identifying Cause and Effect** How did Peter's rule change Russia?

Catherine the Great

Peter was succeeded by his second wife, Catherine I. Other Romanov rulers followed. Peter's grandson, Peter III, married Catherine II, a German princess. Peter III was unpopular and in 1762 was murdered by nobles who supported Catherine II. Known as **Catherine the Great,** she ruled from 1762 to 1796.

Catherine's policies. Catherine supported art, science, literature, and theater. These efforts meant nothing, however, to most Russians, who lived in great poverty and ignorance. In fact, Catherine extended serfdom into new Russian territories. The common people therefore remained poor. The nobles, meanwhile, thrived and became more westernized. Many began speaking French and lost touch with the Russian people.

Catherine's real greatness and her most important contributions to Russia's development lay in her foreign policy. She continued the expansion begun by Peter the Great. Russia still wanted control of the Sea of Azov and the Black Sea. In a successful war against the Turks, Catherine gained control of most of the northern shore of the Black Sea and the region of the Crimea.

Poland. Catherine also gained new territory to the west. The kingdom of Poland was large but weak. Polish nobles argued with each other over electing a king. Their legislature was not efficient. Historically, moreover, Poland had seen much conflict with people of different ethnic and religious backgrounds. This tended to promote suspicion of others. Most Poles were Roman Catholic, and their leaders often discriminated against other groups. Sometimes these minority groups would ask Prussia, Austria, or Russia for help. In 1772 these three nations took advantage of Poland's weakened condition. All three seized slices of Polish territory for themselves in an action known as the First Partition of Poland.

Polish attempts to strengthen their nation failed. In 1793 Russia and Prussia took over more Polish lands in the Second Partition. With the Third Partition in 1795, Russia, Prussia, and Austria divided what was left. Poland disappeared from the map of Europe until 1919.

The Partitions of Poland, 1772–1795

Interpreting Maps Poland was divided among Russia, Austria, and Prussia in a series of three partitions.

■ **Skills Assessment: The World in Spatial Terms** By 1795, which country had acquired most of Poland?

Catherine The Great
(1729–1796)

Although born in Germany, Catherine the Great dedicated herself to Russia and its growth. She was in touch with western European ideas about political reforms. She considered a new law code that would make all people equal before the law.

However, Catherine knew that her power depended on the support of the Russian nobles. Thus, instead of focusing on social reforms within Russia, Catherine concentrated on making Russia one of the great European powers. **What political factor influenced Catherine's decisions about affairs within Russia?**

With her successes in the Black Sea and Poland, Catherine added more than 200,000 square miles to her empire. Russia's borders now reached well into central Europe. Russia had become a force to consider in the European balance of power.

Expansion eastward. Russia's expansion differed from that of western European nations. Instead of expanding overseas, Russia successfully expanded overland. Even before Catherine, Russian settlers, led by Cossacks, moved eastward. In 1581 the Cossacks captured the Mongol city of Sibir. This gave Russia access to Siberia, the huge region east of the Ural Mountains. Here, a rich fur trade attracted growing numbers of settlers. Much like the pioneers of the American West, the early Russian settlers in Siberia built small posts for trade and defense. Despite the harsh climate of the region, many of these settlements thrived and became important links in Russia's continuing economic development. The opening of Siberia, with its wealth of natural resources and its vast space, added much to Russia's growing power and influence.

At the Amur River, Russians came into contact with the Chinese, who resisted Russian expansion into their lands. In 1689 the two nations signed a treaty that fixed the Amur River as the border between them and established trade relations.

By 1741 the Russians had crossed the Bering Strait to North America. They set up a colony in Alaska. Later Russian trading posts expanded southward.

✔ **READING CHECK: Drawing Inferences** In what ways was Catherine more skilled in foreign, rather than domestic, policy?

Catherine the Great's horse-drawn coach reflected the luxury and wealth of the Russian court.

SECTION 2 REVIEW

1. **Identify** and explain the significance:
   Michael Romanov
   Peter the Great
   Catherine the Great

2. **Comparing and Contrasting** Make a chart like the one below. List the strengths and the weaknesses of Peter the Great and Catherine the Great.

Peter	Catherine
Strengths	Strengths
Weaknesses	Weaknesses

3. **Finding the Main Idea**
   a. How did Russia overcome its isolation from Europe?
   b. In what ways were Peter and Catherine the Great absolute monarchs?

4. **Writing and Critical Thinking**
   Supporting a Point of View Write a brief essay from the point of view of the serfs in Russia under Catherine the Great. Explain why, in your opinion, Catherine was not "great."
   Consider:
   • how conditions changed for Russian serfs under Catherine's rule
   • the gap between Catherine's treatment of the nobility and the serfs
   • why Catherine might be considered "great"

Homework Practice Online
keyword: SH3 HP10

Central Europe in the Age of Absolutism

READ TO DISCOVER
1 How did the Habsburgs gain and hold power?
2 How did the Hohenzollerns rise to power?
3 What factors contributed to the conflicts between Prussia and Austria?

IDENTIFY

Maria Theresa
Pragmatic Sanction
Great Elector
Frederick William I
Frederick the Great
Diplomatic Revolution
Seven Years' War

WHY IT MATTERS TODAY

The map of Europe has been drawn and redrawn almost countless times. Use or other **current event** sources to compare national boundaries today with those mapped in this chapter. Record your findings in your journal.

The Main Idea
The Habsburgs of Austria and the Hohenzollerns of Prussia vied for power in Central Europe.

The Story Continues *The Habsburgs had risen from a family of local princes with little influence beyond their immediate region to become one of the most powerful families in Europe and the rulers of Austria. A typical day in the life of one Habsburg monarch of Austria, Maria Theresa, meant consulting with ministers, giving audience to courtiers and visitors, reading, and spending time with family, including her numerous children.*

Habsburg Austria

The Austrian Habsburgs lost much territory in Germany during the Thirty Years' War in the early 1600s. Over the next 100 years, however, they acquired new lands, both from the Turks and as a result of the Treaty of Utrecht. The Habsburg empire now stretched into the Balkans, Hungary, and the Italian Peninsula.

In 1740 the Holy Roman Emperor Charles VI died, leaving only his 23-year-old daughter **Maria Theresa** to inherit Austria and the other Habsburg lands. In some of these lands the law stated that the inheritance had to go to a male. Therefore, before his death Charles urged other European rulers to accept a statement called the **Pragmatic Sanction.** This agreement would allow Maria Theresa to inherit all the Habsburg lands. The laws of the Holy Roman Empire also prevented her from being elected empress. She became empress in 1745 when her husband was elected emperor.

Maria Theresa's empire was a patchwork of regions and peoples. It included Belgians, Bohemians, Croatians, Germans, Hungarians, Italians, Poles, Romanians, Serbs, and Slovenes. This variety led to many conflicts of language, religion, and nationality. Several German states became resentful of the Habsburgs' power. For example, Bavaria, which is located in southern Germany, jealously guarded its lands and independence. At times, Bavaria allied with France against the Habsburgs. Austria's chief rival was the small but rising north German state of Brandenburg-Prussia. The character and size of the Habsburg empire, with its geographic, cultural, and historic diversity, made it extremely difficult to rule effectively.

✔ **READING CHECK: Drawing Inferences** What factors made it difficult for the Habsburgs to rule?

Maria Theresa made improvements in education, medicine, and military affairs.

The Rise of the Hohenzollerns

Brandenburg-Prussia, a small north German state ruled by the Hohenzollern family, became Austria's chief rival. The Hohenzollerns were an ambitious family who had originally ruled a small territory in southern Germany. However, they wanted to increase their power and gain more land. One branch of the family settled in Brandenburg, in northern Germany. The ruler of Brandenburg eventually became an elector of the Holy Roman Empire.

Many of the Hohenzollerns were Protestants. During the Reformation they seized lands that had once belonged to the Catholic Church in their territories. By 1648 they ruled several territories in Germany, including Prussia, which bordered the Baltic Sea.

One of the greatest Hohenzollern rulers was Frederick William, called the **Great Elector.** He ruled Brandenburg-Prussia at the end of the Thirty Years' War. After the war he worked to rebuild his state. Frederick William unified the armies of all his lands into one strong force. He also improved the tax system, agriculture, industry, and transportation.

In 1688 Frederick I succeeded the Great Elector as ruler. From then on, all the Hohenzollern lands in northern Germany were unified in practice under the rule of Prussia. This greatly consolidated Hohenzollern power. Frederick I gained the title of King of Prussia. He tried to imitate Louis XIV of France, maintaining a large, lavish court.

Frederick William I. In 1713 Frederick I's son became king. **Frederick William I** did not like French ways. He ended much of his father's lavish spending. Instead, Frederick William I used the money to make Prussia stronger. He doubled the size of the Prussian army and made it the most efficient fighting force in Europe.

Prussian society in general was militarized under the king, who overhauled the government and brought the state as a whole under his control. "At the table," his daughter once wrote, "nothing else was talked of but economy and soldiers." Frederick William ensured that the Prussian army was well equipped and thoroughly trained. Discipline within the army was rigid, punishments were harsh, and soldiers were expected to obey orders instantly.

By 1740 the Prussian army was among the most powerful military forces in Europe. It had become a well-designed tool with which Prussia could both defend its borders and expand its interests.

Frederick William I also created an efficient system of government for Prussia. Tax collecting and government spending were carefully planned. Frederick William I also encouraged trade and the development of new industries. Believing that all children should have a primary education, he required that all parents send their children to school.

Dressing for Success

Frederick I was not the only monarch who tried to copy the style of Louis XIV. When France was the greatest power on the continent, Louis XIV's style of clothing was copied throughout Europe. Royalty and nobles mirrored the French king with elaborate wigs and rich fabrics. Color and pattern were very important. **How is the clothing style of Frederick I in the image at right similar to that of Louis XIV below?**

Louis XIV

The coronation of Frederick I (shown holding crown)

Frederick the Great. Frederick William I worried that his son, Frederick II, did not seem interested in military or government affairs. Instead the youth wrote poetry, played the flute, and read philosophy. The king used harsh methods, including prison, to try to change his son. Once Frederick II and a companion tried to escape Prussia, but both were caught. King Frederick William I forced his son to watch as the friend was executed.

Despite Frederick William's fears, Frederick II turned out to be an even stronger ruler than his father. He became king of Prussia in 1740, the same year Maria Theresa became the ruler of Austria. Frederick II, or **Frederick the Great,** as he came to be called, was highly intelligent and worked to expand the territory and prestige of Prussia.

✔ **READING CHECK: Finding the Main Idea** What did the Hohenzollerns hope to accomplish? Were they successful?

Conflict Between Prussia and Austria

Frederick William I had signed the Pragmatic Sanction allowing Maria Theresa to inherit all the Habsburg lands. Shortly after becoming king, however, Frederick II marched his powerful Prussian army into Silesia, one of Maria Theresa's most valuable territories. Prussia had only a weak claim to Silesia, but Frederick the Great wanted the territory for its farmland and iron deposits.

The Prussians seized Silesia easily. This conquest started the War of the Austrian Succession, which lasted from 1740 to 1748. On one side Bavaria, Spain, and France joined Prussia to fight Austria, Great Britain, the Netherlands, and Russia. Austria and its allies lost, and Silesia was ceded to Prussia.

The Diplomatic Revolution. After the War of the Austrian Succession, a major "reversal of alliances" occurred in Europe. This shift was known as the **Diplomatic Revolution.** Ever since the time of Louis XIV, Austria and Great Britain had been allied against the French. In 1756, however, Great Britain allied itself with Prussia. To keep Prussia from becoming too powerful, France joined with Austria and Russia. A new balance of power saw France and Austria opposed to Prussia and Great Britain.

The Hohenzollerns
1640–1688 Frederick William, the Great Elector
1688–1713 Frederick I
1713–1740 Frederick William I
1740–1786 Frederick II (the Great)

Interpreting the Chart
Between 1640 and 1786, Hohenzollern rulers added substantially to the strength and efficiency of Prussia's government. *What might be inferred about support for Hohenzollern rule on the basis of this chart?*

INTERPRETING THE VISUAL RECORD

Prussian troops In this painting, Frederick the Great inspects his troops. *What impression does this painting create of the Prussian army?*

The Seven Years' War. These rivalries led to another major European war called the **Seven Years' War,** which lasted from 1756 to 1763. Almost all of Europe became involved in this war. Battles took place on the continent and in European colonies overseas. In fact, the fighting actually began in North America, where it was called the French and Indian War.

Major alliances characterized the Seven Years' War. Prussia was supported by Great Britain, while Austria formed partnerships with France and Russia. In 1757 Frederick II's Prussian army defeated the French forces in Saxony and prevented Austria from reclaiming Silesia. Two years later, however, in 1759, the Prussians were badly defeated by a combined Austrian-Russian force.

Frederick struggled to regain the upper hand. His efforts met with success when mistrust and financial problems began to weaken the alliance that opposed him. At the same time, Prussia's British allies won several major victories against the French in Canada and India. A turning point was reached when the Empress of Russia, Elizabeth, died. Her successor, Czar Peter III, was a great admirer of Frederick II and had no desire to continue supporting Prussia's enemies. He broke from the alliance with Austria and France and, in 1762, made a separate peace with Prussia. At the same time, Britain's new ruler, King George III, made clear his intention to withdraw from the global conflict.

The Seven Years' War ended with no clear winner. A treaty signed in 1763 confirmed Prussia's hold on Silesia—a great loss for Austria. In that same year, the Treaty of Paris gave most of France's North American colonies to Britain, which also maintained its dominant position in India.

European Possessions, 1763

Interpreting Maps The Seven Years' War realigned power throughout the world.

■ **Skills Assessment: The World in Spatial Terms** Which country controlled the most land within the Holy Roman Empire?

The years of peace. The Seven Years' War had caused widespread destruction and loss of life in many parts of Europe, North America, and India. Prussia and Russia had drained their treasuries during the war. Prussia also had lost many people. As they realized the costs of war in both lives and wealth, the European powers became reluctant to fight again. A period of peace descended on a war-weary Europe that was eager to recover. Nevertheless, European monarchs continued to search for ways to expand their national boundaries, find new sources of wealth, and extend their powers.

In Prussia, Frederick the Great had spent the first 23 years of his reign at war. He spent the next 23 years working to rebuild and strengthen his kingdom. Frederick had great organizational skills and governed Prussia effectively. He expanded and improved public education and the already excellent Prussian civil service system. He also made important legal and court reforms and encouraged economic development through increased trade and manufacturing. Frederick also supported tolerance for religious minorities. Under his leadership, Prussia regained the economic prosperity it had lost during the Seven Years' War.

Frederick the Great (center) and his nobles are shown here dining at the Prussian palace with the French philosopher Voltaire (leaning forward at left) as a special guest.

Prussia also continued to gain new territory during these years. Frederick the Great helped to bring about the First Partition of Poland. By acquiring Polish territory along the Baltic coast, Frederick linked Prussia with East Prussia. By the time Frederick the Great died in 1786, Prussia had emerged as a major European economic and political power.

✔ **READING CHECK: Identifying Cause and Effect** What effect did the Prussian invasion of Silesia have on Europe?

SECTION 3 REVIEW

1. **Identify** and explain the significance:
   Maria Theresa
   Pragmatic Sanction
   Great Elector
   Frederick William I
   Frederick the Great
   Diplomatic Revolution
   Seven Years' War

2. **Identifying Cause and Effect**
   Copy the graphic organizer below. Use it to explain the causes and effects of the Diplomatic Revolution.

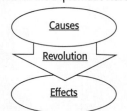

   Causes
   Revolution
   Effects

3. **Finding the Main Idea**
   a. In what ways were the Habsburgs and the Hohenzollerns driven by similar motives?
   b. How did Frederick William I differ from his father?

4. **Writing and Critical Thinking**
   Decision Making Write a paragraph examining whether Frederick the Great was justified in invading Silesia.
   Consider:
   • how Austria had come to possess Silesia
   • whether or not Prussia had any claim to the territory
   • why Frederick the Great wanted Silesia

Homework Practice Online
keyword: SH3 HP10

READ TO DISCOVER

❶ How did Mary Tudor rule England?

❷ How did Elizabeth I rule England?

❸ Why did James I have trouble ruling England?

DEFINE

gentry
burgesses

IDENTIFY

"Bloody Mary"
Elizabeth I
Mary Queen of Scots
Spanish Armada
Puritans
James I

WHY IT MATTERS TODAY

England today maintains its monarchy, although it is different from the monarchy of Elizabeth I. Use **CNN** or other **current event** sources to find out how much power the British monarchy has today as compared with the 1600s. Record your findings in your journal.

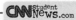

The English Monarchy

The Main Idea
Monarchs in England tried to rule with absolute power, but met with serious opposition from Parliament.

The Story Continues *"I am your anointed Queen. I will never be by violence constrained to do anything." So goes a famous statement by Queen Elizabeth I, one of England's strongest monarchs. Yet in England, unlike countries on the continent, the absolute monarchy would never quite take hold.*

The House of Tudor

In the late 1400s a new royal family, the Tudors, became England's rulers. The Tudors tried to increase their power in England just as the rulers of France and Spain had. The first Tudor king was Henry VII, who made England stable and prosperous. His son, Henry VIII, established a new official church for England, the Anglican Church, when the Roman Catholic pope would not grant him a divorce. Henry's sickly son, Edward VI, succeeded him but ruled for only six years.

Mary I, the oldest daughter of Henry VIII, took the throne in 1553 to become the first reigning queen of England. Mary, a devoted Catholic, was determined to make England a Catholic nation again. Her Protestant subjects were outraged when Mary married Philip II of Spain. Philip had helped lead the Counter-Reformation against Protestantism.

The queen did not lack courage or a sense of kindness. Nevertheless, she proved to be utterly ruthless in her aim to destroy the Anglican Church. Mary tried to do away with clergy who did not follow the laws of the Catholic Church. She had more than 300 people burned at the stake, including Thomas Cranmer, the archbishop of Canterbury. These persecutions earned Mary the nickname **"Bloody Mary"** and provoked rebellion. They also failed to destroy Protestantism in England.

✔ **READING CHECK: Problem Solving** How did Mary Tudor try to promote Catholicism in England? Why do you think her efforts failed?

During the reign of the Tudors, political prisoners were confined in the Tower of London.

The Reign of Elizabeth I

When Mary I died in 1558, her Protestant half-sister **Elizabeth I** became queen. Elizabeth was an able politician who used the monarchy and Parliament to prevent conflict and to strengthen Protestantism. Elizabeth was also in touch with the English people. As the early twentieth century writer Lytton Strachey described her,

❝[T]he ordinary Englishman saw in King Hal's full-blooded daughter a Queen after his own heart. She swore; she spat; she struck with her fist when she was angry; she roared with laughter when she was amused. . . . A radiant atmosphere of humour coloured and softened the harsh lines of her destiny.**❞**

Lytton Strachey, *Elizabeth and Essex: A Tragic History*

Elizabeth and Mary Queen of Scots. In a monarchy, the oldest child usually inherits the throne. Elizabeth, however, never married and had no children. Her closest relative and heir was Catholic—Mary Stuart, the queen of Scotland, who was also known as **Mary Queen of Scots.** The idea of another Catholic queen horrified English Protestants. However, it also delayed the plans of Philip II of Spain to invade England. He had been planning to force a Catholic ruler on the English people.

When Mary fled to England in 1568 to escape problems in Scotland, Elizabeth put her in prison. Later Mary plotted with Philip II's ambassadors in England to kill Elizabeth and seize the throne. Elizabeth found out about the plan and ordered Mary's death. In 1587 the Scottish queen was beheaded. Philip II, meanwhile, was angered by English raiders at sea and by the help Elizabeth gave to Protestants in his lands. He planned another invasion of England.

The Spanish Armada. In 1588 Philip launched a fleet of 130 ships toward England. This **Spanish Armada** was so impressive that it was called the Invincible Armada.

The English sent out their whole fleet to meet the Spanish Armada. The English ships were smaller and swifter, and their guns could shoot faster and farther than those on the Spanish ships. As a result, the English slipped through the Spanish formation of ships and damaged and sank some of the lumbering vessels. The Spanish tried to escape to the North Sea and then sail back around the British Isles. Storms, navigation errors, and lack of supplies worked against them. Many Spanish ships crashed on the shores of Scotland and Ireland. Only about half of the Invincible Armada made it back to Spain. After this defeat, Spain was no longer a threat to England, and Elizabeth's Protestant rule was secure. However, she still faced two major problems at home.

Religious problems. Religion still caused unrest in England. Henry VIII had broken with the pope when he made Anglicanism the religion of England. However, some people thought Henry had not gone far enough. They wanted to "purify" the new church even more. These people, called **Puritans,** or Separatists, objected to the fact that the Anglican Church kept some Catholic practices. For example, the Anglican Church had bishops and Anglican priests dressed in traditional vestments. Puritans thought these and other Anglican customs were too similar to those of the Catholic Church.

Elizabeth and other Tudor monarchs thought that religious disunity threatened England. They wanted to unite their subjects under the Anglican faith. Therefore, the Tudors persecuted not only Catholics but also non-Anglican Protestants, including the Puritans. For example, people who did not attend the Anglican Church had to pay fines. This angered the Puritans and failed to end the disputes. The Puritans became

Holt Researcher

go.hrw.com
KEYWORD: Holt Researcher
FreeFind: Mary I
      Elizabeth I

After reading more about Mary I and Elizabeth I on the Holt Researcher, create a compare-and-contrast chart listing the political, economic, and cultural influence they each had on England.

HISTORY MAKER

**Elizabeth I
(1533–1603)**

Brave and shrewd, Elizabeth I was one of the greatest rulers in English history. She changed England from an island kingdom to a world power.

Elizabeth never married because she did not want to lose her power or tie England to a foreign country. Elizabeth's self-confidence gave the English a deep sense of national pride and made her one of England's most enduring symbols. **Why did Elizabeth never marry?**

The Globe Theatre

In ancient Greece and Rome, plays were staged in large open-air arenas. By the time of Elizabethan England, however, special buildings—theaters—were constructed for plays. The most famous theater in history is the Globe Theatre of London, which was built in the 1500s. Most of William Shakespeare's plays were performed there. Ordinary people stood in an open area, while nobles and the wealthy sat in boxes. Although the original Globe Theatre was torn down, a new theater was recently built to reflect the original design.

How did the seating arrangement in the Globe Theatre reflect English society?

more and more unhappy with the Anglican Church and its clergy. Elizabeth, however, refused to allow further changes to the church. Her religious policies were tolerant compared with those of other rulers at the time. However, they were still objectionable to Catholics on one side and Puritans on the other.

Relations with Parliament. England's Parliament included representatives from the entire country who had the power to pass laws and approve all taxes. In the 1530s Henry VIII had used Parliament to pass the laws that made England a Protestant nation. These acts increased the power and prestige of Parliament. Moreover, people viewed Parliament as a check on the power of the monarchy because it represented the wishes of people outside the central government.

Parliament had two houses. The House of Lords was made up of nobles and clergy. The House of Commons represented two other classes—gentry and burgesses. The **gentry** were landowners who had social position but no titles. Sometimes younger sons of nobles, who could not inherit their father's titles or positions, became gentry. The **burgesses** were merchants and professional people from towns and cities. Sometimes the line between the gentry and the burgesses became blurred. For example, a wealthy merchant who owned land might be considered gentry. Younger sons of nobles might enter a profession and be considered burgesses. Together the gentry and the burgesses had considerable power that the monarch had to respect.

Elizabeth managed Parliament skillfully. She consulted Parliament often and gave the appearance of taking its advice. She obtained the taxes she needed without letting members influence policy too directly. She usually allowed freedom of speech in Parliament. Even so, despite her skill Elizabeth could not prevent some members, particularly Puritans, from questioning her policies. Parliament became even more challenging to the monarchs who followed Elizabeth.

✔ **READING CHECK: Categorizing** What were some of Elizabeth's accomplishments and successes? What were some of her unsolved problems?

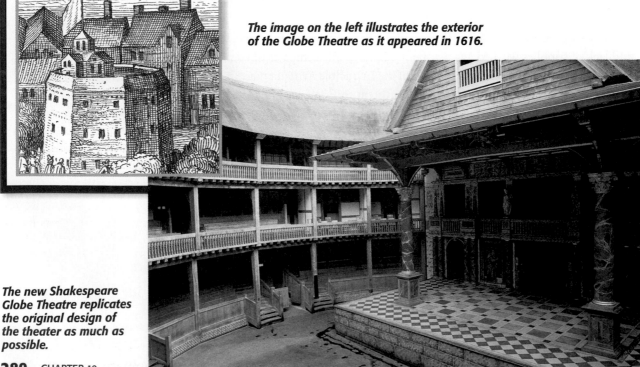

The image on the left illustrates the exterior of the Globe Theatre as it appeared in 1616.

The new Shakespeare Globe Theatre replicates the original design of the theater as much as possible.

James I

When Elizabeth died in 1603, she had no heir to succeed her. King James VI of Scotland, the son of Mary Queen of Scots, became King **James I** of England in 1603. Thus England and Scotland came under the rule of the same monarch.

King James was from the Stuart family, not the Tudors. He was intelligent and educated, but lacked common sense in financial and diplomatic matters. According to Henry IV of France, he was "the wisest fool in Christendom." Although James had experience ruling Scotland, many English suspected that he did not entirely understand their parliamentary system. James strongly believed in the divine right of kings and tried to intervene in the House of Commons.

James was a strong supporter of the Anglican Church. This often placed him in conflict with the Puritans, who continued to ask for religious reforms. The only change in church doctrine that James agreed to was a new translation of the Bible, the King James Version. Also known as the Authorized Version, the King James Version is still favored by some Christians today.

The main opposition to James I came from Parliament, where the Puritans had a strong voice. Because of this opposition, James could never collect enough taxes to pay for his programs. He had to raise money by other means, such as selling titles of nobility, granting monopoly rights, and raising customs duties. Parliament objected to these methods. They also opposed James's efforts to create an alliance with England's old enemy, Spain. When James's negotiations with Spain broke down, the two nations went to war. At the time of James's death in 1625, he had an uneasy relationship with the English people. The growing tension between the Stuart ruler and his English subjects would explode during the reign of James's son, Charles I.

These portraits show James I of England and his wife, Anne of Denmark.

✔ **READING CHECK: Drawing Inferences** How did James I's background contribute to his problems as a ruler?

SECTION 4 REVIEW

1. **Define** and explain the significance:
   gentry
   burgesses

2. **Identify** and explain the significance:
   "Bloody Mary"
   Elizabeth I
   Mary Queen of Scots
   Spanish Armada
   Puritans
   James I

3. **Categorizing** Copy the flowchart below. Use it to list actions taken by the English monarchy over religious divisions and responses to these actions by others.

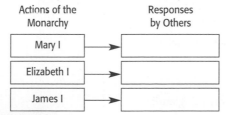

Actions of the Monarchy	Responses by Others
Mary I →	
Elizabeth I →	
James I →	

4. **Finding the Main Idea**
   a. What marked Elizabeth as a strong ruler?
   b. In what ways did James I behave like an absolute monarch?

5. **Writing and Critical Thinking**
   Supporting a Point of View In a diary entry, describe the feelings of a Puritan toward the English monarchy during the reign of James I.
   Consider:
   • how the Puritans felt about Catholicism
   • what the Anglican Church was like
   • the actions of the monarchy

Homework Practice Online
keyword: SH3 HP10

Creating a Time Line

Copy the time line below onto a sheet of paper. Complete the time line by filling in the events, individuals, and dates from the chapter that you think were significant. Pick three events and explain why you think they were significant.

| 1500 | 1600 | 1700 | 1800 |

Writing a Summary

Using standard grammar, spelling, sentence structure, and punctuation, write an overview of the events in the chapter.

Identifying People and Ideas

Identify the following terms or individuals and explain their significance:

1. Cardinal Richelieu
2. divine right of kings
3. Louis XIV
4. Peter the Great
5. Catherine the Great
6. Diplomatic Revolution
7. Frederick the Great
8. Elizabeth I
9. gentry
10. James I

Understanding Main Ideas

SECTION 1 *(pp. 262–266)*

France in the Age of Absolutism

1. How did Cardinal Richelieu strengthen France?
2. In what ways did Louis XV differ from Louis XIV?

SECTION 2 *(pp. 267–272)*

Russia in the Age of Absolutism

3. How did Peter the Great attempt to end Russian isolation?
4. What foreign policy successes did Catherine the Great have?

SECTION 3 *(pp. 273–277)*

Central Europe in the Age of Absolutism

5. How did the Hohenzollerns strengthen Prussia?
6. What wars did the Prussian invasion of Silesia trigger?

SECTION 4 *(pp. 278–281)*

The English Monarchy

7. Why did Philip II of Spain attempt to invade England? What was the result?
8. Why did James I clash with the English Parliament?

Reviewing Themes

1. **Government** How did the government of Louis XIV negatively affect the people of France?
2. **Culture** How did Elizabeth I try to control religious disunity in England?
3. **Economics** How did Peter the Great's rule affect Russian serfs?

Thinking Critically

1. **Identifying a Point of View** Why might a noble agree with Catherine's nickname of "the Great"?
2. **Identifying Cause and Effect** What happened to the French economy as a result of the construction of the palace at Versailles?
3. **Sequencing** How did Prussia prepare itself for the invasion of Silesia?
4. **Comparing** In what ways were Elizabeth I and James I similar?

Writing About History

Evaluating Absolute monarchies dominated Europe for many years. In general, do you think they affected European nations positively or negatively? Support your opinion with facts from the chapter. Use the following chart to organize your thoughts before you begin writing.

Positive effects	Negative effects

Interpreting a Graph

Study the graph below. Then use the information on the graph to answer the questions that follow.

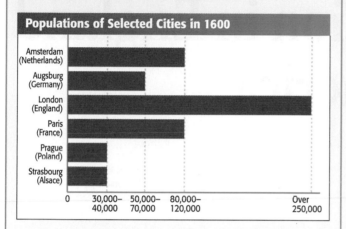

Populations of Selected Cities in 1600

- Amsterdam (Netherlands)
- Augsburg (Germany)
- London (England)
- Paris (France)
- Prague (Poland)
- Strasbourg (Alsace)

0   30,000–40,000   50,000–70,000   80,000–120,000   Over 250,000

1. Which of the following lists the three cities on the European continent with the largest populations in 1600?

   a. London, Amsterdam, Paris

   b. Paris, Amsterdam, Augsburg

   c. Amsterdam, Augsburg, London

   d. Paris, Augsburg, Prague

2. Which city—London or Augsburg—was probably affected most by the Thirty Years' War? Give specific reasons for your choices.

Evaluating Sources

Read the following excerpt from a travel book describing Louis XIV's palace at Versailles. Then answer the questions.

"You enter the château . . . through the gilt iron gates from huge Place d'Armes. On the first floor of the château, dead center past the Sun King's statue and across the sprawling cobbled forecourt, is Louis XIV's bedchamber. The two wings were occupied by the royal children and princes of the blood, while courtiers made do in the attics. . . . The Grands Appartements (state apartments), which flank the Hall of Mirrors, retain much of their original Baroque decoration: gilt stucco, painted ceilings, and marble sculpture."

3. Which of the following statements best describes the evidence this excerpt provides?

   a. The excerpt is a primary source of evidence.

   b. The excerpt is a secondary source of evidence.

   c. The excerpt is both a primary source and a secondary source of evidence.

   d. The excerpt is not a reliable source of evidence.

4. Explain your choice of statements in question 3. Give specific reasons to support your point of view.

Alternative Assessment

Building Your Portfolio

Link to TODAY

Government

Monarchies still exist throughout the world today, although many rulers do not have the authority of previous monarchs. Find and interpret time-lines that show European monarchies beginning with the 1500s through today. Create a database with the country's name, monarch's name, and title—including a popular name such as "the Great"—their length of rule, and the scope of their power.

internet connect

Internet Activity: go.hrw.com
KEYWORD: SH3 WH10

Choose a topic on Monarchs of Europe to:

- create a pamphlet on the impact on Russian society of the reigns of Peter the Great and Catherine the Great.

- write a biography of the Sun King.

- explore the propaganda of William Shakespeare's historical plays.

CHAPTER 11

1550–1789

Enlightenment and Revolution in England and America

1600
Business and Finance
The British East India Company is chartered.

c. 1619
Business and Finance
Tobacco becomes Virginia's most valuable export.

c. 1651
Business and Finance
The Navigation Act is passed in England.

1667
The Arts
John Milton publishes *Paradise Lost.*

1687
Science and Technology
Isaac Newton publishes *Principia.*

| 1600 | 1650 |

1588
Global Events
The Spanish Armada is defeated by the English navy.

1607
Daily Life
Jamestown, Virginia, is founded.

1640
Politics
The Long Parliament convenes.

1665
Science and Technology
Robert Hooke publishes the first significant work on microscopic observation.

1688
Politics
The Glorious Revolution occurs in England.

Battle of the Spanish Armada

Title page from Robert Hooke's **Micrographia**

Build on What You Know

M odern nation-states, most of which were governed by monarchs, developed first in Europe between 1500 and 1800. With the new governments came new ideas concerning the nature and the organization of the state. New relationships between the nations' people and their rulers also spread. The monarchs who led these new states increasingly sought absolute control over their governments and their subjects. A growing number of those subjects, however, had begun to dispute the ideas of absolutism. In this chapter, you will learn about revolutionary ideas that brought sweeping political and social change to England and America.

Signing of the U.S. Constitution

Jean-Jacques Rousseau

1762
The Arts
Jean-Jacques Rousseau publishes *The Social Contract.*

1707
Politics
The Act of Union unites England and Scotland.

1731
Daily Life
The first colonial subscription library opens in Philadelphia.

1763
Global Events
The Treaty of Paris leaves the British in control of North America.

1789
Politics
The U.S. Constitution is ratified.

1700

1750

1800

c. 1742
Science and Technology
Benjamin Franklin invents the Franklin stove.

1776
Politics
The United States declares independence from Great Britain.

John Milton

American teapot with anti-Stamp Act slogan

What's Your Opinion?

Themes Journal *Do you **agree** or **disagree** with the following statements? Support your point of view in your journal.*

Citizenship People have a right to determine their own form of government and to insist that their leaders conform to the popular will.

Constitutional Heritage Stable governments are based on clear principles that define the relationship between rulers and ruled.

Global Relations The people of both a colonial power and its colonies can benefit from their economic and political relations.

Civil War and Revolution

READ TO DISCOVER

❶ What led to the conflicts between Charles I and Parliament?

❷ How did the rebellion in Ireland help start the English Civil War?

❸ Who would have supported the two sides in the English Revolution?

❹ What led to the downfall of the republican government in England?

DEFINE

commonwealth
constitution

IDENTIFY

Charles I
Petition of Right
Long Parliament
Cavaliers
Roundheads
Oliver Cromwell
New Model Army
Rump Parliament
Navigation Act of 1651

WHY IT MATTERS TODAY

Constitutionalism is an important form of government in today's world. Use CNN.com or other **current event** sources to identify countries that have a formal constitution. Record your findings in your journal.

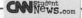

The Main Idea
Parliament's opposition to the concept of royal supremacy led to conflict and rebellion in England.

The Story Continues *Increasingly, the English monarchs of the early 1600s claimed absolute power over Parliament and the law. Their claim echoed the ideas of French philosopher Jean Bodin, who argued that "A prince is bound by no law of his predecessor, and much less by his own laws. . . . He may repeal, modify, or replace a law made by himself and without the consent of his subjects." King Charles I of England certainly held this belief. Throughout the early 1600s tensions grew between Charles and Parliament.*

Charles I and Parliament

Like his father, James I, King **Charles I** believed in the divine right of kings. This belief put Charles out of touch with the people and politics of England. His marriage to a French Catholic princess isolated him even further.

Charles I could not get funds from Parliament. He tried forcing people to loan him money and imprisoned some who refused. Parliament objected to his actions and presented Charles with a document called the **Petition of Right.** This petition stated four ancient liberties: (1) the king could not tax the people without the agreement of Parliament; (2) he could not declare martial law; (3) he could not board soldiers in private homes during peacetime; and (4) he could not imprison a person without a specific charge. Charles signed the Petition of Right, but continued to impose taxes anyway. When members of the House of Commons protested, Charles dismissed Parliament.

For 11 years Charles refused to call Parliament into session. During this time he used drastic means to collect money. The economy improved, but discontent grew over issues like religion. Charles liked the formal religious ceremonies of the Anglican Church. These ceremonies seemed too Catholic to Puritans, however. As a result of this conflict, many Puritans became determined opponents of the king. They increasingly dominated the House of Commons. These Puritans—and many others in Parliament—felt that Charles was becoming a tyrant. Charles began to use royal courts against his enemies. These courts did not guarantee civil liberties. Judges, not juries, made decisions in secret. One of these courts, called the Star Chamber, harshly punished Puritans and critics of the government. People worried that Charles was imposing absolute rule on England.

This portrait of Charles I and his queen, Henrietta, was painted by Anthony Van Dyck in about 1632.

The state religion of Scotland was a form of Protestantism called Presbyterianism. When Charles tried to force Scottish churches to follow Anglican practices, rebellion broke out. The Scots felt that the changes Charles wanted were too Catholic. In 1638 many Scots signed a statement called the National Covenant. In this solemn agreement, Scots swore that any changes to the Scottish church would violate their religion as well as their political freedom. To Scottish Presbyterians, loyalty to their church came before loyalty to the king.

Charles took troops to Scotland but could not put down the rebellion. Seeking more funds for his army, he called Parliament into session. However, the members of Parliament insisted on discussing their complaints before anything else, so Charles dismissed them again. Then the Scots handed Charles's troops a second defeat, this time within England itself. Realizing that he could not defend England without new taxes, Charles called Parliament into session once more in 1640.

✔ **READING CHECK: Summarizing** Why did Charles I close down Parliament?

The Long Parliament

Because the Parliament that Charles convened in 1640 met on and off for 20 years, it came to be known as the **Long Parliament.** Charles wanted Parliament to let him raise money to put down the rebellion in Scotland. Instead, the Puritan-controlled House of Commons ended the king's power to dissolve Parliament. It passed a law that Parliament must meet at least once every three years. It kept the king from raising taxes on his own and even forced the execution of two of his advisors for treason. When Parliament also tried to make changes in the Anglican Church, however, public support began shifting to the king.

While Charles I struggled with the Long Parliament, a rebellion broke out in Ireland. When England had conquered parts of Ireland in the late 1100s, Irish land was given to English settlers. Under James I, the mostly Anglican settlers controlled most of Ireland's wealth. Scottish Presbyterian farmers and merchants later settled in the northern region of Ulster. The native Irish Catholics worked as tenant farmers and laborers. The British treated them brutally, as a conquered people. The Irish had few rights or freedoms and lived in constant fear of being dispossessed by their English landlords. Resistance to British policies grew and, in 1641, a bloody rebellion led by Irish Catholics began against English rule.

Charles I opens a session of Parliament.

Parliament needed a big army to put down the Irish rebellion. Not trusting the king, they proposed that Parliament be in command of the army, but Charles refused. He led troops to the House of Commons to arrest some of his opponents. With neither side compromising, a civil war began in 1642.

✔ **READING CHECK: Identifying Cause and Effect** What factors contributed to the conflict between native Irish people and British settlers in Ireland?

English Civil War

The citizens of England were sharply divided. Those who supported the king included Anglicans, Roman Catholics, nobles, and other opponents of Parliament's reforms. They were called royalists or **Cavaliers.** Those who supported Parliament included Puritans and other non-Anglican Protestants. They were called **Roundheads,** after the close haircuts of the Puritan soldiers.

Oliver Cromwell, a rising Puritan leader, organized his troops into a powerful army. Cromwell's **New Model Army** defeated Charles in 1645. Oxford, the royalist headquarters, surrendered the next year. The king fled to Scotland, but the Scots turned Charles over to Parliament.

In November 1647 Charles escaped and rallied his Scottish supporters to fight again. Cromwell's army crushed them, however, and moved on Parliament, keeping the king's supporters out. The Cromwell-controlled Parliament, known as the **Rump Parliament,** abolished the monarchy and the House of Lords. It proclaimed England a **commonwealth,** or republic. A special court tried Charles for treason. This was its verdict:

 Primary Source

"Whereas Charles Stuart, King of England, is, and standeth convicted, attained, and condemned of high treason, and other high crimes; and sentence upon Saturday last was pronounced against him by this Court, to be put to death by the severing of his head from his body; of which sentence, execution yet remaineth to be done; there are therefore to will and require you to see the said sentence executed in the open street before Whitehall, upon the morrow, being the thirtieth day of this instant month of January, between the hours of ten in the morning and five in the afternoon of the same day, with full effect."

John Bradshaw, Thomas Grey, Oliver Cromwell, et al., *The Death Warrant of Charles I*

Charles was beheaded in front of the palace at Whitehall in 1649. His son fled to France, and Oliver Cromwell took control of England.

✔ **READING CHECK: Analyzing Information** What were the most significant actions of the Rump Parliament?

The death warrant of Charles I was signed and sealed by members of Parliament.

Cromwell's Commonwealth

Oliver Cromwell was an honest and devout Puritan, a powerful speaker, and a skilled leader. He was also unbending in his belief that divine providence had brought him to power. Thus, Cromwell often acted harshly to suppress resistance to his rule. Despite his dictatorial approach to leadership, however, Cromwell was fairly tolerant of others' religious views. Nevertheless, rigid Puritan followers sometimes forced Cromwell to respond to dissent with extreme force.

Cromwell ruled England as lord protector from 1653 until his death in 1658. This five-year period of English history is often known as the Protectorate. During this time, Cromwell was virtually a military dictator, since he based his rule on the support of the army. Despite his great power, however, Cromwell aimed to bring about a parliamentary republic in England. He wanted to create a representative form of government, but continuing unrest and disorder in the English commonwealth prevented this. Nevertheless, Cromwell tried twice to establish a **constitution**— a document outlining the basic laws and principles that govern a nation. The Instrument of Government of 1653 was the first written constitution of any major European nation. It provided that landowners would elect members of Parliament.

The government of the Protectorate was unpopular in England, and discontent became increasingly widespread. Cromwell's government might have been overthrown except for three factors: (1) It raised enough money from taxes and royalist land sales to support itself and its army. (2) The army was disciplined and powerful. It discouraged other groups from acting against the government. (3) Its enemies had no organized army and could never take effective action to resist the lord protector. Cromwell's control over the Irish, for example, was brutally effective, and the royalists never posed a serious threat to his rule.

Cromwell's policies toward other countries supported his aim of encouraging trade and manufacturing at home. Dutch merchants and shipowners had taken advantage of England's civil turmoil to establish a profitable oceangoing trade. Cromwell challenged the Dutch by having Parliament pass the **Navigation Act of 1651,** requiring that all goods shipped to England from other countries be carried by English ships or by ships of the producing country. This law led to war with the Dutch between 1652 and 1654. Although the war ended with no clear victor, the English navy gained prestige, and Cromwell showed that England could support its commerce with naval power.

CONNECTING TO
Civics

Constitutionalism

Constitutionalism is a form of government in which a nation follows a written constitution. No one person or group has all the power in a constitutional government. Instead, power is shared by different parts of the government. For example, the United States has a president, a two-house congress, and courts. Each of these branches has independent powers, but each is also limited by the others. Many countries today have a constitutional form of government.

Understanding Civics

What is constitutionalism and what are its advantages?

INTERPRETING THE VISUAL RECORD

Preamble This document shows the beginning of the Preamble to the U.S. Constitution. *How do the first three words of the Preamble reflect the ideas of constitutionalism?*

End of the Revolution

The experiment with republican government in England eventually failed. Cromwell quarreled with Parliament, which resented his power. He eventually dissolved Parliament and ruled alone. After Cromwell died in 1658, his son Richard became lord protector. Richard was a weak leader, however, and lost the army's support.

By 1660 the English people had begun to turn against Cromwell's republican government. Many had favored Charles I's execution 11 years earlier, but they recognized that the commonwealth had failed to settle the nation or to solve its problems. In 1660, after much debate and with the army's support, Parliament invited Charles II, the Stuart son of Charles I, to return to England. Cheering crowds greeted Charles II when he reached London. People throughout the country hoped that the restoration of the monarchy would bring peace and progress to England once again. As one observer noted,

 Primary Source ❝This day came in his Majesty Charles the Second to London after a sad and long exile. . . . This was also his birthday, and with a Triumph of above 20,000 horse and foot, brandishing their swords and shouting with unexpressable joy. The ways strewed with flowers, the bells ringing, the streets hung with tapestry, fountains running with wine.❞

John Evelyn, *Diary entry,* May 29, 1660

Some historians call the period from 1642 to 1660 the English Revolution. It includes the civil war years from 1642 to 1649, as well as the changes that continued until the monarchy was restored in 1660. Peace returned to England, but 30 years would pass before king and Parliament could work closely together.

✔ **READING CHECK: Problem Solving** What could Oliver Cromwell have done differently to have helped the republican government succeed in England?

SECTION 1 REVIEW

1. **Define** and explain the significance:
   commonwealth
   constitution

2. **Identify** and explain the significance:
   Charles I
   Petition of Right
   Long Parliament
   Cavaliers
   Roundheads
   Oliver Cromwell
   New Model Army
   Rump Parliament
   Navigation Act of 1651

 Homework Practice Online
keyword: SH3 HP11

3. **Sequencing** Copy the time line below. Use it to identify and place into sequence the major events in the English Revolution.

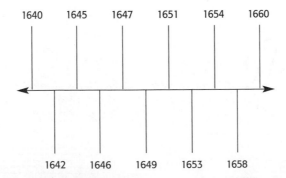

4. **Finding the Main Idea**
   a. Why did Parliament present Charles I with the Petition of Right?
   b. How did rebellion in Ireland help trigger the English Civil War?
   c. Why did England's experiment with republican government under Cromwell fail?

5. **Writing and Critical Thinking**
   Identifying Points of View Who was likely to support Charles I in the English Revolution? Who was likely to support Oliver Cromwell?
   Consider:
   • what Charles I had done to lose the support of the English people
   • the strengths of Cromwell, his army, and his political supporters
   • how Cromwell gained control of the English government

Constitutional Monarchy in England

The Main Idea
Parliament gradually replaced the monarchy as the major source of political power in England.

The Story Continues *A more stable government emerged in England toward the end of the 1600s. It was fueled by new ideas about the relationship between ruler and ruled. These ideas were based, in part, upon the ideas of political thinkers such as John Locke, who wrote that "reason . . . teaches all mankind, who will but consult it, that being all equal and independent, no one ought to harm another in his life, health, liberty, or possessions."*

The Restoration and the Glorious Revolution

The reign of Charles II, when the English monarchy was restored, is called the **Restoration.** This name reflected not only the return to monarchy, but also a rebirth of English culture. Charles II loved entertainment and pleasure. Removing Puritan restrictions on the theater, he made entertainment and the arts more available to the people of England. His subjects named him the "Merry Monarch."

Despite his nickname, however, Charles II had learned much from his father's execution and from his own long years in exile. In reality, Charles was personally cynical and cautious. He avoided fights with Parliament when his policies met with opposition, but he was quite willing to use secrecy and roundabout methods to gain his ends.

Charles continued Cromwell's bold commercial policies, which eventually led to another series of conflicts with the Dutch. During these wars, England won control of the Dutch settlement of New Amsterdam in North America, renaming it New York. Charles tried, as well, to form a new alliance between England and France. Widespread protest in Parliament and throughout England, however, forced him to end his efforts. As a result, England and France began 150 years of rivalry to win control of the seas and to gain overseas colonies and resources.

Charles sought to increase toleration for Catholicism and worked to lift some of the legal restrictions that Parliament had imposed against the faith. His attempts to do so, however, met with such strong parliamentary opposition that he was forced to abandon the effort.

Charles II (shown here as a boy) became king following the fall of Cromwell's commonwealth in 1660.

Political parties develop. Charles II and his Portuguese queen, Catherine of Braganza, had no children. It appeared that Charles's younger brother James, a Roman Catholic, would succeed him. The two political parties developing in Parliament at this time had opposing ideas about this royal succession.

The two parties, the **Tories** and the **Whigs,** were about equal in strength. Their names were first used as insults. In Catholic Ireland the word *tory* meant an outlaw. In England, the name was given to one who believed James had a hereditary right to rule. Tories usually supported the Anglican Church. As believers in a hereditary monarchy, however, they would be willing to accept a Roman Catholic king.

The term *Whig* originally meant horse thief. Later applied to Scottish Presbyterians, the name suggested a group that was rebellious. The Whigs claimed the right to deny the throne to James. They wanted a strong Parliament and opposed having a Catholic ruler.

The Glorious Revolution. When Charles II died in 1685, his Catholic brother came to the throne as **James II.** He was humorless and less flexible than Charles was. James's belief in absolute royal rule antagonized both Whigs and Tories. His attempts to help Catholics frightened Protestants and spurred them to resist his rule.

Succession to the throne remained an important issue during James II's reign. His daughters, Mary and Anne, had both been raised as Protestants and had married Protestant princes. When their mother died, James married Mary of Modena, who was Catholic. In 1688 she had a son, who by law would succeed his father as monarch before his older half sisters would. Protestants feared the boy would begin a whole line of Catholic rulers on the English throne.

Both the Whigs and Tories in Parliament called on James II to step down. Leaders in Parliament then invited James's daughter, Mary, and her Dutch husband, William of Orange, to replace James on the throne. In their letter of invitation to William, the English leaders described the reasons for their opposition to James's rule.

This plate made in 1691 celebrates the coronation of William III and Mary II.

Analyzing Primary Sources

Identifying Cause and Effect
What causes did the English leaders cite for their opposition to King James II?

❝ . . . the people are so generally dissatisfied with the present conduct of the Government in relation to their religion, liberties and properties . . . and they are in such expectation of their prospects being daily worse, that your Highness may be assured there are nineteen parts of twenty of the people throughout the kingdom who are desirous of a change and who, we believe, would willingly contribute to it. ❞

"The Letter of Invitation from the Immortal Seven," quoted in
The Glorious Revolution of 1688 by Maurice Ashley

William of Orange was a famous soldier who had defeated the powerful French. When he landed in England at the head of a Dutch army in 1688, James fled to exile in France. Parliament gave the crown of England to William and Mary as joint rulers, known from that point on as **William III** and **Mary II.** The opponents of James II had combined to bring about what is known as the **Glorious Revolution,** a bloodless transfer of power in the English monarchy.

✔ **READING CHECK: Drawing Conclusions** How did religious attitudes affect the rule of Charles II and James II?

Changes in English Government

The English Civil War and the events that followed led to important changes in the government. These events also changed the ways people thought about government. English philosopher **Thomas Hobbes,** who lived through the civil war, was disturbed by the chaos it created. He outlined his political philosophy in 1651 in a book called *Leviathan.*

Hobbes explained that the first people on Earth lived in anarchy, which he believed to be a state of nature. To avoid the resulting violence and danger, Hobbes said, people chose a leader to rule them. They made an unwritten social contract, giving the leader absolute power. The people kept only the right to protect their own lives.

Hobbes was strongly influenced by the chaos and destruction of the English Civil War. The ideas that he expressed in *Leviathan* reflected his belief that people acted from self-interest and without regard for the rights or welfare of others. In Hobbes's view, the natural world was a place in which only the strong would survive unless order was imposed by the greater power of a ruler. The social contract described by Hobbes was based on the exchange of individual liberty for group safety and social order.

John Locke, another English philosopher, disagreed. He accepted the idea of the social contract but believed that people had given up only some of their individual rights. Those they kept included the right to live, to enjoy liberty, and to own property. He said they could expect their rulers to preserve these rights. A ruler who violated these rights thus violated natural law and broke the social contract.

Locke, in contrast to Hobbes, believed that the contract between ruler and ruled could not limit the individual's natural right to enjoy life, political equality, and the ownership of property. In his *Two Treatises of Government,* Locke argued that these individual rights were superior to laws and governments. Governments existed for the sole purpose of protecting those rights. Thus, a ruler's claim to absolute power contradicted the natural order because people would not—and could not—willingly surrender their fundamental natural rights. A ruler who denied people their basic rights was a tyrant and could justly be overthrown.

Habeas Corpus Act and Declaration of Rights. Following the ideas of Locke, Parliament passed laws attempting to safeguard against arbitrary rule. In 1679 Parliament passed the Habeas Corpus Act to protect people who had been arrested. They could obtain a writ, or order, demanding to be brought before a judge. The judge would decide whether the prisoner should be released or charged and tried for a crime. The writ itself was called **habeas corpus,** Latin for "you shall have the body." The Habeas Corpus Act protected individuals against unfair arrest and imprisonment.

A document called the Declaration of Rights was read to William and Mary before they were given the throne in 1689. That year, Parliament formalized the document, calling it the **English Bill of Rights.** It declared that Parliament would choose who ruled the country. The ruler would be subject to parliamentary laws and could not proclaim or suspend any law. The ruler could not impose taxes or maintain an army in peacetime without Parliament's consent. Parliament would meet frequently and the ruler could not interfere with the election of its members. The Bill of Rights guaranteed free speech for members of Parliament.

The Bill of Rights also protected private citizens. Any citizen could petition the government for relief of injustice. No citizen could be forced to pay unfairly high bail or face cruel or unusual punishment.

HISTORY MAKER

**John Locke
(1632–1704)**

John Locke was an important English philosopher. He believed in private property and was against taxation without representation. Locke's writings influenced the Americans who framed our Declaration of Independence and Constitution.

Locke thought that a contract existed between monarch and subjects. He said the people had the right to change their government if it became oppressive. **How did John Locke's writings affect the United States?**

Holt Researcher

go.hrw.com
KEYWORD: Holt Researcher
FreeFind: John Locke
After reading more about John Locke on the Holt Researcher, write a summary identifying the impact of the legal and political ideas contained in his *Two Treatises of Government.*

Contrasting Views of Individual Liberty: Hobbes and Locke

The era following the English Revolution saw a continuing debate concerning the ideal form of government. Many thinkers favored centralized rule by a monarch who held absolute power over people, land, and property alike. Others, in contrast, believed that natural law gave the individual the right to govern himself or herself. Thomas Hobbes and John Locke came to symbolize opposing sides of this argument. By identifying the different points of view between Hobbes and Locke, one can better understand the political debates that led to many different experiments with government in England.

Thomas Hobbes

The natural condition of humans is one of continuous conflict and competition: "In such condition, there is no place for industry, because the fruit thereof is uncertain; and consequently no culture of the earth, . . . no knowledge of the face of the earth, no account of time, no arts, no letters, no society; and which is worst of all, continual fear and danger of violent death; and the life of people, solitary, poor, nasty, brutish, and short."

John Locke

The natural condition of humans is ". . . a state of perfect freedom to order their actions, and dispose of their possessions and persons as they think fit, . . . without asking leave or depending upon the will of any other man . . . . A state also of equality, wherein all the power and jurisdiction is reciprocal [shared equally], no one having more than another. . . ."

Thomas Hobbes (1588–1679), above, and John Locke (1632–1704), left, were leading English political philosophers. Their strongly contrasting views concerning the nature of government and its proper limits have influenced political thought from the 1600s to the present.

Skills Reminder

To identify a writer's point of view, you should first define the topic—the central idea—on which the writer is focusing. Then, read carefully to determine the writer's position—his or her point of view—toward that idea. Think about what you have learned from the writer before accepting or rejecting the point of view. When studying sources by different authors writing about the same topic, decide if their points of view are similar or opposing. Then decide which source makes the strongest case.

Skills Practice

❶ Summarize the points of view that Hobbes and Locke held about the natural condition of human beings.

❷ Which view do you find the most convincing? Why?

❸ Search recent media sources to find two editorials that express differing views on a common political subject. Choose which view you find the most convincing and explain why. Be sure to cite specific evidence from the editorials to justify your conclusion.

Toleration Act and Act of Settlement. In 1689 Parliament passed the **Toleration Act.** It granted some religious freedoms to Dissenters, Protestants who were not members of the Anglican Church. The Toleration Act did not protect Roman Catholics or Jews, however. It also barred Dissenters from holding public office.

In 1701 Parliament passed the Act of Settlement to keep Catholics from the English throne. The act stated that should William III die with no heir, Mary's sister Anne would inherit the throne. Should Anne have no children, the throne would go to another Protestant granddaughter of James I.

✔ **READING CHECK: Analyzing Information** How did Parliament reduce the power of the monarchy after the Restoration?

Parliamentary Rule

The Bill of Rights and the Act of Settlement marked a turning point in the history of England. The long struggle between the monarch and Parliament over who would rule the country had finally come to an end. Parliament had emerged as clearly supreme to the monarchy. The rights of individuals, moreover, and the limits on government powers had also become better defined. The long process of political development in Britain, however, was far from complete. Views of personal liberty and of the individual's right to participate in a government that was truly representative continued to grow and change.

Growing power of Parliament. By 1700 England was still a monarchy, but Parliament held most of the power. Parliament did not represent most of the people of England, however. The House of Lords consisted only of hereditary nobles and higher clergy. Even the House of Commons, which was gradually becoming the more powerful of the two houses, represented a small minority of the population. Only the landowning male gentry and wealthy merchants and professionals could vote for representatives to the Commons.

In the 50 years following the Glorious Revolution, Parliament continued to gain importance as the real power in Britain's government. During this time, the organization and institutions characteristic of today's British government gradually emerged. Two of the most important government institutions to develop between about 1690 and about 1740 were the cabinet and the office of prime minister.

William and Mary The Glorious Revolution led to Protestant rule by William III and Mary II. *Why might the artist have included so many of the trappings of monarchy in this portrait of William and Mary?*

English monarchs always had met with advisers to discuss problems of government. After the Restoration and the Glorious Revolution, parliamentary leaders had the power to get things done for the monarchs. William III chose his officers of state from among these leaders, who were often heads of government departments. They became known as the **cabinet.**

At first cabinets included both Whigs and Tories. This changed during William III's reign. It was decided that the government would run more smoothly if cabinet ministers belonged to the majority party in Parliament. Sometimes, to make working with Parliament possible, monarchs had to accept a cabinet they did not like. During and after William's reign, Parliament continued to win more authority, including the power to declare war. The king also no longer tried to veto acts of Parliament.

Act of Union. In 1707 the parliaments of England and Scotland passed the Act of Union. This law united England and Scotland into one kingdom, known as Great Britain. It was intended as a measure to strengthen England in its growing conflict with France. Many in Scotland opposed the union. This was partly because it abolished Scotland's parliament, even though Scots now took seats in the English House of Lords and House of Commons.

The union proved beneficial, however. By removing trade barriers, it encouraged commerce and brought wealth to both England and Scotland. The Scottish town of Glasgow grew from a fishing village into a great port city. The Universities of Edinburgh and Glasgow became major centers of learning during the 1700s.

Queen Anne, who ruled from 1702 to 1714, had seventeen children. None survived her. Sophia of Hanover, granddaughter of James I, would have been next in line to the throne. She also was dead. That is how Sophia's son George, the first of the Hanoverian dynasty, became King George I of Great Britain.

Both George I and his son George II were born in Germany. Neither was familiar with British government or customs. George I, who ruled until 1727, did not even speak English. George II, who ruled until 1760, spoke fluent English, but depended heavily on cabinet ministers such as Sir Robert Walpole to manage the government's administration. Walpole served as the king's chief minister until 1742. During these years, he used his knowledge of the House of Commons to work for peace at home and overseas. Walpole also strengthened the British economy, although several of his tax measures were unpopular in Great Britain and in the kingdom's American colonies. Under Walpole's leadership, the British cabinet became increasingly important and necessary, and he is generally viewed as Great Britain's first effective **prime minister,** or first minister. His strong hand helped to stabilize the British political scene.

The British Isles, 1707

Interpreting Maps The Act of Union of 1707 united England and Scotland into one kingdom—the Kingdom of Great Britain.

■ **Skills Assessment: 1. Locate** What small mountain range separates England from Scotland? **2. Analyzing Information** What were the advantages and disadvantages of uniting England and Scotland into Great Britain?

Constitutional monarchy. From 1721 to 1742 the Whigs controlled the House of Commons, led by Walpole, the government's prime minister. Under the rule of the Hanoverian monarchs, the prime minister, who usually held the title of first lord of the treasury during these years, was the real head of government. By this point in its history, the nation had become a **limited constitutional monarchy.** The monarch remained as Britain's head of state. Royal powers, however, were clearly limited by the British constitution, which required the king or queen to consult with Parliament and which reserved certain important powers for Parliament alone. The British system of limited constitutional monarchy has changed very little since the 1700s.

Great Britain has one of the world's oldest constitutional governments. It has been a model for other nations that have wanted to end absolute monarchies. The British constitution is not a single document. Instead, it consists partly of several great documents. Among them are the Magna Carta, the Petition of Rights, the Habeas Corpus Act, the Bill of Rights, and the Act of Settlement. It also includes acts of Parliament, which can be changed by later Parliaments. Some features of the British government have never been written down. The powers of the prime minister and the cabinet are based largely on tradition. The prime minister rather than the monarch selects the other ministers. Together the prime minister and the cabinet plan and carry out government policies.

This image portrays Sir Robert Walpole, Britain's first prime minister, discussing policy with his cabinet.

✔ **READING CHECK: Summarizing** What are the principal features of Britain's limited constitutional monarchy?

SECTION 2 REVIEW

1. Define and explain the significance:
   habeas corpus
   cabinet
   prime minister
   limited constitutional monarchy

2. Identify and explain the significance:
   Restoration
   Tories
   Whigs
   James II
   William III
   Mary II
   Glorious Revolution
   Thomas Hobbes
   John Locke
   English Bill of Rights
   Toleration Act

3. Categorizing Copy the organizational chart below. Use it to identify the relationships between the various elements of the British government.

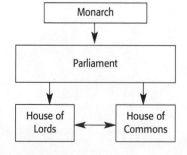

4. **Finding the Main Idea**

a. In what major ways did Parliament's Tories and Whigs differ in their view of the English monarchy?

b. What role did religion play in the reigns of Charles II and James II?

c. What was the "social contract" of Hobbes and Locke, and how did the two thinkers disagree in their view of it?

d. Why was the Parliament of the early 1700s not truly a "representative legislature"?

5. **Writing and Critical Thinking**

Analyzing Information Imagine that you are a member of Parliament during the early 1700s. Write a speech for delivery to your fellow members in which you describe the progress of representative government in England after the English Revolution.
Consider:
• what measures Parliament took to reduce the power of the monarchy after the Restoration
• to what degree the British constitutional system protected the rights of citizens

Homework Practice Online
keyword: SH3 HP11

ENLIGHTENMENT AND REVOLUTION IN ENGLAND AND AMERICA **297**

English Colonial Expansion

READ TO DISCOVER

❶ Who were the sea dogs and what did they accomplish?

❷ What were the results of British mercantilist policy?

DEFINE

sea dogs

IDENTIFY

John Cabot
Sir Francis Drake
Henry Hudson

▶ **WHY IT MATTERS TODAY**

Great Britain still follows the mercantilist policy of importing raw materials and exporting manufactured goods. Use or other **current event** sources to identify which four or five countries are Great Britain's main trading partners today. Record your findings in your journal.

The Main Idea
After defeating the Spanish Armada, the British began to establish a colonial empire based on trade.

The Story Continues *The defeat of the Spanish Armada in 1588 encouraged the English to compete with other European powers for control of overseas raw materials and markets. England's growing imperialism after 1588 brought criticism from other nations. ". . . I must not omit to say that the English through their rapacity [greed] and cruelty have become odious [hated] to all nations," complained a Venetian diplomat in London in 1603.*

The Beginnings of the British Empire

While Spain and Portugal were creating overseas empires during the 1500s, England was busy with problems at home. During the 1600s, however, English explorers began claiming and conquering land overseas. English merchants, who had been trading in Russia and the Baltic, now moved into the Americas and Asia. At the same time, the English navy had become a major force. English merchant shipping replaced the Dutch as a leader in foreign trade. By the 1760s Great Britain's colonial empire was the greatest in the world.

Explorers and sea dogs. Soon after Christopher Columbus sailed from Spain in 1492, King Henry VII of England entered the contest for American colonies. He hired Venetian captain **John Cabot,** who explored the coasts of Newfoundland, Nova Scotia, and possibly New England. Cabot's voyages in 1497 and 1498 gave England its first claim in North America.

During Queen Elizabeth I's reign in the second half of the 1500s, an adventurous group of English sea captains called the **sea dogs** appeared. These traders and pirates included Sir John Hawkins, **Sir Francis Drake,** and Sir Walter Raleigh. With the backing of the crown, they challenged the Portuguese and Spanish monopolies of sea trade.

Francis Drake was knighted by Queen Elizabeth I when he returned from his three-year voyage around the world.

The sea dogs also made important voyages of exploration. Drake, for example, sailed west from England across the Atlantic Ocean. He continued around South America to the west coast of North America. He then crossed the Pacific and Indian Oceans, rounded southern Africa, and returned to England in 1580. Drake was the first English sea captain to sail around the globe.

The sea dogs were best known for plundering foreign ships. Their repeated raids of Spanish slave ships from Africa greatly angered King Philip II of Spain. However, these attacks were part of a larger effort to undermine Spain's empire in the Americas. As Richard Hakluyt, an English historian of the day, observed:

History Makers Speak

❝If you touch him [King Philip II of Spain] in the [West] Indies, you touch the apple of his eye; for take away his treasure . . . [and] his old bands of soldiers will soon be dissolved, his purpose defeated, his power and strength diminished, his pride abated, and his tyranny utterly suppressed . . . .❞

Richard Hakluyt, *A Discourse on Western Planting*

Analyzing Primary Sources

Finding the Main Idea What did Hakluyt think the British could accomplish by attacking Philip's ships in the West Indies?

Philip protested to Queen Elizabeth, who claimed she was helpless to stop the raids. Secretly, Elizabeth supported the sea dogs and shared the profits from selling the slaves. Both pirates and patriots, the sea dogs helped England defeat the Spanish Armada in 1588. They strengthened the nation's seafaring tradition.

The British in India. The defeat of the Spanish Armada encouraged the British to establish colonies overseas. In 1600 Queen Elizabeth I granted a charter to a trading group that came to be known as the British East India Company. Over the course of its long life—it continued for nearly 260 years—the company played a major role in the development of Great Britain's overseas power. During its early years, the company worked to build and expand overseas trade, making no attempt to gain territory. It set up trading posts at Bombay, Calcutta, and Madras in India. These posts gradually became centers of power from which the British were able both to defend their trade interests and to expand their influence. Over time, in fact, the British East India Company became an unofficial extension of the British government. Throughout its history, the company did much to shape and apply Britain's colonial and commercial policies.

Given the decline of the once-mighty Mughal Empire by the 1600s, the British East India Company dealt mainly with local rulers during its early years. The company worked to win the support and loyalty of these rulers in several ways. It helped those who were weak, used force without hesitation against those who opposed the company's aims, and bribed those who were willing to accept its generous "gifts."

By the mid-1700s the British East India Company had established trading posts in Malaya and the East Indies, as well as in India. As it grew, the company came into increasing contact—and conflict—with French traders who had built a similar company. Increasing competition between the two trading companies, and between the British and the French in general, eventually led to open conflict. The British emerged supreme from this struggle. By the late 1750s the company had become the dominant

INTERPRETING THE VISUAL RECORD

The British in India This is a painted wooden model from the early 1800s. It depicts an Indian court called the Cutcherry. *What evidence is there that officers of the British East India Company were in charge?*

European trade interest in India. At the same time, it had become extremely powerful and wealthy and enjoyed strong support in Parliament.

✔ **READING CHECK: Evaluating** What role did the English sea dogs play in England's larger quests for power?

The British in America

England was slow to establish colonies in North America. At first, the British explored the continent in hope of finding the Northwest Passage. This would have been a northern water route to Asia through or around North America. Spain controlled the southern route around Cape Horn in South America. Unfortunately, the Northwest Passage could not be found.

Henry Hudson was one of the first to search for the Northwest Passage. In 1609 he sailed on behalf of the Dutch. He charted much of the coast of eastern North America and explored the river that now bears his name. The next year he sailed on behalf of the English. He explored the bay in northern Canada also named for him.

British settlements. As they searched for the Northwest Passage, the British began settling along the eastern coast of North America. Private companies or individuals founded the first of these colonial settlements. In 1607 they established Jamestown, in what is now Virginia. Jamestown was the first permanent English settlement in North America. In 1620 settlers founded Plymouth, in what is now Massachusetts.

The founders hoped that these settlements would make money for the home country. Few investors, however, made any profit from the colonies. The colonists themselves settled in North America for other reasons. Some came to find greater political or religious freedom. Others simply wanted better lives for their families.

Many settlers did not come voluntarily. As in other colonial empires, the English brought slaves to their colonies. Slavery was most common in the southern colonies and in the West Indies. Barbados, in the Caribbean, was a huge commercial success largely because slaves did most of the work.

The model pictured below is of Henry Hudson's ship, the **Half Moon.** *Although they appear tiny and fragile by today's standards, ships like this carried European explorers to new lands around the world.*

INTERPRETING THE VISUAL RECORD

Henry Hudson This image shows Henry Hudson landing on Manhattan Island. *How does this image reflect a European perspective?*

Most European colonies were ruled from the home country. Self-government set England's empire apart. Most English colonies had some form of representative assembly. Official control, however, remained firmly with England.

Mercantilism and the British colonies. The British government tried to make the colonies more profitable. Its policy of mercantilism held that the colonies existed for the economic benefit of the home country. Mercantilists believed that for a nation to become wealthy, it must export more goods than it imported. They saw colonies as sources of raw materials for the factories of the home country and as markets for the products of those factories.

Parliament passed laws to enforce this policy beginning in the 1650s. One law required colonists to sell certain products only to Britain—even if better prices were available in another country. Other laws discouraged colonists from manufacturing their own goods. For example, the British government forbade colonists to ship woolen cloth that they had manufactured to places outside their own colony.

Colonists resented the British trade regulations, and they found many ways to evade the laws. For example, they avoided paying taxes whenever and however they could. Smuggling became a respectable occupation in the colonies. This practice was hard to prevent because the long, indented coastline of North America had many harbors and inlets where ships could hide. Until the mid-1700s, moreover, the British government did not try very hard to enforce its colonial trade restrictions.

✔ **READING CHECK: Analyzing Information**
What were the results of British mercantilist policy?

Britain's mercantilist policies attempted to assure a flow of gold into the nation's treasury.

Mercantilism
Mercantilism was a theory that favored the extension of a nation's economic power beyond its borders. Mercantilists realized that a strong colonial power would benefit from having a large population to provide the workers, consumers, and soldiers needed by a growing economy. They also believed that gold and silver were important measures of national wealth.

Understanding Economics

Why might merchants in the colonies object to mercantilism?

SECTION 3 REVIEW

1. **Define** and explain the significance:
   sea dogs

2. **Identify** and explain the significance:
   John Cabot
   Sir Francis Drake
   Henry Hudson

3. **Sequencing** Copy the diagram below. Indicate with an arrow for each item the direction—to or from the home country—in which British mercantilist policy would have this item shipped.

   gold

   Great Britain

   raw materials

   silver

   manufactured goods

4. **Finding the Main Idea**
   a. What was the importance of the sea dogs to British hopes for empire?
   b. What were the results of British mercantilist policy?

5. **Writing and Critical Thinking**
   Drawing Conclusions Why did Elizabeth I support the activities of the English sea dogs?
   Consider:
   • how the sea dogs attacked Spanish shipping
   • the results of the sea dogs' attacks
   • how the sea dogs supported English policies against the Spanish

Homework Practice Online
keyword: SH3 HP11

READ TO DISCOVER

❶ What were the principal characteristics of Enlightenment thinking?

❷ What were the similarities and differences in the ideas of important Enlightenment philosophers?

DEFINE

rationalism
philosophes
popular sovereignty
enlightened despotism

IDENTIFY

Enlightenment
The Encyclopedia
Denis Diderot
Baron de Montesquieu
Voltaire
Jean-Jacques Rousseau
Mary Wollstonecraft

▶ WHY IT MATTERS TODAY

The idea that science can help explain human behavior has persisted. Use CNNStudentNews.com or other **current event** sources to find an example of how the scientific method is used to give information about group behavior. Record your findings in your journal.

Shown here are a few pages from a rare first edition of **The Encyclopedia** *published by the French philosophes.*

The Enlightenment

The Main Idea
Enlightenment thinkers examined and challenged traditional views of government.

The Story Continues *Increasingly during the 1600s and the 1700s, the ancient European social and political order, in which a small but privileged minority controlled the majority, came under attack. Critics of the old order complained that the privileged few took much and gave back little. Noted one French thinker, "If [a great lord] . . . can conceal the fact that he has nothing to do by looking busy, . . . he thinks himself the most fortunate of men."*

Crusaders of the Enlightenment

The 1700s have been called the Age of **Enlightenment.** Some people believed that reason and the scientific method could logically explain human nature. This belief that truth can be determined solely by logical thinking was called **rationalism.**

Thinkers of the Enlightenment believed in natural law. Objects in nature were expected to act in ways that were predictable. During the 1700s many people came to believe that laws of nature governed the universe and all its creatures. These beliefs formed the foundation of the modern natural sciences.

These advanced thinkers also believed that God had created the world and all living things. Just as the law of gravity governed the movement of planets, other laws governed human behavior. To live in harmony, people must live according to natural law. However, many believed that God did not act directly in human affairs and that individual human actions mattered most in determining the future. Some thinkers downplayed the importance of religion, a view that became known as secularism. Enlightenment ideas about secularism and individualism would later influence some ideas about the separation of church and state in government.

Thinkers of the Enlightenment were called **philosophes** (fee·luh·ZAWFS), after the French word for philosopher. They were not only philosophers but also critics of society. They wrote to one another and published their ideas in books, plays, pamphlets, and newspapers. Their most famous and ambitious project was *The Encyclopedia,* a sort of handbook describing the ideas of the Enlightenment that became the most famous publication of the period.

INTERPRETING THE VISUAL RECORD

Enlightenment salons Marie-Thérèse Geoffrin's salon in the Hotel Rambouillet provided a weekly opportunity for artists and writers to meet with one another and to discuss the ideas of the Enlightenment. *How might the salon pictured to the left encourage the free exchange of ideas?*

The Encyclopedia was edited by philosopher **Denis Diderot** (dee·DROH). He and co-editor Jean d'Alembert (dah·lem·BER) published the first edition in 28 volumes between 1751 and 1772. Leading philosophes contributed articles covering nearly every possible subject. Many of the articles were very technical. Others criticized many things in society. They attacked the church, the government, the slave trade, torture, taxes, and war. The French authorities frowned on critical writings, however. They imprisoned Diderot and several other philosophes. Nevertheless, people throughout Europe read *The Encyclopedia* and adopted its ideas.

✔ **READING CHECK: Finding the Main Idea** What were the main characteristics of Enlightenment thinking?

Holt Researcher

go.hrw.com
KEYWORD: Holt Researcher
FreeFind:
   Marie-Therese Geoffrin
After reading more about Marie-Thérèse Geoffrin on the Holt Researcher, write an imaginary dialogue that she might have had in her salon about political issues of the time.

Political Criticism

Based on the democratic-republican governments that had evolved in classical Greece and Rome, the philosophes examined the governments of their time. They criticized the power of kings and the privileges of clergy and nobles.

A number of the philosophes adopted the ideas of John Locke. One of them was **Baron de Montesquieu** (MOHN·tes·kyoo). In 1748 Montesquieu published *The Spirit of the Laws*. In this book he tried to describe the perfect government. He concluded that Great Britain had the best. He wrote that the British system's greatest strength was the division of government into three branches. He believed that the balance between the executive, legislative, and judicial branches provided checks to political power.

Although Montesquieu was wrong about how government was divided in Britain, his ideas carried great weight. His idea of checks and balances would influence the framing of the U.S. Constitution in 1787.

French writer Francois-Marie Arouet, best known as **Voltaire,** exemplified the spirit of the Enlightenment. Voltaire wrote clever and stinging satires on the French monarchy, the nobility, and the religious controls of the church. Twice imprisoned in the Bastille for his attacks on the old order, Voltaire fled for a time to Britain. He was especially critical of intolerance and of attempts to suppress personal freedoms. In defense of the freedom of speech, Voltaire wrote, "I [may] disapprove of what you say, but I will defend to the death your right to say it." In his book *Philosophical Letters*, Voltaire wrote that he, too, was impressed by the British political system.

**Mary Wollstonecraft
(1759–1797)**

During the Enlightenment, British author Mary Wollstonecraft argued for the equality of women with men. Wollstonecraft sought personal freedom and economic independence, working as a schoolteacher and a governess before turning to writing. In her most well-known work, *A Vindication of the Rights of Woman* (1792), Wollstonecraft argued that women should enjoy the same educational opportunities and political rights as men, including the right to vote. **What did Mary Wollstonecraft want for women?**

Back in France, Voltaire continued his criticism. He attacked everything he considered a sham or superstition. His novel *Candide* ridiculed prejudice, bigotry, and oppressive government. Voltaire became famous as a champion of religious freedom and freedom of thought.

In 1762 **Jean-Jacques Rousseau** (roo·SOH) published *The Social Contract*. He wrote that people are naturally good, but that environment, education, and laws corrupt them. He believed that people could preserve their natural state only if they could choose their own government. He wrote that good government must be based on **popular sovereignty.** By this he meant that government must be created by and controlled by the people.

History Makers Speak

"Man is born free; and everywhere he is in chains. One thinks himself the master of others, and still remains a greater slave than they."

Jean-Jacques Rousseau, *The Social Contract*

Unlike other philosophes, Rousseau did not trust reason. He believed that it brought corruption and misery. Rousseau's opposition to a strong government also set him apart. Although philosophes disliked absolute monarchy, most of them favored the idea of **enlightened despotism.** This was a system of government in which an absolute monarch would rule, but according to the principles of the Enlightenment.

By the 1780s many people had come to accept Rousseau's philosophy and his distrust of reason. His ideas on government and individual freedom became most influential during the later years of the Enlightenment.

Although most of the philosophes were men, women also participated in the Enlightenment. English author **Mary Wollstonecraft** became an early spokesperson for women's rights. Wollstonecraft argued that Enlightenment ideals of equality should be extended to women as well as men.

✔ **READING CHECK: Comparing and Contrasting** Compare and contrast the ideas of the following philosophes: Montesquieu, Voltaire, and Rousseau.

SECTION 4 REVIEW

1. **Define** and explain the significance:
   rationalism
   philosophes
   popular sovereignty
   enlightened despotism

2. **Identify** and explain the significance:
   Enlightenment
   The Encyclopedia
   Denis Diderot
   Baron de Montesquieu
   Voltaire
   Jean-Jacques Rousseau
   Mary Wollstonecraft

3. **Categorizing** Copy the diagram below. Draw lines to match the principles on the right with the names on the left.

Montesquieu	popular sovereignty
Voltaire	women's rights
Rousseau	checks and balances
Wollstonecraft	freedom of speech

4. **Finding the Main Idea**

   a. What were the main characteristics of Enlightenment thinking?

   b. How did the ideas of secularism and individualism that arose during the Enlightenment affect later governments?

5. **Writing and Critical Thinking**

   Evaluating Select one of the philosophes. Explain why you believe his or her views on government are correct or incorrect.
   Consider:
   • the type of government championed by the philosophe you have selected
   • whether or not his or her ideas and approaches were realistic

Homework Practice Online

keyword: SH3 HP11

READ TO DISCOVER

❶ How did Americans respond to British policies after the French and Indian War?

❷ What type of government did Americans set up after the American Revolution?

IDENTIFY

Stamp Act
King George III
Lord North
Patriots
Loyalists
Thomas Jefferson
George Washington
Benjamin Franklin
Articles of Confederation
Bill of Rights

WHY IT MATTERS TODAY

In modern times people have often rebelled against tyrannical governments. Use or other **current event** sources to find several examples of recent political revolutions. Record your findings in your journal.

CNN Student News.com

The American Revolution

The Main Idea
In the late 1700s the United States of America broke from Britain to form a new kind of government.

The Story Continues *In the American colonies, Enlightenment thinking inspired new beliefs based upon the ideals of popular sovereignty. A growing number of people in Britain's North American colonies held that they should be governed by the same standards of law and liberty that governed people in Great Britain. They insisted that ". . . his majesty's subjects in these [American] colonies are entitled to all the inherent rights and privileges of his natural born subjects within the kingdom of Great Britain."*

Empire and Conflict

New ideas about government were not confined to Europe in the 1700s. In far-off North America, British colonists had developed a new way of life. They were creating a new relationship with the home country. Their first concern was with British trade laws, but they also disliked the French along their borders.

British-French rivalry. The British colonies sat along the Atlantic coast of North America. French settlements were to the north and west, in what was called New France. In the 1700s British-American settlers moved westward across the Appalachian Mountains. Conflict with the French seemed inescapable.

France and Britain had fought in Europe for decades. The conflict spilled over into North America and in 1754 resulted in the French and Indian War. In Europe this sparked the Seven Years' War, which raged from 1756 to 1763. British victory in these conflicts was confirmed by the Treaty of Paris of 1763. The British had won control of much of North America. They ruled from the Atlantic Ocean to the Mississippi River and from the Gulf of Mexico to the Arctic Ocean. British power had reached a new height.

Increased imperial control. The war with France left Britain with a huge debt. British politicians had defended the colonists. They now expected the colonists to repay this effort.

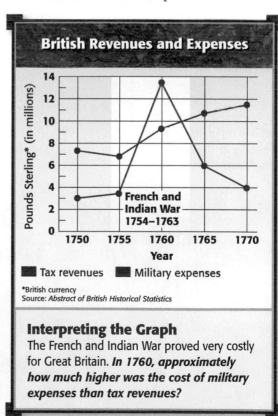

British Revenues and Expenses

French and Indian War 1754–1763

■ Tax revenues ■ Military expenses

*British currency
Source: *Abstract of British Historical Statistics*

Interpreting the Graph
The French and Indian War proved very costly for Great Britain. *In 1760, approximately how much higher was the cost of military expenses than tax revenues?*

Stamps such as this were required by the Stamp Act to be put on all commercial and legal papers.

British policy toward the colonies in the 1760s was uneven. In 1763 after an American Indian uprising, the British barred colonists from settling west of the Appalachians. The government also began enforcing its mercantilist trade laws. The Sugar Act of 1764, for example, imposed taxes on sugar and other imports from non-British colonies. The colonists saw this as a threat to their liberties.

In 1765 Parliament passed the **Stamp Act.** This law imposed a tax, in the form of a special stamp, on all sorts of documents, including wills, contracts, mortgages, newspapers, and pamphlets. The colonists opposed the tax. When they boycotted British goods, Parliament backed down and repealed the Stamp Act.

With each new tax law, colonial resistance increased. Some laws were repealed, but others were not. With no representatives in the British Parliament, the colonists argued against this "taxation without representation." They called it tyranny. Relations between Britain and the colonies grew steadily worse.

Intensified conflict. Reigning from 1760 to 1820, **King George III** was the first Hanoverian monarch to be born in England. He believed that Parliament had too much power. He wanted to select his own ministers. Six prime ministers came to power in just eight years. It was during this unsettled time that the final break with the American colonies occurred.

As the colonists hardened their resistance to British policies, George III was determined to force their obedience. In 1770 he found a new prime minister, **Lord North,** who was willing to carry out his policies.

Many American colonists were coming to believe that breaking away from British rule was necessary to guarantee their rights. The colonists were far from united for independence, however. About one third, called **Patriots,** wanted independence. Another third, called **Loyalists,** or Tories, opposed independence. The rest of the colonists did not take sides.

In 1773 Lord North's government gave the British East India Company a monopoly to ship tea directly to the colonies. Angry colonists threw a shipment of tea into Boston Harbor, an event that became known as the Boston Tea Party. Parliament responded by closing the port of Boston. Colonists called this and several other laws passed in 1774 the Intolerable Acts.

The Patriots took action. In the fall of 1774, delegates from 12 of the 13 colonies met in Philadelphia in the First Continental Congress. They demanded that the colonists be granted the full rights of British citizens. They agreed to meet again the following year if the British Parliament did not repeal the Intolerable Acts.

By April 1775 British troops in Boston had begun to feel threatened by the colonists' growing resistance. In response the British tried to seize colonial guns and gunpowder stored nearby. At the towns of Lexington and Concord, the British fought with groups of armed colonists. The American Revolution had begun.

✔**READING CHECK: Evaluating** How did colonists in America respond to changing British policy in the years between 1763 and 1775?

INTERPRETING THE VISUAL RECORD

The Stamp Act This British cartoon celebrates the repeal of the Stamp Act by showing members of Parliament carrying the "dead" act in a coffin. *What other imagery in the cartoon reflects the "death" of the act?*

American Independence

Delegates to the Second Continental Congress met in Philadelphia in May 1775. Many still hoped to avoid conflict. When they received news of the fighting at Lexington and Concord, their attitudes quickly changed. They prepared for war.

The Declaration of Independence. Delegates met again the following year. They voted to declare their freedom from Great Britain. On July 4, 1776, they adopted the Declaration of Independence. This established the United States of America as an independent nation. **Thomas Jefferson** was the Declaration's principal author. The Declaration of Independence showed the influence of Enlightenment philosophers such as John Locke. It declared that all men are created equal and have the right to "life, liberty, and the pursuit of happiness."

In his first draft of the Declaration, Jefferson had denounced slavery. But other delegates—primarily slaveholders from the southern American colonies—objected strongly to Jefferson's attack on their rights as "property owners." In order to secure the support of slaveholders in the southern colonies, therefore, delegates to the Congress removed the passage from the Declaration. Thus the ideal of individual liberty was only applied in a limited manner. Neither women nor slaves were included in the provisions of the Declaration of Independence. Nevertheless, the Declaration represented a milestone in the struggle for broader equality and justice.

The Declaration stated that all powers of government come from the people. It said that no government can exist without the consent of its citizens and that government is created to protect individual rights. If a government fails to protect these rights, the Declaration said, the people may alter or abolish it and set up a new government. These were extreme ideas. It was one thing to reject absolute monarchy. It was quite another to say people have the right of revolution.

> **Primary Source**
>
> **"We hold these truths to be self-evident, that all men are created equal, that they are endowed by their Creator with certain unalienable Rights, that among these are Life, Liberty, and the pursuit of Happiness. That to secure these rights, Governments are instituted among Men, deriving their just powers from the consent of the governed, That whenever any Form of Government becomes destructive of these ends, it is the Right of the People to alter or to abolish it, and to institute a new Government . . . "**
>
> The *Declaration of Independence*

The American Declaration of Independence was a remarkable and powerful political statement. It was also an elegant summary of many of the ideals and values that influenced Europe and America during the Enlightenment.

✔ **READING CHECK Summarizing** What new political and legal ideas were contained in the Declaration of Independence?

YOUNG PEOPLE IN HISTORY

Young Patriots

Patriots of all ages fought in the American Revolution. Many young boys between the ages of 14 and 16 enlisted in the American army. Other boys, some as young as six, served as drummers for the troops, like the one pictured here. Their job was to signal commands, which sometimes put them in the midst of battle.

The American navy had its share of young sailors as well. Small boys served as deckhands or "powder monkeys." They carried ammunition to the gunners during battle. **How did young boys serve during the American Revolution?**

Analyzing Primary Sources

Drawing Conclusions According to the Declaration of Independence, why are governments established, and what rights do people have when their government becomes oppressive and unjust?

The war for independence. It was not clear who would win the Revolutionary War. Each side had strengths and weaknesses. The Americans were defending their own homes in well-known territory. The British, however, had a superior military force. Their army and navy were well trained. The British fleet was the strongest in the world. The British had to cross an ocean, however, and bring in most of their military supplies and equipment.

The war against the colonists was not popular in Great Britain. Some British even sympathized with the Americans. Britain had no allies to help it in the war. As a result, King George III had to hire some of his soldiers. Many of these mercenaries were Germans from Hesse, a state in the southwestern region of Germany. These mercenaries, known as Hessians, aroused a great deal of anger among the American colonists, who viewed their use by the British as especially brutal.

3 Captured by Americans, Nov. 12, 1775.

1 War begins, April 19, 1775.

Ft. Ticonderoga May 10–12, 1775

4 First great American victory, Oct. 17, 1777.

2 British defeat Americans, June 17, 1775.

5 Campaign of Sept. 1777 to June 1778. Washington spends terrible winter at Valley Forge.

6 George Rogers Clark defeats British along Ohio River, 1778–1779.

10 French blockade, Sept. 1781.

11 General Cornwallis surrenders to Washington, Oct. 19, 1781.

9 French forces join Washington's army, July 1781–Sept. 1781.

7 Controlled by British, Feb. 1781–Nov. 1781.

8 Occupied by British, May 12, 1780. Recaptured by American general Nathanael Greene, Dec. 14, 1782.

Vincennes Feb. 25, 1779

Guilford Courthouse March 15, 1781

Kings Mountain Oct. 7, 1780

Camden Aug. 16, 1780

Wilmington

Charleston

Montreal

Saratoga

Lexington and Concord

Bunker Hill

Boston

Germantown Oct. 4, 1777

Valley Forge

Brandywine Sept. 11, 1777

Philadelphia

New York

Yorktown

QUEBEC

ME (MA)

NH

MA

CT

RI

NY

PA

NJ

MD

DE

VA

NC

SC

GA

APPALACHIAN MOUNTAINS

SPANISH LOUISIANA

Lake Superior

Lake Michigan

Lake Huron

Lake Erie

St. Lawrence River

Ohio River

Mississippi River

Gulf of Mexico

ATLANTIC OCEAN

60° W

40° N

30° N

90° W

80° W

70° W

	American campaign
	British campaign
☼	American victory
☼	British victory
▲▲▲	Blockade

0   125   250 Miles
0   125   250 Kilometers
Albers Equal-Area Projection

Military Campaigns of the American Revolution, 1775–1783

Interpreting Maps The Battle of Saratoga in October 1777 marked the first great American victory of the Revolutionary War.

■ **Skills Assessment: Physical Systems** What geographic feature marked the western boundary of the middle colonies?

At first, a lack of unity among the colonies helped the British. The weakness of the American government was a serious problem. The colonies sent representatives to the Continental Congress voluntarily. Proposals governing the conduct of the war had to be passed unanimously. These proposals involved critical issues such as the purchase of weapons and equipment, food supplies for the army, the appointment of officers, and campaign plans. At a time when speedy decisions were necessary, a single opposing voice within the Congress could halt action. Under these conditions delegates might be forced to spend much time in negotiation with one another to reach agreement and unanimity. The Congress also had to borrow money and print paper currency to finance the war. This need created many problems, however, because the Congress's credit was poor and lenders were difficult to find. In many cases troops and suppliers grumbled that they were being paid with money that was basically worthless.

Under these circumstances it was difficult to build a strong army. At first the American forces were poorly trained volunteers who did not do well in battle against the British soldiers. Fortunately they had good leaders, such as **George Washington,** commander of the American forces. Some help came from other nations, such as France, that opposed British interests on an international scale. These countries helped to provide military officers, troops, weapons, ships, and money for the colonists. Meaningful support from European powers, however, was not seen by the Americans until relatively late in the war.

The Siege of Yorktown, 1781

Interpreting Maps At Yorktown, the British were trapped against the York River by American and French forces.

■ **Skills Assessment: 1. Human Systems** From what countries did the naval ships that engaged in battle at Yorktown sail? **2. Drawing Inferences** Why might the British forces have found it impossible to escape to their home country?

War and peace. Most of the fighting took place between 1776 and 1781. A major turning point came in October 1777, when the Americans defeated a British force under General John Burgoyne at Saratoga, New York. Now that the colonists seemed to have a chance of winning, the French jumped into the fray. Eager to weaken the British Empire, France agreed to an alliance with the United States. Spain and the Netherlands also joined the colonists' efforts. In 1781 the Americans and their French allies trapped and defeated the main British army at Yorktown, Virginia. The Americans had won the Revolutionary War.

Peace negotiations between the Americans and their former British rulers lasted two years. **Benjamin Franklin** was the chief American negotiator. In 1783 the British and the Americans and their allies signed the Treaty of Paris. The Americans had won their independence. They had also won a territory much larger than the original thirteen colonies.

✔ **READING CHECK: Contrasting** What advantages and disadvantages did each side have in the American Revolutionary War?

Holt Researcher

go.hrw.com
KEYWORD: Holt Researcher
FreeFind: Benjamin Franklin
Thomas Jefferson
After reading more about Benjamin Franklin and Thomas Jefferson on the Holt Researcher, write a script for a debate they might have had over the legalization of slavery in the United States.

Governing a New Nation

The new American government had a daunting task. It had to get the various states to work together. It also had to meet the goals of each group that had joined in winning the Revolutionary War.

The Articles of Confederation. The Second Continental Congress adopted the **Articles of Confederation** in 1777. This plan of government was ratified by the American states in 1781. The Articles set up a central government, with a one-house Congress in which each state had a single vote. Congress had the authority to declare war and make peace. It could also deal with other nations and settle disputes between the states. However, under the Articles of Confederation the central government was weak. The weakness of the new nation's government under the Articles was deliberate. Americans feared a strong central government that could quickly become repressive. They wanted to ensure that the individual rights and liberties for which they had fought were safeguarded. Thus Congress had no power to enforce its laws, which had to be approved by at least nine of the states.

Congress could not levy taxes or coin money. It could not regulate trade with foreign nations or among the states. Moreover, the Articles provided for no chief executive, and the only courts were state courts. Clearly, the Articles of Confederation were designed to place power in the hands of the individual states. State governments were seen as closer to the people and the popular will than the central government. Americans believed, too, that state governments were less likely to become repressive than the central government. Almost immediately, however, Americans began to realize that the Articles made it difficult to build an effective and stable government.

The Constitution. Many Americans were unhappy with the weakness of the new government. In May 1787 delegates from the states met again in Philadelphia to revise the Articles. The delegates soon realized, however, that a mere revision would not be enough. They decided instead to write a constitution.

After unanimously choosing George Washington as presiding officer, the delegates went to work. They wanted a strong central government. They also wanted some powers kept for the states. As a result, the Constitution they adopted provided for a **federal system of government.** The central, or federal, government was given many important powers. It could declare war, raise armies, and make treaties. It could coin money and regulate trade with foreign countries. The states and the people retained all other powers.

The federal government had three branches. The **executive branch,** headed by the president, enforced the laws. The **legislative branch,** consisting of the Congress, made the laws. The **judicial branch,** consisting of the federal courts, interpreted the laws. Each branch acted as a check on the power of the others.

The United States in 1783

Interpreting Maps The Treaty of Paris of 1783 gave the United States a large area of land beyond the boundaries of the original 13 colonies.

■ **Skills Assessment: Places and Regions** What nation controlled the region to the south of the United States? To the north? To the west?

Delegates to the Constitutional Convention signed the new document in September 1787. After the Constitution was ratified by the necessary nine states, it went into force in 1789.

Some Americans did not like the Constitution. They feared that it did not protect the rights of individuals. As a result, ten amendments were added in 1791. Together these amendments are known as the **Bill of Rights.** They guarantee freedom of religion, speech, the press, assembly, and petition. They also guarantee freedom from illegal search and seizure and the right to a jury trial.

Effects of American independence. The American Revolution was a major event in world history. It put into practice the ideas of John Locke and other political philosophers of the Enlightenment. The American example of democratic government was a landmark in world history and an important influence. People in other countries still suffered under absolute monarchs and privileged classes. The American Revolution gave them hope.

The American democracy of 1789 was hardly perfect. The states restricted voting to adult males. Most required that voters own property. Women could not vote. African Americans held in slavery had no political rights at all. Clearly many liberties still had to be won. Nonetheless, the American Revolution created a government with a new, democratic relationship among citizens. Not all Patriots agreed on the final form of government created by the Constitution. Still, their common beliefs and the economic and political needs of the new nation held them together. They had created a country that inspired loyalty.

✔ **READING CHECK: Summarizing** Describe the government created by the U.S. Constitution in 1789.

HISTORY MAKER

George Washington (1732–1799)

After the U.S. Constitution was ratified, George Washington was elected as the first president of the United States. Washington had led the American troops to victory in the Revolution. **Why might the American people have wanted Washington as their first president?**

SECTION 5 REVIEW

1. **Define** and explain the significance:
   federal system of government
   executive branch
   legislative branch
   judicial branch

2. **Identify** and explain the significance:
   Stamp Act
   King George III
   Lord North
   Patriots
   Loyalists
   Thomas Jefferson
   George Washington
   Benjamin Franklin
   Articles of Confederation
   Bill of Rights

Homework Practice Online
go.hrw.com
keyword: SH3 HP11

3. **Comparing and Contrasting** Copy the chart below. Use it to compare and contrast the Articles of Confederation and the Constitution.

FEATURE	ARTICLES OF CONFEDERATION	CONSTITUTION
Strong executive branch	no	yes
Power to tax		
One legislative vote each state		
Bill of Rights		
Federal courts		

4. **Finding the Main Idea**
   a. How did the ideas of the Enlightenment influence the leaders of the American Revolution?
   b. How did Americans respond to changes in British colonial policy after 1763?
   c. What were the central features of the government created by the U.S. Constitution?

5. **Writing and Critical Thinking**
   Identifying Cause and Effect Imagine you are one of the signers of the Declaration of Independence. After the Revolutionary War, write a summary of the effects of the Declaration.
   Consider:
   • the legal and political ideas in the document
   • how they differed from previous systems
   • how they affected the creation of the U.S. government

CHAPTER 11 Review

Creating a Time Line

Copy the time line below onto a sheet of paper. Complete the time line by filling in the events, individuals, and dates from the chapter that you think were significant. Pick three events and explain why you think they were significant.

| **1550** | **1700** | **1800** |

Writing a Summary

Using standard grammar, spelling, sentence structure, and punctuation, write an overview of the events in the chapter.

Identifying People and Ideas

Identify the following terms or individuals and explain their significance:

1. Oliver Cromwell
2. Glorious Revolution
3. John Locke
4. habeas corpus
5. Sir Francis Drake
6. Act of Union
7. sea dogs
8. Enlightenment
9. Jean-Jacques Rousseau
10. Stamp Act
11. George Washington
12. Articles of Confederation

Understanding Main Ideas

SECTION 1 (pp. 286–290)

Civil War and Revolution

1. What were the immediate causes of the English Revolution?
2. Who in England was likely to oppose the execution of Charles I?

SECTION 2 (pp. 291–297)

Constitutional Monarchy in England

3. What were the differences between the Tories and the Whigs?
4. What role did religion play in English politics after the Restoration?

SECTION 3 (pp. 298–301)

English Colonial Expansion

5. How did England become the dominant naval power in the 1500s?
6. What was the British policy of mercantilism?

SECTION 4 (pp. 302–304)

The Enlightenment

7. What ideas did Montesquieu, Voltaire, and Rousseau contribute to political philosophy?
8. How did Enlightenment thinking affect some people's views of church and state?

SECTION 5 (pp. 305–311)

The American Revolution

9. What issues led to the American Revolution?
10. What were the differences between the Articles of Confederation and the United States Constitution?

Reviewing Themes

1. **Citizenship** How did many political writers and philosophers of the 1700s see the relationship between people and their government?
2. **Constitutional Heritage** What were the sources of the political ideas that led to the American Revolution and the United States Constitution?
3. **Global Relations** Why did British policy anger many Americans in the years following 1763?

Thinking Critically

1. **Identifying Cause and Effect** What features of British policy probably led Americans to design the government created by the Constitution?
2. **Supporting a Point of View** Although the United States was created with the Declaration of Independence, how could it be argued that the country was really launched in 1789?

Writing About History

Comparing and Contrasting Compare and contrast the British and American governments. Use the chart below to organize your thoughts before writing.

Elements	British Government	American Government
Constitution		
Legislature		
Executive		
Protection of individual liberties		

Reading a Chart

Study the chart below. Then answer the questions that follow.

Great Britain's Constitutional Monarchy

1. Which general statement correctly describes a relationship shown on the chart?
   a. The members of the cabinet choose the prime minister.
   b. The monarch has direct power over the prime minister.
   c. Members of the House of Lords are direct representatives of the people.
   d. The prime minister is a member of the majority party in the House of Commons.

2. Which branch of government has the most power in Great Britain? Give specific reasons for your choice.

Summarizing

Read the paragraph below. Then answer the questions that follow.

During the Enlightenment, the ideas of philosophers were widely read. Montesquieu published *The Spirit of the Laws* in 1748, describing what he thought was a perfect government. From 1751 to 1772 the *Encyclopedia* was published in France. Edited by Diderot and d'Alembert, it examined government, war, taxes, human rights, and the church. In 1759, Voltaire published *Candide,* which satirized oppressive government and prejudice. *The Social Contract,* published in 1762 by Rousseau, argued that government should be created by and subject to the will of the people.

3. The statement that best summarizes this reading is:
   a. Voltaire was more popular than was Rousseau.
   b. The *Encyclopedia* collected all the knowledge that was available during the 1700s.
   c. Rousseau and Montesquieu held opposing ideas regarding the best form of government.
   d. Some Enlightenment writers were concerned with issues of government and society.

4. What effect did the ideas of these thinkers have on the people of their time? Give specific examples.

Alternative Assessment

Building Your Portfolio

Link to TODAY

Constitutional Heritage

The ideas about democratic-republican government that inspired the Enlightenment and the revolutions in England and its colonies had many of their roots in ancient Greece and Rome. Using your textbook and other sources, create a flowchart that traces the process by which democratic-republican government evolved from its beginnings in classical Greece and Rome.

🔌 internet connect

Internet Activity: go.hrw.com
KEYWORD: SH3 WH11

Choose a topic on Enlightenment and Revolution in England and America to:
- understand how the ideas of the Enlightenment have influenced institutions and societies.
- create a recruitment poster for the New Model Army.
- identify political ideas in John Locke's *Two Treatises of Government* and its influence on the Declaration of Independence.

1789–1815

The French Revolution and Napoléon

Rosetta Stone

c. 1790
Science and Technology
Antoine-Laurent Lavoisier publishes *Table of Thirty-One Chemical Elements.*

1792
Global Events
Denmark is the first nation to abolish slavery.

1795–1799
Politics
The Directory rules France.

1796
Science and Technology
An English physician introduces a small pox vaccine.

1785   **1790**   **1795**   **1800**

1789
Global Events
The first U.S. Congress meets in New York.

1794
Global Events
France abolishes slavery in French colonies.

1794
Science and Technology
France establishes the world's first telegraph communications line.

1793
The Arts
The Louvre in Paris becomes France's national art gallery.

1793
Politics
The French government bans Roman Catholicism.

1799
Global Events
French soldiers in Egypt find the Rosetta Stone.

1799
Science and Technology
A perfectly preserved mammoth is found in Siberia.

1799
Science and Technology
The first gas lighting fixture is patented by French chemist Philippe Lebon.

Model of guillotine

Model of the French inventor Claude Chappe's overhead telegraph

Build on What You Know

*I*nspired by Enlightenment ideas as well as trade concerns, the American Revolution forever changed the course of history for the colonies in North America. However, the revolution's influence did not end there. Across the Atlantic in France, people were growing more and more dissatisfied with the monarchy and with how their society was structured. Drawing from the Enlightenment, people continued to call for changes to combat inequalities and injustice. In this chapter, you will learn how the success of the American Revolution inspired similar efforts in France, and how a powerful new empire rose and fell there.

Portrait of Napoléon as emperor of France

1804
Politics
The French uncover a plot to assassinate Napoléon in Paris.

1805
The Arts
French author François-Auguste-René de Chateaubriand publishes the romantic novel *René*.

1810
Science and Technology
Nicolas-François Appert develops techniques for canning foods.

1815
Science and Technology
French scientist Jean-Baptiste de Monet de Lamarck publishes *Natural History of Animals*.

c. 1800
Business and Finance
England begins to export iron.

1806
The Arts
Construction begins on the Arc de Triomphe in France.

1810
Business and Finance
The French government gives itself a monopoly on the sale of tobacco.

1805	**1810**	**1815**

1808
Daily Life
Pigtails disappear as a fashion for men's hair in Europe.

1813
Daily Life
The waltz is popular in European ballrooms.

1807
Politics
England prohibits the slave trade.

1812
Politics
Napoléon enters Russia with the Grand Army.

Arc de Triomphe in Paris

Pearl and diamond tiara of Empress Joséphine

What's Your Opinion?

Themes Journal *Do you* **agree** *or* **disagree** *with the following statements? Support your point of view in your journal.*

Government A government that represents the people can be run by only a few people.

Constitutional Heritage Once it has been written, the constitution of a nation should never be changed.

Citizenship Freedom of speech can be granted only by a government.

READ TO DISCOVER

❶ How was the Old Regime structured?

❷ Why did discontent begin to grow in the mid-1700s?

❸ Why did Louis XVI want to call the Estates General?

❹ How did the meeting of the Estates General push France toward revolution?

DEFINE

bourgeoisie

IDENTIFY

Louis XV
Louis XVI
Marie-Antoinette

WHY IT MATTERS TODAY

The French government started to go through many changes in the 1700s. Use CNN News.com or other **current event** sources to investigate how the French people are represented in government today. Record your findings in your journal.

CNN student News.com

The Roots of Revolution

The Main Idea
The French Revolution was a struggle between a powerful monarch and the people.

The Story Continues *As Americans gained independence from Great Britain, the people of France were also struggling against oppression. As Thomas Jefferson observed after visiting France in the 1780s, "Out of a population of twenty millions of people . . . there are nineteen millions more wretched [poor], more accursed in every circumstance of human existence, than the most conspicuously wretched individual of the whole United States."*

The Old Regime

For more than 100 years, France had been the largest and most powerful nation in Europe, ruled by a monarch who claimed absolute power. When the French Revolution began in 1789, however, the king lost all power within months. The great changes brought by the Revolution made the French feel that they were living in a whole new society. People began to refer to the time before 1789 as the Old Regime. Under the Old Regime, society had been divided into three estates, or classes.

The privileged estates. The First Estate was made up of the clergy of the Roman Catholic Church, less than 1 percent of the French population. The church had been powerful and wealthy ever since the Middle Ages. By the late 1700s the church owned about 15 percent of all the land in France, and so collected vast amounts of money from rents, taxes, and fees. Most of this wealth was held by the higher clergy— bishops, archbishops, and abbots—who did not have to pay taxes themselves. Many of these higher church officials became materialistic and neglected their spiritual duties. The lower clergy, such as parish priests, performed most of the church's work and received little pay.

The nobility, less than 2 percent of the population, made up the Second Estate. These nobles enjoyed many privileges left over from feudal times. They paid few if any taxes, collected dues from peasants, and held the highest positions in the army and government. Eldest sons had the right to inherit titles and lands. Although some nobles cared about the welfare of France, as a group they were irresponsible.

This drawing shows one artist's representation of French society during the Old Regime—the clergy, nobles, peasants, and bourgeoisie (from left to right).

The Third Estate. The rest of the people of France, about 97 percent, belonged to the Third Estate. At the top of the Third Estate were the **bourgeoisie** (boorzh·wah·ZEE), or urban middle class. The bourgeoisie included merchants, manufacturers, and professional people such as doctors and lawyers. Many were educated and wealthy.

Below the bourgeoisie in the Third Estate came three groups who were usually very poor: city workers, artisans, and rural peasants. Peasants made up the largest group. In the 1700s most peasants still owed feudal dues and labor services. They paid heavy taxes as well as rent for the land they worked. They were also forced to pay a tithe—that is, one tenth of their income—to the church. Although they worked long and hard, peasants had no voice in making or changing laws. They remained under the absolute control of their landlords and king.

✔ **READING CHECK: Finding the Main Idea** How was French society organized in the Old Regime?

Growing Discontent

In the mid-1700s discontent in France began to grow. Several factors explain this discontent. The first resulted from the growth of the French population. Families had more children to support, and they needed more food and money. Changing economic conditions in France also spurred discontent. The nobles, clergy, and some of the bourgoisie who owned land pressed the peasants for higher rents. In the cities, laborers found food prices rising higher and higher, but wages were not going up as quickly. The artisans and peasants resented the rich, who collected their rents, lived in big houses, and had plenty to eat. The poor blamed the king for allowing prices to get so high. They hated having to pay taxes when the nobles and clergy did not. Sometimes the poor took to the streets and rioted against these higher prices and taxes. The worsening economic conditions also reinforced the determination of the first two estates to protect their most important privilege: freedom from taxation.

The bourgeoisie prospered during the 1700s, and now they wanted political power to go with their economic strength. Merchants and manufacturers resented paying taxes when nobles and clergy did not. They wanted to be able to conduct business without interference from the government. The bourgeoisie also wanted their sons to have important positions in the church, army, and government—positions that only nobles were allowed to hold.

Although the peasants, workers, and bourgeoisie had different complaints, they shared the same ideas and used the same words to express them. They spoke of "liberty" and "equality" as their natural rights. These ideas may have meant different things to different people, but they were enough to unify France's various groups in a challenge to the king's power.

✔ **READING CHECK: Summarizing** Why did discontent grow in France during the mid-1700s?

Peasants This picture is meant to show an idealized view of peasant life in France. *What things in the picture might be different if it were a true representation of peasant life?*

This political cartoon from about 1790 illustrates the growing conflict between "The Powers"—the nobles, clergy, and bourgeoisie— and the National Assembly.

**Marie-Antoinette
(1755–1793)**

As the wife and queen of Louis XVI, Marie-Antoinette became the most hated woman in France. Her wild spending and refusal to support reforms made her many enemies. During the French Revolution, she spent several months in prison. Finally in October 1793 she was put to death at the guillotine. **Why did the French people dislike Marie-Antoinette?**

The Financial Crisis

The actions of French monarchs stoked the fires of public anger. The 59-year reign of **Louis XV** was one of the longest in France's history. While the country enjoyed nearly 20 years of peace under Louis XV, debts inherited from Louis XIV continued to grow, creating an economic crisis. Louis XV's expensive habits also turned the people against him. When taxes did not provide enough money to meet expenses, Louis XV borrowed more and more from bankers. Warned that his actions were harming France, he is said to have replied, "It will survive for my time. After me, the deluge."

In 1774 **Louis XVI** succeeded Louis XV as king. To strengthen an alliance with Austria, Louis XVI married **Marie-Antoinette,** the daughter of the Austrian empress Maria Theresa. The French people soon came to resent Marie-Antoinette's Austrian connection and her involvement in French politics.

Under Louis XVI France's debts continued to grow, due in large part to the country's assistance to the United States during the American Revolution. To raise money, Louis tried to tax the first two estates. Whenever new taxes were proposed, however, the nobles refused to cooperate and sometimes led riots. By 1787 bankers resisted lending the government more money. France faced financial disaster. In August of 1788 Louis called for a meeting of the Estates General to be held at Versailles. He hoped that by calling together the representatives of all three estates he could get approval for new taxes.

✔ **READING CHECK: Identifying Cause and Effect** What events led to the meeting of the Estates General?

The Meeting of the Estates General

The French people hoped their problems would finally be addressed at the planned meeting of the Estates General. Emmanuel-Joseph Sieyès (syay·YES), a clergyman who became a revolutionary, expressed the complaints of the Third Estate:

Finding the Main Idea What does Sieyès mean when he says nothing will go well without the Third Estate?

History Makers Speak

"What then is the Third Estate? All. But an 'all' that is fettered [chained] and oppressed. What would it be without the privileged order? It would be all; but free and flourishing. Nothing will go well without the Third Estate; everything would go considerably better without the two others."

Joseph Sieyès, from *What Is the Third Estate?*, quoted in *Sources of the Western Tradition*, edited by Marvin Perry, Joseph R. Peden, and Theodore H. Von Laue

This building in Paris, the Conciergerie, was used as a prison and housed Marie-Antoinette during the French Revolution.

In the past the three estates had always met separately, and each estate had cast one vote. Thus the First and Second Estates could always get together and outvote the Third Estate. The Third Estate had as many representatives as the other two estates combined. Therefore, to have a real voice in government, the Third Estate wanted representatives to vote as individuals.

The Estates General met on May 5, 1789. Louis XVI then instructed the delegates to follow the old custom of meeting separately and voting as one body. The representatives of the Third Estate refused to obey. They argued that the Estates General represented the French people, not the three classes. When Louis failed to respond, the Third Estate declared itself to be the National Assembly and invited the other two estates to work with it. This act marked the real beginning of the French Revolution. The representatives declared that they would not stop meeting until they had written a constitution for France and seen it adopted. Finally Louis XVI allowed the estates to meet together.

✔ **READING CHECK: Analyzing Information** Why did the Third Estate refuse to follow the tradition of each estate having one vote?

When the Third Estate was locked out of the Estates General meeting, its representatives gathered nearby in an indoor tennis court. The oath they took there to continue meeting until a constitution was written became known as the Tennis Court Oath.

SECTION 1 REVIEW

1. **Define** and explain the significance:
   bourgeoisie

2. **Identify** and explain the significance:
   Louis XV
   Louis XVI
   Marie-Antoinette

3. **Summarizing** Copy the diagram and use it to show whom the three estates represented and how power was distributed.

Most Power

Least Power

4. **Finding the Main Idea**
   a. How did France's social structure lead to discontent and financial crisis?
   b. Why did Louis XVI take the unusual step of calling all three estates together?

5. **Writing and Critical Thinking**
   Drawing Inferences Imagine you are a representative from the Third Estate at the Estates General meeting. Write a letter to a friend explaining what the Third Estate representatives want.
   Consider:
   • how peasants, noble, and clergy lived
   • how the Third Estate differed from the other two estates

Homework Practice Online
keyword: SH3 HP12

The French Revolution

READ TO DISCOVER

❶ Why and how did the French Revolution spread?

❷ How did a constitution change French government?

❸ Why did the monarchy and the Legislative Assembly come to an end?

DEFINE

émigrés
departments
conservatives
radicals
moderates

IDENTIFY

Olympe de Gouges

The Main Idea
The French Revolution spread quickly and violently, and it changed the government dramatically.

The Story Continues *Early in the morning of July 15, 1789, King Louis XVI was awakened by an official. The king was told that the Bastille prison had fallen to rioters. "Is this a rebellion?" the king is said to have asked. "No Sire," replied the official. "It is a revolution."*

The Spread of the Revolution

King Louis XVI allowed the Estates General to meet together, but during the meeting he moved troops into Paris and Versailles. Fearing that Louis was going to drive out the National Assembly by force, the people of Paris took action. On July 14, 1789, they captured the Bastille prison, a symbol of royal oppression. The crowd looted the Bastille for weapons, then destroyed it.

This outbreak of violence led to the formation of a new government in Paris. General Lafayette—the French hero who had fought in the American Revolution—formed a people's army called the National Guard. A new flag of red, white, and blue stripes replaced the old flag of France.

Events in Paris were repeated all over France as the "Great Fear" swept across the land. The peasants believed that the nobles were planning to crush them and stop the revolution. They also became angry as food shortages worsened. As rumors and fear spread, the peasants attacked local manor houses and monasteries. They destroyed possessions and burned documents recording rents, feudal dues, and other obligations.

✔ **READING CHECK: Identifying Cause and Effect** How did the events of July 14, 1789, change France?

WHY IT MATTERS TODAY

Monarchs still exist in Europe today. Use CNNStudentNews.com or other **current event** sources to investigate which European countries still have monarchs and what powers they have. Record your findings in your journal.

CNN Student News.com

The destruction of the Bastille prison, a symbol of royal oppression, marked the spread of revolutionary fervor.

INTERPRETING THE VISUAL RECORD

Women march This engraving shows a mob of angry Parisian women marching to Versailles on October 5, 1789. They demanded relief from Louis XVI for the nationwide food shortage. *What items are the women carrying and why?*

The End of The Old Regime

Many members of the National Assembly believed that they could stop the violence through reforms. The assembly outlawed the tithe, canceled all feudal dues and services owed by peasants, and removed the privileges that the First and Second estates had previously enjoyed. By August 4, 1789, the National Assembly had formally done away with feudalism in France.

The Declaration of the Rights of Man. Following these reforms, the assembly adopted the Declaration of the Rights of Man and of the Citizen. This document dealt with basic human rights and political powers.

The Declaration of the Rights of Man and of the Citizen stated that men are born equal and remain equal before the law. It granted freedom of speech, of the press, and of religion. It guaranteed the right to take part in government, declaring that all men had an equal right to hold public office. The document also guaranteed the right to a fair trial. The declaration embodied the principles that became the slogan of the French Revolution: "liberty, equality, fraternity."

These rights, however, did not apply to women. A group of women led by Parisian playwright **Olympe de Gouges** wrote their own document, the Declaration of the Rights of Women and Citizenesses. The National Assembly rejected it. The leaders of the Revolution believed in equality for men, but did not believe that women were the equals of men.

Émigrés and royalists. The Old Regime did not die easily. Many nobles fled to Great Britain, Switzerland, and Germany. There they plotted constantly to overthrow the Revolution. These **émigrés**—French for "emigrants"—became a source of trouble for France in years to come.

Some nobles remained at Versailles with the king. They sided with Louis XVI in favor of a return to the Old Regime. They held a banquet at which they praised the king and queen and insulted the National Assembly. When the people learned of this banquet, a crowd led by angry women stormed the palace and forced Louis XVI, Marie Antoinette, and their family to return to Paris with them.

Reforms in government. Between 1789 and 1791 the National Assembly passed more laws aimed at correcting past abuses and setting up a new government. First, it reformed France's administrative structure by dividing the country into 83 equal districts, called **departments.** It called for the election of all local officials. In 1789 the

Holt Researcher

go.hrw.com

KEYWORD: Holt Researcher

FreeFind: Olympe de Gouges

After reading more about Olympe de Gouges on the Holt Researcher, write a letter she might have written to the National Assembly urging support for the Declaration of the Rights of Women and Citizenesses.

Two Declarations of Freedom

In the last decades of the 1700s, revolutions shook both sides of the Atlantic. Two documents expressed the political changes brought on by these revolutions.

Both documents were influenced by the English philosopher John Locke. Almost a hundred years earlier, Locke had argued that men are "by nature, all free, equal, and independent."

In America, the Declaration of Independence was written when the colonies were rebelling against British rule. The document explained the colonies' actions to the outside world. The French document, the Declaration of the Rights of Man and of the Citizen, reminded people of the "sacred rights of man."

Understanding Civics

How were the American and French declarations both similar and different?

National Assembly also seized lands owned by the Catholic Church. This property was sold to the public; some of it was bought by the peasants who had formerly rented it. The proceeds were used for paying down the national debt.

The leaders of the Revolution saw the Catholic Church as a part of the Old Regime, and so they sought to reform it as well. In 1790 the National Assembly issued the Civil Constitution of the Clergy. This law stated that people in parishes and dioceses would elect their own clergy. In return for seizing church lands, the government would pay the salaries of priests and bishops. The pope, however, forbade the clergy to accept this arrangement, and most obeyed him. Because the Civil Constitution of the Clergy placed the church under the control of the French government, many Catholics came to oppose the Revolution.

✔ **READING CHECK: Summarizing** How did the National Assembly try to put the Revolution's ideas into practice?

The Constitution of 1791

In 1791 the National Assembly finished writing a constitution for France. This constitution limited the authority of the king and divided the government into three branches—executive, legislative, and judicial.

The constitution greatly limited the powers of the king. He could no longer make or block laws on his own. Tax-paying male voters elected members to a new legislative body called the Legislative Assembly. The National Assembly was dissolved, and no one who had been a member could run for election to the Legislative Assembly. However, despite these reforms, wealthy men still held most of the political power under France's new system.

Louis XVI reluctantly agreed to his new limited powers. At the same time, he secretly plotted with émigrés to overthrow the new government and restore the Old Regime. Some of Louis's advisers urged him to flee and seek help from foreign governments friendly to the monarchy. In 1791 Louis and his family did try to escape. Even though he wore a disguise, Louis was recognized. He and his family were arrested and sent back to Paris.

People had hoped that under the new constitutional monarchy, France could recover without further disturbances. The king's attempted escape, however, marked a turning point. People no longer trusted Louis, and they publicly discussed creating a republic.

✔ **READING CHECK: Analyzing Information** What kind of government did the Constitution of 1791 provide?

This illustration, possibly from an early printing of the Declaration of the Rights of Man and of the Citizen, dramatically portrays a symbol of one of the Declaration's key ideals—equality.

The Legislative Assembly and War

The new government outlined in the Constitution of 1791 went into effect in October, but lasted less than a year. The revolutionaries had not created a sound government. They had set up a weak executive branch and a powerful but inexperienced legislature elected by only a minority of the population. Moreover, not all the French people supported the Revolution. Catholic priests and nobles opposed the new order. There was also discontent among the poorest members of French society, who had been hurt by a rise in the cost of living. These groups, along with the continuing activities of émigrés, added to the new government's troubles.

The Legislative Assembly became divided into three groups with differing attitudes. One of these groups, the **conservatives,** felt the revolution had gone far enough. Their ideal government was one in which the king had limited authority. The group known as **radicals** wanted more drastic changes than those proposed by the National Assembly. They wanted to get rid of the king, set up a republic, and make broad reforms. The third group, the **moderates,** had no extreme views. They sided with either conservatives or radicals depending on the issue at hand. In the hall where the Legislative Assembly met, each group sat in its own section. The conservatives sat on the right, the moderates in the center, and the radicals on the left. Today we still use the terms *right* to describe a conservative opinion, *center* for a moderate opinion, and *left* for a liberal opinion.

Paris, 1789

Interpreting Maps Louis XVI and his family were imprisoned in the Temple.

■ **Skills Assessment: Locate** In which direction is the Temple from the Tuileries?

These three groups within the Legislative Assembly frequently deadlocked on domestic issues. They united, however, when they were faced with the threat of attack from other European powers that sought to restore the French monarchy. Marie-Antoinette's brother was Emperor Leopold II of Austria, and together with King Frederick William II of Prussia he issued the Declaration of Pillnitz. This declaration invited other European rulers to support the return of royal rule in France.

The threat of foreign invasion brought the Legislative Assembly to attention. Many groups within France were in favor of going to war. Each group in the assembly hoped that a successful foreign war would increase its own influence. Louis XVI favored war because he hoped that foreign armies would defeat the French army and restore him to power. Some people may have worried that war would lead to dictatorship. In April 1792, with only a few members opposing, the Legislative Assembly voted to declare war on Austria. The Assembly had hoped to keep Prussia and the other German states out of the war, but it failed in that objective. Other European monarchies, including Prussia and Sardinia, came to Austria's support. Soon afterward an army of Austrian and Prussian troops invaded France.

✔ **READING CHECK: Making Generalizations** In what ways was the first government after the revolution a weak one?

This poster summarizes the French Revolution's message of liberty, equality, and fraternity—or death.

The End of the Monarchy

The French did not do well in the initial fighting with the Austrian and Prussian armies. French citizens grew alarmed and searched for someone to blame for the defeats. As one observer noted,

Primary Source

"**Everywhere you hear the cry that the king is betraying us, the generals are betraying us, that nobody is to be trusted; . . . that Paris will be taken in six weeks by the Austrians . . . we are on a volcano ready to spout flames.**"

Quoted in William Doyle, *The Oxford History of the French Revolution*

Failures in war, along with economic shortages at home, led to mass uprisings in Paris. A group of radicals seized control of the Commune, Paris's city government.

The Prussians vowed to destroy Paris and punish the revolutionaries if any harm came to the royal family. Upon hearing this the Commune demanded that the Legislative Assembly abolish the monarchy. The Commune rightly accused Louis XVI of plotting with foreign powers to overthrow the Constitution of 1791. Revolutionary troops arrived from the city of Marseilles to defend Paris against the invading armies. Their marching song, "La Marseillaise," became France's national anthem.

Finally on August 10, 1792, the Legislative Assembly suspended the office of king. Armed Parisians marched on the Tuileries Palace, the Paris home of the royal family. They killed many of the king's guards and imprisoned Louis and his family in the Temple. The Commune now ruled Paris, and the Legislative Assembly tried to govern France.

With the monarchy suspended, France needed a new constitution. The Legislative Assembly voted itself out of existence and set a date for election of delegates to a National Convention. These delegates would draw up a new constitution. Thus, in the midst of a foreign war and political turmoil, France faced a complete change of government.

✔ **READING CHECK: Drawing Inferences** Why did the Legislative Assembly exist for so short a period of time?

SECTION 2 REVIEW

1. **Define** and explain the significance:
   émigrés
   departments
   conservatives
   moderates
   radicals

2. **Identify** and explain the significance:
   Olympe de Gouges

3. **Analyzing Information** Copy the diagram and use it to show the factions in the Legislative Assembly.

Left	Center	Right

4. **Finding the Main Idea**
   a. What did the assemblies accomplish?
   b. Why is the year 1789 significant in French history?

5. **Writing and Critical Thinking**
   Supporting a Point of View The French Revolution was based on the ideas of liberty, equality, and fraternity. Write a political pamphlet encouraging fellow Parisians to support the Commune and abolish the monarchy.
   Consider:
   • the actions of Louis XVI
   • the constitutional monarchy established by the Constitution of 1791

Homework Practice Online
keyword: SH3 HP12

The French Republic

READ TO DISCOVER

❶ How did the National Convention rule France?

❷ How did the Reign of Terror affect France?

❸ What was the Directory and how did it rule?

❹ Why was Napoléon able to come to power?

DEFINE

universal manhood suffrage
conscription
counterrevolutionary
coup d'état

IDENTIFY

Georges-Jacques Danton
Maximilien Robespierre
Jean-Paul Marat
Reign of Terror
Napoléon Bonaparte
Joséphine de Beauharnais

WHY IT MATTERS TODAY

Napoléon seized control of power with a coup d'état. Use CNN Student News.com or other **current event** sources to investigate whether coups d'état are happening or have recently happened in other countries. Record your findings in your journal.

CNN Student News.com

The Main Idea
Radical revolutionaries led France through terror and war, while Napoléon rose to power.

The Story Continues *"During the greater part of the day, the guillotine had been kept busy at its ghastly work; all that France had boasted of in the past centuries of ancient names and blue blood had paid toll to her desire for liberty and fraternity." These lines from the novel* The Scarlet Pimpernel *capture the terror of those days when the French Revolution turned bloody.*

The National Convention

The National Convention held its first meeting in September 1792. Delegates were elected to this convention by **universal manhood suffrage.** This meant every adult male could vote, whether he owned property or not.

As in the Legislative Assembly, delegates in the National Convention were divided into three main groups. This time, however, fewer supported the king. The Girondins, republicans named for the department of the Gironde in southwestern France, feared the domination of France by Paris. The second group was the Jacobins, republicans who favored domination by Paris. **Georges-Jacques Danton** and **Maximilien Robespierre** were two of the most powerful Jacobins. Some of the Jacobins were extreme radicals and wanted reforms that would benefit all classes of society. **Jean-Paul Marat,** a doctor from Paris, led these radicals. The third group in the National Convention consisted of delegates who had no definite views. Later, most of these delegates came to favor the Jacobins.

The National Convention governed France for three years. Its first act was to declare the end of the monarchy and the beginning of a republic. The delegates also had to write a new constitution while trying to keep order at home and fight foreign invaders.

The National Convention brought Louis XVI to trial, charging him with plotting against the security of the nation. It found him guilty and sentenced him to death. On January 21, 1793, Louis XVI was beheaded by the guillotine. The rest of Europe found this execution of a monarch shocking. Even in the United States, people were disturbed by the National Convention's radical methods.

✔ **READING CHECK: Comparing and Contrasting** In what ways was the National Convention similar to and different from the Legislative Assembly?

At the time of the French Revolution, the guillotine was a new device that republicans believed would allow a quick and humane execution.

Exporting the Revolution

Even before Louis XVI's execution, the National Convention had some good news. The French army had defeated the Austrian and Prussian forces, stopping the foreign invasion. The French built on these victories by invading the Austrian Netherlands.

The monarchs of Europe now feared that the French would try to overthrow royalty outside France. Great Britain, the Netherlands, Spain, and the kingdom of Sardinia joined Austria and Prussia in an alliance against France. Together they drove the French out of the Austrian Netherlands and invaded France again.

Committee of Public Safety. In 1793 the National Convention took steps to meet the threat of invaders. It set up the Committee of Public Safety to direct the army in crushing foreign invaders. The National Convention also established a special court, the Revolutionary Tribunal, to try "enemies of the Revolution."

To prepare itself against foreign invasion, the Committee of Public Safety adopted **conscription**—the draft. All unmarried, able-bodied men between 18 and 25 were subject to military service. As a force of patriotic young men, the French army took on a new, nationalistic spirit. In the new army, men from any class who proved their ability could become officers. During the 1800s conscription became common in Europe.

Opposition. Some French people rose up against the revolutionary government. In western France the "Royal and Catholic" army fought against the revolutionary army. We call their activities **counterrevolutionary,** meaning their aim was counter to, or against, the Revolution. Counterrevolutionary groups supported the Old Regime.

Jacobins, including Danton and Robespierre, controlled the National Convention. They arrested many Girondin delegates who opposed their policies. Meanwhile Charlotte Corday, a young woman influenced by Girondin ideas, assassinated Marat.

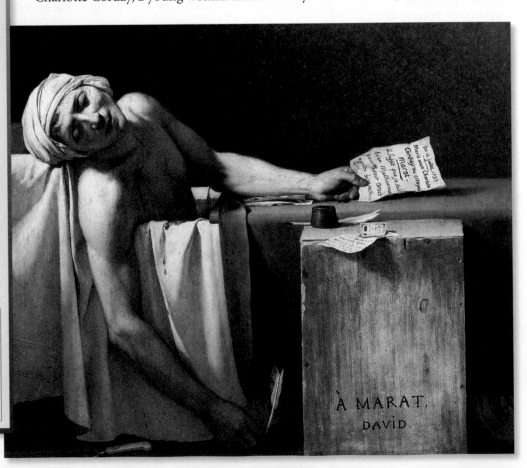

CONNECTING TO Art

Painting:
The Death of Marat
French art reflected changes caused by the French Revolution. Artists began to use different subjects, moods, and techniques.

This painting by Jacques-Louis David demonstrates this new style. Traditionally an assassination would not have been considered a suitable subject for a painting. However, the artist succeeded in painting a moving portrayal of Marat's death. In Marat's hand is a letter from his assassin, Charlotte Corday. On the floor lies the knife that she plunged into his chest.

Understanding the Arts

How do the details such as the knife and letter add to the drama of Jacques-Louis David's painting?

She stabbed him to death as he was bathing. The Revolutionary Tribunal sent her to the guillotine for her crime.

✔ **READING CHECK: Analyzing Information** What happened when the new French government tried to invade other countries?

The Reign of Terror

The National Convention worked to suppress all opposition and revolts within France. The **Reign of Terror,** as it became known, lasted from September 1793 to July 1794. As Robespierre wrote, "It is necessary to annihilate [completely destroy] both the internal and external enemies of the republic or perish with its fall." The Law of Suspects issued in 1793 defined these suspected enemies:

❝Those who have shown themselves the enemies of liberty, those who cannot justify their means of existence and the performance of their civic duties, . . . those of the former nobles who have not constantly manifested their attachment to the revolution, and those who have emigrated during the interval between July 1, 1789, to April 8, 1792.❞

quoted in *The Law of Suspects,* 1793

As leader of the Committee of Public Safety, Robespierre helped to lead the Reign of Terror.

The Revolutionary Tribunal punished the enemies of the Republic and occasionally executed people who were simply suspected of counterrevolution. Marie-Antoinette became an early victim of the Reign of Terror. However, the Jacobins directed the Reign of Terror not only against the nobility, but also against anyone suspected of disloyalty. Robespierre and Danton began by sending their Girondin opponents to the guillotine, along with Olympe de Gouges. In fact, the revolutionaries executed twice as many bourgeoisie as nobles, and more than twice as many peasants and workers as bourgeoisie.

By the spring of 1794, the French army had gained the advantage in the war against the foreign powers. With the republic thus out of danger, Danton declared that he thought the Reign of Terror had met its goal and should be relaxed. In contrast Robespierre became even more fanatical and accused Danton of disloyalty to the Revolution. He had Danton and his followers put to death. This caused even Robespierre's colleagues to fear for their own safety.

For several months Robespierre continued the brutal suppression. He believed that only he could protect the Revolution from its enemies. Finally a few members of the National Convention called a halt. In July 1794 they arrested Robespierre and guillotined him.

With Robespierre's death, the Reign of Terror came to an end. People throughout Paris felt a sense of relief. The Jacobins lost power, and in fact a reaction began against their ideas. The wealthy middle class took control of the National Convention. Fashions changed as people rebelled against the strict Jacobin values. People went back to wearing luxurious dresses and hats. However, prices again rose sharply, causing hardship for the poor. Riots were put down by the army but feelings of unrest persisted. By 1794 many French people even favored a return to monarchy.

✔ **READING CHECK: Summarizing** What did the supporters of the Reign of Terror hope to accomplish?

Holt Researcher

go.hrw.com
KEYWORD: Holt Researcher
FreeFind:
   Maximilien Robespierre
After reading more about Maximilien Robespierre on the Holt Researcher, create a political tract explaining why he supported the Reign of Terror.

Work of the National Convention

Despite the dangers and difficulties of the time, the National Convention met from 1792 to 1795 and made many democratic reforms. These changes affected every level of French society. The Convention created a body called the Committee of Public Safety. Controlled by Jacobins, this committee tried to establish what it called a "Republic of Virtue." By this it meant a democratic republic in which people would act according to the principles of good citizenship. To accomplish this the Committee opened new schools and supported the idea of universal elementary education. To aid the economy the Committee established wage and price controls intended to stop inflation. Even during the Reign of Terror, the Committee worked to address human rights concerns. It abolished slavery in France's colonies and encouraged religious toleration.

In addition, the National Convention replaced the monarchy's confusing system of weights and measures with the metric system. Based on the number ten, this system reflected the interest in rational thinking of the era. Today most parts of the world use the metric system. The Convention also created a new calendar, naming September 22, 1792—the date of the republic's creation—as the first day of the First Year of Liberty. This calendar used colorful names that reflected the seasons. For example, *Thermidor* indicated the warm month (roughly July) and *Ventôse* was the windy month (roughly March). This calendar also increased the number of days in a week, or "decade", from seven to ten. The calendar did not survive, but it does reflect the French people's hope that their republic would mark the dawn of a new era.

Meanwhile the French army went on to victory. By 1795 the French had driven invaders from French soil and conquered territory as far as the Rhine River in Germany. Even more important, the coalition of European countries against France began to break up. A new militaristic spirit swept the country. The National Convention used the army to quell opposition at home. It crushed an uprising in Paris in October 1795. This demonstrated that the new government would not accept any opposition.

✔ **READING CHECK: Summarizing** What were some of the changes the National Convention put into effect?

The French adopted a new calendar in 1793. The year was broken into twelve months of three "decades" (instead of weeks) each. A decade equaled ten days. Five or six extra days were added at the end of each year.

INTERPRETING THE VISUAL RECORD

The people's army The National Convention created a revolutionary army to defend France. This painting shows French citizens enlisting in the new army. *How does the artist show that the recruits are enthusiastic about joining the army?*

The Directory

In 1795 the National Convention completed another constitution. The government established by the new constitution took office in November of that year. It included a two-house legislature. The 500-member lower house proposed laws, while the smaller but more powerful 250-member upper house accepted or rejected the proposed legislation. The upper house also had the power to select the new government's executive branch, which consisted of five individuals known as directors. This gave the new government its name—the Directory. The nation's new constitution also eliminated universal manhood suffrage. Only male property owners could vote. In effect, then, the wealthy once again controlled France's government, as they had under the National Assembly.

The Directory governed France for four years. However, neither radicals nor conservatives were pleased with it. The economy improved somewhat but peasants, workers, and poor people still suffered. The five directors quarreled among themselves and were weak, corrupt rulers. When crowds protested, the directors used the army to stop the unrest.

The Directory was soon as unpopular as the Old Regime had been. Like the Old Regime, it had financial difficulties. Its failure paved the way for a military dictatorship in France.

✔ **READING CHECK: Comparing** How was the National Convention similar to the previous National Assembly?

Napoléon Bonaparte

Under the Directory, ongoing wars with Great Britain, Austria, and Sardinia offered opportunities for able military leaders. Between 1795 and 1799 a young general named **Napoléon Bonaparte** came to the public's attention. Born in 1769 on the French island of Corsica, Napoléon attended military school in France. Already a general at age 26, Napoléon had stopped an uprising in Paris that would have prevented the creation of the Directory.

Napoléon was only five feet two inches tall but had an extremely strong personality. He was ambitious and energetic. He had great organizational skills and was a good manager of both political and military affairs. One of his smartest personal moves was marrying **Joséphine de Beauharnais,** a leader of French society, in 1796. Two days after the marriage, Napoléon won command of the French army that was fighting the Austrians in Italy.

Rise of Napoléon. Napoléon Bonaparte is considered one of the greatest generals of all time. Because of the dominant role that he played starting in 1796, the wars that France fought from then until 1815 are called the Napoléonic Wars. Napoléon's genius lay in his ability to move troops rapidly to the most critical points on the battlefield. His opponents' tactics were older and slower.

Napoléon proved his ability in Italy. The French army there was weak and poorly equipped. Napoléon improved conditions for the troops, gaining their support and boosting morale. With these newly inspired soldiers, Napoléon forced the Sardinians to make peace. He then went on to defeat the Austrians four times. In 1797 Napoléon forced the Austrians to sign a treaty that gave France control of all of northern Italy.

HISTORY MAKER

**Napoléon Bonaparte
(1769–1821)**

Napoléon Bonaparte defeated the most powerful armies in Europe and established a vast empire. He was known for his military skills as well as for his charm and intelligence.

After his death, Napoléon was often memorialized in French art and literature. He was usually shown standing proudly, with one hand resting inside his jacket. **Why is Napoléon popular in French art and literature?**

Napoléon the hero Napoléon had a great talent for seizing public attention and for making himself popular with the French people. *How does this painting show an idealized view of Napoléon?*

The Directory worried that the popular Napoléon might try to seize power. Meanwhile, Napoléon continued to make new conquests, keeping his name before the French people. He proposed attacking the British in Egypt to cut off British trade with India. The Directory quickly agreed, as this would keep Napoléon out of Paris.

At first Napoléon won victories on land against Egyptian forces. However, Napoléon's military campaign in Egypt ended in disaster. The British destroyed the French fleet near Alexandria, isolating the French army in Egypt. Napoléon left his army to take care of itself and returned to France. He hid the truth and exaggerated his victories in Egypt.

Napoléon takes power. Although Napoléon became a hero, France was in a dangerous situation. The British had organized an alliance of nations to oppose France, including Austria and Russia. These forces drove the French armies out of Italy, and French control over other conquered territories slipped.

Napoléon's supporters believed that only he could win victories abroad and restore order at home. Fearing that royalists might seize control, they developed a plan to overthrow the government and put Napoléon in power. These supporters wanted France to be stable because they feared losing the property and power they had gained during the Revolution.

In 1799 the legislature did away with four out of the five directors. Armed troops surrounded the legislature and forced most of its members to leave. Those who stayed turned the government over to Napoléon and his fellow plotters. Seizing power by force like this is referred to as a **coup d'état,** French for a "stroke of state." As Napoléon later said, "I found the crown of France lying on the ground, and I picked it up with my sword."

✔ **READING CHECK: Summarizing** How did Napoléon seize power?

SECTION 3 REVIEW

1. **Define** and explain the significance:
   universal manhood suffrage
   conscription
   counterrevolutionary
   coup d'état

2. **Identify** and explain the significance:
   Georges-Jacques Danton
   Maximilien Robespierre
   Jean-Paul Marat
   Reign of Terror
   Napoléon Bonaparte
   Joséphine de Beauharnais

3. **Analyzing Information** Copy the diagram and use it to show the balance of power under the Directory.

   Hall of Legislative Assembly

4. **Finding the Main Idea**
   a. How did the National Convention change France?
   b. How did the Reign of Terror and foreign wars affect the people of France?
   c. How did Napoléon Bonaparte rise to power?

5. **Writing and Critical Thinking**
   Identifying Points of View Conscription is one way to provide a military with soldiers. Write a dialogue between a teenager who is against the draft and a representative of France hoping to make conscription a policy.
   Consider:
   • what the teenager's life could be like as a soldier
   • how conscription could help the country

Homework Practice Online
keyword: SH3 HP12

READ TO DISCOVER

❶ In what ways was Napoléon's government successful?

❷ How did France became an empire?

❸ How did Napoléon reorganize Europe?

❹ What events led to Napoléon's final defeat at Waterloo?

DEFINE

plebiscite
nationalism
scorched-earth policy

IDENTIFY

Napoléonic Code
Concordat
Horatio Nelson
Duke of Wellington

WHY IT MATTERS TODAY

Napoléon's conquest of Europe stirred up feelings of nationalism in European countries. Use CNN or other **current event** sources to investigate how feelings of nationalism affect world affairs today. Record your findings in your journal.

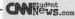

The Napoléonic Era

The Main Idea
As emperor, Napoléon dominated Europe until other major powers joined forces to defeat him.

The Story Continues *After meeting Napoléon in person, French author Madame de Staël analyzed the source of his greatness: "He did not hate any more than he loved; for him nothing existed but himself; . . . His successes depended as much on the qualities which he lacked as on the talents which he possessed. Neither pity, nor religion, nor attachment to any idea whatsoever, could [deflect] him from his principal direction."*

Napoléon as Dictator

Although Napoléon's government kept the form of a republic, the coup d'état of 1799 made him dictator of France. The period from 1799 to 1814 is known as the Napoléonic Era, or Age of Napoléon, because his influence in France and the rest of Europe was so great during this time.

The Consulate. The people of France accepted Napoléon's dictatorship. Many people wanted stability after the years of chaos. Others were simply afraid to protest. Napoléon supported many of the changes brought by the Revolution. He respected the ideals of the Declaration of the Rights of Man and did not restore any feudal practices. However, while Napoléon allowed freedom of opportunity, he firmly believed that the people should obey orders given by their leader.

Napoléon reorganized and centralized the government to give himself unlimited power. The first five years of Napoléon's rule were called the Consulate. This name comes from the executive branch of the government, which was made up of three consuls with Napoléon as First Consul. Napoléon commanded the army and navy.

He had the power to appoint or dismiss most officials and to propose all new laws. All the Consulate's legislative bodies could do was approve or reject Napoléon's decisions.

Napoléon put the constitution of his new government before the people for a vote. Under this procedure, called a **plebiscite,** people could vote only yes or no and could not suggest any changes. Even so, the vast majority of French voters approved the new constitution.

This painting by Jacques-Louis David captures the glory of Napoléon's military victories.

The coronation This painting shows Napoléon crowning his wife Joséphine empress after crowning himself emperor, while behind him the pope and clergy look on. The coronation ceremony took place in Notre Dame Cathedral, Paris. *How does the artist suggest that power rested with Napoléon and not with the church?*

Accomplishments in government. While Napoléon is remembered most for his military leadership, his work in government had a more lasting effect. Under Napoléon's direction scholars organized all French law into a system called the **Napoléonic Code.** Napoléon established the Bank of France to act as a central financial institution. He also put into effect the system of public education planned by the National Convention. This system included high schools, universities, and technical schools. Elementary education was left in the control of churches and local governments.

The Civil Constitution of the Clergy in 1790 had strained relations between the French government and the Roman Catholic Church. In 1801 Napoléon ended this conflict by reaching an agreement with the pope called the **Concordat.** The Concordat recognized that most French citizens were Catholic, but it still allowed religious freedom. Most important, the church gave up claims to the property that the government had seized and sold during the Revolution.

Using skillful diplomacy Napoléon undid the alliance of France's foreign enemies. By 1802 Russia, Austria, and Great Britain had either deserted the alliance or made peace with France. It looked as though Napoléon had brought France peace, a stable government, and economic prosperity.

✔ **READING CHECK: Summarizing** What were some of Napoléon's achievements in government?

Napoléon as Emperor

Holt Researcher

go.hrw.com
KEYWORD: Holt Researcher
FreeFind:
     Napoleon Bonaparte
     Josephine de
     Beauharnais
After reading more about Napoléon and Joséphine on the Holt Researcher, describe how their coronation marked the end of the French Revolution.

Napoléon's supporters wanted to make his power permanent and hereditary. In another plebiscite in 1804, the French people voted to declare France an empire. Napoléon became Emperor Napoléon I and his wife became Empress Joséphine. To mark the beginning of the empire the pope came to Paris to crown the couple. However, just as he was about to place the crown on Napoléon's head, Napoléon took the crown and put it on himself. Thus Napoléon showed that the power and authority he had were not given to him by anyone but himself.

The empire extended far beyond France's old borders. The British now felt that France threatened their own empire and their control of the seas. Great Britain renewed war with France in 1803. Austria, Russia, and Sweden joined with Great Britain. Spain sided with France. Napoléon aimed to defeat the British navy and invade Great Britain.

However, in 1805 a British fleet led by Vice Admiral **Horatio Nelson** defeated a combined French and Spanish fleet off the coast of Spain. Vice Admiral Nelson was killed in the battle, but he had saved Britain from invasion. Napoléon did win great victories in land battles against Austria and Russia.

Napoléon ordered a blockade of the British Isles and forbade the French Empire and its allies from trading with Britain. This blockade was known as the Continental

System, because Napoléon controlled so much of the continent of Europe. The British responded with a blockade against the French. The blockade hurt France, but Napoléon continued to win battles on land. In December 1805 he crushed Russian and Austrian forces, leading to the collapse of the coalition against France.

✔ **READING CHECK: Sequencing** What steps did Napoléon take as emperor?

The Reorganization of Europe

By 1809 Napoléon dominated Europe. He forced Austria and Prussia to sign peace treaties that benefited France, while Russia and Denmark allied themselves with Napoléon. He directly ruled the Netherlands and Spain and forced the Papal States into an alliance. He abolished the Holy Roman Empire and unified the northern Italian states into the Kingdom of Italy, under his control.

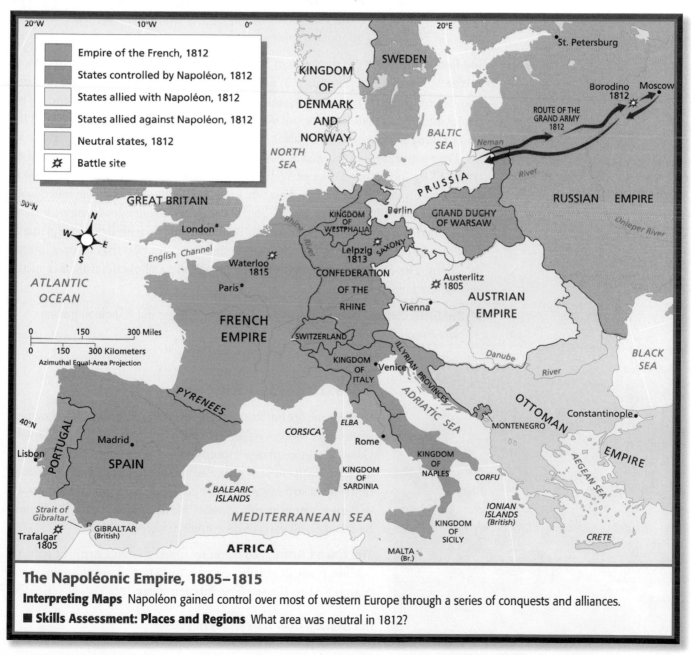

The Napoléonic Empire, 1805–1815

Interpreting Maps Napoléon gained control over most of western Europe through a series of conquests and alliances.

■ **Skills Assessment: Places and Regions** What area was neutral in 1812?

Napoléon secured his power by placing members of his large family as monarchs of the countries he conquered. However, he felt that the best way to secure the empire was to produce an heir. When he and Joséphine failed to have a child by 1809, he had their marriage annulled. He quickly married Austrian princess Marie-Louise, who gave birth to a son, Napoléon II, in 1811.

Increased nationalism. Napoléon made far-reaching changes in the lands he controlled. Wherever he conquered he put the Napoléonic Code into effect, abolishing feudalism and serfdom. He also introduced modern military techniques throughout Europe.

Without intending to, the French increased feelings of nationalism in the people they conquered. **Nationalism** refers to love of one's country rather than one's native region. In France the Revolution, as well as the Declaration of the Rights of Man, made people think of their country and ideals as things worth fighting for. Now these same feelings of loyalty and patriotism appeared among the people Napoléon had conquered. In some places this increased opposition to French rule. Over time, the armies of Napoléon's opponents' grew stronger.

The Peninsular War. To the south of France, on the Iberian Peninsula, lay Spain and Portugal. In 1807 Portugal refused to follow the Continental System because its economy depended upon trade with Great Britain. Napoléon responded by sending his armies into Portugal and driving out its king. He also conquered Spain and forced the Spanish king to step down. Napoléon then made his brother Joseph king of Spain.

The Spanish people revolted against this foreign rule in 1808. The British sent an army led by the future **Duke of Wellington** to help the Spanish and Portuguese people rise up against the French. This war, known as the Peninsular War, lasted from 1808 to 1814. During this time Napoléon still controlled Spain's government, but the war drained France's military resources. In 1813 the Spanish, with British help, finally drove out Joseph Bonaparte. They then wrote a new constitution that set up a limited monarchy. The revolt in Spain, and this new constitution, show the influence of the ideas of the French Revolution.

✔ **READING CHECK: Finding the Main Idea** What changes did Napoléon put into place in countries he conquered?

This painting from 1808 shows Napoléon commanding his forces at the Battle of Eylau.

Catastrophe in Russia

Czar Alexander I of Russia was alarmed by Napoléon's domination of Europe. Moreover, Russia had long depended on trade with Great Britain for manufactured goods. In 1812 the czar began trading again with Great Britain. Because the blockade was Napoléon's only way of striking at the British, he was angry that Russia, an ally of France, would openly ignore it. He decided to invade Russia, and he called on all parts of his empire to supply soldiers.

The Grand Army. Napoléon recruited a Grand Army of 600,000 soldiers from all over his empire. In 1812 this army began a long march east to Russia. The Russian defenders slowly retreated, drawing Napoléon's army deep into their country. As the Russians retreated they practiced a **scorched-earth policy,** burning or destroying crops and everything else the Grand Army might need.

The French eventually captured Moscow, but it was a hollow victory. As soon as the French entered the city, the Russians set it on fire. The fire destroyed so many buildings that the French troops had no housing, and the harsh Russian winter was coming. Napoléon had already lost many soldiers to disease, cold, and hunger, as well as battle. He finally ordered a retreat on October 19, 1812.

Napoléon's retreat from Moscow remains one of the greatest military disasters of all time. Napoléon's troops tried to make their way back to France through the bitter Russian winter without proper clothing and supplies. Many soldiers died from cold and starvation. Furthermore, the French were constantly under attack from Russian soldiers as they passed through the destroyed countryside. By the time the Grand Army reached Prussia, it had lost two thirds of its troops. The Russians followed and invaded the French Empire.

Final defeat. Monarchs in western Europe took advantage of Napoléon's defeat in Russia. They quickly broke their alliances with Napoléon. Prussia, Austria, and Great Britain joined Russia in a final alliance to crush France. In October 1813 Napoléon's army met these allied forces in Leipzig in Saxony. The allies won, and Napoléon retreated into France. The allies captured Paris in March 1814.

Napoléon agreed to give up all claims to the throne for himself and his family. The allies gave him a pension and allowed him to retire to the small island of Elba off the west coast of Italy.

The allies wanted to make sure that France would no longer disrupt Europe's affairs. They agreed that France could keep the boundaries of 1790. They also restored the Bourbon monarchy. Louis XVIII, the brother of Louis XVI, came to the throne. France had a king again.

✔ **READING CHECK: Identifying Cause and Effect** What factors led to Napoléon's defeat in Russia?

The Hundred Days

During 1814 and early 1815, the restored king and his family made many enemies among the French people. Learning of this discontent, Napoléon escaped from Elba and landed in France on March 1, 1815. Louis XVIII sent soldiers to capture Napoléon. Napoléon met them saying, "If there be one among you who wishes to kill his Emperor, he can. I come to offer myself to your assaults." The soldiers' resistance disappeared, and Napoléon led the army into Paris on March 20, beginning a period called the Hundred Days. Frightened, Louis XVIII fled into exile. Napoléon once again ruled France.

Napoléon hoped that disputes among his opponents would keep them from opposing his return, but he was wrong. Prussia, Great Britain, and the Netherlands sent armies toward France. Napoléon assembled an army to stop them.

Government of France, 1774–1814	
1774	Louis XVI became king.
1789	Third Estate, as National Assembly, assumed power.
1791	Legislative Assembly, with Louis XVI as constitutional monarch, began rule.
1795	Directory took control.
1799	Consulate was established, with Napoléon as First Consul.
1804	Napoléon was crowned emperor.
1814	Napoléon was defeated and Bourbon monarchy was restored.

Interpreting the Chart
After being ruled as a republic and then an empire, France returned to monarchy in 1814. *What can you tell about political stability in France during this time?*

King Louis XVIII retained many of Napoléon's reforms in the law, church, and education.

On June 18, 1815, the allied and the French armies met at Waterloo. The British—under the command of the Duke of Wellington—and their Prussian allies dealt Napoléon his final defeat. Napoléon gave up the throne, and the Bourbon monarchs once again took power.

Napoléon asked to be allowed to go to the United States. However, the British sent him to St. Helena, a small, lonely island in the South Atlantic, where he lived under constant guard. In 1821 Napoléon died there.

As the years passed, Napoléon's legend grew. People forgot his failures and remembered his glories and victories. Napoléon and his achievements came to be memorialized in French literature and art. In 1840 the British allowed the French to bring Napoléon's remains back to Paris, where they lie to this day.

✔ **READING CHECK: Summarizing** How was Napoléon finally defeated?

Waterloo Scottish troops clash with charging French cavalry in this painting of Napoléon's defeat at Waterloo. *How does this painting create a sense of the confusion and chaos of battle?*

SECTION 4 REVIEW

1. **Define** and explain the significance:
   plebiscite
   nationalism
   scorched-earth policy

2. **Identify** and explain the significance:
   Napoléonic Code
   Concordat
   Horatio Nelson
   Duke of Wellington

Homework Practice Online
keyword: SH3 HP12

3. **Analyzing Information** Copy the model and use it to show the allies who joined forces against Napoléon in Leipzig.

Leipzig

4. **Finding the Main Idea**
   a. Describe Napoléon's achievements through 1804.
   b. How did Napoléon establish an empire?
   c. How and by whom was Napoléon finally defeated?

5. **Writing and Critical Thinking**
   Drawing Inferences In a short script for a play, have Napoléon saying goodbye to his troops before he is taken to St. Helena.
   Consider:
   • Napoléon's triumphs
   • the loyalty and patriotism of his troops
   • the great change from being emperor to living on a small island

READ TO DISCOVER

1 How did the Congress of Vienna attempt to restore stability to Europe?

2 Why did politicians practice conservative policies?

3 How did Metternich influence conservative politics and stop revolution?

DEFINE

legitimacy
indemnity
reaction
reactionaries
liberalism

IDENTIFY

Charles-Maurice de Talleyrand-
Périgord
Prince Metternich

WHY IT MATTERS TODAY

Alliances in Europe helped to uphold the Congress of Vienna. Use CNNStudentNews.com or other **current event** sources to investigate alliances between countries today and what goals they have. Record your findings in your journal.

CNN student News.com

A Return to Peace

The Main Idea
After 1815 European governments took a conservative approach in restoring stability to Europe.

The Story Continues *After defeating Napoléon, the major European powers wanted to stamp out the ideas of the French Revolution. Nevertheless, the words from the Declaration of the Rights of Man and of the Citizen—"men are born and remain free and equal in rights"—still echoed in people's minds throughout Europe.*

The Congress of Vienna

Napoléon had not always upheld the ideals of the French Revolution—liberty, equality, and fraternity—but he did extend their influence throughout Europe. This led other governments to fear that rebellions against monarchy might spread beyond France. Having defeated Napoléon, the major European powers wanted to restore order, keep the peace, and suppress the ideas of the Revolution.

The principles of the Congress of Vienna. Stability could not be achieved until territorial questions were settled. To resolve these questions hundreds of delegates met at the Congress of Vienna, in Austria. Most decision-making authority rested with Great Britain, Austria, Prussia, and Russia. However, the representative of France, **Charles-Maurice de Talleyrand-Périgord,** also played an important role.

Three principles guided the decisions of the Congress of Vienna. (1) The countries that had suffered the most at the hands of Napoléon had to be paid back for what they had lost. (2) The balance of power had to be restored in Europe, so that no single nation would become too powerful. (3) All decisions would follow the rule of **legitimacy,** which meant that all former ruling families should be restored to their thrones.

Compensations. Countries were reshuffled in an attempt to gain back losses. The Netherlands, conquered early on by French forces, received the Austrian Netherlands. In return, Austria gained two northern Italian states. Because Sweden had fought against Napoléon, it received Norway, formerly a Danish possession. This was also intended to punish Denmark for cooperating with Napoléon. Prussia received some territory along the Rhine River. Although Great Britain did not receive any lands in Europe, it did gain several islands in the French West Indies and in the Mediterranean.

INTERPRETING THE VISUAL RECORD

Restoring order The work of the Congress of Vienna continued throughout the Hundred Days of Napoléon's return to power and after his final defeat at Waterloo. *What does the presence of military officers in this painting say about politics at the time?*

The winning powers also argued over territory. Napoléon had once given part of Poland to his allies in the German state of Saxony. Now Russia and Prussia both claimed parts of Poland. Other countries feared that either outcome would upset the balance of power, and for a time tensions increased. Finally Talleyrand resolved the dispute with a distribution of land that everyone could accept.

In the end France was surrounded by a ring of strong states so that it could not again threaten the peace of Europe. France's boundaries were returned to where they had been in 1790. France also had to pay a large **indemnity**—a financial reward to other countries for the damages it had caused.

At Talleyrand's urging the Congress of Vienna made settlements based on legitimacy. The Bourbon monarchy, already restored in France, also regained power in Spain and in the Kingdom of the Two Sicilies. This principle was not applied everywhere, however. The Austrian Habsburgs, for example, now dominated Italy because of new territorial gains.

✔ **READING CHECK: Summarizing** What were the three principles that guided the Congress of Vienna?

Reactionary Alliances

A time of **reaction** followed the Napoléonic Era, meaning that people in authority wanted a return to the way things had been before. **Reactionaries** are people who not only oppose change but would also like to actually undo certain changes. After 1815 the victors in Europe attempted to restore a balance of power, or stability, and to emphasize a conservative view toward politics.

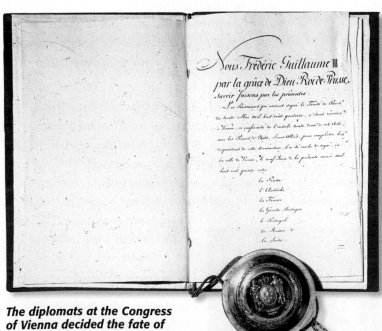

The diplomats at the Congress of Vienna decided the fate of Europe with the ratification of documents such as the Treaty of Paris.

In Spain and the Two Sicilies, the restored monarchs abolished existing constitutions and gave themselves absolute power. Switzerland alone kept its constitutional government but had to promise to remain neutral in European wars.

Napoléon's conquests had resulted in the spread of new political ideas and the rise of nationalism. Groups that shared a common language, history, and culture now wanted to unite under their own governments. Reactionary powers considered this nationalism dangerous and tried to halt it. Therefore European governments took special steps to prevent revolution, and the Congress of Vienna left nationalist groups disappointed.

The four allies that had defeated Napoléon —Austria, Great Britain, Prussia, and Russia— agreed in 1815 to continue their alliance. Known as the Quadruple Alliance, they agreed to hold periodic conferences to discuss common interests. In 1818 France was allowed to join the Quadruple Alliance, making it the Quintuple Alliance.

Czar Alexander of Russia held strong religious ideals and urged the other leaders to sign an agreement called the Holy Alliance. By signing they promised to rule as Christians. Most rulers signed this reactionary document—evidence of the extreme conservatism that existed at the time.

Out of these alliances grew what was called the Concert of Europe—a form of international governance by concert, or agreement. The aim of the Concert was to maintain the balance of power set up by the Congress of Vienna. The Concert of Europe proved effective until 1848.

✔ **READING CHECK: Drawing Conclusions** In what ways were alliances after 1815 helpful to Europe?

Europe After the Congress of Vienna, 1815

Interpreting Maps The Congress of Vienna, meeting between 1814 and 1815, attempted to settle political and territorial questions arising from the Napoléonic Wars.

■ **Skills Assessment: Locate** France's territory was greatly reduced by the actions of the Congress of Vienna. What island remained under French rule?

Europe after Napoléon

The Congress of Vienna succeeded in addressing the concerns of the major European powers after the defeat of Napoléon. Afterward, the Concert of Europe continued to enforce the terms agreed to by delegates at the Congress. Using an outline can help you to understand the terms of a complex document like the Concert of Europe.

An Eyewitness's View:

Prince Metternich, who coordinated much of this diplomatic cooperation, described his main goals in the following way:

"Liberty for every Government to watch over the well-being of its own people; a league between all Governments against factions in all States; . . . respect for the progressive development of institutions in lawful ways . . . such are happily the ideas of the great monarchs: the world will be saved if they bring them into action—it is lost if they do not."

I. Congress of Vienna addresses three main issues
  A. Compensating countries for losses
    1. France pays indemnity for damages caused
    2. Congress awards territories
      a. Austria gains two northern Italian states
      b. Great Britain gains island possessions
  B. Restoring a balance of power
    1. Officials strip France of conquests
      a. Congress restores French borders to 1792 status
      b. France surrounded by strong states
    2. Prussia and Russia reach a compromise
  C. Maintaining legitimacy of ruling families
    1. Louis XVIII rules France
    2. Bourbon monarchs restored in Spain and Two Sicilies

Much of Europe's royalty came to Vienna during the winter of 1814–15. They carried on a lively social life while diplomats and rulers discussed the state of Europe after Napoléon.

Skills Reminder

Most writers follow a standard format to create an outline. They label main heads with Roman numerals, subheads with capital letters, and details with Arabic numerals and lowercase letters. The information in the details should be more specific than at any other level. Each level should have at least two entries and be indented from the level above. Organized in such a way, an outline serves as a blueprint to help you keep track of important information and write a more well-structured research paper.

Skills Practice

❶ Study the partial outline above. What is the main topic of this outline?

❷ Suppose you wanted to add a fact about how Denmark was penalized for cooperating with Napoléon. Where would you place it in the outline?

❸ Choose one section from this chapter and outline it using the format shown above. Your thesis statement should be the main idea of the section. The section's main headings could serve as the major ideas in the outline.

The Age of Metternich

For 30 years after the Congress of Vienna, **Prince Metternich** of Austria influenced European politics so strongly that this period is sometimes known as the Age of Metternich. A reactionary, Metternich believed in absolute monarchy. He feared the movement known as **liberalism,** which extended the ideas of the American and French revolutions. Liberals believed in individual rights and the rule of law. Metternich believed in suppressing such ideas as freedom of speech and of the press. He aimed to prevent war or revolution and to preserve absolutism. Metternich had little difficulty achieving these goals in Austria. He set up a central investigating commission to spy on revolutionary organizations and individuals. He also persuaded the rulers of most German states to adopt the same methods. In France King Louis XVIII was cautious in domestic affairs, but joined in suppressing revolutions elsewhere.

Liberals reacted strongly to the Congress of Vienna and to Metternich's actions. A number of uprisings occurred in Europe, and the Concert of Europe worked to suppress them. Austria, Russia, and Prussia, in particular, were very determined in their efforts to thwart revolutions. Great Britain, however, did not want to intervene in other nations' affairs. Having a representative form of government themselves, the British were sympathetic to liberal movements in other countries. For this and other reasons, Great Britain did not join the Holy Alliance.

For a time Metternich's system of suppression worked well. As repression increased, however, underground movements of resistance began. In the early 1820s allied armies had to put down popular uprisings in the Two Sicilies. In 1821 nationalism flared again as the Greeks revolted against their Ottoman Turk rulers. Under Metternich's influence European rulers ignored Greek calls for aid. Many individuals across Europe, however, supported Greece and even fought as volunteers. Finally Russia, Great Britain, and France brought pressure on the Ottomans. With the signing of the treaty of Adrianople in 1829 Greece won its independence. This successful uprising showed that feelings of nationalism could not be suppressed forever.

Prince Metternich, shown here, used harsh means to stop revolutionary movements. He encouraged governments to place university students and faculty members under strict watch, to censor newspapers and magazines, and to search for secret revolutionary activities.

✔ **READING CHECK: Summarizing** How did Metternich try to stop liberalism?

SECTION 5 REVIEW

1. **Define** and explain the significance:
   legitimacy
   indemnity
   reaction
   reactionaries
   liberalism

2. **Identify** and explain the significance:
   Charles-Maurice de Talleyrand-Périgord
   Prince Metternich

Homework Practice Online
keyword: SH3 HP12

3. **Summarizing** Copy the model and use it to show the three principles guiding the Congress of Vienna.

Congress of Vienna

4. **Finding the Main Idea**

   a. Why was the Congress of Vienna so concerned with the balance of power?
   b. Why was nationalism a threat to reactionaries?
   c. How were Metternich's ideas different from Great Britain's?

5. **Writing and Critical Thinking**

   Analyzing Information Write a letter from Metternich to Austria's allies explaining his system to keep the peace.
   Consider:
   • what monarchs had to fear from liberalism
   • the effectiveness of the Metternich system

Creating a Time Line

Copy the time line below onto a sheet of paper. Complete the time line by filling in the events, individuals, and dates from the chapter that you think were significant. Pick three events and explain why you think they were significant.

| 1789 | 1799 | 1815 |

Writing a Summary

Using standard grammar, spelling, sentence structure, and punctuation, write an overview of the events in the chapter.

Identifying People and Ideas

Identify the following terms or individuals and explain their significance:

1. bourgeoisie
2. Marie-Antoinette
3. Napoléon Bonaparte
4. radicals
5. conscription
6. coup d'état
7. Horatio Nelson
8. plebiscite
9. Duke of Wellington
10. Prince Metternich

Understanding Main Ideas

SECTION 1 *(pp. 316–319)*

The Roots of Revolution

1. List three underlying causes of the French Revolution.
2. What role did the meeting of the Estates General in 1789 play in bringing about the Revolution?

SECTION 2 *(pp. 320–324)*

The French Revolution

3. Describe the accomplishments of the National Assembly.
4. What effect did the Legislative Assembly have on France?

SECTION 3 *(pp. 325–330)*

The French Republic

5. What was the purpose of France's foreign wars and the Reign of Terror?
6. What abilities helped Napoléon rise to power?

SECTION 4 *(pp. 331–336)*

The Napoléonic Era

7. How did Napoléon build his empire?
8. List three of Napoléon's most important defeats.

SECTION 5 *(pp. 337–341)*

A Return to Peace

9. How did the Concert of Europe become an instrument of suppression?

Reviewing Themes

1. **Government** Was the National Convention truly a representative form of government?
2. **Constitutional Heritage** How did the Constitution of 1791 change the status of the French monarchy?
3. **Citizenship** Compare and contrast the attitude of the Jacobins, Napoléon, and Prince Metternich toward freedom of speech.

Thinking Critically

1. **Drawing Inferences** How did the structure of French society lend itself to a revolution?
2. **Making Generalizations** How did Napoléon gain control over Europe?
3. **Contrasting** How was the French Revolution different from the American Revolution?

Writing About History

Categorizing In a paragraph, describe what were the lasting social, political, and cultural effects of the French Revolution. Use the chart below to help you organize your thoughts before writing.

Social Effects	Political Effects	Cultural Effects

Interpreting Maps

Study the map below. Then use the information from the map to answer the questions that follow.

Napoléon in Russia

Analyzing Historical Context

Read the following quote from Comte de Mirabeau, who was trying to calm the people of Marseille after a riot in March, 1789. Then answer the questions.

> "My good friends, I have come to tell you what I think about the events of the past three days in your proud city. . . . Let us first consider bread. . . . At the present time, dear friends, since wheat is expensive everywhere, how could it be cheap at Marseille? . . . The town of Marseille, like every other town, pays something toward the expenses of the kingdom and the support of our good king. Money is taken from this source and a little from that. . . ."

1. Which of the following statements accurately reflects the information shown on the map?

   a. Napoléon's march into Russia reached as far east as Moscow.

   b. Napoléon's army moved from east to west during its march into Russia.

   c. Napoléon's army was well supplied throughout its campaign in Russia.

   d. Weather was never an issue during the French invasion of Russia.

2. Napoléon's campaign in Russia was viewed with horror by many in the years after 1812. Why was this so? Give specific reasons.

3. Which of the following statements best summarizes the situation in Marseille at the time Mirabeau spoke these words?

   a. The people of Marseille were unhappy because the price of wheat was rising.

   b. Marseille paid more taxes than other cities in France at the time.

   c. Food was scarce and very expensive, and the people of the Third Estate had begun to rebel.

   d. The people of Marseille were glad to help support France and the king.

4. What was the main point that Mirabeau was making in this quote?

Alternative Assessment

Building Your Portfolio

Link to TODAY

Constitutional Heritage

The French Revolution took many of its ideas from previous revolutions. Using your textbook and other sources, create a chart summarizing the ideas from the English, American, and French Revolutions concerning separation of powers, liberty, equality, democracy, popular sovereignty, human rights, constitutionalism, and nationalism.

internet connect

Internet Activity: go.hrw.com
KEYWORD: SH3 WH12

Choose a topic on the French Revolution and Napoléon to:

- analyze artistic renderings and evaluate the historical accuracy of key events in Napoléon's life.
- evaluate the differences among the American, French, and Russian Revolutions.
- research the rise and fall of the Jacobins.

Political Satire

The pointed humor of political satire makes fun of politicians' behavior and the failings of social institutions. By making leaders and institutions look ridiculous, satirists hope to inspire people to attack social problems. To shock readers into taking action, satirists often use exaggeration and irony—saying the opposite of what is meant. When he worked in Ireland during the early 1700s, Jonathan Swift (1667–1745) saw many people, particularly children, living in dreadful conditions. Swift proposed several ways to address poverty and lack of political rights in Ireland. After his straightforward suggestions were ignored, Swift wrote the savagely ironic A Modest Proposal. Mercy Otis Warren (1728–1814) wrote some of the first plays to attack England's "imperialistic rule" in America. Her characters in The Group, all based on recognizable British officials and their Tory supporters, have names like Dupe, Spendall, Hum-bug, and Hateall. Warren's stage directions compare them to a swarm of locusts eating everything in its path. Warren's satiric plays, published in newspapers instead of being produced in the theater, contributed to Thomas Hutchinson's removal as governor of Massachusetts.

A Modest Proposal *by Jonathan Swift*

I HAVE been assured by a very knowing American of my Acquaintance in London; that a young healthy Child, well nursed, is, at a Year old, a most delicious, nourishing, and wholesome Food; whether Stewed, Roasted, Baked, or Boiled....I DO therefore humbly offer it to publick Consideration, that of the Hundred and Twenty Thousand children, already computed, Twenty thousand may be reserved for Breed.... That the remaining Hundred thousand, may, at a Year old, be offered in Sale to the Persons of Quality and Fortune, through the Kingdom; always advising the Mothers to . . . render them plump, and fat for a good Table. A child will make two Dishes at an Entertainment for Friends; and when the Family dines alone, the fore or hind Quarter will make a reasonable Dish; and seasoned with a little Pepper or Salt, will be very good boiled on the fourth Day, especially in Winter. . . . I GRANT this Food will be somewhat dear [expensive], and therefore very proper for Landlords; who, as they have already devoured most of the Parents, seem to have the best Title to the Children.

The Group *by Mercy Otis Warren*

The Group enter attended by a swarm of court sycophants [insincere flatterers], hungry harpies [predators who relentlessly pursue their prey], and unprincipled danglers [hangers-on] . . . hovering over the stage in the shape of locusts; led by Massachusettensis in the form of a basilisk [a fierce, sharp-toothed lizard]; the rear brought up by Proteus [someone who allies with a side in a conflict for money], bearing a torch in one hand and a powder flask in the other, the whole supported by a mighty army and navy from Blunderland, for the laudable [admirable—used here in a satirically sarcastic way] purpose of enslaving its best friends.

Understanding Literature

What are the problems that Swift and Warren attack? Do you think they use effective techniques to bring about change? Explain your answer.

Government

The English, American, and French Revolutions shared many of the same principles, even though all three had different outcomes. Create a chart summarizing the ideas from these three revolutions concerning separation of powers, liberty, equality, democracy, popular sovereignty, human rights, constitutionalism, and nationalism.

The Boston Massacre in the American colonies, March 1770 (above), and the storming of the Bastille by French revolutionaries, July 1789 (right), symbolized the power of Enlightenment ideas.

The Battle of Marston Moor in 1644 was a turning point in the English Civil War. The development of constitutionalism in England had a long and sometimes violent history.

Further Reading

Erickson, Carroly. *Great Catherine.* New York: St. Martin's Press, 1995. The life and times of Russia's Catherine the Great.

Hibbert, Christopher. *The Days of the French Revolution.* New York: Quill, 1999. An overview of people and events during the French Revolution.

Sweetman, John. *The Enlightenment and the Age of Revolution, 1700–1850.* New York: Addison Wesley, 1998. A survey of politics, people, culture, and society during the Ages of Enlightenment and Revolution.

Wheeler, Richard, ed., and Bruce Catton. *The Voices of 1776: The Story of the American Revolution in the Words of Those Who Were There.* New York: Meridian, 1996. First person accounts from both sides by men and women who witnessed the Revolutionary War.

Zienert, Karen. *Those Remarkable Women of the American Revolution.* Brookfield, CT: Millbrook Press, 1996. An overview of the role women played during the war.

Constitutional Heritage

Many of the ideas that influenced constitutional governments had roots in ancient civilizations. Create a time line tracing the historical development of the rule of law and of rights and responsibilities, beginning in the ancient world and continuing to the first modern constitutional republics. The time line should include the influence of ideas about rights and responsibilities, such as equality before the law, that originated in Greco-Roman and Judeo-Christian ideals.

🖅 **internet** connect

Internet Activity
KEYWORD: SH3 U3

In assigned groups, develop a multimedia presentation about the era from Absolutism to Revolution. Choose information from the chapter Internet Connect activities and the Holt Researcher that best reflects the major topics of the period. Write an outline and a script for your presentation, which may be shown to the class.

Industrialization and Nationalism

1600–1928

Main Events

- The Industrial Revolution changes the global economy
- The Age of Reform seeks to address problems from the Industrial Revolution
- Nationalism grows in Europe
- Nations compete for overseas empires

Main Ideas

- Why was the Industrial Revolution so important?
- In what ways did life change during the Industrial Age?
- What was the Age of Reform?
- How did nationalism help to unify countries?
- What is imperialism? How did it affect the world?

This Fabergé Easter egg, commissioned in 1898 by Czar Nicholas II, was a gift for his wife.

This 1850 painting by Godfrey Sykes of the interior of an ironworks captures the spirit of the Industrial Revolution. **347**

CROSS-CULTURAL CONNECTIONS

Focus On: Science, Technology, and Society

Main Idea **How did new technologies of the Industrial Revolution change the world?** The Industrial Revolution transformed economies and societies throughout the world. Beginning in England, the technology that started the movement quickly spread throughout Europe and the United States. To support their new industries, many nations began to seek overseas empires for raw materials. The competition for empires fueled already growing nationalism within Europe.

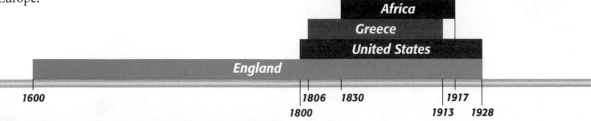

		Africa		
		Greece		
		United States		
England				

| 1600 | | 1806 | 1830 | 1917 | |
| | | 1800 | | 1913 | 1928 |

The Power of Steam The steam engine was one of the most important inventions of the Industrial Age. The first steam engines, developed in the late 1600s, simply pumped water. Scottish engineer James Watt developed the first modern steam engine in 1769. Then British inventor Richard Trevithick designed a high-pressure steam engine to power the first railroad locomotive in 1804. In 1829 the first locomotive carried passengers and freight. Soon after, railroad construction took off at an rapid pace in Britain and the United States. Railways quickly became an important source of transportation for both goods and passengers. British artist William Frith captured the noise and bustle of a British railway station in this painting from 1862.

England, 1600–1928

In 1829, the "Rocket" won a competition sponsored by the Liverpool and Manchester Railroad in England. The steam-powered locomotive pulled three times its own weight at 12.5 mph. It carried passengers at about 24 mph.

Increased Mobility The development of steamship travel during the second half of the 1800s allowed for an enormous increase in immigration to the United States and Canada. Some people called steamship transportation between Europe and North America "the Atlantic Ferry." Faster travel times meant that shipping companies had to provide little more than minimal living space in steerage for poorer passengers, who were required to supply their own food, bedding, and other necessities. In this image from the late 1800s, immigrants in search of new opportunities and a better life come ashore at Ellis Island, New York.

United States, 1800–1928

Global Nationalism Throughout the 1800s and continuing uninterrupted into the 1900s, the forces of nationalism increasingly shaped world events. In Europe, Latin America, the Middle East, and Asia, rising nationalism led to major change, in many cases sweeping away centuries-old political and social structures. Nationalism was stimulated, in part, by the material and technological progress of the Industrial Revolution, and by the general economic growth that resulted. Increased global communication and contact, also products of industrialization, helped to spread ideas of national identity and opposition to the "old order." The English poet Lord Byron, pictured here, championed nationalistic movements in Italy and in Greece, where he died of a fever in 1824.

Greece, 1806–1913

Africa, 1830–1917

Tools of Imperialism One result of technological growth in the 1800s was a rapid change in the weapons of warfare. The invention of the machine gun by Hiram Maxim in 1884 gave imperialistic countries a significant advantage over less-developed nations. Advanced weapons allowed European countries to establish colonial empires in Asia and Africa during this period. German imperialism in Africa, for example, began in the early 1880s. In this painting, created by an East African artist, German officers watch the slaughter of native Africans in the German protectorate of Tanganyika [present-day Tanzania], as German-trained African soldiers use modern weapons to defeat native warriors armed with shields and spears.

The invention of the machine gun in 1884 made for a more portable weapon that could fire 11 rounds per second.

Why It Matters Today

Historically, new technology has had the power both to help and to hurt societies. As a result, people sometimes greet technological growth with mixed emotions.
In what ways does modern technology both help and harm society? How have people in your society reacted to recently developed technology?

1600–1901

The Industrial Revolution

Early hand-cranked cotton gin

1600
Daily Life
The enclosure movement in England continues.

1675
Science and Technology
The Royal Observatory at Greenwich, England, is founded by King Charles II.

1713
Politics
The Treaty of Utrecht is signed.

c. 1733
Science and Technology
John Kay invents the flying shuttle.

1600 ———————————————— **1700**

c. 1633–1637
Business and Finance
Wild speculation in tulip bulbs ultimately ruins many Dutch investors.

c. 1701
Science and Technology
Jethro Tull invents the seed drill.

1721
The Arts
Johann Sebastian Bach's *Brandenberg Concertos* are completed.

1769
Science and Technology
Richard Arkwright patents a water-powered spinning frame.

Painting of a tulip by a Dutch artist

Portrait of Johann Sebastian Bach

Build on What You Know

*T*he discoveries of Galileo Galilei, Sir Isaac Newton, and other pioneering thinkers of the Scientific Revolution led to a deeper understanding of the natural world. By the early 1700s people began to apply these scientific advances in a practical way. This led to the creation of new machines and businesses. Major developments in technology were aimed at producing and moving goods. These products were designed to meet the needs of a fast-growing population. In this chapter, you will learn about how industrial developments took place and what effect they had on society.

Steam locomotive

c. 1785
Science and Technology
Englishman Edmund Cartwright patents the power loom.

c. 1794
Science and Technology
The American inventor Eli Whitney patents the cotton gin, a machine for cleaning seeds from cotton fibers.

c. 1814
Science and Technology
George Stephenson invents the locomotive.

c. 1817
Business and Finance
The New York Stock Exchange opens.

c. 1838
The Arts
Charles Dickens publishes *Oliver Twist*.

c. 1866
Daily Life
The first transatlantic cable is completed.

c. 1889
The Arts
The Eiffel Tower is completed in Paris.

Portrait of Charles Dickens

1800

1900

c. 1801
Politics
Great Britain and Ireland form the United Kingdom.

1848
Politics
Karl Marx and Friedrich Engels publish the *Communist Manifesto*.

1901
Business and Finance
United States Steel is founded.

c. 1790
Business and Finance
The U.S. patent office is established.

1828
The Arts
Noah Webster publishes *An American Dictionary of the English Language* in two volumes.

1776
Business and Finance
Adam Smith publishes *Inquiry into the Nature and Causes of the Wealth of Nations*.

This sequence of images shows various stages in the construction of the Eiffel Tower in Paris.

What's Your Opinion?

Themes Journal *Do you* **agree** *or* **disagree** *with the following statements? Support your point of view in your journal.*

Science, Technology & Society A society's development depends on its ability to understand and use science and technology.

Citizenship The roles that people play in society are related to the distribution of wealth in that society.

Economics The workers who produce goods and services, and so create wealth, deserve a say in how that wealth is distributed.

351

Origins of the Industrial Revolution

READ TO DISCOVER

❶ Why did the Industrial Revolution begin in Great Britain?

❷ How did inventions in the textile industry lead to other new inventions?

❸ What effects did developments in transportation and communication have on the spread of the Industrial Revolution?

DEFINE

enclosure movement
crop rotation
Industrial Revolution
factors of production
mechanization
factory system
vulcanization

IDENTIFY

Jethro Tull
Richard Arkwright
Eli Whitney
James Watt
Henry Bessemer
Robert Fulton
Samuel Morse

WHY IT MATTERS TODAY

Increased demand for some product or service often promotes the development of new technology. Use CNNstudentNews.com or other **current event** sources to find some type of new technology that developed to meet a need of society. Record your findings in your journal.

CNNstudentNews.com

The Main Idea
Conditions in Great Britain led to revolutionary new methods of agriculture and manufacturing.

The Story Continues *A new era of peace after 1815 brought growing prosperity to western Europe. New agricultural methods and improved systems of transportation and communication helped to stimulate progress. One well-known writer noted that "The benefit of . . . Turn-pikes [toll roads] appears now to be so great, and the People in all Places begin to be so sensible of it, that it is incredible what Effect [turnpike construction] has already had upon Trade in the Countries where it is more completely finish'd . . ."*

The Agricultural Revolution

Before the 1600s most European villagers worked their own plots of land in order to grow food for their families. They also used common public lands for grazing animals such as sheep and cattle. In the 1500s and 1600s common lands in England began to be enclosed, or fenced off, into individual plots. At the same time, smaller landholdings were being combined into more efficient, larger holdings. This **enclosure movement** continued into the 1700s. It reached its height by the early 1800s in Great Britain, as a growing population increased demand and raised prices for agricultural products. Wealthy landholders benefited from this movement, while many small landowners lost their lands and their traditional livelihood.

The enclosure movement had several effects. As large landowners added to their holdings, former small-plot owners were forced to become tenant farmers or move to the cities. Also, with the common lands vanishing, farmers no longer had to get permission from other villagers to try new farming methods. In the early 1700s, for example, landowner **Jethro Tull** was concerned about the amount of seed wasted by hand-scattering it over the fields. Tull invented a seed drill that made it possible to plant seeds in straight rows. He also made a horse-drawn hoe to dig up weeds between the rows and break up soil before planting.

Another English landowner, Charles "Turnip" Townshend, copied a successful Dutch practice. English farmers usually left some fields unplanted for a year to let the soil rebuild its nutrients. Townshend found that planting different crops in the fields each year had the same result. For example, he planted wheat or barley one year and root crops such as turnips the next. This system, called **crop rotation,** helped farmers to produce more crops using the same amount of land.

During this Agricultural Revolution, other improvements increased production and made farm labor easier. Iron plows replaced wooden ones. An American, Jethro Wood, invented a plow with a replaceable blade, which eliminated the need to buy a whole new plow. Some of these improvements were very expensive. Only wealthy farmers could afford them. By the 1800s many farm workers, replaced by machines and forced off the land, were moving to the cities. They formed a huge labor force.

✔ **READING CHECK: Identifying Cause and Effect** How did the enclosure movement lead to the development of improved technology in agriculture?

Factors of Production

An era of rapid industrial development known as the **Industrial Revolution** followed the Agricultural Revolution. It began in Great Britain, which had a favorable combination of needed factors—land, capital, and labor. Economists call these the **factors of production.** Land refers to all natural resources. Great Britain had a rich supply of such resources, particularly coal and iron ore. Its many rivers provided waterpower and inland shipping routes, and its many harbors encouraged trade both within and beyond the British Isles. Great Britain also had rich sources of capital, including the tools, machinery, equipment, and inventory used in production. Capital also included money, which those who had grown rich during the 1700s used to invest in new businesses. Great Britain also had a large supply of labor for industry, fueled by the growth in population and migration into cities.

✔ **READING CHECK: Finding the Main Idea** Why did the Industrial Revolution begin in Great Britain?

The Industrial Revolution in Great Britain, 1715–1851

Interpreting Maps In most cases, industrial centers in Britain developed around rich coal deposits and navigable rivers. Canal systems helped to link these areas to markets and shipping points.

■ **Skills Assessment: Physical Systems** What geographical factors may have helped to speed industrial development in the city of Liverpool?

The Textile Industry

In the 1600s men and women in England spun thread and wove cloth by hand in their homes. It was a slow process. England could not meet the growing demand for cloth. As a result, automatic machinery was used to increase production. This was known as **mechanization.** Author Daniel Defoe, writing in the early 1700s, described an enormous silk-spinning machine that automatically performed in minutes operations that took many workers days to complete by hand.

"This engine contains 22,586 wheels and 97,746 movements, which work 73,726 yards of silk thread every time the wheel goes round, which is three times in one minute, and 318,504,960 yards in 24 hours. The water-wheel gives the motion to all the rest of the wheels and movements, of which any one may be stopped separately.**"**

Daniel Defoe, from *The British Revolution, 1750–1970: A Social and Economic History,* by Michael St. J. Parker and D. J. Reid

DAILY LIFE

Industrialization and Sports

By the late 1800s, sports and industry had much in common. Like work, sports became more specialized. Players had specific positions that required specific skills. Players, like factory workers, followed standard rules of conduct. Organized sports also made use of new technologies. New types of sporting equipment, for example, became available as a result of industrialization. **How were organized sports like industry?**

New inventions. A first step toward mechanization was the invention of a mechanized loom for weaving cloth. A loom is a frame with threads stretched lengthwise from top to bottom. These threads are known as "warp" threads. A worker pushed a shuttle holding another thread—the "weft" thread—over and under the warp threads to weave cloth. In about 1733 British engineer John Kay invented the flying shuttle, which moved the weft-carrying shuttle quickly across the loom. Weavers could now make cloth so fast they outran the supply of thread from the old-fashioned spinning wheels.

In the 1760s British weaver James Hargreaves invented the spinning "jenny." This machine could produce eight times more thread than a single spinning wheel. **Richard Arkwright** later invented a way to drive the machine by waterpower. Arkwright brought workers and waterpower together and opened a spinning mill during the 1780s. Workers put in a certain number of hours each day for a fixed pay. This spinning mill was the beginning of the modern **factory system.**

Improvements in the spinning process followed, but workers still could not meet the demand for cloth. In about 1785 English minister Edmund Cartwright invented a water-powered loom. One person could now weave as much cloth as 200 hand-loom operators. This rapid change in spinning and weaving showed how inventions built on one another. The flying shuttle created a need for more thread, which faster spinning produced. This was followed by improved weaving machines. Each invention created a new need, and human ingenuity filled the gap.

Effects of mechanization. As supply increased, the price of cotton cloth went down. As a result, demand increased and so did the need for more raw cotton. Raw cotton imports by England went from 4 millions pounds in 1761 to 100 million pounds in 1815. Most of it came from the southern United States. Cleaning seeds from the cotton fiber was slow, manual work. In 1793 American **Eli Whitney** invented the cotton gin, a machine that could clean much more cotton in a day than hand laborers could. With Whitney's invention, the southern United States became the cotton-producing center of the world. As production soared, so did the profits made by using slave labor to plant and pick cotton. Thus, the cotton gin had the unintended side effect of helping to expand slavery in the United States.

✔ **READING CHECK: Analyzing Information** Why were there so many new inventions in the textile industry in such a short period of time?

Steam Engines, Iron, and Steel

Early machines in the Industrial Revolution were driven by waterpower. Although much better than human, animal, and wind power, waterpower had its drawbacks. A factory had to be located on a stream or river, preferably next to a waterfall or dam. Often this site was not near raw materials, a labor supply, overland transportation, or markets. Water flow also varied from season to season. A more portable and dependable power supply was needed. It was found in steam.

The power of steam had been known since ancient times. Not until about 1712, however, did English engineer Thomas Newcomen harness that power in an engine. The first, crude steam engines were expensive to operate. Scotsman **James Watt** studied and improved on Newcomen's machine. In about 1769 he patented the modern steam engine. British engineer Matthew Boulton financed the first factory to manufacture steam engines. Industry quickly adapted the engine to drive the new spinning and weaving machines. Steam replaced water as industry's major power source.

Iron and steel. More machines meant more iron was needed to make them. From early times, people in Britain had separated iron from its ore using wood or charcoal to fuel the forges. Coal worked even better because it generated more heat. Iron and coal became the two major raw materials of modern industry. Great Britain had plenty of both.

Early steam engines often exploded, however, because iron could not withstand high steam pressure. Steel, an iron alloy, was much stronger, but it was expensive to produce. In the 1850s American William Kelly and Englishman **Henry Bessemer,** working independently, developed what came to be known as the Bessemer process—a cheaper and more efficient method of making steel. The process injected air into molten pig iron, the material from which steel was produced, in order to remove impurities. The injection of air also increased the temperature at which the conversion of pig iron into steel took place. This prevented the molten metal from solidifying during production.

✔ **READING CHECK: Identifying Cause and Effect** How did developments in the textile industry result in inventions in steelmaking?

Other Industrialization

British manufacturers applied new technology to other industries. Production of shoes, clothing, ammunition, and furniture was mechanized. Machines were used for printing, papermaking, lumber and food processing, and making other machines. Some new processes had important by-products. Gases released from coal were burned to give light. In the 1810s London was one of the first cities to burn gas in street lamps. By the 1850s gaslight was common in city streets.

American Charles Goodyear discovered how to make rubber less sticky. This **vulcanization** process is the basis of the modern rubber industry. The oil industry began around the mid-1800s, when people began using crude oil to make paraffin for candles, lubricating oil for machinery, and kerosene for lighting and heating.

✔ **READING CHECK: Drawing Conclusions** What were several ways in which industrialization spread?

Holt Researcher

go.hrw.com

KEYWORD: Holt Researcher

FreeFind: James Watt

After reading more about James Watt on the Holt Researcher, write a summary of his contributions to science and technology.

A Bessemer furnace changed molten iron into steel by forcing air through the iron to burn away carbon and other impurities.

This scene of steamboats on the Mississippi River was produced in the mid-1800s.

Holt Researcher

go.hrw.com

KEYWORD: Holt Researcher

FreeFind: Robert Fulton

After reading more about Robert Fulton on the Holt Researcher, create a time line of how he developed his inventions and what impact they had on society.

Transportation

Transportation had changed little between the Middle Ages and the beginning of the Industrial Revolution. Stagecoaches, packhorses, and heavy, clumsy horse-drawn wagons were common. As industrial production increased, factories needed more raw materials and finished goods had to reach markets quickly. Improvements such as stone-topped roadways were built. Canals were dug to link rivers. The newer canals had locks to regulate the level of water.

Watt's steam engine was used to speed transportation, both on land and water. In about 1814 English engineer George Stephenson perfected a steam locomotive that ran on rails. About 15 years later, a locomotive pulled a line of railway cars from Liverpool to Manchester. Railways soon were being built all over the world.

American engineer **Robert Fulton** was the first to build a profitable steamboat. In 1808 his boat, the *Clermont*, began regular trips on the Hudson River between New York City and Albany. Soon steamboats appeared on rivers and lakes all over the world. In the 1830s a steam-powered ship crossed the Atlantic Ocean. The voyage took about 17 days, less than half the time of a sailing ship. Soon Samuel Cunard of Great Britain was providing regular steamboat service across the Atlantic. Ships built of iron and steel now moved goods all over the world quickly and cheaply.

✔ **READING CHECK: Making Generalizations** What invention stimulated the rapid improvement of transportation around the world?

The Communications Revolution

Early inventions such as the steam engine were mainly the work of amateur engineers. In communications technology, however, scientific research played a more important role.

Prior to the 1800s people may have known that electricity and magnetism were related, but they had not found a practical use for this knowledge. Then in about 1800 Italian scientist Alessandro Volta built the first battery, providing a steady flow of electric current for the first time. In the 1820s André Ampère of France worked out principles governing the magnetic effect of electricity. American **Samuel Morse** put this work to practical use. Morse sent an electric current through a wire, causing a machine at the other end to click. By about 1838 Morse had worked out a system of dots and dashes—the Morse code—by which these clicks could be translated into letters of the alphabet. By 1844 Morse's invention, the telegraph, had become a practical communications device. Telegraph wires soon stretched across continents and oceans, spreading ideas at the speed of electricity.

✔ **READING CHECK: Contrasting** What was a major difference between new inventions in textiles and transportation and new inventions in communication?

Effects of Industrialization on Lancashire

Industrialization in Great Britain had many effects. The economic and social life of some regions of the country were forever changed by new technologies and industries. Lancashire County in northwest England experienced some of the greatest change. Anchored by the manufacturing towns of Manchester and Liverpool, Lancashire became a major industrial center.

Identifying the causes of historical events and determining their effects helps us understand history. Historical events usually have several causes. Underlying causes are long term. Immediate causes lead directly to the event. Cause-and-effect relationships can be shown in many different kinds of diagrams including concept maps, sequences, and webs.

Lancashire County and Surrounding Areas, c. 1850s

- Canal
- Railroad
- CF Cotton factories
- Coalfield

0 10 20 Miles
0 10 20 Kilometers
Lambert Conformal Conic Projection

Skills Reminder

To determine cause and effect, identify the focus of your study—for example, the outcome of an election. This is the effect in question. Then determine the underlying, or most basic, causes. For example, how satisfied were voters with the present office holder? Next, identify the immediate causes—those occurring near at hand. For example, did the weather affect who voted? Form a conclusion about the relative importance of the various causes you have identified.

Skills Practice

Study the information above.

❶ What factors of physical geography may have been underlying causes of industrial development in Lancashire County?

❷ What were the probable immediate causes of railroad and canal construction in Lancashire County?

❸ Draw a diagram that summarizes the probable short-term and long-term causes and effects of industrialization in Lancashire County.

At Promontory Point, Utah, on May 10, 1869, the Union Pacific and Central Pacific railroads met, joining East Coast to West.

The Spread of Industry

Industrial growth in other European countries lagged behind Great Britain. They had not developed their raw materials or markets for their products. The wars following the French Revolution also disrupted their economies.

The French government helped local industry by imposing high tariffs on foreign goods. They also encouraged the building of railroads. However, in the 1800s, most French workers were still farmers and peasants. Germany did not have a central government to aid industrial growth. Not until the 1870s did German industrialization approach that of Great Britain.

The United States had both a strong central government and rich natural resources. It also had a rapidly increasing population. British inventions and methods were adopted in the United States. Inventions like the cotton gin and mechanical reaper boosted agricultural production. Canals and railroads were built, and the steel and machinery industries boomed. By 1869 a railroad stretched from the East Coast to the West Coast. America had joined the Industrial Revolution.

✔ **READING CHECK: Sequencing** List some of the principal developments that led to industrialization in the United States.

SECTION 1 REVIEW

1. **Define** and explain the significance:
   enclosure movement
   crop rotation
   Industrial Revolution
   factors of production
   mechanization
   factory system
   vulcanization

2. **Identify** and explain the significance:
   Jethro Tull
   Richard Arkwright
   Eli Whitney
   James Watt
   Henry Bessemer
   Robert Fulton
   Samuel Morse

3. **Categorizing** Copy the web diagram below. In each box, list some of the advances made during the Industrial Revolution.

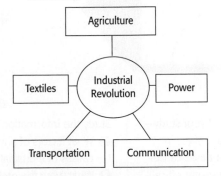

Agriculture

Textiles — Industrial Revolution — Power

Transportation — Communication

4. **Finding the Main Idea**
   a. Which inventions of the late 1600s and the 1700s do you think had the greatest influence on industrialization? Why?
   b. Why was Great Britain an ideal place for the start of the Industrial Revolution?

5. **Writing and Critical Thinking**
   Analyzing Information Imagine that you are a journalist on the staff of a magazine for young people. Write a 150-word article explaining the factors of production that influenced the start of the Industrial Revolution.
   Consider:
   • the great variety of resources included in the factors of production: land, capital, and labor
   • how the absence or shortage of some of these resources would have made industrialization more difficult

Homework Practice Online
go.
hrw
.com
keyword: SH3 HP13

The Factory System

The Main Idea
New lifestyles and living conditions grew out of the Industrial Revolution as society began to change.

The Story Continues *During the 1700s new factory jobs lured thousands of British farm workers to the cities. Many critics feared that urban growth and changing labor patterns would create dangerous social injustice. In 1848 John Stuart Mill wrote, "[Industrialization has] enabled a greater proportion [of workers] to live the same life of drudgery and imprisonment and an increased number of manufacturers and others to make fortunes."*

How Machines Affected Work

The introduction of steam-powered machinery made work easier to do. Instead of spending several years as an apprentice learning a trade, a person could learn to perform a task or operate a machine in a few days.

Employers now wanted people who could learn a few simple tasks. They soon discovered that women and children could operate machines as efficiently as men. Employers preferred to hire young men and women rather than older, skilled people. Young people did not have set working habits and did not expect high wages. Women and children would work for lower wages than men. As a result the early textile factories employed mainly children and young women.

As machines became more widely used, older, skilled workers often found themselves unemployed. Factories no longer needed their abilities as weavers or spinners and would not hire them for simpler work. To make up for their lost income, many of these people sent their children to look for work in textile factories. They themselves were reduced to looking for odd jobs in cities or on farms.

✔ **READING CHECK: Finding the Main Idea** How did the production of goods change as work became mechanized?

The Wage System

The factory system differed significantly from the domestic system. Under the domestic system, workers had usually worked unsupervised in their homes. They turned over finished products, such as thread or cloth, perhaps once a week, and were paid for the number of items completed. In factories, instead of working on a product from beginning to end, each worker performed only a small part of the entire job. Under the factory system, dozens or hundreds of laborers worked in the same room under the watchful eyes of supervisors. Everyone was employed by the factory owners. The owners paid their workers wages based on the number of hours worked or the amount of goods produced.

Several factors determined workers' wages. First and foremost, factory owners wanted to produce goods as cheaply as possible. Thus employers set wages in relation to other costs of production. For example, if the cost of land or capital increased, the owners lowered wages.

Thonet Rocker

Michael Thonet, a cabinet-maker living in Austria in the mid-1800s, invented a process that revolutionized furniture making. He made the bentwood rocker shown here. Thonet bent solid wood by steaming it and clamping a thin strip of steel along one side. Complex joining and carving were no longer needed. Thonet was able to hire local people rather than costly artisans. By 1870 Thonet's factory was making about 1,300 pieces of furniture a day. With six-day workweeks, this was an incredible 400,000 pieces a year.

Understanding Science and Technology

What was the technological significance of the Thonet rocker?

In addition, the number of workers available affected wages. An oversupply of workers brought wages down. By the same token, wages often rose when there were not enough workers to do a particular job.

Also, wages often depended on what people could expect to earn at other kinds of work. For example, early employers in textile factories wanted to attract young women as workers. Therefore they offered a wage higher than what women could earn as household servants.

Wages, moreover, were higher for men than for women. For example, in cotton mills and the London clothing trades in Great Britain, men were paid as much as twice what women earned. It was generally thought that women went to work merely to add "a little something" to their family's income. In reality, however, a woman was sometimes the only wage earner for her family.

Factory workers acquired skills and were paid accordingly. However, they had little else to show for their work. They did not own their tools or equipment, as domestic workers had. Furthermore, there were few opportunities for workers to advance within the factory.

✔ **READING CHECK: Summarizing** What four factors generally determined a factory worker's wages?

The Lives of Factory Workers

Factory workers had many rules to follow. They had to arrive at the factory on time. They could eat or take breaks only at set times. They could leave only with permission. They worked whether it was hot or cold, summer or winter, day or night. Breaking any rules could result in heavy fines, pay cuts, or even job loss.

Factories were cold and damp in winter and steamy in summer. Sanitary facilities were poor. Early machines had no safety devices, so accidents occurred frequently. Employers provided no compensation if a worker was hurt on the job. Workers spent up to 14 hours a day, six days a week, on the job. They had to adjust their lives to the demands of machines that never needed to rest. Some people may have thought that they were expected to become machines themselves.

Abuses in factories soon scandalized Great Britain. In about 1832 a parliamentary committee investigated working conditions for children. One worker that the committee spoke to was 23-year-old Elizabeth Bently, who began to work in a flax mill when she was six years old. Bently described how she and other children had been forced to work from five in the morning until nine at night and had been beaten for being late or working too slowly. Parliament then passed the Factory Act of 1833, which allowed for factory inspection and enforcement of child labor laws.

Life in workers' homes was not much better than in the factories and mines. Workers lived in shabby apartment buildings called **tenements.** A dozen people might be crammed into a single room. As late as 1840, up to 50,000 workers in Manchester, England, lived in cellars. A popular British novelist of the mid-1800s described the below-ground dwelling in which a fictitious working-class Manchester family lived.

"It was very dark inside. The window-panes many of them were broken and stuffed with rags. . . . the smell was so fetid [foul] as almost to knock the two men [observers who were shocked by these living conditions] down. . . . they began to penetrate the thick darkness of the place, and to see three or four little children rolling on the . . . wet brick floor, through which the stagnant, filthy moisture of the street oozed up."

Elizabeth Gaskell, *Mary Barton*, 1848

Over time, conditions improved slightly as consumer goods became cheaper and more available to workers. Wages increased somewhat, but the lower economic classes continued to suffer.

✔ **READING CHECK: Analyzing Information** What were the living conditions of factory workers like during the Industrial Revolution?

Development of the Middle Class

During the Industrial Revolution, the balance of economic and political power shifted from agriculture to manufacturing. As industries and cities grew, a new, well-educated middle class thrived. It consisted of bankers, manufacturers, merchants, lawyers, doctors, engineers, professors, and their families. Many members of this middle class served in management or other types of administrative jobs that helped keep industries running. Over time, this class—based upon economic standing, rather than upon birth—gained increasing social influence and political power. To many workers, the middle class represented a social stepladder. Each generation hoped that the next one would be able to rise a rung higher than they had been. As the middle class expanded, many families were able to do just that.

Lifestyles and living conditions at the lower levels of the middle class often differed very little from those of working-class people. As the finances of middle-class families improved, their lifestyles began to reflect their rising social status. Many middle-class families could afford to live in larger homes and less-crowded neighborhoods. Middle-class men wore business suits and women wore frills and lace. Many people in the upper tiers of the middle class owned property, hired servants, and ate well. Their children attended good schools, where they were trained for higher-level jobs. Middle-class children might also inherit money and social position from their parents. Aristocratic government leaders sought the advice of middle-class economists. Soon government leaders became as concerned about the future of industry as they were about agriculture.

✔ **READING CHECK: Drawing Inferences** What factors led to the rise of the middle class?

YOUNG PEOPLE IN HISTORY

Young Factory Workers
For many people in industrial England, working for a living began at an early age. Children as young as six worked in factories for 12 to 16 hours a day, six days a week. At lunchtime, children often ate food covered with factory dust. In general, factory conditions for children in industrializing England were brutal and often hazardous. **What were working conditions like for the youngest factory workers?**

Holt Researcher go.hrw.com

go.hrw.com
KEYWORD: Holt Researcher
FreeFind: Elizabeth Gaskell
After reading more about Elizabeth Gaskell on the Holt Researcher, assess how her writings about the working class might have affected views of factory life by middle-class readers.

The Singer Automatic
LATEST AND BEST

THE SINGER MANUFACTURING CO.

Inventions like the sewing machine eased work for many women.

Effect of Industrialization on Women's Lives

Throughout history, women had worked hard. They worked in the fields, spun yarn, made clothing, and prepared meals. They produced goods for sale and worked with their husbands in family businesses. As the Industrial Revolution moved production into factories, many working families moved to cities. As city dwellers, many women no longer had the resources or the need to grow food or make clothing.

As the need for farm labor decreased due to improved farming methods and equipment, some women took jobs in textile mills or factories. Many young women, however, continued to work at a traditional woman's job—domestic service. Moving to the cities, they found jobs with middle- and upper-class families, who hired them as maids, cooks, and nannies for their children. They lived with the families and were provided food and shelter. Some of these women later took jobs in shops or factories.

Many middle-class families had enough money so that women did not need to work outside the home. They stayed at home and, often with hired help, cleaned, cooked, and took care of the children. It was often said that a woman's nature equipped her only for these tasks. In the mid-1800s, however, middle-class women began speaking out for roles outside the home.

For some women a life outside the home meant independence. It was also a way to earn a living. During the late 1800s, jobs as nurses, secretaries, and telephone operators opened up to women. Women's colleges were founded to improve their educational levels. With the growth of public schools, many women became teachers. By the end of the 1800s, most elementary school teachers were women.

✔ **READING CHECK: Identifying Points of View** What might each of the following groups have thought about women's roles in society: working-class men, working-class women, middle-class men, middle-class women?

SECTION 2 REVIEW

1. **Define** and explain the significance:
   tenements

2. **Contrasting** Copy the table below. List and contrast the ways in which the rise of the factory system affected each of these groups.

Factory System		
Working-class children	Middle-class families	Women

3. **Finding the Main Idea**
   a. How might some of the changes that affected women in the 1800s have affected the roles that women play in society today?
   b. What factors led to the increased hiring of women and children in factories?

4. **Writing and Critical Thinking**
   Summarizing Choose a well-known melody that you think suits the conditions of early factories. Write lyrics for the music expressing the feelings of a young person working in one of those factories.
   Consider:
   • details of the worker's daily life
   • what the future might hold for them

go.hrw.com **Homework Practice Online**
keyword: SH3 HP13

New Methods and Business Organizations

The Main Idea
Improved production methods helped to speed industrialization during the late 1800s.

The Story Continues *The 1800s were marked by new inventions and new methods of production and distribution. At the same time, new approaches to organizing businesses led to great wealth for some and to poverty for others. Some viewed the gulf between rich and poor as a danger, while others argued that, "The price which society pays for the law of competition . . . is . . . great; but the advantages of this law are . . . greater still, for it is to this law that we owe our wonderful material development . . . ."*

Capitalism and Changing Production Methods

The late 1800s in western Europe and the United States were characterized by a growing spirit of individual enterprise that we know today as capitalism. The term **capitalism** describes an economic system in which individuals or corporations, rather than governments, control the factors of production. In a capitalist system, businesses and the means of production are privately owned and operated. Before the Industrial Revolution, most capitalists were merchants who bought and sold goods. This was called **commercial capitalism.** During the Industrial Revolution, capitalists became more involved in producing and manufacturing goods. This was called **industrial capitalism.**

Division of labor and interchangeable parts. Industrialization changed the way people worked. Factory owners divided the manufacturing process into steps. They hired unskilled labor and assigned a step to each worker. This division of labor increased production. The use of machines in many of the steps helped the workers produce more in a shorter time. The lowered cost of production made more profit for the owners.

This painting of a factory shows one artist's view of the Industrial Revolution.

American inventor Eli Whitney used division of labor to make muskets in the late 1700s. Previously, an entire gun was made by skilled artisans. Each gun was slightly different. If a part broke, a new one had to be handmade. Whitney invented machines that made parts that were all alike. Unskilled workers could now turn out identical, **interchangeable parts.** Whitney's system resulted in speedy production of inexpensive muskets that could be easily repaired. Other factory owners soon saw the benefit of interchangeable parts. They adopted the idea for their own products.

The assembly line. The system of producing large numbers of identical items is known as **mass production.** Division of labor, the use of interchangeable parts, and an assembly line are essential for mass production. Into the 1800s each part of an item was made in a different location in the factory. All the parts were brought together and assembled at a single location. Manufacturers then devised the assembly line, by which the parts were carried from worker to worker. Each worker performed a certain task on the part. This saved time and energy. The number of times per hour that a worker could perform a task increased.

Henry Ford saw a great potential in the assembly line. He used a conveyor belt to carry automobile frames from one worker to the next. Each worker added one or more of the numerous parts in the finished automobile. By using the assembly line for the production of automobiles, he founded one of the largest industries in the world.

American and European industrialists began to mass-produce many other items, such as clothing, furniture, and machinery. By reducing production costs, manufacturers were able to lower prices. More and more people could afford to buy a greater variety of goods and enjoy a higher standard of living.

✔ **READING CHECK: Making Generalizations** How did changes in production methods lead to an improved standard of living?

Assembly line This image shows a Ford assembly line in the early 1900s. *How do you think the assembly line might have made work easier for these Ford employees?*

Rise of the Corporation

Before the Industrial Revolution, most businesses were very small. A business owned and run by just one person was called a sole proprietorship. One owned and run by two or more people was called a partnership. Owners of both types of businesses were free to make business decisions. Each owner was personally responsible, however, for any debts the business had. In addition, sole proprietorships and partnerships usually remain small. Small companies with few workers typically cannot afford mass-production methods or the machinery necessary for large-scale production.

As businesses grew during the 1800s, another form of business organization became common. Businesses formed groups called **corporations** and allowed people to buy stock in their companies. This made it much easier to raise the money needed to run and expand a business. Stockholders elected directors to run the corporation. They shared in its profits, depending on how many shares of stock they owned. A stockholder's financial responsibility was limited to the amount he or she had invested. This made corporations attractive to investors. Banks played an increasingly important role in financing corporations. By the late 1800s some corporations had become very large and powerful. In 1901 American financier **J. P. Morgan** founded the United States Steel Company, one of the first of many billion-dollar corporations.

Increasing the size of a corporation did not necessarily increase its profits, however. To take advantage of mass production, factories attempted to work at full capacity. Sometimes they produced more goods than they could sell. Competition for customers was very keen between corporations making the same product. Cutting prices to sell more products could mean smaller profits. Smaller businesses often sold out to larger ones or even failed.

As a result, although the size of individual corporations increased steadily, the number of individual corporations in some industries decreased. Sometimes a corporation gained almost complete control of the production or sale of a single good or service. This was called a **monopoly.** During the late 1800s and the early 1900s, several gigantic corporations in the United States grew into monopolies or near-monopolies.

By 1900 several giant corporations in Germany had combined to control every stage of entire industries. They did this in the steel industry, for example, by owning coal and iron mines, steel mills, and factories. Such business combinations were known as **cartels.** French novelist Émile Zola described the growing size and complexity of such organizations in a dialogue in which one character describes his investment in a coal-mining cartel to another character.

Steel Production in the United States, 1865–1895

Tons (in millions)

Source: *Historical Statistics of the United States*

Interpreting the Graph

Steel production changed dramatically in the late 1800s. *How might trends in steel production have affected investment in J.P. Morgan's company?*

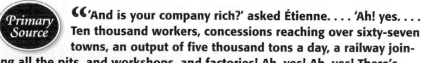

Primary Source

❝'And is your company rich?' asked Étienne.... 'Ah! yes.... Ten thousand workers, concessions reaching over sixty-seven towns, an output of five thousand tons a day, a railway joining all the pits, and workshops, and factories! Ah, yes! Ah, yes! There's money there!'❞

Émile Zola, *Germinal*

Analyzing Primary Sources

Drawing Conclusions What evidence does the character give to show that he has made a wise investment?

✔ **READING CHECK: Comparing** What advantages did corporations have over sole ownerships and partnerships?

This painting from 1879 depicting "bulls" and "bears" in Wall Street is meant to suggest the forces at play in the stock market. Bulls implied a strong market, while bears implied a sluggish one.

Business Cycles

As industry became more and more important, it influenced the economies of many nations. The Industrial Revolution brought alternating periods of prosperity and decline—a pattern that came to be called the **business cycle.**

The success or failure of one industry often affected others. For example, a rising demand for goods increased the demand for machines to make the goods. Factories making machines then required more steel. This increased the need for coal and iron to make steel. To keep up with the cascading demand for goods, more workers were needed. This led to higher wages and increased purchasing power and demand. On the other hand, a falling demand for goods had the opposite result. Industries laid off workers, who, with less money to buy goods, further reduced demand. Many factories might close. When this happened, the entire economy would sink into a **depression.** Eventually demand rebounded, closed factories often reopened, and workers were rehired. The economy then moved back toward prosperity, completing the business cycle.

✔ **READING CHECK: Identifying Cause and Effect** How did the business cycle work after the Industrial Revolution?

SECTION 3 REVIEW

1. **Define** and explain the significance:
   capitalism
   commercial capitalism
   industrial capitalism
   interchangeable parts
   mass production
   corporations
   monopoly
   cartels
   business cycle
   depression

2. **Identify** and explain the significance:
   Henry Ford
   J. P. Morgan

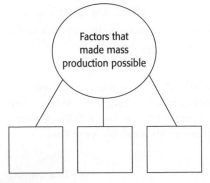

Homework Practice Online
keyword: SH3 HP13

3. **Summarizing** Copy the diagram below. In the boxes, list and describe the three factors that made mass production possible.

Factors that made mass production possible

4. **Finding the Main Idea**

   a. What role did the division of labor play in helping to increase production during the Industrial Revolution?

   b. In what way did the use of the assembly line allow Henry Ford to reach a new level of mass production?

   c. How might monopolies and cartels have affected a nation's economy?

   d. Draw a diagram that shows the steps in the business cycle.

5. **Writing and Critical Thinking**

   Making Generalizations Write an essay explaining how mass production affected people's lives.
   Consider:
   • changes in working conditions
   • changes in economic opportunities
   • changes in what people valued

Living and Working Conditions

READ TO DISCOVER

❶ What were Adam Smith's ideas and how did they affect people's views of industrialism?

❷ Why did reform movements arise?

❸ How did workers try to improve their lives?

DEFINE

free enterprise
laissez-faire
humanitarians
utilitarianism
strike
unions
collective bargaining

IDENTIFY

Adam Smith
Thomas Malthus
David Ricardo
Charles Dickens
Jeremy Bentham
John Stuart Mill

> ### WHY IT MATTERS TODAY
>
> Labor disputes and strikes are common in today's businesses. Use CNN**Student**News.com or other **current event** sources to find examples of a current or recent labor dispute. Record your findings in your journal.
>
> CNN**Student**News.com

The Main Idea
New theories helped shape the Industrial Revolution and its impact upon society.

The Story Continues *As industrialization continued, some thinkers argued that business should be free to grow and change without any sort of government restrictions. Others, however, wanted workers to be granted the political and economic power needed to shape their own lives. British reformer J. R. Stephens held that ". . . every working man in the land has the right to have a good coat . . . a comfortable abode . . . a good dinner . . . and so much wages . . . as should keep him in plenty . . . ."*

Economic Theories

During the Enlightenment of the 1700s, a group of economists called the Physiocrats attacked the ideas of mercantilism. Mercantilism was the economic theory based on the belief that the world contained only a fixed amount of wealth. In order to increase its wealth, mercantilists argued, a country had to take some wealth away from another country. The Physiocrats disagreed with this. They believed that natural laws should be left to govern economic life. Any attempt to interfere with these natural economic laws, they felt, was certain to bring disaster. Scottish economist **Adam Smith** accepted some of the ideas of the Physiocrats. He stated his views in his book *Inquiry into the Nature and Causes of the Wealth of Nations,* which was published in 1776. In this book Smith focused on the creation of wealth, noting the importance of manufacturing as well as agriculture. Today Smith is considered the founder of classical economics.

Laws of economics. Smith reasoned that two natural laws governed all business and economic activity. The first was the law of supply and demand. Smith said that prices and profits depended on both the amount of available goods and the demand for those goods. If an item was scarce and in great demand, people would pay a high price for it and profits would rise. As manufacturers then invested money to make more of the product, supplies would soon exceed the demand.

The result of this supply-and-demand system was tied to Smith's second natural law—the law of competition. He said that as manufacturers compete with each other to sell their products, they must reduce prices. Manufacturers who cut prices too much, however, might lose money and even go out of business. Supply then tends to go down and prices rise. The most efficient manufacturers will survive.

This Scottish penny, bearing the words "Wealth of Nations," is a memorial to Adam Smith.

History Makers Speak

❝Every individual is continually exerting himself to find out the most advantageous employment for whatever capital he can command. It is his own advantage, indeed, and not that of the society, which he has in view. But the study of his own advantage, naturally, or rather necessarily, leads him to prefer that employment which is most advantageous to the society.❞

Adam Smith, *Inquiry into the Nature and Causes of the Wealth of Nations*

Adam Smith was interested in how countries create wealth through industry and farming. He also noted that the division of labor was important to the increase of wealth. In his book, *Inquiry into the Nature and Causes of the Wealth of Nations,* Smith argued that the economy worked best when government involvement was limited. He favored free economic competition. Smith's ideas formed the basis of classical economics. **Why was Adam Smith's work important?**

Laissez-faire economic policies helped transform the small city of Sheffield, England into a major center of industry and production.

Smith also believed that people should be free to engage in whatever business they chose. They should be able to run the business for their greatest advantage. The result would be that investors and owners would make profits, laborers would have jobs, and consumers would buy better goods at lower prices. Smith argued that mercantilist laws and regulations hindered natural economic forces. His system was one of complete **free enterprise.** Many industrialists were attracted to Smith's ideas. In the system he described, economic forces worked automatically and naturally. Free enterprise justified competition unrestricted by laws, regulations, or government controls. Producers were free—in fact, were *required*—to do business solely for their own gain.

✔ **READING CHECK: Making Predictions** What might be some outcomes of implementing Adam Smith's theories about free enterprise?

Malthus and Ricardo. Smith's ideas received strong support from other economists. One was **Thomas Malthus,** an Anglican clergyman who became a professor of economics. In his book *An Essay on the Principle of Population,* published in 1798, Malthus wrote that population increases present the greatest obstacle to human progress. Despite famines, epidemics, and wars, he argued, people still multiply more rapidly than the food supply increases. Thus, Malthus believed that human misery and poverty are inevitable.

British economist **David Ricardo** wrote that working-class poverty is inevitable. In his book *Principles of Political Economy and Taxation,* published in 1817, Ricardo stated that supply and demand determine wages. When labor is plentiful, wages remain low. When labor is scarce, wages rise. As population grows, Ricardo wrote, more and more workers become available, and wages drop. Ricardo's idea became known as the iron law of wages.

Malthus and Ricardo painted a grim picture of workers as inevitably poor and suffering. Not surprisingly, the new social science of economics became known as the "dismal science."

Laissez-faire. The theories of economists such as Smith supported employers, who wanted to buy labor as cheaply as possible. They also wanted government not to meddle in the operations of business. These ideas were summed up in the French phrase **laissez-faire** (leh·say·FAR). This meant "let it be," or "leave things alone."

In Great Britain, craft and merchant guilds had regulated the quality of goods—and in many cases, their prices—until well into the 1800s. Working hours and wages were also controlled. Beginning in the early 1800s, however, most regulations were dropped. Tariffs were eliminated and trade became almost completely unregulated. Laissez-faire economic ideas spread to the rest of Europe and to the United States.

✔ **READING CHECK: Summarizing** What does the theory of laissez-faire say should be done to achieve the most successful economy?

Reformers Arise

Some people argued that businesses could not be left entirely alone. **Humanitarians**—people who work to improve the conditions of others—urged reforms. Ministers preached against the selfish practices of business people. Famous writers of the day made the public aware of the terrible working conditions in mines and factories. English writer **Charles Dickens** used his novels to attack greedy employers. In *David Copperfield*, Dickens described his own wretched childhood experiences. Other writers such as Thomas Carlyle and John Ruskin, and artists such as Gustave Doré, criticized society's obsession with money and neglect of spiritual values.

This illustration from an early edition of Dickens's **David Copperfield** *gives a view of urban life in Great Britain during the Industrial Revolution.*

Many people argued that laws were needed to regulate work hours and set basic standards for wages and working conditions. They insisted such laws would not interfere with the economy.

In Great Britain, some reformers adopted the theory of **utilitarianism** put forth by philosopher **Jeremy Bentham**. Bentham argued that a law was useful, and therefore good, if it led to "the greatest happiness of the greatest number" of people. He believed that people should be educated so that they could decide what things were good for them or would make them happy. Bentham and his followers also called for reform of the nation's justice and prison system.

English philosopher **John Stuart Mill** also believed that a government should work for the good of all its citizens. He rejected economic systems that left workers trapped in poverty. Mill called for government to protect working children and to improve housing and factory conditions. Mill argued for full democracy and for equality for all men and women, regardless of their social class or economic power. In about 1869 he wrote *On the Subjection of Women*, a ground-breaking call for support of women's rights. Mill believed that government should promote education and guarantee individual liberty. This included the right to think as one pleased and to freely express one's views. In about 1861 Mill wrote that all human beings "have equal need of a voice in [government] to secure their share of its benefits."

✔ **READING CHECK: Identifying Cause and Effect** Why would improving education and guaranteeing individual liberty help the working class?

Child labor Young people made up a large part of the labor force in many areas. Many early reforms centered on children. *What reforms are these young workers demanding?*

Early Reform Laws

Working conditions, particularly for women and children, greatly troubled the British public. Parliament began reform efforts with the Factory Act of 1802, which shortened hours and improved conditions for children working in cotton mills. It proved ineffective, however, because it had no means of enforcement. The Factory Act of 1833 corrected this omission and extended the law to all textile mills.

The laws prohibited mills from employing children under 9 years of age. Children between the ages of 9 and 13 could work no more than 8 hours a day, 6 days a week. Older children could work no more than 12 hours a day. A later law said coal mines could not employ any women or any children under the age of 10. A great advance came with the Ten Hours Act in 1847, which set a 10-hour working day for women and for children under the age of 18. Because most workers were women and children, factory owners extended the 10-hour day to everyone. The laws were poorly enforced, however, and conditions remained harsh. Moreover, the reform laws did nothing to improve wages. That would have to be up to the workers themselves.

✔ **READING CHECK: Drawing Inferences** Why did children in the 1800s work long hours in factories when the same is not true today?

Collective Action

To improve their own lives, many workers banded together to demand reform. Such efforts are known as collective action.

Strikes. Workers protested working conditions and low wages by refusing to work. When a large group of workers stops working, it is called a **strike.** Workers often made a list of their demands, refusing to work until the demands were met. Employers sometimes gave in to the workers. Other times they fired the workers and hired new ones. Often they waited until economic needs forced the strikers to return to work.

Numerous strikes took place in industrial countries during the 1800s. The workers usually demanded higher wages and better working conditions. Some strikes began over wages but spread to general working and living conditions of the working class. Some strike leaders called for reorganizing society to end the differences between rich and poor. Strikes grew to large protest movements in the textile and mining areas of England, France, and eastern Europe. These demonstrations often were put down when governments used troops to arrest protesting workers.

Unions. Workers felt that their protests would be more successful if they were organized. They began to form associations called **unions.** These unions would collect dues from members and then use that money to pay workers if they went on strike. The unions planned actions and combined the demands of different kinds of workers in the same factory.

This Italian painting entitled The Human Tide *depicts workers banding together to voice their protests.*

Workers' associations were considered illegal by British, French, and German law. When workers organized anyway, the British Parliament passed the Combination Acts of 1799 and 1800. These laws said that workers who united to demand higher wages, shorter hours, and better working conditions could be imprisoned.

Eventually workers began to make some progress. In about 1825 the Combination Acts were repealed, and in the 1870s Parliament passed laws legalizing strikes. Now unions had real power. In some cases, factory owners began to acknowledge that unions spoke for all the workers. Management and union representatives began to discuss wages, hours, and working conditions. Agreements were written into contracts lasting for a fixed period of time. This process of negotiation is called **collective bargaining.**

✔ **READING CHECK: Finding the Main Idea** How were workers able to get higher wages and better working conditions by forming unions?

SECTION 4 REVIEW

1. **Define** and explain the significance:
   free enterprise
   laissez-faire
   humanitarians
   utilitarianism
   strike
   unions
   collective bargaining

2. **Identify** and explain the significance:
   Adam Smith
   Thomas Malthus
   David Ricardo
   Charles Dickens
   Jeremy Bentham
   John Stuart Mill

Homework Practice Online
keyword: SH3 HP13

3. **Problem Solving** Copy the web diagram below. Fill in the top boxes by listing what employers and workers wanted regarding wages and working conditions. Then fill in the compromise box by suggesting how agreements could have been reached through collective bargaining.

What employers wanted

What workers wanted

Compromise

4. **Finding the Main Idea**
   a. How did Adam Smith's ideas influence employers' treatment of workers?
   b. Why was it easier for the government to pass laws about working hours than about wages?

5. **Writing and Critical Thinking**
   Evaluating Write a brief article in which you identify the strong and weak points in the ideas of economist Adam Smith or reformer Jeremy Bentham.
   Consider:
   • the advantages and disadvantages of allowing business and the economy to go unregulated
   • the advantages and disadvantages of government trying to create conditions to ensure justice for workers

Socialism

READ TO DISCOVER

❶ What type of society did early socialists want to establish?

❷ How did Robert Owen put his socialist beliefs into action?

❸ What did Karl Marx believe would happen to the capitalist world of the 1800s?

❹ What were some competing ideas that arose out of Marxism?

DEFINE

means of production
socialism
utopian socialists
proletariat
communism
democratic socialism

IDENTIFY

Robert Owen
Karl Marx
Friedrich Engels

▶ **WHY IT MATTERS TODAY**

Some countries of the world have socialist governments. Use CNN student News.com or other **current event** sources to find examples of socialist countries. Record your findings in your journal.

The Main Idea
The Industrial Revolution gave rise to new ideas about economic, political, and social justice.

The Story Continues *As the Industrial Revolution progressed, a growing number of people became concerned with economic and social injustice. Many believed that the interests and needs of employers naturally conflicted with those of workers. As early as 1798, one writer noted that: "The increasing wealth of the nation has had little or no tendency to better the conditions of the labouring poor." As industrialization continued, demands for reform and justice based upon the new realities of the marketplace became stronger.*

Socialism

In the economy that resulted from the Industrial Revolution, a few people became enormously rich. Most, however, remained poor, including the workers whose labor drove the economy. This uneven distribution of wealth disturbed many people. Some reformers became convinced that laissez-faire capitalism was not the best economic system. They argued that laws could not do enough to remedy inequalities. The only way to distribute wealth more evenly, they felt, was to change the ownership and operation of the means of production. The **means of production** include the capital and equipment used to produce and exchange goods—for example, land, railroads, mines, factories, stores, banks, and machines.

Some of these reformers advocated a political and economic system called **socialism.** Under socialism, governments own the means of production and operate them

The political cartoon above satirizes German leader Otto von Bismarck, who passed a law trying to contain socialism. At right is a poster urging workers of the world to unite under international socialism.

for the benefit of all people, rich or poor. These reformers, called socialists, wanted to establish an economic system that would do away with the profit motive and competition. They believed everyone, not just capitalists and factory owners, had a right to share in the profits.

Utopian socialists. Early socialists believed that people could live peacefully with each other in small cooperative settlements in which everyone would work for the common good. They would own all the means of production in common and share the products. Socialists worked out plans for model towns and encouraged people to set them up. Some were modeled after the ideal community described in 1516 in Sir Thomas More's *Utopia*. For this reason, early socialists were sometimes called **utopian socialists.**

✔ **READING CHECK: Contrasting** How did socialism differ from capitalism?

Owen. In Great Britain, the most influential utopian socialist was **Robert Owen,** who lived from 1771 to 1858. He quit school at age 10 and went to work. By 19, he managed a large cotton mill and later purchased a spinning mill. In 1814 Owen entered a partnership with Jeremy Bentham.

Owen believed that people who lived in a good environment would stop acting selfishly. He felt responsible for his workers and spent much time and money to make their lives happier and more secure. Owen built good homes for them, set up schools for their children, and made inexpensive food and clothing available. Owen believed, however, that workers should not be dependent on their employers. He encouraged them to form unions. He proposed the formation of "villages of cooperation" in which the unemployed would be self-supporting instead of relying on aid. From 1825 to about 1829 Owen lived in the United States, where he tried unsuccessfully to set up cooperative communities run along socialist lines. Only later in the 1800s and early 1900s did the cooperative movement spread in Europe and America.

✔ **READING CHECK: Drawing Conclusions** What do you think Owen hoped to gain by making his employees' lives more secure?

The Theories of Karl Marx

Some thinkers, such as **Karl Marx,** believed that utopian socialism was impractical. They said that the entire capitalist system should be destroyed. Marx believed that all great changes in history had come from changes in economic conditions. With fellow German **Friedrich Engels,** Marx published *The Communist Manifesto* in 1848. Marx and Engels summed up their view of human history in one sentence: "The history of all hitherto existing society is the history of class struggles." Marx and Engels went on to support their view:

❝Free man and slave, patrician and plebeian, lord and serf, guild master and journeyman, in a word, oppressor and oppressed, stood in constant opposition to one another, carried on an uninterrupted, now hidden, now open fight, a fight that each time ended either in a revolutionary reconstitution of society at large or in the common ruin of the contending classes.❞

Karl Marx and Friedrich Engels, *The Communist Manifesto,* 1848

HISTORY MAKER

Karl Marx (1818–1883)

As a young man, Karl Marx became involved with socialist political groups in Germany and France. Marx's radical views and his attacks on government led to his expulsion from several European countries. He eventually settled in London and lived there the rest of his life.

Marx believed that economics was central to human life. He dreamed of a revolution in which the workers of the world would unite to gain political power. Marx's theories inspired the communist movements of the 1900s. **What did Marx hope for?**

Karl Marx predicted that socialist revolutionaries would clash violently with government forces. This 1905 painting shows the aftermath of one such conflict.

Marx said that each stage of history involved inequality, and therefore struggle, between those who owned property and those who did not. In the capitalist stage of the 1800s, for example, the struggle existed between the owners, or bourgeoisie, and the working class, or **proletariat.** Marx argued that all wealth is created by labor. Under capitalism, however, labor receives only a small fraction of the wealth it creates. Most of the wealth goes to the owners in the form of profits. As a result of this unequal distribution of wealth, Marx thought the time would soon come when society would divide into two classes—a few capitalists and a vast mass of workers. Marx predicted that the capitalists would continue to amass wealth while driving the proletariat deeper and deeper into poverty. Finally, the proletariat in the most advanced and industrialized nations would unite and seize power in a socialist revolution.

At first the revolutionaries would have to control the government by force, Marx said, because many people would not accept socialism. He called this the "dictatorship of the proletariat." Eventually, after people learned the benefits of working together cooperatively, the state would "wither away." Marx called this truly classless society "pure communism." He believed it was the inevitable outcome of human history. In this society, Marx believed, each person would contribute what he or she could, and would receive what he or she needed. Marx said, "From each according to his abilities, to each according to his needs."

✔ **READING CHECK: Analyzing Information** What do you think Marx meant when he said that all wealth was created by labor?

Variations of Socialism

In the mid-1800s socialists in several European countries formed political parties. They were influenced by the ideas of Marx and Engels. Marxist socialists often believed that violent revolution was required to get rid of capitalism. They believed this was probably the only way to establish governments that owned the means of production and controlled all economic planning. Today, this economic and political system is called authoritarian socialism, or **communism.**

Another group of socialists, though influenced by Marx, believed that socialism could develop gradually through education and democratic forms of government. These moderate socialists believed that when enough people became educated about socialism, they would elect socialist representatives to their government. Then government would take over the means of production peacefully. The owners would be paid for their property and government would operate the means of production in the interests of all people. Today this type of socialism is called **democratic socialism.** Under democratic socialism, unlike communism, the people retain partial control over economic planning through the election of government officials. Individuals may own private property, but the government owns at least some of the means of production. The ideas of democratic socialism went on to influence many governments in northern and western Europe.

Marx believed that workers had to unite to fight capitalism successfully. During the 1800s several organizations for workers emerged. In 1864 Marx helped establish the International Working Men's Association, or First International. This organization disbanded, however, in 1876. A Second International was formed in 1889, after Marx's death. Torn by disagreements between moderate and radical socialists, the Second International survived only into the early 1900s. However, elsewhere, particularly in Russia, Marx's ideas would go on to have profound effects.

✔ **READING CHECK: Contrasting** How did democratic socialism differ from communism?

Friedrich Engels's socialist activism is evidenced by his membership in the International Working Men's Association.

SECTION 5 REVIEW

1. **Define** and explain the significance:
   means of production
   socialism
   utopian socialists
   proletariat
   communism
   democratic socialism

2. **Identify** and explain the significance:
   Robert Owen
   Karl Marx
   Friedrich Engels

3. **Evaluating** Copy the table below. Complete the table by listing the effects of socialism on each sector of society.

Working people	Business or factory owners	Factors of production	Government

4. **Finding the Main Idea**
   a. According to Karl Marx, what causes conflict within a society?
   b. How did the political and economic system of communism develop?

5. **Writing and Critical Thinking**
   Comparing Write a brief comparison of Marxist socialism with moderate socialism.
   Consider:
   • how each wanted to change capitalism to socialism
   • what effects each might have on the rights of individuals
   • how each proposed to solve the problems of unequal distribution of wealth

go. hrw .com Homework Practice Online
keyword: SH3 HP13

CHAPTER 13 Review

Creating a Time Line

Copy the time line below onto a sheet of paper. Complete the time line by filling in the events, individuals, and dates from the chapter that you think were significant. Pick three events and explain why you think they were significant.

1600   **1776**   **1901**

Writing a Summary

Using standard grammar, spelling, sentence structure, and punctuation, write an overview of the events in the chapter.

Identifying People and Ideas

Identify the following terms or individuals and explain their significance:

1. Industrial Revolution
2. factors of production
3. James Watt
4. Robert Fulton
5. capitalism
6. mass production
7. laissez-faire
8. Adam Smith
9. socialism
10. Karl Marx

Understanding Main Ideas

Section 1 *(pp. 352–358)*

Origins of the Industrial Revolution

1. What were some of the important inventions and scientific discoveries of the Industrial Revolution?

Section 2 *(pp. 359–362)*

The Factory System

2. How did the lives of women change during the Industrial Revolution?

Section 3 *(pp. 363–366)*

New Methods and Business Organizations

3. How did methods of production change during the Industrial Revolution?

Section 4 *(pp. 367–371)*

Living and Working Conditions

4. What role did unions play in improving wages and working conditions?

Section 5 *(pp. 372–375)*

Socialism

5. What led to the development of socialism and communism?

Reviewing Themes

1. **Science, Technology & Society** How did the Industrial Revolution influence other areas of society?
2. **Citizenship** How did the distribution of wealth affect the roles that people played in society?
3. **Economics** How did the needs of different groups influence the development of economics?

Thinking Critically

1. **Sequencing** Trace the events leading to the mechanization of the textile industry.
2. **Drawing Inferences** What factors influenced the rise of capitalism?
3. **Making Generalizations** What factors forced employers to improve wages and working conditions?
4. **Comparing and Contrasting** Compare and contrast capitalist and socialist economies.

Writing About History

Evaluating American companies sometimes have goods assembled in other countries in order to cut their production costs. American workers protest that this is unfair to them. Use a problem-solving and decision-making process to decide what, if any, action you believe the government should take to address these issues. Write an editorial arguing for that action. Use the following chart to organize your thoughts before you begin writing.

Possible government action	Effect on businesses	Effect on consumers	Effect on workers
No action			
Working with other governments			
Tariffs or subsidies			
Other			

Building Social Studies Skills

Using Artifacts as Historical Evidence

Study the photograph and then answer the questions below.

Hand-cranked sewing machine from the 1850s

1. Which of the following most accurately describes the historical significance of this artifact?

   a. The artifact probably represents a significant technological advance.

   b. The artifact was probably too cumbersome to be used effectively.

   c. The artifact proves that electrical power was available to some as early as the 1850s.

   d. The existence of this artifact proves that sewing machines were widely used during the 1850s.

2. What can you infer about life in the 1850s from this artifact? Give specific examples.

Distinguishing Fact from Opinion

Read the following quote from the American industrialist, Andrew Carnegie. Then answer the questions.

> "This, then, is held to be the duty of the man of wealth: To set an example of modest, unostentatious [simple] living, shunning display or extravagance . . . the man of wealth thus becoming the mere trustee and agent for his poorer brethren . . . . In bestowing [giving] charity, the main consideration should be to help those who will help themselves; . . . to give those who desire to rise the [assistance] by which they may rise."

3. Which of the following statements best describes an opinion held by Carnegie?

   a. Charity should be given by the wealthy to all who are less financially fortunate.

   b. In a capitalist society, one must look out for oneself, without regard for others.

   c. Those who are wealthy owe nothing to their society or to the people around them.

   d. Wealth brings a responsibility to set a positive example for other, less wealthy people.

4. What is your opinion of the views described in this quote? Give specific reasons to support your point of view.

Alternative Assessment

Building Your Portfolio

Link to TODAY

Economics

Adam Smith said that the law of supply and demand and the law of competition automatically determined business and economic trends. Use your textbook, the Internet, and other sources to identify examples of how the two laws operate today. Write an article for a young people's magazine that uses examples of products and services in today's world to explain Smith's ideas.

⁊ internet connect

Internet Activity: go.hrw.com
KEYWORD: SH3 WH13

Choose a topic on the Industrial Revolution to:

- identify the historic origins of capitalism and socialism.
- compare and contrast modern labor unions with early unions.
- write a biography of a female writer who lived and wrote during the Victorian Age.

1800–1928

Life in the Industrial Age

Charles Darwin

1803
Science and Technology
John Dalton outlines a method of "weighing" atoms.

1805
Politics
Thomas Jefferson begins his second term as U.S. president.

1817
Daily Life
Construction begins on the Erie Canal in Buffalo, N.Y.

1831
Science and Technology
Michael Faraday produces an electric current in wire.

1835
Science and Technology
Halley's Comet reappears.

1859
Science and Technology
Charles Darwin publishes *On the Origin of Species by Means of Natural Selection.*

1800	1820	1840	1860

1808
Business and Finance
Captain S. Brown of the British Royal Navy receives a patent for a design of iron anchor chains.

1819
The Arts
Ludwig van Beethoven goes deaf but continues to compose.

1830
Daily Life
Ladies' skirts get shorter, sleeves become wider, hats are very large.

1845
Politics
Texas and Florida become states.

1842
Global Events
Riots and strikes occur in industrial areas of northern England.

1841
Daily Life
P.T. Barnum opens his "American Museum" to exhibit curiosities.

1865
Daily Life
George Pullman introduces the first railroad sleeping cars.

1865
Business and Finance
Thaddeus Lowe invents an ice machine.

1865
The Arts
Yale University opens the first Department of Fine Arts.

Circus producer P. T. Barnum (left) is shown here with Charles Stratton, who became known as Tom Thumb.

Build on What You Know

The Industrial Revolution's effects did not begin and end with inventions. Advances in technology led to new advances in all sciences. New sources of power fueled factories and forever changed the way we live and how we communicate. Cities grew as people from all over the world flocked to the thriving new centers of industry. The world of ideas also moved into the modern age as artists and writers wrestled with the ever-changing industrialized society. In this chapter, you will learn how lifestyles and living standards changed as a result of the Industrial Revolution.

Wilbur Wright pilots a glider in 1902.

1874
The Arts
The first impressionist exhibition takes place in Paris.

1875
Politics
The Public Health Act is passed in Britain.

1876
Science and Technology
Alexander Graham Bell patents the telephone.

1876
The Arts
Mark Twain publishes *The Adventures of Tom Sawyer.*

1893
Daily Life
Americans build the first successful gasoline-powered automobile.

1903
Daily Life
First World Series of baseball is held with more than 100,000 fans in attendance.

1928
Science and Technology
Alexander Fleming discovers penicillin.

1870 | **1890** | **1910** | **1930**

1888
Business and Finance
George Eastman markets a box camera.

1879
Science and Technology
American inventor Thomas Edison produces an electric light bulb that burns for two days.

1905
Science and Technology
Albert Einstein develops the special theory of relativity.

1903
Science and Technology
The Wright Brothers make the first successful airplane flight.

1902
Daily Life
Coal strikes occur in the United States.

c. 1900
The Arts
Ragtime jazz develops in the United States.

The electric light bulb invented by Thomas Edison

1910 Chicago White Sox baseball card

What's Your Opinion?

Themes Journal *Do you **agree** or **disagree** with the following statements? Support your point of view in your journal.*

Science, Technology & Society Advances in one area of the sciences do not affect other fields of study.

Citizenship Equality of education is all that is necessary to make people within a society equal.

Culture Changes in the arts reflect what is happening in society.

Advances in Technology and Communication

The Main Idea
Significant inventions in communications and technology followed the first wave of the Industrial Revolution.

The Story Continues *"The telephone is a curious device that might fairly find place in the magic of Arabian Tales. Of what use is such an invention?"* This was one newspaper reporter's reaction to the invention of the telephone in 1876. Although some inventions of the Industrial Revolution seemed odd at first, they soon had a great effect on how people lived, worked, and thought.

Electricity

Beginning in the early 1800s, manufacturers increasingly applied the findings of science to their businesses, thus generating new industrial growth. The application of scientific solutions to industrial problems had three main results. First, it encouraged the development and use of new sources of power. This was necessary for industry to grow. Second, it gave rise to inventions that could provide rapid communication over long distances. Finally, it led to the creation of new products and materials and the improvement of old ones.

Development of electricity. As industry grew during the 1800s, manufacturers continued to search for new and better sources of power. In the 1870s a tremendous new power source—electricity—was developed.

The English scientist **Michael Faraday** made key discoveries about electricity in the 1820s and 1830s. Faraday concentrated mainly on exploring the nature of electricity. Before Faraday, many scientists had believed that electricity was a sort of fluid that flowed through wires like water through a pipe. Faraday rejected this traditional view and argued that electricity was a form of force or vibration that passed from one particle of matter to another.

From the work of André Ampère and other scientists, Faraday already knew that electricity could produce magnetism. However, Faraday wanted to find out whether magnetism could produce electricity. He discovered that by moving a magnet through a coil of wire, he could generate an electric current in the wire. Using this research Faraday developed the first **dynamo,** or electric generator. This was the direct ancestor of all electric motors. Driven either by a steam engine or by waterpower, the dynamo transformed mechanical power into electrical energy. In turn, this energy could generate power to run machines in factories. By the late 1800s, other inventors had found ways to use electricity as a new power source for industry and even to light up whole cities.

All electric generators and transformers work on the principle of Faraday's dynamo, shown here.

Edison and the light bulb. British and American inventors worked on developing another practical use of electricity. They knew that an electric current passing through certain kinds of wire made the wire glow. This could be a new source of light for streets, homes, and factories. Electric light bulbs were first produced in the 1840s, but they burned out in a matter of minutes. In 1879 American inventor **Thomas Edison** created a bulb that glowed for two days before burning out. As it improved over the next few decades, electric lighting came to replace other sources of illumination.

To make electricity practical, it had to be transmitted efficiently from where it was generated to where it would be used. Edison developed a system for successfully transmitting electricity from a central powerhouse. In 1882 this transmission system was put into use in New York City and London. Other places soon followed.

The electrical industry quickly grew. Waterfalls were used to power huge dynamos. This water-generated power, called hydroelectric power, was sent long distances through wires. Dams were built in many countries to provide artificial sources of waterpower. In the late 1800s large-scale production and transmission of electricity became a reality. Electric motors replaced steam engines in factories. Steam engines were likely used only in those places where hydroelectric power was unavailable or too expensive.

✔ **READING CHECK: Problem Solving** How were Thomas Edison's light bulbs an improvement over the ones that came before?

Holt Researcher

go.hrw.com
KEYWORD: Holt Researcher
FreeFind: Thomas Edison
After reading more about Thomas Edison on the Holt Researcher, write a paragraph identifying which of his inventions you think was most important and explain why.

The Spread of Electricity in the United States

Interpreting Maps During the 1920s annual electrical production in the United States rose dramatically until, by 1930, more than two thirds of American homes had electricity. An abundant supply of energy as well as a large network of power plants led to this expansion.

■ **Skills Assessment: 1. The World in Spatial Terms** Which regions of the United States were among the earliest to receive electrical lines? **2. Human Systems** How do you think this probably affected the economies of those regions?

Communications

The development of electrical power inspired other inventions. In the 1870s American inventor **Alexander Graham Bell** made an important advance in the field of communications. Bell transmitted the human voice over a long distance by means of an electrical circuit through a wire. Bell patented his telephone in 1876. Then in 1895 an Italian named **Guglielmo Marconi** developed a way to send messages through space without wires.

Marconi's invention was based on the work of two earlier scientists, James Clerk Maxwell of Great Britain and Heinrich Rudolph Hertz of Germany. Maxwell had made a mathematical study of electricity and magnetism. In 1873 he asserted the existence of invisible electromagnetic waves that travel through space at the speed of light. In the 1880s Hertz proved the existence of such waves by sending and receiving them. Hertz also measured the length and speed of the electromagnetic waves.

Marconi invented instruments for sending and receiving these radio waves, as they came to be called. His wireless telegraph became very important for ship-to-ship and ship-to-shore communication. In 1901 Marconi sent the first wireless message across the Atlantic ocean. This is how he later described the event:

Analyzing Primary Sources

Finding the Main Idea According to Marconi, in what way did this wireless transmission represent more than just a successful experiment?

66**Shortly before mid-day I placed the single earphone to my ear and started listening. . . . The answer came at 12:30 when I heard, faintly but distinctly, pip-pip-pip. . . . The result meant much more to me than the mere successful realization of an experiment. . . . I now felt for the first time absolutely certain that the day would come when mankind would be able to send messages without wires not only across the Atlantic but between the farthermost ends of the earth.**99

Guglielmo Marconi, from *Scrapbook 1900–1941*

✔ **READING CHECK: Drawing Conclusions** How did Marconi's method of communication build on that of Alexander Graham Bell?

Italian electrical engineer and inventor Guglielmo Marconi is shown here in 1896 with his wireless telegraph machine.

The Internal Combustion Engine

Electricity was not the only type of power that became important in the 1800s. The electric motor, although useful, was limited because it had to remain connected to its power supply. This made electric motors impractical for moving vehicles.

Automobiles. In the late 1800s several European inventors developed engines that carried their own supply of oil or gasoline to power a vehicle. These devices were called internal combustion engines because the combustion, or burning, of fuel took place inside a closed cylinder. Thus they differed from the steam engine, in which combustion takes place outside the cylinder. Pioneers in this field included Gottlieb Daimler and Karl Benz of Germany and Etienne Lenoir of France. In 1893 Charles and Frank Duryea built the first successful gasoline-driven automobile in the United States. Fifteen years later American inventor Henry Ford produced his first commercially successful automobile, the Model T.

Airplanes. Since the 1700s people had been using balloons filled with gases lighter than air to float above the ground. Beginning in the 1800s, inventors tried to create a heavier-than-air machine that would actually fly. The first people to achieve a sustained, controlled flight in a powered airplane were **Wilbur and Orville Wright.** Their historic flight took place in Kitty Hawk, North Carolina, in 1903.

The Wright brothers succeeded by combining science with technology. They had studied **aerodynamics**—the scientific principles governing the movement of air around objects. They then used the technology of the internal combustion engine to propel their plane through the air.

✔ **READING CHECK: Contrasting** How was the internal combustion engine different than engines that came before it?

Petroleum represented a new industry in the 1870s, when John D. Rockefeller organized the Standard Oil Company. It quickly became an essential element of American and worldwide industrialization.

CONNECTING TO
Science and Technology

Petroleum and the Industrial Age

Petroleum—that is, crude oil—and its products have been in use for thousands of years. Ancient Egyptians occasionally used pitch, a thick, sticky form of oil, as a coating for mummies. The Babylonians used pitch to build walls and pave streets.

During the 1800s the kerosene lamp and the internal combustion engine created a great demand for petroleum. Today petroleum powers cars, airplanes, and ships. It generates heat and electricity. Petroleum products include detergents, plastics, cosmetics, and fabrics.

Understanding Science and Technology

In what ways did new technologies create a demand for petroleum?

SECTION 1 REVIEW

1. **Define** and explain the significance:
   dynamo
   aerodynamics

2. **Identify** and explain the significance:
   Michael Faraday
   Thomas Edison
   Alexander Graham Bell
   Guglielmo Marconi
   Wilbur and Orville Wright

3. **Sequencing** Copy the diagram below. Use it to identify the pioneers of the internal combustion engine and the inventors who built on their work.

   Internal combustion engine

   Automobile   Airplane

4. **Finding the Main Idea**
   a. In what way did Faraday further the development of electrical power?
   b. In what ways were Bell's and Marconi's inventions similar and different?
   c. How do new sources of power assist in the development of inventions?

5. **Writing and Critical Thinking**
   Making Predictions Write an editorial about possible uses of the telephone and wireless telegraph from the point of view of someone living at the time these inventions were new.
   Consider:
   • how the telephone allowed the human voice to be transmitted
   • how communication changed because of the wireless telegraph

Homework Practice Online
keyword: SH3 HP14

Advances in Science and Medicine

READ TO DISCOVER

❶ How did cell theory change over time?

❷ Why was Darwin's theory so significant and controversial?

❸ How did scientific discoveries change the nature of medicine and surgery?

❹ What advances were made in the field of physics?

DEFINE

biological sciences
physical sciences
evolution
genetics
pasteurization
antisepsis
radioactivity
quantum theory
special theory of relativity

IDENTIFY

Charles Darwin
Louis Pasteur
Alexander Fleming
Dmitry Mendeleyev
Wilhelm C. Röntgen
Pierre and Marie Curie
Max Planck
Albert Einstein

▶ WHY IT MATTERS TODAY

Many advances in the biological and physical sciences were made in the late 1800s and early 1900s. Use **CNN** Student News.com or other **current event** sources to investigate what current research is happening in these sciences today. Record your findings in your journal.

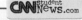
CNN Student News.com

The Main Idea
During the Industrial Age advances were made in the biological, physical, and medical sciences.

The Story Continues *"Einstein is one of the most original thinkers I have ever met. . . . He does not remain attached to classical principles, and when presented with a problem in physics he quickly envisages [imagines] all its possibilities. . . . This is exactly how one should proceed."* This is how a colleague described the work of physicist Albert Einstein. In the 1800s and early 1900s, Einstein was just one of many innovative thinkers exploring new frontiers in science and medicine.

Cell Theory in Biology

The **biological sciences,** such as biology and genetics, deal with living organisms. The **physical sciences** are concerned with the properties of nonliving matter and of energy. Physical sciences include astronomy, geology, physics, and chemistry. During the 1800s and early 1900s, scientists made great strides in both of these branches of science, as well as in medicine.

Scientists of the 1800s were as interested in explaining the nature of life as they were in exploring the nature of nonliving matter. Biologists had long been familiar with the idea of cells, tiny units of living matter. Scientists in the 1600s examined living matter under their microscopes and saw what we now know to be plant and animal cells. Those early observers noticed that the cells of different species are of different shapes and sizes. However, they did not fully understand what they saw and did not draw any general conclusions about cells. It was not until 1838 that German botanist Mathias Schleiden and biologist Theodor Swann clearly expressed cell theory. They stated that all living things are made up of these tiny units of living matter. They also discovered that all cells divide and multiply, causing organisms to grow and mature.

In the 1850s the work of German scientist Rudolf Virchow expanded cell theory. Virchow showed that disease in living organisms came about when cells were changed or destroyed by some outside force. From his study of cells, Virchow also came to the important conclusion that every new cell must come from some older cell. Therefore only living matter can produce new living matter. Thus, by the late 1800s, scientists generally accepted the cell as the basic unit of living matter.

✔ **READING CHECK: Analyzing Information**
What had scientists before Virchow noticed about cells?

Scientists of the 1800s used microscopes like the one shown here to study cell structure.

Evolution and Genetics

Cell theory did not explain the rich variety of plants and animals on Earth. The religious beliefs of many cultures hold that a divine being or beings created all things on Earth. One group of scientists, however, argued that modern plants and animals had evolved, or developed, from common ancestors long ago. This kind of development through change is called **evolution.**

Lamarck's theory of inheritance. In the early 1800s French biologist Jean-Baptiste Lamarck suggested that living things changed their form in response to their environment. For example, giraffes developed long necks because they always had to stretch to eat leaves high up in trees. Such changes were then passed on by inheritance to descendants. Other characteristics might gradually disappear if they were never used. Lamarck thought that these kinds of changes, over millions of years, could have produced present-day plants and animals. Most of Lamarck's ideas were later proved wrong and did not become a part of modern biology. However, Lamarck did influence other scientists, including a British naturalist named **Charles Darwin.**

Darwin's theory of evolution. By 1859 Darwin had spent 30 years studying plant and animal life. He published his theory of evolution in a book called *On the Origin of Species by Means of Natural Selection.*

Darwin began with a well-known biological fact: no two living things are exactly alike, not even a parent and its offspring. Darwin combined this fact with the idea that as a result of natural dangers and limits, there were always more creatures born than could survive. Those who survive will, in general, be those whose characteristics are best adapted to their environment. This idea is known as survival of the fittest, or natural selection. The strongest survivors will live to produce offspring, who will tend to possess the same advantages as their parents. These offspring can in turn pass successful characteristics on to a new generation. In this way, Darwin thought, one could explain the evolution of all forms of life from earlier forms.

Darwin's theory inspired a great deal of activity as scientists worked to either prove or disprove it. Some looked for evidence in fossils as well as living organisms. The theory of natural selection was controversial, however, for two reasons. First, it stated that human beings developed from animals. This idea offended some people. Also, many people thought that Darwin's theory contradicted the story of creation told in the Bible. However, Darwin felt that the theory of evolution did not necessarily challenge the existence of God.

❝There is grandeur in this view of life . . . having been originally breathed by the Creator into a few forms or into one; and that . . . from so simple a beginning endless forms most beautiful and most wonderful have been, and are being evolved.❞

Charles Darwin, *On the Origin of Species by Means of Natural Selection*

Genetics. Darwin's theory left an important question unanswered: why were offspring not exactly like their parents? Unknown to Darwin, an Austrian monk named Gregor Mendel had been gathering evidence that would answer this question. Mendel founded **genetics**—the study of how the inborn characteristics of plants and animals are inherited by their descendants. Mendel did much of his research in the 1850s and 1860s, working with plants. He mated tall plants with short ones. Instead of producing

Charles Darwin gathered most of the material for his theory of evolution during a five-year expedition off the coast of South America and in the Pacific Islands. Upon his return to England, he spent 20 years writing his theory. Shown here is the book's title page.

Then & Now

Science Fiction

The spirit of discovery of the scientific and industrial ages was reflected in a type of literature that we today call science fiction.

Stories similar to today's science fiction were popular in the 1700s and 1800s. The French philosopher Voltaire imagined a visit to Earth by a native of the star Sirius. Mary Shelley imagined a medical student named Victor Frankenstein, who created a living monster out of dead bodies. In the late 1800s French writer Jules Verne wrote about incredible journeys by balloon, rocket, and submarine. British novelist H. G. Wells wrote tales of time machines, invisible men, and invaders from Mars. **Why did science fiction grow during the scientific and industrial ages?**

medium-sized plants, this combination produced tall plants. Then Mendel fertilized these tall offspring with their own pollen. To his surprise, this produced a new mixed generation of tall and short plants.

From his experiments, Mendel concluded that inborn characteristics, or traits, were not necessarily blended or mixed together. Instead, he believed, they were all inherited as if they were separate particles. In some cases a trait could be carried but not expressed. For example, tall plants could carry and pass on to the next generation the particles that would cause shortness.

✔ **READING CHECK: Finding the Main Idea** How did the theory of evolution change science?

The Fight Against Disease

During the Industrial Age remarkable breakthroughs in medicine helped to prolong human life. Until the late 1800s as many as 50 percent of all people born died within the first five years after birth. Disease likely killed more people than did wars, famines, or natural disasters. Little was known about the causes of disease. Scientists had seen bacteria under the microscope as early as the 1600s but did not connect them with disease.

The smallpox vaccine. Smallpox was one of the deadliest diseases of the time. It often swept through cities in epidemics. English physician Edward Jenner investigated smallpox in the late 1700s in hopes of finding a way to prevent it. He learned that milkmaids who had once had cowpox—a disease similar to smallpox but milder—did not get smallpox even when there was an epidemic. After years of experimenting, Jenner developed a safe way to prevent smallpox. In 1796 Jenner made a vaccine from the fluid in cowpox sores and scratched it into a boy's arm. The boy developed a mild case of cowpox but quickly recovered. When the boy was later exposed to smallpox, he did not contract the disease.

Still from War of the Worlds, *a movie based on a story from H.G. Wells*

Illustration for Jules Verne's A Trip from the Earth to the Moon, *1865*

Bacteria and germs. Although Jenner had developed a vaccine for preventing smallpox, he did not know why it worked. Later, French chemist **Louis Pasteur** discovered the scientific principle at work. Pasteur identified microorganisms called bacteria. His experiments showed that bacteria reproduce like other living things. They can travel from place to place in the air or on peoples' hands.

Pasteur also discovered that bacteria cause fermentation—the process that turns grape juice into wine and makes milk go sour. In the 1860s Pasteur developed a process of heating liquids to kill bacteria and prevent fermentation. This process was named **pasteurization** in his honor. Pasteur also discovered that some bacteria cause illness in animals and humans. These harmful bacteria are called germs or microbes.

In 1881 Pasteur experimented with the germ that causes anthrax, a disease that can kill animals and humans. He made a vaccine that contained weakened anthrax germs and injected it into animals. The vaccine prevented the animals from catching anthrax. Pasteur determined that when weakened germs enter the body, the system builds up substances called antibodies to fight them. These antibodies remain in the body and can then defend against the more deadly germs. Thus Pasteur showed why Jenner's vaccine had worked. Pasteur used this same technique to fight rabies, a fatal disease that humans can catch from dogs or other infected animals.

✔ **READING CHECK: Identifying Cause and Effect** How did Jenner's vaccine work?

Holt Researcher
go.hrw.com
KEYWORD: Holt Researcher
FreeFind: Louis Pasteur
After reading more about Louis Pasteur on the Holt Researcher, create a cause-and-effect chart showing how Pasteur's discoveries have affected life in the United States today.

Advances in Surgery and Other Areas

Through the centuries, surgery had always been a last resort. It was always painful and often fatal. Surgeons usually performed only operations that could be completed in a few minutes, such as tooth extractions and limb amputations. Sometimes more complicated procedures were attempted. During many surgical operations patients had to be held down or have their senses dulled with liquor or opium.

The development of surgery. In the 1840s it was discovered that ether and chloroform could cause unconsciousness and eliminate pain. These anesthetics made longer operations possible. Even after anesthetics came into use, however, people still frequently died from infections soon after an operation. Pasteur's discoveries about germs helped here too. Joseph Lister, an English surgeon, studied Pasteur's findings. Lister developed **antisepsis**—the use of chemicals to kill disease-causing germs. The use of such chemicals, called antiseptics, helped to reduce infections in surgery, childbirth, and the treatment of battle wounds.

Other medical advances. The work of German physician Robert Koch further confirmed Pasteur's findings. He found the germs that cause tuberculosis and cholera. He developed sanitary measures, such as water filtration, to prevent disease.

INTERPRETING THE VISUAL RECORD

Operations In the 1800s physicians began to use nitrous oxide, ether, and chloroform to deaden pain during surgery.

Link to Today How does this image differ from operating rooms in the United States today?

The discoveries of Pasteur, Lister, and Koch were the starting point for an international fight against disease. Now that scientists could identify the causes of illness, they could develop vaccines. For example, scientists were able to trace malaria and yellow fever to germs carried in mosquitoes and transmitted by their bites. So the battle against these diseases could now extend to the mosquitoes that carried them. Bubonic plague was found to be carried by fleas on rats. Rat-extermination programs brought this disease under control.

During this time scientists invented and tested many new medicines. Aspirin, which became available in the late 1800s, reduced pain and fever. Insulin, isolated in the 1920s, helped people with diabetes survive and lead more normal lives. Other medicines were developed to fight bacterial infections. **Alexander Fleming** of Great Britain discovered penicillin in 1928. Sulfa drugs were developed in Europe in the 1930s. However, neither penicillin nor sulfa drugs became widely available until about the 1940s.

✔ **READING CHECK: Drawing Conclusions** How did advances in medicine help to fight disease worldwide?

The Atom and Its Structure

According to modern atomic theory, all matter in the universe is made up of very small particles called atoms. The various arrangement and structure of these atoms yields all the different materials that make up our world. The beginning of atomic theory can be traced back to ancient Greek philosophers such as Democritus. During the Scientific Revolution of the 1500s and 1600s atomic theory became widely accepted, although it had yet to be proven.

Atomic weight and the periodic table. An English chemist and schoolteacher named John Dalton was the first scientist to obtain convincing data about atoms. In 1803 Dalton designed a method for "weighing" atoms. First he studied the ratios of elements in different gases. As a starting point Dalton assigned the weight of "1" to the lightest gas, hydrogen. He then expressed the weights of all other known elements in relation to how much heavier they were than hydrogen. Dalton opened up paths for other scientists to explore. In 1869 the Russian chemist **Dmitry Mendeleyev** (men·duh·LAY·uhf) made the first workable classification of the elements. A modified version of Mendeleyev's periodic table is still used in chemistry today.

Modern atomic theory originated in the study of chemistry. However, it soon became a part of physics—the science

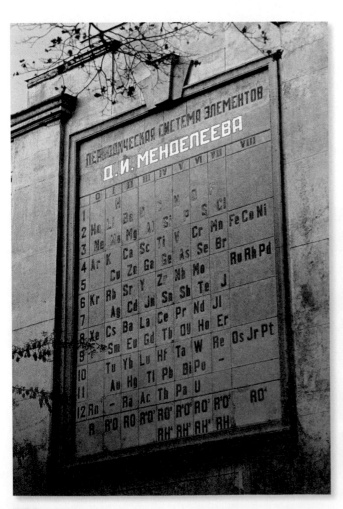

Dmitry Mendeleyev's classification of the elements—the periodic table—is engraved on a wall of the Mendeleyev Institute in St. Petersburg, Russia.

of matter and energy. Scientists came to explain their findings about heat and gases in terms of atoms in motion. In the 1800s scientists began to think of heat as the result of the motion of atomic particles. In a cold substance, such as ice, atoms move relatively slowly. In a hot substance, such as hot water, atoms move much faster, even colliding with one another. When water boils, its atoms move so fast that the water turns into a gas—steam, or water vapor.

Structure of the atom. In 1895 German physicist **Wilhelm C. Röntgen** (RENT·guhn) discovered a new form of ray. These rays could go through many substances, including human skin and tissue. The rays could also leave an impression on photographic paper. Because he did not know what caused this powerful penetrating radiation, Röntgen named the rays X-rays. These rays became widely used in medicine as a diagnostic tool. The existence of this radiation raised more questions about the physical world.

The English physicist J.J. Thomson further studied the nature of matter. In 1897 he discovered the electron—a tiny particle with a negative electrical charge. Thomson found that the electron was 1,000 times lighter than the smallest known atom. From this he concluded that all atoms contained electrons. Therefore subatomic particles— particles inside atoms—must be the true building blocks of all matter in the universe.

Most physicists gradually accepted the electron's existence. However, a French husband-and-wife chemist team, **Pierre and Marie Curie,** provided evidence that atoms were not as simple as earlier scientists had thought. The Curies experimented with the elements polonium and radium. They found that these elements constantly break down and release energy on their own. This process is called **radioactivity.** Elements that release energy in this way are called radioactive elements.

Based on the work done by Thomson and the Curies, Ernest Rutherford of Great Britain developed a new theory of the atom. Rutherford held that at the center of every atom lay a very small but very heavy core, called a nucleus. Electrons orbit around the nucleus. Rutherford then discovered that the nucleus is made up of positively-charged particles, which he called protons. After this, scientists no longer thought of the atom as a solid piece of matter. Later scientists also found a particle inside the nucleus, which they called the neutron. Many more subatomic particles were eventually discovered.

✔ **READING CHECK: Drawing Inferences** What do the discoveries about the structure of the atom imply about the scientific process?

Planck and Einstein

Before 1900 many scientists believed that energy was a continuous substance and that it could be divided into any number of smaller units. In 1900 the German physicist **Max Planck** disproved this commonly held idea. Through his research Planck proved that energy could be released only in definite "packages." He called these units *quanta,* based on *quantum,* the Latin word meaning "how much." Planck's **quantum theory** formed the basis for a completely new approach to the study of matter and energy. However, even this groundbreaking theory was not Planck's only contribution to the field of physics. In another important work, he put forth the theory that light was a continuous wave-like phenomenon.

HISTORY MAKERS

**Pierre Curie (1859–1906)
Marie Curie (1867–1934)**

Pierre and Marie Curie headed one of the most famous families in modern science. Their work on radioactivity defined the field. In fact Marie Curie invented the term "radioactivity" in 1898. In 1903 the Curies shared the Nobel Prize in physics. In 1911 Marie won the Nobel Prize in chemistry.

The Curies' daughter, Irene, formed a similar partnership with her husband. In 1935 they shared the Nobel Prize in chemistry for their work on radioactive materials. **What contributions did Pierre and Marie Curie make to the history of modern science?**

Holt Researcher

go.hrw.com
KEYWORD: Holt Researcher
**FreeFind: Marie Curie
      Albert Einstein**
After reading more about Marie Curie and Albert Einstein on the Holt Researcher, explain how they contributed to the history of science in the 1900s.

$E = mc^2$

One of the most famous mathematical equations in history, $E = mc^2$ means that a little bit of mass can be transformed into an enormous amount of energy. This idea laid the groundwork for the development of the atomic bomb. The bomb explodes when a tiny atom is split, releasing a great amount of energy. Einstein's research showed that such weapons were possible, but he refused to take part in the building of the bomb.

Understanding Math

How does $E = mc^2$ show that mass and energy can each be transformed into the other?

In 1905 **Albert Einstein,** a young German scientist, published four papers that forever changed physics. His first paper examined some of the basic concepts of mechanics and tried to prove the existence of atoms. In his second paper, Einstein built on Planck's theory to describe the nature of light. In his third paper, Einstein developed his **special theory of relativity.** He concluded that no particles of matter can move faster than the speed of light. Einstein also stated that motion can be measured only relative to some particular observer. According to Einstein's theory, then, it does not make sense to speak of absolute motion, space, or time.

In the fourth paper Einstein developed his famous equation $E = mc^2$. This equation expresses the relationship between energy and mass. According to the formula, energy (E) equals mass (m) multiplied by the speed of light squared (c^2). This means that mass can be transformed into energy, and energy into mass.

Einstein's theories overturned long-held ideas. Isaac Newton and other scientists of the past had thought of the universe in terms of three dimensions: length, breadth, and depth. Einstein's theory of relativity declared that all events occur not only in these three dimensions of space but also in a fourth dimension—time. Einstein called this four-dimensional system the space-time continuum. Einstein's theories, as well as Planck's, paved the way for much important work.

Albert Einstein joined the Institute for Advanced Study in Princeton, New Jersey, in 1933.

✔ **READING CHECK: Summarizing** What were Einstein's major contributions to physics?

SECTION 2 REVIEW

1. **Define** and explain the significance:
   biological sciences   antisepsis
   physical sciences   radioactivity
   evolution   quantum theory
   genetics   special theory of
   pasteurization   relativity

2. **Identify** and explain the significance:
   Charles Darwin
   Louis Pasteur
   Alexander Fleming
   Dmitry Mendeleyev
   Wilhelm C. Röntgen
   Pierre and Marie Curie
   Max Planck
   Albert Einstein

3. **Comparing and Contrasting** Copy the diagram and use it to show the contrast between how Newton and Einstein thought about the universe.

   The Physical Universe

Newton	Einstein

4. **Finding the Main Idea**

   a. In what way were Virchow's ideas about cells different than the ideas that had existed before?
   b. Why did Darwin's theory inspire so much scientific activity?
   c. In what ways do Pasteur's discoveries affect life today?
   d. How did scientific theories about atoms change ideas about the universe?

5. **Writing and Critical Thinking**

   Supporting a Point of View From the point of view of a doctor in the mid-1800s, write a newspaper editorial explaining why surgery at that time was safer than ever before.
   Consider:
   • what surgical procedures were like up until the 1800s
   • the advances in surgery and medicine made during the 1800s

Homework Practice Online
keyword: SH3 HP14

Social Sciences in the Industrial Age

READ TO DISCOVER

❶ How did science influence the study of politics, economics, and history?

❷ How did archaeology, anthropology, and sociology explore cultures?

❸ How did the study of the human mind develop?

DEFINE

social sciences
social Darwinism
psychoanalysis
psychiatry

IDENTIFY

E.B. Tylor
James George Frazer
Auguste Comte
Herbert Spencer
Ivan Pavlov
Sigmund Freud

WHY IT MATTERS TODAY

Archaeology has always made use of new scientific methods to better explore and record the past. Use CNN**News**.com or other **current event** sources to investigate current archaeological finds and the techniques used to discover them. Record your findings in your journal.

CNN**News**.com

The Main Idea
Scientists studied human societies and the human mind in an effort to understand human behavior.

The Story Continues *"The decisive moment had arrived. . . . At first I could see nothing . . . but . . . as my eyes grew accustomed to the light, details of the room within emerged slowly from the mist, strange animals, statues, and gold—everywhere the glint of gold."* This is how Howard Carter described his first glimpse of the tomb of King Tutankhamen in 1922. Carter's discovery was just one of the exciting events that brought new insight into human societies during the Industrial Age.

Rise of the Social Sciences

During the 1800s interest in a new field of study, the **social sciences,** grew rapidly. The social sciences are those branches of knowledge that scientifically study people as members of society. The social sciences cover such topics as economics, history, political institutions, and human relations. The idea of making the study of these subjects objective and factual—of treating them like sciences—was new in the 1800s.

The study of politics dates back to the Greek philosophers Plato and Aristotle. Later it became a subject for thinkers like Machiavelli, Locke, and Rousseau. In the 1800s the study of politics became known as political science. Scholars attempted to study law and politics with the same scientific manner that physicists and biologists brought to their own fields of study.

Another social science, economics, had already been well developed in the work of Adam Smith and others. It was not until the late 1800s, however, that economists began to follow the practice of scientists by collecting and arranging statistics in order to test their theories.

The study of history, like political science, dates back to the ancient Greeks. As with political science and economics, the study of history changed in the 1800s. Influenced by nationalism, many scholars wrote histories detailing the accomplishments and glories of their native countries. In addition, historians increasingly based their writings on the systematic study of original materials and the careful organization of facts. They began a massive search for evidence of the past in documents, diaries, letters, and other written sources. New views of history began to emerge from their research.

One of these new trends in history was the study of all people in a society. The French philosopher Voltaire influenced this type of research. In the 1700s Voltaire became known for his attention to social and intellectual history. His work inspired historians to focus less on wars and great leaders and more on the study of ordinary people and how they lived. Another trend at this time—influenced by Darwin—was the interpretation of historical events in terms of evolution.

✔ **READING CHECK: Comparing** How was the development of history like that of political science? Why?

Archaeology, Anthropology, and Sociology

Archaeology is the study of human culture through the artifacts people leave behind. Archaeology became a separate field of study in the mid-1800s. It was in the 1800s that scientists began to learn how old Earth was and how long humans had lived on it. Archaeologists found prehistoric cave paintings in Spain and France. Careful digging of sites uncovered remains of Egyptian, Sumerian, and Assyrian cultures. Excavation techniques allowed scientists to determine the sequence of events in such ancient cities as Troy and Mycenae.

Anthropology. Anthropology is the study of different societies, both past and present. Anthropologists in the 1800s began to explore similarities in the attitudes of human societies and in the ways people relate to one another. The British anthropologist **E.B. Tylor** adopted the German term *kultur* to describe the set of beliefs and behaviors that a society shares. Tylor discussed the concept of *kultur* in his book *Primitive Culture* (1871), in which he looked at religion and how it evolved in all human cultures.

Another British anthropologist, **James George Frazer,** took this approach further in 1890 with his book *The Golden Bough.* Frazer compared the customs of different societies and tried to show links between those societies. The study of similarities and differences among various societies is still a major interest of anthropologists.

Sociology. Sociology—the study of human relationships in society—also first appeared in the 1800s. The French philosopher **Auguste Comte** (KOHNT) was one of the founders of sociology. Comte argued that society, like nature, operated by certain laws. Therefore sociologists should follow scientific methods by using objective facts, not personal interpretations.

In the 1800s sociologists became very interested in adopting the theories of the biological sciences. **Herbert Spencer,** for example, used evolution as the basis for studying human communities. Spencer applied Darwin's theory of natural selection to human societies, coining the phrase "survival of the fittest." Spencer believed that human society, like plant and animal life, had evolved from lower to higher forms through natural selection. He wrote,

❝The individuals best adapted to the conditions of their existence shall prosper most, and the individuals least adapted to the conditions of their existence shall prosper least. . . . Pervading all Nature we may see at work a stern discipline which is often a little cruel that it may be very kind.❞

A History of Civilization, 2nd ed., edited by Crane Brinton, John B. Christopher, and Robert Lee Wolff

Spencer's theory became known as **social Darwinism.** According to this theory, those who had acquired wealth and power had done so because of their superior abilities. Poverty, on the other hand, supposedly proved that people or groups were unfit. Spencer's view came to be seen as simplistic, however, as society became more complex. As people became more aware of how social problems occur, social Darwinism lost much influence.

✔ **READING CHECK: Contrasting** How do archaeology, anthropology, and sociology differ?

Psychology

Another new science of the 1800s, psychology, studies the mind and human behavior. In the mid-1800s scientists began to approach psychology as an experimental science like biology.

Influenced by Darwin, some psychologists studied animal behavior and applied the results to humans. In the 1890s Russian physiologist **Ivan Pavlov** discovered the conditioned reflex. Psychologists had long known that some behavior is automatic. For example, a dog does not have to be taught to salivate, or water at the mouth, when eating food. Psychologists call this kind of response a reflex action. By experimenting with dogs, Pavlov concluded that human actions are responses to outside stimuli and can be changed by training.

In the early 1900s **Sigmund Freud** (FROID), an Austrian doctor, introduced the idea of the unconscious as a determining factor in human behavior. The unconscious mind contains the mental processes of which a person is unaware. Freud learned that under hypnosis, some of his patients could remember past experiences that they otherwise could not recall. Freud believed that these early experiences had led to their illnesses. Freud treated his patients by identifying their unconscious fears or desires. To do this, he studied their dreams and encouraged them to talk freely about whatever came into their minds.

Freud called this process of revealing and analyzing unconscious motivations **psychoanalysis.** Freud founded modern **psychiatry,** the study and treatment of mental illness. People working in other social sciences also borrowed from Freud's theories. They began to see certain social behaviors and cultural attitudes as driven by unconscious psychological motives.

✔ **READING CHECK: Analyzing Information** According to Freud, how can one's unconscious fears and desires be revealed and examined by means of psychoanalysis?

HISTORY MAKER

Sigmund Freud (1856–1939)

Sigmund Freud was one of the most important thinkers of his time. Because of Freud's pioneering studies, doctors could better understand the causes of mental illness.

Freud believed that dreams express unconscious fears or desires. Even now, Freud's work continues to be influential, although some people believe his findings to be old-fashioned. **Why was Sigmund Freud's work important?**

SECTION 3 REVIEW

1. **Define** and explain the significance:
   social sciences
   social Darwinism
   psychoanalysis
   psychiatry

2. **Identify** and explain the significance:
   E.B. Tylor
   James George Frazer
   Auguste Comte
   Herbert Spencer
   Ivan Pavlov
   Sigmund Freud

3. **Summarizing** Copy the diagram and use it to show the fields of study that came to use scientific methods.

Biological and Physical Sciences

4. **Finding the Main Idea**
   a. In what way did the study of history become more scientific during the Industrial Age?
   b. What was Auguste Comte's contribution to sociology?
   c. How were Pavlov's ideas about the basis of human behavior different from Freud's?

5. **Writing and Critical Thinking**
   Supporting a Point of View Write a letter to Freud expressing doubt about his theories.
   Consider:
   • Freud's argument that the unconscious mind controls much human behavior
   • Freud's reliance on dreams and hypnosis to reveal unconscious feelings

READ TO DISCOVER

❶ Why did people emigrate?
❷ Why was the growth of cities so great and how did they change as they grew?
❸ In what ways did public education change society?
❹ How did the leisure activities we know today begin to develop?

▶ **WHY IT MATTERS TODAY**

Cities and suburbs continue to experience change. Use CNN student News.com or other **current event** sources to investigate a city near you and how it interacts with surrounding suburbs. Record your findings in your journal.

CNN student News.com

Society and Culture in the Industrial Age

The Main Idea
During the 1800s increases in population changed the nature of cities, education, and leisure activities.

The Story Continues *During the Industrial Age, improved living conditions caused the populations of metropolitan areas to boom as never before. This rapid growth prompted newspaper editor Horace Greeley to comment that "We cannot all live in cities, yet nearly all seem determined to do so."*

Emigration

During the 1800s improvements in medicine, sanitation, and food distribution helped lead to an increase in population. In the United States and Europe, population growth was fastest in the more industrialized regions. As the population grew, it also became more mobile. Large numbers of people began to move across national boundaries and oceans to foreign lands.

Such movements of people away from their native lands are called **emigrations.** The largest emigrations were from Europe to North and South America, Africa, Australia and New Zealand. Between 1870 and 1900 more than 10 million people left Europe for the United States alone. This was one of the greatest mass movements of people in history. Many people fled from countries with poor economic conditions, such as Ireland and Italy. Other people, such as Jews, Armenians, and Slavs, fled oppression and discrimination.

Within Europe, large numbers of people moved to the areas of greatest industrialization. Rapid industrialization in northern and western Europe had created a great demand for factory labor. In these areas higher wages attracted workers. Also steamships and trains made travel safer and more affordable.

✔ **READING CHECK: Analyzing Information** What characterized many of the people who emigrated during the 1800s?

Between 1892 and 1943, approximately 17 million people with hopes of a better life entered the United States at New York's Ellis Island.

The Growth of Cities

As the population increased, changes in agriculture and industry led to the rapid growth of cities. Employment on farms declined as developing industries in or near cities offered new jobs. The factory system became the greatest cause of city growth.

Many factories were located in already established cities, which then grew greatly. Manchester, England, for example, grew from 10,000 people in 1717 to 303,000 in 1851. When factories were built in rural areas, cities grew up around them.

Before the Industrial Revolution, most people lived in rural areas or small villages. By the early 1900s, however, in many nations more people lived in or near cities than in the countryside. No city in the Western

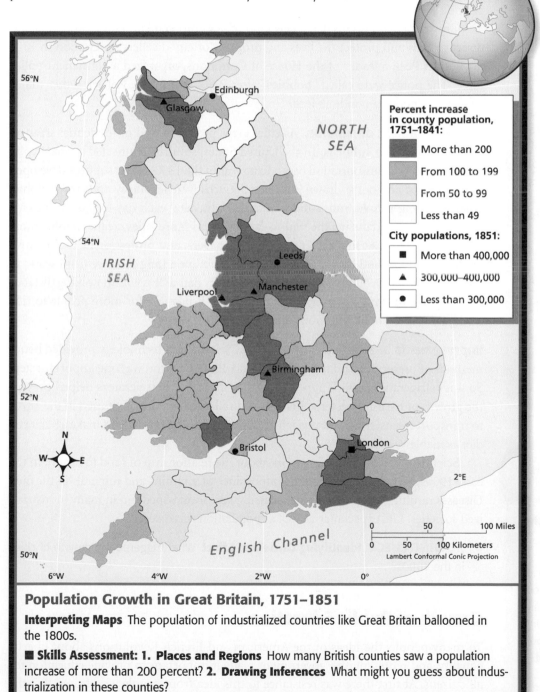

Population Growth in Great Britain, 1751–1851

Interpreting Maps The population of industrialized countries like Great Britain ballooned in the 1800s.

■ **Skills Assessment: 1. Places and Regions** How many British counties saw a population increase of more than 200 percent? **2. Drawing Inferences** What might you guess about industrialization in these counties?

Jane Addams grew up in a wealthy Illinois family, but she dedicated her life to helping the poor. In 1889 she helped open Hull House in an immigrant neighborhood of Chicago. Hull House, which provided education, job training, and cultural events, soon became the model for community service centers throughout the United States.

Addams also crusaded for world peace. In 1915 she became chairwoman of the Women's International League. She later went on a peace mission to Europe. In 1931 she became the second woman ever to win the Nobel Peace Prize. **What were some of Jane Addams's accomplishments?**

**Holt
Researcher**

**go.hrw.com
KEYWORD: Holt Researcher
FreeFind: Jane Addams
       Emily Davies**
After reading more about Jane Addams and Emily Davies on the Holt Researcher, write an imaginary dialogue between the two that reflects their political, economic, and cultural contributions to the world.

world had a population of 1 million in 1800. Yet just 100 years later, cities such as New York, London, Paris, and Berlin each had more than 1 million residents.

Sanitation and public order. European and American cities of the 1800s were very different than they are today. Houses did not have running water. Until the late 1800s most cities did not have sewers. People dumped garbage in the streets. This pollution combined with the smoke from factories made cities foul smelling and unhealthy.

After the 1870s technological advances brought improvements, such as iron pipes, flush toilets, and running water. Cities installed public sewers, paved streets, and street lights. Governments passed laws requiring better heating systems and better construction. Through the efforts of reformers like **Jane Addams,** cities began to provide social services.

Growing cities also needed a new kind of law enforcement. Police officers had to direct crowds and protect the lives and property of city dwellers. In London in 1829 **Sir Robert Peel,** a leader of the House of Commons, organized a permanent police force. The police were called "**bobbies**" after Peel's first name, Robert. Other major cities soon followed London's lead.

The development of suburbs. As cities grew, people moved to residential areas on the outskirts called **suburbs.** In the United States, suburbs connected to the city by streetcar or ferry transportation began to appear in the 1800s. Later suburbs developed along railroad and horse-drawn bus lines. Suburbs were less noisy and crowded than cities. Working people from suburban families traveled each day to jobs in the city.

Suburbs spread during the mid-to-late 1800s, as more cities created public transportation systems. At first only merchants, managers, and professionals could afford the fare for trains and buses. They could afford to live a long distance from work, in the new suburbs. Ordinary factory workers usually had to live within walking distance of their jobs. In time, however, lower fares made it possible for more people to ride trolleys or other public transportation to work.

Improvements in diet and food storage. Science and technology provided better methods of preserving and transporting food. Pasteurization was one important step. So was refrigeration, which appeared in the late 1800s. Refrigerators helped prevent the growth of harmful bacteria. Refrigerated railroad cars were first used in the 1870s to transport meats, fruit, and vegetables. These developments helped make a balanced diet available year-round.

Scientists were also learning more about the relationship of food to health. In the early 1900s scientists discovered the importance of vitamins and minerals in the diet. Diseases resulting from vitamin deficiencies were soon wiped out in many industrialized societies. Life expectancy as well as population increased.

✔ **READING CHECK: Identifying Cause and Effect** What triggered the growth of cities in the 1800s?

Growth of Public Education

To many people, the ideas of the American and French Revolutions about liberty, equality, and representative government made it important to provide education for all citizens. At first there was resistance to this idea from people who feared that the cost of education would mean increased taxes. However, other factors encouraged the development of free public education. Industrialists wanted workers who could read and write. They needed engineers, scientists, and skilled technicians. Other people believed that state-sponsored schools would produce patriotic citizens. Military leaders wanted educated soldiers. Ordinary people thought that an education would improve their children's chances for a better life.

After 1870 governments in western Europe and the United States passed laws requiring education for all children. In some European nations, the central government controlled schools. In the United States, individual states administered schools and levied taxes to support them. Also many school systems grew to include kindergarten for young children and state universities for advanced study. New subjects, particularly in the sciences, were offered. Vocational and technical training were also introduced.

Education for women changed greatly during the 1800s. The women shown in this classroom are studying geography and science.

In general, children of the lower classes attended school only for as long as the law required. They then went to work to help support their families. Middle-class children usually went on to high school and often attended college.

Education for women. By the end of the 1800s, many countries offered elementary education for girls but secondary education was limited. Some people argued that many subjects were not necessary or proper for women. In the United States, Great Britain, and France, secondary education for girls focused on languages, literature, and home economics—not on the sciences, mathematics, or philosophy. Some people objected to these differences. A British woman named Emily Davies urged her government to prepare women to attend universities. In 1865 she argued,

History Makers Speak

❝We are not encumbered [burdened] by theories about equality and inequality of mental power in the sexes. All we claim is that the intelligence of women, be it great or small, shall have full and free development. And we claim it not specially in the interest of women, but as essential to the growth of the human race.❞

Thoughts on Some Questions Relating to Women, 1860–1908, by Emily Davies

Few colleges admitted women as students during the 1800s. Therefore during the 1800s colleges just for women began to appear in Great Britain and the United States.

Effects of education. The spread of education had many positive results. People knew more about current issues and could participate more in government. Because people of all ages could read, more newspapers, magazines, and books were published.

Newspapers, which were not widely read before 1800, became popular and important. During the 1800s they began to cover such topics as politics, foreign affairs, art, and science. Sometimes newspapers supported or criticized certain political parties or government figures. Political cartoons began to appear. New communications technology, such as the telegraph, allowed papers to print the latest news. Newspapers began to send reporters to distant places to get important stories from far away.

Analyzing Primary Sources

Drawing Conclusions According to Emily Davies, who would benefit from increased education for women?

As greater numbers of people learned to read, newspapers competed for their attention with sensational stories and cartoons.

In the Industrial Age shorter workdays and higher wages gave people more free time. Team sports, reflected in the detail from Henri Rousseau's *The Football Players,* shown below, quickly became favorite pastimes. As these sports became more popular, increased numbers of people came to cheer their team. Families played games together or went bicycling. Trips to the beach, parks, and museums were also popular activities. **How did higher wages contribute to the increase in leisure activities?**

As newspapers grew, jobs for editors and writers increased. In the past, writing was something people did in addition to work. Now it became full-time work. Journalism—writing and editing for newspapers and magazines—became an accepted profession.

✔ **READING CHECK: Drawing Conclusions** What effects did increased education have on society?

Leisure and Cultural Activities

Many of today's popular forms of entertainment developed during the 1800s. People had long enjoyed concerts, games, plays, and sports. But as cities grew during the industrial age, the number and types of entertainment activities increased. Large audiences now paid to hear professional musicians perform or to watch professional athletes compete.

Sports. People had participated in athletic events since ancient times. However, during the 1800s many games became more organized. In Great Britain, "football"—known as soccer in the United States—was among the first games to become a professional spectator sport. Rugby and American football evolved from soccer.

In the 1860s the London Football Association drew up rules for the games of soccer and rugby. By the mid-1880s many soccer and rugby players in England were full-time athletes. Football clubs for working-class people were created in the 1870s. By that time, laws in England granted factory workers Saturday afternoon and Sunday as rest days. In the 1880s an American named **Walter Camp** adapted rugby into an early form of the game known as football in the United States. A professional league was set up in 1920.

In the 1890s bicycling began to experience great popularity in the United States. By 1896 there were hundreds of manufacturers of bicycles. These manufacturers used machine technology and assembly-line systems. In the late 1800s New York City introduced a traffic code to regulate bicycle and horse traffic.

Baseball also became popular in the late 1800s in the United States. English children's games using a bat and ball dated back to the 1700s. However, it was not until 1845 that a written set of rules gave baseball its modern form. The game became popular with troops in the Civil War. In the late 1860s the first professional baseball team, the Cincinnati Red Stockings, was formed. Baseball quickly grew in popularity at both the amateur and professional levels.

Concert halls, museums, and libraries. Before the 1800s individuals and private groups sponsored most cultural activities. Musicians performed concerts in the homes of the rich or as part of religious services. Artists and sculptors produced works for wealthy families or individuals. Religious and civic organizations sometimes commissioned artwork for display in churches or clubs.

During the 1800s art and music became available to more people. Forms of popular entertainment had been available in taverns in England for many years. The growing population in cities created a greater demand for such entertainment, and music and concert halls began to appear. Music halls combined musical and comic entertainment. In the late 1800s in the United States, a light entertainment known as vaudeville became popular in cities as well as frontier towns. Vaudeville consisted of light, often comical skits that combined music, dialogue, dancing, and singing.

During the 1800s some art collections displayed in private homes or churches were moved to public museums. The Louvre museum in Paris, for example, had originally contained the art collections of French kings. After the French Revolution it became a public museum and began to collect artwork from all over the world.

Public libraries also began to appear in such cities as London and Paris. In the United States, the wealthy industrialist Andrew Carnegie donated money to open free public libraries in many cities.

Public parks and urban planning. Crowded cities had few places for outdoor recreation. When railroads were built, people often rode trains out into the country for a day. People began to demand that city governments provide parks in cities for recreation.

By the end of the 1800s, many cities had playgrounds for children. Private lands were donated or purchased by city governments and given to the people. Large areas inside city limits, such as Central Park in New York, were set aside as public parks.

✔ **READING CHECK: Sequencing** What conditions made the rise of leisure activities possible in the 1800s?

This painting of a croquet game in a public park reflects the increased participation in leisure activities during the late 1800s.

SECTION 4 REVIEW

1. **Define** and explain the significance:
   emigrations
   bobbies
   suburbs

2. **Identify** and explain the significance:
   Jane Addams
   Sir Robert Peel
   Walter Camp

3. **Sequencing** Copy the chart below and use it to show how changing educational opportunities affected different groups in society.

	Children	Women	Journalists
Public education			
College education			

4. **Finding the Main Idea**
   a. Why did people move from one place to another within Europe?
   b. How did public museums' collections grow?

5. **Writing and Critical Thinking**
   Supporting a Point of View Imagine that you are a resident of a large city during the Industrial Age. Write a letter to your mayor arguing for the need for public parks.
   Consider:
   • what living conditions were like as cities grew rapidly
   • the need for recreation

Homework Practice Online
go.hrw.com
keyword: SH3 HP14

READ TO DISCOVER

❶ What ideas drove the romantic movement?

❷ Who were the artists, writers, and musicians of the romantic movement?

❸ How does realism differ from romanticism?

❹ What other artistic movements emerged during this time?

DEFINE

romanticism
realism
regionalism
naturalists
impressionists

IDENTIFY

Sir Walter Scott
Grimm brothers
James Fenimore Cooper
Ludwig van Beethoven
Pyotr Ilich Tchaikovsky
Mark Twain
Emile Zola
Paul Cézanne

▶ WHY IT MATTERS TODAY

The art produced in the late 1800s is still valued today. Use CNN[student.com] or other **current event** sources to investigate how artists like Cézanne and Matisse are considered today. Record your findings in your journal.

Literature, Music, and Art in the Industrial Age

The Main Idea
Some artists of the 1800s glorified the past, while others embraced modern industrial life.

The Story Continues *During the Industrial Age some artists turned away from the modern world in favor of the imagination. Romantic poet Samuel Taylor Coleridge, in his famous poem "Kubla Khan," displays this fascination with exotic places and ancient times: "In Xanadu did Kubla Khan / A stately pleasure-dome decree; / Where Alph, the sacred river, ran / Through caverns measureless to man / Down to a sunless sea."*

Romanticism

Literature, music, and art reflected the dramatic social and economic changes of the Industrial Age. Many writers of the early 1800s, reacting against the age of reason and science, joined an artistic movement known as **romanticism.** The work of these artists appealed to the imagination and a spirit of individuality. These artists were interested in showing the life as they thought it should be rather than as it really was. Romantics valued emotion and instinct above reason.

In Great Britain, the most famous romantics were a group of young poets, including William Wordsworth, John Keats, and Lord Byron. Their works were filled with a love for beauty and nature. As Wordsworth wrote in one verse,

Primary Source

**❝One impulse from a vernal wood
May teach you more of man,
Of Moral Evil and of good,
Than all the sages can.❞**

William Wordsworth, "The Tables Turned," from *Poems of Wordsworth,* edited by Matthew Arnold

Other writers concentrated on the glories of the past, especially medieval times. For example, in *Ivanhoe* the Scottish author **Sir Walter Scott** wrote about the days of knighthood. Inspired by the growing nationalism of the times, other writers turned to the folklore, songs, and history of their own countries. In Germany the **Grimm brothers** collected fairy tales that continue to be well known. German author Johann Wolfgang von Goethe (GUHR·tuh) was a master of poetry, drama, and the novel. His drama *Faust,* the story of a man's bargain with the devil, is his most famous work. Romanticism also influenced American writers of the early 1800s. **James Fenimore Cooper** wrote adventure stories that idealized the American Indian and the frontier. Washington Irving used New York's Hudson River valley as the setting for his romantic stories, such as *The Legend of Sleepy Hollow.*

✔ **READING CHECKS: Making Generalizations** What themes did most romantic literature share?

Romantic Music, Painting, and Architecture

In music, like in literature, the 1800s began with a shift toward romanticism. Although romantic music was inspired by the cultures from which the composers arose, the beauty of the music is still universally appreciated. Romantic music is still heard today throughout the world. One of the inspirations for this transition was the German composer **Ludwig van Beethoven** (BAYT·hoh·vuhn). Beethoven brought to music some of the same aims that the British poets of his time brought to literature. He expressed his love of nature in the *Pastoral Symphony*. A call for liberty and freedom dominates his one opera, *Fidelio,* as well as the final movement of his ninth, and last, symphony. Beethoven's music became known for its powerful and passionate emotions.

The romantic movement produced a great outpouring of musical composition, especially in Austria and Germany. Johannes Brahms composed powerful symphonies and concertos that surge with rich, intensely emotional music. Franz Schubert, Robert Schumann, and Felix Mendelssohn brought to their music the lyric quality of romantic poetry. Frédéric Chopin (SHOH·pan), a Polish-born composer who lived in France, wrote expressive and beautiful piano works. Franz Liszt of Hungary used gypsy songs and dances in some of his compositions. He also developed the tone poem, a symphonic piece based on a theme from literature or philosophy.

In Russia **Pyotr Ilich Tchaikovsky** (chy·KAHF·skee) wrote ballet music, operas, and symphonies. His works were often built around stories, such as the ballet *The Sleeping Beauty* and the overture fantasy *Romeo and Juliet.* His *1812 Overture* commemorates Napoléon's defeat in Russia.

Perhaps the greatest composer of operas in the 1800s was Giuseppe Verdi. His best operas, such as *Othello* and *Aïda,* contain some of the most beautiful and dramatic vocal music ever written. The stories and themes of his operas were very nationalistic. Verdi's music inspired nationalist feelings in Italians even before Italy itself became politically united.

La Scala opera house in Milan, Italy, opened in 1778. Many romantic operas of the 1800s, including Giuseppe Verdi's, are still heard there today.

Richard Wagner (VAHG·nuhr) was the best known composer of operas in Germany. He referred to his operas as music dramas. His work combined singing, dancing, costumes, and scenery to create a very intense experience for his audience. Like others at the time, Wagner was very nationalistic. Many of his operas are based on Germanic myths.

In the 1820s and 1830s, romantic painters, like romantic writers, chose subjects from the past. Their paintings were full of drama and action. Eugène Delacroix (del·uh·KRWAH) of France painted this way. John Constable and J.M.W. Turner of Great Britain were landscape painters whose works reflected the romantic interest in nature. They often painted outdoors instead of in a traditional artist's studio. As a result, their work shows intense color and vitality.

Romanticism in architecture expressed itself in the so-called Gothic revival of the mid-1800s. The Gothic revival was an attempt to recreate the great architectural style of the Middle Ages. The British houses of Parliament reflect a Gothic style, as do many churches, colleges, and public buildings in the United States.

✔ **READING CHECK: Summarizing** In what ways did other arts reflect the same themes as romantic literature?

Photography

The age of photography began in 1839 when Louis-Jacques-Mande Daguerre introduced his daguerreotype, an early type of photograph. Photography has since had a great impact on society. In the 1800s photographs showed the world to people in new ways. Photographs taken by William Jackson influenced Congress to make Yellowstone the first national park. Mathew Brady's Civil War photographs showed the realities of war. Like the novels of Charles Dickens, the photographs of Jacob Riis showed the lives of poor people in very dramatic ways. The camera's ability to capture such scenes helped give rise to a movement known as realism.

✔ **READING CHECK: Making Generalizations** In what ways did the goals of early photographers differ from those of romantic artists?

Romantic art This painting by artist Hans Dahl, entitled *Girl with Goats by a Fiord,* is typical of the romantic style. ***What characteristics of romanticism can you identify in this painting?***

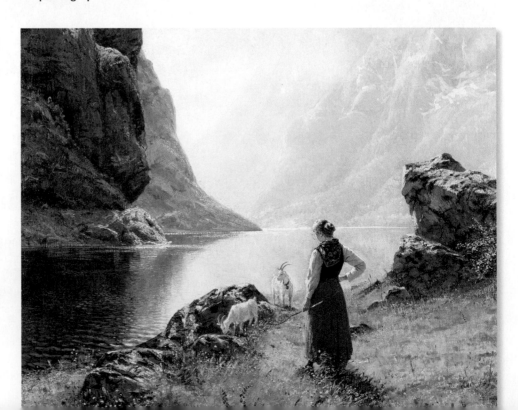

Art of the Industrial Age

Works of art always reflect in some way not only the values of the artist, but also the society in which the artist lives. The artist may agree or disagree with the rules of his or her society, or its political beliefs. By paying close attention to detail and the themes in a painting, you can better understand the historical period in which the artist was working, such as the Industrial Age.

An Artist's View

Honoré Daumier's painting *The Washerwoman* was created during the Industrial Revolution. Daumier rebelled against the romantic notions of art. Instead of dreaming about nature or the past, his art reflected social realities of the Industrial Revolution, which had created an urban working class that worked long and hard.

Paint box of an artist of the 1800s

Skills Reminder

To use art as a historical document, first identify the historical period in which the art was created. Try to identify some major trends affecting daily life during that time. Then determine the theme of the painting. Connect the theme to the historical period. What forces in society might the artist have been responding to? Finally, think about what the artwork is saying about society.

Skills Practice

❶ Who are the subjects of the painting? What are they doing?
❷ What is the mood of the painting?
❸ What is Daumier saying about the Industrial Revolution and the people involved in it?
❹ Using library or Internet resources, find a painting by another famous artist. Try to determine how the work of art could be used as a historical document.

The Rise of Realism

The subject matter of romantic art and literature had little to do with the lives of ordinary people. In the mid-1800s some writers and artists began to deal with everyday life and social settings, an approach called **realism.** One of the most important realists was Gustave Flaubert (floh·BAIR) of France. His novel *Madame Bovary* described the life of an ordinary woman with very close attention to detail. In Great Britain, Mary Ann Evans wrote realistic novels under the name George Eliot. Her greatest work, *Middlemarch,* analyzed different classes in Victorian society.

Realists often dealt with social and economic themes. In *War and Peace,* Russian writer Leo Tolstoy showed war not as a romantic adventure but as misery and death. The Norwegian playwright Henrik Ibsen brought human problems to the stage. His play *A Doll's House* argued for equality between a husband and wife in marriage.

In the United States one form of realism was **regionalism,** which focused on everyday life in particular places. For example, in his novels *The Adventures of Tom Sawyer* and *The Adventures of Huckleberry Finn,* **Mark Twain** described life along the Mississippi River.

In the late 1800s the **naturalists** took realism even further. They showed the ugly or unpleasant aspects of everyday life. The French novelist **Emile Zola** was a leader of this approach. He wrote as if he were a scientist carefully studying human activity. Although some people objected to his frankness, his exposure of social problems helped bring about reform. Another realist was the British novelist Charles Dickens, who often wrote about the poor in London.

In painting, artists such as Gustave Courbet (koor·BAY) and Honoré Daumier (dohm·YAY) tried to depict the everyday realities of life in the Industrial Age. Another type of realism was attempted by a group of painters called the **impressionists.** Impressionist painting flourished during the 1860s and 1870s in France. Impressionist

This painting by Pierre-Auguste Renoir, depicting an outdoor café scene in Paris, demonstrates the impressionists' attention to light and color.

painters tried to paint vivid impressions of people and places. To do this they carefully studied light and color. Claude Monet (moh·NAY) and Pierre-Auguste Renoir (ren·WAHR) were leading impressionist painters. Painters in England and the United States also took up the style.

✔ **READING CHECK: Finding the Main Idea** With what were the realists concerned?

Experiments in Art Forms

Like writers and musicians, painters and sculptors often rebelled against the industrial world. There was less nationalism in art than in literature and music. There was also more individual experimentation.

The landscapes and still lifes of painter **Paul Cézanne** explored the form and shapes of his subjects. He moved away from recognizable, realistic scenes. Cézanne's work influenced a group of painters who are often called the postimpressionists. Another artist, Paul Gauguin (goh·GAN), left Europe to live in Tahiti. His art stressed color and simple, flat shapes. French artist Henri-Émile-Benoît Matisse and Dutch painter Vincent Van Gogh (van·GOH) also emphasized color design over realism. Edgar Degas (deh·GAH), Henri de Toulouse-Lautrec (too·LOOZ·loh·TREK), and Édouard Manet all painted scenes of Parisian life in very personal styles.

The sculptor Auguste Rodin (roh·DAN) also broke with tradition. Some of his statues included unworked portions of marble to give the work an unfinished quality. Like many artists of the time, Rodin rejected the idea that art had to show things as they appear in real life.

✔ **READING CHECK: Analyzing Information** How did the work of Cézanne, Gauguin, and Rodin show their individual styles?

Edgar Degas worked with the human form in both paintings and sculpture. Shown here is his Little Fourteen-Year-Old Dancer.

SECTION 5 REVIEW

1. **Define** and explain the significance:
   romanticism
   realism
   regionalism
   naturalists
   impressionists

2. **Identify** and explain the significance:
   Sir Walter Scott
   Grimm brothers
   James Fenimore Cooper
   Ludwig van Beethoven
   Pyotr Ilich Tchaikovsky
   Mark Twain
   Emile Zola
   Paul Cézanne

3. **Sequencing** Copy the diagram and use it to chart the progression of artistic styles during the Industrial Age.

4. **Finding the Main Idea**
   a. How did music of the 1800s express romanticism?
   b. In what way was realism in art and literature a departure from romanticism?
   c. In what ways did Cézanne and the postimpressionists rebel against industrialism?

5. **Writing and Critical Thinking**
   Identifying Points of View Write a dialogue between a romantic artist or writer and a realist, expressing what each one hoped to accomplish.
   Consider:
   • what the romantics felt we could learn from nature
   • the ways in which realist authors and artists could sometimes bring about social change by exposing harsh conditions

Homework Practice Online
keyword: SH3 HP14

Creating a Time Line

Copy the time line below onto a sheet of paper. Complete the time line by filling in the events, individuals, and dates from the chapter that you think were significant. Pick three events and explain why you think they were significant.

1800	1840	1880	1928

Writing a Summary

Using standard grammar, spelling, sentence structure, and punctuation, write an overview of the events in the chapter.

Identifying People and Ideas

Identify the following terms or individuals and explain their significance:

1. Alexander Graham Bell
2. pasteurization
3. antisepsis
4. Pierre and Marie Curie
5. social sciences
6. Sigmund Freud
7. psychoanalysis
8. romanticism
9. realism
10. Paul Cézanne

Understanding Main Ideas

SECTION 1 *(pp. 380–383)*

Advances in Technology and Communication

1. Record the sequence of events that followed Faraday's discovery that magnetism could generate electricity.
2. Why did Orville and Wilbur Wright succeed where others failed?

SECTION 2 *(pp. 384–390)*

Advances in Science and Medicine

3. What progress was made in the area of biological sciences?
4. Explain how advances in medicine benefited society.
5. What advances were made in atomic theory?

SECTION 3 *(pp. 391–393)*

Social Sciences in the Industrial Age

6. How did Darwin's theory of evolution influence the field of sociology?

SECTION 4 *(pp. 394–399)*

Society and Culture in the Industrial Age

7. What factors led to the rapid growth of cities in the 1800s?
8. What effect did improved food storage have on population growth?

SECTION 5 *(pp. 400–405)*

Literature, Music, and Art in the Industrial Age

9. How did the work of the postimpressionist sculptors and painters step away from realism?

Reviewing Themes

1. **Citizenship** How did education change during the 1800s?
2. **Science, Technology & Society** How did electricity affect communication?
3. **Culture** How was romanticism a response to industrialized society?

Thinking Critically

1. **Drawing Inferences** How did the public education systems that developed in France and the United States help to fulfill the ideas of equality and a representative government?
2. **Making Predictions** How might innovations in transportation and communication affect social mobility?
3. **Comparing and Contrasting** How did the ideas and works of realists differ from those of the romantics?

Writing About History

Summarizing The 1800s saw great changes in the sciences and arts and in where and how people lived. Write a page from a memoir of a person who has lived through some of these significant changes. Use the following chart to organize your thoughts before you begin writing.

Advances of the Industrial Age	Technology	Medicine	Social sciences	Arts
Effect on daily life				

Connecting Architecture to History

Study the glass building shown. It was built to house an exhibition celebrating new industrial products. Then answer the questions.

Interior of the Crystal Palace, built for the Great Exhibition, London, 1851

1. Which is the best general statement about this building's place in history?

   a. It was the first modern building, and from then on all buildings were built in a similar style.

   b. The design of the building and the materials used in its construction were intended to celebrate the spirit of "progress."

   c. The building's architectural style and construction materials were typical of the times.

   d. Not many people saw the building in 1851 because they weren't interested in an industry exhibition.

2. Explain your choice of statements in question 1. Give specific examples to support your point of view.

Understanding Frames of Reference

Read this quote from Mark Twain's *Life on the Mississippi,* published in 1883. Then answer the questions.

> "When I was a boy, there was but one permanent ambition among my comrades in our village on the west bank of the Mississippi River. That was, to be a steamboatman. . . . By and by one of our boys went away. At last he turned up as an apprentice engineer . . . on a steamboat. . . . And whenever his boat was laid up he would come home and swell around the town in his blackest and greasiest clothes, so that nobody could help remembering that he was a steamboatman; . . . If ever a youth was cordially admired and hated by his comrades, this one was."

3. Which is the best statement of what this quote implies about Twain's social class when he was a boy?

   a. He and his friends were from families of steamboat workers.

   b. He and his friends were from families that worked hard and had very little money.

   c. He was from a wealthy family that traveled often.

   d. He was from a middle-class family that valued cleanliness.

4. Do you think any of the "comrades" mentioned in this quote were girls? Give specific reasons for your answer.

Alternative Assessment

Building Your Portfolio

Link to TODAY

Culture

Writers and artists can often help bring about social reform by exposing harsh conditions through their works. Compile a list of realist writers and artists who addressed such themes during the Industrial Age. Create a chart to summarize your findings.

internet connect

Internet Activity: go.hrw.com
KEYWORD: SH3 WH14

Choose a topic on Life in the Industrial Age to:

- explore Thomas Edison's inventions.
- research the immigrant experience in America during the 1800s.
- learn about contemporary women's colleges.

1791–1911
The Age of Reform

Immigrants to the United States in the mid-1800s

1804
Global Events
Haiti becomes the first independent nation in Latin America.

1814
Global Events
The Treaty of Ghent ends the War of 1812.

1831
Daily Life
German immigrants to America number about 15,000.

1790   **1815**   **1840**

1797
Politics
John Adams becomes president of the United States.

1838
Politics
Chartists in Great Britain demand universal suffrage and vote by ballot.

1828
Business and Finance
Construction begins on the Baltimore and Ohio Railroad, the first railroad to carry passengers and freight.

The second president of the United States, John Adams, and wife, Abigail

An early passenger train

Build on What You Know

*T*he Industrial Revolution that began in England in the mid-1700s marked a major turning point for European society. It soon transformed the ways in which people in Europe and America lived, worked, and thought. Changes in occupations and living conditions brought more leisure time as well as social problems. Life had become very different. These major changes led to calls for reform to make life better as well. In time, those calls would spread beyond Europe. In this chapter, you will learn how people in various nations worked to reform their governments and societies in the name of Enlightenment ideals.

U.S. president Abraham Lincoln

1852
Science and Technology
The French chemist Charles-Frédéric Gerhardt publishes his theory of organic compounds.

1853
Global Events
The Crimean War begins.

1863
Politics
U.S. president Abraham Lincoln issues the Emancipation Proclamation.

Cover of Upton Sinclair's The Jungle

1896
Global Events
The Klondike gold rush begins in Bonanza Creek, Canada.

1906
The Arts
Upton Sinclair's *The Jungle* is published.

1907
Global Events
New Zealand joins the British Empire.

1911
Daily Life
The British Official Secrets Act becomes law.

1911
Politics
Great Britain enacts the Parliament Act of 1911.

1865   **1890**   **1915**

1856
Daily Life
The 13.5-ton clock popularly known as Big Ben is crafted for the British Parliament.

1856
Science and Technology
The Bessemer converter changes the steel-making process.

1866
Business and Finance
"Black Friday" occurs at the London Stock Exchange.

1888
Science and Technology
Louis Pasteur founds the Pasteur Institute in Paris.

1910
The Arts
Igor Stravinsky's *The Firebird* ballet debuts in Paris.

1909
Daily Life
London hairdressers give the first permanent waves.

1904
Science and Technology
Work begins on the Panama Canal.

1903
Business and Finance
Henry Ford founds the Ford Motor Company.

Louis Pasteur in his laboratory

What's Your Opinion?

*Do you **agree** or **disagree** with the following statements? Support your point of view in your journal.*

Citizenship There should be no restrictions on who may vote in a society.

Government The interests of private individuals in a society cannot come before the interests of the government.

Constitutional Heritage Established laws, not powerful individuals, should guide a nation.

READ TO DISCOVER

❶ How did British government and social welfare change in the 1800s?

❷ What policies did Disraeli and Gladstone follow in Britain?

❸ How did British government and social welfare change in the early 1900s?

❹ What changes occurred in other areas of the British Empire during the 1800s and 1900s?

DEFINE

suffrage
suffragettes

IDENTIFY

Queen Victoria
Benjamin Disraeli
William Gladstone
Emmeline Pankhurst
Lord Durham
Aborigines
Maori

WHY IT MATTERS TODAY

Liberalism continues to be a key political philosophy in the United States and elsewhere in the world. Use CNN Student News.com or other **current event** sources to see what issues liberals are interested in today. Record your findings in your journal.

CNN Student News.com

Liberal Reforms in Great Britain and Its Empire

The Main Idea
Reform movements arose in Great Britain in response to the problems of the Industrial Revolution.

The Story Continues *During the 1800s and 1900s, reformers in Britain worked to extend civil rights. Women especially fought hard for the right to vote and were often arrested. Emmeline Pankhurst, one of the leaders of this movement, noted that "Over one thousand women . . . have suffered their imprisonment . . . weakened in body, but not in spirit. We are . . . convinced that this is the only way in which we can win power to alter what for us are . . . absolutely intolerable conditions."*

Reforms of the 1800s

The Industrial Revolution had brought wealth and power to Great Britain. It had also created many economic and social inequalities. As the Industrial Revolution spread, a political philosophy grounded in the Enlightenment and the French Revolution emerged. In general this philosophy, called liberalism, supported government protection of individual rights and civil liberties.

During the 1800s individuals who believed in liberalism were very active in politics. British liberals helped enact numerous reforms to protect individuals' political and civil liberties. Some reforms were aimed at extending **suffrage,** or the right to vote. Others focused on correcting social and economic problems. The abolition of slavery and the slave trade was among these reforms.

Voting restrictions. Great Britain was one of the first European nations to limit the power of the monarchy. Since the Glorious Revolution of 1688, Parliament was the real ruler of Great Britain. The House of Commons was supposed to represent all British people. Voters in each district elected a representative to serve them.

There were many restrictions, however, on the right to vote and hold office. Only people who owned property could vote. People voted in the open, so that others could see how they voted. Therefore, voters could be bribed or intimidated. In some districts the nobles controlled who would be the representative in the House of Commons. District boundaries no longer represented how the population was distributed. Only men who owned a great deal of property could be elected to the House of Commons. No Catholics, Jews, or Dissenters—non-Anglican Protestants—could hold political office.

The Reform Bill of 1832. Workers and the middle class began to demand changes in this voting system. The members of the upper class resisted because they feared political reform would not only take power away from them, but could also bring about a reign of terror, as it had in France.

In 1829, however, Parliament passed the Catholic Emancipation Act. This law allowed Roman Catholics to serve in Parliament if they recognized the Protestant monarch as the ruler of Great Britain. By 1830 the middle class and laborers were demanding more wide-ranging reforms. Several times in the past the House of Commons had passed a bill that extended voting rights and redrew district boundaries more fairly. However, the House of Lords refused to let the bill pass until 1832.

This Reform Bill of 1832 took seats in the House of Commons away from less populated areas and gave them to the industrial cities. It also gave people with less property the right to vote. The middle class now had a voice in Great Britain's government and power in Parliament.

By forcing passage of the Reform Bill of 1832, the Whig Party had won the strong support of these new voters. Now the Whigs joined with some Radicals, and with liberals from the Tory Party, to form the Liberal Party. The Tory Party of wealthy landowners became known as the Conservative Party.

Social and economic change. Major social and economic changes took place in Great Britain after 1832. The Factory Act of 1833 and other laws were aimed at reforming the horrible working conditions of women and children. Slavery was abolished in all British colonies in 1833. That same year the Liberal Party took a first step toward free public education by winning financial support for private and church schools.

In 1844 a London hatter placed this illustration inside his hats to show his support for free trade and the Anti-Corn-Law League.

The Liberal Party also helped eliminate the unpopular Corn Laws. These laws placed high taxes on grain imported by Britain, enabling British landowners to sell their grain at high prices. As a result, British workers had to pay high prices or starve. After a bitter fight, Parliament repealed the Corn Laws in 1846. This was Britain's first step toward free trade.

The Chartist movement. As the spirit of reform began to spread in Great Britain during the 1830s, members of the working class felt that their voices had gone unheard. In response, a cabinetmaker named William Lovett founded the London Workingmen's Association in 1836. Among the reforms that Lovett and his group demanded were universal male suffrage and a secret ballot. The group called for electoral districts in Great Britain to be redrawn in order to equalize parliamentary representation throughout the country. It also wanted salaries for members of Parliament so that workers could afford to enter politics. These reforms were proposed in a document known as the People's Charter. Supporters of Lovett and his calls for reform were called Chartists.

The Chartist movement became widely popular among British workers. As social and economic conditions gradually improved, however, its power declined. By the late 1840s, the Chartist movement had effectively ended, but over time, many of the reforms it had backed became law. In 1867, for example, a major reform bill was passed, nearly doubling the number of British voters. Yet while most urban industrial workers could now vote, women and many lower-class workers still could not.

✔ **READING CHECK: Making Generalizations** What was the overall aim of the liberal reforms of the 1800s?

Benjamin Disraeli was Queen Victoria's favorite prime minister.

CONNECTING TO

GEOGRAPHY

The Irish Potato Famine

Both Ireland and the United States were changed forever when a fungus struck the Irish potato crop in 1845. The fungus returned year after year, causing plants to wilt and rot. In the already poor nation, hunger led to disease and starvation.

Unable to work or pay rent, many families were evicted from their homes. Many died in the streets or countryside as relief efforts proved insufficient. Famine and disease probably killed more than 1 million people. More than 2 million people left Ireland between 1845 and 1855, many for the United States.

Understanding Geography

How did a crop fungus in Ireland affect the United States?

Disraeli and Gladstone

When King William IV died in 1837 with no heirs, his 18-year-old niece Victoria became queen. The rule of **Queen Victoria** lasted 63 years and is known as the Victorian Age. Victoria gave her prime ministers a free hand and did not interfere. Between 1868 and 1894, two prime ministers dominated British affairs.

A leader of the Conservative Party, **Benjamin Disraeli** twice served as prime minister. He was a master politician interested in guiding foreign affairs and expanding Britain's empire. Disraeli first became prime minister in 1868, but his term lasted only a few months before the Liberal Party defeated his party in a general election. During his second term, from 1874 to 1880, Britain gained control of the Suez Canal and Queen Victoria became the Empress of India.

A leader of the Liberal Party, **William Gladstone** served four terms as prime minister. Gladstone was concerned mainly with domestic and financial affairs. Under his leadership, Parliament made many reforms. Gladstone first became prime minister in 1868. One of his achievements was passage of the Education Act of 1870, which created a national elementary education system. Working-class children could now receive a basic education for a small fee. Elementary education became free in 1891. Also under Gladstone, in 1872 Britain began to use a secret ballot. This reform reduced bribery and political pressure on voters. In 1884 Gladstone and the Liberal Party passed a third reform bill that gave the vote to male agricultural workers. In 1885 voting districts were redrawn to be approximately equal in population.

Despite their many reforms, Gladstone and the Liberal Party failed to solve the "Irish question." In 1801 the Act of Union had linked Ireland to Great Britain and disbanded Ireland's Parliament. Most Irish people hated British rule. The Irish had little representation in the British Parliament. Because most Irish were Catholic, they were upset at having to pay taxes that supported the Anglican Church. The Liberals wanted Ireland to have home rule, which would allow the Irish people to rule themselves. Conservatives, however, did not want Britain to give up control.

British policies that were designed to help British industry hurt Irish farmers. The poor were left to suffer. When the Irish potato crop failed in the mid-1800s, famine swept Ireland. Many Irish fled to the United States. Gladstone unsuccessfully fought for home rule. To ease tensions Conservatives agreed to some land reforms in the 1890s.

✔ **READING CHECK: Contrasting** How did the positions of Gladstone and the Liberals differ from those of Disraeli and the Conservatives?

Reforms of the Early 1900s

Political reform was accompanied by social reform. During the late 1800s and early 1900s, the labor union movement grew stronger in Great Britain. Socialism, too, attracted more and more followers. In 1884 a group of intellectuals formed the Fabian Society. This organization aimed to improve society through socialist ideas and education. The Fabians tried to spread their ideas through established political parties. In 1906 they helped workers, who were frustrated with the Liberal and Conservative parties, form the British Labour Party.

In 1905 the Liberal Party returned to power. Under Prime Minister Herbert Asquith, the Liberals passed numerous social welfare laws. New laws provided for old-age pensions, health insurance, and unemployment insurance. To pay for these new programs, Parliament raised taxes. In 1909 Parliament's budget called for higher taxes on the wealthy. This angered the House of Lords, which fought against the plan. Liberals then took steps to limit the power of the lords. The Parliament Act of 1911 took away the lords' power to veto any tax or spending bills. It allowed them only to delay other bills. Many nobles bitterly opposed the act. George V, however, who had become king in 1910, supported the Liberals. He suggested he would create enough new Liberal lords to pass the act. The House of Lords gave in and reluctantly passed it.

Less than a month later, a law was passed that gave members of the House of Commons a salary of 400 pounds a year. That was a good salary at the time. It meant that a person without an independent income could serve in Parliament.

Beginning in the late 1800s, many women in Great Britain became **suffragettes**— women who campaigned for their right to vote. They were led by energetic and outspoken women like **Emmeline Pankhurst** and her daughter Christabel.

HISTORY MAKER

Emmeline Pankhurst (1858–1928)

For forty years Emmeline Pankhurst worked on behalf of the women's suffrage movement in Great Britain. Among her accomplishments was the passage of a bill allowing married women to vote in local elections. She also established the Women's Social and Political Union.

The Union's early tactics included demonstrations and marches. Later it became more militant. Pankhurst went to jail numerous times and suffered ill health from her many hunger strikes. Shortly before her death, women won the right to vote in Britain. **How did Emmeline Pankhurst work to achieve the vote for women?**

	Reforming the British Parliamentary System
1829	The Catholic Emancipation Act permitted Roman Catholics to be elected to Parliament.
1832	The Reform Bill of 1832 redistributed seats in Parliament and lowered property qualifications for voting.
1867	The Reform Bill of 1867 further lowered property qualifications, almost doubling the electorate.
1872	The secret ballot was adopted.
1884	The Reform Bill of 1884 gave the right to vote to most farmworkers.
1885	The Redistribution Bill divided Britain into approximately equal electoral districts.
1911	The Parliament Act of 1911 took away the power of the House of Lords to veto parliamentary bills.
1928	All British women over age 21 were granted voting rights.

Interpreting the Chart
Over the course of 100 years, many changes took place in Britain's parliamentary system. *What general trend does this chart indicate?*

The suffragettes petitioned Parliament and demonstrated. They became increasingly determined and disruptive. Women's suffrage, however, was not won until after World War I.

✔ **READING CHECK: Summarizing** How was Parliament changed during the 1900s?

Changes in the British Empire

What If? What if Great Britain had not experienced the American Revolution? How might its policies toward Canada and other colonies have differed?

Settlers in other areas of the British Empire—Canada, Australia, and New Zealand—also benefited from the liberal reforms in Great Britain.

Canada. In the early 1800s, Canadians were not happy with British rule. British settlers in Upper Canada—now part of Ontario—wanted more self-rule. French Canadians in Lower Canada—now part of Quebec—disliked being controlled by the British.

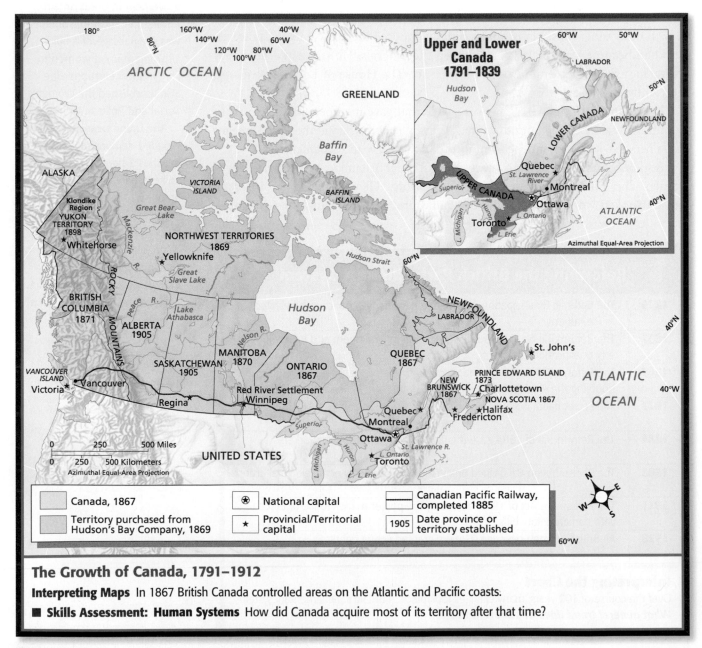

The Growth of Canada, 1791–1912

Interpreting Maps In 1867 British Canada controlled areas on the Atlantic and Pacific coasts.

■ **Skills Assessment: Human Systems** How did Canada acquire most of its territory after that time?

During the 1830s a depression, unemployment, and crop failures led to failed uprisings in both parts of Canada.

Britain was anxious not to repeat the mistake that had cost it the American colonies, in which the British government had not treated the colonists as full citizens. It had been too far away to fully understand their situation or enforce its authority.

In 1838 the British government sent **Lord Durham** to Canada. A member of the Liberal Party, Durham was given broad powers to reform Canada's government. Durham suggested that Great Britain could keep colonies such as Canada in the empire by granting them self-government and that Canada be united into one state. In 1841 the British Parliament unified British Upper Canada and French Lower Canada by passage of the Act of Union. A parliament was formed in which both regions were represented equally. From 1846 to 1848, the British expanded the power of Canada's Parliament and granted Canada self-government.

Uniting Upper and Lower Canada was a failure. The equally divided Parliament resulted in gridlock. This problem was solved when the British Parliament passed the British North America Act of 1867, creating the Dominion of Canada with four provinces—Ontario, Quebec, Nova Scotia, and New Brunswick. Each province had its own legislature for local affairs. A federal Parliament dealt with national issues.

Canada expanded by purchasing the Northwest Territories in 1869 and 1870 from the Hudson's Bay Company, creating the province of Manitoba. In the 1870s British Columbia and Prince Edward Island became provinces. In the late 1890s the discovery of gold brought many people to northwestern Canada, leading to the organization of the Yukon Territory in 1898. The Canadian Pacific Railway opened western Canada to immigration, and Alberta and Saskatchewan joined the Dominion in 1905.

Australia. While early history is obscure, scientists believe the earliest settlers of Oceania, which includes Australia and New Zealand, came from Asia over 40,000 years ago and lived simply off the land. In 1770 Captain James Cook, a British sailor, claimed the eastern shore of Australia for Great Britain. This area is now known as New South Wales. After the American Revolution Britain began to use Australia as a penal colony. The first convicts arrived in 1788 and soon founded the town of Sydney. Free settlers arrived shortly thereafter. Convicts who served their sentences could stay in Australia and own land, but the two groups of settlers did not always get along.

These women and men working a Canadian mine in about 1900 dreamed of finding fortunes in gold.

Australia and New Zealand, c. 1800s

Interpreting Maps Britain established six colonies across the Australian continent.

■ **Skills Assessment: Places and Regions** What island off the southern coast of Australia did the British also colonize?

The Maori A New Zealand photographer captured this image of a Maori chief in about 1880. *What does this image tell you about the chief and his people?*

The early 1800s were a lawless period in Australia. Immigrants, ex-convicts, and gangs of escaped convicts clashed. The original inhabitants of Australia, the **Aborigines,** were pushed into the interior of the country. The Aborigines population was greatly reduced by British settlement. Many died from new diseases brought by the Europeans. British ideas of racial superiority also led to brutal violence against the Aborigines.

Britain claimed the entire continent of Australia in 1829. By 1836 the colonies of Tasmania, Western Australia, and South Australia had been organized. Victoria was formed in 1851, and Queensland was added in 1859. The colonies developed independently of each other. However, to guard against territorial expansion by other European powers the colonies united in 1901 as the Commonwealth of Australia, a self-governing part of the British Empire. As Australia's economy grew, trade unions and the Labor Party influenced Parliament. Social welfare laws were passed concerning issues such as old-age pensions and wage fixing.

New Zealand. Like Australia, New Zealand had been sighted by Captain James Cook. Private companies developed the islands in the 1820s and 1830s. In 1840 the British took control of New Zealand when they signed a treaty with the **Maori** (MOW·ree), the original inhabitants. The British Parliament granted New Zealand a constitution in 1852, and the islands became a self-governing colony.

Like the Aborigines in Australia, however, the Maori were hurt by European settlement. British settlers and the native inhabitants fought over land, and several wars took place in the 1860s and early 1870s. Many Maori died from warfare and disease.

The discovery of gold in 1861 brought new waves of immigrants. In 1893 New Zealand became the first country in the world to grant women the right to vote. In 1907 New Zealand joined the British Empire as a dominion.

✔ **READING CHECK: Identifying Cause and Effect** How were the original inhabitants of Australia and New Zealand affected by European settlement?

SECTION 1 REVIEW

1. **Define** and explain the significance:
   suffrage
   suffragettes

2. **Identify** and explain the significance:
   Queen Victoria
   Benjamin Disraeli
   William Gladstone
   Emmeline Pankhurst
   Lord Durham
   Aborigines
   Maori

3. **Categorizing** Copy the chart below. Use it to organize the conditions and reforms in Great Britain in the 1800s and 1900s.

Condition	Reform

4. **Finding the Main Idea**
   a. Why was the Reform Bill of 1832 needed? How did it affect British government?
   b. Compare the views and achievements of British prime ministers Benjamin Disraeli and William Gladstone.
   c. What steps did Britain take in Canada, Australia, and New Zealand to ensure that the colonists there would not rebel?

5. **Writing and Critical Thinking**
   Supporting a Point of View Write a policy statement that expresses the Conservative Party's point of view on reforms in Britain in the 1800s.
   Consider:
   • what conditions existed that prompted the reforms
   • what reforms were enacted
   • the cost of the reforms

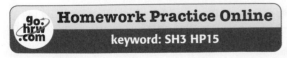
Homework Practice Online
keyword: SH3 HP15

READ TO DISCOVER

❶ How did the United States expand westward?

❷ Why did the United States fight a civil war?

❸ In what ways did the United States change after the Civil War?

DEFINE

sectionalism
secede
total war

IDENTIFY

Northwest Ordinance
Abraham Lincoln
Emancipation Proclamation
Lucretia Mott
Elizabeth Cady Stanton

WHY IT MATTERS TODAY

The extension of suffrage and civil rights that began in the 1800s affects elections, job opportunities, housing, and education to this day. Use CNN or other **current event** sources to see how the "equal protection" clause has affected policies such as affirmative action. Record your findings in your journal.

CNN Student News.com

Expansion and Reform in the United States

The Main Idea
During the 1800s the United States expanded greatly, but a civil war divided the nation.

The Story Continues *As the United States gained more territory in North America, people argued bitterly over whether to abolish or continue slavery. President Abraham Lincoln promised to both stop slavery and keep the country together, saying, "I believe this government cannot endure permanently half slave and half free. I do not expect the Union to be dissolved; . . . but I do expect it will cease to be divided."*

Territorial Growth

While Great Britain was reforming its social, economic, and political systems, the United States was growing larger and more populated. In 1788 the United States was made up of 13 states and had a population of almost 4 million people, most living in small farming communities in the east. Most Americans wanted to avoid European affairs and focused on building their lives within the new country. By 1900 the United States had grown to almost four times its original size and its population was about 60 million.

The Northwest Territory. Individual colonies had once claimed the land bordered by the Appalachian Mountains, Mississippi and Ohio Rivers, and Great Lakes. When the Articles of Confederation were ratified, this land—called the Northwest Territory—was turned over to the United States. Thousands of settlers moved into the territory, and in 1787 Congress passed the **Northwest Ordinance** to provide some form of government for them.

The ordinance guaranteed that the settlers would receive the same rights as the citizens in the original 13 states. It also stated that the Northwest Territory would be divided into states that would be admitted into the Union. Once 5,000 males lived in a territory, it could start its own legislature. When 60,000 people lived there, it could

This painting shows people from Connecticut moving to the Northwest Territory in the late 1700s.

adopt a constitution and apply for statehood. Many people left their homes on the east coast to settle the Northwest Territory. Of the ten new states that were added to the United States between 1791 and 1836, three were part of the Northwest Territory.

Continued expansion. In 1803 the French emperor Napoléon sold the United States the vast Louisiana Territory, which almost doubled the size of the nation. The country also purchased Florida from Spain in 1819. In 1836 American settlers in Mexican territory declared themselves independent and formed the Republic of Texas. When the United States took control of Texas, war with Mexico began. The United States won and received the Mexican Cession, a huge tract of land.

The nation continued to expand. An 1846 treaty with Great Britain gave the United States the Oregon Territory. In 1853 the country completed the Gadsden Purchase,

U.S. Territorial Expansion, 1785–1898

Interpreting Maps By the 1850s the nation stretched from Mexico to Canada and from one ocean to the next. This expansion led to conflicts with the Mexicans as well as American Indians.

■ **Skills Assessment: Physical Systems** How many present-day states were entirely or partially included in the Louisiana Purchase?

which expanded its southern border. Over the next 50 years Americans would move west to search for gold or to settle the land as farmers or ranchers. Their movements pushed American Indians off most of the land and onto reservations.

✔ **READING CHECK: Summarizing** In what ways did the United States acquire western lands?

Slavery and Civil War

Although unified politically, the United States was hurt by **sectionalism,** or competition among sections or regions of the country. In the early 1800s three major sections emerged: the industrial Northeast, the agricultural South, and the largely frontier West. People from these three regions had different ways of life and different views on issues. The issue that divided them most was slavery.

Slavery was legal in the United States, but each individual state could allow or abolish it. Some southerners believed they needed African American slaves to harvest their cotton and tobacco crops. As the nation expanded, Americans began to question whether slavery should be allowed in the new territories. Southerners said that Congress had no power to prohibit it. Northerners disagreed. In time, however, more and more people began to think that slavery should be abolished altogether. Throughout the early 1800s these arguments led to bitter sectional quarrels. Southern states sometimes threatened to **secede,** or withdraw from the Union.

In 1860 **Abraham Lincoln** was elected president. His Republican Party had already vowed to stop the spread of slavery to new territories. In response to the election South Carolina seceded from the Union. Other southern states followed, and together they formed the Confederate States of America.

President Lincoln argued that these states had no constitutional right to secede. Therefore they were rebelling, and the federal government had a constitutional duty to end all rebellions. In 1861 the Union and the Confederacy began a bloody war that continued for four long years. Military leaders employed the new strategy of **total war,** in which both the enemy's military and civilian resources were targets of destruction. The use of new and vastly more lethal weapons made this the first "modern" war.

As the war continued, it became clear that the South lacked the troops and industrial resources needed to overcome the power of the North. In April 1865 the Confederacy surrendered, ending the war. The Civil War was the most costly conflict in which the United States has ever been involved. More than 600,000 people lost their lives. Families were torn apart, property was destroyed, and bitterness endured well into the 1900s.

In 1863 President Lincoln had issued the **Emancipation Proclamation,** freeing slaves in those parts of the country still in rebellion. Although it had little immediate effect, the proclamation signaled that slavery would end everywhere with the end of the war. Following the war, Congress passed three amendments to the Constitution, abolishing slavery and guaranteeing rights to former slaves. In many places, however, the law was not followed. Freedom did not necessarily ease the lives of the former slaves.

✔ **READING CHECK: Identifying Cause and Effect** How did the election of Abraham Lincoln influence the start of the Civil War?

Major Civil War Battles

Interpreting Maps Not all the states that permitted their citizens to hold slaves moved to secede from the Union after the election of Abraham Lincoln.

- **Skills Assessment: 1. Places and Regions** Which slave states remained in the Union?
2. **Using Geography** Why did Union forces aim to capture Vicksburg, Mississippi?
3. **The World in Spatial Terms** About how far apart from one another were the capital cities of the two opposing sides?
4. **Making Generalizations** Which side, the North or the South, likely sustained more property damage from the war? Explain your answer.

Growth through Immigration

As the United States expanded during the 1800s, patterns of immigration changed. From 1800 to 1880 more than 10 million people came to the United States. Many of these immigrants were from northwestern Europe, including Great Britain, Ireland, and Germany. Later in the century, the rate of immigration increased. Between 1891 and 1910, some 12 million immigrants arrived, mainly from southern or eastern Europe. Most of these newer immigrants were Czech, Greek, Hungarian, Italian, Polish, Russian, and Slovak. People from the Middle East, Asia, and North and South America arrived in smaller numbers. Reading graphs can help in understanding these changes in immigration trends.

Total Immigration to the United States, 1860–1900

Source: *Historical Statistics of the United States*

An Immigrant's View

Most immigrants came to America either to seek economic opportunities or to escape religious or political persecution at home. Romanian immigrant Esther Gidiwicz recalled her feelings upon arriving in the United States:

> "All of a sudden, we heard a big commotion and we came to America and everybody started yelling—they see the Statue of Liberty. . . . I remember my father putting his arms around my mother and the two of them standing and crying and my father said to my mother, 'You're in America now. You have nothing to be afraid of.'"

Origin of Immigrants

- Great Britain
- Ireland
- Scandinavia
- Germany
- Italy
- Russia
- Other European Countries
- Asia
- North and South America
- Other

Data reflect 1900 and 1998. Due to rounding, numbers may not add up to 100 percent.

1900   **1998**

Historical Statistics of the United States; Statistical Abstract of the United States, 2000

Skills Reminder

To accurately interpret a graph, first read the title. The title of the graph indicates the graph's main idea and focus. Then study the labels to identify the type of information presented in each section or along each axis. Analyze the information in the graph carefully. Take note of time intervals, increases or decreases in quantities, and proportions. Use appropriate math skills as needed. Look for trends and changes in the data. Use the results of your analysis, along with your knowledge of the historical period, to sum up the data, identify trends, and draw conclusions.

Skills Practice

Examine the graphs shown above. Based on the information shown, answer the following questions.

❶ What types of graphs are represented?

❷ What does each graph show about immigration?

❸ Write one conclusion you can draw from the graphs.

❹ Using information from the library or the Internet, create a graph that shows other trends in the population of the United States over time. Write a series of questions to go with it.

Elizabeth Cady Stanton (1815–1902)

At the Seneca Falls Convention in 1848, Elizabeth Cady Stanton asked women to organize themselves and assert their rights. Her efforts helped launch the women's suffrage movement in the United States. **What impression of Stanton does this photograph create?**

A Changing Nation

After the Civil War, immigration and territorial expansion brought political and social change to the United States.

Suffrage and political growth. In the original 13 states, only white males who owned property could vote. However, states carved from new territories had few property requirements for voters. In time the eastern states also dropped their property restrictions. In the 1820s and 1830s, more and more political officials were elected rather than appointed. Political candidates came to be chosen by party conventions rather than a small group of legislators. More voters than ever before decided elections.

Those voters did not include women, however. In 1848 a women's rights convention was held in Seneca Falls, New York, organized by **Lucretia Mott** and **Elizabeth Cady Stanton.** The delegates drew up a list of demands, including the right to vote. Many women who campaigned for the abolition of slavery also insisted on equality for women. Their efforts gained strength after African American men were granted the right to vote. In the 1890s and early 1900s, the movement for women's suffrage grew stronger. Finally, in 1920, the ratification of the Nineteenth Amendment gave women the right to vote.

Growth in diversity. Between 1865 and 1900, cities doubled or tripled in size, connected by a network of railroads. Part of this growth was due to immigration. For decades many people had come to America from England and Scotland. In the mid-1800s, however, heavy waves of immigrants reached the United States from Ireland and Germany. During the late 1800s immigration from southern and eastern Europe greatly increased. By about 1900 many immigrants were also arriving from Latin America. Large-scale immigration during these years helped make the population of the United States more diverse.

✔ **READING CHECK: Categorizing** In what ways did the United States change after the Civil War?

SECTION 2 REVIEW

1. **Define** and explain the significance:
   sectionalism
   secede
   total war

2. **Identify** and explain the significance:
   Northwest Ordinance
   Abraham Lincoln
   Emancipation Proclamation
   Lucretia Mott
   Elizabeth Cady Stanton

3. **Sequencing** Copy the time line below. Use it to list three events that helped expand the borders of the United States.

1775   1800   1825   1850   1875

Event	Territory gained

4. **Finding the Main Idea**
   a. Why did a growing number of Americans choose to relocate to the western regions of the country throughout the 1800s?
   b. What factors prompted the South to secede from the Union in 1860?
   c. In what significant ways did patterns of immigration to the United States change during the course of the 1800s?

5. **Writing and Critical Thinking**
   Decision Making Write a letter from the point of view of a U.S. senator in the late 1800s considering whether to support suffrage for women.
   Consider:
   • why women wanted suffrage
   • why some men might have opposed female suffrage

Homework Practice Online
keyword: SH3 HP15

Revolution and Reform in France

READ TO DISCOVER

❶ Why did the rule of Louis Philippe lead to a revolution in 1848?

❷ How did Louis-Napoléon start a second empire in France?

❸ What characterized France's relations with Germany and other countries?

❹ How did the Third Republic maintain political stability in France?

DEFINE

anarchists
coalitions

IDENTIFY

Louis Philippe
Louis-Napoléon
Crimean War
Florence Nightingale
Otto von Bismarck
Franco-Prussian War
Communards
Alfred Dreyfus

WHY IT MATTERS TODAY

Socialism continues to be a force in today's French government. Use CNN.com or other **current event** sources to see how much power socialists have in the French legislature. Record your findings in your journal.

CNN student News.com

The Main Idea
Constitutionalism was an underlying force in the turmoil that characterized France during the 1800s.

The Story Continues *"To arms, citizens! / Form your battalions, / Let us march, let us march!" These lyrics from "The Marseillaise"— the anthem of the French revolution—first called French citizens to battle in 1792. In 1879 the song once again became France's national anthem, as the French continued their long fight for political and social change.*

Discontent and Revolution

As the United States expanded its borders and endured a costly civil war, France was experiencing its own troubles. The Congress of Vienna had restored Louis XVIII to the throne after Napoleon's second exile. Louis accepted a constitution that limited his power and kept many of the reforms set from 1789 to 1815. He tried to balance between those who wanted a return to absolute monarchy and those who wanted a more liberal government.

When Louis XVIII died in 1824, his brother Charles X became king of France. Charles believed in absolute monarchy and abolished most of the liberal reforms. He also taxed the people in order to pay back nobles whose estates had been seized and sold to the peasants. When the French people revolted in July 1830, Charles gave up his throne.

The "Citizen King." The leaders of the revolution of 1830 could not agree on what kind of government to set up once Charles X left. Those who favored a republic did not have the power to create one. Eventually all groups agreed to choose another king. They decided on **Louis Philippe,** a member of the Bourbon family whom they believed to be liberal.

Louis Philippe was king of France, but one approved of by the French Parliament. To help win the support he needed from the people, he called himself the "citizen king." In reality, Louis Philippe's actions helped the upper middle class most of all. Although the number of people allowed to vote had more than doubled after the revolution of 1830, landowners still held most of the power. Workers were not allowed to organize, and labor unions were illegal. High tariffs placed on imported goods kept the prices of domestic goods high. These high prices benefited industrialists but hurt workers and peasants.

Louis Philippe sought to secure his position as France's elected king with policies that favored powerful, conservative interests.

RÉPUBLIQUE FRANÇAISE.

Combat du peuple parisien dans les journées des 22, 23 et 24 Février 1848.

Revolution Discontented French citizens rose up to battle the government of Louis Philippe and set up a republic. *What mood does this image reflect?*

Republicanism under Louis-Napoléon

Louis-Napoléon fixed many elections so that most of the candidates directly supported his government. His half-brother remarked:

"In voting for the friends of Louis-Napoléon, one will have a second chance to vote for the prince himself."

How did Louis-Napoléon undermine the idea of republicanism?

Monarchists who wanted a direct descendant of Charles X to be king opposed Louis Philippe. The Bonapartists also opposed Louis Philippe, because they wanted to revive Napoléon's empire. At the same time, republicans believed that France should become a republic, grant political rights, and make reforms. Most French workers agreed. Food shortages and unemployment between 1846 and 1848 heightened tension and discontent.

The revolution of 1848. France finally erupted in 1848 after Louis Philippe issued a decree that, in effect, restricted citizens' free speech. The decree led to rioting in the streets. When National Guard troops were summoned to restore order, they joined the rioters. Louis Philippe decided he had no choice but to give up the throne. He abdicated and left for England.

The people of Paris established a temporary government and proclaimed the Second French Republic. Active in the new government were urban workers who believed in socialism. To combat widespread unemployment and end economic depression, the government organized "national workshops" that gave people work. This action was an early instance of a modern government trying to remedy chronic unemployment in a country.

The Second Republic allowed all men in France to vote. Elections were held to choose a National Assembly that would write a new constitution. Conservative members of that National Assembly, however, voted to end the national workshops. Violent rioting erupted in Paris in response. The army was called in, and Paris became a battlefield. Within three days the rebellion was crushed, and its socialist leaders were executed, imprisoned, or exiled. The founder of modern socialism, Karl Marx, was expelled from France.

✔ **READING CHECK: Finding the Main Idea** Which groups divided France during the early 1800s?

Louis-Napoléon and the Second French Empire

The new constitution written by the National Assembly gave France a republican form of government. A president would be elected to serve one, and only one, four-year term. The legislature would be elected by all French males of voting age.

Louis-Napoléon. The first election was held in December 1848. Rather than electing someone who had been part of the Second Republic, however, the voters chose **Louis-Napoléon,** the nephew of Napoléon Bonaparte. Louis hoped to restore the empire eventually. He tried to build support all over France, particularly among the military and French Catholics.

The republic's constitution did not allow Louis-Napoléon to serve more than one term. He hoped the National Assembly would amend the constitution to change this law. When he saw that he did not have enough votes to pass the amendment, he decided to take matters into his own hands. The writer Victor Hugo described the night of December 2, 1851, when "Paris slumbered, like a sleeping eagle caught in a black snare."

That night Louis-Napoléon's troops marched into Paris and arrested 70 members of the National Assembly who had opposed his aims. Widespread rioting both in opposition to and in support of Louis-Napoléon's actions broke out in the streets of Paris. Promising to put the issues to a plebiscite—a yes-or-no vote on his actions—and to create a new constitution for France, Louis-Napoléon portrayed himself as a defender of order. Because of Louis-Napoléon's famous name and his promises of order, the people voted almost 12 to 1 in his favor. Like his uncle before him, Louis-Napoléon's coup d'état and plebiscite enabled him to win control of France.

The Second French Empire. A new constitution for France was written, giving Louis-Napoléon a ten-year term as president. He now had great power but had an even greater goal in mind: to restore the empire of his uncle, Napoléon I. In 1852 another plebiscite was held for yet another constitution. The Senate passed a resolution to restore the empire, and Louis-Napoléon was elected Emperor Napoléon III.

Although Napoleon III pretended to champion democracy, he acted to crush those who opposed him. He censored and exiled his critics. The Second French Empire appeared to be a parliamentary regime, with wide voting rights and an elected legislature. In reality, it was an authoritarian regime. The legislature could pass only laws proposed by the emperor. People lost many of their rights. Newspapers were censored and could be shut down. Liberal university professors lost their jobs. Freedom of speech did not exist, and it was impossible to organize political opposition against the government.

On the other hand, Napoléon III did try to develop France by modernizing it. He encouraged the development of railroads and manufacturing, which helped the middle class. He set up public works programs, which helped the lower class. Domestic affairs became more stable.

✔ **READING CHECK: Summarizing** What actions did Louis-Napoléon take to gain absolute power in France?

Foreign Conflicts

Napoléon III wanted Europe to recognize him as the head of France. He also wanted to improve relations with Britain. To achieve these ends, he involved France in a foreign dispute that ultimately led to war.

The Crimean War. Russia claimed authority over certain holy places in Palestine, an area that was part of the Ottoman Empire. France disputed this claim. At the same time, Russia claimed the right of protection over Orthodox Christian subjects within the Ottoman Empire. These disputes among Russia, the Ottomans, and France became increasingly heated during the early 1850s. In 1854 France, Great Britain, and the Ottoman Empire formed an alliance and declared war on Russia. The fighting took place mostly in the Crimea, a peninsula in southern Russia. Over the course of two years, both sides in the **Crimean War** suffered massive losses. In the end Russia was defeated and France won glory—but little else.

Two important developments grew out of the Crimean War. Modern field hospitals to care for those wounded in battle came into use, and **Florence Nightingale** introduced professional nursing of the wounded. Cecil Woodham Smith described the admiration Nightingale received from doctors and soldiers.

Primary Source

❝She was the rock to which everyone clung. . . . Her calmness, her resource, her power to take action raised her to the position of a goddess. The men adored her. . . . The doctors came to be absolutely dependent on her.❞

From *Florence Nightingale,* by Cecil Woodham Smith

An overseas empire. After the war Napoléon III turned to building a French colonial empire. In North Africa he strengthened French control over the nation of Algeria. French engineers began constructing the Suez Canal in Egypt in 1859. In Asia France took control of Cambodia. Napoléon III also tried to control Mexico, but his appointed emperor there, Archduke Maximilian of Austria, was overthrown by Mexicans led by Benito Juárez and executed in 1867.

Back home in France, Napoléon III faced mounting pressure. Although he had relaxed controls on the press and public and had begun other reforms, the elections of 1869 showed that his opponents were growing stronger. Napoléon III had to choose between becoming more liberal or more authoritarian. He chose to be more liberal, and the voters approved. Meanwhile, a crisis with Prussia was looming.

The Franco-Prussian War. Prussia was working to unite all German states under its leadership. Napoléon III and the French people were against a union because they did not trust Prussia's motives. To prepare for war, Napoléon III tried but failed to draft army troops. Meanwhile, the head of Prussia's government, **Otto von Bismarck,** decided that a war with France would help him unite the German states. Bismarck made a series of clever diplomatic moves to insult the French and goad them into war. The plan worked. In July 1870 France declared war on Prussia.

The **Franco-Prussian War** was a disaster for France from the start. Its troops suffered defeat after defeat. Napoléon III took control of the army himself and was promptly captured. The National Assembly immediately proclaimed the fall of the Second French Empire and established the Third Republic. The new government tried to defend the nation, but the Prussians invaded France and began a siege of Paris. In January 1871 Paris fell to the Prussians, and the war was over.

HISTORY MAKER

Florence Nightingale (1820–1910)

In 1854 Florence Nightingale headed a group of nurses sent to the Crimean War. For the next two years she worked tirelessly to care for the wounded, control the spread of disease, and improve morale. Her reports about bad conditions in the hospitals led to reforms.

Nightingale later achieved professional training for nurses and established a nursing school. She is credited with creating the modern profession of nursing. **What were Florence Nightingale's contributions to nursing?**

Artist Richard Woodville captured the ferocity of fighting during the "Charge of the Light Brigade" at the Battle of Balaclava in 1854.

France under German domination. Bismarck presented France with the Treaty of Frankfurt, which dictated harsh terms. It forced France to give up Alsace and the eastern part of Lorraine, two regions on the French-German border. Also, German troops would not leave until France made large payments to Germany. A new National Assembly was elected to decide whether to accept the terms. Most republicans wanted to continue to fight; most monarchists did not. Because the French people wanted peace, they elected a majority of monarchists, and the National Assembly voted to accept the treaty.

The surrender angered the people of Paris, who were strongly republican. They had fought almost alone to defend themselves against the Prussians. In March 1871 socialists and radical republicans in Paris set up a council to govern the city. It was called the Commune, and its members, called **Communards,** proposed to change France. The Communards wanted a decentralized government, separation of church and state, and other reforms.

The Communards destroyed famous Parisian buildings such as the Tuileries royal palace, shown burning in this illustration, during the fighting of 1871.

The French government, now in Versailles, decided to disarm the Parisians. Troops entered the city and fought the Communards from street to street. By May 1871 the Communards were defeated, but in the process of retreat they executed their hostages. In the end, more than 20,000 Communards were killed by government troops. France borrowed the money to pay Germany, and German soldiers left France in 1873.

 READING CHECK: Problem Solving How could the French have avoided war with Prussia?

The Third Republic

The National Assembly was not able to agree on a new constitution until 1875. The Constitution of 1875 officially made France a republic. Under the Third Republic, a president would be elected by the legislature for a term of seven years. The legislature was made up of the Senate, whose members were elected indirectly, and the Chamber of Deputies, whose members were elected by male voters. Although there were many changes of government over time, the Constitution of 1875 stood for nearly 70 years.

In the late 1800s the legislature was made up of various factions, or opposing sides. One group wanted to strengthen the military in case another conflict broke out with Germany. Another faction wanted to weaken the powers of the Catholic Church. Still another wanted France to expand its overseas empire, as Napoléon III had been doing. The conservative republicans managed to steer a course that avoided extremes. They legalized trade unions and expanded education by establishing free, required schools for children under 13, but they did not really address the country's most serious social problems.

Another threat to the government came from extremists in the labor movement. Boycotts, strikes, and sabotage disrupted the economy. In addition, political extremists called **anarchists,** who opposed all government, waged terrorist campaigns in France and throughout Europe.

The Dreyfus case Alfred Dreyfus was not only wrongfully convicted, but he was also forced to endure public humiliation. *What are the soldiers doing to symbolically strip Dreyfus of his power?*

Scandals. In the 1890s a financial scandal rocked the nation. A French company had started work on building the Panama Canal, and thousands of French citizens had invested money in the project. When the project failed, the resulting accusations of bribery threatened the French government.

Another serious danger to the Third Republic arose in 1894. French army Captain **Alfred Dreyfus** was accused and convicted of giving French military secrets to Germany. Dreyfus, a Jew, was sentenced to life in prison, even though evidence surfaced that he was innocent. The French army would not allow anyone to criticize its actions. Monarchists and anti-Semites—people who are prejudiced against Jews—supported the army. Even when the real traitor was discovered, the army cleared him rather than admit it had the wrong man. Émile Zola, a French author, wrote an open letter, "*J'accuse*" ("I accuse"), in which he blamed the army and its supporters for covering up the truth. Finally in 1906 Dreyfus's name was cleared. By then, the case had increased tensions between the republicans and conservatives in France.

Reform and coalition. After the Dreyfus case, French republicans began to make more reforms. They ended the favored position of the Catholic Church. In 1905 church and state were separated, and the French had complete religious freedom.

Different factions still caused friction in the country. Groups ranged from monarchists on the far right to radical socialists on the far left. No one party ever had complete control of the government. In order to get things done, parties would temporarily unite to form **coalitions.** These were political groups organized to support a common cause.

✔ **READING CHECK: Summarizing** What political problems hurt France during the Third Republic?

SECTION 3 REVIEW

1. **Define** and explain the significance:
   anarchists
   coalitions

2. **Identify** and explain the significance:
   Louis Philippe
   Louis-Napoléon
   Crimean War
   Florence Nightingale
   Otto von Bismarck
   Franco-Prussian War
   Communards
   Alfred Dreyfus

3. **Sequencing** Copy the flowchart below. Use it to list the events that led to Louis-Napoléon becoming Emperor of France.

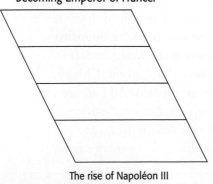

The rise of Napoléon III

4. **Finding the Main Idea**
   a. How did monarchists and republicans differ on their visions for France?
   b. What did the Treaty of Frankfurt force France to do?
   c. How did French conservative republicans help the Third Republic remain politically stable?

5. **Writing and Critical Thinking**
   Identifying Points of View Consider the following opinion: "We need a king to maintain the peace and control the nation." Write a paragraph explaining whether a monarchist or republican would make such a statement, and whether you agree with it.
   Consider:
   • what monarchists believed
   • what republicans believed
   • what you believe about how a nation should be governed

Homework Practice Online

keyword: SH3 HP15

Latin Americans Win Independence

READ TO DISCOVER

❶ What was life like in the Spanish and Portuguese colonies of Latin America?

❷ Why did Latin Americans begin to oppose colonial rule?

❸ How did Latin American colonies win their independence?

❹ How did the new nations fare after independence?

DEFINE

haciendas
peninsulares
creoles
mestizos
mulattoes

IDENTIFY

Simón Bolívar
Toussaint-Louverture
Miguel Hidalgo y Costilla
Monroe Doctrine

WHY IT MATTERS TODAY

Some nations in Central and South America continue to have political instability. Use CNN or other **current event** sources to see which regions or nations are in the midst of political turmoil. Record your findings in your journal.

CNNstudentNews.com

The Main Idea
Inspired by revolutions in North America and France, Latin Americans overthrew European rule.

The Story Continues *Inspired by political reforms in Europe and North America, Venezuelan general Simón Bolívar dreamed of an independent, united South America. As one French observer commented, "The ideas of the Liberator [Bolívar] are like his imagination: full of fire, original, and new. . . . He is a lover of truth, heroism, and honor and of the public interest and morality."*

Life in Colonial Latin America

By the 1800s the American and French Revolutions were inspiring people in Latin American colonies to consider freedom of their own. In time, a series of independence movements swept the entire region, from Mexico to the tip of South America.

Colonial economy. Portugal had colonized the region of Brazil. Spain controlled most of the rest of South America, Central America, and southwestern North America. Over several centuries, a distinct colonial life in Latin America developed and thrived. Both Spain and Portugal based their colonial empires on the principle of mercantilism. They believed that a nation gained wealth by obtaining gold and silver. As a result, the two nations took these precious metals from their colonies and used the areas as markets for their own goods. The colonies could not trade freely with other nations.

Certain colonists, usually conquistadors or favorites of the monarch, were given huge estates on which they set up large, self-sufficient farms. These were called **haciendas** (hah·see·EN·duhz) in Spanish America and *fazendas* in Brazil. The estates produced a variety of goods, such as meat, hides, and sugar.

American Indians were used as slave farm workers, miners, or servants. They were often overworked and mistreated. In addition, European diseases wiped out whole Indian settlements in some areas and led to drastic population declines in others. As the Indian population decreased and the need for labor increased, the Spanish and Portuguese began to import slaves from Africa.

Meanwhile Spanish wealth in the colonies grew. Mexico City, Lima, and other cities became centers of commerce. Imposing public buildings, cathedrals, and palaces were constructed. Fortresses protected cities from pirates and sea dogs.

INTERPRETING THE VISUAL RECORD

Slavery Africans were brought to Latin America to work as slaves, as on this sugar plantation. *How does the sugar-cane-processing machine being used by the man work?*

Simón Bolívar
1783–1830

Simón Bolívar was born into an aristocratic Venezuelan family of Spanish descent. Raised in wealth and privilege, Bolívar received an excellent education, in the course of which he was influenced by the thinking of Locke, Hobbes, and the French writers of the Enlightenment. He led popular revolutions against Spanish rule in what is now Bolivia, Colombia, Ecuador, Peru, and Venezuela. Today Bolívar is known throughout Latin America as *El Libertador*—"The Liberator." **What factors helped to shape Simón Bolívar's revolutionary thinking?**

Holt Researcher
go.hrw.com
KEYWORD: Holt Researcher
FreeFind: Simon Bolivar
After reading more about Simón Bolívar on the Holt Researcher, write a newspaper article identifying the changes that resulted from the revolutions he helped lead.

Colonial society. In the highest ranks of colonial society were royal officials and owners of large estates and mines. At the lower end were the workers, peasants, and slaves. An enormous social gap existed between the two groups.

Racial discrimination was a fact of colonial life. Society was ruled by **peninsulares,** Europeans who were born on the Iberian Peninsula—Spain or Portugal. White people born in the colonies were called **creoles.** Although some creoles enjoyed great wealth, most suffered social and job discrimination from the peninsulares. By the 1700s the majority of the colonial population was of mixed ancestry. **Mestizos** were of American Indian and European background; **mulattoes** were of European and African ancestry. Both groups faced racial and social barriers but still had more opportunities than Africans or American Indians.

The Catholic Church had great power and influence in the colonies. Missionaries converted American Indians to Catholicism. While some missionaries helped exploit the Indians, others took an interest in their cultures and tried to prevent abuses by the government and individuals.

Women's roles were determined by ethnic or family background. Spanish women— a relatively small segment of the colonial population—enjoyed some economic freedom because they could own property. In addition, some Spanish women managed family businesses, ranches, and estates with their husbands or, if widowed, by themselves.

✔ **READING CHECK: Contrasting** What was life in the colonies like for peasants and workers compared with life for the peninsulares?

Discontent and the First Rebellion

In the 1600s and 1700s, Spain began to relax its control of the colonies. As a result, creoles began to assume more power, both politically and economically. When King Charles III of Spain tried to regain control, many colonists objected.

Causes of discontent. When Charles III took the Spanish crown in 1759, he had several goals in mind. The new king wanted to establish royal control over the Catholic Church in Spain and its overseas lands. In particular, Charles sought to weaken the wealthy and powerful Jesuits. In 1767 the king succeeded in expelling the Jesuits from Spain.

Charles moved to restore Spanish authority in Latin America by creating an intendancy system. He appointed peninsulares as intendants, or governors, in the colonies. As royal appointees, these officials were loyal to the Spanish crown rather than to the colonial viceroys. Their policies were designed to benefit the home country of Spain, and its ruler, at colonial expense. This system greatly angered many colonists in Latin America, as did Charles's economic policies. The king moved to strengthen the Spanish economy by limiting competing colonial industries. Charles also forced the colonists in Latin America to pay heavy taxes in support of Spain's European wars. These policies caused bitter resentment throughout the colonies.

Colonists responded to Charles's actions with calls for independence. Growing feelings of nationalism were fueled by the revolutionary events in France and in the British colonies in North America. **Simón Bolívar,** who would go on to lead several revolutions in Latin America, said, "The hatred that the Peninsula [Spain and Portugal] has inspired in us is greater than the ocean between us."

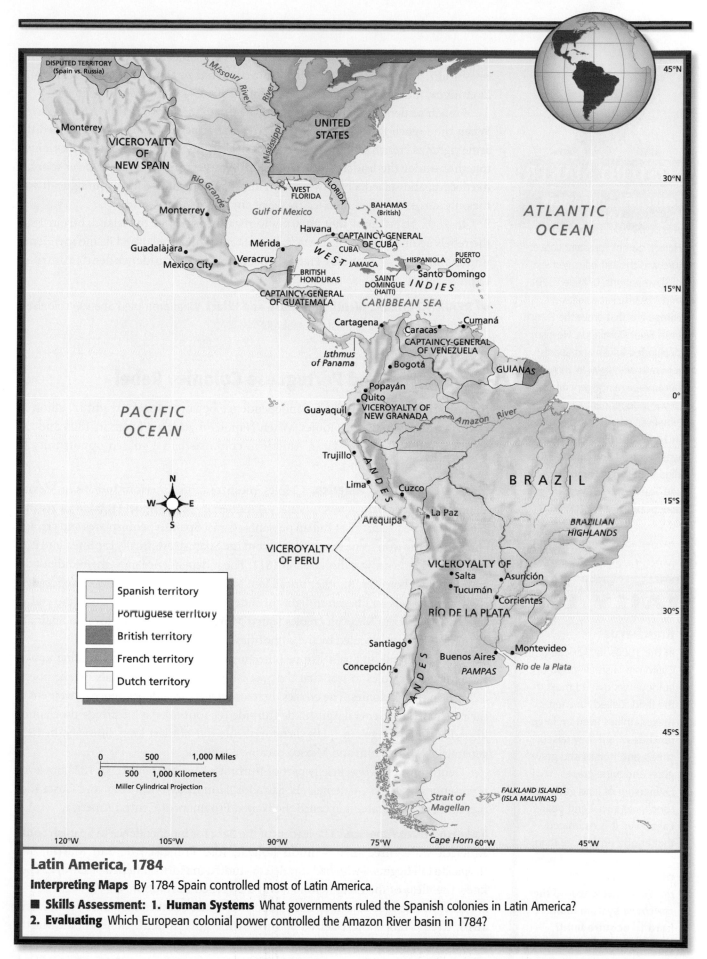

Latin America, 1784

Interpreting Maps By 1784 Spain controlled most of Latin America.

■ **Skills Assessment: 1. Human Systems** What governments ruled the Spanish colonies in Latin America?

2. Evaluating Which European colonial power controlled the Amazon River basin in 1784?

HISTORY MAKER

Toussaint-Louverture (c. 1743–1803)

Haitian patriot Toussaint-Louverture was the self-educated son of slave parents. Between 1791 and 1793 he led a series of campaigns that drove the French from Saint Domingue. He also persuaded British and Spanish forces to withdraw. In 1800 he became governor-general of the newly independent country. However, when France attacked in 1802 Toussaint-Louverture was betrayed and captured. He died in prison in France. **How did Toussaint-Louverture gain independence for Haiti?**

DAILY LIFE

Rancheros

In the 1800s in Mexican California, a small group of landowners owned most of the land. Called *rancheros,* these families lived on large ranches where they raised sheep and horses and grew grain and wine grapes. Ownership of land gave the *rancheros* social and political power. It is estimated that at one time more than 8 million acres of land were controlled by only 800 *rancheros.* **How would the *ranchero* system make it hard to acquire land?**

Haiti's slave revolution. By the early 1800s the Spanish colonies were ripe for revolution. Yet the first successful revolt occurred in the French colony of Saint Domingue, the western half of the island of Hispaniola in the West Indies.

French settlers in Saint Domingue owned plantations worked by African slaves. When the French Revolution broke out, free mulattoes in the colony demanded the same rights as French settlers. The settlers resisted. In 1791 mulattoes and slaves joined together under the leadership of **Toussaint-Louverture** (TOO·san LOO·ver·toor), a freed slave, and staged a bloody revolt. They won control of Saint Domingue. It was the only successful revolution led by slaves anywhere in the world.

In 1802 Napoléon I sent an army to regain control of the island, but in 1804 the rebels again defeated the French. Saint Domingue proclaimed its independence under the ancient name of Haiti. It became the first independent country in Latin America.

✔ **READING CHECK: Identifying Cause and Effect** What prompted Spanish colonists to think of rebelling against colonial rule?

The Spanish and Portuguese Colonies Rebel

In the early 1800s the desire for independence began to fuel outright rebellion in Spanish and Portuguese colonies. When Napoléon attacked Spain in 1808 and the Spanish fought back, the Latin American colonists had a golden opportunity to declare their independence.

Mexico and Central America. Creoles, mestizos, and American Indians in Mexico all began to participate in revolutionary activities. In 1810 **Miguel Hidalgo y Costilla,** a local priest, led an army of Indian peasants against Spanish peninsulares and creoles. Hidalgo's army won some early victories, but the Spanish eventually captured and executed him. His army was dispersed in 1811. The independence movement did not die with Hidalgo, however. Another priest, José María Morelos y Pavón, assumed leadership of the rebels and began to fight for independence, land reform, and the end of slavery. Upper-class Mexican creoles feared Morelos and remained loyal to Spain. In 1815 Morelos was executed by the authorities.

In 1820 liberals in Spain stripped the king of some of his powers, leading upper-class Mexican creoles to fear that the Spanish government would also make liberal changes in their colonies. The creoles therefore staged an independence movement of their own, led by General Agustín de Iturbide (ee·toor·BEE·day). Iturbide proclaimed himself Emperor Agustín I. His dictatorial rule did not last long, however. In 1823 generals overthrew him and Mexico became a republic.

Central America was briefly part of Iturbide's Mexican empire. In 1823 however, representatives from Guatemala, El Salvador, Honduras, Nicaragua, and Costa Rica met to form a federal union called the United Provinces of Central America.

Spanish South America. The leaders of the fight for independence in Spanish South America were three men—Simón Bolívar, José Francisco de San Martín, and Bernardo O'Higgins—who had traveled or studied in North America or Europe. They knew the ideas of the Enlightenment and the French Revolution.

One of the first revolts against Spain was in the southern region of La Plata in 1810. Creole rebels there seized control of the government. General San Martín led the fighting against the Spanish. Six years later the colonials declared the independence of what would later be called Argentina. Paraguay, another region of La Plata, achieved its independence from Spain in a bloodless revolution in 1811.

Independence for the rest of South America came only after a long, bloody civil war. Simón Bolívar—nicknamed "the Liberator"—started the revolt in Venezuela in 1810, destroying Spanish power there by 1821. Bolívar became the president of a new nation called Gran Colombia, which included the present-day countries of Colombia, Venezuela, Ecuador, and Panama. Meanwhile, San Martín gathered troops and made a difficult crossing of the Andes into Chile. There he joined with forces led by Bernardo O'Higgins to defeat the Spanish in 1818.

San Martín and his army then sailed north to capture the city of Lima in Peru. The Spanish government there fled, and San Martín declared Peru independent in 1821. However, royalist forces remained in some parts of Peru until Simón Bolívar took charge and drove the Spanish out for good in 1824. The following year the northern territory of Upper Peru became a separate republic, named Bolivia in honor of Bolívar.

José Francisco de San Martín (left), an Argentine general, led independence movements in Argentina, Chile, and Peru.

Brazil. When Napoléon's army invaded Portugal in 1807, the prince regent Dom João and his family fled to Brazil. His rule in the colony benefited Brazil, as he opened ports to trade and encouraged industry. After Napoléon was overthrown, Dom João—now called King John VI and monarch of both Brazil and Portugal—at first remained in Brazil. When a revolt broke out in Portugal in 1820, however, Dom João returned home. He tried to control Brazil from across the ocean, angering many Brazilians. They encouraged Dom João's son, who had stayed in Brazil, to declare independence. Dom Pedro did so in 1822 and ruled as emperor until 1831. His son, Dom Pedro II, succeeded him, ruling until 1889.

The new nations of Brazil and Argentina began to argue over land that lay between them. Settlers in this disputed territory gained its independence in 1825 and called their new nation Uruguay.

By this point, almost all of Latin America was independent. Portugal lost its entire empire, and Spain held only Cuba and Puerto Rico. Very little land in the region remained under colonial rule.

✔ **READING CHECK: Drawing Inferences** Why was Simón Bolívar nicknamed "the Liberator"?

Latin America After Independence

Independence opened Latin American markets to trade, but the United States at first paid little attention to the region. However, when in the 1820s Spain tried to regain its lost colonies, the United States took note. In 1823 President James Monroe issued the **Monroe Doctrine.** The doctrine stated that the United States would not interfere in European affairs or with Europe's remaining colonies in the Western Hemisphere. At the same time, it would oppose any attempts by European nations to take back former colonies, create new ones, or interfere with any government in the hemisphere. European nations denounced the doctrine, but none challenged it.

In addition to expanded trade, independence brought some social benefits. Some groups, particularly mestizos, were better able to advance socially. Tribute payments by Indians were ended. Slavery was abolished throughout Latin America by 1888.

Latin American unity. It was difficult for the states of Latin America to unite because of vast distances, geographical barriers, and regional rivalries. Only Brazil managed to maintain national unity. Ecuador and Venezuela broke away from Gran Colombia. The United Provinces of Central America crumbled into five separate countries. Argentina was threatened by divisions within its own territory. In 1826 Bolívar called a congress of Latin American nations to meet in Panama to promote unification. Although the Panama Congress failed, many Latin Americans cherished the idea of unity.

Latin America, 1830

Interpreting Maps Within 50 years, the huge Spanish empire in Latin America had broken into many independent nations.

■ **Skills Assessment: 1. Places and Regions** What islands remained under Spanish or British rule in 1830?

2. Drawing Inferences Why might the United States have felt the need to issue the Monroe Doctrine?

Internal problems. Conflict between liberals and conservatives kept many countries in a state of turmoil. The conflict tended to follow class lines. Upper-class creoles were usually conservative. They wanted to keep as much of their European heritage as possible, including a strong Catholic Church and government control of the economy. Mestizos had liberal values. They favored separation of church and state, democratic republics, and a laissez-faire economy.

These conflicts made it hard to establish orderly rule. Latin American governments came to power through rebellion as often as through election. Creoles often retreated to their haciendas while *caudillos*—ambitious mestizo military leaders—became presidents. *Caudillo*-led governments gave the people stability but not freedom, and usually lasted only as long as the dictator lived.

Liberals and conservatives also battled over the role of the Catholic Church. Republican governments often took positions against the church. However, educational systems that had been run by the church were neglected, and there was little public education to replace them. Upper-class conservatives opposed the loss of church power, and the lower classes remained solidly Catholic in faith. This conflict added to Latin America's internal difficulties.

The first 50 or 60 years, then, of Latin American independence were difficult. By the late 1800s growing industry and trade helped distribute wealth more evenly. Development was rapid, and cities grew. Political unrest was still common, but over time many nations began to achieve stability and economic growth.

✔ **READING CHECK: Contrasting** How did creoles and mestizos differ politically in the new Latin American countries?

Hacienda owners This early-1800s watercolor shows the wealthy creole owners of a hacienda meeting with a laborer. *How does the artist indicate the hacienda owners' high status?*

SECTION 4 REVIEW

1. **Define** and explain the significance:
   haciendas
   peninsulares
   creoles
   mestizos
   mulattoes

2. **Identify** and explain the significance:
   Simón Bolívar
   Toussaint-Louverture
   Miguel Hidalgo y Costilla
   Monroe Doctrine

3. **Categorizing** Copy the pyramid below. Use it to explain the social classes that existed in Latin America.

Colonial society

4. **Finding the Main Idea**
   a. What were some of the causes of the discontent that led to revolutions in Latin America?
   b. How would you describe the revolutions for independence in Latin America?
   c. What problems did Latin Americans face after independence?

5. **Writing and Critical Thinking**
   Problem Solving Take the viewpoint of a Spanish official living in a colony. Write a letter to the king explaining what he should do to prevent the colonists from fighting for independence.
   Consider:
   • what life was like in the colony
   • what options the Spanish had for governing the colonies

Homework Practice Online
keyword: SH3 HP15

Creating a Time Line

Copy the time line below onto a sheet of paper. Complete the time line by filling in the events, individuals, and dates from the chapter that you think were significant. Pick three events and explain why you think they were significant.

1790	1830	1870	1910

Writing a Summary

Using standard grammar, spelling, sentence structure, and punctuation, write an overview of the events in the chapter.

Identifying People and Ideas

Identify the following terms or individuals and explain their significance:

1. Queen Victoria
2. suffrage
3. William Gladstone
4. Northwest Ordinance
5. total war
6. Louis-Napoléon
7. Communards
8. creoles
9. Simón Bolívar
10. Monroe Doctrine

Understanding Main Ideas

SECTION 1 *(pp. 410–416)*

Liberal Reforms in Great Britain and Its Empire

1. What were some of the governmental and economic changes that took place in Great Britain in the 1800s and 1900s?
2. How did European settlement change the lifestyles of the original inhabitants of New Zealand and Australia?

SECTION 2 *(pp. 417–422)*

Expansion and Reform in the United States

3. After 1783, how did the United States acquire most of its territory?
4. What factors led to the Civil War?

SECTION 3 *(pp. 423–428)*

Revolution and Reform in France

5. In what ways were French republicans and monarchists different?
6. What helped the Third Republic last for about 70 years despite its many problems?

SECTION 4 *(pp. 429–435)*

Independence Movements in Latin America

7. Why did creoles want independence from Spain?
8. What benefits and what problems resulted from independence?

Reviewing Themes

1. **Citizenship** How did the reform movement in Britain and the anti-slavery movement in the United States influence women's suffrage?
2. **Government** How did the creoles in Latin America respond when Spain tried to regain control of its colonies there?
3. **Constitutional Heritage** How did most workers in France want the government to be structured? Why?

Thinking Critically

1. **Comparing and Contrasting** Compare the changes that took place in Great Britain and France during the first half of the 1800s.
2. **Decision Making** Should the French people have voted for Louis-Napoléon? Why do you think they did?
3. **Sequencing** What major territories were gained by the United States during the 1800s, and in what order were they obtained?
4. **Problem Solving** Would it have been possible for the newly formed Latin American nations to unify? If so, how? If not, why not?

Writing About History

Comparing Write a dialogue between a republican and a monarchist in France or between a mestizo and a creole in Latin America in which the two debate the way they believe government should be structured. Use the following chart to organize your thoughts before you begin writing.

	Republican or Mestizo	Monarchist or Creole
Government structure		
Leader		
Voting rights		

Interpreting a Time Line

Study the time line below. Then answer the questions that follow.

1838 Lord Durham becomes governor-general of the two Canadian provinces.

1898 The Yukon Territory is organized.

1800 — **1850** — **1900**

1867 The British North America Act creates the Dominion of Canada.

1. Which statement correctly summarizes the time line?

   a. It runs from when Canada becomes a Dominion to when the Yukon Territory is formed.

   b. It runs from when Lord Durham recommends self-government to when the Yukon becomes a province.

   c. It runs from when Britain passes the Act of Union to when Canada is divided into territories.

   d. It runs from when Canada consisted of two provinces to Canada's expansion into the Yukon.

2. What are some other events in Canadian history that could be placed on this time line? Give specific dates for the events.

Making Generalizations

Read the following quote by Thomas Carlyle about Queen Victoria at age 18. Then answer the questions.

> "Yesterday, going through one of the Parks, I saw the poor little Queen. She was in an open carriage, preceded by three or four swift red-coated troopers. . . . It seemed to me the poor little Queen was a bit modest, nice sonsy [sweet] little lassie; blue eyes, light hair, fine white skin; of extremely small stature: she looked timid, anxious, almost frightened; for the people looked at her in perfect silence; one old livery-man alone touched his hat to her: I was heartily sorry for the poor bairn [child] . . . It is a strange thing to look at the fashion of this world!"

3. Which is the best general statement about why Carlyle felt sorry for Queen Victoria?

   a. He thought she looked shy and uncomfortable, and it was only fate that she had become a public figure.

   b. He thought people along her route should have waved or bowed to her.

   c. He thought she looked ill.

   d. He thought she was too young and inexperienced to be Queen.

4. How would you evaluate Queen Victoria's reign? Give specific reasons to support your answer.

Alternative Assessment

Building Your Portfolio

Link to TODAY

Citizenship

During the 1800s people fought for the extension of suffrage to include more and more different groups in the population. Using your textbook and other sources, find out about other groups that have more recently won the right to vote, in the United States and elsewhere. Look also for problems that arise when the right to vote has been denied or hindered. Present your findings in the form of an oral report to your classmates.

internet connect

Internet Activity: go.hrw.com
KEYWORD: SH3 WH15

Choose a topic on The Age of Reform to:

- create a scrapbook that highlights the history of Mexico, El Salvador, Nicaragua, Colombia, Chile, or Argentina since independence.
- collect information on the status of native peoples today.
- search letters and diary entries from soldiers who served in the U.S. Civil War.

CHAPTER 16

1806–1913

Nationalism in Europe

This Penny Black stamp shows Queen Victoria in profile

1808
The Arts
Johann Wolfgang von Goethe's *Faust, Part I* is published.

1811
Science and Technology
Luddites riot against English textile mills that have replaced people with machines.

1815
Global Events
Napoléon I is defeated at Waterloo.

1828
Daily Life
Noah Webster publishes the first *American Dictionary of the English Language.*

1840
Daily Life
The world's first adhesive postage stamp, the Penny Black, goes on sale in Great Britain.

1849
Politics
Hungary enjoys a brief period of independence.

1800   **1820**   **1840**

1807–1813
Global Events
Napoléon I dominates Prussia.

1818
The Arts
Mary Wollstonecraft Shelley publishes her novel *Frankenstein.*

1831
Business and Finance
The McCormick reaper allows one person to do the work of five.

1848
Global Events
Revolutions break out in Italy, France, Germany, and the Austrian Empire.

Mary Wollstonecraft Shelley

The original McCormick reaper

Build on What You Know

During the 1800s reforms in Great Britain made the government more democratic. Changes in France led to a republic that was governed by a coalition of parties. Monarchist, liberal, and socialist beliefs were all represented. During the same period, other European countries were having their own problems. Nationalism became a driving force for change in Italy, Germany, Russia, and other European regions. In this chapter, you will learn about those developments and what effects they had on the people and political futures of those countries.

This emblem bears the symbol of the International Red Cross.

Egg-shaped clock by Peter Carl Fabergé

1861
Politics
The serfs are emancipated in Russia.

1862–1890
Politics
Otto von Bismarck serves as prime minister of Prussia.

c. 1863
Global Events
The International Red Cross is founded in Switzerland.

1873
Science and Technology
Scottish physicist James Clerk Maxwell describes electromagnetism.

1878
Global Events
The Congress of Berlin takes place.

1893
Politics
New Zealand becomes the first country to grant women suffrage.

1905
Politics
The Revolution of 1905 occurs in Russia.

1912–1913
Global Events
The Balkan Wars take place.

| 1860 | 1880 | 1900 |

1859
Business and Finance
Construction on the Suez Canal begins, funded by French and Egyptian investors.

1872
The Arts
James Whistler paints a famous portrait of his mother.

1867
Politics
The Austrian Empire forms the Dual Monarchy.

1882
Science and Technology
Robert Koch discovers the tuberculosis bacillus.

1896
The Arts
Puccini's *La Bohème* is produced in Turin, Italy.

1901
Science and Technology
The first Nobel prizes are awarded.

1908
Business and Finance
Henry Ford introduces the Model T.

Gold coin of Emperor Francis Joseph I of Austria-Hungary

The Artist's Mother by James Whistler

What's Your Opinion?

Themes Journal

Do you **agree** *or* **disagree** *with the following statements? Support your point of view in your journal.*

Global Relations Threats from outside forces are not usually a factor in the unification of a country.

Government The goals and ideals of different political groups often make a move toward unification difficult.

Culture A shared history and common traditions may lead to a desire for the establishment of a unified nation.

The Unification of Italy

READ TO DISCOVER

❶ What events led to nationalistic movements for unification in Italy?

❷ Who were the important leaders in the fight for the unification of Italy?

❸ What problems did Italy face after unification?

DEFINE

risorgimento

IDENTIFY

Carbonari
Giuseppe Mazzini
Young Italy movement
King Victor Emmanuel II
Camillo Benso di Cavour
Napoléon III
Giuseppe Garibaldi

WHY IT MATTERS TODAY

In the 50 years following Italian unification, more than 5 million people emigrated from Italy to the United States. Use CNNstudentNews.com or other **current event** sources to identify recent problems in the world that have led to similar emigrations. Record your findings in your journal.

CNNstudentNews.com

The Main Idea
During the 1800s liberal and nationalist leaders established a unified and independent Italy.

The Story Continues *Throughout most of the 1800s, Italy was shaken by turmoil as its citizens struggled to throw off foreign rule and establish a free, united nation. As revolutionary leader Giuseppe Mazzini wrote, the Italians were fighting for "the eternal right which God has implanted in the peoples, that of appreciating and defining for themselves their own life, and governing themselves in accordance with their own appreciation of it."*

Liberals and Nationalists in Italy

In the 1790s many Italians had been inspired by the ideals of the French Revolution. Conquest by Napoléon had unified Italy for a brief time. However, the Congress of Vienna again divided Italy into several large and small states. Austria ruled the territories of Lombardy and Venetia, and reactionary monarchs in other states tried to undo the reforms made during Napoléon's time.

Despite this division, nationalism continued to grow. In the early 1800s many thinkers and writers tried to revive interest in Italy's traditions. This nationalist movement became known as **risorgimento**—the Italian word for "resurgence." Its goals were liberation and unification. Nationalists could not work openly and had to form secret societies. One such group was the **Carbonari.** One of the most famous Carbonari was **Giuseppe Mazzini.** In 1831 Mazzini called for all Italian patriots to join his **Young Italy movement,** dedicated to spreading the ideas of the risorgimento. Mazzini insisted that "neither pope nor king," but rather a republic, should rule Italy.

In 1848 liberals and nationalists led revolts in several Italian states. They overthrew Austrian rule in Lombardy and Venetia and forced some rulers in other states to agree to constitutions. In 1849 the revolutionaries seized Rome, setting up a republic governed by Mazzini and two other leaders. However, these victories did not last long. In 1849 Austria recaptured some of its former possessions in the north. Monarchs in the other states returned to power, revoking the new constitutions. Only the Kingdom of Sardinia remained a completely independent state.

After the failure of the revolts of 1848 and 1849, Italian liberals had little success. Conservative and clerical elements among the nationalists called for a federation of Italian states ruled by the pope. Liberals opposed this, partly because the pope had not supported their revolt in 1849. Other Italians

King Victor Emmanuel II of Sardinia sought to add to his kingdom's territory.

wanted a constitutional monarchy under **King Victor Emmanuel II** of Sardinia. This king was not especially sympathetic to the liberals, but he did want to expand Sardinian territory. His chief minister, **Camillo Benso di Cavour** (kahv·OOHR), was a republican and an Italian patriot. Cavour and the Sardinian parliament supported the goals of the liberals.

✔ **READING CHECK: Drawing Conclusions** How effective were the efforts of Italians to nationalize in the first part of the 1800s?

Sardinia, France, and Austria

As chief minister it was Cavour, and not King Victor Emmanuel II, who actually governed the kingdom of Sardinia. Cavour admired the British system of parliamentary government. He wanted Sardinia to lead the way in uniting and industrializing Italy.

A well-educated and widely traveled aristocrat, Camillo Benso di Cavour had once edited a nationalist newspaper, El Risorgimento, a page of which is shown below. Cavour also took part in the revolt of 1848.

Cavour's Sardinia. Cavour reorganized and strengthened the Sardinian army. He helped to establish banks, factories, and railroads and improved trade with other countries. Believing in the separation of church and state, Cavour tried to reduce the political influence of the church. He even tried to suppress the politically powerful Jesuit order. He increased Sardinia's political influence by siding with France and Great Britain during the Crimean War and participating in the 1856 peace conference that ended that war.

Napoléon III. Cavour saw Austria as the greatest barrier to Italian unification. He proposed an alliance of France and Sardinia against Austria. French emperor **Napoléon III** wanted to increase French influence. He thought that if the Austrians were driven from Italy, France might be able to dominate the Italian states. Cavour, on the other hand, hoped that with Austria out of Italy, other Italian states might join Sardinia in a strong alliance against both France and Austria.

In 1858 Cavour and Napoléon III met secretly to plan their strategy against Austria. Napoléon III agreed that if Austria could be provoked into declaring war on Sardinia, France would send troops to help drive the Austrians from Lombardy and Venetia. In return Cavour promised to give the French-speaking regions of Nice and Savoy—then Sardinian possessions—to France.

War with Austria. In 1859 Cavour began military preparations for war. In response Austria declared war, just as Cavour had hoped. At first the war went according to plan. Sardinian and French forces drove the Austrians out of Lombardy and marched into Venetia. Italian patriots in Tuscany, Modena, and Parma overthrew their Austrian rulers and asked to be annexed to the kingdom of Sardinia.

Napoléon III had not expected the Italians to unite in this way. Fearing that Prussia might join with Austria and not wishing to fight their combined forces, Napoléon III signed an armistice with Austria. According to this agreement, Sardinia received Lombardy, but Austria kept Venetia. Austrian rulers were also returned to power in Tuscany, Modena, and Parma. Although he had delivered on only part of his bargain, Napoléon III insisted on receiving Nice and Savoy. Afraid of losing what gains Sardinia had made, Victor Emmanuel II agreed to the French terms.

**Giuseppe Garibaldi
(1807–1882)**

Born in Nice, Giuseppe Garibaldi joined the Young Italy movement while in his twenties. He was forced to flee Italy several times because of his revolutionary activities. Garibaldi spent 12 years in South America, learning the art of guerrilla warfare.

With help from Cavour, Garibaldi was able to return to Italy in 1854. He then formed an army of volunteers, called "Red Shirts" because of their colorful uniforms. This army conquered southern Italy, helping to unite the country. The feat made Garibaldi a national hero. **Why is Garibaldi important in Italian history?**

The Red Shirts Giuseppe Garibaldi and his supporters, known as Red Shirts, conquered the Kingdom of the Two Sicilies in 1860, adding this area to the kingdom of Italy. *Was the artist who created this illustration a supporter or an opponent of the Red Shirt cause? Explain.*

The Italian people, however, would not abandon the idea of unity. Rebellions in Parma, Modena, and Tuscany again expelled the Austrian rulers. The people of Romagna, a province in the Papal States, also revolted. Each of these areas held a plebiscite, in which the people overwhelmingly voted to join the kingdom of Sardinia.

✔ **READING CHECK: Finding the Main Idea** How did Cavour work to unite and industrialize Sardinia?

Garibaldi and the Thousand

The southern half of the Italian Peninsula, together with the island of Sicily, made up the kingdom of the Two Sicilies. This area now became the target of the Italian nationalists. **Giuseppe Garibaldi,** a man devoted to Italian freedom, led the way.

With Cavour's knowledge, Garibaldi recruited an army of more than 1000 soldiers. In the spring of 1860, Garibaldi and his "Expedition of the Thousand" invaded and captured Sicily. Crossing to Italy's mainland, Garibaldi's forces seized Naples, the capital city. They then drove King Francis II and his troops north to the border of the Papal States. Celebrated for his military skill, Garibaldi became a hero both within and outside of Italy.

Garibaldi planned to continue north to capture Rome and then Venetia. Cavour, however, now feared that Garibaldi might displace Victor Emmanuel II as Italy's leader and set up a republic of his own. Therefore Cavour sent an army south to stop Garibaldi's advance. In the process, Sardinia annexed most of the territory of the Papal States.

In the fall of 1860 Garibaldi and Emmanual II met in Naples. Garibaldi promised to support the establishment of the kingdom of Italy, with Victor Emmanuel II as king. He asked only to serve as governor of Naples. Fearing Garibaldi's great popularity, the king refused.

✔ **READING CHECK: Drawing Conclusions** Why did Cavour send an army to stop Garibaldi?

Financing a New Nation

Problem solving is the process of reviewing a troubling situation and then making decisions and recommendations for resolving that situation. Throughout history leaders have had to solve problems faced by their countries. Generally they do not develop solutions out of thin air. Rather, resolutions are developed through the use of problem-solving processes. The leaders of Italy faced many problems in the early 1800s. One of the biggest was how to raise money. The building of a new nation is an expensive process, and Italy was poor. Italian leaders arrived at a solution to this problem by working through a problem-solving process.

The Italian Process

To raise revenue, Italy's leaders knew they had to continue collecting taxes. Some officials argued for a tax system based on wealth, which would lessen the economic burden placed on the poor. Others argued that such a system would take too long to implement, because it meant determining the value of everyone's property. Instead, they called for continuing to tax food and other basic goods. While such taxes hurt the poor, they provided the government with money much more quickly. The minister of finance chose this option. As a result, many citizens accused him of insensitivity to the poor. However, the minister replied that by putting the new nation on solid financial footing, he was serving the interest of all citizens.

Problem:
Italy's lack of finances necessary to build a nation

Option 1
Tax each person based on wealth

Advantage: alleviates the burden placed on the poor

Disadvantage: takes too long to generate revenue

Option 2
Tax food and other necessities

Advantage: provides government with money more quickly

Disadvantage: hurts the poor

Solution Decided Upon:
Tax on food and other goods

Result:
Criticism from some; solid financial footing for nation

Southern Italy was a rural and agricultural land in which people led simple, traditional lives as peasants or artisans. Some leaders feared such people would be unfairly burdened by a tax on food and other similar items.

Skills Reminder

To use a problem-solving process, first identify the problem. Then gather information and examine the options. Note what steps the group or person is considering to solve the problem. Analyze the advantages and disadvantages of each action the group is considering. Note that different members of the group may hold differing opinions about an option. Then choose and implement the solution. Recognize what solution the group implemented and evaluate its success based on the results.

Skills Practice

❶ Based on the results, was the solution chosen by the minister of finance a wise one?

❷ What might have happened if he had chosen the other option?

❸ Choose a problem that another group in this chapter faced. Use the problem-solving process to describe how the group determined a solution. Consult library materials or the Internet if necessary.

Unification and its Problems

During 1860 people everywhere in Italy, except Venetia and Rome, held plebiscites. They voted overwhelmingly for national unity under the king of Sardinia. Meeting in Turin in 1861, representatives of the various states confirmed Victor Emmanuel II as king of Italy. In 1866 Italy gained Venetia in a war with Austria, and in 1870 Rome's citizens voted for union with Italy. The following year Rome was proclaimed the capital of the kingdom of Italy.

Although politically united, Italy still faced many problems. Few Italians had experience with self-government. Regions of the country remained divided by cultural traditions, and tensions grew between the industrialized north and the agricultural south. The standard of living of most Italians was low and labor problems arose.

Attempting to build a colonial empire, Italy engaged in several military ventures in Africa in the 1880s. A brief war against the Ottoman Empire in 1911 brought little gain. The conquest of Libya in 1912 strengthened Italy's position in the Mediterranean region but divided the nation.

✔ **READING CHECK: Analyzing Information** What was a major reason that unification did not result in political stability for Italy right away?

Unification of Italy, 1858–1870

Interpreting Maps Italy was united into a single kingdom over a 12-year period.

■ **Skills Assessment: The World in Spatial Terms** What territories did Italy cede to France in 1860?

Map legend:
- Kingdom of Sardinia, 1858
- Austrian territory annexed by Sardinia, 1859
- Territory annexed by Sardinia to form kingdom of Italy, 1860
- Austrian territory annexed by Italy, 1866
- Territory annexed by Italy, 1870

SECTION 1 REVIEW

1. **Define** and explain the significance:
   risorgimento

2. **Identify** and explain the significance:
   Carbonari
   Giuseppe Mazzini
   Young Italy movement
   King Victor Emmanuel II
   Camillo Benso di Cavour
   Napoléon III
   Giuseppe Garibaldi

3. **Categorizing** Make a cluster drawing like the one below. Fill in the cluster drawings by identifying the different problems of a unified Italy.

   Problems of a unified Italy

4. **Finding the Main Idea**
   a. What two events led to new nationalist movements for unification in Italy?
   b. Who were the important leaders in the fight for Italian unification?
   c. Why did the kingdom of Sardinia take the lead in Italian unification?

5. **Writing and Critical Thinking**

   Supporting a Point of View Decide whether you agree with Napoléon III's actions during the Italian movement for unification. Write arguments supporting your point of view.
   Consider:
   • the agreement Napoléon III made with Cavour
   • Napoléon III's failure to achieve his goals in his alliance against Austria
   • Napoléon III's fear of having to fight both Austria and Prussia

Homework Practice Online
go.hrw.com
keyword: SH3 HP16

READ TO DISCOVER

❶ How did Prussia replace Austria as the leading German state in Europe?

❷ In what ways did German unification differ from Italian unification?

❸ What changes in German government occurred as a result of unification?

DEFINE

kaiser

IDENTIFY

Junkers
Zollverein
William I
Treaty of Prague
Bundesrat
Reichstag

WHY IT MATTERS TODAY

The Zollverein was a major step toward German unity. The member states benefited from an agreement for a free market and tariff protection against foreign competitors. Use CNN News.com or other **current event** sources to find out with what countries the United States has tariff agreements. Record your findings in your journal.

CNN student News.com

The Unification of Germany

The Main Idea
Prussian leader Otto von Bismarck used war to bring his own brand of nationalism to Germany.

The Story Continues *In the 1800s nationalist feelings grew in Germany as the liberal ideas of the French Revolution swept across Europe. As one German student explained, "We want Germany to be considered one land and one people.... We want a constitution for the people that fits in with the spirit of the times and with the people's own level of enlightenment, rather than what each prince gives his people." However, the type of nationalism that emerged in Germany did not include the liberal reforms for which people had hoped.*

Prussia as Leader

In the mid-1800s Germany remained what it had been for centuries—a patchwork of independent states. Each had its own laws, currency, and rulers. In the late 1800s Prussia led the fight for unification of these states.

Prussia had become strong in the 1700s during the reigns of Frederick William I and his son Frederick the Great. However, Napoléon I defeated Prussia in 1806 and dominated the country for seven years. He seized Prussian lands, limited the size of Prussia's army, and forced Prussia to contribute money and soldiers to France.

The Prussians found ways around Napoléon's restrictions. The army drafted soldiers for short periods of intensive training. These soldiers then went into the reserves and a new group took their place. In this way Prussia trained a large force while still observing the limits Napoléon had placed on their standing army. These Prussian troops helped to defeat the French at Leipzig in 1813 and fought at Waterloo in 1815. Prussia became one of the four great powers at the Congress of Vienna and joined the Quadruple Alliance.

In 1815 the Congress of Vienna created the German Confederation, a group of states that included Prussia. The Congress granted Prussia important territories in Saxony and along the lower Rhine River. Prussia absorbed these regions into its efficient government and strong economy. Austria was Prussia's greatest German rival. An Austrian Habsburg had held the position of Holy Roman Emperor since the 1400s, giving Austria influence over the German states. Napoléon, however, had abolished the Holy Roman Empire, and the Congress of Vienna did not restore it.

This German illustration from 1850 depicts the Prussian cavalry in action.

Moreover, Napoléon's rule had inspired nationalism in the German states. German nationalism favored Prussia more than Austria. In Prussia almost everyone was German. Austria, although ruled by Germans, contained many other nationalities, such as Hungarians, Romanians, Italians, and Slavs. After Prussia's gains at the Congress of Vienna, Austria's focus moved south and east, toward Italy and the Balkans.

✔ **READING CHECK: Finding the Main Idea** What factors influenced Prussia's rise to power over the German states more than Austria?

The Zollverein

After the Congress of Vienna, the first major step in German unification involved the economy. Tariffs imposed by the German states made trade between states costly, forcing up the price of goods. Prussians even placed tariffs on goods moving from one Prussian possession to another.

A class of aristocratic landowners called the **Junkers** (YOOHNG·kuhrz) complained that tariffs were hurting sales of farm products. Joining with tradespeople, intellectuals, financiers, and manufacturers, the Junkers campaigned for freer movement of goods. In 1818 they persuaded the king of Prussia to abolish tariffs within his territories. By 1834 German states had agreed to treaties that resulted in a customs union called the **Zollverein** (TSOHL·fer·yn). By 1854 the Zollverein included most of the German states, but not Austria.

The Zollverein made prices lower and more uniform. Industrialization spread in the German Confederation due to free markets for goods and protection from foreign competition. The states adopted uniform systems of weights, measures, and currency. Manufacturers produced and sold more goods. The German economy moved toward unification.

Powerful German aristocrats promoted the customs union known as the Zollverein to abolish trade barriers within the German Confederation. The union did much to encourage industrial growth and economic unity among its member German states.

Politically, however, each state in the German Confederation continued to act independently. Strong nationalistic and democratic movements emerged within the Confederation. When uprisings broke out in France in 1848, demands for liberal reforms followed throughout the German states. Elections were held for representatives to a National Assembly in Frankfurt to try to unify Germany. The National Assembly drafted a constitution that provided for a hereditary monarchy with powers limited by a popularly elected legislature. However, liberal demands for a representative government were not met, so that the German system remained absolutist. German unification would be accomplished by a king and his aggressive prime minister.

✔ **READING CHECK: Identifying Cause and Effect** How did the formation of the Zollverein move the German states toward economic unity?

Bismarck and Prussian Strength

In 1861 **William I** became king of Prussia. The next year he appointed Otto von Bismarck to head the Prussian cabinet. A conservative Junker politician, Bismarck built the Prussian army into a powerful war machine.

Bismarck opposed democracy and the idea of a parliament. He believed that the state, not the people, should hold authority. Bismarck wanted to expand Prussia. He may also have believed it was Prussia's destiny to lead the German people to unification.

 "Prussia must build up and preserve her strength for the favorable moment which has already come and gone many times. Her borders under the treaties of Vienna are not favorable to the healthy existence of the state. The great questions of the day will not be settled by speeches and majority decisions—that was the great mistake of 1848 and 1849—but by blood and iron."

Otto von Bismarck, quoted in
The Origins of the Wars of German Unification, by William Carr

Bismarck and William faced opposition from the Prussian parliament. When the parliament refused to approve money for a military buildup, Bismarck simply collected the taxes without their approval. Claiming that the government had to keep functioning even without agreement, he ignored the constitution, outraging the liberals. As protests grew Bismarck hoped that successful foreign policy would calm an increasingly hostile public.

✔ **READING CHECK: Analyzing Information** In what ways did Bismarck act to undermine the power of Prussia's parliament?

Wars of Unification

To increase the power and size of Prussia, Bismarck first had to drive Austria from its position of leadership in the German confederation. Second, Prussia had to overcome Austria's influence over the southern German states, which opposed Prussian leadership. He accomplished these objectives in three wars.

The Danish War. On the border between Denmark and Germany lay two small states—the duchies of Schleswig and Holstein. The population of Holstein was entirely German. Schleswig's population included a mixture of Germans and Danes. The Danish king ruled the two duchies even though their constitutions made them separate from Denmark. In 1863 King Christian IX took the Danish throne. At the insistence of many Danes, he proclaimed a new constitution in which he tried to annex Schleswig for Denmark.

Both Prussia and Austria protested the new Danish constitution. Together they demanded that it be revoked. When Denmark refused, Prussia and Austria declared war on Denmark. Denmark hoped for help from France and Great Britain, but neither of those countries acted. In 1864, after three months of fighting, Denmark surrendered.

The peace treaty gave the two duchies to Prussia and Austria jointly. That arrangement produced conflict between Austria and Prussia. Austria wanted the two duchies to form a single independent state within the German Confederation. Prussia opposed the idea. After a bitter quarrel, Prussian and Austrian leaders decided that Prussia would control Schleswig and Austria would control Holstein.

Analyzing Primary Sources

Summarizing How would you describe Bismarck's approach to German unification?

HISTORY MAKER

**Otto von Bismarck
(1815–1898)**

Known for his strong will and determination, Bismarck worked hard to unite Germany. However, he was always against any form of popular government.

Bismarck introduced a number of reforms that helped bring together the German states. Bismarck also went to war to win territory that he believed belonged to Germany. Because of Bismarck, Germany became a major power. **How did Bismarck help to unify Germany?**

Nationalism

In the early 1800s Germans began to take a new interest in their national traditions, language, and customs. This spirit expressed itself in art, literature, and music, and helped inspire political steps toward unification.

Many Germans associated nationalism with liberalism. They believed that representative government and individual freedoms would advance along with nationalistic principles. However, Bismarck used nationalism mainly as a tool to help Prussia gain control over the rest of Germany.

Understanding Civics

How did different people view the connection between nationalism and government rule in Germany?

The Seven Weeks' War. As Prussian influence expanded, Bismarck prepared for conflict with Austria. He first persuaded Napoléon III of France to remain neutral, then formed an alliance with the new nation of Italy. Finally Bismarck provoked Austria into declaring war on Prussia in 1866 over the ongoing Schleswig and Holstein dispute.

Prussia's efficient conduct during the war startled the whole world. Prussian forces took advantage of technology—moving by train, communicating by telegraph, and using modern weaponry. They defeated the once-powerful Austrians in only seven weeks. The balance of European power dramatically shifted.

The **Treaty of Prague** ended the Seven Weeks' War in 1866. Under the terms of the treaty, the German Confederation was dissolved. Austria surrendered Holstein to Prussia, and Italy gained Venetia. A year later several north German states united with Prussia to form the North German Confederation. The king of Prussia was president of this confederation, but each state had self-government. As the largest and most powerful state, Prussia dominated the legislature of the Confederation.

The Franco-Prussian War. To complete the unification of Germany, Bismarck had to persuade the independent states in southern Germany to join the North German Confederation. His opportunity came in 1870 when he received a telegram from King William. Bismarck edited the telegram so that it sounded as though the king had insulted the French ambassador. When the telegram was published, it so enraged the French that in July of 1870 they declared war on Prussia.

As Bismarck had expected, the southern German states united against the French threat. No outside nation came to France's aid. The Franco-Prussian War was short but decisive. The superb Prussian army defeated the French in a few months of hard fighting. Napoléon III surrendered in September, and his government fell. Paris remained under siege until it surrendered in January 1871. A treaty followed in May. Much of France was occupied by German troops. France lost Alsace and part of Lorraine, and had to pay a huge indemnity.

✔ **READING CHECK: Making Generalizations** What was Bismarck's primary method of achieving unification?

King William I of Prussia (above right) helped Bismarck create a form of nationalism that suppressed democratic and liberal activities.

Prussian soldiers with cannons (right) quickly defeated the French.

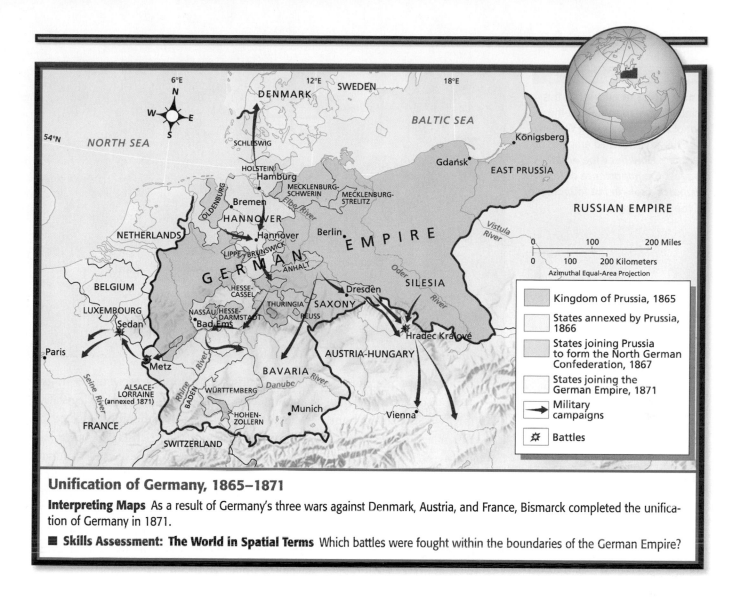

Unification of Germany, 1865–1871

Interpreting Maps As a result of Germany's three wars against Denmark, Austria, and France, Bismarck completed the unification of Germany in 1871.

■ **Skills Assessment: The World in Spatial Terms** Which battles were fought within the boundaries of the German Empire?

Formation of the German Empire

For Germany the treaty ending the Franco-Prussian War was not as important as an event that took place before its signing. On January 18, 1871, representatives of the allied German states met in the Hall of Mirrors at the Palace of Versailles near Paris. There they declared the formation of the German Empire, including all German states except Austria. The Prussian capital of Berlin became the empire's capital. King William I of Prussia was proclaimed German emperor. Bismarck was named chancellor, or chief minister, of the empire, and continued as prime minister of Prussia as well. His nickname became the "Iron Chancellor."

Although he disliked constitutions, Bismarck accepted a constitution that united the 25 German states in a federal form of government. Each state had its own ruler as well as the right to handle its own domestic matters, such as education, law enforcement, and local taxation. Southern states had some special rights, such as Bavaria's right to control its own military. The federal government controlled all common matters, such as national defense, foreign affairs, and commerce. The emperor, called the **kaiser,** headed the government. The kaiser held tremendous power. He appointed the chancellor and commanded the military in times of war. He could declare a defensive war on his own and an offensive war with legislative approval.

A new German empire In this painting, Bismarck stands at the foot of the throne as King William I of Prussia is crowned emperor of Germany. *How does the artist suggest the importance of Bismarck's role in the founding of the new empire?*

The legislative branch consisted of two houses. The **Bundesrat,** or upper house, was a federal council made up of 58 appointed members. The **Reichstag,** or legislative assembly, was the lower house. It consisted of almost 400 members elected by universal male suffrage. Supposedly a representative body, the Reichstag, however, had limited powers. It could approve military budgets only once every seven years and saw only those bills that the Bundesrat had already approved. These restrictions made it almost impossible for the Reichstag to effect any liberal or democratic change not supported by the emperor or the Bundesrat.

The German constitution strongly favored the interests of Prussia. The king of Prussia was also kaiser of Germany. Prussia had the most delegates in the Bundesrat. They were appointed by Prussia's state government. As the most populous state, it also had the most representation in the Reichstag.

✔ **READING CHECK: Categorizing** In what ways did Prussia remain the most powerful force in the German Empire?

SECTION 2 REVIEW

1. **Define** and explain the significance:
   kaiser

2. **Identify** and explain the significance:
   Junkers
   Zollverein
   William I
   Treaty of Prague
   Bundesrat
   Reichstag

3. **Analyzing Information**
   Copy the table below. Identify how each of the wars fought by the Prussians contributed to the unification of Germany.

Unification of Germany	
The Danish War	
The Seven Weeks' War	
The Franco-Prussian War	

4. **Finding the Main Idea**
   a. How did Prussia replace Austria as the leading German state in Europe?
   b. Contrast the ways in which German unification differed from Italian unification.
   c. After unification, what was the makeup of the German government?

5. **Writing and Critical Thinking**
   Identifying Bias Explain how Bismarck's policies supported his belief in action rather than words.
   Consider:
   • the way he dealt with the Prussian parliament
   • the way he provoked other countries into war
   • how he kept liberals from carrying out reforms in the new German Empire

Homework Practice Online
keyword: SH3 HP16

SECTION 3

Opposition to Bismarck

READ TO DISCOVER

1 What problems did Bismarck face as chancellor of the German Empire?

2 How did Germany become industrialized under Bismarck's leadership?

3 What factors led to the decline of Bismarck's power as chancellor?

IDENTIFY

Kulturkampf
Social Democratic Party
William II

▶ WHY IT MATTERS TODAY

Germany has gone on to become a highly respected industrial nation. Use **CNN** or other **current event** sources to find out in what industries and technologies Germany has taken the lead. Record your findings in your journal.

CNN Student News.com

The Main Idea
Bismarck encountered opposition from groups within the German Empire and a new monarch.

The Story Continues *When William II became kaiser of the German Empire, he regarded it as his sacred duty to help the German people prosper. "Those who are willing to help me in this work will be heartily welcomed by me, no matter who they be," William II declared. "But those who should oppose me in this work I will crush." The new kaiser's words were put to the test when he soon came into conflict with Otto von Bismarck.*

Problems for the Empire

Because the constitution did not give Bismarck the absolute monarchy he wanted, he tried to achieve it in other ways. However, after the formation of the German Empire, he had to compromise to make the political system work. The constitution gave the people little voice, and dissatisfied groups formed political parties that opposed Bismarck's policies. Bismarck's government was increasingly forced to attend to these demands. Some groups demanded a more liberal and democratic government. Others feared Bismarck's military policy and the ever-growing army.

Representatives in the Prussian legislature were conservative. They were elected by a special system that gave more representation to voters from the upper class. However, politicians from other areas of the empire were more likely to oppose Bismarck. The growing power of political groups in other parts of the empire increased tension between Prussia and the other German states.

Relations with the Catholic Church presented special problems for Bismarck. He was a Protestant and did not trust the loyalty of Catholics to the empire. Many Catholics were also members of the Centre Party, which Bismarck regarded as an enemy.

Bismarck began the anti-Catholic program of **Kulturkampf**—German for "culture struggle." Germany passed strict laws to control Catholic clergy and schools. The laws expelled the Jesuits and forbade political expression from the pulpit. They required that all Catholic clergy be Germans educated in German schools. Diplomatic relations with the Vatican were broken as part of the Kulturkampf. Eventually even church property was confiscated.

These policies created opposition. The Centre Party doubled in size, and many non-Catholic liberals joined the opposition. By 1878 Bismarck began to

INTERPRETING THE VISUAL RECORD

Bismarck's enemies This French political cartoon shows Bismarck as his enemies saw him. *What qualities of Bismarck does this drawing emphasize?*

NATIONALISM IN EUROPE **451**

modify the Kulturkampf because he needed the support of the Centre Party against a growing socialist presence. He reestablished diplomatic relations with the pope and had laws against Catholics eased or repealed. Kulturkampf ended in failure in 1887.

✔ **READING CHECK: Identifying Cause and Effect** Why did Kulturkampf fail?

Industrial Development under Bismarck

During Bismarck's time the German Empire changed into an industrial giant. Germany had rich stores of natural resources, including great coal and iron deposits. The German government managed railroads to promote industrial development, and a system of canals provided cheaper transportation.

Industrialization came later in Germany than in Great Britain or France, which proved to be an advantage. German industries could use the best methods and most advanced machinery that had been developed elsewhere. German scientists then worked out further improvements.

Under Bismarck's leadership the government helped industry in many ways. Money and banking laws were standardized throughout the empire. Postal services, by which so much business was conducted, were centralized. The government encouraged German industrialists to form cartels—groups of companies that combine together for greater power in the marketplace—to control prices. The government adopted a high-tariff policy to protect industries from foreign competition. Germany soon rivaled Great Britain and France as an industrial power.

✔ **READING CHECK: Finding the Main Idea** How did Germany's government under Bismarck help Germany to become industrialized?

Socialism in Germany

As chancellor of the German Empire, Bismarck started several industrial reforms, including the standardization of money and improved transportation. This photo shows the German industrial city of Dresden in 1875.

With the growth of German industry, cities grew rapidly, and a class of factory workers appeared. German laborers, like those in other nations, wanted decent working conditions. Some people believed that the actions of the cartels led to lower wages for workers and higher prices for consumers. Many felt that these problems required government action to regulate industry.

Some social reformers, as they had in other countries, went further. They called for government ownership of major industries. German socialists banded together in 1869 to form what would become the **Social Democratic Party** (SDP). The party grew quickly, most of its members coming from the ranks of urban workers. By 1877 the SDP had elected 12 members to the Reichstag.

Even if the SDP had gained a much greater representation, it would have accomplished very little. The Reichstag could not pass any laws that the Bundesrat opposed. Because the Bundesrat represented aristocratic rulers, they were unlikely to support or pass any laws that the socialists wanted. The Reichstag, however, served as a limited public forum in which socialist members could express grievances. Socialists explained what they would do if they were given power, thus catching the interest and support of the workers.

✔ **READING CHECK: Drawing Inferences** Why were socialists unable to get reform laws passed?

Bismarck's Antisocialist Campaign

Every gain in socialist voting strength—and every socialist demand for reform—alarmed Bismarck. When the SDP won more than 490,000 votes in 1877, Bismarck decided to use all his power to fight them. He got his opportunity in 1878 when two assassination attempts were made against the emperor.

Bismarck knew that neither of the would-be assassins had any connection with socialism. However, he took advantage of public concern by accusing the Social Democrats of plotting the attempts. The emperor and the Bundesrat dissolved the Reichstag and called for new elections. A widespread campaign against socialists and their ideas followed.

The election did not change the strength of the SDP in the Reichstag. However, Bismarck pushed through laws that prohibited newspapers, books, or pamphlets from spreading socialist ideas. He banned public meetings of socialists. Despite such restrictive laws, socialists increased their support with each election. As he had done with the Kulturkampf, Bismarck changed tactics to keep control in the face of growing opposition.

Bismarck decided to grant many of the reforms the socialists proposed, so that fewer people would have reason to support the socialists. Beginning in 1883 he endorsed laws that gave workers insurance against sickness, then against accidents—both paid for by employers. Other laws limited working hours, provided for certain holidays, and guaranteed pensions for disabled and retired workers. Thus Germany initiated a pioneering program of government-directed social reforms. The reforms did not end socialism in Germany, but they did reduce the workers' grievances. Many other industrial nations later adopted similar programs.

✔ **READING CHECK: Identifying a Point of View** What did Bismarck think that government directed social reforms would accomplish?

What If? What if Bismarck had not begun a program of social reform in Germany in the 1880s? How might the history of Germany and other industrial nations have been different?

The Reichstag building in Berlin, Germany

The Resignation of Bismarck

Kaiser William I died in 1888 at the age of 91. Crown Prince Frederick III, who was more sympathetic to liberalism, succeeded him. However, Frederick III died after only a few months in office. As a result Frederick's son, **William II,** became emperor in 1888. He was 29 years old at the time of his coronation.

William II held strongly conservative opinions. He believed in the absolute authority of the emperor. This soon brought the young monarch into conflict with Bismarck. William II felt that Bismarck had too much power. Bismarck resented the way the young emperor reduced powers that the chancellor had wielded effectively for years. He also resented William II's involvement in political affairs that previously had been under his control.

In 1890 the socialists scored huge gains in the elections. Bismarck considered convening the Bundesrat to come up with a new constitution. William II realized that this would create governmental chaos at the beginning of his reign. Under William I, Bismarck had often gotten his way by threatening to resign. When Bismarck offered his resignation in 1890, however, the kaiser accepted it. With great bitterness Bismarck resigned.

Bismarck's policies had left Germany strong, but had frustrated the German people. Bismarck had never allowed the development of a parliamentary democracy. With Bismarck gone, William II was able to pursue his own policies. He set out to expand Germany's influence in the world, and during his reign Germany became a leading industrial and military power. William II increased the size and strength of the German army and expanded the German navy. He signed new agreements with neighboring nations. By the early 1900s Germany was stronger than ever before. However, this soon brought Germany into conflict with Great Britain, the world's leading naval power at the time.

Shortly after becoming emperor of Germany, William II (left) forced Bismarck to resign as chancellor.

✔ **READING CHECK: Contrasting** How did William II's relationship with Bismarck differ from that of his grandfather, William I?

SECTION 3 REVIEW

1. **Identify** and explain the significance:
   Kulturkampf
   Social Democratic Party
   William II

2. **Categorizing** Copy the diagram below. On the left side, indicate the actions of Bismarck that resulted in positive effects for the German Empire. On the right side, indicate Bismarck's actions that resulted in opposition to his actions.

   Actions of Bismarck

3. **Finding the Main Idea**
   a. What problems did Bismarck face as chancellor of the German Empire?
   b. What did Bismarck do to help Germany become industrialized?
   c. What factors led to the decline of Bismarck's power as chancellor?

4. **Writing and Critical Thinking**
   Analyzing Information Explain why it was an advantage for Germany to industrialize after Great Britain and France.
   Consider:
   • what resources a country needs to industrialize
   • what machinery and processes a country needs when it industrializes
   • the role that scientists played in industrialization

Homework Practice Online
keyword: SH3 HP16

Reform and Revolution in Russia

READ TO DISCOVER

❶ What geographical and cultural factors made Russia different from the rest of Europe?
❷ What were the characteristics of Russian domestic and foreign policies?
❸ What types of reform movements occurred in Russia, and what were their results?

DEFINE

autocrat
nihilists
terrorism
pogroms

IDENTIFY

"Russification"
Pan-Slavism
Alexander II
Emancipation Edict
People's Will
Social Democratic Labor Party
Duma

The Main Idea
A series of conflicts between the monarchy and radical liberals led to revolution in Russia.

The Story Continues *In the 1800s liberal ideas from western Europe stirred up unrest among the Russian people. The Russian czars tried to shut the door to Western influence and preserve their own power. As one official wrote, "[I]n view of the sad occurrences that surround us on all sides, it was necessary to fortify our Fatherland. . . . Russia lives and is preserved by the spirit of a strong, humane, enlightened autocracy." This autocracy would soon clash with a new wave of political radicals.*

The Russian Empire

By the mid-1800s Russia had the largest territory and population of any European nation. Yet industrial development, which so strengthened the West, lagged in Russia. Most of Russia's extensive natural resources lay undeveloped. Ports were blocked by ice for much of the year and exits from the seas were controlled by other countries. This left Russia virtually landlocked. Efforts to win access to the Mediterranean led to conflicts with the Ottoman Empire.

Unlike Great Britain or France, the huge Russian Empire included a great variety of peoples and national groups. The largest ethnic groups in the European part of Russia were the Belorussians or White Russians in the west, the Ukrainians in the agricultural south, and the Great Russians in north and central Russia. These groups were descended from common Slavic ancestors, but each had its own language, customs, and history. These main Slavic groups were also divided by geography.

Scattered throughout the empire were various minorities who spoke many languages. Many of these groups, such as the Poles and Finns, had been conquered by the Russians and disliked Russian rule. Russia had also conquered peoples of Central Asia and Caucasia. This diversity of ethnic, national, and religious groups made unification difficult.

✔ **READING CHECK: Finding the Main Idea** What were some issues that made industrialization and unification difficult for Russia in the 1800s?

Village life in many parts of Russia reflected centuries-old Slavic customs and traditions.

Russian Domestic and Foreign Policies

The liberal movement that influenced other European nations so strongly in the 1800s made little progress in Russia. The czar ruled the huge Russian empire as an **autocrat,** one who holds absolute power. Although the czars tried to maintain autocracy, liberal political developments in Europe affected Russia.

Russia had struggled with the influence of the West from before the time of Peter the Great a century earlier. Nationalistic ideas appealed to the ethnic minorities within the Russian Empire, especially to the strongly patriotic Poles and Finns. By the early 1800s liberalism had also begun to attract some of the educated members of the Russian aristocracy.

Faced with problems caused by liberal ideas and restless nationalities, the czars took harsh measures. To counteract liberalism the government strictly censored speech and the press and rejected all demands for a constitution. In the 1830s Czar Nicholas I began a program of **"Russification."** This program forced non-Russian peoples in the empire to use the Russian language, accept the Orthodox religion, and adopt Russian customs in place of their traditional ones.

Russian foreign policy had two primary features. The first branch of Russian foreign policy was designed to increase Russian influence among the Slavic peoples of the Balkans, to the west of Russia. In this sometimes troubled region, Russia promoted **Pan-Slavism,** the union of all Slavic peoples under Russian leadership. The second main feature of Russian foreign policy addressed Russian interests to the south and east. Russia sought to continue the expansion that had begun under the first czars, pushing east into Asia and south toward the Ottoman Empire. Expansion southward, however, was halted with a defeat in the Crimean War in the 1850s. In that disastrous war, Russia lost crucial border territory.

✔ **READING CHECK: Drawing Inferences** Why did Russian foreign policy focus on expanding their territory to the east?

Alexander II and Reforms

In 1855 **Alexander II** became czar. Although basically conservative and autocratic, Alexander paid attention to public opinion. He responded, although cautiously, to the movement for freedom for all serfs. His actions were the first steps toward modernization for a country that had realized its backwardness with its defeat in the Crimean War.

Emancipation for the serfs. Serfdom took a different form in Russia than it had in the rest of Europe. After the time of Peter the Great, serfs were bound to persons and not to the land. They could not leave their villages or masters' homes without their owners' permission or a government order.

Czar Nicholas I ordered Russian soldiers to imprison the sons of a Polish fugitive.

Statue of Czar Alexander II in Helsinki, Finland

Toward the middle of the 1800s, reform of serfdom became clearly necessary. Serfdom obstructed development by restricting the labor pool. Factory owners would benefit if the serfs were freed. The industrialists did not believe in liberal ideas; they simply needed workers for their factories. Moreover, some nobles felt that a great nation should not allow the ownership of people. These nobles began to support a campaign against serfdom. Another group of government officials, most notably in the ministry of the interior, sought reform for the serfs. They persuaded Alexander II to consider abolishing the institution.

Finally in 1861 Alexander II issued the **Emancipation Edict,** which freed all serfs. The czar decided that "It is better to abolish serfdom from above than to wait until the serfs begin to liberate themselves from below." The terms of the Emancipation Edict compensated nobles for land, which peasants could buy in small tracts from the government.

However, emancipation did not solve all problems for the former serfs. Land was sold to them in tiny plots at high prices. Most serfs could not afford enough land to earn the payments for the land, pay taxes, and still make a living. Therefore they had to rent more land from their former owners, at high rents. As one British observer wrote,

❝The Emancipation Law did not confer on [give] the peasants as much land as they require, and consequently the peasant who has merely his legal portion has neither enough of work nor enough of revenue.❞

from *Russia in Revolution,* by Stanley W. Page

Some former serfs were unable to either buy or rent land. These people and their families moved from the country to growing towns and cities. There they became cheap sources of labor for factories.

Alexander II's other reforms. Alexander II attempted other liberal reforms, looking to modernize his nation. Because the Emancipation Edict took control of the provinces away from the landowners, it also created the need for a new system of local government. An 1864 law created this new system. Beginning in that year, Alexander allowed rural districts to elect *zemstvos.* These were councils at the provincial and county levels. Three groups had the right to vote in the *zemstvo* elections: the nobles, the middle class, and the peasants. However, the votes were still counted in a way that allowed the nobles and rich taxpayers to dominate the elections. *Zemstvos* could levy taxes and controlled programs such as public health, education, assistance for the poor, local crafts, and some public works programs. Alexander also reformed the courts. He modeled civil and criminal courts after European courts. He created courts of appeal and local justices of the peace. This helped reduce delays and corruption. In political cases, however, the ministry of the interior still held power beyond the reach of the courts. Alexander limited the powers of the secret police, gave the press greater freedom, and expanded education. He also reorganized the military, reducing the period of active service from 25 years to 6 years.

It was customary for the czar and his family to exchange eggs like this one on Easter.

Holt Researcher

go.hrw.com

KEYWORD: Holt Researcher

FreeFind: Peter Carl Faberge

After reading about Peter Carl Fabergé on the Holt Researcher, sketch a design for an egg that would have special significance to you.

CONNECTING TO

Art

Metalworking: Fabergé Egg

This unusual piece of art is an enameled gold egg containing an accurate model of the Gatchina Palace near St. Petersburg. Only inches in height, it even includes a tiny flag flying from the palace tower. The egg is decorated with pearls and diamonds.

The Gatchina egg was created in the jewelry firm of Peter Carl Fabergé in St. Petersburg. Founded in 1842 the company employed the finest jewelers and goldsmiths in all of Europe. In 1918 the house of Fabergé was closed by officials of a new government. To raise money the government sold many of the eggs. Many of these priceless eggs are now housed in private collections and museums.

Understanding the Arts

Why are Fabergé eggs so valuable today?

Alexander's reform policies did not please everyone. Conservatives tried to convince the czar that such actions threatened the position of the ruler and the nobles. In their minds, this endangered the stability of the nation. Liberals considered Alexander's reforms to be mere first steps. They pointed out the need for further changes. Radicals criticized Alexander even more strongly.

✔ **READING CHECK: Making Generalizations** Why did the Emancipation Edict fail to solve the problems of serfdom?

Radicals and Government Reaction

Several radical political groups were active in Russia. In the 1860s some middle-class and upper-class intellectuals became **nihilists**—from the Latin word *nihil*, meaning "nothing." They believed a just society could be created only by building a completely new Russia. This meant abolishing the existing political, economic, and social structures.

Terrorist attacks. In the 1870s another group, the Populists, urged their followers to live among peasants as teachers and doctors. Some believed that the large estates of nobles should be seized and the land divided among the peasants. After the government arrested many Populists, some Russian radicals turned to violent action, forming a movement called **People's Will.** This group used **terrorism**—bombings and assassinations by political groups—to try to force the government to grant its demands.

Radical activity made Alexander II more conservative. After an attempt on his life in 1866, he repressed radical groups but continued his reforms. In 1870 major cities were granted limited elected government, followed by military reforms in 1874. After repeated assassination attempts, which Alexander faced with great courage, he was finally killed in a bomb attack by People's Will in 1881.

On March 1, 1881, a bomb thrown at Alexander II's coach injured several of his attendants. Alexander was killed by a second bomb thrown at the coach.

Time of repression. The assassination of Alexander II ended liberal reform and led to an era of intense repression. Alexander III and his successor, Nicholas II, used every available means to stamp out liberalism. Many of Alexander II's reforms were overturned. His successors used censorship, control of the church and education, spies and informers, and imprisonment and exile. Discriminating against minority groups, they revived and intensified Russification. Jews were massacred in riots called **pogroms** (POH·gruhmz). In the pogroms of 1881, the government failed to intervene as more than 100 Jewish villages and towns were pillaged and many residents were murdered or forced to flee.

This attempt to preserve the old order met with much opposition. Industrialization in Russia had produced a class of workers who wanted the right to form unions and to strike. Liberals and radicals found ready support from these often-exploited workers.

The Russian government's attempts to block all change produced an explosive situation. Terrorism increased. In 1898 socialists formed the **Social Democratic Labor Party,** modeled after the German SDP. This group grew increasingly radical. The government's repressive policies had backfired.

✔ **READING CHECK: Identifying Cause and Effect** What were the effects of the Russian government's actions after the assassination of Alexander II?

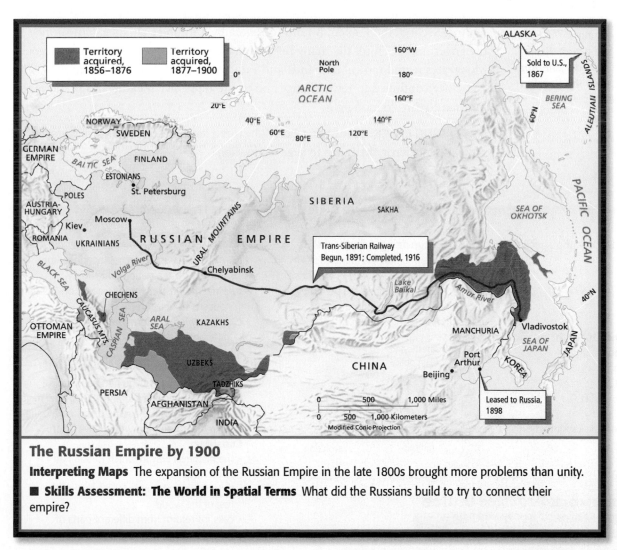

The Russian Empire by 1900

Interpreting Maps The expansion of the Russian Empire in the late 1800s brought more problems than unity.

■ **Skills Assessment: The World in Spatial Terms** What did the Russians build to try to connect their empire?

The Revolution of 1905

In 1904 and 1905 Russia went to war with Japan over territories in China and Korea. To the surprise of the world, the Japanese dealt the Russians a humiliating defeat. The defeat spurred discontented groups into action. Russia's loss exposed a government that was corrupt and inefficient, as well as oppressive. Renewed pogroms against Jews were rampant.

On January 22, 1905—"Bloody Sunday"—the dissent came to a head. The czar's troops shot unarmed strikers on their way to deliver a petition to him. This incident triggered the Revolution of 1905. Workers struck and held demonstrations. Street fighting was especially violent in non-Russian areas. There were mutinies in the army and navy. Finally the czar issued a decree called the October Manifesto, which promised individual liberties. The decree also called for the election of a parliament called the **Duma.** After more bloody fighting, the government finally halted the revolution with severe repression and executions.

Despite the October Manifesto, autocracy continued. The czar dismissed a session of the Duma because members insisted that the czar's ministers answer to them. A 1907 law increased the representation of large landowners and restricted the voting rights of others. This resulted in a more conservative Duma.

The revolutionary movement of 1905 failed to overthrow the czar for three main reasons. First, much of the army remained loyal and would not end the czar's regime. Second, the French, bound to Russia by a military alliance, lent money to the government. Third, the many revolutionary groups were divided in their goals. Moderates feared radical demands and radicals disagreed among themselves. The autocracy continued to resist change and to use repressive measures to preserve the thousand-year-old monarchy.

✔ **READING CHECK: Identifying Bias** Why was a law passed in 1907 giving greater representation in the Duma to large landowners?

Bloody Sunday On Bloody Sunday, January 22, 1905, Russian troops fired shots at a group of peaceful demonstrators. The Revolution of 1905 had begun. *Based on the picture, why do you think the attack angered the Russian people so much?*

SECTION 4 REVIEW

1. **Define** and explain the significance:
   autocrat
   nihilists
   terrorism
   pogroms

2. **Identify** and explain the significance:
   "Russification"
   Pan-Slavism
   Alexander II
   Emancipation Edict
   People's Will
   Social Democratic Labor Party
   Duma

3. **Categorizing** Copy the web diagram below. Fill in the circles by identifying the actions of the Russian government during the period of reform and revolution.

Domestic and foreign policy

The serfs

Russian government actions

Reaction to radicals

Reaction to the revolution

4. **Finding the Main Idea**
   a. Why did Russia's geography and culture make industrialization difficult?
   b. How did Russia try to force its non-Russian citizens to be more "Russian"?
   c. What types of reform did Alexander II attempt?

5. **Writing and Critical Thinking**
   Decision Making If you had been czar of Russia at the beginning of the 1800s, how might you have dealt with the issue of industrialization? Explain the actions you would have taken.
   Consider:
   • the historical way in which Russia had been ruled
   • the problem of Russia falling behind the rest of the world
   • calls for reform from different parts of Russian society

Homework Practice Online
keyword: SH3 HP16

READ TO DISCOVER
❶ What led to the formation of the Dual Monarchy and what problems did it face?
❷ How did the decline of the Ottoman Empire affect European politics?
❸ How did ethnic clashes in southern Europe set the stage for a showdown among the major powers?

IDENTIFY

Francis Joseph I
Treaty of San Stefano
Balkan League

▶ **WHY IT MATTERS TODAY**

In recent years, several Balkan countries have reasserted their independence. Use CNNfyi.com or other **current event** sources to find out which Balkan countries have changed their names or manner of government in the past several decades. Record your findings in your journal.

CNN student News.com

Unrest in Austria-Hungary

The Main Idea
Nationalist groups in Austria-Hungary and the Balkans struggled violently for independence.

The Story Continues *"A troubled, sinister mood prevails here in all circles. The Paris revolution has illuminated the obscurity of our position like a thunderbolt. The suburbs are said to be in a very irritated state. . . . Discontent is general, and I only fear it is not recognized by the authorities as it ought to be."* This is how one observer described the mood in Vienna as demands for liberal reforms swept the Austrian Habsburg Empire.

Results of the Uprisings

By 1848 uprisings in France had set off revolts in almost every other European nation. In the city of Vienna demonstrators and the army clashed. A concerned Emperor Ferdinand ordered Prince Metternich, his chief minister, to resign. After dominating European affairs for more than 30 years, Metternich fled the country. "When France sneezes, all Europe catches cold," he remarked. Later in the year, Emperor Ferdinand himself stepped down, turning over the throne to his 18-year-old nephew.

Uprisings also occurred in Hungary, one of the largest parts of the Austrian Empire. The people of this region resented Austrian rule. A significant portion were Magyars (MAG·yahrz), descendants of nomadic warriors who had migrated to Hungary from Russia and Romania in the 900s. The Magyars spoke a language unlike most other European languages and had their own culture. A strong nationalist movement centered on throwing off Austrian rule and making the Magyars dominant in Hungary.

Hungarian patriot Lajos Kossuth led a revolt in 1848. For a time it looked as if Hungary would gain its independence. Kossuth was elected "responsible governor president" by the Hungarian Diet in 1849. However, Austria soon drove out the

These Hungarian troops fought for independence against Austrian and Russian forces in 1849.

Ethnic Groups in Austria-Hungary, 1867

Interpreting Maps While Austria and Hungary joined together under the Dual Monarchy, they kept separate parliaments and languages.

■ **Skills Assessment: Human Systems** Which non-Slavic peoples lived throughout Austria-Hungary?

revolutionaries. Czar Nicholas I of Russia sent troops to help because he feared that revolution might spread to Russian-controlled Poland. Kossuth fled to Turkey, ending for a time Hungarian attempts at independence.

✔ **READING CHECK: Drawing Inferences** How did the French revolts in 1848 influence the resignation of Metternich and the abdication of Ferdinand?

Formation of the Dual Monarchy

After its defeat by Prussia in 1866, Austria responded to Hungarian demands for independence in 1867 by forming the Dual Monarchy—also called Austria-Hungary. The Dual Monarchy had a common ruler, **Francis Joseph I.** His title was Emperor of Austria and King of Hungary. Three ministries controlled war, finance, and foreign affairs for the whole empire, but Austria and Hungary each had its own parliament. The Austrian Parliament met in Vienna; the Hungarian one met in what became the city of Budapest.

The Dual Monarchy was also a practical economic arrangement. Hungary, chiefly agricultural, furnished raw materials and food. Austria, strongly industrial, produced manufactured goods. Each provided a market for the other.

The Dual Monarchy did not solve all problems, however. Austria wanted high tariffs for its manufactured goods. Division by nationalities also remained. Austrian Germans and Hungarian Magyars spoke different languages. Ethnic minorities such as the Czechs, Slovaks, Serbs, Croats, Romanians, Poles, Slovenes, Ukrainians, and Italians existed in both Austria and Hungary. These people benefited little from the Dual Monarchy and continued to press for self-government.

The defeat in the Seven Weeks' War in 1866 also forced Austria from its leadership of Europe. Hoping to gain influence and territory, the Dual Monarchy turned toward the Balkans, a region to the southeast controlled by the Ottoman Empire.

✔ **READING CHECK: Drawing Conclusions** In what way did the Dual Monarchy fail to solve some of the problems in Austria and Hungary?

The Ottoman Empire and the Balkans

By the 1800s the once-powerful Ottoman Empire had declined substantially. Military defeats had decreased the empire's territory. Ottoman rulers could no longer afford many improvements in agriculture, roads, or hospitals. Many people living in the empire were Christians and Jews. The Turks granted religious and cultural freedom to these non-Muslim minorities, but did not make them social or political equals.

In the early 1800s the rise of nationalism increased discontent in the Balkan area of the Ottoman Empire. This region contained Serbs, Bulgarians, Romanians, Albanians, and Greeks. All of these diverse peoples wanted to govern themselves. Despite Turkish efforts to suppress nationalism, Greeks and Serbs revolted during the 1820s. Helped by outside powers, Greece gained independence in 1829. Serbia achieved a degree of self-rule.

Foreign countries stepped in to promote their own interests. Russia supported Balkan nationalists, many of whom were fellow Slavs and Orthodox Christians. Also, Russia stood to gain a water route from the Black Sea to the Mediterranean if the Ottoman Empire collapsed. Great Britain did not want the Russians in the Mediterranean, so they supported the Turks. It was a strange arrangement. Autocratic Russia promoted independence for the Balkans, while Great Britain, although democratic, supported the Turks in suppressing self-rule.

✔ **READING CHECK: Analyzing Information** What was unusual about the support of other countries for the Balkan nationalists and Ottoman Turks?

The Balkans

For centuries the Balkans have been an area of conflict. This is because they are strategically located where Europe and Asia meet. Since 300 B.C., they have been invaded and controlled by many different groups. The Roman, Byzantine, Slav, and Ottoman empires have all ruled the region. Only a few times in their history have the people there ruled themselves.

Today, the Balkans are still a region in conflict. They are no longer controlled by foreign powers. Instead, different ethnic groups struggle to control territory there. **What has contributed to a history of conflict in the Balkans?**

A well-armed Serbian soldier holds a defensive position in the area of Panonia, Serbia, in March 1992.

The Congress of Berlin and the Balkan Wars

In 1875 revolts broke out in several Turkish provinces in the Balkans. Two years later Russia, in support of the rebels, declared war on the Ottoman Empire. The Turks were defeated and forced to sign the **Treaty of San Stefano** in 1878. The treaty granted independence to Romania, Serbia, and Montenegro. It also gave self-rule to Bulgaria, which Russia then occupied for some years. Bulgaria extended to the Aegean Sea in the eastern Mediterranean.

This sudden increase of Russian influence in the Balkans alarmed other European nations. Before the Treaty of San Stefano went into effect, the major European powers forced Russia to meet with them at the Congress of Berlin in 1878. The Congress dealt with several territorial issues. Serbia, Montenegro, and Romania retained their independence.

Decline of the Ottoman Empire, 1699–1913

Interpreting Maps Throughout the 1800s and early 1900s many territories of the Ottoman Empire became independent or were annexed by other countries.

■ **Skills Assessment: Using Geography** What are the approximate latitude and longitude coordinates for the capital of the Ottoman Empire?

Bulgaria was granted self-government, but it was divided and reduced in size. Moreover, Bulgaria was kept within the Ottoman Empire, thus removing Russia's access to the Aegean Sea. Austria continued to govern Bosnia and Herzegovina but was not permitted to add them to its own territory. Great Britain won the right to occupy the island of Cyprus. This gave the British a naval base in the eastern Mediterranean and kept Russia out of the region. Over time, Great Britain and Italy each seized Ottoman territories in Africa.

In 1908 Austria broke the agreement of the Congress of Berlin by annexing Bosnia and Herzegovina. In 1912 and 1913 two wars between independent Balkan nations and the Ottomans further altered national boundaries. Bulgaria, Serbia, Greece, and Montenegro, known together as the **Balkan League,** declared war on the Ottoman Empire and won. However, the winners quarreled over division of the lands, leading to a second war. This time Serbia, Greece, Montenegro, Romania, and the Ottoman Empire attacked Bulgaria. Bulgaria suffered humiliating losses in this second war and was left with only a small outlet on the Aegean Sea.

By the end of 1913, the Ottoman Empire in Europe included only the city of Constantinople and enough land to control the water route from the Black Sea to the Mediterranean. Other important outcomes of the Balkan Wars included Bulgaria's new alignment with Austria, and Serbia's growing hostility toward Austria. These greatly contributed to heightened political tension in the Balkans.

✔ **READING CHECK: Identifying Cause and Effect**
Why did the European nations force Russia to accept changes in the Treaty of San Stefano?

INTERPRETING THE VISUAL RECORD

Violence in the Balkans This 1913 illustration shows an artillery crew preparing to fire during the Balkan Wars. *What does this picture suggest about the way the wars were fought?*

SECTION 5 REVIEW

1. **Identify** and explain the significance:
   Francis Joseph I
   Treaty of San Stefano
   Balkan League

2. **Sequencing** Copy the diagram below. Create as many boxes as you need. In the boxes, sequence the actions that led to the loss of territory and power in the Ottoman Empire during the 1800s.

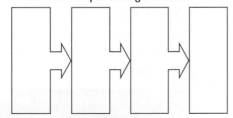

3. **Finding the Main Idea**
   a. What were the strengths and weaknesses of the Dual Monarchy?
   b. How did the decline of the Ottoman Empire influence European politics?
   c. How did ethnic clashes in the Balkans increase tensions toward the end of the 1800s?

4. **Writing and Critical Thinking**
   Contrasting Explain why revolts in Russia failed to produce reforms while those in the Ottoman Empire resulted in the decline of the empire.
   Consider:
   • the reasons why the revolution of 1905 failed in Russia
   • the difficulty of ruling an empire the size of the Ottoman Empire
   • involvement of other nations in the revolutions

Homework Practice Online
keyword: SH3 HP16

CHAPTER 16 Review

Creating a Time Line

Copy the time line below onto a sheet of paper. Complete the time line by filling in the events, individuals, and dates from the chapter that you think were significant. Pick three events and explain why you think they were significant.

1806	1913

Writing a Summary

Using standard grammar, spelling, sentence structure, and punctuation, write an overview of the events in the chapter.

Identifying People and Ideas

Identify the following terms or individuals and explain their significance:

1. Young Italy movement
2. Giuseppe Garibaldi
3. Zollverein
4. William I
5. Bundesrat
6. Social Democratic Party
7. "Russification"
8. terrorism
9. Francis Joseph I
10. Balkan League

Understanding Main Ideas

SECTION 1 (pp. 440–444)
The Unification of Italy

1. Who were some of the important leaders in Italy's fight for unification, and what did they do to achieve the goal of Italian unity?
2. What were some of the problems faced by Italy after unification?

SECTION 2 (pp. 445–450)
The Unification of Germany

3. What actions allowed Prussia to replace Austria as the leading German state in Europe?
4. What changes in German government occurred as a result of unification?

SECTION 3 (pp. 451–454)
Opposition to Bismarck

5. What problems did Bismarck have to overcome as chancellor of the German Empire?
6. What factors led to Bismarck's decline in power and to his subsequent resignation?

SECTION 4 (pp. 455–460)
Reform and Revolution in Russia

7. Why did the liberal movement make little progress in Russia during the 1800s?
8. How did the Russian government deal with reform movements?

SECTION 5 (pp. 461–465)
Unrest in Austria-Hungary

9. What were the strengths and weaknesses of the Dual Monarchy?
10. Why were the early 1900s filled with tension among nations of Europe?

Reviewing Themes

1. **Government** How did differences in the goals of different political groups affect the unification and nationalization of countries such as Germany and Russia?
2. **Global Relations** To what extent did threats from other countries influence unification movements?
3. **Culture** In what countries did common cultural backgrounds play a role in unification efforts?

Thinking Critically

1. **Comparing** Compare the way the Italians and Germans went about unification.
2. **Summarizing** Explain how liberalism affected Russia's domestic policy.
3. **Drawing Inferences** Why did Western nations fear Russian influence in the Balkans?

Writing About History

Supporting a Point of View As nationalist movements increased in countries such as Prussia and Russia, they were met with repression. Write an article that presents arguments for or against the use of repression to silence protests. Use the following chart to organize your thoughts before you begin writing.

Effects of repression on reform movements in Prussia and Russia	
Positive	**Negative**

Building Social Studies Skills

Interpreting Maps

Study the map below. Then use the information to answer the questions that follow.

Prussia in 1815

Kingdom of Prussia, 1815

1. Which of the following areas might Prussia annex to gain two rivers with direct access to the North Sea?
   a. Hesse
   b. Hannover
   c. Saxony
   d. Schleswig

2. Why might it be important for Prussia to have direct access to the North Sea? Give specific reasons.

Identifying Point of View

Read the excerpt below, from an account of the Italian nationalist leader Giuseppe Garibaldi's actions as he led his Red Shirt army to victory at the Battle of the Volturno in 1860.

> "Nothing but the genius of Garibaldi in that terrible hour could have turned his fortunes so far . . . I saw Garibaldi, with his red shirt wringing wet with perspiration, his eye sternly gleaming, his face flushed with the heat of conflict, and blackened by the smoke and dust. I heard his voice commanding—but it was no longer now the calm, clear voice of quieter times. It was hoarse and guttural, and choked with emotion. For the good general saw his gallant band unfalteringly pouring out their life-blood."

3. Which of the following statements best describes the writer's point of view?
   a. Garibaldi's actions had little effect on the battle.
   b. The Red Shirts were little more than bandits.
   c. Garibaldi's actions turned the tide of battle in favor of the Red Shirt cause.
   d. Garibaldi was a poor leader who failed to inspire his followers.

4. Is this account a primary or a secondary source? What evidence can you cite to justify your answer?

Alternative Assessment

Building Your Portfolio

Link to TODAY

Culture

The Balkan countries continue to struggle over territory and independence. Cultural and religious differences fuel many of these struggles. Use the Internet and other sources to identify Balkan countries that are still in conflict with one another. Make a chart showing the countries and what each country is trying to achieve.

🔲 internet connect

Internet Activity: go.hrw.com
KEYWORD: SH3 WH16

Choose a topic on Nationalism in Europe to:
- compare and contrast modern nationalist movements with a nationalist movement discussed in the chapter.
- write a biography of a leader of a nationalist movement in Italy or Germany.
- research the suppression of radical groups and writers in Russia in the 1800s.

1830–1917
The Age of Imperialism

A commemorative plate portraying Queen Victoria of Great Britain

1830
Politics
France occupies Algiers.

1830
Business and Finance
Chile begins to export nitrates for gunpowder.

1834
The Arts
Eugène Delacroix paints *Algerian Women at Home*.

1848
The Arts
Japanese printmaker Katsushika Hokusai finishes *Mount Fuji Seen Below a Wave at Kanagawa*.

1854
Global Events
The Crimean War begins.

1867
Global Events
Canada becomes a self-governing dominion.

1871
Daily Life
Sir Henry Stanley finds Dr. Livingstone in Africa.

1830 **1845** **1860**

1837
Global Events
Queen Victoria begins her reign.

1849
Daily Life
Cape Colony forbids the landing of convicts.

1869
Science and Technology
The Suez Canal is completed.

1835
Politics
The Boers begin the Great Trek in Africa.

1868
Politics
The Meiji era begins in Japan.

1831
Daily Life
The French Foreign Legion is formed.

1866
Science and Technology
The first transatlantic telegraph cable is laid.

The Great Wave of Kanagawa, by the Japanese artist Katsushika Hokusai

Build on What You Know

*I*n 1815 Europe reached a turning point. Napoléon had been defeated. The rulers hoped to return their empires to the old ways. The ideas of nationalism, though, swept through Europe. Many people thought the unified nation-state was the best way to gain individual rights. This nationalism led to unrest and revolutions. Those European countries that accepted change and reform emerged as stronger and more unified states. The strongest of these began to expand their empires across the globe. In this chapter, you will learn how the great European powers and the United States came to control a large part of the world.

Pineapples were a major crop in Hawaii during the late 1800s.

British writer Rudyard Kipling

1898
Politics
The United States annexes Hawaii.

1899
Global Events
The Boer War between the British and the Transvaal's Dutch settlers starts in South Africa.

1907
The Arts
Rudyard Kipling wins the Nobel Prize for literature.

1890
Daily Life
Influenza epidemics occur worldwide.

1901
Science and Technology
Mosquito controls rid Havana of yellow fever.

1910
Global Events
The Mexican Revolution begins.

1916
The Arts
Frank Lloyd Wright designs the Imperial Hotel in Tokyo.

1877
Business and Finance
Frozen meat is shipped from Argentina to Europe for the first time.

1891
The Arts
French painter Paul Gauguin settles in Tahiti.

1875

1890

1905

1920

1886
Business and Finance
Gold is discovered in the Transvaal in Africa.

1904
Politics
The Roosevelt Corollary is adopted.

1914
Science and Technology
The Panama Canal opens, linking the Caribbean and Pacific Oceans.

1913
Science and Technology
Dr. Albert Schweitzer opens a hospital in the French Congo.

Self-Portrait With Palette by French artist Paul Gauguin

The U.S.S. Maine

What's Your Opinion?

Themes Journal *Do you* **agree** *or* **disagree** *with the following statements? Support your point of view in your journal.*

Global Relations An industrialized country can easily control a country that is not industrialized.

Geography Imperialists should expand into locations that benefit their need to transport goods and raw materials.

Economics Imperialists should expand into areas that have natural resources they can use.

READ TO DISCOVER

❶ What is imperialism, and how have imperialists sought to control other peoples?

❷ What were the economic causes of Western imperialism?

❸ In what ways was Western imperialism a product of cultural differences?

DEFINE

imperialism
settlement colonies
dependent colonies
protectorates
spheres of influence

IDENTIFY

"The White Man's Burden"

WHY IT MATTERS TODAY

Imperialism is still common in the world today. Use CNN student News.com or other **current event** sources to find three instances of one country taking control of another country. Record your findings in your journal.

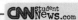

The Roots of Western Imperialism

The Main Idea
Imperialism among the great powers grew out of a complex mixture of political, economic, and social forces.

The Story Continues *During the 1800s, Europeans continued their expansion. At first the Europeans had little influence in the places where they settled. In about 1870, though, they began to take control of these new areas, viewing expansion as a right and a responsibility. "It is our duty," explained a famous supporter of expansionism, "to seize every opportunity of acquiring more territory. . . ."*

Modern Imperialism

The years between 1870 and 1914 were the height of the age of **imperialism.** Imperialism is when one country takes control of another country. One country might control the other's government, trade, or culture. This was not a new idea. Empires had controlled other countries before the 1800s. What was new was the strength of the modern nations. By 1914 the great powers of Europe, Japan, and the United States controlled almost the entire world.

In the beginning, major European governments such as France, Germany, and Great Britain did not plan their imperialism. Often it started when merchants or explorers went to foreign lands. Sometimes the Europeans were not welcome. Then European soldiers would arrive to protect their citizens. After a while, engineers and builders would come. They would open mines, build roads, and make other improvements. The area would be developed, but only for the benefit of the Europeans. The local people had very little say in this process.

Types of control. In some places Europeans had **settlement colonies.** These were large groups of people from one country living together in a new place. For example, Australia was a settlement colony of Great Britain. In other areas Europeans set up **dependent colonies.** In these, a few European officials ruled the non-European people. India, for example, was a dependent colony of Great Britain.

Imperialism often started with the merchant trade. These foreign merchant ships are arriving at a harbor in China.

Europeans set up **protectorates** in some areas. Here, the local ruler kept his title. The Europeans, however, really controlled the area. Other nations were kept out. Areas that were not colonies or protectorates were often in **spheres of influence.** A sphere of influence was an area in which one nation had a special interest. Other nations agreed to respect those special interests.

National rivals. Nationalism was a powerful force between 1870 and 1914. Nations believed that others would respect them more if they had colonies. They also saw colonies as places to get troops for bigger armies. Gurkhas, soldiers from Nepal, joined Australians and New Zealanders in British armies. Troops from West Africa fought for the French.

Nations thought a large navy was as important as a large army. Navies protected widely scattered colonies as well as the nation's merchant ships. During this time, steam-powered ships burned coal. The range of a steamship was "from coal to coal." That made a coaling station, a place where ships could refuel, very important. Tiny islands with nothing to offer except their strategic locations became coaling stations or naval bases. Often these islands became objects of fierce competition among naval powers.

By 1914 there were bitter rivalries among the imperial powers. Nations had colonies all over the world. They had huge armies and navies. They had also created hatred among the colonized people. Eventually this led to world conflict.

✔ **READING CHECK: Comparing and Contrasting** What were the similarities and differences among the four ways imperialists controlled their colonies?

U.S. imperialism This political cartoon represents the United States gathering the fruits of imperialism. *What does the image imply about the ability of Western powers to take the countries they wanted?*

Economic Motives for Imperialism

Industrialization spurred imperialism. After 1850 technology grew rapidly. There were new kinds of energy, new machines, and new industries. The industrialized nations needed a lot of raw materials, such as copper and rubber, to make products. None of the nations wanted to depend on others for raw materials. Their leaders were afraid that in the event of war their countries would not be able to fight off an enemy. To protect themselves, the countries tried to control regions that had the raw materials they needed.

New technology also brought a need for new markets. It was now possible to produce huge amounts of goods. There was also an increased demand for products, particularly in Europe and the United States. Even so, Europe and the United States could not use all the goods produced. Industrialists began to look for new markets in Asia, Africa, and Latin America.

BUY INDIAN TEA

The desire for raw materials and trade goods fueled colonization among many European powers. This advertisement for Indian tea appeared in Britain.

THE AGE OF IMPERIALISM **471**

Europeans and Americans believed that if other people knew their goods were available, they would buy them. Some imperialists went further. They believed they could create new markets by changing people's habits. For example, they would convince the people of central Africa to wear shirts and ties. This would create more business for European and American clothes factories. The factories would hire more people and everyone would make more money.

Industrialists thought they should control their new markets, just as they controlled the sources of their raw materials. They wanted their governments to give them exclusive rights to sell in these markets. At the same time, they demanded protective tariffs to ensure that they would not lose their home markets to foreign competition.

Rapid population growth accompanied industrialism. This provided another economic motive for imperialist expansion. Some historians estimate that the world's population doubled between 1800 and 1900. Industrial development created many jobs, but in Europe there was not enough work to employ all the new job seekers. Displaced farmers and laborers often found it necessary or desirable to go elsewhere. As a result, Europeans left their home countries in record numbers in the 1880s. For Great Britain, France, and Germany, overseas migration was not a new phenomenon. For such countries as Italy, Spain, and Austria-Hungary, however, the emigrations of the 1880s marked the first mass movements of their peoples. The populations of North America, South America, and Australia swelled with settlers from Europe.

✔ **READING CHECK: Summarizing** What were the two main economic motives for Western imperialism?

Cultural Motives for Imperialism

Many people in the industrialized nations thought they had a duty to spread Western ideas and knowledge around the world. People were considered lacking if their religion or culture differed from that of the West.

"The White Man's Burden." British poet Rudyard Kipling is widely considered to be the most powerful voice in favor of British imperialism. The title of one of his best-known poems is **"The White Man's Burden."** This phrase is often used to sum up the Western attitude toward non-Western people. This is the first stanza of the poem.

Advertising This soap advertisement appeared in the 1800s. *How does this advertisement reflect the ideas of "The White Man's Burden"?*

The first step towards lightening

The White Man's Burden

is through teaching the virtues of cleanliness.

Pears' Soap

is a potent factor in brightening the dark corners of the earth as civilization advances, while amongst the cultured of all nations it holds the highest place—it is the ideal toilet soap.

Finding the Main Idea What did Kipling mean by the phrase, "Go bind your sons to exile"?

History Makers Speak

❝Take up the White Man's burden—
Send forth the best ye breed—
Go bind your sons to exile
To serve your captives' need;
To wait in heavy harness,
On fluttered folk and wild—
Your new-caught, sullen peoples,
Half devil and half child.❞

from "The White Man's Burden," by Rudyard Kipling

Many Europeans agreed with Kipling's poem. They thought non-Western people were primitive—"half devil and half child." These wrong ideas caused Europeans to change the way of life for countless people. They were "helping" or "improving" them. Europeans also used the idea of their "burden" to justify imposing their own values and cultural ideas on other peoples.

People who were against imperialism claimed that the only burden the white man wanted to take up was the burden of colonial wealth. Such opponents, however, had very little effect on the imperialist policies of Western nations.

Missionaries. Christian missionaries were very active throughout many areas of the world during the age of imperialism. Churches in Europe and the United States sent a growing number of people to the colonies. Although they hoped to convert people to Christianity, the missionaries did other work as well. Many had been trained as teachers. They helped build schools and taught in them. Others had medical training. They cared for the sick and helped to establish and operate hospitals. Through the efforts of these missionaries, knowledge of medicine, hygiene, and sanitation spread along with Christianity.

✔ **READING CHECK: Identifying Bias** How did the attitudes and beliefs of Western people affect imperialism?

This photo shows a missionary classroom in the Philippines. Missionaries spread learning and modern medical practices, as well as Christianity, during the age of imperialism.

SECTION 1 REVIEW

1. **Define** and explain the significance:
   imperialism
   settlement colonies
   dependent colonies
   protectorates
   spheres of influence

2. **Identify** and explain the significance:
   "The White Man's Burden"

Homework Practice Online
keyword: SH3 HP17

3. **Categorizing** Copy the chart below. Use it to organize the economic and cultural effects of imperialists and the types of control they used.

```
              Imperialism
         ┌────────┼────────┐
   Types of   Economic   Cultural
   control    effects    effects
```

4. **Finding the Main Idea**
   a. Why did imperialism lead to dissent among colonized people?
   b. What evidence would you give that the most important motive of imperialists was economic?
   c. How did the ideas expressed in "The White Man's Burden" affect the lives of colonized people?

5. **Writing and Critical Thinking**
   Identifying Cause and Effect Explain the factors that caused the Western imperialists to take over other areas of the world.
   Consider:
   • economic causes
   • national rivalries
   • cultural motives

READ TO DISCOVER
❶ Why did the French want to gain control of North Africa?
❷ What events and aims promoted British expansion in North and East Africa?

IDENTIFY
Suez Canal
al-Mahdī
Fashoda crisis

▶**WHY IT MATTERS TODAY**

The Suez Canal has been very important to world shipping. It is used just as much today as it was in the 1800s. Use CNN or other **current event** sources to find out about the canal and what has happened to it since 1900. Record your findings in your journal.

CNN Student News.com

European Claims in North Africa

The Main Idea
Imperialism motivated both France and Great Britain to establish colonies in North Africa.

The Story Continues *Some European nations sought to expand overseas not only out of a concern for national security but also from a sense of national identity and pride. Jules-François-Camille Ferry, who became France's Minister of Foreign Affairs in 1883, explained his motives for empire-building. "France . . . cannot be merely a free country. . . ," Ferry insisted. "She ought to propagate [spread] [her] influence throughout the world and carry everywhere that she can her language, her customs, her flag, and her genius."*

The French in North Africa

The French looked toward North Africa to expand their empire. In 1830 a French force occupied Algiers, a Muslim state of the Ottoman Empire. The Algerians did not want French rule. For more than 40 years, the French fought against almost continuous local rebellions. The French thought Algiers was worth the trouble. Many French people and other Europeans moved there. French officials took over Algerian land and settled many colonists there.

The small state of Tunis was east of Algiers. Tunis was also part of the Ottoman Empire, but it had an independent government. In 1881 France found a weak excuse to stage a military action against Tunis, which became a French protectorate. The Turkish governor stayed as ruler, but the French controlled the country. Like the Algerians, the Tunisians resented French control. Many people were inspired to work toward independence.

Morocco's strategic location on the Strait of Gibraltar made it another appealing prize. In 1904 France made an agreement with Britain, Spain, and Italy. According to the agreement, France took control of Morocco. In return, France promised not to get in the way of Britain's plans for Egypt or Italy's plans for Libya. Spain was allowed to keep a sphere of influence in northern Morocco for trading purposes. In 1909 Morocco became a French protectorate.

✔ **READING CHECK: Making Generalizations** How did the people of North Africa react to the French expansion?

France held Tunis (now Tunisia) as a protectorate from 1881 until granting it independence in 1956. This illustration shows French troops storming Tunis in 1881.

Morocco and France

France's takeover of Morocco was not an invasion by force. Rather, the leader of Morocco, facing enormous pressure from many sides, made the decision to ask for French intervention. Making decisions like this one involves choosing between two or more courses of action. The decisions that people and nations make have played a significant role in the shaping of history. Thus, an important part of understanding the events of the past is the ability to analyze and evaluate the decisions that historical figures have made. The factors that go into choosing a course of action make up what is known as the decision-making process. Familiarity with such a process will not only help you to better understand history, but may also help you improve your own decision-making skills.

A Historian's Account

The text below describes the events that led to Moroccan sultan Moulay Abd al-Hafid asking for French control of his country.

In 1911 Moulay Abd al-Hafid found himself besieged in his capital, Fez, by hostile tribesmen. He quickly considered appealing to France for assistance. If he brought in the French to help restore order, they would seize control of the country—something for which his countrymen would never forgive him. As one prominent Moroccan put it, "Foreigners are the original cause of all our troubles." If the sultan did not seek French help, however, he might lose his throne and the country might sink deeper into violence and turmoil. In the end, Moulay Abd al-Hafid decided to invite the French in. As a result, France made Morocco a protectorate and set about governing the nation's affairs. Moroccans responded by branding the sultan a traitor and embarking on a years-long rebellion against French rule.

Sultan Moulay Abd al-Hafid (above, right) appealed to the French to help restore order in Morocco. At the left, French and Spanish delegates are shown at the signing of the treaty that made Morocco a French protectorate.

Skills Reminder

To use a decision-making process, identify the decision by determining the situation that calls for a decision to be made. Recognize the options. Note what different courses of action the person, group, or nation may choose. Then assess the possible outcomes of the different courses of action. Take into consideration the advantages and disadvantages of each option. Analyze the decision. Determine what course of action the person or group chose and evaluate it based on the actual consequences it brought about.

Skills Practice

❶ Read the account of Moulay Abd al-Hafid's decision. Identify the situation, the options, and possible outcomes.

❷ Identify the decision he made and evaluate its wisdom based on the outcomes it produced.

❸ Choose another situation from this chapter in which a person, group, or nation had to make a decision. Consult the library or Internet for more information if necessary. Using the decision-making process, write a paragraph analyzing and evaluating the decision.

The British in North Africa

Egypt had been part of the Ottoman Empire for centuries. By the mid-1800s, though, the empire was weakening. The Ottoman rulers in Egypt had become nearly independent.

Egypt and the Suez Canal. In 1854 the Egyptian government allowed a French company to start building a canal. The **Suez Canal** would go through the Isthmus of Suez to connect the Mediterranean Sea and the Red Sea. Egypt bought almost half of the stock in the company.

Building the canal cost Egypt a lot of money. At the same time, the Egyptian ruler had an extravagant lifestyle. Soon Egypt was deeply in debt. To avoid bankruptcy, Egypt decided to sell its stock in the Suez Canal. This action gave the British a great opportunity. They wanted to control the canal. It would give them a more direct sea route to their colonies in India, Australia, and New Zealand. In 1875 Great Britain bought the Egyptian stock. Because the British now owned so much stock, they gained control of the canal.

At about the same time, an international committee was set up to manage Egypt's huge debt. Many Egyptians did not want to be controlled by foreigners. Egyptian army leader 'Urabi Pasha tried to explain their view to a European.

Analyzing Primary Sources

Supporting a Point of View
How does Pasha appeal to the Europeans' sense of fairness in explaining the Egyptian viewpoint?

History Makers Speak

❝Without doubt it will please every free man to see men free . . . truthful in their sayings and doings, and determined to carry out their high projects for the benefit of mankind generally, and the advantage of their own country in particular.❞

'Urabi Pasha, from *Secret History of the Occupation of Egypt* by Wilfred Scawen Blunt

'Urabi Pasha's words fell on deaf ears, however, and in 1882 a rebellion began. The British navy attacked Alexandria to put down the rioting. Britain then sent troops to stop another rebellion near the Suez Canal. Although Egypt seemed to be independent, the British actually ruled it for many years.

INTERPRETING THE VISUAL RECORD

Suez Canal This illustration shows the first voyage through the Suez Canal on November 17, 1869. *How might the Egyptian people in the crowd have viewed the opening of the Suez Canal?*

The Fashoda crisis. To the south of Egypt was the Sudan. The Sudan was an Egyptian colony. Both Great Britain and France were interested in controlling this area. The upper Nile River flowed through the Sudan. The British wanted to build dams along the river. They hoped to store water for irrigation and to manage the flow of water into the lower Nile. The French wanted to add the Sudan to the colonies they already controlled in the area.

Before the Europeans could act, there was a revolution in the Sudan. In 1881 a Muslim leader named Muhammad Ahmad led a revolt against Egyptian rule. He called himself **al-Mahdī,** a title meaning "the expected one." Followers of the Mahdi gained control of several major cities. In early 1885 they captured Khartoum, the capital of the Sudan. The British decided to act to stop the Mahdists. They also wanted to prevent the French from gaining control in the Sudan. In 1898 Great Britain invaded the Sudan. Under General Horatio Herbert Kitchener, British troops quickly defeated a large Mahdist army.

Meanwhile, the French had also decided to act. Two years earlier they had sent an expedition to Africa under Captain Jean-Baptiste Marchand. Their goal was to gain control of the upper Nile at Fashoda. Starting from the French Congo, Marchand and his small force of Senegalese soldiers made a daring 3,000-mile journey through tropical Africa. In July 1898 Marchand reached Fashoda. Kitchener's British forces arrived at Fashoda two months later. The French and British troops waited for orders from their governments. Both countries prepared for war. Finally, France realized that neither its army nor navy could defeat the British. France yielded the Sudan to Great Britain.

These events became known as the **Fashoda crisis.** The outcome was that Great Britain and Egypt won joint control of the area, with Great Britain clearly the dominant partner. The region became known as Anglo-Egyptian Sudan.

✔ **READING CHECK: Finding the Main Idea** What was the main reason Great Britain and France became involved in the Fashoda crisis?

Holt Researcher

go.hrw.com

go.hrw.com
KEYWORD: Holt Researcher
FreeFind:
   Muhammad Ahmad
After reading more about Muhammad Ahmad on the Holt Researcher, write an outline for a speech he might have given to his followers explaining why they should oppose the British.

The powerful British lion forces the game but weaker French rooster to withdraw from Fashoda in this 1898 cartoon.

FASHODA

DOINGS IN THE DESERT.

SECTION 2 REVIEW

1. **Identify** and explain the significance:
   Suez Canal
   al-Mahdī
   Fashoda crisis

2. **Sequencing** Copy the organizer below. Use it to place into sequence the important events in the record of British imperialism in North and East Africa.

	Date	Describe
Isthmus of Suez		
Tunis		
Khartoum		
Algiers		
Fashoda		

3. **Finding the Main Idea**
   a. What attitude did the French seem to have toward the people of North Africa?
   b. Why was Great Britain interested in controlling Egypt and the Sudan?

4. **Writing and Critical Thinking**
   Supporting a Point of View Imagine it is the 1800s. You are against imperialism in North Africa. Write a letter to your local newspaper persuading others to support your views.
   Consider:
   • the rights of colonists
   • how North Africans reacted to the French
   • how Egyptians reacted to the British
   • who benefited from the Suez Canal

Homework Practice Online
keyword: SH3 HP17

European Claims in Sub-Saharan Africa

READ TO DISCOVER

❶ What patterns of colonization did Europeans follow in West Africa?

❷ What did Europeans gain by colonizing central and East Africa?

❸ Why was South Africa so important to the colonial powers?

❹ What effect did imperialism have on all of Africa?

DEFINE

paternalism
assimilation

IDENTIFY

Samory Touré
Sir Henry Stanley
Leopold II
Boers
Afrikaans
Shaka
Cecil Rhodes
Boer War
Menelik II

WHY IT MATTERS TODAY

Today, Africa is still struggling with problems that are a result of imperialism. Use CNN or other **current event** sources to identify one of these problems and explore how one African country is trying to solve that problem. Record your findings in your journal.

CNN student News.com

The Main Idea
By 1914 most of the major European industrial powers had colonies in sub-Saharan Africa.

The Story Continues *By about 1900, European powers had carved most of sub-Saharan Africa into colonies and settlements. They justified colonization as a humanitarian need, rather than a drive for profit. ". . . Europe was impelled to the development of Africa primarily by the necessities of her people, and not by the greed of the capitalists," explained one British observer.*

Competition for West Africa

West Africa had been a major center of the slave trade. Europeans had slave trading posts along the coast. In the early 1800s, however, most European countries abolished the slave trade. These former slaving centers turned to other types of trade, such as palm oil, feathers, ivory, rubber, and other products from the interior. By the late 1800s, the Europeans had started to push inland. They were eager to control the sources of the products they traded.

Europeans did not gain African land easily. Often they met with fierce resistance. For example, the French fought for control of Senegal for several years. **Samory Touré** led a revolt against the French in Senegal. He continued fighting off and on from 1883 until 1898 when he was finally captured. By 1900 the French had claimed not only Senegal but also a vast area called French West Africa.

Great Britain also met resistance. When the British moved inland from the Gold Coast (modern Ghana), they came up against the powerful African kingdom of Ashanti. The Ashanti fought hard to keep their land. In the end Great Britain ruled all Ashanti territory, and the Gold Coast became a British colony.

By the early 1900s, France, Great Britain, Germany, Spain, and Portugal had claimed almost all of West Africa. Liberia, which had become a republic in 1847, was the only independent state in that area. Because former slaves from the United States had settled Liberia, the United States helped keep the country from becoming a European colony.

✔ **READING CHECK: Finding the Main Idea** Why did the Europeans want to control the interior of West Africa?

Competition for Central and East Africa

Journalist **Henry Stanley** fueled interest in central Africa. In 1869 the *New York Herald* hired Stanley to find Dr. David Livingstone, a missionary who had disappeared in central Africa. In 1871 Stanley finally found him, with a greeting that became famous throughout the world: "Dr. Livingstone, I presume?"

Stanley wrote many newspaper articles about his search for Dr. Livingstone. Stanley thought Europeans should develop the huge area he had explored. He tried but failed to interest the British government. Then he turned to King **Leopold II** of Belgium. Leopold, acting as a private citizen, carved out a personal colony of 900,000 square miles.

Leopold's rule of the Congo is an example of imperialism at its worst. His only interest was in getting as much wealth as possible. He sold business people the rights to take raw materials. They took great amounts of the Congo's natural rubber. Leopold also used slave labor. Other countries were outraged by what was happening in the Congo. Leopold finally turned over his private colony to the Belgian government and it became the Belgian Congo in 1908.

Just as in West Africa, the European nations divided East Africa into colonies. A famine helped the Europeans colonize East Africa. In the 1890s most of the cattle in East Africa died from rinderpest, a disease carried by cattle imported from Europe. After the disease killed their herds, the East Africans began to starve. The people were too weak to resist the Europeans.

✔ **READING CHECK: Identifying Cause and Effect** What did Sir Henry Stanley's writing have to do with the colonization of the Congo?

Competition for Southern Africa

European settlement in South Africa began in 1652. Dutch settlers founded Cape Town as a supply station for ships sailing to the East Indies. The Dutch settlement grew into a large colony called Cape Colony. In the early 1800s the British seized Cape Colony and it became a British possession.

African Boundaries, 1883–1914

Interpreting Maps Between the 1880s and 1914 European powers divided Africa among themselves without regard for native rights.

■ **Skills Assessment: Human Systems** What native African state had direct access to the Red Sea coastal trade in 1883?

Africa in 1914

Interpreting Maps By about 1914, most of the major European countries held colonies throughout Africa.

■ **Skills Assessment: 1. Human Systems** What native African states remained independent of European control during the colonial era? **2. Using Geography** What colony along the African coast of the Red Sea was held by France? **3. Drawing Inferences** Why might the location of this French colony along the Red Sea coast have had great economic and military importance?

The Boers. When the British government took over, many people left the colony. They moved to the north and east in a mass migration. The move is known as the Great Trek. These people were descendants of the original Dutch settlers. They were called the **Boers.** The Boers spoke their own language, known as **Afrikaans.** In the new territories, the Boers carved out three colonies—Natal (nuh·TAHL), on the southeast coast, the Orange Free State to the west, and the Transvaal to the north.

As the Boers moved into the new territories, they came in contact with the Zulu who lived in the region. Under the great leader **Shaka,** the Zulu had created a thriving empire with a strong army. For years this army fought the Boers for control of the region. In 1879 the British joined in the war, defeating the Zulu and destroying their empire.

Rhodes and his influence. The discovery of diamonds in the Orange Free State and gold in the Transvaal increased competition in southern Africa. Germany hoped to find rich mineral reserves. In 1884 Germany declared a protectorate over the territory of South-West Africa. In the same year, Great Britain began moving inland from Cape Colony. British businessman **Cecil Rhodes** led this inland move.

Rhodes arrived in Cape Colony in 1870. He was a sickly young man who hoped the climate would improve his health. A short time later, Rhodes moved to the diamond fields in the Boer-controlled Orange Free State. He showed a great talent for business. Within 20 years of his arrival, Rhodes completely controlled South African diamond production. Later, Rhodes organized a huge colony farther north. This area was named Rhodesia (now Zimbabwe) after him. Rhodes hoped that one day Britain's control would extend from Cape Colony in South Africa to Cairo, Egypt, in the north.

The Boer War. In 1895 Rhodes sponsored a group who tried to overthrow the Transvaal government. The Boers in the Transvaal had kept the British from opening mines. The attempt failed, and relations between the Boers and the British became openly hostile. In 1899 the **Boer War,** known to modern South Africans as the South African War, broke out. After three years of costly fighting, the British defeated the Boers. As part of the settlement, the British were allowed to begin mining in the Transvaal.

To make sure the Boers stayed peaceful, the British allowed them to keep using the Afrikaans language in their schools and courts. The British also provided funds for Boers—though not for Africans—to rebuild their destroyed farms. In 1910 the British united Cape Colony and the three Boer colonies. It became the Union of South Africa. The new constitution made it almost impossible for nonwhites to ever get voting rights. This was the beginning of South Africa's system of racial segregation.

✔ **READING CHECK: Contrasting** In what ways did the British treat the Boers differently from the way they treated Africans?

INTERPRETING THE VISUAL RECORD

Zulu warrior This drawing from about 1875 depicts a Zulu warrior with shield, spears, and traditional dress. *Based on this drawing, how effective do you think Zulu weapons were against European firearms?*

Holt Researcher

go.hrw.com
KEYWORD: Holt Researcher
FreeFind: Shaka
After reading more about Shaka on the Holt Researcher, create a time line of the significant events in his battle against the British.

The Effect of Imperialism on Africa

Imperialism was a difficult experience for all of Africa. In most areas, Europeans controlled all levels of government. This meant they controlled the lives of the people. Europeans based this type of government on their belief that Africans were not able to rule themselves. This way of ruling is called **paternalism.** Europeans governed their colonies in the same way that parents guide their children.

It is true that Africa did get some benefit from imperialism. New crops and new ways of farming were introduced in many areas. European medicine helped people live longer and healthier lives. Roads and railroads were built all over Africa.

The Berlin Conference

In 1884 European leaders met in Germany to resolve potential conflicts over African colonies. With no regard for the boundaries the Africans already had in place (which were often based on the location of ethnic groups), the Europeans carved up Africa among themselves. The decisions made at the Berlin Conference continue to hamper the continent's development.

Understanding Geography

How might the boundaries created by European leaders at the Berlin Conference have caused problems for the nations and people of Africa?

Even though the roads were mostly for European use, they did make it possible to get African products to the world markets. To some degree, too, this helped to improve communication in parts of Africa. It also helped to break down some of the barriers that had traditionally separated African peoples.

Some African leaders even sought out alliances with Europeans to benefit their countries. Often, however, the Europeans tried to take advantage of these alliances to the detriment of the Africans. For example, in 1889 Emperor **Menelik II** of Ethiopia negotiated a treaty with Italy. Menelik discovered, however, that the Italians were trying to trick him by showing him a copy of the treaty in his language that was different from the treaty in Italian, which gave the Europeans more power. Menelik's wife, Taitu, summed up her response to the Italians, "You wish Ethiopia to be represented before the other Powers as your protectorate, but this shall never be." When Italy tried to invade Ethiopia in 1896, Menelik's forces successfully fought them off.

Most other African nations were unable to stop the advance of outsiders. Instead, many resisted imperialism by insisting on maintaining their own identity. In spite of many years of control, most Africans never accepted European culture, even though Europeans hoped they would do so. The French even hoped for **assimilation**, which happens when people give up their own culture completely and adopt another culture.

It is not so surprising that the Africans did not accept European culture. After all, nearly everything the Europeans did was for their own benefit, not that of the Africans. Europeans did not think the Africans deserved to be treated equally. For their part, the Africans continued to live much as they had lived for centuries.

Emperor Menelik II of Ethiopia successfully resisted European imperialism.

✔ **READING CHECK: Making Generalizations** What effect did European colonization have on the African people?

SECTION 3 REVIEW

1. **Define** and explain the significance:
   paternalism
   assimilation

2. **Identify** and explain the significance:
   Samory Touré
   Sir Henry Stanley
   Leopold II
   Boers
   Afrikaans
   Shaka
   Cecil Rhodes
   Boer War
   Menelik II

3. **Categorizing** Copy the model below. Use it to organize examples of African resistance to European expansion.

   Who Resisted
   ↓
   Reason(s)
   ↓
   Result(s)

4. ### Finding the Main Idea
   a. What were the similarities and differences between Senegal and Liberia?
   b. What role did slavery play in the colonizing of Africa?
   c. How did imperialism affect Africa?

5. ### Writing and Critical Thinking
   Identifying a Point of View Imagine that you are a European correspondent assigned to cover events in South Africa during the Boer War. Write a newspaper column in which you explain Great Britain's views of the actions and policies that led to war in South Africa.
   Consider:
   • British treatment of native Africans
   • British attitudes toward the Boers
   • how the British aimed to exploit Africa's natural resources

Homework Practice Online
keyword: SH3 HP17

READ TO DISCOVER

❶ What role did Great Britain play in the development of India?

❷ How did Japan change its ancient and tradition-based culture in response to Western imperialism?

❸ How did Western imperialism affect the peoples of Southeast Asia?

❹ Why were European and American imperialists interested in the Pacific islands?

IDENTIFY

Meiji Restoration
Diet
Sino-Japanese War
Treaty of Shimonoseki
Mongkut
Liliuokalani
Emilio Aguinaldo

WHY IT MATTERS TODAY

The culture of modern India shows the effects of British imperialism. Use or other **current event** sources to explore the ways that Indian culture has been influenced by British rule. Record your findings in your journal.

Expansion in Asia

The Main Idea
Western imperialism affected Asia and the Pacific in a variety of ways during the 1800s and 1900s.

The Story Continues *As Western imperialism reached into Asia and the Pacific during the 1800s, native peoples often responded with resistance and conflict. One Indian writer described the nationalist ideals that grew in his country in the face of British imperialism: "The double policy of self-development and defensive resistance [against British colonial rule] is the common standing-ground of the new spirit all over India."*

British Imperialism in India

During the early to mid-1800s, the British East India Company controlled a large area of India. This trading company treated India as a private colony. In 1857 Indian soldiers rebelled against the company. After that, the British government took direct control. Great Britain ruled about three-fifths of the Indian subcontinent. The rest was divided up into more than 550 states. An Indian prince headed each of these states.

The nature of British rule. Great Britain wanted to control both British India and the Indian states. The British used the old Roman method of divide and rule. It granted favors to those princes who cooperated with British rule and dealt harshly with those who did not. It treated Hindus and Muslims equally but did little to ease religious hatred between them.

The British were active rulers in India. They kept public order and ended the many local wars among the other states. They built roads, bridges, and railroads, established factories, hospitals, and schools, and tried to improve Indian farming methods. Many British families went to India and made it their permanent home.

By the early 1900s, British rule in India had created an unusual situation, with the people of two very different cultures living side by side. However, the two groups had little social contact with each other. The British had put themselves above Indian society.

INTERPRETING THE VISUAL RECORD

British colonials in India Members of an aristocratic British family in India, surrounded by their Indian servants, pose before their elegant estate. *How might an image such as this provoke feelings of resentment and nationalism among native Indians?*

These Indian and British teachers worked together at a school in India in the late 1800s.

They thought they were a superior race. They had private social circles that were open to any European, but closed to any Indian. For many years Indians were treated this way, regardless of their social status, education, or abilities.

Although the British did not socialize with Indians, the British system of education had a powerful impact on India. From 1899 on, the British colonial administration worked to establish Western-style schools of all levels throughout India. The classes were mostly taught in English. Students learned about Western ideas, such as democracy and socialism, along with the regular school subjects.

The rise of Indian nationalism. A movement for Indian self-rule began in the late 1800s. Not all Indian nationalists supported the same approach. Some wanted to move toward independence gradually. These were usually people who had been educated in British schools. They also wanted to keep certain aspects of Western culture that they thought could benefit India.

Other Indians wanted to break all ties with Great Britain and sweep away the Western influence. The views of this second group alarmed Indian Muslims, who were a minority in the land. British rule protected them from violence. They feared that if British rule were removed their future might be in danger. The independence movement in India gathered strength very slowly. The British kept the country under a tight rein.

✔ **READING CHECK: Identifying Bias** How did the attitudes of the British affect the way they ruled in India?

Japanese Responses to Imperialism

While Britain was firmly in control of India, Japan was taking a different course. Westerners did not rule in Japan. Japan controlled its own government. However, the Japanese had been influenced by Western ideas. In response, Japan changed its form of government and began to industrialize.

The Meiji Restoration. In 1868 a group of samurai overthrew the Tokugawa shogunate. Then they returned the emperor to power. This change is called the **Meiji Restoration.** The samurai took action because they had grown impatient with Japan's old ways. They wanted a government and social system more like those in the West. They convinced the Meiji government to make broad changes.

One of the most important changes was to do away with the old system of social classes. Now all Japanese were free to choose what kind of work they wanted to do. The government also required that everyone should go to school. With this program, Japan almost wiped out illiteracy.

In 1899 the Japanese put into effect a new constitution that gave the Japanese people a say in their country's government by giving voting rights to some Japanese. However, only those people who owned a large amount of property were allowed to vote. Although the constitution gave the emperor supreme power, he did not use it. The new constitution also created a two-house national assembly called the **Diet.** One house of the Diet was made up of people who were elected. In the beginning, the elected house had very limited power. A small group of leaders acting in the name of the emperor held the real power in Japan.

Industrialization. Japan modernized very quickly. The government bought new factory machinery from Western countries and passed laws to encourage private citizens to start businesses. Also, in the 1880s the government sent students and leaders to the Western countries. They were to learn as much as they could about Western ideas. One of these leaders was Prince Itō Hirobumi. He was an outstanding statesman during this period. One trip he made was to the United States. While he was in San Francisco, he described Japan's hopes for the future.

History Makers Speak

❝Today it is the earnest wish of both our Government and people to strive for the highest points of civilization enjoyed by more enlightened countries. Looking to this end, we have adopted their military, naval, scientific, and educational institutions, and knowledge has flowed to us freely in the wake of foreign commerce. . . . Japan cannot claim originality as yet, but it will aim to exercise practical wisdom by adopting the advantages and avoiding the errors. . . .❞

Prince Itō Hirobumi from an 1880s speech given in San Francisco

Analyzing Primary Sources

Drawing Inferences What did Prince Itō mean when he said Japan "cannot claim originality as yet"?

By 1900 Japan had become the first country in Asia to industrialize. Japanese cities were linked together by railroads and telephones. Factories were making goods that could be sold to other countries. The textile industry was particularly strong. Japan exported machine-made cotton cloth and silk. The money the Japanese got from these exports paid for the imports they needed. They bought raw materials such as iron ore and crude oil. Japan used these raw materials to make steel and build ships. The country was much stronger than it had been before the Meiji Restoration.

The Sino-Japanese War. Even though Japan had modernized, it feared the imperialists in Asia. This fear led the Japanese to become imperialists themselves.

The area that most interested Japan was nearby Korea, which had been a dependent colony of China for a long time. China did not allow other countries to enter Korea. However, Russia, France, and the United States were all interested in trading there. Japan did not want these Western countries to have control of a country so near to their own.

This was the scene at Yokohama in 1871 as Prince Iwakura left on Japan's foreign mission to learn about Western countries.

In 1894 a rebellion broke out in Korea. The rebels wanted their people to be free from Chinese control. Both Japan and China sent armed forces to Korea. The situation exploded into the **Sino-Japanese War** (*sino* means Chinese). Foreigners predicted an easy victory for the large Chinese army. The Japanese, however, had done a better job of modernizing than China. They were well equipped and prepared. Japanese troops scored quick victories on both land and sea. In a surprisingly short time, Japan had defeated China.

In 1895 the **Treaty of Shimonoseki** ended the Sino-Japanese War. China was forced to give Korea its independence. Japan gained control of the island of Taiwan (Formosa) and some other small islands next to it. Japan also gained control of an area along the coast of Manchuria. In addition, Japan won the right to trade in China. This war between Japan and China marked the beginning of Japan as a major world power.

✔ **READING CHECK: Summarizing** How did Japan respond to Western imperialism?

Territory Claimed by:

France
Germany
Great Britain
Japan
Netherlands
United States
⊙ Chinese treaty port
• Other city

RUSSIAN EMPIRE

TRANS-SIBERIAN RAILWAY

CHINESE EASTERN RAILWAY

SAKHALIN

45°N

MONGOLIA

Manchuria

Harbin

Vladivostok

Lůshun (Port Arthur)

Beijing

Liaodong Pen.

KOREA

SEA OF JAPAN

JAPAN

Edo (Tokyo)

Tianjin

WEIHAI (Br.)

Seoul

Yokohama

Huang River

Shandong Peninsula

QINGDAO (German)

YELLOW SEA

AFGHANISTAN

PERSIA

CHINA

Chongqing

Nanjing

Hankou

Shanghai

Nagasaki

30°N

Chang River

Hangzhou

Ningbo

NEPAL

Indus River

Fuzhou

Wenzhou

P'ENG-HU IS. (Japanese)

RYUKYU IS.

Ganges River

BHUTAN

Guangzhou (Canton)

Xiamen

BRITISH INDIA

BURMA

Xi River

HONG KONG (Br.)

MACAO (Port.)

FORMOSA (TAIWAN)

PACIFIC OCEAN

DIU (Port.)

DAMAN (Port.)

ZHANJIANG (Fr.)

HAINAN

YANAON (Fr.)

Bay of Bengal

SIAM

FRENCH INDOCHINA

Manila

PHILIPPINES

MARIANA ISLANDS (German)

15°N

GOA (Port.)

ARABIAN SEA

ANDAMAN IS. (Br.)

Mekong River

SOUTH CHINA SEA

GUAM (U.S.)

MAHÉ (Fr.)

PONDICHERRY (Fr.)

KARIKAL (Fr.)

NICOBAR IS. (Br.)

CEYLON

BRITISH NORTH BORNEO

CAROLINE ISLANDS (German)

MALDIVES (Br.)

Strait of Malacca

MALAY STATES

Singapore

SARAWAK

BORNEO

Equator   0°

SUMATRA

NETHERLANDS EAST INDIES

Sulawesi

BISMARCK ARCH.

NEW GUINEA

JAVA

TIMOR (Port.)

135°E

15°S

N
W   E
S

INDIAN OCEAN

120°E

150°E

0   500   1,000 Miles
0   500   1,000 Kilometers
Miller Cylindrical Projection

AUSTRALIA

75°E   90°E   105°E

Imperialism in East Asia to 1914

Interpreting Maps Western imperial powers controlled much of East and Southeast Asia by the early 1900s.

■ **Skills Assessment: 1. The World in Spatial Terms** Which European power controlled the most area in this region? **2. Analyzing Information** Why were China's treaty ports important to the Western powers?

Imperialism in Southeast Asia

In the late 1800s, European imperialism made its way to Southeast Asia as it did to nearby India. The area became an important source of spices and tea. Later, valuable products such as tin and oil came from this area.

British colonies. Great Britain had control of two important colonies in Southeast Asia—Burma and Singapore. It was natural that the British should take an interest in Burma, as it was on the eastern border of India. By 1886 all of Burma had come under British control.

The island of Singapore is on the tip of the Malay Peninsula. It guards the entrance to the Strait of Malacca. This is one of the world's most vital trade routes. Britain's first recorded contact with Singapore was in 1819, when a ship belonging to the British East India Company landed there. When the company representative learned that there were only a few residents he decided to purchase land for a factory site. The spot grew into the city of Singapore, which became an important naval base in the British Empire.

French gains. The eastern part of Southeast Asia contained three small nations, none of which had stable governments. At times they were under the influence of neighboring Siam (modern-day Thailand). In the 1800s, the French military took over the region and claimed it for France. Under French rule the governments of the three nations became more stable and their economies improved. The area became known as French Indochina. The original three nations regained their independence in the 1950s. Today they are the nations of Laos, Cambodia, and Vietnam.

The kingdom of Siam had a more stable government than the other parts of Southeast Asia. The country was well organized and well run. However, Siam had to deal with two European powers on its borders. The British had interests on one border and the French had interests on another. Both Great Britain and France nibbled at the borders of Siam. To keep their independence, Siamese rulers skillfully played British interests against French interests. King **Mongkut,** who ascended to power in 1851, was particularly good at such diplomacy. Mongkut studied Western ideas to understand his enemies and help modernize his country.

The British and French finally agreed that an independent Siam was useful as a buffer state between them. A buffer state is a country located between two hostile powers that serves to decrease the chance of war between the two powers.

The Dutch East Indies. The Dutch East Indies, now Indonesia, are a series of islands that run from the East Asian mainland 3,200 miles to the coast of Australia. The islands of Java, Sumatra, and Borneo are the largest of these islands. The Dutch first colonized the East Indies in the 1600s. In the late 1800s, several revolts convinced the government of the Netherlands to change the way they governed their richest colony. The Netherlands gradually reformed their colonial policies. The Dutch East Indies became the nation of Indonesia in 1949.

✔ **READING CHECK: Drawing Conclusions**
Why was Siam able to remain independent during the age of imperialism?

Holt Researcher
go.hrw.com
KEYWORD: Holt Researcher
FreeFind: Mongkut
After reading more about Mongkut on the Holt Researcher, write an evaluation of his best and worst policies as king.

INTERPRETING THE VISUAL RECORD

King Mongkut Siam's King Mongkut worked hard to protect his country's independence in the 1800s. *How does this painting reflect the king's acceptance of some aspects of Western society?*

Chinese porcelain was imported to Europe, where it was considered quite valuable. This punch bowl depicts trading centers in Canton.

Imperialism in the Pacific to 1914

Interpreting Maps After its war with Spain in 1898 the United States became a greater imperial power in the Pacific.

■ **Skills Assessment: 1. Locate** What group of islands under U.S. control was closest to the treaty ports of mainland China?

U.S. Interests in the Pacific Islands

The imperialist powers were interested in only a few of the Pacific islands. Some islands had valuable natural resources. However, the Western powers mostly wanted islands for coaling stations and naval bases.

The Samoa Islands. In the late 1800s, a serious rivalry developed in the Samoa Islands. The United States had gained the right to use the harbor city of Pago Pago (PAHNG·oh PAHNG·oh) on the island of Tutuila (too·too·WEE·luh). Americans used it as a trading post, coaling station, and naval base. Great Britain and Germany had gotten similar rights in other parts of the Samoa Islands.

The rivalry among the three foreign powers continued for a number of years until the three came close to going to war. Finally, in 1899 the rivals signed a treaty. Great Britain, preoccupied with the Boer War, withdrew its interests. The United States received firm control of Tutuila and six other small islands. Together these islands became American Samoa. Germany gained control of all the other islands in the Samoan group. They eventually became known as Western Samoa.

The Hawaiian Islands. The Hawaiian Islands were very important to the United States. They had an excellent harbor for a naval base, as well as rich soil, good rainfall, and a mild climate. After 1865 business people from the United States and other nations began to arrive. They started huge sugarcane and pineapple plantations. Soon they wanted more control over the island's government.

Hawaii's Queen **Liliuokalani** did not want foreigners to control Hawaii. She tried to change the treaties that allowed them to stay. In 1893 the business leaders gained enough power to end the queen's reign. The United States took over Hawaii in 1898.

The Philippines, Guam, and Wake Island. When Spain and the United States went to war in 1898 (see section 5), U.S. naval forces all over the world were ordered into action. The first battle of the war took place in the Spanish-controlled Philippines. Six ships under the command of Commodore George Dewey steamed from Hong Kong to Manila, the capital of the Philippines. Dewey's ships attacked the Spanish fleet in Manila harbor. The Spanish fleet was in poor repair and was destroyed in just a few hours. United States land forces followed. Within a few months, the Philippine Islands came under the control of the United States. At about this time, U.S. forces also took Guam, a small island east of the Philippines that Spain also controlled.

Some Filipinos welcomed the Americans. Some even fought with them against the Spanish. Many Filipinos, though, saw no reason to change one master for another. **Emilio Aguinaldo** led the Filipinos in a fight for independence. The Filipinos used guerrilla warfare against the better-equipped United States army. The war lasted for three hard years. The Filipinos were finally defeated in 1902.

Besides taking over the Philippine Islands and Guam, the United States also took control of Wake Island. This gave the United States a chain of islands running from its west coast across the Pacific to Asia.

✔ **READING CHECK: Making Predictions** What benefit do you think the United States gained from its Pacific islands later in the 1900s?

HISTORY MAKER

Queen Liliuokalani (1838–1917)

Queen Liliuokalani was the first woman ever to become ruler of the Hawaiian Islands. She was also the last.

As queen, Liliuokalani faced increasing pressure from American businessmen who wanted the islands to be a part of the United States. In order to avoid bloodshed, she agreed to step down from the throne. In so doing, she opened the way for the United States to annex Hawaii, a move she bitterly opposed. After leaving the throne, she withdrew from public life. **Why did Liliuokalani give up control of Hawaii?**

SECTION 4 REVIEW

1. Identify and explain the significance:
Meiji Restoration
Diet
Sino-Japanese War
Treaty of Shimonoseki
Mongkut
Liliuokalani
Emilio Aguinaldo

2. Evaluating Copy the web below. Use it to analyze and evaluate the ways in which each Asian region was affected by Western imperialism.

India — Western Imperialism — Japan
Pacific Islands — Southeast Asia

3. **Finding the Main Idea**
a. How did British rule affect India?
b. Why were the Japanese able to reform and industrialize their nation so quickly?
c. How did United States expansion in Hawaii differ from its expansion in the Philippines?

4. **Writing and Critical Thinking**

Comparing and Contrasting Write two paragraphs about Western and Japanese imperialism in Asia. In the first paragraph describe the positive effects of imperialism in Asia. In the second paragraph describe the negative aspects of imperialism in the region.
Consider:
• improvements in Asia during the age of imperialism
• the effects of imperialism on Asian people
• how the imperialist powers exploited Asian land and resources

Homework Practice Online

keyword: SH3 HP17

Imperialism in Latin America

The Main Idea
Imperialist powers controlled Latin America with economic influence and political intervention.

The Story Continues *The Monroe Doctrine kept European powers from colonizing Latin America. The United States flexed its military muscle to support its interests in Latin America. "In the Western Hemisphere the . . . Monroe Doctrine may force the United States . . . to the exercise of an international police power,"* President Theodore Roosevelt once threatened.

Economic Imperialism

By the end of the 1800s, the United States and Europe were buying many products from Latin America. Americans ate bananas from Central America, drank coffee from Brazil, and smoked Cuban cigars. Great Britain bought large amounts of wool and beef from Argentina. Any Latin American country with products to trade found people to buy them.

Europeans and Americans began to invest money in Latin America. They built factories and textile mills; bought ranches, plantations, and mines; and even owned railroads. Latin American governments thought it was a good idea to allow foreigners to buy land and spend money in their countries. They hoped these businesses would help their economies. The foreign investors, however, usually did not keep their money in Latin America. Instead they sent the money they made back to their own countries. This limited growth in the Latin American countries.

Some Latin American countries borrowed money from Europe or the United States. They used the money to make public improvements or strengthen their armies and navies. Sometimes a country could not pay back its loans. Foreign banks and business leaders persuaded their own governments to pressure any country that did not pay. Sometimes they sent ships and troops to force a country to pay.

✔ **READING CHECK: Finding the Main Idea** How did the Europeans and Americans control the economies of Latin American countries?

Britain and the United States funded many railroads in Latin America. This railroad was constructed through a banana plantation in Costa Rica.

The Spanish-American War

In 1898 the United States became deeply involved in Latin America. The problem grew out of disagreements with Spain over Cuba. The Caribbean island had been a Spanish colony for many years, but the Cubans were unhappy under Spanish rule. A rebellion had failed, and the situation was tense. This alarmed Americans who had businesses in Cuba. Also, many Americans thought Cuba should be free.

Anger boiled over in 1898. The **Maine,** an American battleship, exploded in Havana harbor, killing some 260 Americans. The *Maine* had been sent to Cuba to protect American citizens and their property. No one knew the cause of the explosion. Many in the United States assumed that the Spanish were to blame.

Spain wanted to avoid war, but it would not withdraw from Cuba. The United States declared war in April 1898. Congress stated that the United States was fighting only on behalf of Cuban independence and that America had no intention of taking the island for itself.

By May the war had started. The first battle ended with the defeat of the Spanish fleet in the Philippines. In July U.S. troops arrived in Cuba. With Cuban help, U.S. troops quickly defeated the Spanish. American writer Stephen Crane reported on the war for the *New York World* newspaper. Here he sums up the battle in which Theodore Roosevelt and his Rough Riders took part.

This painting depicts Theodore Roosevelt leading the Rough Riders into battle during the Spanish-American War.

> **History Makers Speak** **❝No doubt when history begins to grind out her story we will find that many a thundering, fine, grand order was given for that day's work; but after all there will be no harm in contending that the fighting line, the men and their regimental officers, took the hill chiefly because they knew they could take it, some having no orders and others disobeying whatever orders they had. . . . It will never be forgotten as long as America has a military history.❞**
>
> Stephen Crane in the *New York World*, July 14, 1898

Analyzing Primary Sources

Drawing Inferences What did Stephen Crane imply when he said the Americans "took the hill chiefly because they knew they could"?

The Treaty of Paris ended the war in December 1898. By the terms of the peace treaty, Spain gave up its claim to Cuba. It also gave the United States another of its colonies, Puerto Rico, which became a commonwealth of the United States. In the Pacific, Spain gave up the Philippines and Guam.

Following the war, United States troops controlled Cuba. Americans started schools, built roads, and tried to improve health care. Doctors and nurses worked to wipe out yellow fever. After two years the United States allowed Cubans to elect their own government. A new Cuban assembly wrote a constitution, which included the **Platt Amendment**. This amendment said that Cuba could not transfer any land except to the United States. In addition, it gave the United States the right to intervene in Cuba. This could happen whenever the United States thought the stable government was in danger. The United States also insisted on having a permanent naval base in Cuba at Guantánamo Bay. In this way the United States continued to exert influence over Cuba.

✔ **READING CHECK: Identifying Cause and Effect** What were the effects of the Spanish-American War?

The Panama Canal

Before the war, the American battleship *Oregon* had been stationed on the Pacific coast of the United States. When war became likely, the *Oregon* was sent to the Caribbean Sea. To reach the Caribbean, the battleship had to race around the entire South American continent. This was a distance of almost 13,000 miles. The United States realized it had a problem. It would either have to build two complete navies or find a quicker way to move ships between the Atlantic and Pacific Oceans.

The idea of a canal across the Isthmus of Panama was not new. The French company that built the Suez Canal had tried to build a canal across Panama, but their attempt had failed. In the late 1800s, the United States began talks with Colombia, which controlled Panama at that time. The United States wanted to lease a strip of land across the isthmus, but the Colombian government would not approve the lease. This angered people in the United States and Panama. Some business leaders in Panama led a revolt to gain freedom from Colombia.

American naval forces prevented Colombia from putting down the revolt in Panama. The revolution succeeded. In 1903 the new government gave the United States the rights to build the canal. Work began in 1904.

The **Panama Canal** opened in 1914. It was one of the world's great engineering feats. It might have been impossible to build without new power shovels and other machines. Science, too, played an important part. A Cuban doctor named **Carlos Juan Finlay** discovered that mosquitoes carry yellow fever. The disease had killed many workers attempting to build the canal. By destroying the mosquitoes, scientists controlled the spread of the disease. This allowed construction crews to work in the Panamanian jungles.

The new canal shortened the sea route from New York to San Francisco by about 8,000 miles. Merchant ships of all nations paid a toll to use the canal. However, the greatly shortened route saved time and operating costs.

✔ **READING CHECK: Making Generalizations**
Why was the Panama Canal important for the United States?

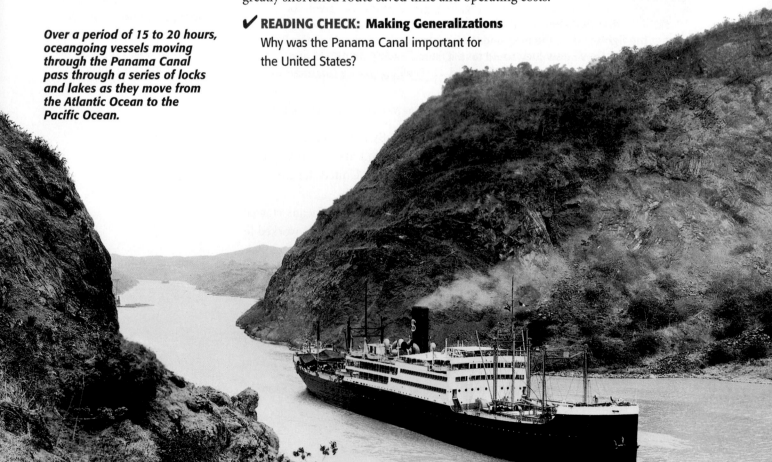

Over a period of 15 to 20 hours, oceangoing vessels moving through the Panama Canal pass through a series of locks and lakes as they move from the Atlantic Ocean to the Pacific Ocean.

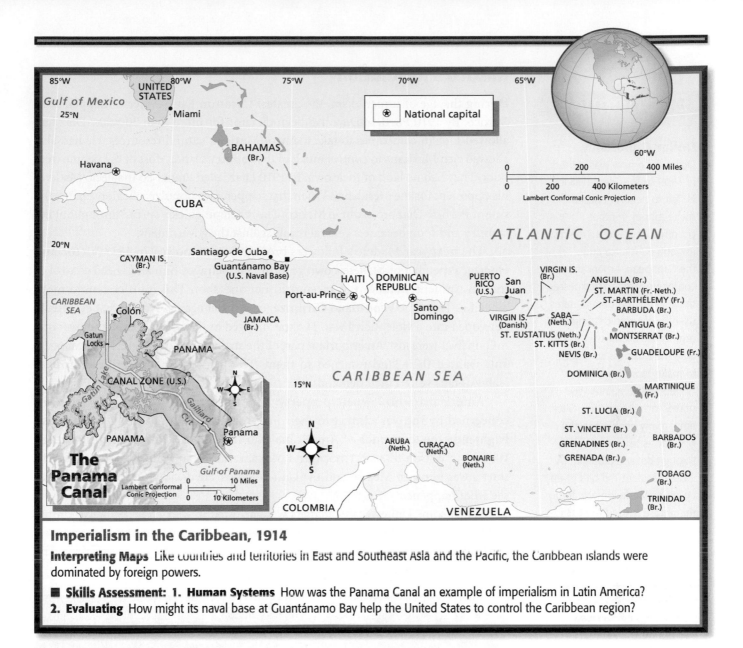

Imperialism in the Caribbean, 1914

Interpreting Maps Like countries and territories in East and Southeast Asia and the Pacific, the Caribbean islands were dominated by foreign powers.

■ **Skills Assessment: 1. Human Systems** How was the Panama Canal an example of imperialism in Latin America?
2. Evaluating How might its naval base at Guantánamo Bay help the United States to control the Caribbean region?

The Roosevelt Corollary

The United States knew it would have to protect the Panama Canal. It also knew Europeans might send armed forces to Latin America. To prevent this, the United States took a strong stand.

In 1904 President Theodore Roosevelt said that if the independence of any country in the Western Hemisphere were in danger, the United States would act to prevent other countries from entering. Also, the United States would make sure that Latin American countries would repay their loans. This is known as the **Roosevelt Corollary**. The corollary angered Latin Americans. To them, it sounded as if they could not manage their own governments. They were also against Americans forcing them to pay back their loans. In spite of this, the United States acted several times. It maintained a nearly continuous military presence in Nicaragua from 1912 to 1933. It did the same in Haiti and the Dominican Republic at about the same time. American troops were in Cuba from 1906 to 1909 and also intervened on other occasions.

✔ **READING CHECK: Drawing Conclusions** What effect do you think the Roosevelt Corollary had on relations between the United States and Latin America?

Dollar Diplomacy

Dollar diplomacy was started in 1909 by President William H. Taft to help Americans make money in other countries. It was used mainly in Central America and the Caribbean. American companies started businesses there. Then, the United States used its economic strength to protect the businesses. In this way, the business continued to make money and the United States maintained power in these nations. Over time, many people resisted U.S. efforts to control them through dollar diplomacy. By 1912 President Taft had given up on dollar diplomacy. Today the phrase is used to describe efforts by one country to control another through money.

Understanding Economics

How might American loans help a foreign country today?

Mexico's Revolution

During the age of imperialism, the greatest unrest in Latin America happened in Mexico. By 1910 **Porfirio Díaz** had been dictator for more than 30 years. Díaz had allowed foreign companies to take many of Mexico's natural resources. He had also allowed rich Mexicans to control much of the country's land. Most of the people were poor. They had no land of their own. In 1910 Díaz jailed Francisco Indalécio Madero, his opponent for the presidency. When that happened, a popular rebellion against the rule of Porfirio Díaz broke out in Mexico. The rebellion quickly spread throughout the country and soon became a general revolt against the government.

The next year Madero's followers brought him to power. In 1913 **Victoriano Huerta,** a member of Madero's own government, betrayed him and seized control of the government. Madero was taken prisoner and shot. This murder caused more rebellion. This time **Venustiano Carranza** led a revolt against Huerta that eventually developed into a violent civil war. The war dragged on for several years, and over one million lives were lost. An important part of the struggle was over land. Mexican peasants wanted their land returned to them. The peasant leader **Emiliano Zapata** (sah·PAH·tah) voiced their demands.

Americans who owned property and businesses in Mexico were very concerned by the war's threat to their investments. The continuing conflict also frightened the thousands of Americans who lived there. They wanted President Woodrow Wilson to send troops into Mexico. President Wilson did not want to start a war between Mexico and the United States. He decided instead to wait and see what happened.

When some United States soldiers were arrested in Mexico in 1914, the United States finally decided to act. Marines took control of Veracruz, an important port on the Gulf of Mexico. This cut off supplies and money to the Huerta government. The action helped Carranza's forces win the war.

Mexican artist Diego Rivera painted murals dealing with the history and social problems of his country. Struggle of the Classes *is in Mexico City.*

Women played an important role in Mexico's revolution, as this photograph from 1911 illustrates.

The colorful rebel leader **Pancho Villa** (VEE·yah) continued to fight Carranza for control of the revolution. Villa led effective guerrilla attacks against the new government. He also attacked large landowners in Mexico, taking property and money to finance and supply the revolutionary army. In 1916, for reasons that are still not clearly understood, Villa moved his troops across the border into the United States. He raided the small town of Columbus, New Mexico, killing more than a dozen Americans. President Woodrow Wilson reluctantly sent troops under the command of General John Pershing into Mexico to capture Villa. As the U.S. force went deeper into Mexico, Carranza's government became more and more concerned. For a time there was a threat of war between Mexico and the United States. In 1917, however, the United States withdrew its troops from Mexico. Americans had started to pay attention to the world war that was taking place in Europe.

Pancho Villa was a Mexican revolutionary and guerrilla leader.

✔ **READING CHECK: Summarizing** What were the main causes of unrest and revolution in Mexico?

SECTION 5 REVIEW

1. **Identify** and explain the significance:
   Maine
   Platt Amendment
   Panama Canal
   Carlos Juan Finlay
   Roosevelt Corollary
   Porfirio Díaz
   Victoriano Huerta
   Venustiano Carranza
   Emiliano Zapata
   Pancho Villa

2. **Identifying Cause and Effect**
   Copy the chart below. Use it to identify the causes and effects of United States military interventions in Latin America from 1898 to about 1933.

   Where → Reason → What Happened

3. **Finding the Main Idea**
   a. Why were European and American investments no help to the economies of Latin American countries?
   b. What evidence shows that the United States wanted control over Cuba after the Spanish-American War?
   c. How might the United States and Mexico be different if the two countries had gone to war in 1916?

4. **Writing and Critical Thinking**
   Summarizing Imagine you are a reporter in Panama during the building of the Panama Canal. Write an article describing what you observe.
   Consider:
   • working and living conditions in the Panamanian jungle
   • physical health of the workers
   • purposes of the canal

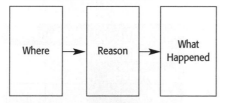
Homework Practice Online
go.hrw.com
keyword: SH3 HP17

CHAPTER 17 Review

Creating a Time Line

Copy the time line below onto a sheet of paper. Complete the time line by filling in the events, individuals, and dates from the chapter that you think were significant. Pick three events and explain why you think they were significant.

1830   **1875**   **1917**

Writing a Summary

Using standard grammar, spelling, sentence structure, and punctuation, write an overview of the events in the chapter.

Identifying People and Ideas

Identify the following terms or individuals and explain their significance:

1. imperialism
2. dependent colonies
3. Fashoda crisis
4. paternalism
5. Leopold II
6. Boers
7. Meiji Restoration
8. *Maine*
9. Roosevelt Corollary
10. Venustiano Carranza

Understanding Main Ideas

Section 1 (pp. 470–473)

The Roots of Western Imperialism

1. Why did the imperialists want to control regions with raw materials?
2. Why were coaling stations important to the imperialists?

Section 2 (pp. 474–477)

European Claims in North Africa

3. How would British control of the Suez Canal affect world trading patterns?
4. What role did the al-Mahdt play in the history of the Sudan?

Section 3 (pp. 478–482)

European Claims in Sub-Saharan Africa

5. Why was Leopold's rule in the Congo an example of imperialism at its worst?
6. What role did Cecil Rhodes play in South Africa?

Section 4 (pp. 483–489)

Expansion in Asia

7. What effect did British schools have in India?

8. What did the Japanese do to industrialize their country?

Section 5 (pp. 490–495)

Imperialism in Latin America

9. Why did Venustiano Carranza lead a revolt in Mexico?

Reviewing Themes

1. **Global Relations** What evidence is there that an industrialized country can control a country that is not industrialized?
2. **Geography** What evidence is there to show that areas were colonized because they met the transportation needs of other, more powerful countries?
3. **Economics** What evidence is there to show that areas were colonized for natural resources?

Thinking Critically

1. **Summarizing** Why did the industrialized nations of the West move to become imperialist powers?
2. **Comparing and Contrasting** What are the similarities and differences between the Platt Amendment and the Roosevelt Corollary?
3. **Drawing Inferences** How did the Sino-Japanese War mark Japan's growth as a world power?
4. **Supporting a Point of View** What evidence would you give that money was an effective means of control in Latin America?

Writing About History

Identifying a Point of View Write a report explaining the reasons for Western expansion into Africa, Asia, Latin America, and the Pacific, and describe what happened as a result of this expansion. Use the chart below to organize your thoughts before you write.

	Africa	Asia	Latin America	Pacific
Raw materials and products				
Resistance and rebellions				
Imperialist competition				

Reading a Chart

Study the chart below. Then answer the questions that follow.

Foreign Investment in 1914
(in millions of U.S. dollars)

Area	British Investments	French Investments	American Investments
North America	7,000	500	900
Latin America	3,700	1,600	1,200
Africa	2,400	900	—
Asia	3,500	1,200	100

1. Which statement correctly describes a relationship shown on the chart?

   a. In 1914, the British and French invested more in North America than any other area.

   b. In 1914, British investments worldwide were less than they had been in 1900.

   c. French and American investments in Asia were increasing in 1914.

   d. In 1914, Americans invested more in Latin America than all other areas combined.

2. Why do you think British investments were greater world-wide than those of the French or the Americans? Give specific reasons for your viewpoint.

Categorizing Information

Read the paragraph below. Then answer the questions that follow.

> As the great powers expanded their influence, scientists and adventurers explored uncharted territories. Arctic explorer Robert Edwin Peary from the United States is thought to be the first to reach the North Pole (April 6, 1909). Norwegian explorer Roald Amundsen was the leader of the first expedition to reach the South Pole, accomplished on December 14, 1911. In 1912, American archaeologist Hiram Bingham discovered the lost cities of the Inca in the Andes Mountains of Peru. Between 1875 and 1915, Prince Albert I of Monaco conducted surveys of the world's oceans. He collected marine specimens and took soundings.

3. Which of the following gives the best categories for organizing the information in the paragraph?

   a. Place Explored, Date Explored, Type of Exploration

   b. Name, Where From, Place Explored, Date Explored

   c. Name, Profession, Place Explored

   d. Place Explored, Date Explored, Importance

4. Do you think these explorations and others like them were important? Give specific reasons to support your point of view.

Alternative Assessment

Building Your Portfolio

Link to TODAY

Global Relations

Imperialism still exists in the world today. Use your textbook and other sources to find examples of imperialism today. Then, using knowledge you have gained by evaluating the actions of individuals, groups, and nations during the Age of Imperialism, write an analysis of why some nations still maintain colonies and how the colonized peoples have reacted to it.

🔲 internet connect

Internet Activity: go.hrw.com
KEYWORD: SH3 WH17

Choose a topic on the Age of Imperialism to:

• create an annotated time line on the political changes experienced by the territory once known as the Congo.

• write a report on the impact of colonization on the African people.

• write a series of journal entries from the point of view of Dr. Livingstone.

CROSS-CULTURAL CONNECTIONS *Literature*

Nationalism and Literature

Literature gives historians insight into past events and into people's feelings about those events. Leo Tolstoy (1828–1910) wrote about Napoléon's 1812 invasion of Russia in his novel War and Peace. *He described how the Russians reacted to Napoléon's capture of their capital. In contrast, Giuseppe Garibaldi (1807-1882) used a speech to inspire troops, known as Red Shirts, fighting for Italian independence. He urged Italians to unite and fight for the new kingdom of Italy under King Victor Emmanuel II.*

War and Peace *by Leo Tolstoy*

When half of Russia was conquered, and the inhabitants of Moscow were fleeing to remote provinces, and one levy of militia after another was being raised for the defense of the country, we not living at the time cannot help imagining that all the people in Russia, great and small alike, were engaged in doing nothing else but making sacrifices, saving their country, or weeping over its downfall. . . . In reality, it was not at all like that. . . . The majority of the people of that period took no heed of the general progress of public affairs, and were only influenced by their immediate personal interests. . . . The significance of the drama taking place in Russia at that time was the less easy to grasp, the closer the share a man was taking in it. In Petersburg, and in the provinces remote from Moscow, ladies and gentlemen in volunteer uniforms bewailed the fate of Russia and the ancient capital, and

talked of self-sacrifice, and so on. But in the army, which had retreated behind Moscow, men scarcely talked or thought at all about Moscow, and, gazing at the burning city, no one swore to be avenged on the French, but every one was thinking of the next quarter's pay due to him, of the next halting-place, . . . and so on.

Giuseppe Garibaldi speaks to his soldiers

We must now consider the period which is just drawing to a close as almost the last stage of our national resurrection, and prepare ourselves to finish worthily the marvelous design of the elect of twenty generations, the completion of which Providence has reserved for this fortunate age.

Yes, young men, Italy owes to you an undertaking which has merited the applause of the universe. You have conquered and you will conquer still. . . .To this wonderful page in our country's history another more glorious still will be added, and the slave shall show at last to his free brothers a sharpened sword forged from the links of his fetters.

To arms, then, all of you! all of you! And the oppressors and the mighty shall disappear like dust. . . .

Providence has presented Italy with Victor Emmanuel. Every Italian should rally round him. By the side of Victor Emmanuel every quarrel should be forgotten. Once more I repeat my battle-cry: "To arms, all—all of you."

Understanding Literature

How do both Tolstoy and Garibaldi attempt to inspire feelings of nationalism in people?

Science, Technology, and Society

The Industrial Revolution brought about a number of important developments in technology, communications, science, and medicine. Imagine that you are a student of history at Cambridge University in England during the late 1880s. You and your friends are making a "time capsule" that will contain artifacts, drawings, and descriptions of industrial life in the late 1800s. Your task is to create a list of the different items you would include. What would these items reveal about the role of technology and industry in the late 1800s? Use the bibliography below to help you.

This cartoon caricature shows Bismarck "sweeping away" German opposition to his policies of unification.

Artifacts of the Industrial Age: a typewriter of 1874 (above) and a telegraph receiver of 1840 (right)

Government

During the second half of the nineteenth century a number of European countries underwent dramatic political change. Imagine that you are a newspaper editor in Berlin in 1870. You are a strong supporter of Otto von Bismarck and the cause of German national unification. Write an editorial in which you answer Bismarck's critics and those who oppose unification of the German states under Prussian leadership. Explain why you support unification and admire Bismarck.

Further Reading

Corrick, James. *The Industrial Revolution.* San Diego: Lucent Books, 1998. A survey of the Industrial Revolution and its effects on Europe and the United States.

Dersin, Denise, ed. *What Life Was Like: In the Jewel of the Crown, British India, A.D. 1600–1905.* Alexandria, Virginia: Time-Life Books, 1999. A broad survey of political, social, and cultural life in British India.

Shelston, Dorothy and Alan Shelston. *The Industrial City, 1820–1870.* New York: Macmillan, 1990. A look at how industrialization changed the city.

Smith, Bonnie G. *Imperialism: A History in Documents.* New York: Oxford University Press, 2000. First-person accounts and political documents outlining the history of imperialism during the period 1850–1945.

Tilly, Louise A. and Joan W. Scott. *Women, Work and Family.* New York: Routledge, 1987. Discusses how the Industrial Revolution affected women in France and England.

internet connect

Internet Activity
KEYWORD: SH3 U4

In assigned groups, develop a multimedia presentation that describes lifestyles of the Industrial Revolution. Choose information from the chapter Internet Connect activities and the Holt Researcher that best reflects the major topics of the period. Write an outline and a script for your presentation, which may be shown to the class.

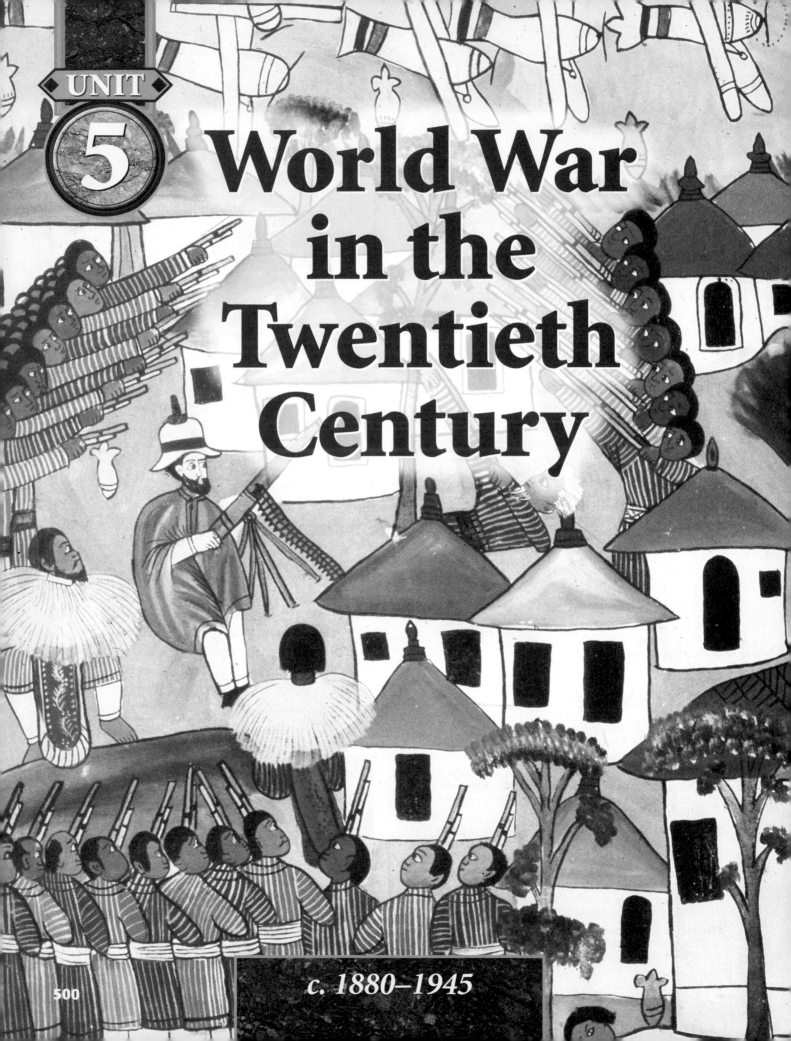

World War in the Twentieth Century

c. 1880–1945

Main Events

- World War I and the Russian Revolution occur
- The Great Depression affects countries around the globe
- New political forces emerge in Europe, Africa, Asia, and Latin America
- World War II and the Holocaust occur

Main Ideas

- What were the causes of World War I?
- What was the Russian Revolution?
- Why did the Great Depression occur?
- What is a totalitarian form of government?
- What political changes took place in Asia, Africa, and Latin America?
- What were the causes of World War II?
- What was the Holocaust?

World Wars I and II affected the entire populations of the countries involved. These two posters from 1943 encouraged American women to work in industries that would help the war effort.

Fascist Italy used aircraft and other modern weapons to invade Ethiopia during the mid-1930s.

501

Focus On: Global Relations

Main Idea **How did conflicts between countries lead to two world wars?** Relations between countries during the late 1800s and early 1900s were marked by distrust, hostility, and war. Internal conflicts also plagued many nations, as various groups struggled to control national governments. In some places, new political forces arose that worsened, rather than strengthened, relations with other nations. This led to more international conflicts.

Asia
Africa
The Americas
Europe

1880   1898   1919   1938   1945

World War I in Europe, 1914–1918

World War I In 1914 Europe exploded into a war of unprecedented devastation and fearsome new weapons. The effects of poison gas, illustrated in this painting by John Singer Sargent, indicated a new level of brutality. It affected not only soldiers on the front but also civilians, who were bombarded from the air. In addition, the production of new weapons required the output of factories in industrial nations throughout the world. The devastation caused by these weapons affected postwar economic recovery.

The Great Depression The financial collapse of the Great Depression was a global crisis that shattered national economies and brought hardship to millions. Nations and markets around the world experienced drastically reduced banking, manufacturing, and commercial activity and consumer spending. Unemployment became widespread. Some countries sought to help their citizens by providing government-supported jobs, food, and other essentials, but many of these programs did little to correct the basic economic causes of the depression. Soup kitchens and breadlines became common sights in many industrialized nations, such as Austria, where this busy kitchen served people from all walks of life and all social levels.

The Great Depression, 1929–1939

Expansion in Africa The Italian fascist dictator Benito Mussolini believed overseas expansion could ease his country's economic problems during the Great Depression. Mussolini's expansionist plans led to a dispute between Italy and Ethiopia in 1934. One year later, Italy invaded the poorly armed country and defeated its army. This photograph shows Ethiopia's Emperor Haile Selassie seated in the center, surrounded by Ethiopian dignitaries and supporters. In 1936 Selassie went into exile in England, where he began planning a campaign with the British to defeat the Italians. He and the Allies accomplished this goal in 1942 when Selassie returned to power.

Ethiopia, 1934–1942

Fascist dictators Benito Mussolini (left) and Adolf Hitler (right) formed a partnership called the Rome-Berlin Axis.

World War II in the Pacific, 1939–1945

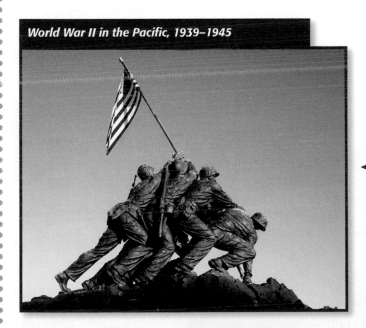

World War II The war continued in the Pacific after it had ended in Europe. The capture of Iwo Jima by U.S. Marines, memorialized in the sculpture shown here, followed some of the most intense fighting of the war. The war ended less than six months later, but its effects would shape the future of the world. World War II was not only the most destructive war in history, but it also marked the beginning of the nuclear age.

Why It Matters Today

The hostilities that provoked World War I led to future wars. They also helped spark a revolution, a push for overseas empires, and the redrawing of boundaries that affected peoples throughout the world. Global relations are still affected by these events. **What current international conflicts still threaten global security?**

C. 1880–1920

World War I and the Russian Revolution

*Impressionist painting by
French artist Edgar Degas*

1884
Science and Technology
The modern machine gun
is invented.

1891
Science and Technology
Construction begins on the
Trans-Siberian railroad.

1900
Daily Life
The "Cake Walk"
becomes a
popular dance.

1880

1890

1900

1882
Politics
The Triple Alliance
affects the balance
of power in
Europe.

1882
Global Events
The British occupy
Cairo, Egypt.

1886
The Arts
The eighth impressionist
art exhibition opens in
Paris.

1895
The Arts
Pyotr Ilich Tchaikovsky's
Swan Lake is performed
in St. Petersburg.

*Workers building a section of
the central Siberian railway*

Build on What You Know

*T*ensions among the world's advanced industrialized powers increased rapidly during the last half
of the 1800s. These nations sought new sources of raw materials for their growing industries and
competed with one another for control of overseas markets. In some cases competition among
the industrialized powers reached the point of military threats and confrontations. Tension was
particularly high in Europe, where major nations such as Great Britain, France, and Germany
vigorously pursued economic expansion. In this chapter, you will learn about how these
developments led to a global war and to great social changes.

A naval airship in the Dardanelles, World War I

Artist's conception of Grand Central Terminal, New York

1913
Daily Life
The Grand Central Terminal is completed in New York.

1913
Business and Finance
Henry Ford's assembly line makes the Model T.

1918
Global Events
Millions die of influenza in America, Europe, and Asia.

1915
Science and Technology
Germany becomes the first nation to use poison gas in a war.

1920
Politics
The League of Nations holds its first meeting.

1920
Daily Life
Women win the right to vote in the United States.

1908
Global Events
Austria-Hungary annexes Bosnia and Herzegovina.

1910

1920

1905
Global Events
Japan wins the Russo-Japanese War.

1919 Politics
The major powers sign the Treaty of Versailles.

1917
Global Events
The Russian Revolution begins.

German U-boat poster from World War I

Women vote in the United States, c. 1920.

1914
Global Events
World War I begins in Europe.

1914
Science and Technology
Germans introduce submarine warfare.

1913
The Arts
Charlie Chaplin begins making movies.

What's Your Opinion?

Themes Journal *Do you* **agree** *or* **disagree** *with the following statements? Support your point of view in your journal.*

Government Every ethnic group, no matter how small, should have its own independent government.

Global Relations No group of nations should have the right to tell another country what it can and cannot do.

Economy A nation's government should control the production and distribution of goods within that nation.

Setting the Stage for War

The Main Idea
In the late 1800s and early 1900s, conflicting interests in Europe set the stage for war.

The Story Continues *European monarchs came together in 1910 for the funeral of the king of England. This unity, however, would soon be shattered by rivalry. "So gorgeous was the spectacle . . . when nine kings rode in the funeral of Edward VII of England . . . Together they represented seventy nations in the greatest assemblage of royalty and rank ever gathered in one place and, of its kind, the last."*

Nationalism, Imperialism, and Militarism

For a time after the Congress of Vienna in 1815, relations among European countries were relatively harmonious. Beginning in the mid-1800s, however, cooperation broke down. Growing rivalries were especially keen in the Balkan region of Europe and in the competition for overseas colonies. By the early 1900s the great powers of Europe were plunging toward war. Four factors fueled this: nationalism, imperialism, militarism, and the system of alliances.

Nationalism in Europe had emerged in the 1800s as various ethnic groups tried to gain more political unity. This desire was an explosive one in a Europe where several nationalities were often ruled by a single regime. The European imperialist states had already come close to war as they competed for control of Africa, Asia, and other parts of the world.

The glorification of armed strength, or **militarism,** was very important to many European leaders before World War I. They believed they could achieve their goals through the threat or use of force. By the late 1800s European nations had built large, well-trained armies. If one nation were to **mobilize,** or prepare its army for war, other nations would mobilize in self-defense.

As rivalries among European nations grew, armies also grew. In the 1890s Germany began enlarging its navy to rival Great Britain's. In 1906 Great Britain launched the *Dreadnought,* the world's first modern battleship. Germany rushed to build similar ships.

✔ **READING CHECK: Making Generalizations** How did militarism grow out of the conflicts among European nations?

INTERPRETING THE VISUAL RECORD

Battleships The *Dreadnought* was the first battleship to feature turbine power and rotating batteries of guns. *How does this photograph suggest the technical achievement that the* Dreadnought *represented?*

The System of Alliances

In the period from 1861 to 1871, the unification of Germany and that of Italy had changed the balance of power in Europe. The unification of Germany, especially, created an entirely new situation. In place of a group of relatively weak states, a powerful German Empire, under the leadership of Prussia, emerged. Otto von Bismarck, the skillful and strong-willed German chancellor, shaped its ambitious foreign policy.

The Triple Alliance. Bismarck had reason to fear that France would seek revenge for its 1871 defeat in the Franco-Prussian War. Perhaps France would do this by trying to regain Alsace-Lorraine, the region it had lost to Germany in that war. Bismarck therefore set his foreign policy to keeping France diplomatically isolated and without allies. Bismarck particularly wanted to prevent an alliance between France and Russia. Such an alliance would isolate Germany diplomatically. At worst, it could even mean that Germany would have to fight a war on both its eastern and western borders.

In 1881 Bismarck formed an alliance with Austria-Hungary and Russia. Known as the Three Emperors' League, it bound each member to remain neutral if any one of them went to war. The next year Bismarck persuaded Italy to join Germany and Austria-Hungary in the **Triple Alliance.** In this move to isolate France, he had now secured Germany's eastern and southern flanks.

The Three Emperors' League ended due to rivalry between Austria-Hungary and Russia over the Balkans. Bismarck managed to make a new agreement with Russia. In this Reinsurance Treaty of 1887, both countries again promised neutrality.

The Triple Entente. In 1888 William II became kaiser of Germany. By 1890 he had dismissed Bismarck as chancellor and abandoned Bismarck's policies. In the meantime, France had been trying to avoid diplomatic isolation. France helped Russia out of a financial crisis, and the two countries had signed a military alliance by 1894. Germany now faced enemies to both the east and the west.

During this time competition for overseas colonies grew between Germany and Great Britain. Troubled by the German naval buildup, the British searched for allies. After settling their conflicting claims in Africa, France and Great Britain soon became allies. In 1907, after agreeing to recognize each other's spheres of influence in Asia, Russia and Great Britain also became allies. The alliance between France, Russia, and Great Britain was called the **Triple Entente.** Both France and Russia also had secret understandings with Italy, giving the Italians a foot in both rival camps.

By 1907 the powers of Europe had divided into two armed camps. These rival alliances threatened world peace. Should fighting break out between two rival powers, all six nations were almost certain to become involved.

✔ **READING CHECK: Summarizing**
Why did European nations form alliances?

Kaiser William II surveys German troops in 1916.

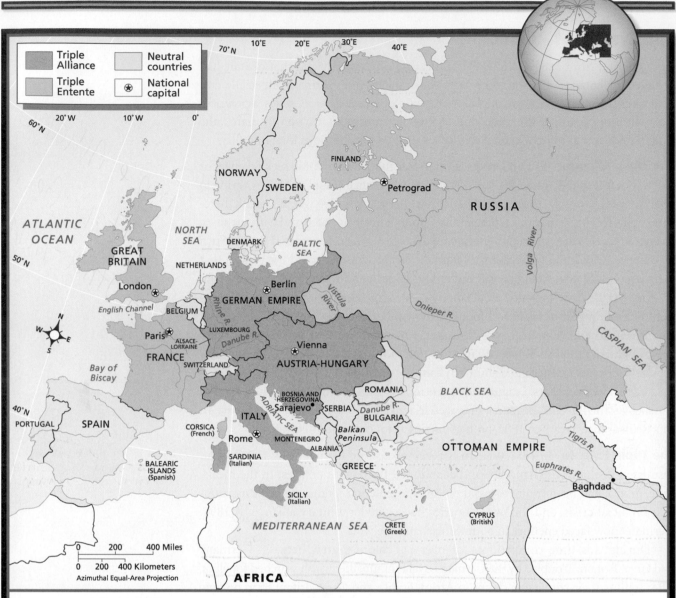

Legend:
- Triple Alliance
- Triple Entente
- Neutral countries
- ⊛ National capital

Europe and the Middle East on the Eve of World War I, 1914

Interpreting Maps The Triple Alliance and the Triple Entente divided Europe into two hostile camps.

■ **Skills Assessment: 1. Places and Regions** Which military alliance was split by the territory of the other?

2. Categorizing Copy the following graphic organizer and fill in the names of the members of the Triple Alliance, the Triple Entente, and the neutral countries of Europe in 1914. Which alliance had more European members?

Triple Alliance	Triple Entente	Neutral Countries

The Balkan "Powder Keg"

Serbia's independence from the Ottoman Empire had been recognized by the Congress of Berlin in 1878. Now, nationalists in Serbia hoped to make their country the center of a larger Slavic state. The Serbian nationalists especially wanted to gain the provinces of Bosnia and Herzegovina, because Serbia was landlocked and these two territories would provide an outlet on the Adriatic Sea. However, the Congress of Berlin had made these two provinces protectorates of Austria-Hungary. This bitterly disappointed the Serbs. After Austria-Hungary went one step further by annexing Bosnia and Herzegovina in 1908, angry Serbian nationalists increased their activities.

Russia, the largest Slavic country, saw itself as the protector of the Balkan Slavs. Russia supported Serbia's goals. The nationalist movement that pressed for the political and cultural unity of all Slavs under Russian leadership was called Pan-Slavism. This contributed to a rivalry between Great Britain and Russia. The British did not want the Russians to gain access to the Mediterranean Sea.

Kaiser William II failed to take advantage of the Anglo-Russian rivalry. Instead, he tried to bring the Ottoman Empire, an old enemy of Russia, into the Triple Alliance. He planned to extend German influence into the Balkans and the Middle East by building a railroad from Germany through Constantinople to Baghdad. Both Great Britain and Russia were alarmed by possible German expansion. As a result, British-Russian ties were strengthened. Germany, on the other hand, supported Austria-Hungary in its opposition to Slavic nationalism.

The spark that ignited the **Balkan "powder keg"** came on June 28, 1914. The heir to the Austro-Hungarian throne, Archduke **Francis Ferdinand,** and his wife were visiting Sarajevo, the capital of Bosnia and Herzegovina. As they rode in an open automobile, Gavrilo Princip, a member of a Serbian nationalist group, assassinated them both. Some Serbian officials were implicated in the terrorist plot.

Austria-Hungary angrily vowed to punish the Serbs. Afraid that Russia would support Serbia, however, it first secured the support of Germany. Austria-Hungary then sent an ultimatum to the Serbian government. In an **ultimatum** one party threatens harmful action if the demands it has made are not met. The Austro-Hungarian ultimatum included these demands: 1) The Serbian government must suppress all groups that opposed the Austro-Hungarian government; 2) Serbia must dismiss school teachers and ban books that did not support Austria-Hungary; 3) Serbia must dismiss government officials who spoke out against Austria-Hungary; and 4) Austro-Hungarian officials must be allowed to participate in the trials of those accused in the assassination. If Serbia did not agree to the ultimatum's terms, Austria-Hungary would use military action.

The Serbian government accepted the first three of these terms. It rejected the last term, but offered to submit it to the International Court at The Hague. Expecting a rejection of its offer, however, the Serbian government mobilized its troops. When the ultimatum deadline expired on July 28, Austria-Hungary declared war on Serbia. Austro-Hungarian leaders expected a quick victory.

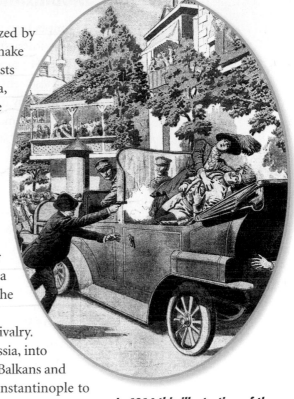

In 1914 this illustration of the assassination of Archduke Francis Ferdinand and his wife appeared in French newspapers.

✔ **READING CHECK: Finding the Main Idea** Why were the Balkans at the center of the conflict between European powers?

Mobilization of Europe

Attempts to persuade Austria-Hungary to continue negotiating with Serbia were useless. Russia prepared to support Serbia by moving troops toward its border with Austria-Hungary. Since Germany had mobilized in support of Austria-Hungary, Russia also sent troops to its border with Germany.

Germany demanded that Russia stop its mobilization or face war. Russia ignored this ultimatum. On August 1, 1914, Germany declared war on Russia. Convinced that France would side with Russia, and hoping to gain an advantage, Germany declared war on France two days later. A former president of the United States, William Howard Taft, expressed the surprise and fear many Americans felt at the news of war in Europe.

Analyzing Primary Sources

Drawing Inferences Why might former president Taft have thought that the war would spread to all of Europe?

History Makers Speak

❝As I write, Germany is reported to have declared war against Russia and France. . . . Nothing like it has occurred since the great Napoleonic wars. . . . All of Europe is to be a battleground. . . . The future looks dark indeed.❞

William Howard Taft, "A Message to the People of the United States"

In 1839, shortly after Belgium's independence, the great powers of Europe had guaranteed its neutrality. Under terms of the guarantee, Belgium agreed to stay out of any European war. It agreed not to help any **belligerents,** or warring nations. In turn, the great powers agreed not to attack Belgium.

When war began in 1914, however, Belgium's location between Germany and France became important. The Germans wanted to defeat France quickly so that they could then focus on Russia. The border between France and Germany was heavily fortified, so the Germans demanded to cross Belgian territory. The British protested, insisting that Germany honor the 1839 guarantee of Belgian neutrality. Germany scoffed at this "scrap of paper." On August 4, 1914, German soldiers marched into Belgium. Great Britain declared war on Germany later that day.

✔ **READING CHECK: Summarizing** What event led to Great Britain's entering the war against Germany?

This photo shows Belgian volunteers mobilizing to resist Germany.

The War Expands

Later in August, Japan entered the war on the side of Great Britain and France. Japan was motivated by a desire to gain German possessions in China and the Pacific. In Europe all the nations of the Triple Alliance and the Triple Entente except Italy were now at war. The Italian government took the position that the Austro-Hungarians had acted as aggressors when they declared war on Serbia. Thus, the Triple Alliance, which was meant for defense only, did not require Italy to give aid to its allies.

Italy remained neutral for 10 months. Finally, it signed a secret treaty with Great Britain, France, and Russia. This treaty guaranteed Italy a share of the spoils after the expected defeat of Germany and Austria-Hungary. In May 1915, Italy entered the war against Germany and Austria-Hungary, its former allies in the Triple Alliance.

Meanwhile, Germany had been trying to gain other allies. In October 1914 the Ottoman Empire entered the war on the side of Austria-Hungary and Germany. The Ottoman Turks were not a strong military power but occupied a strategic position. They controlled the Dardanelles, the strait between the Black Sea and the Mediterranean. Turkish control of this important waterway meant that now Germany and Austria-Hungary could keep Russia's Black Sea fleet bottled up. They could also block the allies from sending supplies to Russia through the Mediterranean and the Black Sea. Germany also persuaded Bulgaria, a Slavic rival of Serbia, to enter the war on its side in October 1915.

✔ **READING CHECK: Analyzing Information**
Why did Italy join the war against Germany and its allies?

Turkish soldiers pose with their rifles, c. 1910; above right, a French magazine cover from 1915

SECTION 1 REVIEW

1. **Define** and explain the significance:
   militarism
   mobilize
   ultimatum
   belligerents

2. **Identify** and explain the significance:
   Triple Alliance
   Triple Entente
   Balkan "powder keg"
   Francis Ferdinand

3. **Comparing and Contrasting** Copy the diagram and use it to show which countries belonged to the Triple Entente and which to the Triple Alliance by October 1915.

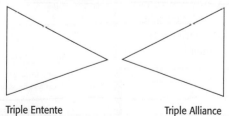

Triple Entente   Triple Alliance

4. **Finding the Main Idea**
   a. What underlying factors led to World War I?
   b. Why were the Balkans called a "powder keg"?

5. **Writing and Critical Thinking**
   Identifying a Point of View Write a short speech, expressing the view of a Serbian nationalist, to the Congress of Berlin in 1878.
   Consider:
   • the ideals of the Pan-Slavism movement
   • the result of Bosnia and Herzegovina becoming protectorates of Austria-Hungary

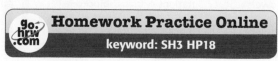

Homework Practice Online
keyword: SH3 HP18

World War I: A New Kind of War

READ TO DISCOVER

❶ What advantages did each side have in World War I?

❷ How did new technology affect the way in which World War I was fought?

❸ What led the United States to join the Allied Powers?

DEFINE

propaganda
war of attrition
contraband
atrocities

IDENTIFY

Central Powers
Allied Powers
U-boats
Woodrow Wilson
Arthur Zimmermann

WHY IT MATTERS TODAY

With advancements in technology, innovations in warfare continue to this day. Use **CNN**Student News.com or other **current event** sources to investigate what new weapons are being developed and used today. Record your findings in your journal.

CNN Student News.com

The Main Idea
World War I dragged on in Europe and other regions of the world for four long, bloody years.

The Story Continues *Writer Erich Maria Remarque vividly described the horror of an artillery bombardment during World War I. "The thunder of the guns swells to a single heavy roar and then breaks up again into separate explosions. The dry bursts of the machine-guns rattle. Above us the air teems with invisible swift movement, with howls, pipings, and hisses. They are the smaller shells;—and amongst them, booming through the night like an organ, go the . . . heavies [largest, most explosive artillery shells]."*

The Belligerents

The soldiers who marched off to war in the summer of 1914 thought they would win a quick victory. However, the war lasted four years and was filled with horrors never before seen.

The warring countries formed two powerful sides. Germany, Austria-Hungary, Bulgaria, and the Ottoman Empire became known as the **Central Powers.** Their territory extended from the North Sea to the Middle East. This helped them with both easy communication and rapid troop

Europe in 1916–1917

Interpreting Maps Britain set up a blockade of Germany's North Sea coast. Germany countered with a U-boat blockade off Britain's west coast.

■ **Skills Assessment: The World in Spatial Terms** Why was control of the North Sea critical for both Germany and Great Britain?

| Central Powers | Neutral nations | British blockade |
| Allied Powers | German U-boat blockade | |

movement. The Central Powers also had the advantage of Germany's well-trained and well-equipped army.

Great Britain, France, Russia, and their partners became known as the **Allied Powers,** or the Allies. They had more soldiers and a greater industrial capacity than the Central Powers. They also had the advantage of Britain's navy, the largest in the world. This allowed the Allies to get food and raw materials from around the world more easily. It also gave them the ability to blockade the Central Powers. Eventually, 32 countries made up the Allied Powers.

✔ **READING CHECK: Comparing and Contrasting** How did the military capabilities of the Central Powers and Allied Powers differ?

Innovations in Warfare

World War I was an industrialized war. Its weapons were mass-produced by the same efficient methods used for manufacturing other products of the new industrial age. Both sides used weapons that had never been tried before. Germany became the first nation to effectively use submarines in naval warfare. **U-boats** (from the German word *Unterseebooten*, meaning "underwater boats") caused extensive losses to Allied shipping. The Germans also introduced poison gas as a weapon against enemy infantry.

Among the new weapons were machine guns and long-range artillery. A machine gun had the firepower of many rifles. It fired rapidly and almost without interruption. Although by the end of the war lighter machine guns had been developed, the first ones were very heavy. They could be fired by

CONNECTING TO
Science and Technology

U-boats

U-boats greatly strengthened German sea power. U-boats armed with torpedoes sank hundreds of Allied ships during World War I. They reduced the amount of supplies being shipped to the Allies from overseas and allowed Germany to make surprise attacks on surface shipping.

A U-boat had two hulls. The inner hull protected the ship from the pressure of the sea. The outer hull fit around it. The space between the two hulls held water. Pumping water in and out of this space made the ship dive and rise.

Forward torpedo tubes

Mine tubes

U-boats fired torpedoes, which exploded when they hit an enemy ship. Torpedoes were stored in tubes between the two hulls of a U-boat. A door at each end of the tube allowed the crew to fire and reload torpedoes without taking on water.

Understanding Science and Technology

How did the crew control the depth of a U-boat under the ocean surface?

Holt Researcher

go.hrw.com
KEYWORD: Holt Researcher
FreeFind:

Manfred von Richthofen

After reading more about Manfred von Richtofen on the Holt Researcher, write a summary of how the airplane changed warfare.

one man, but a team of several men was needed to move and load them. Machine guns killed in great numbers. They made infantry attacks on strongly defended positions very costly. To counter both machine guns and artillery, protective trenches were dug.

Another new weapon was the airplane. Airplanes were mainly used for observing enemy troop movements. At this early stage in their development, they were neither fast nor easy to maneuver. However, they were sometimes used against enemy airplanes in air battles called dogfights. They were also used for dropping bombs on enemy targets. Several skilled dogfight pilots, called aces, became legends. The most famous flying ace was Baron Manfred von Richthofen of Germany, who was nicknamed "The Red Baron." He reportedly shot down some 80 enemy aircraft during the war.

In 1916 Britain introduced the tank, a heavily armored vehicle with guns mounted on it. Running on treads, it could move easily over rough ground. Tanks enabled troops to tear through barbed wire and cut into enemy defenses. One British observer recalled seeing a tank in action for the first time:

History Makers Speak

❝Instead of going on to the German lines the three tanks assigned to us straddled our front line, stopped and then opened up a murderous machine-gun fire, enfilading [covering] us left and right. There they sat, squat monstrous things, noses stuck up in the air, crushing the sides of our trench out of shape with their machine-guns swiveling around and firing like mad.❞

Bert Chaney, quoted in *People at War, 1914–1918,* edited by Michael Moynihan

Analyzing Primary Sources

Drawing Inferences Based on this observer's description, how effective were tanks in trench warfare?

Even the types of soldiers in the war changed. Previously in Europe wars were fought mainly by professional soldiers. Their only source of income was their military pay and rations of food and clothing. In contrast, soldiers in World War I were mostly drafted civilians. Men who were not drafted worked at home to help their country's war effort. Many women, too, worked in arms factories. A war in which nations turn all their resources to the war effort became known as "total war."

To stir the patriotism of their people, governments made wide use of **propaganda.** This was the use of selected bits of information, both true and false, to get people to back their country's war effort. Governments set up agencies whose only purpose was to control news about the war. Newspapers and popular

Then & Now

Women in Wartime

When war began in 1914, the countries of Europe desperately needed war materials. Women poured into the work force, replacing the men who had gone off to war. Many women ran farms and worked in factories or offices. This experience gave women a new sense of confidence and economic independence. *What roles did women play in the wartime economy?*

These English women worked in a factory making arms and ammunition during World War I.

magazines, especially those of the Allies, showed the enemy as brutal and sub-human while praising their own countries.

✔ **READING CHECK: Analyzing Information** What new weapons had been developed as a result of technological advances?

Early Years of the War

Germany launched its main attack on France across neutral Belgium. By September 1914 German troops had reached the Marne River near Paris. The French and British armies fought back. In fierce battles they managed to hold the line. Paris was saved.

France's success in the Battle of the Marne changed the entire nature of the war. Germany's hope of a quick victory ended. Both sides dug in. Trenches lined the western front, which stretched from Switzerland to the English Channel and the North Sea.

On the eastern front, the Russians had mobilized their troops. The French asked Russia to help divert the German forces from the western front. The Russians launched an attack into East Prussia from the east and the south.

Late in August 1914 the Russians battled a German force at the Battle of Tannenberg. The Russian army suffered a humiliating defeat. About half its force was lost, including more than 90,000 prisoners. The German losses were less than 15,000. With this victory, the Germans launched an offensive, moving into Russian Poland.

Fighting on Gallipoli. Although Russia had a huge army, it lacked the guns and ammunition to equip its soldiers properly.

Map legend:
- Central Powers
- Allied Powers
- Neutral nation
- ☼ German victory
- ☼ Russian victory
- Farthest Russian advance, February 1915
- Farthest German advance, May 1918
- Boundary according to the Treaty of Brest Litovsk, March 3, 1918
- Marsh
- ⊛ National capital

The Eastern Front, 1914–1918

Interpreting Maps During World War I, the Germans advanced much farther than the Russians did.

■ **Skills Assessment: The World in Spatial Terms** What battle on the Baltic Sea did the Germans win in 1917?

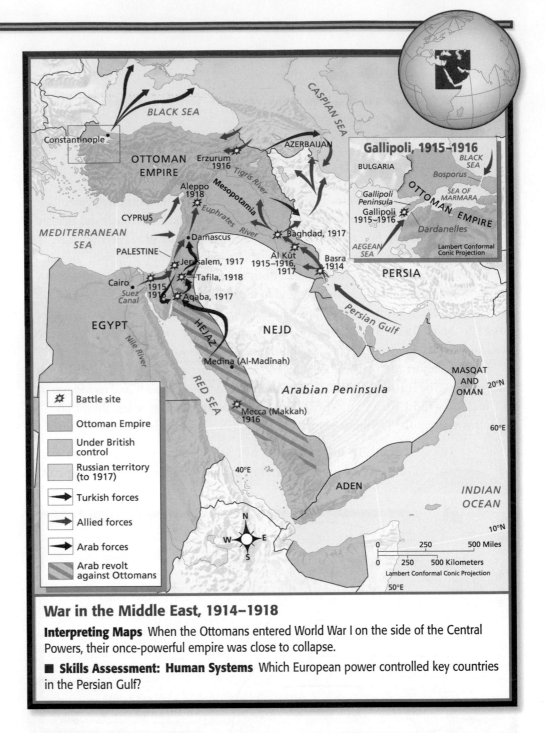

War in the Middle East, 1914–1918

Interpreting Maps When the Ottomans entered World War I on the side of the Central Powers, their once-powerful empire was close to collapse.

■ **Skills Assessment: Human Systems** Which European power controlled key countries in the Persian Gulf?

In 1915 Great Britain and France tried to change this situation. They decided to try to force their way through the Dardanelles so they could capture Constantinople. They hoped to remove the Ottoman Empire from the war. Then they would be able to get needed supplies to the Russians.

The British and French sent heavily armed battleships to bombard Ottoman artillery on the Gallipoli Peninsula. When after several days the bombardment failed to destroy the enemy positions, British and French troops were sent in. However, they were able to gain only a shallow foothold inland. Heavy resistance from the Turks brought the bloody fighting to a stalemate. After eight months and the loss of hundreds of thousands of lives on both sides, the Allies withdrew from Gallipoli. The plan to capture Constantinople had failed, largely due to mismanagement and bad timing.

Naval warfare. The British decided to blockade the North Sea to keep merchant ships from reaching Germany. At first the blockade was aimed at cutting off the flow of raw materials to German factories. Eventually the blockade became an attempt to ruin the German economy and starve the German people.

Germany also set up a blockade. It used U-boats to sink ships that were carrying food and arms to the British. In May 1915 a German submarine sank the British passenger liner *Lusitania* off the coast of Ireland. The *Lusitania* was carrying a cargo of war materials as well as passengers to England. Nearly 1,200 people were killed, including 128 Americans. **Woodrow Wilson,** the U.S. president, denounced the attack. He warned Germany that the United States would not tolerate another such incident. Wary of provoking the neutral Americans into entering the war, Germany cut back its submarine attacks.

In May 1916 the only large naval battle of the war was fought, at the Battle of Jutland, in the North Sea off the coast of Denmark. Both Germany and Great Britain claimed victory. However, the German navy remained in port for the rest of the war.

The stalemate. By late 1915 the war in the west had become a stalemate on land as well as on sea. Military leaders on both sides began to wonder whether they could ever break through the other's line of trenches. As both armies continued their attacks, small areas of land changed hands again and again. Thousands and thousands of lives were snuffed out. The conflict had become a **war of attrition**—a slow wearing-down process in which each side was trying to outlast the other.

✔ **READING CHECK: Sequencing** Describe the progress of the war from 1914 to 1916.

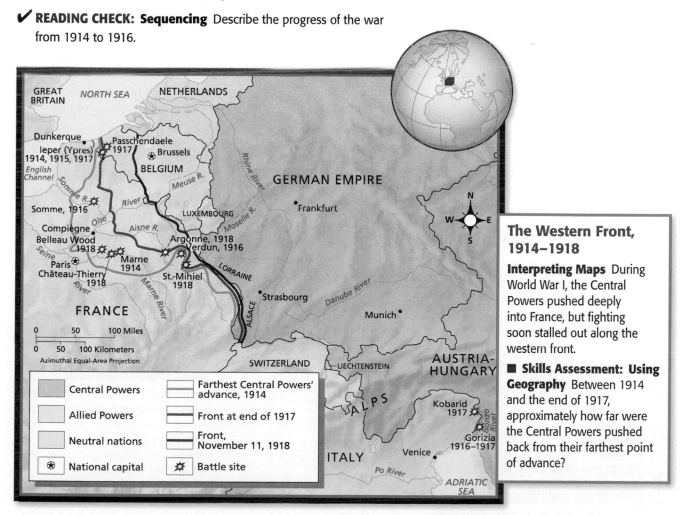

The Western Front, 1914–1918

Interpreting Maps During World War I, the Central Powers pushed deeply into France, but fighting soon stalled out along the western front.

■ **Skills Assessment: Using Geography** Between 1914 and the end of 1917, approximately how far were the Central Powers pushed back from their farthest point of advance?

The United States and World War I

Most Americans had agreed with President Wilson's declaration in 1914 that the United States should be neutral and that the war was strictly a European affair. Nevertheless, the war soon affected the United States. As the most highly industrialized neutral nation, it supplied food, raw materials, and munitions to both sides. According to international law, however, if a ship carried **contraband**—war materials supplied by a neutral nation to a belligerent one—the goods could be seized. At first American investors and business people dealt with both sides. As the British blockade of Germany tightened, however, Americans traded more and more with the Allies.

British propaganda had a great influence on Americans. Stories about German **atrocities**—brutal acts against defenseless civilians—angered Americans. They did not realize that many of the stories were exaggerated or not true.

Early in 1917 several developments pushed the United States toward war. One incident involved a high official in the German foreign ministry, **Arthur Zimmermann.** In January, Zimmermann sent a secret telegram to the German ambassador in Mexico proposing an alliance between Germany and Mexico. Germany offered to help Mexico regain Arizona, New Mexico, and Texas if it would fight on Germany's side. The British intercepted the telegram and decoded it. It was then published in American newspapers. Americans were enraged.

Another development was the resumption of unrestricted submarine warfare by the Germans, who declared a "war zone" around Britain. German U-boats sank many ships. Many Americans died as a result of these attacks.

Then, in March, revolutionaries in Russia overthrew the autocratic czarist government. All the major Allied countries had now moved toward democracy, while none of the Central Powers had. Americans were more likely to participate in a war fought for democratic ideals. President Wilson addressed Congress, saying that "the world must be made safe for democracy." On April 6, 1917, Congress voted to declare war on Germany.

This coded telegram from Berlin to the German embassy in Mexico proposed an alliance between Mexico and Germany.

✔ **READING CHECK: Analyzing Information** How was the United States affected by the war before 1917?

SECTION 2 REVIEW

1. **Define** and explain the significance:
   propaganda
   war of attrition
   contraband
   atrocities

2. **Identify** and explain the significance:
   Central Powers
   Allied Powers
   U-boats
   Woodrow Wilson
   Arthur Zimmermann

Homework Practice Online

keyword: SH3 HP18

3. **Comparing and Contrasting** Copy the diagram and use it to show the advantages and disadvantages each side had at the beginning of the war.

   Central Powers

   Allied Powers

4. **Finding the Main Idea**
   a. How did new technology change the way the war was fought?
   b. What principles were proclaimed by the United States for declaring war?

5. **Writing and Critical Thinking**

   Supporting a Point of View Design a poster encouraging Americans to support the war.
   Consider:
   • the atrocities committed, such as the sinking of the *Lusitania*
   • the idea of making the world "safe for democracy"

SECTION 3

READ TO DISCOVER

❶ What events led to the Russian Revolution?

❷ How did the Communists come to power?

❸ How did its revolution affect Russia's participation in World War I?

IDENTIFY

Mensheviks
Bolsheviks
Vladimir Lenin
Communist Party
Red Army

WHY IT MATTERS TODAY

Russia continues to undergo dramatic changes. Use **CNN**🅝🅔🅦🅢.com or other **current event** sources to investigate what Russia's government is like today. Record your findings in your journal.

CNN student News.com

The Russian Revolution

The Main Idea
Growing problems in Russia came to a crisis during World War I, finally leading to revolution.

The Story Continues *Years of war, poverty, and class struggle had brought an end to the czarist regime in Russia. One Russian described how the revolution began for him. "The streets were full of people. The trams [streetcars] weren't running, overturned cars lay across the tracks. I did not know it then, I did not understand what was happening. I yelled along with everyone, 'Down with the czar!' . . . I yelled again and again. . . . I felt that all of my familiar life was falling apart, and I rejoiced in its destruction."*

Russia in World War I

World War I showed Russia's economic weaknesses. The huge country did not have sufficient food, appropriate armaments, or adequate roads to supply its army. When the Ottoman Empire entered the war on the side of the Central Powers, supplies from outside Russia were sharply cut. The Allies had counted on the large number of Russian soldiers. However, Russia's army was not only poorly equipped but also poorly led. The corrupt, inefficient government could not deal with the problems of modern warfare. Russian war losses were enormous.

By the spring of 1917 the Russian people had lost faith in their government and in the czar. The elected legislative body, the Duma, had little power. Although serfdom had been abolished in 1861, debts, rents, and taxes kept most Russian peasants poor. Strikes and street demonstrations broke out in Petrograd, the capital. When the Duma demanded government reforms, the czar dissolved it.

In the past the government had always been able to use the army against disturbances. This time, however, the soldiers sided with the demonstrators. Encouraged by the army's defiance of the czar, the Duma refused to disband. In March 1917 the czar abdicated, giving up the throne. He and his family were soon imprisoned. The Russian monarchy, and with it the rule of the Russian aristocracy, had come to an end.

✔ **READING CHECK: Identifying Cause and Effect** What were the problems that led to the Russian Revolution?

Lenin and the Bolsheviks

With the overthrow of the czar a temporary government was set up. It would rule Russia until a constitutional assembly could be elected. While the new rulers of Russia tried to restore order, however, another group was working for more radical change.

The Petrograd Soviet of Workers' and Soldiers' Deputies had been organized when unrest had begun in Russia. *Soviet* is the Russian word for "council." The leaders of the Petrograd Soviet were socialists. They believed that political equality must be coupled with economic equality. Similar soviets were organized elsewhere in Russia. Radical members called for immediate peace and land reforms.

Holt Researcher

go.hrw.com

KEYWORD: Holt Researcher

FreeFind: Vladimir Lenin

After reading more about Vladimir Lenin on the Holt Researcher, write an analysis of his influence on political events of the 20th century.

The provisional government, however, pledged to continue the war. It also opposed the changes demanded by the more radical revolutionaries.

Two factions fought for control of the soviets. The moderate **Mensheviks** lost out to the more radical **Bolsheviks.** The leader of the Bolsheviks was **Vladimir Lenin,** a revolutionary socialist. Lenin demanded that all governing power be turned over to the soviets. The Bolsheviks' slogan of "peace, bread, and land" appealed to the war-weary and hungry Russian people. Lenin was a Marxist—a follower of Karl Marx. However, Russia had comparatively little industry and only a small working class. Lenin believed, therefore, that social forces in Russia might not move as Marx had predicted. He set up a small group of leaders to train Russian workers to become a revolutionary force. Lenin's version of Marxism formed the basis of communism.

Revolutionary Russia, 1917–1921

Interpreting Maps The Bolsheviks faced opposition from some foreign forces as well as from internal opponents.

■ **Skills Assessment: Locate** What major cities were in the area controlled by the Bolsheviks?

On November 7, 1917, the Bolsheviks overthrew the provisional government and took control of Russia. This is sometimes called the October Revolution for the month that it happened in the Russian calendar. In 1918 the Bolsheviks renamed themselves the **Communist Party** and dissolved the constitutional assembly because they did not have a majority in it.

✔ **READING CHECK: Finding the Main Idea** Why did the Bolsheviks come to power?

Peace and Civil War

Despite continuing losses, the provisional government had kept Russia in the war. Lenin's new government, however, signed a peace treaty with the Central Powers in March 1918 at the city of Brest Litovsk. Desperate for peace, the Russians accepted the harsh terms dictated by the Germans. Russia agreed to give up a lot of territory.

The new regime then turned its attention to Russia's internal political problems. The Communists faced great opposition. Their opponents included the Mensheviks and other socialist factions, and groups who wanted to restore the monarchy. Civil war broke out early in 1918. To prevent any chance of the monarchy coming back to power, the Communists executed the imprisoned czar and his entire family in July 1918.

The civil war lasted about three years. The Communists forces were called the **Red Army,** adopted from the symbolic color of the European socialist revolutionaries. Their right-wing, counter-revolutionary opponents were known as the Whites. The destruction of the civil war mirrored that caused by World War I.

The Allies were angered by the separate peace treaty Communist Russia had signed with the Central Powers. They tried to get Russia to renew fighting Germany, but the Communists stood by the treaty they had signed. The Allies also feared that the Communists would encourage the spread of revolution to their own countries. The Allies sent troops to Russia and financial aid. By 1921, however, the Communists had won. In 1922 the Communists renamed the land they ruled the Union of Soviet Socialist Republics, or the Soviet Union.

✔ **READING CHECK: Evaluating** Why did the peace treaty between Communist Russia and the Central Powers anger the Allies?

HISTORY MAKER

Vladimir Lenin (1870–1924)

Vladimir Lenin's life changed when his older brother was executed for conspiring to overthrow the emperor. Throwing himself into revolutionary activities, Lenin was arrested and exiled. After his return he became the first leader of the new Soviet Union, which championed the ideals of socialism. Considered one of the greatest revolutionaries of all time, Lenin became a hero for many later communist leaders. **Why is Lenin important?**

SECTION 3 REVIEW

1. **Identify** and explain the significance:
   Mensheviks
   Bolsheviks
   Vladimir Lenin
   Communist Party
   Red Army

2. **Sequencing** Copy the diagram and use it to show what led to the czar's abdication.

   ☐ ☐ ☐ ☐
   ↓ ↓ ↓ ↓
   | Czar Nicholas II abdicates |

3. **Finding the Main Idea**
   a. How did Lenin and the Bolsheviks come to power in Russia?
   b. Why did the Russians pull out of the war?

4. **Writing and Critical Thinking**
   Analyzing Information Design a flyer that the Bolsheviks might have used to organize a rally during 1917.
   Consider:
   • what issues they thought were important
   • the conditions in Russia during World War I

Homework Practice Online
keyword: SH3 HP18

READ TO DISCOVER

❶ What were the Fourteen Points?

❷ How did the war end?

❸ What disagreements did the peacemakers face?

DEFINE

armistice
reparations

IDENTIFY

Fourteen Points
Ferdinand Foch
Paris Peace Conference
League of Nations

▶ **WHY IT MATTERS TODAY**

After World War I many territories were transferred from one power to another. Alsace-Lorraine is a region in France that before World War I was part of Germany. Use CNNStudentNews.com or other **current event** sources to describe life in Alsace-Lorraine today. Record your findings in your journal.

The Terms of Peace

The Main Idea
With the end of World War I, the United States and European nations worked to ensure peace.

The Story Continues *Americans did not have to be soldiers to join the war effort. One woman noted, "Billy, my nephew, is twelve years old. . . . They call the suburb in which Billy lives one hundred percent patriotic. Everybody is in war work. . . . Billy's crowd is indefatigable [tireless] in its labors. . . . The boys usher at meetings, assist in parades, deliver bundles and run errands. They are tireless collectors of nutshells, peach pits [for gas masks] and tinsel paper."*

The Fourteen Points

President Woodrow Wilson's idea that by joining the war America was helping to safeguard democracy established a high, idealistic purpose for World War I. Russia's separate peace with the Central Powers, however, dampened Allied morale. The bloody stalemate on the western front continued. Many people feared that the war would last for many more years.

In January 1918 President Wilson spoke to Congress. He outlined a set of ideas for a more just world once the war ended. His plan became known as the **Fourteen Points.** Six of the points contained plans of a general nature. The eight remaining points dealt with specific countries and regions, such as Russia, Belgium, Alsace-Lorraine, and the Balkans.

The six general points could be summarized as follows: 1) no secret treaties; 2) freedom of the seas for all nations; 3) removal of all economic barriers, such as tariffs; 4) reduction of national armaments; 5) adjustment of colonial claims so they were fair to both the imperialist powers and the colonial peoples; 6) establishment of "a general association of nations" to guarantee political independence and protection to small and large states alike.

The Fourteen Points caught the imagination of people everywhere. Even some people of Germany, tired of the hardships of war, were impressed by Wilson's proposals.

✔ **READING CHECK: Making Generalizations** What was the overall purpose of the Fourteen Points?

More than 2 million American soldiers served in France in World War I. Some are seen here marching through the Arc de Triomphe in Paris.

Defeat of the Central Powers

The Treaty of Brest Litovsk with Russia allowed the Germans to pull troops from the eastern front. They now could concentrate on a huge offensive on the western front in the spring and summer of 1918. This was a last attempt to break through the Allied lines and capture Paris. Meanwhile Allied forces held out for U.S. troops to arrive.

At the end of May the Germans again reached the Marne River. They were just 37 miles from Paris. By this time, however, thousands of American troops were landing every day in France.

An Allied force under the command of French marshal **Ferdinand Foch** (FAWSH) stopped the Germans at Château-Thierry. In July the Allies began a counterattack. Major offensives in August and September forced the Germans back toward their own border. It also became worse elsewhere for the Central Powers. Bulgaria surrendered at the end of September. The Turks, too, soon asked for peace. By October the old Habsburg empire in Austria-Hungary had broken up. Austria and Hungary stopped fighting and formed separate governments.

President Wilson had told the German leaders that he would deal only with a government that truly represented the German people. In the face of growing German military and civilian unrest, the kaiser gave up the throne in early November and a German republic was announced.

In November 1918 a German delegation signed an **armistice,** an agreement to stop fighting. The armistice provided that at 11:00 A.M. on November 11, 1918, all fighting would cease. Under the terms of the armistice, Germany canceled the Brest Litovsk treaty with Russia. Germany had to give up a large part of its fleet, including all submarines. It had to turn over much of its munitions and release war prisoners. The Allies would occupy German territory west of the Rhine River.

The costs of World War I were very high. It is estimated that the war left more than 8.5 million (perhaps 10 million) soldiers dead. About 21 million more were wounded, many crippled for life. Militarily, Germany suffered the most severely, losing more than 1.8 million soldiers. Russia lost almost as many, and France and its colonies lost over 1.4 million. Austria and Hungary counted over 1 million dead, and Great Britain lost almost 1 million. The United States lost over 110,000 soldiers. Civilian deaths and injuries were also very high. Naval blockades, military encounters, famine, and disease had all taken their toll. The financial loss, too, was enormous. Historians have estimated that the total cost was more than $300 billion, a huge amount for the time.

✔ **READING CHECK: Identifying Cause and Effect** What events in Europe helped end the war?

What If? How might world history have been different if the United States had not fought in World War I?

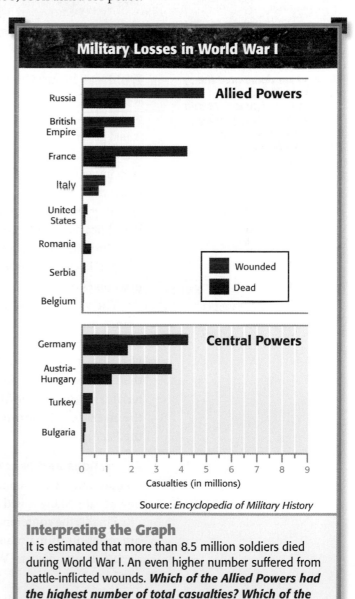

Military Losses in World War I

Allied Powers

Russia
British Empire
France
Italy
United States
Romania
Serbia
Belgium

■ Wounded
■ Dead

Central Powers

Germany
Austria-Hungary
Turkey
Bulgaria

0 1 2 3 4 5 6 7 8 9
Casualties (in millions)

Source: *Encyclopedia of Military History*

Interpreting the Graph
It is estimated that more than 8.5 million soldiers died during World War I. An even higher number suffered from battle-inflicted wounds. *Which of the Allied Powers had the highest number of total casualties? Which of the Central Powers had the highest casualties?*

The Big Four dominated the Paris Peace Conference. Seated left to right are Vittorio Orlando, David Lloyd George, Georges Clemenceau, and Woodrow Wilson.

The Paris Peace Conference

After the armistice in November 1918, the Allies faced the task of arranging peace terms. In January 1919 the victorious Allied nations met at Versailles, outside Paris, for what came to be known as the **Paris Peace Conference.** The meeting was dominated by the leaders of the four major Allied Powers. The group—which included U.S. President Woodrow Wilson, British Prime Minister David Lloyd George, French Premier Georges Clemenceau, and Italian Prime Minister Vittorio Orlando—came to be known as the Big Four.

Problems facing the peacemakers. Problems began almost immediately when some countries were excluded from the peace process. President Wilson had spoken of a peace conference that would write a treaty that was fair to all, but the European Allied governments were not very forgiving of their losses. They insisted on dictating the peace settlement. Russia, under Communist rule and beset by civil war, was not even invited. Representatives of the defeated Central Powers were allowed little role in writing the peace terms.

After World War I Europe faced a radically new and confusing political situation. Republics had replaced monarchies in Austria-Hungary, Germany, and Russia. The Ottoman Empire was on the brink of collapse. Various ethnic groups pressed for independence, self-government, and unified states. The spirit of nationalism also grew in colonies overseas.

The victorious nations had many conflicting territorial demands. Above all, France wanted security against another German attack. It insisted on moving its border eastward to the Rhine River. It wanted the return of the region of Alsace-Lorraine. It also wanted the coal-rich Saar valley. Italy claimed the Tirol region and the cities of Fiume and Trieste. Belgium wanted two small portions of German territory along the border. Great Britain wanted Germany's African colonies and the near destruction of the German navy. Japan wanted German colonies in the Pacific.

Reparations and peacekeeping. The destruction caused by the war also brought up questions about **reparations**—payment for war damages. Who should pay? And how much? Many Allied leaders wanted Germany to bear the cost of the war.

Finally, the conference considered President Wilson's plan for setting up a world organization to maintain peace—a **League of Nations.** This idea had widespread appeal. It was dear to Wilson's heart but many people doubted how practical it would be.

✔ **READING CHECK: Drawing Inferences** Why did the European Allies insist on setting the terms of the peace settlement?

What Kind of Peace?

Early in the Paris Peace Conference, two very different, conflicting viewpoints surfaced. Wilson believed the peace settlement should be fair and not so harsh that it would kindle future wars. On the other hand, many of the Allies felt hatred toward Germany. They believed that Germany had started the war and should pay for it. The British, French, and Italian governments did not officially object to Wilson's Fourteen Points. Yet they had never given up the aims of their secret treaties—to divide territory taken from the Central Powers among themselves after the war. Many Allied leaders believed the only way to ensure a lasting peace was to prevent Germany from ever being powerful again.

Some countries, particularly France, wanted concrete guarantees that Germany would never again be able to threaten their security. Georges Clemenceau, the premier of France, admired Wilson's ideals, but believed the U.S. president was being naive in trusting Germany. "Hopes without certainty cannot suffice to those who suffered the aggression of 1914," he said. Clemenceau argued that the only way to ensure France's future security was to break up Germany and have Allied forces occupy its various regions. The future of Germany would rest on the decisions made at the Paris Peace Conference.

✔ **READING CHECK: Finding the Main Idea** Why did some victors in the war want to break up Germany?

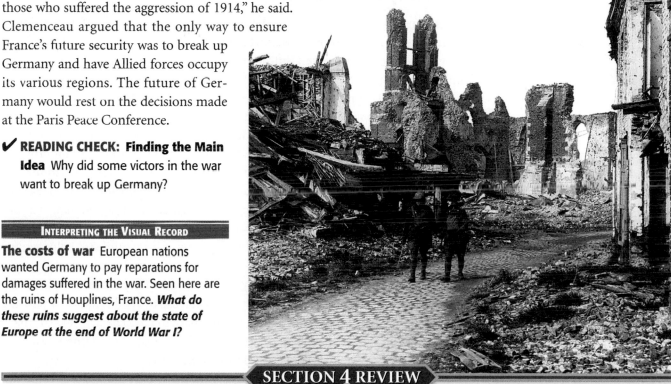

INTERPRETING THE VISUAL RECORD

The costs of war European nations wanted Germany to pay reparations for damages suffered in the war. Seen here are the ruins of Houplines, France. *What do these ruins suggest about the state of Europe at the end of World War I?*

SECTION 4 REVIEW

1. **Define** and explain the significance:
   armistice
   reparations

2. **Identify** and explain the significance:
   Fourteen Points
   Ferdinand Foch
   Paris Peace Conference
   League of Nations

3. **Summarizing** Copy the diagram and use it to show the six general ideas in the Fourteen Points.

FOURTEEN POINTS					

4. **Finding the Main Idea**
   a. How did World War I come to an end in 1918?
   b. What were some problems facing the peacemakers?

5. **Writing and Critical Thinking**
   Supporting a Point of View Write a letter to a newspaper editor supporting Wilson's view or Clemenceau's view at the Paris Peace Conference.
   Consider:
   • the cost of the war to both the Allied and Central Powers
   • how Wilson proposed to prevent future global wars
   • why Clemenceau feared German power

go.hrw.com **Homework Practice Online**
keyword: SH3 HP18

READ TO DISCOVER
❶ What were the terms of the Treaty of Versailles?
❷ How were territories redivided after the war?
❸ How was the League of Nations structured?

DEFINE

genocide
economic sanctions
mandate

IDENTIFY

Treaty of Versailles
World Court

▶**WHY IT MATTERS TODAY**

The League of Nations was the forerunner of the United Nations. Use CNN or other **current event** sources to investigate the structure and work of the United Nations. Record your findings in your journal.

Creating a "New" Europe

The Main Idea
The Treaty of Versailles rearranged territories and brought great changes to Europe after World War I.

The Story Continues *After World War I, world leaders gathered to try to arrive at a settlement that would keep such a war from happening again. As one participant described the proceedings, "We were preparing not Peace only, but Eternal Peace. There was about us the halo of some divine mission. . . . For we were bent on doing great, permanent and noble things."*

The Treaty of Versailles

After six months of negotiations, the delegates to the peace conference finally hammered out an agreement. The victorious Allied Powers made separate peace treaties with each of the five Central Powers—Germany, Bulgaria, the Ottoman Empire, and Austria and Hungary (now two separate nations).

In May 1919 representatives of the new German Republic were called in and presented with a peace treaty. The treaty with Germany was signed at Versailles, near Paris. It was known as the **Treaty of Versailles.** To Wilson's disappointment, the treaty dealt very harshly with Germany. The Germans complained bitterly that the treaty did not follow the Fourteen Points. The treaty made Germany admit that it was guilty of starting the war and must alone pay reparations. The Treaty of Versailles carved large chunks of territory from Germany and placed many restrictions on the German government. However, it also provided for the formation of the League of Nations. Wilson hoped this dream of his would still help create a lasting peace.

The Germans strongly objected to paying reparations. They denied that Germany alone was responsible for starting the war. Moreover, the treaty did not even state the total amount of reparations that Germany would have to pay. The defeated Germans had no choice, however. In late June 1919 they signed the treaty. One witness described the scene as the German delegates arrived to sign the treaty:

❝Through the door . . . isolated and pitiable, come the two German delegates. . . . The silence is terrifying. . . . They keep their eyes fixed away from those two thousand staring eyes, fixed upon the ceiling. They are deathly pale.❞

Harold Nicolson, *Peacemaking 1919*

As a result of the Versailles treaty, many territorial changes were made at Germany's expense. Alsace-Lorraine was returned to France. Belgium gained some small territories along its borders. Germany agreed not to fortify the Rhineland, which Allied troops would occupy for an unspecified period of time. Moreover, Poland was restored as an independent nation. An area called the Polish Corridor cut off East Prussia from the rest of Germany and gave Poland an outlet to the Baltic Sea. The port of Danzig became a free city under the League of Nations. Some territory of the new Polish state also had been part of Russia.

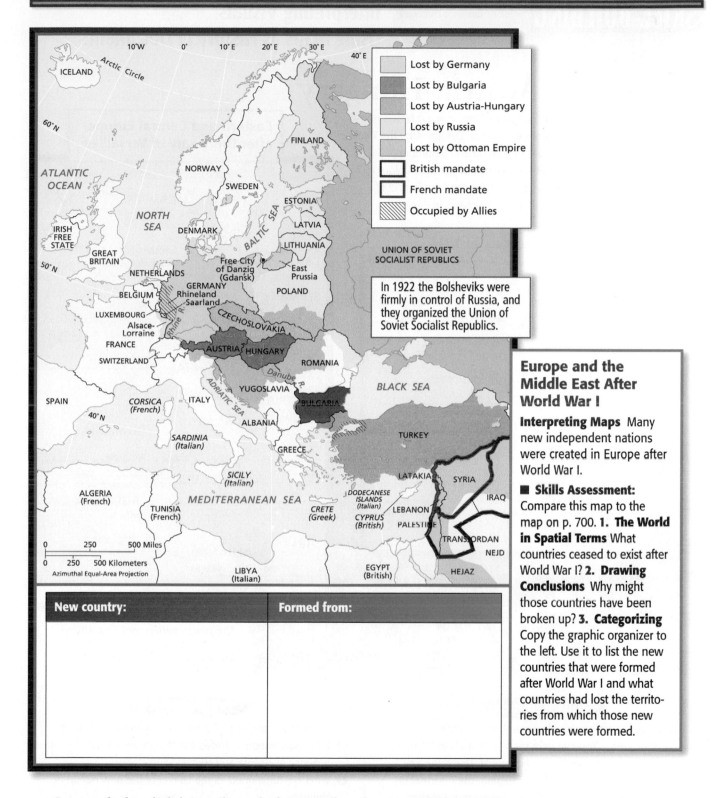

Legend:
- Lost by Germany
- Lost by Bulgaria
- Lost by Austria-Hungary
- Lost by Russia
- Lost by Ottoman Empire
- British mandate
- French mandate
- Occupied by Allies

In 1922 the Bolsheviks were firmly in control of Russia, and they organized the Union of Soviet Socialist Republics.

Europe and the Middle East After World War I

Interpreting Maps Many new independent nations were created in Europe after World War I.

■ **Skills Assessment:** Compare this map to the map on p. 700. **1. The World in Spatial Terms** What countries ceased to exist after World War I? **2. Drawing Conclusions** Why might those countries have been broken up? **3. Categorizing** Copy the graphic organizer to the left. Use it to list the new countries that were formed after World War I and what countries had lost the territories from which those new countries were formed.

New country:	Formed from:

Germany had to abolish its military draft. It was allowed an army of just 100,000 men. The Germans were not allowed to manufacture heavy artillery, tanks, or military airplanes. The German navy could have a few warships but no submarines. These peace terms were meant to ensure that Germany would be unable to start a war. The Allies, however, lacked the ability to enforce them.

✔ **READING CHECK: Categorizing** What limits were placed on the German military by the peace treaty?

**Interpreting Visuals:
Using Maps as Historical Documents**

Changes in Austria-Hungary

From 1867 until 1919 the Austro-Hungarian Empire, ruled by the Habsburg monarchs, covered much of eastern and central Europe. After the Treaty of Versailles, however, the empire was broken up and a number of smaller countries were created. Studying maps of this area before and after the Treaty of Versailles helps you to understand the impact of World War I on political and historical developments in Europe.

Austria-Hungary in 1914

Eastern and Central Europe after the Treaty of Versailles

The peace settlement that ended World War I was drafted by the Allies at Versailles beginning in December 1918.

Skills Reminder

To use a map as a historical document, first identify the subject of the map. You can gain more information from the map by identifying its historical context. Using the key that is given with the map will help explain the information about the subject included on the map and connect that information to the historical context of the subject. Determine how the map helps to show a particular historical pattern, change, or event. Finally, compare the map with other maps—what are some of the differences between the maps? This will help you build an overall understanding of how the pattern, change, or event that it shows produced a new historical reality.

Skills Practice

Study the maps above and answer the following questions:

❶ What new nation included the former Serbia and the former province of Bosnia and Herzevonia?

❷ What city functioned as the capital of the new nation of Hungary?

❸ Compare the two maps. Then write a general statement describing the historical patterns, changes, or events revealed by your analysis.

❹ Using an atlas or other map sources, find a current map of this region of Europe. Has it changed or stayed the same? What might that indicate about the political situation of the region since World War I?

Fates of Former Territories

The Allied victors wrote separate peace treaties with the new nations of Austria and Hungary. The treaty with Austria was signed in September 1919, with Hungary in June 1920. The two countries kept only a small part of the pre-war Austro-Hungarian Empire. Austria surrendered the southern Tirol and the city of Trieste to Italy. Hungary lost some of its territory to the newly independent nations of Czechoslovakia and Yugoslavia. Brought together in Yugoslavia were Serbia, Slovenia, Croatia, Montenegro, and Bosnia and Herzegovina. Hungary also lost territory to Romania, Poland, and Russia.

Ethnic populations. The peace treaties solved many problems but also created new ones. One of the most difficult problems was that of national self-determination. This was especially true in Austria and Hungary, where nationalist movements had been encouraged by Wilson's Fourteen Points. Often the new boundaries did not match natural ethnic divisions. For example, the new national frontiers left about 3 million Germans in Czechoslovakia and Hungarians in Romania. Poland also gained access to the Baltic Sea through the Polish Corridor, a section of land inhabited by Germans. This angered many Germans in the area. Ferdinand Foch predicted that the Polish Corridor would be "the root of the next war."

Some ethnic groups, like the Armenians in Turkey, were brutally oppressed. During World War I the Turks had launched a **genocide,** or systematic extermination, of the Armenians in the Ottoman Empire. Foreign outcry against these atrocities caused a halt to the practice once the war ended, but the Turks resumed their repression in 1920. In 1915 the Armenian population of the Ottoman Empire had stood at some 2 million. About 1.5 million were killed, the rest deported. By 1923 the Armenian population of Asia Minor was almost nonexistent.

Bulgaria, the Ottoman Empire, and Russia. The victors also punished Bulgaria. In its 1919 treaty with the Allies, Bulgaria ceded territory to Greece, losing its outlet to the Aegean Sea.

The Ottoman Empire also paid a high price for being on the losing side. By the treaty of 1920, it was stripped of almost all territory but Turkey itself. Several new

Wagons loaded with supplies, these Armenian refugees are shown here fleeing from Turkish persecution in 1920.

nations were formed from the Ottoman lands east of the Mediterranean. They included Palestine, Transjordan, Syria, and Iraq. They were to be administered by Great Britain and France for the League of Nations. The Dardanelles and Bosporus remained in Turkey. However, these strategic waterways could not be fortified and were to be under international control.

Although it had fought for the Allies, Russia also suffered territorial losses. Its early withdrawal from the war and the rise of the Bolsheviks isolated Russia from the rest of the Allies. By 1918 the Baltic states of Finland, Estonia, Latvia, and Lithuania had declared their independence from Russia. The Allies recognized them as independent. In addition, Russia not only lost land to Poland but also lost the province of Bessarabia to Romania.

✔ **READING CHECK: Drawing Conclusions** What were some problems created by the peace treaties?

The League of Nations

During talks among Allied leaders over the peace settlements, President Wilson made some compromises in the Fourteen Points. He realized that the treaties themselves did not fully provide a "peace of justice." He thought, however, that the new League of Nations would be able to fix any injustices the treaties created. A special commission, which included Wilson, wrote the Covenant of the League of Nations. This agreement, adopted by the Paris Peace Conference, became part of the Versailles treaty.

Organization. According to the Covenant, the League of Nations had two main aims: (1) to promote international cooperation and (2) to keep peace among nations, by settling disputes and reducing armaments. Three main agencies would conduct League business: an assembly, a council, and a secretariat. The League was to work closely with a related but independent body, the Permanent Court of International Justice, or **World Court.** This court would determine cases involving international law. Today the court is located at The Hague in the Netherlands.

The Assembly would be composed of representatives of all member nations. Regardless of size, each nation would have one vote. The Council, the main peacekeeping body, would consist of 9 member nations (later increased to 14). Five members would be permanent—Great Britain, France, Italy, Japan, and the United States—the victors in the war. The remaining seats on the Council were to be filled by the other member nations on a rotating basis.

The members of the League of Nations agreed not to go to war over any disputes. Instead they would submit a dispute to the World Court or other special commission. If a nation broke this agreement, the League could

This was the first public session of the League of Nations, in 1920.

impose penalties such as breaking diplomatic relations. They also could impose **economic sanctions,** such as blocking trade with the offending nation. Military force would be only a last resort.

Mandates. The League of Nations provided a way to deal with the overseas colonies of the defeated powers. Until the people of a colony were considered "ready for independence," the League would hold the colony in trust and take responsibility for it. The League set aside the colony as a **mandate,** to be ruled by the government of an "advanced" nation. The ruling nation would promise to "prepare" the people there for independence. It would make annual reports to the League about the mandate's progress.

German possessions in Africa and the Pacific and Ottoman territories in the Middle East were given as mandates to Great Britain, France, Australia, New Zealand, Belgium, or Japan. The mandate for South-West Africa was given to South Africa.

The start of the League. Although the League of Nations had been strongly promoted by President Wilson, the United States never became a member. Some Americans were wary of the League's powers. Some wanted changes in the Versailles treaty, which included the League Covenant. Because of the League's peacekeeping commitments, some Americans feared being dragged into another war over issues that did not concern them. As a result of this strong opposition, the U.S. Senate did not ratify the Versailles treaty. Instead the United States eventually signed a separate peace treaty with Germany.

Despite the absence of the United States, the 42 member nations at the League's first meeting in Geneva in November 1920 were hopeful for the future. Germany joined in 1926. The Soviet Union became a member in 1934. By the 1940s some 59 nations had joined the League of Nations.

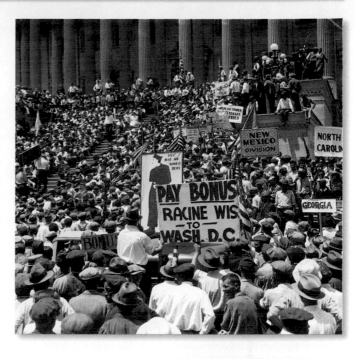

✔ **READING CHECK: Identifying Bias** What did the system of mandates reveal about the Allies' attitude toward colonial peoples?

◀ SECTION 5 REVIEW ▶

1. Define and explain the significance:
genocide
economic sanctions
mandate

2. Identify and explain the significance:
Treaty of Versailles
World Court

Homework Practice Online
keyword: SH3 HP18

3. Analyzing Information Copy the diagram and use it to show the organizational structure of the League of Nations.

League of Nations

4. **Finding the Main Idea**

a. How did the Treaty of Versailles deal with Germany's colonies?

b. What were the aims of the League of Nations?

5. **Writing and Critical Thinking**

Drawing Inferences Write a speech to the U.S. Senate opposing joining the League of Nations. Use the Armenian genocide as an example of the weaknesses of the League.

Consider:
• what happened in the Armenian genocide
• how the League was limited in its ability to respond to it

CHAPTER 18 Review

Creating a Time Line

Copy the time line below onto a sheet of paper. Complete the time line by filling in the events, individuals, and dates from the chapter that you think were significant. Pick three events and explain why you think they were significant.

| 1882 | 1916 | 1920 |

Writing a Summary

Using standard grammar, spelling, sentence structure, and punctuation, write an overview of the events in the chapter.

Identifying People and Ideas

Identify the following terms or individuals and explain their significance:

1. belligerents
2. Allied Powers
3. propaganda
4. Woodrow Wilson
5. Vladimir Lenin
6. Communist Party
7. armistice
8. League of Nations
9. Treaty of Versailles
10. economic sanctions

Understanding Main Ideas

SECTION 1 *(pp. 506–511)*
Setting the Stage for War

1. What was Bismarck's purpose in forming the Triple Alliance of 1882?
2. What event exploded the Balkan "powder keg" and began World War I?

SECTION 2 *(pp. 512–518)*
World War I: A New Kind of War

3. How was new technology used in World War I?
4. What led the United States to declare war?

SECTION 3 *(pp. 519–521)*
The Russian Revolution

5. What were the conditions in Russia that led to revolution?
6. How did signing the Treaty of Brest Litovsk help the Communist regime in Russia?

SECTION 4 *(pp. 522–525)*
The Terms of Peace

7. What were the six general proposals of the Fourteen Points?
8. What problems did the peacemakers try to solve?

SECTION 5 *(pp. 526–531)*
Creating a "New" Europe

9. Why was President Wilson disappointed with the Treaty of Versailles?
10. How was the League of Nations organized?

Reviewing Themes

1. **Government** What role did propaganda play in World War I?
2. **Global Relations** How did World War I affect relations between the world's great powers?
3. **Economy** How was industry affected by World War I?

Thinking Critically

1. **Analyzing Information** What role did economic conditions play in World War I?
2. **Making Predictions** What did the Armenian genocide indicate about human rights after World War I?
3. **Drawing Conclusions** How did the period from 1914 to 1918 mark the end of the old world and the beginning of a new world?
4. **Identifying Cause and Effect** What effect might the March 1917 revolution in Russia have had on the decision of the United States to join the war?

Writing About History

Summarizing World War I greatly affected the borders of many countries in and near Europe. Write a description of the changes for Germany, Russia, Austria-Hungary, Turkey (Ottoman Empire), and Poland. Refer to the maps in the chapter and use the following chart to organize your thoughts before you begin writing.

Countries that gained territory	Countries that lost territory	Countries that ceased to exist

Analyzing Historical Statistics

Study the bar graph below. Then use the information to answer the questions that follow.

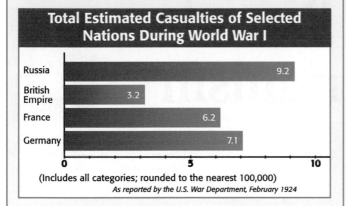

Total Estimated Casualties of Selected Nations During World War I

Russia	9.2
British Empire	3.2
France	6.2
Germany	7.1

(Includes all categories; rounded to the nearest 100,000)
As reported by the U.S. War Department, February 1924

1. Which of the following statements is most accurate?

a. Total Russian casualties were more than three times the number of total British Empire casualties.

b. France suffered 1 million more total casualties than did Germany.

c. Russia suffered nearly as many total casualties as did France and the British Empire combined.

d. Total German and Russian casualties were about equal.

2. Use the statistical information shown in the graph to write a paragraph about the war's impact on postwar recovery and development. Be sure to use correct grammar, spelling, punctuation, and writing style.

Evaluating Sources

Read the following advertisement. On May 1, 1915, the German government placed it in several American newspapers. On May 7, 1915 a German submarine sank the *Lusitania,* a British passenger liner. Then answer the questions.

> "NOTICE! Travellers intending to embark on the Atlantic voyage are reminded that a state of war exists between Germany and her allies and Great Britain and her allies; that the zone of war includes the waters adjacent to the British Isles; that, in accordance with formal notice given by the Imperial German Government, vessels flying the flag of Great Britain, or of any of her allies, are liable to destruction in those waters and that travellers sailing in the war zone on ships of Great Britain or her allies do so at their own risk."

3. Which of the following describes the type of evidence this advertisement provides?

a. This is a secondary source of evidence.

b. This is an unreliable source of evidence.

c. This is a primary source of evidence.

d. This is both a primary source and a secondary source of evidence.

4. The attack on the *Lusitania* killed 1,198 people, including 128 Americans. Do you think the U.S. had a basis for protesting the attack? Explain your reasoning.

Alternative Assessment

Building Your Portfolio

Government

The United States and Russia have often conflicted over ideological issues rooted in their respective revolutions. Write an evaluation of how the American Revolution differed from the Russian Revolution. Then create a compare-and-contrast chart that summarizes the ideas of both revolutions concerning separation of powers, liberty, equality, democracy, popular sovereignty, human rights, constitutionalism, and nationalism.

Link to TODAY

🔲 internet connect

Internet Activity: go.hrw.com
KEYWORD: SH3 WH18

Choose a topic on World War I and the Russian Revolution to:

• create a propaganda poster supporting the Allied Powers or the Central Powers.

• learn about social issues and events that were causes or effects of the war.

• understand the strengths and weaknesses of the Versailles treaty.

1919–1936

The Great Depression and the Rise of Totalitarianism

Striking dockworkers in Great Britain, c. mid-1920s

1920
Daily Life
The first commercial radio broadcasting station goes on the air in the United States.

1922
Politics
Benito Mussolini heads a coalition government in Italy.

1924
Politics
Lenin's death leads to a political struggle for leadership in the Soviet Union.

1926
Business and Finance
A general strike brings Great Britain to a halt, May 3–12.

1919

1924

1919
Science and Technology
The influenza pandemic responsible for more than 20 million deaths finally begins to subside.

1922
The Arts
T. S. Eliot publishes the poem *The Waste Land.*

1921
Business and Finance
Vladimir Lenin announces the New Economic Policy, which allows for some free enterprise in communist Russia.

1923
Business and Finance
Germany informs the Allies that it cannot make war reparations payments on schedule.

1923
Global Events
France and Belgium occupy the Ruhr Valley in Germany.

1925
The Arts
Czech writer Franz Kafka's novel *The Trial* is published.

1925
Science and Technology
German chemists discover the element rhenium.

1927
Daily Life
Charles Lindbergh becomes a worldwide celebrity after completing a solo flight across the Atlantic Ocean.

T. S. Eliot's
The Waste Land

Charles Lindbergh's airplane
Spirit of St. Louis

Build on What You Know

World War I destroyed lives, property, and national identities on a scale never before experienced. The Treaty of Versailles forced defeated European countries to pay enormous reparations to the victors and limited their freedom to rebuild. This drained their resources, destabilized their governments, and affected their sense of national pride. New governments created under the treaty were particularly fragile. In this chapter, you will learn how the war's aftermath led to anxiety, conflict, and, in some parts of Europe, the rise of totalitarian governments.

**The Persistence of Memory
by Salvador Dali**

**1936
Global Events**
Germany occupies the Rhineland.

**1929
Global Events**
The Great Depression
begins.

**1929
The Arts**
Ernest Hemingway's
novel *A Farewell to Arms,*
expressing postwar
disillusionment, is
published.

**1931
The Arts**
Salvador Dali's painting
*The Persistence of
Memory* illustrates the
surrealistic style.

**1933
Business and Finance**
A world economic
conference held in
London fails to solve
the Great Depression.

**1933
Politics**
Adolf Hitler becomes
chancellor of Germany.

**1935
Global
Events**
Italian
forces
invade the
African
nation of
Abyssinia
(Ethiopia).

**1936
Politics**
Léon Blum becomes premier of
France.

**1936
The Arts**
Charlie Chaplin's motion picture
Modern Times, a satire on
industrialization, is released.

1929

1934

**1930
Science and
Technology**
U.S. astronomer
Clyde Tombaugh
discovers the planet
Pluto.

**1933
Daily Life**
The Eighteenth
Amendment,
which bans the
sale of alcoholic
beverages in the
United States, is
repealed.

**1935
Science
and
Technology**
A British
inventor
develops a
wearable
hearing aid.

**1936
Daily Life**
African American Jesse Owens
wins four gold medals in the
Olympics in Berlin.

*A relief line in
New York City
during the Great
Depression*

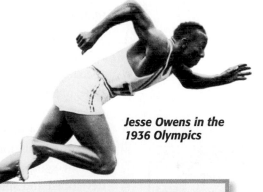

*Jesse Owens in the
1936 Olympics*

What's Your Opinion?

**Themes
Journal** *Do you* **agree** *or* **disagree** *with the
following statements? Support your point
of view in your journal.*

Global Relations Nations should always defend
international treaties.

Government Democratic practices can always
be relied on to prevent dictators from coming
to power.

Culture Scientific and technological advances
do not affect culture.

The Postwar Era

READ TO DISCOVER

❶ How did scientific theories affect thinking in other areas of life?

❷ How did writers, musicians, painters, and architects experiment with new forms?

❸ How did popular culture and consumerism affect societies?

DEFINE

influenza pandemic
surrealism
jazz
cubism
dadaists
functionalism
international style
flappers
prohibition

IDENTIFY

Gertrude Stein
Lost Generation
Franz Kafka
James Joyce
T. S. Eliot
Igor Stravinsky
Pablo Picasso
Salvador Dali
Ch'i Pai-shih
Louis Sullivan
Frank Lloyd Wright

▶ WHY IT MATTERS TODAY

Motion pictures remain important to popular culture in the world today. Use CNN Student News.com or other **current event** sources to learn more about the types of films that are popular with audiences today. Record your findings in your journal.

CNN Student News.com

The Main Idea
The work of artists, musicians, and writers in the postwar era reflected global anxieties.

The Story Continues *World War I profoundly disrupted European and American society. The mass destruction caused by the war changed ideas about nations and people. Many people felt a sense of anxiety and concern for the future. New scientific discoveries added to the concern. A journalist writing in 1938 noted that, "Marx, Freud, [and] Einstein all conveyed the same message to the 1920s: the world was not what it seemed. The senses [that] shaped our ideas of time and distance, right and wrong, law and justice, and the nature of man's behaviour in society, were not to be trusted."*

The Effects of Scientific Events and Ideas

In the wake of World War I, with its mass destruction and wholesale slaughter, many people lost faith in the Enlightenment ideal of ongoing human progress. They felt a sense of disconnection and doubt about the future. New events and ideas in science raised even stronger doubts about the predictable nature of the world.

A global epidemic. Although the death and destruction of World War I was difficult for many people to accept, at least they understood what had caused most battlefield deaths. In the midst of the fighting, however, the world was hit by a mysterious illness that caused more deaths than the war itself and showed how little doctors still understood about disease.

In the spring of 1918 many soldiers fighting in France began to complain of flu-like symptoms. The disease spread, but few patients died from it. Then, in the summer and fall of 1918, a second, more deadly wave of this flu appeared and quickly became global in nature. In all, three waves of the **influenza pandemic** hit the world between 1918 and 1919. A pandemic is an epidemic that occurs over a large geographic area and affects a significant portion of the population. The disease spread with terrifying speed, in part because of the rapid movement of people during the global war. At the time, many doctors referred to it as the "Spanish influenza" because news of the deadly disease spread quickly throughout Spain, where wartime censorship was limited.

No inhabited continent was safe from this flu, which quickly spread into the civilian population. It could kill some victims within two or three days of the first sign of symptoms. Doctors still knew relatively little about how such illnesses developed and spread. They were unable to overcome the deadly disease. Then, just as mysteriously as it had appeared, this strain of influenza disappeared, and the pandemic stopped. It is uncertain exactly how many people died from the influenza pandemic, but most estimates put the death toll well above 20 million.

Scientific and social theories. Events like the influenza pandemic increased many people's feelings that the world was a frightening and unpredictable place. Some looked to the ideas of Sigmund Freud, founder of the modern field of psychology, to ease some of this uncertainty. Freud's claim that the unconscious—not the rational mind—often controlled people's actions seemed to explain many confusing and irrational events in life.

Interpreting Maps World War I contributed to the rapid global spread of influenza.

■ **Skills Assessment:**
1. Places and Regions What continent suffered the most deaths from the influenza pandemic? **2. Drawing Inferences** Why might estimates of the number of deaths from the influenza pandemic vary so much?

Map labels:
- INDIAN OCEAN
- ASIA 19.5–33.5 million
- EUROPE 1.9 million
- ARCTIC OCEAN
- AFRICA 1.9–2.3 million
- NORTH AMERICA 903,000–1.1 million
- PACIFIC OCEAN
- AUSTRALIA less than 100,000
- ATLANTIC OCEAN
- SOUTH AMERICA 466,000–666,000
- Azimuthal Equidistant Projection

Extent of epidemic by:
- August
- September
- October
- November
- Migration of epidemic

19.5–33.5 million — Total estimated influenza deaths per continent (from all three waves)

Some people used Freud's ideas to understand the dreadful destruction of World War I and the continued uneasiness that confronted people around the world.

Other people looked to scientific theories to support their disillusion with the attitudes that some felt had led to war. People who believed that social standards of morality or artistic taste were not absolute pointed to Albert Einstein's argument that even such definite concepts as motion, space, and time were relative. These people argued that values differ greatly in different societies. No one could say that one set of principles was good for all groups. This idea became known as moral relativism.

✔ **READING CHECK: Identifying Cause and Effect** How did scientific events and ideas shape views in the postwar era?

New Directions in Literature

The major writings of World War I and the postwar years show dissatisfaction with traditional ideas. Some writers tried to offer a new vision. German historian and philosopher Oswald Spengler expressed one mood of the era in his *Decline of the West*. Spengler argued that civilizations pass from youth to maturity to old age and then to death. Spengler claimed that European civilization would disintegrate. His view matched the sense of disillusionment of the era.

One group of Americans who expressed such disillusionment included several writers who continued to live in Europe after the war. American **Gertrude Stein** hosted many of these authors in her Paris home. "All of you young people who served in the war, you are all a lost generation," she once said. After that, this group, which included Ernest Hemingway, F. Scott Fitzgerald, and John Dos Passos, became known as the **Lost Generation**. Their novels, such as Hemingway's *The Sun Also Rises*

The "Lost Generation" of American writers included such literary giants as Ernest Hemingway (top) and F. Scott Fitzgerald (bottom).

and Fitzgerald's *The Great Gatsby,* reflected a generation that had lost its moral grounding during the war.

Other writers reflected a new era by experimenting with form. The influence of Freud led many authors to examine unconscious motivations. French novelist Marcel Proust believed that reality is a world of memory and sensation lost in daily life. Proust vividly brought to life the sensory impressions of a disappeared past in the novel *Remembrance of Things Past.* This first part of the novel appeared in 1913. Most of it, however, was published after World War I. Thomas Mann, a German contemporary of Proust, wrote about the constant presence of death amid life and the disconnection of the writer from society. Mann's *The Magic Mountain* (1924), which is set in a hospital, deals symbolically with the moral state of Europe. Mann's novels reflected the era's mood of decay and sadness.

Most of the works of **Franz Kafka,** a Czech writer, were unknown before his death in 1924. Kafka used **surrealism** in his work. Surrealism brings conscious and unconscious ideas together to portray life in a dreamlike way. In *The Castle* (1926), a man searches for an authority in a castle. He travels through endless corridors and deals with many people, but never finds the authority he seeks. These stories of struggle to find meaning, and Kafka's unique way of telling them, later influenced many writers.

Ireland's **James Joyce** caused a great stir during this period. Joyce's *Ulysses* (1922) was a revolutionary book that broke from the traditional novel. In this work, Joyce used a technique called "stream of consciousness." This technique attempts to record everything that comes into a character's mind. Many readers found *Ulysses* difficult to understand. It lacks normal punctuation and the story seems to skip about. Joyce's experimentation with language and form was characteristic of post–World War I artists.

Similarly, many poets of this period abandoned traditional forms such as rhyming lines. Instead they wrote poetry without rhyme that had lines of varying lengths. They also experimented with punctuation and even with the physical appearance of their poems. American-born poet **T. S. Eliot** expressed the negative outlook of the postwar years. In his long poem *The Waste Land* (1922), Eliot described a world without faith, where moral and spiritual values could not be restored.

✔ **READING CHECK: Summarizing** How did the work of leading writers reflect changes in society during the postwar era?

New Directions in Music, Painting, and Architecture

Musicians and painters of this period, like novelists and poets, experimented with creative new forms and styles. Some new artistic ideas were developed before World War I. These ideas, however, did not take hold until the unsettled postwar years.

Music. One of the pioneers of a new direction in music was Russian-born composer **Igor Stravinsky.** His ballet *The Rite of Spring* (1913) caused a major uproar at its first performance. It broke completely with traditional musical composition. This musical piece featured different instruments playing in different keys at the same time. Many people found the sound disturbing. The Austrian Arnold Schoenberg and his students were more revolutionary than Stravinsky. Schoenberg abandoned the usual eight-tone musical scale, using instead a twelve-tone scale. In addition, Schoenberg and his followers avoided traditional forms such as the large symphony. They wrote pieces for unusual groups of instruments, such as *Quartet for Violin, Clarinet, Tenor Saxophone, and Piano.*

CONNECTING TO

Science and Technology

The Development of Radio

Up to the end of World War I, radio technology had been used mainly to send Morse code. In 1920 the Radio Corporation of America (RCA) began manufacturing "radio music boxes." These inexpensive radios were easily affordable for most families. Almost overnight, the radio became a popular consumer item in industrialized nations. In the United Kingdom, radio ownership soared, with a radio in three of every four households by the late 1930s.

Understanding Science and Technology

How did the radio affect the culture of industrialized countries?

An early radio system

Technology influenced music during this time. In industrialized countries a growing number of households had radios in the 1920s and 1930s. Music aimed at a mass audience filled the airwaves. This medium helped give rise to the popularity of new music such as **jazz.** This form of music originated among the African American community in New Orleans. It fused styles from West Africa and Latin America with sounds from African American folk music and some European styles. The lively music soon swept the United States and Europe, giving rise to numerous "jazz clubs." Jazz performers like Louis Armstrong, Billie Holiday, and "Jelly Roll" Morton became famous throughout the world.

Painting. Like writers and musicians, painters also experimented with forms and styles. Two artists working in Paris, **Pablo Picasso** and Georges Braque, created a new style called **cubism.** This style, which was influenced by traditional African art, emphasized geometric designs, using shapes such as cubes, flat planes, and spheres. Cubist painters often showed objects from several different viewpoints at the same time. For example, a painting might show half a face in profile and half from the front.

Other artists moved beyond traditional forms in various ways. Surrealistic painters attempted to represent the unconscious. Their works featured objects that did not seem to relate to one another. The Spanish surrealist **Salvador Dali** painted *The Persistence of Memory* (1931). It is a dreamlike landscape that appears to consist of liquid clocks draped over a tree branch and the edge of a shelf. Other artists, such as Russian painter Wassily Kandinsky and Dutch painter Piet Mondrian, created purely abstract designs. One group of painters called the **dadaists** used random images to reflect what they considered the insanity of the war.

Some places like China witnessed a struggle between modern and more traditional artists. While some Chinese artists embraced new experimental forms, others, like Ch'i Pai-shih, praised traditional Chinese art. Ch'i Pai-shih was the last great painter of the older school of Chinese art.

Architecture. Advances such as the use of structural steel caused remarkable changes in architecture. American **Louis Sullivan** pioneered the new architecture. Sullivan helped develop the skyscraper. He also created a new style called **functionalism.** With functionalism, a building is designed for its specific use instead of in a particular style. **Frank Lloyd Wright,** a student of Sullivan, adopted many of Sullivan's ideas and added his own. Wright believed that buildings should fit into their environment. In the 1920s Wright completed the Imperial Hotel in Tokyo, Japan. Adapting the hotel to its location, he designed a way to "float" the building's foundation, rather than to anchor it in rock. Thus, the Imperial Hotel was one of the few large buildings in Tokyo to survive a major earthquake in 1923.

Holt Researcher

go.hrw.com
KEYWORD: Holt Researcher
FreeFind: Pablo Picasso
Salvador Dali
After reading more about Pablo Picasso and Salvador Dali on the Holt Researcher, create a comparison chart noting similarities and differences in their artistic styles, including universal themes in their art.

INTERPRETING THE VISUAL RECORD

Prairie house Between 1900 and 1910, Frank Lloyd Wright developed many prairie houses in the American Midwest. This image shows an example of the outside of Wright's prairie house design. *Why might the prairie house be considered an example of functionalism?*

European architects, influenced by Sullivan and Wright, also developed a new style of architecture called the **international style.** This style included uninterrupted sheets of steel and glass. German architect Walter Gropius later described changes in architecture.

 ❝The great technical inventions and social developments of the last hundred years set off a stream of changes in our way of living and producing. . . . [T]here has been a steady movement toward a less rigid . . . style of living and building. The skeleton structures enabled us to introduce large window openings and the marvel of glass curtain walls . . . which transformed the rigid compartmental character of buildings into a transparent fluid one.❞

Walter Gropius, from *Four Great Makers of Modern Architecture*

✔ **READING CHECK: Finding the Main Idea** How did architecture change after the war?

Popular Culture and Consumerism

The era of the 1920s was marked by the rise of leisure activities and purchases of consumer goods in industrialized nations. Shorter workdays and slowly improving economies gave people more money and free time. After years of war, many were ready to enjoy life. Feats like Charles Lindbergh's first solo flight across the Atlantic in 1927 seemed to many to signal a new era of progress.

Entertainment. The chief entertainment for popular audiences of the 1920s and 1930s was the motion picture. Developed in about 1900, motion pictures were first shown publicly about 10 years later. By the 1920s millions of moviegoers regularly flocked to theaters to see their favorite films. By the late 1930s, for example, 40 percent of British adults said they went to the movies once a week. Some 25 percent said they went twice a week. While some films reflected the darker feelings of the postwar years, most movies offered viewers escape and entertainment. Slapstick comedies were among the most popular films of the era. The 1927 film *The Jazz Singer* further revolutionized film by introducing sound.

Playing and watching sports became very popular throughout the world. Baseball was popular in the United States and Japan. Golf was widely played and followed in both countries, as well as in parts of Europe. Tennis was another popular sport, attracting players and spectators throughout the United States and Europe.

Europe and Latin America enjoyed soccer, also called football. The game became so popular internationally that the World Cup soccer tournament was established in 1930. The modern Olympics also grew in popularity. The ancient Greek athletic contest was revived in 1896 and held every four years. Amateur athletes from around the world competed in the games. Many Olympic athletes became instant heroes in their home countries. Countries around the world vied for the privilege of hosting the games, which brought revenue and great prestige to the sponsoring nation.

Consumer culture. The decade of the 1920s brought enormous changes to people's lifestyles. As economies improved, more people began to purchase consumer goods. The price of many goods once considered luxury items, like automobiles, dropped significantly.

As more people purchased such items, the whole structure of society began to change. One woman described how owning a car had affected her family.

History Makers Speak ❝We'd rather do without clothes than give up the car. We used to go to [my husband's] sister's to visit, but by the time we'd get the children shoed and dressed there wasn't any money left for carfare. Now no matter how they look, we just poke 'em in the car and take 'em along.❞

from *Middletown: A Study in Modern American Culture*, by Robert S. Lynd and Helen Merrell Lynd

Companies came up with new techniques to get consumers to buy more goods. Radio advertising brought commercials right into people's homes. Companies also began offering to sell more goods on credit. Buying on credit allowed people to instantly purchase goods they wanted instead of saving up for them, as they had in the past.

The expanded use of credit reflected a gradual change in attitudes and values of the times. Increasingly people were focused on the present moment instead of planning for the future. At the same time, the questioning of traditional values was bringing other changes. Increasingly the younger generation began to challenge "proper" societal norms. For example, in industrialized nations many women started wearing short hair and skirts and going out to public places like jazz clubs. These young women were nicknamed "**flappers.**" Women were also asserting their independence by voting and joining the work force in greater numbers than ever before.

Some younger people rebelled against the older generation's efforts to curb their behavior. In the United States, the Eighteenth Amendment of the Constitution established **prohibition,** making alcoholic beverages illegal, in 1920. Many people ignored prohibition, however, and it proved too difficult to enforce. The amendment was repealed in 1933.

✔ **READING CHECK: Drawing Conclusions** How did popular culture and consumerism in industrialized nations reflect a shift in values?

A stylishly dressed woman of the flapper era

SECTION 1 REVIEW

1. **Define** and explain the significance:

   influenza pandemic
   surrealism
   jazz
   cubism
   dadaists
   functionalism
   international style
   flappers
   prohibition

2. **Identify** and explain the significance:

   Gertrude Stein
   Lost Generation
   Franz Kafka
   James Joyce
   T. S. Eliot
   Igor Stravinsky
   Pablo Picasso
   Salvador Dali
   Ch'i Pai-shih
   Louis Sullivan
   Frank Lloyd Wright

3. **Categorizing** Copy the web diagram below. Use it to explain how each discipline reflected the anxieties and experimentation of the postwar years.

   Music — Painting — Mood of the 1920s — Literature — Architecture

4. **Finding the Main Idea**

   a. How were popular culture and architecture affected by new technology following the end of the war?

   b. How did people's social behavior reflect a change in values in many societies?

5. **Writing and Critical Thinking**

   Analyzing Information Write an essay that explains how science and art reflected the uncertainty of the postwar years.

   Consider:
   • the ideas of Freud and Einstein
   • the work of novelists such as Mann and Kafka
   • the music of Stravinsky and Schoenberg

Homework Practice Online
keyword: SH3 HP19

READ TO DISCOVER

❶ What weaknesses appeared in the global economy during the postwar era?

❷ How did nations initially respond to the Great Depression?

❸ How did the New Deal mark a shift in the U.S. government's relationship with its citizens and the economy?

DEFINE

economic nationalism
market speculations

IDENTIFY

Black Tuesday
Great Depression
Herbert Hoover
Franklin D. Roosevelt
New Deal
Social Security Act

WHY IT MATTERS TODAY

The stock market remains an important indicator of economic well-being. Use CNN News.com or other **current event** sources to learn more about the stock market today. Record your findings in your journal.

CNN Student News.com

Postwar Prosperity Crumbles

The Main Idea
Nations responded to the global economic crisis of the 1930s by protecting their own economies.

The Story Continues *Postwar prosperity turned to worldwide economic depression by the end of the 1920s. Unemployment soared around the world. On the high plains of the United States, overcultivation and drought turned farmlands into one large Dust Bowl. In this excerpt from* The Grapes of Wrath, *author John Steinbeck describes dust bowl families as they abandon their homes. "In the little houses the tenant people sifted their belongings and the belongings of their fathers and of their grandfathers. . . . They piled up the goods in the yards and set fire to them. They stood and watched them burning, and then frantically they loaded up the cars and drove away, drove in the dust."*

Signs of Economic Troubles

Many nations never fully recovered from the economic effects of World War I. Others relied heavily on Western industrialized nations like the United States. Although Western industrialized nations generally prospered during the 1920s, some economic problems existed. As the decade of the 1920s continued, therefore, the global economy became increasingly vulnerable to disaster.

Farmers. Much of the prosperity of the 1920s was fueled by industry. Meanwhile, many farmers were suffering. Much European farmland had been destroyed during the war. During that time farmers in other areas, such as Africa, Australia, India, New Zealand, North America, and South America, increased food production to sell to Europe. American farmers took out loans to buy modern machinery and additional land. With the return of peace in 1918, the worldwide demand for certain crops like grain fell, and agricultural prices dropped. Farmers made very little money. Those who had borrowed money to expand now had problems paying their debts.

Protectionism. In the postwar world the economies of different countries were linked more closely together than at any time before. In this situation the promotion of **economic nationalism,** or protectionism, caused problems. This occurred when nations tried to protect domestic industries by limiting trade with others. To protect their industries from foreign competition, nations established tariffs on the import of goods. This policy usually failed. For example, high American tariffs made it hard for Europeans to sell their goods in the United States. Thus, they could not purchase goods from the United States or pay off their debts. American bankers and business leaders loaned money to Europeans to buy American goods. This practice, however, drove the Europeans further into debt.

Speculation and panic. During the 1920s millions of Americans engaged in **market speculations,** or risky investments, in the stock market. The stock market is an organization through which shares of stock in companies are bought and sold. A company issues shares of stock to raise money for its business. Investors who buy the stock are actually buying shares of the company. As long as investors hold the shares of stock, they can share in the company's earnings. They can also profit by selling the shares at prices above their original purchase cost if the company's stock increases in value.

During the 1920s stock prices soared. Many investors made large profits and believed that stock prices would continue to rise. This confidence led investors to borrow money to buy more stock. When the stock's value rose, the stock could be sold at a higher value. The investor could then repay the loan and still enjoy a profit. If the value of the stock fell, however, problems arose. By the late 1920s the stock prices of many companies had become wildly overvalued.

On October 29, 1929—**Black Tuesday**—investors on the New York Stock Exchange panicked in the face of bad economic news. Fearing a drop in stock prices that were artificially high, investors rushed to sell their shares. The sudden sell-off drove stock prices tumbling. Many stocks on the exchange became virtually worthless overnight. At the same time, many of the economy's underlying problems and weaknesses surfaced as investor confidence fell. Savers rushed to their banks to withdraw their savings, only to find that the banks had not maintained adequate cash reserves to honor mass withdrawals. Banks, in turn, demanded that borrowers repay their loans, but borrowers had no money. A major financial crunch resulted. In a very short time, thousands of banks and their customers—factories, farms, and individuals—were forced into bankruptcy.

✔ **READING CHECK: Finding the Main Idea** What economic weaknesses appeared in the global economy during the 1920s?

The crash Crowds gather along Wall Street during the Stock Market crash. *What does this gathering reflect about the crash?*

The Great Depression

The collapse of the New York Stock Exchange marked the beginning of the worldwide **Great Depression.** Prices and wages fell, business activity slowed, and unemployment rose, all in a very brief period of time. By 1932 more than 30 million workers in countries throughout the industrialized world could not find jobs. Poverty during the depression, however, occurred in the midst of great productivity. Goods were available and their prices fell to very low levels, but people had no money to buy them. Some countries tried to force prices up by destroying farm surpluses. For example, Brazil burned excess coffee for years.

Most nations, including the United States, initially tried to protect themselves from the Great Depression through economic nationalism. In reality, however, this usually made economic recovery more difficult.

Great Britain tried to create jobs by granting low-interest loans to its industries. In 1931 the British government raised tariffs against foreign goods. Great Britain also formed a system of economic cooperation within its empire. France was less industrialized than Great Britain. This helped protect it from the effects of the Great Depression for a couple of years. French trade eventually declined, however, while unemployment rose and industrial production dropped sharply. The uncertainty of the depression years caused political instability in France. In 1933 alone there were three changes of government. Elsewhere in the world, the Great Depression caused unrest and violence. In Germany it helped destroy the Weimar Republic.

✔ **READING CHECK: Summarizing** How did some nations deal with the onset of the Great Depression?

The New Deal

The United States lagged behind most other industrialized nations in creating social programs to help its citizens in troubled times. Americans did not have publicly funded unemployment insurance or government relief programs that could help during periods of economic struggle. As a result, when the Great Depression began, American workers who lost their jobs had to rely on personal savings, if any, or on charity. People who could not afford to buy food stood in breadlines to receive a bowl of soup. Some people sold apples on street corners to earn money.

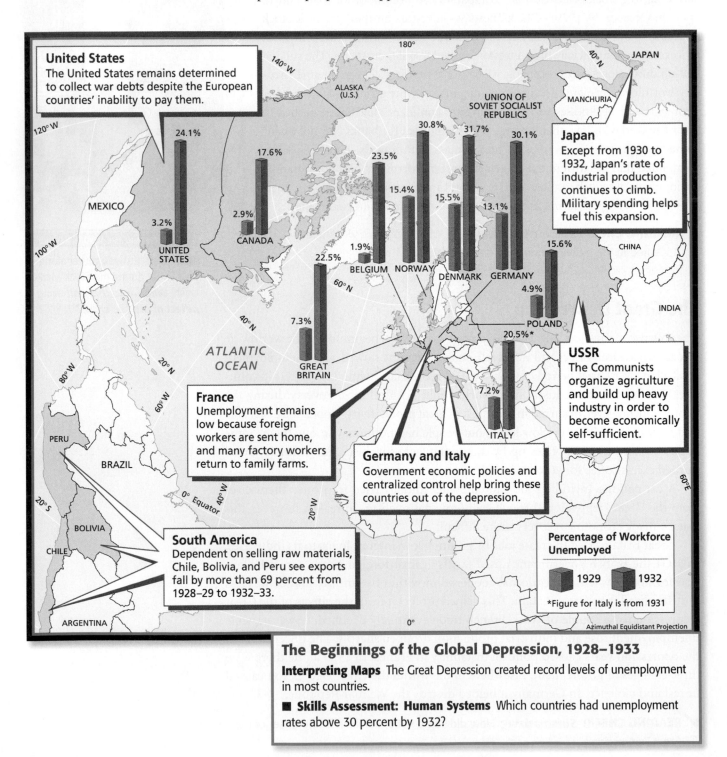

United States
The United States remains determined to collect war debts despite the European countries' inability to pay them.

Japan
Except from 1930 to 1932, Japan's rate of industrial production continues to climb. Military spending helps fuel this expansion.

France
Unemployment remains low because foreign workers are sent home, and many factory workers return to family farms.

Germany and Italy
Government economic policies and centralized control help bring these countries out of the depression.

USSR
The Communists organize agriculture and build up heavy industry in order to become economically self-sufficient.

South America
Dependent on selling raw materials, Chile, Bolivia, and Peru see exports fall by more than 69 percent from 1928–29 to 1932–33.

Percentage of Workforce Unemployed
1929   1932
*Figure for Italy is from 1931

UNITED STATES 3.2% / 24.1%
CANADA 2.9% / 17.6%
GREAT BRITAIN 7.3% / 22.5%
BELGIUM 1.9% / 15.4%
NORWAY 23.5%
DENMARK 15.5%
GERMANY 13.1% / 30.1%
NORWAY 30.8%
DENMARK 31.7%
POLAND 4.9% / 15.6%
ITALY 7.2% / 20.5%*

Azimuthal Equidistant Projection

The Beginnings of the Global Depression, 1928–1933

Interpreting Maps The Great Depression created record levels of unemployment in most countries.

■ **Skills Assessment: Human Systems** Which countries had unemployment rates above 30 percent by 1932?

President **Herbert Hoover** was said to believe that prosperity was "just around the corner." Hoover tried to revive the American economy, but his efforts had little effect in the face of so massive an economic collapse. In 1932 the American people elected a new president, **Franklin D. Roosevelt.** The new president immediately created a program of relief and reform called the **New Deal.** The federal government granted money to each state to provide the needy with clothing, food, and shelter. To create jobs, the government began a program of public works. The program hired people to construct public buildings, roads, and other projects.

Congress followed Roosevelt's emergency relief program by reforming the economic system. Banks and stock exchanges were placed under stricter regulation. The **Social Security Act** of 1935 provided for unemployment and old-age benefits. Congress established a 40-hour workweek and minimum wages. It also guaranteed workers the right to form unions.

Under the New Deal, the United States became deeply involved in the welfare of its citizens. The New Deal did not, however, completely end the Great Depression in the United States. Government efforts to restore prosperity were not enough to solve the economic crisis.

✔ **READING CHECK:**
Problem Solving How did the New Deal mark a dramatic change in the U.S. government's approach to economic crisis?

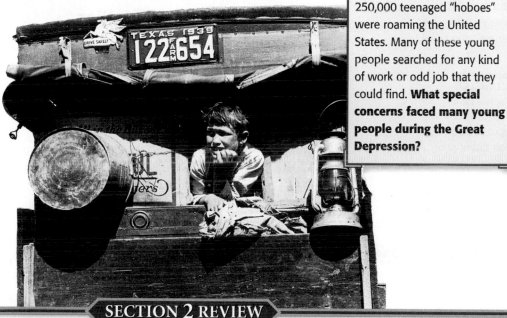

This migrant child rides in the backseat of the family car as his parents travel to look for work in 1939.

YOUNG PEOPLE IN HISTORY

Growing Up During the Depression

During the Great Depression, young people faced special problems. In some cases, parents expected children to work when the parents themselves could not.

Children were often a burden in poor families. For many youngsters, running away seemed the only solution. At one point, almost 250,000 teenaged "hoboes" were roaming the United States. Many of these young people searched for any kind of work or odd job that they could find. **What special concerns faced many young people during the Great Depression?**

SECTION 2 REVIEW

1. Define and explain the significance:
economic nationalism
market speculations

2. Identify and explain the significance:
Black Tuesday
Great Depression
Herbert Hoover
Franklin D. Roosevelt
New Deal
Social Security Act

3. Identifying Cause and Effect
Copy the graph below. Use it to describe the effects of the Great Depression.

International relations
Human suffering
Government reactions

4. **Finding the Main Idea**

a. What weaknesses in the global economy led to the Great Depression?

b. How effective was the New Deal in responding to the problems of the Great Depression?

5. **Writing and Critical Thinking**

Drawing Inferences Imagine that you are a young American living during the Great Depression. Write a journal entry discussing President Roosevelt's approach to correcting the problems of the economy and explaining why Roosevelt called his package of legislation a "New Deal" for Americans.

Consider:
• the underlying problems that contributed to the Great Depression in America
• the hardships that the depression caused
• government efforts to assist Americans

Homework Practice Online
keyword: SH3 HP19

Political Tensions After World War I

READ TO DISCOVER

① What difficulties did France face during the postwar years?

② How did the British government deal with its domestic problems?

③ What problems weakened eastern European governments?

DEFINE

general strike
nationalization

IDENTIFY

Maginot Line
Locarno Pact
Popular Front
Léon Blum
Ramsay MacDonald
Easter Rising
Sinn Fein
Irish Republican Army

▶ WHY IT MATTERS TODAY

Northern Ireland remains a region troubled by violence today. Use **CNNNews.com** or other **current event** sources to learn about the conflict in Northern Ireland. Record your findings in your journal.

CNN student News.com

The Main Idea
Western Europe weathered the crisis of the 1920s, but eastern Europe did not fare as well.

The Story Continues *At war's end, European lands and economies were in ruins. France was especially hard hit. One observer described the landscape of northern France: "For mile after mile nothing was left. No building was habitable and no field fit for the plow. . . . One devastated area was exactly like another—a heap of rubble, a morass [jumble] of shell-holes, and tangle of wire." The unparalleled destruction caused by World War I, and the need to rebuild in the face of rapidly changing political, social, and economic conditions, strained many European nations.*

✎ France's Postwar Difficulties

France emerged from World War I victorious but weakened. During the four years of war, northern France had been a major battleground. At war's end, farmland and even entire cities lay in ruins. Trenches and shell holes scarred the land. The most modern parts of France's agriculture and industry had been destroyed. Most tragic of all, a large number of France's young men had died in the war.

The economy. France also faced severe economic problems. High prices hurt industrial workers and the lower middle class. At the same time, the expenses of the French government rose. After the war France owed money to its citizens and to the United States for war materials. The government had to pay the war debt and the interest on the debt. It also financed a rebuilding program for the war-damaged areas.

Military security was another major expense for the French. Twice in less than 50 years, Germany had invaded France. The French were determined to prevent another invasion from the east. France rebuilt its army and constructed a series of steel and concrete fortifications. This system, called the **Maginot** (MA·zhuh·noh) **Line,** stretched nearly 200 miles along the borders of Germany and Luxembourg. Construction of the Maginot Line was enormously costly, further weakening the French economy.

The Maginot Line was an enormously costly defense system that was ultimately useless. When World War II broke out, Germany invaded France from the vantage point shown here, north of the Maginot Line.

International affairs. The political situation in Europe improved during the mid-1920s. In 1925 Belgium, Czechoslovakia, France, Germany, Great Britain, Italy, and Poland met at a conference held at Locarno in Switzerland. Delegates to the conference signed a number of treaties that together became known as the **Locarno Pact.** Delegates pledged that their countries would peacefully settle all future disputes. They also guaranteed the existing boundaries between France and Germany.

France also signed mutual assistance treaties with Czechoslovakia and Poland. These defensive alliances soon weakened, however. In the mid-1930s, Belgium declared that it would be neutral in any war. Italy, a wartime ally with France, returned to its traditional opposition to France. The French formed a shaky alliance with Russia, now under a communist government. To encircle Germany, France also made alliances with Romania and Yugoslavia. Along with Czechoslovakia and Poland, these nations shared France's mistrust of Germany.

Political unrest. As the Great Depression began to affect France, many people lost confidence in the government. In early 1934 rioters in Paris called for an end to republican government. They favored a strong government headed by a dictator who would protect the nation. French trade unions responded to these right-wing demands by calling for a **general strike.** Workers in various industries refused to work until their demands were met. Left-wing parties in France then organized a government called the **Popular Front.** Its leader, the socialist **Léon Blum,** became premier of France in 1936.

To prevent the conservatives from seizing power by force, Blum's government carried out many reforms. The Popular Front first persuaded leaders of French industries to grant pay increases to end the strike. The government then established a 40-hour workweek and guaranteed workers the right to paid vacations. It also set up a system to negotiate labor disagreements. The Bank of France came under government control. The weapons industry underwent partial **nationalization,** meaning that it was placed under government control. Prices, however, continued to rise. Wage increases did little to help French workers. Divisions within the Popular Front also made governing difficult. Blum's government lasted only a year.

After the fall of the Popular Front, the new French government canceled many of the reforms that had helped labor. As a result, many workers came to oppose the government. Many new political and social groups developed, some of which followed extreme approaches. Although France remained a democracy, traditional French systems of government and society were questioned. Bitter divisions grew among the French people.

✔ **READING CHECK: Summarizing** What economic and political problems did France experience after World War I?

Léon Blum's short-lived Popular Front government tried to cope with the effects of the Great Depression.

Great Britain After World War I

Like France, Great Britain faced serious economic problems after World War I. The money it had used to finance industrial expansion was gone and the government had to borrow money. After the war Britain's outdated factories and machinery had trouble competing with newer American and Japanese technology. In addition, high tariffs due to economic nationalism damaged British trade.

Labor troubles. British workers suffered after the war. Disarmament left many factory workers without jobs. By 1921 nearly a quarter of Great Britain's work force was unemployed. The government provided unemployment benefits, but the high unemployment rate led to labor unrest. Labor unions tried to keep the high wages and employment rates of the war years. Industry leaders opposed these union demands.

Ramsay MacDonald, leader of the Labour Party, spoke out for the workers, but the Labour Party did not have a majority in the House of Commons. MacDonald formed a coalition government with the Liberal Party. A coalition government is made up of several parties that agree to work together. The government set a tight budget. It also protected British industry from foreign competitors and helped the construction industry. These measures helped the economy recover. They also helped Britain avoid the social unrest that toppled democratic governments elsewhere.

Ireland. In the 1920s Great Britain faced serious problems in Ireland, a country it had ruled for centuries. During the 1800s Irish nationalists demanded the right to rule themselves. By 1914 the demand for Irish independence was still not met, although the British government promised Ireland home rule once World War I was over. Many Irish nationalists, however, wanted complete independence from Great Britain. During the war Irish nationalists revolted in the **Easter Rising** on Easter Monday, April 24, 1916. The British ended the bloody revolt and executed many of its leaders.

The Irish nationalist Padraic Pearse was executed by the British following the Easter Rising of 1916.

INTERPRETING THE VISUAL RECORD

Easter Rising A citizen army parades outside Liberty Hall during the Easter Rising of 1916. *What does the banner on Liberty Hall mean?*

Michael Collins, an Irish nationalist, explained the importance of the 1916 uprising. Collins noted that the execution of the Easter Rising's leaders fueled Irish nationalism.

History Makers Speak

"It [the Easter Rising of 1916] appeared at the time of the surrender to have failed, but that valiant effort and the martyrdoms [killings] which followed it finally awoke the sleeping spirit of Ireland."

Michael Collins, from *The Path to Freedom*

Analyzing Primary Sources

Drawing Inferences Why would Michael Collins regard the failed Easter Rising as a victory for the Irish people?

In 1918 members of an Irish nationalist party called **Sinn Fein** (SHIN·FAYN) dominated the election for Irish seats in the British Parliament. Instead of taking their seats in Parliament, the Sinn Fein representatives declared themselves the representative government for an independent Irish republic. When Britain refused to recognize this new government, fighting broke out again. For several years Sinn Fein's military, the **Irish Republican Army** (IRA), battled British troops in a series of violent and bitter struggles. The British received little support from the Irish people.

Finally, with a full-scale war looming, British officials offered to compromise. A settlement was ratified in 1922, dividing Ireland in two. Catholic southern Ireland became the self-governing Irish Free State, with loose ties to Great Britain. Six northern counties with a Protestant majority remained in the United Kingdom. They were known as Northern Ireland. Many Irish nationalists refused to accept this arrangement, and civil war raged again. Just a few months after the settlement was finalized, Michael Collins, who had helped negotiate the agreement, was assassinated by nationalists who felt he had betrayed his people.

In the 1930s nationalist Eamon de Valera was elected prime minister of the Irish Free State. Under his leadership, the Free State began to break away from Great Britain. By 1949 the Irish Free State had become completely independent, calling itself the Republic of Ireland. For many nationalists, however, Ireland would only be free when both north and south were reunited.

✔ **READING CHECK: Finding the Main Idea** What kinds of domestic unrest affected Great Britain during and after the war?

Eastern Europe

As western European nations tried to recover from the war, new nations in eastern Europe built new governments. Instability and cultural tensions in eastern Europe had led to World War I. These problems had not disappeared with the end of the war. They reappeared in new political conflicts among nations that had little experience with democracy. In addition, these nations suffered severe economic problems. The breakup of the Austro-Hungarian and Russian Empires disrupted old trading patterns. Policies of economic nationalism further weakened eastern European economies. Several of the new governments formed in eastern and southeastern Europe after World War I angered the land-owning classes by breaking up some estates owned by the old aristocracy and redistributing the land to peasants. However, despite cultural, economic, and political problems, many of the new nations kept democratic governments.

Postwar Austria was a small, poor nation. Many Austrians wanted to unite with Germany, but peace treaties prohibited the union. Conflicts between socialists and conservatives weakened efforts to create a democracy. A third of Austria's population

Then & Now

Northern Ireland
The division of Ireland in 1922 did little to resolve tensions between pro-British Protestants and nationalist Catholics in Northern Ireland. Conflict grew in the late 1960s, when civil rights groups demanded voting reforms to eliminate discrimination against Catholics. Ongoing violence caused Great Britain to impose direct rule over Northern Ireland in 1972, but the shooting and bombing continued. In 1998 the British agreed to let Northern Ireland govern itself. Despite the 1998 peace accord, political unrest continues.
What issue led to increased violence in Northern Ireland during the 1960s and after?

lived in Vienna. They struggled for control against the rest of the country's people, who saw the nation's needs differently. Opposing groups created private armies, leading many people to desire authoritarian rule. Austria gradually became less democratic.

Hungary became a republic in November 1918. In March 1919, Béla Kun, a Hungarian communist, overthrew the weak republic. Kun had embraced communism while in Russia during the war. Now he tried to establish a system modeled on Russia's new government. He nationalized the land, which made many Hungarians angry. He also failed to distribute food to the people. When Russia did not provide promised assistance, Kun's government fell.

Admiral Miklós Horthy, a member of the military class, then ruled Hungary. He found postwar reconstruction very difficult. Parts of Hungary's prewar empire had been given to Austria, Italy, Poland, and Romania. The new boundaries cut off factories from supplies and markets. During the Great Depression, Hungary sought economic help from the League of Nations, and then from Germany and Italy. Hungary found itself with less and less control over its destiny.

Poland was located between Germany and Russia. Faced with serious economic troubles, Poland had little chance at becoming a democracy. Despite the new Polish democratic constitution, many groups bitterly opposed the government. High German tariffs crippled the Polish economy. The government became more and more unstable. In 1926 Marshal Józef Pilsudski (peel·SOOT·skee) installed a military dictatorship. By that time Bulgaria, Romania, and Yugoslavia had all replaced their democratic governments with conservative military dictatorships or monarchies.

✔ **READING CHECK: Analyzing Information** What role did geography play in the problems that eastern European nations faced?

Soldier-statesman Józef Pilsudski ruled Poland with an iron hand.

SECTION 3 REVIEW

1. **Define** and explain the significance:
   general strike
   nationalization

2. **Identify** and explain the significance:
   Maginot Line
   Locarno Pact
   Popular Front
   Léon Blum
   Ramsay MacDonald
   Easter Rising
   Sinn Fein
   Irish Republican Army

3. **Analyzing Information** Copy the chart below. Use it to explain the problems each nation faced after World War I.

Country	Problems
Great Britain	
France	
Austria	
Hungary	
Poland	

4. **Finding the Main Idea**
   a. What problems did France and Great Britain face during the years following World War I?
   b. Why did some new European governments survive and others fail during the 1920s?

5. **Writing and Critical Thinking**
   Supporting a Point of View Imagine you are a laborer in Paris in 1934. Write a broadsheet that explains why you want people to strike.
   Consider:
   • France's economic troubles during the Great Depression
   • political threats to stability

Homework Practice Online
go.hrw.com
keyword: SH3 HP19

Fascist Dictatorships in Italy and Germany

READ TO DISCOVER

❶ How did Benito Mussolini transform Italy into a fascist state?

❷ Why did the Weimar Republic fail?

❸ How did Adolf Hitler become an important figure in Germany?

❹ How did the Nazis use power in Germany?

DEFINE

fascism
corporatist state

IDENTIFY

Benito Mussolini
Black Shirts
Adolf Hitler
Nazi Party
Third Reich
Rome-Berlin Axis

▶ **WHY IT MATTERS TODAY**

Fascist and pro-Nazi groups still exist in Germany, the United States, and other nations today. Many people oppose these groups, and keep track of their activities. Use CNN Student News.com or other **current event** sources to learn more about opposition to such hate groups. Record your findings in your journal.

CNN Student News.com

The Main Idea
Political and economic crises after World War I helped totalitarian regimes take control in Germany and Italy.

The Story Continues *After World War I, high unemployment and economic problems helped to pave the way for the rise of totalitarian dictatorships. In Italy, Benito Mussolini played upon his country's problems to gain power, becoming the first of Europe's fascist leaders. One writer compared Mussolini to Napoleon: ". . . like Napoleon, he [Mussolini] could strike fear into men twice his size with a direct glance from those astonishing eyes."*

The Rise of Fascism in Italy

As it did elsewhere, the war and its aftermath took its toll in Italy. The Italian government, a constitutional monarchy, seemed unable to respond effectively to these problems. One person who did offer a clear response to Italy's troubles was **Benito Mussolini.** As a young man, Mussolini had edited a socialist newspaper. During World War I, however, his views changed, and he became an extreme nationalist. When Mussolini returned from the war, he organized his own political party. He called it the Fascist Party and called its doctrine **fascism** (FASH·iz·uhm). The words *fascist* and *fascism* come from the Latin word *fasces.* It refers to a bundle of rods bound tightly around an ax that symbolized the authority of the government.

Fascist doctrine. Fascism relied on dictatorship and totalitarianism. It was strongly nationalistic and militaristic and opposed to communism as well as most democratic principles. In practice, fascist and communist governments seemed much alike, in that both tried to control people through force and censorship. There were important differences between fascism and communism, however. Communism appealed to workers and promised ultimately to achieve a society without social classes in which all property is shared communally. Fascism, on the other hand, appealed to the upper and middle class. Fascism promised to preserve existing social classes and the ownership of private property. The difference in views of private property placed fascism and communism in direct opposition to one another.

Mussolini criticized democracy as a weak and ineffective form of government. When he became dictator, he took the title Il Duce (il DOO-chay), Italian for "the leader."

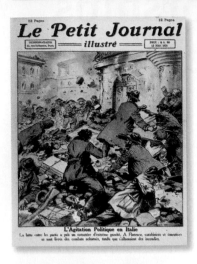

This illustrated cover of Le Petit Journal portrays fighting between communists and fascists in Florence, Italy, in 1921.

Among Mussolini's first followers were discontented nationalists and soldiers returning from the war. Gradually, however, the Fascists attracted shopkeepers, artisans, and wealthy landowners. Large manufacturers interested in blocking communist gains among workers were especially drawn to fascism. These new supporters provided financial assistance to the Fascists. The lower middle class, which had been hurt by inflation, and the unemployed also supported the Fascists.

Mussolini recognized the appeal of anticommunism. He emphasized it in his programs and promised to prevent a communist revolution. Fascism began to stand for the protection of private property and the middle class. Mussolini proposed cooperation between labor and management to restore and protect the Italian economy. He stressed national pride, pledging to return Italy to the military glories of the Roman Empire.

Mussolini's rise to power. The Fascists conducted a violent campaign against their opponents, especially communists and socialists. Known as **Black Shirts** for the color of their uniforms, Fascists broke up strikes, intimidated voters, and drove elected socialist officials from office. In October 1922, Black Shirt groups from all over Italy met in Rome. They claimed their purpose was to defend Italy against a communist revolution. In response, liberal members of the Italian parliament called upon the king to declare martial law. When the king refused, the cabinet resigned. Conservative advisers then persuaded the king to appoint Mussolini premier and to ask him to head a coalition government.

Once in office Mussolini began to destroy democracy in Italy and to set up a dictatorship. He appointed Fascists to all official positions in the central government and pushed a new election law through parliament. Under it, the party receiving the most votes would automatically gain two thirds of the seats in the lower house of parliament.

The Fascists won the election of 1924. In 1925 Mussolini was made "head of the government." While the king was allowed to reign as a figurehead, real power was held by the Fascist Party. Mussolini took over the Ministry of War and controlled the police. A Grand Council of the Fascist Party set government policy, but it usually deferred to Mussolini.

With Mussolini firmly in control, outward signs of dictatorship appeared. Parties opposed to Fascist rule were disbanded. The government suspended basic liberties, such as freedom of speech, freedom of the press, and trial by jury. Labor unions came under government control. Strikes were outlawed. Uniformed and secret police spied on everyone. Under Fascist rule, Italy rapidly became a police state.

Sons of the Wolf Mussolini established an organization for young people called "Sons of the Wolf," in which children were taught fascist ideas. *Why might Mussolini think it was important to recruit youths to the fascist movement?*

The corporatist state. Mussolini introduced a new and complicated system of government called corporatism, making Italy a **corporatist state.** Representation was determined by area of economic activity. Major economic activities including agriculture, commerce, manufacturing, and transportation were formed into organizations similar to corporations. By about 1934 Italy had 22 of these corporations. Within each corporation, representatives of government, labor, and management met to establish wages and prices and to agree to working conditions.

Labor unions and business leaders were expected to submit to Mussolini's government and to cooperate with one another for the goals of the state. Private property and limited profits were permitted, however.

✔ **READING CHECK: Finding the Main Idea** What are some aspects of fascism and corporatism?

The Weimar Republic

As in Italy, Germany underwent great political change after World War I. In early 1919, following the kaiser's abdication, Germany became a republic. The following year, an assembly met in the city of Weimar (VY·mar) and drafted a constitution. The German federal republic became known as the Weimar Republic.

The German people were unhappy with the Weimar Republic because it had signed the humiliating Treaty of Versailles. Many Germans considered the Weimar Republic to be a traitor to Germany's interests. The government faced some of the same economic, political, and social problems that all Europe faced after World War I. Unemployment was extremely high, and inflation soared. Money lost value so rapidly that printers stopped putting numbers on bills.

Both right-wing groups and communist groups tried to overthrow the republic. For example, in 1923 an uprising known as the Beer Hall Putsch occurred in Munich. It was led by a group of extreme nationalists. Although the government put down the uprising and jailed its leaders, the Beer Hall Putsch highlighted the weaknesses of the government and the growing frustrations of the German people. **Adolf Hitler,** a leader of the Beer Hall Putsch, seized on these frustrations to gain support for his political party—the Nazis.

✔ **READING CHECK: Identifying Cause and Effect** Why was the Weimar Republic so weak?

The Nazis and Hitler

Many political parties formed in Germany after World War I. One was the National Socialist German Workers' Party, or **Nazi Party.** The party was extremely nationalistic, anti-Semitic, and anticommunist. It promised to protect Germany from communism. As a result, the Nazis eventually attracted the support of some wealthy business leaders and landowners. One of the first Nazi recruits was Adolf Hitler. By 1921 he was head of the Nazi Party. In 1923, while imprisoned for his role in the Beer Hall Putsch, Hitler wrote *Mein Kampf* (*My Struggle*). The book expressed the spirit of the Nazi movement. In it, Hitler outlined his plan for racial purity through the total elimination of all Jews and

Holt Researcher

go.hrw.com
KEYWORD: Holt Researcher
FreeFind: Benito Mussolini
Adolf Hitler
After reading more about Benito Mussolini and Adolf Hitler on the Holt Researcher, create a Venn diagram comparing the ideology and actions of the two leaders.

INTERPRETING THE VISUAL RECORD

Inflation in Germany Inflation soared in Germany during the early 1920s. The value of the German mark fell so low that people bundled the money and sold it by weight as wastepaper instead of using it as currency. *What does this picture reveal about economic conditions in Germany during the 1920s?*

others that he considered "impure." By 1927 Hitler's anti-Semitic ideology, shared by the Nazi Party, began to be transformed into active discrimination against Jews, which soon grew increasingly violent. Hitler left no doubt as to his goals for the German nation.

Analyzing Primary Sources

Drawing Conclusions What was Hitler's primary goal for Germany?

 History Makers Speak **"If the National Socialist movement really wants to be consecrated [honored] by history with a great mission for our nation . . . it must find the courage to gather our people and their strength for an advance along the road that will lead this people from its present restricted living space to new land and soil."**

Adolf Hitler, from *Mein Kampf*

Hitler's emotional speeches attracted many listeners. He promised to repeal the Treaty of Versailles and to restore Germany's military power. He pledged, too, to lead the nation in the recovery of its lost territory and to build a "Greater Germany." To these promises Hitler added his racial doctrine. According to Hitler the Germans were the "master race." All others were inferior. Many Germans were eager to follow a leader who pledged to restore their country's lost glory.

✔ **READING CHECK: Drawing Conclusions** What does the popularity of Hitler's message reveal about the attitudes of many German people during the 1920s?

The Nazis in Power

In 1925 the Nazi Party had just 25,000 members. By 1929 the party had grown to 180,000 members. In the 1930 election, the Great Depression and continuing social and civil unrest caused many workers and middle-class voters to turn to the Nazi Party. In 1932 the party won 230 seats in the Reichstag, one house of the German parliament.

By late 1932 the Nazis held more seats in the Reichstag than any other party. They did not have enough votes to claim a majority, however. In January 1933 the president of the republic appointed Hitler as chancellor. Hitler then used the private Nazi army to frighten members of the Reichstag. In 1933 someone set fire to the Reichstag building. Hitler blamed the communists and received emergency powers to deal with the supposed communist revolt. He used these powers to make himself a dictator.

A formation of uniformed German workers gives the Nazi salute to Adolf Hitler, standing in the open automobile, at Nürnberg, Germany, in 1937.

HISTORY MAKER

Adolf Hitler (1889–1945)

Following Germany's humiliating defeat in World War I, Adolf Hitler set out to establish an iron dictatorship that would rule Germany and the world "for a thousand years." Like Mussolini in Italy, Hitler rose to power through a combination of masterful crowd manipulation, fiery speaking ability, and emotional appeal to German fears. He twisted facts and used Germans' frustrations over World War I to convince Germans that they were victims of international injustice and conspiracy. **What tactics did Hitler use to gain power?**

Adolf Hitler's Rise to Power

Adolf Hitler rose from obscurity during the bleak postwar period in Weimar Germany to become an all-powerful dictator. Hitler was expert at creating "the big lie," claiming that the greater the falsehood, the more likely it would be accepted without question. He sought to destroy Germany's postwar parliamentary democracy from within, through policies of intimidation and violence and by using the republic's laws and practices against it. Hitler learned to cover his drive for absolute power at any cost with a thin cloak of legality. A careful study of documents from the period of Hitler's rise to power reveals how he used the law to undermine Germany's democratic institutions in order to control the political system.

The Historical Background

The documents below include a chart showing the results of elections for seats in Germany's Reichstag (representative parliament) in 1932 and 1933. Document 2 is an excerpt from Hitler's Emergency Decree, which was based on the burning of the Reichstag in 1933. The Nazis blamed the fire on the Communists. The Decree played on Germans' fear of disorder and revolution, which many believed was caused by the Communists. The Emergency Decree placed severe restrictions on the Communists, who were the Nazis' biggest rivals and to whom they had lost seats in the Reichstag in the election of 1932.

Party Name	Nov. 1932	Mar. 1933
THE NAZI TAKEOVER OF GERMANY'S GOVERNMENT, 1932–1933 Seats in the German Reichstag by Political Party		
National Socialists (Nazis)	196	288
Nationalists	52	52
People's Party and Bavarian People's Party	31	21
Catholic Center	90	92
Socialists	121	120
Communists	100	81

Excerpt from The Emergency Decree:

"The following is decreed as a defensive measure against Communist acts of violence, endangering the state: Sections 114, 115, 117, 118, 123, 124, and 153 of the Constitution of the German Reich are suspended until further notice. Thus, restrictions on personal liberty, on the right of free expression of opinion, including freedom of the press, on the right of assembly . . . association . . . warrants for house-searches, . . . are also permissible beyond the legal limits otherwise prescribed."

Adolf Hitler delivers an impassioned speech to the Reichstag in 1939. Hitler frequently provoked Germans' anger and resentment toward the international community by claiming that Germany was "stabbed in the back" by cowardly, hidden enemies during World War I.

Skills Reminder

Historians use documents as basic sources of information and evidence. Documents answer questions, support or disprove assumptions, and help historians to build theories concerning the historical record. They take many forms— written, printed, and visual. To analyze documents, first identify the opinion, fact, or issue that is the document's subject. Then determine the document's source, validity, and bias. Finally, place the document in its historical context and draw conclusions based upon the information that it provides.

Skills Practice

❶ Study the statistical data shown in the chart above. Recognize that for any single party to gain control of the German Reichstag, it had to have a clear majority of seats. Write a paragraph describing the trends shown by the chart and what the Nazis might have done to win control of the legislature.

❷ Analyze the excerpt from Hitler's Emergency Decree. Write a general explanation of the meaning of the excerpt, including its effects on individual rights and liberties. Then describe how this document might have used German laws to reinforce Hitler's totalitarian rule.

Once in power, Hitler took the title *der Führer* (FYOOR·ur), German for "the leader." He turned Germany into a police state, banning labor unions, opposition newspapers, and opposition political parties. He gave the Gestapo, a secret police force, wide-ranging powers. Members of so-called inferior races, especially Jews, suffered persecution. In some places the Nazis forced the Jews to live in separate neighborhoods called ghettos. Many Jews were forced to wear the Star of David, a six-pointed star that is the symbol of Judaism, on their clothing. The Nazis' political opponents were harshly suppressed or sent to concentration camps. In Nazi Germany, concentration camps were initially set up to isolate all people suspected of opposing Hitler's regime. However, in accordance with Hitler's plan to rid Germany of its Jewish population, the camps soon developed into a network for the systematic suppression and extermination of millions of Jews and other so-called "impure" population groups in Nazi-occupied countries.

Like Mussolini, Hitler promised to revive his nation's economy. He also reminded Germans of their nation's former glory. He called his rule the **Third Reich.** *Reich* is the German word for "empire." The first German empire had been the Holy Roman Empire. The second was the German Empire of the Hohenzollerns. Hitler declared that the Third Reich would last 1,000 years.

During the early 1930s Germany began secretly rebuilding its military. In early 1936 Hitler ordered troops into the Rhineland. This act violated the Treaty of Versailles, which prohibited Germany from keeping troops there. Neither France nor Great Britain reacted to this treaty violation. In part, this was because neither of the two powers believed that the violation was worth going to war. Hitler was encouraged by his easy success in the Rhineland. He sought an alliance with Mussolini. In the fall of 1936, the two dictators formed the **Rome-Berlin Axis.**

✔ **READING CHECK: Summarizing** How did Hitler come to power in Germany, and how did he use that power to become a dictator?

Book burnings Nazis and German students carry books and pamphlets to be burned during a demonstration against literature they believed to be anti-Germanic. *What do the participants' physical actions in this image reveal about their attitude toward the burning of books?*

SECTION 4 REVIEW

1. **Define** and explain the significance:
   fascism
   corporatist state

2. **Identify** and explain the significance:
   Benito Mussolini
   Black Shirts
   Nazi Party
   Adolf Hitler
   Third Reich
   Rome-Berlin Axis

3. **Comparing and Contrasting** Copy the chart below. Use it to compare and contrast fascism with communism.

Fascism	Communism	
		Class
		Property
		Government power

Homework Practice Online
keyword: SH3 HP19

4. **Finding the Main Idea**
   a. How did World War I contribute to the rise of fascism in Italy and Germany?
   b. How did the dictators use their power in Italy and Germany?

5. **Writing and Critical Thinking**

   Supporting a Point of View Imagine that you are an American journalist in Germany during the 1930s. Write a newspaper column persuading readers that the Nazis are determined to destroy democracy.
   Consider:
   • the Nazis' use of military troops
   • Nazi attacks on minority groups

SECTION 5

READ TO DISCOVER

❶ What were the terms of the New Economic Policy?

❷ How did Stalin shape the Soviet economy?

❸ Why did Stalin imprison and execute millions of Soviet people?

DEFINE

collective farms
command economy
purge

IDENTIFY

New Economic Policy
Leon Trotsky
Joseph Stalin
Five-Year Plan
Politburo
Comintern

WHY IT MATTERS TODAY

Communism remains a powerful political force in what was once the Soviet Union. Use **CNN** or other **current event** sources to learn more about communism's influence in the former Soviet Union. Record your findings in your journal.

The flag of the USSR was bright red to symbolize revolution. The hammer and sickle symbolized worker and peasant unity, while the star stood for the Communist Party.

Dictatorship in the Soviet Union

The Main Idea
Under the leadership of Joseph Stalin, the Soviet Union became a powerful police state.

The Story Continues *In 1917 the Communists seized power and imprisoned Czar Nicholas II, his wife Alexandra, and their five children. On the night of July 18, 1918, the royal family was taken to the basement of the house where they were being held. There, the entire family was shot to death. Many Communists thought they had ended centuries of oppression under czarist rule. Within a few years, however, Russia was once again at the mercy of an absolute ruler. Joseph Stalin would prove to be one of the most brutal dictators Russia had ever experienced.*

Russia Under Lenin

In 1922 the Communist leaders renamed Russia the Union of Soviet Socialist Republics (USSR). The people of the USSR became known as the Soviet people. The country's name indicated that the soviets, or revolutionary councils, now held power. The USSR was divided into separate political republics joined in a federal union. Eventually the USSR included 15 of these republics.

Between 1918 and 1921, Russian leader Vladimir Lenin followed a policy known as War Communism. This policy nationalized Russian industries. Social and economic measures were not based on a long-range plan, however. Communist leaders had to develop a program to build their new society in Russia.

War Communism did little to improve the Russian economy. In 1920 Russian farmers produced significantly less grain than they had grown before World War I. Factory production was less than one-sixth of its prewar levels. By 1921 the Communist leadership faced economic collapse and social disorder. In response, Lenin announced the **New Economic Policy** (NEP). The major industries—heavy industry, communications, transportation, and the credit system—remained under government control. The NEP allowed some free enterprise, however. Individuals could buy, sell, and trade farm products. Some private business, especially among peasants, was allowed. A new class of small businessmen, the Nepmen, arose. The Nepmen traded in domestic goods and helped manufacturers secure needed materials.

Soviet agriculture made important changes in this period. During the revolution farmlands had been seized from wealthy landlords and divided among the peasants. The government tried to persuade peasants to form **collective farms.** Land was pooled into large farms on which people worked together as a group. On a collective farm, peasants shared the scarce modern farm machinery.

Women's roles. The Communists claimed to believe that men and women in Soviet society should be equal. In 1917 they declared that women should receive equal pay for work equal to that of men. Women were also granted time off from work to take care of newborn babies. In addition, the Soviet government made it much easier to obtain a divorce. As a result, the Soviet Union had one of the highest divorce rates in Europe.

Many male Communist Party members and peasants who preferred traditional values tried to limit women's gains, however. Many women still received lower pay than men. They faced higher rates of unemployment. Few women held positions of authority within the Communist Party and the Soviet government.

Soviet women served in Red Army combat units in the 1920s.

Education. Soviet leaders emphasized education. They hoped to increase literacy rates and to teach socialist doctrine in the schools. In addition, they established technical schools to train industrial workers. Educators had limited success, however, partly because they lacked funds. Students lacked supplies such as pencils and notebooks. Some schools closed in the winter because they lacked heat. Moreover, the government emphasized higher education, often ignoring the needs of elementary schools. As a result, in 1925 Soviet students averaged fewer than three years in school.

✔ **READING CHECK: Finding the Main Idea** What reforms took place in the USSR under Lenin?

The Five-Year Plan

When Lenin died in 1924, a power struggle took place within the Communist Party. The main rivals for power were **Leon Trotsky** and **Joseph Stalin.** Trotsky was a talented party organizer. He had almost single-handedly created the Red Army that defended the Bolshevik Revolution. Stalin was a leader of the party.

Trotsky and Stalin had differing views regarding the best way to make Communism succeed. Trotsky followed the strict Marxist belief that revolution should take place among workers all over the world. Stalin broke with this doctrine and advocated "socialism in one country." Stalin argued that after socialism succeeded in the Soviet Union, revolution would spread to the rest of the world. A merciless struggle began between Trotsky and Stalin and their followers within the Communist Party. By 1928 Stalin had emerged as the leader. Trotsky, in turn, was exiled from the Soviet Union. He was later murdered in Mexico on Stalin's orders.

Stalin believed the economy was not growing quickly enough. Peasants were refusing to sell wheat at the low prices set by the government. In 1928 Stalin ended the NEP. He returned to a **command economy,** in which the government controlled all economic decisions. Stalin wanted to make government control of the economy a permanent part of Soviet life.

In 1928 the government released the first **Five-Year Plan** for economic growth. The plan set ambitious agricultural, industrial, and social goals for the next five years. Stalin wanted to double the production of oil and coal, and triple the output of steel.

Early Communist leader Leon Trotsky was killed in 1940 following a power struggle with Joseph Stalin.

Stalin intended the Five-Year Plan to turn the Soviet Union into a modern, industrialized society. The planners hoped that collective farming would produce enough food for the Soviet people as well as a surplus for export. Money received from farm exports would help pay for modern machinery. This new machinery would advance the growth of Soviet industry.

The Five-Year Plan caused hardships for the Soviet people. Government efforts to have peasants voluntarily join collective farms failed. The government then forced people to accept the policy. All farms were to be merged into collectives. Peasants had to join or suffer severe punishment. Those who tried to keep their lands faced execution, exile, or imprisonment. The government turned about 90 percent of the productive farmland into collective farms. The Five-Year Plan actually decreased agricultural production, however, and millions of people died as a result of famine and crop failure.

Despite such failures, the Soviet economy grew under the Five-Year Plan. For example, steel production increased dramatically. A second Five-Year Plan, even broader than the first, went into effect in 1933. Soviets who expected an increase in consumer goods or food supply as a reward for their hard work were disappointed. Production of consumer goods actually decreased. The government focused its efforts on expanding heavy industry, especially military production. Rather than a reward, the Soviet people faced harder times as consumer goods and food became scarcer.

✔ **READING CHECK: Evaluating** What effect did Stalin's Five-Year Plan have on Soviet life?

Stalin's Dictatorship

Before communism, the czars had used secret police and spies to maintain their absolute rule. Stalin, like Lenin, used similar tactics. Under Stalin the Soviet people were ruled by fear. People had to obey the demands of the Communist Party without complaint or face punishment such as imprisonment or death.

Religion and art were two areas of Soviet life that the government attempted to control. Soviet officials discouraged religious worship and seized the property of the Orthodox Church. Churches and Jewish houses of worship were destroyed or converted into public buildings. Government officials ordered the imprisonment and execution of many ministers, priests, and rabbis. They outlawed religious instruction in schools. The works of artists, musicians, and writers were subjected to government control and censorship. Artists were ordered to produce works of "socialist realism" as proof of their loyalty to the state.

The Great Kremlin Palace in Moscow, once the sprawling home of the Romanov czars, became a government office building under the Communists.

Government under Stalin. In 1936 Stalin proclaimed a new Soviet constitution. This constitution kept the basic framework of government that had existed under Lenin. The Supreme Soviet, the parliamentary body, met twice a year. The Council of People's Commissars, which later was renamed the Council of Ministers, held executive and administrative authority. On paper the Soviet government appeared to be democratic. In reality, however, most power lay in the hands of the **Politburo** (Political Bureau) of the Communist Party. The Supreme Soviet elected members to the Politburo, which was a small committee. Stalin controlled the Politburo. He was a dictator with almost complete authority.

Stalin's dictatorship grew harsher over time. In 1934 an important official in the Communist Party was assassinated. Stalin responded with a **purge**—a large-scale elimination—of party members who were supposedly disloyal to him. He used brutality, intimidation, and public trials staged for show to rid the party of members who he claimed were disloyal or were working against the interests of the state. The purge expanded to include the general population. People could be imprisoned without a trial for the most minor offenses.

The Soviet Union in 1936

Interpreting Maps The USSR included Russia, as well as as Azerbaijan, Uzbek, Kirghiz, and Georgia, among others.

■ **Skills Assessment: Human Systems** What cities' names show the influence of the Revolution?

Scholars estimate that by 1939 more than 5 million people had been arrested, deported, imprisoned in forced labor camps, or executed. One Soviet author recalled the injustice that a peasant experienced.

History Makers Speak

❝Another peasant, with six children, met a different fate. Because he had six mouths to feed he devoted himself whole-heartedly to collective farm work, and he kept hoping he would get some return for his labor. And he did—they awarded him a decoration. They awarded it at a special assembly, made speeches. In his reply, the peasant got carried away. He said, 'Now if I could just have a sack of flour instead of this decoration! Couldn't I somehow?' A wolflike laugh rocketed through the hall, and the newly decorated hero went off to exile, together with all six of those dependent mouths.❞

Aleksandr I. Solzhenitsyn, from *The Gulag Archipelago*

Foreign policy. The Soviet Union's foreign policy during the 1920s and 1930s was confusing. On the one hand, the new Communist government wanted other established nations to accept it. On the other hand, the Soviets supported the Communist International or **Comintern.** Lenin had founded this organization to spread the Communist revolution throughout the world. The Comintern worked to overthrow democracies by urging workers in other countries to rebel. These open calls for revolution caused fear and suspicion outside the Soviet Union.

✔ **READING CHECK:**
Summarizing What was the relationship between the ordinary Soviet citizen and the state during the era of Stalin's rule?

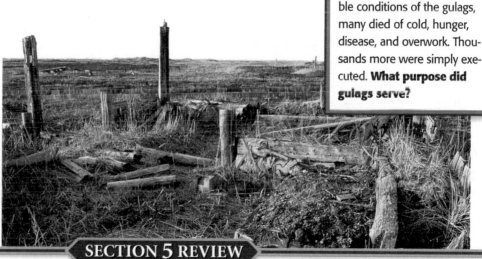

Remains of a Soviet gulag

SECTION 5 REVIEW

1. **Define** and explain the significance:
   collective farms
   command economy
   purge

2. **Identify** and explain the significance:
   New Economic Policy
   Leon Trotsky
   Joseph Stalin
   Five-Year Plan
   Politburo
   Comintern

3. **Comparing** Copy the chart below and use it to compare the NEP and the first Five-Year Plan.

	NEP	5 Yr. Plan
Consumer goods		
Economic freedom		
Agriculture		
Successes		
Failures		

4. **Finding the Main Idea**
   a. How did Joseph Stalin rise to power?
   b. Why did the Soviet system of government make the development of a police state possible?

5. **Writing and Critical Thinking**
   Drawing Inferences Imagine that you are a Soviet citizen living under Stalin's rule. Write a letter that you secretly smuggle to a friend in the United States. Your smuggled letter describes Soviet life.
   Consider:
   • Stalin's economic policies
   • life in the Stalinist police state

Homework Practice Online
keyword: SH3 HP19

Creating a Time Line

Copy the time line below on to a sheet of paper. Complete the time line by filling in the events, individuals, and dates from the chapter that you think were significant. Pick three events and explain why you think they were significant.

1920	1929	1936

Writing a Summary

Using standard grammar, spelling, sentence structure, and punctuation, write an overview of the events in the chapter.

Identifying People and Ideas

Identify the following terms or individuals and explain their significance:

1. Igor Stravinsky
2. cubism
3. economic nationalism
4. Franklin Roosevelt
5. general strike
6. Popular Front
7. fascism
8. Third Reich
9. collective farms
10. command economy

Understanding Main Ideas

Section 1 *(pp. 536–541)*
The Postwar Era

1. How did Freud's notion of the irrational and the subconscious influence postwar literature?
2. How did technology lead to advances in architecture?

Section 2 *(pp. 542–545)*
Postwar Prosperity Crumbles

3. What was the effect of the U.S. stock market crash in 1929?
4. What New Deal programs led to reforms in the American economy?

Section 3 *(pp. 546–550)*
Political Tensions After World War I

5. What economic and political problems did France face after World War I?
6. What economic and political problems did eastern European nations face after World War I?

Section 4 *(pp. 551–556)*
Fascist Dictatorships in Italy and Germany

7. What role did communism play in Mussolini's rise to power?

8. How did Hitler turn Germany into a police state after 1933?

Section 5 *(pp. 557–561)*
Dictatorship in the Soviet Union

9. What was the goal of the first Five-Year Plan?
10. How did Stalin insure loyalty from government and party officials and from the Soviet people?

Reviewing Themes

1. **Global Relations** Why did western European nations and the United States fail to respond to Germany's violations of the Treaty of Versailles?
2. **Government** How did Hitler use Germany's democratic system to gain control over the country?
3. **Culture** How did the work of Freud and Einstein influence culture during the 1920s?

Thinking Critically

1. **Evaluating** Why were Allied nations in western Europe more successful at remaining democratic after World War I?
2. **Drawing Conclusions** Why did nations practice economic nationalism if this policy only prolonged the depression?
3. **Identifying Cause and Effect** Why might there be a relationship between communist or fascist doctrines and the development of a police state?
4. **Finding the Main Idea** What was life like for the average Soviet citizen during the 1930s?

Writing About History

Comparing and Contrasting Use the chart below to explain similarities and differences between communism and fascism.

	Fascism	Communism
Class		
Private property		
Government authority		
Individual rights		

Using Artifacts as Historical Evidence

Study the photograph below. Then answer the questions that follow.

Classic 1920s U.S. touring car

1. Which of the following statements best summarizes the historical evidence this artifact gives?
    a. Some automobiles of this period were meant to be driven over long distances.
    b. All automobiles of this period were large.
    c. Only very wealthy people could afford to own an automobile.
    d. Some automobiles of this period may have been designed to be symbols of comfort and luxury.

2. What can you infer about 1920s lifestyles in the United States from this artifact? Give specific examples.

Linking Literature to History

Read the following excerpt from the 1934 "Ballad of Roosevelt" by poet Langston Hughes, a leader of the Harlem Renaissance. Then answer the questions.

> "Sister got sick
> And the doctor wouldn't come
> Cause we couldn't pay him
> The proper sum—
> A-waitin' on Roosevelt,
> Roosevelt, Roosevelt,
> A-waitin' on Roosevelt.
> Then one day
> They put us out o' the house.
> Ma and Pa was
> Meek as a mouse
> Still waitin' on Roosevelt,
> Roosevelt, Roosevelt."

3. Which statement best describes the author's main point?
    a. Many families lost their homes during the depression.
    b. Roosevelt's relief programs did not do enough to help.
    c. Even though many people were poor during the depression, they did not complain.
    d. Medical services were almost nonexistent during the depression.

4. How does the author's view of the depression compare with what really happened? Give specific examples.

Alternative Assessment

Building Your Portfolio

Link to TODAY

Life for many during the years of the Great Depression was a struggle to survive in the face of nearly overwhelming economic hardship. Use the library, the Internet, and other sources to research living conditions in the United States, Great Britain, France, or another industrialized nation during the depression. Then use pictures, drawings, or other visual images to build a collage that reflects your findings.

internet connect

Internet Activity: go.hrw.com
KEYWORD: SH3 WH19

Choose a topic on the Great Depression and the Rise of Totalitarianism to:
- create a pamphlet on the Spanish Civil War.
- create a graph and database on U.S. economic cycles.
- write journal entries from the point of view of a teenager living in the Great Depression.

1898–1938

Nationalist Movements Around the World

Empress Dowager Tz'u-hsi

c. 1906
Politics
Mohandas Gandhi begins his first campaign of non-violent resistance to British colonial rule.

Cartoon depicting European countries dividing China

1909
Business and Finance
The Anglo-Persian Oil Company is formed.

1900
Global Events
The Boxer Rebellion is suppressed.

1910
Global Events
Japan annexes Korea.

1900

1910

1898
Politics
Empress Dowager Tz'u-hsi begins her rule of China.

c. 1898
Science and Technology
Japanese scientist Kiyoshi Shiga discovers the bacteria responsible for dysentery.

1902
Science and Technology
The Aswan Dam in Egypt opens.

1904–1905
Global Events
The Russo-Japanese War occurs.

1908
Daily Life
Cairo University opens.

1912
Politics
The Republic of China is formed.

Aswan Dam, Egypt

Build on What You Know

The world struggled to recover after World War I. However, just as the economies of many countries were beginning to fully recover from the war, the Great Depression struck. The United States dealt with the Depression by instituting President Franklin Roosevelt's New Deal. In some European countries the economic turmoil of the 1930s helped lead to the rise of dictatorships. In this chapter, you will learn about revolutionary movements that took place in other parts of the world and what effects they had on the politics and economies of the countries.

Reza Shah Pahlavi of Persia

1921
Politics
Reza Shah Pahlavi takes control of Persia.

1923
Politics
Transjordan is proclaimed an independent state under the British Mandate.

1923
Daily Life
Mustafa Kemal begins a program of sweeping civil and cultural change in Turkey.

c. 1928
Business and Finance
Overproduction of coffee disrupts Brazil's economy.

1931
Politics
The Statute of Westminster grants autonomy within the British Commonwealth to Australia, New Zealand, Canada, and South Africa as independent nations.

Red and green coffee beans still on the branch

1935
Global Events
Great Britain grants India a constitution.

1920 | **1930** | **1940**

1919
Global Events
Nationalist uprisings against British rule begin in Egypt.

1919
Politics
British troops kill 400 Indian demonstrators for self-government at Amritsar.

1922
Science and Technology
The tomb of King Tutankhamen is discovered.

1922
The Arts
Mori Ogai, creator of modern Japanese literature, dies.

c. 1922
The Arts
Diego Rivera begins his first mural, *Creation*.

1922–1930
Science and Technology
Dinosaur fossils are found in the Gobi Desert.

1925
Politics
Universal men's suffrage is granted in Japan.

1938
Business and Finance
Oil companies in Mexico are nationalized.

1936
Global Events
King Farouk begins ruling Egypt under a newly established constitutional monarchy.

1934–1935
Politics
Mao Zedong emerges as a leader during the Long March in China.

Mao's statue in Kashgar, China

What's Your Opinion?

Themes Journal *Do you **agree** or **disagree** with the following statements? Support your point of view in your journal.*

Government The military should have an active role in government.

Culture The intensity of people's nationalistic feelings can be influenced by their culture.

Economics An economic crisis in a nation is distinct from a political crisis.

The British Empire in the Postwar Era

READ TO DISCOVER

❶ What caused British rule in Egypt and the Middle East to end?

❷ How did the people of India pursue their desire for independence?

❸ How did the British respond to calls for change in other parts of the empire?

DEFINE

passive resistance

IDENTIFY

Wafd Party
Anglo-Egyptian Treaty
Zionism
Balfour Declaration
Mohandas Gandhi

▶**WHY IT MATTERS TODAY**

The Suez Canal remains an important pathway for international trade. Use or other **current event** sources to identify the role of the Suez Canal in the world economy today. Record your findings in your journal.

CNN ᔆᵗᵘᵈᵉⁿᵗNews.com

The Main Idea
After World War I, British colonies in many parts of the world began to demand more freedom.

The Story Continues *During the height of British imperialism a popular expression said, "The sun never sets on the British Empire." In the late 1800s and early 1900s, that statement was true. The British Empire was so widespread that, at any given moment, some part of the empire somewhere in the world was having daylight. This fact, however, would begin to change after World War I, as Britain began to lose control over parts of its vast empire.*

Egypt and the Middle East

After World War I many of Britain's colonies began demanding self-rule. Dealing with these nationalist movements was difficult because of the vastness of the empire.

Independence for Egypt. Although the Ottoman Empire officially ruled Egypt, the British had in fact controlled the country since 1882. When the Ottomans joined the Central Powers in 1914, the British declared Egypt a protectorate. After World War I a strong nationalist movement developed in Egypt, led by the **Wafd Party.** In 1919 the party led a popular revolt against the British. Although the British quickly put down this revolt, calls for independence continued. Finally, in 1922, the British declared Egypt independent. However, the British government would leave military forces there to defend Egypt and the Suez Canal. Britain also maintained administrative control over the Sudan, which included the Upper Nile, and wanted to oversee Egypt's foreign policy.

During the 1920s and early 1930s, the Egyptian independence movement grew stronger. Egyptian nationalists wanted complete freedom from Britain. After Italy invaded Ethiopia, an alarmed Egypt and Britain forged the **Anglo-Egyptian Treaty** of 1936, which gave Egypt greater independence. The treaty provided the British military with a garrison in Egypt for 20 years. The two nations pledged to support each other if war broke out in the Middle East, and Britain sponsored Egypt's membership in the League of Nations. Many Egyptians, however, were not satisfied because British troops were still stationed throughout Egypt.

INTERPRETING THE VISUAL RECORD

The Suez Canal The Suez Canal (circled in the photo at the left) connects the Mediterranean Sea and the Red Sea. *Based on this picture, why would the British consider it important to retain control of the Suez Canal?*

The Size of the British Empire

Graphs, as you have learned, are visual presentations of information. Just as interpreting graphs is an important part of reading and comprehending history, so too is the ability to create them. The ability to make graphs allows you to organize material in a way that often makes it easier to understand and remember. Making graphs out of information, such as the population of the British Empire, can help you gain a better understanding of the topic.

The British Empire was vast not only in territory, but also in population. The mandates following World War I increased the empire to its fullest extent. But the British government and military was not as strong as it had been during the buildup of its empire. As nationalist movements arose in its colonies, the British were unable to maintain their grasp on the empire.

Size and Population of Selected Dominions within the British Empire, c. 1920		
Country	Area under British control (in square miles)	Population under British control (approximate)
India	1,802,629	306,000,000
Australia	2,967,909	5,000,000
Canada	3,851,809	8,788,000
South Africa	471,445	6,250,000
Rest of empire	3,006,208	69,962,000
British Empire total	12,100,000	396,000,000

Shown above are Indians protesting the Simon Commission, which was appointed by the British government to examine British rule in India. The commission met with opposition because it included no Indians.

Skills Reminder

To create a graph from written text, determine the focus and title of the graph. Then decide which type of graph will provide the best visual summary of the material. A line graph plots changes in quantities over time. A bar graph is most often used to compare amounts within categories. A pie graph, or circle graph, divides a circular whole into sections, with the whole equaling 100 percent. Identify the necessary data. Create the graph.

Skills Practice

❶ Using the data above, build a graph showing the percentage of the land area of the British Empire represented by each country. Build another graph showing the percentages of the empire's population by country.

❷ Using your library or the Internet, research other statistical data about one of the countries discussed in this chapter and use that information to create a graph.

The Middle East. Middle Eastern Arabs had helped the British during World War I. They therefore felt betrayed when both Britain and France imposed control on them after the war. Britain eventually recognized the independence of both Transjordan and Iraq, but maintained a strong military presence in both kingdoms. Meanwhile, the British kept complete control over Palestine because of its strategic location. Events in Palestine, however, soon presented Britain with a serious problem.

Since the late 1800s, Jews from Europe had been establishing small colonies in Palestine. A nationalist movement called **Zionism** aimed to build a Palestinian homeland for Jews. In 1917 Britain was seeking support among Jews for the Allied war effort. To win it, British foreign secretary Arthur Balfour wrote to a Zionist leader, expressing British support for a Jewish homeland. Balfour's statement later became known as the **Balfour Declaration.** It became the basis of Great Britain's mandate for Palestine and, for the next 30 years, strongly shaped British policies in the region.

"His Majesty's Government view with favour the establishment in Palestine of a national home for the Jewish people, . . . it being clearly understood that nothing should be done which may prejudice the civil and religious rights of existing non-Jewish communities in Palestine. . . ."

Lord Balfour, Balfour Declaration

The British had also promised to allow the creation of an independent Arab state that included parts of Palestine in exchange for helping defeat the Ottomans. After World War I, both the Jews and Arabs expected Great Britain to make good on its promises. Tensions rose and clashes erupted between the two groups. To calm Arab fears, the British limited the number of Jews allowed to immigrate to Palestine. The Jews resented this policy. When the Nazis began persecuting them, Jewish immigration to Palestine increased. In 1937 the British declared that a Zionist homeland and Arab independence were incompatible. It recommended dividing the land between the groups. World War II delayed action on this plan.

✔ **READING CHECK: Analyzing Information** Why did the British make promises to both the Arabs and Jews?

The Independence Movement in India

India was Great Britain's largest colony. In return for Indian troops and money during World War I, Britain had promised India more self-government. After the war, however, the British were divided on the issue. Some felt that Indian self-rule would lead to the empire's destruction. Others believed that self-rule should be granted to India as it had been to other parts of the British Empire.

Indians, too, disagreed on independence. Some Indians, including some who had been educated in the West, wanted to continue under British rule. Indian nationalists called for complete independence. Any settlement would have to accommodate the diverse views in India—of both Muslims and Hindus, of both upper castes and lower castes, and of different regions.

The leader of the Indian nationalist movement was **Mohandas Gandhi.** Many Indians revered Gandhi as a spiritual as well as a political leader. Gandhi opposed violence. He urged the people to gain independence by nonviolently refusing to

HISTORY MAKER

**Mohandas Gandhi
(1869–1948)**

A member of an Indian merchant class family, Mohandas Gandhi became a lawyer. While practicing law in South Africa, however, he confronted racist attitudes. Beginning in about 1906 Gandhi began his first campaign of non-violent resistance to achieve justice.

In 1914 Gandhi returned to India. A massacre of Hindus by British authorities convinced him that India must strive for complete independence. As a leader in the Indian National Congress, Gandhi worked toward that goal. His humble manner and attire inspired millions and earned him great respect. His followers called him Mahatma, or "Great Soul." Gandhi was assassinated in 1948. **How would you characterize Gandhi's life and work?**

cooperate with the government, a form of civil disobedience called **passive resistance.** Gandhi described his feelings about passive resistance as follows:

History Makers Speak

"I believe in the doctrine of non-violence as a weapon of the strongest. I believe that a man is the strongest soldier for daring to die unarmed with his breast bare before the enemy."

Mohandas Gandhi, quoted in *The Story of a Nation,* by Gulam Ali Alanna

Passive resistance included boycotting British goods and refusing to pay taxes. To control this nationalist movement, the British restricted civil liberties and forcibly broke up political gatherings. Many moderate Indians turned against British rule.

In 1935 Great Britain allowed India to elect representatives. However, it still controlled India's defense, revenue, and foreign policy. The British could also veto laws proposed by the representatives. Efforts for complete independence continued.

✔ **READING CHECK: Drawing Inferences** What factors within Indian society contributed to diverse views on Indian independence?

> **Analyzing Primary Sources**
>
> **Making Predictions** How might a nonviolent refusal to cooperate with a ruling government produce victory for nationalists?

The Commonwealth Expands

Even in parts of the British Empire that had some self-government, the people sought more. After World War I, the dominions of Canada, Australia, New Zealand, and South Africa wanted complete self-government. Great Britain agreed and in 1931 granted these four dominions autonomy. They joined with Great Britain as equal partners in the British Commonwealth of Nations. Each member became responsible for its own policies. Over the years, other British colonies became independent and joined the Commonwealth. Favorable trade agreements among member nations helped their economies during the depression that faced many countries after World War I. The Commonwealth, therefore, worked well economically for both Great Britain and its former colonies.

✔ **READING CHECK: Identifying Cause and Effect** Why did colonies that had achieved independence agree to join in the British Commonwealth?

> **Holt Researcher**
> go.hrw.com
> **KEYWORD:** Holt Researcher
> **FreeFind:** Mohandas Gandhi
> After reading more about Mohandas Gandhi on the Holt Researcher, write an analysis of his influence on events of the 20th century.

SECTION 1 REVIEW

1. **Define** and explain the significance: passive resistance

2. **Identify** and explain the significance:
   Wafd Party
   Anglo-Egyptian Treaty
   Zionism
   Balfour Declaration
   Mohandas Gandhi

3. **Sequencing** Make a flowchart like the one below. Use it to list the important stages of Egypt's national status after World War I.

1919   1922   1920s–30s   1936

4. **Finding the Main Idea**
   a. How did Great Britain's relationship with Egypt change over time?
   b. What role did Zionism play in Palestine's efforts toward independence?
   c. How did the people of India work for self-rule?
   d. How did the British respond to calls for change in other parts of their empire?

5. **Writing and Critical Thinking**
   Identifying Bias Write a brief explanation of what various groups might gain or lose by making India independent or by having it remain under British rule.
   Consider:
   • how independence would benefit citizens of India
   • why the existence of different religious and social groups presented a problem for independence

Homework Practice Online
keyword: SH3 HP20

Turkey, Persia, and Africa

The Main Idea
After World War I nationalist movements gained political influence in Turkey, Persia, and Africa.

The Story Continues *The nationalist ideas that swept the Middle East and India after World War I did not stop there. New political forces began to stir in other colonies and remnants of old empires. Change would not come easily, however. As one new leader would declare, "We must teach our people to be free."*

Turkey Under Kemal

After its defeat in World War I, the once mighty Ottoman Empire was stripped of all its land except Turkey. Greek troops arrived to impose the peace treaty's terms, and the weak Ottoman government could do nothing to prevent their increasing grip on the country.

Then **Mustafa Kemal,** a hero of the fighting at Gallipoli, stepped forward. Kemal and his nationalist followers took control of the assembly. Declaring that the sultan was controlled by Turkey's enemies, the assembly appointed a council headed by Kemal to run the country. Kemal's forces drove the Greeks from Turkey in 1922. That same year the assembly did away with the sultanate. In 1923 it established the Republic of Turkey and moved the capital to Ankara. Kemal became the republic's first president. The government became a one-party system led by the president.

Kemal believed that the war had shown the superiority of Western technology and Western ideas of nationalism. He worked to modernize and westernize Turkey. Believing that Islam was a roadblock to modernization, he drew up a new constitution that ended the long union of Islam and the government. He abolished the position of caliph, imposed broad civil and social reforms, and abandoned the Islamic calendar.

Kemal ordered the Turkish people to adopt Western ways. He prohibited the wearing of traditional clothing and decreed that all Turks take surnames. He himself took the name Atatürk, meaning "father of the Turks." Kemal also established secular schools and colleges and replaced the Arabic-based Turkish alphabet with the Latin alphabet. He supported laws that gave women the right to vote and hold office. His economic programs included state-run industries and subsidized farming. Under Kemal, Turkey became more prosperous.

✔ **READING CHECK: Drawing Inferences** Why did Mustafa Kemal feel it was necessary to separate the government from Islam in order to carry out his programs?

INTERPRETING THE VISUAL RECORD
Mustafa Kemal It was Mustafa Kemal who declared that the people must be taught to be free. *What does Kemal's appearance here tell you about his view of Western things?*

Modernizing Persia

Turkey's neighbor, Persia, had never been under the control of the Ottoman Empire. Shahs of the Qajar dynasty had ruled Persia since the 1700s. By about 1900, however, both Great Britain and Russia had begun to exert a strong influence on the Persian government.

In 1921 Reza Khan, a Persian army officer with strong nationalist feelings, seized control of the government. Four years later, he deposed the ruling shah and took the throne, taking the title **Reza Shah Pahlavi.**

Like Mustafa Kemal, Reza Shah wanted to modernize his country and free it from foreign domination. He strengthened the army and broke the power of rebellious tribes. Under a massive reform program, he built roads and hospitals, established a university, and gave women more rights. Transportation and communication were improved, and new industries were begun. In 1935 Reza Shah announced that the country would be officially called what its people called it—Iran.

Iran's constitution called for a limited monarchy, but Reza Shah held most of the power. He strictly controlled the press and suppressed political parties. His secret police ruthlessly put down any opposition to his government. Reza Shah's foreign policy of balancing British and Russian interests led him to seek closer ties with Germany. This alliance would eventually cause his downfall.

✔ **READING CHECK: Supporting a Point of View** How would you support the view that Reza Shah was effective in modernizing Persia?

New Nations in the Middle East, 1922–1939

Interpreting Maps With the formation of new countries in the Middle East, control over vital areas, such as the Strait of Hormuz, became important.

■ **Skills Assessment:**
1. The World in Spatial Terms What two countries controlled the land surrounding the Strait of Hormuz?
2. Analyzing Information Why would the Strait of Hormuz be important?

YOUNG PEOPLE IN HISTORY

Missionary Schools
The first experience that many Africans had with Western ideas and culture came from Christian missionary schools. Students learned to read and write in English and were taught the Christian faith with stories from the Bible. Many missionaries learned the languages and the customs of the Africans in order to live and work among them. **What did students learn in missionary schools?**

Holt Researcher

go.hrw.com
KEYWORD: Holt Researcher
FreeFind: Nnamdi Azikiwe
Jomo Kenyatta
After reading more about Azikiwe and Kenyatta on the Holt Researcher, create a time line marking the major events in their anticolonial movements.

Africans Call for Change

The many Africans who fought in the armies of Great Britain and France during World War I expected to be rewarded. They wanted greater political freedom after the war. Like the Indians, they were disappointed.

Increased political activity. The war had broadened the experience of many Africans. For the first time, they encountered the world beyond their villages and families. When these former soldiers returned home, they brought with them new ideas about freedom and nationalism. In time, they put these ideas to work organizing anticolonial protest movements. Colonial education also moved many Africans to become politically active. Missionary and government schools taught African students Western ideals of equality and self-rule. At the same time, the colonial governments denied Africans these rights. More and more Africans personally experienced the contradiction between Western teaching and their lives under colonialism. They became determined that change must come. Racism and political repression made many Africans actively seek reform and even independence.

New political associations and leaders. Africans began to organize. Tanganyika, for example, was a former German colony whose mandate had been given to Britain. Tanganyikans formed a civil servants' association. Open to all Africans, it overcame traditional ethnic barriers and became a center of anticolonial protest. Other labor unions and workers' associations also became important forums for African complaints. In response, colonial governments strengthened the authority of tribal chiefs, who generally favored colonial rule. Colonial rulers also agreed to some reforms. However, these small efforts could not stem the rising tide of opposition to colonialism. By the 1930s Africans increasingly demanded independence rather than reform.

The loudest calls for independence came from a group of young men who had been educated in the West. **Nnamdi Azikiwe** (ah-ZEEK-wah) of Nigeria, **Jomo Kenyatta** of Kenya, and **Léopold Senghor** of Senegal led the anticolonial movement. Following Gandhi's example, they organized demonstrations and other actions against colonial rulers. They used Western methods of political organization to attract support.

✔ **READING CHECK: Summarizing** What factors contributed to the increase in political activity and calls for nationalism in Africa after World War I?

SECTION 2 REVIEW

1. **Identify** and explain the significance:
   Mustafa Kemal
   Reza Shah Pahlavi
   Nnamdi Azikiwe
   Jomo Kenyatta
   Léopold Senghor

2. **Analyzing Information** Copy the chart below. Use it to note the main steps toward nationalization and modernization after World War I.

Turkey	Persia	Africa

↓   ↓   ↓
Nationalization and modernization

3. **Finding the Main Idea**
   a. Compare and contrast the modernization programs of Mustafa Kemal and Reza Shah Pahlavi.
   b. What factors aided the struggle for independence in Africa after World War I?

4. **Writing and Critical Thinking**
   Making Generalizations Write a summary explanation of why the period after World War I led to a rise in nationalist movements in Turkey, Persia, and Africa.
   Consider:
   • the experiences that people had during the war
   • how the success of Western technology influenced both citizens and leaders

Homework Practice Online
keyword: SH3 HP20

READ TO DISCOVER

❶ How did resentment of foreign interests lead to the downfall of the Qing dynasty?

❷ In what ways did the nationalist movement in China change under the leadership of Sun Yixian and Chiang Kai-shek?

❸ How did communism develop in China?

IDENTIFY

Open Door Policy
Empress Dowager Tz'u-hsi
Boxer Rebellion
Kuomintang
Sun Yixian
Chiang Kai-shek
Long March
Mao Zedong

▶ WHY IT MATTERS TODAY

Today the Nationalist Chinese occupy the island of Taiwan off the coast of mainland China. Use CNN NEWS.com or other **current event** sources to identify the issues that exist between the People's Republic of China and Taiwan. Record your findings in your journal.

CNN student News.com

Unrest in China

The Main Idea
In the early 1900s Chinese nationalists fought foreign influence in their country and then each other.

The Story Continues *The increasing influence of Western powers in China caused divisions within the country. Increasingly dissatisfied with the monarchy, some Chinese launched a nationalist movement to regain Chinese power and glory through Western ideals of government. "In comparison with other nations, we have the greatest population and the oldest culture, of four thousand years' duration," noted one nationalist leader. The nationalists hoped that their movement would continue this great tradition.*

The End of the Qing Dynasty

By about 1900 the imperialist powers of France, Germany, Great Britain, Japan, and Russia enjoyed substantial spheres of influence in China. The foreign powers stayed mainly on the coast and along the Chang River. At the turn of the century, however, foreign traders increasingly moved deeper into China's interior.

The United States was concerned that American merchants would be excluded from Chinese trade. In 1899 the U.S. government appealed to other nations to recognize what it called the **Open Door Policy.** Under this policy, all nations would have equal rights to trade in China. Other countries, however, were vague in their responses to the U.S. appeal. The scramble for trade privileges continued.

The Boxer Rebellion. By the end of the 1800s, foreign powers had won numerous trade concessions and privileges. Foreign interests dominated the Chinese economy and government. Traders and missionaries traveled the country at will. China's fate as a secondary nation seemed sealed.

In 1898 the young Qing emperor hoped to reduce foreign interference by revitalizing his government and modernizing China. The country's conservative leaders were offended by these drastic cultural changes. The emperor's aging aunt, the **Empress Dowager Tz'u-hsi** (TSOO·SHEE), took action. The emperor was imprisoned, and for the next ten years Tz'u-hsi ruled China.

Tz'u-hsi's officials encouraged anti-foreigner movements that were breaking out, including a group called the Society of the Righteous and Harmonious Fists. In the English language the members of this group became known simply as Boxers. The Boxers attacked first Chinese Christians and, later, foreign missionaries. When they began attacking foreigners throughout China, the uprising became known as the **Boxer Rebellion.** The Boxers destroyed churches, railways, mines—anything connected with outsiders. Many foreigners fled to embassies in Beijing. There they came under siege by an army of angry Boxers.

Determined to protect their interests in China, imperialist nations sent an army to Beijing. Soldiers from Great Britain, France, Germany, Russia, Japan, and the United States put down the Boxer Rebellion in 1900. The foreign powers then imposed heavy penalties on the Chinese, including fines for destroyed property. They also claimed the right to maintain troops in Beijing and along the Beijing-Tianjian

Empress Dowager Tz'u-hsi (1835–1908)

As a young girl growing up in the imperial court, Tz'u-hsi witnessed the effects of the Opium War and the Taiping Rebellion. She was also present when the British and French occupied Beijing in 1860 and destroyed the emperor's summer palace. She became a bitter opponent of Western influence.

As regent for Chinese emperors, Tz'u-hsi dominated China for decades. Called "Old Buddha" by Westerners, she prevented many reforms. For example, she diverted funds for a new navy to rebuild the summer palace. **Why might the Empress Dowager Tz'u-hsi have opposed Western reform?**

Foreign Influence in China, 1839–1912

Interpreting Maps European powers claimed control over large portions of China.

■ **Skills Assessment: Human Systems** Which country with a sphere of influence in China was least likely to be affected by the Boxer Rebellion?

Railway to the coast. The crushing of the Boxer Rebellion brought China completely under foreign domination.

Overthrow of the dynasty. The Boxer Rebellion failed to drive foreigners from Chinese soil. It did, however, encourage nationalist sentiment among the Chinese people, especially the young and well educated. A new political party, the **Kuomintang,** or Chinese Nationalist Party, grew out of the nationalists' desire for reform. The party's director was **Sun Yixian** (also known as Sun Yat-sen). He had lived in the United States, attended school in Hawaii, and studied medicine at two medical schools in Hong Kong. Sun Yixian described the necessity of nationalism to his fellow Chinese:

History Makers Speak

❝The Chinese people have only family and clan groups; there is no national spirit. Consequently, . . . we are the poorest and weakest state in the world. . . . If we do not earnestly promote nationalism and weld together . . . we face a tragedy—the loss of our country and the destruction of our race.❞

Sun Yixian, quoted in *A Treasury of the World's Great Speeches,* edited by Houston Peterson

The nationalists were influenced by the Western ideas of Sun Yixian and others. They wanted a constitutional government with civil liberties guaranteed by a bill of rights. They also wanted China to become industrialized so that it could defend itself economically against imperialist powers. The nationalists believed that China could protect itself against foreign control only if it became a modern nation.

Pressured by the nationalists, the Qing rulers attempted reforms, including the promise of a new constitution. Nationalists, merchants, and powerful rural families, however, wanted a complete break from "Old China" and an end to the Qing dynasty. In 1911 army officers supporting Sun Yixian led a series of revolts in southern China. The leader of the imperial army, Yuan Shikai, did not respond with force. Instead he negotiated, hoping for a new dynasty with himself in a position of power. No agreement was reached, however, and the 268-year Qing dynasty ended.

✔ **READING CHECK: Drawing Inferences** Why might Chinese nationalists have wanted a leader who had been educated by the Western nations from which they wanted freedom?

Sun Yixian, pictured here with his wife, worked to create a national spirit among the Chinese.

Forming the Chinese Republic

In February 1912 the Kuomintang forced the last Qing emperor to abdicate. It then proclaimed China a republic. Sun Yixian described the Kuomintang philosophy as the "Three Principles of the People"—the people's government, the people's rights, and the people's livelihood. The principles called for (1) political unification and an end to foreign influence; (2) a gradual change to democratic government, with full personal liberties and rights for all Chinese people; and (3) economic improvements that included industrialization and a more equal distribution of land.

Problems with the warlords. Revolution and assassination marked the early years of the Republic of China. Yuan Shikai became president, and Sun Yixian fled to Japan. Yuan tried to start his own imperial dynasty. He failed, but China was in turmoil. Powerful warlords ruled most of the country with their personal armies.

The Nationalists—as members of the Kuomintang called themselves—hoped to defeat the warlords and establish a strong central government for the Republic of China. They asked for help from foreign powers, but only the Soviet Union responded. In the early 1920s, the Soviets sent technical, political, and military advisers to help build a modern Chinese army.

Under Chiang Kai-shek, the Nationalist army slowly unified China, but political forces split.

A split in the Kuomintang. When Sun Yixian died in 1925, military commander **Chiang Kai-shek** (CHANG KY·SHEK) took over leadership of the Nationalists. Under Chiang the Nationalist army grew stronger. In 1926 Chiang began a military campaign against the warlords called the Northern Expedition. Warlord resistance collapsed against the efficient, highly motivated Nationalist troops. The Nationalists quickly gained control of Hunan province and the cities of the Wuhan area.

Not all members of the Kuomintang were satisfied. The left wing of the party, made up of socialists and Communists, wanted more power for the peasants and workers. The conservative right wing opposed such radical change, particularly redistributing land to the peasants. Chiang became leader of the right wing.

In 1927 Chiang expelled all Soviet advisers from the country and moved against the party's left-wing members. Troops loyal to Chiang attacked the Communist stronghold of Shanghai. They arrested and executed large numbers of Communists. Chiang now believed that the Communists were no longer a threat to his leadership. He established a Nationalist government in Nanjing.

The Nanjing government. Chiang and his followers wanted a strong, efficient government. They did not, however, want a democratic one. They set up a one-party system with Chiang as virtual dictator.

Chiang's attempts to promote industrialization were limited by a lack of capital. Much government revenue was spent on defense. Foreign control of China's natural resources also slowed economic development. Even so, the areas of China under Nationalist control made progress. Massive construction projects of roads and railroads were begun. A national bank was established, and education was improved.

The Nationalists failed to deal with two crucial problems, however. They did not change the oppressive system of land ownership because they wanted the support of landowners and merchants. They also failed to change tax collection methods. In short, they did little to eliminate the suffering and discontent of Chinese peasants.

✔ **READING CHECK: Making Predictions** How might the peasants react to the Nationalists' failure to help them?

The Growth of Chinese Communism

In July 1921 a small group of Chinese intellectuals met in Shanghai and founded the Chinese Communist Party. They were inspired by the example of the Russian Revolution and the ideas of Marx and Lenin. The founders of Chinese communism hoped to free their country from foreign domination and economic backwardness. At first, they set about building strong party organizations and labor unions in the cities. They cooperated with the Kuomintang to defeat the regional warlords.

When the Kuomintang was weak and in need of support, the Nationalists welcomed Communists. As the Communist Party grew stronger, however, conservative Nationalists became alarmed. The 1927 executions of the Shanghai Communists by Chiang's troops ended the alliance. In the early 1930s, when Chiang realized that he had failed to destroy the Communists, he undertook several large-scale military operations to eliminate communism for good.

The Long March. The Communists who escaped the purge of 1927 fled first to Jiangxi province in southeastern China. There they set up their own government, modeled after the Russian communist regime. Nationalist forces repeatedly attacked the Communists in 1934. As the Nationalists' assaults became more destructive, the Communists were forced to evacuate from Jiangxi.

In the now-famous **Long March,** which lasted more than a year, about 100,000 Communists made their way on foot from Jiangxi to Shaanxi province in northwestern China. They were chased by Nationalist troops and strafed by aircraft while crossing 18 mountain ranges and 24 rivers. Many died on the 6,000-mile trip. Those who survived, along with Communists already in Shaanxi, established their headquarters in the isolated mountain town of Yan'an. On this trip, a charismatic young man named **Mao Zedong** (MOW ZUH·DUHNG) established himself as a leader.

Mao Zedong. Mao was born in the countryside of southeastern Hunan province. He had long argued that Chinese peasants, not the urban proletariat, could provide the best basis for a communist revolution in China. Finally, in a rural area far from the major cities of China, he had a chance to prove his argument. In Shaanxi province, Mao and his followers put the programs of land and tax reform advocated by the Communists into practice. To help ensure success, they met with peasants and listened to their problems. The Communists also explained China's problems at a national level to the peasants and urged them to support the revolution.

At first the peasants, suspicious of outsiders, did not trust the Communists. When they found that the Communists were trying to understand and help them, however, the peasants joined their cause. Many volunteered to serve in the Communist army, called the Red Army. Others provided useful information about the location and movement of Nationalist troops. With peasant support, the Communists rebuilt their strength and resisted Nationalist attempts to destroy them.

In addition, there was a growing threat from Japanese militarism. Many Chinese felt that Chiang Kai-shek should face this threat instead of fighting other Chinese. Support for communism grew among those who believed that Japan was the true enemy.

✔ **READING CHECK: Identifying Cause and Effect** What problems helped the Communists take hold in China?

Civil War in China, 1925–1935

Interpreting Maps In the cities and countryside, the Chinese people suffered tremendous upheaval as Nationalists, Communists, and warlords vied for control.

■ **Skills Assessment: Human Systems** What does the difficult and indirect path of the Long March suggest about the conditions the Communists faced?

Map legend:
- ▨ Area controlled by Kuomintang, 1925
- → The Long March, 1934–1935
- ✷ Kuomintang victories over the warlords
- ✷ Kuomintang strikes against the Communists
- ▨ Japanese territory

SECTION 3 REVIEW

1. Identify and explain the significance:
Open Door Policy
Empress Dowager Tz'u-hsi
Boxer Rebellion
Kuomintang
Sun Yixian
Chiang Kai-shek
Long March
Mao Zedong

2. Summarizing Copy the diagram below. Use it to summarize the roles and actions of Chinese leaders in the early 1900s.

Tz'u-hsi — Sun Yixian
Chinese leaders
Chiang Kai-shek — Mao Zedong

3. **Finding the Main Idea**
a. What were some of the factors that led to the fall of the Qing dynasty?
b. How did the Nationalist movement grow and change under the leadership of Chiang Kai-shek?
c. What factors led to the rise of communism in China?

4. **Writing and Critical Thinking**

Supporting a Point of View Imagine that you are a member of either the Nationalist or Chinese Communist Party. Write a speech to convince others of the value of what you are working for.
Consider:
• what each party wanted to accomplish
• the methods each party used to achieve its goals

Homework Practice Online
go.hrw.com
keyword: SH3 HP20

READ TO DISCOVER

❶ Why and how did the Japanese pursue a policy of expansion beginning in the late 1800s?

❷ How did Japanese life change during rapid modernization?

❸ What effect did the military begin to have on Japan during the 1920s and the 1930s?

IDENTIFY

Russo-Japanese War
Treaty of Portsmouth

▶ **WHY IT MATTERS TODAY**

The success of Japan's military in the early 1900s led to further attempts at expansion and aggression. Their defeat in World War II forced them to change direction. Use CNN or other **current event** sources to find out what Japan's goals are today. Write your findings in your journal.

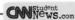

Imperialism in Japan

The Main Idea
A policy of expansion, along with a growing militarism, marked Japan in the early 1900s.

The Story Continues *Dancing the fox trot. Listening to jazz. Playing baseball. This was Japan in the 1920s. Japan had begun to modernize as early as the late 1800s. Over the next 50 years many Japanese adopted Western ideas concerning industry, democracy, and society, as well as arts and entertainment. They would also take on imperialist ideas of their own.*

Japanese Expansion

The reforms begun by the Meiji Restoration changed Japan into a modern industrial and military power. This power allowed Japan to begin a policy of expansion in the late 1800s. Japan wanted to extend its influence for two reasons. First, new territory would provide both raw materials for Japan's growing industries and markets for its products. Second, expansion would show Western nations just how far Japan had progressed.

Korea and Manchuria. Japan had long been interested in Korea. The Treaty of Shimonoseki that ended the Sino-Japanese War in 1895 provided for Korean independence. Soon, however, Japan dominated the Korean government.

Japan then looked to Manchuria. After the Boxer Rebellion, most foreign powers withdrew their troops from China. However, many Russian troops stayed in Manchuria. Russia had forced a lease from the Chinese to extend a railway line across Manchuria. It had leased a port from China as well. To Japan, the Russians looked set to dominate Manchuria.

In 1902, believing that war with Russia was likely, Japan signed an alliance with Great Britain. They agreed that both countries had the right to protect their interests in China, Manchuria, and Korea against a third power. If either country went to war with a single power, the other would remain neutral. If a third power joined the conflict, they would aid each other. Russia was the obvious target of the alliance.

The Japanese 1st Infantry in battle

The Anglo-Japanese alliance meant great prestige for Japan. It now had the support of one of the world's great powers. The alliance increased pressure on Russia to withdraw from Manchuria. Diplomatic attempts failed, however. In January 1904 Japan issued an ultimatum to Russia. Russia refused to answer Japan's demands.

The Russo-Japanese War. In February 1904, without declaring war, Japan attacked and badly damaged the Russian fleet at Port Arthur in Manchuria. Soon after, the Japanese military overran Korea and, throughout the summer of 1904, pushed the Russians back through Manchuria. In February and March of 1905, some 330,000 Russian troops and 270,000 Japanese troops fought a great battle at Mukden. Losses were heavy on both sides, and the Russians pulled back. Then in May 1905 the Japanese navy stunned the world when it completely destroyed the Russian Baltic fleet at the Battle of Tsushima.

The Russo-Japanese War In this painting, the Japanese navy attacks Russian forces at Port Arthur. *What is happening in the picture that shows Japanese bravery?*

Although the Japanese were winning the **Russo-Japanese War,** the costs of the war—in lives and money—were a strain. They asked U.S. president Theodore Roosevelt to mediate the conflict. Roosevelt reluctantly agreed. In 1905 he invited Japanese and Russian representatives to negotiations at Portsmouth, New Hampshire.

The Treaty of Portsmouth. Late in 1905, the **Treaty of Portsmouth** ended the Russo Japanese War. Under the agreement, Russia ceded to Japan its lease on the Liaodong Peninsula, including Port Arthur. They also gave Japan the southern half of the Russian island of Sakhalin, north of Japan. Russia gave up control of the southern branch of the Beijing-Tianjian Railway and recognized Japan as the dominant power in Korea. In addition, Russia agreed to withdraw all troops, except for railway guards, from Manchuria.

The Treaty of Portsmouth eliminated Japan's competition in Manchuria. It forced other powers to respect Japan's strength. When Japan annexed Korea in 1910, none of the other imperialist powers protested.

What If? Japan's startling victory in the Russo-Japanese War made it the equal of other imperialist powers competing in the Pacific. How might history have changed if Russia, not Japan, had won the war in 1905?

✔ **READING CHECK: Finding the Main Idea** How did Japan position itself to be an important power during the early 1900s?

Problems of Modernization

In less than 50 years, Japan had gone from a feudal agricultural nation to one of the world's leading industrial and military powers. This leap created problems for the island nation.

Increasing population. Industrialization and scientific development brought higher standards of living and new forms of medical care to Japan. These spurred population growth. Cities grew rapidly, and every inch of suitable land was cultivated.

Even so, the increased food supply could not match the rapid increase in population. Japanese people emigrated to Korea and Taiwan, as well as to Hawaii and other Pacific islands. Thousands more left for the United States. In time, the United States prohibited the immigration of Asians but still allowed Europeans to enter the country. Japan deeply resented this policy.

The Westernization of Japan

Beginning in the late 1800s, the Japanese became more interested in the ways of the West. As a Japanese prince explained: "We sent talented young students to Europe and America to master various fields of science and technology." The Japanese also borrowed and adapted elements of American popular culture, in particular sports such as baseball and entertainment such as music, dance, and films. Women's roles became more westernized too, and a feminist movement, though unsuccessful, began. **What effect do you think Western ideas might have on a traditional society such as Japan's?**

Economic trouble. Japan's industrialization created another problem. Because of its small size, Japan did not have many of the raw materials needed in modern industry. It had to import them. To pay for these raw materials, it had to sell goods abroad. In trying to export its goods, however, Japan met with restrictions in the rough world of international trade. Many countries passed tariff laws to protect their own products and markets against Japanese competition. They argued that Japanese goods had an unfair advantage because cheap labor in Japan allowed Japanese manufacturers to charge lower prices. The Japanese economy had to expand or collapse.

Social tensions. The Meiji era was a time of social and political stability. Customs and law allowed for little dissent. By the 1920s, however, economic development, universal education, and new ideas from the West had changed Japanese attitudes. Many believed it was time for the people to benefit from Japan's economic advances.

Industrial workers organized labor unions. They called strikes for higher wages and better working conditions. Tenant farms demanded lower agricultural rents. Urban intellectuals and students were inspired by the victory of the Western democracies in World War I. They argued that democracy was the wave of the future. Universal men's suffrage was granted in 1925, but women would not win the right to vote until years later. Other Japanese turned to socialism or communism.

Some young Japanese began to question the traditional values of their society. The center of Japanese society, once agricultural, became the modern city. New ideas and arts entered Japan from the West. Work roles shifted as well. People from farm villages now worked in factories. Women took jobs in manufacturing, textile, and office work. These changes did not come without resistance. When world financial markets collapsed in 1929, many felt that the focus away from traditional Japanese interests had corrupted the country economically and morally.

✔ **READING CHECK: Categorizing** What types of problems did modernization produce in Japan?

Growing Influence of the Military

Japan's political leaders of the 1920s had difficulty answering the concerns of the Japanese people. Opposition to westernization grew. This atmosphere of turmoil and dissatisfaction on the part of many Japanese provided opportunities for Japan's military to increase its influence.

The constitution of 1889 had given top-ranking military officers great power. Civilian authorities had almost no control over military affairs. Until the 1920s military ministers usually cooperated with civilian members of government. However, during World War I, the military had seen a new kind of war. Victory had depended not only on troops, but also on controlling the entire spiritual and material resources of the nation. Because military ministers believed that victory in any future war would require the same unity, they saw discontent in Japan as a serious problem. As a result, throughout the 1920s and the 1930s, Japan was increasingly influenced by attitudes of militarism, a point of view in which military needs, values, and goals shape a nation's civil lifestyles and its domestic and international policies. Much like the rising fascist governments in Europe, Japan's increasingly militaristic government ever more strongly influenced Japanese social, economic, and political development.

Japan's economic problems in the late 1920s also drove the military officers to take a greater role in government. Army and navy officers believed that Western nations would never treat Japan as an equal. They pointed to Western restrictions on Japanese immigration and exports as proof. Groups that believed in the "purity" of Japanese culture influenced young officers. They felt that Japan should pursue a more independent course, particularly in Asia.

In time, the military insisted that the Japanese people return to traditional values. They called for a larger army and a stronger navy. In addition, they supported a Japanese "Monroe Doctrine" that gave them powers in Asia similar to those exercised by the United States in the Western Hemisphere. In particular, they looked to Manchuria as a target for future expansion. The growing influence of the military would have far-reaching consequences, not only for Japanese society but for the rest of the world as well.

✔ **READING CHECK: Analyzing Information** How did World War I contribute to the rise of military influence over the Japanese government?

Japanese Emperor Hirohito salutes as he rides past his troops.

SECTION 4 REVIEW

1. **Identify** and explain the significance:
   Russo-Japanese War
   Treaty of Portsmouth

2. **Categorizing** Copy the web diagram below. Use it to identify the influence of each factor on Japan from 1900 through the 1920s.

   Russo-Japanese War
   Modernization
   Japan
   Social tensions
   Military

3. **Finding the Main Idea**

   a. Why did Japan pursue a policy of expansionism?
   b. What were the causes of the Russo-Japanese War?
   c. How was Japan's militaristic government similar to fascist governments in Europe?

4. **Writing and Critical Thinking**

   Supporting Points of View Write a dialogue between a young Japanese student who favors Western ideas and a young Japanese soldier who does not.
   Consider:
   • the benefits of industrialization, democracy, and new ideas in the arts
   • the benefits of traditional Japanese values

Homework Practice Online
keyword: SH3 HP20

Latin America Between the Wars

READ TO DISCOVER

❶ In what significant ways did Latin American nations change after World War I?

❷ Why were authoritarian regimes able to come to power in many Latin American nations?

❸ What kind of relationship did Latin America have with the United States?

IDENTIFY

Diego Rivera
Rafael Trujillo Molina
Anastasio Somoza
Good Neighbor Policy
Fulgencio Batista
Lázaro Cárdenas

▶ **WHY IT MATTERS TODAY**

Relations between the United States and Latin American countries are an important focus of U.S. foreign policy. Use **CNN**Student**News**.com or other **current event** sources to find out recent developments in U.S. policy toward Mexico, Cuba, or some other Latin American nation. Record your findings in your journal.

CNN student News.com

The Main Idea
General prosperity in Latin America gave way to economic and political crises in the 1930s.

The Story Continues *Nationalism had blossomed and borne fruit in Latin America in the 1800s, when nations gained their independence from Spain and Portugal. Democracy, however, had not as yet gained as strong a hold. In fact, many Latin Americans would find themselves under the strong-arm rule of military dictators when the Great Depression threw their countries into turmoil.*

Economic, Social, and Political Developments

After World War I Latin America appeared to be headed for prosperity. The area's growing economic strength led to changes in other areas of Latin American life, as well.

Economic changes. As the 1920s began, agricultural products dominated Latin American economies. Beef, wheat, sugar, coffee, and fruits were the principal exports. Yet during the early 1900s, Mexico also became a leading oil exporter. Oil was discovered in Venezuela, Peru, Bolivia, and Colombia. The mining of copper in Chile and Peru, tin in Bolivia, and bauxite in Guiana grew rapidly, too. Most of the oil and mining operations, however, were owned by British and American companies.

The 1920s also saw a rapid expansion in electric and hydroelectric power generation in Latin America. Foreign investors financed these industries too. The energy allowed many Latin American countries to industrialize. Larger countries began producing textiles, construction materials, machinery, and automobiles. Oil refining and food processing became important. Heavy industrialization, however, would not come to Latin America until after World War II.

The growth of Mexico City in the 1920s and 1930s reflected the increasing economic strength of Latin America.

Social changes. Industrialization contributed to the growth of cities. By 1935 Mexico City, Rio de Janeiro, São Paulo, and Buenos Aires each had 1 million or more people.

Industrialization also helped change the social-economic structure. To provide labor for growing industries, countries such as Argentina, Brazil, and Chile had encouraged immigration from Europe since the late 1800s. The number of Latin American workers swelled.

With growth in the working class came an increase in labor union activity. The 1920s saw a surge in union membership. Latin American unions were largely socialist or anarchist in their views. They used strikes as the primary way to achieve their goals. As a result, by the late 1920s, many cities in Latin America had been hit by general strikes. Many governments called out police and army troops to put down strikes violently. Some governments outlawed both strikes and labor unions.

The middle class, too, began to grow as new jobs opened up in the professions, government service, and commerce. Changes in university programs created opportunities for middle-class youths in engineering, business, and public administration. Such developments gave the middle class greater access to power.

Political changes. Political life in Latin America underwent sweeping changes in the early 1900s. For example, political parties backed by the middle class emerged in Chile, Argentina, Peru, and Brazil. Torn by regional disputes, Mexico went to a single-party political system in hopes of guaranteeing stability. In Uruguay, leaders enacted a broad reform program that included free elections, social security, and nationalization of railroads and public utilities.

Democracy still eluded most Latin American nations. Concerns of the growing working class could not be ignored, however. Many Latin American artists, such as Mexico's Diego Rivera, addressed these concerns in their work. Middle-class politicians, struggling for control with upper-class landowners, turned to the working class for support in elections. An election did not always mean a smooth transition of power, however. In some countries, the way to change the government was still to overthrow it.

✔ **READING CHECK: Summarizing** How did Latin American nations change after World War I?

Economic Crisis and Authoritarianism

At the end of the 1920s, prices began to fall for Latin America's major agricultural exports, such as sugar and coffee. Chile's major export was nitrates, used in fertilizers and explosives. When German scientists developed a process for making synthetic nitrates, Chile's export economy suffered a crippling blow.

The effects of the Great Depression. Prices fell even more during the worldwide economic depression in the 1930s. Because they received little for their exports, many Latin American nations found it impossible to import any but the most essential goods. Some countries stopped paying their foreign debts. As national economies faltered, unemployment spread. So too did worker unrest.

Economic crisis led to political crisis. Coup d'états overthrew constitutional governments that had existed for 30 or 40 years. Most of the nations of Latin America experienced major political upheaval. Planters and exporters lost not only their fortunes to the depression but also their political power as middle classes rebelled.

Painting:
Fruits of Labor
One of Mexico's finest artists, Diego Rivera recorded the dramatic changes in his country after World War I. A follower of the art movement known as social realism, Rivera produced paintings that dealt with contemporary problems. Among his best are works that show the plight of Mexican peasants. The Mexican government commissioned Rivera to paint many murals for schools and government buildings. Shown here is a detail from his fresco *Fruits of Labor* in Mexico City, which honors working people and their children. The fresco took Rivera and his assistants six years to complete.

Understanding the Arts

In what ways did the work of Diego Rivera reflect Latin American social issues during the 1920s and the 1930s?

Authoritarian regimes. The military strongly influenced or controlled many new governments. In some countries, U.S.-trained military leaders ruled. In the Dominican Republic, General **Rafael Trujillo Molina** began a dictatorship in 1930 that would last 31 years. In Nicaragua, General **Anastasio Somoza** seized power in 1936, two years after assassinating his chief rival.

Many of the new authoritarian governments suppressed any attempt at dissent. They limited the influence of landowners and broke the power of labor unions. Some simply abolished workers' organizations, jailing their leaders. In Brazil, President Getúlio Vargas dismantled any framework of democracy. In El Salvador, the army massacred more than 10,000 peasants to destroy a popular communist movement.

Some military leaders tried to gain support through persuasion rather than terror. They gave favors just to union members loyal to the military. Some even responded to the needs of the people by enacting land reforms and passing minimum wage and pension laws. These actions limited the appeal of left-wing movements.

✔ **READING CHECK: Categorizing** In what two ways did military leaders attempt to gain control and support in Latin American nations?

Relations with the United States

Earlier United States intervention in Latin America had created ill will and suspicion. President Franklin D. Roosevelt tried to undo these feelings. During the 1930s, Roosevelt began a program he called the **Good Neighbor Policy.** It stressed cooperation and noninterference by the United States in Latin American affairs.

In 1933 the Pan American Conference met in Montevideo. There the United States pledged not to interfere in the internal or external affairs of Latin American nations. It recalled army units that had occupied Haiti since 1915. It also surrendered its right to interfere in the affairs of Panama.

The Cuban test. That same year a situation in Cuba tested Roosevelt's commitment to the Montevideo agreement. A group of radical reformers overthrew Cuban dictator Gerardo Machado. The new government declared a socialist revolution and nationalized some American-owned companies. In response the United States refused to give diplomatic recognition to the new government, but it did not intervene directly. When Cuban army sergeant **Fulgencio Batista** decided to overthrow the reformers, however, the U.S. envoy to Cuba encouraged him.

Social and political disorder spread throughout Cuba in 1933. Here citizens in Havana celebrating the rumor that President Machado has resigned react to police gunfire.

Although the United States no longer directly intervened in Latin American affairs, it still held considerable influence. In Cuba, Batista remained the power in the background while a series of civilian governments ruled in name only. In 1934 the United States recognized the stability that Batista had brought to Cuba. It canceled the Platt Amendment, which had given the United States the right to interfere in Cuban affairs.

Economic nationalism. During the 1930s, most Latin American governments worked to make their countries more self-sufficient by encouraging industry. Given the dismal economic picture caused by the global depression of the 1930s, international markets for their goods were weak. Imported goods, moreover, were generally costly. Countries therefore had no choice but to develop their own industries for manufactured goods. This economic nationalism joined with growing feelings of political nationalism. The middle class, in particular, no longer wanted to be dependent on the United States or Europe.

The most important example of economic nationalism occurred in Mexico in 1938. American- and British-owned oil companies in Mexico had become involved in a wage dispute with their workers. They refused to accept a Mexican Supreme Court ruling in favor of the workers. As a result, President **Lázaro Cárdenas** intervened and nationalized the oil industry.

The British angrily broke off diplomatic relations. The United States, however, tried to get Mexico to pay the oil companies what they claimed their holdings were worth. The two governments eventually reached a compromise. Mexicans regard March 13, 1938—the day when President Cárdenas nationalized the oil companies—as the birth date of Mexican economic independence.

Mexican president Lázaro Cárdenas, a revolutionary general and son of a poor family, carried out promises of economic reform and nationalized Mexico's petroleum industry in the 1930s.

✔ **READING CHECK: Making Generalizations** How did Latin American countries generally view the United States and Europe?

SECTION 5 REVIEW

1. Identify and explain the significance:
Diego Rivera
Rafael Trujillo Molina
Anastasio Somoza
Good Neighbor Policy
Fulgencio Batista
Lázaro Cárdenas

2. Identifying Cause and Effect Copy the table below. Use it to show the causes or effects of each factor on Latin America.

Cause	Effect
Increase in exports and generation of electricity	
Industrialization	
Middle-class access to greater political power	
	The Good Neighbor Policy
	Economic nationalism

3. **Finding the Main Idea**
a. What caused a change in the economies of Latin American countries after World War I?
b. How did authoritarian regimes come to power in many Latin American countries?
c. How did the United States react to events in Latin American countries in the 1930s?

4. **Writing and Critical Thinking**
Decision Making Use a decision-making process to determine whether President Roosevelt honored the Montevideo agreement when he supported Batista's revolt in Cuba.
Consider:
• how United States economic interests were affected by socialist reforms
• what the United States had agreed to in the Montevideo agreement

Homework Practice Online
go.hrw.com
keyword: SH3 HP20

CHAPTER 20 Review

Creating a Time Line

Copy the time line below onto a sheet of paper. Complete the time line by filling in the events, individuals, and dates from the chapter that you think were significant. Pick three events and explain why you think they were significant.

| 1898 | 1913 | 1938 |

Writing a Summary

Using standard grammar, spelling, sentence structure, and punctuation, write an overview of the events in the chapter.

Identifying People and Ideas

Identify the following terms or individuals and explain their significance:

1. Zionism
2. Mohandas Gandhi
3. passive resistance
4. Mustafa Kemal
5. Open Door Policy
6. Chiang Kai-shek
7. Mao Zedong
8. Long March
9. Treaty of Portsmouth
10. Good Neighbor Policy

Understanding Main Ideas

SECTION 1 *(pp. 566–569)*

The British Empire in the Postwar Era

1. What influence did Mohandas Gandhi have on the way the people of India sought independence?

SECTION 2 *(pp. 570–572)*

Turkey, Persia, and Africa

2. In what way did World War I change the attitude of Africans about colonial government?

SECTION 3 *(pp. 573–577)*

Unrest in China

3. Why was the United States concerned about the influence of imperialist powers in China?

4. What factors led to the development of communism in China?

SECTION 4 *(pp. 578–581)*

Imperialism in Japan

5. Why did Japan pursue a policy of expansionism after World War I?

SECTION 5 *(pp. 582–585)*

Latin America Between the Wars

6. How did the economies of Latin American countries change after World War I?

Reviewing Themes

1. **Government** How did the military affect Japan's government?

2. **Culture** How did cultural issues affect nationalistic movements in Africa?

3. **Economics** How did economic issues influence political events in Latin America?

Thinking Critically

1. **Contrasting** Contrast the British reaction to demands for Indian independence with their reaction to similar demands from Canada, Australia, and New Zealand.

2. **Evaluating** How would you evaluate the effectiveness of Mustafa Kemal's attempt to modernize Turkey?

3. **Sequencing** Trace the events leading to the rise of communism in China.

4. **Identifying Cause and Effect** What factors influenced the expansionist efforts of Japan after World War I?

Writing About History

Categorizing The United States has tried to influence the political and economic activities of other countries. Some argue that the United States must do this to protect its own interests, while others believe that every nation has the right to make its own decisions. Write an informative article presenting both sides of this issue. Use the following chart to organize your thoughts.

U.S. action	Effects—U.S.	Effects—other country
Supporting revolution		
Imposing economic sanctions		
Conducting military action		
Other types of action		

Analyzing Statistical Data

Study the information provided below. Then use the information to answer the questions that follow.

The Population of Palestine in 1914 (Estimated)

- About 535,000 Muslims
- About 70,000 Christians (mostly Arabs)
- About 85,000 Jews
- Estimated total population: 690,000

1. Which of the following best describes the population of Palestine in 1914?

   a. Muslims greatly outnumbered Christians and Jews in Palestine in 1914.

   b. Most Christians in Palestine in 1914 were immigrant farmers from Europe.

   c. Christians and Jews together slightly outnumbered Muslims in 1914 Palestine.

   d. Farmers represented the largest segment of the Palestinian population in 1914.

2. Convert the statistics above into a pie graph on the population of Palestine. How might this information have influenced Palestinian views in 1914 on who should rule the area?

Problem Solving

Read the following quote from an essay by a commentator published in 1936. Then answer the questions.

"Negotiation between two Western states is the mutual attempt to approach common ground. Its essence is compromise. But the concept of compromise is quite foreign to the Japanese. To them, diplomatic negotiation means the effort of each national representative to put over his own plan intact, the end in view being that one shall win and the other shall lose. The Naval Conference this year has been an illustration of Japan's attitude. Arriving at London with a fixed determination to obtain parity or nothing, the Japanese were not prepared to yield a single ton, regardless of what was proposed."

3. Which of the following is the best statement of the problem described in the excerpt?

   a. There was no word for "compromise" in the Japanese language.

   b. All the Western countries had a common goal.

   c. The Japanese thought of themselves as superior.

   d. Japan and the West had very different understandings of the word "negotiate."

4. In today's world, Japan and the Western powers have become allies and active trading partners. How do you think the problem described in the quote was solved?

Alternative Assessment

Building Your Portfolio

Link to TODAY

Global Relations

Great Britain's efforts to try to direct the future of Palestine led to increased tensions in the region after World War I. Use the Internet and other sources to identify how other countries, such as the United States, have tried to assist in recent disputes within this region. Using what you have learned from Britain's example, evaluate the effectiveness of these efforts in bringing a peaceful resolution to conflict.

internet connect

Internet Activity: go.hrw.com
KEYWORD: SH3 WH20

Choose a topic on Nationalist Movements Around the World to:

- write a biography of Mustafa Kemal.
- investigate the British Commonwealth of Nations and how the member nations interact.
- create a poster on wars of independence in the Philippines and Nicaragua.

1921–1945

World War II

The cover and the
sheet music to
George Gershwin's
"Rhapsody in Blue"

Adolf Hitler

1921
Business and Finance
The German mark falls rapidly and inflation begins.

1923
The Arts
American composer George Gershwin writes "Rhapsody in Blue."

1926
Science and Technology
American scientist Robert H. Goddard fires the first liquid fuel rocket.

1929
Business and Finance
A world economic crisis begins after the U.S. stock market crashes.

1933
Politics
Adolf Hitler is appointed chancellor of Germany.

1933
The Arts
Books by Jewish and other non-Nazi authors are burned in Germany.

1920 — **1925** — **1930**

1922
Politics
Benito Mussolini forms a fascist government in Italy.

1924
Daily Life
More than two million radios are in use in the United States.

1926
The Arts
Ernest Hemingway publishes his novel *The Sun Also Rises.*

1928
Global Events
The Kellogg-Briand Pact is signed, making war "illegal."

1931
Global Events
The Japanese attack Manchuria.

1928
Science and Technology
American aviator Amelia Earhart becomes the first woman to fly across the Atlantic.

A radio from the 1920s

Amelia Earhart

Build on What You Know

*A*fter World War I, bitterness and distrust continued to divide Europe. Under the Treaty of Versailles, Germany and its allies had to accept blame for starting the war and pay for damages to the countries they had invaded. The treaty also greatly reduced Germany's size and put limits on the size of its military. These measures were designed to keep Germany from waging another war. When Germany began violating the terms of the treaty, however, Great Britain and France took no action. In this chapter, you will learn how German, Japanese, and Italian aggression led to the outbreak of a new world war. You will also learn how the Allies fought this aggression and defeated the Axis Powers.

A page from a child's sugar ration book from Great Britain

These suitcases were taken from prisoners upon their arrival at the Auschwitz-Birkenau concentration camp.

1934
Global Events
The Soviet Union is admitted to the League of Nations.

1935
Science and Technology
Robert Watson-Watt builds radar equipment to detect aircraft.

1936
Politics
The Spanish Civil War begins.

1936
Global Events
Mussolini and Hitler form the Rome-Berlin Axis.

1937
Politics
President Franklin Roosevelt signs the U.S. Neutrality Act.

1937
The Arts
Pablo Picasso paints *Guernica* for the Paris World Exhibition.

1940
Daily Life
Bacon, butter, and sugar are rationed in Great Britain.

1939
Global Events
Germany invades Poland.

1939
Business and Finance
The U.S. economy begins to boom from European orders for arms and war equipment.

1941
Politics
Hitler orders the "Final Solution"—a program to kill the entire Jewish population in Europe.

1941
Global Events
The United States and Great Britain sign the Atlantic Charter.

1941
Global Events
The Japanese make a surprise attack on the U.S. naval base at Pearl Harbor, Hawaii.

1941
Science and Technology
The U.S. "Manhattan Project" of intensive atomic research begins.

1943
The Arts
Casablanca wins the Academy Award™ for best film.

1945
Politics
Roosevelt, Churchill, and Stalin meet at the Yalta Conference.

1945
Global Events
The Allies achieve victory in Europe on May 8, V-E Day.

1945
Science and Technology
The first atomic bomb is exploded near Alamogordo, New Mexico, on July 16.

1945
Business and Finance
Black—or illegal—markets for food, clothing, and cigarettes develop throughout Europe.

1935 — **1940** — **1945**

Poster for the movie Casablanca

What's Your Opinion?

Themes Journal *Do you* **agree** *or* **disagree** *with the following statements? Support your point of view in your journal.*

Global Relations Regional conflicts in one part of the world can spread to affect the rest of the world.

Government Racial prejudice within a nation can be used as a political weapon by the government of that nation.

Science, Technology & Society Technology developed during wartime can be both beneficial and destructive.

Threats to World Peace

READ TO DISCOVER

❶ Why were Japan and Italy able to carry out aggressive territorial policies in the 1930s?

❷ Why was the League of Nations unable to stop international aggression?

❸ How did Spain's civil war lead to a fascist dictatorship there?

IDENTIFY

Kellogg-Briand Pact
Osachi Hamaguchi
Falange
Spanish Civil War
Francisco Franco
International Brigades

▶ WHY IT MATTERS TODAY

Today the United Nations works to keep international peace. Use CNN Student News.com or other **current event** sources to find out what recent peace efforts the UN has undertaken. Record your findings in your journal.

CNN Student News.com

The Main Idea
During the 1930s aggression by Japan and Italy and civil war in Spain threatened world peace.

The Story Continues *After World War I, the role of the League of Nations as an international peacekeeper was challenged. When Italy invaded Ethiopia in 1935, Ethiopia's former leader Haile Selassie explained the threat to international peace. "It is not merely a question of a settlement in the matter of Italian aggression. It is a question of collective security; of the very existence of the League . . . ."*

Japanese Aggression in Asia

In 1928 the U.S. secretary of state, Frank B. Kellogg, and the French foreign minister, Aristide Briand, met in Paris. Together they created an agreement that made war "illegal." Eventually more than 60 nations signed the **Kellogg-Briand Pact.** During the 1930s, however, it became clear that world powers would not be able to put such an agreement into effect. Japan made one of the first challenges to this pact.

The Japanese military began gaining power in the late 1920s. Then in 1930 Japan's liberal prime minister, **Osachi Hamaguchi,** was fatally shot. Political chaos followed the assassination. Within two years, a group of military leaders controlled the Japanese government. In September 1931 a small group of Japanese army officers staged a fake attack on the railway near Mukden, in China's province of Manchuria. Blaming the attack on China, Japanese forces in Manchuria quickly took control of the entire province. The major nations in the League of Nations condemned Japan's aggression but were not willing to take military action to protect China. Japan responded to the condemnation by withdrawing from the League of Nations.

The lack of enforceable opposition encouraged Japan, which announced its intention of extending its influence not only to all of China, but also throughout East Asia and the western Pacific. Six years later, in 1937, the Japanese army captured the city of Beijing. While Chinese forces fought hard to protect their country, Japan slowly gained more territory. By 1939 the Japanese controlled about one fourth of China, including all seaports.

✔ **READING CHECK: Finding the Main Idea** What was the result of Japanese aggression during the 1930s?

Victorious Japanese troops celebrate the conquest of Manchuria.

The Expansion of Japan, 1928–1941

Interpreting Maps When the Japanese took over Manchuria, they declared it the independent nation of Manchukuo and installed a puppet government led by the former emperor of China. Within a ten-year period, Japan occupied about one fourth of China. Then the Japanese fought to gain control over Southeast Asia and to establish a large island empire in the Pacific.

■ **Skills Assessment:** 1. **Human Systems** Through what two cities in Manchuria did the Japanese advance?
2. **Drawing Inferences** Why do you think Japan chose Manchuria as its first site of expansion?

Italy's Conquest of Ethiopia

Benito Mussolini came to power in Italy in 1922 and ruled as a fascist dictator. Mussolini worked to improve the nation's economy. He may have believed that overseas expansion would help ease some of Italy's economic problems. Ethiopia, one of the few independent nations in Africa, became the target of Mussolini's aggressive goals.

When a border dispute with Italy broke out in 1934, Ethiopia called on the League of Nations to help. The League could not offer military protection to Ethiopia, however, because it maintained no armed forces. A year later Italian forces invaded and defeated the poorly equipped Ethiopian army. The League declared Italy an aggressor and placed economic sanctions on the country. The weak boycott on trade had little effect on Italy, however. In the spring of 1936, Mussolini announced Ethiopia was part of the Italian Empire.

Most countries did not agree with Italy's actions. However, no major power was willing to enforce the League's sanctions. Horrible memories of World War I made countries such as Great Britain and the United States unwilling to risk another war. In addition, many countries were busy dealing with the problems created by the Great Depression. As a result, Italy and Japan realized they could continue their acts of aggression with little real threat of opposition.

✔ **READING CHECK: Analyzing Information** Why was the League of Nations unable to stop aggression in both Italy and Japan?

Civil War in Spain

After World War I political instability increased in Spain. In 1923 rebels overthrew the government and set up a military dictatorship. This government fell in 1931 when the army withdrew its support. Spain's new leaders formed a government called the Second Spanish Republic. They planned to establish freedom of religion and to separate church and state issues. Education came under government control and members of the clergy were not allowed to teach. The new government also took land from the Catholic Church and the nobility and gave it to the peasants. Workers received new benefits such as shorter hours, better wages, and the right to organize.

Nationalists versus Loyalists. These dramatic new changes angered many Spanish conservatives. They quickly gave their support to a fascist party called the **Falange.** Using terrorism, the Falange worked to preserve the power of the army, landowners, and the church. Members of the Falange became even more active after a group of socialists and Communists, called the Popular Front, won a major election in February 1936. In the summer of 1936, Falangist uprisings led to the outbreak of the **Spanish Civil War.** The Falangist rebels were led by General **Francisco Franco** and called themselves Nationalists. Those who supported the republic were known as Loyalists, or Republicans. By the end of 1936, the Nationalists controlled most of northern Spain. The Loyalists controlled the east and southeast. They also had power over most of the northern coastline and the capital city of Madrid.

Foreign assistance to Spain. The Spanish Civil War soon grew into a small European war. Germany and Italy saw a fascist Spain as a part of their plan to surround France with unfriendly powers and threaten Great Britain. They sent fully equipped military units to bolster Nationalist forces. The Soviet Union sympathized with the republican government. Soviets sent planes, technicians, and military advisers

CONNECTING TO Art

Painting: *Guernica* by Pablo Picasso

Although Pablo Picasso lived in France, he was born in Spain. He strongly supported the Loyalist cause during the Spanish Civil War. Picasso's painting *Guernica* expresses his outrage over the bombing of the Spanish town of Guernica, which had no strategic value in the war. Picasso's broken figures show war victims' fear and suffering. They twist in pain under a bright electric light. Picasso asked that *Guernica* be kept in the United States until democracy returned to Spain. In 1981 the painting was placed in a museum in Madrid.

Understanding the Arts

What techniques does Picasso use to express the pain and horror of war?

to Spain. Their support, however, was not nearly as great as what Franco received from his fascist allies.

Volunteers from France, Great Britain, and the United States also rushed to help the Spanish Republic. These idealistic antifascist volunteers became known as the **International Brigades.** The French and British feared that the Spanish Civil War might spread to the rest of Europe. Spain's civil war illustrated a wider conflict between communism and fascism throughout Europe. English writer George Orwell described the antifascist city of Barcelona.

❝Practically every building of any size had been seized by the workers and was draped with red flags . . . ; every wall was scrawled with the hammer and sickle and with the initials of the revolutionary parties; almost every church had been gutted and its images burnt.❞

George Orwell, *Homage to Catalonia*

Nationalist forces defeated the Loyalists in the spring of 1939. Franco set up a fascist dictatorship. He became Spain's head of state and had unlimited power. Franco's government and economic structure began to look a lot like Mussolini's in Italy. Franco brought an end to all free elections and most civil rights. Spain's old ruling groups—the army, the landowners, and the Roman Catholic Church—all held positions of power under Franco's rule.

During the three years of the Spanish Civil War, Spain and its people suffered greatly. The war caused considerable destruction and loss of life. Estimates of Spain's war dead during these years range from 500,000 to 1 million. Over the course of the war, moreover, the bitter differences that had separated the various opposing groups in 1936 became deeper and even more divisive.

✔ **READING CHECK: Sequencing** How did Spain become a fascist dictatorship?

Analyzing Primary Sources

Identifying a Point of View Why would antifascists in Spain have destroyed churches?

INTERPRETING THE VISUAL RECORD

Spanish Civil War Europe's larger conflict between communism and fascism was demonstrated in the Spanish Civil War. *Why do you think these antifascists barricaded the streets of Barcelona?*

SECTION 1 REVIEW

1. **Identify** and explain the significance:
   Kellogg-Briand Pact
   Osachi Hamaguchi
   Falange
   Spanish Civil War
   Francisco Franco
   International Brigades

2. **Identifying Cause and Effect**
   Copy the chart below. Use it to explain how militarism and fascism affected Japan, Italy, and Spain in the 1930s.

	Japan	Italy	Spain
Militarism and Fascism			

3. **Finding the Main Idea**
   a. Why was the League of Nations unable to stop the aggression of Japan and Italy?
   b. How did Francisco Franco become a fascist dictator in Spain?

4. **Writing and Critical Thinking**
   Making Predictions Describe what might have happened differently during the 1930s if the League of Nations had been a more effective international peacekeeper.
   Consider:
   • Japan's aggression in the 1930s
   • Italy's aggression in the 1930s
   • the effects of not opposing such aggression

Homework Practice Online
go.hrw.com
keyword: SH3 HP21

Hitler's Aggressions

READ TO DISCOVER

❶ How was Adolf Hitler able to take over Austria and Czechoslovakia?

❷ How and why did Great Britain and France attempt to avoid another war in Europe?

❸ How did Great Britain and France prepare for war in the face of German aggression?

❹ Why did Hitler and Stalin create the Nazi-Soviet Pact, and how did Western nations respond to Hitler's invasion of Poland?

DEFINE

appeasement

IDENTIFY

Axis Powers
Anti-Comintern Pact
Munich Conference
Neville Chamberlain
Édouard Daladier
German-Soviet nonaggression pact

WHY IT MATTERS TODAY

Today, world powers often get involved when one country acts aggressively against another. Use CNN student News.com or other **current event** sources to find an aggressive act during recent years that the United States has taken action against. Record your findings in your journal.

The Main Idea
Adolf Hitler led Germany in its aggressive acts to expand the territory of the German empire.

The Story Continues *Militarism and fascism also grew in Germany. Under Adolf Hitler's leadership, Germany began a plan to acquire "living space" for the "superior" German race. "An additional 500,000 kilometers [almost 200,000 square miles] in Europe can provide new homesteads for millions of German peasants . . . ," Hitler wrote.*

Austria and Czechoslovakia

In 1933 Adolf Hitler announced that he would rearm the country. He then took Germany out of the League of Nations. In March 1936 German troops marched into the Rhineland, violating the Treaty of Versailles. In October 1936, Hitler and Mussolini created an alliance called the Rome-Berlin Axis. They began calling themselves the **Axis Powers.** Shortly afterward, Japan and Germany promised to work together. They signed an agreement called the **Anti-Comintern Pact,** pledging to stop the spread of communism. Italy later signed the pact. By the end of 1936, the three nations who would later enter World War II as the Axis Powers had hidden their aggressive intentions under the cover of fighting communism.

Annexing Austria. A Nazi Party had been formed in Austria in the late 1920s. By the early 1930s, the extremely conservative Austrian government was doing little to resist Nazi inroads. By 1938 threats from both Hitler and Mussolini forced the Austrian government to include Nazi members in its cabinet.

Although the Austrian chancellor had made an agreement with Hitler on union with Germany, he regretted the agreement and suggested that the Austrian people be allowed to vote on the issue. Hitler refused, preferring instead to take Austria with a show of force. The Austrian chancellor resigned, and a German army marched into Austria unopposed. In March 1938 Hitler declared Austria to be part of the Third Reich. This was in violation of the Treaty of Versailles, which had specifically forbidden any union between Germany and Austria. Even so, Great Britain and France did nothing more than send protests to Hitler, which he ignored. The League of Nations took no action.

Mussolini and Hitler at a 1937 conference in Munich.

The addition of Austria increased the size of Germany's population, territory, and resources. It also increased Hitler's power in Europe. Strategically, Germany controlled the heart of central Europe. Germany now had a common border with its ally Italy and it nearly encircled Czechoslovakia. Hitler identified this country as his next area of expansion.

Crisis in the Sudetenland. More than 3 million Germans lived in the Sudetenland (soo·DAYT·uhn·land), a region around the western rim of Czechoslovakia. The Sudetenland included a chain of mountains that provided a natural defense for Czechoslovakia. They were heavily fortified as a very important defensive line.

These Sudeten women express strong emotions as they salute German troops in Czechoslovakia.

The Czech government tried to protect the rights of Germans living in this area. However, many still wanted union with Germany. As a result the Nazi Party grew in strength there. When riots broke out in September 1938, Czechoslovakia placed the region under martial law. Hitler then announced he would invade and annex the Sudetenland to protect fellow Germans. The loss of this heavily armed mountain region would mean disaster for Czechoslovakia since it would leave the country defenseless against Germany.

Appeasement. As tensions grew in Europe, Hitler held a meeting on September 29, 1938, called the **Munich Conference.** He invited British prime minister **Neville Chamberlain** and French premier **Édouard Daladier** (dah·lahd·yay). Also in attendance was Mussolini. Chamberlain and Daladier accepted Hitler's demand that the Sudetenland be joined with Germany. Britain and France feared Germany's military strength. In addition, they knew their own countries were not prepared for war. This policy of trying to keep the peace by accepting some of the demands of the aggressor is called **appeasement.**

Upon returning to London, Chamberlain spoke triumphantly to a cheering crowd. He announced that he had achieved "peace in our time." France announced it would not honor its agreement to defend Czechoslovakia. Germany began to occupy the Sudetenland. Abandoned by its allies, Czechoslovakia was left defenseless. The United States also tried to avoid the conflict. Famous pilot Charles Lindbergh expressed the feelings of many Americans.

History Makers Speak

❝If we are forced into a war against the wishes of an overwhelming majority of our people, we will have proved democracy such a failure at home that there will be little use fighting for it abroad.❞

Charles A. Lindbergh, *The New York Times,* April 24, 1941

Analyzing Primary Sources

Finding the Main Idea According to Lindbergh, in what sense would democracy have failed if the United States went to war?

In March 1939 German troops invaded Czechoslovakia. Within six months this independent republic had been erased from Europe's map. Germany also gained the port city of Memel, Lithuania, in the spring of 1939. Yet another country lost its independence when Mussolini invaded Albania in April 1939. The Italians took this small country on the east coast of the Adriatic Sea in only a few days. Once again the League of Nations had failed to be effective. Its complete helplessness in the face of aggression was now obvious.

✔ **READING CHECK: Summarizing** How did Hitler conquer Austria and Czechoslovakia, and what role did Great Britain and France play?

Preparations for War

After Hitler took over Czechoslovakia, British and French leaders could no longer ignore the fascist dictators. Britain and France therefore began to prepare for war. Neville Chamberlain ordered that Britain's rearmament program be stepped up. He also rushed through Parliament a law drafting men into the military. Great Britain joined France in a promise to protect Poland if Germany attacked.

Negotiating with Stalin. Great Britain and France asked Soviet leader Joseph Stalin to become part of an alliance against Germany. The Soviet Union had joined the League of Nations while Japan, Germany, and Italy had

German and Italian Expansion, 1935–1941

Interpreting Maps Within six years of expansion, Germany and Italy controlled much of Europe and North Africa.

■ **Skills Assessment: 1. Places and Regions** What regions did Germany and Italy control by December 1941?

2. Analyzing Information What countries remained neutral during this period?

dropped out. However, Soviet leaders still did not trust the Western democracies. Western nations were fearful of communism. Until this time they had kept the Soviet Union out of all major decisions. Soviet leaders in turn feared that the Western powers would welcome a chance to turn Hitler loose on them.

The Soviets required that any agreement with the West guarantee the independence of Poland, Finland, and the Baltic countries of Estonia, Latvia, and Lithuania. All but Lithuania had common borders with the Soviet Union. The Soviets also wanted a military alliance with these countries. This would allow an immediate response if Germany attacked. The Baltic states immediately protested the Soviets' idea. A military agreement would mean that Soviet armies would have the right to move into their countries to fight off a German attack. As a result the talks dragged on without any agreement.

✔ **READING CHECK: Summarizing** What preparations did Great Britain and France make for war when Hitler's plans became clear?

The Nazi-Soviet Pact. At the same time that Stalin was negotiating with Great Britain and France, he was carrying on secret talks with Germany. In August 1939 the Western democracies received a huge shock when Hitler proudly announced a **German-Soviet nonaggression pact.** Also called the Nazi-Soviet Pact, this agreement publicly stated that Germany and the Soviet Union would never attack each other. Each would remain neutral if the other went to war.

The reasons for this agreement were not clear at the time. Both Hitler and Stalin may simply have been playing for time. Hitler wanted to make sure the Soviets would be neutral if Great Britain or France took action against Germany. Stalin hoped that Hitler's attention would be focused on events in the West. This would give the Soviet Union enough time to prepare for a conflict with Germany.

Secretly, however, Hitler and Stalin had agreed to divide eastern Europe into spheres of influence. Germany was to take western Poland. The Soviet Union was to have a free hand in the Baltic countries. It would also control eastern Poland and the province of Bessarabia. Little doubt existed as to the meaning of the agreement. The Western nations had lost a possible ally in the East, and Germany had arranged for the Soviet Union to be neutral. This gave Germany a huge military advantage.

✔ **READING CHECK: Finding the Main Idea** Why did Hitler and Stalin create the Nazi-Soviet Pact?

Shown here is Joseph Stalin (second from right) with other Russian and German diplomats concluding the German-Soviet nonaggression pact.

Danzig and the Polish Corridor. The crisis that finally touched off World War II began in Poland. Hitler wanted Germany to control the seaport city of Danzig—modern day Gdańsk. Danzig was a free city, protected by the League of Nations. Poland and Germany both had rights to use the busy and strategically important port of Danzig, located at the mouth of the Vistula River on the coast of the Baltic Sea. A strip of land about 90 miles long and between 25 and 55 miles wide allowed Poland access to the port of Danzig. This land ran through what had been German Prussia. It had been granted to Poland in 1919 by the Treaty of Versailles in order to provide Poland with a direct opening to the Baltic. This strip of land, known as the Polish Corridor, became a growing source of conflict between Poland and Germany during the years following World War I. After Hitler came to power in 1933, he acted to claim Danzig for Germany because it had a large German population. It also had a strong and growing Nazi Party that by 1937 had taken control of the city government.

On September 1, 1939, Hitler announced the annexation of Danzig to the German Reich. At the same time, without warning, his air force began a massive attack on Poland. Nazi tanks sped across the border and swiftly drove toward Warsaw and the Polish heartland. The Poles were relentlessly attacked by German forces equipped with modern weapons and technology, and a strategy of total war. Polish troops made a courageous but hopeless defense against the German onslaught. Two days later Great Britain and France decided that they would not stand for any further Nazi aggression. They kept their promises to Poland and declared war on Germany. Within 48 hours the unannounced attack on Poland had become the beginning of World War II.

✔ **READING CHECK: Drawing Conclusions** How did the Nazi-Soviet Pact and Hitler's attack on Poland lead to World War II?

SECTION 2 REVIEW

1. **Define** and explain the significance:
   appeasement

2. **Identify** and explain the significance:
   Axis Powers
   Anti-Comintern Pact
   Munich Conference
   Neville Chamberlain
   Édouard Daladier
   German-Soviet nonaggression pact

3. **Summarizing** Copy the graphic organizer below. Use it to identify the steps Hitler took to annex Austria and Czechoslovakia.

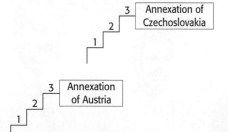

4. **Finding the Main Idea**
   a. How and why did France and Great Britain try to avoid war with Hitler?
   b. Why might British and French policies during the 1930s have encouraged German aggression?
   c. How did the Western powers react to Hitler's invasion of Poland?

5. **Writing and Critical Thinking**
   Identifying Cause and Effect Explain how Great Britain and France prepared for war after Hitler overtook Czechoslovakia.
   Consider:
   • building their military strength
   • the protection of Poland
   • negotiating with Stalin

go.hrw.com
Homework Practice Online
keyword: SH3 HP21

Axis Gains

READ TO DISCOVER

❶ How did German control of Norway, Denmark, and the Low Countries benefit Hitler?

❷ What success did German forces experience in France?

❸ What was the Battle of Britain, and why were the Germans unable to achieve victory?

❹ What role did the United States play at the beginning of the war, and how did that role change?

DEFINE

blitzkrieg
"phony war"
collaborators
maquis
isolationists

IDENTIFY

Winston Churchill
Philippe Pétain
Charles de Gaulle
Luftwaffe
Battle of Britain
Neutrality Acts
Lend-Lease Act
Atlantic Charter

► WHY IT MATTERS TODAY

Great Britain and the United States continue to work together on international issues. Use **CNN**News.com or other **current event** sources to find a recent issue that these two countries have addressed. Record your findings in your journal.

CNN Student News.com

The Main Idea
Striking quickly and forcefully, the Axis Powers gained military control over most of Europe.

The Story Continues *After France and Great Britain agreed to Hitler's demands at the Munich Conference, the German leader believed he had little to fear from the Western leaders. "I saw them at Munich," he said. "They are little worms." Germany's invasion of Poland brought declarations of war from Great Britain and France. Hitler already had the advantage, however, and continued his conquest of European nations.*

The "Phony War"

Hitler's invasion of Poland introduced the world to a new kind of warfare. The attack was a **blitzkrieg** (German for "lightning war"), meaning it took place with great speed and force. After a month of fighting, Poland surrendered to Hitler. While Germany attacked Poland, France moved its army up to its chain of fortifications along the Maginot Line. British forces landed on the northern coast of France and the British navy blockaded Germany's ports. The Germans placed troops in the Siegfried Line, the system of fortifications they had built in the Rhineland. There were a few attacks on British battleships. Otherwise, however, there was little action on the western front. While there was an increase in troop movement and arms production, newspapers began to speak of the **"phony war"** in western Europe. Some people still hoped that an all-out war could be avoided.

As the Germans marched into Poland from the west, the Soviet army built up on the Soviet-Polish border. Then following the secret deal made in the Nazi-Soviet Pact, the Soviets invaded eastern Poland on September 17. Once again Poland disappeared from the map of Europe. The Soviets also took control of Estonia, Latvia, and Lithuania. On November 30, 1939, the Soviet Union attacked Finland. The Finns appealed to the League of Nations. However, the League could do nothing more than expel the Soviet Union for its aggression against another member nation. Although the Finns fought bravely, their struggle ended in March 1940.

Scandinavia and the Low Countries. On April 9, 1940, the "phony war" ended with a sudden German invasion of Denmark and Norway. The Germans sometimes depended on help from **collaborators,** people who were willing to help their country's enemies. A leader of the Norwegian Fascist Party named Quisling proved to be an important collaborator for Germany. He provided information to the Germans before the invasion and aided the occupying forces. In a single day German troops took control of some of Norway's strategic ports. Both Norway and Denmark fell to German control.

By taking these countries, Germany gained an outlet to the Atlantic Ocean. The Scandinavian coastline and landscape gave Germany very good submarine bases and airfields. This put shipping to France and Great Britain in serious danger. The British realized that Hitler was now an immediate threat to their safety. In May 1940 **Winston Churchill** replaced Neville Chamberlain as prime minister. Churchill had been one of the few politicians to speak out against the policy of appeasement in the 1930s.

Citizens of Warsaw, Poland, flee the German Blitzkreig as fire consumes their neighborhood.

Hitler, meanwhile, continued to attack. On May 10, 1940, German armored units invaded the Low Countries—the Netherlands, Belgium, and Luxembourg. By the end of May, all three countries had surrendered. Hitler's forces were now in a position to outflank France's Maginot Line. German armored units drove westward toward the English Channel. Reaching the coast, they cut off a large number of British, Belgian, and French troops from the main French force to the south. Outnumbered and with no room to change their position, the encircled Allied troops tried to escape from the French seaport of Dunkerque.

Evacuation of Dunkerque. The British air force, badly outnumbered, struggled to help the trapped forces in Dunkerque. Fortunately the German ground forces stopped their advance. Every available ship and boat in Britain was ordered to Dunkerque. Even fishing and rowboats fell under attack by aircraft, submarines, and artillery as they picked up forces from the beaches. Between about May 27 and June 4, about 338,000 men were safely transported across the channel to England. However, they did lose all their heavy equipment.

The reason why Hitler did not attack the retreating Allies is not known for certain. He may have believed his air force could finish off the Allied forces. This decision would later be seen as a costly mistake. It allowed Britain to regain its strength. Although the Allies were defeated at Dunkerque, the success of the rescue effort helped raise British spirits.

✔ **READING CHECK: Evaluating** How did Hitler benefit from taking control of Norway, Denmark, and the Low Countries?

The Fall of France

After the evacuation of Dunkerque, the French were left to fight alone on the European continent. The Maginot Line was useless. Having taken Belgium, the Germans were in a position to attack France from the north, where there were few fortifications. Germany turned southward to attack the heart of France early in June 1940. The French fought a difficult, losing battle. The French army expected stationary battles such as those in World War I. They were not trained or equipped for this new kind of war. German planes bombed and machine-gunned civilians who tried to escape the attack, causing great panic and disorder.

In June 1940 northern France became a scene of absolute confusion. Carrying whatever belongings they could, civilians crowded roads as they tried to escape to the south.

Mussolini quickly took advantage of France's weakness. He declared war on France and Great Britain on June 10, and Italian forces attacked southern France. On June 14 the Germans entered Paris, and the French armed resistance in the north fell apart. Rather than surrender, the French cabinet resigned.

Some French leaders, however, were willing to surrender. **Philippe Pétain** (PAY·tan), a hero of World War I, formed a government and assumed dictatorial powers. Late in June, Hitler forced the Pétain government to sign a peace agreement with Germany and Italy. The terms of the agreement were severe. German troops were to occupy northern France, including Paris, and a strip of territory along the Atlantic coast southward to Spain. France had to pay the costs of this occupation. The French navy was to be disarmed and not allowed out of French ports. Pétain's government moved to the city of Vichy (VISH·ee), in the south. Thus France was divided into occupied France, administered by the Germans, and Vichy France, which collaborated with the Germans. The Vichy government also controlled most French possessions in North Africa and the Middle East.

The French Resistance. Some of the French who wanted to continue to fight against Germany escaped to Africa or to Britain. Under the leadership of General **Charles de Gaulle** (duh·GOHL), they formed the Free French government. It set up headquarters in London. Britain, and later the United States, equipped the Free French army. As the war went on, this army played a part in several campaigns.

In France itself a resistance movement worked underground, or in secret. Similar movements developed in other German-occupied countries as well. Members of some of these groups were called **maquis** (mah·KEE)—the French term for the scrubby undergrowth common in the areas where resistance fighters hid. The maquis fought the Germans from within their occupied lands. They undermined the Nazi war effort by engaging in acts of sabotage such as blowing up bridges, wrecking trains, and cutting telephone and telegraph lines.

✔ **READING CHECK: Summarizing** What success did Hitler have in France?

The Battle of Britain

After France fell, many predicted that Britain would prove to be even weaker than France. Little by little, Hitler began scattered bombing raids on Great Britain, gradually increasing them in intensity. When he offered to negotiate a peace settlement, Churchill refused. At the end of June 1940, Churchill braced the British people for the dangerous battle that he felt sure would come.

> *History Makers Speak*
>
> **"Hitler knows that he will have to break us in this island or lose the war. If we can stand up to him, all Europe may be free and the life of the world may move forward into broad, sunlit uplands. But if we fail, then the whole world, including the United States, including all that we have known and cared for, will sink into the abyss of a new Dark Age. . . . Let us therefore brace ourselves to our duties, and so bear ourselves that, if the British Empire and its Commonwealth last for a thousand years, men will say, 'This was their finest hour.'"**
>
> Winston Churchill, quoted in *A Treasury of the World's Great Speeches,* edited by Houston Peterson

Hitler ordered his air force, the **Luftwaffe,** to soften up Britain for invasion. He moved the Luftwaffe units to airfields in France and Belgium, closer to their targets.

HISTORY MAKER

Winston Churchill (1874–1965)

Winston Churchill is generally considered to be one of Great Britain's most outstanding leaders. As prime minister during World War II, Churchill is best remembered for helping to boost British hopes of victory.

Churchill also recognized the importance of maintaining close ties with the United States. Throughout the war, he worked hard to promote good relations between the two countries. His distrust of Stalin and the Soviet Union emphasized his concern about the spread of communism. **What were Churchill's goals and concerns?**

Analyzing Primary Sources

Evaluating Why do you think Churchill's speech made a difference in the war?

The Battle of Britain Between about September 1940 and May 1941, Britain suffered regular nighttime air raids by German bombers. Some 43,000 civilians died and thousands were left homeless. *Why might this British family need the wooden shutters that they are making?*

The first German air attacks were on British military sites. Later they struck railroads and civilian and industrial targets. These raids, along with British efforts to counter them, became known as the **Battle of Britain.** This fighting continued non-stop during September and October. Hitler believed his airforce would destroy the people's will to fight. The British, however, dug out of their ruins and carried on. The Royal Air Force—or RAF—continued fighting to defend the island country. The growing success of these fighter planes gave the British hope.

Outnumbered by the Luftwaffe, British pilots flew combat missions day after day, night after night. The RAF also had a new electronic tool called radar. This helped identify enemy aircraft or ships as they came near. The early warning provided by radar gave British fighters time to counterattack and kept the Germans from making surprise attacks. The RAF's control of the air also meant that Germany could not invade across the English Channel.

The Germans continued their night bombing for many months. At the same time, British bombers made stronger and heavier attacks on German cities. By the middle of 1941, air warfare had peaked. Germany began sending some of its war resources to the east. However, Germany's blockade of British shipping meant there was a chance that Great Britain could be starved into surrendering. This might have happened had it not been for the United States.

✔ **READING CHECK: Finding the Main Idea** Why was Germany unable to win the Battle of Britain?

United States Involvement

In the **Neutrality Acts** passed between 1935 and 1937, the United States had stated its wish to stay neutral in future wars. These laws said Americans could not sell war equipment to warring nations. Americans could not make loans to these nations or sail on their ships. In addition, American ships were restricted from entering war zones.

Many people worried that Nazi Germany would hurt not only Europe, but also civilization itself. Most Americans, however, believed that Europe's wars should not concern the United States. These **isolationists,** as they were called, had come to power at the end of World War I. Their power began to fade as fears grew that the Nazis would take over the world. In 1939 a revised Neutrality Act allowed American firms to sell munitions to warring nations on a cash-and-carry basis. Great Britain still controlled sea routes between the United States and Great Britain. Therefore, the effect of this law was to allow the sale of arms only to Great Britain.

After the rescue from Dunkerque and the fall of France, American sympathy for the British grew. President Franklin D. Roosevelt believed that Britain was the front line of a war that would involve the United States sooner or later. In September 1940 President Roosevelt moved 50 old American warships to Great Britain. In exchange Great Britain gave the United States use of several naval and air bases. In that same month Congress passed the first national draft law in the United States during peacetime. Early in 1941 Churchill said to the United States: "Give us the tools, and we will finish the job." In March Congress passed the **Lend-Lease Act,** authorizing the president to supply war materials to Great Britain on credit. Now the direction of America's involvement became clear.

✔ **READING CHECK: Sequencing** What was the U.S. position on foreign wars during the 1930s and how did it begin to change?

Holt Researcher

go.hrw.com
KEYWORD: Holt Researcher
FreeFind: Winston Churchill
Franklin Roosevelt
After reading more about Winston Churchill and Franklin Roosevelt on the Holt Researcher, create a Venn diagram comparing their accomplishments in office. Then assess which one you think had the greatest impact on the 20th century.

The Atlantic Charter

President Roosevelt and Prime Minister Churchill met in August 1941. Together they created a statement that became known as the **Atlantic Charter.** This document stated that the United States and Great Britain (1) sought no territorial gain, (2) would allow no territorial changes without the consent of the people concerned, (3) respected the right of all people to choose their own form of government, (4) believed that all nations should have equal rights to trade and to raw materials, (5) wanted nations to cooperate on economic matters to ensure everyone a decent standard of living, (6) believed people everywhere should have the right to security and freedom from want and fear, (7) believed freedom of the seas should be guaranteed, and (8) believed that nations must abolish the use of force and establish a system of general security, suggesting the creation of an international organization.

During the fall of 1941, the United States Navy helped the British in many ways. It fought against German submarines and protected ships in the western Atlantic. Isolationist opinion was still strong in the United States. By November 1941, however, the United States was giving the British all aid short of joining the war.

✔ **READING CHECK: Summarizing** In what ways did the United States become involved in the war?

In August 1941 Roosevelt and Churchill met aboard a British battleship off the coast of Newfoundland. Their Atlantic Charter publicly announced the democratic goals shared by Great Britain and the United States.

SECTION 3 REVIEW

1. Define and explain the significance:
   blitzkrieg
   "phony war"
   collaborators
   maquis
   isolationists

2. Identify and explain the significance:
   Winston Churchill
   Philippe Pétain
   Charles de Gaulle
   Luftwaffe
   Battle of Britain
   Neutrality Acts
   Lend-Lease Act
   Atlantic Charter

Homework Practice Online
keyword: SH3 HP21

3. Sequencing Copy the time line below. Use it to describe German progress in the war through the first half of 1941.

```
                April      June
                1940       1940
                 |          |
  _____
        |                |            |
   September           May          mid-
     1939             1940          1941
```

4. **Finding the Main Idea**

a. How did Hitler gain control over France and how did some French people continue to resist German rule?

b. How was British airpower able to prevent a German invasion across the English Channel?

5. **Writing and Critical Thinking**

Sequencing Describe the progression of the involvement of the United States in World War II.
Consider:
• the original Neutrality Acts and the revised Neutrality Act of 1939
• why Americans sympathized with the British
• the Atlantic Charter and U.S. aid to the British in the fall of 1941

The Soviet Union and the United States

READ TO DISCOVER

1 What steps did the Axis Powers take to gain control of eastern Europe, the Middle East, and North Africa?

2 How did Germany plan to gain control of the Soviet Union, and how successful was the Soviets' defense?

3 How did Japan's goals in the Pacific lead to war with Britain and the United States?

IDENTIFY

Erwin Rommel
Hideki Tōjō

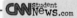
The Main Idea
The Soviet Union entered the war against Germany, while the United States fought Germany and Japan.

The Story Continues *In the Atlantic Charter, Franklin D. Roosevelt and Winston Churchill called for the destruction of "Nazi tyranny." They pledged to create a postwar world in which "all men in all the lands may live out their lives in freedom from fear and want." The loyalty of the United States to the Allied cause now was obvious.*

Eastern Europe and the Mediterranean

In the fall of 1940, Germany held almost all of western Europe. It controlled the Atlantic coastline from the tip of Norway to southern France. Spain, under Franco's rule, remained neutral but allowed German submarines to use its ports. Italy and Germany also controlled much of the western Mediterranean coastline. This was an important advantage. Great Britain still held Gibraltar, on the southern coast of Spain. It also held the islands of Malta and Cyprus, in the Mediterranean, and Alexandria in Egypt. British troops were stationed in Palestine and in Egypt, protecting the Suez Canal. In September Japan joined the Rome-Berlin Axis, allying itself with Hitler and Mussolini.

Mussolini hoped to build a Mediterranean empire for Italy. In the fall of 1940 he sent his troops into Egypt and Greece. The decision proved to be unwise. Italy's attack on Greece did not go well. The British stopped the Italians' advance into Egypt and took Tobruk, a port city of Libya. They also liberated Ethiopia and turned the Italians back from British Somaliland.

The Axis powers had more success in and around the Balkans. By April 1941, Hungary, Romania, Slovakia, and Bulgaria had all joined the Axis side. That same spring, Germany took Yugoslavia, Greece, and the island of Crete. This gave the Germans control over the Balkan Peninsula except for European Turkey. In June 1941 Germany and Turkey signed a treaty that said Turkey would remain neutral. The Balkan victories put Germany in a position to attack the Soviet Union and the Middle East. Controlling the region's rich oil fields would give Hitler a huge advantage. If Britain lost the Suez Canal, its position in India, Southeast Asia, and the Pacific would be threatened.

The Axis Powers had the support of many citizens in Iraq and Egypt who wanted to be rid of their British occupiers. The French Vichy government controlled Lebanon and Syria. In May 1941 British and Indian troops crushed a pro-Axis coup d'etat in Iraq. In July British and Free French forces drove the Vichy French out of Lebanon and Syria. Meanwhile, the Allied situation in Africa grew worse.

An Ethiopian chief addresses his troops before battle.

German troops commanded by General **Erwin Rommel** moved across the Mediterranean to take control of Libya in early 1941. However, by the summer of 1942, the British were having success in the naval and air war in the Mediterranean. This allowed the British to build up troops and equipment in North Africa. They also were able to cut off Axis supplies. In October Rommel's forces were soundly beaten at the Battle of El Alamein. Now the Axis forces, unable to make up their losses, retreated to Tunisia.

✔ **READING CHECK: Comparing** What were the results of Axis Powers trying to take control of eastern Europe, the Middle East, and North Africa?

World War II in Europe and North Africa, 1939–1945

Interpreting Maps World War II made Europe and North Africa one huge battlefield.

■ **Skills Assessment: 1. The World in Spatial Terms** What two battles took place along the 50° N parallel in Europe?

2. Drawing Conclusions What physical feature affected fighting in southern Europe and North Africa?

Germany's Attack on the Soviet Union

The Soviet Union reacted to German victories in the Balkans with alarm and anger. It believed the Balkans should be within the Soviet sphere of influence. The Soviet Union demanded that certain parts of this region be kept in their sphere of influence. Hitler suggested instead that Germany should have Europe and the Soviet Union should create a sphere in Asia. The Soviets rejected this idea.

On June 22, 1941, the war began a new phase. Without declaring war, German armies invaded the Soviet Union. Hitler had opened a huge new front in the east. It was 2,000 miles long from north to south. Churchill offered aid to the Soviet Union. The United States also said it was willing to help. Sending aid to the Soviets, however, was very difficult. Shipping across the Mediterranean ran the risk of submarine and air attacks. The route through the Baltic Sea was impossible. Reaching Soviet ports on the Arctic required passing the long, German-held coast of Norway. As a result, the Allies started a new route. They moved supplies from the Persian Gulf across Iran by train and truck to the southern part of the Soviet Union.

The Soviet defense. The Germans' first movements into the Soviet Union had great success. Everywhere the Soviet armies were driven back. Soviet defenders used the same scorched-earth methods against Hitler that their ancestor had used against Napoléon. The retreating soldiers and civilians carried away what they could. They destroyed everything else. Many Soviet soldiers stayed hidden in forests, making daring guerrilla attacks on railroads, bridges, and trains.

Soon, however, Moscow and Leningrad were under attack. Hitler had expected the Soviet Union to surrender quickly. The Soviets were able to hold off German control of Moscow and Leningrad, however. As a result, the German army had to stay longer than expected. The delay forced the Germans to fight during the bitterly cold Russian winter. When the Soviets chose the winter for a counterattack, the Germans were forced to retreat.

In the spring of 1942, Hitler ordered a new offensive to the south. He hoped to take the oil-producing area around Baku, on the shore of the Caspian Sea. To protect the troops in that main attack, part of the German army was to capture the city of Stalingrad. German troops pushed into Stalingrad in September 1942. There, however, Soviet fighting grew stronger. Hitler now

These photographs show women on the eastern front coping with the devastation of war.

made capture of Stalingrad the main objective of the offensive. Stalin ordered that the city be held at all costs. The battle of Stalingrad had begun.

✔ **READING CHECK: Sequencing** How did Hitler try to gain control of the Soviet Union, and how did the Soviets defend themselves?

Japanese Aggressions in the Pacific

The struggle against the Axis Powers took another important turn in December 1941 when events in the Pacific drew the United States into the war. Japanese militarism and aggression had increased throughout the 1930s. Japanese armies pushed farther and farther into China, although the Chinese continued to resist. Early in 1939, with the situation in Europe growing increasingly tenser, Japan saw a chance to extend its control over Southeast Asia. Japan first captured several small islands off the coast of French Indochina. The effect was to cut off the British sea route between Hong Kong and Singapore. Neither France nor Great Britain could act in time to prevent this move.

The Japanese used fighter planes like the ones shown here to expand their empire in the Pacific.

After both the Netherlands and France fell, Japan made further aggressive moves in East Asia. The Japanese government announced that the Netherlands East Indies was under Japanese "protective custody." The Japanese also forced the Vichy government to allow French Indochina to become a Japanese protectorate.

In September 1940 Japan formed an alliance with Germany and Italy. In April 1941 Japan and the Soviet Union signed a five-year nonaggression treaty. Soon after, the Japanese moved farther south to occupy lands in French Indochina.

The United States responded to Japanese aggressions in three ways. First, it protested Japan's violations of the Nine-Power Pact of 1922. Second, it provided assistance to Chinese Nationalists. Third, it placed an embargo on the sale to Japan of steel and scrap iron, and then of oil. These actions made Japan even more intent on expanding in East Asia. Now only the American-held Philippines and the Hawaiian Islands threatened Japanese rule in the Pacific. The United States, meanwhile, had already moved a large part of its Pacific Fleet to Hawaii.

Relations between the United States and Japan continued to worsen. An even more militaristic government came to power in Japan under Premier **Hideki Tōjō.** Early in 1941 the Japanese government realized that their most dangerous potential enemy was the United States. Believing that their best chance for victory was to knock out the U.S. Pacific Fleet quickly, the Japanese commanders began to plan a surprise attack on the U.S. fleet, based at Pearl Harbor in Hawaii.

✔ **READING CHECK: Analyzing Information** How did relations between Japan and the United States worsen between 1939 and 1941?

American Entry into the War

On December 7, 1941, the Japanese launched a surprise bombing raid on the American naval base at Pearl Harbor, Hawaii. They planned to strike such a severe blow that the United States would be unable to fight the Japanese in the Pacific. Several U.S. battleships were sunk. Others were badly damaged. American military dead totaled more than 2,300.

On December 8, 1941, Congress declared war on Japan, as did the British Parliament. Three days later, Germany and Italy declared war on the United States, and Congress replied with its own declaration of war. The Japanese quickly took advantage of American unreadiness. On the same day as the attack on Pearl Harbor, Japan captured the American island of Guam. They also began aerial attacks on the Philippines. Soon afterward, Japan took control of Luzon, Burma, Thailand, and Malaya.

Japan went on to conquer what became a widespread island empire. Most of the Netherlands East Indies (Indonesia), the Philippines, and the Gilbert Islands came under Japanese rule. Australia was the last stronghold of resistance in the southwest Pacific. The landing of the Japanese on New Guinea and the Solomon Islands threatened to cut off Australia's important supply routes from Hawaii.

✔ **READING CHECK: Identifying Cause and Effect** How did Japan's goals in the Pacific lead to war with Britain and the United States?

INTERPRETING THE VISUAL RECORD

Pearl Harbor Americans were shocked and outraged by the Japanese attack on Pearl Harbor. *What do these headlines suggest about public concern over the bombing?*

SECTION 4 REVIEW

1. **Identify** and explain the significance:
   Erwin Rommel
   Hideki Tōjō

2. **Identifying Cause and Effect** Copy the graphic organizer below. Use it to describe the results of the Axis attacks on eastern Europe, the Middle East, and North Africa.

   Axis attacks →
   - Eastern Europe → Results
   - Middle East → Results
   - North Africa → Results

3. **Finding the Main Idea**

   a. What steps did Hitler take to gain control over the Soviet Union, and how did the Soviets respond?

   b. Why did the Japanese attack Pearl Harbor, and what was the result?

4. **Writing and Critical Thinking**

   Sequencing Describe the results of Axis aggressions from late 1940 through 1942.

   Consider:
   - Italy's actions
   - Germany's expansion
   - Japan's actions in the Pacific

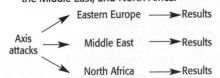

Homework Practice Online

keyword: SH3 HP21

The Holocaust

READ TO DISCOVER

❶ How was the Final Solution developed?

❷ What were conditions like in concentration camps?

❸ In what ways did different people resist the Holocaust?

IDENTIFY

"New Order"
Final Solution
Heinrich Himmler
SS
Wannsee Conference
Auschwitz
Holocaust
Anne Frank

▶ **WHY IT MATTERS TODAY**

The oppression and persecution of people based on ethnicity or race continues today. Use CNNStudentNews.com or other **current event** sources to find at least two recent examples of racial or ethnic discrimination in the world. Record your findings in your journal.

CNNstudentNews.com

The Main Idea
Hitler led the Nazi effort to kill all European Jews and others who were not members of the "Aryan race."

The Story Continues *Holocaust survivor Elie Wiesel remembered his arrival at the death camp Auschwitz. "A German officer gave the order: 'Men to the left! Women to the right!' Eight words spoken quietly, indifferently, without emotion. . . . I walked on with my father and the other men. And I did not know that in that place, at that moment, I was parting from my mother and [sister] Tzipora forever."*

Hitler's "New Order"

The invasion of the Soviet Union was part of Hitler's master plan for a European **"New Order."** Hitler wanted to make the European continent into a single political and economic system. He planned to gain "living space" in Eastern Europe. Then his pure "Aryan race" could colonize the new area. According to Hitler's plan, the land in the Soviet Union would supply Germany with food and raw materials. Hitler expected tens of millions of Russians to starve to death. According to Nazi beliefs, all Slavs were "racially inferior."

The Nazis increasingly practiced anti-Semitism during the 1930s. Then in 1941 Hitler ordered the destruction of Europe's entire Jewish population. The Nazis called this program the **Final Solution** to the "Jewish question." In Germany this genocide was made possible by the passionate racist beliefs of some people. Hitler used past genocides that had gone unpunished as examples. Some of Hitler's officers had witnessed the Armenian genocide in Turkey. As Hitler sent his generals to run the death camps in Poland, he said, "Go, kill without mercy . . . who today remembers the annihilation [total destruction] of the Armenians?"

Heinrich Himmler, the head of the the Schutzstaffel, or **SS,** the military branch of the Nazi Party, headed the Final Solution. At first the SS simply rounded up Jews and shot them in large groups. Soon, however, they turned to using poison gas as a more efficient method of execution. At a January 1942 conference in Wannsee, Germany, officials met to formalize their plans. The **Wannsee Conference** set out a systematic plan for exterminating Jews in concentration camps.

✔ **READING CHECK: Evaluating** How was the Final Solution an extension of Nazi philosophy?

The sign over the gate of this concentration camp translates to "Work makes you free."

Concentration Camps, 1933–1945

Interpreting Maps As the German army invaded surrounding countries, Hitler ordered the construction of concentration camps, which became sites of enforced labor and death.

■ **Skills Assessment: Locate** Which European country contained the most labor camps? The most death camps?

Map legend:
- ▲ Labor camp
- ■ Death camp
- 1935 Date founded
- Border, 1933

Holt Researcher

go.hrw.com
KEYWORD: Holt Researcher

FreeFind: Fania Fenelon
After reading more about Fania Fenelon on the Holt Researcher, write a diary entry about her experiences at Auschwitz.

Analyzing Primary Sources

Drawing Inferences What does Primo Levi's account reflect about the methods of the SS?

Concentration Camps

The Nazis moved Jews by the hundreds of thousands to concentration camps in Germany and Poland. Dachau and Buchenwald in Germany were two of the largest labor camps. In Poland the Germans built Treblinka and **Auschwitz**—huge death camps in which people were systematically murdered. At first the Nazis buried their victims in mass graves. Eventually they used huge ovens to cremate the dead.

Not everyone who arrived at the camps was killed immediately. As prisoners arrived, SS officers sorted them into groups by age, health, and sex. Some groups, especially those unable to do much physical work, were immediately sent to "showers" for cleaning. These "showers" were really gas chambers. Primo Levi, a survivor of Auschwitz, recalled the selection process when he arrived at the camp.

❝The SS man . . . judges everyone's fate, and in turn gives the card to the man on his right or his left, and this is the life or death of each of us. . . .

Even before the selection is over, everybody knows that the left was effectively the 'schlechte Seite,' the bad side.**❞**

Primo Levi, from *Survival in Auschwitz*

Those Jews who were not killed soon after arrival lived in unspeakable conditions. The combination of forced labor, brutal treatment, starvation, filth, and disease killed thousands of other people in the camps.

During the war, people in some western European countries tried to protect Jews. In eastern Europe, however, a long tradition of anti-Semitism made the Nazi program easier to carry out. Its results there were even more devastating. By the time the Nazi government fell, its leaders and its followers had murdered 6 million European Jews. The Nazi genocide of the 1930s and 1940s is called the **Holocaust.** Millions of Slavs, Gypsies, and others who did not conform with the Nazi idea of "purity" were also murdered.

✔ **READING CHECK: Making Generalizations** What was life like in concentration camps during the Holocaust?

Resisting the Holocaust

At first most Jews obeyed the orders of the SS. Some went into hiding, including the family of **Anne Frank,** a teenager who kept a diary of her experiences during the Holocaust. As many people began to realize what the Nazis were doing, some Jews fought back. The fiercest resistance came from those in the Jewish ghetto in Warsaw, Poland. A band of Jews resisted Nazi efforts to evacuate the ghetto to concentration camps. In the end, however, the poorly armed group could not hold off the German forces. Eventually the Jewish rebels were killed and the ghetto was destroyed.

Many other Europeans quietly ignored what was happening to the Jews. Some non-Jews, however, did try to help save some people from the Holocaust. After the Germans occupied Denmark, for example, Danes helped some 7,000 Jews escape into neutral Sweden. In Hungary, Swedish diplomat Raoul Wallenberg saved countless Jews by declaring them under the protection of the Swedish embassy. In Poland and Czechoslovakia, German industrialist Oskar Schindler saved many Jews by employing them in his factories.

✔ **READING CHECK: Summarizing** How did some people resist the Holocaust?

HISTORY MAKER

Anne Frank (1929–1945)

One of the most powerful and haunting documents of World War II is the diary of teenager Anne Frank. Anne's diary, containing her thoughts and feelings, has come to represent for many the horrors of the Holocaust.

Anne's German-Jewish family fled Nazi Germany for Amsterdam, where they hid in a friend's home. Eventually, however, the Nazis found the Franks' hiding place and sent the entire family to a concentration camp, where Anne later died. **What does Anne Frank's diary symbolize?**

The Nazis forced Jews to wear the Star of David (shown here) to identify themselves.

SECTION 5 REVIEW

1. Identify and explain the significance:
"New Order"
Final Solution
Heinrich Himmler
SS
Wannsee Conference
Auschwitz
Holocaust
Anne Frank

2. Evaluating Copy the graphic organizer below. Use it to show the role of aggression and anti-Semitism in the Nazis' "New Order."

3. **Finding the Main Idea**
   a. How did the Nazis carry out the Final Solution?
   b. What were concentration camps like?

4. **Writing and Critical Thinking**
   Identifying a Point of View Imagine you are a resistance fighter in the Warsaw ghetto. Write a letter to a friend explaining why you are fighting the evacuation of the ghetto, even though you realize that you have little chance of defeating the Germans.
   Consider:
   • why the ghetto was evacuated
   • what the fate of the fighters would be if they complied with German orders
   • the odds of succeeding

Homework Practice Online
keyword: SH3 HP21

The End of the War

READ TO DISCOVER

❶ What were the outcomes of Allied military actions in the Soviet Union, North Africa, Italy, and the Atlantic?

❷ How were the Allies able to achieve victory in Europe?

❸ What steps did the Allies take to end the war with Japan?

DEFINE

"soft underbelly of the Axis"
island hopping

IDENTIFY

Battle of Stalingrad
Dwight D. Eisenhower
Battle of Midway
Operation Overlord
D-Day
V-E Day
V-J Day
Bataan Death March

The Main Idea
Allied victories in North Africa, Europe, and the Pacific led to the end of World War II.

The Story Continues *After France fell, French generals had predicted that Britain would "have her neck wrung like a chicken" in three weeks. Churchill later commented: "Some chicken! Some neck!" The British had survived Hitler's aggression. Now, with the help of the United States, they stood ready to turn the tide of war in the Allies' favor.*

Important Offensives

Representatives of 26 nations came together in Washington, D.C., in January 1942. Each nation promised to use all its resources to defeat the Axis. They also agreed to not sign any separate peace treaties and to follow the Atlantic Charter.

In the summer of 1942, the Germans pushed the Soviets back to Stalingrad. The **Battle of Stalingrad** went on for six long and bloody months. German forces pushed inside the city, suffering terrible losses on the way. Instead of falling back, the determined Soviets defended the city street by street and house by house. In November 1942 the Soviets began a counterattack. They circled around the German troops, trapping them in Stalingrad. Those who were left of Hitler's troops surrendered on February 2, 1943. Stalingrad became a major turning point in the war as the Germans never fully recovered from their defeat.

The Allies also made progress in North Africa during 1942. General **Dwight D. Eisenhower** of the United States landed his American and British troops in Africa in November 1942. Eisenhower's army and British General Bernard Montgomery's forces in Tunisia trapped Rommel's army between them. By the middle of May 1943, the Axis forces in North Africa were forced to surrender. As a result of Rommel's defeat, North Africa was completely under Allied control. Italy's African empire disappeared. Control of the French colonies in Africa passed to the Free French government. Moreover, the Allies had kept control of the Suez Canal. This made the Mediterranean safer for Allied navies.

After the Allied victory in North Africa, Stalin demanded that British and American troops open a second front in Europe. He wanted to lessen the German pressure on the Soviet Union. Churchill suggested attacking what he called the **"soft underbelly of the Axis"**—through Italy and the Balkans. American and British forces took the island of Sicily in the summer of 1943. Then they made plans to invade the Italian mainland. When the Allies landed on Sicily, Mussolini was forced to resign. Marshal Pietro Badoglio (bah·DOHL·yoh) became premier. His first act was to dissolve the Fascist Party. Then he began secret talks with the Allies. When the Allied army landed on the southwestern tip of Italy in September 1943, the Italians agreed to stop fighting the Allies. In fact Italy declared war on Germany. German troops still present in Italy, however, continued to resist Allied troops.

✔ **READING CHECK: Summarizing** What did the Allies gain as a result of their victories in the Soviet Union, North Africa, and Italy?

The War at Sea and in the Air

During 1943 American and British bombing attacks against Germany and the occupied countries increased. The Allies bombed nearly every German city. Many were greatly damaged. The Allies were also gaining strength in the Atlantic. Beginning in 1939, German submarines had sunk many Allied ships. In the spring of 1943, however, destroyers and other armed ships safely led troop and supply ships from the United States. Planes also protected the shipping routes. Improved sonar technology located submarines. This took away much of their advantage.

The Japanese advance in the Pacific took its first loss in May 1942. In the Battle of the Coral Sea, American and Australian air and naval forces defeated a Japanese fleet headed for Australia. Soon afterward an American fleet met a larger Japanese fleet pushing eastward to try to capture Midway Island, northwest of Hawaii. The Americans defeated the Japanese in the important **Battle of Midway** in June. With these two victories, the United States Navy began to turn the tide in the war against Japan.

In August 1942 American marines took the airfield on Guadalcanal. This was the first invasion of Japanese-held territory. Winning control of Guadalcanal was important because it protected the Australian supply line. It also gave the Americans a huge lift in confidence. As Japan tried to reclaim the territory during the next three months, both sides suffered great losses. In 1943 the Allies took the offensive in the Pacific. Forces from Australia and New Zealand helped those from the United States. Together they fought to drive the Japanese out of the Solomon Islands. Then they began a strategy called **island hopping.** Under this policy, only certain Japanese islands were captured. Others were skipped and left without supplies.

During 1944 the Americans cleared the Japanese from the Marshall Islands, New Guinea, and the Marianas. In October 1944 an American army under General Douglas MacArthur landed in the Philippines. Shortly afterward, the Japanese suffered a crushing defeat in a great air and sea fight, the Battle of Leyte Gulf. In six months the Allies gained control of the Philippine Islands.

✔ **READING CHECK: Analyzing Information** What victories did the Allies achieve at sea, and what was the turning point in the war in the Pacific?

INTERPRETING THE VISUAL RECORD

Midway The U.S. victory in the Battle of Midway crippled the Japanese navy. *From the painting, what can you determine about the type of fighting that took place during the Battle of Midway?*

Victory in Europe

British and American troops slowly fought their way up the Italian Peninsula. However, most German troops remained locked in bloody battles with the Soviet Union. It was clear that another, larger invasion of Europe was needed to create the hoped-for "second front." Plans were started for **Operation Overlord,** the invasion of northwest France.

On June 6, 1944—**D-Day** as the military called it—the long-awaited landing began on France's Normandy coast. Within a month, more than 1 million Allied troops had landed. After heavy fighting Allied troops moved into northern France. Shortly afterward, Allied forces landed on the Mediterranean coast of France and fought their way northward. On August 25, 1944, Allied troops entered Paris. By September they faced the strongly fortified Siegfried Line along Germany's western edge.

Winston Churchill: Symbol of Wartime Britain

The quality of its leadership, as well as its military and industrial might, help to explain why a nation wins or loses a war. During World War II, the personalities of Allied and Axis leaders played a major role in the war's outcome. Under the exceptional leadership of Prime Minister Winston Churchill, Great Britain was able to overcome staggering odds as it battled the concentrated power of the German war machine. Churchill inspired his nation to victory. His greatest service may well have been his ability to symbolize—through speeches and personal actions—the characteristics of courage, endurance, and determination that his nation so badly needed in the face of German aggression.

Reading biographical accounts of Churchill's life helps us to understand this important man. A biographical account is a secondary source that describes all or part of an individual's lifetime. The source represents the opinions of the writer, and readers must be alert for evidence of bias—either for or against the individual whose life and work is being described. A biographical account is one of several sources that can be used to gather information about a historical figure. The reliability of a biographical account depends upon the biographer's approach—careful or careless, objective or subjective—to the subject. One of the best ways to determine the value of the account is to analyze several different types of evidence, primary and secondary alike, to develop as complete a picture of the subject as possible.

Churchill made clear his vision of Britain's wartime aims in a speech broadcast to the nation during the darkest days of the war.

> **"You ask what is our policy? I will say: It is to wage war, by sea, land and air, with all our might and with all the strength that God can give us . . . You ask, What is our aim? I can answer in one word: Victory—victory at all costs, victory in spite of all terror, victory, however long and hard the road may be; for without victory, there is no survival."**
>
> Winston Churchill,
> Speech to the House
> of Commons,
> May 1940

Churchill as a Symbol—A Biographer's View:

> **"One of Churchill's greatest gifts . . . was his ability to use his exceptional mastery of words and love of language to convey detailed arguments and essential truths; to inform, to convince, and to inspire. . . . His dislike of unfairness, of victimization, and of bullying—whether at home or abroad—was the foundation stone of much of his thinking. His finest hour was the leadership of Britain when it was most isolated, most threatened, and most weak; when his own courage, determination, and belief in democracy became one with that of a beleaguered [threatened with destruction] nation."**
>
> Martin Gilbert, "Churchill, Winston," *The Oxford Companion to Politics of the World*

Churchill's bulldog appearance, coupled with his gift of oratory and his unswerving determination to defeat the "monstrous tyranny" of Hitler's Germany, symbolized Britain's dedication to victory. He became the visible image of Allied determination.

Skills Reminder

To understand a biographical account, carefully assess the account to identify the writer's underlying bias. Is the biographical account balanced in its treatment? Does it provide a complete picture, placing equal emphasis on the subject's strong and weak points, contributions and failures, and positive and negative traits? Note what kind of language—positive, negative, or neutral—the writer uses to describe the subject. Are descriptors chosen to build a certain "image" of the subject?

Skills Practice

❶ Analyze Martin Gilbert's description of Churchill above. Can you infer Gilbert's general opinion of Churchill based on the excerpt?

❷ What clues regarding Gilbert's view of Churchill can you identify?

❸ Read a biography of a person mentioned in this chapter, then write a book review assessing its value in understanding the person and their importance to history.

Several weeks after D-Day, the Soviets began a major drive against Germany from the east. By the end of 1944, they had taken Finland, Estonia, Lithuania, Latvia, Romania, and Bulgaria. After five weeks of fighting, the Americans broke through the Siegfried Line in October. After a costly 10-day battle—the Battle of the Bulge—the Allies turned back the German drive. Finally, in early spring 1945, German defenses fell apart. At the end of April, the German army in Italy surrendered. The Soviet and American armies made their first contact in eastern Germany in April of 1945. It was agreed that the Soviets would take Berlin. On April 30—two days before the Soviets captured the ruined city—Hitler committed suicide. Within a week the German high command surrendered unconditionally. May 8, 1945 became **V-E Day,** the day of victory in Europe.

✔ **READING CHECK: Sequencing** What events led to the Allied victory in Europe?

World War II in the Pacific, 1941–1945

Interpreting Maps In 1943 the Allies waged a series of battles against the Japanese in the Pacific.

■ **Skills Assessment: The World in Spatial Terms** Where did the two northernmost Pacific battles take place?

Victory Over Japan

Although the war had ended in Europe, it continued in the Pacific. American marines captured the island of Iwo Jima after a month of the most bitter fighting in the war. The Allies took the island of Okinawa next. One marine later remembered his dreadful experience in the battle.

History Makers Speak

❝The mud beneath our feet was deeply veined with blood. It was slippery. Blood is very slippery. So you skidded around, in deep shock, fighting as best you could until one side outnumbered the other. The outnumbered side would withdraw for reinforcements and then counterattack.❞

William Manchester, *The New York Times Magazine*

In this battle about 263 Allied ships were sunk or damaged by suicide attacks of Japanese pilots. The only goal for these young kamikaze pilots was to find a good target and dive into it. The Japanese continued their resistance under heavy Allied bombing. Japan's ports were blocked and their navy could not move. The Japanese refused to surrender, however, and the Allies prepared for a major invasion of the home islands.

Yalta and Potsdam. In February 1945, Roosevelt and Churchill met with Stalin at Yalta, in the Soviet Union. They agreed that Germany would be divided and occupied by Allied troops. The Soviets agreed to enter the war against Japan. In return for their help, the Soviet Union would receive several Japanese territories. Another meeting began on July 17, 1945, at Potsdam, Germany. Roosevelt had died in April and Harry Truman was now president of the United States. Britain's new prime minister, Clement Attlee, had replaced Churchill. The leaders planned for the occupation of Germany and demanded an unconditional surrender from Japan.

Japanese surrender. When Japan again refused to surrender, President Truman made an important decision—to use the atomic bomb against Japan. On August 6, 1945, an American B-29 bomber dropped the deadly weapon on the city of Hiroshima. The impact of the bomb demolished everything in the area and started a spontaneous fire that destroyed the city. About 80,000 people were killed instantly, with many more injured. Countless more people later died from radiation sickness. The effects of the bomb were unlike anything ever seen before. In Tokyo, government officials at first had difficulty comprehending the scale of the damage.

On August 8, the Soviet Union declared war on Japan. Soviet armies swept into Manchuria, meeting little resistance. On August 9, an American plane dropped a second atomic bomb on Japan. This time the target was Nagasaki, where 40,000 people died instantly. Finally, on August 14, the Japanese surrendered unconditionally, asking only that the emperor be allowed to retain his title and authority. The Allies agreed, on the condition that the emperor accept the orders of the top Allied commander in the Pacific, General Douglas MacArthur. On September 2, 1945, known as **V-J Day,** both sides signed the Japanese surrender documents.

Costs of the war. World War II was the most destructive war in history. More than 22 million military personnel died and more than 34 million were wounded. In Europe and Asia, upward of 16 million civilians died. As the war progressed, weapons and tactics became more devastating. People began to feel that killing civilians was acceptable if it weakened the enemy.

The war also violated human rights on a scale never before seen. The Nazi Holocaust was only the most extreme of the war's atrocities. The Japanese and Soviets also committed acts of cruelty. Viewing conquered enemies as people without honor, Japanese troops often treated soldiers and civilians alike with great brutality. When the Japanese occupied the Chinese city of Nanjing in 1937, they burned stores and homes, eventually massacring about 250,000 people. In the Philippines in 1942, Japanese soldiers forced some 78,000 prisoners of war to march more than 55 miles up the Bataan Peninsula, killing more than 600 Americans and as many as 10,000 Filipinos. The incident became known as the **Bataan Death March.**

Soviet policy in occupied Poland was similar to that of the Nazis. The Soviets did not single out Jews, but instead attacked specific groups including landowners, local officials, clergy, teachers, and intellectuals. The Soviets sent about 1.5 million Poles to labor camps. When the Soviets retreated during the German invasion of 1941, they simply began shooting many of the imprisoned Poles. Close to 100,000 of those prisoners were executed.

The American use of nuclear weapons ushered in the atomic age and with it, many new questions and fears. How would the world deal with these powerful new weapons? What effect might they have on future wars? In the aftermath of World War II, leaders throughout the world struggled with these questions.

✔ **READING CHECK: Summarizing** How was World War II like no other war?

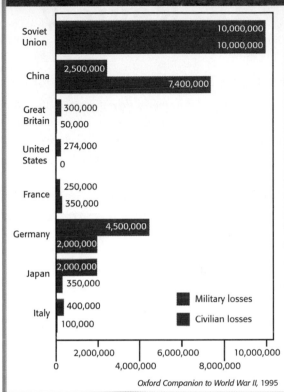

Losses of the Major Wartime Powers in World War II, 1939–1945

Country	Military losses	Civilian losses
Soviet Union	10,000,000	10,000,000
China	2,500,000	7,400,000
Great Britain	300,000	50,000
United States	274,000	0
France	250,000	350,000
Germany	4,500,000	2,000,000
Japan	2,000,000	350,000
Italy	400,000	100,000

Oxford Companion to World War II, 1995

Interpreting the Graph
More than 50 million people were killed during World War II. Overall, more civilians were killed than soldiers. *What three countries had the highest civilian losses? What factors do you think contributed to these losses?*

SECTION 6 REVIEW

1. **Define** and explain the significance:
   "soft underbelly of the Axis"
   island hopping

2. **Identify** and explain the significance:
   Battle of Stalingrad
   Dwight D. Eisenhower
   Battle of Midway
   Operation Overlord
   D-Day
   V-E Day
   V-J Day
   Bataan Death March

3. **Sequencing** Copy the graphic organizer below. Use it to show the events that led to the Allies' victory in World War II.

V-E Day (May 8, 1945)
① ② ③ ④ ⑤ ⑥ ⑦

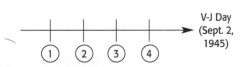
V-J Day (Sept. 2, 1945)
① ② ③ ④

4. **Finding the Main Idea**
   a. Why were Allied victories in the Soviet Union, North Africa, Italy, and the Atlantic necessary to win World War II?
   b. Why were the American victories in the Battle of the Coral Sea and the Battle of Midway important?
   c. Why was an Allied invasion of Europe necessary for achieving victory in Europe?
   d. What was unique about World War II?

5. **Writing and Critical Thinking**
   Supporting a Point of View Do you think the Allies were right to use the atomic bomb on Japan? Why or why not?
   Consider:
   • the benefits of getting Japan to surrender more quickly
   • the great destruction and loss of civilian life caused by the two atomic bombs

Homework Practice Online
keyword: SH3 HP21

CHAPTER 21 Review

Creating a Time Line

Copy the time line below onto a sheet of paper. Complete the time line by filling in events, individuals, and dates from the chapter that you think were significant. Pick three events and explain why you think they were significant.

| 1921 | 1933 | 1945 |

Writing a Summary

Using standard grammar, spelling, sentence structure, and punctuation, write an overview of the chapter.

Identifying People and Ideas

Identify the following terms or individuals and explain their significance:

1. Kellogg-Briand Pact
2. Francisco Franco
3. Munich Conference
4. Winston Churchill
5. Atlantic Charter
6. Hideki Tōjō
7. genocide
8. Holocaust
9. Dwight D. Eisenhower
10. D-Day

Understanding Main Ideas

Section 1 *(pp. 590–593)*

Threats to World Peace

1. Why was the League of Nations unable to keep Japan and Italy from taking over other countries?

Section 2 *(pp. 594–598)*

Hitler's Aggressions

2. How and why did Great Britain and France follow a policy of appeasement with Hitler?

Section 3 *(pp. 599–603)*

Axis Gains

3. How did the U.S. role in World War II change between the late 1930s and the fall of 1941?

Section 4 *(pp. 604–608)*

The Soviet Union and the United States

4. What were Japan's goals in the Pacific and how did they affect the United States?

Section 5 *(pp. 609–611)*

The Holocaust

5. How did some people try to resist the Holocaust?

Section 6 *(pp. 612–617)*

The End of the War

6. How did the Allies win the war with Japan?

Reviewing Themes

1. **Global Relations** How did regional conflicts grow to involve many nations in World War II?
2. **Government** How did Hitler use prejudice as a tool?
3. **Science, Technology & Society** How was the technology of World War II both beneficial and destructive?

Thinking Critically

1. **Making Generalizations** How was the era from 1939 to 1945 unique?
2. **Identifying Cause and Effect** How did the rise of nazism, fascism, and militarism in Germany, Italy, and Japan, as well as communism in the Soviet Union, contribute to the outbreak of World War II?
3. **Summarizing** What violations of human rights took place during World War II?

Writing About History

Problem Solving Review the failure of the League of Nations to end Italian and Japanese aggression during the 1930s. Then use a problem-solving process to write a peace-keeping plan for a new organization that would make it better equipped to keep international peace. Use the following diagram to organize your thoughts before you begin writing.

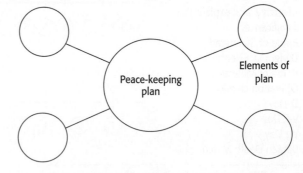

Reading a Chart

Study the chart below. Then answer the questions that follow.

Major Stages of World War II

Date	Europe and North Africa	The Pacific Theater
1939	Germany invades Poland.	—
1940	"Battle of Britain" occurs.	—
1941	U.S. enters war against the Axis.	Japan attacks Pearl Harbor.
1942	Allies invade North Africa.	U.S. lands on Guadalcanal.
1944	Allies land in Normandy.	U.S. lands in Philippines.
1945	Germany surrenders to the Allies.	U.S. drops atomic bombs on Japan. Japan surrenders.

1. Which statement correctly describes a relationship shown on the chart?

   a. The war in Europe and North Africa was shorter than the war in the Pacific.

   b. Hitler invaded Poland two years after Japan attacked Pearl Harbor.

   c. The U.S. landed in the Philippines one year after the Allies invaded North Africa.

   d. The war in the Pacific started two years after the war began in Europe.

2. Which of the events that occurred in 1945 was most responsible for Japan's surrender to the Allies? Give specific reasons to support your view.

Identifying Bias

Read the following quote from a message that Winston Churchill sent to Franklin Roosevelt in February, 1941. Then answer the questions.

> **"Some believe that Japan in her present mood would not hesitate to court an attempt to wage war both against Great Britain and the United States. Personally, I think the odds are definitely against that, but no one can tell. Everything that you can do to inspire the Japanese with fear of a double [two-front] war may avert the danger. If however they come in against us and we are alone, the grave character of the consequences cannot easily be overstated."**

3. Which of the following best describes how Churchill's experience influenced his viewpoint?

   a. Churchill had experience dealing with the Japanese, and he thought they feared a two-front war.

   b. Churchill welcomed the chance to show the world that Britain could defeat Japan.

   c. He had seen the war damage in his country, and he knew that Britain could not hold off Japan alone.

   d. Churchill was a soldier and wanted to command the Allied troops.

4. What events of World War II had Churchill already witnessed before he sent this message? Give specific examples.

Alternative Assessment

Building Your Portfolio

Link to TODAY

Global Relations

Interview a friend or relative who remembers the World War II years. Ask this person to explain the meaning of the following words or phrases: victory garden, ration books, blackouts, dog tags, Rosie the Riveter, war bonds, C-rations, and black market. During your interview, try to discover other World War II terms that you might add to the list.

🖅 **internet** connect

Internet Activity: go.hrw.com
KEYWORD: SH3 WH21

Choose a topic on World War II to:

• write a biography of Raoul Wallenberg.

• write a report on the historical information and legacy of Anne Frank.

• write a report about a landing beach on D-Day that includes a map, a description of what happened there, photographs, and eyewitness accounts.

CROSS-CULTURAL CONNECTIONS *Literature*

Hope Amid Turmoil

Erich Maria Remarque (1898–1970) wrote All Quiet on the Western Front *to overcome his depressing memories of trench warfare in World War I. In the excerpt below, German Paul Baumer has stabbed a French soldier after he fell on top of Baumer in a shell-hole. Later, Baumer regrets his enemy's death. Despite Remarque's hopes for a peaceful future, the world was soon at war again. As Allied armies advanced toward Germany in World War II, eight Jews hiding above a Dutch factory hoped for liberation. One of them was Anne Frank (1929–1945), who had received a diary for her 13th birthday. She hoped her diary would one day become a record of the Holocaust. Twenty days after the excerpt below was written, the Germans found the Frank's hiding place. Sent to the Bergen-Belsen concentration camp, Anne died of typhoid just weeks before the camp's liberation in April 1945.* The Diary of a Young Girl *has sold millions of copies since Anne's father published her diary in 1947.*

All Quiet on the Western Front
by Erich Maria Remarque

The silence spreads. I talk and must talk. So I speak to him and say to him: "Comrade, I did not want to kill you. If you jumped in here again, I would not do it, if you would be sensible too. But you were only an idea to me before, an abstraction that lived in my mind and called forth its appropriate response. It was that abstraction I stabbed. But now, for the first time, I see you are a man like me. I thought of your hand-grenades, of your bayonet, of your rifle; now I see your wife and your face and our fellowship. Forgive me, comrade. We always see it too late. Why do they never tell us that you are just poor devils like us, that your mothers are just as anxious as ours, and that we have the same fear of death, and the same dying and the same agony— Forgive me, comrade; how could you be my enemy? If we threw away these rifles and this uniform you could be my brother just like Kat and Albert."

The Diary of a Young Girl
by Anne Frank

Anyone who claims that the older folks have a more difficult time in the Annex doesn't realize that the problems have a far greater impact on us. We're much too young to deal with these problems . . . It's difficult in times like these: ideals, dreams and cherished hopes rise within us, only to be crushed by grim reality. It's a wonder I haven't abandoned all my ideals, they seem so absurd and impractical. Yet I cling to them because I still believe, in spite of everything, that people are truly good at heart. It's utterly impossible for me to build my life on a foundation of chaos, suffering and death. I see the world being slowly transformed into a wilderness, I hear the approaching thunder that, one day, will destroy us too, I feel the suffering of millions. And yet, when I look up at the sky, I somehow feel that everything will change for the better, that this cruelty too shall end, that peace and tranquility will return once more.

Understanding Literature

How do Remarque's and Frank's writings reflect hope? Why do you think Frank's diary has remained a bestseller for more than 50 years?

Economics

The Great Depression of the 1930s not only influenced the world economy, it also played an important role in shaping political events. Imagine that you are a German student living in Berlin. You have faithfully kept a journal throughout your life, taking special care to note the changing economic and political trends in Germany. Create seven journal entries detailing national events taking place in 1933. You can write entries for seven consecutive days or select seven dates from throughout the year. Remember to consider the state of the German economy and its influence on German political life during the early 1930s.

Hitler youth propaganda poster

Global Nationalism

Nationalist movements brought about change in many parts of the world, including Africa, Asia, and Latin America, during the early 1900s. The influence of strong leaders inspired calls for independence, modernization, and other political, social, and economic change. Imagine that you are an international correspondent assigned to interview a nationalist leader for a feature article on revolutions. Create a list of questions you would ask. The questions should indicate your understanding of the conditions in the country as well as the goals and methods of the person you are interviewing.

Chinese leader Chiang Kai-shek, shown here in about 1935, was head of the Chinese Nationalist Army. He later became president of Taiwan.

Further Reading

Holliday, Laurel, ed. *Children in the Holocaust and World War II: Their Secret Diaries.* New York: Simon and Schuster, 1995. First-person accounts of events during the Second World War as seen by young people.

Lang, Sean. *The Second World War: Conflict and Co-Operation.* London: Cambridge University Press, 1993. Presents an overview of the people, places, and events of the war.

Terkel, Studs. *Hard Times: An Oral History of the Great Depression in America.* New York: New Press, 2000. Classic featuring the voices of Americans who lived during the Great Depression.

Wepman, Dennis. *Africa: The Struggle for Independence.* New York: Facts on File, 1994. A history of African responses to imperialism and colonial rule.

Winter, J. M. *The Experience of World War I.* New York: Oxford University Press, 1989. A survey history of the First World War.

☑ internet connect

Internet Activity
KEYWORD: SH3 U5

In assigned groups, develop a multimedia presentation about the era from World War I to World War II. Choose information from the chapter Internet Connect activities and the Holt Researcher that best reflects the major topics of the period. Write an outline and a script for your presentation, which may be shown to the class.

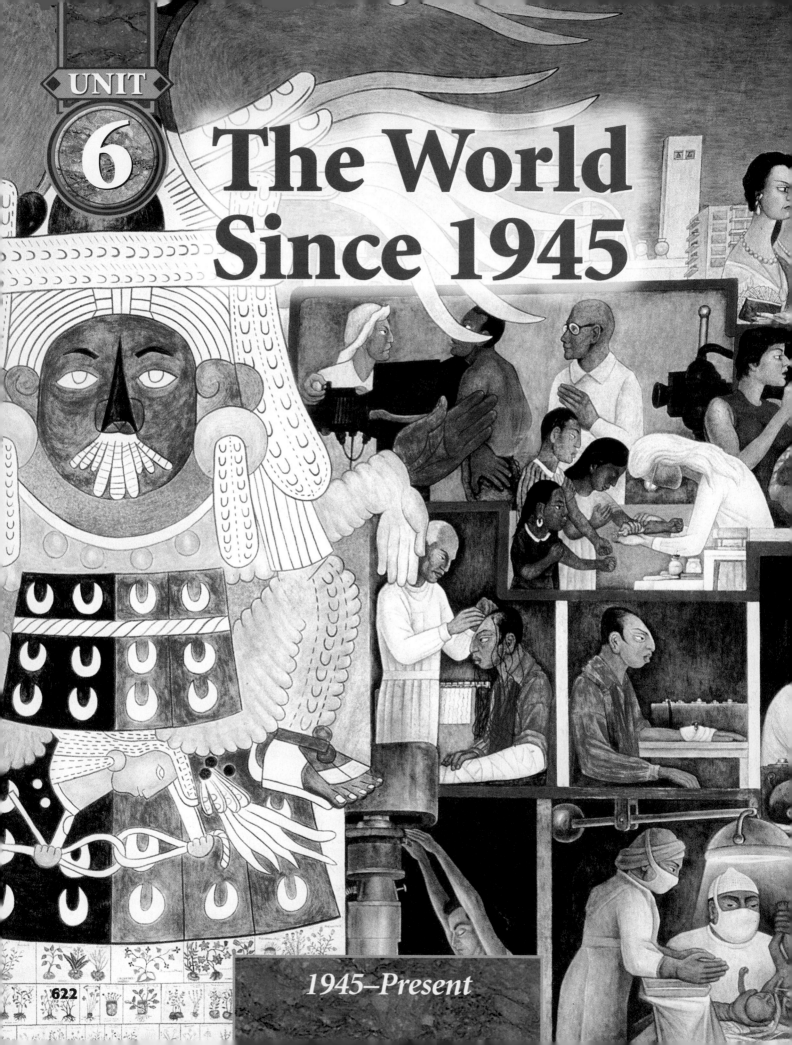

UNIT 6

The World Since 1945

1945–Present

622

Main Events

■ The Cold War occurs
■ Independence movements arise
■ The communist bloc collapses
■ The world becomes increasingly interconnected

Main Ideas

■ What were the Cold War's origins and outcomes?
■ How did postwar political realities encourage independence movements?
■ What factors promoted global economic change?

Ant carrying computer chip

Mexican muralist Diego Rivera created this striking composition, entitled The History of Medicine in Mexico, *in 1953.* **623**

CROSS-CULTURAL CONNECTIONS

Focus On: Citizenship

Main Idea **What are the rights of citizens?** A citizen is a member of a political community. He or she enjoys certain rights and privileges, such as the right to vote, and certain responsibilities, such as the defense of the community. The nature of citizenship changed dramatically in many nations after 1945.

Asia	
Europe and North America	
Latin America	
Africa and the Middle East	

1945   present

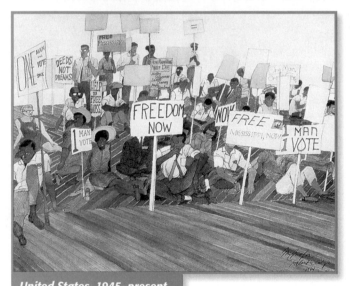

United States, 1945–present

Civil Rights Movement Although thousands of African-Americans fought for freedom in Europe and the Pacific during World War II, they returned to a nation that still practiced segregation in schools, stores, and jobs. During the postwar years African-Americans began a nationwide crusade for civil and political rights. The 1950s and the 1960s were particularly turbulent. This painting by Franklin McMahon, entitled *Civil Rights Protestors at the 1964 Democratic National Convention,* captures a moment in the long struggle for equality.

Communist China On October 1, 1949, Communist leader Mao Zedong proclaimed the new People's Republic of China. Mao used the Soviet Union as a model to begin a series of socialist actions designed to redistribute land, eliminate rural landlords, and promote industrial production. When Mao's policies failed, he silenced his critics by launching the Cultural Revolution in 1966. During this period Mao brutally suppressed political opposition by mobilizing youth in the Red Guards, such as those pictured here, to attack his enemies. In the years following Mao's death in 1976, however, demands for democratic reform began to be heard in China.

China, 1945–present

Statue of "Goddess of Democracy" erected in 1989 in Tiananmen Square during demonstrations for reform

Creating Israel The nation of Israel was created on May 14, 1948. Eight months later, in January 1949, Israelis held their first general election to establish the new nation's government. Political leaders, including the prime minister, who heads the government, and members of the Israeli Knesset, the nation's legislature, are elected by popular vote. Representatives to the Knesset meet in the starkly impressive building pictured at right. The Knesset has supreme political authority in Israel, including the power to oust the prime minister and dissolve the government.

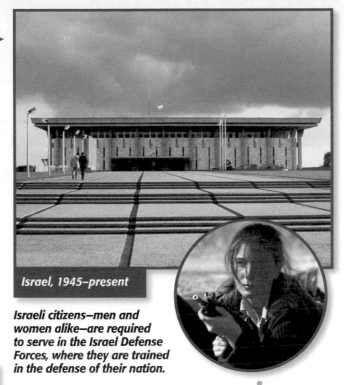

Israel, 1945–present

Israeli citizens—men and women alike—are required to serve in the Israel Defense Forces, where they are trained in the defense of their nation.

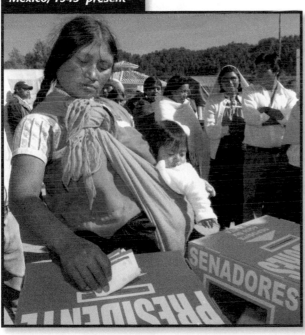

Mexico, 1945–present

Mexico's Peaceful Revolution On July 2, 2000, Mexican citizens brought an end to the 71-year rule of the PRI—the Institutional Revolutionary Party. By electing Vicente Fox president of Mexico, citizens sought to rid their country of a corrupt government. Some Mexicans compared Fox's election in 2000 to the storming of the Bastille in 1789, when French citizens overthrew their unjust monarchy. The Totzil Mayan woman pictured here voting in Mexico's 2000 elections is exercising the citizen's power to choose political representatives.

Why It Matters Today

After World War II people around the globe experienced many different forms of citizenship. As political transformations took place in the late 1900s, the nature of citizenship changed in many countries. **In what countries has citizenship recently changed? Where are people continuing to fight for rights as citizens?**

1945–1968

Europe and North America in the Postwar Years

1955
Global Events
The Warsaw Pact
is established.

1945
Global Events
The United
Nations is
established.

1950
The Arts
Construction begins
on Le Corbusier's
Notre Dame du Haut.

1953
Politics
Joseph Stalin dies.

1955
**Business and
Finance**
Egypt agrees to trade
cotton with Romania
and the Soviet Union.

1945

1950

1955

1945
The Arts
Jazz saxophonist Charlie
Parker popularizes "bebop."

1945–1946
Global Events
The Nürnberg trials are held.

1949
Global Events
NATO is formed.

1949
Politics
The Federal Republic of
Germany is founded.

1948
Global Events
The Berlin blockade and airlift begin.

1954
Daily Life
U.S. Supreme
Court bans
school
segregation.

1953
**Science and
Technology**
Biologists discover the
double helix structure of
DNA.

1956
The Arts
Spanish poet
Juan Ramón
Jiménez
receives the
Nobel Prize
for literature.

*Cover of a
Charlie Parker album*

DNA molecule

Build on What You Know

*I*n order to defeat the Axis Powers in World War II, Western nations had allied themselves
with the Soviet Union. This alliance proved effective, and in 1945 Soviet troops entered
Berlin, bringing the fighting in Europe to an end. With the war over, however, prewar
differences that had divided the Western European democracies from the communist
Soviet Union reemerged. Moreover, much of Europe had been devastated in the fury of
World War II. In this chapter, you will learn about economic and political conditions in
Europe and North America in the decades following World War II.

Newspaper headline following the 1963 Kennedy assassination

A still from the movie 2001: A Space Odyssey

1957
Business and Finance
The Common Market is created.

1957
Science and Technology
The Soviets launch *Sputnik I.*

1959
Politics
The Cuban government falls to Marxist rebels.

1959
Science and Technology
The St. Lawrence Seaway is completed.

1964
Politics
Soviet leader Nikita Khrushchev is forced to resign.

1964
Daily Life
Martin Luther King Jr. receives the Nobel Peace Prize.

1964
The Arts
The Beatles make their first tour of the United States.

1968
Global Events
Warsaw Pact troops invade Czechoslovakia, ending the Prague Spring.

1968
The Arts
Stanley Kubrick's film *2001: A Space Odyssey* is released in Britain.

1960

1965

1958
Business and Finance
West Germany is the leading industrial power in Western Europe.

1961
Global Events
The Berlin Wall is built.

1963
Politics
Lyndon Johnson becomes president after John F. Kennedy is assassinated.

1968
Science and Technology
The Soviet *Zond* becomes the first spacecraft to fly around the moon.

1968
Daily Life
Vietnam War protesters clash with police in the streets of Chicago.

Antiwar protesters face troops at the 1968 Democratic Party Convention in Chicago.

What's Your Opinion?

Themes Journal

Do you **agree** *or* **disagree** *with the following statements? Support your point of view in your journal.*

Economics National economies grow more quickly when all economic decisions are made by the government.

Government People should always be allowed to determine who governs them and what kind of government they have.

Citizenship Public protests can be an effective way to bring about change and progress in a democracy.

SECTION 1

READ TO DISCOVER

1. What were the origins of the postwar settlement for Europe?
2. Why was Germany divided into four occupation zones and what developed as a result?
3. How is the United Nations organized?
4. What problems did the Allies face in keeping peace in Europe?

DEFINE

veto power

IDENTIFY

United Nations
Nürnberg trials
Eleanor Roosevelt
General Assembly
Security Council

WHY IT MATTERS TODAY

The United Nations remains active today in efforts to promote peace. Use CNNstudentNews.com or other current event sources to learn more about United Nations peacekeeping efforts today. Record your findings in your journal.

CNNstudentNews.com

Aftermath of the War in Europe

The Main Idea
At the end of World War II, the Allied nations had trouble determining how to keep peace in Europe.

The Story Continues *Harry Hopkins, an American who attended the Yalta Conference, later recalled participants' optimism. "We were absolutely certain we had won the first great victory of the peace—and, by 'we,' I mean all of us, the whole human race." The dangerous waters of the postwar world, however, proved far more difficult to navigate than Hopkins or others imagined.*

Wartime Conferences and Postwar Problems

Victory over the Axis powers brought on a whole new set of problems for Allied leaders. To a degree, these problems were the result of decisions they had made during the war.

In November and December of 1943, the "Big Three" Allied leaders—Churchill, Roosevelt, and Stalin—had met at Tehran, the capital of Iran. At this meeting, they decided to defeat Germany by carrying on the war on two fronts. Western Allied forces would attack Germany from the west, while Soviet forces would attack from the east. This decision meant that Western forces would meet the Soviets somewhere in the middle of Germany.

In February 1945, Churchill, Roosevelt, and Stalin had met at the Black Sea resort town of Yalta. With victory clearly in sight, the three leaders agreed to divide Austria and Germany into zones of military occupation. Armies from each of the Allied nations would be responsible for the territories they liberated from Nazi control. Berlin would lie entirely within the Soviet zone, but it would be divided into four parts. The Soviets would control East Berlin, and the Western Allies would create their own zones in West Berlin. Vienna was to be divided in a similar manner. The Allied leaders regarded the division of Germany as only a temporary measure, however. They foresaw that a final peace settlement would be arranged later.

The Allies seemed to reach agreement on Poland and territories that the Soviets had already taken in Eastern Europe. Churchill and Roosevelt believed these countries should be allowed to determine their own futures. They obtained Stalin's promise that

Two months after the Yalta Conference, President Roosevelt died. Millions in the United States and around the world mourned his death.

he would allow free elections and the establishment of democratic governments. In return, they agreed with Stalin that governments in these eastern countries must be friendly to the Soviet Union. Each side left Yalta believing its viewpoint had won.

For Stalin, however, friendly governments meant governments under Soviet control. In addition, he believed that free elections could take place only after eastern Europeans had learned socialist principles. As a result, Stalin's promise of free elections was meaningless from a Western point of view.

The three leaders also considered how to prevent another war. They disagreed considerably on this issue. Churchill and Stalin wanted the Allies to divide the world into spheres of influence. Roosevelt, however, called for an internationalist approach similar to that used for the League of Nations after World War I. He proposed a **United Nations** organization that would keep the peace through collective security arrangements. The initial plans for such an organization had already been worked out at a 1944 conference. At Yalta, the three leaders discussed the proposed charter for the organization and agreed on voting procedures to be followed.

✔ **READING CHECK: Identifying Cause and Effect** How did decisions made during the war affect the situation in postwar Europe?

Map legend:
- ⊛ National capital
- Zones:
  - U.S.
  - Soviet
  - British
  - French

Occupied Berlin: West Berlin, East Berlin, Potsdam

Scale: 0 100 200 Miles / 0 100 200 Kilometers
Azimuthal Equal-Area Projection

Occupied Germany, 1945–1955
Interpreting Maps The Allies decided to divide Germany into zones of military occupation after the war.

■ **Skills Assessment: Using Geography** Why did the Soviet Union control the eastern portion of Germany?

The Occupation of Germany

After Germany's surrender in 1945, the Allies occupied their military zones and established temporary military governments. In July Allied leaders met at Potsdam, outside Berlin, to discuss a postwar settlement. Churchill, and later Clement Attlee, who had replaced Churchill as prime minister, represented Great Britain. Harry Truman, who became president after Roosevelt's death in April 1945, represented the United States. Stalin remained the Soviet representative.

Decisions at Potsdam. At Potsdam, the three leaders agreed on several basic principles: (1) Germany should remain a single country, although for the time being it would be divided, (2) Germany must be demilitarized, (3) the Nazi party must be outlawed, (4) German political structure should be rebuilt on a democratic basis, and (5) individuals responsible for war crimes should be brought to trial.

To oversee the occupation governments, the Allied leaders established the Allied Control Council. They also agreed that a Council of Foreign Ministers representing China, France, Great Britain, the Soviet Union, and the United States should write the peace treaties. As the councils began their work, however, it became clear that the Western democracies and the Soviet Union had very different plans for a postwar settlement. The major disagreements centered on two points: the boundaries of postwar Germany and war reparations.

Redrawing borders. Stalin now insisted that the Soviet Union would retain territories in Poland and on the Baltic Sea gained as a result of the Nazi-Soviet Pact. To make up for lost territory, Poland should receive German territory to its west. The Allies agreed to the new western border for Poland. Both Poland and the Soviet Union took parts of East Prussia. This transfer of territory stripped Germany of one fourth of its land.

These territorial adjustments also led to a large increase in Germany's population. The Poles and Soviets evicted Germans from the lands they acquired. In addition, Czechoslovakia insisted that Sudeten Germans who had supported Hitler's invasion in 1938 must leave the country. The burden of feeding, housing, and employing these refugees fell on a shrunken and divided postwar Germany.

Demilitarization and reparations. The Allies swiftly disbanded all German land, air, and sea forces. They also demanded that all factories used in the war industry be dismantled. This plan proved difficult to enforce. The Allies had to determine what constituted a war industry. For example, a factory that manufactures tractors can easily be converted to produce tanks.

The Allies disagreed on German economic recovery. The United States and Britain concluded that German industry must be revived if Europe was to become prosperous again. France initially preferred to keep German industry weak to prevent future rearmament. The Soviets saw reparations as more important than reviving German industry. They demanded that Germany pay them $10 billion in reparations.

In the end, Western leaders agreed that the Soviets could claim reparations, mostly in the form of industrial equipment from all the military zones. The Soviets dismantled and moved hundreds of industrial plants from Germany to the Soviet Union. This practice severely hurt German industry's chances to recover. Eventually, the Western Allies halted the flow of reparations to the Soviet Union.

With such problems, the Allied Control Council found it increasingly difficult to reach decisions. The occupation governments soon began to ignore it and administered their territories as they saw fit.

The Nürnberg trials. After the war the full horror of the German concentration camps and the terrible consequences of Nazi racial purification were revealed to the world. Although Hitler was dead and many high-ranking Nazi officials had fled to South America, many Nazi leaders had been captured. The Allies were determined to bring them to trial. In 1945 and 1946, a special international court met at Nürnberg, Germany (also known as Nuremberg). At the **Nürnberg trials** the court charged 22 Nazi leaders with crimes against peace and humanity. In the end, 12 were sentenced to death, 7 were sentenced to life imprisonment, and 3 were acquitted. The court also declared the Nazi Party a criminal organization.

War Crimes

A "war crime" refers to any crime that violates the laws of war. Murder and mistreatment of a nation's civilian population are usually considered war crimes. Others include theft, racial or religious persecution, and the killing of hostages. The Nürnberg trials of 1945 helped nations agree on how to try suspected war criminals. International war crimes trials were held in 1996, when Bosnian Serb Dusko Tadic was sentenced to 20 years in prison for the torture and murder of prisoners of war. In 1999 former Yugoslav leader Slobodan Milošević was also indicted for war crimes in the Balkans. Milošević was taken into UN custody in June of 2001 and his trial began in 2002. **What actions taken during a war would be considered crimes?**

✔ **READING CHECK: Making Predictions** What might result from the temporary division of Germany?

This October 1946 photo was taken at the Nürnberg trial of the Nazi leaders.

The United Nations

In April 1945 representatives from 51 nations met in San Francisco. This General Assembly agreed on a charter for the United Nations (UN). By October 1945, enough nations had ratified the charter to establish the UN. The primary purpose of the UN was to maintain international peace and security. It was also designed to foster international cooperation to solve cultural, economic, and social problems. A UN official explained why the organization's headquarters would be in the United States.

"It was of paramount importance that the nerve-centre [of the United Nations] be located as close as possible to the new economic and political centre. . . . The challenging question of the future was how to secure the fullest possible U.S. participation in whatever international organizations might emerge.**"**

Trygve Lie, from *A History of the United States*

Even so, many Americans looked with skepticism at the UN. One person responsible for persuading many skeptics to support the new organization was former First Lady **Eleanor Roosevelt.**

The two most important bodies within the UN were the **General Assembly** and the **Security Council.** Any nation that wished to join would be admitted to the General Assembly. Each nation in the Assembly, regardless of its size or power, would have the same rights and voting power as any other nation. The Assembly was responsible for drawing up the UN budget and determining each member's share of the cost. The General Assembly also elected the secretary-general and the judges of the International Court of Justice.

The Security Council included 10 temporary members elected from the General Assembly for two-year rotating terms. Five nations—Britain, China, France, the Soviet Union, and the United States—were permanent members. Each permanent member could prevent the council from taking action by using its **veto power**—the power to defeat a measure with a single vote. The Security Council was designed to satisfy those who felt some members should have more influence than others.

✔ **READING CHECK: Drawing Inferences** Why did the planners of the United Nations make some nations permanent members of the Security Council?

HISTORY MAKER

Eleanor Roosevelt (1884–1962)

As the niece of one president of the United States and the wife of another, Eleanor Roosevelt grew up with politics in her blood. Her willingness to tackle tough issues made Roosevelt one of the most admired first ladies ever.

Roosevelt also wrote more than a dozen books and a weekly newspaper column. She later served as the U.S. delegate to the United Nations. Her good works and compassion earned her the nickname "First Lady of the World." **Why was Eleanor Roosevelt admired?**

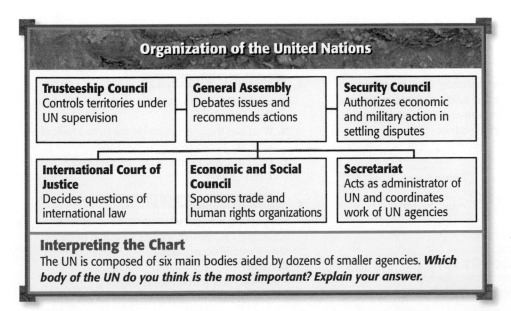

Organization of the United Nations

Trusteeship Council Controls territories under UN supervision	**General Assembly** Debates issues and recommends actions	**Security Council** Authorizes economic and military action in settling disputes
International Court of Justice Decides questions of international law	**Economic and Social Council** Sponsors trade and human rights organizations	**Secretariat** Acts as administrator of UN and coordinates work of UN agencies

Interpreting the Chart
The UN is composed of six main bodies aided by dozens of smaller agencies. *Which body of the UN do you think is the most important? Explain your answer.*

Peacemaking Problems

The war undermined or destroyed many governments in Europe. As they emerged from the shambles of the war, many European states established new forms of government. In 1946 the Italian people voted to abolish the monarchy and become a republic. In France Charles de Gaulle headed a temporary government until a new constitution was adopted in 1946.

In Eastern Europe the Soviets established temporary governments in the countries they had liberated. These governments were dominated or controlled outright by communists, despite the anticommunist feelings of the majority of the population. It soon became clear that the Soviet Union and the Western Allies had conflicting goals for postwar Europe.

In February 1947 the Council of Foreign Ministers reached agreement on several peace treaties. Italy gave up claims in countries it had invaded during the war and lost other territory. Its colonies were placed under the authority of the United Nations. Bulgaria, Finland, Hungary, and Romania also had to return territory and accept changes to their prewar boundaries. In addition, they had to reduce their armed forces and pay reparations to invaded nations.

The peace negotiations exposed growing differences between the Soviet Union and the Western Allies. The Soviets insisted that communists control the governments of Eastern European nations so that the Soviet Union would be safe from future invasion. The Western Allies wanted free elections and representative governments. In the end, a compromise was reached. The Soviets agreed to allow a few representatives of noncommunist parties to participate in the new Eastern European governments.

The Allies could not reach agreements on the most important treaties. The four-way occupation of Austria continued until 1955. That year a treaty restored Austria as an independent, sovereign republic within its 1930 boundaries. For its part, Austria had to agree to remain neutral. In the case of Germany, the Allies never reached a final settlement. The division of Germany into eastern and western parts eventually became a formal division into two countries.

As the Red Army rolled across Eastern and Central Europe, Stalin insisted on placing governments friendly to Soviet interests in power in the liberated nations.

✔ **READING CHECK: Contrasting** How did Soviet plans for the future of Europe differ from those of the Western Allies?

SECTION 1 REVIEW

1. **Define** and explain the significance:
   veto power

2. **Identify** and explain the significance:
   United Nations
   Nürnberg trials
   Eleanor Roosevelt
   General Assembly
   Security Council

Homework Practice Online
keyword: SH3 HP22

3. **Summarizing** Copy the graphic organizer below. Use it to summarize the agreements made at Yalta that affected postwar Europe.

```
              Germany
            ↗          ↘
   Yalta → Eastern Europe → Postwar
            ↘          ↗     Europe
             Future security
```

4. **Finding the Main Idea**
   a. What were the key decisions made at the Postdam Conference?
   b. What was the goal in forming the United Nations and what are its two most important bodies?
   c. What postwar events led to the spread of communism?

5. **Writing and Critical Thinking**
   Supporting a Point of View Write an editorial supporting the Western nations' view that Germany should rebuild economically.
   Consider:
   • the Allied plan for rebuilding Germany
   • the conflict over territorial adjustments and reparations

Origins of the Cold War

READ TO DISCOVER

❶ How and why did the alliance between the Western Allies and the Soviet Union end?

❷ How did the United States attempt to stop the spread of communism and aid Europe?

❸ How did Germany become two separate countries?

❹ What Cold War alliances developed in Europe?

DEFINE

containment

IDENTIFY

Cold War
Truman Doctrine
Marshall Plan
Cominform
Berlin Airlift
NATO
Warsaw Pact

▶ **WHY IT MATTERS TODAY**

The North Atlantic Treaty Organization still exists today. Use CNN*News*.com or other **current event** sources to learn which nations currently belong to NATO and what recent actions it has taken. Record your findings in your journal.

CNN*Student News*.com

The Main Idea
The wartime alliance between the Soviet Union and Western powers ended, leading to a Cold War.

The Story Continues *At one meeting during the 1943 conference in Tehran, President Roosevelt teased Winston Churchill so much that Joseph Stalin laughed. Roosevelt recalled, "From that day on our relations were personal. . . . The ice was broken and we talked like men and brothers." Friendly relations between the United States and the Soviet Union, however, soon proved impossible to maintain.*

The End of the Alliance

Disagreements between the Soviet Union and the Western Allies eventually caused the alliance that had defeated the Axis Powers to dissolve. In its place, a new rivalry emerged. On one side was the Soviet Union, supported by the communist nations of the world. The Soviet Union and its allies were sometimes called the Eastern bloc. On the other side was the United States, supported by the Western democracies and other noncommunist nations.

This struggle between communism and democracy occasionally led to bloody local wars. For the most part, however, it was a war of ideas and worldviews waged by the two superpowers, the Soviet Union and the United States. As a result, the struggle quickly became known as the **Cold War.**

The two sides in the Cold War had completely different economic and political systems. Each side naturally believed that its own system should be the model for European reconstruction. In addition, each side was concerned with its own future security. The Soviet Union was determined to protect itself from any future attack from the West. Thus, Stalin created a buffer zone of communist nations along the western frontier of the Soviet Union.

The Western powers regarded Stalin's buffer zone as evidence that the Soviets hoped to expand and one day dominate all of Europe. Soviet actions fueled their fears. Stalin insisted that the Soviet Union retain territories it had gained in the Nazi-Soviet Pact, and he installed a pro-Soviet government in Poland. This seemed to violate the agreement Stalin made at Yalta regarding free elections.

Shown here is a Soviet propaganda poster from the mid-1940s. The theme of this poster reflects the military and industrial buildup that would continue throughout the Cold War.

In 1947 President Truman speaks to Congress.

Holt Researcher

go.hrw.com

KEYWORD: Holt Researcher

FreeFind: Harry Truman

After reading more about Harry Truman on the Holt Researcher, analyze one of his controversial political decisions, taking historical context into account.

Analyzing Primary Sources

Contrasting How did Truman summarize the different ways of life of communist and democratic countries?

More militaristic actions followed. Stalin massed troops along the border of Turkey. He demanded the return of territory in Caucasia that had once been taken by the czars. Stalin also insisted upon joint Soviet-Turkish control over the straits that connected the Black Sea to the Aegean and Mediterranean Seas. Such control would guarantee the Soviet Union's naval fleet an outlet to the Mediterranean. In February 1946 Stalin announced that the communist struggle for worldwide revolution would continue. In March Soviet forces that had occupied Iran during the war refused to withdraw. Instead, they supported the establishment of a communist party in Iran.

To the West, Soviet policy seemed to be based on expansion, not self-defense. Pressure from the United States and Britain forced Stalin to back down from his positions on Turkey and Iran. When a political crisis broke out in Greece in 1947, the United States finally decided to intervene.

✔ **READING CHECK: Summarizing** What actions led Western nations to believe that the Soviets wanted to dominate Europe?

The United States Aids Europe

By 1944 the Nazis had withdrawn from Greece. A civil war then broke out between communists and conservatives loyal to the monarchy. Great Britain, which supported the royalists, negotiated a truce in 1945. In the summer of 1946, however, the communists renewed the civil war. They received aid from the new communist governments in Albania, Bulgaria, and Yugoslavia. The Greek government turned once again to the British for help.

Britain was exhausted and almost bankrupted by the war. In February 1947 the British informed the United States that they would end financial aid to Greece and Turkey and withdraw their troops from Greece. Britain hoped the United States would come to aid those countries to prevent communist domination of the region.

The Truman Doctrine. On March 12, 1947, President Harry Truman spoke before Congress. He offered his perception of the postwar world.

 ❝At the present moment in world history nearly every nation must choose between alternative ways of life. . . . One way of life is based upon the will of the majority, and is distinguished by free institutions, representative government, free elections, guarantees of individual liberty, freedom of speech and religion, and freedom from political oppression. The second way of life is based upon the will of a minority forcibly imposed upon the majority. It relies upon terror and oppression, a controlled press and radio, fixed elections, and the suppression of personal freedoms.❞

Harry Truman, from *Public Papers of the Presidents*

Truman went on to set forth a policy that is called the **Truman Doctrine.** He declared that the United States must consider the continued spread of communism to be a threat to democracy. He argued that the United States must "support free peoples who are resisting attempted subjugation [takeover] by armed minorities or by outside pressures." Truman asked Congress to provide $400 million to help defend Greece and

Turkey from communist aggression. Congress agreed. With U.S. technical and financial assistance, the Greek government ended the rebellion.

To carry out the Truman Doctrine, the United States would not try to stamp out communism in countries where it already existed. If a country requested assistance to prevent a communist takeover, the United States would offer materials, money, and technical knowledge. Thus, the United States committed itself to contain, or restrict, the spread of communism. This policy became known as **containment.**

The Marshall Plan. Western leaders feared that ongoing poverty in war-torn Europe would drive Europeans into communist parties. Thus, the United States announced a new plan of massive economic assistance. Called the **Marshall Plan** after U.S. Secretary of State General George Marshall, the European Recovery Program also encouraged European nations to work together. They were to determine their needs and remove trade barriers so that goods could flow freely across the continent. Eventually, 17 European nations participated in the Marshall Plan. The United States also offered aid to the Soviet Union and Eastern European nations under Soviet control, but those nations rejected the offer.

Between 1948 and 1952, the United States spent over $13 billion on the Marshall Plan. By 1952 European farm and industrial production was above prewar levels. Europe was on the road to prosperity. The United States also benefited from the Marshall Plan, as it supplied export goods to the recovering European economies.

In 1949 as a response to the Marshall Plan, the Soviet Union founded the Council for Mutual Assistance, COMECON, to develop economic cooperation among Eastern European nations. Because the Soviet Union could not adequately fund the program, it did not suceed.

✔ **READING CHECK: Finding the Main Idea** In what ways did the United States aid Europe after the war?

The Cold War in Europe

The Soviets regarded the Truman Doctrine as an effort to encircle and undermine the Soviet Union. They denounced the Marshall Plan as an American capitalist effort to dominate Europe economically. In September 1947 the Soviets established the Communist Information Bureau, or **Cominform,** to oppose the Marshall Plan. This organization included all European communist parties. The Cominform, however, was unsuccessful in opposing Marshall Plan aid. Its major effect was to create tension between communist and noncommunist parties in Europe.

Eastern and Central Europe. As the West put its containment policy into place, the Soviets tightened their grip on Eastern and Central Europe. In 1948 communists overthrew the democratic government of Czechoslovakia. They turned the nation into a one-party communist state and a member of the Eastern bloc. Only one break appeared in the division between East and West. Marshall Tito of Yugoslavia, a devoted communist, objected to Soviet domination. He announced that Yugoslavia would follow an independent path. By June 1948 Yugoslavia was expelled from Cominform.

The Marshall Plan The photo below shows a shipment of sugar provided under the Marshall Plan arriving in London. *What does this image tell you about the types of aid needed by people in European countries?*

FOR EUROPEAN RECOVERY SUPPLIED BY THE UNITED STATES OF AMERICA

FIRST CARGO OF CARIBBEAN SUGAR SHIPPED UNDER MARSHALL AID

Problems in Germany. By 1948 it was clear that joint government in Germany by the four former Allies was impossible. The three Western powers had taken steps to reunite their zones economically and to revive democracy in Germany. It became clear that they were moving toward a unified German state.

The Soviets bitterly opposed reunification. In June 1948 they blockaded the East German border to all land and water traffic into Berlin from the west. The people of West Berlin soon faced starvation. Western nations reacted swiftly. The United States and Great Britain organized an airlift to supply West Berlin. The **Berlin Airlift** provided food and supplies daily to the inhabitants of the western part of the city. One inhabitant of West Berlin recalled those times:

❝Early in the morning, when we woke up, the first thing we did was listen to see whether the noise of aircraft engines could be heard. That gave us the certainty that we were not alone, that the whole civilized world took part in the fight for Berlin's freedom.❞

Anonymous Berliner, quoted in *Bridge in the Sky,* by Frank Donovan

The airlift operated so efficiently that raw materials were also supplied to West Berlin factories. As a warning to the Soviets, the United States also stationed long-range bombers in Great Britain. The Soviets made no real efforts to stop the airlift and in May 1949 lifted the blockade.

The division of Germany. The Berlin blockade might be seen as the "official" beginning of the Cold War. It also had one immediate and important consequence—the division of Germany. With the approval of the Western Allies, in May 1949 a constitutional assembly declared the Federal Republic of Germany. Popularly known as West Germany, the nation had its capital in Bonn. The Soviet Union followed suit, establishing the German Democratic Republic—also known as East Germany—in October 1949. The division of Germany became a symbol of the East-West division of the Cold War.

✔ **READING CHECK: Problem Solving** Was the division of Germany the best solution to disagreements over its future? Explain.

Supplies were airlifted into an isolated West Berlin by the United States and Great Britain.

During the airlift, each child's ration consisted of just a slice of dark bread and margarine.

Cold War Alliances

When the United States and its allies formed NATO, an alliance for mutual protection, the Soviet Union and its allies did the same through the Warsaw Pact. As the United States became more important to global defense, the country wound up spending more money on military defense even during times of relative peace.

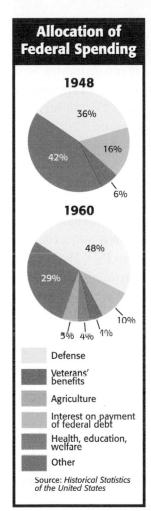

Allocation of Federal Spending

1948
- 36%
- 16%
- 42%
- 6%

1960
- 48%
- 29%
- 10%
- 5%
- 4%
- 1%

- Defense
- Veterans' benefits
- Agriculture
- Interest on payment of federal debt
- Health, education, welfare
- Other

Source: *Historical Statistics of the United States*

- NATO nations
- Warsaw Pact nations
- Other Communist nations
- Neutral nations
- Iron Curtain
- Other cities
- National capital

The United States and Canada are the North American members of NATO.

European Alliances, 1955

Skills Reminder

Information about a complicated historical topic such as the Cold War is often conveyed through various media: verbal, visual or graphic, and statistical. The ability to transfer information from one form to another—writing a paragraph to summarize a chart or graph, for example—will help you more easily comprehend and remember the information. To transfer information from one medium to another, identify the main idea. Choose the necessary details appropriate for the medium you are going to use. Create the new form of information. In making charts, maps, or graphs, use the steps you have learned. Finally, evaluate the new medium. Make sure you have accurately and clearly conveyed the original information.

Skills Practice

❶ Study the map above. Make a chart that lists the members of NATO and the Warsaw Pact by 1955.

❷ Study the graph above. Why do you think the portion of U.S. spending devoted to defense increased so much between 1948 and 1960?

❸ Using databases on the Internet, find information about Soviet defense spending in the late 1940s and 1950s and create a graph that illustrates this information.

❹ Using all the information you have gathered, write a short essay explaining how the formation of NATO and the Warsaw Pact affected government spending in the United States and the Soviet Union.

NATO and the Warsaw Pact

The division of Germany was one of a series of events in 1949 and 1950 that made clear the split between East and West. In the summer of 1949, the Soviets detonated their first atomic bomb. In October 1949 armies of the Chinese Communist Party defeated the Chinese Nationalist Government, driving the Nationalists off the mainland to the island of Taiwan. In 1950 North Korean communist forces invaded South Korea. These events reminded the world that the Cold War might all too quickly grow hot.

Because of the East-West split, new political and military alliances formed. In April 1949 twelve Western nations signed the treaty creating the North Atlantic Treaty Organization (**NATO**). Signers agreed that if one member nation were attacked, all members would take united action against the aggressor. Greece and Turkey joined NATO in 1952, and West Germany followed in 1955. All member nations contributed to a NATO military force. Eventually the organization came to rely heavily on U.S. nuclear weapons to deter Soviet invasion of Western Europe.

After West Germany joined NATO, the Soviet Union responded by creating a formal alliance of its own. In May 1955 a meeting was held with representatives of the Eastern bloc. These nations adopted a 20-year mutual defense agreement called the **Warsaw Pact.** The Warsaw Pact troops greatly outnumbered NATO troops in Europe. The overwhelming difference in ground troops between NATO and the Warsaw Pact reinforced the Western powers' reliance on using nuclear weapons as a deterrent.

✔ **READING CHECK: Identifying Cause and Effect** Why did Western nations and nations of the Eastern bloc form alliances?

In this picture U.S. President Harry Truman signs the North Atlantic Pact, which created NATO. Shown above is the NATO emblem.

SECTION 2 REVIEW

1. **Define** and explain the significance:
   containment

2. **Identify** and explain the significance:
   Cold War
   Truman Doctrine
   Marshall Plan
   Cominform
   Berlin Airlift
   NATO
   Warsaw Pact

3. **Sequencing** Make a flowchart like the one below to sequence the main events that led to the Cold War.

4. **Finding the Main Idea**
   a. Why did Stalin want to control Eastern Europe? How did Western nations perceive his actions?
   b. How were the Truman Doctrine and the Marshall Plan part of the containment policy?
   c. What happened in Germany as a result of the Cold War?

5. **Writing and Critical Thinking**
   Identifying a Point of View Write a paragraph explaining why NATO and the Warsaw Pact were formed.
   Consider:
   • the goal of NATO
   • the purpose of the Warsaw Pact

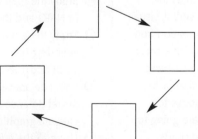

Homework Practice Online
keyword: SH3 HP22

READ TO DISCOVER

❶ What was the West German "miracle"?

❷ Why did the British meet with mixed success in stimulating economic growth?

❸ How did France maintain an independent position in European affairs?

❹ How did the Soviet Union change under new leadership?

❺ What problems did Eastern European nations face?

DEFINE

welfare state

IDENTIFY

Berlin Wall
Common Market
European Community
Nikita Khrushchev

WHY IT MATTERS TODAY

European integration remains an important issue today. Use CNN student News.com or other **current event** sources to learn about recent efforts at cooperation and integration between European nations. Record your findings in your journal.

CNN student News.com

Reconstruction, Reform, and Reaction in Europe

The Main Idea
While many Western European nations prospered after World War II, Eastern Europe faced difficulties.

The Story Continues *Author Marion Dönhoff described the devastation he witnessed in Germany as the war came to an end. "We spent the nights around camp fires on the road or else in the barns of abandoned farmyards; every dawn brought the same scene: dying children and old people closing their eyes which reflected the fear and anxiety and suffering of generations." Would it be possible for a nation in such ruin to rebuild after the war?*

The West German "Miracle"

After the war the Western Allies remained committed to democracy and the principle of majority rule. Economically, they continued to accept the basic principles of capitalism. They believed in some form of a market economy. In a market economy, competition among private businesses and individuals determines what goods will be produced, how they will be produced, and what they will cost.

West German economic recovery. West Germany followed this free-market policy. The reconstruction and industrial development of the nation progressed at a remarkably rapid rate. In fact, some people called it the German "miracle."

During the postwar years, the West German government provided housing and jobs to many refugees from East Germany and other Eastern European nations. The labor of these refugees contributed to West Germany's rapidly growing economy. German industry flourished, thanks to technological innovation, a commitment to quality, and few labor troubles. The West German unit of currency, the Deutsche mark, became one of the most stable in the world. By 1958 West Germany was the leading industrial nation in Western Europe.

The West German automobile industry was one of the business successes that helped boost economic recovery after World War II.

Politics. West Germany had also become one of the world's most stable democracies. In the postwar era two parties, the Christian Democrats and the Social Democrats, dominated West German politics. The first West German chancellor, Konrad Adenauer, was a Christian Democrat. Adenauer was committed to a market economy and establishing the rule of law as a principle of the German state.

A dedicated anticommunist and anti-Soviet, Adenauer also closely aligned with the West. Under his guidance, Germany joined NATO in 1955. He also encouraged Germans in the Soviet bloc to escape to the West. Many did so, particularly in Berlin. In response, in 1961 the East German government erected a wall separating the two halves of the city. Anyone caught trying to escape over the wall was shot. The **Berlin Wall,** with its cap of barbed wire, became a major symbol of the Cold War.

Adenauer retired from office in 1963. Another Christian Democrat, Ludwig Erhard, became chancellor. Erhard had in many ways been the architect of the free-market polices that produced the "German miracle." Under Erhard's leadership, West Germany continued to prosper, but the rate of economic growth slowed. In 1966 the country experienced a mild recession, or economic slowdown. Worries over the economy and the Christian Democrat's foreign policy of complete alignment with the United States caused many Germans to turn to the Social Democrats. In 1969 the Social Democrats won a national majority under their leader, Willy Brandt.

In 1961 more than 1,000 East Germans were fleeing to West Berlin every day. To halt the flow, East Germany built the Berlin Wall. After its construction, more than 170 people died trying to escape over it.

✔ **READING CHECK: Analyzing Information** What elements of Adenauer's leadership helped economic growth and democracy in West Germany?

Postwar Britain

As West Germany pursued free-market polices, Great Britain moved in the opposite direction. In 1945 British voters rejected Winston Churchill's Conservative Party. The Labour Party, a moderate socialist party, formed Britain's postwar government.

Under Labour Party leadership, Great Britain became a **welfare state**—a state in which the government takes primary responsibility for the social welfare of its citizens. The British government provided free medical care for everyone. It nationalized the Bank of England, coal mines, railroads, and utilities. It did not, however, interfere with most industry, which remained privately owned.

For years after the war, Great Britain faced economic problems. Its industrial equipment was inefficient and outdated. Many workers had died in the war. Some scientists and managers had emigrated to Australia, Canada, or the United States. After the war Great Britain lost valuable colonies and possessions. The cost of its remaining overseas commitments was a heavy burden.

Clement Attlee (front row, center) is surrounded by supporters after his Labour Party wins the 1945 election and Attlee becomes prime minister.

In 1951 voters elected a new Conservative government to power. As prime minister once again, Winston Churchill reversed some of the Labour government's nationalization policies. However, the general outlines of the British welfare state remained in place under the Conservatives.

Britain continued to lag behind the rest of Europe in economic recovery. Industrial growth was much slower than in other countries. In fact, in the 1960s Great Britain's industrial productivity fell to one of the lowest national levels in the industrialized world.

One cause of this decline was the shift in the world economy from coal to oil and nuclear power as energy resources. Britain's strength had long been its coal reserves. The Labour Party blamed the Conservatives for the poor economy, but it did no better when holding the majority itself.

✔ **READING CHECK: Identifying Cause and Effect** Why did the British economy face continuing difficulties in the postwar era?

New Republics in France

Postwar France also faced difficulties. During the war France had suffered considerable damage. Towns and cities were destroyed; farmlands were ravaged. At war's end inflation caused even more hardship for the French people. Jean Monnet, a French economist, crafted policies to revive the economy. In addition the Marshall Plan provided economic assistance. Slowly French agriculture and industry began to recover and even modernize.

After the war French voters adopted a new constitution and proclaimed the Fourth Republic. However, this government was politically unstable. It fell during the late 1950s over a crisis that brought France to the brink of civil war. The crisis involved the French army's attempt to restore its prestige after the defeat of 1940.

The French considered Algeria, in northern Africa, an important part of France. In 1954, however, Algerian nationalists began a bloody war for independence. After several years of extreme violence, many people in France wanted to let Algeria go, but others strongly opposed such a course. In 1958 the French legislature turned to General Charles de Gaulle to save the nation from civil war. De Gaulle was authorized to write a new constitution and to rule by decree until its ratification. The new constitution created France's Fifth Republic and a strong presidency.

De Gaulle became the first president of the Fifth Republic. To the surprise of the army, he accepted Algerian independence. He also moved to peacefully transform the French empire into a voluntary association of self-governing nations known as the French Community.

In foreign policy de Gaulle was a nationalist. He believed Europe would prosper only as an alliance of strong nations with individual identities and freedom of action. Although France remained a political member of NATO, de Gaulle withdrew French forces from NATO command. He opposed U.S. and British influence in Europe and established close relations with West German Chancellor Adenauer to offset it.

In the late 1960s political conditions within France became unstable. Militant students demanded reforms in the educational system. Workers held strikes, calling for higher wages and better working conditions. To meet the crisis, de Gaulle dissolved the National Assembly and called for general elections. In April 1969 the French people rejected de Gaulle's proposed reforms, and de Gaulle resigned from office.

✔ **READING CHECK: Sequencing** What events led to de Gaulle's rise and fall from power in France?

Western Europe and Integration

Recovery in other Western European nations took many different paths. To solidify economic health, some nations sought cooperation within the European community.

HISTORY MAKER

Charles de Gaulle (1890–1970)

Charles De Gaulle was one of the great military heroes of France during World War I. Between the wars, he pushed for a small, but more mobile and technically advanced, army. After France fell to the Germans in World War II, de Gaulle led the Free French forces. Upon liberation, he helped rebuild the French government.

De Gaulle retired from politics in 1946, but was called back into service during the crisis of the late 1950s. As a politician, he believed in strong national government, with as few alliances as possible. He also granted independence to 12 French territories in Africa. **How might de Gaulle's treatment of French territories in Africa have related to his views about alliances?**

Architecture: Chapel by Le Corbusier

World War II damaged or destroyed numerous European works of art, including many old and beautiful churches. Many Europeans, then, hailed the construction of a new church that was built from 1951 to 1955 and designed by renowned architect Charles-Édouard Jeanneret, better known as Le Corbusier. Called Notre Dame du Haut, the chapel (at right) is located on a mountaintop in Ronchamp, France. Its massive walls seem to curl like paper. Its doors are almost concealed. According to one art historian, its interior evokes "a nostalgia for the certainties of a faith that is no longer unquestioned. Ronchamp mirrors the spiritual condition of the modern age."

Understanding the Arts

How does Le Corbusier's construction give an impression of hope?

Analyzing Primary Sources

Identifying a Point of View Why did Adenauer see European integration as necessary?

Recovery elsewhere in Europe. Denmark, Norway, and Sweden had strongly entrenched democracies and greater political stability than other countries. Their economies prospered during the 1950s and 1960s. This prosperity allowed them to establish extensive welfare states. In Italy the Christian Democratic Party dominated politics during the 1950s and 1960s and the country experienced major agricultural and industrial growth. By the 1960s, however, the communist and socialist parties had gained considerable strength because of labor unrest. By the end of the 1960s, Italy's economic growth declined sharply. This decline led to political instability.

Greece, Portugal, and Spain all developed free-enterprise systems. Their economic programs, however, met with varying degrees of success. Portugal and Spain were the only Western European nations that did not establish democratic governments after the war. Governments in the two nations remained authoritarian.

Economic integration. In the 1950s the French proposed that the nations that produced most of Western Europe's coal and steel unite their facilities. In 1952 Belgium, France, Italy, Luxembourg, the Netherlands, and West Germany formed the European Coal and Steel Community (ECSC). A central authority regulated production and prices. Member nations did not charge each other tariffs on coal or steel. Konrad Adenauer explained the reason for the international cooperation.

History Makers Speak

❝These West European countries are no longer in such a position that each can defend itself on its own; they are no longer in such a position that each can save European culture by itself. These aims, which are common to all of us, can only be attained, if West European countries join together, politically, economically, and culturally . . .❞

Konrad Adenauer, from *The Adenauer Era*

In 1957 the same six nations established the European Economic Community (EEC)—usually called the **Common Market.** The six members agreed to gradually abolish import quotas and tariffs within the Common Market. They also agreed to a common tariff on goods coming into the market from nonmember nations.

In 1967 the Common Market adopted a five-year plan to provide greater price and wage stability and more uniform tax levels among member nations. That same year, the EEC merged with the ECSC and another multinational group, the Atomic Energy Community, to form the European Communities. Later called the **European Community,** or EC, the organization was headquartered in Belgium.

In the 1950s Britain had refused to join the EEC. In the 1960s, however, the EEC prospered, while Britain lagged behind. Eventually the British applied for admission. Still worried about British influence in Europe, French president Charles de Gaulle vetoed Britain's application. Not until de Gaulle's retirement and death did Britain gain admission to the EEC in 1973.

✔ **READING CHECK: Problem Solving** Why did Western European nations seek to integrate economically?

The Soviet Union After Stalin

In 1953 Joseph Stalin, who had ruled the Soviet Union with an iron hand for three decades, died. His death led to a power struggle for control of the Soviet government. Eventually **Nikita Khrushchev** (kroosh·CHAWF), former secretary of the Communist party in the Ukraine, emerged as Stalin's successor.

In a 1956 speech, Khrushchev shocked the Soviet leadership when he denounced Stalin's policies. He condemned Stalin for the murder of hundreds of thousands of innocent Soviet citizens and a host of other crimes against the Soviet people. This speech marked the beginning of the policy of "destalinization." Khrushchev lifted restrictions on intellectuals and artists, freed many political prisoners, and ended some of the terrorism of the secret police.

Khrushchev also enacted economic reforms. He loosened somewhat the central government's tight grip on the economy. Local factory and farm managers were given more control to help meet production quotas. Khrushchev's primary economic goal was to make more consumer goods available to the Soviet people. Continued spending on heavy industry and the military prevented any substantial increase in consumer goods, however. In addition, Soviet industry had been rebuilt after the war, but largely with prewar technology. The only real Soviet innovations were in military and space technology. In 1957 the Soviets launched the first orbiting satellite, *Sputnik I.*

Despite problems, the Soviet economy did expand, and living conditions of the people rose considerably. The Soviet Union gradually became a modern industrial society.

For a time Khrushchev attempted to improve relations with Western powers. This thaw in East-West relations lasted until 1960, when the Soviets shot down a U.S. spy plane. The building of the Berlin Wall in 1961 and a crisis over Soviet missiles in Cuba in 1962 worsened relations even further. After Khrushchev's economic reforms also failed to produce results, he was forced to resign from office. His successor, Leonid Brezhnev, tightened domestic and foreign polices once more.

✔ **READING CHECK: Drawing Inferences** Why did Khrushchev criticize Stalin's rule?

Eastern Europe

Like the rest of Europe, the new satellite countries of the Eastern bloc also had to rebuild after World War II. Communist bloc leaders accepted the Marxist-Leninist

The successful launch of the Sputnik I satellite (shown above) by the Soviet Union helped spark the international race to put a man on the moon.

The Hungarian revolt In these photos Hungarians in Budapest topple a statue of Stalin during the 1956 uprising. *What have the protesters done with the statue?*

doctrine that ordinary people did not always know what was best for society. In keeping with this principle, communist countries practiced a command economy, in which the government made all economic decisions.

The Soviet-controlled governments in Eastern Europe attempted to implement collective farming. Bulgaria collectivized over half its available farmland. The Poles, however, resisted collectivization so forcefully that most land remained in private hands. Collectivization delayed economic recovery in Eastern Europe.

Soviet-style Five-Year Plans and central planning made the industrialization of Eastern Europe more successful. East Germany became the leading industrial power in the region. Consumer goods remained a low priority, however. Living standards rose in Eastern Europe, but remained low when compared with those in the West.

During the early postwar years, the Communist bloc seemed a solid group of nations with common goals. However, rifts soon appeared. Yugoslavia's growing independence from the Soviet Union inspired people in other satellite countries. In 1953 Soviet forces put down a revolt in East Germany. Poland threatened a revolt in 1956, and as a result gained a small amount of independence in domestic affairs. Hungarians revolted against Soviet domination in 1956. Soviet troops violently repressed the revolt.

Dissatisfaction with communism and Soviet domination continued in Eastern Europe throughout the 1960s. In 1968 Alexander Dubcek (DOOB·chek) began a program of reforms in Czechoslovakia. Dubcek promised civil liberties and democratic political reforms. This short-lived period of freedom became known as the Prague Spring. Warsaw Pact troops invaded Czechoslovakia, seized reform leaders, and replaced them with pro-Soviet people.

✔ **READING CHECK: Drawing Conclusions** Why did the Soviets suppress political freedoms in Eastern Europe?

SECTION 3 REVIEW

1. **Define** and explain the significance: welfare state

2. **Identify** and explain the significance:
   Berlin Wall
   Common Market
   European Community
   Nikita Khrushchev

3. **Categorizing** Copy the chart below. Use it to explain the economic policies of Western and Eastern European nations and the Soviet Union.

	Market economy	Command economy
Defined		
Example nations		
Results		

4. **Finding the Main Idea**
   a. What is a welfare state? What welfare program did the British government establish?
   b. What moves toward economic integration did some European nations take in the 1950s?
   c. Why did Khrushchev's efforts to reform the Soviet economy meet with limited success?

5. **Writing and Critical Thinking**
   Contrasting Write an economic analysis contrasting the West German "miracle" with the performance of the Soviet economy.
   Consider:
   • the differences between a command economy and a market economy
   • the type of goods that each nation produced

Homework Practice Online
keyword: SH3 HP22

SECTION 4

READ TO DISCOVER

1 What major domestic problems did the United States face in the postwar era?
2 How did the policy of containment lead to foreign conflicts?
3 What challenges did the Canadian people respond to in the postwar era?

IDENTIFY

Joseph McCarthy
John F. Kennedy
Lyndon Johnson
NAACP
Martin Luther King Jr.
Southeast Asia Treaty Organization
Cuban missile crisis
DEW Line

WHY IT MATTERS TODAY

The United States and Canada remain close allies today. Use or other **current event** sources to learn more about relations between the United States and Canada. Record your findings in your journal.

CNN Student News.com

The United States and Canada

The Main Idea
The United States and Canada prospered in the postwar era, but both nations faced internal difficulties.

The Story Continues *On January 20, 1961, the new president John F. Kennedy spoke to the American people. Kennedy declared, "Ask not what your country can do for you; ask what you can do for your country. . . . Ask not what America will do for you, but what together we can do for the freedom of man." Kennedy's call for dedication and sacrifice inspired many Americans as they faced a difficult period in their history.*

Domestic Challenges Face the United States

During the postwar era, the United States had a strong economy and a leading role in world affairs. However, the nation still faced difficulties. Internal conflicts, political problems, and the growing realization that there are limits to economic growth marked the years following the war.

Between 1945 and 1968 three Democrats and one Republican served as president of the United States. These four presidents often had similar goals, but they differed on how to achieve those goals. The decisions they made shaped the way in which the American people viewed both the world and themselves during a critical period in American history.

The economy and the Cold War at home. After World War II the U.S. economy reached new peaks of productivity, with huge new industries and rapid growth of new construction. Several minor recessions, in which business slowed and unemployment increased, occurred during the 1940s and 1950s. The 1960s, however, were a period of continuous economic growth. Only toward the end of the decade did rising inflation foreshadow economic problems to come.

Economic prosperity led to a rising standard of living in the United States. However, the Cold War made some Americans feel anxious and insecure. Many people did not understand why the United States allowed the Soviet Union to dominate Eastern Europe. Eventually a climate of anticommunist hysteria developed. Some Americans came to believe that Soviet gains occurred because certain people in the United States were sympathetic to communism.

Senator **Joseph McCarthy** of Wisconsin became the leading spokesman for this conspiracy belief. Between 1950 and 1954 McCarthy questioned the loyalty of some government officials. Without presenting any real evidence, he accused people of communist activities. In the process he ruined the careers and destroyed the reputations of many Americans. A Senate

This Time *magazine cover from 1954 reveals the great impact Senator Joseph McCarthy had on the politics of his day.*

Dr. Martin Luther King Jr. delivered his "I Have a Dream" speech at the Lincoln Memorial in Washington, D.C.

subcommittee in 1950 found the charges false. Although he had a large following, the senator was again investigated. In late 1954 the Senate voted 67-22 to condemn McCarthy's conduct. He soon lost influence, but the Cold War, especially the threat of nuclear conflict, continued to concern many Americans.

Domestic reforms and civil rights. Following the example of the New Deal, postwar presidents created new programs to address social problems. President **John F. Kennedy** introduced a broad program of domestic reforms. Before Congress passed much of his proposed legislation, however, Kennedy was assassinated on November 22, 1963.

Kennedy's successor, **Lyndon Johnson,** offered an even more sweeping vision of social reform. Johnson hoped to create what he called the Great Society. His program included a war on poverty and other major reforms, including important civil rights legislation.

As the United States grew more affluent, minorities began to demand equal civil rights with the rest of the population. For example, African Americans lived under many political, economic, and social restrictions. In parts of the United States, black Americans could not vote or obtain decent educations, jobs, and housing. In response to racial discrimination, African Americans had formed organizations in the early 1900s, such as the National Association for the Advancement of Colored People (**NAACP**), to secure civil rights.

A turning point in the civil rights movement took place in 1954. In the landmark case *Brown v. Board of Education of Topeka*, the U.S. Supreme Court declared that state laws requiring black children to attend separate schools were unconstitutional. The court ordered states that had such laws to integrate their schools. This important decision encouraged the growing civil rights movement of the late 1950s and 1960s. In the 1960s Congress passed several civil rights and voting rights acts that guaranteed political equality for African Americans and other minorities.

The best-known civil rights leader of this time was **Martin Luther King Jr.,** a Baptist minister. King called for the use of nonviolent methods, such as boycotts, marches, and sit-ins, to bring about change. African Americans and their supporters held peaceful demonstrations and mass protests against discrimination. For his efforts, King received the Nobel Peace Prize in 1964. Four years later he died violently at the hands of an assassin. His murder dealt a severe blow to the civil rights movements and sparked a wave of riots across the country.

The U.S. civil rights movement had global effects as well. People protesting for their rights throughout the world found inspiration from the civil rights movement. One Catholic woman in Northern Ireland compared the struggles of her people to African Americans. "Like . . . the blacks [in the United States], we were poor, virtually disenfranchised, and very angry." Some Irish Catholics tried to emulate the style of African American civil rights activists, even borrowing their use of the African American spiritual "We Shall Overcome." When Martin Luther King Jr. was killed, he was mourned throughout the world.

✔ **READING CHECK: Identifying Cause and Effect** How did the civil rights movement affect the world?

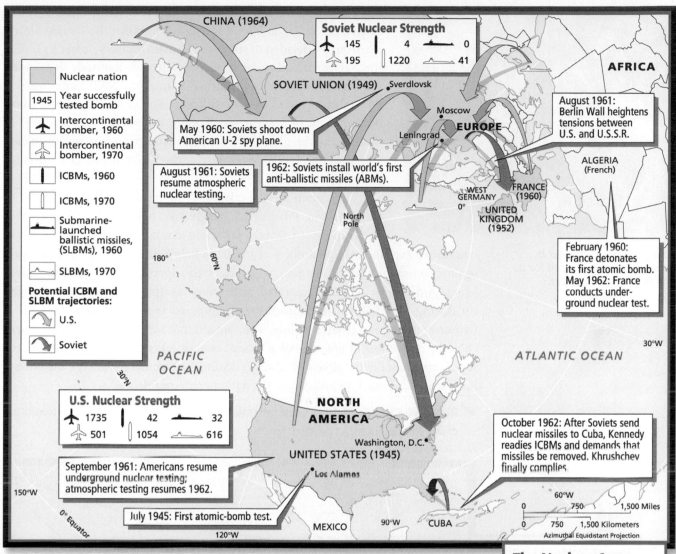

Nuclear nation

1945 Year successfully tested bomb

✈ Intercontinental bomber, 1960

✈ Intercontinental bomber, 1970

▌ ICBMs, 1960

⬭ ICBMs, 1970

⬛ Submarine-launched ballistic missiles, (SLBMs), 1960

⬛ SLBMs, 1970

Potential ICBM and SLBM trajectories:

↩ U.S.

↩ Soviet

Soviet Nuclear Strength
| ✈ 145 | ▌ 4 | ⬛ 0 |
| ✈ 195 | 1220 | 41 |

CHINA (1964)

SOVIET UNION (1949) • Sverdlovsk

• Moscow

May 1960: Soviets shoot down American U-2 spy plane.

EUROPE

Leningrad

August 1961: Berlin Wall heightens tensions between U.S. and U.S.S.R.

AFRICA

August 1961: Soviets resume atmospheric nuclear testing.

1962: Soviets install world's first anti-ballistic missiles (ABMs).

ALGERIA (French)

WEST GERMANY 0° FRANCE (1960)

UNITED KINGDOM (1952)

North Pole

February 1960: France detonates its first atomic bomb. **May 1962:** France conducts underground nuclear test.

180°

60°N

30°W

PACIFIC OCEAN

ATLANTIC OCEAN

30°N

U.S. Nuclear Strength
| ✈ 1735 | ▌ 42 | ⬛ 32 |
| ✈ 501 | 1054 | 616 |

NORTH AMERICA

October 1962: After Soviets send nuclear missiles to Cuba, Kennedy readies ICBMs and demands that missiles be removed. Khrushchev finally complies.

Washington, D.C.•

UNITED STATES (1945)

September 1961: Americans resume underground nuclear testing; atmospheric testing resumes 1962.

• Los Alamos

150°W

0° Equator

July 1945: First atomic-bomb test.

MEXICO   90°W   CUBA

60°W

0 ——— 750 ——— 1,500 Miles
0 ——— 750 ——— 1,500 Kilometers
Azimuthal Equidistant Projection

120°W

Foreign Policy and the Cold War

For the most part U.S. foreign policy during the postwar period focused on the containment of communism. In Asia the United States sent troops to South Korea in a "police action" to stop North Korean Communists from taking over the country. President Dwight D. Eisenhower created the **Southeast Asia Treaty Organization** (SEATO) in an attempt to halt further communist advances in the region. He also announced the Eisenhower Doctrine, which provided economic and military assistance to noncommunist nations in the Middle East. Efforts to ease Cold War tensions during this period failed. In 1961 the construction of the Berlin Wall made it clear that the Cold War would continue in full force. The greatest fear was that the war would turn hot and result in nuclear conflict.

In 1959 a Marxist named Fidel Castro led rebel forces that overthrew the corrupt government of Cuba. The Eisenhower administration feared that a communist Cuba would become a base of Soviet operations. In April 1961 newly elected President Kennedy authorized an invasion of Cuba by anti-Castro forces who received training and equipment from the Central Intelligence Agency (CIA). However, U.S. air support for the invasion was canceled, and Cuban forces

The Nuclear Arms Race, 1945–1970

Interpreting Maps
Throughout the postwar era, the United States and the Soviet Union were locked in a deadly nuclear arms competition. Flashpoints, such as the U-2 spy plane crisis in 1960, increased global tensions and spurred ongoing weapons development and deployment.

■ **Skills Assessment:**
Using Geography How did Soviet nuclear arms strength compare to that of the United States in 1960? In 1970?

Young citizens gathered in Washington, D.C., to call for an end to the Vietnam War.

captured or killed the invaders. After the failed invasion, Castro turned to the Soviet Union for support against the United States. Khrushchev decided to strengthen Soviet military power by building nuclear missile sites in Cuba. Alarmed, Kennedy demanded that the Soviet Union withdraw its missiles. NATO and Warsaw Pact military forces went on full alert. For 13 days the world stood on the brink of nuclear war. Finally, the Soviet Union agreed to remove the missiles, if the United States promised not to invade Cuba. Kennedy also privately agreed to remove U.S. missiles from Turkey.

The **Cuban missile crisis** was the most dangerous moment of the Cold War. From a U.S. perspective, however, the Vietnam War in Southeast Asia was far more damaging. The United States committed ever-increasing numbers of troops to help South Vietnam in its struggle against communist North Vietnam, which received support from the Soviet Union. Many Americans became frustrated and angry as the Vietnam War dragged on during the 1960s. Antiwar protesters expressed their discontent by staging demonstrations on college campuses. They argued that U.S. involvement in Vietnam caused needless loss of life. In 1968 a violent confrontation broke out between protesters and police in the streets of Chicago during the Democratic Party Convention. Such scenes did much to undermine the nation's self-confidence.

✔ **READING CHECK: Making Generalizations** What problems did Cold War tensions create for the American people?

Radar Systems and Defenses in North America, 1959–1964

Interpreting Maps During the Cold War the United States invested enormous amounts of money to build nuclear warning and defense systems. Many of these systems ran through Canada.

■ **Skills Assessment: The World in Spatial Terms** Why was the DEW Line considered to be America's first line of defense against a Soviet nuclear attack?

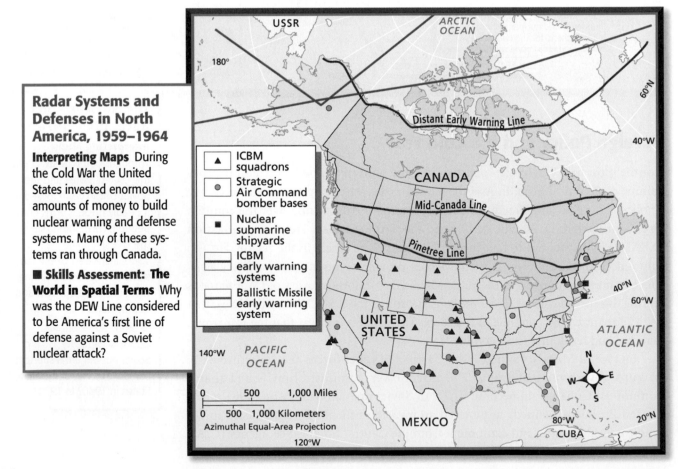

Canada's Challenges

For more than a century, Canada and the United States had maintained a close relationship. During and after World War II this relationship grew stronger, especially with regard to economic and military affairs. Canada relied heavily on the United States for its national defense. Together the two nations built a line of radar installations called the Distant Early Warning Line, or **DEW Line,** designed to give early warning of air attacks. Together, Canada and the United States also established the North American Air Defense Command.

Active participation in two world wars ended the isolation policy that Canada had maintained for many years. After World War II, Canada became a vigorous supporter of the United Nations and NATO. Canadians loaned billions of dollars to other countries and welcomed refugees from Europe. Like the United States, Canada experienced considerable economic development after World War II. Much of the country remained agricultural, producing corn, feed grains, and wheat. However, industry also grew after the war. The large Canadian forests provided wood products, and the wood pulp and paper industries expanded. Development of electrical power and improvements in transportation stimulated the mining of coal, iron, and uranium. Oil and gas production increased. Aircraft, automobile, and electrical industries developed in the provinces of Quebec and Ontario.

During the 1960s a new challenge appeared in Canadian life. Many French-speaking Canadians, particularly those living in the province of Quebec, desired to separate from the rest of Canada. Feelings of French nationalism were not new, but grew more intense at this time. The movement received a boost from the 1967 visit of French president Charles de Gaulle. A new political party, the Parti Quebecois, (par•TEE kay•bay•KWAH) called for secession from the Canadian Confederation. The party gained 24 percent of the vote in Quebec in the 1970 elections, and in 1976 won control of Quebec's government. In 1980 the Parti Quebecois put the issue of separation to voters. The referendum failed, but in 1995 a similar vote showed 49.4 percent of Quebecois in favor of separation, indicating that the challenge to Canadian unity will not vanish soon.

✔ **READING CHECK: Making Predictions** What challenges might a separatist movement create for a nation such as Canada?

CONNECTING TO
Civics

Separatism

Quebec's separatist movement is just one of many that have occurred throughout history. Over time, various ethnic, national, cultural, and religious groups have expressed a desire to be free from the larger groups to which they belong. Because of their wish to separate from this larger group, they are often referred to as separatists. Separatist movements continue throughout the world today. The Kurds, a Middle Eastern cultural group of 20 to 25 million people, want their own nation. The Basque people, a small cultural group in Spain, have turned to violence in their bid to be free from Spanish control.

Understanding Civics

Why might political leaders oppose separatist movements in their nations?

SECTION 4 REVIEW

1. **Identify** and explain the significance:
   Joseph McCarthy
   John F. Kennedy
   Lyndon Johnson
   NAACP
   Martin Luther King Jr.
   Southeast Asia Treaty Organization
   Cuban missile crisis
   DEW Line

2. **Identifying Cause and Effect** Copy the graphic organizer below. Use it to explain the effect that the Cold War had on domestic concerns in the United States.

Effects of the Cold War	
Economic	
Political	
Security	
Civil Rights	

3. **Finding the Main Idea**
   a. What domestic issues caused conflicts in the United States during the postwar era?
   b. How did Canada's foreign policy change in the postwar era?
   c. What did the separatist movement reflect about Canada?

4. **Writing and Critical Thinking**
   Finding the Main Idea Write an essay about the importance of the U.S. civil rights movement.
   Consider:
   • the effect of the movement on the United States
   • how it affected other movements throughout the world

Homework Practice Online
go.hrw.com
keyword: SH3 HP22

CHAPTER 22 Review

Creating a Time Line

Copy the time line below onto a sheet of paper. Complete the time line by filling in the events, individuals, and dates from the chapter that you think were significant. Pick three events and explain why you think they were significant.

1940	1950	1960	1970

Writing a Summary

Using standard grammar, spelling, sentence structure, and punctuation, write an overview of the events in the chapter.

Identifying People and Ideas

Identify the following terms or individuals and explain their significance:

1. United Nations
2. Cold War
3. containment
4. Marshall Plan
5. NATO
6. European Community
7. Nikita Khrushchev
8. Joseph McCarthy
9. John F. Kennedy
10. Martin Luther King Jr.

Understanding Main Ideas

SECTION 1 *(pp. 628–632)*

Aftermath of the War in Europe

1. How did unresolved issues following World War II contribute to postwar tensions between the United States and the Soviet Union?
2. How did territorial adjustments affect the German economy?

SECTION 2 *(pp. 633–638)*

Origins of the Cold War

3. How did the Truman Doctrine reflect the goal of containment?
4. What were the causes and effects of the Berlin blockade?

SECTION 3 *(pp. 639–644)*

Reconstruction, Reform, and Reaction in Europe

5. What was the West German "miracle" and what produced it?
6. What was the economic situation in the Soviet Union and Eastern Europe after the war?

SECTION 4 *(pp. 645–649)*

The United States and Canada

7. What was the goal of the civil rights movement in the United States?
8. Why did the United States become involved in the conflict in Vietnam?

Reviewing Themes

1. **Economics** How effective were command economies in the postwar era?
2. **Government** What problems regarding democracy did the separatist movement in Canada raise?
3. **Citizenship** What sort of protests did civil rights activists rely upon in the 1960s?

Thinking Critically

1. **Summarizing** What are the responsibilities of the UN Security Council and the General Assembly?
2. **Identifying Cause and Effect** How did American political ideas shape events in the postwar era?
3. **Evaluating** Why did Nikita Khrushchev denounce Stalinism?
4. **Contrasting** How were the market economies of most Western European nations different from the command economies of the Soviet Union and Eastern European nations?

Writing About History

Summarizing Suppose you are a foreign correspondent in Europe after the war. Write a report that informs about economic and political development in Europe and the Soviet Union after World War II. Use the following chart to organize your thoughts before you begin writing.

	Economics	Politics
Germany		
Great Britain		
France		
Eastern Europe		
Soviet Union		

Interpreting a Chart

Study the chart below. Then use the information on the chart to answer the questions that follow.

Growth in World Energy Demand, 1940-1970*

Year	Form of energy			
	Coal	Oil	Natural Gas	Hydroelectric
1940	1.0	0.33	0.1	0.25
1950	1.0	0.5	0.25	0.15
1960	1.5	1.0	0.5	0.15
1970	1.75	2.25	1.0	0.25

*Values are approximate and expressed as "thousand million tons oil equivalent."

1. Which statement correctly describes a relationship shown on the chart?

   a. In 1940 the demand for coal was greater than for oil, but by about 1960 the demand for both was the same.

   b. Between 1960 and 1970 the demand for natural gas and hydroelectric was greater than for coal or oil.

   c. In the 1950s the demand for coal was about the same as it had been in the 1940s.

   d. In the 1940s the demand for hydroelectric became greater than the demand for natural gas.

2. What trends account for the difference in world energy demand between 1940 and 1970? Give specific examples.

Drawing Inferences

Read the following comment made by Robert McNamara in 1988 on the Cuban missile crisis. McNamara had been the United States Secretary of Defense during the crisis. Answer the questions that follow.

> "At the time, we had 5,100 nuclear weapons that we could deliver onto the Soviet Union and they had only 300 they could deliver onto the U.S. We knew that, and we knew our knowledge was reliable. And that was strategic parity. We were prevented from using our 5,100 nuclear weapons because we knew that whatever damage we did to you, you would have enough left to inflict unacceptable damage on the United States. So that was parity."

3. Which of the following is the best statement of what the author's comment implies?

   a. The U.S. could not afford to use all of its nuclear weapons.

   b. The U.S. looked for ways other than using nuclear weapons to solve the crisis.

   c. The U.S. was not concerned about the 300 nuclear missiles the Soviets had.

   d. The U.S. did not like the concept of "strategic parity."

4. Why is the Cuban missile crisis considered by many to have been the most dangerous period of the Cold War? Give specific reasons.

Alternative Assessment

Building Your Portfolio

Link to TODAY

Citizenship

The right to assemble and to protest are long-standing rights enjoyed by Americans. The civil rights movement of the late 1950s and 1960s was just one area of protest in U.S. history. Research to find out what other movements have inspired large-scale protests in recent history and how successful these protest have been. Compile your findings in a chart.

internet connect

Internet Activity: go.hrw.com
KEYWORD: SH3 WH22

Choose a topic on Europe and North America in the Postwar Years to:

- research the Cold War and look for elements of popular culture that reflect Cold War anxieties.

- assess how human rights and democratic ideals have been advanced by the United Nations.

- learn about McCarthyism and its effects on the United States.

CHAPTER 23

1945–Present

Asia Since 1945

1945
Global Events
The United Nations is established.

1947
Politics
India gains independence from Britain.

1950
Daily Life
Mother Teresa founds a religious order in Calcutta.

Sitar musician Ravi Shankar of India

1968
The Arts
Japanese writer Yasunari Kawabata wins the Nobel Prize for literature.

1968
Business and Finance
The United States relaxes trade restrictions with China.

1971
Politics
Bangladesh becomes independent from Pakistan.

1950

1960

1970

1946
Science and Technology
The electric rice saucepan revolutionizes Japanese cooking.

1954
The Arts
The Japanese movie *The Seven Samurai* becomes popular in the West.

1954
Politics
The Geneva Accord divides Vietnam.

1961
Daily Life
China's population reaches 650 million.

1960
The Arts
Indian musician Ravi Shankar becomes popular in the West.

1960
Business and Finance
A Tokyo company introduces the world's first felt-tip pen.

1965
Daily Life
Pakistan and much of India suffer starvation because of drought.

1967
Global Events
Israel wins the Six-Day War in the Middle East.

1969
Science and Technology
The *Apollo 11* mission lands Americans on the moon.

1972
Business and Finance
Indian entrepreneur Ravi Tikkoo founds Globtik Tankers.

Poster advertising the Japanese movie classic,
The Seven Samurai

Build on What You Know

Before World War II most of the countries of Asia were colonies of European powers. During the war, some Asian countries provided supplies or arms to the war effort. Some sent troops to join the fighting. Some, because of their strategic locations, were invaded and occupied. After World War II the Asian world changed greatly. The European empires in Asia began to crumble as nationalist sentiments grew and new political parties gained influence. In this chapter, you will learn how the nations of Asia made the transition from colonial possession to independent statehood.

Chinese students celebrate as Hong Kong returns to Chinese control.

1997
Global Events
The former British colony of Hong Kong is returned to Chinese control.

1986
Science and Technology
The Chernobyl nuclear disaster occurs in USSR.

1986
Politics
Corazon Aquino is elected president of the Philippines.

1998
Business and Finance
Economic problems in Japan spread to other Asian economies and to markets worldwide.

1998
The Arts
The Petronas Twin Towers, the world's tallest buildings, are completed in Kuala Lumpur, Malaysia.

1976
Daily Life
The World Health Organization reports Asia is free of smallpox for first time in history.

1991
Global Events
The Soviet Union breaks up.

1980

1990

2000

1984
The Arts
Chinese writers call for greater artistic freedom.

1989
Politics
A pro-democracy movement is repressed in China.

2001
Global Events
A mid-air collision between a U.S. intelligence-gathering aircraft and a Chinese jet fighter creates new international tensions.

2000
Daily Life
Two pandas on loan from China arrive at the National Zoological Park in Washington, D.C.

A lone man stands before a line of tanks as Chinese troops move toward student demonstrators in Tiananmen Square in 1989.

Chinese pandas relax at the National Zoological Park in Washington, D.C.

What's Your Opinion?

*Do you **agree** or **disagree** with the following statements? Support your point of view in your journal.*

Government The more controls a government puts in place, the fewer civil rights the people have.

Global Relations Communist and noncommunist countries clash whenever they are located near each other.

Economics A new or developing nation can only succeed if its economy grows.

READ TO DISCOVER

1 How did differences between Hindus and Muslims lead to a divided India?

2 What problems did India face after independence?

3 How did Pakistan and Bangladesh develop after the partition of India?

DEFINE

nonalignment
mixed economy

IDENTIFY

Muslim League
Muhammad Ali Jinnah
Jawaharlal Nehru
Indira Gandhi
Mother Teresa
Dalai Lama
Awami League
Benazir Bhutto

▶ **WHY IT MATTERS TODAY**

India, Pakistan, and Bangladesh regularly experience natural disasters. Use CNNstudentNews.com or other **current event** sources to find recent examples. Record your findings in your journal.

CNNstudentNews.com

South Asia After Empire

The Main Idea
India and Pakistan emerged from British control as independent nations divided along religious lines.

The Story Continues *In the years following World War II, India and Pakistan gained their independence from British rule. The change, however, was not an easy one. Two months after Independence Day, Mohandas K. Gandhi commented sadly, "What sin have I committed that He should have kept me alive to be witness of these horrors?"*

The End of British Rule

The movement for Indian self-rule grew after World War I. Many Indians agreed with the nationalists. They wanted complete freedom from British rule. The nationalists continued to work for self-rule throughout World War II.

Wartime developments. Many Indians refused to back Britain in World War II. They were angry because Great Britain would not meet their demands for self-rule. Also, the British had said that India was at war with Germany without asking the Indian National Congress. Ministers of the Congress resented this action, and the entire Congress resigned in 1939. They called for immediate self-rule.

When Japan entered the war on the side of Germany, the Allies needed India as a base. The pressure on Britain to reach a settlement with India increased. In March 1942, Britain sent Sir Stafford Cripps to work out the terms for India's independence. This would only happen, though, once the war ended. The Indian National Congress rejected his plan. So did the **Muslim League,** a group of Muslim leaders formed to protect the rights of Indian Muslims.

Soon after the Cripps plan failed, nationalist leader Mohandas Karamchand Gandhi started the "Quit India" movement. He insisted that complete separation was the only answer. Great Britain should leave India at once. Britain treated the "Quit India" campaign as a rebellion. Gandhi and some 60,000 of his followers were arrested.

While the Hindus continued to resist the British, the Muslim League made different demands. Led by **Muhammad Ali Jinnah,** they wanted a Muslim state separate from India. This new state would be Pakistan. They believed a separate country would better protect the interests of India's Muslims. The Muslim League wanted Britain to divide the country and then leave. Talks between Gandhi and Jinnah failed to resolve the differences. By 1946 bloody riots had broken out between Hindus and Muslims.

Indian statesman Muhammad Ali Jinnah was the driving force in the creation of the independent Muslim state of Pakistan.

The partition of India. In March 1947, Lord Louis Mountbatten became British viceroy in India. His strategy was to set a short deadline for Britain to grant independence and force the leaders to reach agreement. The decision to partition, or divide, India was made difficult by the fact that the Muslim and Sikh minorities lived next to Hindus in some areas. Division of the minorities would cause dislocation and tension. Police and military forces would have to be divided, weakening these forces when they would be needed most. In the Punjab, nationalist Sikhs wanted their own state.

Independence was declared in August according to the borders defined by a British-led commission, but without enough preparation for keeping the peace. The celebrations were hardly over before the tragedy began. Citizens fled their homes in the chaos that followed. Violence and massacres erupted. Millions, primarily Muslims, lost their homes or were killed in the following months.

On August 15, 1947, the two nations of India and Pakistan were born. Just before midnight **Jawaharlal Nehru,** India's first prime minister, rose to speak.

History Makers Speak

❝At the stroke of the midnight hour, when the world sleeps, India will awake to life and freedom. A moment comes, which comes but rarely in history, when we step out from the old to the new, when an age ends, and when the soul of the nation, long suppressed, finds utterance. . . .❞

Jawaharlal Nehru, "Tryst with Destiny"

Less than six months later, Mohandas Gandhi was assassinated. The assassin was a Hindu extremist who resented Gandhi for his tolerant attitude toward Muslims.

✔ **READING CHECK: Identifying Cause and Effect** What caused the violence in India after partition?

Independent India

In 1950 India's new constitution went into effect. The government became a republic. It has an elected president and parliament. Although the president is the head of state, the prime minister and cabinet members hold the real power.

Government leaders and policies. Jawaharlal Nehru faced a difficult task as the first prime minister of India. Many forces divided his country from the start. There were several religions, many languages, and the caste system. Nehru hoped to unite India. He wanted to separate religion from government and give people more individual rights. Nehru also set India on its path of **nonalignment.** This meant that India did not ally with either the United States or the Soviet Union.

Nehru died in 1964. Two years later his daughter, **Indira Priyadarshini Nehru Gandhi,** became the prime minister. Her goal was to carry out her father's ideas. Indira Gandhi ran the Indian government for nearly 20 years. Some of her actions, however, angered people. Many Indians turned against her. In 1977 they voted her out of office. Three years later voters elected her prime minister again.

Analyzing Primary Sources

Analyzing Information What did Nehru mean when he said "the soul of the nation, long suppressed, finds utterance"?

India's first prime minister, Jawaharlal Nehru, and his daughter, Indira Gandhi, made a state visit to the United States in December 1956.

Major religious areas:

- Over 90% Muslim
- 70%–90% Muslim
- Over 90% Hindu
- 60%–90% Hindu
- 30%–40% Sikh
- 80%–100% Buddhist
- Over 30% Christian
- National boundary
- Disputed border
- Cease-fire line
- ⊛ National capital

India and West Pakistan fought for control of this area.

In 1971 East Pakistan became the independent nation of Bangladesh.

Religious Divisions and the Partitioning of India, 1947

Interpreting Maps The partitioning of India created conflicts among the country's main religious groups.

■ **Skills Assessment: Human Systems** Which two religious groups were fighting for control of Kashmir?

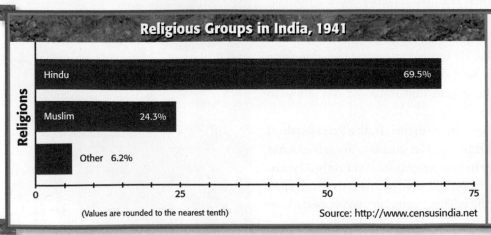

Religious Groups in India, 1941

Religions

- Hindu — 69.5%
- Muslim — 24.3%
- Other — 6.2%

(Values are rounded to the nearest tenth)

Source: http://www.censusindia.net

Interpreting the Graph
Religious groups in India identified by the 1941 British census included Hindu, Muslim, Christian, Sikh, Buddhist, and Jain faiths. Most of the former British colony's Muslims became citizens of Pakistan as a result of the partition of 1947. *Which religious group probably dominated India's political scene following independence?*

Gandhi faced a difficult problem on her return. Sikhs from the province of Punjab were fighting for self-rule. They had killed a number of government officials. In 1984 Gandhi ordered the Indian army to storm the Sikh base, which was the Golden Shrine in Amritsar, their holiest place of worship. About 1,000 people died in the attack. The Sikhs promised to get revenge. A few months later, two of Gandhi's Sikh bodyguards assassinated her. Her son, Rajiv Gandhi, took over as prime minister. He was a popular leader, but his party lost power.

In 1989 a new prime minister, V. P. Singh, was elected. He wanted to improve the rights of the lower castes. Violent protests forced him to resign in 1990. Most people thought voters would return Rajiv Gandhi to power. Before the election, though, Gandhi was assassinated. Several years of unrest followed as more than 20 political parties fought for power. In 1998 Atal Bihari Vajpayee was elected prime minister. Vajpayee, like his predecessors, expressed his desire for better relations with Pakistan. In spite of this, clashes between troops from both countries continued. By 2000 the fighting between India and Pakistan had taken a frightening turn. Both countries had built and tested nuclear weapons.

Social and economic problems. Nehru followed socialist ideas for India's economy. From 1947 onward, India has had a **mixed economy.** This occurs when private companies own some industries and the government owns the rest. To help the economy grow, India followed a series of Five-Year Plans. These plans worked very well. By the end of the 1980s, Indian farms were growing more food. The textile and steel industries were strong. The country also was exporting many finished products, such as clothing and bicycles.

In spite of this growth, India still had a huge problem. Its population was growing too fast. In 1950 the Indian population was about 360 million. Within about 30 years, it had grown to about 685 million. The nation's economy could not keep up with the population increase. By the late 1980s, the average annual income was $300. Millions of Indians had no jobs. Cities were crowded and housing was short. Many millions barely managed to stay alive from day to day.

In the 1990s, India tried to find new solutions to its problems. As the government became more open to foreign investors and trade, the economy grew. At the same

HISTORY MAKER

**Indira Gandhi
(1917–1984)**

Indira Gandhi was involved in India's political scene for most of her life. Gandhi was the daughter of Jawaharlal Nehru. Like her father, she became involved in nationalist activities while India was fighting for its independence.

Indira Gandhi followed in her father's footsteps when she became India's prime minister in 1966. She surprised many people who believed she was incapable of doing the job. Instead, Gandhi showed herself to be a powerful ruler whose leadership helped India to become a key force in world affairs. **How might Indira Gandhi's childhood have prepared her for political leadership?**

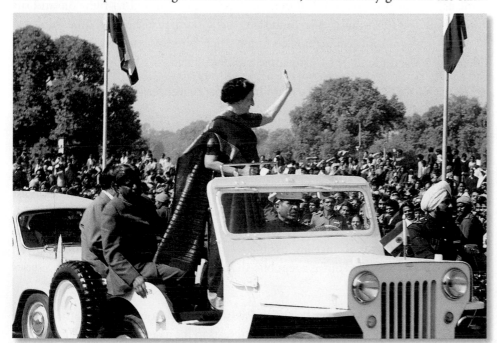

Indira Gandhi, India's prime minister from 1966 to 1977 and again from 1980 to 1984, bridged the country's transition from colony to independent republic.

time, though, the population continued to grow. By 2000 India had over 1 billion people. If this rate continues, India will have more people than any other country by 2050. These people will live on just 2 percent of the world's land area.

✔ **READING CHECK: Making Predictions** What effect do you think India's population growth will have on the nation's future?

Foreign relations. In world affairs, India tried to build friendships with both communist countries and the West. This nonalignment became a model for other countries. A number of new African and Asian nations followed India's lead. By staying neutral, these countries hoped to get aid from both sides.

India's foreign policy did not solve all its problems. In 1950 China occupied Tibet. The Tibetans rebelled, but the Chinese crushed the revolt. For a long time before this, India had backed the **Dalai Lama,** Tibet's Buddhist religious leader and political head. When the Chinese took control of Tibet, the Dalai Lama and some of his Buddhist followers fled to India. There they formed a government in exile. During the next few years, relations between India and China became even more difficult.

India began to move away from nonalignment in the 1970s and established close ties with the Soviet Union. Then, in the 1980s, India became interested in better relations with the United States. Even so, India would not take sides in the Cold War. By the 1990s, India's policies had changed, and it began to take a more open approach to foreign affairs.

The continuing problem of Kashmir. India and Pakistan faced a difficult problem in the northern state of Kashmir. The problem began with partition in 1947. Kashmir's ruling prince, who was Hindu, at first tried to avoid joining either country. On the one hand, Pakistan claimed Kashmir because three quarters of its people were Muslim. On the other hand, Nehru's family was from Kashmir and he had ties with the area. He sent Indian troops to back the Hindu prince.

Muslims and Hindus in Kashmir fought each other for control. This led to fighting between Indian and Pakistani soldiers. In 1949 the United Nations set a cease-fire line. At that point, India held two thirds of Kashmir. Still, the question of Kashmir's nationality was not answered. India and Pakistan continued to fight on and off throughout the 1950s and 1960s. In the late 1980s, border clashes and other violence between rebel groups became more common. Such flare-ups continued into the early 2000s. By 2004, more than 20,000 people had been killed.

✔ **READING CHECK: Finding the Main Idea** What challenges with foreign affairs did India face?

The Division of Pakistan

When British rule ended, Pakistan became a two-part country. West Pakistan and East Pakistan were separated by India. The two parts were about 1,000 miles from each other. The differences between them were huge. They had different languages, cultures, and geography. It was almost impossible to govern the two parts as one country. Although Pakistan started out as a republic, the government soon lost control to a series of military leaders.

Independence for Bangladesh. When Pakistan held elections in 1970, the **Awami League** won the majority of the East Pakistani seats in the assembly. The Awami League was a political party that wanted self-rule for East Pakistan. When Pakistan's central government refused to accept the election result, riots broke out in East Pakistan. The central government sent troops to put down the riots. They arrested the leaders of the Awami League. The situation soon became a civil war in which thousands of people were killed. India sent arms and troops to help East Pakistan. Ten million people from East Pakistan fled to India. Late in 1971 the West Pakistanis were defeated and East Pakistan became the new nation of Bangladesh.

Bangladesh and Pakistan today. Bangladesh had been torn apart by war. It also suffered famines, floods, and tropical storms. The new government was not equal to the huge task of rebuilding the country. In the mid-1970s, it was taken over in a military coup. In the 1991 elections, the Bangladesh National Party (BNP) won a victory over the Awami League. The BNP leader, Khalida Zia, became the country's first woman prime minister. In 1996 new elections brought the Awami League back into power. Bad feelings between the two parties continued, and the country faced huge challenges. In 1998 floods covered almost all of Bangladesh. More than 1 million people died, and at least 30 million people lost their homes.

Pakistan, too, faced political unrest. In 1977 General Mohammed Zia ul-Haq took control of the government. He had the prime minister, Zulfikar Ali Bhutto, arrested. Bhutto was put to death two years later. Zia finally allowed elections in 1988. **Benazir Bhutto,** the daughter of Ali Bhutto, was elected prime minister. She became the first woman to serve as head of a Muslim nation. The army removed her from office in 1990, but she was elected again in 1993. Three years later she was defeated. In 1999 the army took control, and General Pervez Musharraf became prime minister. General Musharraf has been active in removing Taliban allies from the Pakistani military forces and in 2002, Pakistan's participation in the war against terrorism led to the repeal of U.S. economic embargoes imposed on the country in 1998.

✔ **READING CHECK: Contrasting** In what ways are Pakistan's current problems different from those of Bangladesh?

HISTORY MAKER

**Benazir Bhutto
(1953–   )**

Benazir Bhutto graduated from Radcliffe College, in the United States. When she was sworn in as the prime minister of Pakistan, she became the first woman to govern a Muslim country. **How do the experiences of Benazir Bhutto reflect the changing roles and influence of women in modern Asia?**

SECTION 1 REVIEW

1. **Define** and explain the significance:
   nonalignment
   mixed economy

2. **Identify** and explain the significance:
   Muslim League
   Muhammad Ali Jinnah
   Jawaharlal Nehru
   Indira Gandhi
   Mother Teresa
   Dalai Lama
   Awami League
   Benazir Bhutto

3. **Summarizing** Make a chart like this one to summarize how India, Pakistan, and Bangladesh became independent nations.

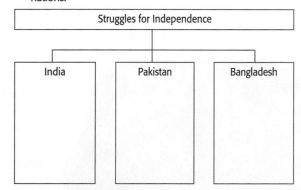

Struggles for Independence

India | Pakistan | Bangladesh

4. **Finding the Main Idea**
   a. What effect did religion have on the way India and Pakistan were established?
   b. How did nonalignment affect India's foreign relations?
   c. What have been the greatest domestic challenges for India, Pakistan, and Bangladesh?

5. **Writing and Critical Thinking**
   Supporting a Point of View Write a paragraph explaining why you think it was a good or bad idea to divide India before independence.
   Consider:
   • the fighting between Hindus and Muslims
   • relations between India and Pakistan since partition

Homework Practice Online
go.hrw.com
keyword: SH3 HP23

SECTION 2

READ TO DISCOVER

1 How did Mao Zedong's government try to rebuild China after World War II?
2 What occurred at Tiananmen Square, and what were the consequences for China?
3 Why was Korea divided, and how have the two Koreas developed since 1953?
4 Why have China and Taiwan been in conflict?

IDENTIFY

Great Leap Forward
Cultural Revolution
Red Guards
Jiang Qing
Gang of Four
Deng Xiaoping
Tiananmen Square Massacre
Kim Il Sung
Syngman Rhee

WHY IT MATTERS TODAY

The pro-democracy movement in China is still active today. Use CNN.com or other **current event** sources to find out what has happened to the movement since 2000. Record your findings in your journal.

CNN Student News.com

Communist China and Its Influence

The Main Idea
China and North Korea became communist, while South Korea and Taiwan remained non-communist.

The Story Continues *Unlike India, China did not have to fight for self-rule. In the 1930s, however, conflicts inside China had grown into a bloody civil war. According to one observer, "We need only look at . . . the uprisings by the peasants, the mutinies of soldiers and the strikes of students . . . to see that it cannot be long before a 'spark' kindles 'a prairie fire.'" By the time the civil war ended, China was devastated.*

China Under Mao Zedong

During World War II, the Chinese Nationalists and Chinese Communists had agreed to temporarily stop their civil war in the face of the common threat posed by Japanese aggression. Throughout the war years, the Nationalists and the Communists joined in an uneasy alliance against the Japanese. Their combined forces fought an effective guerrilla campaign until Japan surrendered in 1945. Following the war, however, bitter fighting broke out once again as China's destructive civil war resumed.

In 1949 the Communists under the leadership of Mao Zedong finally drove the Nationalists from power. Chiang Kai-shek, the Nationalists' leader, fled with his supporters to the island of Taiwan. Chiang and the Nationalists formed a government there. On the Chinese mainland Mao Zedong's Communists formed the People's Republic of China. About 1 million Chinese were killed during the communist takeover. The United States, which had supported the Nationalists, refused to recognize the new Chinese Communist government.

The People's Republic of China. The Communists wanted to turn China into a modern, industrialized nation. Because of the damage from the civil war, this was a huge task. In 1953 the Communists began their first Five-Year Plan for economic growth. It was modeled on similar Soviet plans. Part of the plan was to build up China's industry. Another part was land reform. The Communists forced landlords to give their land to the peasants. Millions of people were killed during this violent change. The peasants organized their new land into collective farms. The government operated state farms on much of the land that was left. The first Five-Year Plan was a success, as both agricultural and industrial output increased.

The flag of the People's Republic of China, designed after the communist takeover of the Chinese mainland in 1949.

Revolution in China, 1945–1949

Interpreting Maps Communists gained control over China over a four-year period.

■ **Skills Assessment: Places and Regions** What city was a communist capital until 1949?

Map legend:

Areas occupied by Communists:
- By 1945
- 1945–June 1946
- July 1946–June 1948
- July 1948–June 1949
- July–Sept. 1949
- After October 1949

- National boundary
- ⊙ Communist capital until 1949
- ✪ National capital since 1949
- ★ Nationalist capitals
- • Other city

Map callout: The People's Republic of China is proclaimed on October 1, 1949.

Map callout: In late 1949, Chiang Kai-shek's Nationalist government flees to Taiwan, where it re-establishes the Republic of China.

0   250   500 Miles
0   250   500 Kilometers
Robinson Projection

The Great Leap Forward. To speed up progress, in 1958 Mao's government announced a second Five-Year Plan called the **Great Leap Forward.** The Chinese government hoped to increase industrial output to the point where it matched that of the West. To reach this goal, China bought modern machinery and ran it almost continuously. The government encouraged people to produce their own iron and steel in small backyard blast furnaces.

The Great Leap Forward created huge farm communities called people's communes. These included farms and small industries. Single people lived in dormitories, meals were served in mess halls, and children were cared for in nurseries while their parents worked long hours in the fields and factories. Workers were paid based on "work points," which were set based on gender, age, skills, type of job, and region.

The Red Guards

In 1966 almost 11 million Chinese students from all across China banded together to form a political group known as the Red Guards. The students marched to the capital of Beijing, where they held mass demonstrations in support of the Communist Party. According to Chinese officials, the aim of the Red Guards was to "purify" China's political scene by ridding it of opponents to the rule of Mao Zedong. The Red Guards were responsible for the execution of thousands of Chinese who disagreed with Mao and his government. The group did not last long. By 1968 the Red Guards had diminished in power and prestige. **How did the Red Guards show their support for the Communist government?**

The Great Leap Forward was a terrible failure. Industrial output decreased, and there were constant food shortages. As many as 20 million people starved to death between 1958 and 1960. The government abandoned the program in the early 1960s.

The Cultural Revolution. After the failure of the Great Leap Forward, Mao's leadership of the Communist Party was in question. He fought back in 1966 by launching the **Cultural Revolution,** a violent attempt at social change. Mao aimed to rid China of its old customs, habits, and thoughts. He wanted to replace them with a new socialist culture. Mao's ideas were collected in a little red book. For example, Mao spoke against intellectuals.

History Makers Speak

❝The . . . intellectuals who are hostile to our state . . . will stir up trouble and attempt to overthrow the Communist Party and restore the old China. . . . Such people are to be found in political circles and in . . . educational, scientific . . . and religious circles, and they are extremely reactionary.❞

from Mao Zedong, *Quotations from Chairman Mao*

Mao chose China's young people to lead this revolution. These radical students soon became known as the **Red Guards.** They went on rampages throughout China. They ruined ancient works of art, burned books, and destroyed anything from the "old way." They also beat, tortured, or killed some people who did not follow Mao's teachings completely.

The Cultural Revolution and the mass murders it involved had a disastrous effect on China. Agricultural and industrial production fell sharply. Chinese society was in chaos. In late 1968 Mao took control and broke up the Red Guards.

✔ **READING CHECK: Summarizing** What did Mao do to try to solve China's problems?

China After Mao

Mao Zedong died in 1976. After his death, a struggle began between moderate Communists and a radical group led by Mao's widow, **Jiang Qing** (jee·AHNG CHING), who was sometimes known as Madame Mao. The moderates wanted to restore order and economic growth. Jiang Qing's group, known as the **Gang of Four,** wanted to continue the Cultural Revolution. In time, the moderates won control and placed the Gang of Four on trial for numerous crimes, including treason. They were found guilty and given life sentences.

Holt Researcher

go.hrw.com

KEYWORD: Holt Researcher

FreeFind: Jiang Qing

After reading more about Jiang Qing on the Holt Researcher, create a chart comparing China under her influence with China under Mao.

At a 1966 rally, thousands of Red Guards wave Mao Zedong's "little red book," which was a collection of his political ideas.

By the late 1970s, **Deng Xiaoping** (DUHNG SHOW·PING) had become leader of the moderates. He directed a complete reform of the economy. Deng's plan was called the Four Modernizations. The goal was to improve agriculture, industry, science and technology, and national defense. China began to move toward a market economy. This led to a more open society in which there were cultural and scientific exchanges with Western countries. China also began importing technology from the West. This new direction led to major economic gains. From the mid-1980s to the early 1990s, China had one of the world's fastest-growing economies.

The new direction encouraged many Chinese to speak out. Some called for a "fifth modernization"—democracy. In the spring of 1989, hundreds of thousands of pro-democracy demonstrators occupied Tiananmen Square, Beijing's central gathering place. They wanted an end to corruption in the ruling party, a greater say in government, and better conditions in the universities.

Thousands of students staged a hunger strike and ignored government orders to leave. In early June tanks and armed troops began to move toward Tiananmen Square, opening fire on the protesters. Hundreds were killed and thousands wounded. This incident became known as the **Tiananmen Square Massacre,** and it stunned the West. Most Western nations and international aid agencies stopped or cut back on loans to China. Tourism halted. Since China needed to replace this lost income, Jiang Zemin, China's president from 1993 to 2003, proposed a new plan. In 1997 the government turned over control of thousands of failing state-owned businesses to private owners. Although few of the companies made money at first, the plan did give China some much-needed income. As memories of the Tiananmen Square Massacre faded, foreign investment revived and foreign trade surged to new highs. By 2003 China had become the world's second-largest economy. Even so, many of China's economic problems persisted. Unemployment remained high and millions of people continued to live in poverty.

Chinese human-rights demonstrators and uniformed soldiers mingle during a 1989 protest in Beijing's Tiananmen Square.

Foreign relations since 1949. In the early 1950s the Soviet Union and China were allies, but before long, the two nations developed differences. China began to view the Soviet Union as a threat, and during the 1960s the two countries clashed along their common border. As the split with the Soviet Union deepened, China turned to the United States. Following President Nixon's visit to China in 1972, the two nations began to allow exchanges, increasing travel back and forth. In 1979 the United States officially recognized the People's Republic of China and ended recognition of Taiwan. China's improving relations with the West through the 1980s led to trade agreements with several countries and increased financial aid and technical help.

By the late 1990s China had largely recovered from the results of Tiananmen Square. In 1997, neighboring Hong Kong, which had been a British colony since the 1840s, was returned to Chinese rule. Although China's human rights record and the status of Taiwan, which has resisted reunification efforts, are issues of disagreement between the United States and China, relations between the two countries have improved since President Hu Jintao and Premier Wen Jiabao were elected in 2003.

What If? How would U.S. relations with China be different if the Chinese had not been in conflict with the Soviet Union?

✔ **READING CHECK: Drawing Inferences** Why did the Chinese government crack down on the students in Tiananmen Square?

Vladivostok

SOVIET UNION

CHINA

42° N

Ch'öngjin

Yalu River

Ch'osan

Tumen River

NORTH KOREA

40° N

Taedong R.

Hungnam

Korea Bay

Wonsan

P'yöngyang ✪

SEA OF JAPAN

Imjin R.

P'anmunjöm
Kaesöng

38th Parallel
Boundary est. 1945   38°N

Seoul ✪

Inch'on

Han R.

YELLOW SEA

SOUTH KOREA

Kum R.

Taejon

Naktong R.

36°N

Taegu

Pusan

Korea Strait

JAPAN

126°E   128°E   130°E

	Farthest North Korean advance, Sept. 15, 1950		Cease-fire line, July 27, 1953
	Extent of UN advance, Nov. 25, 1950	✪	National capital
	Farthest Chinese/North Korean advance, Jan.1951	•	Other city

Korean War, 1950–1953

Interpreting Maps North Korea and South Korea were initially divided along the 38th parallel.

■ **Skills Assessment: 1. Locate** Where was the cease-fire line established? **2. Drawing Conclusions** What does this indicate about the effect of the war on the geographic boundary of the two countries?

A Korean family flees the fighting in April 1951.

A Divided Korea

Relations between China and the United States were tense in the 1950s and 1960s. A major cause of the tension was Korea. After World War II Korea had been divided at the 38th parallel (north latitude). The Soviet Union occupied the area north of this line. American troops controlled the southern part. The division was meant to be temporary. The two powers agreed that a government should be formed to rule the entire country. That never happened, and Korea remained divided. In North Korea, a communist government led by **Kim Il Sung** took power. In South Korea a republic was created with **Syngman Rhee** as president. Both leaders wanted to reunite Korea, by force if necessary. In June 1950 North Korea invaded South Korea. The Communists quickly captured Seoul (SOHL), the South Korean capital. The United Nations Security Council condemned the attack. It called on UN members to furnish troops and supplies to stop the invasion. Most of the troops came from the United States. In September the United States and South Korea launched an attack. The North Koreans fell back behind their border, with U.S. troops in pursuit.

As the U.S. troops approached the border between Korea and China, China felt threatened. It sent several hundred thousand Chinese soldiers to join those of North Korea. This combined force drove the U.S. troops back south of the 38th parallel. In response, some U.S. military leaders wanted to bomb China directly. President Harry Truman opposed these actions. He thought it might lead to a third world war. Bitter fighting continued for two more years. The two sides finally signed a cease-fire agreement in July 1953. The dividing line was almost exactly where it had been before the war.

Although South Korea was a republic, it was not democratic. Syngman Rhee and the leaders who followed him ran the country as dictators. They used their power, however, to promote economic growth. Both industry and foreign trade increased. South Korea had one of the fastest-growing economies in the world from the 1960s to the 1990s. At the same time, South Koreans had little political freedom.

In 1998 Kim Dae Jung was sworn in as president of South Korea. Kim placed great importance on bringing democracy to South Korea. He also made a point of reaching out to North Korea.

North Korea had severe problems. Terrible famines plagued the nation. The United States and other nations sent massive amounts of food aid to North Korea. Faced with famine and economic collapse, North Korea finally agreed to a meeting with South Korea.

The Two Koreas

On June 14, 2001, North Korea and South Korea observed the first anniversary of the Korea Summit. At this important summit, leaders of the two nations signed the North Korea-South Korea Joint Declaration, beginning a new phase in the history of the divided peninsula. Here is how one reporter described the mood at the summit in June of 2000:

> "The Korea Summit appears to have gone better than most had hoped. No one expected such genuine warmth to be generated between the two presidents. Reunification of Korea is still on a distant horizon, and the journey to that day will not be smooth and easy. But the fact that reunification is now discussed as a tangible possibility instead of an abstract dream is significant. Almost as significant is the impact this new relationship will have on the United States. . . .
>
> Less than a year ago [June 1999] there was a confrontation between North Korea and South Korea on the high seas. The conflict ended with the sinking of a North Korean ship. Less than two years ago [August 1998] North Korea tested a missile which could threaten South Korea, Japan, and other neighbors. . . .
>
> Now the president of North Korea and president of South Korea are meeting in Pyongyang, the North Korean capital. This is the first inter-Korean summit since a 1953 cease-fire put the Korean War on hold."

The North Korea-South Korea Joint Declaration, with the two leaders' signatures

South Korean President Kim Dae Jung (left) and North Korean leader Kim Jong Il (right) raise their arms together before signing the joint declaration.

Skills Reminder

Students today have more ways to find information than ever before. One traditional way of finding information is by consulting books and periodicals in a library. Check the library's card catalog or computerized records to find out how the library organizes its materials. The World Wide Web can also be a great research tool. Search engines can provide you with a list of Web sites that contain keywords relating to your topic. Use the skills you have developed for evaluating sources to judge the validity of any Web site you access.

Skills Practice

Consult three or more reference sources to answer the following questions.

❶ What types of information about the two Koreas can you get from a library's card catalog, whether traditional or electronic?

❷ What kinds of references contain information about the geography and political boundaries of the Korean Peninsula?

❸ Where would you look to find the most recent coverage of developments in the relationship between North Korea and South Korea?

In June 2000 Kim Jong Il of North Korea and Kim Dae Jung of South Korea held a summit meeting. They agreed that families who had been separated could visit each other. The leaders also made plans for future meetings. In October Kim Dae Jung was awarded the 2000 Nobel Peace Prize for his contributions to democracy and human rights in South Korea and for his efforts to reunify Korea.

✔ **READING CHECK: Comparing and Contrasting** What were the similarities and differences between North Korea and South Korea after the Korean War? North was communist, South was a republic, but there was little political freedom in either place.

The Nationalists in Taiwan

Since World War II, Taiwan has become a leading nation in the shipbuilding industry.

The Chinese Nationalists had fled to Taiwan in 1949 and formed a new government. Although China considered Taiwan a Chinese province and most countries never recognized it as an independent nation, Taiwan was generally allowed to govern itself. The government formed on the island seemed to be democratic, but actually Chiang Kai-shek and other Nationalist Party members held all the power. In spite of this, the United States gave aid to Taiwan for many years. The United States also had army and navy bases on the island and kept social and economic ties with Taiwan. By the 1990s Taiwan had become a leading economic power in Asia, even though the island had few natural resources. Instead, the island became one of the world's major producers of manufactured goods, many of which went to the United States. The people of Taiwan enjoyed a high standard of living.

In the early 1980s the Nationalists agreed to allow other parties to form. In 1989 Taiwan had open elections for the first time. Then in 2000 the Nationalist Party lost the election to another party. The new president was Chen Shui-bian, whose party strongly believed that Taiwan should become an independent nation. China, though, insisted that Taiwan was a Chinese province. This position has been a key part of China's foreign policy since the late 1940s. The status of Taiwan continues to cause tension between China and the United States.

✔ **READING CHECK: Drawing Conclusions** Why might the United States keep military and economic ties with Taiwan? to have an ally near China

---

SECTION 2 REVIEW

1. **Identify** and explain the significance:
   Great Leap Forward
   Cultural Revolution
   Red Guards
   Jiang Qing
   Gang of Four
   Deng Xiaoping
   Tiananmen Square Massacre
   Kim Il Sung
   Syngman Rhee

2. **Sequencing** Make a chart like the one below. Use it to list in chronological order the main events that happened in China since 1949.

Date	Event
1949	Communists form People's Republic of China

3. **Finding the Main Idea**
   a. How did the Great Leap Forward and the Cultural Revolution affect China?
   b. How did Cold War politics affect the future of Korea after World War II?
   c. What is the main reason for tensions between Taiwan and China?

4. **Writing and Critical Thinking**
   Making Generalizations Imagine that you are a student protesting in Tiananmen Square. Write a pamphlet explaining why you are protesting despite government calls to stop.
   Consider:
   • the issues that concerned students
   • the possible response of the government
   • the views of the outside world

Homework Practice Online
go.hrw.com
keyword: SH3 HP23

The Japanese Miracle

READ TO DISCOVER

1 What factors allowed Japan to recover as effectively as it did after World War II?
2 What economic and social changes occurred in Japan from the 1950s onward?
3 How has the relationship between Japan and the United States changed in the years since World War II?

DEFINE

zaibatsu

IDENTIFY

SCAP
"MacArthur Constitution"
Liberal-Democratic Party

WHY IT MATTERS TODAY

The emperor is still the official head of state in Japan. Use CNN News.com or other **current event** sources to find out who the emperor is and what his role is in modern Japan. Record your findings in your journal.

The Main Idea
Japan grew into a major international and economic power after recovering from World War II.

The Story Continues *After World War II Japan was in ruins. Many homes and factories had been destroyed. There were severe shortages of food, clothing, and fuel. The Japanese emperor told his people that they should pave the way for future generations by "enduring the unendurable and suffering what is insufferable." Much of their help would come from their former enemies.*

The Occupation of Japan

After World War II American troops occupied Japan under the command of General Douglas MacArthur, the Supreme Commander for the Allied Powers. His offices became known as **SCAP,** after his title. MacArthur's first task was to demilitarize Japan. He removed the people who had been powerful in government and business during the war. Some top leaders were tried for war crimes. Several were executed for their crimes. More than 5 million troops were disarmed and released from military service.

At first SCAP had planned to take over the war industries that were still left in Japan. Taking the factories, however, would have created difficulties. The Allied Powers did not want to support Japan indefinitely. The Japanese had to be given the chance to provide for themselves. In the end, the Japanese were allowed to keep most of their factories and switch them to peacetime activities.

SCAP's second task was to create a new Japanese government. Under MacArthur's direction, the Japanese set up a nonmilitary and democratic government. The "**MacArthur Constitution**" created a parliamentary democracy that called for the direct election of the Diet, or parliament. All Japanese adults now had the right to vote. It also made it clear that the emperor was not divine. He was now a symbol of state who had little power. Finally, the constitution included an important clause that said the Japanese people gave up war as a natural right of their country. The Japanese adopted their new constitution in 1947.

✔ **READING CHECK:**
Summarizing What were the two main tasks SCAP undertook at the beginning of the occupation of Japan?

General MacArthur and Emperor Hirohito, c. 1945

Japanese women in the electronics industry contributed to their country's economic revival after World War II.

Postwar Developments

Before World War II Japan had been the most industrialized of the Asian nations. Afterwards, its economy was badly damaged. Japan, however, made a surprisingly rapid recovery.

Economic development. Several SCAP policies helped Japan recover after the war. One important program was land reform. For the first time, many small farmers were able to own the land they worked. New farm machinery and improved seeds helped them grow and harvest more. Farm output increased very quickly.

Another SCAP program broke up some of the **zaibatsu.** These were huge industrial firms controlled by powerful families. They were so big they prevented free trade. Some of the zaibatsu, such as Mitsubishi and Mitsui, survived the breakup. None, however, had the power they had before the war.

In the 1960s Japan changed its economic focus and started to take advantage of its highly skilled work force. It began to produce advanced technology for the world market. With government support, the new approach was very successful. By the 1980s Japan had become Asia's leading economic power.

In the 1990s the pace of Japan's economic growth slowed. Some companies had grown too fast and had financial problems. Also, there was more competition from other countries. The government tried to revive the economy, but it had only limited success.

Social changes. The economic growth after World War II brought Japan a much higher standard of living. Most families had lived modestly before the war. Now they were able to buy modern household appliances and new automobiles. Also, more women began to join the workforce. This caused a major shift in Japanese society. Women won greater legal, political, and social freedom. At the same time, the importance of the family began to decline. It was no longer the center of all Japanese life.

The higher standard of living did not always mean a better quality of life. The Japanese worked longer hours than people in the West, and the cost of living was much higher. Both the number of factories and the number of people grew. Land to build on became very scarce. From the 1960s onward, prices for land and housing soared. Factories created another problem—pollution. Many Japanese called on their government to pay more attention to quality of life and less to economic growth. In 1974 a young political party member told an American reporter:

History Makers Speak

❝If we get too rich, prosperous, and materialistic, all we do is create more unhappiness. We must therefore return to the true Japanese moral standards, including respect for our ancestors, compassion, gratitude, courage, cooperation, and obligation—all virtues neglected since the war. Only in this way will we regain the confidence of the people.❞

from "Letter from Tokyo," *The New Yorker,* May 1974

Analyzing Primary Sources

Identifying Bias How did the young person's attitude toward the quality of life in Japan affect his comments?

✔ **READING CHECK: Finding the Main Idea** What effect did economic growth have on Japanese society?

Foreign Relations and Political Life

The "MacArthur Constitution" had limited Japanese armed forces and military production. In addition, the Japanese had signed a treaty agreeing to renounce war as a political tool. Within a few years, however, the Cold War between the United States and the Soviet Union led to a reversal in U.S. policy toward Japan. The communist victory in China and the stalemate in North Korea had changed the balance of power in Asia. The United States viewed these communist states as a threat. The U.S. government felt that Japan should be able to defend itself in case of war and urged Japan to increase its armed forces.

The Japanese did not want a return of the militaristic governments of prewar days. They had no wish to rearm. They spent their money to build peacetime industries and to increase exports. Raising the standard of living was more important than raising an army. In spite of pressure from the West, Japan resisted increased military spending. Finally in 1997 the United States and Japan reached an agreement. In case of a conflict near Japan, Japan would provide the United States with supplies and assistance, but not armed forces.

A more independent stance. After World War II Japan and the United States kept friendly ties. At times, there was stress between the two countries. For example, the Japanese resented the U.S. pressure to build up their armed forces. Many Japanese also disliked having American troops stationed in Japan. The U.S. forces on the island of Okinawa had been a sore point since the 1960s. Toward the end of 2000, the United States finally began to reduce the number of troops stationed there.

During the 1980s Japan began to follow its own course in world affairs and make decisions apart from the United States. Japanese leaders wanted the country to become the economic and political leader in Asia. Part of their plan was to help developing countries by giving them large amounts of money and technical aid. By the end of the 1980s, Japan was giving more aid than any other country in the world.

In the early 1990s Japan began to rethink its relations with the nations of the former Soviet Union. In 1996 the leaders of Japan and Russia met for talks. Even after the meetings, however, relations between the two countries were strained. Japan and Russia had an ongoing dispute over the Kuril Islands. The Soviet Union had occupied the islands after World War II, and Russia still claimed them. Japan insisted that four small islands in the southern Kuril chain belonged to Japan because they were part of the Japanese-controlled island of Hokkaido. The Russians insisted the islands were part of the Kurils and thus fell under their control. The Japanese were not willing to give Russia any aid until the problem was solved.

Toshiki Kaifu and Mikhail Gorbachev signed a joint declaration in April 1991.

Japan's national legislature, the Diet, meets in this impressive building in Tokyo.

Politics in Japan. After World War II a large number of political parties were active in Japan. The most powerful was the **Liberal-Democratic Party** (LDP), which controlled the government from the 1950s until the 1990s. The Socialists and others strongly disagreed with LDP policy and voiced their dislike of Japan's defense agreement with the United States. They also were against having American armed forces stationed in Japan.

In 1989 Japan faced a government crisis when a financial scandal rocked the LDP. It involved many top LDP members. A few months after the scandal broke, Toshiki Kaifu became prime minister. People trusted him even though he was a member of the LDP. By 1991, however, he had been forced out of office. In the 1993 elections, the LDP lost its majority in the Diet, ending the party's almost 40-year rule. Political turmoil continued, however.

In 1998 Keizo Obuchi, a member of the LDP, was chosen to be prime minister. Obuchi focused on ways to revive the economy and his programs had some success. After Obuchi died in early 2000, Yoshiro Mori became prime minister. When Mori resigned a year later, Junichiro Koizumi was elected prime minister. Koizumi promised to thoroughly reform the government and bring an end to political corruption. Although he has had only limited success in his efforts, he was re-elected in 2003.

✔ **READING CHECK: Identifying Cause and Effect** How did the Liberal-Democratic Party's policies affect Japanese relations with the United States? made defense agreement

SECTION 3 REVIEW

1. **Define** and explain the significance:
   zaibatsu

2. **Identify** and explain the significance:
   SCAP
   "MacArthur Constitution"
   Liberal-Democratic Party

3. **Categorizing** Copy the chart below. Use it to organize the changes that occurred in Japan after World War II.

Changes in Japan after WWII		
Economics	Society	Foreign Relations

4. **Finding the Main Idea**
   a. What were the characteristics of the postwar Japanese government?
   b. How did the life of an average Japanese person change after World War II?
   c. What have been the main causes of tension between Japan and the United States in the postwar years?

5. **Writing and Critical Thinking**

   Making Predictions Describe what the results might have been if the Allied Powers had not helped Japan after World War II.

   Consider:
   • the destruction in Japan after the war
   • land ownership and the control of industry
   • the social structure of Japan

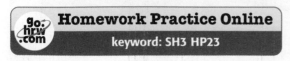

Homework Practice Online

keyword: SH3 HP23

READ TO DISCOVER

❶ What were the causes and effects of dictatorships in the Philippines and Indonesia?

❷ How did the Vietnam War affect Vietnam, Laos, and Cambodia?

❸ What problems did the nations of Southeast Asia face as they struggled to create stable governments?

DEFINE

domino theory

IDENTIFY

Ferdinand Marcos
Corazon Aquino
Aung San Suu Kyi
Ho Chi Minh
Geneva Accord
Tet Offensive
Paris Peace Accords
Ho Chi Minh Trail
Khmer Rouge
Pol Pot

▶ **WHY IT MATTERS TODAY**

Each Southeast Asian country has had ongoing political problems. Use or other **current event** sources to find out about the political situation in one of these countries. Record your findings in your journal.

CNN student News.com

Independence Struggles in Southeast Asia

The Main Idea
After World War II all the former colonies in Southeast Asia became independent countries.

The Story Continues *Almost all the countries in Southeast Asia were once colonies. After World War II these countries gained their independence. Some did so peacefully, while others resorted to violent means. An interviewer asked one revolutionary leader how his people could expect to win against a well-armed Western power. He replied, "Our secret weapon is nationalism. To have nationhood…is greater than any weapons in the world."*

The Philippines

The United States controlled the Philippines from the time of the Spanish-American War in 1898 until early 1946. Then, on July 4, 1946, the Philippines became an independent nation with a government modeled after that of the United States. The new nation had an elected president and congress. Economic and political relations between the Philippines and the United States continued to be close, and the Philippines continued to play a key role in U.S. policy toward Asia.

In the 1970s the Philippines were in turmoil. Communists were rioting in some areas. Muslims were fighting for self-rule. Philippine president **Ferdinand Marcos** needed to gain control. He placed the country under martial law and had hundreds of his enemies arrested. In 1973 Marcos put a new constitution in place that gave him even more powers. Although these were the actions of a dictator, U.S. officials continued to support Marcos because of his anticommunist and pro-Western policies.

Ferdinand Marcos gained much wealth through his corrupt government. He and his wife, Imelda, lived extravagantly while the country was mired in poverty. One example of their wasteful lifestyle was Imelda Marcos's collection of over 1,000 pairs of shoes.

Under Marcos the Philippine economy weakened and protests against his rule began to grow. In 1983 the leader of an opposing party, Benigno Aquino, was assassinated. His death sparked riots all over the country. In 1986 Aquino's widow, **Corazon Aquino,** ran against Marcos in a special election. Although Marcos claimed that he won the election, it soon became clear that Aquino was the real winner. Marcos and his family were forced to leave the country.

When Aquino took office, the economy was very weak, and many people were living in poverty. Aquino was able to make some gains. She did bring democracy back after the Marcos years. She also promoted new business. Aquino, however, was not able to carry out all of her programs. Her government began to lose power as it failed to manage the nation's huge debt and poor economy.

In 1992 Fidel Ramos became president, and the economy finally began to improve. Then in 1998 former movie actor Joseph Estrada was elected president. Within two years his government was in deep trouble as Estrada was accused of taking large sums of money in bribes. By 2000 the Philippines were torn by mass protests once again.

✔ **READING CHECK: Comparing and Contrasting** What were the similarities and differences between the presidencies of Ferdinand Marcos and Corazon Aquino?

Burma (Myanmar)

Since medieval times the area known as Burma has been a strategically important region, an area of important trade routes. During World War II the British colony served as an important route for getting supplies to China until the Japanese occupied the region in 1942. In 1948 Great Britain gave Burma its independence. The new nation faced difficulties that included the lack of a strong central government, a scarcity of trained civil servants, tribal and political dissension, and communist attempts to seize the country. The first premier, U Nu, headed a coalition government that brought some order to the country. However, the coalition soon broke into factions and the army, led by General Ne Win, seized control of the government.

Ne Win ruled Burma from 1962 to 1988. His government took total control of the economy, a move that almost destroyed Burma's economy. Farm production fell, and consumer goods became scarce. In 1988, violent riots forced Ne Win to resign, but other military leaders seized power. To show that they wanted to make a fresh start, the new leaders renamed the country Myanmar.

The first free elections in 30 years took place in 1990. When the opposing party won, the military refused to give up power. Instead it cracked down on everyone it considered a threat. In 1991 **Aung San Suu Kyi** won the Nobel Peace Prize for her efforts to reform her country. She was kept under house arrest for several years. Many of her supporters were killed or put in prison. The government's crackdown only added to the unrest in Burma. Still, the military ruled the country throughout the 1990s.

The United States limited its contact with Myanmar during this period. In other Western nations, many criticized Myanmar's poor record in human rights. Though some political prisoners were released from house arrest in 2003, the U.S. and some Asian countries continue to push for the reform of Myanmar's government.

✔ **READING CHECK: Supporting a Point of View** What evidence would you give to show that people in Myanmar have few civil rights?

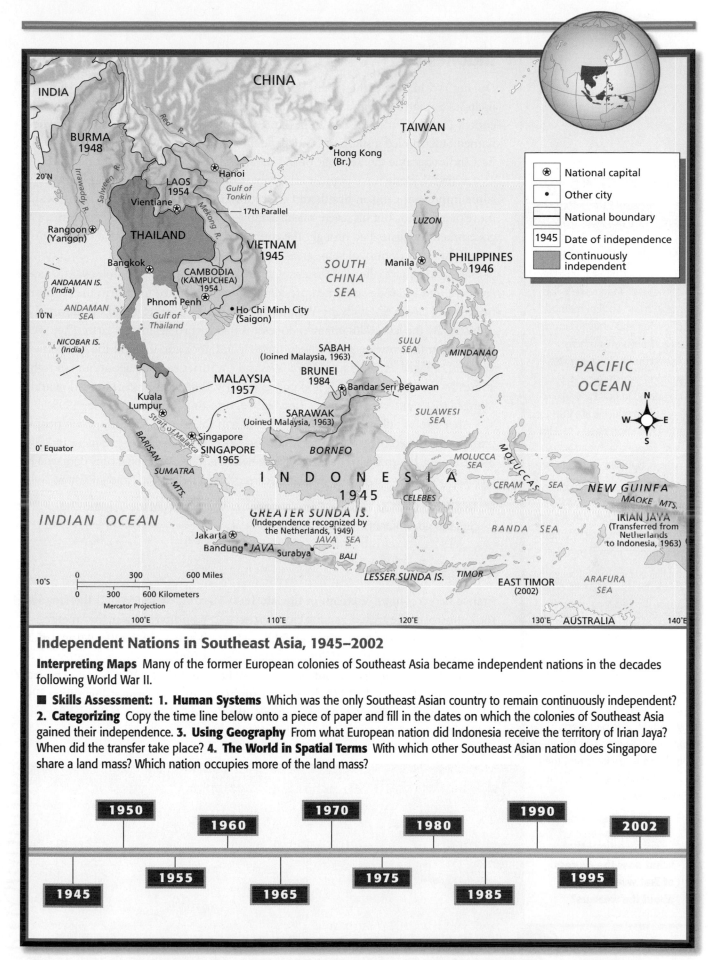

Independent Nations in Southeast Asia, 1945–2002

Interpreting Maps Many of the former European colonies of Southeast Asia became independent nations in the decades following World War II.

■ **Skills Assessment: 1. Human Systems** Which was the only Southeast Asian country to remain continuously independent?
2. Categorizing Copy the time line below onto a piece of paper and fill in the dates on which the colonies of Southeast Asia gained their independence. **3. Using Geography** From what European nation did Indonesia receive the territory of Irian Jaya? When did the transfer take place? **4. The World in Spatial Terms** With which other Southeast Asian nation does Singapore share a land mass? Which nation occupies more of the land mass?

1950 1960 1970 1980 1990 2002
1945 1955 1965 1975 1985 1995

Indonesia

During World War II the Japanese occupied the East Indies, an island group that includes Sumatra and Java. The Dutch expected to take control again when the war ended. They had ruled the East Indies since the 1600s. Instead, an Indonesian engineer named Sukarno led a successful independence movement against them. In 1949 the East Indies became the Republic of Indonesia, with Sukarno as its first president.

At first Sukarno was a popular leader able to unite the Indonesian people and make some important gains in health and education. In the early 1960s, Sukarno became more of a dictator, but his severe rule failed to solve Indonesia's growing problems. The government's policies had brought the country close to bankruptcy, and Communists were fighting for control of some areas.

General Suharto, head of the army, acted against Sukarno. He took over the government and in 1968 was named president. Suharto planned to reform the economy by creating closer ties with the West and using Western aid to build up Indonesia's industry. By the late 1980s, many Indonesians had turned against Suharto. They were angry about the growing gap between the rich and poor and thought the government was mismanaged and corrupt. Several Western countries worried about human rights abuses by the Indonesian army and police. In early 1998 a major economic downturn plunged the country into turmoil. President Suharto finally resigned in May 1998.

After two of Suharto's successors failed to win the trust of the Indonesian people, parliament named Megawati Sukarnoputri—Sukarno's daughter—president in 2001. Sukarnoputri has struggled to lead a diverse nation and revive an economy damaged by terrorist bombings carried out by Islamic extremists in Bali in 2002 and Jakarta in 2003.

✔ **READING CHECK: Making Generalizations** What effect did the Sukarno and Suharto governments have on Indonesia?

Vietnam

France had colonized Vietnam in the late 1800s. During World War II the Japanese took control of the area. When the French tried to return after the war, they met resistance from a group of communist guerrilla fighters. These were the Viet Minh, led by **Ho Chi Minh.** Ho declared Vietnam independent in 1945.

In 1946 fighting broke out between the French and the Viet Minh. The war dragged on for years. In 1954 the French suffered a major defeat at Dien Bien Phu (dyen byen FOO). The Viet Minh captured thousands of French troops. After this defeat, the French agreed to peace talks.

Division and war. The **Geneva Accord,** signed in 1954, ended the war. After the French withdrew their forces, Vietnam was divided into two zones at the 17th parallel. Elections were planned for 1956 to select one government for the whole country. With Chinese and Soviet help, Ho Chi Minh began to build a communist state in the north zone. Ngo Dinh Diem was president of the non-communist government in the south. Diem put down all opposition to his government. He showed little interest in reforms or in fixing government corruption. He refused to participate in the elections planned for 1956. As a result, no elections were ever held.

By the late 1950s the Viet Minh had formed the National Liberation Front (NLF). The NLF soon became known as the Viet Cong, or Vietnamese Communists. Their goal was to overthrow Diem and reunite Vietnam. The Viet Cong began a guerrilla war in rural South Vietnam. Diem's answer was to crack down on the Viet Cong and anyone else who opposed him. In 1963 a military group assassinated Diem and took control of the government.

American involvement. American leaders did not want South Vietnam to fall to communism. If that happened, they thought all of Southeast Asia would follow. This idea was called the **domino theory.** The United States government decided to get directly involved in the war. In January 1965 President Johnson ordered air attacks on North Vietnam. By the late 1960s more than 500,000 U.S. troops were in Vietnam.

At the beginning of 1968, North Vietnam launched a major attack called the **Tet Offensive,** named for the Vietnamese New Year on which it began. Although American and South Vietnamese forces drove the Communists back, many Americans who saw the fierce fighting on television began to openly oppose U.S. involvement in the war.

The **Paris Peace Accords** of 1973 ended American involvement in the war. The South Vietnamese army could not hold back the enemy after the United States pulled out its troops. In April 1975 South Vietnam surrendered to North Vietnam. More than 1.3 million Vietnamese and nearly 58,000 Americans had lost their lives during the war.

A reunited Vietnam. In 1976 the two Vietnams united as one country, with Hanoi in the north as the capital. The former southern capital, Saigon, was renamed Ho Chi Minh City. After Saigon fell, more than 1 million Vietnamese fled their country. Some left because they feared the North Vietnamese. Most left because they did not want to live under a communist government. These refugees faced a dangerous sea voyage to one of the other Southeast Asian countries. Many of these "boat people" died at sea. Those who survived spent months in crowded camps. They had to wait for permission to settle in another country. The largest number, about 725,000, came to the United States.

War in Southeast Asia, 1954–1975

Interpreting Maps As with Korea, Cold War political concerns led to the division of Vietnam and eventually to war.

Skills Assessment: Physical Systems Through what countries did the Ho Chi Minh Trail run?

Holt Researcher

go.hrw.com
KEYWORD: Holt Researcher
FreeFind: Ho Chi Minh
After reading more about Ho Chi Minh on the Holt Researcher, write a pamphlet describing his views on Vietnamese independence.

After the Vietnam War, more than one million people left Vietnam by boat as refugees.

After 1975 Vietnam struggled financially. The country was deeply in debt and most people lived in poverty. To solve its problems, the Vietnamese government began to allow private businesses to develop. At first, progress under this program was slow. In the 1990s, though, the economy boomed as the country started to attract foreign investors and open diplomatic ties. In 1995 the United States even restored diplomatic relations with Vietnam. In 2000 the two nations signed a trading pact.

✔ **READING CHECK: Identifying Cause and Effect** What were the main causes of the Vietnam War? How did it change the country?

Laos and Cambodia

Like Vietnam, Laos and Cambodia were French colonies that gained their independence after World War II. Later, both nations were drawn into the Vietnam conflict.

Laos. Laos gained independence from France in 1954. Almost immediately, however, civil war broke out among the country's political factions. This turmoil continued for almost 20 years.

In the midst of this internal chaos, Laos began to feel the effects of the Vietnam War, even though it officially was neutral in the conflict. The **Ho Chi Minh Trail,** the Viet Cong's major supply route from North to South Vietnam, wound through the mountain valleys of eastern Laos. To break this supply line, the United States bombed the Laotian countryside, causing heavy property damage and many civilian casualties.

In 1975 the struggle for power in Laos ended when the Pathet Lao set up a communist government called the Lao People's Democratic Republic. Although the Pathet Lao tried to follow a policy of nonalignment, this proved impossible in the complicated politics of Asia. Laos had to call on the Vietnamese for help in controlling anticommunist factions in its northern provinces. In return it allowed Vietnam to station 50,000 troops on Laotian soil. These troops were not withdrawn until 1989. Then in the early 1990s Laos began to go its own way as Laotian leaders worked to improve relations with Thailand and China. They also signed trade and financial aid agreements with the United States, Japan, and Russia. By the mid-1990s, Laos had attracted a significant amount of foreign investment, which helped its economy grow.

Human skulls were gathered as a memorial in the Cambodian city of Phnom Penh. The grisly display honors the victims of Khmer Rouge genocide that took place during the mid-1970s.

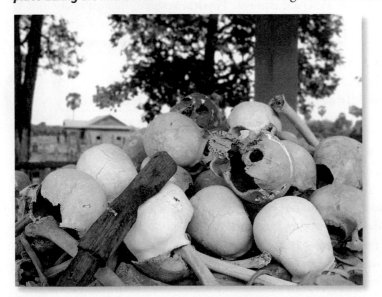

Cambodia. Cambodia gained its independence from France in 1953. As with Laos, Cambodia tried to remain neutral in the Vietnam War but was drawn into it because the Ho Chi Minh Trail ran inside its eastern border. Also, Viet Cong troops had established supply lines in Cambodia. In response the United States bombed the Ho Chi Minh Trail and sent troops into Cambodia.

During the war, the Viet Cong began arming and training a group of Cambodian Communists called the **Khmer Rouge.** In 1975 the Khmer Rouge seized the Cambodian capital of Phnom Penh and set up a new Cambodian government under their leader, **Pol Pot.**

The Khmer Rouge enforced a brutal plan that resulted in a massive genocide of Cambodia's population. The government emptied all the cities and forced people to do manual labor on farms. No one had any tools or farming experience, however, and many of these former city dwellers died of starvation. The Khmer Rouge also undertook a systematic program to execute almost all of Cambodia's government officials, army officers, teachers, and intellectuals. This survivor describes the constant fear.

Primary Source
"Angkar [the name of Cambodia's Communist party] was everywhere, a pervasive presence that none could escape. . . . Husbands and wives spoke . . . only in private, in a whisper, fearful of being overheard. . . . No one criticized Angkar in public; even the minimally critical passing allusion could be enough to ensure arrest, interrogation and subsequent disappearance for re-education."

M. Stuart-Fox, *The Murderous Revolution*

Analyzing Primary Sources

Drawing Inferences What did this survivor mean by the phrase "disappearance for re-education"?

Between 1975 and 1977, more than 1 million Cambodians—one fifth of the population—died under Pol Pot's regime. Thousands more fled to makeshift refugee camps in neighboring Thailand.

Border disputes that were centuries old soon brought Cambodia into conflict with Vietnam. In 1978 Vietnam invaded Cambodia. Although China threw its support to the Khmer Rouge, in 1979 the Vietnamese overthrew Pol Pot's government and installed one friendly to them. With Pol Pot in exile, fighting continued throughout the 1980s. Finally, in 1991 the UN brought an end to the fighting and the leading parties agreed to share power. Free elections were held in 1993, but the government continued to be unstable. By the late 1990s, however, opposition from the Khmer Rouge began to weaken. The group weakened even further after it was announced in 1998 that the notorious Pol Pot had died.

✔ **READING CHECK: Evaluating** What led to mass murder in Cambodia?

This former Khmer Rouge soldier defected to Cambodian government forces during fighting in 1998.

SECTION 4 REVIEW

1. **Define** and explain the significance:
   domino theory

2. **Identify** and explain the significance:
   Ferdinand Marcos
   Corazon Aquino
   Aung San Suu Kyi
   Ho Chi Minh
   Geneva Accord
   Tet Offensive
   Paris Peace Accords
   Ho Chi Minh Trail
   Khmer Rouge
   Pol Pot

3. **Identifying Cause and Effect** Use a chart like this one to organize details of times when existing governments in Southeast Asia were taken over without consent or election.

Who Took Over Where	→	Reasons

	→	Results

4. **Finding the Main Idea**

   a. What effect did government have on the economic growth of the Philippines and Indonesia?

   b. What effect did the Vietnam War have on countries other than Vietnam?

   c. How does Cambodia's history differ from other Southeast Asian countries?

5. **Writing and Critical Thinking**

   Decision Making Decide whether you agree or disagree with U.S. involvement in the Vietnam War. Write a short article explaining your position.
   Consider:
   • the domino theory
   • the number of U.S. troops involved and the loss of life
   • how the war ended

go. hrw .com
Homework Practice Online
keyword: SH3 HP23

READ TO DISCOVER

❶ What led Asian governments to impose tight controls in their countries?

❷ What problems did Asian countries face as they tried to develop their economies, and how did they solve those problems?

❸ How has economic success in Asian countries affected the West?

IDENTIFY

ASEAN

"Four Tigers"

▶**WHY IT MATTERS TODAY**

Many products we use every day are made in Asia. Use CNN student News.com or other **current event** sources to trace an Asian product you own from the place it was made to the store where you bought it. Record your findings in your journal.

CNN student News.com

Asian Paths to Prosperity

The Main Idea
By the year 2000 some of the fastest-growing economies in the world were in Asia.

The Story Continues *The newly independent Asian nations were soon in the midst of great changes. As one Asian leader told young people at a conference, "You have tilled the earth the way your ancestors have always done and eked out a living of some sort. . . . And the world has, meanwhile, passed you by. Then, all of a sudden, you decide that you must also join this race to the moon. . . ."*

Political Development

Many of the new Asian nations set up democratic governments. As time passed, however, democracy faded and some governments became communist. Others were highly authoritarian. Loss of human rights was a constant threat. This tight government control was common in Asia for three main reasons.

First, most Asian nations faced conflicts between people of different ethnic backgrounds. Most Asian countries have populations of different races and cultures. In Malaysia, for example, there are Malays, Chinese, and Indians. Often there had been hatred between one group and another for centuries. From time to time these tensions erupted into fighting. Government leaders relied on their armies and police forces to maintain control. Usually this meant loss of civil rights.

Second, governments worried about their national security. Some leaders in the Philippines, Indonesia, and other countries opposed communism. Some of these leaders did little to restrain violence against people who were thought to be communists, and many people were killed. In communist countries it was the reverse. Leaders of these countries fought anticommunists within their own borders. Their strong central governments allowed little talk of reform.

Third, the Asian countries wanted rapid economic growth. Many Asian leaders thought a democratic government was slow and inefficient in promoting economic growth. They believed that government control would allow their countries to grow faster.

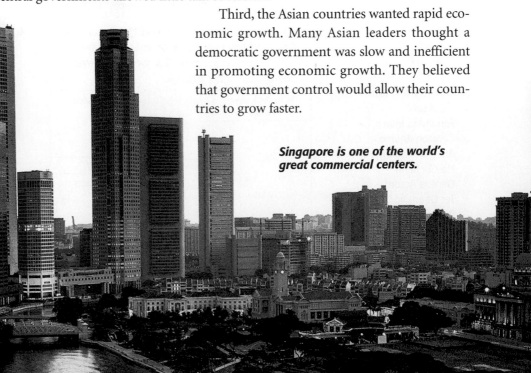

Singapore is one of the world's great commercial centers.

An example of the effect of these ideas was Singapore. From the time Singapore became independent in 1965, one man ran the government. He was Prime Minister Lee Kuan Yew. Throughout his time in office, Lee imposed strict controls on labor unions, political activity, and the media. When Lee stepped down in 1990, he left Singapore with one of the world's most stable governments. It was also one of the wealthiest countries in Asia. Lee described his government this way.

History Makers Speak

"We have departed in quite a number of material aspects . . . from the principles of justice, and the liberty of the individual. . . . We have had to adjust, to temporarily deviate from ideas and norms. This is a heavy price. . . . So let us always remember . . . the price we have had to pay in order to maintain normal standards in the relationship between man and man, [and] man and authority . . ."

from a speech by Lee Kuan Yew, Singapore, 1967

Analyzing Primary Sources

Evaluating Does Lee Kuan Yew think individual rights are important or unimportant?

✔ **READING CHECK: Summarizing** What were the three reasons Asian countries imposed tight government controls?

Economic Development

By the year 2000, more than 3.5 billion people lived in Asia. That was 60 percent of the world's total population. Although millions of Asian people still lived in poverty, the continent was home to some of the fastest-growing economies in the world.

Barriers to economic development. With a few exceptions, the economies of most Asian countries started their postwar growth slowly. In part, this was because many Asian countries emerged from the colonial era with little wealth of their own. It took huge amounts of money to develop industry. They needed machinery, factories, and transportation networks. Some Asian countries did not have the money needed to bring their industries up to the level of the world's more advanced nations.

The Asian countries had two ways to get the money they needed. They could get loans from international agencies and other countries and encourage investment by foreign individuals or foreign corporations. Or, they could export their agricultural goods and natural resources. They could sell tea, spices, timber, rubber, minerals, and other goods. In the 1950s and 1960s, however, these items brought low prices in the world markets. Sometimes, too, their trading partners would have economic downturns. Then demand for Asian goods would drop. Reliance on foreign investment could also cause economic downturns. Just as capital could come in, financial investors would withdraw it suddenly when they lost confidence in a country. Such dependence on foreign capital helped to bring about a major crisis for Asian economies during the 1990s.

In the years immediately following World War II, most Asian countries lacked managers and skilled workers. To solve this problem,

The containers stacked on the deck of this Japanese freighter hold just a fraction of the billions of dollars worth of goods that the United States imports every year from Asian countries.

The logo of the Association of Southeast Asian Nations symbolizes ASEAN's goals of unity, growth, and peace.

many nations completely reformed their education systems. They opened vocational schools to train workers and started on-the-job training programs.

Cooperating for development. In the 1970s, some Asian countries began to find answers to their problems. They began to form loose economic groups among themselves. This helped them get higher prices for their exports. Asian countries also joined with developing nations in other parts of the world. Together they were able to get better loan terms. Most of these loans were from agencies such as the World Bank and the International Monetary Fund.

In 1967 Southeast Asian countries joined together in an association to develop trade and economic policies for the whole region. They started the Association of Southeast Asian Nations (**ASEAN**). Its goals were to promote economic growth and social progress in Southeast Asia. In addition, ASEAN hoped to improve peace and security in the area.

Several Asian nations tried to speed up economic growth through greater government control. Some governments took over and ran important industries. For example, the Indonesian government took over the oil industry. These governments wanted to see that the profits went back into the country's development. Other countries passed laws against labor unions and strikes. They wanted to make sure that nothing would stop work in the factories. In some cases these actions might have led to more rapid economic growth. The growth, however, was at the expense of individual rights.

Economic expansion. By the beginning of the 1990s, some Asian countries had made a great deal of progress. Japan, for example, ranked as one of the world's major economic powers. South Korea, Taiwan, Singapore, and Hong Kong all had very strong economies. They played important roles in the world markets. Together, these four became known as the **"Four Tigers."**

By the mid-1990s, all of Asia was a region of powerful economic growth. Observers began to call this growth "the Asian miracle." Many Asian nations were growing at annual rates of 6 percent to 10 percent. China's growth was dramatic. Its gross national product multiplied by four in just twenty years. Even so, millions of Asian people still lived in poverty. The numbers of poor, though, had decreased. In East and Southeast Asia, the number dropped by 50 percent between 1975 and 1995.

Nevertheless, there are significant problems in the region, including political instability, overpopulation, and a growing gap between rich and poor. In 1997 a financial crisis in Thailand began to spread to neighboring nations. By 2000 many Asian economies were experiencing economic crises. However, many experts predict that Asia will continue to gain strength. Some expect that by about 2025 China may surpass the United States as the largest economy in the world.

✔ **READING CHECK: Making Generalizations** How did Asia become a region of powerful economic growth?

Asian Cultural Diffusion

For hundreds of years, Asia has exercised a powerful influence over the West. The ancient religions, philosophies, and martial arts of China and Japan have long fascinated many Westerners. Exhibits of ancient Asian porcelain, carpets, manuscripts, and other arts and crafts have drawn huge crowds to Western art galleries. More recently, Asia has exerted an economic influence on Western consumers through Asian-made products. Asian electronics, for example, own a large share of the world market. Many Asian televisions, computers, cameras, and video equipment are in American stores. Asian cars and trucks, too, find ready markets in Western countries. A few Asian companies have opened automobile factories in the West. Asia has also supplied parts to Western companies. A great number of products constructed in the West have been made from Asian parts.

This economic competition from Asia has both alarmed and fascinated Western business leaders. Since the late 1970s, Western economists have traveled throughout Japan trying to discover why Japanese goods sell so well in world markets. Many economists have suggested that the answer lies in the cooperative relationship between management and workers. Others have noted that government assistance and low-interest business-development loans enable Japanese companies to buy the latest machinery. Still others have pointed out that the Japanese educational system emphasizes the study of science and math. This focus has produced a force of scientists and engineers who have been able to develop better, more competitive products.

✔ **READING CHECK: Analyzing Information**
How has Asian economic success influenced the West?

This skilled Japanese worker uses high-technology tools and instruments to assemble and test cameras.

SECTION 5 REVIEW

1. **Identify** and explain the significance:
   ASEAN   "Four Tigers"

2. **Categorizing** Copy the chart below. Use it to organize the economic problems Asian countries had and how they were solved.

Economic problems in new Asian countries
1.
2.
3.

Solutions to economic problems
1.
2.
3.

   Homework Practice Online
   go.hrw.com
   keyword: SH3 HP23

3. **Finding the Main Idea**
   a. In general, what have been the effects of tight government controls and restrictions on individual human rights in many Asian countries since the end of World War II?
   b. In what ways did efforts to build cooperation and alliances among the countries of Southeast Asia help to promote economic development and growth throughout the region?
   c. In what ways have the United States and other countries of the West been influenced by Asian nations' economic growth and competition since the end of World War II?

4. **Writing and Critical Thinking**
   Supporting a Point of View Imagine that you are a journalist working in today's Asia. Write a newspaper editorial in which you analyze the loss of individual rights in some Asian nations, and explain why you think this is an important issue.

   Consider:
   • what actions resulting in the loss of individual rights have taken place in the region
   • why some Asian governments have moved to put tight controls in place in their countries
   • why many people in Asia see a need for increased individual rights
   • what these people might do to promote the growth of individual political and human rights

Creating a Time Line

Copy the time line below onto a sheet of paper. Complete the time line by filling in the events, individuals, and dates from the chapter that you think were significant. Pick three events and explain why you think they were significant.

| 1945 | 1960 | 1975 | Present |

Writing a Summary

Using standard grammar, spelling, sentence structure, and punctuation, write an overview of the events in the chapter.

Identifying People and Ideas

Identify the following terms or individuals and explain their significance:

1. nonalignment
2. Indira Gandhi
3. Red Guards
4. Tiananmen Square Massacre
5. SCAP
6. MacArthur Constitution
7. domino theory
8. Ho Chi Minh
9. Tet Offensive
10. Khmer Rouge

Understanding Main Ideas

SECTION 1 *(pp. 654–659)*

South Asia After Empire

1. Why did Great Britain partition India before independence?
2. What problems did Pakistan face after it became independent?

SECTION 2 *(pp. 660–666)*

Communist China and Its Influence

3. How did life in China differ after Mao Zedong's death from what it had been before?
4. In what ways have the histories of the two Koreas differed?

SECTION 3 *(pp. 667–670)*

The Japanese Miracle

5. What happened in Japan during the Allied occupation following World War II?
6. What steps did Japan take to become a major world economic power?

SECTION 4 *(pp. 671–677)*

Independence Struggles in Southeast Asia

7. What were the results of strong government control in the Philippines and Indonesia?
8. What were the causes and results of the Vietnam War?

SECTION 5 *(pp. 678–681)*

Asian Paths to Prosperity

9. What problems did the Asian countries face as they worked toward economic development?

Reviewing Themes

1. **Government** What evidence is there that people had fewer civil rights in Asian countries that had strong controlling governments?
2. **Global Relations** List examples of clashes between neighboring communist and noncommunist Asian nations.
3. **Economics** What are examples of Asian countries whose economic growth has led to outstanding success?

Thinking Critically

1. **Summarizing** What problems did the new independent nations of Asia have in common?
2. **Comparing** What are the similarities and differences between the Korean and Vietnam wars?
3. **Drawing Inferences** How do the World Bank and the International Monetary Fund affect Asian growth?
4. **Supporting a Point of View** What evidence would you give that a democratic government does not slow economic progress as some Asian leaders thought?

Writing About History

Comparing Write a short essay comparing events in China and Cambodia in the late 1900s, noting how their policies violated political, economic, social, and human rights. Use the chart below to help organize your thoughts.

	China	Cambodia
Political rights		
Economic rights		
Social rights		
Human rights		

Determining Chronological Sequences

Study the chronological data below.

The Vietnam Conflict: Selected Events

1967—389,000 U.S. troops in Vietnam by end of year

1967—Anti-war protests increase in the U.S.

1968—North Vietnam launches the Tet Offensive

1969—First withdrawals of U.S. troops announced

1970—U.S. troops move into Cambodia

1973—U.S. Congress prohibits further U.S. military activity in Indochina

1. Determine if each of the statements that follows is true, false, or unknown based on the information provided by the data only.

 a. Anti-war protests in the United States grew until the early 1970s.

 b. The number of U.S. troops in Vietnam was never greater than 350,000.

 c. U.S. troops moved into Cambodia about two years after the Tet Offensive.

 d. After 1976 U.S. military activity in Indochina was prohibited by the U.S. Congress.

2. Today, some Americans believe that the United States should work to build closer cultural and economic ties with the people of Vietnam. What factors do you think might limit or prevent the growth of such ties?

Identifying a Point of View

Read the following description by a North Vietnamese soldier about using elephants to improve the Ho Chi Minh Trail. Then answer the questions.

> "Thuan, the commander of the unit, sent men to fell trees in the forest to fill up the swamp. The elephant quickly understood: it grabbed hold of the logs with its forelegs and gradually pulled itself from the mud and out of danger. We were all overjoyed and set off immediately . . . but somehow we were detected and our convoy was shelled. We were worried that our animals, because of their size, were not safe. . . . I still wonder how no elephants were hit."

3. Which of the following statements best describes the author's perspective toward the situation?

 a. He was most comfortable in the forests and swamps along the trail.

 b. He would rather have been fighting than working with elephants.

 c. He was more focused on building the trail and caring for elephants than on fighting a war.

 d. He was surprised the convoy was shelled.

4. Why might the North Vietnamese have been improving the Ho Chi Minh Trail? Give specific reasons.

Alternative Assessment

Building Your Portfolio

Link to TODAY

Government

Loss of individual rights is still a problem in the world today. Use your textbook and other sources to find examples of countries where strong government control has meant loss of civil rights. Then write a newspaper article about your findings. Illustrate your article with drawings, photographs, or maps.

🖪 **internet connect**

Internet Activity: go.hrw.com
KEYWORD: SH3 WH23

Choose a topic on Asia Since 1945 to:

- create a chart comparing the population growth of the United States and India by analyzing factors such as death rates, birthrates, and immigration statistics.

- research the Association of Southeast Asian Nations (ASEAN), and write a persuasive report on why or why not to join the association.

- write a biography of an Asian leader.

CHAPTER 24

1945–Present

Africa and the Middle East Since 1945

Rough, uncut diamond from Sierra Leone

1956
Politics
The Suez Crisis erupts in Egypt.

Late 1950s
Business and Finance
Oil is discovered in the Niger Delta of Nigeria.

1967
Politics
Civil war erupts in Nigeria.

1967
Global Events
Israel fights the Six-Day War against Arab neighbors.

1975
Science and Technology
Mary Leakey discovers hominid footprints in Tanzania that are estimated to be more than 3.6 million years old.

1976
Politics
Violence erupts in Soweto, South Africa.

1950   **1960**   **1970**

1948
Global Events
The state of Israel is declared; war begins with neighboring Arab states.

Abebe Bikila

1960
Business and Finance
OPEC is formed.

1960
Daily Life
Abebe Bikila of Ethiopia wins the first of two Olympic gold medals in the marathon.

1960
Science and Technology
Jane Goodall begins research on chimpanzees in Tanzania.

1965
Politics
Joseph Mobutu takes full control of the Congo.

Jane Goodall

1972
Business and Finance
History's third largest diamond is discovered in a Sierra Leone mine.

1979
Politics
The shah of Iran is overthrown.

1979
Global Events
The Iran hostage crisis begins.

1979
Daily Life
Strict Islamic customs are enforced in Iran.

1979
Global Events
Israel and Egypt sign the Camp David Accords.

Build on What You Know

World War II produced great political, economic, and social change throughout Europe, Asia, and the Americas. The formation of the United Nations brought with it the hope that further wars could be avoided through peaceful negotiation. The nationalist movements that had begun in Africa and the Middle East after World War I increased after World War II. In Africa, radical young leaders demanded independence from European colonial powers. New Middle Eastern leaders were determined to break free from European domination. In this chapter, you will learn how Africa and the Middle East have changed since 1945.

Wole Soyinka

**1986
The Arts**
Nigerian Wole Soyinka becomes the first African to win the Nobel Prize in literature.

Nighttime bombing of Baghdad during the Persian Gulf War

**1990
Politics**
Nelson Mandela is released from a South African prison after 27 years of confinement.

**1980–88
Global Events**
The Iran-Iraq War is fought.

**1990
Politics**
The African National Congress is legalized.

**1997
Politics**
Mobutu Sese Seko is forced out of power in Zaire.

**1981
Politics**
Anwar Sadat is assassinated.

**1991
Global Events**
The Persian Gulf War occurs.

**2001
Science and Technology**
Scientists determine that the glacier on Mount Kilimanjaro is melting.

1980   **1990**   **2000**

**1980
Politics**
Rhodesia becomes the independent nation of Zimbabwe.

**1989
The Arts**
Salman Rushdie's novel *The Satanic Verses* is condemned by Iran's Ayatollah Khomeini.

**1994
Politics**
The first multiracial national elections are held in South Africa.

South Africans lined up to cast their votes in 1994.

What's Your Opinion?

*Do you **agree** or **disagree** with the following statements? Support your point of view in your journal.*

Government The process that a country uses to achieve its independence has little effect on its later history.

Culture The presence of different ethnic groups within a country has little effect on that country's government.

Economics The discovery of an important resource in a country has little effect on the development of the country's economy.

1 What factors led to a rise of African nationalism after World War II?

2 How did the processes that ended colonial rule in British, French, Belgian, and Portuguese colonies differ?

3 How was South Africa's move to independence different from that of other African nations?

apartheid

Pan-Africanism
Kwame Nkrumah
Mau Mau
Robert Mugabe
Nelson Mandela
Desmond Tutu
Steven Biko
F. W. de Klerk

▶ WHY IT MATTERS TODAY

Some African nations are still experiencing problems in achieving democratic government and peaceful rule. Use [CNN news.com] or other **current event** sources to identify the present areas of conflict. Record your findings in your journal.

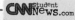

African Independence After World War II

The Main Idea
African nationalists demanded freedom from European colonial powers after World War II.

The Story Continues *"The social and economic development of Africa will come only within the political kingdom, not the other way around." With these words, Kwame Nkrumah expressed the belief that political unity in Africa was the key to success. Before unity could come, however, Africans had first to satisfy their growing desire for independence.*

Nationalism

The 1930s had seen Africans increasingly demand independence from the European colonial powers. This movement strengthened when colonial governments cut back wages for African civil servants during the Great Depression. It was fueled even more by the 1935 Italian invasion of Ethiopia, the last great independent African state.

World War II was a turning point in African history. During the war thousands of Africans served in the armies of the European colonial powers. The continent itself became a source and a route for supplies. At the same time declarations such as the Atlantic Charter seemed to promise self-determination for all peoples after the war. When the war finally ended, many Africans were no longer satisfied to remain under European control. A new wave of nationalism began to sweep the continent. A group of young African leaders headed movements to end colonial rule.

These African nationalists were heavily influenced by the Pan-African movement. **Pan-Africanism** promoted the cultural unity of people of African heritage in their struggle for freedom. It began among people of African descent in North America and the West Indies, but the movement sought equality for black people throughout the world. Ending African colonial rule was central to this goal. Many young Africans were drawn by the Pan-African call "Africa for the Africans at Home and Abroad." In 1945 a Pan-African Congress was held in Manchester, England. Some of its delegates would go on to lead independence movements.

Africans expected that their demands for freedom would soon be met. The colonial powers did not plan to give up their empires in Africa easily, however. Some colonies followed a slow constitutional process with popular elections and a peaceful transfer of power. Others suffered long wars of national liberation.

✔ **READING CHECK:**
Summarizing What were some reasons that Africans demanded independence after World War II?

These Congolese soldiers fought for the Allies in World War II.

The British Colonies

In February 1960 British prime minister Harold Macmillan addressed the South African Parliament. He warned that "winds of change" sweeping through Africa would blow away colonialism. In fact, the British had been the first to recognize this change. The first sub-Saharan colony to gain independence under majority rule was the British colony of the Gold Coast. When it became independent, the country was given a historically African name—Ghana.

Ghana. One young nationalist leader was **Kwame Nkrumah** (en·KROO·muh) of the Gold Coast. Nkrumah received his higher education in the United States and worked in Great Britain. In 1945 he attended the Pan-African Congress in Manchester. In late 1947 he returned to the Gold Coast to become general secretary of the United Gold Coast Convention. This was a political party of the westernized African upper class. From this position Nkrumah began to build a national following. He believed that political unity in Africa was the key to liberation.

Soon Nkrumah called on people to begin a campaign of civil disobedience, including strikes and boycotts of British goods. In this charged atmosphere in 1948, riots broke out in Accra, the colony's capital city. They soon spread to other towns. It took colonial authorities several days to restore order. The riots did much to convince the British that they must make some concessions to nationalist demands.

Nkrumah's radical tactics and demands alarmed more conservative African leaders. After they expelled him from his post, Nkrumah founded his own political party, the Convention People's Party. The CPP was dedicated to achieving immediate self-government. Under Nkrumah's guidance, it soon became a major political party.

Under constant pressure from the CPP, the British agreed to hold a national election in the Gold Coast in 1951. Nkrumah's party won a huge victory, but Nkrumah continued to press for full independence. In 1957 the Gold Coast achieved that status. Nkrumah renamed the newly independent nation Ghana to commemorate the ancient African kingdom of Ghana.

Kenya. The example of Ghana became an inspiration to African nationalists in other colonies. In some, however—particularly those with significant numbers of white settlers—the movement toward independence was more difficult and complicated. Kenya in East Africa, for example, took a very different road to independence.

By the early 1950s, the British government was willing to grant an increasing political role for Africans in the East African colony of Kenya. Many white settlers there, however, rejected any kind of reform. They feared that African self-government would threaten their ownership of huge fertile tracts of land in the central highlands on which they grew valuable cash crops like coffee.

Rapid population growth after World War II had led to land shortages. As a result, Africans demanded to settle in the highlands, although they were not allowed to own land there.

CONNECTING TO GEOGRAPHY

Pan-Africanism

Pan-Africanism refers to the movement whose goal has been to improve the lives of all people of African descent. The word *Pan-Africanism* was chosen to describe the movement because it means "all African." American intellectual W. E. B. Du Bois and Jamaican Marcus Garvey were leaders of the movement. While Pan-Africanism sought to end colonial control of Africa, it had as its larger goal the unification of people of African descent throughout the world. It was, then, a movement that went beyond geographical boundaries. The Organization of African Unity (OAU) was founded in 1963 to promote Pan-Africanism. It had 53 member nations by the year 2000.

Understanding Geography

How is Pan-Africanism different from a single nation's independence movement?

The flag of the Organization of African Unity

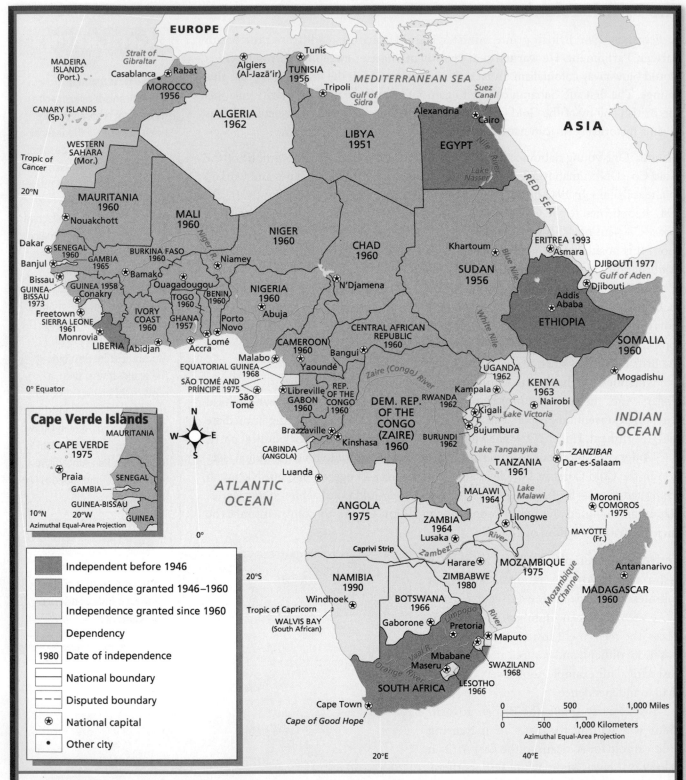

African Independence, 1946–2000

Interpreting Maps Within 15 years of the end of World War II, many colonial powers had granted independence to their African colonies. By the 1990s all of Africa was free from colonial rule.

■ **Skills Assessment: 1. Locate** What country remained a dependency in 1993? Of what colonial power was it a dependency? **2. Making Generalizations** What year seems to have been a watershed for independence for western and central African nations?

The Kikuyu, Kenya's largest ethnic group, saw this area as their ancestral homeland. Kikuyu leader Jomo Kenyatta explained:

History Makers Speak ❝It is the key to the people's life; it secures them that peaceful tillage [cultivation] of the soil which supplies their material needs and enables them to perform their magic and traditional ceremonies in undisturbed serenity [happiness].❞

Jomo Kenyatta, *Facing Mount Kenya: The Tribal Life of the Gikuyu*

The Kikuyu continued to be excluded, however. The situation exploded into violence in the early 1950s. In a four-year guerrilla campaign, a secret Kikuyu organization known as the **Mau Mau** brought terror and destruction to the central highlands. About 100 Europeans and at least 2,000 Africans loyal to the British government were killed. When the British took military action against the movement, more than 11,500 Kikuyu were killed. Thousands more were jailed in detention camps. Although the British had put down the rebellion, they had not ended the drive for Kenyan independence.

In 1961 Kenyatta, who had been jailed as a suspected Mau Mau leader, was freed. He emerged as a popular and forceful leader of the independence movement. Despite ethnic rivalries, Kenyatta created a shared sense of Kenyan nationalism. He won an easy victory in national elections held in May 1963. Later that year Kenya gained its independence and Jomo Kenyatta became its first prime minister. In 1964 he became president and held that position until his death in 1978.

British central Africa. British colonies in central Africa also experienced both guerrilla warfare and peaceful constitutional change. Southern Rhodesia's large white population had achieved internal self-government in the 1920s. Northern Rhodesia and Nyasaland were governed by the British.

In an attempt to create a multiracial state, the British created the Federation of Rhodesia and Nyasaland. Many white settlers had lobbied for this set-up. However, African nationalist leaders saw the federation as a way for white settlers to continue to control the black majority populations of the territories. After 10 years, in 1963, the African majorities in Northern Rhodesia and Nyasaland voted to withdraw from the federation. In 1964 these areas became the independent states of Zambia and Malawi. Both were under majority African rule. Although Britain tried to force Southern Rhodesia toward majority rule, the white population, led by Prime Minister Ian Smith, refused to cooperate.

In 1965 Smith declared Rhodesia an independent state. Great Britain and much of the rest of the world refused to recognize this illegal act and cut off trade relations. Smith still refused reforms, and guerrilla warfare broke out. Eventually Smith was forced to work with moderate African leaders to form a new government under African leadership. However, the privileged status of whites was still guaranteed.

The guerrilla warfare therefore continued. The Rhodesian government finally agreed to hold free elections open to all, including the guerrilla leaders. **Robert Mugabe,** considered the most radical of the candidates, won. In April 1980 Rhodesia became the new nation of Zimbabwe—after the ancient southern African kingdom of Great Zimbabwe.

✔ **READING CHECK: Making Generalizations** What kinds of changes occurred in British Africa?

Analyzing Primary Sources

Identifying a Point of View Why were the Kikuyu willing to fight for the right to occupy Kenya's central highlands?

Jomo Kenyatta, a member of the 1945 Pan-African Congress in England, was jailed on charges of leading the Kenyan Mau Mau rebellion of 1951. He became the prime minister of Kenya in 1963 and president a year later.

This **Time** *magazine cover from 1959 demonstrates the world-wide attention that African independence movements drew.*

The French Colonies

French colonies in Africa took a somewhat different path toward independence than British colonies. Unlike the British, the French had always insisted that their goal was to incorporate their African colonies into France itself.

Before World War II most of France's African colonies had been organized in two administrative units. These were French West Africa and French Equatorial Africa. The colonial governors of French West Africa remained loyal to Vichy during the war. French Equatorial Africa, led by Chad's governor Félix Éboué, supported the Free French forces of General Charles de Gaulle. In 1944, with de Gaulle's approval, the governors of French Equatorial Africa met to announce liberal reforms. The Brazzaville Declaration also made it clear, however, that the colonies should not expect independence.

After the war France adopted a new constitution. Under this constitution the French empire became the French Union. The vote was extended to more Africans, who were now eligible to elect African representatives to the French National Assembly in Paris. Other Africans were also elected to the Assembly of the French Union.

Although this system provided many Africans with political experience, it fell short of true independence. Many Africans felt that their interests were second to those of France. In response, African leaders such as Léopold Senghor of Senegal, Felix Houphouet-Boigny of the Ivory Coast, and Sékou Touré of Guinea began to develop the same kind of popular parties that were emerging in British colonies. At first the new political parties only sought self-government within the French Union. As it became increasingly clear that France was not interested in granting anything but limited control over the colonies, however, many African nationalists became more radical in their demands.

In 1958 French president de Gaulle gave the African colonies a choice. They could be members of a new organization called the French Community and accept French control of their foreign affairs. Or they could become independent. By remaining with the French, they would continue to receive French aid. Those that chose independence would be immediately cut off from all aid and contacts with France. Only Guinea, under Sékou Touré, chose complete independence.

History Makers Speak

❝We have to tell you bluntly, Mr. President, what the demands of the people are. . . . We have one prime and essential need: our dignity. . . . But there is no dignity without freedom. . . . We prefer freedom in poverty to opulence [wealth] in slavery.❞

Sékou Touré, quoted in *Africa Since 1875: A Modern History,* by Robin Hallett

The other French colonies accepted de Gaulle's new French Community. Guinea was immediately isolated, both politically and economically. It turned to the Soviet Union for help. Alarmed, de Gaulle reversed his position. Two years later, in 1960, the African colonies that had accepted membership in the French Community were granted independence without losing their close French ties.

✔ **READING CHECK: Drawing Conclusions** Why did many African colonies decide against accepting France's offer of complete independence?

Analyzing Primary Sources

Decision Making Do you agree with Touré's decision to become independent? Why or why not?

Belgian and Portuguese Colonies

Unlike Britain and France, Belgium and Portugal at first opposed any form of self-rule in their African colonies. As a result, the struggle for African nationalism in these colonies was more difficult. Perhaps the most frightful journey to independence occurred in the Belgian Congo.

The Belgian Congo. Belgium opposed independence because of its colony's great wealth in timber and mineral resources. It therefore provided little opportunity for Africans to develop skills in self-government.

The Congo was home to many groups of people, with different languages and customs. Belgian rule reinforced these differences. During World War II, however, many Congolese left their villages and flocked to the cities to help produce goods for the war effort. There they met other Congolese and established cultural clubs.

In the 1950s events in neighboring British and French colonies introduced nationalistic ideas into the Congo. After 1955 Belgian authorities even allowed new political parties to form. Most remained committed to their local regions, but a few parties encouraged national unity. At first the Belgian government resisted. It proposed a gradual 30-year timetable to prepare the Congo for independence. In 1959, however, violent protests erupted in the capital city of Léopoldville. Alarmed, Belgian authorities announced that the Congo would become independent on June 30, 1960.

African leaders were not prepared for independence to come so quickly. Various political parties—representing different ethnic groups, geographical regions, and political beliefs—participated in the first elections. Patrice Lumumba (lu·MUHM·buh), an outspoken critic of European influence, became premier. The vast majority of Belgian technicians and experts feared his anti-European views and left the country. With few trained Africans to replace them, the Congo descended into chaos.

In July 1960 Congolese soldiers mutinied against their Belgian officers. A period of violence, aimed mostly at white people, followed. To make matters worse, the copper-rich province of Katanga seceded from the Congo. As civil war broke out, first Belgium and then the United Nations intervened. The Congolese army, under Colonel Joseph Mobutu, overthrew Lumumba, who was assassinated in 1961.

Fighting wracked the country until 1965, when Mobutu himself took full control. He established a ruthless military dictatorship that lasted into the 1990s. His long rule was due in part to the Cold War. Western countries supported Mobutu as a counterweight against other African countries that were leaning toward the Communists. In 1971 Mobutu Africanized the name of the country to Zaire and his own name to Mobutu Sese Seko.

The Portuguese colonies. While many African colonies were winning their independence, Portugal continued to oppose it for Portuguese Guinea, Portuguese West Africa, and Portuguese East Africa. In desperation, African leaders in these colonies organized "liberation armies." Long, bloody wars, in which nationalists gained control of much of the countryside, followed.

The Congo was a Belgian colony from 1908 until 1960. Violence broke out across the country after independence. Here UN troops arrive in the Congo in 1961.

The wars ended only when the military in Portugal staged a coup in 1974 and announced that Portugal would withdraw from Africa. Within months the three former colonies became the independent nations of Guinea-Bissau, Angola, and Mozambique. None had the time to build firm foundations for their economies or governments. Portugal, the first European power to establish colonies in Africa, was also the last to give them up. Enormous pressure was now placed on the last remaining holdout of minority white rule in Africa, the Republic of South Africa.

✔ **READING CHECK: Identifying Cause and Effect** Why did the Congo and Portuguese colonies have a difficult time with independence?

South Africa

South Africa was created in 1910 from the union of two British and two Boer territories. It was a white-ruled nation with dominion status, linked to Great Britain only in foreign affairs. Internally, it ruled itself as it saw fit.

Apartheid. Before World War II English-speaking whites dominated the South African government. By custom, whites and nonwhites were segregated socially. Nonwhites had fewer educational opportunities. By law, they could get only low-paying manual work. Africans made up about 75 percent of the population, but were restricted by law to just 13 percent of the land.

In 1948 the National Party—dominated by Afrikaans-speaking descendants of the original Dutch settlers—came to power. Segregation and economic exploitation became a government policy called **apartheid**—the Afrikaans word for "apartness." Separate tribal states, known as homelands, were founded for Africans. After a brief period of self-government, these homelands were supposed to become independent. Afrikaaner leaders insisted that under apartheid each race would develop separately. However, the homelands were in the most barren areas of the country. Even after independence, they remained completely dependent on South Africa.

Protests against apartheid. The African National Congress (ANC) was just one group that fought apartheid, but it was the best-known group. In the 1950s it launched a campaign of civil disobedience in which ANC members openly violated apartheid laws. The South African government responded swiftly and brutally. In 1960 police fired on peaceful demonstrators in Sharpeville. More than 60 died and more than 180 were wounded. World opinion condemned the massacre. Some ANC leaders—among them black lawyer **Nelson Mandela**—now felt that they would have to confront violence with violence. In response, the government banned the ANC.

In 1961 Prime Minister Hendrik Verwoerd proclaimed South Africa a republic, and it withdrew from the British Commonwealth. The government arrested Mandela and other ANC leaders in 1962. Found guilty of treason, they all received life jail terms. Yet the ANC continued to operate, primarily from bases outside South Africa. Inside the country leaders such as **Desmond Tutu, Steven Biko,** and others continued to speak out against apartheid. Some, such as Biko, paid with their lives. An increasing number of white South Africans joined the antiapartheid movement.

Meanwhile the government continued its policy of repression. In 1976 it passed a law that Afrikaans must be spoken in all South African schools. Black schoolchildren in Soweto were peacefully marching in protest when police fired on them, killing many.

Holt Researcher
go.hrw.com
KEYWORD: Holt Researcher
FreeFind: Desmond Tutu
          Nelson Mandela
After reading more about Desmond Tutu and Nelson Mandela on the Holt Researcher, analyze their influence on events of the 20th century.

HISTORY MAKER

Desmond Tutu (1931–   )

Although he originally wanted to be a doctor, Desmond Tutu could not afford the tuition. Instead, he became a teacher and, later, a priest. He also became the first black Anglican bishop of South Africa and the first black archbishop.

Tutu knew firsthand what it was like to live under apartheid. His opposition to apartheid earned him the Nobel Peace Prize in 1984.

What were some of Desmond Tutu's accomplishments?

Over the next months outraged Africans rioted all over the country. Many were no longer willing to wait for change.

In the 1980s, faced with protests at home and abroad, the government began to retreat from its strict apartheid policies. Constitutional reforms gave some political voice to "Colored," or mixed race, and Asian South Africans. Black Africans, however, were still denied any political participation. To pressure South Africa to change its racist policies the international community imposed economic sanctions.

A change of direction. In September 1989 **F. W. de Klerk** was elected president of South Africa. De Klerk lifted a 30-year ban on antiapartheid rallies and legalized the ANC and other banned organizations. He also ordered the release of Nelson Mandela. On his release Mandela repeated the words he had spoken at his trial:

❝I have cherished the ideal of a democratic and free society in which all persons live together in harmony and with equal opportunities. It is an ideal which I hope to live for, and to see realized. But . . . if needs be, it is an ideal for which I am prepared to die.❞

Nelson Mandela, quoted in *Higher than Hope*, by Fatima Meer

De Klerk hoped that Mandela and other opposition leaders would meet with him to discuss ways to build a new South Africa. The promise of reform, however, did not end the violence. A fight for leadership of the black population broke out between the ANC and the largely Zulu Inkatha Freedom Party. Thousands of black South Africans died in the next 15 months. In addition, not all whites supported de Klerk.

In 1994 South Africa held its first all-races elections. Nelson Mandela was elected president. He called on the people to "heal the wounds of the past." However, Mandela's government faced the challenges of desperate poverty and an AIDS epidemic. Mandela retired in 1999 and was succeeded by Thabo Mbeki.

✔ **READING CHECK: Evaluating** How did reforms in South Africa expand civic participation by citizens?

HISTORY MAKER

Nelson Mandela (1918–   )

After serving 27 years in prison for his activism, Nelson Mandela became the first black president of South Africa. **How did the slogan on Mandela's campaign button reflect the expansion of democracy in South Africa?**

SECTION 1 REVIEW

1. **Define** and explain the significance:
   apartheid

2. **Identify** and explain the significance:
   Pan-Africanism
   Kwame Nkrumah
   Mau Mau
   Robert Mugabe
   Nelson Mandela
   Desmond Tutu
   Steven Biko
   F. W. de Klerk

3. **Sequencing** Make a cluster drawing like the one below. Use it to identify the events leading to African independence.

4. **Finding the Main Idea**
   a. How and why did African nationalism grow after World War II?
   b. In what different ways did British, French, Belgian, and Portuguese colonies achieve their independence?
   c. Why was South Africa's experience of independence different from that of other African nations?

5. **Writing and Critical Thinking**

   Supporting a Point of View Many people within the African nations were willing to face imprisonment or violence to achieve independence. Write a list of reasons that either support these actions or argue against them.
   Consider:
   • the failure of colonial governments to keep promises of independence made to African nations
   • the resistance of white settlers to black Africans occupying lands the Africans considered sacred
   • repression of nationalist movements by colonial governments
   • the legalization of segregation and other apartheid laws in South Africa

go.hrw.com **Homework Practice Online**
keyword: SH3 HP24

Africa Since Independence

READ TO DISCOVER

1 What challenges did newly independent African countries face?

2 How did rivalry between the Cold War superpowers affect Africa?

3 In what ways did Africa experience a revival of African culture?

DEFINE

desertification

IDENTIFY

Jerry Rawlings
Laurent Kabila
Shaaban Robert
Wole Soyinka

WHY IT MATTERS TODAY

Since African nations achieved independence, there has been a great surge of interest in the cultures of Africa. Use CNN **News**.com or other **current event** sources to identify some of the African art forms and cultural practices that have become popular. Record your findings in your journal.

CNN student **News**.com

The Main Idea
After achieving independence African nations faced many political and economic problems.

The Story Continues *In the 1960s Obafemi Awolowo, a political leader from western Nigeria, spoke about human rights in his newly independent homeland: "Every member of any human association has rights, intangible though they are, which are sacred and inalienable, and which must be protected against any invasion, at all costs." Awolowo believed that it was the duty of the state to preserve these rights. However, in newly independent African nations, that was more easily said than done.*

Political Challenges

Africans greeted independence with high hopes. The end of colonial rule, however, brought with it many serious problems. New African leaders were inexperienced in politics and in governing the new states. When they failed to improve conditions as quickly as people wanted, the military often stepped in. Soon many African countries were being ruled by military dictatorships.

Ghana is a good example of the pattern that emerged in many African states after independence. During the early years of Kwame Nkrumah's rule, Ghana's main cash crop—cocoa—sold for high prices on world markets. The resulting prosperity helped make Nkrumah popular. He used that popularity to gain absolute power.

In 1964 a new constitution made Ghana a one-party state, and any challenge to Nkrumah was seen as treason. "All Africans know that I represent Africa," Nkrumah said, "and that I speak in her name. Therefore no African can have an opinion that differs from mine." That did not stop people from criticizing, particularly when the price of cocoa dropped on the world market. This drop, combined with government debt and corruption, caused Ghana's economy to collapse. Nkrumah became more and more ruthless and his popularity fell rapidly. In 1966 he was ousted in a military coup. Over the next 12 years Ghana shifted between civilian and military rule. Political instability was linked to shifts in the economy that resulted from changing cocoa prices.

Kwame Nkrumah reviews an honor guard in 1961. He led Ghana to independence, but his thirst for power resulted in his eventual removal from office.

In 1979 a young air force pilot, **Jerry Rawlings,** led a takeover. Rawlings claimed that the present military leaders were corrupt and had to go. After public trials several leading military officers were executed. Rawlings then allowed elections to take place, and the country returned to civilian rule.

A little more than a year later, Rawlings dissolved the civilian government. He claimed it was worse than the military junta it had replaced. Rawlings tried socialist policies to improve the economy, but they too failed. A new course toward free enterprise worked. By 1990 Ghana's rate of economic growth was one of the highest in Africa.

To achieve this success, however, the people of Ghana had to pay high import, sales, and income taxes. Subsidies on food and fuel were reduced. The currency was devalued to stimulate exports. Ghanaians grew tired of these measures and of Rawlings's rigid governing style. A new constitution was adopted, and civilian rule was established. Resigning from the military, Rawlings ran for the presidency and won.

✔ **READING CHECK: Making Generalizations** What kinds of political problems—exemplified by Ghana—did new African nations face?

Ethnic Violence

Ghana's political experience was typical of many African nations. Some nations, however, had to deal with special problems left over from colonial rule. National boundaries had been drawn by imperialist powers for their own convenience. People of similar cultural backgrounds were often separated, while people of different cultures were grouped together. In some places, such as Nigeria, this led to civil war.

Nigeria. By 1963, four years after independence, Nigeria was a federation of four regions. Each had a large degree of local independence. The government hoped that this loose federation would satisfy people's ethnic and regional differences and prevent conflicts. It did not.

In 1966 the military took over the government but still could not overcome the ethnic and regional tensions. In 1967 the Eastern Region seceded from the federation and declared itself the independent Republic of Biafra. A two-year civil war followed that resulted in the deaths of several million Biafrans from starvation and disease. After Biafra surrendered, the Nigerian government gradually restored stability. Ethnic and regional tensions continued, however.

The Nigerian civil war showed what ethnic conflict could do within a country. Such violence also spilled over national borders and threatened whole regions.

Rwanda, Burundi, and Zaire. In the 1990s in Rwanda and Burundi, tensions between the two major ethnic groups, the Tutsi and the Hutu, exploded into violence. In late 1993 about 50,000 Burundians—mostly Hutu—lost their lives in violence following a Tutsi-sponsored coup attempt. Marie Kaboinja, a survivor of the massacres, told of the violence:

❝Tutsis charged us with spears and pangas [machetes]. . . . We ran away with my family. But many of us were killed, including my grandfather, father, mother, aunt and my three children.❞

Marie Kaboinja, quoted in
"Burundi Still Bleeding," *The Economist*

During the Nigerian civil war with Biafra, millions of people like the refugees shown here died of starvation and disease.

These Rwandan refugees are shown here waiting to cross the border into Zaire to escape the ethnic civil war in their own country.

In 1994 an estimated 500,000 Rwandans were killed. Most were Tutsi slaughtered by Hutu. A Tutsi army then captured the capital of Rwanda. About 2 million people fled to refugee camps in Zaire and in other neighboring countries. Many refugees died of disease and starvation. The killing in Rwanda continued.

The presence of so many Rwandan refugees destabilized Zaire. In 1995 the government stood by as Hutu refugees forcibly expelled Tutsi whose ancestors had settled in the eastern Congo as early as the 1700s. The Tutsi responded with force. It was feared that the Tutsi-Hutu conflict would engulf the entire central African lakes region. The Tutsi rebels were joined by forces who opposed Zaire's Mobutu Sese Seko. The Tutsi and the anti-Mobutu forces, led by **Laurent Kabila,** marched on the capital city of Kinshasa. In May 1997 they forced Mobutu to flee the country. Kabila renamed Zaire the Democratic Republic of the Congo. He promised to rebuild the country and halt foreign interference. After Kabila was assassinated in a failed coup attempt in 2001, his son Joseph took his place as head of the government.

✔ **READING CHECK: Problem Solving** How might ethnic conflicts have been reduced in Africa?

Economic and Environmental Problems

Almost all new African nations experienced economic difficulties. Their colonial economies had been tied to their imperialist rulers. After independence, they lacked the balance between agriculture and industry that is needed for economic stability.

Limited economies. Many new African nations depended on a single crop or mineral resource. For example, Ghana depended on cocoa, Zambia on copper, Sudan on cotton, Zaire on cobalt, and Nigeria on oil. All these products were subject to large price swings in the world market. Dependence on one product puts an economy at risk. When prices for that product drop, the whole economy—and therefore the nation—suffers. This is what happened in Ghana when cocoa prices dropped. A similar situation occurred in Nigeria.

By 1979 Nigeria had returned to a democratically elected civilian government. Because of the country's oil wealth, Nigerians had the chance to escape the poverty that threatened most other African nations. Industrialization looked promising. Then in the 1980s the international price of oil dropped. Oil had accounted for 95 percent of Nigeria's export revenues. With the drop in oil prices, the country's economy faltered. As in Ghana, the military took over in 1983 and introduced strict new measures to try to turn

Nigerians voted in a 1992 election, as the military government tried to return the country to civilian rule after an economic crisis.

the economy around. In 1985 this government was itself overturned by Major General Ibrahim Babangida. He introduced bold reforms to restore economic and political stability. Babangida renegotiated the country's foreign loans and applied for assistance from international financial organizations. In the 1990s he and other generals tried to return the country to civilian rule.

Like Nigeria, many new African countries turned to international organizations such as the World Bank for loans. However, bad planning, poor management, and corruption often left the countries worse off than before. Soon most African countries were deeply in debt. In addition, their economies remained highly vulnerable to changes in the global economy. Rising prices often forced Africans to pay huge amounts for imported goods.

Population and environment. Under colonial rule improvements in health care, disease control, and nutrition led to population growth. After independence this growth continued. To provide food farmers overused their land and planted crops on dry areas where fierce winds stripped away the topsoil. Acres of trees were cut down for firewood. The combined effect of these practices was **desertification**—the spread of the desert. In addition, severe droughts have brought starvation to millions.

Beginning in the 1970s and 1980s, new diseases emerged and new strains of viruses appeared. AIDS, for example, spread rapidly through many regions of the African continent. By 2003, approximately 30 million Africans were infected with HIV or AIDS. In 1995 the deadly Ebola virus struck in Zaire, causing the government to close the borders of an entire province.

✔ **READING CHECK: Identifying Cause and Effect** What has been one of the main causes of economic problems in Africa nations since their independence?

Superpower Rivalries

As African nations pursued peace and stability, they sought assistance from both the Soviet Union and the United States. The Cold War between these two superpowers added to Africans' problems.

When civil war broke out in Angola after independence in 1975, the United States, the Soviet Union, and Cuba rushed military support to the rival factions. For the next 12 years, Angola became a battleground, or "hot war," for the Cold War. When tensions between the two superpowers eased, attempts were made to end the Angolan civil war. A regional agreement linking the independence of Namibia to the withdrawal of Cuban troops was reached in 1988. In 1991 the rival sides agreed to hold free elections the following year. Tensions still remain, however.

Soviet-American rivalry was even more complex in the Horn of Africa, the area that includes Ethiopia and Somalia. The Horn borders the Red Sea as well as the Indian Ocean sea-lanes to the oil-rich Persian Gulf.

When Ethiopian emperor Haile Selassie was overthrown in 1974, a Marxist regime came to power. The Soviet Union provided military aid. Ethiopia's traditional enemy, Somalia, was also a socialist country supported by the Soviet Union. When Somalia invaded Ethiopia in 1977, the Soviet Union sided with Ethiopia. Somalia was defeated by Cuban troops with Soviet weapons.

African nations, however, often sought aid for practical reasons rather than ideological beliefs. A worldwide relief effort tried to help Ethiopia during a severe drought in 1984. Somalia, also devastated by drought, called on its Arab neighbors as well as the United States for aid.

In 1991 after the Cold War had ended, the military dictatorships in both Somalia and Ethiopia collapsed. Somalia descended into civil war as different clans and rival warlords fought for power. The fighting prevented aid from reaching victims of the drought. In 1992 a United Nations force intervened. Unable to stop the bloodshed, it withdrew in frustration in 1995. Although warring factions reached agreement in 1998, fighting continued. Many Somalis have sought refuge in other countries.

✔ **READING CHECK: Drawing Inferences** What are some reasons that the world's powerful nations have taken an interest in Africa?

Revival of African Culture

This Kenyan harpist is one of many musicians and artists keeping the traditional arts of Africa alive.

Despite the political and economic problems that followed independence, the people of Africa have experienced a rebirth of cultural self-confidence. During the colonial era, some Africans adopted European attitudes toward their own cultures. African art and music were considered primitive and crude. The literature of Africa—a treasury of oral traditions including myths, proverbs, and folktales—was of little interest.

Not all Africans turned away from their own history and cultural heritage, however. Written records of Swahili poetry and tales in this Bantu language go back to the 1600s. Swahili has continued to evolve. The father of modern Swahili literature was **Shaaban Robert,** a Tanzanian poet, essayist, and novelist.

In West Africa a new literary tradition developed using the colonial languages of English and French. The poems of Léopold Senghor, who later became president of independent Senegal, described the hardships of colonialism. Senghor celebrated his deep sense of pride in being a black African. The works of Senghor, novelist Camara Laye, and others also proudly point to the deep spiritual traditions of Africa. In 1986 Nigerian playwright and poet **Wole Soyinka** became the first African to win the Nobel Prize in literature.

Similarly, an interest in African music and sculpture was reawakened. African artists began to produce traditional pieces—ceremonial masks, decorated weapons, traditional musical instruments, wood and bronze statues—for a growing world market. In many places African artists combined age-old techniques with new materials and artistic ideas. In addition, a film industry has developed. Throughout the continent, this mixture of African and outside influences has revitalized African art.

✔ **READING CHECK: Drawing Conclusions** Why would some Africans lose their pride in their culture and artistic traditions?

SECTION 2 REVIEW

1. **Describe** and explain the significance:
desertification

2. **Identify** and explain the significance:
Jerry Rawlings
Laurent Kabila
Shaaban Robert
Wole Soyinka

3. **Categorizing** Copy the diagram below. List some of the factors that caused problems for African countries after independence.

Ghana	Nigeria	Angola
Somalia	Rwanda	Zaire

4. **Finding the Main Idea**
   a. What economic and environmental challenges did some of the newly independent African countries face?
   b. Why were the superpowers eager to help some of the African nations?
   c. How has African culture revived in the last half of the 1900s?

5. **Writing and Critical Thinking**
   Identifying Cause and Effect Explain how ethnic conflicts contributed to problems in the independent countries of Africa.
   Consider:
   • the problems in Nigeria left over from colonial rule
   • the rivalry between the Tutsi and Hutu
   • battles for power between rival warlords and clans in Somalia

go. hrw .com **Homework Practice Online**
keyword: SH3 HP24

1 How did France's position in the Middle East and North Africa change after World War II?

2 How did Britain's position in the Middle East and Egypt change after World War II?

3 What political and social changes did independence bring to Egypt and the Middle East?

4 What major issues did Iran and Turkey face after World War II?

DEFINE

kibbutz

IDENTIFY

Menachem Begin
Gamal Abdel Nasser
Suez Crisis
Mohammad Mosaddeq

WHY IT MATTERS TODAY

Tensions continue in the Middle East. Use **CNN** student news.com or other **current event** sources to identify the conflicts that exist between Israelis and Palestinians today. Record your findings in your journal.

CNN student news.com

Nationalism in the Middle East and North Africa

The Main Idea
Nationalist pressures created conflicts in the Middle East and North Africa after World War II.

The Story Continues *New nations emerging in the Middle East after World War II confronted a host of regional problems. One of the greatest ongoing conflicts was between the newly formed state of Israel and its Arab neighbors. In 1948 Azzam Pasha, the secretary of the Arab League, predicted, "This will be a war of extermination and momentous [extraordinary] massacre." Israeli extremists responded with their own threats. "We intend to attack, conquer and keep [territory] until we have the whole of Palestine," declared one group.*

The French Withdraw

Even before the French colonies in sub-Saharan Africa gained their independence, France was confronted with independence struggles in other colonies. In fact, the first successful challenges to French colonialism came in Syria and Lebanon in the Middle East.

France had gained control of Syria and Lebanon as a mandate after World War I. During World War II British and Free French troops had taken control of both countries from the Vichy government. After the war, despite promises of independence, French troops remained. After British pressure and several bloody battles with Arab nationalists, French troops withdrew. Syria and Lebanon became fully independent republics in the mid-1940s.

The heart of the French colonial empire in Africa was Algeria. In fact, Algeria was more than a colony. It had been assimilated, or legally absorbed, into France, like other parts of West Africa. Algerian voters elected representatives to the French National Assembly in Paris. However, voting restrictions were placed on the large majority of Muslim Arabs. Algeria had a community of Europeans known as *colons*. The *colons* accounted for about 10 percent of the population but owned most of Algeria's industries and its best land.

The success of Arab nationalism in Syria inspired many Algerians, who began to demand independence. When both the *colons* and the French authorities resisted these demands, nationalists formed the Algerian National Liberation Front (the French initials are FLN) to fight for independence. The FLN launched its revolution on November 1, 1954.

French police troops occupied streets in Algiers during a 1961 demonstration. The Algerian Revolution ended with the 1962 referendum on independence.

The Algerian war became brutal as both sides committed atrocities and used torture. The FLN waged a campaign of terror against both the French and the less radical Algerian Arabs who opposed independence. The war was so severe that in 1958 an uprising among the *colons* in Algiers contributed to the downfall of the French Fourth Republic. In France Charles de Gaulle returned to power.

The *colons* and the military leaders who supported them expected de Gaulle to crush the rebels. Instead he chose to negotiate with them. Despite resistance, including attempts on his life, de Gaulle granted Algeria independence in 1962.

The Algerian war influenced French colonialism elsewhere. In 1958 it motivated de Gaulle to offer terms for independence to the French colonies south of the Sahara. It was also partly responsible for independence in its two Muslim neighbors, Morocco and Tunisia.

Tunisia had become a French protectorate in 1883. Morocco had only become a protectorate in 1912. In 1954 nationalists from both countries launched guerrilla campaigns to drive out the French. In 1956, while fighting the war in Algeria, France gave in. Morocco became a constitutional monarchy, and Tunisia became a republic.

✔ **READING CHECK: Identifying Cause and Effect** How did events in Syria and Lebanon affect French colonialism in Africa?

British Withdrawal

At the end of World War II, Britain's control over the Middle East seemed solid. During the war the British had stationed huge numbers of troops in Egypt to protect their interests. With their allies, they had occupied much of Iran to keep supply lines to the Soviet Union open. They had forced Reza Shah Pahlavi to step down and placed his son, Mohammad Reza Pahlavi, on the throne. British troops had occupied Syria along with the Free French and had established control over Iraq. In addition, the British still held their mandate for Palestine, despite opposition from both Jews and Arabs. Britain's control over the Middle East, however, was about to slip away.

The creation of Israel. In 1939 the British reversed the Balfour Declaration, which had pledged to secure a Jewish national homeland. Instead they favored an end to Jewish immigration and the creation of an Arab Palestinian state. The Jewish Agency, which oversaw the affairs of the Jewish community in Palestine, supported increased Jewish immigration as survivors of the Nazi Holocaust fled Europe. The Holocaust had left hundreds of thousands of Jewish refugees stranded. Once the war was over, the Jewish Agency withdrew its support for the British mandate because Britain refused to allow Holocaust survivors to resettle in Palestine.

CONNECTING TO Art

Stained Glass: Windows in Jerusalem

As Jews settled in Palestine and, later, in the Jewish state of Israel, they constructed houses, schools, and other facilities. One of these was a hospital in Jerusalem. Shown in the picture are stained-glass windows from the hospital's synagogue. There are 12 windows in all, each devoted to one of the 12 tribes of Israel. Marc Chagall, a Russian Jewish artist who settled in France, designed the windows. By Jewish law, images of people cannot appear in synagogues. The artist therefore cleverly used symbols of animals, birds, plants, and fish to tell Jewish stories and convey his faith.

Understanding the Arts

How did Marc Chagall convey his faith through his art?

Meanwhile extremist Zionist groups waged a terrorist campaign against British authorities. In 1946 a group called the Irgun, led by **Menachem Begin** (BAY·guhn), blew up the King David Hotel in Jerusalem. Eventually a virtual state of war existed between the British and the Zionists.

In 1947 Britain gave up its Palestinian mandate and referred the entire problem to the United Nations. In November of that year the UN voted to partition Palestine into separate Jewish and Arab states. Jerusalem would be an international city. The Arabs unanimously rejected the UN plan, while the Zionist leaders accepted it. In May 1948 Israel declared its independence as a sovereign Jewish state. Chaim Azriel Weizmann became its first president and David Ben-Gurion its first prime minister.

The establishment of a Jewish nation infuriated Palestinian Arabs. As soon as British troops withdrew from the area, armies from neighboring Arab countries moved against Israel. Although outnumbered, the determined Israelis won. When the war ended in early 1949, Israel had won more territory than it had been given in the UN partition plan. The Arabs accepted a cease-fire, but UN-sponsored efforts to negotiate permanent peace failed.

One Arab nation gained land from the 1948 war. What remained of the proposed Palestinian state was officially annexed by Transjordan (now Jordan) in 1950. Other Arabs, including many Palestinians, bitterly opposed this action. Hundreds of thousands of Palestinians who had been expelled from the land claimed by Israel were living as refugees in camps. The Israeli government would not allow the return of the Palestinians, nor would it pay the Palestinians for lands seized. Palestinian lands were given to Jewish immigrants. Most Arab countries refused to resettle the Palestinians, arguing that such a move would justify the seizure of their lands or lessen the pressure on Israel to return the lands.

From 1948 to 1960 Israel absorbed about 1.3 million immigrants. That number almost tripled the Jewish population of the country. The use of the **kibbutz,** a type of collective farm that exists in Israel, helped turn desert areas into productive land.

Egypt. In addition to their problems in Palestine, the British also faced Egyptian demands for true independence. The presence of large numbers of British troops in Egypt after the war angered many Egyptian nationalists. So, too, did Britain's continuing control of the Sudan, which Egypt considered an Egyptian province. Between 1945 and 1952, efforts to negotiate a complete British evacuation from Egypt failed.

Meanwhile King Farouk I of Egypt headed a corrupt and inefficient government that came under fire from both nationalists and reformers. In 1952 a group of army leaders toppled the monarchy and made Egypt a republic. A popular young officer, **Gamal Abdel Nasser**, emerged as Egypt's new leader.

Nasser decided to rid Egypt of foreign domination once and for all. In 1954 Great Britain agreed to evacuate the Suez base and to allow free elections in the Sudan. Sudan chose independence rather than union with Egypt. In domestic affairs Nasser emphasized land reform, industrialization, greater government control over the economy, and expanded rights for women. His development projects to modernize Egypt were expensive, and he soon decided to seek aid from both the East and West. His efforts led to a crisis over the Suez Canal.

What If? If the Holocaust had not occurred during World War II, do you think the United Nations would have supported the creation of Israel? Why or why not?

General Gamal Abdel Nasser (seated second from left) invited members of the world's media to see Egypt celebrate the first anniversary of the 1952 revolution that deposed King Farouk.

The Suez Crisis The picture shows ships blocking the Suez Canal during the Suez Crisis. *What problems would sinking these ships create for both sides when the crisis finally ended?*

The Suez Crisis. In 1955 Nasser announced an arms agreement between Egypt and Czechoslovakia (acting for the Soviet Union). The United States and Britain became alarmed over the possibility of an alliance between Egypt and the Eastern bloc. They offered funds for Nasser's most ambitious project—the construction of a dam at Aswan on the Nile. The Aswan High Dam would irrigate new lands for farming and produce hydroelectric power. United States and British leaders hoped that this offer would keep Egypt from slipping further under Soviet influence.

Nasser hesitated, hoping for a better offer from the Soviets. He also recognized the communist People's Republic of China. When he finally agreed to the U.S. and British offer, he was told it had been withdrawn. Nasser viewed this as an insult to Egyptian national dignity. In response, he nationalized the Suez Canal in 1956.

The canal had been controlled primarily by British and French shareholders since the 1800s. This control had long been resented by Egyptians, whose labor had built the canal. Many felt that foreign funding of the canal had cost the country its independence. Nasser planned to use the revenues from the canal to fund the Aswan High Dam. His action was also a public way to assert his independence from European domination of Egypt. To Arabs and anticolonial nationalists, Nasser became a great hero. To the West, he became a demon. Nationalization of the canal led to a confrontation with old colonial powers.

Britain, France, and Israel felt the most threatened by the move. The Egyptians refused to allow Israeli ships to pass through the canal. Britain and France were outraged because they both had a stake in the company that built the canal. They worried that Egypt, which was friendly to the Soviet Union, now controlled a waterway through which much of the world's trade passed.

Israel, Britain, and France conspired to overthrow Nasser and take control of the canal. They agreed that Israel should launch a lightning attack across the canal into Egypt. Britain and France would then intervene, supposedly to separate the Israelis and Egyptians. In reality, they would help destroy the Egyptian armed forces and reestablish European control over Suez.

At first the plan went well. Israel advanced through the Gaza Strip and into the Sinai Peninsula, moving toward the canal. Great Britain and France demanded an Egyptian cease-fire and insisted on temporary control of the Canal. When Egypt refused, British and French troops seized the Mediterranean end of the canal. Both sides sank ships in the canal to block it.

The United States, under President Dwight Eisenhower, worried that the Soviets would be drawn into the crisis. With that fear in mind, the United States intervened. Privately, Eisenhower threatened to cut off all U.S. aid to Britain unless the invasion ended and the Anglo-French forces withdrew. The British agreed, and the invasion collapsed.

In a UN-negotiated settlement, Britain and France withdrew their forces. The Israelis withdrew after gaining a vague guarantee that Egypt would allow Israeli ships through the canal. Later, however, Egypt blockaded the canal. A UN force was sent to patrol the cease-fire line between the Israelis and the Egyptians in the Sinai Desert. The **Suez Crisis** was seen as the final defeat of European imperialism. Nasser became the most popular leader in the Arab world. Many Middle Eastern countries now turned toward their political and social development.

✔ **READING CHECK: Sequencing** What were the major events in the British sphere of influence in the Middle East and North Africa from the end of World War II to Egypt's victory in the Suez Crisis?

Political and Social Change

In Africa younger, Western-educated leaders had led the movements for independence. In contrast, most of the new Middle Eastern states became independent under an older, traditional, upper-class or even royal generation. Iraq and Jordan became Arab kingdoms under the sons of Sharif Husayn of Mecca. They had been installed as monarchs by the British after World War II. Saudi Arabia was a traditional Arab kingdom ruled by the house of Ibn Saʻud. Syria and Lebanon were both ruled by wealthy landowning and merchant elites. Only in Egypt, where army officers overthrew King Farouk and negotiated Britain's withdrawal, did revolution precede independence.

Nasser developed a political ideology that bound together not only Egypt but also the entire Arab world. Nasser always made his appeals for support in Islamic terms that would appeal to the people. However, he insisted that modernization along socialist lines was the key to independence.

History Makers Speak **❝Revolution is the way in which the Arab nation can free itself of its shackles, and rid itself of the dark heritage which has burdened it. . . . [It] is the only way to overcome underdevelopment which has been forced on it by suppression and exploitation . . . and to face the challenge awaiting the Arab and other underdeveloped nations; the challenge offered by the astounding scientific discoveries which help to widen the gap between the advanced and backward countries. . . . Freedom today means that of the country and of the citizen. Socialism has become both a means and an end: sufficiency and justice. ❞**

Gamal Abdel Nasser, quoted in *A History of Arab Peoples,* by Albert Hourani

A common practice in Egypt was absentee land ownership, in which wealthy city people owned rural farmland and made fortunes from tenants who actually worked the land. Under Nasser the Egyptian government ended this system. It took control of most industries and businesses such as banks and insurance companies. The government also passed laws limiting work hours, establishing a minimum wage, and creating many social services. Education was extended, and the government tried to improve the status of women.

Similar reforms were embraced by the Ba'ath Party, which first emerged in Syria. Initially the Ba'athists emphasized a kind of Pan-Arab nationalism. By the mid-1950s, however, they had also adopted socialism. This party appealed primarily to the new generation of Western-educated Arab intellectuals.

Ba'athism, whose name means rise or rebirth, took on many characteristics of dictatorial rule as it spread to neighboring countries such as Iraq and Lebanon.

Analyzing Primary Sources

Identifying a Point of View By which means did Nasser feel Arab nations could overcome underdevelopment and meet the challenge of scientific advances?

'Abd al-'Aziz Ibn Sa'ud unified Arabian domains into the Kingdom of Saudi Arabia in 1932.

In 1957 a Ba'athist government took over in Syria, and in 1958 a Ba'athist-inspired coup took place in Iraq. A new generation of leaders emerged in the Middle East and North Africa that believed in socialism as the best way to modernize their countries. The socialism practiced by these governments, however, proved to be the first step toward dictatorship.

Meanwhile Nasser began to preach a new brand of Pan-Arabism combined with socialism. In 1958 he persuaded Syria to merge with Egypt in the United Arab Republic, or UAR. As new Arab leaders emerged in Syria and Iraq, their fears of Egyptian domination grew. In 1961, despite all the talk of Pan-Arabism, Syria broke away from the UAR. The only point of agreement between Egypt and Syria was their opposition to Israel.

✔ **READING CHECK: Drawing Inferences** Why did changes occur in Egypt differently from in other Middle Eastern states?

Iran and Turkey

Unlike other Middle Eastern nations, Iran and Turkey had strong ties to the West. They also faced challenges after World War II.

Iran. At the end of World War II, Great Britain and the Soviet Union occupied Iran. Although U.S. and British pressure eventually forced the Soviet Union to withdraw, Iran remained under heavy British influence. Britain owned the majority of the Anglo-Iranian Oil Company, which controlled Iran's oil industry. Iranian nationalists resented British domination of their country. They believed that Iranian development could be achieved through democratic, constitutional means.

Iranians cheer as their flag is raised over an oil company nationalized by the Iranian government in 1951.

In 1951 the popular Iranian nationalist leader **Mohammad Mosaddeq** (MOHS·ad·dek) became Iran's prime minister. Mosaddeq's two goals were to establish constitutional government in Iran and to free Iran from foreign interference. He tried to limit the power of the shah and to strengthen the Majlis, the Iranian parliament. He also established Iran's sovereignty over the country's primary source of income, the oil industry. Shortly after coming to power, he nationalized the Anglo-Iranian Oil Company. These moves outraged both the British and Iranian conservatives, who supported a strong monarchy.

The British called the nationalization illegal and organized a worldwide boycott of Iranian oil. United States officials were alarmed by claims that Mosaddeq accepted political support from Iranian communists. They feared that the Soviet Union might gain control of Iran. For this reason, in 1953 the U.S. Central Intelligence Agency helped Mosaddeq's opponents engineer a coup and restore power to Mohammad Reza Pahlavi. The young shah of Iran worked to reestablish his power and to modernize Iran rapidly. He relied on close ties with the United States and on his army and secret police. By the early 1960s the shah controlled Iran and ran it as a dictatorship.

Turkey. Following World War II the secular and progressive policies of Turkey's leader, Mustafa Kemal, were continued under his successor, Ismet Inönü (i·nuh·NOO). Through careful diplomacy, Inönü kept Turkey neutral during the war. Turkey declared war on Germany and the other Axis Powers only when it became clear that they were going to lose.

After the war Turkey came under increased pressure from the Soviet Union, which continued to push south just as imperial Russia had done. In response, Turkish leaders allied themselves more closely with the United States and the Western world. In 1952 Turkey joined NATO.

Meanwhile Inönü moved away from Kemal's autocratic rule toward a more democratic government. In 1945 he announced the end of the one-party state and allowed other political parties to form. In May 1950 the first free elections brought the opposition party to power under its leader, Adnan Menderes. After Menderes began to lose support, he restricted groups that opposed him, and threatened to undo some of the reforms made by Kemal. In 1960 the Turkish army overthrew Menderes, who was later executed. The army soon restored civilian rule. It also made it clear that it would resist any attempts to stray from the path of reform begun by Kemal and Inönü.

Turkey continued to industrialize like European nations. Education continued to be extended, and the Turkish economy generally prospered. One source of conflict, however, was continued restrictions on religion. Eventually some Turks organized in an attempt to lift the restrictions and restore Islam to a central role in national life.

Ismet Inönü, president of Turkey

✔ **READING CHECK: Contrasting** Why were events in Iran and Turkey after the war different from those in other Middle Eastern countries?

SECTION 3 REVIEW

1. **Define** and explain the significance:
   kibbutz

2. **Identify** and explain the significance:
   Menachem Begin
   Gamal Abdel Nasser
   Suez Crisis
   Mohammad Mosaddeq

3. **Sequencing** Copy the flowchart below. Use it to identify the events leading up to the Arab-Israeli war of 1948–1949.

Causes → Arab-Israeli war of 1948–1949 → Effects

4. **Finding the Main Idea**

   a. How did nationalism in the Middle East influence French colonialism in Africa?

   b. How did Israel and Egypt come to be independent nations?

   c. Why did the United States support a monarchy instead of a democratic, constitutional government in Iran?

5. **Writing and Critical Thinking**

   Evaluating Of the changes described in this section, which do you think has had the greatest impact on the rest of the world? Explain your reasoning.
   Consider:
   • the liberation movement in Algeria that led to war
   • the UN decision to create an Israeli state within Palestine
   • Nasser's actions in ridding Egypt of European domination
   • the Iranian nationalization of the Anglo-Iranian Oil Company

Homework Practice Online
go.
hrw.
.com
keyword: SH3 HP24

READ TO DISCOVER

❶ How have Arab-Israeli conflicts shaped the recent history of North Africa and the Middle East?

❷ How did the presence of rich oil fields affect the Middle East?

❸ What was the revolution in Iran and why did it occur?

❹ What types of leadership emerged in the Arab world in the 1960s and after?

DEFINE

intifada

IDENTIFY

PLO
Yasir Arafat
Anwar Sadat
Golda Meir
Camp David Accords
OPEC
Ayatollah Khomeini
Saddam Hussein

WHY IT MATTERS TODAY

OPEC, the Organization of Petroleum Exporting Countries, sets the prices for much of the oil used in the world. Use CNNStudentNews.com or other **current event** sources to find out how OPEC actions have affected the United States in the past and recently. Record your findings in your journal.

CNN Student News.com

Jerusalem has historical significance for Judaism, Christianity, and Islam.

War, Revolution, and Oil in the Middle East and North Africa

The Main Idea
Bitter ethnic, religious, and political disputes continued to disrupt peace throughout the Middle East.

The Story Continues *The Arab-Israeli war of 1948–1949 was only the beginning of postwar conflict and upheaval in the Middle East. In August 1990 the Iraqi army of Saddam Hussein launched a major attack against other Middle Eastern states. Yet it, too, was not the last disturbance in this turbulent area of the world.*

The Arab-Israeli Confrontation

After the breakup of the union between Egypt and Syria in 1961, Gamal Abdel Nasser worked to keep his country's leadership role in the Arab world. He faced a difficult choice when tension arose along Israel's border with Syria and Jordan in the late 1960s. If Nasser supported his Arab neighbors, he risked war with a powerful Israeli military. If he held back, he risked his leadership standing.

In May 1967 Nasser made his choice. He demanded the withdrawal of UN troops that had been policing the Egyptian-Israeli border since the end of the Suez Crisis in 1956. He also blockaded the Gulf of Aqaba to cut Israel's direct sea route to Africa and Asia. In mid-May Egyptian troops began mobilizing in large numbers near Israel's southern border. Syrian forces mobilized along the Golan Heights at Israel's northern frontier.

The Six-Day War. Realizing the danger of delay, Israel launched an attack, on June 5, 1967. In six days of fighting, Israel captured the Sinai Peninsula and the Gaza Strip from Egypt. Driving back Syrian and Iraqi armies on its northern border, Israel seized the Golan Heights from Syria. It pushed back invading Jordanian forces and took the entire West Bank of the Jordan River from Jordan. Israel also captured East Jerusalem, which had been occupied by Jordan since the 1948 war.

The events of the Six-Day War radically changed Middle Eastern politics. Many displaced Palestinians lost faith in the Arab governments' ability to recapture what had been Palestine. They began to rely on their own guerrilla organization, the Palestine Liberation Organization (**PLO**), led by **Yasir Arafat.** The United States and the Soviet Union realized that they might be drawn into an Arab-Israeli conflict. Both therefore actively sought peace in the Middle East. Egypt, Syria, and Jordan wished to regain lost territory. Mutual suspicions and fears, however, doomed peace efforts.

Egypt under Sadat. When Nasser died in September 1970, **Anwar Sadat** succeeded him. Under Sadat's leadership, Egypt and Syria began a war against Israel on October 6, 1973, the Jewish holy day of Yom Kippur. The attack caught Israeli prime minister **Golda Meir** and her military off guard. At first the Arabs pushed Israeli troops back. Then Israel rallied to cross the Suez Canal and occupy Egyptian land.

All sides had reason to seek a settlement. U.S. Secretary of State Henry Kissinger used shuttle diplomacy—trips back and forth between Egypt and Syria—to obtain an agreement. He eventually achieved two, one between Israel and Egypt and one between Israel and Syria. Then moves toward peace stalled.

In November 1977, however, Sadat surprised the world. He went to Israel to speak in person to the Israeli parliament and to then Israeli prime minister Menachem Begin. In his speech, Sadat explained that peace must be won by all:

"It is not my battle alone. Nor is it the battle of the leadership in Israel alone. It is the battle of all and every citizen in all our territories, whose right it is to live in peace. It is the commitment of conscience and responsibility in the hearts of millions."

Anwar Sadat, *In Search of Identity: An Autobiography*

Supported by the United States, many months of delicate negotiations followed. In September 1978 U.S. president Jimmy Carter invited the two leaders to Camp David, the presidential retreat in Maryland. Sadat and Begin eventually agreed on the framework for a peace settlement. The **Camp David Accords** were followed by a peace treaty signed by Egypt and Israel in March 1979.

Many people doubted that this breakthrough would end the Arab-Israeli confrontation. Palestinian terrorist attacks and calls by the Palestinian leadership for Israel's demise continued. As a result, Israelis resisted any idea of a Palestinian state. Sadat's opponents claimed that he had sold out the Palestinians to regain Egyptian territory. In 1981 peace hopes dimmed when Sadat was assassinated.

The conflict continues. The Camp David Accords established peace on Israel's western border, but they did not address the problem of Palestinian refugees in neighboring countries or Israel's occupation of the West Bank and Gaza Strip. From bases in Lebanon the PLO launched guerrilla attacks on northern Israel. Israel retaliated by invading Lebanon in 1982. For two months Israel bombed Lebanon's capital, Beirut, where the PLO had its headquarters. After a settlement the PLO withdrew its forces to Tunisia. However, the Israeli invasion was not successful politically, and resulted in enormous suffering by Palestinians and Lebanese. It actually strengthened the PLO's standing among Palestinians and intensified an already bitter civil war in Lebanon. Although the Palestinians were exiled to Tunisia, they were not removed as a political force. Because many Israelis had opposed the invasion, it also caused a deep split within Israeli society.

Israelis also disagreed on how to handle the territories acquired during the Six-Day War. Since the 1970s Israelis had been establishing settlements in these zones. Palestinians living there demonstrated against the settlements. In December 1987 they

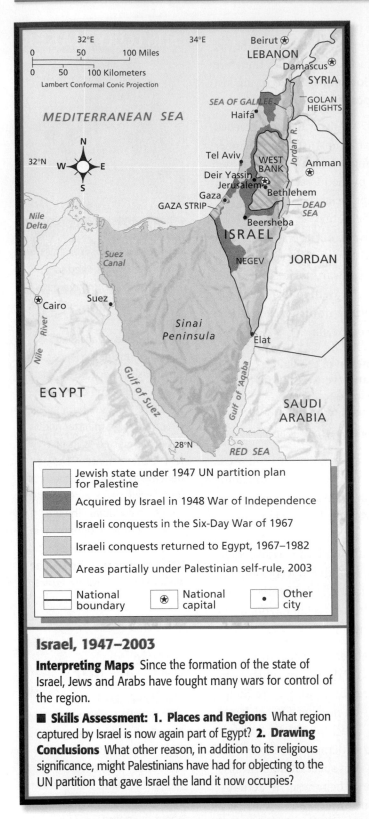

Israel, 1947–2003

Interpreting Maps Since the formation of the state of Israel, Jews and Arabs have fought many wars for control of the region.

■ **Skills Assessment: 1. Places and Regions** What region captured by Israel is now again part of Egypt? **2. Drawing Conclusions** What other reason, in addition to its religious significance, might Palestinians have had for objecting to the UN partition that gave Israel the land it now occupies?

Map legend:
- Jewish state under 1947 UN partition plan for Palestine
- Acquired by Israel in 1948 War of Independence
- Israeli conquests in the Six-Day War of 1967
- Israeli conquests returned to Egypt, 1967–1982
- Areas partially under Palestinian self-rule, 2003
- National boundary
- National capital
- Other city

began a violent uprising called the **intifada** (Arabic for "shaking"). Young Palestinians threw rocks, bottles, and homemade weapons at army patrols and other Israeli authorities. The Israeli army responded with arms. In the first year alone, the intifada claimed more than 300 Palestinian lives. Another 20,000 were wounded; almost 12,000 were imprisoned. Although some Israelis supported these harsh measures, others believed that the Israelis should withdraw from the occupied zones and exchange land for a peace settlement with the Palestinians.

Moves toward peace. Despite the continuing intifada, a growing Israeli peace movement and the Israeli election of 1992 shifted the situation. Yitzhak Rabin (rah·BEEN), a former army chief who had led Israeli forces in the Six-Day War, became prime minister. Rabin authorized secret negotiations with Palestinian leaders.

After negotiations in Oslo, Norway, during 1993, Israeli foreign minister Shimon Peres met with PLO Chairman Arafat. Israel agreed to Palestinian self-government in the West Bank and Gaza Strip. The PLO officially recognized Israel's right to exist. On September 13, 1993, Rabin, Peres, and Arafat met in Washington, D.C., to sign a preliminary agreement.

Extremists on both sides opposed parts of the peace process. Many Israelis who had settled on the West Bank feared violence at the hands of the self-governing Palestinian Authority. In 1994 a radical Israeli settler killed 29 Palestinians in the West Bank city of Hebron. At the same time, a radical Palestinian organization known as Hamas launched a terrorist campaign within Israel.

An Israeli radical opposed to giving land to Palestinians assassinated Rabin in 1995, further disrupting peace plans. In 2001 Israeli military leader Ariel Sharon was elected prime minister. His reputation for harsh treatment of Palestinians in previous wars, however, led to more Palestinian violence, which Israeli troops met in return. In April 2003, the United States, Russia, the European Union, and the United Nations presented a joint peace plan to the Israelis and Palestinians. Nicknamed the "road map," the plan spells out steps for the two sides to take to work toward a final peace settlement. Although both sides have pledged to follow the plan, each continues to blame the other for a lack of progress. In the meantime Palestinian suicide bombers continue to blow themselves up in Israel in an effort to kill Israelis. Israeli security forces respond by targeting suspected terrorists for assassination.

✔ **READING CHECK: Making Generalizations** What are the major reasons why efforts to bring about an Arab-Israeli peace failed?

Mideast Oil and World Energy Needs

During the early 1900s the manufacture of cars, ships, and aircraft increased greatly. These vehicles relied on petroleum for fuel. The demand for petroleum threatened to outrun production from existing oil fields. New sources of oil were needed, and the Middle East was where oil prospectors looked. Many countries in this region granted prospecting companies—mostly from Britain or the United States—land-use permits called concessions to search for oil. Beginning in the early 1900s, major oil fields were discovered in countries around the Persian Gulf and then in Libya in North Africa.

The rulers of these countries—many of them monarchies established by colonial powers under protectorates—received a share of the oil companies' profits. After World War II oil production increased, and the rulers and many of their subjects became very rich. Some critics pointed out that oil profits, called petrodollars, mainly increased the personal fortunes of local rulers. However, much of the money did go to improve the lives of the citizens. Petrodollars paid for social welfare systems and huge economic developments throughout the Persian Gulf region. They provided funds to build roads, schools, and desalinization plants to supply precious fresh water to desert regions.

As nationalism grew following World War II, many oil-producing countries demanded a larger share of the profits. Foreign companies were often unwilling to grant their demands. When the Iranian government nationalized the country's oil industry in 1951, the Anglo-Iranian Oil Company organized an international boycott of Iranian oil. Because oil from other countries was plentiful, the world market did not suffer from the loss of Iranian oil.

Iran's experience showed oil-producing countries that, individually, they had little power in dealing with the oil companies. In 1960 Middle East and Latin American oil-producing nations such as Venezuela created the Organization of Petroleum Exporting Countries (**OPEC**). Other oil-producing nations later joined the organization. As the bargaining agent for oil-producing nations, OPEC worked to set oil production levels and world oil prices. Its power soon became apparent. During the Arab-Israeli War of 1973, Arab OPEC members used oil as an economic weapon. They temporarily cut off shipments to the United States as punishment for supporting Israel. The price of oil rose sharply, from about $3 to more than $12 a barrel. This boycott was later eased, partly because it also hurt OPEC members.

The discovery and development of new oil fields in Alaska and the North Sea helped Western nations reduce their dependency on Middle Eastern oil after 1973. The Persian Gulf oil fields, however, remain the world's largest. They are a critical source of energy for the industrialized world. Production is expected to decline in oil fields outside the Middle East. Experts therefore predict that oil produced in Iran, Iraq, Kuwait, Saudi Arabia, and the United Arab Emirates will become even more important to the world economy. There may also be huge oil reserves in the newly independent Central Asian states, which are close to the Middle East in religion and culture.

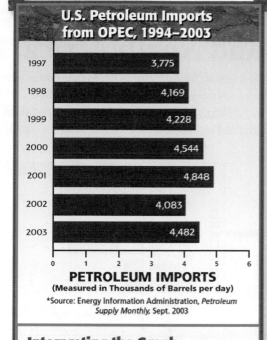

U.S. Petroleum Imports from OPEC, 1994–2003

Year	Thousands of Barrels per day
1997	3,775
1998	4,169
1999	4,228
2000	4,544
2001	4,848
2002	4,083
2003	4,482

PETROLEUM IMPORTS
(Measured in Thousands of Barrels per day)
*Source: Energy Information Administration, *Petroleum Supply Monthly,* Sept. 2003

Interpreting the Graph
The United States, like other highly industrialized nations, consumes a great deal of petroleum to meet its energy needs. Much of the oil that drives the American economy is purchased from OPEC nations. *What trend in U.S. petroleum consumption is shown by the graph, and how does this trend influence U.S. relations with the nations of OPEC?*

✔ **READING CHECK: Finding the Main Idea** How is the oil produced in the Middle East important to Arab countries? How is it important to the rest of the world?

Oil Deposits in the Middle East and North Africa, 1970s

Oil is vital to the economy of the Middle East as well as to the world economy. It is possible to use a special-purpose map to understand how vital it is. A special-purpose map provides data about factors such as natural resources. It also shows the relationship of these factors to geographical regions. It can be used to visualize data, to draw conclusions, and to make predictions.

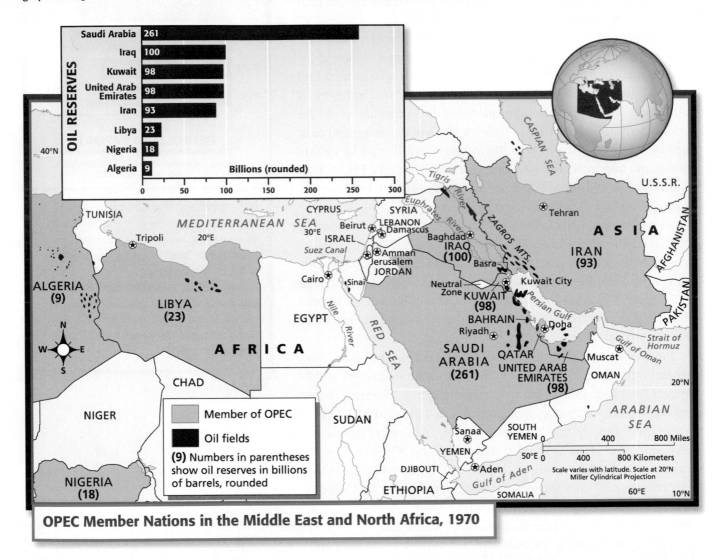

OIL RESERVES

	Billions (rounded)
Saudi Arabia	261
Iraq	100
Kuwait	98
United Arab Emirates	98
Iran	93
Libya	23
Nigeria	18
Algeria	9

Legend:
- Member of OPEC
- Oil fields
- (9) Numbers in parentheses show oil reserves in billions of barrels, rounded

OPEC Member Nations in the Middle East and North Africa, 1970

Skills Reminder

To read a special-purpose map, first determine the purpose of the map. Is it designed to give you information on troop movements? Resources? Land use? Then formulate conclusions about the information presented on the map. For example, if the map shows troop movements, can you learn why the troops took the particular routes they did?

Skills Practice

❶ Study the map above. What is the purpose of the map?

❷ What conclusions can you draw from the map?

❸ Use the map to predict what might happen if the Strait of Hormuz were blocked.

❹ Identify another map in this book as a special-purpose map and explain what conclusions you can draw from it.

The Iranian Revolution

By 1971 Britain had withdrawn most of its troops from the Persian Gulf region, leaving Iran as the leading power in the area. Western nations, including the United States, looked to the shah of Iran, Mohammad Reza Pahlavi, to guarantee the region's security. Discontent, however, was growing in Iran.

Socialists and Islamic traditionalists opposed the shah's ties with the West. In addition, an economic slump in the 1970s frustrated millions of Iranians who had moved from the countryside to the cities to look for work. The brutality of the shah's secret police only increased anger against his rule.

Many of those who opposed the shah took a renewed interest in Islam. Conservative Islamic leaders led by the **Ayatollah Khomeini** (koh·MAY·nee) opposed the shah's modernization efforts. Banished from Iran since 1964, the 76-year-old religious leader had continued to speak out against the shah. By 1978 discontent with the shah's rule erupted in riots and demonstrations. Unable to contain the unrest, the shah left Iran in early 1979. Khomeini returned in February. He demanded abolition of the monarchy and the establishment of an Islamic republic. Iranians elected a president in January 1980, but Khomeini held the real power. His supporters eliminated other political forces in the country.

Meanwhile the shah had entered the United States for medical treatment. On November 4, 1979, Iranian militants captured the U.S. embassy in Tehran and seized more than 60 American hostages. They demanded that Mohammad Reza Pahlavi be returned to Iran to stand trial. The shah quickly left the United States. He died in Egypt in 1980, but the Iranians continued to hold the hostages until January 1981.

Trouble for Iran came in September 1980, when its neighbor Iraq attacked. Iraq wanted to control a waterway between the two countries. A bitter war raged. Both sides suffered heavy casualties but made little territorial gain. The war posed a serious threat to the Persian Gulf region until a cease-fire was agreed upon in 1988.

Khomeini died in 1989, and more moderate leaders took over. However, Iran continued to call for Islamic revolution in other Middle East countries. Relatively liberal Islamic leaders were elected in 1997, but relations with the United States remained strained. Following a devastating earthquake in the city of Bam in December 2003, however, the United States sent relief supplies and lifted some economic sanctions against Iran. The moves raised hopes for improved relations between the two countries.

✔ **READING CHECK: Sequencing** List the events that led up to and followed the revolution in Iran.

The hostage crisis Images of the Ayatollah Khomeini were posted outside the U.S. embassy in Tehran, where Iranian revolutionaries held 60 Americans hostage. *What does this picture tell you of the Iranian revolutionaries' view of Khomeini?*

Struggle for Leadership in the Arab World

After the Camp David Accords, most Arabs rejected Anwar Sadat and Egypt's leadership. A struggle over which country would lead the Arab world began.

Syria. In 1970 General Hafiz Asad took control in Syria. He ruthlessly put down any challenges to his authority. After Syria's defeat in the Yom Kippur War, Asad turned his attention to building his influence in the Arab world. He aided and helped train Palestinian guerrilla groups. During the civil war in Lebanon in 1975, he first acted as mediator and then sent a large peacekeeping force to Lebanon. These troops gave the Lebanese people real hope for a lasting peace. Some wondered, however, what Asad

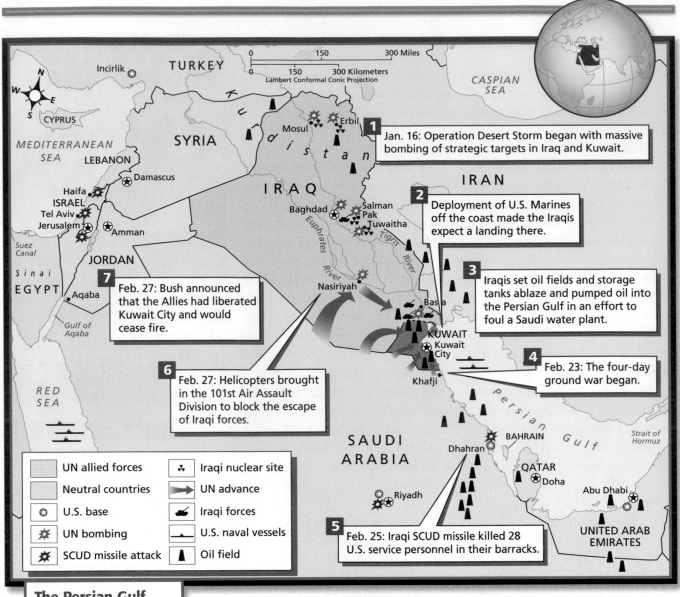

The Persian Gulf War, 1991

1 Jan. 16: Operation Desert Storm began with massive bombing of strategic targets in Iraq and Kuwait.

2 Deployment of U.S. Marines off the coast made the Iraqis expect a landing there.

3 Iraqis set oil fields and storage tanks ablaze and pumped oil into the Persian Gulf in an effort to foul a Saudi water plant.

4 Feb. 23: The four-day ground war began.

5 Feb. 25: Iraqi SCUD missile killed 28 U.S. service personnel in their barracks.

6 Feb. 27: Helicopters brought in the 101st Air Assault Division to block the escape of Iraqi forces.

7 Feb. 27: Bush announced that the Allies had liberated Kuwait City and would cease fire.

Legend:
- UN allied forces
- Neutral countries
- U.S. base
- UN bombing
- SCUD missile attack
- Iraqi nuclear site
- UN advance
- Iraqi forces
- U.S. naval vessels
- Oil field

The Persian Gulf War, 1991

Interpreting Maps Iraq's attack on Kuwait brought about a quick response from UN allied forces.

■ **Skills Assessment: Places and Regions** From what country did most UN allied troops advance during the ground war?

would ask in return. In 1980 Asad supported Iran in the Iran-Iraq War. In 1990 he again opposed Iraq when it invaded Kuwait. After Asad's death in 2000, his son Bashar Al-Asad became president, maintaining the policy of little tolerance for any opposition.

Iraq. When the nationalist Ba'ath Party seized power in Iraq in 1968, **Saddam Hussein** was one of the driving forces. Using execution and imprisonment, Saddam removed anyone who threatened the party. In 1979 he took control of the government. When the Kurds, a minority group in northern Iraq, called for a degree of self-rule, he used chemical weapons against them. When the Iran-Iraq War ended in 1988, Iraq had the largest and best-equipped army in the Arab world. It also had enormous debts and economic problems because Iran had destroyed Iraqi oil facilities during the war. Saddam began a program of reconstruction. In August 1990 Saddam attacked Kuwait. He charged the Kuwaitis with pumping Iraq's share of oil from a jointly owned oil field. Kuwait's high level of production was driving down the price of oil. Iraq quickly took possession of the smaller country and formally annexed Kuwait on August 8.

World opinion was solidly against the Iraqi invasion. When Iraq seemed poised to invade Saudi Arabia, a coalition of about 30 nations launched Operation Desert Shield. They sent more than 600,000 troops to defend Saudi Arabia. The UN imposed economic sanctions on Iraq and set a date for Iraqi withdrawal. If Iraq failed to withdraw, military action would result. The deadline passed, and the next day Desert Shield became Desert Storm. Coalition forces led by the United States launched an air attack. Iraq launched missile attacks against Saudi Arabia and Israel. Coalition air attacks continued for nearly 40 days. Then ground forces began to move into Kuwait and southern Iraq.

Worn down by weeks of bombing and surrounded by Allied forces, the Iraqi soldiers retreated from Kuwait City across the desert. Kuwait was liberated within weeks. Hoping that Saddam would fall, Iraqis in the south and the north rebelled. The rebellions failed, however, and Saddam remained in power. To prevent Iraq from launching another war, stiff sanctions on oil and other goods continued. The UN ordered Iraq to stop producing weapons of mass destruction. When UN inspectors arrived to see that Saddam had complied, the Iraqis made inspections difficult.

Iraq's continued resistance to inspections, repeated violations of UN sanctions, and suspected development of prohibited weapons led the United States in 2002 to threaten an invasion of the country to force its compliance with the UN sanctions program. Saddam's delay in allowing unobstructed inspections to resume convinced the U.S. government that the Iraqi ruler would never fully comply with the sanctions program and would continue to pose a threat to neighboring countries and to the United States.

As a result, the United States led a coalition of forces in an invasion of Iraq in March 2003. Major combat was declared over in early May after Iraq's armed forces had been defeated and Saddam had fled from power. In December 2003, Saddam was located in hiding and captured by U.S. troops. The U.S.-led coalition remains in Iraq and is working to maintain order until a democratically chosen government is ready to assume the administration of the country.

✔ **READING CHECK: Summarizing** What reasons led the United States and its coalition partners to invade Iraq in 2003?

While many women in the Middle East today wear the traditional body veil demanded by some Islamic leaders, others have adopted Western-style clothes.

SECTION 4 REVIEW

1. **Define** and explain the significance:
   intifada

2. **Identify** and explain the significance:
   PLO
   Yasir Arafat
   Anwar Sadat
   Golda Meir
   Camp David Accords
   OPEC
   Ayatollah Khomeini
   Saddam Hussein

3. **Categorizing** Copy the web diagram below. Use it to identify the causes of unrest in each of the areas shown.

4. **Finding the Main Idea**
   a. How did conflicts between Arabs and Israelis influence the history of North Africa and the Middle East?
   b. How did the presence of rich oil fields in the Middle East affect the region?
   c. What were the causes and effects of the revolution in Iran?
   d. How has the leadership of countries in the Middle East and North Africa changed since World War II?

5. **Writing and Critical Thinking**
   Comparing and Contrasting Write an article comparing the ways Iran and Iraq developed after World War II.
   Consider:
   • the political and economic issues that each country dealt with
   • the type of leadership each country had
   • the results of internal dissent

go.hrw.com Homework Practice Online
keyword: SH3 HP24

Creating a Time Line

Copy the time line below onto a sheet of paper. Complete the time line by filling in the events, individuals, and dates from the chapter that you think were significant. Pick three events and explain why you think they were significant.

1945	present

Writing a Summary

Using standard grammar, spelling, sentence structure, and punctuation, write an overview of the events in the chapter.

Identifying People and Ideas

Identify the following terms or individuals and explain their significance:

1. Pan-Africanism
2. apartheid
3. Nelson Mandela
4. desertification
5. Gamal Abdel Nasser
6. PLO
7. Camp David Accords
8. OPEC
9. Ayatollah Khomeini
10. Saddam Hussein

Understanding the Main Ideas

SECTION 1 *(pp. 686–693)*

African Independence After World War II

1. How did nationalists after 1945 differ from earlier African leaders?
2. How did South Africa's experience of colonialism and independence differ from that of other nations of Africa?

SECTION 2 *(pp. 694–698)*

Africa Since Independence

3. How does Ghana represent the post-independence experience of most African countries?
4. How did ethnic diversity contribute to political instability in independent African nations?

SECTION 3 *(pp. 699–705)*

Nationalism in the Middle East and North Africa

5. How did the rise of Arab nationalism affect France's and Britain's positions in North Africa and the Middle East?
6. What major issues confronted Turkey and Iran after World War II?

SECTION 4 *(pp. 706–713)*

War, Revolution, and Oil in the Middle East and North Africa

7. What were the causes of Arab-Israeli disputes?
8. Why is the Middle East still a source of major concern?

Reviewing Themes

1. **Government** How did the way the people of the Belgian Congo achieved their independence affect their nation?
2. **Culture** In which countries have the presence of different cultures contributed to unrest and civil wars?
3. **Economics** How have the rich oil fields of the Middle East and North Africa affected the lives of people there?

Thinking Critically

1. **Comparing and Contrasting** Compare and contrast the way colonial rule ended in British, French, and Belgian colonies after World War II.
2. **Summarizing** What factors have troubled the Middle East and North Africa?
3. **Sequencing** Trace the events leading to the rise and fall of apartheid in South Africa.
4. **Identifying Cause and Effect** What were the causes and results of the Arab-Israeli war of 1948–1949?

Writing About History

Supporting Points of View Many problems that still exist in Africa and the Middle East stem from differences in cultures. The civil wars in Kenya and Nigeria, apartheid in South Africa, the Arab-Israeli disputes, and the rise of Islamic fundamentalism all have a basis in cultural and religious differences. Select one of these issues. Write a dialogue between two persons on opposite sides in which they try to explain and resolve their differences. Use the following chart to organize your thoughts before you begin writing.

What the culture on one side of the dispute believes	
What the culture on the other side of the dispute believes	
Previous results of attempts to reach an agreement	
Action to be taken	

Building Social Studies Skills

Using Art to Understand History

Study the painting below. Then answer the questions that follow.

South African Family at Home, by Franklin McMahon

1. Which statement best describes what you can conclude from the painting about contemporary daily life in South Africa?

   a. Most South Africans live in one-room houses.

   b. In South Africa, women live separately from men.

   c. Everyone in South Africa is very poor.

   d. Some South African women are very poor and struggle to care for their children.

2. Why do you think the artist chose the subject he did for his painting? Give specific reasons to support your point of view.

Analyzing Primary Sources

Read the following quote. Then answer the questions.

"In a large desert tent in war-torn Ajeip, Sudan, doctors and nurses . . . hover over starving Sudanese children, administering high-calorie biscuits and sugar water in an effort to revive them. . . . Half a world away, patients arrive at the cardiac ward of Mt. Sinai hospital in Manhattan, many complaining of chest pains. Doctors and nurses prepare some for open-heart surgery, . . . In contrast to the Sudanese children, many of whom will not pull through, most of the New Yorkers will survive."

3. Which of the following statements best describes the issue introduced in the excerpt?

   a. People are dying from not enough food and from too much food, and both situations are preventable.

   b. Children in the Sudan are dying of starvation, while people in New York are surviving heart disease.

   c. The money spent on heart surgery in New York could be used to feed the children in the Sudan.

   d. Doctors and nurses in both the Sudan and New York should have more recognition for saving lives.

4. Do you think the issue presented in the quote is an important one? Give specific reasons for your viewpoint.

Alternative Assessment

Building Your Portfolio

Link to TODAY

Economics

America's dependence on foreign oil makes this country vulnerable to disputes in oil-producing countries. Some possible solutions are developing more of the oil resources on U.S. land and using energy sources that do not require oil. Use the Internet and other sources to find out the pros and cons of each solution. Make a chart that displays your results.

✓ internet connect

Internet Activity: go.hrw.com
KEYWORD: SH3 WH24

Choose a topic on Africa and the Middle East Since 1945 to:

- write a biography of Desmond Tutu which highlights his influence on events in South Africa during the 1900s.

- create a time line sequencing the major events of apartheid in South Africa.

- learn about recent developments in the Israeli-Palestinian peace process.

CHAPTER 25

1945–Present

Latin America Since 1945

Eva Perón

1945
Global Events
World War II ends.

1948
Global Events
The OAS is founded.

1952
Politics
Eva Perón dies.

1959
Global Events
Fidel Castro becomes the leader of Cuba.

1963
Daily Life
A hurricane kills more than 4,000 people in the Caribbean.

1963
Politics
Fidel Castro visits the Soviet Union.

1967
The Arts
One Hundred Years of Solitude by Gabriel García Márquez is first published.

1945	1955	1965

1946
Politics
Juan Perón is elected president of Argentina.

1946
Daily Life
Brazil's population reaches 45 million.

1950
Science and Technology
Mario Pani and Enrique del Moral begin designing University City, Mexico.

1958
Daily Life
Pelé helps Brazil win the first of three World Cup soccer championships.

1961
Global Events
The Bay of Pigs invasion occurs.

University City building in Mexico

Brazilian postage stamp celebrating soccer star Pelé's 1,000th career goal in 1969.

Build on What You Know

The end of World War II marked a turning point in world history. The upheaval caused by the war resulted in a new world order and a new balance of economic and political power. While Europe struggled to rebuild its shattered cities and towns, the countries of Asia and Africa tried to address fundamental challenges by revamping their struggling economies, fighting for independence, and overcoming the long-term effects of colonialism. In this chapter, you will learn how the nations of Latin America struggled to establish and gain economic and political stability after World War II.

Vicente Fox

**Cover of Gabriel García Márquez's
One Hundred Years of Solitude**

1992
Business and Finance
The United States increases trade sanctions against Cuba.

1992
Science and Technology
Brazil hosts a world environmental conference.

1987
Science and Technology
A portion of Ecuador's main oil pipeline is destroyed in an earthquake.

2000
Politics
Vicente Fox is elected president of Mexico.

1974
Business and Finance
Worldwide inflation occurs.

1982
Politics
The British battle Argentina for the Falkland Islands.

1975

1985

2000

1972
Daily Life
A Nicaraguan earthquake kills more than 10,000.

1976
Politics
Isabel Perón is overthrown in Argentina.

1976
Business and Finance
Argentina devalues the peso.

1983
Global Events
The United States invades Grenada.

1990
The Arts
Mexican poet Octavio Paz wins the Nobel Prize for literature.

1994
Business and Finance
NAFTA goes into effect.

1999
Business and Finance
Panama takes over control of Panama Canal.

Former U.S. president Jimmy Carter turns over control of Panama Canal to Panamanian President Mireya Moscoso.

What's Your Opinion?

Themes Journal *Do you* **agree** *or* **disagree** *with the following statements? Support your point of view in your journal.*

Economics Strong economies make strong governments.

Government In order to run the government efficiently, some governments must restrict basic freedoms.

Global Relations One nation has the right to interfere in the affairs of another nation.

Facing New Challenges

The Main Idea
The nations of Latin America have struggled to establish stable economies since 1945.

The Story Continues *Industrialization in Latin America was a mixed blessing. Carolina Maria de Jesus, a Brazilian slum dweller, supported her three children by recycling trash. In a diary entry she summed up her plight: "I returned home, or rather to my shack, nervous and exhausted. I thought of the worrisome life that I led. Carrying paper, washing clothes for the children, staying in the street all day long. Yet I'm always lacking things."*

Developing New Economies

Before World War II Latin America had been dominated by rural, agricultural societies. During the war the region provided a steady flow of raw materials and foods to the Allies. After the war the demand for these goods increased. Even so, many Latin American nations found it difficult to become economically stable.

Economic instability. Most Latin American political leaders thought the way to solve the region's economic problems was for each nation to develop its own national industries. Such industrial development would provide jobs and consumer goods for the growing population, and it would make the nations less dependent on foreign goods. To pay for industrial development, Latin American governments obtained loans from foreign countries and commercial banks.

Another way to develop economically was to invite foreign corporations to do business in Latin America. Leaders believed these corporations would bring capital and technology into their nations and spur industrialization. Relations between these foreign-owned businesses, known as **multinational corporations,** and their host countries soon became strained, however. Many Latin Americans resented that

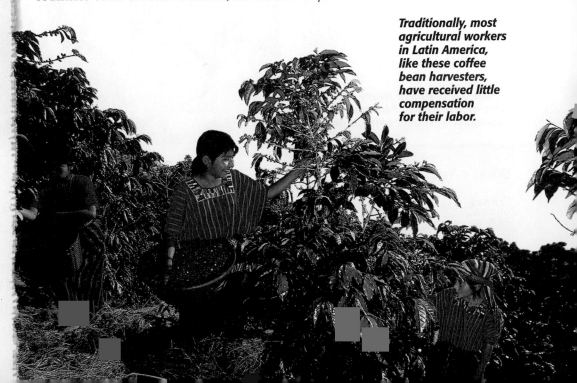

Traditionally, most agricultural workers in Latin America, like these coffee bean harvesters, have received little compensation for their labor.

foreigners owned important factories. In addition, the foreign corporations often took their profits back home instead of investing them in the host nations.

Monoculture. One reason that Latin American economies were unstable was their basis in **monoculture.** In other words, almost every country in the region relied on just one or two crops or minerals for exporting. Venezuela and Mexico relied on oil. Colombia and Central American nations relied on coffee. When world prices for these products rose or fell, the economies of the countries rose or fell. The nations rode an economic roller coaster.

Latin American monocultures favored crops grown on large commercial plantations. Many plantation workers were families who came to the plantation only at harvest time. Writer Rigoberta Menchú, a Maya Indian of the Quiché group, described the childhood experience of being a coffee-bean picker:

❝When I turned eight, I started to earn money on the finca [plantation]. I set myself to the task of picking 35 pounds of coffee a day. In those days, I was paid 20 centavos for that amount. . . . It was very hard on me. I remember very well never wasting a single moment, mainly out of love for my parents and so that they could save a little of their money, although they couldn't really. . . .❞

Rigoberta Menchú, *I, Rigoberta Menchú: An Indian Woman in Guatemala*

Import substitution. You have already read how Latin American nations followed a policy of economic nationalism in the 1930s. They tried to encourage their own industries and reduce foreign imports. After the war the nations took this policy one step further. They tried to identify certain imported goods and replace them with their own manufactured goods. This policy is known as **import substitution.** To make the policy work, Latin American governments granted favors to businesses to encourage them to manufacture these goods. They also imposed tariffs on imported goods, making them more expensive.

This approach worked well in larger nations like Mexico, Argentina, and Brazil because they had enough resources. These countries began to produce steel, heavy machinery, pharmaceuticals, cars, and many consumer goods. From 1950 to 1978 manufacturing grew in Latin America at a steady rate, even among smaller nations like Chile and Guatemala. Industrial growth slowed by the mid-1980s, however. Many Latin Americans did not earn enough money to purchase consumer goods in substantial quantities. In addition, a worldwide recession had begun to affect the region.

Debt problems. In the 1980s Latin America faced another economic problem: debt. Nations such as Argentina, Brazil, and Mexico had borrowed huge sums of money from foreign nations and commercial banks to help them industrialize. Many of these loans were made in the 1970s, when interest rates were rising. When their economies began to decline in the early 1980s, the nations had a hard time making their loan payments. The lenders of the money took steps to make it easier for the nations to repay the money they owed. Even so, the nations still owed hundreds of billions of dollars.

This huge debt led to inflation. The Latin American nations had to pay interest on foreign loans as well as keep their industries and governments running. To do this they printed more and more money. When too much money is in circulation, its value decreases and more money is needed to buy the same goods. In other words, prices rise and inflation occurs. By the 1980s several Latin American countries had annual inflation rates of over 1,000 percent.

Guatemalan writer and civil rights activist Rigoberta Menchú received the Nobel Peace Prize in 1992.

Analyzing Primary Sources

Drawing Inferences Is 20 centavos a day a small or large amount of money? How can you tell?

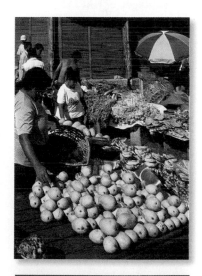

INTERPRETING THE VISUAL RECORD

Markets Street vending is common in many Latin American countries and helps to keep consumer prices down. *How do markets such as this help consumers?*

NAFTA

The North American Free Trade Agreement was designed to promote free trade between the United States, Canada, and Mexico. NAFTA officially went into effect on January 1, 1994. By dropping trade barriers such as tariffs, the agreement makes it easier for the three nations to buy and sell their products to each other. For example, Mexico now purchases 75 percent of its agricultural products from the United States. Special NAFTA rules promote the purchase and use of home-grown North American products.

Understanding Economics

What might be the advantages and disadvantages of NAFTA?

A migrant farmworker from Mexico harvests apples on a farm in the United States.

To combat such high inflation, most nations raised taxes, cut spending, and stopped aiding industries. They also reduced the number of government workers and controlled their wages. The nations still had high inflation rates, however, and the actions taken to cut inflation slowed down economies. Hardest hit was the working class.

Economic alliances. After World War II Latin American countries explored new forms of economic relations. They wanted to lessen their dependence on industrialized countries and achieve greater cooperation in areas of tariffs and trade. In 1969 the nations of Bolivia, Chile, Colombia, Ecuador, and Peru put into effect the Andean Pact. This agreement was designed to restrict foreign investment, improve tariff coordination, and increase economic cooperation among these nations. Many Latin American countries strengthened their economies in the 1990s by making agreements with the United States and establishing regional free-trade alliances with each other. For example, the North American Free Trade Agreement, or **NAFTA,** which took effect in 1994, economically united Mexico with Canada and the United States, creating a large free-trade zone. Argentina, Brazil, Paraguay, and Uruguay formed a similar alliance known as Mercosur, which took effect in 1995. In Miami at the end of 2003, trade ministers from 34 nations in North, Central, and South America participated in talks to set up a Free Trade Area of the Americas (FTAA).

✔ **READING CHECK: Identifying Cause and Effect** What factors affected the economies of Latin American nations?

Changes and Challenges of Industrialization

Industrialization created higher standards of living and better health care for some Latin Americans. It also created many new challenges.

Population growth and poverty. When nations industrialize, their populations show a typical pattern of change. Before industrialization a nation's birthrate and death rate are usually high. Industrialization lowers the death rate because it brings better living conditions, sanitation, nutrition, and health care. Eventually birthrates will lower too, as women have fewer babies. During the period of transition, however, when death rates lower but birthrates stay high, a population boom occurs. Since World War II the Latin American population has skyrocketed. By the mid-1990s the population had tripled to nearly 470 million people. It is expected to continue growing through the year 2025.

An increasing percentage of Latin Americans live in poverty. More than one-third of the people in Latin America were poor in 1997. That figure was an increase of almost 60 million in 10 years. This situation was made worse by widespread unemployment. At the same time the gap between rich and poor grew, leading to much discontent. Many Latin Americans moved to the United States and to cities in search of better jobs and better lives.

Urban growth. In addition to overall population growth, Latin American cities began to grow as more and more people moved to them to find work. The cities also offered schools, social services, hospitals, and entertainment. Since 1945 urban populations have grown much faster than national populations, often twice as fast. The largest cities, such as Lima, Mexico City, and São Paulo, have grown the most.

As Latin American cities grew, governments had to install sewage systems, water mains, electrical lines, roads, and public transportation. These projects often caused financial burdens. Also, severe housing and job shortages existed. Governments were able to provide only a limited amount of housing, and most of the migrants who did find work in the cities did not make enough money to pay for housing. People began to live on empty land without permission. They built shacks of scrap metal and other cast-off materials. Many newcomers to Latin American cities today end up living in these shantytown slums. Because the urban slums have inadequate sewer systems and no running water, they are ideal places for diseases to spread. A cholera outbreak in Peru in 1991 spread to Brazil, Chile, Colombia, and Ecuador, killing more than 3,000 people.

Environmental problems. Growing urban populations cause environmental damage too. Mexico City's many cars and factories, for example, have led to high levels of pollution, endangering health and life. Many infants there have harmful levels of toxins in their blood.

In addition to the pollution caused by urban growth, the development of resources has led to other environmental problems. Millions of acres of land—including valuable rain forests—have been cleared to make room for buildings, roads, industry, and farms. In Central America alone more than two thirds of the rain forests have been destroyed. Many plant and animal species have become extinct, and there has been significant soil erosion. Also, dangerous pesticides, many of which have been banned in the United States, are still being used in Latin America.

✔ **READING CHECK: Problem Solving** What did Latin American leaders need to do in response to the problems caused by growing cities and industrialization?

Population Growth in Selected Latin American Countries, 1900–2025

Legend: Argentina, Brazil, Chile, Mexico, Peru

y-axis: 250,000,000 / 200,000,000 / 150,000,000 / 100,000,000 / 50,000,000 / 0
x-axis: 1900, 1950, 1988, 2000, *2025
*Projected figures

Source: Population Reference Bureau

Interpreting the Graph
The populations of Latin American countries have grown dramatically, in part because of better nutrition and health care for some in the region. *In addition to having more people than the other countries shown, what else is different about the population projections for Brazil and Mexico?*

New Political and Social Forces

As Latin American nations changed and developed, so too did their political structures. By the mid-1990s most of the nations had democratic governments, and increasingly people began to make their voices heard in government.

Women, workers, and the Catholic Church. In Latin America today women are emerging as a political force. They began their struggle for the right to vote around World War I, but were not successful region-wide until 1961. Though their voting power has increased their influence in society, they still struggle for full equality. In southern Latin American countries, women have led the fight against military dictatorships and abuses of human rights. In Argentina a group of women whose family members had disappeared due to government-sanctioned violence formed **Mothers of the Plaza de Mayo** to oppose abuses of government and military power.

To gain land for agriculture and development, some Latin American rain forest lands have been cleared.

Union members demonstrate in protest of worker lay-offs by a Brazilian auto-making plant in January 1999.

Workers have gained power also. As industrialization spread and immigration declined, workers began to organize into unions. They fought for better working conditions by striking. Today a significant portion of the workforce belongs to unions.

The Roman Catholic Church, which has always been a strong presence in Latin America, has increasingly supported political change in Latin America. Following a meeting of Catholic bishops in 1968, church leaders began to oppose certain governments on issues such as welfare and human rights. They fought for social justice against oppressive economic and political systems.

International alliances. During and just after World War II, Western nations entered into several mutual defense pacts. Many political leaders viewed such pacts as necessary to prevent communist powers from gaining more territory. Inter-American cooperation was taken a step further in 1948. In that year delegates from the nations of the Western Hemisphere met in Bogotá, Colombia and founded the **Organization of American States** (OAS). The organization's aim was to foster economic, military, and cultural cooperation among the hemisphere's nations. The OAS works to prevent outside states from intervening in the Western Hemisphere and to maintain peace among member nations. The group currently has 35 members, including most of the independent nations in the hemisphere.

The founding of the OAS represented a continuation of the Good Neighbor Policy, through which the United States sought cooperation with its southern neighbors. This ideal, however, proved difficult to achieve. For example, in 1965 the U.S. intervened in a revolution in the Dominican Republic. The OAS gave its approval to this military action. Despite this official support, however, the incident caused some local resentment and soured U.S.-Latin American relations.

✔ **READING CHECK: Finding the Main Idea** Which groups have gained political influence in Latin America?

SECTION 1 REVIEW

1. **Define** and explain the significance:
   multinational corporations
   monoculture
   import substitution

2. **Identify** and explain the significance:
   NAFTA
   Mothers of the Plaza de Mayo
   Organization of American States

Homework Practice Online
keyword: SH3 HP25

3. **Categorizing** Copy the chart below. Use it to categorize the positive and negative effects of industrialization on Latin American countries.

Attempts at economic development	Economic problems experienced

4. **Finding the Main Idea**
   a. What economic measures did Latin American leaders take to industrialize?
   b. Why did the populations of Latin American cities increase?
   c. What role do women, workers, and the church play in Latin American politics?

5. **Writing and Critical Thinking**
   Decision Making Pretend you are writing to a poor friend who is moving to a Latin American city to find work. Tell your friend whether he or she is making a good decision. Explain your reasoning.
   Consider:
   • what the housing is made of
   • what sewage and water systems they have
   • what the countryside can and cannot offer

READ TO DISCOVER

❶ How did Mexico's fortunes rise and fall after World War II?

❷ How did economic conditions influence political events in Central America?

❸ How have Central American nations moved toward democracy?

DEFINE

contras

IDENTIFY

PRI
Carlos Salinas de Gortari
Vicente Fox
Sandinistas
Daniel Ortega
Violeta Barrios de Chamorro
Contadora Principles
Oscar Arias

WHY IT MATTERS TODAY

The Central American nations have worked toward peace and democracy since the 1990s. Use or other **current event** sources to find out which Central American nations are democracies today. Record your findings in your journal.

CNN student News.com

Mexico and Central America

The Main Idea
Mexico and the nations of Central America have experienced political and economic problems.

The Story Continues *Mexico rang in a new millennium with a new president and a new, more hopeful attitude about the future. Launching the New Development Plan, government spokeswoman Martha Sahagun said it called for "good government, healthy public finances, a revolution in education and great social development." These advances, she said, would "permit each Mexican to have a dignified life" by at least the year 2025.*

Mexico

Mexico was a stable nation right after World War II. The Institutional Revolutionary Party (its initials are **PRI** in Spanish) had firm control over the civilian government. A succession of presidents ran the nation effectively. The party, however, became entrenched in power. It refused to allow opposition and resisted demands for reform.

By the late 1960s student protests racked Mexico, just as they did in many nations at that time. There were numerous confrontations between protesters and police. In 1971 an anti-government guerrilla campaign began. The government hunted down the guerrillas, ending the threat by the late 1970s.

Economic problems. Mexico experienced economic ups and downs after World War II. Its leaders tried to remedy these problems by lowering the value of the currency, the peso, and cutting back on government spending. Then in the 1970s the economy was boosted significantly when huge oil reserves were discovered. Mexico's earnings from petroleum and petroleum-based products soared from about $544 million in 1976 to more than $16 billion in 1981. Believing its economic problems were over, the nation borrowed great sums of money to fund development projects.

Things took a turn for the worse, however, in the 1980s. Financial problems in the state-owned oil company, PEMEX, led the government to reduce investments in the company. Then the world oil market slumped, reducing Mexico's income. The nation still had major debts from the money it had borrowed, and inflation skyrocketed.

The 1985 Mexico City earthquake killed approximately 10,000 or more people and left tens of thousands homeless.

In Tijuana, Mexico, a group of would-be immigrants waits for nightfall to cross the fence into the United States.

Another blow came in 1985, when a massive earthquake rocked Mexico City. The nation needed to rebuild the shattered capital as well as provide for the thousands of citizens who were now homeless.

President **Carlos Salinas de Gortari** took office in 1988. He tried to solve the economic crisis by loosening government controls on the economy and selling some government-owned businesses to encourage foreign investors. He also encouraged free trade, working hard for NAFTA. He hoped it would lead the United States and Canada to invest in Mexico and stimulate economic growth.

Salinas's plan to decrease government control over the economy did not improve the situation, however. In December 1994 the next president, Ernesto Zedillo Ponce de León, lowered the value of the peso again. Confidence in the Mexican economy plummeted and many questioned Mexico's ability to repay its loans. U.S. president Bill Clinton pulled together a multibillion-dollar aid package, but the Mexican economy remained in trouble. Inflation rose roughly 50 percent, and Mexico suffered its worst recession in its history. Finally, with government-ordered spending cuts, the economy began to recover in 1996.

Emigration. Another problem in Mexico was unemployment. The economy did not grow as quickly as the population, and too many people could not find jobs. As a result, thousands of Mexicans began entering the United States illegally to look for work. Relations between the two countries suffered. In 1986, however, the United States granted legal status to some who had entered illegally. Tensions eased. Illegal immigration into the United States has continued, however, in part because of Mexico's economic problems.

Political consequences. Mexico's problems in the 1980s and 1990s had political consequences for the PRI. Despite having held power since 1929, the party began to lose its grip on Mexico. More groups opposed the party in elections, and many observers felt that President Salinas had won the presidency in 1988 only through fraud.

In 1994 an uprising of peasant farmers in Chiapas led to clashes with government troops. That same year the PRI presidential candidate was assassinated. By 1997 the PRI's hold was broken. For the first time other political parties took control of Mexico's congress. In the 2000 election, the PRI lost the presidency after holding it for more than 70 years, when opposition candidate **Vicente Fox** was victorious. Fox ushered in a new approach to governing.

✔ **READING CHECK: Finding the Main Idea** How did the political domination of the PRI affect Mexico after 1945? What finally broke the power of the party?

Mexico's oil deposits, processed at refineries such as this, are found along the Gulf of Mexico from Tampico to Campeche.

Recent Mexican History

Multimedia resources are sources of information that incorporate words, sounds, and images in a single package. They include, among other things, television documentaries, CD-ROMS, and Internet presentations. Multimedia resources often include ideas and data on historical topics from a variety of primary and secondary sources. Such resources can help you better understand events like the recent political changes in Mexico.

Television is symbolic of the endless possibilities of modern multimedia technology. TV can inform, entertain, and educate us.

This compact disc can store and deliver huge quantities of data in many different forms.

This small television camera is a marvel of optical, electronic, and audio performance.

Skills Reminder

To use a multimedia resource, take note of its title, publication date, and the people or organization that produced it. Study the resource, listening, watching, and reading carefully. Identify the main ideas and the specific means it uses to convey each piece of information. As you examine the information, use the skills you have developed in evaluating sources of evidence and identifying bias. This will help you identify any factual inaccuracies or general biases. Then put the information to use. Use the results of your analysis to form generalizations and draw conclusions based on the multimedia resources.

Skills Practice

In your local library or through the Internet, examine a multimedia source on recent Mexican history. Answer the following questions about the multimedia source you examined.

❶ What was its title? Who produced or created it? When?
❷ What types of evidence does the source provide to convey its main ideas?
❸ How does the source handle any differing points of view? What biases, if any, does the source display?
❹ How does the source contribute to your understanding of the topic you chose?

Central American Conflicts

After World War II Central America enjoyed economic growth. From 1950 to 1970 the nations cooperated, allowing industry to grow and highways and other trade routes to be built. People began to move to the cities in great numbers. Urban populations grew steadily in the 1970s and 1980s.

This economic growth, however, benefited only a small section of the population. Campesinos, the region's poor peasants, did not enjoy the prosperity. In many cases, the best farmlands stayed in the hands of the rich, while the number of landless farm workers grew. Then even more poor citizens became homeless when devastating earthquakes and hurricanes struck the region.

Nicaragua. One nation where people joined efforts in a revolutionary movement was Nicaragua. By the late 1970s much of the nation had risen up against its oppressive dictator, Anastasio Somoza Debayle.

The anti-Somoza revolution was led by a Marxist group called the **Sandinistas.** When Somoza fled the country in 1979, the Sandinistas took control of the government. Led by **Daniel Ortega,** they set up a ruling council, or junta.

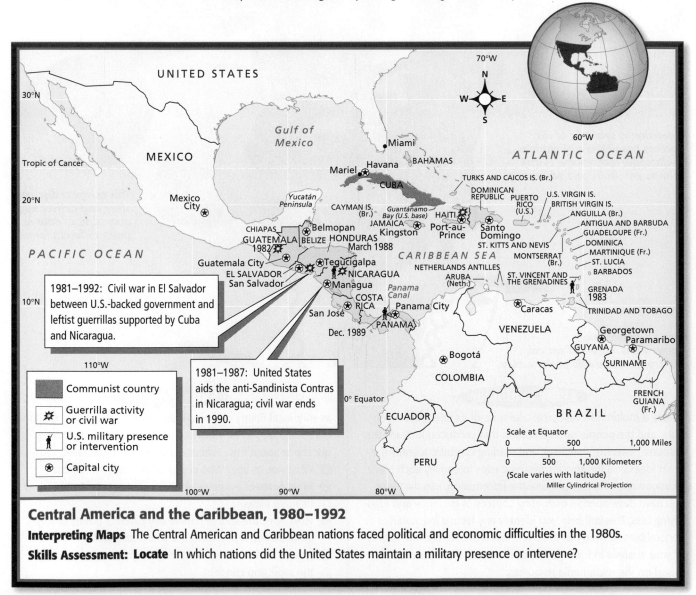

Central America and the Caribbean, 1980–1992

Interpreting Maps The Central American and Caribbean nations faced political and economic difficulties in the 1980s.

Skills Assessment: Locate In which nations did the United States maintain a military presence or intervene?

The Sandinistas forged close ties with Cuba and began to move Nicaragua toward communism. They adopted programs to help the poor and spent money on health and education. They also restricted civil rights and limited political opposition.

In the early 1980s opposition to the Sandinistas grew inside Nicaragua. In addition, the United States under President Ronald Reagan charged that the Sandinistas were aiding other Marxist rebels in Central America. A U.S.-funded group called the **contras** began a guerrilla war to overthrow the Sandinistas. Although they were aided by the Soviet Union and Cuba, the Sandinistas had to devote more and more government money to their army. As the civil war raged, the economy of the country suffered severely. Shortages of goods were common. The fighting wore on and cost many lives.

Faced with trade embargoes and a weak economy, the Sandinistas could no longer carry on the fight. In 1990 the fighting between the Sandinistas and the contras ended when Daniel Ortega conducted free elections. He gave up power peacefully after losing the election to **Violeta Barrios de Chamorro.** The United States quickly lifted the trade embargo it had placed on Nicaragua in 1985. The new government also received foreign economic aid.

The change of government, however, did little to help Nicaragua. Under Barrios de Chamorro the country faced political instability, foreign debt, and high inflation and unemployment. The Sandinistas in the National Assembly challenged many of her reforms. The presidents who followed Barrios de Chamorro also had to deal with high inflation, unemployment, and other continuing problems.

El Salvador. Northwest of Nicaragua lies El Salvador. From the 1940s to the 1970s, this Central American nation was ruled by wealthy citizens or military dictatorships. In the 1970s guerrilla groups began to mobilize people to demonstrate against the government. Some Catholic clergy supported these protests.

In 1979 civil war broke out between the government and a leftist guerrilla group called the Farabundo Martí National Liberation Front (its initials are FMLN in Spanish). The FMLN waged a campaign of urban terrorism and fierce battles against government forces. In response, right-wing "death squads"—many of them backed by the army—attacked anyone who expressed any kind of support for the FMLN's aims. In 1980 Catholic archbishop Oscar Romero was assassinated, and three American nuns and a volunteer were murdered.

José Napoleón Duarte was appointed president in December 1980 and elected in 1984. Throughout most of the 1980s, his government was supported and aided by the United States. Duarte was a civilian and a moderate who tried to enact reforms. The violence continued during his administration, however.

The right-wing ARENA party won control of the government in the late 1980s. The FMLN responded with even more violence. Guerrillas attacked urban centers, including the capital of San Salvador, in 1989. Right-wing death squads reacted. In November 1989 one such squad murdered six Catholic priests. By 1992 more than 80,000 Salvadorans had been killed in the continuing violence.

Alfredo Cristiani succeeded Duarte as president in 1989. Cristiani and FMLN leaders took steps toward peace. A peace agreement, reached through UN mediation, was signed in 1992. The first postwar elections were held in 1994. The ARENA candidate, Armando Calderón Sol, became president. In the 1997 elections ARENA maintained a strong presence in the national legislature, even though FMLN showed strength among the voters. ARENA candidate Francisco Flores won the presidency in 1999.

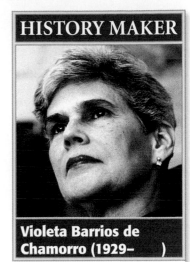

HISTORY MAKER

Violeta Barrios de Chamorro (1929–)

When the husband of Violeta Barrios de Chamorro was killed—probably by agents of Somoza—she took a leading role in the struggle against Somoza. Barrios de Chamorro was part of the government that took power after Somoza fled. She became unhappy with the Sandinistas, however. When she won the presidency in 1990, she became a symbol of the triumph of democracy. Barrios de Chamorro also promoted peace when she declared amnesty for many who had fought in the civil war. **Why would Barrios de Chamorro declare amnesty after the civil war?**

Holt Researcher

go.hrw.com
KEYWORD: Holt Researcher
FreeFind:
  Violeta Barrios de Chamorro
After reading more about Violeta Barrios de Chamorro on the Holt Researcher, create a campaign poster for her explaining why she is a symbol of democracy.

Panama. The nation of Panama endured its own political and economic problems. One complicating factor there was that the United States controlled the Panama Canal and the land around it. The two nations signed a treaty in 1978 that would give Panama control of the area by the end of 1999. Many Americans, though, were concerned that U.S. interests would be threatened if Panama controlled the canal.

By the late 1980s relations between the two nations had deteriorated. United States officials believed that Manuel Noriega, the Panamanian dictator, was helping South American nations bring drugs into the United States. President Ronald Reagan urged Noriega to resign, but he refused. To pressure him further, the Reagan administration cut off aid to Panama. Later, when Panamanian soldiers killed a U.S. soldier and harassed others, President George Bush sent U.S. troops in to restore order. Noriega was captured, convicted of drug trafficking, and sentenced to 40 years in prison.

Panama had its first democratically elected government in years, after the U.S. invasion in 1989. The country worked hard to maintain its democracy and avoid a return to military dictatorship. Major economic and social problems, though, persisted. In 1999 Mireya Moscoso became Panama's first female president. As promised by the United States, the Panama Canal was turned over to Panama that same year.

✔ **READING CHECK: Identifying Cause and Effect** How did economic factors play a role in the conflicts that took place in Central America?

A freighter in the Miraflores Locks of the Panama Canal

Moves Toward Peace and Democracy

After years of turmoil in Central America, several Latin American countries tried to find a peaceful solution to the region's problems. In 1983 Colombia, Mexico, Panama, and Venezuela agreed to the **Contadora Principles.** This document promoted negotiations rather than violence as the way to settle regional conflicts. It also called for a reduction in foreign military presence.

In 1987 representatives from throughout Central America met in Guatemala for a regional peace conference. Costa Rican president **Oscar Arias** proposed a peace plan that called for an end to all fighting in the region, an end to foreign aid to rebels, and economic reforms. As the following excerpt from a speech by Arias shows, he believed that there would be no peace in the region without democracy:

Oscar Arias's peace plan was endorsed by five Latin American nations.

History Makers Speak

"Freedom works miracles. For free men everything is possible. The challenges confronting us can be overcome by an America which is democratic and free. When I assumed the Presidency of Costa Rica, I called for an alliance for freedom and democracy in the Americas. I said then, and I repeat today, that we cannot ally ourselves either politically or economically with governments which oppress their peoples. Latin America has never known a single war between two democracies. That is reason enough for every person of good faith, for every government with good intentions, to supports the efforts to stamp out tyranny."

Oscar Arias, "Nobel Peace Prize Acceptance Speech"

Costa Rica, El Salvador, Guatemala, Honduras, and Nicaragua all supported the proposal. For his efforts, Arias received the Nobel Peace Prize in 1987. Political instability, however, caused in part by deeply rooted social and economic divisions, continued to plague parts of Central America throughout the 1980s. Peace would not seem to be a likely prospect in the region until the 1990s.

✔ **READING CHECK: Making Generalizations** What political changes swept through Central America in the 1990s?

Analyzing Primary Sources

Identifying a Point of View
Would military dictators agree with Arias's viewpoint?

SECTION 2 REVIEW

1. **Define** and explain the significance:
   contras

2. **Identify** and explain the significance:
   PRI
   Carlos Salinas de Gortari
   Vicente Fox
   Sandinistas
   Daniel Ortega
   Violeta Barrios de Chamorro
   Contadora Principles
   Oscar Arias

3. **Sequencing** Make a flowchart like the one below. Complete it to show how world oil prices affected Mexico.

```
Mexico has
economic
problems
    └── Oil is
        discovered
            └── [       ]
                    └── [       ]
```

4. **Finding the Main Idea**
   a. What events showed that the PRI was losing its political hold on Mexico?
   b. How did the United States influence events in Nicaragua and Panama in the 1980s?
   c. What did Oscar Arias propose in his plan?

5. **Writing and Critical Thinking**
   Supporting a Point of View Pretend you are an editor of a newspaper in Central America in the 1980s and are opposed to your nation's dictatorship. Write an editorial explaining why you believe the government must be changed.
   Consider:
   • what the economy and society of the nation are like
   • what life is like under a dictatorship

go.hrw.com Homework Practice Online

keyword: SH3 HP25

READ TO DISCOVER

1 How did Fidel Castro's rule affect Cuba?
2 What key issue has caused ongoing debate in Puerto Rico?
3 What problems have the smaller Caribbean nations faced?

DEFINE

dissidents

IDENTIFY

Fidel Castro
Ernesto "Che" Guevara
Luis Muñoz Marín
Operation Bootstrap
Jean-Claude Duvalier
Jean-Bertrand Aristide

WHY IT MATTERS TODAY

The U.S. economic boycott of Cuba has gone on since the early 1960s. Use CNN.com or other **current event** sources to find information about the current status of the boycott. Record your findings in your journal.

Nations of the Caribbean

The Main Idea
Political affairs in Caribbean nations have been strongly influenced by the United States.

The Story Continues *The nations of the Caribbean experienced their own political upheavals, revolutions, and attempted rebellions. When young revolutionary Fidel Castro was on trial in Cuba for his raid on a military barracks, he stated confidently, "History will absolve me."*

The Cuban Revolution

Fulgencio Batista was a Cuban army officer who had taken control of the island nation of Cuba. In 1959 Batista was overthrown in the Cuban revolution, one of the greatest political upheavals in Latin American history.

Fidel Castro. The leader of the Cuban revolution was **Fidel Castro.** Castro's anti-Batista campaign began in 1953, when he led an attack on a military barracks. Castro was jailed, but later went into exile in Mexico, where he trained a group of revolutionaries. He returned to Cuba with a band of followers in 1956. Along with his brother Raúl and a young Argentine revolutionary named **Ernesto "Che" Guevara,** Castro led guerrilla operations against the corrupt Batista government.

Batista responded with brutal and oppressive measures. As a result, many Cubans began to support the revolutionaries. In 1958 the United States decided to cut off its support of Batista, and stopped shipping arms to his government. Realizing he had no chance of surviving, Batista fled Cuba in 1959. Castro took control of the government. A young schoolgirl described the scene as Fidel Castro led his victorious troops into the Cuban capital of Havana:

History Makers Speak

❝Out in the street all the cars were flying pennants, people sang and whistled, strangers embraced each other, and everybody was shouting, 'Viva Cuba libre!' [Long live free Cuba!]❞

from *Four Women: Living the Revolution,* by Oscar Lewis et al.

Life under Castro. The lower and middle classes at first supported Castro. They approved of his promises to reform education and agriculture, improve health care, restore civil liberties, and hold open elections. His desire to build a new Cuba free of American influence was welcomed by many Cubans.

INTERPRETING THE VISUAL RECORD

Castro Huge crowds welcomed Fidel Castro upon his arrival in the town of Cienfuegos. *Does this picture support the schoolgirl's account of the people's response to Castro?*

Soon, however, the new government veered toward communism and the Soviet bloc. By the end of 1959 Castro's openly communist regime became dictatorial. Freedom of the press was denied, and some of Castro's opponents were executed. Castro began to make Marxist land reforms that redistributed income and property. His government took control of U.S.-owned agricultural estates and businesses. Castro did make many of his promised social reforms. His education policy boosted Cuba's literacy rate to 96 percent, the highest in Latin America.

Although the poor generally supported Castro, he lost the backing of many upper- and middle-class Cubans. Businesspeople and landowners were angry that their property had been seized. Middle-class intellectuals and liberal politicians were shocked by Castro's authoritarianism. In time more and more Cubans began to flee the country. Many settled in Florida.

The Bay of Pigs. Cuba's growing relationship with the Soviet Union troubled the U.S. government. Concerns about this relationship grew in 1960, when Castro ordered U.S.-owned oil companies in Cuba to process fuel supplied by the Soviets. The companies refused, and Castro seized their refineries. To strike back, the United States refused to import sugar from Cuba. Castro responded by seizing other U.S. properties in Cuba. Relations between the countries took a turn for the worse. In January of 1961 President Eisenhower broke off U.S. diplomatic relations with Cuba.

The U.S. Central Intelligence Agency (CIA) began to provide support for Cuban exiles in Guatemala and to train them for an uprising against Castro. A rebel invasion landed at the Bay of Pigs in April 1961. However, the U.S. military support that was key to the invasion never came. Nor did the expected anti-Castro uprising among Cubans. The invasion failed miserably. Castro's forces killed or captured many rebels, several of whom were Batista supporters. The failed invasion only pushed Castro even closer to the Soviets.

Cuba and the Cold War. After the Bay of Pigs invasion, Castro was concerned that the United States would attempt another attack on Cuba. He therefore allowed the Soviets to build nuclear missile sites on the island. The crisis that followed brought the world to the brink of nuclear war. The two superpowers eventually agreed the missile sites would be removed if the United States promised not to invade Cuba.

Castro's Cuban troops easily repelled the Bay of Pigs invasion force.

Che Guevara was an Argentine doctor who became a revolutionary after witnessing a U.S.-backed overthrow of the Guatemalan president in 1954. He served in various posts under Fidel Castro and was killed while leading a guerrilla attack in Bolivia.

In the mid-1960s Castro began a program to assist communist revolutions in other nations. He sent arms, soldiers, and military advisers to Latin American countries such as the Dominican Republic and Nicaragua, and to African countries such as Angola and Ethiopia.

As he had with the revolution in Cuba, Che Guevara helped Castro in these efforts. While leading a guerrilla operation in the mountains of Bolivia in 1967, he was killed by Bolivian rangers.

Because of Cuba's efforts to "export" revolution, the United States urged the Organization of American States to expel Cuba. It also encouraged other nations in the region to participate in an economic boycott of Cuba. The boycott isolated Cuba and its economy from the United States.

Problems at home. Cuba's economy was hurt as a result of this isolation. Industrialization did not proceed as planned. Production of Cuba's main crop, sugar, fell. As a result, Cuba became more dependent on aid from the Soviet Union.

The economic difficulties and shortages of goods created dissatisfaction and unrest. Many Cubans sought political asylum in other countries. The number of **dissidents**—those who disagree with a government—grew. Castro agreed to let anyone who wanted to leave Cuba do so, as long as the authorities were informed. About 125,000 people left, most of them on boats provided by Cuban exiles in Miami. Castro used the opportunity to empty Cuba's prisons and mental hospitals, forcing the inmates onto boats heading to the United States.

The recent past. Despite being isolated, Cuba maintained its support of revolutions. Throughout the 1980s it aided communist regimes in Angola and Ethiopia and remained opposed to the United States.

Cuba also remained economically dependent on the Soviet Union. In the late 1980s, however, the Soviets drastically reduced aid to Cuba. With little aid and with the economic boycott still in effect, the Cuban economy nearly collapsed in the early 1990s. Basic goods were in short supply. The Cuban government began a rationing program and imposed restrictions on the purchase of consumer goods.

In the face of economic disaster, Castro insisted that Cuba would remain a communist nation. In the mid-1990s, however, he allowed a limited number of private businesses. He also enacted other economic reforms. The Cuban economy slowly

Thousands of Cubans took advantage of the opportunity to leave their country when Castro loosened emigration restrictions. These people fled in 1994.

began to show signs of recovery due to increased tourism and foreign investment. In 1998 Pope John Paul II visited Cuba. He called for an end to U.S. trade sanctions and asked Castro to allow religious freedom and social justice in Cuba. The United States eased trade restrictions on agriculture products in 2000, and Cuba began purchasing U.S. farm goods in 2001.

✔ **READING CHECK: Summarizing** What kind of economic relationship does Cuba have with the United States and other capitalist countries?

Puerto Rico

The island of Puerto Rico has been associated with the United States since 1898. In that year the United States took control of the island following the Spanish-American War. By 1917 the U.S. Congress had made Puerto Rico a U.S. territory and given all Puerto Ricans U.S. citizenship. In the early 1930s Puerto Ricans led by **Luis Muñoz Marín** began to call for greater autonomy from the United States. The United States granted Puerto Rico a degree of self-government in 1947, and Muñoz Marín became the island's governor one year later.

This was not enough for Muñoz Marín. He pushed for even greater freedom for Puerto Rico. The U.S. Congress responded in 1950 by allowing Puerto Rico to write its own constitution. Two years later Puerto Rico was given commonwealth status.

Muñoz Marín had worked since the 1940s to boost Puerto Rico's economy. His plan for outside investment and industrialization was called **Operation Bootstrap.** Aided by tax breaks for investors from the United States, it was a great success. The economy thrived over the next two decades. Once-poor Puerto Rico raised its per capita income—the amount of money each person earns on average—dramatically.

Good economic times did not last, however. There were not enough jobs for the island's growing population. Many Puerto Ricans left for the continental United States to find work. More than 2 million Puerto Ricans live on the U.S. mainland today.

There has been constant debate in Puerto Rico about whether the island should become one of the states in the United States or remain a commonwealth. In a 1993 nonbinding vote on the issue, about 48 percent preferred to stay a commonwealth, while about 46 percent favored statehood. A small percentage—less than 5 percent—voted for independence.

✔ **READING CHECK: Making Predictions** Based on what you know, do you think Puerto Ricans will ever choose U.S. statehood? Why or why not?

Luis Muñoz Marín (shown with hands raised) initially supported independence for Puerto Rico. He was later elected governor of the U.S. commonwealth and made economic and social reforms on the island.

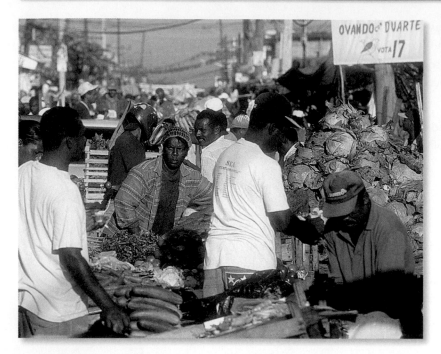

The Mercado Nuevo is the main fruit and vegetable market in Santo Domingo, Dominican Republic.

Other Caribbean Nations

Cuba was not the only troubled island nation in Latin America. In the 1960s in particular other Caribbean islands faced political changes, challenges, and violence.

The Dominican Republic. The Dominican Republic occupies two thirds of the Caribbean island of Hispaniola. Haiti occupies the other third. The country occupies a strategic position on major sea routes leading from Europe and North America to the Panama Canal. The Dominican Republic, despite its name, was for many years ruled as a dictatorship. A constitutional government had been set up in 1924 after a period of occupation by U.S. forces who had been sent to maintain stability in the troubled nation. In 1930, however, the dictator Rafael Trujillo overthrew this government. Trujillo's military dictatorship lasted until he was assassinated in 1961. Trujillo was succeeded by Juan Bosch, the first democratically elected president in over 30 years.

A coup overthrew Bosch in 1963. Military leaders formed a three-member ruling junta. Bosch's followers, some of whom were said to be communists, started an uprising to return him to power. U.S. president Lyndon Johnson feared that the Dominican Republic would become, like Cuba, another communist nation in the Western Hemisphere. In 1965 he sent thousands of U.S. marines to the Dominican Republic to support the military government in case of an attempted communist takeover.

After 1965 the nation's political situation and economy saw some degree of improvement. A new constitution was introduced in 1966. Democracy began to advance again within the country. Throughout the 1970s and 1980s, the island was stable. Although the economy depended heavily on sugar exports, the government also developed some tourism and light industry.

The Republic's economy declined slightly in the 1970s, fluctuated during the 1980s, and then took a downturn in the early 1990s, as the nation suffered through an energy crisis. The utilities that provided power could generate just a fraction of what the country needed. Business and industry were disrupted. Unemployment and inflation soared.

By the mid-1990s, however, the economy had improved somewhat. More and more people visited the island as tourists. The inflation rate was down well below earlier levels. The Republic's unemployment rate, however, was still high. Millions of Dominicans lived in poverty. Democratic elections were held in 1996, and Leonel Fernandez Reyna became president without incident. The country still had major economic problems to be solved, and anti-government feelings persisted. In May 2000 Hipólita Mejía Domínguez was elected president. He promised to fight corruption and expand the economy.

Haiti. The nation of Haiti occupies the western third of the island of Hispaniola. Haiti originally became an independent nation in 1804 after the island's population of slaves successfully rebelled against the French. However, the history of republican government in Haiti has often been interrupted. From 1957 to 1971 the country was dominated by President François Duvalier, who ruled with an iron hand. He was succeeded by his son, **Jean-Claude Duvalier,** who declared himself "President for Life." Jean-Claude was forced into exile in 1986 and the military took power.

The rule of the Duvalier family had left Haiti the poorest country in the Western Hemisphere. The Haitian people hoped that a new government would help improve their lives. However, the military regime that had forced Duvalier out of power was reluctant to hold elections. It finally agreed to do so in 1987, but when violence flared between rival political groups the elections were canceled. Free elections in 1988 brought a civilian government council to power, but they in turn were followed by a series of military coups and more violence.

The government remained in the hands of the military until 1990, when elections were held. In December of 1990 **Jean-Bertrand Aristide** became the nation's first democratically elected president. Aristide, a former Catholic priest, did not last long, however. In September of 1991 rebel troops took over the government, forcing Aristide to flee the nation. International aid was suspended and trade sanctions imposed against the new government of Haiti. The United States intervened, and nearly four years later Aristide was able to return to Haiti and take office.

In the 1995 election René Préval was elected president. It marked the first time in Haiti's history that one elected Haitian official, Aristide, had completed his term in office and peacefully passed power on to his successor. In 2000 Aristide's party, the Lavalas Political Organization, swept parliamentary elections that many argued were marred by fraud. Although opposition parties protested by boycotting the presidential elections later that year, Aristide won the vote. As Haiti continued to suffer from poverty, crime, and corruption, however, opposition to the president grew. When armed rebels advanced on the capital in February 2004, Aristide was forced to resign.

Smaller nations of the Caribbean. After being colonized by European powers more than 200 years ago, most Caribbean islands today have their own governments. Many are independent nations.

Democratic elections brought Jean-Bertrand Aristide to Haiti's presidency in 1990. Although he was re-elected in 2000, armed opposition to his rule forced Aristide to resign in early 2004.

Holt Researcher
go.hrw.com
KEYWORD: Holt Researcher
FreeFind:
Jean-Bertrand Aristide
After reading more about Jean-Bertrand Aristide on the Holt Researcher, write a memo by a U.S. official explaining why the United States intervened to help him take office.

In the 1990s the presence of U.S. troops in Haiti helped restore Haitian president Jean-Bertrand Aristide to power.

In 1958 most of the British islands of the Caribbean were joined together into a country called the West Indies Federation. The federation was dissolved in 1962, after Jamaica seceded. Jamaica was then granted status as an independent dominion within the Commonwealth of Nations, an association consisting primarily of former members of the British Empire. Soon afterward Barbados and Trinidad and Tobago also became independent nations. In 1967 some nations attempted to create a Federation of the East Caribbean. When these efforts failed, some smaller islands temporarily became "associated states of the United Kingdom." However, a number of small islands have gained their independence in recent decades. For example, Grenada became independent in 1974, Antigua and Barbuda in 1981, and St. Kitts and Nevis in 1983. Other new members of the Commonwealth include Dominica, Saint Vincent and the Grenadines, and Saint Lucia.

In 1983 a coup overthrew the Marxist government of Grenada. The rebels themselves were also communists. Neighboring Caribbean nations asked the United States to help restore order. President Ronald Reagan sent troops on October 25. Aided by small numbers of troops from several Caribbean nations, the U.S. forces quickly took control of Grenada. A democratic government was restored in 1984.

The invasion of Grenada was carried out by a multinational force led by U.S. troops to restore order after a bloody coup.

The invasion of Grenada was an unusual instance of cooperation among Caribbean nations. Despite sharing certain physical, historic, and economic traits, the islands have not developed much cohesiveness. In the late 1980s regional groups and associations such as the Caribbean Community and Common Market (Caricom) did begin to advance island trade and business. This organization now has 14 members. Agriculture and tourism are important to the economies of many Caribbean nations.

✔ **READING CHECK: Making Generalizations**
What role has the military played in many Caribbean nations since the end of World War II?

SECTION 3 REVIEW

1. **Define** and explain the significance:
   dissidents

2. **Identify** and explain the significance:
   Fidel Castro
   Ernesto "Che" Guevara
   Luis Muñoz Marín
   Operation Bootstrap
   Jean-Claude Duvalier
   Jean-Bertrand Aristide

3. **Summarizing** Copy the graphic organizer below. Complete it to show the economic problems Central American and Caribbean nations faced after World War II.

   Nations

4. **Finding the Main Idea**
   a. Which Cuban citizens tended to support Castro, and which did not?
   b. What political freedoms has Puerto Rico won from the United States since 1898?
   c. How did the Haitian military respond to attempts at democracy in the 1980s and 1990s?

5. **Writing and Critical Thinking**
   Problem Solving Imagine you are a U.S. government adviser in the 1960s. Write a memo to the president explaining how the United States can support democracy in Latin America.
   Consider:
   • what economic conditions the Latin American nations faced
   • what effect communism had on the U.S. government's thinking

Homework Practice Online
keyword: SH3 HP25

DEFINE

desaparecidos

IDENTIFY

Fernando Henrique Cardoso
Eva Perón
Juan Perón
Shining Path
Alberto Fujimori
Salvador Allende
Augusto Pinochet

▶ WHY IT MATTERS TODAY

To increase industrialization and agriculture, Brazil has allowed parts of the Amazon rain forest to be cleared. Use **CNN**News.com or other **current event** sources to find out how this has affected Brazil both economically and environmentally. Record your findings in your journal.

CNNStudent News.com

South America

The Main Idea
Revolution and political turbulence swept the continent of South America in the years after World War II.

The Story Continues *As in the Caribbean and Central America, military control of the government became common in South American nations. Marcio Moreira Alves, a Brazilian citizen, described the frightening aspects of military rule: "The military could rule by decree, arrest whom they pleased, abolish political rights and electoral posts. Their acts could not be examined by the courts."*

Brazil

The Brazilian dictator Getúlio Vargas, who had taken power in 1930, was ousted by the army at the close of World War II in 1945. He was elected president again in 1950 and again was ousted by the military, four years later. His successor continued Vargas's policy of industrialization and modernization. He also borrowed heavily from foreign banks to build a splendid new capital in the interior called Brasília.

In 1961 João Goulart became president of Brazil with strong support from the labor movement. The military distrusted Goulart because they believed he sympathized with left-wing causes. Inflation grew and industrialization slowed under Goulart's rule. To improve the economy and head off a threat from the political left, the army overthrew Goulart in 1964.

The military government forced wages down and pressured labor unions to cooperate in the effort to cut production costs. In addition, foreign corporations were encouraged to invest in Brazil. This policy worked. The nation's economy grew so fast that it was called "the Brazilian Miracle." People migrated to the cities to get jobs. However, civil rights were lost amid the economic prosperity. The government suppressed all dissent and banned political parties. It also went heavily into debt. By the late 1980s Brazil had the highest foreign debt of all the developing nations in the world.

A civilian government took office in 1990. President Fernando Collor tried to strengthen the Brazilian economy by reducing government spending, selling state-owned industries to private businesses, and even freezing most savings and checking accounts. His actions, however, pushed Brazil into a recession. Collor resigned in 1992, and his vice president, Itamar Franco, took over. President for 24 months, Franco could not turn the economy around, either. Meanwhile, corruption and crime flourished.

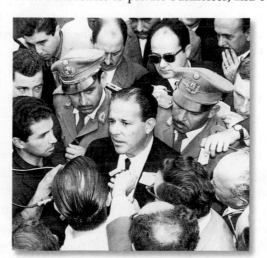

Brazilian president Goulart fled to Uruguay after he was ousted from power in 1964. His overthrow was an example of authoritarian rule replacing democratically elected leaders in South America in the several decades after World War II.

Then in 1994 Franco's finance minister, **Fernando Henrique Cardoso,** devised economic reforms so successful that in 1995 Cardoso himself went on to become president. Under his government economic production increased and inflation decreased. In the late 1990s changes in world markets challenged Brazil's ability to maintain this economic progress.

✔ **READING CHECK: Identifying Cause and Effect**
How did the state of Brazil's economy affect the nation's politics?

Brazil's new postwar capital, Brasília, boasts examples of stark modern architecture.

Argentina

Like Brazil, Argentina had political and economic problems. Yet a powerful, popular woman added a bit of glamour to Argentina's post–World War II difficulties. Her name was **Eva Perón.**

The Peróns. Colonel **Juan Perón** steadily rose to power in Argentina in the 1940s with strong support from lower-class workers and the growing middle class. He became Argentina's president in 1946. Perón, however, was greatly overshadowed by his wife, Eva. "Evita," as she was called, was a former film and radio actress. Through her skillful political use of the media, she developed a huge following and was considered the hero of the working class. Juan Perón held the title of president, but it was Evita who was loved by the people.

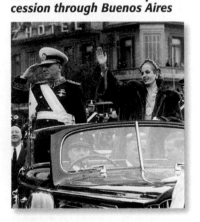

Juan and Eva Perón in a procession through Buenos Aires

The Peróns helped the working class and soon had the support of much of Argentina. With little opposition, they built up a dictatorship. Political dissent was suppressed. By the early 1950s, Argentina had developed many economic troubles. Even so, the adoration for Evita did not wane. In 1951, an ill Eva Perón made a public appearance to decline the nomination of vice president. The following is a description of the event:

History Makers Speak

❝The woman who mounted the steps and looked out upon the frenzied crowd was a far cry from the fledgling first lady of 1946, or the glamorous queen of the Rainbow Tour. The blonde curls and gaudy attire had long since given way to what one scholar called 'the streamlined, eternally classic style which was to be hers—and uniquely hers at that time—until her death.' Her hair was pulled back severely, accentuating the growing gauntness of her features. Tears flooded her eyes. She raised her arms in response to the delirium, and a look of uncertainty clouded her expression.❞

from *Péron: A Biography,* by Joseph A. Page

When Evita died of cancer in 1952, Juan Perón lost his greatest political weapon. While Evita's popularity became legendary after her death, Juan's fell dramatically. By 1955 he was forced into exile after a military coup.

For the next 18 years Argentina endured a series of military and civilian governments struggling against both political and economic difficulties. A terrorist campaign waged by leftist guerrillas added to the chaos. By the early 1970s the Argentines had begun to look back fondly on the Perón years as a time of peace and prosperity. Juan Perón seized the opportunity and in 1973 returned from exile. He won a landslide victory and become Argentina's president once more. His third wife, Isabel, was his vice president.

Juan Perón immediately set out to wage war against the leftist guerrillas and to improve Argentina's poor economy. He died before he was able to make any progress, however. Isabel succeeded him, becoming the first woman president in the Americas. Her government was incapable of dealing with Argentina's many problems and was overthrown in 1976. The military seized control once again.

Two wars. To end the guerrilla attacks once and for all, the military regime launched an all-out assault on its opponents. The army and police arrested and imprisoned not only opposition leaders but also anyone who criticized the government. As many as 15,000 people or more were taken away in the night and never seen again. Most of these **desaparecidos,** or "disappeared persons," were tortured before being killed. The military government's campaign became known as the "dirty war."

Because of the dirty war, as well as ongoing economic problems, public support for the military government weakened. To regain its popularity, the military decided in 1982 to invade the Falkland Islands off the coast of Argentina. These islands were owned by Great Britain, but Argentina had long laid claim to them. The Argentine military leaders thought the British would not bother to defend them. They anticipated an easy victory that would be popular among the Argentines.

The generals were wrong. The British sent an armada of ships and thousands of soldiers to reclaim the islands. In a matter of weeks, the British had won decisively. The Argentines were embarrassed by the defeat.

A return to democracy. The Falklands defeat was the end of the military government. Free elections were held in 1983, and Raúl Alfonsín was elected president. He promised to bring to justice all those who had been involved in the dirty war. Hundreds of military personnel were put on trial. Three former presidents and several high-ranking officials were convicted. This unkept promise, as well as ongoing economic problems, hurt Alfonsín's party. Its presidential candidate lost the 1989 election.

Carlos Menem became president and faced massive problems. Inflation was high. The country had difficulty making its foreign payments. The threat of still another military takeover was constant. To aid the economy, Menem set wage and price controls and sold state-owned businesses to private owners. To soothe the military, he pardoned many of those found guilty of crimes during the dirty war. This last act angered some Argentines, but Menem was reelected in 1995. His economic policies helped return Argentina to economic growth. Fernando de la Rua became the new president in 1999.

✔ **READING CHECK: Summarizing** What role did the military play in Argentina's recent past?

Then & Now

The Falklands

The Falkland Islands have remained an object of dispute for many years. In 1764 and 1765 the French and the British made rival claims to parts of the island group. When British priorities changed, however, the islands were abandoned. Spain also had a small settlement in the island group until 1811. The new nation of Argentina took over in 1820, but in 1833 the British reclaimed the islands, an action the Argentines have long considered to be illegal. This disputed claim of ownership set the stage for the Falkland Islands War of 1982. With the Argentine defeat, the islands remain in British hands. **What ongoing dispute led to the Falkland Islands War?**

Port Howard settlement on East Falkland is one of the two main islands of the Falklands.

This Peruvian police building was bombed by Shining Path guerrillas protesting government actions.

Peru

Peru was similar to other Latin American nations during this time period. The nation had economic problems—soaring inflation, unemployment, crushing poverty, and increasing foreign debt. It suffered an economic depression in the 1980s. The government was run by either military dictators or conservative civilians. Another threat to democracy in Peru came from communist guerrilla groups that waged war against the government.

Guerrillas. There were two major groups of guerrillas. The Tupac Amarú Revolutionary Movement (its initials are MRTA in Spanish) was an urban group. It bombed public buildings and utility companies in cities and assassinated police and other public officials. A second group, *Sendero Luminoso,* or **Shining Path,** carried out its terrorist campaign in the rural highland areas. Shining Path was a Maoist group. Like Mao Zedong of China, they believed that Peruvian society must be destroyed and a new, socialist society built on its ruins.

Drug trafficking complicated Peru's situation even more. The country is Latin America's leading producer of coca, the plant from which cocaine is made. The MRTA and Shining Path both accepted money and weapons in exchange for helping protect the profitable cocaine business.

Alberto Fujimori. Things began to change in 1990, when the son of a Japanese immigrant was elected president. **Alberto Fujimori** took over a country in chaos. His austere economic measures lowered the astronomically high inflation rate (7,650 percent in 1990) to a manageable level. By the end of 1994, terrorism and violence had also decreased. With a growing economy, Fujimori easily won reelection in 1995.

By mid-1996, however, Fujimori's popularity was on the decline. Economic growth had slowed. Charges of corruption were leveled at his government. Then in December of that year, MRTA guerrillas invaded the Japanese embassy in Lima, Peru. For months, they held people hostage inside. The crisis did not end until April 1997, when Fujimori ordered Peruvian soldiers to storm the embassy. All the guerrillas were killed, along with two soldiers. One hostage died of heart failure. Fujimori's popularity rose again, at least for a time. Then, in November 2000 Fujimori fled the country amid a growing corruption scandal. A few months later the Peruvian congress charged him with crimes against humanity for his involvement with death squads in the early 1990s.

✔ **READING CHECK: Comparing and Contrasting** How did MRTA and Shining Path differ? In what ways were they similar?

Colombia

Colombia was a nation in turmoil immediately following World War II. A series of military and civilian dictators ruled. Civil strife and economic problems plagued the nation. Fighting between political factions was so intense that Colombians call this time *La Violencia,* meaning "The Violence."

In 1957 the situation was so bad that the two major political parties agreed to form a coalition government. They shared political offices and alternated holding the office of president. By the early 1970s the economy had stabilized. Colombia's future appeared brighter. In fact, the country was considered one of the models of democracy in Latin America.

The drug trade. Drugs, however, changed Colombia's fortunes. When illegal drug use in the United States and Europe increased in the 1970s, Colombians realized they could make money growing marijuana and coca. Drug producers and dealers began making huge profits. More and more marijuana and coca were grown. As rival groups tried to control the drug trade, violence and crime soared. The industrial city of Medellín became the headquarters of the Medellín cartel, a group that ran the Colombian drug trade. The cartel used assassination and other threats to gain control of law enforcement agencies. Lower-level officials were bribed or threatened until they cooperated with the cartel.

Adding to Colombia's problems were terrorist campaigns waged by both political sides. Left-wing groups such as M-19 kidnapped and sometimes murdered public officials. Right-wing death squads, many connected with the army, killed people who sympathized with the leftists. Politically and economically motivated murder and intimidation became commonplace in Colombia. Behind this political violence stood the drug lords, who financed it.

The war on drugs. In the late 1980s Colombian authorities declared war on the drug cartels. They asked U.S. law officers and the military to help them. They also promised to turn over to the United States any drug traffickers they captured. The result was open warfare on the streets of Medellín and Cali, headquarters of another drug cartel.

Despite efforts by the government to end drug trafficking, it continued into the 1990s. By 1995 the Cali cartel was believed to control perhaps 70 percent of the world trade in cocaine. Part of the problem was extensive corruption, as drug lords continued to funnel large sums of money in the form of "campaign contributions" into the hands of selected political leaders. Colombian president Ernesto Samper himself was accused of having accepted millions of dollars from the Cali cartel for his 1994 election campaign. In 1996 the Colombian legislature considered impeaching Samper, but chose not to.

Colombia's economic and political problems continued into the late 1990s. In June 1998 Andrés Pastrana Arango succeeded Samper as president.

✔ **READING CHECK: Summarizing** How did the Colombian drug cartels affect the government?

Colombian drug enforcement officers patrol fields and destroy illegal crops.

CARIBBEAN SEA

⊛ Caracas
VENEZUELA
GUYANA
Georgetown ⊛
Paramaribo ⊛
⊛ Bogotá
COLOMBIA
SURINAME
Cayenne ⊛
FRENCH GUIANA (Fr.)

Orinoco R.

0°
⊛ Quito
ECUADOR

ATLANTIC
OCEAN

Amazon River

PERU
BRAZIL

Lima ⊛

La Paz
⊛ BOLIVIA
Brasília ⊛

20°S
Sucre ⊛

PACIFIC
OCEAN

PARAGUAY
Asunción ⊛

N
W   E
S

ARGENTINA
URUGUAY

Santiago ⊛
CHILE
Buenos
Aires ⊛
⊛ Montevideo

Río de la Plata

40°S

FALKLAND
IS. (Br.)

| 0 | 400 | 800 Miles |
| 0 | 400 | 800 Kilometers |

Modified Chamberlin Trimetric Projection

80°W   60°W   40°W   20°W

■ Elected civilian government, 1975

Date of transition from military to civilian rule:

| ■ 1976– 1980 | ■ 1981– 1985 | ■ 1986– 1990 | ■ 1991– 1995 |

⊛ National capital

Democratic Transition in South America, 1975–1995

Interpreting Maps During the postwar period, many South American countries underwent military coups. Beginning in 1975, however, the nations gradually moved from military to civilian rule.

Skills Assessment: 1. Human Systems What was the last South American country to end military rule? **2. Making Generalizations** In general, which nations first adopted civilian rule?

Chile

Chile had long been noted as a model of stable democracy in Latin America. In the 1970s and 1980s, that changed. In 1970 Chileans elected **Salvador Allende** as president. Allende was the first Marxist to come to power peacefully in the Western Hemisphere. As a socialist, Allende nationalized the country's copper mines and other industries, broke up large estates, and increased wages across the board. His more radical followers seized farms and factories. Before long the Chilean economy was in a dramatic decline, and food shortages had spread. Hard pressed for funds, Allende's government printed more money to meet its needs. By 1972 inflation was rampant. All segments of the Chilean population suffered.

As the economy worsened, discontent and unrest spread. In 1973 military leaders who opposed Allende overthrew the government, with the support of the United States. Allende died in the bloody coup.

Once in control, the military worked quickly to crush opposition. The government jailed or executed many who had opposed the coup. Fearing for their lives, thousands fled into exile. The leader of the coup, **Augusto Pinochet,** dissolved the national legislature, outlawed all political parties, and restricted civil liberties.

The beauty and geographic diversity of Chile is illustrated in this striking image of the Torres del Paine National Park.

Pinochet also ended all government interference in the nation's economy. He allowed it to operate under free-market forces of supply and demand. The high inflation that was common under Allende declined significantly, but unemployment rose. During the early 1980s unemployment ranged at or near 20 percent throughout Chile. At the same time, however, increased foreign investment helped Pinochet's economic program to take hold. By the late 1980s prosperity had returned to Chile.

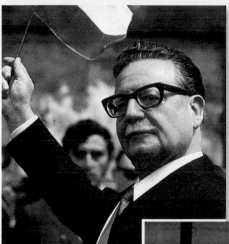

Salvador Allende (top) was killed in a military coup that brought Augusto Pinochet (below) to power.

Even so, civil unrest plagued the country. Pinochet responded with repressive measures. Then, to strengthen his hold on power, he called for a plebiscite, or special vote, in 1988 to determine whether he should remain in power. Pinochet expected to win, but nearly 55 percent of the voters called for him to step down. Accepting defeat, Pinochet set an election for 1989. A coalition candidate, Patricio Aylwin Azócar, was elected president. Pinochet, however, remained in control of Chile's army until 1998.

The nation's economy continued to grow under Aylwin Azócar and his successor, Eduardo Frei Ruiz-Tagle. Although the nation struggled with poverty and widespread pollution, the Chilean economy grew for 14 straight years and became one of the strongest in Latin America. In January 2000 Ricardo Lagos Escobar, a socialist, became president. He was the nation's first socialist president since Allende. Two years earlier Pinochet had been arrested in Great Britain on charges of torture and human rights abuses. A Chilean court found Pinochet unfit to stand trial, however, and few people expected that the aging former dictator would ever be tried for his role in violating the rights of his people.

✔ **READING CHECK: Analyzing Information** What measures helped make the Chilean economy one of the most prosperous in Latin America?

SECTION 4 REVIEW

1. **Define** and explain the significance:
   desaparecidos

2. **Identify** and explain the significance:
   Fernando Henrique Cardoso
   Eva Perón
   Juan Perón
   Shining Path
   Alberto Fujimori
   Salvador Allende
   Augusto Pinochet

3. **Sequencing** Copy the chart below. Complete it to show the order of Brazil's leaders and the dates they took power.

Leader	Leader	Leader	Leader
Jaõa Goulart			Fernando Cardoso
Year	Year	Year	Year
1961			1994

4. **Finding the Main Idea**

   a. Why did the Argentine military's "dirty war" occur?

   b. What did MRTA and Shining Path hope to achieve in Peru?

   c. What role did Augusto Pinochet play in recent Chilean history?

5. **Writing and Critical Thinking**

   Identifying Cause and Effect Imagine you are a reporter. Write an article detailing the reasons for and the effects of the drug trade in Colombia.
   Consider:
   • why Colombians started growing crops for drugs
   • what has happened in Colombia as a result
   • how the Colombian government has been affected

Homework Practice Online
go.hrw.com
keyword: SH3 HP25

Creating a Time Line

Copy the time line below onto a sheet of paper. Complete the time line by filling in the events, individuals, and dates from the chapter that you think were significant. Pick three events and explain why you think they were significant.

| 1945 | 1975 | present |

Writing a Summary

Using standard grammar, spelling, sentence structure, and punctuation, write an overview of the events in the chapter.

Identifying People and Ideas

Identify the following terms or individuals and explain their significance:

1. monoculture
2. NAFTA
3. Sandinistas
4. contras
5. Oscar Arias
6. Fidel Castro
7. Operation Bootstrap
8. Eva Perón
9. desaparecidos
10. Augusto Pinochet

Understanding the Main Ideas

SECTION 1 *(pp. 718–722)*

Facing New Challenges

1. What political forces emerged in Latin America after World War II, and how did they affect each region?
2. What economic struggles did the nations face after World War II?

SECTION 2 *(pp. 723–729)*

Mexico and Central America

3. How did Mexico's economic problems affect emigration?
4. How was wealth distributed in Central America? Who had it and who did not have it?

SECTION 3 *(pp. 730–736)*

Nations of the Caribbean

5. How have Cuba and Puerto Rico differed since World War II?
6. What economic and political problems have affected Haiti and the Dominican Republic since World War II?

SECTION 4 *(pp. 737–743)*

South America

7. What were the successes and failures of Juan Perón's first presidency?
8. What caused the Colombian drug trade to increase, and how did it affect the country?

Reviewing Themes

1. **Economics** How did poor economic conditions affect political events in Latin America?
2. **Government** What methods did Latin American dictators use to retain their control of a country?
3. **Global Relations** Why has the United States sometimes gotten involved in Latin American political situations?

Thinking Critically

1. **Identifying Cause and Effect** What caused the general population increase in Latin America, and what were its consequences?
2. **Comparing and Contrasting** How were the revolutions in Cuba and Nicaragua similar? How were they different?
3. **Problem Solving** How did Fidel Castro deal with the large number of dissidents in Cuba? Was this a successful approach?
4. **Evaluating** What economic reforms seemed to work best in Latin America? Which seemed to be least effective?

Writing About History

Evaluating Violeta Barrios de Chamorro declared amnesty for many involved in the Nicaraguan civil war. Carlos Menem in Argentina pardoned many of those found guilty of crimes during his country's "dirty war." Write an essay analyzing the effects of these actions and whether they were proper given the historical context. Use the following chart to organize your thoughts before you begin writing.

	Negative	Positive
Effects of amnesty/ pardons		

Building Social Studies Skills

Interpreting a Chart

Study the chart below. Then use the information to answer the questions that follow.

Populations of Selected Latin American Nations, 2003		
Nation	**Population, 2003 (est.)**	**Population Growth Rate (est.)**
Argentina	38.7	+1.0%
Brazil	182.0	+1.1%
Chile	15.7	+1.0%
Mexico	104.9	+1.4%
Peru	28.4	+1.6%

(All figures are projected, shown in millions, rounded to nearest 100,000)

1. Which statement is most accurate based on the information in the chart?

   a. Peru is the fastest-growing nation in Latin America.

   b. Chile is growing at a faster rate than is Peru.

   c. Brazil's population is more than twice as large as Mexico's population.

   d. Not all the nations shown experienced increased population growth between 2000 and 2001.

2. What impact might population growth in Latin America have on the developing economies of the region? Give specific examples.

Identifying a Point of View

Read the following quote by anthropologist Jason Clay about indigenous—or native—people living in Brazil. Then answer the questions.

> "Modern technology in the form of helicopters, satellite surveys, and telecommunications equipment has enabled states and corporations to make detailed surveys of the Earth. Even the most isolated indigenous societies are now being probed in a one-sided, involuntary exposure to the rest of the world. . . . For example, in late 1987 gold was found on the lands of the 8,000 forest-dwelling Yanomami Indians of northern Brazil. Within eight months nearly 30,000 Brazilian prospectors had invaded the region to seek their fortunes."

3. Which of the following statements best describes the author's point of view?

   a. He is against the use of helicopters, satellite surveys, and telecommunications equipment.

   b. He does not like the fact that modern society is destroying the land and lifestyles of indigenous people.

   c. He is against states and corporations surveying the Earth.

   d. He thinks Brazil allowed too many prospectors into the region where the Yanomami live.

4. Why might the Brazilian government have a viewpoint different from the author's concerning indigenous people? Give specific reasons.

Alternative Assessment

Building Your Portfolio

Link to TODAY

Government

Political power has changed hands frequently in Latin America. Using your textbook and other sources, find out how many governments in the region came to power from coups or revolutions, whether these governments are secure, and if any are dictatorships. Make a chart that shows the nations, their leaders, how they gained power, and whether or not they are dictatorships.

🖃 internet connect

Internet Activity: go.hrw.com
KEYWORD: SH3 WH25

Choose a topic on Latin America Since 1945 to:

• learn about current events in Latin America.

• analyze Mexico's political choices and decisions since 1945 and how they are reflected in Mexico today.

• research current statistics on per capita gross domestic product, major exports, and major imports of Mexico, Honduras, El Salvador, Belize, Costa Rica, Nicaragua, and Haiti. Create a database for comparison.

1969–Present

The Superpowers in the Modern Era

Apollo *and* Soyuz *crew members during docking.*

1970
Politics
National Guard troops fire on students protesting the Vietnam War at Kent State University.

1973
Global Events
U.S. combat troops withdraw from Vietnam.

1973
Business and Finance
An OPEC oil embargo leads to a U.S. energy crisis.

1976
Daily Life
The United States celebrates its bicentennial.

c. 1978
The Arts
"Disco" music and dancing are popular.

1980
Politics
Ronald Reagan becomes president of the United States.

1982
Global Events
Argentina and Great Britain fight the Falklands War.

1970   **1980**

1970
The Arts
Russian writer Aleksandr Solzhenitsyn wins the Nobel Prize for literature.

1972
Politics
The Watergate break-in occurs.

1975
Science and Technology
The *Apollo* and *Soyuz* space-craft dock in orbit.

1974
Politics
Richard Nixon resigns as U.S. president.

c. 1979
Global Events
Diplomatic relations officially open between China and the United States.

1979
Politics
Margaret Thatcher becomes prime minister of Great Britain.

Vietnam War Memorial

President Richard M. Nixon

Build on What You Know

As the nations of Latin America struggled to develop their economies after World War II, they endured political upheaval. In this chapter, you will learn how the final decades of the 1900s were also turbulent times in the industrialized nations of North America and Europe. The Soviet Union, formerly one of the world's superpowers, dissolved into separate states. The nations of Western Europe moved closer toward union, and the fall of communism reawakened ethnic divisions in Eastern Europe. The United States and Canada confronted challenges at home.

Russian president Boris Yeltsin at a Moscow rally, 1993

Newspaper headline announcing the election of George W. Bush

1991
Global Events
The Soviet Union dissolves.

1991
Global Events
The United States leads the Persian Gulf War against Iraq.

2001
Politics
George W. Bush becomes president of the United States after a disputed election.

1986
Science and Technology
The Chernobyl nuclear accident occurs in the Soviet Union.

1992
Politics
Bill Clinton becomes the president of the United States.

1995
Science and Technology
The U.S. space shuttle *Atlantis* docks with the Russian space station *Mir*.

1990

2000

1990
Global Events
East and West Germany reunite.

1993
Business and Finance
The nations of the European Economic Community implement the Maastricht Treaty, ending trade barriers.

2001
Global Events
On September 11, terrorists attack the World Trade Center and the Pentagon.

New York City's Manhattan Island following the terrorist attack on September 11, 2001

What's Your Opinion?

Themes Journal *Do you* **agree** *or* **disagree** *with the following statements? Support your point of view in your journal.*

Government A nation that maintains strong government control over the people is a strong nation.

Economics Wealth should be shared equally by all members of a society.

Global Relations It is permissible to dominate another country for its own good.

The Industrial Powers of North America

READ TO DISCOVER

1. How did the Vietnam War and the Watergate scandal affect political attitudes in the United States?
2. What changes have occurred in the economy of the United States since 1970?
3. How did American foreign policy change in the 1970s, 1980s, and 1990s?
4. What major challenges did Canada face in the late 1900s?

DEFINE

détente
weapons of mass destruction

IDENTIFY

Richard Nixon
Vietnamization
Watergate scandal
Jimmy Carter
Ronald Reagan
Iran-contra affair
Bill Clinton
George W. Bush
Carter Doctrine
Pierre Trudeau
Meech Lake Accord

WHY IT MATTERS TODAY

Watergate was only one scandal to affect American presidents in recent times. Use CNNnews.com or other **current event** sources to find out about investigations the U.S. Congress conducted during the Reagan and Clinton administrations. Record your findings in your journal.

CNN student News.com

The Main Idea
The United States and Canada faced challenging political, economic, and foreign policy issues in the 1970s, 1980s, and 1990s.

The Story Continues *"Our constitution works. Our great republic is a government of laws and not of men. Here the people rule."* *With these words, President Gerald Ford tried to renew the American people's faith in their government following a national scandal. The next few decades would see the United States confront other challenges both within and outside its borders.*

Ending the Vietnam War

The war in Vietnam was still raging when Republican **Richard Nixon** became President in 1969. Hoping to avoid complete defeat, Nixon searched for ways to end America's involvement in the conflict "with honor."

Nixon planned to withdraw American forces from Vietnam. In a process called **Vietnamization,** he planned for the South Vietnamese to take over the fighting as American troops gradually withdrew. By 1973 there were only about 40,000 American troops left in Vietnam. At the same time Nixon used military pressure to force communist leaders to accept peace on American terms. He ordered the invasion of Cambodia in 1970 and increased the bombing of North Vietnam. On January 27, 1973, communist leaders accepted an agreement called the Paris Peace Accords. This agreement stated that all U.S. and allied forces would leave Vietnam in exchange for the release of all prisoners of war. Within months all major combat units were back home, although some troops remained until 1975.

The Vietnam War had a negative impact on the United States. It cost many lives and strained the nation's economy. Moreover, communist forces won control of South Vietnam in 1975. Thus the United States failed to achieve its main goal in the war—preventing the unification of a communist Vietnam.

The war also divided the American people. During the Nixon administration the antiwar movement gained strength. Actions such as the invasion of Cambodia appeared to contradict Nixon's promise to end the war. Demonstrations against the war at college campuses became common. Some of these protests turned violent or even deadly. In 1970 National Guard troops fired on students at Kent State University in Ohio, killing four people. Eleven days later two more students were killed in a protest at Jackson State

The image of young woman crying over the body of a student killed at Kent State University expressed the horror of the event.

College in Mississippi. The government's claims of success in Vietnam proved to be exaggerated. Many Americans began to question the trustworthiness of their leaders.

✔ **READING CHECK: Problem Solving** How did Nixon attempt to end American involvement in Vietnam?

Watergate and Its Legacy

After Vietnam many Americans had become disillusioned with their government. This situation worsened as a result of a major political scandal involving President Nixon.

In 1972 burglars were caught breaking into the headquarters of the Democratic National Committee at the Watergate hotel in Washington, D.C. The *Washington Post* newspaper charged that officials of President Nixon's reelection campaign had planned the break-in. A U.S. Senate investigation revealed that an illegal secret fund had been used to conceal the burglary's connection to high-level White House aides. It soon became clear that Nixon had known about and approved this cover-up. Facing impeachment by Congress, Nixon resigned his office in August of 1974. His vice president, Gerald R. Ford, took power.

The **Watergate scandal** shook many Americans' faith in their government. President Ford's decision to pardon Nixon did not help restore public confidence. As a result of Watergate, many people began to associate Washington politics with dishonesty and corruption. To combat this perception several candidates for the presidency after Watergate campaigned as "outsiders" with no ties to Washington. They promised to clean up corruption in the political system. In 1976 Democrat **Jimmy Carter,** a former governor of Georgia, was elected president. Carter proved to be a man of high integrity, but his presidency was troubled. The U.S. economy remained sluggish, and Carter suffered setbacks in foreign policy. In 1979 Muslim militants seized the American embassy in Iran, leading to a lengthy hostage crisis.

In 1980 Carter lost to another Washington outsider—conservative Republican **Ronald Reagan,** the former governor of California. Reagan's optimistic slogans lifted the spirits of many Americans, helping him win reelection in 1984. However, during Reagan's second term a scandal known as the **Iran-contra affair** came to public attention. Members of Reagan's National Security Council staff had arranged the sale of weapons to Iran in exchange for the release of U.S. hostages in Lebanon. Money from these sales was then used to fund Nicaraguan rebels called contras, against the wishes of Congress.

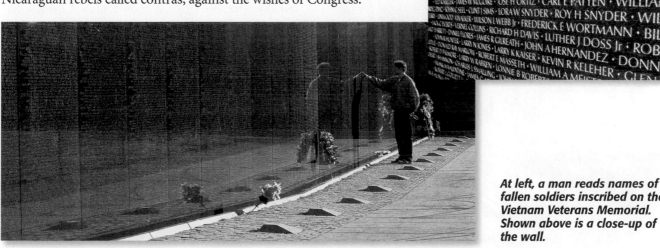

At left, a man reads names of fallen soldiers inscribed on the Vietnam Veterans Memorial. Shown above is a close-up of the wall.

Holt Researcher

go.hrw.com

KEYWORD: Holt Researcher

FreeFind: George W. Bush

After reading more about George W. Bush on the Holt Researcher, write an outline for a campaign commercial explaining how his background prepared him for the presidency.

Reagan's vice president, George Bush was elected in 1988. Although Bush won praise for his leadership during the Persian Gulf War, an economic recession caused growing concern among voters. In 1992 **Bill Clinton,** the Democratic governor of Arkansas, became president. Clinton proved popular with the public and won a second term in 1996. However, his image was harmed by questionable financial dealings and accusations of sexual misconduct. In December 1998 the Senate voted to impeach Clinton for lying to a grand jury. In February 1999 the Senate acquitted Clinton of the charges against him, but the scandal had weakened Clinton's administration. In November 2000 Bush's son, **George W. Bush,** ran against Clinton's vice president, Al Gore. After a closely disputed election that took several weeks to resolve, Bush won the presidency.

✔ **READING CHECK: Identifying Cause and Effect** How did the Watergate scandal affect American politics?

The U.S. Economy

During the late 1960s government spending soared to finance the Great Society programs and the Vietnam War. At the same time energy costs and prices for other goods were rising. This led to inflation—a general increase in prices and a decline in the buying power of the dollar. The instability of the U.S. economy became a cause for concern in the 1970s.

Attempts to stabilize the economy. Efforts made throughout the 1970s to stabilize the economy were unsuccessful. President Nixon tried to stimulate the economy with tax changes. However, his policies led to stagflation, a combination of decreased economic activity, high unemployment, and rising prices. Presidents Ford and Carter tried to fight stagflation through tax cuts, but the problem persisted throughout the 1970s.

A recession in the early 1980s finally brought inflation down as Ronald Reagan took office. To increase economic activity Reagan called for tax cuts that would encourage consumer spending and business investment while borrowing heavily from the national debt. By the mid-1980s unemployment had dropped and the economy began a period of sustained growth. However, the debts of the U.S. government had grown greatly. Until the late 1980s the government spent more money than it took in through taxes. To make up the difference the government had to borrow money, often from foreign lenders. As the debt and interest on it grew, many American leaders became increasingly concerned.

Finally in the late 1990s, economic growth made a balanced budget possible for the first time in almost 30 years. After a brief downturn in the early 1990s, the economy stayed strong for the rest of that decade. Boosted by growth in technology industries and a record rise in the stock market, the boom of the 1990s marked one of the longest and strongest periods of economic growth the country had ever seen.

The changing U.S. economy. Changes in the world economy significantly affected the U.S. economy. In the 1970s and 1980s, the United States began to lose its lead in heavy industry. American shipbuilders, automakers, and steel companies found it more difficult to compete with

The computer industry helped fuel the economic boom of the 1990s.

companies in countries such as Germany and Japan, resulting in job loss in the 1980s. The decline in heavy industry meant that the United States had to import more goods than it exported, creating a trade deficit. Through the 1980s and 1990s, American products dominated the fields of aerospace engineering, pharmaceuticals, and information technology, creating new jobs that outpaced the loss of jobs in heavy industry.

By the end of 2000 a downturn in Asian economies affected the U.S. economy, and worried investors sold off stocks, leading to a decline in U.S. stock market prices. A slowdown in growth among technology companies marked a gradual end to the boom and despite high expectations among Internet entrepreneurs, the "dot-com" bubble burst, weakening the economy and causing widespread job loss.

As unemployment and corporate fraud rose, consumer confidence and the stock market dropped in 2002. Two multi-billion dollar companies, Enron and WorldCom, were forced to declare bankruptcy when the discovery of illegal accounting practices in their operations caused their stock prices to plummet. The stock market climbed back up by the end of 2003 as economic growth improved and business profits rose. The unemployment rate, however, remained stubbornly high.

✔ **READING CHECK: Comparing** How did the U.S. economy of the 1970s compare with the U.S. economy of the 1990s?

Energy. The cost and availability of energy plays a large role in the U.S. economy. Fossil fuels such as coal, natural gas, and oil have generally been the nation's main sources of energy. By the 1970s the United States was importing much of its oil, particularly from the Middle East. This created problems. An embargo by oil producing countries in 1973 and the Iranian revolution of 1979 each caused oil shortages and price hikes. These events added to U.S. economic instability in the years following Vietnam.

Americans began to look to other sources of energy. Greater use of coal was one possibility, but would cause further air pollution. Some Americans pushed for the development of clean, renewable sources of energy, such as solar and wind power. Nuclear power was considered as an alternative to oil, but critics worried about its safety. After serious accidents at the Three Mile Island power plant in Pennsylvania and the Chernobyl plant in the Soviet Union, support for nuclear energy eroded.

In the 1990s oil companies began to tap into new oil deposits in Alaska, the Gulf of Mexico, and the Caspian Sea. Oil remained the main source of energy for the United States and the world. Despite concerns over dependency on foreign oil, American consumption of oil continued to increase. The economic prosperity of the 1990s did little to encourage energy conservation and sales of sport utility vehicles that got very poor gas mileage increased. In 2001 gas prices soared to record levels. This increase, coupled with the slowing economy, may have led some people to trade in their large vehicles for more fuel-efficient cars.

While gasoline prices for vehicles increased, some parts of the country experienced power outages due to a shortage of energy sources. To save power, California instituted "rolling blackouts," planned power outages designed to preserve the overall amount of energy available. In August 2003, an overloaded electrical grid in the eastern United States caused a power surge that resulted in a blackout in the country's northeast region and portions of Canada.

✔ **READING CHECK: Problem Solving** How should U.S. leaders deal with energy concerns in the coming years?

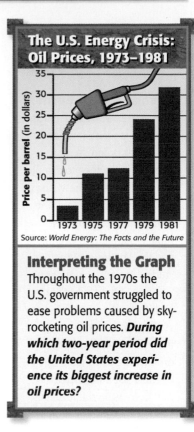

The U.S. Energy Crisis: Oil Prices, 1973–1981

Source: *World Energy: The Facts and the Future*

Interpreting the Graph
Throughout the 1970s the U.S. government struggled to ease problems caused by skyrocketing oil prices. *During which two-year period did the United States experience its biggest increase in oil prices?*

Gasoline Consumption 1970 vs. 2000

Total gas consumption	
Then	92.3 billion gallons
Now	162.3 billion gallons

Average annual consumption per car	
Then	688 gallons
Now	547 gallons

Average gas mileage	
Then	
cars	13.5 miles per gallon
trucks	5.5 miles per gallon
Now	
cars	22.0 miles per gallon
trucks	5.8 miles per gallon

Interpreting the Chart
Despite concerns over dependency on oil, total American gasoline consumption for vehicles increased between 1970 and 2000. *What does the chart imply about the reasons why gasoline consumption has increased?*

During the 1960s and 1970s, both the United States and the Soviet Union sent out deep-space probes to explore the solar system. The *Viking* probes landed on Mars. The *Voyager* vehicles flew by Jupiter, Saturn, and Uranus, and the *Venera* explorations studied the surface of Venus.

In 1973 the United States built the first successful space station, *Skylab*. A space station is a manned outpost in orbit where astronauts can conduct scientific experiments. In 1986 the Russians sent up the space station *Mir*.

Other U.S. unmanned explorations of Mars include the *Pathfinder,* the rover vehicles *Sojourner* in 1997, and *Spirit* and *Opportunity* in 2004. In 2003, China launched its first manned spacecraft.

Understanding Geography

What can scientists learn from studying the geography of places beyond the earth?

Changes in American Foreign Policy

American foreign policy underwent several changes in the late 1900s. In the 1970s, American leaders sought to ease the tensions of the Cold War by improving relations with communist countries.

U.S.-Soviet relations. In 1972 President Nixon became the first American president to visit Moscow. During that visit Nixon and Soviet leader Leonid Brezhnev signed the Strategic Arms Limitation Treaty, or SALT. This treaty limited each nation's nuclear weapon supplies. The two nations also agreed to cooperate in other areas. This general improvement in Soviet-American relations became known as **détente,** a French word meaning "easing of strain."

Presidents Ford and Carter continued the policy of détente throughout the 1970s. By the end of that decade, however, tensions flared again. President Carter, who felt strongly about human rights, protested the harsh way that the Soviet government treated those who opposed its policies. He also criticized Soviet and Cuban involvement in civil wars in Angola and Ethiopia. In December 1979 the Soviets invaded nearby Afghanistan. This invasion threatened the security of the oil-rich Persian Gulf. In 1980 President Carter made a statement called the **Carter Doctrine.** He declared that the United States would regard any attempts by outside forces to control the Persian Gulf as an assault on U.S. interests. The United States, he said, might even respond with military force. Carter then limited trade with the Soviets and called for a boycott of the 1980 Olympic Games in Moscow.

Détente came to an end. Some Americans believed the reduction in U.S. military forces after Vietnam had encouraged Soviet aggression. In the early 1980s President Reagan increased military spending, updated the U.S. nuclear arsenal, and boosted aid to anticommunist forces overseas. The Soviet Union tried to keep up with U.S. military spending.

By the mid-1980s new Soviet leadership pursued a friendlier relationship with the United States. American and Soviet leaders met several times and finally agreed to eliminate certain nuclear weapons. The Soviet Union reduced its military presence around the world, withdrawing from Afghanistan in 1989. When the Soviet Union officially dismantled in 1991, the United States was left as the world's only superpower.

The "new world order." Threats to world security existed throughout the world. Iraq and other countries tried to acquire **weapons of mass destruction**—nuclear, chemical, and biological weapons. The spread of such weapons remained a major concern throughout the 1990s. President George Bush urged the United Nations to work toward a "new world order," in which nations would cooperate to defend weaker countries.

The United States played an active role in world politics in the mid-1990s. Presidents George Bush and Bill Clinton both attempted to settle the ongoing Arab-Israeli dispute. U.S. policy also concerned itself with the international issues of trade, terrorism, and the environment.

Earth, as viewed from the space shuttle

Shown at left is a photo of the damaged U.S. spy plane that landed in the Hainan province of China in 2001. Below, members of the crew describe their experience during a press conference after their return to U.S. territory.

Relations with China. U.S. relations with the People's Republic of China improved steadily during the 1970s and 1980s. In 1972 President Nixon visited China, beginning a new period of diplomacy. By 1979 the U.S. had established full diplomatic relations with China. Many Americans saw opportunities for investment and trade in China's rapidly growing economy. The fact that China and the United States both distrusted the Soviet Union also helped bring the two nations together.

By the late 1980s, however, the nations found themselves at odds over China's treatment of its own citizens. Many Americans criticized China's record on human rights, especially after the Chinese government killed and wounded perhaps thousands of pro-democracy demonstrators at Tiananmen Square in 1989. Moreover, China continued to sell advanced weapons to potentially hostile nations like Iran, while building up its own military. Such issues became part of a larger debate among U.S. politicians. Some wanted to improve trading relations between the two countries, while others wanted to wait until China had improved its human rights record.

Tensions between China and the United States spiked in 2001 when a U.S. spy plane collided with a Chinese fighter jet, killing the Chinese pilot. After the United States apologized for the incident, relations improved. They continue to do so, despite ongoing differences over human rights, trade, missile defense, and the status of Taiwan.

✔ **READING CHECK: Identifying Cause and Effect** What issues affected U.S. foreign policy from the 1970s through the year 2001?

Canada

Geographically, Canada is the world's second-largest country. It possesses a wealth of raw materials, and its citizens enjoy a high standard of living. Still, Canada faced political and economic challenges in the late 1900s.

The leader of the Liberal Party, **Pierre Trudeau,** was prime minister of Canada from 1968 to 1979, when he was defeated by Joseph Clark, a Progressive Conservative. Trudeau won re-election in 1980. Trudeau focused on maintaining Canada's federal union. In the early 1980s a recession led many Canadians to call for economic reforms. In 1984 the Progressive Conservative Party won a general election. The new prime minister, Brian Mulroney, attempted to strengthen the economy, but the recession deepened into the early 1990s. In 1993 the Conservatives replaced Mulroney with Kim Campbell, Canada's first woman prime minister. Later that year, the Conservatives lost a general election and Jean Chrétien of the Liberal Party became Canada's new prime minister. Chrétien served for 10 years and in 2003 was succeeded by Paul Martin, leader of the Liberal Party.

Separatism. One of the major issues facing Canada was that of French Canadian separatism. Most Canadians are of English-speaking descent. However, in the province of Quebec, French-speaking Canadians form the majority. Throughout Canada's history this group has struggled to preserve its distinct culture, which is based heavily on French traditions.

In the 1960s French Canadians began to demand cultural recognition, as well as more power in local and national government. Prime Minister Trudeau promised to protect French Canadian culture while still keeping Canada united. In 1969 he helped pass the Official Languages Act, making both French and English official languages of Canada.

For many French Canadians this was not enough. The Parti Québécois wanted complete separation of Quebec from Canada. In 1976 this party won control of the government of Quebec. The Parti Québécois explains their goals in the following way:

❝Our program proposed two elements of association between Quebec and Canada [after independence]: first a customs union, then a monetary union.

The customs union recognizes simply that Quebec exports an important part of its production to the other Canadian provinces and that these provinces have essential markets in Quebec. Nothing would be more ridiculous than to begin independence with a tariff war between the two countries....In the event of a monetary union. . . . [all] that is required is that, when Quebec becomes independent, the two new countries—each with its own monetary institutions—agree to coordinate their policies closely....❞

Pierre Vallieres, *The Revolutionary Process in Quebec*

Canadian leaders met at Meech Lake in 1987. In an agreement known as the **Meech Lake Accord,** they agreed to accept Quebec as a "distinct society" within Canada. However, the accord failed to become part of Canada's constitution. Many Canadians felt that it gave too much power to Quebec. The separatists renewed their efforts and in 1995 held a referendum on separation. The result was very close—

just under 50 percent of the people of Quebec voted in favor of separation. French Canadian separatism remains a hotly debated issue.

Relations with the United States. Most Canadians live within several hundred miles of the border with the United States. This border is the longest undefended international frontier in the world. Relations between Canada and the United States became very close during the 1900s. The flow of trade across the Canadian-United States border remains the heaviest bilateral trade in the world.

Officials from Mexico, the United States, and Canada sign the North American Free Trade Agreement (NAFTA) in 1992.

Even so, the two countries have at times had disagreements. Disputes sometimes arise over fishing rights in the Atlantic and Pacific. Environmental concerns were raised when pollution from American smokestacks was found to be contributing to acid rain in northeastern Canada. The greatest strain, however, stems from Canada's concern about U.S. involvement in its economy.

Many Canadians have been unsure about free trade. In 1988 the United States-Canada Free Trade Agreement proposed to eliminate almost all tariff barriers between the two nations. Opponents worried that the agreement would give the United States too much control over the Canadian economy. The debate grew even more heated in the early 1990s, when the United States suggested adding Mexico to the agreement at a time when Canada had just gone into a deep recession. In the end Canada joined with the United States and Mexico in 1992 to sign the North American Free Trade Agreement (NAFTA). This agreement went into effect on January 1, 1994.

✔ **READING CHECK: Summarizing** How have U.S.-Canadian relations been throughout the 1990s? How can you tell?

SECTION 1 REVIEW

1. **Define** and explain the significance:
   détente
   weapons of mass destruction

2. **Identify** and explain the significance:
   Richard Nixon
   Vietnamization
   Watergate scandal
   Jimmy Carter
   Ronald Reagan
   Iran-contra affair
   Bill Clinton
   George W. Bush
   Carter Doctrine
   Pierre Trudeau
   Meech Lake Accord

3. **Categorizing** Copy the chart below. Use it to describe the U.S. economy during the 1970s, 1980s, and 1990s.

	1970s	1980s	1990s
Economic activity			

4. **Finding the Main Idea**
   a. How did many Americans feel about political leaders after Watergate?
   b. What actions of the Chinese government have created tension with the United States?
   c. Why were the Meech Lake Accords not approved in Canada?

5. **Writing and Critical Thinking**
   Supporting a Point of View Imagine that you are a Canadian citizen who opposes the separatist movement in Quebec. Write a newspaper editorial explaining your opposition to independence for Quebec.
   Consider:
   • why many French Canadians seek independence
   • why many Canadians oppose Quebec independence
   • how Quebec's independence would affect Canada

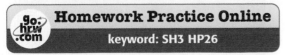

Homework Practice Online

keyword: SH3 HP26

SECTION 2

Europe

READ TO DISCOVER

❶ How did Margaret Thatcher's leadership affect Great Britain?

❷ What challenges did European nations face in the late 1900s?

❸ What steps did European nations take toward unity in the late 1900s?

IDENTIFY

Margaret Thatcher
Tony Blair
Georges Pompidou
François Mitterand
Willy Brandt
Ostpolitik
Helmut Kohl
Juan Carlos
Helsinki Accords
Maastricht Treaty

▶ WHY IT MATTERS TODAY

The European Union has stirred controversy. Use **CNN Student News.com** or other **current event** sources to find out how Europeans today feel about the union. Record your findings in your journal.

CNN Student News.com

The Main Idea
Many nations in Europe moved toward political and economic integration in the late 1900s.

The Story Continues *By the end of the 1960s, Great Britain faced severe economic problems. Outdated factories and low productivity made it hard to compete with other industrialized nations. The economy was further strained as the government raised taxes and increased borrowing. Unemployment and inflation remained high throughout the 1970s. Into this situation came a new leader with a new vision for Britain. "Let me give you my vision," Margaret Thatcher once said, "A man's right to work as he will, to save what he earns, to have property, to have the state as a servant and not as a master; these are the British inheritance."*

Great Britain

With a decisive victory in the 1979 election, the Conservative Party came to power. The party's leader, **Margaret Thatcher,** became the first female prime minister in Britain's history. Thatcher argued that the government regulated industry too closely and taxed people too heavily. She worked to reduce the role of the government in the economy.

Thatcherism. Thatcher reduced government funding of many social programs, and eliminated some completely. This prompted her critics to charge that her real goal was to abolish the British welfare system. Thatcher continued to ease government controls on business, converting many government-owned industries into private companies. She also reduced the power of labor unions in the economy.

The economy had begun to improve by the mid-1980s, especially in southern England. The development of new oil fields in the North Sea helped in this recovery. However, many areas of northern England did not benefit from the economic rebound. In this industrial region unemployment remained very high. This was partly the result of the same economic shift seen in the United States, from heavy industry to an economy based on services. Thatcher's critics charged that her policies favored the wealthy and created an unequal society.

Thatcher brought the same tough approach to her foreign policy. In 1982 she ordered troops to defend the British-held Falkland Islands after Argentina invaded them. She maintained close ties to the United States. In 1990 she played an important role in forming the international coalition that forced the Iraqi army out of Kuwait.

Prime Minister Margaret Thatcher and President Ronald Reagan were similar in their approaches to politics and economics.

In the late 1980s Thatcher began to lose support as the British economy weakened. Her downfall came when she implemented the so-called poll tax. This tax replaced property taxes as the source of funds for local government. The poll tax charged all taxpayers the same percentage, regardless of their income level. The tax proved very unpopular with the British people. Opponents within her own Conservative Party challenged Thatcher's leadership. Realizing she could not win reelection, Thatcher resigned in November 1990.

To replace Thatcher the Conservatives chose John Major, a member of her cabinet. On many issues Major was more moderate than Thatcher. He believed in forging closer ties with Europe. The British economy began to pick up again. However, scandals and incompetence in the government led many in Britain to seek new leadership. In 1997 the Labour Party, led by **Tony Blair**, came to power. Blair faced many challenges such as the ongoing conflict in Northern Ireland and the 2003 war in Iraq.

Northern Ireland. When the Republic of Ireland gained independence in 1922, only the territory of Northern Ireland remained part of Britain. People hoped that the ancient ill will between Ireland and Britain would diminish. However, new disagreements emerged. Within Northern Ireland Protestants are in the majority. Over time this majority came to control the government and the economy of Northern Ireland. Lack of political power and economic opportunity created resentment among the Northern Irish Catholics.

In the late 1960s Catholic protests began to turn violent. In the early 1970s the British government sent troops to Northern Ireland to keep the peace. The presence of British soldiers in Northern Ireland soon became permanent.

Throughout the 1970s Catholic and Protestant groups used violence to further their causes. The Irish Republican Army (IRA) has been the most active group. Almost entirely Catholic, the IRA wanted to drive the British out of the north and unite all of Ireland. The IRA took its war beyond Irish borders, staging bombings in British cities and attacking British soldiers in other parts of Europe.

Aside from military force, the British tried to resolve the conflict through political means. The Republic of Ireland gained a voice in the affairs of Northern Ireland with the Anglo-Irish Agreement of 1985, but over time both Protestants and Catholics opposed the pact. In 1993 the British and Irish prime ministers pledged to give Northern Ireland the right to decide its own fate. The IRA declared a cease-fire the following year. Peace talks followed, and in 1998 the Good Friday Peace Accords were signed. Despite efforts to instill power sharing in Northern Ireland, Catholic-Protestant government has been suspended several times since the transfer of power from London in 1999.

✔ **READING CHECK: Summarizing** What caused Margaret Thatcher to lose her political support in Great Britain?

INTERPRETING THE VISUAL RECORD

IRA violence The IRA claimed responsibility for this bus bombing, which occurred in London. *What does the damage seen here suggest about IRA methods?*

France

In 1969 **Georges Pompidou** replaced Charles de Gaulle as president of France. Because the two men had worked together for years, they viewed French interests somewhat similarly. De Gaulle had seen France as a major player in world affairs. Pompidou worked to widen French trade involvement overseas and focused on domestic issues.

Pompidou believed that France should continue to cooperate with its traditional allies. He strengthened ties with the United States and ended French opposition to British membership in the European Economic Community, or EEC. Pompidou also introduced social programs designed to ease the problems that had led to widespread protests in the 1960s. He began an ambitious plan of renovation for the city of Paris. However, he had to curb many of his plans due to an economic crisis brought on by the OPEC oil embargo of 1973.

Pompidou died unexpectedly in 1974, and Valery Giscard d'Estaing became president. He continued Pompidou's foreign policy of cooperation with other countries. Domestically, Giscard d'Estaing reduced state controls on the economy. However, high inflation and unemployment made it impossible for him to implement his programs for social change.

Disappointed with Giscard d'Estaing's failure to bring about prosperity and social change, in 1981 the French people elected socialist **François Mitterand.** France still faced severe economic problems—high inflation, trade deficits, and rising unemployment. Mitterand sought to strengthen the economy by increasing the role of government. Several industries and banks were nationalized, and taxes on the wealthy were raised. Mitterand also expanded government programs for the unemployed. However, by the 1990s Mitterand had moved away from traditional socialist policies.

French foreign policy once again became aggressive under Mitterand. France often provided military assistance to its former colonies in Africa. Mitterand contributed troops to peacekeeping missions in Lebanon and Bosnia in the 1980s and 1990s. French troops also participated in the Gulf War coalition against Iraq.

However, uncertainty about the future affected French voters in the 1990s. Economic problems such as unemployment and recession remained. Immigration of Arabs from North Africa into France became a source of social tension. The French also worried about their ability to compete with the new, powerful Germany. In 1995 Jacques Chirac, the conservative mayor of Paris, became president. Chirac promised a fresh approach to France's economic problems, but encountered difficulty. Many people feared the loss of jobs and income as France dropped barriers to trade with other European countries. Moreover, in 1996 Chirac provoked international protests by testing nuclear weapons in the South Pacific. Chirac's party suffered a setback in the elections of 1997, and as a result a coalition government was formed. Chirac, a conservative, remained president, while Lionel Jospin, a socialist, became prime minister

✔ **READING CHECK: Finding the Main Idea** What was the main factor preventing French leaders from attaining their goals for the country?

François Mitterand, the first socialist president of France, served for two six-year terms.

Germany

By the late 1960s West Germany had become a major economic power. Even so, it faced political problems. Relations with East Germany, the Soviet Union, and other communist countries posed challenges.

A member of the liberal Social Democratic Party, **Willy Brandt** was elected Chancellor in 1969. He believed West Germany had to stay allied with the rest of Western Europe and the United States. However, he also wanted to reduce tensions between his country and the communist nations of Eastern Europe. His effort to improve these relations was called **Ostpolitik,** German for "Eastern Policy." This policy led to treaties with Poland and the Soviet Union in 1970, and to other agreements. In 1974 Helmut Schmidt succeeded Brandt and continued Ostpolitik. He also pursued closer political and economic ties with Western Europe. In the early 1980s, however, an economic recession hit West Germany. The people faced rising unemployment and inflation.

The economic troubles led to political change. In 1982 the Christian Democrats, led by **Helmut Kohl,** took power. Kohl promised to return the country to prosperity by following conservative policies like those of Ronald Reagan and Margaret Thatcher. He also made changes in foreign policy, committing more firmly to the NATO alliance and strengthening relations with the United States.

Kohl's greatest challenge was the reunification of Germany. After the Berlin Wall fell in 1989, talks were held between the two Germanies, Britain, France, the Soviet Union, and the United States. In October of 1990 East and West Germany became one nation again. The goodwill generated by this great change helped Kohl win reelection two months later. However, Kohl began to lose popularity as German citizens faced the difficult realities of reunification. Revitalizing the former East Germany became a great burden on the German economy in the 1990s. Kohl remained in power until 1998, when he was defeated by Gerhard Schroeder of the Social Democratic Party. Schroeder pledged to reduce unemployment and stimulate the economy.

✔ **READING CHECK: Summarizing** What was the goal of the policy of Ostpolitik?

Young people in Berlin wave German flags in celebration as the reunification of Germany takes effect in October of 1990.

Northern and Southern Europe

The other nations of Europe confronted their share of problems brought on by the postwar period, the Cold War, and economic instability. The late 1900s brought prosperity to the smaller nations of northern Europe.

Northern Europe. The tiny principalities of Monaco and Liechtenstein kept their autonomy. Belgium, Luxembourg, and the Netherlands worked together to foster European unity. During the Cold War, NATO members Denmark, Iceland, and Norway played an important role in helping defend Western Europe. The nations of Finland, Sweden, Austria, and Switzerland chose to remain neutral throughout the Cold War, but stayed on good terms with the rest of Western Europe.

Italy. The worldwide economic recession of the 1970s hit Italy hard, leading to high unemployment and runaway inflation. This created great political turmoil. Of the 14 political parties, none could gain a majority in the Italian parliament. Therefore governments had to be formed through coalitions. Few of these coalitions lasted very long, making it difficult to solve the nation's problems. A wave of terrorism at the end of the decade only added to Italy's problems.

Italy's situation improved during the 1980s. Many terrorist organizations were defeated, and free-market reforms stimulated the economy. However, the economy was also strained by Italy's huge national debt. Moreover, a huge gap in wealth existed between the industrialized north and the poor, mostly rural south. Political instability continued into the 1990s. Corruption scandals, some involving organized crime, shook the government. By 1997 reforms in parliament had restored some stability to Italian politics.

Portugal. Portugal made the transition from dictatorship to democracy in the late 1900s. In 1974 a military coup led by Antonio de Spinola ousted dictator Marcello Caetano. Spinola granted independence to most of Portugal's remaining colonies, including Angola and Mozambique. He then resigned, calling for free elections. Portugal faced serious political and economic instability over the next several years. In 1986 Portugal joined the EEC and implemented a series of free-enterprise reforms. These measures helped spur economic growth. Lisbon mayor Jorge Sampaio won the presidency in 1996, and the strong economy continued into the late 1990s.

Juan Carlos is the king of Spain, but his power is limited by parliament and a constitution.

Spain. When dictator Francisco Franco died in 1975, **Juan Carlos** became king. He began restoring democracy to Spain. In 1977 Spain held its first free democratic elections in 40 years. Moderate political parties led by socialists won most of the seats in the Cortes, or Spanish parliament. In 1981 a group of army officers tried to seize control of the government. The attempt failed, but demonstrated the fragility of the new democracy.

Another challenge came from the ongoing separatist movement in the Basque region of Spain. The Basque people, with their own distinct culture and language, have long pushed for independence. In 1980 they won self-government within Spain, but some separatists remain unsatisfied. The Basque separatist group ETA demanded complete independence and used terrorism throughout the 1980s.

Spain faced the same economic problems as other European nations—high inflation and unemployment. Spanish leaders sought to improve their economy through trade. In 1986 Spain joined the EEC. Despite the ongoing Basque separatist issue and lingering economic problems, Spain has become one of the leading democracies in Europe. Conservative Prime Minister José Maria Aznar's Popular Party won a majority in the Cortes in March 2000.

Greece. Greece endured a dark political period during the late 1900s. In 1967 a repressive military group known as the "Colonels" overthrew King Constantine II in a coup. In 1974 the Colonels supported a revolt against the democratically elected government of nearby Cyprus. When this revolt failed, however, the rule of the Colonels in Greece collapsed. In 1974 Greek voters chose to make their country a republic rather than return to monarchy. Andreas Papandreou, a socialist, was elected prime minister in 1981. That same year Greece joined the EEC, but economic problems persisted. Also, in the 1990s Greece's relations with its neighbors Turkey and Macedonia worsened. Papandreou resigned in 1996 due to ill health, and Costas Simitis became prime minister. His new, more conservative government promised closer cooperation with the West.

✔ **READING CHECK: Summarizing** What major political changes took place in Italy, Greece, Spain, and Portugal during the late 1900s?

European Cooperation

In the years after World War II, cooperation between the nations of Europe increased. Organizations such as NATO and the European Economic Community grew in strength and membership. Political changes within Europe in the late 1900s created the possibility for even greater cooperation and union.

The Helsinki Accords. In 1975 some 35 nations—including the United States and the Soviet Union—met in Helsinki, Finland. They discussed topics of security and cooperation in Europe. The meeting resulted in a series of agreements known as the **Helsinki Accords.** These accords gave European nations a new framework for

Living in the Pyrenees Mountains on both sides of the French-Spanish border, the Basque people maintain their own culture and government.

economic and technological cooperation, and provided a peaceful means for settling certain boundary disputes. The agreements also called on all nations to respect basic human rights, such as freedoms of speech and worship. The Helsinki Accords were largely symbolic. However, they provided an important foundation for the democratic movements that swept across Eastern Europe in the 1980s.

NATO. The North Atlantic Treaty Organization (NATO), which had kept Western Europe safe during the Cold War, remained the cornerstone of security in the region as the 1900s drew to a close. However, the organization's policies and future role increasingly came into question. Tensions between Greece and Turkey, both NATO members, eventually led to Greece quitting NATO in 1974. Greece later rejoined, but its relations with other NATO countries remained strained. The United States provoked controversy by deploying nuclear weapons within Europe during the Cold War. Many European nations did not want American nuclear weapons on their soil. At the same time, the United States demanded that other NATO nations pay a larger share of the expense of defending Europe.

NATO's future grew uncertain following the collapse of the Soviet Union in the early 1990s. With no great military threat from the East, critics charged that NATO was no longer needed. Eastern European countries, however, were eager to join NATO to protect against any possible Russian effort to reassert control in the region. Poland,

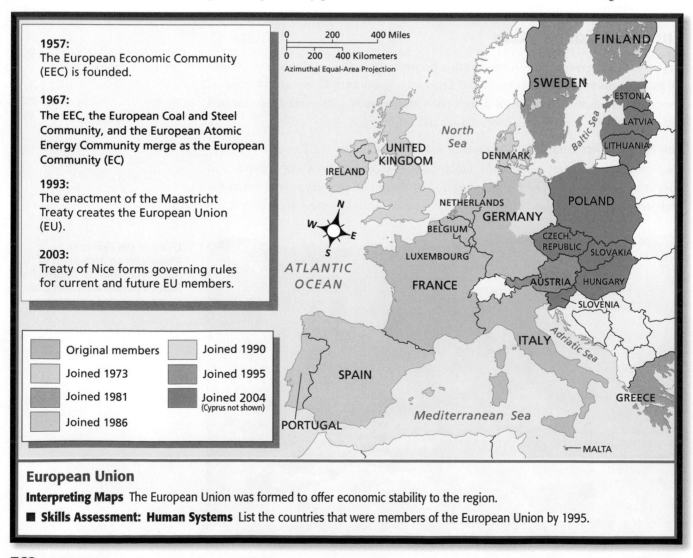

1957:
The European Economic Community (EEC) is founded.

1967:
The EEC, the European Coal and Steel Community, and the European Atomic Energy Community merge as the European Community (EC)

1993:
The enactment of the Maastricht Treaty creates the European Union (EU).

2003:
Treaty of Nice forms governing rules for current and future EU members.

Original members
Joined 1973
Joined 1981
Joined 1986
Joined 1990
Joined 1995
Joined 2004 (Cyprus not shown)

European Union

Interpreting Maps The European Union was formed to offer economic stability to the region.

■ **Skills Assessment: Human Systems** List the countries that were members of the European Union by 1995.

Hungary, and the Czech Republic were welcomed into the alliance in 1999. In 2002, three ex-Soviet republics—Estonia, Latvia, and Lithuania—along with Bulgaria, Romania , Slovakia, and Slovenia were invited to join in 2004.

From EEC to EU. In the 1990s the European Economic Community evolved into the more closely knit European Union (EU). During the 1970s and 1980s, the EEC grew from 6 members to 12. Britain joined, after lengthy negotiations, in 1973, as did Ireland and Denmark. They were followed by Greece in 1981, Spain and Portugal in 1986, and Austria, Finland, and Sweden in the early 1990s. As the EEC grew, members began to work toward common practices regarding taxation, credit, trade, and monetary policy.

In 1993 the EEC countries implemented an agreement called the **Maastricht Treaty,** creating the European Union. With the Maastricht Treaty, members ended trade barriers between their countries, agreed to pursue closer cooperation in defense and foreign relations, and accepted the idea of a common currency. Implementation of the treaty in the 1990s proved difficult, however. Several members of the EEC worried that the EU would undermine their sovereignty. British leaders were especially concerned. Voters in Denmark just barely ratified the Maastricht Treaty, and in Norway EU membership was rejected. By 1995, however, 15 nations had joined the EU. In 2004, 10 more countries joined the EU, bringing the number of member nations to 25. Europe continues to achieve a remarkable degree of unity as it moves forward in the new century.

✔ **READING CHECK: Finding the Main Idea** What were the goals of the Maastricht Treaty?

Shown here are some of the coins and bills of the European Union's currency system.

SECTION 2 REVIEW

1. **Identify** and explain the significance:
   Margaret Thatcher
   Tony Blair
   Georges Pompidou
   François Mitterand
   Willy Brandt
   Ostpolitik
   Helmut Kohl
   Juan Carlos
   Helsinki Accords
   Maastricht Treaty

2. **Sequencing** Copy the chart below. Use it to explain how the move toward European cooperation led from the European Economic Community (EEC) to the European Union (EU).

   EEC → ☐ → ☐ → ☐

3. **Finding the Main Idea**
   a. What issues led to the rise and fall of Margaret Thatcher's party?
   b. What issues universally concerned European countries in the late 1900s?
   c. What problems did NATO encounter in the late 1900s?

4. **Writing and Critical Thinking**
   Contrasting Write an imaginary dialogue between someone who supports the EU concept and someone who opposes it.
   Consider:
   • what European countries can gain from membership in the Union
   • what many Europeans fear losing

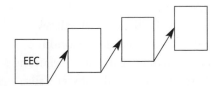

Homework Practice Online
keyword: SH3 HP26

READ TO DISCOVER

❶ What events led to the fall of the Soviet Union?

❷ How did Russia fare under Boris Yeltsin?

❸ How was Eastern Europe affected by the fall of communism?

DEFINE

perestroika
glasnost
ethnic cleansing

IDENTIFY

Leonid Brezhnev
Brezhnev Doctrine
Mikhail Gorbachev
Boris Yeltsin
Commonwealth of
  Independent States (CIS)
Lech Walesa
Vaclav Havel
Dayton Accord

WHY IT MATTERS TODAY

When the Soviet Union dissolved, the former republics were left to fend for themselves economically. Use CNN**News**.com or other **current event** sources to gather information about economic conditions in former Soviet territories. Record your findings in your journal.

CNN**News**.com

The Fall of Communism

The Main Idea
After influencing international politics for half a century, communism lost its hold in Eastern Europe.

The Story Continues *During the 1980s widespread political protests in Poland brought about radical change. As one reporter commented, "Communist reforms, prodded by popular pressure, have moved even faster there than in the Soviet Union. Just weeks ago, Poland's Solidarity union was illegal. Now, [the president of Poland] is ready to ask Solidarity to lead the next government." Similar reforms swept other Eastern European countries at a rapid pace, bringing both promise and risk.*

The Soviet Union Under Brezhnev

Throughout the 1970s **Leonid Brezhnev** led the Soviet Union. He proved to be a forceful leader. With the invasion of Czechoslovakia in 1968, Brezhnev demonstrated that the Soviet government would tolerate no dissent among its satellite nations. He issued the **Brezhnev Doctrine,** stating that the Soviet Union would intervene in any satellite nation that seemed to be moving away from communism. As a result, no satellite government attempted reforms on the scale of the Prague Spring during the Brezhnev years. Brezhnev also suppressed dissent at home. He restricted such basic human rights as freedom of speech, worship, and movement.

While seeking to crush all opposition both domestically and in the Soviet satellites of Eastern Europe, Brezhnev worked to strengthen his country's position in the balance of world power. Through the policy of détente, he tried to stabilize relations with the United States. However, world leaders found it difficult to believe the Soviet Union was working toward peace when it continued to build up its military and support anti-Western movements. The 1979 Soviet invasion of Afghanistan further strained relations with the West.

Meanwhile, the Soviet economy remained inefficient and troubled. Most Soviets experienced a decline in their standard of living under Brezhnev. Agricultural failures, inadequate transportation, and outdated factories all contributed to the dire state of the Soviet economy. Heavy military spending compounded the problem severely. By the time Brezhnev died in 1982, the need for economic reform had become clear and relations with the United States had substantially deteriorated.

Brezhnev and Nixon in 1973

A new debate about the future ensued after Brezhnev died. Older Soviet leaders worried that reform would weaken the nation. They sought to improve the economy without abandoning communism. They named Yuri Andropov, former head of the secret police, to succeed Brezhnev. In poor health, Andropov held office for only about 15 months and was replaced by the aging Konstantin Chernenko, who lasted for little more than a year. After Chernenko's death, a younger generation of leaders finally gained control of the government.

✔ **READING CHECK: Summarizing** What problems did the Soviet Union face under Leonid Brezhnev?

Holt Researcher go.hrw.com

go.hrw.com
KEYWORD: Holt Researcher
FreeFind: Mikhail Gorbachev
After reading more about Mikhail Gorbachev on the Holt Researcher, write a memo as an American diplomat noting how he is different from previous Soviet leaders.

Gorbachev and Reform

In 1985 **Mikhail Gorbachev** became the new leader of the Soviet Union. Gorbachev had a background in agricultural and economic affairs. He began to overhaul the Soviet political and economic systems.

Perestroika and glasnost. Gorbachev began a series of reforms known as **perestroika** (per·uh·STROY·kuh), or "restructuring," and **glasnost** (GLAZ·nohst), meaning "openness." Gorbachev relaxed government control of the economy and eased restrictions on dissent, allowing people to speak freely and read whatever they liked. Recognizing the burden that military spending placed on the Soviet economy, he planned to reduce the size of the armed forces. He also looked for a way to end the unpopular Soviet occupation of Afghanistan.

Gorbachev's reforms won him international praise. Relations improved with the United States, and Gorbachev met with President Reagan. The two signed several arms-reduction agreements. In 1989 Soviet forces withdrew from Afghanistan. At home, however, Gorbachev's programs were slow to take effect and sometimes caused hardship. Perestroika made more consumer goods available, but there were still shortages of basic necessities. In 1990 Gorbachev introduced a plan for a mixed economy, combining private ownership with government control. Hard-line communists, though, pressured him to drop the plan. In 1991 conservative members of the government and military attempted a coup. They arrested Gorbachev, but the president of Russia, **Boris Yeltsin,** raised opposition to the coup. The coup failed, but Gorbachev never recovered his former popularity. Yeltsin emerged as the new leader of reform.

The end of the Soviet Union. Keeping the Soviet Union together became increasingly difficult as Gorbachev's reforms took effect. The freedom of speech provided by glasnost increased tensions between the various Soviet ethnic groups and nationalities. Rival groups could now express opinions they would otherwise have kept to themselves. Ethnic fighting broke out between the Muslim Soviet republic of Azerbaijan and the Christian Soviet republic of Armenia.

Some Soviet republics began to demand independence. In 1990 the Baltic republics—Latvia, Lithuania, and Estonia—tried to secede from the Soviet Union. Gorbachev attempted an

What If? What might have happened if Gorbachev had achieved his goals and had not been forced to resign in 1991? How might the Soviet Union and Eastern Europe be different?

Mikhail Gorbachev won the Nobel Peace Prize in 1990 for his reform work in the Soviet Union. He is shown here with his wife, Raisa.

In May of 1990, Boris Yeltsin (center, holding papers) became the first popularly elected leader in the history of Russia.

economic and military crackdown, drawing criticism both at home and abroad. In 1991 more and more Soviet republics demanded independence. It soon became clear that the Soviet Union could not last. In December of 1991 Gorbachev stepped down as president of the Soviet Union. By the end of the year the Soviet Union had ceased to exist.

✔ **READING CHECK: Identifying Cause and Effect** How did Gorbachev's reforms lead to the breakup of the Soviet Union?

Russia's New Leadership

After the breakup of the Soviet Union, the Federation of Russia emerged as the largest and most powerful of the newly independent states. Under Boris Yeltsin's leadership, Russia began to make the transition to democracy, though high inflation and unemployment strained the Russian economy. Yeltsin privatized many industries and opened Russia to foreign investment, but Russia's economic troubles continued throughout the 1990s.

Political and social troubles. The ongoing economic problems led to political turmoil. In the early 1990s Yeltsin was strongly challenged by the Russian legislature, which still included many communists. When Yeltsin attempted to dissolve the legislature in 1993, its members declared the move unconstitutional and announced a new government. Yeltsin kept power only by ordering a military assault against the legislative building.

At the same time, Yeltsin's nationalist and communist opponents began to win more support. The military became increasingly dissatisfied over low pay and poor living conditions. There was danger of a coup. Amid questions about his health, Yeltsin faced a strong challenge in the election of 1996. Only by making concessions to the conservatives did Yeltsin manage to win reelection.

Russia's diverse challenges continued. The Orthodox church experienced renewed growth and power and did not always agree with democratic reformers. In addition, the fall of communism sparked an increase in organized crime in Russia, with criminal gangs dealing in illegal enterprises such as drugs, prostitution, and black-market goods.

Another challenge came from increased separatist movements among Russian minority groups. The most serious case involved the small southern region of Chechnya. The Chechens, a Muslim people, had long fought their Russian conquerors. With the breakup of the Soviet Union, Chechnya declared its independence. Yeltsin, however, refused to let the oil-rich region break away, and in 1994 sent in the army. The brutal war provoked international criticism and caused heavy casualties on both sides. In 1996 a peace treaty was signed and Russian and Chechen leaders pledged to work out the final status of Chechnya in later negotiations. After these negotiations faltered and Chechen rebels were blamed for a series of bombings in Moscow and other cities in 1999, Russian troops again invaded. The renewed fighting has degenerated into a stalemate. Russian forces are not strong enough to defeat the Chechen fighters, and the Chechens are too weak to turn back the Russians.

Russia and the world. The breakup of the Soviet Union created 15 independent republics. To coordinate defense and economic policies for the new nations, Russia established the **Commonwealth of Independent States (CIS).** Relations between Russia and the republics were often strained. A major concern was the perception that Russia was trying to dominate the new republics near the oil-rich Caspian Sea.

Needing financial assistance, Yeltsin's government cooperated with the West and reached important agreements with the United States on arms reduction. NATO expansion into eastern Europe and Western fears over the security of Russia's nuclear weapons caused some tension, but Russia and the West tried to focus on matters of agreement.

When Yeltsin resigned in late 1999, Prime Minister Vladimir Putin became acting president. The following March, Putin was formally elected to the presidency. His hard line against Chechnya and his efforts to further reform a once again growing Russian economy have been the focus of his term in office.

✔ **READING CHECK: Categorizing** What types of problems did Russia face under Boris Yeltsin?

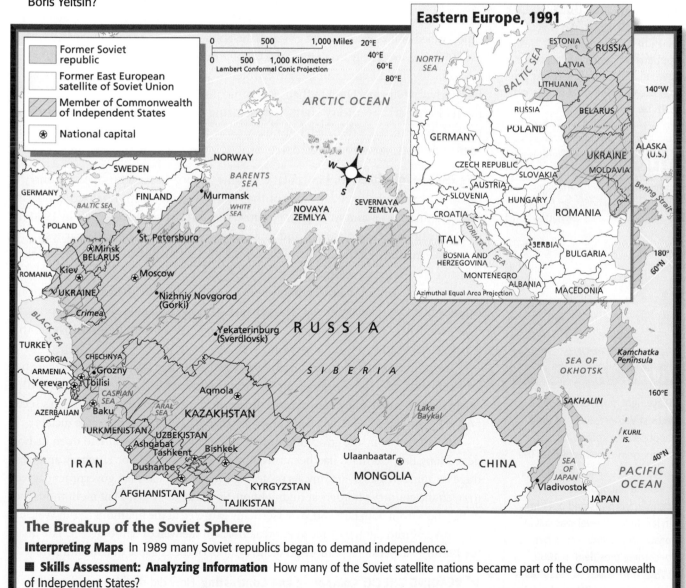

The Breakup of the Soviet Sphere

Interpreting Maps In 1989 many Soviet republics began to demand independence.

■ **Skills Assessment: Analyzing Information** How many of the Soviet satellite nations became part of the Commonwealth of Independent States?

Dissent and Revolution in Eastern Europe

During the 1960s and 1970s, the Brezhnev Doctrine had prevented any real dissent in nations under Soviet control. Gorbachev's reforms, however, gave encouragement to democratic movements in Eastern Europe. In 1989 a tide of democratic reform swept communist governments from power across Eastern Europe.

Growing dissent. The announcement of the Helsinki Accords in the late 1970s improved the climate for dissidents in Eastern European countries. Those who opposed totalitarian rule called on their governments to abide by the human rights articles of the accords. In Poland economic troubles also fueled the growth of dissent. Huge price increases in 1980 sparked massive labor strikes. Led by an unemployed electrician named **Lech Walesa** (LEK vah·LEN·suh), the strikers demanded political and economic reforms. They formed an independent trade union called Solidarity. Aided by glasnost, the Solidarity protests continued throughout the 1980s and eventually led to the downfall of Poland's communist government.

Initially, both communist governments and dissidents were skeptical of Gorbachev's reforms. Despite their economic problems, Eastern European governments were perhaps uneasy about restructuring along Soviet lines. Dissidents may have at first expressed disbelief, but finally came to support glasnost and perestroika as the best hope for winning freedom.

The 1989 revolutions. In 1989 Poland became the first Eastern European country to throw off communist rule. In April of that year the government legalized Solidarity. Poland's first non-communist prime minister in forty years was elected. In 1990 the Communist Party was dissolved and replaced by two social democratic parties.

Other nations followed Poland's example. In Czechoslovakia, protesters took to the streets to demand reform. When they lost the support of the workers, who went on a national strike, the government quickly gave in. Shortly thereafter the national legislature selected **Vaclav Havel,** a writer and former dissident leader, as the country's new president. The transition to democracy was so smooth in Czechoslovakia that people called it the "Velvet Revolution."

The transition to noncommunist rule was less peaceful in Romania. People there had long suffered under the repressive rule of dictator Nicolae Ceausescu (chow·SHES·koo). A brief civil war broke out as pro-reform demonstrators clashed with Ceausescu's secret police. By the end of 1989, pro-democracy forces captured and executed the dictator.

In East Germany the government came under increasing pressure to open its borders. Many East Germans had been traveling to Czechoslovakia or Hungary and from there escaping to West Germany. As protests grew, the East German government agreed to open the country's borders at midnight on November 9, 1989. That night thousands of Berliners from both East and West Germany gathered at the infamous Berlin Wall. On the stroke of midnight, they raced to break holes in the wall or climb over it. The fall of the Berlin Wall became the most powerful symbol of the collapse of communism.

✔ **READING CHECK: Comparing and Contrasting** How did dissidents and government leaders in Eastern Europe view Gorbachev's reforms?

INTERPRETING THE VISUAL RECORD

Berlin Wall The Berlin Wall, which had divided East and West Germany for nearly 30 years, came down in 1989. *What feelings are expressed in the grafitti and artwork on the wall?*

HISTORY MAKER

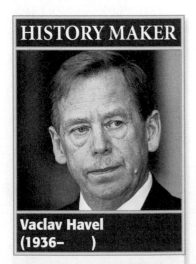

Vaclav Havel (1936–   )

Playwright, poet, and political activist Vaclav Havel had long opposed the communist government in Czechoslovakia. The government, calling Havel a threat to national security, banned his plays and put him in jail. In fact, Havel was still in prison only a few weeks before becoming president in 1989. **What happened to Havel as a result of his political views?**

The Aftermath of Communism

The end of communism in Eastern Europe promised new prosperity. The new governments of Eastern Europe adopted democratic policies and free-market reforms. Many hoped for closer cooperation with the West.

The challenges of change. However, change was not easy. The Eastern European countries had lost their largest trading partner, the Soviet Union. Their inefficient industries could not compete with those of the West. Furthermore, the years of communist rule had left Eastern Europe one of the world's most polluted regions.

The new freedoms gained in Eastern Europe also released old ethnic tensions. In 1992 Czechoslovakia peacefully split into two separate countries, as Slovak nationalism grew. This created the more prosperous Czech Republic and the poorer country of Slovakia. Other countries, such as Albania, experienced more violent unrest.

Yugoslavia's breakup. In Yugoslavia, ethnic tensions led to one of the bloodiest civil wars of modern times. Yugoslavia was made of six republics and many different ethnic groups, including Serbs, Croats, Slovenians, Macedonians, and Albanians. The Serbs were mainly Eastern Orthodox, and Croats and Slovenians Roman Catholic. In the republic of Bosnia and Herzegovina, Muslims were the largest group.

As communism fell, Serbia, under President Slobodan Milošević (SLOH•buh•dahn muh•LOH•suh•vich), tried to dominate the rest of Yugoslavia. This inspired intense nationalism among the Croats and Slovenians. In 1991 Croatia and Slovenia declared their independence. Fighting broke out between Serbia and Croatia, ending in a truce mediated by the United Nations and enforced by UN peacekeepers. Croatia and Slovenia had won their freedom. In 1992 Bosnia similarly declared its independence.

Strife in Bosnia. Bosnia's greatest challenge was its diverse ethnic and religious mix. Muslims formed the largest single group, but still did not make up a majority of the entire population. Nearly one third of Bosnia's population identified themselves as Serbian, while about one fifth claimed Croatian descent. Many Bosnian Serbs wished to remain part of Serbian-dominated Yugoslavia. Receiving aid from the Yugoslavian government in Belgrade, Bosnian Serbs began a program of **ethnic cleansing**—a campaign of terror and murder intended to drive the Muslims out of areas the Bosnian Serbs claimed.

In an effort to end the fighting, the United Nations stopped the flow of weapons into the region. However, this only made it harder for the Muslim-controlled Bosnian government to fight off the better-armed Serbs. As Serb attacks continued, the UN set up certain protected "safe haven" areas. This did not stop the Serbs, who continued to bomb the Bosnian capital of Sarajevo as well as UN "safe havens." NATO responded by bombing Serbian targets in 1995.

The Bosnian Serbs finally agreed to enter into U.S.-led peace talks in Dayton, Ohio. These talks resulted in the **Dayton Accord.** This

Children are seen here playing in a suburb of Sarajevo. This area was surrounded by Serb forces for at least six months during the campaign of ethnic cleansing.

Transition to Democracy

After throwing off communist rule, Eastern European countries faced a sometimes rough road to economic and social recovery. In his first presidential address to the people of Czechoslovakia, Vaclav Havel did not hide the truth from them:

> **"Our country is not flourishing. . . . Entire branches of industry are producing things for which there is no demand while we are short of things we need. . . . We have spoiled our land, rivers and forests, inherited from our ancestors, and we have, today, the worst environment in the whole of Europe. . . . If we accept [the heritage of the last 40 years] in such a way, we shall come to understand it is up to all of us to do something about it."**

	Poland	Czech Republic	Romania	Albania
Conditions in 1989				
Present conditions				

The city of Budapest, shown here, is the capital of Hungary, one of the formerly communist countries of Eastern Europe.

Skills Reminder

Before writing a paper, choose a topic of interest. Determine what you wish to describe, explain, or prove. Decide what questions you hope to answer.

Begin to collect facts about the topic. Then use the information you have gathered and your stated purpose to formulate a thesis statement.

Determine what ideas and evidence you will need to use to support your thesis statement. Organize the collected facts and discard those that have no bearing on the general statement.

Skills Practice

Pick one of the following Eastern European countries and use the process of historical inquiry to research it. Use and interpret multiple sources of evidence about the country. Then write a five-page research paper on its progress since achieving independence. Maintain standard grammar, spelling, sentence structure, and punctuation in your report. Use the graphic organizer above to help prepare your outline before you begin writing.

- Poland
- Czech Republic
- Romania
- Albania

U.S. troops were part of the UN peacekeeping force sent to Bosnia to enforce the Dayton Accord.

agreement gave the Bosnian Serbs control over certain areas while still recognizing the overall sovereignty of Bosnia's Muslim-led government. The UN sent a joint military Implementation Force to Bosnia in December 1995 to enforce the new peace.

In 1998, however, the Yugoslav government cracked down on ethnic Albanian rebels seeking independence for the province of Kosovo. NATO responded to Yugoslavia's actions with air strikes in March 1999. After 11 weeks of bombing, the Yugoslavian government finally allowed a NATO peacekeeping force into Kosovo and withdrew its own troops from the province. Kosovo now operates under UN rule.

Following protests over fraudulent elections in Serbia in 2000, Slobodan Milošević was forced to resign as president. The following year he was turned over to international authorities to face trial on charges of crimes against humanity for his role in directing the wars in Bosnia and Kosovo. In 2003, Yugoslavia dropped its old name and adopted the name of the only two republics that still make it up—Serbia and Montenegro.

✔ **READING CHECK: Identifying Cause and Effect** How did the fall of communism contribute to the resurgence of ethnic tensions in Eastern Europe?

SECTION 3 REVIEW

1. **Define** and explain the significance:
   perestroika
   glasnost
   ethnic cleansing

2. **Identify** and explain the significance:
   Leonid Brezhnev
   Brezhnev Doctrine
   Mikhail Gorbachev
   Boris Yeltsin
   Commonwealth of
     Independent States (CIS)
   Lech Walesa
   Vaclav Havel
   Dayton Accord

Homework Practice Online

keyword: SH3 HP26

3. **Identifying Cause and Effect** Copy the chart below. Use it to explain the causes and results of the fall of communism.

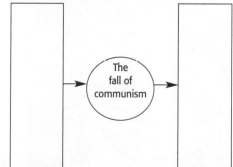

The fall of communism

4. **Finding the Main Idea**

   a. Compare and contrast the reforms that Gorbachev and Yeltsin implemented.

   b. How did Eastern European countries throw off communist rule?

   c. What factors led to strife in Bosnia?

5. **Writing and Critical Thinking**

   Supporting a Point of View Write a speech to be given by Mikhail Gorbachev in 1985, telling why perestroika and glasnost will benefit the nation.
   Consider:
   • the purpose of the reforms
   • what problems the Soviet Union had at the time
   • effect on international relations

READ TO DISCOVER

1 How was the United States attacked on September 11, 2001, and how did people respond?

2 How did the events of September 11, 2001 affect the U.S. economy?

3 What immediate steps did U.S. leaders and their allies take to find those responsible for the attacks and bring them to justice?

IDENTIFY

World Trade Center
Pentagon
Rudolph Giuliani
Tom Ridge
Donald Rumsfeld
Colin Powell

WHY IT MATTERS TODAY

The terrorist attacks of September 11, 2001, continue to affect American life and U.S. foreign policy. Use CNN student News.com or other **current events** sources to learn about the latest issues and events stemming from this national tragedy.

A Day That Changed the World

The Main Idea
The United States suffered a devastating terrorist attack by Islamic extremists on September 11, 2001.

The Story Continues *On Tuesday morning, September 11, 2001, it was business as usual in the downtown financial district of New York City. In the World Trade Center complex, some of the 50,000 employees were starting their workday, most of them within the Twin Towers that dominated the Manhattan skyline. Others were still on their way to work. On Fifth Avenue a group of pedestrians noticed a large airplane pass by. "We all looked up," recalled one man. "We all thought it would be unusual for a plane to be flying so low over the city." Moments later they witnessed a terrible disaster unfold.*

The Attack

At 8:45 A.M., the daily routine of a city and a nation was shattered when an American Airlines passenger jet crashed into the north tower of the **World Trade Center.** The impact was devastating, as though a bomb had struck the 110-story building. Lynn Simpson, who was working on the 89th floor, recalled, "I heard an enormous crash. The ceiling fell in, the lights went out and the sprinklers went on. . . . I told everyone to get out." Stunned men and women began evacuating the building as emergency crews rushed to the scene. Then at about 9:00 A.M. a second plane—United Airlines Flight 175—slammed into the south tower of the WTC complex.

Shocked Americans began to realize that these were deliberate attacks when it was learned that both planes had been hijacked by terrorists. Moreover, it was soon clear that New York was not the terrorists' only target. At approximately 9:40 A.M. a third plane, American Airlines Flight 77, hit the west side of the Pentagon. Located just outside Washington, D.C., the **Pentagon** is the headquarters of the U.S. military leadership. The impact of the crash caused massive damage and started fires deep within the huge, five-sided building. Hundreds of military personnel and civilians were killed.

At the World Trade Center complex, hundreds of rescue workers struggled to aid victims and firefighters tried to control the raging fires. In the midst of their efforts, further disaster struck. At 10:00 A.M. the south tower suddenly collapsed, followed half an hour later by the fall of the north tower. "It [the south tower] just fell down in perfect symmetry, one floor, then another

Columns of thick smoke billow from the wreckage of the World Trade Center's twin towers on September 11, 2001, after hijacked commercial airliners piloted by Islamic extremists dove into the buildings, killing thousands.

floor, then another," said a stunned witness. The collapse of the massive buildings killed or trapped thousands of people still inside or near the towers, including hundreds of firefighters, police officers, and other rescuers.

A fourth plane—United Airlines Flight 93—was also hijacked and still in the air over southern Pennsylvania. Cell phone calls from passengers aboard the plane indicate that they learned of the other attacks and decided to stop the terrorists on board from hitting their next target. Flight 93 crashed southeast of Pittsburgh sometime around the time of the collapse of the World Trade Center's towers.

In downtown New York City, clouds of smoke, dust, and ash drifted through the streets along with thousands of battered and dazed survivors. Thousands more people were unaccounted for in the wreckage. Meanwhile, emergency teams battling fires in the Pentagon were unable to search for survivors. As many as 266 passengers and crew aboard the four hijacked flights had been killed. Americans everywhere were shocked, wondering what was to come.

✔ **READING CHECK: Sequencing** In what order did the events of the morning of September 11, 2001, take place?

In the aftermath of the terrorist attacks, members of New York City's fire and police departments mounted a heroic effort to rescue victims trapped in the rubble of the World Trade Center.

The World Responds

Government officials raced to mount rescue efforts and placed the U.S. military on full alert. The Federal Aviation Administration temporarily grounded air traffic nationwide and closed airports. Key government centers, such as the White House, were briefly evacuated.

Rescue and relief. New York hospitals mobilized hundreds of doctors but found, tragically, that there were relatively few survivors to care for. Within hours, firefighters and other rescue workers from across the nation came to New York to join state and city emergency personnel searching the rubble for survivors. Their efforts were hampered by the tons of unstable debris and by the intense heat from underground fires. Three weeks after the attack there were still more than 5,900 people missing, all presumed dead. New York mayor **Rudolph Giuliani** said of the final death toll, "It will be more than we can bear." In all, about 2,500 people were killed at the World Trade Center, including more than 300 firefighters and many other rescue workers. At the Pentagon, 184 military and civilian personnel, including those on the hijacked plane, had been killed.

Congress swiftly approved a $40 billion relief package to help the nation recover from the attacks. The money would fund emergency assistance and national security measures. The government also passed legislation that provided compensation to the families of victims. Democrats and Republicans displayed an unusual degree of cooperation in pushing through such measures. "I think the message is very simply we are united . . . when it comes to a national threat as great as this," said Senate Majority Leader Tom Daschle of South Dakota.

People unite. Political leaders also tried to rally Americans' spirit on the day of the attack. Mayor Giuliani assured fellow New Yorkers, "We're going to rebuild and rebuild stronger." President George W. Bush, who had been in Florida visiting an elementary school, was moved to a safe location. From there, he

Americans such as these middle school students from Burnet, Texas, united to demonstrate patriotism and support for the victims of the September 11 terrorist attacks.

In the days following the terrorist attacks, Americans across the nation came together in a series of interfaith memorial services to honor the victims and to demonstrate unity and faith.

gave a brief speech to the nation. "Freedom itself was attacked this morning by a faceless coward," he declared. Republican and Democratic members of Congress issued a joint declaration to the country from the Capitol steps. They said that the United States would not be intimidated by terrorism. The members then sang a chorus of "God Bless America."

The tragic events of September 11, 2001, drew sympathy and support from around the world. Citizens of more than 40 countries were among the missing. The European Union declared September 14 a day of mourning throughout its 15 member states. British prime minister Tony Blair called the terrorist acts "an attack on the free and democratic world everywhere." The French newspaper *Le Monde* ran a headline saying, "WE ARE ALL AMERICANS." Russian and Chinese leaders gave their condolences. Even traditional opponents of the United States, such as Cuba and Iran, expressed their sympathy and regret. U.S. leaders gave thanks for these gestures and worked to form an active coalition against terrorism.

Perhaps the greatest show of unity came from the American people themselves. Many were inspired to displays of charity and patriotism. Within two days Wal-Mart, the nation's largest retail chain, had sold its entire stock of half a million American flags. Charitable groups across the country moved swiftly to raise funds for relief efforts. Thousands of people went to Red Cross centers to donate blood. "It's just amazing," said one nurse in New York. "There'll be a three- or four-hour wait, and just look at all of these people standing here." Actors and musicians held a special telethon, "America: A Tribute to Heroes," on September 21. The effort raised some $150 million to benefit the families who had lost loved ones in the attacks.

People also came together in public to heal their wounds and show their strength. When professional sports leagues resumed their schedules, stadiums were filled with patriotic tributes and fans waving flags. Actor James Earl Jones drew cheers as he opened a mass prayer service held in New York City's Yankee Stadium.

History Makers Speak

"Our spirit is unbroken. In fact, it is stronger than ever. Today we reaffirm our faith in the essential dignity of every individual. What we share as Americans and as human beings is far greater than what divides us."

James Earl Jones, September 23, 2001

Spiritual leaders representing many faiths led prayers for the victims and called for unity as a nation. The Boys and Girls Choir of Harlem sang a stirring rendition of "We Shall Overcome," with its refrain, "We are not afraid. . . . We shall live in peace."

✔ **READING CHECK: Finding the Main Idea** In what ways did Americans first respond to the terrorist attacks?

The Investigation

Immediately after the attacks, the largest criminal investigation in U.S. history began. Within 48 hours the Federal Bureau of Investigation (FBI) placed more than 4,000 special agents on the case. The FBI soon released the names of 19 suspected hijackers from several Middle Eastern nations. Investigators gathered evidence suggesting that each group of hijackers included trained pilots and that some of these men had been living and training in the United States for months. Even more crucial was the identity of those who had planned these acts of terror.

A prime suspect surfaced almost immediately—Osama bin Laden. This wealthy Saudi Arabian exile was already wanted for his suspected role in earlier terrorist attacks against U.S. forces overseas. A supporter of an extreme form of Islamic fundamentalism, bin Laden had publicly called for attacks on the United States, which he claimed had corrupted and oppressed Muslims. Officials believed that bin Laden's global terrorism network, known as al Qaeda, or "the Base," was one of the few terrorist groups with the resources and organizational structure to have carried out the attacks.

Experts also agreed that the attacks of September 11 probably involved the cooperation of more than one terrorist group. Investigators from a broad range of federal agencies, with assistance from other nations, began a global manhunt for anyone with knowledge of the attacks. They sifted through debris at the crash sites to find physical evidence and tracked airline, telephone, credit card, and other financial records to trace terrorists' movements. Several hundred suspects were detained at home and abroad for questioning. Although the complexity of the task and the need to protect security and sources forced officials to be cautious, the Bush administration pledged to release conclusive evidence about the attacks as soon as it was feasible to do so.

✔ **READING CHECK: Summarizing** What early conclusions did investigators draw about the source of the attacks, and how did they investigate them?

The Economic Impact

The terrorist strikes on the World Trade Center had a high cost in economic terms as well as in lives. The costs related to the immediate physical damage were estimated at $25 billion. In addition, the New York Stock Exchange (NYSE) had to shut down operations for four days following the attack. When the stock market reopened, concerns about a potential war and poor economic indicators combined to cause one of the worst weeks in the history of the NYSE. European and Asian stock markets also suffered heavy losses. Although stock prices made a modest rally the following week, concerns about the health of the national and global economy remained. "The insecurity is still there," commented one German trader. "There is no way to tell what is going to happen," explained an American trader. The Federal Reserve quickly cut interest rates in an effort to help the economy.

One area of particular concern was the airline industry. Forced to shut down operations for days and facing greatly increased security expenses and a public reluctance to fly, major airlines took heavy financial losses. They laid off thousands of workers, and at least one smaller carrier went out of business. The air-travel crisis caused wider problems as well. Tourism declined severely around the nation, and companies relying on supplies shipped by air endured shortages. Congress and the president rushed to pass a $15 billion bail-out package to help keep the nation's airlines operating.

One of the most difficult economic problems for the government to address was falling consumer confidence. Many Americans had been concerned by the weakness of the economy before the terrorist attacks. Uncertainty and fear raised by

The stock market tumbled sharply when exchanges such as the NASDAQ, pictured here, reopened six days after the September 11 terrorist attacks. National economies around the world were hard hit by the attacks and the threats they posed to global peace.

President George W. Bush addressed a joint session of Congress on September 20, during which he pledged to utilize the full might of the nation in a war on international terrorism.

Analyzing Primary Sources

Identifying a Point of View
What did President Bush call on other nations to do?

the events of September 11 made many Americans believe the country was headed for a recession. "We do have to fear fear itself, it matters, it affects consumer spending," stated one economist. Government officials responded to such concerns by emphasizing that the long-term health of the economy was strong, even if difficult times lay ahead.

✔ **READING CHECK: Identifying Cause and Effect** What immediate effect did the terrorist attacks have on the U.S. economy?

A Call to Action

In a national address on September 20, President George W. Bush called the attacks on the World Trade Center and the Pentagon "an act of war." He promised that the United States would bring those responsible to justice.

A war on terrorism. The president also declared that the United States would wage war on terrorism itself. Bush emphasized that U.S. efforts would be aimed not only against terrorist organizations but also against national governments that supported and protected terrorists. "Either you are with us, or you are with the terrorists," he declared.

History Makers Speak

❝Tonight we are a country awakened to danger and called to defend freedom. Our grief has turned to anger, and anger to resolution. Whether we bring our enemies to justice, or bring justice to our enemies, justice will be done. . . . The enemy of America is not our many Muslim friends; it is not our many Arab friends. Our enemy is a radical network of terrorists, and every government that supports them. . . . Every nation, in every region, now has a decision to make. Either you are with us, or you are with the terrorists. From this day forward, any nation that continues to harbor or support terrorism will be regarded by the United States as a hostile regime. . . . Great harm has been done to us. We have suffered great loss. And in our grief and anger we have found our mission and our moment. Freedom and fear are at war. The advance of human freedom—the great achievement of our time, and the great hope of every time—now depends on us. Our nation—this generation—will lift a dark threat of violence from our people and our future. We will rally the world to this cause by our efforts, by our courage. We will not tire, we will not falter, and we will not fail.❞

George W. Bush, September 20, 2001

In his speech the president singled out one government—the Taliban regime of Afghanistan—as a key sponsor of terror. The Taliban emerged in the mid-1990s as a splinter group of fundamentalist Muslims. Many members had fought against the Soviets during their occupation of Afghanistan. Its leaders had developed ties to Osama bin Laden, whom they later sheltered.

Domestic security. President Bush appointed Governor **Tom Ridge** of Pennsylvania to head the Office of Homeland Security. This office was created to coordinate the domestic national security efforts of various government agencies.

Key goals included improving airport security and protecting vital systems such as transportation and power networks from attack. Proposed airline security measures included background checks on passengers and employees, more-thorough baggage searches, and restricted access to airport facilities. Political leaders such as U.S. Attorney General John Ashcroft also called for expanded law-enforcement powers to combat terrorism.

A difficult mission. Administration officials, including Secretary of Defense **Donald Rumsfeld,** agreed that striking at terrorists outside the United States would be a lengthy and difficult task. Success would require identifying the proper targets as well as finding ways to destroy them.

The Bush administration sought to fight terrorism using economic, diplomatic, and military means. The president froze the assets of individuals, groups, and companies with suspected terrorist ties. Secretary of State **Colin Powell** led U.S. efforts to build an international coalition against terrorism and to isolate the Taliban regime. The leaders of nations such as Great Britain and Russia pledged their support of antiterrorist efforts. For the first time in its existence, NATO invoked Article 5 of its original treaty, under which NATO members are required to come to the defense of an alliance member under attack. Even former allies of the Taliban regime, such as Pakistan and Saudi Arabia, were convinced to support U.S. efforts.

The United States also began mobilizing military forces such as aircraft carrier groups and ground troops in preparation for attacks on terrorism. Less than one month after the terrorists' attacks, the United States and its allies began their offensive. On October 7, the first in a series of powerful air strikes hit al Qaeda bases and Taliban sites in Afghanistan. At the same time, food, medicine, and other supplies were air-dropped to the country's impoverished civilian population. The Northern Alliance, an Afghan group that had fought against the Taliban since the early 1990s, provided ground support. The United States and Great Britain also sent ground troops. The troops slowly drove out the Taliban and captured members of al Qaeda. On December 17, the American flag was raised at the U.S. embassy in Kabul for the first time since 1989. Four days later a new Afghan government was established.

In the days immediately following the attacks of September 11, 2001, the United States began deploying its military arsenal in preparation for a long and difficult struggle against global terrorism. Pictured here is the U.S. aircraft carrier Theodore Roosevelt.

✔ **READING CHECK: Summarizing** What early steps did U.S. leaders take to respond to the terrorist attacks on the United States?

SECTION 4 REVIEW

1. Identify and explain:
 World Trade Center
 Pentagon
 Rudolph Giuliani
 Tom Ridge
 Donald Rumsfeld
 Colin Powell

2. Analyzing Information Copy the graphic organizer below. Use it to explain some of the ways in which the U.S. government responded to protect the United States and bring its attackers to justice.

3. **Finding the Main Idea**

 a. Who did investigators initially suspect of carrying out the terrorist attacks of September 11, 2001, and how did they pursue the investigation?

 b. How did the attacks affect the economy?

4. **Writing and Critical Thinking**

 Evaluating Imagine that you are first learning of the attacks on September 11, 2001, and want to help however you can. Write a paragraph describing possible actions you could take to assist those in need.

 Consider the following:
 • the efforts of relief agencies to help victims
 • the need for national unity
 • the importance of tolerance

Homework Practice Online

keyword: SH3 HP35

CHAPTER 26 Review

Creating a Time Line

Copy the time line below onto a sheet of paper. Complete the time line by filling in the events, individuals, and dates from the chapter that you think were significant. Pick three events and explain why you think they were significant.

| 1969 | 1985 | present |

Writing a Summary

Using standard grammar, spelling, sentence structure, and punctuation, write an overview of the events in the chapter.

Identifying People and Ideas

Identify the following terms or individuals and explain their significance:

1. Watergate scandal
2. détente
3. Margaret Thatcher
4. Helmut Kohl
5. Helsinki Accords
6. European Union
7. Mikhail Gorbachev
8. glasnost
9. ethnic cleansing
10. World Trade Center

Understanding the Main Ideas

SECTION 1 (pp. 748–755)
The Industrial Powers of North America

1. What political problems plagued the United States in the 1970s and 1980s?
2. What did President Bush mean by "new world order"?
3. Why do many people in Quebec desire autonomy?

SECTION 2 (pp. 756–763)
Europe

4. What was Margaret Thatcher's approach to foreign and economic policy?
5. What led to coalition governments in Italy?
6. Why did some European nations oppose entry into the European Union?

SECTION 3 (pp. 764–771)
The Fall of Communism

7. How did the Brezhnev Doctrine affect Eastern Europe?
8. What were perestroika and glasnost intended to do?
9. What factors led to war in the former Yugoslavia?

SECTION 4 (pp. 772–777)
A Day That Changed the World

10. What events took place in the United States on September 11, 2001?
11. How did these events affect U.S. security and the economy?

Reviewing Themes

1. **Economics** How did the government's role in the economy differ in the Soviet Union as compared with Western nations?
2. **Government** How did the communist states suppress dissent?
3. **Global Relations** What political and economic concerns did leaders in the West have regarding Russia after the fall of communism?

Thinking Critically

1. **Comparing and Contrasting** Compare and contrast the political changes that took place in Great Britain and West Germany in the 1970s and 1980s.
2. **Analyzing Information** How did human rights affect U.S. policies toward China and the Soviet Union?
3. **Identifying Cause and Effect** How was the Soviet Union affected by perestroika and glasnost?

Writing About History

Summarizing Not all of the former Soviet republics have joined the Commonwealth of Independent States. Write a brief essay that explains which nations have joined the commonwealth and what the costs and benefits are of joining. Use the following chart to organize your thoughts before you begin writing.

Benefits of joining CIS	Costs of joining CIS

Interpreting a Graph

Study the graph below. Then use the information on the graph to answer the questions that follow.

Nuclear Electricity Generation in Selected Countries (2003)

Percent of electricity generated by nuclear power

China	France	Mexico	Russia	United Kingdom	United States
1.2%	77.1%	4.2%	14.8%	23.7%	20.7%

1. Which of the following is a correct general statement about the data shown on the graph?

   a. The more lakes and rivers a country has, the more nuclear power it uses.

   b. The amount of electricity generated by nuclear power has no relationship to the size of the country.

   c. Electricity generated by nuclear power is expensive.

   d. Some nuclear reactors generate more electricity than can be used by its customers.

2. Of the 32 countries that use nuclear power, some have cut back on their nuclear energy programs. Why do you think the countries cut back? Give specific reasons to support your view.

Understanding Frames of Reference

Read the following excerpt from a speech given by historian Barbara Tuchman in 1966. Then answer the questions.

"I know very little . . . about laboratory science, but I have the impression that . . . from a given set of circumstances a predictable result should follow. The trouble is that in human behavior and history it is impossible to isolate or repeat a given set of circumstances. . . . Tides are so obedient to schedule that a timetable for them can be printed like that for trains, though more reliable. In fact, tides and trains sharply illustrate my point: One depends on the moon and is certain; the other depends on man and is uncertain."

3. Which of the following probably best describes Tuchman's approach to understanding human behavior?

   a. Tuchman sees little difference between the study of history and the study of science.

   b. Patterns of human behavior are predictable.

   c. Tuchman believes that history repeats itself.

   d. Tuchman follows a historical—rather than a purely scientific—approach toward understanding human behavior.

4. Explain your choice of statements in question 3. Give specific examples to support your point of view.

Alternative Assessment

Building Your Portfolio

Link to TODAY

Government

Political systems of the superpowers are based on philosophies and ideas developed throughout history. Use the library and other sources to compile a list of such ideas, including Judeo-Christian ethics and the rise of secularism and individualism in Western civilization, beginning with the Enlightenment. Then write a report that analyzes how at least one of these ideas has influenced governments, institutions, or societies.

internet connect

Internet Activity: go.hrw.com
KEYWORD: SH3 WH26

Choose a topic on the Superpowers in the Modern Era to:

• create a chart about U.S. and Soviet relations after World War II.

• write a biography of former British prime minister Margaret Thatcher.

• create a newspaper of Quebec.

(1945–Present)
The Modern World

1947
Daily Life
More than 1 million U.S. war veterans enroll in colleges under the "G.I. Bill of Rights."

This stamp was issued by the U.S. Postal Service to commemorate the G.I. Bill.

1950
Daily Life
The UN reports that more than half the world's children are undernourished.

1961
Global Events
The UN General Assembly condemns apartheid.

Apollo mission patch

1952
Business and Finance
Germany becomes a member of the World Bank.

1961
Science and Technology
Soviet cosmonaut Yury Gagarin becomes the first person to travel in space.

1969
Science and Technology
The *Apollo 11* mission lands on the moon and Neil Armstrong takes the first human steps there.

1950 — **1960** — **1970**

1949
The Arts
American playwright Arthur Miller wins the Pulitzer Prize for *Death of a Salesman.*

1954
Science and Technology
Jonas Salk's polio vaccine is released for general use.

1965
The Arts
The Beatles' song "A Hard Day's Night" is popular.

1975
Politics
Russian scientist Andrey Sakharov wins the Nobel Peace Prize for his humanitarian efforts.

1946
The Arts
Russian immigrant George Balanchine directs the *Nightshadow* ballet in New York City.

1963
The Arts
New York's Guggenheim Museum holds a show of pop art, including works by Andy Warhol.

1970
Daily Life
About 231 million television sets are in use around the world.

1946
Politics
The UN General Assembly holds its first session in London.

One of Andy Warhol's signature soup can paintings

Build on What You Know

During World War II, many nations suffered from economic hardship, ruined property, and loss of life. After the war's end, nations struggled to rebuild their cities and economies. New tensions surfaced as the political and economic battles of the Cold War began. In this chapter, you will learn how the everyday lives of most of the world's citizens changed dramatically in the years following World War II. Exciting and thoughtful new styles in the cultural arts reflected the world's rapidly changing society. Science, technology, and a new commitment to human rights brought about much of this transformation.

Compact discs became popular in the 1980s.

In 2003 China sent Yang Liwei, its first astronaut, into outer space.

2001
Global Events
United States invades Afghanistan after terrorist attacks on Sept. 11.

1983
Business and Finance
The compact disc is marketed for the first time.

1989
Politics
Czechoslovakia's communist government falls, and playwright Vaclav Havel becomes president.

1980 ———————— **1990** ———— **2000**

1978
Daily Life
The world population is 4.4 billion, with 200,000 people added each day.

1982
The Arts
Colombian author Gabriel García Márquez wins the Nobel Prize for literature.

1986
Science and Technology
An explosion at the Chernobyl nuclear power plant spreads radiation over parts of the Soviet Union and Europe.

1990
Science and Technology
World Wide Web is created.

2000
Global Events
A joint American and Russian crew begin living on the new international space station.

2003
Global Events
United States invades Iraq, and Saddam Hussein is captured.

2003
Science and Technology
China launches first manned spacecraft.

1976
Business and Finance
The world's first supersonic passenger jet service begins when two Concorde jets take off at the same time from London and Paris.

NASA's rover, Spirit, landed on Mars in 2004.

What's Your Opinion?

*Do you **agree** or **disagree** with the following statements? Support your point of view in your journal.*

Science, Technology & Society Technological developments and advances always improve society.

Culture The arts flourish during times of economic prosperity.

Citizenship Citizens of one country cannot stop human rights violations in another country.

The Arts and Literature

The Main Idea
After World War II the arts and literature reflected the political and social changes of the time.

The Story Continues *During the late 1940s Jackson Pollock started a bold new style of painting. He explained why the floor was the best place to create his drip-and-splash art. "On the floor, I am more at ease," he said. "I feel nearer, more a part of the painting, since this way I can walk around in it, work from the four sides and be literally 'in' the painting." Such experimentation was a major trend in the art world after World War II.*

Visual Arts

The period since 1945 has been one of constant change and experimentation in the arts. This experimentation has even led to an expansion of what it means to be an artist.

Painting and sculpture. After 1945 New York City became one of the liveliest centers of new ideas and painting styles. Many painters began to use a new style that came to be known as **abstract expressionism.** American **Jackson Pollock** was one of the leading abstract expressionists. Pollock expressed himself by dripping different colors of paint onto a canvas spread out on the floor. He believed art was a personal expression that came from the artist's unconscious mind.

During the 1950s artists expressed themselves in different ways. Some realists in the United States and Great Britain developed a new style called **pop art.** These artists, such as Andy Warhol, used everyday items such as soup cans, comic strips, or road signs in their art. Experimentation also occurred in sculpture. The American sculptor Louise Nevelson created large wooden sculptures, often as wall units. Her sculpture *Black Chord* is filled with objects placed within boxed compartments.

In the late 1950s and 1960s another group of artists began painting **op art.** Painters of this style worked with brilliant colors and shapes to create optical illusions. Painting realistic scenes, objects, and people, became more common during the 1970s and 1980s. German artist Anselm Keifer, for example, dealt with the moral problems of Nazism.

This painting by Jackson Pollock, Silver Over Black, White, Yellow, and Red (1948), exemplifies the abstract expressionist style.

New types of visual art. As artistic experiments continued, many different kinds of art came to be accepted. One trend of the modern age has been **conceptual art.** Often conceptual art focuses on "environments" made up of relationships among objects and people. Conceptual artists believe that the act of creating the art is more important than the actual art object. In **performance art,** the artist actually becomes a living work of art. The German artist Joseph Beuys, for example, spent a week caged in a New York gallery with a coyote.

Architecture. Architects continued to search for new ideas and techniques after 1945. One popular material was reinforced concrete. French architect Charles-Édouard Jeanneret, known as Le Corbusier, used this material in his buildings. One of the most influential architects of the 1900s, he used clean, precise forms in his designs. Many architects used smooth, polished materials, such as glass. Le Corbusier and a committee of others employed this idea in designing the UN headquarters in New York City. New shapes also appeared in architectural designs. The Sydney Opera House in Australia is one example of an unusually shaped building. American architect Frank Gehry's wildly innovative Guggenheim Museum in Bilbao, Spain, and his Walt Disney Concert Hall in Los Angeles, California, are two others.

New engineering techniques led to the creation of domed stadiums, such as the Astrodome in Houston, Texas. Cities built structures with unique designs, large areas of glass, or shining mirrored tiles. Some homes combined attractive designs with new technologies to save fuel, such as solar panels. However, no single design has been the most popular architecture since 1945. Experimentation has resulted in many different styles standing side by side.

✔ **READING CHECK: Comparing** How were developments in painting, sculpture, and architecture similar?

Music and Dance

Experimentation has also been common in the world of music. After 1945 new kinds of sound were created in serious music. Composers wrote new music that included synthesizers—sounds created by computers. Composers such as John Cage wrote music that gave the performer—and even the audience—a major role in determining how a piece would sound. Other composers, such as Dmitry Shostakovich, wrote important music based on traditional forms. Although he lived under Stalin's repressive rule in the Soviet Union, Shostakovich's orchestral music expressed great emotion. His symphonies continue to attract listeners worldwide.

Popular music broke new ground in the 1950s when a style called rock 'n' roll developed in the United States. Rock music had a heavy, accented beat and a simple, repetitive melody. It grew out of many different styles, including African American rhythm and blues. During the 1960s a rock band of four young men from Liverpool, England, became enormously popular. In their creative style, the Beatles sang about love and finding one's place in the world. These universal themes made the Beatles popular around the world. Other forms of rock also developed, including folk rock, hard rock, punk rock, and disco. Country-western and African American music such as soul, rhythm and blues, and rap were also popular music forms.

The Beatles' creative style had a major influence on popular music in the 1960s.

How Architecture Reflects Society

Architecture often reflects cultural values, environmental characteristics, and historical realities. For example, the Sears Tower in Chicago and the Empire State Building in New York City are symbols of metropolitan society. In the same way, the Cathedral of Notre Dame in Paris reflects the religious focus of medieval society. Linking architecture to history helps historians to explain societies and their environments. Historians can also study architectural styles to analyze people's reactions to their environment and thus to better understand the society's values and the historical conditions in which it existed. By comparing different architectural styles for the same type of structure over time, historians can spot changes in social norms and values.

The Queen's Hall in London (right) presented its first performance in 1893. The hall featured an elaborate and ornate interior (above).

Known for his inventive architectural style, American architect Frank Gehry designed the Walt Disney Concert Hall, which opened in Los Angeles, California, in 2003. The new hall, which is home to the Los Angeles Philharmonic Orchestra, boasts state of the art acoustics and a highly sculptured pipe organ.

Skills Reminder

To link architecture to history, first establish the historical context of the piece of architecture. Identify the society that built the structure. Identify the major characteristics of the piece of architecture. Then describe the characteristics of the environment. Relate the environmental characteristics to the historical context in which the piece of architecture was built. Finally, identify the values expressed by linking the historical context of the piece of architecture with its environmental characteristics.

Skills Practice

❶ Carefully study the two buildings shown above. What do the images reveal about the societies that built them?

❷ What are their most evident similarities and differences?

❸ What do the images tell you about changes in public performance halls and the societies that support them?

❹ Using the library or Internet, research information about another piece of architecture you have seen in this book. Then write a short analysis of what it reflects about the society that built it.

In the 1980s and 1990s music videos became increasingly popular. This spread popular music and created fans worldwide for many musicians. Interest also grew in the music of different cultures. Many Western artists took their ideas from the music of Africa, the Caribbean, South America, and other parts of the world.

The world of dance also followed new directions after 1945. Artists who left Russia after its revolution particularly influenced ballet. Russian exile **George Balanchine** became founder, artistic director, and chief choreographer/director of the New York City Ballet. In the 1960s and 1970s, young ballet stars such as Rudolf Nureyev, Mikhail Baryshnikov, and Nataliya Makarova defected from the Soviet Union. They made new homes and careers in the West. After 1945 the freer and looser forms of modern dance began to affect ballet. As in all the performing arts, new forms of individual expression and experimentation took the place of traditional uniformity. **Martha Graham,** an American, became a leader in modern dance. In the late 1900s American choreographers such as Alvin Ailey Jr., Twyla Tharp, Paul Taylor, and Alwin Nikolais were powerful figures in the world of dance.

✔ **READING CHECK: Summarizing** What universal themes were expressed in music and dance, and who were the most influential figures in these fields after 1945?

INTERPRETING THE VISUAL RECORD

Modern dance Martha Graham's dance choreography expressed powerful emotions. *Why do you think Graham's dancing was influential during this period?*

Motion Pictures

Most filmmakers used traditional subjects after 1945. These included adventures, comedies, and social drama. Spectacular productions—costing millions of dollars—continued to be popular. Other films tried to break free of traditional restrictions. In the 1940s and 1950s, Italian directors such as **Federico Fellini** produced films that sharply criticized social and political injustice.

At the end of the 1950s, a group of young French directors known as the "New Wave" further revolutionized film. New Wave directors included Louis Malle and Jean-Luc Godard. They believed that the director should act as the *auteur,* or author, of a film. That is, a film should reflect one person's idea, rather than be a commercial package put together by a movie studio. The New Wave directors often used nontraditional filmmaking methods, such as hand-held cameras. They also edited their films in new ways. As a result they created a particular visual style for the film, which they believed was more important than the storyline.

Some of the most interesting but disturbing films of the 1960s and 1970s came from Japan. **Akira Kurosawa** and other Japanese directors used violence and a dark atmosphere to create startling and frightening new effects. Meanwhile director Lina Wërtmuller was making deeply satirical films about Italian politics and society as well as the relations between men and women.

Technical skill became an important part of American films after the 1970s. George Lucas's *Star Wars* series, Steven Spielberg's *E.T., The Extraterrestrial* (1982), and James Cameron's *Titanic* (1997) all depended heavily on visual effects. The creative use of computer technology was shown in *Jurassic Park* (1993), *Toy Story* (1995), and *Shrek* (2001). Meanwhile, independent moviemakers took film in a new direction. Largely free of ties to the big studios, they made films with strong social commentary. Director Spike Lee, for example, addressed the experiences of urban African Americans, forcing audiences to think about race relations.

The American filmmaking industry suffered financial setbacks during the 1980s when widespread use of VCRs, videotape rentals, and cable television in private homes gave movie theaters increasing competition. More recently, the influx of DVDs and the ability to download films has raised issues involving copyright law and piracy.

✔ **READING CHECK: Categorizing** Which countries influenced filmmaking the most after 1945?

Drama

Important new developments also occurred in the theater. In East Germany the company founded by playwright **Bertolt Brecht** staged plays that brought attention to their artificiality. Audience members were constantly reminded that they were watching a play. Perhaps the most powerful new outlook on the modern age was the biting social commentary of the playwrights of the so-called "**theater of the absurd.**" Its leaders were Samuel Beckett, an Irishman, and Eugene Ionesco, a Romanian. Both playwrights lived in France. Puzzlement and absurdity run throughout Beckett's works. His most famous play is *Waiting for Godot* (1953).

Other playwrights of the period made more realistic but no less sharp attacks on modern society. The most notable of these dramatists were John Osborne, an Englishman, and Arthur Miller, an American. Osborne wrote about the cruel lives of the British working class. Miller's powerful dramas—particularly *Death of a Salesman* (1949)—explored human weaknesses and the tensions in families. Social themes also entered the world of American musical theater. For example, *West Side Story* (1957), based on Shakespeare's *Romeo and Juliet,* focused on inner-city gangs divided by race and turf wars. Similarly, the hit Broadway musical *Rent* breathed new life into a classic story in the late 1990s. This modernized version of Puccini's opera *La Bohème* dealt with topics such as drug use and AIDS.

While on Broadway for nearly 18 years, the musical Cats was performed 7,485 times.

Other "blockbuster" musicals appeared in the 1980s and 1990s, featuring impressive sets and musical arrangements. Shows by British composer Andrew Lloyd Weber, including *Phantom of the Opera* and *Cats,* enjoyed much success and longevity on Broadway stages. *Cats,* based on a collection of works by British poet T.S. Eliot, closed in 2000 after the longest run in Broadway history. In addition, motion pictures served as inspiration for some Broadway musicals, such as *The Lion King,* based on the popular Disney film, and Mel Brooks's hit musical *The Producers,* which won a record-breaking 12 Tony Awards.

✔ **READING CHECK: Analyzing Information** How did plays and musicals of the postwar years reflect the histories of the cultures in which they were produced?

Poetry and Novels

Protest was a major theme of leading writers in the postwar years. Many poets and novelists took a stand against the comfortable self-satisfaction they saw in the world around them.

Writers. A group of writers called the **Beats** criticized wealthy citizens and their values. Beat novelist Jack Kerouac and poet Allen Ginsberg began writing in the 1950s. Like many Beat writers, they attacked the commercialism, materialism, and insensitivity they saw in the American way of life. With anger and sadness, Ralph Ellison and James Baldwin each wrote about the life of African Americans in the United States. Nigerian novelist Chinua Achebe examined the effects of colonial rule on his native land. Boris Pasternak and Aleksandr Solzhenitsyn addressed the oppression of the Soviet system. Writers from Eastern Europe wrote about the hardships of life under communism. These "underground" works were often the only source of truth for many Eastern Europeans.

Scientific and technological advances after World War II boosted interest in science fiction. Writers filled the imaginations of millions of readers with tales of space travel, robots, and distant planets. Ray Bradbury, Robert Heinlein, and Isaac Asimov were leading science fiction authors. A character in one of Bradbury's short stories gave voice to the excitement many people felt as humans came closer to breaking out of Earth's gravitational field.

"All I know is it's really the end of the beginning. The Stone Age, Bronze Age, Iron Age; from now on we'll lump all those together under one big name for when we walked on Earth and heard the birds at morning and cried with envy [jealousy]. Maybe we'll call it the Earth Age, or maybe the Age of Gravity."

Ray Bradbury, "The End of the Beginning"

Other writers such as American Kurt Vonnegut, Jr. created new views of the real world. These stories and novels also criticized the cold and heartless attitudes of the times. Mexican author Octavio Paz used haunting, lonely images of people in his dreamlike poems. Colombian Gabriel García Márquez wrote dark, mystical stories about everyday subjects. These two Latin American authors won Nobel Prizes for their work.

In recent years the voices of minority women have become increasingly powerful in the United States. Alice Walker (*The Color Purple*) and **Toni Morrison** (*Beloved*) won Pulitzer Prizes for their work. Morrison also won the Nobel Prize for literature. Walker and Morrison wrote about the issues African Americans faced from the period of slavery through the late 1900s. African American writer **Maya Angelou** wrote books and poetry that explored the black experience in the South. In her novels, Laura Esquivel looked at the experience of being a Hispanic woman in her native Mexico.

Criticism. Some writers provoked controversy. For example, in 1988 Western critics hailed Anglo-Indian author Salman Rushdie's satirical novel *The Satanic Verses*. Many Muslims, however, thought the book was extremely offensive. Some governments banned the book, and the Ayatollah Khomeini of Iran issued a death sentence against Rushdie. As a result the writer was forced into hiding. Violent demonstrations against *The Satanic Verses* occurred in Pakistan and other countries.

Controversy led to violence elsewhere as well. In 1994 Egyptian author Naguib Mahfouz became the first Arab writer to win the Nobel Prize. Mahfouz was attacked by an assailant who objected to the author's treatment of Islam in his works.

Holt Researcher

go.hrw.com
KEYWORD: Holt Researcher
FreeFind: Maya Angelou
Toni Morrison
After reading more about Maya Angelou and Toni Morrison on the Holt Researcher, assess how their personal experiences influenced their writing.

Analyzing Primary Sources

Analyzing Information How does this excerpt from Bradbury's science fiction story reflect the time in which it was written?

HISTORY MAKER

**Maya Angelou
(1928–   )**

Maya Angelou grew up in Arkansas. During her childhood, she experienced constant abuse and crushing poverty. Today she is celebrated as one of America's foremost writers and poets. Her books and poems explore racism and oppression of all kinds. **What topics form the focus of Maya Angelou's works?**

In 1988 Naguib Mahfouz became the first Arab writer to be awarded the Nobel Prize for literature.

At the end of the 1900s and as the next century began, novelists and poets continued to share their unique insights and personal experiences with readers around the world. Many of these writers produced works that expressed social commentary and powerful emotions. Some of the most influential writers today include Japanese novelist Kenzaburo Oe, American novelist John Updike, and Irish poet Seamus Heaney.

✔ **READING CHECK: Finding the Main Idea** What themes were important to postwar writers?

The Audience for the Arts

The excitement of postwar artistic and literary activity created great public interest. This was particularly true in the United States. More than half of the existing American museums today were founded since 1970. More Americans pay to go to museums, concerts, operas, ballets, and theaters each year than to attend sporting events.

Around the world today, people's average level of education continues to increase. People also have more time for leisure activities, particularly in industrialized nations. Television allows millions of viewers to see films, plays, concerts, and a wide range of other cultural activities. Many people continue to pursue similar interests outside the home. Thus education, increased leisure time, and expanding cultural awareness have combined to give the arts and literature greater exposure and support than ever before.

✔ **READING CHECK: Analyzing Information** What evidence suggests that more people participated in cultural activities after World War II?

SECTION 1 REVIEW

1. **Define** and explain the significance:
   abstract expressionism
   pop art
   op art
   conceptual art
   performance art
   theater of the absurd

2. **Identify** and explain the significance:
   Jackson Pollock
   George Balanchine
   Martha Graham
   Federico Fellini
   Akira Kurosawa
   Bertolt Brecht
   Beats
   Toni Morrison
   Maya Angelou

3. **Categorizing** Copy the chart below. Use it to identify the leading poets and novelists after 1945.

Theme/Category	Poets	Novelists
Beat generation		
African Americans		
Science Fiction		
Fantasy/Social commentary		
Women		

4. **Finding the Main Idea**
   a. What have been the major developments in painting and sculpture since 1945?
   b. What new techniques and designs have architects used since 1945?
   c. How have music and dance changed since the end of World War II?
   d. What trends developed in film and drama after 1945?

5. **Writing and Critical Thinking**
   Making Generalizations What overall trends have developed in the arts since 1945?
   Consider:
   • the visual arts
   • the performing arts
   • architecture
   • literature
   • public participation

Homework Practice Online
keyword: SH3 HP27

Science and Technology

READ TO DISCOVER

❶ What advances in travel and space exploration have occurred since 1945?

❷ What effect have miniaturization and computerization had on modern life?

❸ What technological improvements have been made in medical science?

❹ What environmental concerns have scientists identified?

DEFINE

miniaturization
supercomputers
laser
antibiotics
DNA
genetic code
cloning
urbanization
biodiversity
acid rain
greenhouse effect

IDENTIFY

Yury Gagarin
Alan Shepard
Neil Armstrong
Columbia
Alpha
Rachel Carson

WHY IT MATTERS TODAY

The United States continues to lead the world in space exploration. Use CNNStudentNews.com or other **current event** sources to learn about current NASA programs. Record your findings in your journal.

CNNStudentNews.com

The Main Idea
Dramatic advances in science and technology after World War II affected all the nations of the world.

The Story Continues *As astronaut Neil Armstrong climbed out of the lunar module and onto the surface of the moon, he spoke to Mission Control in Houston, Texas. "That's one small step for a man, one giant leap for mankind." Armstrong's words described the amazing achievement of putting humans on the moon. His words also speak to the whole of humans' extraordinary achievements in science and technology after World War II.*

Faster Travel

After World War II improvements in airplanes changed travel throughout the world. The first jetliner began passenger service between the United States and Europe in 1958. By the mid-1960s jetliner travel had become commonplace. The first jumbo jet began passenger service in 1970, traveling at speeds of more than 400 miles per hour. Air travel became the most popular and convenient way to visit distant places.

Meanwhile other forms of transportation also advanced rapidly. Trains in Japan and Europe sped through the countryside at more than 150 miles per hour. Automobile use increased throughout the world. In 1994 the Channel Tunnel, nicknamed the "Chunnel," connected Great Britain and France underneath the English Channel.

✔ **READING CHECK: Identifying Cause and Effect** When did the technology for jet airplanes develop, and how did it affect travel in the 1900s?

Space Exploration

The United States and the former Soviet Union led the world in space exploration. However, other countries such as Canada, Japan, and several Western European nations also developed space programs. In 2003, China launched its first manned spacecraft and the United States sent rovers to further Mars exploration.

Advances in air travel were a direct result of World War II. Engineers took the technology developed to build fighter jets in the war and changed it to fit the needs of civilian travel.

On July 20, 1969, the United States won the intense race to put the first person on the moon.

Early successes. The space age began on October 4, 1957, when the Soviet Union launched *Sputnik*—the world's first space satellite—into orbit around Earth. Then the Soviets built a rocket with enough power to put a person into orbit. Soviet cosmonaut **Yury Gagarin** became the first person to orbit Earth. The United States' progress in space exploration closely followed the Soviets. In 1958 the U.S. successfully launched an unmanned satellite into space. **Alan Shepard** became the first American to travel in space in 1961.

Lunar landing. In July 1969 the United States sent three Americans to the moon. They traveled aboard the spaceship *Columbia.* The astronauts on this *Apollo 11* mission were **Neil Armstrong,** Edwin "Buzz" Aldrin, Jr., and Michael Collins. On July 20, Armstrong and Aldrin boarded the lunar module, the *Eagle.* Collins stayed aboard the spaceship to help manage the mission. As the lunar module set down safely on the moon's surface, the crew told Mission Control, "The Eagle has landed." Mission Control responded, "Be advised, there are lots of smiling faces in this room and all over the world."

For the next two hours the astronauts took photographs and collected lunar soil and rocks. They also planted a U.S. flag on the moon's surface and conducted experiments. About 22 hours after the *Eagle* had landed, the astronauts left the moon and returned to the command module. On July 24, 1969, they returned to Earth.

✔ **READING CHECK: Sequencing** Identify the major events in the space race between the United States and the Soviet Union.

Unmanned spacecraft. The United States completed several manned moon landings from 1969 to 1972. Then the U.S. space program began to shift its focus to unmanned spacecraft. These missions explored the solar system. Late in 1973 *Pioneer 10* became the first spacecraft to fly by Jupiter. In mid-1976, *Viking 1* and *Viking 2* landed on Mars, the "red planet." For several years they sent information back to Earth that helped scientists understand the planet's makeup. *Voyager 1* and *Voyager 2,* launched in 1977, explored the more distant planets of the solar system. Both made flybys of Jupiter and Saturn between 1979 and 1981. They sent spectacular photographs back to Earth. Then *Voyager 2* continued to the outer reaches of the solar system. It passed the planet Uranus in 1986 and by 1989 had reached Neptune.

After a break of some years, the United States restarted its unmanned space exploration program in 1989 with the *Magellan* and *Galileo* missions. *Magellan* mapped nearly the entire surface of Venus. *Galileo* went into orbit around Jupiter in 1995, sending back information about the planet and its moons. One of the most exciting accomplishments in the mid-1990s was the landing of another U.S. spacecraft on Mars. The *Pathfinder,* which touched down on July 4, 1997, gave scientists strong proof that there had once been water on Mars. Water is the key item needed to create and sustain life. Scientists launched *NEAR Shoemaker* (Near Earth Asteroid Rendezvous) in 1996. This spacecraft was the first to study asteroids, or deep space geology. *NEAR* spent one year taking 160,000 photographs of the asteroid Eros. At the end of the mission, NASA successfully landed the spacecraft on Eros. This gave scientists even more detailed photographs of the asteroid's surface.

Satellites. Satellites are spacecraft that orbit Earth and include several types—communications, weather, Earth observation, navigation, and military. Communications satellites receive radio signals from one location on Earth and then send the signals to a different location. Recent improvements in this technology have made satellite radio possible, giving listeners far more choices in audio entertainment than available on traditional radio. Advances in navigation satellite technology have resulted in widespread availability of global positioning systems (GPS). Originally designed for military use, GPS technology now allows people to determine their precise location when operating a GPS-equipped car, boat, plane—or even cell phone or wristwatch.

New frontiers in space. A new period of space exploration began in 1981. That year the United States launched the first space shuttle, *Columbia.* By 1986 these reusable shuttles had made two dozen successful missions, so the launch of the *Challenger* on January 28, 1986, seemed routine. However, 73 seconds after liftoff the shuttle burst into flames, killing its seven crew members. The disaster halted U.S. manned space flights until the launch of the space shuttle *Discovery* in 1988. In 1990 the *Discovery's* crew placed the Hubble Space telescope into orbit, allowing astronomers to look deeper into space than ever before.

The United States and the Soviet Union also built space stations. The Soviets led the way with the launch of *Salyut 1* in 1971. Two years later, the United States followed with *Skylab.* These space stations allowed astronauts to do experiments in geography, engineering, medicine, and many other fields. After the Cold War ended, the United States and the former Soviet Union joined some of their space exploration efforts. In 1995 the United States space shuttle *Atlantis* docked with the Russian space station *Mir.* The United States, Russia, and 14 other nations began building an International Space Station (ISS) in 1998. In November 2000 one U.S. astronaut and two Russian cosmonauts began a four-month stay on the ISS. They named their new home *Alpha.*

On February 1, 2003, tragedy again struck the U.S. space program. That morning, the space shuttle *Columbia* disintegrated upon re-entering Earth's atmosphere after a successful space mission. All seven astronauts aboard were killed. Athough U.S. manned space flights were once again suspended until safety improvements could be made, the United States and Russia reaffirmed their commitment to continue work on the ISS.

Sixteen nations worked together to build the International Space Station—now one of the brightest objects in the night sky.

✔ **READING CHECK: Summarizing** How did scientists learn about the solar system after the moon landing?

Miniaturization and Computerization

Advances in air and space travel often involved making machines smaller and lighter. This process is known as **miniaturization.** One of the most helpful products of miniaturization was a tiny electronic device called the transistor, invented in 1947. It took the place of the much larger vacuum tube and could do many times as much work. Within 25 years, many transistors and other components could be placed on an integrated circuit—a tiny wafer of material such as silicon.

ENIAC formally started working in February 1946. The computer contained 18,000 tubes, and its power source was half as large as the machine itself.

Miniaturization made possible dozens of new products that affect the activities of people around the world. Portable radios, pocket calculators, digital watches, and automatic cameras developed from this process. At first these products were expensive and not widely used. However, costs fell quickly as technology advanced and the demand for such products increased.

History of the computer. The most remarkable result of miniaturization was the modern computer. In the 1600s the French scientist Blaise Pascal invented the first automatic calculator. It worked with wheels linked to each other by gears. The idea interested scientists and engineers for the next 300 years. In the 1830s Charles Babbage designed a mechanical calculating machine that he called the "analytical engine." His machine had all of a modern computer's basic parts. These include data storage, memory, a system for moving between the memory and storage components, and an input device. Babbage was not, however, able to build the machine he designed.

ENIAC—Electronic Numerical Integrator and Calculator—was an enormous computer built in 1946. It took up a whole room at the University of Pennsylvania. The discovery of transistors helped make possible much smaller machines that could store and rapidly process information. The later development of integrated circuits also allowed for smaller machines. As scientists improved computers year after year, the new machines quickly began to influence society. Computers became faster and more efficient. Meanwhile they needed less and less space to store gigantic amounts of information. As a result, products ranging from automobiles to self-focusing cameras to microwave ovens began using computers.

Computer uses. Computers made it easier for doctors to diagnose diseases. They also improved patients' treatment. Devices such as CAT (computerized axial tomography) scanners and MRI (magnetic resonance imaging) machines allow doctors to view the human body in incredible detail. These diagnostic tools reduce the need for surgery. Outside the medical field, tasks assigned to computers range from guiding spacecraft, to printing newspapers, to constructing maps. In addition, large and powerful **supercomputers** help to solve complex scientific and engineering problems. Solutions to these problems would have been impossible a short time ago. Supercomputers have more than one processing unit. This means they can do billions of computations per second. Supercomputers have revolutionized the way products are developed, experiments are conducted, and research is performed.

Today computers increasingly affect people's daily lives. Desktop and lightweight laptop computers are common in offices, homes, schools, and libraries. Businesses use computers to process and store enormous amounts of financial and administrative information. The range of activities affected by computers grows daily. Meanwhile, computers continue to increase in power and speed while shrinking in size and cost.

✔ **READING CHECK: Making Generalizations** How have miniaturization and computerization affected modern life?

Communications

After World War II technological advances made radio and then television affordable to more people. Radio and television made it possible to spread ideas and information faster and to more people than ever before.

The Internet. The development of computers further extended the information revolution. The Internet allows computers to communicate with one another over telephone lines. By connecting computer networks, the Internet creates a global network. People all over the world can exchange information—words, pictures, and sound—nearly instantaneously. About 250 million personal computers had access to the Internet by 2000. People spent an average of one hour per day online. Many now communicate with each other through e-mail—electronic messages delivered in a matter of seconds.

In the 1990s companies began using the Internet to do business, market and sell products, and carry out research. As a result, the number of Internet-related jobs in 1999 doubled from the previous year to 2.5 million. The high-tech industry was responsible for nearly a third of real U.S. economic growth in the late 1990s. The fastest growing part of Internet business was the sale of products online, often called e-commerce.

In the 1990s and the years that followed, the Internet (at left) came into worldwide use as both a business and educational tool. Below, women in Somalia use computers.

Other innovations. In addition to desktop computers, many other important methods of communication came into use in the late 1900s. In the 1970s photocopiers became essential business machines. In the 1980s and 1990s fax machines became affordable and widely used. Cellular phones became common in the mid-1990s. Fiber-optic cables also improved communications. These cables use light instead of electricity or radio waves to send information. In 1960 an American scientist built the first **laser.** A laser concentrates light and releases it in an intense beam that travels in a straight line. Lasers are used in communications as well as medicine and industry. Radio, television, and telephone signals are sent with lasers. Doctors use lasers to repair damaged tissue in the eye and to burn away unhealthy tissue. Lasers help manufacturers accurately cut into hard substances, such as metal or diamonds. They can even be used to clean delicate pieces of art.

✔ **READING CHECK: Finding the Main Idea** What new communication tools were developed after World War II?

Medical Science

Not all advances that followed World War II involved physics or electronics. Biologists and other scientists made large gains in their battle against disease.

Treatment of diseases. In 1928 the British scientist Alexander Fleming discovered a substance he called penicillin. He noted that it stopped the growth of many types of bacteria. Fleming believed penicillin could help cure illnesses caused by those bacteria.

Science and Technology

Genetic Engineering

During the 1980s scientists began to use genetic engineering to alter genes in plants and animals. A major goal of this effort was to produce bigger and better food sources.

Today scientists have identified genes that cause or contribute to Alzheimer's disease, breast cancer, skin cancer, and other devastating illnesses. In the photo below, lab technicians analyze a film showing part of a DNA sequence. Scientists are also learning how to use gene therapy—replacing defective genes with normal genes—as a major new approach to medicine.

Our increasing control over the human genetic makeup raises important moral and ethical questions. For example, will people be able to create "designer babies" by selecting specific characteristics such as hair color, eye color, or musical ability? If so, what would the implications be for society? Bioethicists are struggling with such questions as our ability to control our genetic structures continues to increase.

Understanding Science and Technology

What are some potentially positive and negative effects of genetic engineering?

Penicillin and similar substances that can kill or limit bacterial growth are called **antibiotics.** After 1945 these "wonder drugs" transformed the fight against disease. Antibiotics cured some illnesses, such as tuberculosis, that previously had no cure. Medical researchers also made great progress in preventing disease. Jonas Salk's polio vaccine was released for general use in 1954. As a result, polio has been all but wiped out in developed countries. Similarly, a worldwide campaign against smallpox nearly eliminated the disease by the 1980s. Elsewhere, however, overuse of antibiotics for conditions that antibiotics cannot cure (such as the cold or flu) has begun to limit their effectiveness in treating some conditions for which they were designed (various viruses, for example).

The worldwide AIDS (acquired immunodeficiency syndrome) epidemic began in the early 1980s. By the end of 2001 the United Nations UNAIDS program had recorded nearly 22 million deaths from AIDS since the beginning of the epidemic. In 2003, 40 million people were living with HIV/AIDS. Of these cases, Sub-Saharan Africa had about 25 million. There is no known vaccine or cure for AIDS. However, researchers have had increasing success in treating AIDS with a powerful combination of drugs. Making these often-expensive drugs available to poor AIDS patients in Africa and Asia, where the disease continues to accelerate, has proven a major challenge. Fighting the disease requires continuing research and education programs. AIDS education teaches people how HIV, the virus that causes AIDS, is spread and how it can be prevented.

Genetics. In 1953 scientists discovered the structure of **DNA** (deoxyribonucleic acid). DNA is a basic part of genes—the small units of chromosomes that determine hereditary characteristics, such as eye and hair color. In 2001 an international team called the Human Genome Project mapped the chemical structure of DNA. This sequence of DNA's chemical "letters" provides a "recipe" for human life, called the **genetic code.** Understanding this genetic code may lead to new cures for cancer, heart disease, and other illness. One scientist involved in the project explained its importance.

History Makers Speak

"[Mapping human DNA] has been compared with putting a man on the moon, but I believe it is more than that. This is the outstanding achievement not only of our lifetime but perhaps in the history of mankind."

Michael Dexter, "Human Genome to go Public," www.cnn.com

Scientists' knowledge of DNA raised new questions about what could be done with their findings. The process of making a genetically identical copy of an animal's cell is called **cloning.** In 1997 researchers at the Roslin Institute in Edinburgh, Scotland, successfully cloned a sheep. Since then, other species of mammals have been cloned. Some experts believe that within the next decade scientists might have the ability to clone humans.

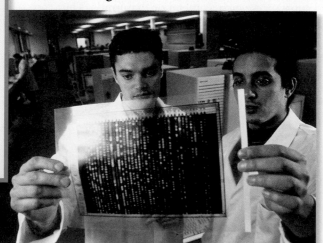

✔ **READING CHECK: Evaluating** What is the significance of developments in medical science and genetic research since 1945?

Technology

With increasingly powerful instruments, physical scientists were able to look at the tiny particles within the atom. They soon learned how to use the energy released when the structure of the atom is changed. Atomic energy was first used to make more powerful bombs. Later it was used to produce electricity for a growing population. Whenever atomic energy is created, dangerous radiation, known as radioactivity, is released. When carefully controlled, radioactivity can have very helpful medical uses. For example, cancer can be treated with radiation. Uncontrolled exposure, however, can be deadly.

An explosion at the Chernobyl nuclear power plant in the Soviet Union in 1986 made radiation's dangers clear. Chernobyl was the world's worst nuclear accident. The explosion spread radioactive material over areas in the Soviet Union and Europe. Many people later died of radiation-related illnesses. Cancer rates and the number of birth defects jumped. Doctors believed these trends would continue for decades. The Chernobyl accident increased opposition to nuclear power. However, researchers continued to find helpful uses for radiation, including treatment of disease and food preservation.

Chemists developed the first synthetic substances—materials that do not occur in nature—in laboratories in the 1800s. It was not until the 1940s, however, that these synthetic substances, called plastics, began to appear in every area of life. Plastics completely changed the way products looked. They also changed how products were manufactured. By the 1990s plastics were being used to create automobiles, desktop computers, clothing, and many other products.

Since 1945 technological advances have dramatically changed the world. Devices such as telephones and refrigerators existed before 1945. However, only after the war were they made cheaply enough for millions of people to buy them. New technological products are more common in industrialized nations. However, they have also had a great influence on life in developing nations. New industries, such as television and computer manufacturing, sprang up. Millions of people were employed in new kinds of jobs. World trade also grew as nations exchanged new products.

Tens of thousands of people living near Chernobyl had to be evacuated after a nuclear accident in 1986.

✔ **READING CHECK: Identifying Cause and Effect** How did technology affect people's lives in the late 1900s?

Science and the Environment

Many scientists are looking at ways to preserve the world's environment. Some scientific advances have had unexpected effects on the natural world. Scientists are helping to find ways to balance human needs with the earth's delicate environment.

Deforestation Around the World, c. 1940–1995

Interpreting Maps In recent years many of the world's tropical rain forests have experienced deforestation, or the loss of trees, due to numerous factors.

■ **Skills Assessment: Places and Regions** What country has the world's largest remaining area of rain forest?

Rachel Carson raised awareness of the effects of pesticides on the environment.

Population issues. An important development in the postwar period was the rapid growth in world population. Between 1930 and 1950, world population grew by about 23 percent. In the next four decades, however, population rose by 112 percent. It reached almost 6.3 billion people in 2003 as medical advances and improvements in health and sanitation lowered death rates. Scientific advances also helped feed people.

Migration from the countryside to the city—a process known as **urbanization**—has swelled urban populations around the world. From Mexico City to Cairo to Calcutta, overcrowding has added to environmental problems such as pollution in those areas. Limiting the birth rate and improving food production are two of the ways people are trying to ease the effects of population growth.

Population growth and industrialization increase the need for land and other natural resources. As a result, forests, wetlands, and other areas are sometimes destroyed, causing the loss of plant and animal habitats. This situation has been a particular problem in the world's rain forests. Some scientists argue that this reduction in **biodiversity**—the variety of plants and animals that naturally occurs in the environment—could have damaging effects on humans as well as the environment. Industrialization and population also increase the amount of waste humans create. Government and industry leaders in many nations continue searching for ways to reduce waste, encourage recycling, and safely dispose of dangerous materials.

Effects of pollution. Air pollution also became an environmental concern. Motor vehicles and factories pollute the air with toxins when they burn fossil fuels. When rain falls through these toxins in the air, **acid rain** is created. Recently many nations have worked together to reduce the production of toxins. After 1945 many farmers began to use pesticides to decrease crop damage caused by insects. **Rachel Carson** warned in her 1962 book, *Silent Spring,* that some pesticides had harmful effects on the environment. As a result, certain pesticides were banned from use. Scientists now pay closer attention to the long-term environmental effects of pesticides.

According to many scientists, the burning of oil, coal, and natural gas has increased the amounts of carbon dioxide and other gases in the earth's atmosphere. At normal levels these gases allow the sun's rays to warm the planet and keep the earth's heat from escaping. This **greenhouse effect** helps keep the earth's temperature at the right levels for plants and animals to live. When the level of greenhouse gases increase, more heat is trapped and global temperatures rise. Scientists do not agree on just how great a danger global warming is, but they are closely monitoring changes in the earth's temperature. The United Nations has also held summits addressing this issue.

Some scientists argue that pollution is causing the ozone layer in the earth's atmosphere to become thinner. Ozone is a gas that shields the earth against the sun's ultraviolet rays. These dangerous rays can cause skin cancer in humans and damage plant and animal life. Some scientists believe that a leading cause of ozone thinning is the use of chemicals called chlorofluorocarbons (CFCs). CFCs are used in aerosol sprays, coolants, and to make electronic parts and plastics. Many countries began to phase out or ban the use of CFCs in the 1980s and 1990s.

✔ **READING CHECK: Categorizing** What environmental problems have scientists been concerned about in recent years?

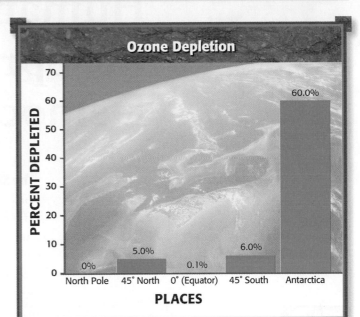

Ozone Depletion

Interpreting the Graph
Many scientists believe that ozone depletion in the atmosphere has been caused by pollution. *How might a person use these same statistics to argue that ozone depletion is not caused by pollution?*

SECTION 2 REVIEW

1. **Define** and explain the significance:
   miniaturization
   supercomputers
   laser
   antibiotics
   DNA
   genetic code
   cloning
   urbanization
   biodiversity
   acid rain
   greenhouse effect

2. **Identify** and explain the significance:
   Yury Gagarin
   Alan Shepard
   Neil Armstrong
   Columbia
   Alpha
   Rachel Carson

3. **Identifying Cause and Effect**
   Copy the graphic organizer below. Use it to identify the effects of World War II and U.S.-Soviet competition on travel and space exploration.

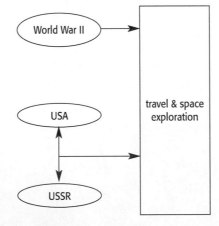

4. **Finding the Main Idea**
   a. Describe the influence of miniaturization and computerization on life in the late 1900s.
   b. List three medical or technological advances made since 1945 and their importance.
   c. How has the rate of growth of the world population changed during the 1900s? What effect might this have on the environment?
   d. What were some of the causes of pollution during the 1900s, and what were some of the solutions scientists proposed for dealing with pollution?

5. **Writing and Critical Thinking**
   Making Generalizations Select one of the technological advances discussed in this chapter and explain ways in which it could have positive and negative effects.
   Consider:
   • genetics
   • nuclear science
   • the environment

READ TO DISCOVER

❶ What are some recent examples of human rights abuses?

❷ How have the nations of the world dealt with human rights violations?

❸ How did democratic ideals and practices spread in the late 1900s?

WHY IT MATTERS TODAY

Abuses of human rights continue today. Use CNN student News.com or other **current event** sources to find out what countries are currently abusing human rights and what people are doing to combat it. Record your findings in your journal.

CNN student News.com

Human Rights and the Spread of Democratic Ideals

The Main Idea
In many parts of the world, respect for human rights and democracy spread after World War II.

The Story Continues *"I have a dream that one day . . . all of God's children . . . will be able to join hands and sing in the words of the old Negro spiritual, 'Free at last! Free at last! Thank God Almighty, we are free at last!'"* Martin Luther King, Jr. spoke these words as he led the fight for African American equality in the United States. Around the world many people worked to protect and advance basic human rights.

Human Rights Issues

The horrors of World War II demonstrated the need to protect human rights around the world. To advance support of human rights, in 1945 the newly formed United Nations made a strong statement.

Primary Source

❝We the people of the United Nations, determined . . . to reaffirm faith in fundamental human rights, in the dignity and worth of the human person, in the equal rights of men and women and of nations large and small, . . . have resolved to combine our efforts to accomplish these aims.❞

from the Preamble to the United Nations Charter

In 1948 the UN adopted the **Universal Declaration of Human Rights.** This document outlined the basic human rights that the international community agreed every person should have. However, the UN did not have any way to enforce the declaration or later agreements on human rights. Indeed, most countries argued that any attempt at enforcement would violate their national sovereignty. This opposition to outside influence remains a major problem for international human rights protection.

Human rights abuses. Even though the United Nations continues to address human rights abuses around the world, such abuses remain all too common. Human rights violations often have political, ethnic, racial, or religious roots. For example,

These refugees fled Bosnia to avoid the ethnic cleansing in that country.

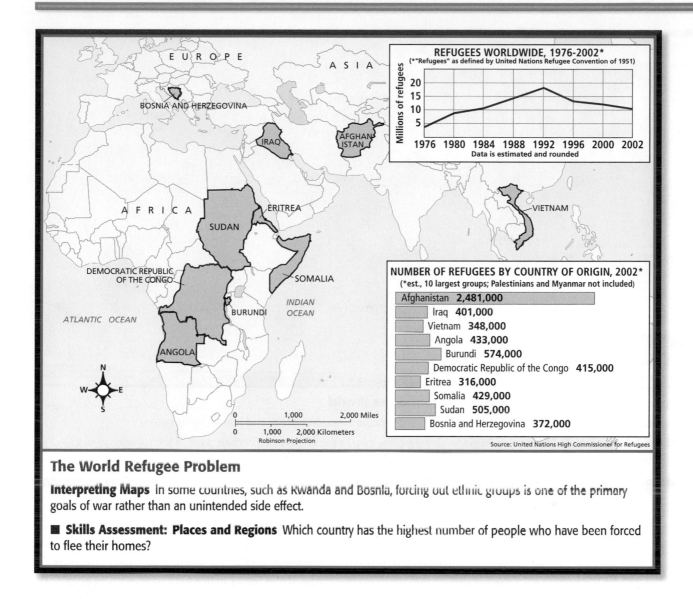

REFUGEES WORLDWIDE, 1976-2002*
(*"Refugees" as defined by United Nations Refugee Convention of 1951)

Millions of refugees: 20, 15, 10, 5
1976 1980 1984 1988 1992 1996 2000 2002
Data is estimated and rounded

NUMBER OF REFUGEES BY COUNTRY OF ORIGIN, 2002*
(*est., 10 largest groups; Palestinians and Myanmar not included)

Country	Refugees
Afghanistan	2,481,000
Iraq	401,000
Vietnam	348,000
Angola	433,000
Burundi	574,000
Democratic Republic of the Congo	415,000
Eritrea	316,000
Somalia	429,000
Sudan	505,000
Bosnia and Herzegovina	372,000

Source: United Nations High Commissioner for Refugees

The World Refugee Problem

Interpreting Maps In some countries, such as Rwanda and Bosnia, forcing out ethnic groups is one of the primary goals of war rather than an unintended side effect.

■ **Skills Assessment: Places and Regions** Which country has the highest number of people who have been forced to flee their homes?

brutal "ethnic cleansing" during the civil war in Bosnia resulted in thousands of deaths. In addition to interethnic war crimes in Kosovo and Rwanda, terrorist acts in Northern Ireland have also killed many innocent people. Elsewhere, repressive governments have imprisoned, tortured, and executed people who have spoken out against them.

✔ **READING CHECK: Summarizing** What are some recent examples of human rights abuses?

Protecting human rights. Still, there has been some progress. International pressure helped bring an end to apartheid in South Africa. In 1994 that nation held its first truly democratic election. Political changes in the former Soviet Union also led to improved human rights, and tensions have eased in Northern Ireland. In addition to the United Nations, many other organizations work to protect human rights. For example, Amnesty International, a private organization, investigates and reports on human rights abuses around the world. International organizations have pressed for officials who abuse human rights to be tried for war crimes. In addition to human rights in general, people in many countries have actively supported the rights of specific groups, such as women and children.

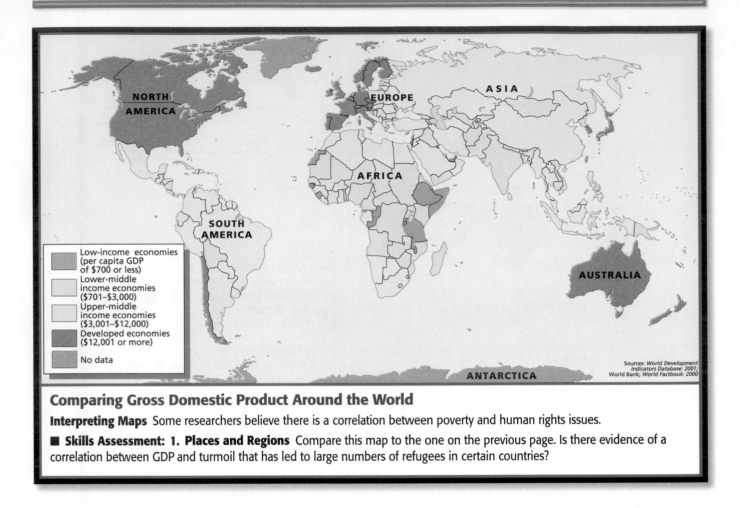

Comparing Gross Domestic Product Around the World

Interpreting Maps Some researchers believe there is a correlation between poverty and human rights issues.

■ **Skills Assessment: 1. Places and Regions** Compare this map to the one on the previous page. Is there evidence of a correlation between GDP and turmoil that has led to large numbers of refugees in certain countries?

One challenge to addressing human rights is that the concept does not have a single, universal meaning. Different cultures look at human rights in different ways. Some people, particularly in non-Western countries, place greater importance on the interests of the community than on the rights of the individual. Many of these people criticize Western nations for expecting other nations to follow their values. Similarly, such concepts as women's rights have different meanings in different societies. In the Islamic world, women's rights are viewed within the context of the Qur'an, the holy book of Islam. Others argue that allowing people to live in extreme poverty is a violation of human rights. They argue that one way to combat human rights abuses is to try to help improve the overall Gross Domestic Product (GDP) of poorer nations.

✔ **READING CHECK: Finding the Main Idea** What are some ways that people have successfully advanced human rights?

The Spread of Democratic Ideals

During the 50-year period after World War II, communism spread to many nations. Then in the early 1990s, the Soviet Union and its former satellite states in Eastern Europe rejected communism. These countries were actually part of a larger trend in world politics that began in the mid-1970s. Authoritarian regimes began to lose control of many countries and democracy began to take hold. For example, after decades of dictatorship in Portugal, a constitutional government finally began in 1976.

In 1975 Spanish dictator Francisco Franco died. Spain returned to democracy under the restored constitutional monarch, King Juan Carlos I. This trend toward democracy continued in the 1980s and grew after the fall of communism in the Soviet Union and Eastern Europe.

Democratic gains. Democracy made significant gains in Asia. South Korea and Taiwan both allowed more popular participation in politics. Democracy returned to the Philippines after nearly 15 years of autocratic rule by Ferdinand Marcos. In Pakistan and Bangladesh, military rulers stepped aside, if not very far and not always for very long. Latin America also experienced a shift toward democracy. Nicaragua, Chile, Brazil, Argentina, Peru, and Mexico moved from various levels of dictatorship and authoritarian rule to more democratic systems of government. In South Africa the formerly powerless black majority elected a government headed by Nelson Mandela. In 1998 Indonesians forced President Suharto to leave office after 32 years of authoritarian rule.

Holdouts on democracy. While many nations moved toward democracy, a few governments continued authoritarian rule. The People's Republic of China began economic reforms to move towards a free market. At the same time, however, hard-line communists cracked down on a growing pro-democracy movement. Living standards in Cuba dropped dramatically after Soviet economic support dried up in the early 1990s. Nevertheless, Fidel Castro continued to hold on to power. Communist rule also continued in North Korea, even though longtime dictator Kim Il Sung died in 1994.

Some other countries also chose not to follow the trend toward democracy. Muslim revolutionaries limited democratic participation in Iran and Sudan. Older revolutionary dictatorships continued in Syria and Iraq. Saudi Arabia remained under the autocratic rule of the Saudi royal family. A military junta continued to repress democracy in Burma. Human rights activist Aung San Suu Kyi lived under house arrest in Burma from 1989 to 1995. Suu Kyi was not allowed to attend the presentation ceremony for her Nobel Peace Prize in 1991. However, she never stopped working for democratic reforms.

✔ **READING CHECK: Finding the Main Idea** What made the spread of democratic ideals and practices possible?

YOUNG PEOPLE IN HISTORY

Children's Rights

Within a century children have gone from having almost no legal rights to having most of the same legal rights as adults. In 1989 the United Nations passed the **"Convention on the Rights of the Child."** This agreement outlines the legal, social, and economic guidelines that each country must follow to protect children. The accord has won support worldwide. **How have views of children's rights changed?**

Holt Researcher

go.hrw.com
KEYWORD: Holt Researcher
FreeFind: Aung San Suu Kyi
After reading more about Aung San Suu Kyi, assess how she helped to advance human rights and democratic ideals.

SECTION 3 REVIEW

1. **Identify** and explain the significance:
   Universal Declaration of Human Rights
   Convention on the Rights of the Child

2. **Making Generalizations** Copy the graphic organizer below. Use it to identify countries that moved toward democracy in the late 1900s.

   Democratization after 1970

3. ### Finding the Main Idea
   a. What areas of the world are still struggling with human rights issues?
   b. How has the international community worked to protect human rights?

4. ### Writing and Critical Thinking
   Supporting a Point of View Imagine you are the U.S. ambassador to the United Nations. Write a speech arguing that nations must work together to advance human rights and democratic ideals.
   Consider:
   • where human rights violations have occurred
   • how knowledge of human rights issues has spread
   • how democracy has spread

Homework Practice Online
go.hrw.com
keyword: SH3 HP27

CHAPTER 27 Review

Creating a Time Line

Copy the time line below onto a sheet of paper. Complete the time line by filling in events, individuals, and dates from the chapter that you think were significant. Pick three events and explain why you think they were significant.

| 1945 | 1985 | present |

Writing a Summary

Using standard grammar, spelling, sentence structure, and punctuation, write an overview of the chapter.

Identifying People and Ideas

Identify the following terms or individuals and explain their significance:

1. abstract expressionism
2. George Balanchine
3. Maya Angelou
4. Yury Gagarin
5. *Alpha*
6. miniaturization
7. genetic code
8. urbanization
9. biodiversity
10. Rachel Carson

Understanding Main Ideas

Section 1 *(pp. 782–788)*

The Arts and Literature

1. What were the major themes in painting, sculpture, and architecture after World War II?
2. How did poetry and novels written in the years after 1945 reflect postwar society around the world?

Section 2 *(pp. 789–797)*

Science and Technology

3. How have major trends and developments in modern technology, such as miniaturization and computerization, changed modern life?
4. What major advances in medical science have taken place since 1945?

Section 3 *(pp. 798–801)*

Human Rights and the Spread of Democratic Ideals

5. Why are human rights difficult to protect?
6. What evidence suggests that democracy has spread in the late 1900s?

Reviewing Themes

1. **Culture** What direction did developments in the arts and literature follow in the years after World War II?
2. **Science, Technology & Society** How can technological change affect ideas and behavior?
3. **Citizenship** What challenges to well-being can people expect in the future?

Thinking Critically

1. **Comparing** How were early successes of the space exploration programs of the United States and the Soviet Union similar?
2. **Evaluating** How might rapid population growth in a developing country slow down other types of growth and development?
3. **Drawing Inferences** What are some of the positive and negative results of genetic engineering?
4. **Identifying Cause and Effect** How did lifestyles in America change after World War II, and what factors caused these changes?

Writing About History

Problem Solving Imagine that you are a journalist who specializes in developing articles about modern issues and challenges. Choose a current environmental problem and write a short paper that describes several ways the world community might deal with the issue. Then predict what the outcomes of your suggested actions might be. Analyze which interest groups might favor your recommendations and which might oppose them, and explain why. Use the following diagram to organize your thoughts before you begin writing.

Comparing and Contrasting

Study the list of modern sources of information below. Then use the information from the list to answer the questions that follow.

Some Typical Sources of Information in Today's World

- The Internet
- Information passed by word of mouth
- Newspapers and magazines
- Public library
- Television and radio

1. Which of the statements below is the most accurate?

   a. The most important source of information among the sources listed above is "The Internet."

   b. Public libraries are the best single source of information because they are so easy to use.

   c. All of the sources listed above are important, and all take different approaches to information sharing.

   d. Television and radio are most important because they rely upon sight and sound.

2. Information is more available in greater quantities today than ever before. Write a brief paragraph explaining why this might actually pose a disadvantage to those who seek information.

Identifying Cause and Effect

Read the following quote from a report about information technology. Then answer the questions.

> "In June 1999, reporters from around the world flocked to Bhutan to watch the tiny Himalayan kingdom officially enter the information age. Bhutan's rulers had long tried to protect the nation's traditional Buddhist culture from outside influence with limits on tourist traffic and bans on satellite television receivers. But now King Wangchuck was . . . inaugurating Bhutan's first Internet hookup and addressing his subjects during the nation's first television broadcast. . . . Bhutan has joined a diverse and rapidly expanding global network."

3. Which of the following correctly states the reason so many reporters went to Bhutan in 1999?

   a. Reporters had not been allowed to visit the small nation of Bhutan for many years, but now they were allowed in to cover this event.

   b. Many of the reporters wanted to see the Himalayas.

   c. This was an important news story because Bhutan's king had rejected Buddhism.

   d. This was an important news story because Bhutan had successfully resisted outside influence for so long.

4. Do you think it is important for all countries to be part of the global information network? Give specific reasons.

Alternative Assessment

Building Your Portfolio

Link to TODAY

Citizenship

Democratic ideals and practices spread to new countries in the late 1900s. Select one country that changed to a democratic government after 1970. Research the reasons for and consequences of this change. Is everyday life for citizens of this country better or worse since democracy took hold? Make an oral presentation of your findings to your class.

internet connect

Internet Activity: go.hrw.com
KEYWORD: SH3 WH27

Choose a topic on the Modern World to:
- investigate global warming.
- learn more about modern world literature by studying contemporary novelists and poets.
- write a biography about one of the artists mentioned in this chapter.

CROSS-CULTURAL CONNECTIONS *Literature*

Cultural Pride

Léopold Senghor and Isabel Allende find inspiration for their literature in their cultural heritage. Born in Senegal and educated in France, Léopold Sédar Senghor explains that many of his poems echo African dance rhythms while they tell of African nations' struggles to overcome hatred of the colonial powers that once ruled them. After leading Senegal's independence movement, Senghor served as the country's first president from 1960 to 1980. Novelist Isabel Allende was forced to leave Chile in 1973 after her uncle, President Salvadore Allende, was assassinated in a military coup. Allende's novel The House of the Spirits *tells the story of several generations of a Latin American family led by Esteban Trueba. Allende uses the conflicts in Trueba's family to mirror issues dividing Latin America in the late 1900s.*

"Prayer to the Masks"
by Léopold Senghor

The Africa of empires is dying—it is the agony
Of a sorrowful princess
And Europe, too, tied to us at
   the navel.
Fix your steady eyes on your
   oppressed children
Who give their lives like the
   poor man his last garment.
Let us answer "present" at the
   rebirth of the World
As white flour cannot rise without
   the leaven.
Who else will teach rhythm to the world
Deadened by machines and cannons?
Who will sound the shout of joy at daybreak to wake orphans
   and the dead?
Tell me, who will bring back the memory of life
To the man of gutted hopes?
They call us men of cotton, coffee, and oil
They call us men of death.
But we are men of dance, whose feet get stronger
As we pound upon firm ground.

The House of the Spirits
by Isabel Allende

Jaime practiced his profession with the vocation of a true apostle. . . . [H]e spent his strength working in the clinic and treating the poor without charge in his spare time.

"You're a hopeless loser, son," Trueba would say, sighing. "You have no sense of reality. You've never taken stock of how the world really is. You put your faith in utopian values that don't even exist."

"Helping one's neighbor is a value that exists."

"No. Charity, like Socialism, is an invention of the weak to exploit the strong and bring them to their knees."

"I don't believe in your theory of the weak and the strong," Jaime replied.

"That's the way it is in nature. We live in a jungle."

"Yes, because the people who make up the rules think like you! But it won't always be that way."

"Oh, yes, it will. Because we always win. We know how to move around in the world and how to use power. Listen to me, son. Pull yourself together and open your own clinic. I'll help you. But cut out your Socialist nonsense!"

Understanding Literature

What evidence of cultural pride can you find in Senghor's and Allende's literature? Why do you think their writings are widely read outside their cultures?

Citizenship

The nature of citizenship changed for many Europeans, Asians, and Latin Americans during the last decades of the 1900s. Imagine that you are an artist living in Buenos Aires, Argentina, in 1983. You have been asked to create a mural for a new civic building. Your task is to create a series of images that depict the new meaning of citizenship in your country compared to other countries. What kinds of images would you show, and what would they reveal about the nature of citizenship in the 1980s?

Miniature flags from some of the world's nations

Demolition of the Berlin Wall

Global Relations

During the second half of the 1900s, sweeping political changes took place in many countries around the world. As a result, our world is a far different place today than it was in the 1950s. Imagine that you are a historian at work on a biographical dictionary. The dictionary will contain entries describing significant political figures on the world stage between the years 1945 and 2000. Your task is to prepare individual sample entries discussing five political figures whom you consider the most important leaders of the period. Which figures would you include? Ask yourself which world leaders had the greatest global impact during the years after World War II. Explain your selections.

Further Reading

Fireside, Harvey and Bryna J. Fireside. *Young People From Bosnia Talk About War.* New York: Enslow Publishing, 1996. First-person accounts from teenagers living in Bosnia during the civil war.

Matthews, John R. *The Rise and Fall of the Soviet Union.* San Diego: Lucent Books, 2000. A comprehensive survey from the beginning of the Soviet Union to its collapse.

Pietrusza, David. *The Chinese Cultural Revolution.* San Diego: Lucent Books, 1997. A history of China focusing on the period between the rise of the Chinese Communist Party and the Tiananmen Square demonstration in 1989.

Roberts, J. M. *The Illustrated History of the World: Volume 10, The Global Age.* New York: Oxford University Press, 2000. A survey of world events from the period 1945 to the present.

Winkler, Alan M. *The Cold War: A History in Documents.* New York: Oxford University Press, 2001. A history of the Cold War told through first-person accounts and government documents.

internet connect

Internet Activity
KEYWORD: SH3 U6

In assigned groups, develop a multimedia presentation about the world from 1945 to the present. Choose information from the chapter Internet Connect activities and the Holt Researcher that best reflects the major topics of the period. Write an outline and a script for your presentation, which may be shown to the class.

The War on Terrorism: A Global View

Prior to September 11, 2001, few people in the United States had been affected by terrorism. From that day forward, however, Americans have turned their full attention to a type of violent, destructive activity that has been happening all too frequently throughout the rest of the world for many years.

Rescuers respond after a car bombing of the Israeli embassy in Buenos Aires, Argentina. Many believe that the bombing was orchestrated by Hezbollah.
Top: World Trade Center, New York City

Terrorism Around the World

As of early 2004, the U.S. State Deparment had identified over 70 terrorist organizations in various parts of the world. These groups have planned and executed wide-scale attacks on public buildings, guerrilla raids on villages, kidnappings, suicide bombings, and airplane hijackings. Between 1998 and 2002 there were over 1,600 terrorist attacks worldwide, and more than 17,000 people lost their lives as a result of terrorist activities.

Terrorism in Latin America and Africa

Since 1998, more than 650 terrorist attacks have been recorded in Latin America. In Colombia, the terrorist groups Revolutionary Armed Forces of Colombia (FARC) and the United Self-Defense Forces of Colombia (AUC) have kidnapped over 3,000 people since 2000. In February 2003, alone, FARC took responsibility for more than 53 deaths.

In Peru, the Sendero Luminoso, or Shining Path, has been active since the 1960s trying to establish a Communist regime. Over 30,000 Peruvians have lost their lives as a result of this group's activities. In the southern Mexican state of Chiapas, the Zapatista National Liberation Army has been waging a campaign against the Mexican government since 1994.

Investigators inspect debris after a terrorist bomb ripped through a busy café in Ankara, Turkey.

This group considers itself a national movement whose goals are to gain land, work, shelter, and respect for indigenous peoples and protection for their cultures.

In Africa, terrorist groups are active in more than 20 countries. Some of the rebel groups, such as the Lord's Resistance Army in Uganda, are well armed, well organized, and have been active for years. Other terrorist groups are smaller bands operating within individual nations or across borders. Terrorist activities in Africa have claimed approximately 6,000 lives since 1998.

Terrorism in Europe

Europe has not been free of terrorist activities. For example, over the past few years Chechen rebels have claimed responsibility for numerous terrorist attacks in various Russian cities. Among these was

A car bomb exploded in Bogotá, Colombia, in October 2003. The bombing was one of a series that occurred just prior to national elections.

the highly publicized occupation of the Dubrovka Theater in Moscow in 2002, which led to the deaths of 170 people. The attacks are part of Chechnya's effort to secede from Russia, which has fought a military campaign in Chechnya for most of the last decade to prevent the breakup.

In the Basque region of northern Spain, the Basque Fatherland and Liberty group, ETA, has waged a violent campaign to establish an independent Basque homeland. More than 800 people have been killed as a result of ETA bombings and assassinations. Many hundreds more have been injured.

Various groups continue to commit terrorist attacks in the struggle over whether Northern Ireland should remain part of the

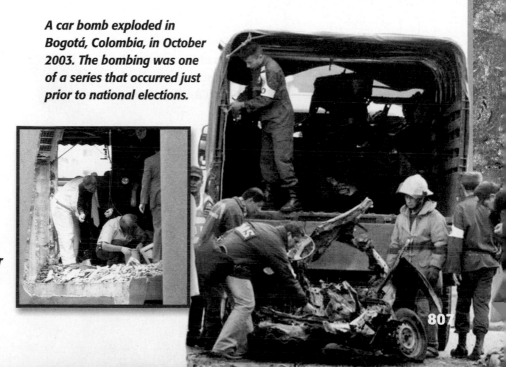

807

United Kingdom. Over the past thirty years, more than 3,500 civilians and soldiers have been killed in the conflict over the territory's fate.

One of the most tragic acts of terrorism in Europe occurred in 1988. That year, PanAm Flight 103 was brought down over Lockerbie, Scotland, by Libyan terrorists who had planted a bomb in a suitcase loaded onto the plane. Two hundred and seventy people lost their lives—259 passengers and crew and 11 people on the ground. Among the 270 dead, 189 were Americans.

Terrorism in the Middle East

In the Middle East, Palestinian groups such as Hamas, Abu Nidal, the Al-Aqsa Martyrs, and Hezbollah continue to conduct terrorist attacks against Israel. These attacks, and Israeli retaliations, have complicated efforts to build a lasting peace and have been a major source of tension in the region. The ongoing conflict between Israel and Palestine has been used by some to justify the horrendous acts of terrorism committed by a few fanatics. Despite

Two nightclubs on the beach in Bali were bombed in October 2002. Rescuers helped search for survivors, but more than 200 people were killed in the blasts.

U.S. efforts to bring all the parties to negotiations to work toward a peaceful solution, suicide bombings and retaliations continue.

Al Qaeda

Few, if any, terrorist groups have carried out attacks in as many different parts of the world as al Qaeda and its allies. In October 2002, a group with links to al Qaeda bombed a nightclub on the Indonesian island of Bali, a popular vacation spot. More than 200 people were killed, including many young Australians. In May 2003, bombings in Morocco attributed to

al Qaeda took 41 lives. In August of that same year, bombings at a Marriott hotel in Jakarta, Indonesia, killed 10 and wounded 150. Soon after, in Ankara, Turkey, two synagogues, the British consulate, and a British bank were bombed. Turkish authorities arrested al Qaeda sympathizers for their suspected role in the plot.

It was the tragic results of al Qaeda's attacks on the United States on September 11, 2001, however, that triggered worldwide outrage over terrorism. The United States was quick to respond to the attacks, both at home and abroad. Buoyed by international sympathy, the United States declared war on terrorism.

An armed member of Fatah marches at the funeral of a Hamas suicide bomber in Gaza City, Palestine.

THINK ABOUT IT

1. What alternatives to terrorism provide a better means of achieving social change?
2. Why are there many more terrorist incidents in Africa and Latin America than in Europe and North America?

Fighting Terrorism in the United States

Following the events of 9/11, the United States took a number of steps to help prevent further terrorist attacks within the nation.

The USA-PATRIOT Act

In October 2001, Congress passed the USA-PATRIOT Act. This sweeping law, a first step in U.S. homeland security, gave the government added powers to investigate persons suspected of planning terrorist acts. It permitted the Department of Justice to intercept e-mail messages, wiretap telephones, search private residences, and even check library users' computer records. Following passage of the act, the Justice Department detained and questioned more than a thousand persons living in the United States.

Stringent security checks mean long lines for passengers at airports.

Imprisoning al Qaeda Suspects

Many al Qaeda suspects, mostly of Middle Eastern origin, were imprisoned at Guantánamo, the U.S. military base in Cuba. By 2004, an estimated 650 prisoners from forty-two countries were being held.

Most of these prisoners were in legal limbo, being held with no charges filed against them and no trials scheduled. In May 2003, Secretary of State Colin Powell urged the Pentagon to decide quickly which Guantánamo prisoners could be released and which prisoners would be charged and tried. Later that year, a federal appeals court ruled that the prisoners should be tried in U.S. civil courts, not by military tribunals as the Pentagon desired. The ruling highlighted America's struggle to protect individual rights while ensuring security.

Airport Security

The 9/11 attackers had used airplanes to carry out their terrible deeds, so airport security in the United States became a high government priority. Congress tightened inspection procedures and imposed stricter standards for security personnel. Most air travelers accepted the resulting long lines. They understood the importance of strengthened air security.

In late 2003 and early 2004, many international flights to the United States were cancelled due to suspected terrorist activity. In addition, the Department of Homeland Security began photographing and fingerprinting visitors from many countries as an additional security precaution.

THINK ABOUT IT

1. Why did Congress pass the USA-PATRIOT Act?
2. The attacks of September 11, 2001, "horrified the nation," as well as people throughout the world. What other one-day events in world history have resulted in worldwide sympathy and reaction?

Fighting Terrorism in Afghanistan

Shortly after the 9/11 attacks were linked to al Qaeda forces operating in Afghanistan, under the protection of the Afghan government, U.S. and allied troops invaded the country. The U.S.-led coalition forces destroyed al Qaeda strongholds and worked with local leaders to begin the process of establishing a stable, democratic government.

Battling al Qaeda and the Taliban

By late 2001, the U.S.-led military operations in Afghanistan had killed or captured many suspected al Qaeda fighters and destroyed their bases and training camps. These military operations also overthrew the Taliban, which had ruled Afghanistan since 1996.

The coalition's efforts left al Qaeda severely weakened, but still a threat. Some al Qaeda loyalists hid out in rugged eastern Afghanistan, where the mountains are riddled with caves. Others slipped across the border into Pakistan.

Searching for Osama bin Laden

The leader of al Qaeda, Osama bin Laden, eluded capture in the initial military operations in Afghanistan. Continuing into 2004, an Arabic-language TV network even broadcast videotapes in which bin Laden urged continued struggle against the United States. His responsibility for the 9/11 attacks became absolutely clear when U.S. forces in Afghanistan discovered a videotape on which he boasted of planning the attacks.

Born around 1957, bin Laden was the son of a fabulously rich Saudi Arabian construction contractor. Over the years, bin Laden had developed a fanatical hatred of the United States. As a strict Muslim fundamentalist, he saw America as morally corrupt and in violation of Islamic law, including the requirement that women be veiled. He was outraged that U.S. troops operated bases in Saudi Arabia, home of the sacred shrine

Afghanistan-Pakistan Border Region

Interpreting Maps Osama bin Laden and members of his al Qaeda forces were believed to be hiding in the caves within the Tora Bora region of Afghanistan.

■ **Skills Assessment Evaluating** Why would the mountainous region between Pakistan and Afghanistan serve as a good hiding place for terrorists?

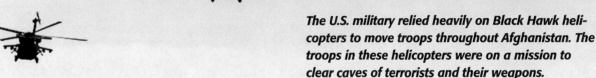

The U.S. military relied heavily on Black Hawk helicopters to move troops throughout Afghanistan. The troops in these helicopters were on a mission to clear caves of terrorists and their weapons.

Right: Delegates of the loya jirga met in Kabul, Afghanistan, in January 2004 to discuss the country's new constitution.

Osama bin Laden

of Mecca. American support for the Jewish nation of Israel infuriated him as well.

Even before 9/11, federal courts had indicted bin Laden for terrorist crimes, including the 1998 bombing of U.S. embassies in Tanzania and Kenya. After the 1998 attacks, President Clinton had ordered missile attacks on al Qaeda camps in Afghanistan.

A New Government in Afghanistan

With the Taliban defeated, U.S. authorities and Afghan leaders worked on plans for a new government. However, conflicts among Afghanistan's regional warlords complicated the task. So did hostility between the country's two major ethnic groups, the Pashtuns and the Tajiks.

In 2002, an assembly of regional Afghan leaders, called the

loya jirga, chose Hamid Karzai as president. Early in 2004, after months of wrangling, the *loya jirga* agreed on a new constitution providing for a democratically elected government, an independent judiciary, and more rights for women and minorities.

The capital, Kabul, remained dangerous, however, with assassination attempts against President Karzai and other officials. Outside the capital, local warlords and diehard Taliban supporters controlled some areas. Soldiers and civilians continued to suffer casualties. Some *loya jirga* members even feared to return home because of death threats. The new constitution was a big step forward, but the future of this troubled land remained uncertain.

An Afghan man watches a group of U.S. soldiers inspect a local bazaar.

THINK ABOUT IT

1. Why did Osama bin Laden focus his hatred on the United States?
2. What problems make it difficult for the new Afghan government to function effectively?

The War in Iraq

With al Qaeda on the run in Afghanistan, the Bush administration and its allies identified Iraq as the next battlefield in the war on terrorism.

Background of the Iraq War

During a war between Iran and Iraq in the 1980s, the United States had supported Iraq and its ruler Saddam Hussein. At that time, Iran, which had held American citizens hostage from 1979 to 1981, seemed the more dangerous foe.

This changed in 1990, when Iraq invaded Kuwait. A multinational coalition drove the Iraqis from Kuwait, but Saddam remained in power. Under the cease-fire terms, however, Saddam agreed to admit UN inspectors to make sure he was not building weapons of mass destruction, or WMDs—chemical, biological, or nuclear weapons capable of killing enormous numbers of people.

The cease-fire also restricted Iraq's oil exports, and "No Fly" zones were imposed in northern and southern Iraq to prevent Saddam from attacking opposition groups: Kurds in the north and Shiite Muslims in the south. U.S. and British warplanes enforced these "No Fly" zones. When fired upon, they bombed Iraqi antiaircraft sites.

Despite obstruction from Saddam, the UN inspectors generally concluded that Iraq had halted its WMD programs. Many U.S. officials disagreed, however, suspecting that Saddam was simply hiding these programs. From 1998 to 2001, U.S. and British bombing of Iraqi military targets increased.

The Bush Administration Focuses on Iraq

In his January 2002 State of the Union address, President Bush accused three nations—Iraq, Iran, and North Korea—of forming an "axis of evil." The phrase stirred memories of World War II, when Germany, Japan, and Italy had been called the "Axis powers."

Of the three countries that Bush named, Iraq topped the list. Saddam's record of aggression and obstructing the weapons-inspection program was clear. In addition, key administration figures believed that Saddam should have been overthrown in the Persian Gulf War. They urged Bush to complete this "unfinished business" from his father's presidency.

Others argued that the United States, as the world's only superpower, should use that power to promote democracy in the Middle East. Ending Saddam's dictatorship, they insisted, could transform the region.

Supporters of overthrowing Saddam also contended that his removal from office could create better conditions for resolving the disputes between Israel and its Arab neighbors and promote peace in the region. The war on terrorism presented an opportunity to pursue all these goals.

Thousands of anti-war demonstrators marched through many cities in Europe protesting the war in Iraq.

Americans Debate War with Iraq

President Bush, Vice President Dick Cheney, and other administration leaders made the case for war. Saddam had links to al Qaeda, they asserted, and had played a role in the 9/11 attacks. They also claimed that Saddam possessed WMDs that endangered America.

For these reasons, they said, the United States was justified in launching a preemptive war—that is, a war against a nation that had not attacked the United States. Cheney declared, "The risks of inaction are greater than the risks of action."

Many Americans, however, did not believe that the administration had offered convincing proof of Saddam's ties to al Qaeda, or of his continuing WMD programs. The critics agreed that Saddam was a brutal tyrant, but they questioned whether this justified a preemptive war against his regime.

Despite these differences, on October 11, 2002, the Congress passed a war resolution authorizing President Bush to "use the Armed Forces of the United States as he determines to be necessary and appropriate" to deal with "the continuing threat" posed by Iraq.

Bush Seeks International Support

President Bush urged America's NATO allies to join in a war to overthrow Saddam Hussein. After initial reluctance, he also sought UN support. Addressing the United Nations in September

Prime Minister Tony Blair addresses members of the British House of Commons.

British Prime Minister Tony Blair spoke with many world leaders, including Jacques Chirac, the president of France, to try to enlist their support for the war.

2002, the president called on the world body to act decisively against Saddam for violating UN resolutions.

After this speech, Saddam pledged full cooperation with the UN weapons inspectors. The inspectors reported better cooperation and asked for more time to complete their task. UN Secretary-General Kofi Annan supported this position. The United States dismissed Iraq's hasty about-face as mere propaganda, however, and continued to press for war.

France, Germany, and other U.S. allies did not agree with the U.S. government's assessment or its call for war. They favored continued diplomatic pressure and UN arms inspections. Russia and China opposed the war as well. "France and Germany have the same point of view on this crisis. Any decision belongs to the Security Council and the Security Council alone," argued Jacques Chirac, president of France. The differences over Iraq severely frayed

American relations with these countries.

A wave of sympathy for America had swept much of the world after 9/11, but world opinion on the war differed. Massive antiwar rallies filled the streets in Rome, Paris, London, and other cities.

Approximately thirty governments did support the United States, however, including Great Britain, Spain, Italy, and Poland. British Prime Minister Tony Blair strongly backed Bush, despite heavy domestic opposition. The Bush administration called these supporters "the coalition of the willing."

813

"This is not the time to falter. This is the time . . . to show that we will stand up for what we know to be right, to show that we will confront the tyrannies and dictatorships and terrorists who put our way of life at risk, to show at the moment of decision that we will have the courage to do the right thing."

British Prime Minister Tony Blair, in a speech to the House of Commons, March 18, 2003

The UN Security Council at UN headquarters in New York City

Assembling troops, planes, and ships in the Middle East, the United States prepared to act without UN or NATO backing. In February 2003, Secretary of State Colin Powell presented the case for war to the UN General Assembly, but few minds were changed.

Senator Robert C. Byrd, a West Virginia Democrat, criticized the administration's decision to proceed without UN authorization or support from key allies. Said Byrd, "Before committing our nation to war with Iraq and the years of occupation that will surely follow, we should repair the damage to our relations with our allies. . . . Our rhetoric has gone over the top, from giving an indication of our strength to giving an indication of recklessness."

Critics recalled how the first President Bush in 1990 had patiently built strong international support for ousting Iraqi troops from Kuwait. They urged the current President Bush to do the same, rather than adopting a go-it-alone approach.

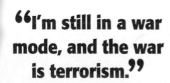

"I'm still in a war mode, and the war is terrorism."

—George W. Bush

America Goes to War

On March 19, 2003, the first air strikes of "Operation Iraqi Freedom" hit targets in and around Baghdad. The following night, U.S. and British ground forces invaded Iraq from the south. While the British secured the oil center of Basra, U.S. forces proceeded north toward Baghdad.

The American troops included Army and Marine forces, as well as reservists and National Guard members called to active duty.

Many left family and jobs behind. Among those called to action were a significant number of women, reflecting the fact that the U.S. military is about 15 percent female.

On March 22, Iraqi troops attacked a U.S. convoy, killing several Americans. Private Jessica Lynch from Palestine, West Virginia, suffered two broken legs and was captured. A few days later, U.S. soldiers rescued her from an Iraqi hospital. Publicized by the Pentagon, Lynch's story caught the nation's imagination. She denied that she was a hero and paid tribute to her fallen comrades. One of these was Private Lori Piestewa, the first American-Indian woman killed in action fighting for the U.S. Army.

Iraqi resistance proved weak, and after three weeks of sporadic fighting, Baghdad was captured. American troops occupied government buildings and Saddam's palaces, pulled down a massive statue of Saddam, and found mass graves of victims of Saddam's murderous regime.

By the end of this stage of the conflict, 140 coalition soldiers had been killed, including 109 Ameri-

Soldiers carry the flag-draped coffins of Italian servicemen who were killed in a terrorist attack in Iraq.

cans. Although precise figures are unknown, more than 2,300 Iraqi military troops had also been killed in the fighting. In addition, over 6,300 Iraqi civilians had died or suffered injuries, despite extensive coalition efforts to spare noncombatants.

On May 1, President Bush, wearing an Air Force flight suit, flew to the U.S. aircraft carrier *Abraham Lincoln* off the coast of San Diego to declare

major combat operations in Iraq completed. In front of a banner proclaiming "Mission Accomplished," the president said, "In the battle of Iraq, the United States and our allies have prevailed." Saddam remained at large, however, and more difficulties lay ahead.

THINK ABOUT IT

1. Why did the United States decide to go to war in Iraq without UN support?
2. What role should the UN play in settling international conflicts?

British Tornado fighter bomber

"America fights wars, but America does not start wars."
—Robert Byrd

With "shock and awe," American and allied forces invaded Iraq and removed Saddam Hussein from power. Iraqi forces were overwhelmed, and within four weeks, the war was over.

The Long Aftermath in Iraq

Major combat was over, but establishing a lasting peace and reconstructing Iraq proved a long and demanding task.

The High Cost of Reconstruction

The United States at once set out to rebuild Iraq's oil industry and restore long-neglected public services, such as telephones, electricity, water, and health care. The U.S. administrator in Iraq, L. Paul Bremer, led this effort.

Reconstruction contracts went to major U.S. companies, such as the Halliburton Corporation and the Bechtel Group. Some critics objected that political influence helped these businesses win the contracts. Vice President Cheney was a former head of Halliburton, and President Reagan's secretary of state, George P. Schultz, was a director of Bechtel. The government official responsible for awarding these contracts denied this charge. "The notion that any of us ... manipulated the process is ridiculous," he said.

The occupation and reconstruction of Iraq involved massive costs. Late in 2003, Bush asked Congress to appropriate $87.5 billion for Iraq-related expenditures. He compared this project to the

Requested Homeland Security Funding by Mission Area for 2004

Amount	Mission Area	Percent
$15,039,000,000	Border and Transportation Security	36%
$12,156,000,000	Protecting Critical Infrastructure and Key Assets	29%
$7,256,000,000	Emergency Preparedness and Response	18%
$3,709,000,000	Domestic Counterterrorism	9%
$2,623,000,000	Defending against Catastrophic Threats	6%
$317,000,000	Intelligence and Warning	1%
$240,000,000	Other	1%

Office of Management and Budget

Marshall Plan, which had helped rebuild Europe after World War II. The costs would likely mount even higher in future years, he warned.

Congress approved the request, but the total shocked even legislators who had supported the war. With federal deficits mounting because of rising Medicare, Medicaid, and social-security expenses, as well as military costs unrelated to Iraq, years of massive spending in Iraq would further strain the budget.

Bush Seeks Other Nations' Assistance

The administration asked other nations to help in the reconstruction effort. Japan pledged $5 billion. Most countries, however, argued that the UN should be more involved in the process.

In December 2003, Bush sent former Secretary of State James Baker abroad to persuade other nations to cancel Iraq's debts to them, or to at least stretch out the time allowed for repayment. These debts totaled $125 billion. Several nations agreed, including some that had opposed the war. Baker's task was complicated, however, by a Department of Defense announcement that only nations that had supported the Iraq war would be permitted to bid on reconstruction contracts. After several nations expressed their concerns, the United States revised its policy, and companies from other nations were allowed to bid on the second round of contracts.

Following the ouster of Saddam, U.S. soldiers and Iraqis worked together to remove giant statues of the tyrant that had adorned his Republican Palace in Baghdad.

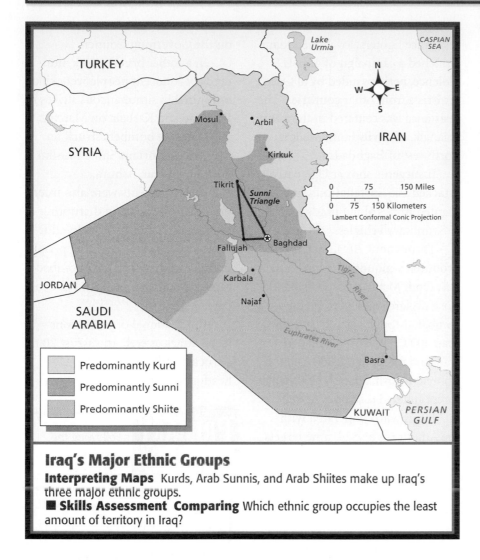

Iraq's Major Ethnic Groups

Interpreting Maps Kurds, Arab Sunnis, and Arab Shiites make up Iraq's three major ethnic groups.

■ **Skills Assessment Comparing** Which ethnic group occupies the least amount of territory in Iraq?

30, 2004, for handing over power to a new Iraqi government. This task proved difficult, however. No census records existed that could establish a list of eligible voters. Furthermore, deep hostilities divided the country's ethnic and religious groups.

Iraq is a predominantly Arab, Islamic nation, but Islam is split into two major groups, the Sunnis and the Shiites. The Sunnis are generally more liberal and more prosperous. The Shiites, numerous among the urban poor, strictly enforce Islamic law and are more hostile to non-Muslim "infidels." Iraq's Arab Shiites, centered in the south and comprising about two-thirds of the population, were oppressed by Saddam and his Arab Sunni supporters in the north. In addition, approximately 5 million Kurds live in northeastern Iraq. Although mostly Sunni, the Kurds are a fiercely independent non-Arab ethnic group. Shiites, Sunnis, and Kurds had very different ideas about Iraq's future government.

Establishing a New Government

After Saddam's overthrow, the United States set up a Governing Council drawn from Iraq's major ethnic and religious groups. At first, however, this body accomplished little and was divided by internal disputes.

In November 2003, amid growing violence in Iraq, President Bush instructed Paul Bremer to move quickly toward creating an Iraqi government, police force, and army to take over security responsibilities and permit coalition forces to withdraw. The administration set a goal of June

Continued Resistance in Iraq

Before the war, top Bush administration officials had predicted that the Iraqis would greet American troops as liberators. As it turned

In March 2004, Iraq's Governing Council, some of whom are shown here, agreed on an interim constitution to govern the country.

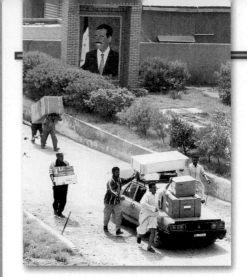

Looters took whatever supplies and equipment they could find.

In addition, insurgents, or resistance fighters, loyal to Saddam launched a campaign of anti-U.S. violence, perhaps aided by al Qaeda terrorists from other countries. The resistance was centered in the Sunni Triangle, a heavily Sunni region northwest of Baghdad.

Insurgents shot at U.S. patrols, attacked U.S. installations, and planted mines along roads used by U.S. military vehicles.

Throughout 2003, such attacks produced a mounting toll of casualties. From May 1, when President Bush declared an end to major combat, through early 2004, more than 400 U.S. GIs were killed in Iraq, and more than 2,000 were injured. British, Spanish, and Italian forces suffered casualties as well.

Iraqis who cooperated with the Americans also became targets. An Iraqi woman on the Governing Council was assassinated, and Iraqi police were often targeted in bombings. Shiites, too, fell victim to Sunni insurgents. A leading Shiite cleric, Mohammed Baqir al-Hakim, was killed when a bomb exploded outside a sacred Shiite shrine in Najaf, taking the lives of 125 wor-

shippers. The cleric's brother was on the Governing Council.

In another brutal attack, hundreds of innocent people were killed or injured in simultaneous strikes in Baghdad and Karbala on March 2, 2004. Suicide bombers struck on the most important Shiite Muslim holy day of year, Ashura.

The insurgents were also intent on creating chaos and disrupting the reconstruction effort. In addition to specifically targeting people in their attacks, they also bombed railroads, oil pipelines, and electric facilities.

International organizations faced attack as well. In August 2003, a truck bomb destroyed the UN headquarters in Baghdad, killing

out, most Iraqis did indeed welcome Saddam Hussein's overthrow, but many also resented the presence in Iraq of 132,000 U.S. troops, 10,000 British soldiers, and 14,000 armed service personnel from approximately thirty other nations.

With Iraq's police forces in disarray, ordinary criminals operated freely for some time. After Baghdad's fall, looters broke into the national museum, stealing priceless objects. Although many of the objects were later returned, lawlessness remained a major problem in Baghdad and other cities.

A car bombing destroyed the Canal Hotel, UN headquarters, in Baghdad.

PRIMARY SOURCE

Following the bombing of UN headquarters in Baghdad, Kofi Annan gave the following statement:

> **Nothing can excuse this act of unprovoked and murderous violence against men and women who went to Iraq for one purpose only: to help the Iraqi people recover their independence and sovereignty, and to rebuild their country as fast as possible, under leaders of their own choosing.**

twenty-three people, including the UN's top envoy to Iraq, Sergio Vieira de Mello. Secretary-General Kofi Annan withdrew the UN mission, citing security concerns.

In October 2003, insurgents bombed the International Red Cross's Baghdad office.

Saddam Is Captured

In the months following the war, Saddam remained at large, and many Iraqis feared that he might return to power.

Then, in December 2003, Saddam was captured. He was found hiding in a hole in a building near his hometown of Tikrit. Paul Bremer announced the capture to the press in simple words: "Ladies and gentlemen, we got him."

Most Iraqis wanted Saddam tried by an Iraqi tribunal because the people of Iraq had suffered so heavily under his regime. Others favored a trial by a UN-appointed tribunal, so that Saddam's punishment would have international authority behind it.

Even with Saddam in custody, Iraq remained turbulent and violent. The attacks on GIs continued, as did the bombings designed to disrupt Iraqi society. The reconstruction effort went forward steadily, but under great difficulties.

President Bush offered assurances that as living conditions improved and a new Iraqi government took power, Iraq would be a better and safer place, and the hopes of those who had planned

This photo of Saddam was taken following his capture in Tikrit. He was the "Ace of Spades" within the deck of cards representing the United States' most wanted list.

the war would be fulfilled. In addition, he continued to emphasize that the war in Iraq had reduced the threat of terrorism in the United States. "In 2003, we've become a safer nation," he said.

However, the debate continued. Opponents of the Bush strategy argued that the war in Iraq may have strengthened support for terrorism in the Muslim world, and in fact made the nation less safe.

Searching for Weapons of Mass Destruction

President Bush had justified the war by claiming that Saddam had links to al Qaeda and, especially, by warning that Iraq possessed weapons of mass destruction that endangered American security. After Saddam's fall, 1,200 U.S. inspectors entered the country to search for WMDs. In January 2004, the team's leader, David Kay, testified before the

Senate Intelligence Committee that no evidence of WMDs had been discovered. "It turns out that we were all wrong, . . . and that is most disturbing."

Critics immediately demanded that an independent panel study why intelligence on Iraq's WMDs had been so flawed. President Bush responded by naming a blue-ribbon panel to investigate U.S. intelligence.

THINK ABOUT IT

1. Does the United States have an obligation to help rebuild Iraq? What previous historical events might serve as a guide?
2. Why would insurgents bomb both the UN and Red Cross headquarters in Baghdad?

Iraqi insurgents repeatedly blew up Iraq's oil pipelines, railroads, electric lines, and police stations.

Fighting Terrorism Worldwide

The effort to combat terrorism and eliminate WMDs was global in scope. A series of attacks, arrests, and diplomatic initiatives made clear the worldwide nature of the danger and the effort to combat it.

Continued Dangers

Many governments have cooperated in the effort to unearth the secretive terrorist networks that are plotting and carrying out terrorist attacks. The governments have worked to trace and shut down these groups' funding sources. The effort, however, has often been frustrating.

Nonetheless, international forces have had some success. In March 2003, Khalid Sheikh Mohammad, an alleged planner of the 9/11 attacks, was captured in Pakistan, and in February 2004, Iraqi police captured Muhammad Ziman Abd al-Razzaq al-Sadun, a wanted senior member of the toppled Ba'ath Party. However, al Qaeda and other terrorist groups continue to wreak havoc in the Middle East and elsewhere.

Combatting Nuclear Threats

A major concern in the battle against terrorism was the increased threat of nuclear weapon proliferation. For example, the creator of Pakistan's first nuclear bomb, Dr. Abdul Qadeer Khan, admitted in 2004 to leaking nuclear weapon information to Iran, Libya, and North Korea. In addition, the United States had long suspected Iran of pursuing nuclear-weapons research. When late in 2003, Iran agreed to inspections by the UN's International Atomic Energy Agency, Washington welcomed the development.

North Korea, an impoverished Communist nation ruled by the unpredictable Kim Jong Il, openly boasted of its nuclear program. Although a North Korean nuclear attack on the United States was unlikely, many feared that North

New Ways of War

The "war on terrorism" differed from other U.S. wars, such as World War I and World War II. In those conflicts, Congress had declared war against specific nations for specific attacks. German U-boats had sunk U.S. ships before America declared war in 1917. The Japanese had attacked Pearl Harbor in 1941. When these nations surrendered, the wars ended. In the new kind of war that followed the 9/11 attacks, the enemy—"terrorism"—was shadowy and elusive. Small groups operated across national boundaries and chose targets throughout the world, often with little coordination. No single moment of victory could be declared. This war could last indefinitely, the president warned, and could take many different forms.

North Korea's leader, Kim Jong Il, oversaw North Korea's military buildup, including the development of a nuclear program.

Pakistani scientist Dr. Abdul Qadeer Khan created an underground network that sold nuclear secrets and equipment to countries such as Syria, Libya, and North Korea.

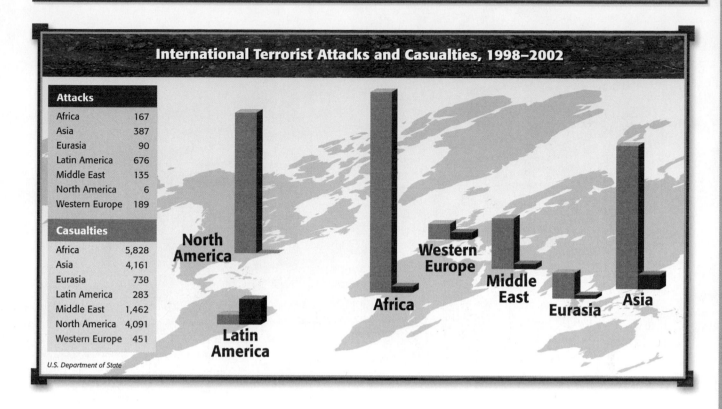

International Terrorist Attacks and Casualties, 1998–2002

Attacks	
Africa	167
Asia	387
Eurasia	90
Latin America	676
Middle East	135
North America	6
Western Europe	189

Casualties	
Africa	5,828
Asia	4,161
Eurasia	738
Latin America	283
Middle East	1,462
North America	4,091
Western Europe	451

U.S. Department of State

Korea's nuclear weapons or materials might fall into the hands of terrorists.

Joining with South Korea, Japan, Russia, and China, the Bush administration pursued diplomatic negotiations with the North Koreans. Progress was slow, but North Korea did express willingness to end its nuclear-weapons program in return for economic aid and security guarantees against attack.

In December 2003, President Bush announced that Mu'ammar Gadhafi of Libya had agreed to UN inspections to verify that he had no WMDs. This, too, was welcome news.

In his statement of U.S. goals for 2004, Secretary of State Colin Powell wrote, "The war on terrorism remains our first priority, but success in that war depends on constructive ties among the world's major powers. These we pursue

without respite." Achieving that goal, in societies that are very different from America's, and in regions of the world torn by conflict and inflamed by hatred and resentment, poses enormous challenges not just for the United States, but for all nations of the world.

THINK ABOUT IT

1. Is it possible to wage a successful international war on terrorism?
2. What steps can a country take to help ensure that terrorist groups do not receive funding from groups inside or outside of the country?
3. What steps should the international community take to prevent terrorist groups from acquiring nuclear technology and weapons?

Providing reconstruction and humanitarian aid was a major goal of the allied forces in Iraq. Many soldiers were warmly welcomed, and their efforts greatly appreciated.

821

HOLT
World History
The Human Journey

Reference Section

Almanac

At 12:00 noon Eastern Standard Time in Washington, D.C., it is . . .

1:00 p.m. in Santiago, Chile
5:00 p.m. in London, United Kingdom
6:00 p.m. in Madrid, Spain
7:00 p.m. in Athens, Greece
7:00 p.m. in Tel Aviv, Israel

8:00 p.m. in Moscow, Russian Republic
8:00 p.m. in Nairobi, Kenya
1:00 a.m. the following day in Beijing, China
2:00 a.m. the following day in Seoul, Korea
3:00 a.m. the following day in Melbourne, Australia

Major World Languages[1]

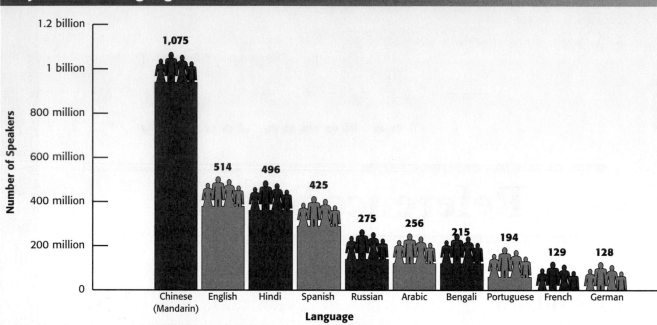

[1]Figures include estimated total number of native and non-native speakers of a given language. A "native" speaker is defined as one for whom the language is his or her first language.

Heights of Selected World Mountains, in Feet

Selected Major Rivers of the World

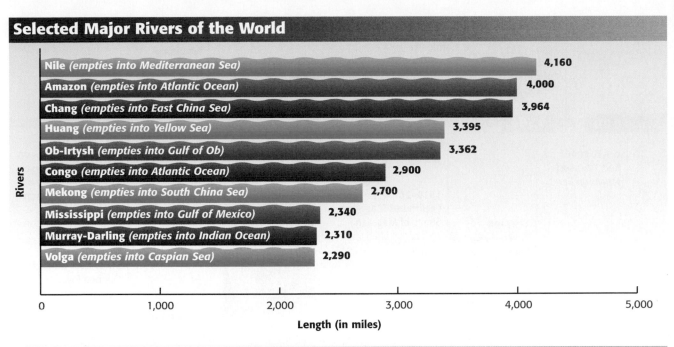

River	Length (in miles)
Nile (empties into Mediterranean Sea)	4,160
Amazon (empties into Atlantic Ocean)	4,000
Chang (empties into East China Sea)	3,964
Huang (empties into Yellow Sea)	3,395
Ob-Irtysh (empties into Gulf of Ob)	3,362
Congo (empties into Atlantic Ocean)	2,900
Mekong (empties into South China Sea)	2,700
Mississippi (empties into Gulf of Mexico)	2,340
Murray-Darling (empties into Indian Ocean)	2,310
Volga (empties into Caspian Sea)	2,290

Length (in miles)

Continental Highs and Lows

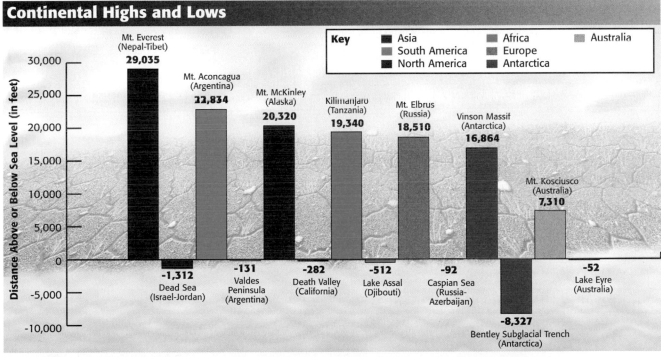

Key: Asia, South America, North America, Africa, Europe, Antarctica, Australia

Mt. Everest (Nepal-Tibet) 29,035
Mt. Aconcagua (Argentina) 22,834
Mt. McKinley (Alaska) 20,320
Kilimanjaro (Tanzania) 19,340
Mt. Elbrus (Russia) 18,510
Vinson Massif (Antarctica) 16,864
Mt. Kosciusco (Australia) 7,310

Dead Sea (Israel-Jordan) -1,312
Valdes Peninsula (Argentina) -131
Death Valley (California) -282
Lake Assal (Djibouti) -512
Caspian Sea (Russia-Azerbaijan) -92
Bentley Subglacial Trench (Antarctica) -8,327
Lake Eyre (Australia) -52

Distance Above or Below Sea Level (in feet)

The World's Largest Natural Lakes

Sea or Lake (Continent)	Area (Sq. Mi.)	Max. Depth (ft.)	Sea or Lake (Continent)	Area (Sq. Mi.)	Max. Depth (ft.)
Caspian Sea (Asia-Europe)	143,244	3,363	Lake Michigan (North America)	22,300	923
Lake Superior (North America)	31,700	1,330	Lake Tanganyika (Africa)	12,700	4,823
Lake Victoria (Africa)	26,828	270	Lake Baikal (Asia)	12,162	5,315
Aral Sea (Asia)	24,904 (est.)	220	Great Bear Lake (North America)	12,096	1,463
Lake Huron (North America)	23,000	750	Lake Malawi (Africa)	11,150	2,280

Some Early Explorers of the Western Hemisphere

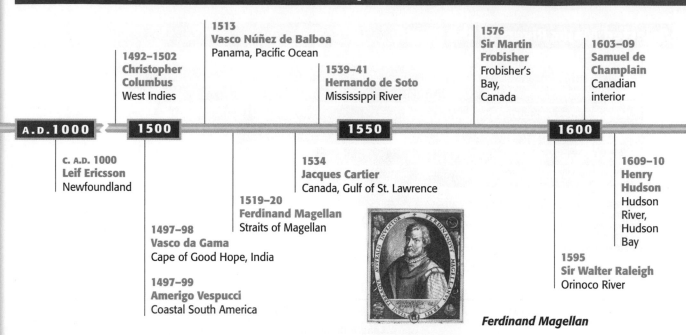

1513
Vasco Núñez de Balboa
Panama, Pacific Ocean

1492–1502
Christopher Columbus
West Indies

1576
Sir Martin Frobisher
Frobisher's Bay, Canada

1539–41
Hernando de Soto
Mississippi River

1603–09
Samuel de Champlain
Canadian interior

A.D. 1000   **1500**   **1550**   **1600**

c. A.D. 1000
Leif Ericsson
Newfoundland

1534
Jacques Cartier
Canada, Gulf of St. Lawrence

1609–10
Henry Hudson
Hudson River, Hudson Bay

1497–98
Vasco da Gama
Cape of Good Hope, India

1519–20
Ferdinand Magellan
Straits of Magellan

1595
Sir Walter Raleigh
Orinoco River

1497–99
Amerigo Vespucci
Coastal South America

Ferdinand Magellan

World Energy Facts

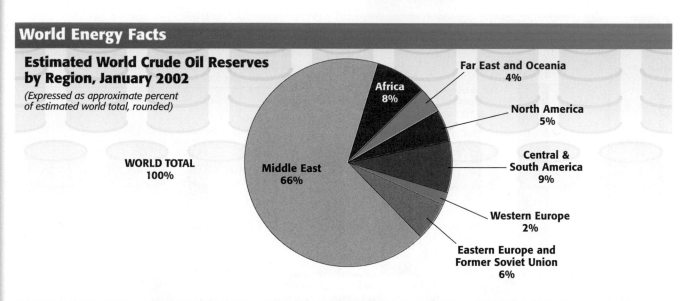

Estimated World Crude Oil Reserves by Region, January 2002

(Expressed as approximate percent of estimated world total, rounded)

Far East and Oceania 4%

Africa 8%

North America 5%

Central & South America 9%

Western Europe 2%

Eastern Europe and Former Soviet Union 6%

Middle East 66%

WORLD TOTAL 100%

Some Great Milestones in Medicine

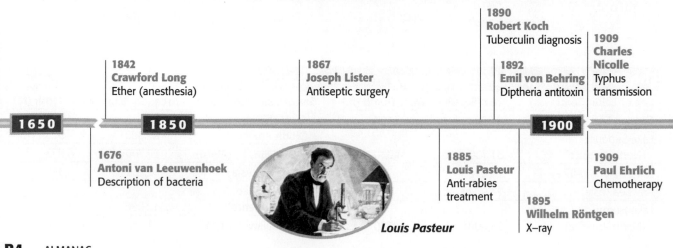

1890
Robert Koch
Tuberculin diagnosis

1909
Charles Nicolle
Typhus transmission

1842
Crawford Long
Ether (anesthesia)

1867
Joseph Lister
Antiseptic surgery

1892
Emil von Behring
Diptheria antitoxin

1650   **1850**   **1900**

1676
Antoni van Leeuwenhoek
Description of bacteria

1885
Louis Pasteur
Anti-rabies treatment

1909
Paul Ehrlich
Chemotherapy

1895
Wilhelm Röntgen
X–ray

Louis Pasteur

1673
Jacques Marquette,
Louis Joliet
Mississippi River

1727–29
Vitus Bering
Bering Strait, Alaska

1804–06
Meriwether
Lewis,
William Clark
Missouri River,
Rocky Mountains

1700 **1750** **1800**

1789
Sir Alexander
Mackenzie
Northwestern Canada

Henry Hudson

Estimated World Population in 2000

(Approximate populations are shown and rounded)

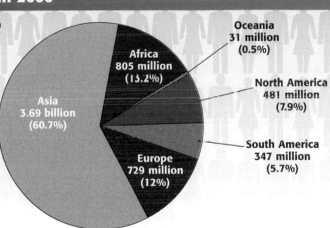

Oceania
31 million
(0.5%)

Africa
805 million
(13.2%)

North America
481 million
(7.9%)

Asia
3.69 billion
(60.7%)

WORLD TOTAL
6.08 billion
(100%)

South America
347 million
(5.7%)

Europe
729 million
(12%)

Model of the
"double helix"
of DNA

1951
Francis Crick, James Watson,
Maurice Wilkins
Structure of DNA

1963
John Enders
Measles vaccine

2001
Joint research effort:
U.S. government
agencies and private
institutions
Human Genome
Project

1928
Alexander Fleming
Penicillin

1950 **2000**

1922
Frederick Banting,
Charles Best,
John Macleod
Insulin

1940
Charles Drew
Storage of
blood plasma

1954
Jonas
Salk
Polio
vaccine

1979
U.N. World Health
Organization
Smallpox eradication

The Human Genome
Project–DNA sequencing

Glossary

This Glossary contains many of the terms you need to understand as you study world history. After each term there is a brief definition or explanation of the meaning of the term as it is used in world history. The boldfaced page number after each definition refers to the page on which the term is boldfaced in the textbook. A phonetic respelling is provided to help you pronounce many of the terms.

Phonetic Respelling Guide

Many of the key terms in the textbook have been respelled to help readers pronounce them. The following Phonetic Respelling and Pronunciation Guide has been adapted from several common dictionaries. Using the guide along with the text respellings will allow readers to pronounce difficult terms, including biographical and place names.

Mark	As In	Respelling	Example
a	alphabet	a	*AL·fuh·bet
ā	Asia	ay	AY·zhuh
ä	cart, top	ah	KAHRT, TAHP
e	let, ten	e	LET, TEN
ē	even, leaf	ee	EE·vuhn, LEEF
i	it, tip, British	i	IT, TIP, BRIT·ish
ī	site, buy, Ohio	y	SYT, BY, oh·HY·oh
	iris	eye	EYE·ris
k	card	k	KAHRD
kw	quest	kw	KWEHST
ō	over, rainbow	oh	OH·vuhr, RAYN·boh
u̇	book, wood	ooh	BOOHK, WOOHD
ȯ	all, orchid	aw	AWL, AWR·kid
ȯi	foil, coin	oy	FOYL, KOYN
au̇	out	ow	OWT
ə	cup, butter	uh	KUHP, BUHT·uhr
ü	rule, food	oo	ROOL, FOOD
yü	few	yoo	FYOO
zh	vision	zh	VIZH·uhn

*A syllable printed in small capital letters receives heavier emphasis than other syllables in a word.

abbess Head of a convent who served a role similar to an abbot. **110**

abbot Head of a monastery who controlled and distributed all property. **110**

Aborigines Original inhabitants of Australia. **416**

abstract expressionism Style of painting after 1945 that involved a personal expression from the artist. **782**

acid rain Rainfall that contains toxins produced from burning fossil fuels. **796**

adobe Sun-dried brick used for building purposes by the Pueblo Indians. **19**

aerodynamics Scientific principles governing the movement of air around objects. **383**

Afrikaans Language of the Boers in South Africa. **481**

Allied Powers Alliance that included Great Britain, France, Russia (later, the Soviet Union), the United States, and other countries during World Wars I and II. **513**

almanacs Books that predict the weather and the prospects for growing crops, and also contain such things as calendars, maps, and medical advice. **183**

Alpha First international space station, as named in November 2000. **791**

anarchists Political extremists who oppose all government. **427**

Anglo-Egyptian Treaty Treaty in 1936 between Egypt and Britain that gave Egypt greater independence. **566**

antibiotics Substances that can kill or limit bacterial growth. **794**

Anti-Comintern Pact Agreement between Japan and Germany pledging to stop the spread of Russian communism. **594**

antisepsis Use of chemicals to kill disease-causing germs. **387**

apartheid Government policy of segregation and economic exploitation in South Africa. **692**

appeasement Policy of trying to avoid war by accepting some demands of the aggressor. **595**

apprentice One who learns a skill under a master. **136**

armistice Agreement signed by leaders of warring nations to stop fighting. **523**

Articles of Confederation Plan ratified by the American states in 1781 that set up a central government with a one-house Congress in which each state had a single vote. **310**

ASEAN Association of Southeast Asian Nations; organization formed to promote economic growth. **680**

Ashikaga Family of shoguns who ruled in Japan for nearly 250 years. **86**

assimilation Process in which people give up their own culture and adopt another culture. **482**

astrolabe Instrument used to calculate latitude by looking at stars. **59**

Atlantic Charter Statement created by Winston Churchill and Franklin Roosevelt that declared their two countries' intentions in 1941. **603**

atrocities Brutal crimes of war, often committed against civilians. **518**

Auschwitz Nazi death camp in which people were systematically murdered. **610**

autocrat Ruler who holds absolute power. **456**

Awami League Political party dedicated to East Pakistan's independence. **658**

Axis Powers Alliance including Germany, Italy, and Japan. **594**

Aztec Wandering warriors who gradually came to rule central Mexico. **19**

B

Babylonian Captivity Years that the pope lived in Avignon, France, instead of Rome, Italy (1309-1377). **150**

balance of power Principle in which countries have equal strength in order to prevent any one country from dominating the others. **265**

Balfour Declaration Statement written by the British foreign secretary to a Zionist leader in Palestine. **568**

Balkan "powder keg" State of unrest in the Balkans that allowed the assassination of the heir to the Austro-Hungarian throne and led to World War I. **509**

Balkan League Balkan nations of Bulgaria, Serbia, Greece, and Montenegro that declared war on the Ottoman Empire. **465**

barter economy Economy of exchanging goods and services for other goods and services without using money. **133**

Bataan Death March Forced march by the Japanese of prisoners of war in the Philippines in 1942. **617**

Battle of Britain Nonstop German air raids on Britain during 1940 and 1941. **602**

Battle of Midway Important battle in which the Americans defeated the Japanese in 1942. **613**

Battle of Stalingrad Battle between Germany and the Soviets in Stalingrad in the summer of 1942; Soviet victory greatly weakened Germany's forces. **612**

Beats Group of writers in the post–World War II years that criticized wealthy citizens and their values. **787**

bedouins Nomadic Arab herders of sheep and camel. **48**

belligerents Warring nations. **510**

Berlin Airlift System of dropping food and supplies by air into West Berlin by the United States and Britain. **636**

Berlin Wall Wall constructed to separate East and West Berlin, to prevent East Germans from escaping to West Berlin. **640**

Bill of Rights Ten amendments of the U.S. Constitution that protect the freedoms and rights of individuals. **311**

biodiversity Variety of plants and animals that naturally occurs in the environment. **796**

biological sciences Sciences that deal with living organisms, such as biology and genetics. **384**

Black Death Terrible plague that swept through Europe, beginning in 1347. **138**

Black Shirts Fascists who conducted a violent campaign against their opponents. **552**

Black Tuesday October 29, 1929, when stock investors rushed to sell their shares, resulting in a major financial collapse. **543**

blitzkrieg German for "lightning war"; fast, forceful style of fighting used by Germany during World War II. **599**

"Bloody Mary" Nickname for Mary I of England. **470**

bobbies Nickname for London police. **396**

Boer War War between the Boers and the British for control in the Transvaal in 1899. **481**

Boers Descendants of the original Dutch settlers in South Africa. **481**

Bolsheviks Radical faction of Russia who won over the Mensheviks for control, led by Lenin. **520**

bourgeoisie (boorzh·wah·ZEE) Urban middle class, including merchants, manufacturers, and professionals. **317**

Boxer Rebellion Uprising in China in which foreigners were attacked and anything connected with outsiders was destroyed. **573**

boyars Nobles who advised the prince in each Kievan city. **39**

Brezhnev Doctrine Doctrine stating that the Soviet Union would intervene in any satellite nation that seemed to be moving away from communism. **764**

broadsides Single printed news sheets sold to the public. **183**

Bundesrat Upper house of the legislative branch of the united German states. **450**

burgesses Merchants and professional people from towns and cities. **280**

Bushido "Way of the warrior"; code of

behavior of the samurai, stressing bravery, loyalty, and honor. **86**

business cycle Alternating periods of prosperity and decline. **366**

C

cabinet Heads of government departments who advise the head of state. **296**

caliph Title meaning "successor to the Prophet" used in government and religion in Islamic society. **51**

Camp David Accords Peace agreement between Egypt and Israel, mediated by the United States. **707**

canon law The code of law in the Catholic Church. **110**

capital Wealth that is earned, saved, and invested to make profits. **134**

capitalism Economic system in which individuals, rather than governments, control the factors of production. **363**

Carbonari Secret society of Italian nationalists in the early 1800s. **440**

cardinals Catholic officials ranking next below the pope. **109**

Carolingians Line of Frankish rulers established by Pepin III's coronation in A.D. 751. **97**

cartels Corporate combinations that control entire industries. **365**

Carter Doctrine Statement declaring that the United States would regard any attempts by outside forces to control the Persian Gulf as an assault on U.S. interests. **752**

caste system Complex form of social organization that began to take shape after the Indo-Aryan migration. **8**

Cavaliers Those who supported the king in the English Civil War; also known as royalists. **288**

Central Powers World War I alliance of Germany, Austria-Hungary, Bulgaria, and the Ottoman Empire. **512**

Children's Crusade Short-lived failed crusade in 1212 by young people from Europe who marched on the Holy Land to regain it for Christianity. **129**

chivalry Code of conduct that dictated knights' behavior toward others. **106**

civilization Complex culture that can produce a surplus of food, establish large towns with a government, and has people who perform different jobs. **4**

cloning Process of making a genetically identical copy of an animal's cell. **794**

coalitions Political groups organized to support a common cause. **428**

Cold War Suspicion and hostility between the communist and Western democratic nations, waged primarily by political and economic means rather than with weapons. **633**

collaborators People who are willing to help their country's enemies. **599**

collective bargaining Process of negotiation between management and union representatives. **371**

collective farms Land pooled into large farms on which people work together as a group. **557**

Columbia Spaceship used for travel for the first United States mission to the moon. **791**

Columbian Exchange Massive exchange of goods, plants, animals, and diseases that took place between the Western and Eastern Hemispheres following Columbus's voyage. **202**

Cominform Communist Information Bureau established by the Soviets to oppose the Marshall Plan. **635**

Comintern Communist International, an organization founded by Lenin to spread the communist revolution throughout the world. **561**

command economy Economy in which the government controls all economic decisions. **558**

commercial capitalism Early economic system in which most capitalists were merchants who bought and sold goods. **363**

Commercial Revolution Era between 1400 and 1750 when Europeans made major changes to their economies due to new exploration. **197**

common law Law based upon customs and judges' decisions rather than upon written codes. **115**

Common Market Officially called the European Economic Community, an organization of six Western European nations established in 1957 for international economic cooperation. **642**

commonwealth A republic. **288**

Commonwealth of Independent States (CIS) Commonwealth established to coordinate defense and economic policies for the new independent republics following the breakup of the Soviet Union. **767**

Communards Paris council members who wanted a decentralized government, separation of church and state, and other socialist reforms. **427**

communism Authoritarian socialism; economic and political system in which governments own the means of production and control economic planning. **374**

Communist Party New name of the Russian Bolsheviks who dissolved the constitutional assembly in 1918. **521**

compass Navigational instrument created in the 1300s that uses a magnetized piece of metal that points to the north. **196**

conceptual art Style of art in which the act of creating the art is more important than the actual art object. **783**

Concordat Agreement between Napoléon and the pope recognizing Catholicism as the religion of most French citizens. **332**

conscription Military draft. **326**

conservatives Group that does not want to change existing conditions. **323**

constitution Document outlining the basic laws and principles that govern a nation. **289**

consulates Foreign diplomatic offices headed by consuls. **235**

Contadora Principles Agreement promoting negotiations rather than violence as a way to settle regional conflicts in Latin America. **729**

containment Policy aimed at restricting the spread of communism. **635**

contraband War materials supplied by a neutral nation to a belligerent one. **518**

contras Group seeking to overthrow Nicaragua's Sandinista government. **727**

Convention on the Rights of the Child An agreement passed by the United Nations in 1989 that outlines the legal, social, and economic guidelines each country must follow to protect children. **801**

corporations Businesses that allow people to buy stock in the company. **365**

corporatist state Nation in which the major economic activities, such as agriculture, transportation, manufacturing, and commerce, are organized into syndicates that resemble corporations. **553**

Council of Trent Meeting of church leaders in the 1500s to clearly define Catholic doctrines for the Counter-Reformation. **177**

Counter-Reformation Attempt by the Catholic Church, following the Reformation, to return the church to an emphasis on spiritual matters. **176**

counterrevolutionary Activities aimed against, or counter to, a revolution, organized by supporters of the Old Regime. **326**

coup d'état (koo day-TAH) Seizure of power by force; in French, a "stroke of state." **330**

craft guilds Associations of skilled workers that set standards for working conditions. **136**

creoles White people born in Spanish or Portuguese colonies. **430**

Crimean War War waged by France, Great Britain, and the Ottoman Empire against Russia. **425**

crop rotation The practice of alternating crops of different kinds to preserve soil fertility. **352**

Crusades Expeditions by Christians to regain the Holy Land from the Muslims. **126**

Cuban missile crisis Situation during the Cold War in which the Soviet Union built nuclear missile sites in Cuba. **648**

cubism Artistic style that emphasizes geometric designs, using shapes such as cubes, flat planes, and spheres. **539**

cultural diffusion Spread of culture from one area of the world to another. **4**

Cultural Revolution Violent attempt at social change in China, launched by Mao Zedong in 1966. **662**

cuneiform (kyoo-NEE-uh-fawrm) Sumerian writing made by pressing a wedge-shaped tool into clay tablets. **5**

curia Group of advisers to the pope drawn from the highest ranks of clergy. **109**

czar Title taken by Ivan the Terrible; Russian for "caesar." **42**

dadaists Group of artists who used random images to reflect what they considered the insanity of war. **539**

daimyo (DY-mee-oh) Powerful local lords in feudal Japan. **88**

Dayton Accord Agreement mediated by the United States that gave Bosnian Serbs a degree of autonomy while recognizing the sovereignty of the Muslim-led government. **771**

D-Day June 6, 1944, the day Allied troops began the invasion on France's Normandy coast. **613**

democratic socialism Political system in which the government takes over the means of production peacefully; people retain basic human rights and partial control over economic planning. **375**

departments Administrative districts in France. **321**

dependent colonies Colonies in which a few officials from one country (usually European) rule (non-European) people of another country. **470**

depression Period in which the decreased demand of goods causes the entire economy to sink. **366**

desaparecidos "Disappeared" people in Argentina who criticized the government and were killed by the military government's campaign. **739**

desertification Spread of the desert. **697**

détente (day-TAHNT) Era of improved Soviet-American relations. **752**

DEW Line Radar installations built by the United States and Canada to give early warning of air attacks. **649**

Diamond Sutra World's first known printed book, a Buddhist text produced in China in A.D. 868. **78**

Diet Japan's two-house national legislature. **484**

Diplomatic Revolution Major reversal of alliances in Europe in the mid-1700s. **275**

direct democracy Form of democracy in which all citizens participate directly in making decisions. **11**

dissidents People who disagree with a government. **732**

divine right of kings Belief that God chooses kings to rule nations. **264**

division of labor Characteristic of civilizations in which different people perform different jobs. **4**

DNA Deoxyribonucleic acid; the small units of chromosomes that convey characteristics from parent to child. **794**

domestic system Method of production that takes place in the worker's home rather than in a shop or factory. **133**

domino theory Idea that if one country falls to communism, surrounding countries will soon follow. **675**

dowry Money or goods a wife brings to a marriage. **30**

Duma Elected parliament for Russia. **462**

dynamo Electric generator. **380**

E

Easter Rising April 24, 1916, when Irish nationalists revolted against Britain. **548**

economic nationalism Policy that a nation uses to try to improve its economic well-being by limiting trade. **542**

economic sanctions Refusal to trade with an offending nation. **531**

Emancipation Edict Proclamation by Czar Alexander in 1861 that freed all Russian serfs. **457**

Emancipation Proclamation Decree issued by President Abraham Lincoln in 1863 that effectively ended slavery at the end of the Civil War. **419**

emigrations Movements of people away from their native lands. **394**

émigrés Nobles who fled France during the Revolution. **321**

enclosure movement Practice of fencing or enclosing common lands into individual holdings. **352**

Encyclopedia, The Reference book describing the ideas of the Enlightenment. **302**

English Bill of Rights Document in 1689 that declared the powers of Parliament and protected private citizens. **293**

enlightened despotism System of government in which an absolute monarch ruled according to the principles of the Enlightenment. **304**

Enlightenment Period in the 1700s when philosophers believed that they could apply the scientific method and use reason to explain human nature logically. **302**

ethical monotheism Religion believing in one god, emphasizing ethics. **6**

ethnic cleansing Campaign of terror and murder intended to drive out certain ethnic groups from a region or an area. **769**

European Community Multinational European economic organization headquartered in Belgium. **643**

evolution Belief that organisms develop through change over time. **385**

excommunication Official edict that bars a person from church membership. **34**

executive branch Branch of government that enforces the laws and is headed by the president. **310**

extraterritoriality Exemption of foreigners from the laws of the country in which they live or do business. **227**

F

factors of production Basic resources for industrialization, such as necessary land, capital, and labor. **353**

factory system Production of goods in a factory through the use of machines and a large number of workers. **354**

Falange Spanish fascist party. **592**

fascism Governmental doctrine that relies on dictatorial rule and a totalitarian regime, in which the state maintains rigid control of the people through force and censorship. **551**

Fashoda crisis Conflict between France and England in the Sudan. **477**

favorable balance of trade Situation that exists when a country sells more goods than it buys. **198**

federal system of government System of government in which power is divided between a central, or federal, government and individual states. **310**

feudalism Political system of local government based on the granting of land in return for loyalty, military assistance, and other services. **102**

fief Grant of land given to a vassal from a lord. **102**

Final Solution Name given to the Nazi attempt to destroy the Jewish population of Europe. **609**

Five-Year Plan Plan of Stalin's government for economic growth during the 1920s. **558**

flappers Young women who challenged the social norms of the 1920s by wearing short hair and skirts and going out to jazz clubs. **541**

Flemish school Group of painters who perfected the technique of oil painting on canvas. **169**

Fourteen Points President Woodrow Wilson's plan for a just world based on the Allies' aims to end World War I. **522**

"Four Tigers" South Korea, Taiwan, Singapore, and Hong Kong; noted for their strong economic growth. **680**

Franco-Prussian War War between France and Prussia that ended in France's defeat in 1871. **426**

free enterprise System in which economic forces work automatically and naturally, without mercantilist laws and regulations. **368**

free trade Practice based on the belief that government should not restrict or interfere with international trade. **226**

Fujiwara First family to gain control over the central government in Japan; had power from the mid-800s to the mid-1100s. **86**

functionalism Style of architecture in which a building is designed for its specific use rather than according to a particular style. **539**

G

Gang of Four Madame Mao's radical communist group who wanted to continue the Cultural Revolution in China. **662**

General Assembly One body of the United Nations, comprised of any nation that wishes to join. **631**

general strike Refusal by workers in various industries to work until their demands are met. **547**

genetic code Sequence of DNA's chemical "letters" that determines the characteristics for each human life. **794**

genetics Study of the ways in which inborn characteristics of plants and animals are inherited by their descendants. **577**

Geneva Accord Agreement signed in 1954 that called for French withdrawal from Vietnam and division of the country into two zones. **675**

genocide Systematic extermination of a people. **529**

gentry Landowners in England who had social positions but no titles. **280**

geocentric theory Theory according to Hellenistic thinker Ptolemy that Earth is the center of the universe. **191**

German-Soviet nonaggression pact 1939 agreement dividing eastern Europe into spheres of influence. **597**

ghazis Warriors for Islam; Turkish soldiers who were the first Ottomans. **240**

glasnost (GLAZ·nohst) Soviet policy of openness under which government controls on the economy were relaxed and restrictions on dissent were eased. **765**

Glorious Revolution Bloodless transfer of power to William and Mary of England in 1688. **292**

Golden Horde Name given by Europeans to the Mongol invaders of the 1200s due to the golden color of their tents. **81**

Good Neighbor Policy U.S. policy during the 1930s that stressed cooperation among Latin American nations. **584**

Gothic Style of church architecture characterized by tall spires and flying buttresses that was developed by master builders during the mid-1100s. **142**

Grand Canal Canal constructed during the Sui dynasty that linked northern and southern China for the first time. **74**

Great Depression Worldwide depression in the early 1930s when prices and wages fell, business activity slowed, and unemployment rose. **543**

Great Leap Forward Mao Zedong's second Five-Year Plan for China in 1958, intended to speed progress. **661**

Great Schism Period of church history from 1378 to 1417 when the church was divided into opposing groups. **150**

Greek fire Flammable liquid used as a weapon by the Byzantine navy. **32**

greenhouse effect Warming of the earth's surface. **797**

Grimm brothers German brothers who collected fairy tales that continue to be well known. **400**

guerilla warfare Military technique relying on swift raids by small bands of soldiers. **211**

H

habeas corpus Legal right protecting individuals from arbitrary arrest and imprisonment. **293**

Habsburg Powerful family of European rulers in the 1200s. **148**

haciendas (hah·see·EN·duhz) Large self-sufficient farms in Spanish America. **429**

Hagia Sophia Great, decorative Byzantine church in Constantinople. **35**

Han Dynasty of rulers that ruled a centralized and growing empire in China. **10**

heliocentric theory Theory developed by Copernicus that the sun is the center of the universe. **191**

Helsinki Accords Series of agreements in 1975 that gave European nations a new framework for economic and technological cooperation, among other democratic agreements. **761**

heresy Opinion that conflicts with official church beliefs. **34**

heretics People who denied the truth of the official church's principles or who preached beliefs not approved by the church. **110**

hijrah (hi·JY·ruh) Migration of Muhammad and his followers in A.D. 622, marking the first year in the Muslim calendar. **49**

Ho Chi Minh Trail Viet Cong's major supply route through Laos from North to South Vietnam. **676**

Holocaust Systematic elimination of European Jews and others by the Nazis. **611**

Hopewell Group of people who settled in the Ohio Valley region sometime from about 300 B.C. to 200 B.C. **19**

Huguenots French people, including high-ranking nobles, who converted to Calvinism. **175**

humanists People who specialize in studying the humanities, which includes grammar, history, poetry, and rhetoric. **163**

humanitarians People who work to improve the conditions of others. **369**

Hundred Years' War War between France and England for the French throne that continued from 1337 to 1453, and introduced the use of new weapons. **144**

icon Holy picture of Jesus, the Virgin Mary, or a saint. **32**

Iconoclastic Controversy Debate between opponents and defenders of icons in the Byzantine Church; one of the issues that led to the split of the Christian church in 1054. **34**

iconoclasts People who opposed the use of icons in worship. **32**

imams Spiritual leaders who, according to some Shi'ah Muslims, should be direct descendants of Muhammad. **52**

imperialism Ambition of a powerful nation to dominate the political, economic, and cultural affairs of another nation or region. **470**

import substitution Economic policy of replacing certain imported goods with

a country's own manufactured goods produced inside the country. **719**

impressionists Group of painters who developed a type of realism by studying light and color to create vivid impressions of people and places. **404**

Inca Civilization in the Andes Mountains in South America that by the end of the 1400s included much of what is now Peru, Ecuador, Bolivia, and Chile. **21**

indemnity Compensation paid to a nation for damage inflicted on it. **338**

indulgences Paid pardons from punishment for sin. **171**

industrial capitalism Type of capitalism that began during the Industrial Revolution when capitalists were involved in producing and manufacturing goods themselves, often using mechanized and industrialized methods of production. **363**

Industrial Revolution Term for changes beginning in the 1700s, when power-driven machines began to do much of the work that people had done before. **353**

influenza pandemic Flu-like epidemic that killed more than 20 million people worldwide during 1918 and 1919. **536**

Inquisition Institution of the Roman Catholic Church that sought to eliminate heresy by seeking out and punishing heretics. **111**

Intendants Regional administrators and representatives of the crown in the provinces of France. **263**

interchangeable parts Identical parts that can replace each other. **364**

interdict The Catholic Church's punishment of a region, involving closing churches and withholding sacraments. **110**

International Brigades Antifascist volunteers from France, Britain, and the United States who participated in the Spanish Civil War. **593**

international style Style of architecture that included uninterrupted expanses of steel and glass. **540**

intifada Violent uprising by Palestinians in the late 1980s. **708**

Iran-contra affair Scandal in which members of President Reagan's national security staff sent money from the sale of weapons to Iran in exchange for hostages to the Nicaraguan contras. **749**

Irish Republican Army (IRA) The military branch of the Irish nationalist group Sinn Fein. **549**

Islam Religion based on Muhammad's teachings and ideas that began spreading throughout Arab tribes in the A.D. 600s. **49**

island hopping Military strategy of capturing only certain islands of a country and bypassing the others. **613**

isolationists Persons who believe that their own country should not become involved in relations with other nations, especially alliances. **602**

Janissaries Highly trained troop of slave soldiers for Ottoman sultans. **240**

jazz New form of music that originated in the 1920s among the African American communities in New Orleans. **539**

Jesuits Catholic religious order founded by Ignatius de Loyola in 1534. **177**

jihad (ji-HAHD) Teaching of Islam to defend the faith. **50**

joint-stock company Business organization developed during the Commercial Revolution in which owners raised money by selling shares, or stock, in the company. **197**

journeyman Skilled worker who was paid wages by a master. **136**

judicial branch Branch of government that interprets and applies the laws. **310**

Junkers Group of aristocratic landowners who campaigned for abolishing tariffs in the early 1800s. **446**

junks Large Chinese ships. **220**

Justinian Code Collection of laws that formed the basis for Byzantine law under Emperor Justinian. **30**

kaiser Title of the German emperor. **449**

kami Japanese gods or nature spirits. **85**

Kellogg-Briand Pact Agreement made between the United States and France in 1928 that made war "illegal." **590**

Khmer Rouge Cambodian Communists trained by the Viet Cong who took over the government and enforced a massive genocide of the Cambodian population. **676**

kibbutz Collective farm in Israel. **701**

kizilbash Military army developed by the Safavids to fight for political power. **244**

Kulturkampf An anti-Catholic program started by Bismarck in Germany in the late 1800s. **451**

Kuomintang Chinese Nationalist Party that grew out of the nationalist desire for reform. **574**

laissez-faire (le-say-FAR) Belief that government should not interfere with the operations of businesses. **368**

laser Device that concentrates light and releases it in an intense beam that travels in a straight line. **793**

League of Nations World organization formed after World War I to maintain peace. **524**

Legalism School of Chinese philosophy concerned with politics. **10**

legislative branch Branch of government that makes the laws. **310**

legitimacy Principle involving restoring former ruling families to their thrones. **337**

Lend-Lease Act 1941 legislation allowing the United States to supply war materials to Great Britain on credit. **602**

Liberal-Democratic Party Most powerful political party in Japan after World War II, which controlled the government from the 1950s to the 1990s. **670**

liberalism Political movement believing in representative government protecting individual rights and the rule of law; also refers to movements to reform government. **341**

limited constitutional monarchy Government in which the monarch remains head of the state, but the king or queen is required to consult Parliament. **297**

Locarno Pact Number of treaties signed in Locarno by delegates of seven European countries in 1925. **547**

Long March 6,000-mile journey by Communist Chinese to escape Nationalist troops. **576**

Long Parliament English Parliament elected in 1640 that convened on and off for 20 years. **287**

Lost Generation Group of American writers whose writings reflected a generation that lost its moral grounding during World War I. **537**

Loyalists American colonists who opposed independence from England. **306**

Luftwaffe German air force in World War II. **601**

Maastricht Treaty Treaty that created the European Union. **763**

"MacArthur Constitution" U.S.-imposed constitution adopted by Japan in 1947. **667**

Maginot Line France's fortifications along the borders of Germany and Luxembourg. **546**

Magna Carta "Great Charter," English document that made the law the supreme power and became a cornerstone of constitutional government. **114**

Magyars Nomadic group who invaded Europe; eventually settled in what is now Hungary. **100**

Maine U.S. battleship that exploded in Havana harbor in 1868, contributing to the Spanish-American War. **491**

mandate Area, usually a former colony, to be administered by the government of another nation. **531**

manorialism Economic system during the Middle Ages that revolved around self-sufficient farming estates where lords and peasants shared the land. **105**

Maori Original inhabitants of New Zealand. **416**

maquis Members of a French underground resistance movement. **601**

market economy Economy in which land, labor, and capital are controlled by individual persons. **134**

market speculations Risky investments in the stock market. **542**

Marshall Plan Massive economic assistance program to European countries by the United States. **635**

mass production System of producing large numbers of identical items. **364**

Mau Mau Kikuyu organization that waged a guerilla campaign against British presence in Kenya. **689**

Maya One of the most advanced early people in the Americas, occupying most of the Yucatán Peninsula. **19**

means of production Everything used to produce and exchange goods. **372**

mechanization Use of automatic machinery to increase production. **354**

medieval Term that describes the period of western European history known as the Middle Ages. **96**

Meech Lake Accord Failed agreement between Canadian leaders to accept Quebec as a "distinct society" within Canada. **754**

Meiji Restoration Change when a group of samurai overthrew the Tokugawa shogunate and restored the emperor to power. **484**

Mensheviks Moderate faction of Russia who fought for control during the early 1900s. **520**

mercantilism Economic theory stating that there is a fixed amount of wealth in the world and that in order to receive a larger share, one country has to take some wealth away from another country. **198, 301**

merchant guild Association of merchants and workers created to protect their rights to trade and to help out members and their families. **135**

Merovingians Clovis and his successors, who were generally weak Frankish rulers who left the job of governing to palace officials. **96**

mestizos People of American Indian and European descent. **430**

Middle Ages Period in western European history between the collapse of the Roman Empire and the Renaissance. **96**

middle class Class of skilled workers between the upper class and the poor and unskilled workers. **136**

Middle Passage Second stage of the triangular trade system, which involved the shipping of slaves across the Atlantic to the Americas. **206**

militarism Glorification of armed strength. **506**

millets Separate, self-governed religious minorities within the Ottoman Empire. **242**

Minamoto Clan reigning in Japan beginning in 1156; changed the way governments were run by introducing the shogun control. **86**

minaret Tower attached to the outside of a mosque, from where a crier would call Muslims to worship. **61**

miniaturization Process of making machines smaller and lighter. **791**

mixed economy Economy in which private companies own some industries, and the government owns the rest. **657**

mobilize Act of preparing a nation's army and other resources for war. **506**

moderates Persons who do not hold extreme political views. **323**

monasticism Way of life in convents and monasteries where nuns and monks withdraw from the world and its temptations. **109**

monoculture Country's reliance on one crop. **719**

monopoly Complete control of the production or sale of a single good or service by a single firm. **365**

Monroe Doctrine Doctrine in 1823 stating that the United States would not interfere in European affairs or with Europe's remaining colonies in the Western Hemisphere, as long as the Europeans did not try to regain or create new colonies in the region. **433**

Moors Muslims who made Spain their home in the A.D. 700s. **53**

mosaic Picture or design made from small pieces of enamel, glass, or stone. **35**

mosques Muslim places of worship. **50**

Mothers of the Plaza de Mayo Group of Argentine women whose family members disappeared due to government-sanctioned violence and abuses that they opposed. **721**

mulattoes People of European and African ancestry in the Spanish American colonies. **430**

multinational corporations Foreign-owned businesses in a host country. **718**

Munich Conference Meeting called by Hitler in 1938 to discuss the Czech problem, which led to the annexation of the Sudetenland by Germany. **595**

Muslim League Political group of Indian Muslims, formed to protect their rights. **654**

Muslims Followers of the religion of Islam. **50**

N

NAACP National Association for the Advancement of Colored People; group that worked for civil rights. **646**

NAFTA North American Free Trade Agreement, linking Mexico, Canada, and the United States in a large free-trade zone. **720**

Napoléonic Code System of French law under Napoléon's direction. **332**

nationalism Love of one's country rather than of one's native region. **334**

nationalization Act of placing an industry under government control. **547**

NATO North Atlantic Treaty Organization; an alliance of twelve Western nations formed in 1949. **638**

naturalists Realists who took the approach one step further to show the ugly or unpleasant aspects of everyday life. **404**

Navigation Act of 1651 Law that required imported goods to be carried in English ships or ships of the country making the goods. **289**

Nazi Party Extremely nationalistic, anti-Semitic, and anticommunist party that rose to power in Germany in the 1920s. **553**

Neutrality Acts Legislation passed between 1935 and 1937 in the United States that stated its wish to stay neutral in future wars. **602**

New Deal Programs by President Franklin D. Roosevelt in which the federal government established public works to create jobs and granted money to each state to provide for the needy. **545**

New Economic Policy Lenin's policy to deal with the economic collapse in Russia that allowed some free trade. **557**

New Model Army Cromwell's powerful army that defeated King Charles in the English Civil War. **288**

"New Order" Adolf Hitler's plan for organizing Europe into a single political and economic system ruled by Germany. **609**

nihilists Political group that believes in abolishing the existing political, economic, and social structures. **458**

nonalignment Nation's policy of refusing to ally with either the United States or the Soviet Union. **655**

Northwest Ordinance Law passed by the U.S. Congress to provide government for the Northwest Territory. **417**

Nürnberg trials Nuremberg trials; postwar trials of Nazi leaders charged with crimes against peace and humanity. **630**

O

op art Art of the 1950s and 1960s in which artists used brilliant colors and shapes to create optical illusions. **782**

OPEC Organization of Petroleum Exporting Countries, created in 1960 to set oil prices and world oil production levels. **709**

Open Door Policy Right of all foreign nations to trade equally in China. **573**

Operation Bootstrap Plan for outside investment and industrialization to boost Puerto Rico's economy. **733**

Operation Overlord Code name for the Allied invasion of northwest France. **613**

Opium War Conflict from 1839 to 1842 between China and Britain that arose due to Britain's export of opium to China. **227**

Organization of American States (OAS); group designed to foster military, economic, and cultural cooperation among nations of the Western Hemisphere. **722**

Ostpolitik Term used to describe Willy Brandt's efforts to improve relations between East and West. **759**

Ottoman Turks Asian people who conquered Constantinople in the 1300s and established a large empire. **36**

P

Pan-Africanism Movement promoting the cultural unity of people of African heritage in their struggle for freedom. **686**

Panama Canal Canal completed in 1914 that connects the Atlantic and Pacific Oceans. **492**

Pan-Slavism Unity of all Slavic peoples under Russian leadership. **456**

Paris Peace Accords 1973 cease-fire agreement calling for withdrawal of U.S. troops from South Vietnam. **675**

Paris Peace Conference Meeting of victorious nations to write terms for the peace following World War I. **524**

passive resistance Nonviolent civil disobedience. **569**

pasteurization Process of heating liquids to kill bacteria and prevent fermentation. **387**

paternalism System of governing colonies in much the same way that parents guide their children. **481**

Patriots American colonists who favored independence from England. **306**

peninsulares Europeans who were born on the Iberian Peninsula of Spain or Portugal. **430**

People's Will Russian movement that tried to use violence and intimidation to bring about reform. **458**

Pentagon Headquarters of the United States military leadership, located near Washington, D.C., and the scene of a terrorist attack on September 11, 2001. **772**

perestroika (per·uh·STROY·kuh) Soviet restructuring policy designed to overhaul the Soviet political and economic systems. **765**

performance art Art form in which the artist becomes a living work of art. **783**

perspective Art technique that involves making distant objects smaller than those in the foreground and arranging them to create the illusion of depth on a flat canvas. **164**

Petition of Right Petition stating four ancient liberties presented to Parliament by Charles I. **286**

philology History of literature and language. **223**

philosophes (fee·luh·ZAWFS) Thinkers of the Age of Enlightenment. **302**

"phony war" Early phase of World War II marked by little activity in western Europe. **599**

physical sciences Sciences concerned with energy and mostly nonliving matter, such as astronomy, geology, physics, and chemistry. **384**

Platt Amendment Provision of the Cuban constitution giving the United States the right to intervene in Cuba. **491**

plebiscite (PLEB·uh·syt) Procedure used to submit the constitution of a new government to the people for a yes-or-no vote. **331**

PLO Palestine Liberation Organization; Palestinian guerilla organization led by Yasir Arafat. **707**

pogroms (POH·gruhmz) Riots in which Jews were massacred in Russia in the 1880s. **459**

Politburo Political Bureau of the Communist Party that held most of the power in the Soviet Union. **560**

Polovtsy Turkish people who after 1055 controlled the area south of Kiev in Russia. **41**

pop art Style used by artists who painted common objects such as soup cans, pictures from comic books, or road signs. **782**

pope Title assumed by the patriarch of Rome and head of the Catholic Church; from the Latin word meaning "father." **15**

Popular Front Left-wing coalition government of France in the late 1930s. **547**

popular sovereignty Governmental principle based on just laws and on a government created by and subject to the will of the people. **304**

Pragmatic Sanction Statement made by Charles VI, urging European leaders to allow Maria Theresa to inherit Habsburg lands. **273**

Pravda Russkia Russia's first law code, created by Yaroslav I. **39**

predestination Belief that at the beginning of time God decided who would be saved. **174**

PRI Mexico's Institutional Revolutionary Party. **723**

prime minister Head of government in Great Britain. **296**

primogeniture (pry·moh·JE·nuh·choohr) System of inheritance from father to eldest son for ownership or possession of land. **102**

prohibition Policy forbidding the manufacture, sale, and transportation of alcoholic beverages. **541**

proletariat (proh·luh·TAYR·ee·uht) Name given by Karl Marx to the working class. **374**

propaganda Ideas, facts, or rumors spread deliberately to further one's cause or to damage an opposing cause. **514**

protectorates Colonies in which the native rulers keep their titles, but officials of the foreign power actually control the regions. **471**

psychiatry Study and treatment of mental illness. **393**

psychoanalysis Process of revealing and analyzing the unconscious. **393**

purge A large-scale elimination of people from an organization or area. **560**

Puritans People who objected to the Anglican Church maintaining some Catholic practices; they wanted to further "purify" the English Church. **279**

Q

Qin Dynasty that came to power in China in 221 B.C. under which the first true empire of China was created. **9**

quantum theory Max Planck's theory stating that energy can be released only in definite "packages," or quanta. **389**

queue Single braid that characterized the hairstyle that all Chinese men were required to wear during the Qing dynasty. **222**

Qur'an Holy book of Islam. **50**

R

radicals Persons who want broad changes made in government. **323**

radioactivity Process in which atoms of certain elements constantly break down and release energy. **389**

Rajputs Indian warrior princes who began challenging Turkish Muslim control in India in the 1500s. **247**

rationalism Belief that truth can be determined solely by logical thinking. **302**

reaction Period of time during which people in authority want a return to the conditions of an earlier time. **338**

reactionaries Extremists who not only oppose change, but also want to undo certain changes. **338**

realism A method of dealing with the realities of everyday life and expressing a keen observation of social settings, characteristic of literature and art in the mid-1800s. **404**

reaya Masses of ordinary subjects in Ottoman society. **242**

Red Army Communist forces. **521**

Red Guards Radical students chosen by Mao Zedong to lead the Cultural Revolution. **662**

Reformation Religious revolution that split the church in western Europe and created a number of new churches. **171**

regionalism Form of realism that focuses on everyday life in particular places. **404**

Reichstag Lower house of the German legislature. **450**

Reign of Terror Period during the French Revolution when the National Convention worked to suppress all opposition. **327**

Renaissance Movement following the Middle Ages that centered on revival of interest in the classical learning of Greece and Rome; French word meaning "rebirth." **162**

reparations Payment for war damages. **524**

republic Form of government in which voters elect officials to run the state. **13**

Restoration Period of the reign of Charles II of England when the monarchy was restored; also the rebirth of English culture during that time. **291**

risorgimento Italian word for "resurgence"; used as a name for the Italian nationalist movement of the 1800s. **440**

romanticism Trend followed by many writers of the early 1800s whose work appealed to sentiment and imagination and dealt with the romance of life. **400**

Rome-Berlin Axis 1936 alliance formed between Mussolini in Italy and Hitler in Germany. **556**

Roosevelt Corollary Extension of the Monroe Doctrine stating that the United States would guarantee that Latin American nations would meet their international obligations. **493**

Roundheads Those who supported Parliament in the English Civil War. **288**

Rump Parliament Parliament controlled by Oliver Cromwell that abolished the monarchy and proclaimed England a republic. **288**

Rus People led by Rurik who came to rule Keiv and the Slavic tribes along the Dnieper River. **38**

"Russification" Program by Czar Nicholas I in the 1830s that forced non-Russian peoples to adopt the Russian language, religion, and culture. **456**

Russo-Japanese War War between Japan and Russia for Manchuria that began with Japan's unannounced attack in 1904. **579**

S

sacraments Ceremonies at which participants receive God's direct favor, or grace, to ward off the consequences of sin. **108**

samurai Japanese warriors hired for protection by wealthy landlords in feudal Japan. **86**

Sandinistas Marxist group who led the revolution against the dictator of Nicaragua. **726**

SCAP "Supreme Commander of the Allied Powers," General Douglas MacArthur and his offices in occupied Japan. **667**

scholasticism Medieval philosophy attempting to bring together faith and reason. **142**

scientific method Method of inquiry that includes carefully conducted experiments and mathematical calculations to verify the results of experiments. **191**

Scientific Revolution Transformation in thinking that occurred during the 1500s and 1600s caused by scientific observation, experimentation, and the questioning of traditional opinions. **190**

scorched-earth policy Tactic of burning or destroying crops and anything else of value to an invading army. **335**

sea dogs Adventurous group of English sea captains who lived in the late 1500s. **298**

secede Withdraw from a union. **419**

sectionalism Competition among sections or regions of a country. **419**

sects Religious societies of a few people, usually with a preacher as their leader. **173**

Security Council Body of the United Nations that includes temporary members elected from the General Assembly for two-year rotating terms. **631**

Seljuq Turks Muslim people from central Asia who gained control of Palestine, or the Holy Land to Christians, during the late 1000s. **126**

seppuku (SE·poo·koo) Form of ceremonial suicide of defeated or disloyal samurai to avoid dishonor; also known in the West as hari-kari. **186**

serfs Peasants who were bound to the land where they worked for a lord. **106**

settlement colonies Large groups of people from one country living together in a new country. **470**

Seven Years' War War from 1756 to 1763 that involved almost all of Europe; the fighting began in North America as the French and Indian War. **276**

Shang Invaders of the Huang River valley who came to power sometime between 1750 B.C. and 1500 B.C. and established the first dynasty in China. **9**

Shi'ah Branch of Islam formed in the A.D. 600s that believed only imams should decide religious and worldly matters. **52**

Shining Path Maoist guerilla group in Peru that carried out its terrorist campaign in the rural highland areas. **740**

Shinto "Way of the kami"; indigenous religion of Japan involving rituals and prayers to appease nature spirits, and veneration of the emperor. **85**

shires Governmental districts in early England; governed by a shire-reeve (sheriff). **112**

shogun Chief military and governmental officer in feudal Japan. **86**

Sikh Religion based on the teachings of Nānak, an Indian mystic in the 1500s, who tried to unite the Hindu and Muslim religions. **249**

simony (SY·moh·nee) Practice of buying high positions in the Catholic Church, common during the Middle Ages. **111**

Sinn Fein Irish nationalist party that in 1918 declared themselves the representative government for an independent Irish republic. **549**

Sino-Japanese War War between China and Japan over Korea in 1894, resulting in a Japanese victory. **485**

social Darwinism Theory developed by Herbert Spencer that applies Darwin's theories to the evolution of human societies. **392**

Social Democratic Labor Party Russian socialist party formed in 1898. **459**

Social Democratic Party German socialist party formed in the late 1800s. **452**

social sciences Branches of knowledge that scientifically study people as members of society, covering such areas as economics, political institutions, history, and relations among people. **391**

Social Security Act U.S. law providing for unemployment and old-age benefits. **545**

socialism Political and economic system in which the government owns the means of production. **372**

"soft underbelly of the Axis" Region of Italy and the Balkans that Churchill believed to be the weak part of the Axis Powers. **612**

Southeast Asia Treaty Organization (SEATO); organization created by President Dwight D. Eisenhower to halt communist advances in Southeast Asia. **647**

Spanish Armada Impressive fleet of ships launched by Philip II of Spain; defeated by England in 1588. **279**

Spanish Civil War War between Falangist Nationalists of Spain and the Republicans during the 1930s. **592**

special theory of relativity Einstein's theory that no particle of matter can move faster than the speed of light and that motion can be measured only relative to a particular observer. **390**

spheres of influence Areas in which one country has a special interest, and other nations agree to respect that interest. **471**

SS Schutzstaffel, or military branch of the Nazi Party. **609**

Stamp Act Law passed by Parliament in 1765 that imposed a tax, in the form of a stamp, on special documents for American colonists. **306**

standard of living Measure of the quality of life. **184**

steppe Large, grassy plain stretching across eastern Europe and central Asia that is ideal for agriculture. **37**

strike Refusal of workers to work until their demands are met. **370**

subsidies Government grants of money. **396**

suburbs Residential areas on the outskirts of a city. **396**

Suez Canal Canal that goes through the Isthmus of Suez to connect the Mediterranean Sea and the Red Sea. **476**

Suez Crisis Conflict between primarily Western powers and Egypt over the possession of the Suez Canal in the 1950s. **702**

suffrage Right to vote. **410**

suffragettes Women who fought for all women's right to vote. **413**

Sufi Muslim mystics who tried to live simple lives. **53**

sultan Ruler of the Turks who claimed to serve the Muslim caliph. **55**

Sunni Branch of Islam formed in the A.D. 600s who believed agreement among Muslim people should settle religious and worldly matters. **52**

supercomputers Powerful computers that help solve complex scientific and engineering problems. **792**

surrealism Artistic style that brings conscious and unconscious ideas together to portray life in a dreamlike way. **538**

Swahili African society that emerged in the late 1100s along the East African coast and combined elements of African, Asian, and Islamic cultures. **18**

taiga (TY-gah) Russian region north of the steppe having great forests, much rainfall, and cold, long winters. **39**

Taiping Rebellion Revolt in China from 1850 to 1864, led by Hong Xiuquan who, influenced by Christian teachings, declared a mission to establish a new dynasty. **229**

Taj Mahal Building constructed under Shah Jahan as a tomb for his wife, which remains one of the architectural wonders of the world. **249**

Tale of Genji, The Story of courtly life in Japan written by Murasaki Shikibu in about A.D. 1000; generally considered the world's first novel. **86**

tariffs Import taxes on foreign goods. **198**

tenements Cramped, shabby apartment buildings where workers lived during the Industrial Revolution in England. **360**

terrorism Bombings, kidnappings, and other acts of violence by political groups or governments, sometimes against innocent people, to force governments to grant their demands. **458**

Tet Offensive Major attack launched on the South Vietnamese by North Vietnam and the Viet Cong in 1968. **675**

theater of the absurd Type of theater characterized by biting social commentary. **786**

theocracy Government ruled by religious leaders claiming God's authority. **175**

Third Reich Adolf Hitler's name for his regime meaning the "third empire." **556**

third Rome Moscow; Russian Orthodox interpretation of the city's leading role in bringing spiritual light to the world. **43**

Thirty Years' War War beginning in Prague in 1618 as a Protestant rebellion against the Holy Roman Empire. **263**

Thousand and One Nights, The Popular collection of Muslim folktales. **61**

Tiananmen Square Massacre Incident in which students staged a hunger strike in Tiananmen Square and ignored government orders to leave, resulting in the death of hundreds. **663**

tithe Church tax collected from Christians in early times that represented one tenth of their income; later became a gift to the church representing one tenth of a person's income. **110**

Toleration Act 1689 act of British Parliament granting some religious freedoms to non-Anglican Protestants. **295**

Tories Political party that supported the monarchy in England in the 1600s. **292**

total war Strategy in which the enemy's military and civilian resources are attacked. **419**

Treaty of Kanagawa Negotiations between Matthew Perry and Japan in 1854 that permitted trade between the two countries. **235**

Treaty of Nanjing Treaty following the Opium War in which China gave Hong Kong to Britain and opened ports to British trade. **227**

Treaty of Portsmouth Agreement that ended the Russo-Japanese War. **579**

Treaty of Prague Agreement at the end of the Seven Weeks' War in 1866 between Prussia and Austria. **448**

Treaty of San Stefano Treaty that forced the defeated Turks to grant independence to Romania, Serbia, and Montenegro. **464**

Treaty of Shimonoseki 1895 treaty forcing China to recognize independence of Korea and make concessions to Japan. **485**

Treaty of Tordesillas Agreement between Spain and Portugal that moved west the line determining the land each country could claim in the Atlantic. **202**

Treaty of Versailles Treaty between Germany and the Allied Powers at the end of World War I. **526**

triangular trade System of trade involving three stages, one of which was the transatlantic slave trade. **206**

Triple Alliance Alliance between Germany, Austria-Hungary, and Italy. **507**

Triple Entente Alliance between France, Russia, and Great Britain in the early 1900s. **507**

troubadours Traveling singers who entertained people during the Middle Ages. **140**

Truman Doctrine Policy declaring that the United States must consider the continued spread of communism as a threat to democracy. **634**

U-boats German submarines used in World War I. **513**

ultimatum Demand in which one party threatens harmful action to another party if the other party rejects its proposals. **509**

"unequal" treaties Trade treaties that China signed under pressure of invasion, giving Western powers trade benefits. **227**

unions Associations of workers that combine forces and demands of different workers. **371**

United Nations Organization of nations to keep peace through collective security arrangements. **629**

Universal Declaration of Human Rights Document adopted by the United Nations in 1948 that outlined the basic human rights every person should have. **798**

universal manhood suffrage Policy that every adult male could vote, whether he owned property or not. **325**

urbanization Migration from the countryside to the city. **796**

usury (YOO-zhuh-ree) Policy of charging high interest on loans. **134**

utilitarianism Belief that a law was useful if it led to "the greatest happiness of the greatest number" of people. **369**

utopian socialists Persons who believe that people can live at peace with each other if they live in small cooperative settlements, owning all of the means of production in common and sharing the products. **373**

vassal Person granted land from a lord in return for services. **102**

V-E Day May 8, 1945, the day of Allied victory in Europe in World War II. **615**

vernacular languages Everyday speech that varies from place to place. **139**

veto power Power to defeat a measure with one single vote. **631**

viceroys Spanish officials who represented the monarchy in Spain's colonial empire. **209**

Vietnamization Process of preparing the South Vietnamese to take over the fighting of the Vietnam War to allow for the withdrawing of U.S. troops. **748**

Vikings Germanic people from Scandinavia who often raided western Europe during the A.D. 800s and 900s. **100**

V-J Day September 2, 1945, the day the Japanese surrendered to the United States in World War II. **616**

vulcanization Process of treating rubber to make it more useful. **355**

Wafd Party Egyptian nationalist party that led a revolt against the British in 1919. **566**

Wannsee Conference Meeting of German officials to plan for systematically exterminating Jews. **609**

war of attrition Slow wearing-down manner of warfare in which each side tries to outlast the other. **517**

War of the Roses War between the York and Lancaster families of England in 1455. **145**

War of the Spanish Succession War in which European countries battled Louis XIV to avoid Bourbon rule in both France and Spain. **265**

Warsaw Pact Mutual defense agreement between the Soviet Union and countries of the Eastern bloc. **638**

Watergate scandal The break-in at the Democratic National Committee headquarters in 1972 that led to President Nixon's resignation. **749**

weapons of mass destruction Nuclear, chemical, and biological weapons of great power. **752**

welfare state State in which the government undertakes primary responsibility for the social welfare of its citizens. **640**

Whigs Political party in England that rebelled against the monarchy, wanted a strong Parliament, and opposed having a Catholic ruler. **292**

White Lotus Rebellion Peasant rebellion against the Qing dynasty led by the Buddhist cult known as the White Lotus Society. **224**

"White Man's Burden, The" Poem by Rudyard Kipling that expressed the European attitude toward non-Western people during the imperialist era. **472**

World Court Permanent Court of International Justice, located at The Hague in the Netherlands. **530**

World Trade Center New York City office complex that was struck by a devastating terrorist attack on September 11, 2001. **772**

Yi Korean dynasty founded in 1392 when Koreans drove out the Mongols; lasted until Korea was annexed by Japan in 1910. **89**

Young Italy movement Group of Italian patriots dedicated to spreading ideas of nationalism. **440**

zaibatsu Huge industrial firms controlled by powerful families in Japan. **668**

Zen Sect of Buddhism that stresses meditation as a means of enlightenment. **77**

Zhou People who overthrew the Shang dynasty of China in 1122 B.C. **9**

Zionism Nationalist movement to build a homeland for the Jews in Palestine. **568**

Zollverein Customs union of most German states in 1834. **446**

Glosario

Este GLOSARIO contiene muchos de los términos que necesitas entender cuando estudias la historia mundial. Cada palabra tiene una breve definición o explicación de su significado, según su uso en historia mundial. El número entre paréntesis al lado de cada definición, se refiere al número de página en la cual esa palabra está marcada en el libro de texto.

A

abbess/abadesa Dirigente de un convento, quien ejerce un rol similar al de un abad. **110**

abbet/abad Dirigente de un monasterio, quien controla y distrubuye la propiedad. **110**

Aborigines/Aborígenes Habitantes originarios de Australia. **416**

abstract expressionism/expresionismo abstracto Estilo de pintura a partir de 1945 que envuelve la expresión personal del artista. **782**

acid rain/lluvia ácida Lluvia que contiene toxinas producidas por el consumo de petróleos fósiles. **796**

adobe/adobe Ladrillo de barro secado al aire, usado para la construcción por los Pueblos Indígenas. **19**

aerodynamics/acrodinámica Principios científicos que regulan el movimiento de aire alrededor de los objetos. **383**

Afrikaans/Afrikaans Aficaans. Lenguaje de los Bóers en Sudáfrica. **481**

Allied Powers/potencias aliados Gran Bretaña, Francia, Rusia, y otros aliados que lucharon unidos durante la Primera Guerra Mundial. **513**

almanacs/almanaques Libros que pronostican el tiempo y las probabilidades de crecimiento de los cultivos, y también contienen cosas como calendarios, mapas, y consejos médicos. **183**

Alpha/Alfa Primer estación espacial internacional, nombrada en noviembre del 2000. **791**

anarchists/anarquistas Extremistas políticos que se oponen al gobierno. **427**

Anglo-Egyptian Treaty/Tratado Anglo-Egipcio tratado entre Egipto e Inglaterra que le entregó a Egipto una mayor independencia, en 1936. **566**

antibiotics/antibióticos Substancias que pueden matar o limitar el crecimiento de bacterias. **794**

Anti-Comintern Pact/Tratado Anti-Comunismo Internacional Acuerdo entre Japón y Alemania comprometiéndose a detener la expansión del comunismo ruso. **594**

antisepsis/antisepsia Uso de químicos que destruyen los microbios que causan enfermedades infecciosas. **387**

apartheid/apartheid Política de gobierno, de segregación y explotación económica en Sudáfrica. **692**

appeasement/pacificación Política que intentar evitar guerras, por medio de la aceptación de algunas de las demandas del atacante. **595**

apprentice/aprendiz El que aprende alguna destreza de su maestro. **136**

armistice/armisticio Acuerdo firmado por países en guerra para detener su lucha. **523**

Articles of Confederation/Artículos de la Confederación Plan ratificado por los estados Americanos en 1781, que establece un gobierno central con un solo Congreso en el cual cada estado tiene un voto. **310**

ASEAN/ASEAN Asociación de Naciones Sudasiáticas. Organización formada para promover el crecimiento economico. **680**

Ashikaga/Ashikaga Familias de shogunes quienes gobernaron Japón durante cerca de 250 años. **86**

assimilation/asimilación Proceso en el cual una persona renuncia a su propia cultura y adopta una cultura diferente. **482**

astrolabe/astrolabio Instrumento usado para calcular la latitud, por medio de la observación de estrellas. **59**

Atlantic Charter/Carta del Atlántico Declaración creada por Winston Churchill y Franklin Roosevelt que declaró las intenciones de sus dos países en 1941. **603**

atrocities/atrocidades Crímenes brutales de guerra, cometidos a menudo contra los ciudadanos. **518**

Auschwitz/Auschwitz Campo de concentración nazi donde las personas eran asesinadas sistemáticamente. **610**

autocrat/autócrata Dirigente con el poder absoluto. **456**

Awami League/Liga Awami partido político dedicado a la independencia de Pakistan del Este. **658**

Axis Powers/potencias del Eje Eje Roma-Berlín. Alianza entre Alemania, Italia, y Japón. **594**

Aztec/Aztecas Guerreros viajantes quienes gradualmente llegaron a gobernar el centro de México. **19**

B

Babylonian Captivity/Cautiverio Babilónico Años durante los cuales El Papa vivió en Avignon, Francia, en lugar de Roma, Italia (1309–1377). **150**

balance of power/balance de poder Principio en el cual los países tienen igualdad de fuerza para prevenir que un país trate de dominar a los otros. **265**

Balfour Declaration/Declaración Balfour Declaración escrita por el Ministro Británico de Asuntos Exteriores a un líder Sionista en Palestina. **568**

Balkan "powder keg"/Balkan "powder keg" Estado de desasosiego en los Balcanes que provocó el asesinato del heredero del imperio Austro-Húngaro e inició la guerra (I Guerra Mundial). **509**

Balkan League/Guerra de los Balcanes Las naciones Balcánicas de Bulgaria, Servia, Grecia, y Montenegro que declararon la guerra en el Imperio Otomano. **465**

barter economy/economía de trueque Economía basada en el intercambio de bienes y servicios, sin usar dinero. **133**

Bataan Death March/Marcha de la Muerte Marcha impuesta por los japoneses a los prisioneros de guerra en las Fili-pinas, en 1942. **617**

Battle of Britain/Batalla de Inglaterra Enfrentamientos aéreos entre la aviación británica y la alemana en 1940 y 1941. **602**

Battle of Midway/Batalla de Midway Importante batalla en la cual los Norteamericanos derrotaron a los Japoneses en 1942. La victoria soviética debilitó grandemente las fuerzas germanas. **613**

Battle of Stalingrad/Batalla de Stalingrado Batalla entre alemanes y soviéticos en Stalingrado, en el verano de 1942 **612**

Beats/Beats Pertenecientes a la Generación Beat. Grupo de escritores que en los años de la Post-Guerra (Segunda Guerra Mundial) criticaban a los ciudadanos ricos y sus valores. **787**

bedouins/beduinos Árabes nómadas del desierto, que llevan manadas de camellos y ovejas. **48**

belligerents/beligerantes Naciones en guerra. **510**

Berlin Airlift/Ayuda aéreade Berlín Sistema de aerotransporte de los Estados Unidos e Inglaterra, de arrojar comida y otros víveres desde el aire, en el sector occidental de Berlín. **636**

Berlin Wall/Muro de Berlín Muro construido para separar el este del oeste de Berlín, para prevenir que los alemanes del este escaparan al oeste de Berlín. **640**

Bill of Rights/Carta de Derechos Diez enmiendas o modificaciones de la Constitución de los Estados Unidos, que protegen la libertad y los derechos de los individuos. **311**

biodiversity/biodiversidad Variedad de plantas y animales que se dá naturalmente en el ambiente. **796**

biological sciences/ciencias biológicas Ciencias que estudian a los organismos vivientes,como la biología y la genética. **384**

Black Death/muerte negra Terrible plaga que devastó Europa a principios de 1347. **138**

Black Shirts/camistas negras Fascistas que dirigieron una violenta campaña contra sus oponentes. **552**

Black Tuesday/martes negro 29 de octubre de 1929, cuando inversionistas de valores se lanzaron a vender sus acciones y esto tuvo como resultado un gran colapso financiero. **543**

blitzkrieg/blitzkrieg Guerra Relámpago que tiene lugar con una gran fuerza y velocidad, empleado por los alemanes durante la Segunda Guerra Mundial. **599**

"Bloody Mary"/"Bloody Mary" Sobrenombre utilizado para Mary I de Inglaterra. **470**

bobbies/bobbies Apodo que recibe la policía de Londres. **396**

Boers/Bóers Sudafricanos de origen holandés. **481**

Boer War/Guerra Bóer Guerra entre los Bóers y los británicos por el control en Transvaal en 1899 **481**

Bolsheviks/bolcheviques Facción radical de Rusia dirigida por Lenin, que ganaron el control contra los Mencheviques. **520**

bourgeoisie/burguesía Clase media urbana, que incluye comerciantes, industriales y profesionales. **317**

Boxer Rebellion/Rebelión de los Bóxers Levantamiento en China en el cual fueron atacadas personas ajenas a esta sociedad secreta y todo lo conectado con ajenos fué destruido. **573**

boyars/boyardos Nobles que aconsejaban al príncipe en cada ciudad Kievan. **39**

Brezhnev Doctrine/Brezhnev, Doctrina Doctrina que establece que la Unión Soviética puede intervenir cuando alguna de las naciones satélites parece estar alejándose del comunismo. **764**

broadsides/broadsides Hojas de papel impreso con noticias, vendidos al público. **183**

Bundesrat/Bundesrat Cámara legislativa de Alemania. **450**

burgesses/burgueses Mercaderes y profesio-nales de pueblos y ciudades. **280**

Bushido/Bushido Código de conducta del samurai, que enfatiza valentía, lealtad y honor. **86**

business cycle/ciclo comerciál Ciclo de los negocios. Períodos alternos de prosperidad y declinamiento. **366**

cabinet/gabinete Cabecillas de los departamentos de gobierno, quienes aconsejan al jefe de Estado. **296**

caliph/califa Título que significa "sucesor del Profeta" usado en el gobierdo y religión de la sociedad Is-lámica. **51**

Camp David Accords/Acuerdos de Campo David Acuerdo de paz entre Egipto e Israel, media-das por los Estados Unidos. **707**

canon law/ley canónica Código de derecho de la Iglesia Católica. **110**

capital/capital Dinero ganado, ahorrado e invertido para conseguir ganancias. **134**

capitalism/capitalismo Sistema económico en el cual los individuos, en vez del gobierno, son quienes controlan los factores de la producción. **363**

Carbonari/Carbonari Sociedad secreta de ita-lianos nacionalistas, a principios de los años 1800. **440**

cardinals/cardenales Rangos oficiales de la Iglesia Católica, que siguen detrás del Papa. **109**

Carolingians/Carolingios Dinastía relativa a Carlomagno, establecida con la coronación de Pipino III como"rey por la gracia de Dios" desde el 751 D.C. **97**

cartels/carteles Combinaciones corporativas que controlan industrias enteras. **365**

Carter Doctrine/Doctrina de Carter Declaración que establece que los Estados Unidos vigilaría cualquier intento de fuerzas ajenas por controlar el Golfo Pérsico, como un asalto a los intereses de Estados Unidos. **752**

caste system/sistema de castas Compleja forma de organización social que comienza a tomar forma después de la migración Indoaria. **8**

Cavaliers/Cavaliers Partidarios del Rey Carlos I en la Guerra Civil Inglesa; también conocidos como "monárquicos". **288**

Central Powers/potencias centrales Alianza entre Alemania, Austria-Hungría, Bulgaria,y el Imperio Otomano, en la Primera Guerra Mundial. **512**

Children's Crusade/Cruzada de los Niños Efímera cruzada en 1212, donde jóvenes de Europa marcharon en la Tierra Santa para recuperar el Cristianismo. **129**

chivalry/Caballería Código o sistema medieval de caballería. **106**

civilization/civilización Cultura compleja que puede producir un excedente de comida, establecer grandes poblaciones con un gobierno, y tener personas que realizan diferentes labores. **4**

cloning/clonación Proceso de hacer una copia genéticamente idéntica, a partir de una célula animal **794**

coalitions/coaliciones Grupos políticos organizados para apoyar una causa común. **428**

Cold War/guerra fría Sospecha y hostilidad entre las naciones comunistas y las naciones occidentales democráticas, que se libró primordialmente, usando medios políticos y económicos, en lugar de armas. **633**

collaborators/colaboradores Personas dispuestas a ayudar a los enemigos de su nación. **599**

collective bargaining/pacto colectivo proceso de negociación entre dirigentes y representantes sindicales. **371**

collective farms/fincas colectivas Tierras mancomunadas en grandes fincas, donde las personas trabajan juntas como un grupo. **557**

Colombia/Columbia Nave espacial usada para el viaje de la primera misión de los Estados Unidos a la luna. **791**

Colombian Exchange/intercambio colonista Intercambio masivo de bienes, plantas, animales, y enfermedades, que tuvo lugar entre los hemisferios Oriente y Occidente, que siguie-ron a los viajes de Colón. **202**

Cominform/Cominform Oficina de Información Comunista establecido por los Soviéticos para oponerse al Plan Marcial. **635**

Comintern/Comintern Comunismo Internacional,una organización fundada por Lenín para esparcir la revolución comunista alrededor del mundo. **561**

command economy/economía de mando Economía en la cual el gobierno controla todas las decisiones económicas. **558**

commercial capitalism/capitalismo comercial Sistema económico temprano, en el cual la mayoría de los capitalistas eran comerciantes que compraban y vendían bienes. **363**

Commercial Revolution/Revolución Comercial Época entre 1400 y 1750 cuando los europeos hicieron cambios ma-yores a sus economías debido a las nuevas exploraciones. **197**

common law/ley común Ley basada en las costumbres y decisiones de jueces, en vez de lo escrito en los códigos. **115**

Common Market/Mercado Común Llamado oficialmente la Comunidad Económica Europea, una organización de seis naciones de Europa Occidental, establecida en 1957 para la cooperación económica internacional. **642**

commonwealth/república Régimen político en Inglaterra. Forma de gobierno. **288**

Commonwealth of Independent States/Comunidad de Estados Independientes (CIS) Sistema establecido para coordinar políticas económicas y de defensa para las nuevas repúblicas independientes, después de la ruptura de la Unión Soviética. **767**

Communards/Comuneros Miembros del concejo local en París quienes querían un gobierno decentralizado, separando la Iglesia del Estado, y otras reformas socialistas. **427**

communism/comunismo Sistema económico y político en el cual los gobiernos poseen los medios de produc-ción y controlan el planeamiento de la economía. **374**

Communist Party/Partido Comunista Nombre nuevo de los rusos Bolcheviques, que disolvieron la asamblea constitucional en 1918. **521**

compass/brújula Instrumento de navegación creado en 1930, que utiliza una pieza de metal magnetizada que apunta al norte. **196**

conceptual art/arte conceptual Estilo de arte en el cual el acto de crear arte es más importante que el mismo objeto artístico. **783**

Concordat/Concordato Acuerdo entre Napoleón y el Papa, reconociendo al Catolicismo como la religión de la mayoría de los ciudadanos franceses. **332**

conscription/reclutamiento Reclutamiento militar. **326**

conservatives/conservadores Grupo que no desea cambiar las condiciones existentes. **323**

constitution/constitución Documento que contiene las leyes y principios básicos que gobiernan una nación. **289**

consulates/consulados Oficinas diplomáticas en el extranjero, dirigidas por un cónsul. **235**

Contadora Principles/Principios de Contadora Acuerdo promoviendo negociaciones en lugar de violencia, como una ma-nera de apaciguar conflictos regionales en América Latina. **729**

containment/contención Política de contención, dedicada a restringir la expansión del comunismo. **635**

contraband/contrabando Materiales bélicos suplidos por una nación neutral a una nación beligerante. **518**

contras/contras Grupos que buscan sustituir el gobierno Sandinista en Nicaragua. **727**

Convention on the Rights of the Child/Declaración de los Derechos del Niño Acuerdo de las Naciones Unidas, en 1989, que apunta las directrices legales, sociales y económicas que cada país debe seguir para proteger a los niños y las niñas. **801**

corporations/corporaciones Negocios en creci-miento desde los años 1800, que permiten a la gente comprar acciones en una compañía. **365**

corporatist state/estado corporativo Nación en la cual la mayor parte de las actividades económicas, como la agricultura, transporte, industria y comercio, están organizadas en sindicatos similares a las corporaciones. **553**

Council of Trent/Concilio de Trento Reunión de líderes de la Iglesia en los años 1500, para definir claramente las doctrinas católicas para la Contrareforma. **177**

Counter-Reformation/Contrareforma Intento de la Iglesia Católica, luego de la Reforma, por devolver a la Iglesia a un énfasis en asuntos espirituales. **176**

counterrevolutionary/contrarrevolucionario Actividades en contra de una revolución,organizadas por los que apoyan el Viejo Régimen. **326**

coup d'etat/coup d'état Toma de poder por la fuerza; en francés, un "ataque al Estado". **330**

craft guilds/gremios de artesanos Asociación de trabajadores manuales para establecer las condiciones de trabajo. **136**

creoles/creoles Personas caucásicas nacidas en colonias españolas o portuguesas. **430**

Crimean War/Guerra de Crimea Guerra decla-rada por Francia, Gran Bretaña y el Imperio Otomano, contra Rusia. **425**

crop rotation/rotación de cultivos La práctica de alternar cultivos de diferentes tipos, para preservar la tierra fértil. **352**

Crusades/Cruzadas Expediciones hechas por los cristianos para recuperar la Tierra Santa de los musulmanes. **126**

Cuban missile crisis/Crisis de los misiles Cuba Situación durante la Guerra Fría en la cual la Unión Soviética construyó zonas de misiles nucleares en Cuba. **648**

cubism/cubismo Estilo artístico que enfatiza diseños geométricos, usando formas como cubos, superficies planas y esferas. **539**

cultural diffusion/difusión cultural Expansión de una cultura de un área del mundo a otra. **4**

Cultural Revolution/Revolución Cultural Intento violento de un cambio social en China, encabezado por Mao Zedong en 1966. **662**

cuneiform/cuneiforme Escritura sumeria en forma de cuñas. **5**

curia/curia Grupo de consejeros del Papa, llevados desde los más altos rangos del clero. **109**

czar/zar Título tomado por Iván el Terrible; palabra rusa para "caesar" o "césar." **42**

dadaists/dadaístas Grupo de artistas que usaban imágenes al azar para reflejar lo que ellos consideraban la insensatez de la guerra. **539**

daimyo/daimyo señores o amos feudales en Japón. **88**

Dayton Accord/Acuerdo de Daytona Acuerdo mediado por los Estados Unidos, mediante el cual se le otorga a los Bosnios–Serbios un grado de autonomía y a la vez se reconoce la soberanía del gobierno de Mahoma. **771**

D-Day/día D 6 de junio, 1944, el día que las tropas aliadas iniciaron la invasión de la costa de Normandía. **613**

democratic socialism/socialdemocracia Sistema político en el cual el gobierno toma posesión pacíficamente de los bienes de producción, la gente conserva los derechos humanos básicos y control parcial de la economía. Tránsito del capitalismo al socialismo por medio de reformas graduales. **375**

departments/departamentos Distritos administrativos en Francia. **321**

dependent colonies/colonias dependientes Colonias en las que unos pocos oficiales de un país (generalmente europeo), gobierna o dirige a otro país no-europeo. **470**

depression/depresión Período en el cual la poca demanda de bienes causa que la economía de un país se hunda. **366**

desaparecidos/desaparecidos Desaparecidos en Argentina, quienes criticaron el gobierno, y fueron asesinados por la campaña del gobierno militar. **739**

desertification/desertificación Expansión del desierto. **697**

détente/détente Era de mejorías de las relaciones Soviético-Americanas. **752**

DEW Line/DEW límite Radares instalados por los Estados Unidos y Canadá, que advierte sobre ataques aéreos. **649**

Diamond Sutra/Diamond Sutra Primer libro impreso del mundo, un texto Budista producido en China en el año 868 A.C. **78**

Diet/Dieta Cámaras legislativas en Japón. **484**

Diplomatic Revolution/Revolución Diplomática Transformación de alianzas en Europa a mediados de los años 1700. **275**

direct democracy/democracia directa Forma de democracia en la que todos los ciudadanos participan directamente en la toma de decisiones. **11**

dissidents/disidentes Personas que no están de acuerdo con el gobierno. **732**

divine right of kings/derechos divinos de los reyes Creencia de que Dios elige a los reyes que reinarán una nación. **264**

division of labor/división de labores Característica de las civilizaciones en la cual diferentes personas realizan diferentes trabajos. **4**

DNA/ADN Ácido desoxirribonucléico, pequeñas unidades de cromosomas que transportan características de padre a hijo. **794**

domestic system/sistema doméstico Método de producción que tiene lugar en la casa del trabajador, y no en una tienda o fábrica. **133**

domino theory/teoría dominó Idea de que si un país cae en el comunismo, los países que lo rodean, eventualmente caerán en él. **675**

dowry/dote Dinero y bienes que una esposa brinda al matrimonio. **30**

Duma/Duma Parlamento elegido por Rusia. **462**

dynamo/dínamo Generador eléctrico. **380**

Easter Rising/Rebelión del Este 24 de abril de 1916, cuando nacionalistas irlandeses se rebelaron en contra de los británicos. **548**

economic nationalism/nacionalismo económico Política económica que usa una nación para tratar de mejorar su economía, por medio de límites en el comercio. **542**

economic sanctions/sanciones económicas Negativa de comerciar con una nación ofensiva. **531**

Emancipation Edict/Edicto de Emancipación Proclamación del Zar Alexander en 1861 que liberó a los siervos rusos. **457**

Emancipation Proclamation/Proclamación de Emancipación Decreto emitido por el presidente Abraham Lincoln en 1863 que acabó efectivamente con la esclavitud, a final de la Guerra Civil. **419**

emigrations/emigraciones Personas que se alejan de su tierra natal **394**

émigrés/émigrés Nobles que dejaron Francia durante la Revolución **321**

enclosure movement/movimiento de encercamiento Práctica de cercar territorios comunes y convertirlas en propiedades individuales. **352**

Encyclopedia, The/Enciclopedia, La Libro de referencia de las ideas de la Ilustración. **302**

English Bill of Rights/Cesión Inglesa de Derechos Documento en 1689 que declaró los poderes del Parlamento y protegía a los ciudadanos particulares. **293**

enlightened despotism/despotismo ilustrado Sistema de gobierno en el cual un monarca absoluto dirigía de acuerdo con la Ilustración o Iluminación. **304**

Enlightenment/Ilustración Período en los años 1700, cuando los filósofos creían que podían aplicar el método científico y el uso de la razón para explicar de manera lógica la naturaleza humana. **302**

ethical monotheism/monoteísmo ético Religión que cree en un sólo Dios, y enfatiza la ética. **6**

ethnic cleansing/limpieza étnica Campaña de te-rror y muerte que intentaba sacar ciertos grupos étnicos de una región. **769**

European Community/Comunidad Europea Organización multinacional europea, con sede en Bélgica. **643**

evolution/evolución Creencia de que los organismos se desarrollan y cambian a traves del tiempo. **385**

excommunication/excomulgación Edicto oficial que expulsa a una persona como miembro de la Iglesia. **34**

executive branch/poder ejecutivo Sección administrativa de gobierno, que refuerza las leyes, y está encabezado por el presidente. **310**

extraterritoriality/inmunidad Exoneración de extranjeros de las leyes del país en el cual viven o trabajan. **227**

factors of production/factores de producción Recursos básicos para la industrialización, tales como tierra necesaria, capital y mano de obra. **353**

factory system/sistema de factoría Producción de bienes en una fábrica, utilizando maquinaria y un gran número de trabajadores. **354**

Falange/Falange Partido fascista español **592**

fascism/fascismo Doctrina gubernamental que se basa en reglas dictatoria-les y en un régimen totalitario, en el cual el Estado mantiene control rígido de la población, por medio de la fuerza y de censura . **551**

Fashoda crisis/crisis Fachoda Conflicto entre Francia, Inglaterra y Sudán. **477**

favorable balance of trade/balance favorable de comercio Situación

favorable que existe cuando un país vende más bienes de los que compra. **198**

federal system of government/sistema de gobierno federal Sistema de gobierno en el cual el poder está dividido entre un poder central, uno federal, gobierno, y estados individuales. **310**

feudalism/feudalismo Sistema de gobierno local basado en la concesión de tierras como pago por lealtad, ayuda militar y otros servicios. **102**

fief/feudo Concesión de tierras de un amo a su vasayo. **102**

Final Solution/Solución Final Nombre dado al intento de los Nazis por destruir la población judía de Europa. **609**

Five-Year Plan/Planes Quinquenales Plan del gobierno de Stalin para el cre-cirmiento económico durante los años 1920. **558**

flappers/agitadoras mujeres jóvenes que desafiaron las normas sociales en los 1920, usando cabello corto, y faldas cortas, y saliendo a clubes de jazz. **541**

Flemish school/escuela Flamenca Grupo de pintores que perfeccionaron la técnica de pintura sobre lienzo. **169**

Fourteen Points/Catorce Puntos Plan del Presidente Woodrow Wilson por un mundo justo basado en los objetivos de los Aliados por terminar la Primer Guerra Mundial. **522**

"Four Tigers"/"Cuatro Tigres" Korea del Sur, Taiwan, Singapur, y Hong Kong; llamados así por el fuete crecimiento de sus economías. **680**

Franco-Prussian War/guerra Franco-prusiana Guerra entre Francia y Prusia, que terminó con la derrota de Francia en 1871 **426**

free enterprise/libre empresa Sistema en el cual las fuerzas económicas trabajan automática y naturalmente, sin leyes mercantilistas ni regulaciones. **368**

free trade/libre comercio Práctica basada en la creencia de que el gobierno no debe restringir o interferir con el comercio internacional. **226**

Fujiwara/Fujiwara Primer familia en ganar control sobre el gobierno central en Japón, desde mediados de los años 800 hasta mediados de los 1100. **86**

functionalism/funcionalismo Estilo arquitectónico en el que un edificio es diseñado basado en su uso específico, y no en un estilo en particular. **539**

Gang of Four/bando de los cuatro Grupo comunista radical de Madame Mao, que querían continuar con la revolución cultural China. **662**

General Assembly/Asamblea General Colectivo de las Naciones Unidas, que consta de cualquier nación que desee unirse a él. **631**

general strike/huelga general Trabajadores de varias industrias, que se niegan a trabajar hasta que sus demandas sean cumplidas. **547**

Genetic Code/código genético Secuencia o cadena de información genética que determinan las características de cada vida humana. **794**

genetics/genética Estudio de cómo las características de plantas y animales sin nacer, son heredadas por sus descendientes. **577**

Geneva Accord/Convención de Ginebra Acuerdo firmado en 1954, que puso fin a la guerra colonial entre Francia e Indonesia. **675**

genocide/genocidio Exterminación sistemática de personas. **529**

gentry/alta burguesía Te-rratenientes en Inglaterra que tenían una buena posición social pero no tenían un título. **280**

geocentric theory/teoría geocéntrica Teoría de acuerdo con el pensador Helenístico Tolomeo, de que la Tierra es el centro del universo. **191**

German-Soviet nonaggression pact/pacto Germanosoviético de no agresión Acuerdo en 1939 dividiendo Europa del este en esferas de influencia. **597**

ghazis/ghazis Guerreros del Islam; soldados turcos quienes fueron los primeras Otomanos. **240**

glasnost/glásnost Política soviética de apertura bajo el cual el gobierno controla que la economía fuera desahogada y las restricciones en desacuerdo fueran disminuidas. **765**

Glorious Revolution/Revolución Gloriosa Traspaso de poder de Guillermo y María de Inglaterra en 1688. **292**

Golden Horde/Horda Dorada Nombre dado por los europeos a los invasores mongoles de 1200, debido al color dorado de sus tiendas. **81**

Good Neighbor Policy/Política del Buen Vecino Política estadounidense durante los años 30 , que promulga la co-operación entre las naciones de América Latina. **584**

Gothic/gótico Estilo arquitectónico de iglesias, caracterizado por arcos apuntados y la bóveda sobre crucería de ojivas. Este estilo fué desarrollado por los maestros constructores de mediados de los 1100. **142**

Grand Canal/Gran Canal Canal construido durante la dinastía Sui que unió el norte con el sur de China por primera vez. **74**

Great Depression/Gran Depresión Depresión mundial a principios de los años 1930, cuando los salarios cayeron, la actividad comercial bajó y hubo mucho desempleo. **543**

Great Leap Forward/Gran Salto Adelante Segundo Plan Quiquenal de Mao Zedong para China, en 1958, para acele-rar el progreso. **661**

Great Schism/Gran Escición Período de la historia de la Iglesia, de 1378 a 1417 cuando ésta fué dividida en dos grupos opuestos. **150**

Greek Fire/Combustible Griego Líquido inflamable usado como arma por la marina bizantina. **32**

greenhouse effect/efecto invernadero Calentamiento de la superficie terrestre. **797**

Grimm brothers/hermanos Grimm Hermanos alemanes que publicaron una famosa colección de cuentos infantiles. **400**

guerilla warfare/guerrilla Técnica que cuenta de invasiones repentinas por parte de pequeñas bandas de soldados. **211**

habeas corpus/habeas corpus Derecho legal que protege a los individ-uos de un arresto arbitrario. **293**

Habsburg/Habsburg Poderosa familia de gobernantes europeos en los años 1200. **148**

haciendas/haciendas Largas fincas autosu-ficientes en América Española. **429**

Hagia Sophia/Hagia Sophia Iglesia decorativa Bizantina en Constantinopla. **35**

Han/Han Dinastía de gobernantes que dirigieron un imperio creciente y centralizado en China. **10**

heliocentric theory/teoría heliocentrista Teoría desarrollada por Copérnico, que dice que el Sol es el centro del universo. **191**

Helsinki Accords/Acuerdo Helsinki Serie de acuerdos en 1975 que dió a las naciones europeas nuevos esquemas de trabajo para la cooperación económica y tecnológica entre otros acuerdos democráticos. **761**

heresy/herejía Opinión que la Iglesia considera contra la fé católica. **34**

heretics/herejes Personas que negaban la veracidad de los principios de la Iglesia, o que predicaban creencias que la Iglesia no aprobaba. **110**

hijrah/hijrah Migración de Muham-mad y sus seguidores en 622 D.C., marcando el primer año en el calendario Musulmán. **49**

Ho Chi Minh Trail/Sendero Ho Chi Min Nombre de la mas importante ruta de abastecimiento de Viet Cong, a través de Laos, del norte al sur de Vietnam. **676**

Holocaust/Holocausto Eliminación sistemática de los judíos en Europa, por parte de los Nazis. **611**

Hopewell/Hopewell Grupo de personas asentados en el Valle de Ohio, aproximadamente entre los años 300 y 200 A.C. **19**

Huguenots/Hugonotes Franceses, entre ellos nobles de alto rango, que se convirtieron al Calvinismo. **175**

humanists/humanistas Personas que se especializan en el estudio del Huma-nismo. Este incluye gramática, historia, poesía y retórica. **163**

humanitarians/humanitarios Personas que trabajan para mejorar las condiciones de otros. **369**

Hundred Years' War/Guerra de los Cien Años Guerra entre Francia e Inglaterra por el trono francés, que continuó desde 1337 a 1435, e introdujo el uso de nuevas armas. **144**

icon/ícono Imagen sacra de Jesús, la Virgen María, o de algún santo. **32**

Iconoclastic Controversy/Controversia Iconoclástica Debate entre oponentes y defensores de iconos en la Iglesia Bizantina. Uno de los motivos que llevó a la división de la Iglesia Cristiana en 1054. **34**

iconoclasts/iconoclastas Personas que se oponían al culto de las imagenes. **32**

imams/imamíes Líderes espirituales, quienes de acuerdo con algunos musulmanes, son descendientes directos de Muhammad. **52**

imperialism/imperialismo Ambición de una nación poderosa por dominar los asuntos políticos, económicos y culturales de otra nación o región. **470**

import substitution/sustitución de importaciones Política económica de reemplazar ciertos bienes importados con bienes fabricados por otra nación, producidos dentro del país. **719**

impressionists/impresionistas Grupo de pintores que desarrollaron un tipo de rea-lismo, mediante el estudio de la luz y el color, para crear vívidas impresiones de personas y lugares. **404**

Inca/Inca Civilización en los Andes en América del Sur, que para fines de 1400 D.C., incluía gran parte de lo que hoy día es Perú, Ecuador, Bolivia y Chile. **21**

indemnity/indemnización Compensación pagada a una nación por algún daño causado a ella. **338**

indulgences/indulgencias Perdonar un castigo o pecado. **171**

industrial capitalism/capitalismo industrial Tipo de capitalismo ocurrido durante la revolución Industrial, cuando los capitalistas estaban involucrados en la producción y manufactura de bienes, utilizando métodos mecanizados e indutrializados de producción. **363**

Industrial Revolution/Revolución Industrial Cambios producidos a principios de los años 1700, cuando las maquinarias empezaban a hacer mucho del trabajo que las personas tenían que hacer antes. **353**

influenza pandemic/influenza pandémica Epidemia de este tipo de gripe, que mató 20 millones de personas alrededor del mundo, entre 1918 y 1919. **536**

Inquisition/Inquisición Institución de la Iglesia Católica Romana que perseguía y eliminaba herejes y castigaba las herejías. **111**

Intendants/Intendentes Administradores regionales y representantes de la corona en las provincias de Francia. **263**

**interchangeable parts/partes inter-
cambiables** Partes idénticas que
pueden ser sustituidas entre ellas.
364

interdict/interdicto Castigo de la Iglesia Católica de una región, que
involucra la clausura de iglesias y la
negación de sacramentos. **110**

**International Brigades/Brigadas
Internacionales** Voluntarios
antifascistas de Francia, Inglaterra y
los Estados Unidos, que participaron
en la Guerra Civil Española. **593**

**international style/estilo interna-
cional** Estilo de arquitectura que
incluye continuas extensiones de
acero y vidrio. **540**

intifada/intifada Violento levantamiento de Palestinos en 1980 **708**

**Iran-Contra Affair/Asunto Irán-Con-
tras** Escándalo en el cual miembros
del consejo de Ronald Reagan,
vendían ilegalmente armas a Irán
como intercambio por los rehenes.
749

**Irish Republican Army (IRA)/Ejército
Republicano Irlandés** Rama militar
del grupo nacionalista irlandés Sinn
Fein. **549**

Islam/islam Religión basada en las
enseñanzas e ideas de Muhammad
que comenzaron a expandirse a
través de las tribus Árabes en los
años 600 D.C. **49**

island hopping/salto de islas Estrategia militar de capturar solo ciertas
islas de un país y saltar las otras.
613

isolationists/aislacionistas Personas
que creen que su propio país no
debe involucrarse en relaciones con
otras naciones, especialmente alianzas. **602**

Janissaries/Janissaries Tropa de soldados esclavos altamente entrenada
por los sultanes Otomanos. **240**

jazz/jazz Nueva forma de música origi-
nada en los años 1920 entre los
afroamericanos en Nueva Orleans.
539

Jesuits/Jesuitas Orden de religiosos
católicos fundada por Ignacio de Loyola en 1534. **177**

jihad/jihad Enseñanzas del Islam de
defender la fé. **50**

**jointstock company/sociedad anón-
ima** Organización de negocios

desarrollada durante la Revolución
Comercial en la que sus dueños acu-
mulan dinero con la venta de
acciones en la compañía. **197**

journeyman/jornalero Trabajador
especializado al que se le pagaba un
salario. **136**

judicial branch/poder Judicial Sector
del gobierno que interpreta y aplica
las leyes. **310**

Junkers/Junkers Grupo de terratenientes aristócratas quienes querían
que se aboliera el pago de aranceles
a principios de los años 1800. **446**

junks/juncos Grandes embarcaciones
chinas. **220**

Justinian Code/Código de Justiniano
Colección de leyes que formaban las
bases de la ley Bizantina, en el imperio de Justiniano. **30**

kaiser/kaiser Título del emperador
Alemán. **449**

kemi/kami Dioses japoneses o espíri-
tus naturales. **85**

**Kellogg-Briand pact/Pacto Kellogg-
Briand** Acuerdo hecho en 1928
entre los Estados Unidos y Francia,
que hizo la guerra "ilegal". **590**

Khmer Rouge/Khmers Rojos Comunistas camboyanos que instauraron
un régimen de terror, tomando el
gobierno y realizaron un genocidio
masivo de la población camboyana.
676

kibbutz/kibbutz Finca colectiva en
Israel. **701**

kizilbash/kizilbash Ejercito militar de
los Safavids para luchar por el poder
político. **244**

Kuturkampf/Kulturkampf Programa
anti-católico iniciado por Bismarck en
Alemania a finales de 1800. **451**

Kuomintang/Kuomintang Partido
Nacionalista Chino que nació del
deseo nacionalista de una reforma.
574

laissez-faire/laissez-faire En francés
"dejad hacer". Creencia de que el gobierno no debe interferir con las
operaciones de negocios. **368**

laser/láser Aparato que concentra luz
y la libera en un intenso rayo que
viaja en línea recta. **793**

League of Nations/Liga de Naciones
Organización mundial formada
después de la Primer Guerra Mundial
para mantener la paz. **524**

Legalism/Legalismo Escuela de
filosofía china concerniente a la
política. **10**

legislative branch/poder legislativo
Área del gobierno que hace las leyes.
310

legitimacy/legitimidad Principio que
envuelve el restablecimiento de
anteriores familias gobernantes a sus
tronos. **337**

Lend-Lease Act/Ley de préstamos En
1941, legislación que permite a los
Estados Unidos suplir materiales de
guerra a crédito a Gran Bretaña. **602**

**Liberal-Democratic Party/Partido
Liberaldemócratico** El mas
poderoso partido político en Japón
después de la Segunda Guerra
Mundial, que controló el gobierno de
1950 a 1990. **670**

liberalism/liberalismo Movimiento
político que cree en un gobierno representativo que defiende los derechos del individuo frente al Estado y
la supresión de trabas a la actividad
económica. **341**

**limited constitutional monarchy/
monarquía constitucional limi-
tada** Gobierno en el cual el
monarca permanece a la cabeza del
Estado pero el rey o reina son
requeridos en el Parlamento. **297**

Locarno Pact/Pacto de Locarno
Número de tratados firmados por
delegados de siete países de
Europa, en Locarno, en 1925. **547**

Long March/Gran Marcha Viaje de
6,000 millas hecho por los comunistas chinos para escapar de las
Tropas Nacionalistas. **576**

Long Parliament/Parlamento Largo
Parlamento Inglés seleccionado en
1640 y que entraban y salían de él
por 20 años. **287**

Lost Generation/Generación Perdida
Grupo de escritores americanos
cuyos escritos reflejaba la experiencia
de una generación que perdió los
fundamentos de su moral durante la
Primera Guerra Mundial. **537**

Loyalistas/Leales Colonistas americanos que se oponían a indepen-
dización de Ingalterra. **306**

Luftwaffe/Luftwaffe Fuerza aérea Alemana en la segunda Guerra Mundial.
601

M

Maastricht Treaty/Tratado Maastricht Tratado que creó la Unión Europea. **763**

"MacArthur Constitution"/"Constitución MacArthur" Constitución impuesta por Estados Unidos, adoptada por Japón en 1947. **667**

Maginot Line/Línea Maginot Sistema defensivo francés, en la frontera con Alemania, construido entre 1927–1932. **546**

Magna Carta/Carta Magna Documento inglés que hizo de la ley un poder supremo y la convirtió en la piedra angular del gobierno constitucional. **114**

Magyars/Magyars Grupo nómada que invadió Europa; eventualmente se establecieron en lo que hoy día es Hungría. **100**

Maine/Maine Barco de guerra estadounidense, que explotó en el puerto de la Habana en 1868, y que sirvió a Estados Unidos para declararle la guerra a España. **491**

mandate/mandato Territorio bajo mandato, usualmente una colonia previa que sería administrada por el gobierno de otra nación. **531**

manorialism/sistema feudal Sistema económico durante la edad Media, desarrollado alrededor de fincas autosuficientes donde los dueños y los campesinos compartían la tierra. **105**

Maori/Maori Habitantes originarios de Nueva Zelanda. **416**

maquis/maqués Miembros de un movimiento encubierto de resistencia francés. **601**

market economy/economía de mercado Economía en la que la tierra, trabajo y capital, son controlados por personas individuales. **134**

market speculation/especulación de mercado Inversiones riegosas en el mercado de valores. **542**

Marshall Plan/Plan Marshall Programa de reconstrucción europea, adoptado en Estados Unidos en 1948. **635**

mass production/producción en serie Sistema de producción de grandes cantidades de productos idénticos. **364**

Mau Mau/Mau Mau Organización Kikuyu que agitó una campaña de guerilla en contra de la presencia británica en Kenya. **689**

Maya/Maya Una de las más avazadas poblaciones de las Américas, que ocuparon gran parte la Península de Yucatán. **19**

means of production/medios de producción Todo lo utilizado para producir e intercambiar bienes. **372**

mechanization/mecanización Uso de maquinaria automatizada para acelerar la producción. **354**

medieval/medieval Término que describe el período de la historia de Europa occidental, conocido como la Edad Media. **96**

Meech Lake Accord/Acuerdo de Meech Lake Acuerdo fallido entre líderes canadienses de aceptar a Québec como una "sociedad distinta". **754**

Meiji Restoration/Restablecimiento de Meiji Cambio cuando un grupo de samurai derrocó el shogunato Tokugawa y restableció el emperador al poder. **484**

Mensheviks/Mencheviques Facción moderada rusa que luchó por el poder a principios de los 1900. **520**

mercantilism/mercantilismo Sistema económico vigente en los siglos XVII y XVIII que atiende en primer término al desarrollo del comercio con intervención del Estado, y que considera la posesión de metales preciosos como signo de riqueza. **198, 301**

merchant guild/gremio mercantilista Asociación de mercaderes y trabajadores, para proteger sus derechos de comerciar y para ayudar a los miembros de su familia. **135**

Merovingians/Merovingios Dinastía de los primeros reyes de Francia. Clodoveo, hijo de Meroveo extendió sus dominios a casi toda la Galia. **96**

mestizos/mestizos Pesonas descendientes de amerindios y europeos. **430**

middle ages/edad media Período de la historia occidental de Europa, comprendido entre la caída del Imperio Romano y el Renacimiento. **96**

middle class/clase media Clase formada por comerciantes, patronos de pequeña y mediana industria y profesiones liberales. Está entre la clase noble y la clase campesina en la Edad Media. **136**

Middle Passage/Pasaje Medio Segunda etapa del sistema de comercio triangular, el cual envolvía el transporte de esclavos a las Américas a través del Atlántico. **206**

militarism/militarismo Glorificación del poder armado. **506**

millets/millets Minorías religiosas separadas y autogobernadas en el Imperio Otomano. **242**

Minamoto/Minamoto Clan que reinaba en Japón en 1156; introdujo el control shogun, y cambió el la forma en que el gobierno era llevado. **86**

minaret/minarete Alminar, torre de la mezquita. **61**

miniaturization/miniaturización Proceso de hacer máquinas más pequeñas y livianas. **791**

mixed economy/economía mixta Economía en la cual empresas privadas son dueñas de algunas compañías y el gobierno es el dueño de las demás. **657**

mobilizer/movilizar Acción de preparar el ejército de una nación y otros recursos de guerra. **506**

moderates/moderados Personas que no mantienen un punto de vista político extremo. **323**

monasticism/monasticismo Modo de vida en conventos y monasterios donde las monjas y monjes eran alejados del mundo y sus tentaciones. **109**

monoculture/monocultura Cuando un país depende de un solo tipo de cultivo. **719**

monopoly/monopolio Control completo de la producción o venta de un solo bien o servicio, por una firma en particular. **365**

Monroe Doctrine/Doctrina Monroe Doctrina en 1823 que establecía que los Estado Unidos no deberían interferir en los asuntos europeos o en las colonias europeas en el hemisferio oeste. **433**

Moors/Moros Musulmanes que hicieron de España su hogar en los años 700 D.C. **53**

mosaic/mosaico Pintura o diseño hecho de pequeñas piezas de esmalte, vidrio o piedra. **35**

mosques/mezquita Edificio que los mahometanos usaban para la oración y las ceremonias religiosas. **50**

**Mothers of the Plaza de Mayo/
Madres de la Plaza de Mayo**
Grupo de mujeres argentinas cuyos familiares desaparecieron debido a las sanciones violentas y los abusos del gobierno a los que ellos se opusieron. **721**

mulattoes/mulatos Personas de antepasados europeos y africanos, en las colonias españolas en América. **430**

multinational corporations/corporaciones multinacionales Empresas en un país, que son propiedad de un país extranjero. **718**

Munich Conference/Conferencia de Munich Reunión llamada por Hitler en 1938 para discutir el problema checo, lo que llevó a la anexión de los Sudetes con Alemania. **595**

Muslim League/Liga Musulmana Grupo de musulmanes hindúes, formado para proteger sus derechos. **654**

Muslims/Musulmánes Seguidores de la religión islámica. **50**

NAACP/NAACP Asociación Nacional de Fomento de las Personas de Color (por sus siglas en inglés). **646**

NAFTA/NAFTA Acuerdo Norteamericano de Libre Comercio. Grupo que trabajaba por los derechos civiles. Este une a México, Canadá y los Estados Unidos, como una sola zona de comercio. **720**

Napoléonic Code/Código Napoleónico Sistema de leyes francesas dirigidas por Napoleón. **332**

nationalism/nacionalismo Apego a los nativos de una nación, a ella propia y a cuanto les pertenece. **334**

nationalization/nacionalización Acto de poner una industria bajo el control del gobierno. **547**

NATO/NATO Tratado de Organización Norte Atlántica. Alianza de doce naciones occidentales, formada en 1949. **638**

naturalists/naturalistas Sistema que atribuye todas las cosas a la naturaleza como primer principio. En la literatura,muestra lo ingrato, crudo o desagradable de la vida diaria. **404**

Navigation Act of 1651/Ley de Navegación en 1651 Ley que requería que los bienes importados fueran transportados en barcos ingleses o barcos del país que produjo los bienes. **289**

Nazi Party/Partido Nazi Nacionalistas extremistas, anti-Semitas, y anticomunistas, que alcanzaron el poder en Alemania en 1920. **553**

Neutrality Acts/Leyes de Neutralidad Legislación pasada entre 1935 1937 en los Estados Unidos, que estableció su deseo de permanecer neutral en guerras futuras. **602**

New Deal/New Deal Programa del presidente Franklin D. Roosevelt en el que el gobierno federal estableció un amplio programa de obras públicas para crear empleo y conceder dinero a cada estado para sus necesidades. **545**

New Economic Policy/Nueva Política Económica Política de Lenín que permitió algo de libre comercio para lidiar con el colapso en la economía rusa. **557**

New Model Army/Nuevo Modelo de Ejército Poderoso ejército de Cromwell, que derrotó al Rey Carlos en la Guerra Civil Inglesa. **288**

"New Order"/"Nuevo Orden" Plan de Adolfo Hitler de organizar Europa en un solo sistema político y económico, dirigido por Alemania. **609**

nihilists/nihilismo Negación de todo principio religioso, político o social. **458**

nonalignment/no-aliados Las naciones que se niegan a ser aliadas de los Estados Unidos o de la Unión Soviética. **655**

Northwest Ordinance/Decreto del Noroeste Ley pasada por el Congreso de los Estados Unidos para proveer gobierno al territorio noroeste. **417**

Nürnberg Trials/Juicio de Nürnberg Juicios de la postguerra contra los líderes nazis, acusados de crímenes contra la humanidad. **630**

op art/op art Movimiento artístico surgido en Estados Unidos en 1960, fundamentado en ilusiones ópticas e impresiones plásticas del movimiento. **782**

OPEC/OPEC Organización de Países Exportadores de Petróleo, creada en 1960 para establecer los precios del petróleo y los niveles de producción de petróleo en el mundo. **709**

Open Door Policy/política de puertas abiertas Derecho de todas las naciones extranjeras de comerciar con China. **573**

Operation Bootstrap/Operación Bootstrap Plan de inversión extranjera e industria-lización, para levantar la economía de Puerto Rico. **733**

Operation Overlord/Operación Overlord Nombre para la invasión aliada al noroeste de Francia. **613**

Opium War/guerra del opio Conflicto entre China e Inglaterra entre 1839 y 1842 que surgió por la oposición china al comercio de opio por los ingleses. **227**

Organization of American States/ Organización de Estados Americanos (OEA) Grupo diseñado para fomentar la cooperación militar,económica y cultural entre las naciones del hemisferio occidental. **722**

Ostpolitik/Ostpolitik Término usado para describir los esfuerzos de Willy Brandt para mejorar las relaciones entre el este y el oeste. **759**

Ottoman Turks/Otomanos Pueblos asiáticos que conquistaron Constantinopla en 1300 y establecieron un gran imperio. **36**

Pan-Africanism/panafricanismo Movimiento que promueve la unidad cultural de los pueblos africanos en su lucha por la libertad. **686**

Panama Canal/Canal de Panamá Canal completado en 1914 que conecta los océanos Pacífico y Atlántico. **492**

Pan-Slavism/paneslavismo Unidad de los países eslavos bajo el liderazgo de Rusia. **456**

Paris Peace Accords/Acuerdo de Paz de París Acuerdo de cese al fuego en 1973, llamando al retiro de los Estados Unidos del sur de Vietnam **675**

Paris Peace Conference/Conferencia de Paz en París Reunión de naciones victoriosas para escribir los acuerdos de paz después de la Segunda Guerra Mundial. **524**

passive resistance/resistencia pasiva Desobediencia civil pacífica. **569**

pasteurization/pasteurización Proceso de calentar líquidos para matar las bacterias y evitar la fermentación. **387**

paternalism/paternalismo Sistema de aplicar a las relaciones sociales, políticas y laborales. formas de autoridad y protección similares a las que ejerce un padre sobre su familia. **481**

patriots/patriotas Colonistas americanos que favorecieron con la independencia de Inglaterra. **306**

peninsulares/peninsulares Europeos que nacieron en la Península Ibérica de España o Portugal **430**

People's Will/voluntad de la gente Movimiento ruso que usaba la violencia e intimidación para realizar reformas. **458**

Pentagon/Pentágono Sede de los jefes mili-tares de los Estados Unidos, loca-lizado en Washington, D.C. Fué escenario de un ataque terrorista el 11 de septiembre, 2001. **772**

perestroika/perestroika Política de restructuración soviética diseñada para revisar el sistema político y económico. **765**

performance art/arte performance Forma de arte en la que el artista es una obra de arte viviente. **783**

perspective/perspectiva Técnica de arte que envuelve hacer los objetos distantes más pequeños que los que están al frente, y acomodarlos de manera que se cree la ilusión de profundidad en un lienzo plano. **164**

Petition of Right/petición de derechos Petición que establecía cuatro antiguas libertades, presentadas al Parlamento por Carlos I. **286**

philology/filología Estudio de literatura y lenguaje. **223**

philosophes/filósofos Pensadores de la era de la Ilustración. **302**

"phony war"/"guerra falsa" Simulacro de guerra. Fase temprana de la Segunda Guerra Mundial, marcada por una poca actividad en el occidente europeo. **599**

physical sciences/ciencias físicas Ciencias concernientes a la energía y materia no viviente, tales como la astronomía, geología, física y química. **384**

Platt Amendment/Enmienda de Platt Disposición de la constitución cubana, dándole derecho a Estados Unidos de intervenir en Cuba. **491**

plebiscite/plebiscito Procedimiento usado para determinar la constitución de un nuevo gobierno por medio del voto. **331**

PLO/PLO Organización Liberación Palestina. Organización de gue-rrilla palestina, liderada por Yasir Arafat. **707**

pogroms/pogromo Movimiento popular antisemítico, donde los judíos eran masacrados, en Rusia en los 1880. **459**

Politburo/Politburo Oficina Política del Partido Comunista, que tenía la mayoría del poder en la Unión Soviética. **560**

Polovtsy/Polovtsios Pueblo turco que después de 1055 controló el área del sur del Kiev en Rusia. **41**

pop art/arte pop Estilo usado por artistas que pintaban objetos comunes como latas de sopa, señales de tránsito, y revistas. **782**

pope/Papa Título asumido por el patriar-ca de Roma y cabeza de la Iglesia Católica. Palabra latina que significa "padre". **15**

Popular Front/Frente Popular Coalición del ala izquierda del gobierno de Francia en 1930. **547**

popular sovereignty/soberanía popular Principio gubernamental basado en leyes justas, y en un gobierno creado y sujeto a la voluntad del pueblo. **304**

Pragmatic Sanction/Sanción Pragmática Declaración hecha por Carlos VI, insistiendo a los líderes europeos permitir a María Teresa heredar territorio de Habsburg. **273**

Pravda Russkia/Pravda Russkia Primer código de leyes ruso, creado por Yaroslav I. **39**

predestination/predestinación Creencia de que al principio del tiempo, Dios decidió quienes iban a salvarse. **174**

PRI/PRI Partido Revolucionario Institucional de México. **723**

prime minister/primer ministro Jefe de gobierno en Gran Bretaña. **296**

primogeniture/primogenitura Sistema de heredar poseciones y tierra de un padre a su hijo mayor. **102**

prohibition/prohibición Política que prohibe la fabricación, venta y distribución de bebidas alcohólicas. **541**

proletariat/proletariado nombre dado por Karl Marx a la clase obrera. **374**

propaganda/propaganda Ideas, hechos, o rumores esparcidos deliberadamente para empujar la causa propia, o dañar causas o puestas. **514**

protectorates/protectorado Colonias en las que las que los gobernadores nativos mantenían sus títulos, pero oficiales de las fuerzas extranjeras controlaban las regiones. **471**

psychiatry/psiquiatría Estudio y tratamiento de enfermedades mentales. **393**

psychoanalysis/psicoanálisis Proceso de revelar y analizar el subconsciente. **393**

purge/purga Eliminación en gran escala de personas de una organización o área. **560**

Puritans/Puritanos Personas que aspiraban a una doctrina más pura que la propuesta por la Iglesia Católica Inglesa. **279**

Qin/Qin Dinastía que llegó al poder en China en 221A.C., bajo la cual el primer imperio chino verdadero fué creado. **9**

quantum theory/teoría cuántica Teoría de Max Planck que dice que la energía solo es liberada en grupos determinados, o quanta. **389**

queue/queue Trenza de cabello que caracterizaba el estilo de peinado que todos los hombres chinos debían usar durante la dinastía Qing. **222**

Qur'an/Corán libro sagrado del Islam. **50**

radicals/radicales Personas que propugnan grandes reformas en distintos órdenes. **323**

radioactivity/radioactividad Proceso en el que los átomos de ciertos elementos constantemente se separan y li-beran energía. **389**

Rajputs/Rajputas Príncipes guerreros indios que empezaron a retar el control turco musulmano en la India en 1500. **247**

rationalism/racionalismo Creencia de que la verdad puede ser determinada solamente por el pensamiento lógico. **302**

reaction/reacción Tendencia tradicionalista que se opone a lo nuevo. Cuando una persona con autoridad desea restablecer lo abolido. **338**

reactionaries/reaccionarios Extremistas que se oponen al cambio, y desean deshacer ciertos cambios. **338**

realism/realismo Doctrina o sistema de los filósofos de atribuir realidad a las ideas generales; atribuido a la literatura, arte y sociedad desde 1800. **404**

reaya/reaya Masas de sujetos ordinarios en la sociedad Otomana. **242**

Red Army/Ejército Rojo Fuerzas comunistas. **521**

Red Guards/Guardia Roja Estudiantes radicales elegidos por Mao Zedong, para dirigir la Revolución Cultural. **662**

Reformation/Reforma Revolución religiosa que dividió la Iglesia en Europa occidental, y creó una cantidad de iglesias nuevas. **171**

regionalism/regionalismo Forma de realismo que se enfoca en la vida diaria de lugares particulares. **404**

Reichstag/Reichstag Casa de la legislatura alemana. **450**

Reign of Terror/Régimen de Terror Período durante la Revolución Francesa cuando la Convención Nacional trabajó para suprimir toda oposición. **327**

Renaissance/Renacimiento Movimiento que precedió a la Edad Media, es el renacer del interés en las enseñanzas clásicas de Grecia y Roma. **162**

reparations/reparaciones Pago por el daño causado por guerras. **524**

republic/república Forma de gobierno representativo en que la soberania reside en el pueblo. **13**

Restoration/Restauración Período en que reinó Carlos II de Inglaterra, cuando la monarquía fué restablecida; se refiere también al nacimiento de la cultura inglesa en ese tiempo. **291**

risorgimento/risorgimento Palabra italiana para resurgimiento, usada como el nombre del movimiento naciona-lista italiano en 1800. **440**

romanticism/romanticismo Corriente seguida por muchos escritores a principios de 1800, cuyos trabajos

apelaban al sentimiento e imaginación y el romance en la vida. **400**

Rome-Berlin Axis/Axis Roma-Berlín (Eje Roma-Berlín) Alianza formada en 1936, entre Mussolini en Italia y Hitler en Berlín. **556**

Roosevelt Corollary/Consecuencia Roosevelt Extensión de la Doctrina de Monroe, que dicta que los estados Unidos garantizarían que las naciones de Latinoameerica cumplirían con sus obligaciones internacionales. **493**

Roundheads/Roundheads Cabezas redondas. Aquellos que apoyaron al Parlamento en la Guerra Civil Inglesa. **288**

Rump Parliament/Parlamento Remanente Parlamento controlado por Oliver Cromwell, que abolió la monarquía y proclamó a Inglaterra como república. **288**

Rus/Rus Región bajo el control de Rurik quines llegaron a gobernar Kiev y las tribus Eslavas a lo largo del Río Dneiper. **38**

"Russification"/"Rusificación" Programa del zar Nicolás I en 1830 que forzó a los pueblos no-rusos a adoptar el lenguaje, religión y cultura rusa. **456**

Russo-Japanese War/Guerra Ruso-Japonesa Guerra entre Japón y Rusia que empezó con un ataque sorpresivo de Japón en 1904 **579**

sacraments/sacramentos Ceremonias en las que los participantes reciben la gracia de Dios para salvarse de las consecuencias de pecar. **108**

samurai/samurai Guerreros japoneses contratados para proteger el bienestar de los terratenientes en Japón feudalista. **86**

Sandinistas/Sandinistas Grupo marxista que dirigió la revolución contra el dictador de Nicaragua. **726**

SCAP/SCAP "Comandante Supremo de las Potencias Aliadas" General Douglas MacArthur, en la ocupación de Japón. **667**

scholasticism/escolasticismo Filosofía medieval que intentara juntar la fé y la razón. **142**

scientific method/método científico Método de investigación que incluye cuidadosos experimentos conduci-

dos y cálculos matemáticos para verificar el resultado de los experimentos. **191**

Scientific Revolution/Revolución Científica Transformación de pensamiebnto ocurrido durante 1500 y 1600, causada por la observación científica, la experimentación, y el cuestionamiento de las opiniones tradicionales. **190**

scorched-earth policy/Política militar de quemar la tierra Táctica de quemar o destruir cultivos y tierras de valor. **335**

sea dogs/perros marinos Grupo de aventureros capitanes marinos, que vivieron a finales de 1500. **298**

secede/separarse Retiro de una unión o nación. **419**

sectionalism/seccionalismo Competencia entre secciones o regiones de un país. **419**

sects/sectas Sociedades religiosas de pocas personas, usualmente con un sacerdote como líder. **173**

Security Council/Consejo de Seguridad Cuerpo de las Naciones Unidas que incluye miembros temporales elegidos por la Asamblea General, por términos de dos años. **631**

Seljuq Turks/turcos Seljuq Musulmanes de Asia central quienes le ganaron el control de Palestina o Jerusalem a los cristianos, a finales de los 1000. **126**

seppuku/seppuku Forma ceremonial de suicidio de samurais derrotados o desleales, para salvar el honor. También conocidos en Occidente como hari-kari. **186**

serfs/siervos Campesinos que debían vivir en la tierra en la que trabajaban para un amo. **106**

settlement colonies/colonias Grandes grupos de personas de un país, que viven en un país diferente. **470**

Seven Years' War/Guerra de los Siete Años Guerra desde 1756 a 1763 que involucró a casi toda Europa; la pelea empezó en Norteamérica como una guerra entre indios y franceses. **276**

Shang/Shang Invasores del valle del río Huang que llegaron al poder entre 1750 y 1500 A.C., y establecieron la primer dinastía China. **9**

Shi'ah/Shi'ah Rama del Islam formada en los 600 D.C., que creía que solo los imams deberían decidir sobre asuntos religiosos y terrenales. **52**

Shining Path/Sendero Luminoso Grupo de guerrilla Maoísta que llevó su campaña terrorista a las zonas altas rurales. **740**

Shinto/Shintoísmo o Sintoísmo Religión indígena de Japón que envuelve rituales y oraciones para apaciguar espítitus de la naturaleza y venerar al emperador. **85**

shires/condados Distritos gubernamentales en la vieja Inglaterra. **112**

shogun/shogun Jefe militar y oficial gubernamental en Japón feudal. **86**

Sikh/Sikh Religión basada en las enseñanzas de Nañak, un místico hindú en 1500, quien trató de unir las religiones hinduista y la musulmana. **249**

simony/simonía Práctica de comprar altos puestos en la Iglesia, actividad común en la Edad Media. **111**

Sinn Fein/Sinn Fein Partido nacionalista Irlandés que en 1918 se declararon a sí mismos, el gobierno representante de una república irlandesa indepen-diente. **549**

Sino-Japanese War/Guerra Sino-Japonesa Guerra entre China y Japón por Corea, en 1894, cuyo resultado fué la victoria de Japón. **485**

social Darwinism/darwinismo social Teoría desa-rrollada por Herbert Spencer que aplica la teoría de Darwin de la evolución de las sociedades humanas. **392**

Social Democratic Labor Party/Partido Laboral Socialdemócrata Partido socialista ruso formado en 1898. **459**

Social Democratic Party/Partido Social Demócrata Partido socialista alemán formado a finales de 1800. **452**

social sciences/ciencias sociales Rama del conocimiento que estudia científicamente a las personas como miembros de la sociedad; cubren áreas tales como la economía, las instituciones políticas, historia, y relaciones entre los individuos. **391**

Social Security Act/Ley de seguridad social Leyes que proveen beneficios a personas desempleadas y a personas ma-yores en los Estados Unidos. **545**

socialism/socialismo Sistema político y económico en el que el gobierno posee los medios de producción. **372**

"soft underbelly of the Axis"/"la parte vulnerable del Axis" Región de Italia y los Balcanes que según Churchill, era la parte débil del Poder Axis. **612**

Southeast Asia Treaty Organization/Organización de Tratados Sudasiáticos (SEATO) Organización creada por el presidente Dwight D. Eisenhower para detener los avances del comunismo en el sureste de Asia. **647**

Spanish Armada/Armada española Impresionante flota de naves enviadas por Felipe II de España para invadir Inglaterra y que fueron de-rrotados por Inglaterra en 1588. **279**

Spanish Civil War/Guerra Civil Española Guerra entre los Falangistas Nacionalistas de España y los Republicanos durante 1930. **592**

special theory of relativity/teoría general de la relatividad Teoría de Einstein, que proporciona la ley de la gravitación y sus relaciones con otras fuerzas de la naturaleza. **390**

spheres of influence/esferas de influencia Áreas en las cuales un país tiene un interes particular y otras naciones respetan ese interés. **471**

SS/SS Schutzstaffel, o rama militar del Partido Nazi. **609**

Stamp Act/Ley del timbre Ley pasada por el Parlamento en 1765, que impuso un impuesto en forma de sello, en documentos especiales, para los americanos colonistas. **306**

standard of living/estándares de vida Medición de la calidad de vida. **184**

steppe/estepa Llanura muy extensa ideal para la agricultura, en el este de Europa y el centro de Asia. **37**

strike/huelga Cuando los trabajadores se niegan a trabajar hasta que sus demandas sean aceptadas. **370**

subsidies/subsidios Concesiones de dinero del gobierno. **396**

suburbs/suburbios Áreas residenciales en las afueras de la ciudad. **396**

Suez Canal/Canal de Suez Canal que va desde el Istmo de Suez y conecta con el Mar Mediterráneo y el Mar Rojo. **476**

Suez Crisis/Crisis de Suez Conflicto entre potencias Occidentales y Egipto, por la posesión del Canal de Suez en 1950. **702**

suffrage/sufragio Derecho al voto. **410**

suffragettes/sufragistas Mujeres que lucharon por el derecho de las mujeres de votar. **413**

Sufi/Sufi Místicos mahometanos que trataban de vivir una vida simple. **53**

sultan/sultán Título del emperador de los Turcos. Príncipe o gobernador mahometano. **55**

Sunni/Sunní Nombre que se le da en el islamismo a los ortodoxos seguidores de la Sunna. **52**

supercomputers/percomputadoras Potentes computadoras que ayudan a resolver complicados problemas científicos y tecnológicos. **792**

surrealism/surrealismo Estilo artístico que junta ideas conscientes e inconscientes para retratar la vida en forma de sueño. **538**

Swahili/Swahili Sociedad africana que emergió a finales de los años 1100 a lo largo de la costa Este africana. Combinaba elementos de las culturas africana, asiática e islámica. **18**

taiga/taiga Región rusa muy lluviosa, al norte de las estapas, con largos y fríos inviernos. **39**

Taiping Rebellion/Rebelión de Taiping Revuelta en China entre 1850 a 1864, guiada por Hong Xiuquan, quien influenciado por las enseñanzas del cristianismo, declaró una misión para establecer una nueva dinastía. **229**

Taj Mahal/Taj Mahal Palacio construido bajo Shah Jahan, como una tumba para su esposa. Actualmente es una de las maravillas arquitectónicas del mundo. **249**

Tale of Genji, The/La Aventura de Genji Historia escrita por Murasaki Shikibu, en Japón, alrededor del año 1000 D.C. Considerada generalmente como la primer novela en el mundo. **86**

tariffs/tarifas Impuestos a la importación de productos extran-jeros. **198**

tenements/viviendas Edificios de apartamentos, muy juntos y en mal estado donde los trabajadores vivían, durante la Revolución Industrial en Inglaterra. **360**

terrorism/terrorismo Bombardeos, secuestros, y otro actos de violencia, llevados a cabo por grupos políticos, muchas veces realizados contra gente inocente, para forzar a un gobierno a conceder demandas. **458**

Tet Offensive/Ofensiva del Tet Ataque iniciado en el sur de Vietnam, por el norte de Vietnam y el Viet Cong en 1968. **675**

"theater of the absurd"/"teatro del absurdo" Tipo de teatro caracterizado por hacer sarcásticos comentarios sociales. **786**

theocracy/teocracia Gobierno dirigido por líderes religiosos, que proclaman la autoridad de Dios. **175**

Third Reich/Tercer Reich Nombre dado por Adolfo Hitler a su régimen, significa "tercer imperio" **556**

third Rome/tercera Romana Interpretación rusa ortodoxa de su rol principal de traer la luz espiritual al mundo. **43**

Thirty Years' War/Guerra de los Treinta Años Guerra iniciada en Praga en 1618, como una rebelión de los Protestantes contra el Santo Imperio Romano. **263**

Thousand and One Nights/Las Mil y Una Noches Colección de cuentos populares musulmanes. **61**

Tiananmen Square Massacre/ Masacre de la Plaza Tianamen Incidente en el que estudiantes iniciaron una huelga de hambre en la Plaza Tianamen, e ignoraron las órdenes del gobierno de retirarse, resultó en la muerte de cientos de personas. **663**

tithe/diezmo Impuesto recogido por los cristianos para la Iglesia en los viejos tiempos, que representaba una décima parte de sus ganancias. **110**

Toleration Act/Ley de Tolerancia Acta del Parlamento Británico en 1689, concediéndo algunas libertades religiosas a los no-protestantes. **295**

Tories/Tories Partido político que apoyaba la monarquía en Inglaterra en los 1600. **292**

total war/Guerra total Estrategia en la que la milicia enemiga y los recursos civiles son atacados. **419**

Treaty of Kanagawa/Tratado de Kanagawa Negociaciones entre Matthew Perry y Japón en 1854 que permitió comerciar entre los dos países. **235**

Treaty of Nanjing/Tratado de Nanjing Tratado que siguió la Guerra del Opio en la cual China cedió Hong Kong a los británicos y abrieron puertos para el comercio británico. **227**

Treaty of Portsmouth/Tratado de Portsmouth Acuerdo que terminó con la guerra ruso-japonesa. **579**

Treaty of Prague/Tratado de Praga Acuerdo para terminar la Guerra de las Siete Semanas entre Prusia y Austria. **448**

Treaty of San Stefano/Tratado de San Stefano Tratado que obligó a los turcos derrotados a conceder la independencia a Rumanía, Serbia y Montenegro. **464**

Treaty of Shimonoseki/Tratado de Shimonoseki Tratado en 1895 obligando a China a reconocer la independencia de Korea y hacer concesiones a Japón. **485**

Treaty of Tordesillas/Tratado de Tordesillas Acuerdo entre España y Portugal que movió hacia el oeste el límite del territorio que cada país podía reclamar en el Atlántico. **202**

Treaty of Versailles/Tratado de Versalles Tratado entre Alemania y los Países Aliados para ponerle fin a la Primer Guerra Mundial. **526**

triangular trade/comercio triangular Sistema de comercio que involucra tres etapas, una de las cuales es la trata de esclavos a traves del Atlántico. **206**

Triple Alliance/Alianza Triple Alianza entre Alemania, Austria-Hungría e Italia. **507**

Triple Entente/Triple Entente Alianza entre Francia, Rusia y Gran Bretaña, a principios de 1900. **507**

troubadours/trovadores Cantantes que viajaban entreteniéndo gente en la Edad Media. **140**

Truman Doctrine/Doctrina Truman Política que declara que los Estados Unidos considera que el continuar con la expansión del comunismo es una amenaza a la democracia. **634**

U-boats/U-boats Submarinos alemanes usados en la Primer Guerra Mundial. **513**

ultimatum/ultimátum Demanda en la que una parte amenaza a la otra si esta no acepta sus propuestas. **509**

"unequal" treaties/trueque desigual Intercambio de bienes que China firmó bajo amenaza de invasión, dándole a las potencias Occidentales los beneficios del intercambio. **227**

unions/uniones Asociaciones de trabajadores, que combinan fuerzas y demandas de diferentes trabajadores. **371**

United Nations/Organización de las Naciones Unidas Organización de naciones para mantener la paz a traves de acuerdos colectivos. **629**

Universal Declaration of Human Rights/Declaración Universal de los Derechos Humanos Documento adoptado por las Naciones Unidas en 1948, que resume los derechos humanos básicos que cada persona debe tener. **798**

universal manhood suffrage/sufragio universal de los hombres Política de que todo hombre adulto podía votar, sin importar si poseía propiedades o no. **325**

urbanization/urbanización Migración del campo a la ciudad. **796**

usury/usura Política de cobrar altos intereses por un préstamo. **134**

utilitarianism/utilitarismo Creencia de que una ley funcionaba si llevaba a "la mayor felicidad al mayor número de personas posible". **369**

utopian socialists/socialistas utópicos Personas que creen que se puede vivir en paz los unos con los otros, si se vive en pequeñas colonias cooperativistas que poseen todos los bienes de producción en común, y comparten los productos. **373**

vassal/vasallo Persona a la que un amo le concedía tierras, como pago por sus servicios. **102**

V-E Day/Día V-E 8 de mayo de 1945, el día de la victoria Aliada en Europa en la Segunda Guerra Mundial. **615**

vernacular languages/lenguaje vernácular Lenguaje doméstico, nativo, propio de un país. **139**

veto/poder de veto Poder de derrotar una medida con un solo voto. **631**

viceroys/virrey El que con ese título gobierna en nombre y con autoridad del rey. Oficiales españoles que representaban a la monarquía en el imperio colonial español. **209**

Vietnamization/Vietnamización Proceso de preparación de los sudvietnamitas para tomar el control de la lucha en la Guerra de Vietnam y permitir la retirada de las tropas de Estados Unidos. **748**

Vikings/Vikingos Pueblo germánico de Escandinavia que atacaban frecuentemente el oeste de Europa durante los años 800 y 900. **100**

V-J Day/Día V-J 2 de setiembre de 1945, el día que los japoneses se rindieron ante los Estados Unidos en la Segunda Guerra Mundial. **616**

vulcanization/vulcanización Proceso de tratar el hule para hacerlo mas usable. **355**

Wafd Party/Partido Wafd Partido nacionalista egipcio que llevó a una revuelta contra los británicos en 1919. **566**

Wannsee Conference/Conferencia Wannsee Reunión de oficiales alemanes para externinar la raza judía. **609**

war of attrition/Guerra de desgaste Lenta manera de debilitar el bienestar en la que que cada parte trata de sobrevivir a la otra. **517**

War of the Roses/Guerra de las Rosas Guerra entre las familias York y Lancaster de Inglaterra en 1455. **145**

War of the Spanish Succession/ Guerra de Sucesión Española Guerra en la que países europeos combatieron a Luis XIV para evitar el dominio Bourbon en Francia y España. **265**

Warsaw Pact/Pacto de Varsovia Acuerdo de mutua defensa entre la Unión Soviética y países del bloque del Este. **638**

Watergate scandal/Escándalo de Watergate La entrada a los cuarteles del Comité Democrático Nacional en 1972 que llevó a la renuncia de Nixon. **749**

weapons of mass destruction/armas de destrucción masiva Armas nucleares, químicas y biológicas de gran poder. **752**

welfare state/estado benefactor Estado en el que el gobierno se hacía responsable primordialmente del bienestar social de sus ciudadanos. **640**

Whigs/Whigs Partido político en Inglaterra, que defendían los derechos del Parlamento y de los sectores protestantes frente a la monarquía. **292**

White Lotus Rebellion/Rebelión de Lotos Blancos Rebelión campesina contra la dinastía Qing, liderada por el culto budista conocido como la Sociedad de Lotos. **224**

"The White Man's Burden"/"La Carga del Hombre Blanco" Poema de Rudyard Kipling que expresó la actitud de los europeos hacia personas no-occidentales durante la era imperialista. **472**

World Court/Tribunal Internacional de Justicia Corte de justicia internacional, ubicada en La Haya, en Holanda. **530**

World Trade Center/Centro de Comercio Internacional (WTC) Complejo de oficinas en la ciudad de Nueva York, que fué destruido por un devastador ataque terrorista el 11 de septiembre del 2001. **772**

Yi/Yi Dinastía coreana en 1392, cuando los coreanos sacaron a los mongoles, y duró hasta que Corea se anexó a Japón en 1910. **89**

Young Italy Movement/movimiento joven italiano Grupo de patriotas italianos dedicados a extender las ideas del nacionalismo. **440**

Z

zaibatsu/zaibatsu Enormes firmas industria-les controladas por familias poderosas en Japón. **668**

Zen/Zen Secta del Budismo que se enfoca en la meditación como método de ilustración. **77**

Zhou/Zhou Los que derrocaron la dinastía china Shang, en 1122 A.C. **9**

Zionism/Sionismo Movimiento nacionalista para construir un hogar para los judíos en Palestina. **568**

Zollverein/Zollverein Unión aduanera de los Estados alemanes creada en 1834 **446**

Index

B

D

G

Europe in 1600, *m*178; Hinduism, 8, *m*64, 66; Islam, 18, *g*64, *m*64; Judaism, 6, 47, *g*64, *m*64, 65; in Kievan Russia, 39; monotheism, 5; Orthodox Christianity, 39; Orthodox Russian, 42–43; polytheism, 5; Shintoism, *m*64, 85, 86; in Soviet Union, 559; in Tang dynasty, 77; world religions overview, 71, *f*71

religious conflicts, 42, 281

religious persecution, colonization and, 199

religious wars, 179, 210

Remarque, Erich Maria, 620, 704

Rembrandt, 211

Remembrance of Things Past (Proust), 538

Renaissance: artists of, 164–166, 169–170; causes of, 163; characteristics of, 162; daily life in, 184–185; economic growth during, 158; education and, 183–184; effects of, 167, 185; High Renaissance, 166; humanities and, 163; Italian Renaissance, 162–166, *f*162, *m*162, *f*165; Northern Renaissance, 167–170; printing and, 167, 168, 183; recreation and, 182; religious reformation, 171–178, 183; violence during, 182; writers of, 163–164, 168–169

René (Chateaubriand), 315

Renoir, Pierre-Auguste, 404, 405

reparations: World War I, 524, 525; World War II, 629, 630, 632

representative democracy, *f*112

republic, 13

Republic of China, 564, 575–576. *See also* China

Republic of Ireland, 549. *See also* Ireland

Restoration, 291–292

Reyna, Leonel Fernandez, 734

Reza Shah Pahlavi, 565, 571, 700

"Rhapsody in Blue" (Gershwin), 588

rhenium, 534

Rhine River, 167, 265

Rhineland, 526, *m*527, 535, 556, 594, 599

Rhodes, Cecil, 481

Rhodesia, 481, 685, 689

Rhone River, 167

rhythm and blues music, 783

Ricardo, David, 368

Ricci, Matteo, 222

rice, 78

Richard I (king of England), 128–129

Richard III (king of England), 145

Richelieu, Cardinal, 262–263, *p*262

Ridge, Tom, 776

Riis, Jacob, 402

rinderpest, 479

Rio de Janeiro, 583

risorgimento, 440

Rite of Spring, The (Stravinsky), 538

river valley civilizations, 4

Rivera, Diego, 494, 565, 583, 623

roads, 356

Robbins, Jerome, 786

Robert, Shaaban, 698

Robespierre, Maximilien, 325, 326, 327, *f*327, *p*327

Rock of Gibraltar, 53

rock 'n' roll music, 783

"Rocket", the, 348

rockets, 588

Rodin, Auguste, 405

"rolling blackouts", 751

Romagna, 442

Roman Catholic Church: authority of, 110–111, 119–121; Babylonian Captivity, 150; Benedictine Rule, 109–110; canon law and, 110; clergy of, 108–109; Council of Constance, 150, 151; Council of Trent, 177; Counter-Reformation, 176–179; excommunication and, 34, 110, 119, 121; family and, 111; feudal warfare and, 103; in France, 314, 316; Galileo and, 193; German Kulturkampf, 451–452; Great Schism, 125, 150; heresy and, 34, 110, 111; hierarchy of, 108–109; Huguenots

and, 175; humanists and, 171; Inquisition, 111, 176, 177; interdict, 110, 121; in Latin America, 722; medieval and modern church compared, 120; monasticism and, 109–110; papacy and, 120; plague deaths and, 138; political power of, 110; Protestant Reformation and, 171–174, 175; sacraments of, 108; simony and, 111; Spanish Inquisition, 210; taxation power of, 110; and Third Republic of France, 427–428; Vatican, 94

Roman Republic and Empire, v, 13–16; architecture and engineering of, 14; eastern or Byzantine Empire, 16; fall of the western empire, 16; government of Roman Empire, 46; leaders of, 13–14, *p*13; literature of Roman Empire, 162, 163; Renaissance interest in Roman Empire, 162–164; rise of Christianity in, 15

Romanesque architecture, 142

Romania, *m*A2, *m*A9; alliance with France, 547; Congress of Berlin and, 464; Dual Monarchy and, 463; German control of, 604; land from Hungary, 529, 550; war with Bulgaria, 465; in World War II, 615, 632

Romanov dynasty, 267–272

romanticism, 400

Rome, 163; as capital of Italy, 444; Germanic settlement in provinces of, 28; influence on Muslim culture, 58; Inquisition and, 176–177; Mazzini government in, 440

Rome-Berlin Axis, 503, 556, 594, 604

Romeo and Juliet (Shakespeare), 169

Romeo and Juliet (Tchaikovsky), 401

Romero, Oscar, 727

Rommel, Erwin, 605, 612

Röntgen, Wilhelm C., 389

Roosevelt, Eleanor, 631, *f*631, *p*631

Roosevelt, Franklin D.: Atlantic Charter and, *f*602, 603, 604; Cuba and, 584; Good Neighbor Policy and, 584; New Deal, 545; U.S. Neutrality Act, 589; Yalta Conference, 589, 616, 628–629

Roosevelt, Theodore: Roosevelt Corollary and, 493; Russo-Japanese War and, 579; in Spanish-American War, 491, *p*491

Roosevelt Corollary, 469, 493

Rosetta Stone, 314, *p*314

Roslin Institute, 794

Rough Riders, *p*491

Roundheads, 288

Rousseau, Jean-Jacques, 285, *p*285, 304, 391

Royal Air Force, 602

rubber, 355

rugby, 398

Ruiz-Tagle, Eduardo Frei, 743

Rump Parliament, 288

Rumsfeld, Donald, 777

Rurik, 38, *f*38

Rus, 38

Rushdie, Salman, 685, 787

Ruskin, John, 369

Russia, *m*A2, *m*A11, 37–43; absolutism in, 258, 270; alliance with France, 507; Balkans and, 509; "Bloody Sunday", 460; Byzantine Empire and, 267; Catherine the Great, 270–272, *p*272; China and, 227; civil war in, 521, 524; Commonwealth of Independent States and, 767; Communist Party and, 521; court reform, 457; Crimean War, 408, 425–426, 456; Duma formed, 460; economy of, *f*37, *f*455; Emancipation Edict, 457; expansion of, *m*268, 271, 272, 456, *m*459; fall of Soviet Union and, 766; France and, 332, 333, 425–426, 460; Germany declares war on, 510; government in,

*f*519; industrialization in, 459; isolation of, 267; Kievan Russia, 38–40, *m*38, 41–42; Lenin and, 520, 521, *p*521; Manchuria and, 578–579; Marxism and, 375, 520; Mongols and, 41–43, 81, 267; Moscow, 42–43; Napoléon I invasion of, 334–335, *m*343, 498; nobility in, 270; organized crime and, 766; Ottoman Empire and, 341, 463–464; Pan-Slavism and, 456, 509; Partition of Poland, 271, *m*271, 277; People's Will, 458; Peter the Great, 268–270, 456; pogroms against Jews, 459, 460; Quadruple Alliance, 338; radical groups, 458–459; reforms in, 456–458; Reinsurance Treaty of 1887, 507; religion in, 267, 456; repression in, 459; revolutions, 460, 505, 518, 519–521, *m*520; Romanov dynasty, 267–272; Russian Orthodox Church in, 270; "Russification", 456, 459; Russo-Japanese War, 579; separatist movements, 766; serfdom and, 270, 271; setting and people, 37–38, 267; as Soviet Union, 521; Three Emperors' League and, 507; Treaty of Portsmouth, 579; Triple Entente and, 507, *m*508; and War of the Austrian Succession, 275; war with Japan, 460; war with Ottoman Empire, 261; westernization of, 268, 270, 456; in World War I, 509, 510, 515, 519, 524; zemstvos, 457. *See also* Union of Soviet Socialist Republics (USSR)
Russian Orthodox Church, 42–43
Russian Revolution, 460, 505, 518, 519–521, *m*520
Russification, 456, 459

Russo-Japanese War, 505, 564, 579
Rutherford, Ernest, 389
Rwanda, *m*A2, *m*A10, 695–696

sacraments, 108
Sadat, Anwar, 685, 707
Safavid Empire, 159, 239, 244–246
Safī od-Dīn, 244
Sahara, 14, 19
Saint Domingue, 432
Sakhalin, 579
Sakharov, Andrei, 780
Saladin, 128, 129
Salinas de Gortari, Carlos, 724
Salk, Jonas, 780, 794
salt, 184
Salyut 1, 791
Samoa Islands, 488–489. *See also* American Samoa
Samoza, Anastasio, 584
Sampaio, Jorge, 760
Samper, Ernesto, 741
samurai, 27; feudal society and, 86, *p*86, 88; Tokugawa shogunate and, 232, *p*232, 233–234, 235; training of, *f*86
San Francisco, 631
San Martín, José Francisco de, 432, *p*433
San Salvador, 201, 727
San Stefano, Treaty of, 464
Sandinistas, 726–727
sanitation, 387, 396
Sanskrit, 90–92
Santa Maria, 201
São Paulo, 583, 720
Sarajevo, 509, 769
Sardinia, 440–442
Sargent, John Singer, 502
Saskatchewan, 415
Satanic Verses, The (Rushdie), 685, 787
satellites, 785
Saudi Arabia, *m*A2, *m*A11, *f*48, 703, 709, 712–713, 777, 801
Savoy, 441
Saxons, 97, 112
Saxony, 445
Scandinavia, Vikings and, 100
SCAP (Supreme Commander for the Allied Power), 667–668

Scarlet Pimpernel, The, 325
Scheherazade, 61
Schindler, Oskar, 611
Schink, Bartholomäus, 597
Schleiden, Mathias, 384
Schleswig, 447, 448
Schmidt, Helmut, 759
Schoenberg, Arnold, 538
scholar-gentry, 221
scholasticism, 142
Schroeder, Gerhard, 759
Schubert, Franz, 401
Schumann, Robert, 401
Schutzstaffel, 609
Schweitzer, Albert, 469
science: communications, 793; discoveries, *f*190; environment and, 795–797; human behavior and, *f*302; Islamic civilization and, 56; medical science, 793–794; in Middle Ages, 142; miniaturization and computerization, 791–792; scientific method, 191, 194, 391, 392; space exploration, 789–791; technology, *f*348, 795; travel, 789. *See also* Scientific Revolution
science fiction, *f*386
scientific method, 191
Scientific Revolution, 190–195, 350; anatomy, 193; astronomy, 191–193; chemistry, 195; mathematics, 191, 194; microscope, 194–195; nature study, 191; printing press and, 194, 195; scientific method and, 191, 194
scientific societies, 195
scorched-earth policy, 335
Scotland, *m*A9; Act of Union, 296; Calvinists and, 175; independence from England, 95; Presbyterianism and, 287; rebellion against Charles I, 287
Scott, Sir Walter, 400
Scribes, 167
sculpture, 782
sea dogs, 298–299
Sears Tower, 784
SEATO. *See* Southeast Asia Treaty Organization
secede, 419
Second Continental Congress, 307, 310

Second International, 375
Secret History, The (Procopius), 33, 35
sectionalism, 419
sects, 173
secular clergy, 109
Security Council (United Nations), 631
Sejong (Korean emperor), 90, *f*90
Selassie, Haile, 503, *p*503, 590, 697
Seljuq Turks, 36; and Crusades, 126–129
Sendero Luminoso. See Shining Path
Seneca Falls Convention, 422
Senegal, 478, 804
Senghor, Léopold, 572, 690, 698, 804, *p*804
Seoul, 665
separatism, 649, 754
seppuku, 86
September 11 attacks, 772–776
sequence, understanding, 54
Serbia, 463, 464, 465, 509, 529, 769
serfs, 136, 184, 334, 457; Emancipation Edict and, 457
serpent mound, *p*207
settlement colonies, 470
Seven Samurai, The, 652
Seven Weeks' War, 448
Seven Years' War, 276, 305
Shaanxi, 576, 577
Shah-nameh (Firdausi), *f*254
Shah's Peacock Throne, 251
Shaka (Zulu leader), 481, *f*481
Shakespeare, William, 167, *f*167, 169, *p*169, 189, *f*254, *p*254, 280
Shang dynasty, 9
Shanghai, 222
Shankar, Ravi, 652, *p*652
Sharon, Ariel, 708
Sharpeville, 692
sheikh, 48
Shelley, Mary Wollstonecraft, 386, 438, *p*438
Shepard, Alan, 790
Shi'ah, 52–53, 244, 251
Shiga, Kiyoshi, 564
Shimonoseki, Treaty of, 485
Shining Path, 740
Shinto religion, 85–86

Acknowledgements

For permission to reproduce copyrighted material, grateful acknowledgment is made to the following sources:

About.Com, Inc.: From "The Korea Summit" June 13, 2000 by Keith Porter, accessed July 19, 2001, from http://worldnews.about.com/library/weekly/aa061300a.htm?terms=korea+summit. Copyright © 2000 by Keith Porter. All rights reserved.

American Heritage Magazine, a division of Forbes Inc.: Quote by Ibn Battuta from *The Horizon History of Africa*, edited by Alvin M. Josephy, Jr. Copyright © 1971 by American Heritage Publishing Co. Inc.

Asian Humanities Press, a division of Jain Publishing Co., Inc.: From "The Yoga of Meditation (Dhyana Yoga)," Part 6, Lines 10-14, from *The Bhagavad Gita: A Scripture for the Future*, translated by Sachindra K. Majumdar. Copyright © 1991 by Sachindra Kumar Majumdar.

Biblioteca Persica: From *Persian Heritage Series, No. 2: The Epic of Kings: Shah-Nama, the national epic of Persia* by Ferdowsi, translated by Reuben Levy. Copyright © 1967 by Center for Iranian Studies.

Cambridge University Press: From Chapter XVII from *The Prince* by Niccolo Machiavelli, edited by Quentin Skinner and Russell Price. Copyright © 1988 by Cambridge University Press.

Peter Coan: From "Esther Gidiwicz" from *Ellis Island Interviews: In Their Own Words* by Peter Morton Coan. Copyright © 1997 by Peter Morton Coan.

Columbia University Press: From "The Russian Law" from *Medieval Russian Laws*, translated by George Vernadsky. Copyright © 1947 by Columbia University Press.

Doubleday, a division of Random House, Inc., www.randomhouse.com: From *The Diary of a Young Girl: The Definitive Edition* by Anne Frank, edited by Otto H. Frank and Mirjam Pressler, translated by Susan Massotty. Copyright © 1995 by Doubleday, a division of Random House, Inc.

Grove/Atlantic, Inc.: From "A Song of War Chariots" by Du Fu, translated by Witter Bynner, from *Anthology of Chinese Literature: From Early Times to the Fourteenth Century*, edited by Cyril Birch. Copyright © 1965 by Grove Press, Inc.

David Higham Associates Ltd.: From *The Song of Roland*, translated by Dorothy L. Sayers (Penguin Classics, 1937). Copyright © 1957 by Executors of Dorothy L. Sayers. Originally published by Penguin Books Ltd.

Hill and Wang, a division of Farrar, Straus & Giroux, LLC.: From *Night* by Elie Wiesel, translated by Stella Rodway. Copyright © 1958 by Les Editions de Minuit; English translation copyright © 1960 by MacGibbon & Kee, renewed © 1988 by The Collins Publishing Group. Originally published as *La Nuit*. All rights reserved. Electronic format by permission of **Georges Borchardt, Inc., for Les Editions de Minuit.**

The Heirs to the Estate of Martin Luther King, Jr., c/o Writers House, Inc. as agent for the proprietor, New York, NY: From "I Have a Dream" by Martin Luther King, Jr. Copyright © 1963 by Martin Luther King, Jr.; copyright renewed © 1986 by Coretta Scott King.

Alfred A. Knopf, a division of Random House, Inc., www.randomhouse.com: From "The Epoch of Decline" from *The House of the Spirits* by Isabel Allende, translated by Magda Bogin. Translation copyright © 1985 by Alfred A. Knopf, Inc., a division of Random House, Inc.

P. Lal: From "The Thousands" from *The Dhammapada*, translated by P. Lal. Copyright © 1967 by P. Lal.

National Geographic Society: From "Viking Trail East" by R. P. Jordan from *National Geographic*, March 1985. Copyright © 1985 by National Geographic Society.

The New York Times Company: Quote by Vaclav Havel from "Speech by the Czech President" from *The New York Times*, January 2, 1990. Copyright © 1990 by The New York Times Company.

Penguin Books Ltd.: From *The Nibelungenlied*, translated by A. T. Hatto (Penguin Classics, 1965, revised edition, 1969). Translation copyright © 1965, 1969 by A. T. Hatto. From *Utopia* by Thomas More, translated by Paul Turner (Penguin Classics, 1965). Copyright © 1965 by Paul Turner. From *The Secret History* by Procopius, translated by G. A. Williamson (Penguin Classics, 1966). Copyright © 1966 by G. A. Williamson.

Estate of Erich Maria Remarque: From *All Quiet on the Western Front* by Erich Maria Remarque. Copyright 1929, 1930 by Little, Brown and Company; renewed © 1957, 1958 by Erich Maria Remarque. "Im Westen Nichts Neues." Copyright 1928 by Ullstein A.G.; renewed © 1956 by Erich Maria Remarque. All rights reserved.

Charles E. Tuttle Co., Inc., Boston, MA, and Tokyo, Japan: Haiku death poem by Banzan from *Japanese Death Poems: Written by Zen Monks and Haiku Poets on the Verge of Death*, compiled by Yoel Hoffmann. Copyright © 1986 by Charles E. Tuttle Co., Inc. From *Hawaii's Story by Hawaii's Queen* by Liliuokalani. Copyright © 1964 by Charles E. Tuttle Co., Inc.

University Press of Virginia: From "Prayer to the Masks" from *The Collected Poetry* by Léopold Sédar Senghor, translated by Melvin Dixon. Copyright © 1991 by the Rector and Visitors of the University of Virginia.

The University of Chicago Press: From "The Fundamental Characteristics of European Feudalism" from *Feudal Society* by Marc Bloch, translated by L. A. Manyon. Copyright © 1961 by The University of Chicago Press.

Verso: From *I, Rigoberta Menchú: An Indian Woman in Guatemala*, edited and introduced by Elisabeth Burgos-Debray, translated by Ann Wright. Copyright © 1983 by Editions Gallimard and Elisabeth Burgos; translation copyright © 1984 by Verso.

Sources Cited:

From *The Murderous Revolution: Life & Death in Pol Pot's Kampuchea* by Martin Stuart-Fox. Published by Alternative Publishing Co-operative Ltd., Chippendale, New South Wales, 1985.

Quote from "Letter from Tokyo" from *The New Yorker*, May 20, 1974. Published by The Condé Nast Publications, Inc., New York, 1974.

From "Unity in Diversity" by Walter Gropius from *Four Great Makers of Architecture: Gropius, Le Corbusier, Mies van der Rohe, Wright.* Published by Da Capo Press, a division of Perseus Books, New York, 1970.

Quote by automobile modern consumer from *Middletown: A Study in Modern American Culture* by Robert S. Lynd and Helen Merrell Lynd. Published by Harcourt, Inc., Orlando, 1929.

Quote by Carmelite cleric from "Half the World (1450-1750)" from *Crossroads of Civilization: 3000 Years of Persian History* by Clive Irving. Published by HarperCollins Publishers, Inc., New York, 1979.

Quote from "A Relativistic World" from *Modern Times: The World from the Twenties to the Nineties*, Revised Edition by Paul Johnson. Published by HarperCollins Publishers, Inc., New York, 1991.

From "Poets, Scholars, and Physicians" from *Islam, from the Prophet Mohammed to the Capture of Constantinople, Part II: Religion and Society*, edited and translated by Bernard Lewis. Published by HarperCollins Publishers, Inc., New York, 1974.

From account regarding Russian collective farming from *The Gulag Archipelago 1918-1956* by Aleksandr I. Solzhenitsyn, translated by Thomas P. Whitney. Published by HarperCollins Publishers, Inc., New York, 1973, 1974.

From funeral oration by the Archbishop of Novgorod, Feofan Prokopovich, from "The Heroic Tsar" (Retitled: "The Great Czar") from *Peter the Great Changes Russia*, Second Edition, edited by Marc Raeff. Published by D. C. Heath and Company, Lexington, MA, 1972.

From "The End of the Beginning" by Ray Bradbury from *The Stories of Ray Bradbury.* Published by Alfred A. Knopf, a division of Random House, Inc., New York, 1980.

From *The Guns of August* by Barbara Tuchman. Published by Macmillan Publishing Company, a division of Simon & Schuster, New York, 1962.

Quote by Guglielmo Marconi from "The First Radio Signal Across the Atlantic, 12 December 1901" from *Scrapbook 1900-1941* by Leslie Bailey. Published by Frederick Muller, 1957.

From "The Bloodiest Battle of All" by William Manchester from *The New York Times Magazine*, June 14, 1987.

From "The Communist Roller Coaster" from *The New York Times*, August 18, 1989.

From "Churchill, Winston" by Martin Gilbert from *The Oxford Companion to Politics of the World*, edited by Joel Krieger. Published by Oxford University Press, New York, 1993.

From military account from "Events of the Year 932" from *The Baburnama: Memoirs of Babur, Prince and Emperor*, edited, translated, and annotated by Wheeler M. Thackston. Published by Oxford University Press, New York, 1996.

From "Twentieth-Century Architecture" from *The History of Art* by H. W. Janson and Anthony F. Janson. Published by Prentice Hall and Harry N. Abrams, Inc., 1997.

From account of exodus of German citizens in January 1945 from "From Collapse to Re-creation" from *Foe into Friend: The Makers of the New Germany from Konrad Adenauer to Helmut Schmidt* by Marion Dönhoff, translated by Gabriel Annan. Published by St. Martin's Press, Inc., New York, 1982.

From description of the Petrograd riots by Alexandra Rodionova from "Working-Class and Peasant Women in the Russian Revolution" from *Signs: Journal of Women in Culture and Society*, No. 2, Winter 1982. Published by the University of Chicago Press, 1982.

From "Paris During the Hundred Years' War" from *The Portable Medieval Reader*, edited by James Bruce Ross and Mary M. McLaughlin. Published by Viking Penguin, a division of Penguin Putnam Inc., New York, 1949.

Photo Credits

(c) Alan Thornton/Stone; 69 (tl) Scala/Art Resource, NY, (tc) PhotoDisc, Inc., (tr) Erich Lessing/ Art Resource, NY, (c) Elio Ciol/Corbis, (b) Mark Thiessen/Corbis; 70 (tl) Ronald Sheridan/ Ancient Art & Architecture Collection, (tc) Werner Forman Archive/Art Resource, NY, (tr) Bonhams, London/Bridgeman Art Library, (c) AFP/ Corbis, (b) Reuters NewMedia Inc./Corbis; 71 Gael Cornier/AP/Wide World Photos; 72 (t) Erich Lessing/Art Resource, NY, (bl) Victoria & Albert Museum, London/Art Resource, NY, (br) British Library, London/Bridgeman Art Library; 73 (t) Sakamoto Photo Research Laboratory/Corbis, (bl) The Art Archive, (br) Michael Bodycomb/Kimbell Art Museum/Corbis; 74 Musée Guimet, Paris, France/Lauros-Giraudon, Paris/SuperStock; 75 Liu Xiasyang/ ChinaStock; 77 The British Library/The Art Archive; 79 (t) The Metropolitan Museum of Art, A.W. Bahr Collection, Fletcher Fund, 1947. (47.18.1) Photography © 1978 The Metropolitan Museum of Art, (b) Photograph Courtesy Peabody Essex Museum; 80 Werner Forman Archive/Art Resource, NY; 82 (t) National Palace Museum, Taiwan/ET Archive, London/SuperStock, (b) Giraudon/Art Resource, NY; 83 Bibliothèque Nationale, Paris, France/Bridgeman Art Library; 84 Janette Ostier Gallery, Paris, France/Giraudon, Paris/SuperStock; 86 Werner Forman Archive/Victoria & Albert Museum, London/Art Resource, NY; 88 Chris Lisle/Corbis; 89 Ronald Sheridan/Ancient Art & Architecture Collection; 90 Boltin Picture Library; 91 (t) Dan McCoy/Rainbow/PictureQuest, (b) Pictor International, Ltd./PictureQuest; 94 (t) Dagli Orti/University Library Heidelberg/The Art Archive, (bl) Eirik Irgens Johnsen/ University Museum of National Antiquities, slo, Norway, (br) The Pierpont Morgan Library/Art Resource, NY; 95 (t) Musée de la Tapisserie, Bayeux, France/Bridgeman Art Library, (bl) Bibliothèque Nationale, Paris/AKG London, (br) Erich Lessing/Art Resource, NY; 96 Pierre Belzeaux/Photo Researchers; 97 (t) AKG London, (b) Bildarchiv Steffens/Bridgeman Art Library; 98 Giraudon/Bridgeman Art Library; 101 Knudsens-Giraudon/Art Resource, NY; 102 Bettmann/Corbis; 103 (t) AKG London, (b) Robert W. Madden/National Geographic Image Collection; 105 Bridgeman Art Library/SuperStock; 106 Bibliothèque Nationale, Paris/AKG London; 107 (l) The Pierpont Morgan Library/Art Resource, NY, (r) New York Public Library/Art Resource, NY; 108 AKG London; 109 British Library/Bridgeman Art Library; 110 Michael Teller/AKG London; 111 Dagli Orti/The Art Archive; 112 Winchester Cathedral, Hampshire, UK/Bridgeman Art Library; 113 Michael Freeman/Corbis; 114 Bettmann/Corbis; 117 AKG London; 118 Erich Lessing/Art Resource, NY; 119, 120 AKG London; 121 Harper Collins Publishers/The British Library/The Art Archive; 124 (t) Archivo Iconografico, S.A./Corbis, (bl) Erich Lessing/Art Resource, NY, (br) The British Library/The Art Archive; 125 (tl) Bibliothèque Royale de Belgique, Brussels, Belgium/Bridgeman Art Library, (tr) Réunion des Musées Nationaux/Art Resource, NY, (b) Bill Bachmann/Index Stock Imagery/PictureQuest; 126 Bridgeman Art Library; 128 Bibliothèque Nationale, Paris, France/Bridgeman Art Library; 130 Ancient Art & Architecture Collection; 133 Giraudon/Art Resource, NY; 134 British Library, London/Bridgeman Art Library, London/SuperStock; 136 Victoria & Albert Museum, London/Art Resource, NY; 137 Mary Evans Picture Library; 138 Giraudon/Art Resource, NY; 139 Giraudon/Art Resource, NY; 140 Archivo Iconografico, S.A./Corbis; 141 (t) Mary Evans Picture Library, (b) Archivo Iconografico, S.A./Corbis; 142 Archivo Iconografico, S.A./Corbis; 143 (t) Mimmo Jodice/Corbis, (b) Massimo Listri/Corbis; 144 Bibliothèque Nationale, Paris/AKG London; 146 Christie's Images/Corbis; 148 Dagli Orti/Musée du Chateau de Versailles/The Art Archive; 149 Giraudon/Art Resource, NY; 150 Gail Mooney/Corbis, NY; 151 Dagli Orti/University Library Prague/The Art Archive; 154 (l) Archivo Iconografico, S.A./Corbis, (r) Eileen Tweedy/Victoria & Albert Museum London/The Art Archive; 155 (t) Dagli Orti/Tiroler Landesmuseum, Innsbruck/The Art Archive, (cl) von Linden/AKG London, (cr) Dagli Orti/The Art Archive; 156-157 Library of Congress, Washington D.C./Bridgeman Art Library; 157 (b) Eileen Tweedy/The Art Archive; 158 (tl) Alinari/Art Resource, NY, (tr) Victoria & Albert Museum/Art Resource, NY, (b) Erich Lessing/Art Resource, NY; 159 (t) Royal Ontario Museum/Corbis, (bl) Dagli Orti/Palace of Chihil Soutoun Isfahan/The Art Archive, (br) Victoria & Albert Museum, London/Bridgeman Art Library; 160 (t) Dagli Orti/Galleria degli Uffizi Florence/The Art Archive, (b) Gary Yeowell/Stone; 161 (tl) Bettmann/Corbis, (tr) Réunion des Musées Nationaux/Art Resource, NY, (b) Scala/Art Resource, NY; 163 Ali Meyer/Bridgeman Art Library; 164 Musée Des Beaux-Arts de Lille, Jardin du Muss/Giraudon/Art Resource, NY; 165 (t) Scala/Art Resource, NY, (b) Araldo de Luca/Corbis; 166 Réunion des Musées Nationaux/Art Resource, NY; 167 The Pierpont Morgan Library/Art Resource, NY; 168 Erich Lessing/Art Resource, NY; 169 (t) Art Resource, NY, (bl, br) Scala/Art Resource, NY, ; 170 Erich Lessing/Art Resource, NY; 171 The Art Archive; 172 Scala/Art Resource, NY; 173 Index/Bridgeman Art Library; 174 Belvoir Castle, Leicestershire/Bridgeman Art Library; 175 British Library, London/Bridgeman Art Library; 176 Erich Lessing/Art Resource, NY; 177 Giraudon/Art Resource, NY; 179 Bridgeman Art Library; 180 Peter Willi/Bridgeman Art Library; 181 Bridgeman Art Library; 182 Kunsthistorisches Museum, Vienna, Austria/Bridgeman Art Library; 184 (t) Phillips, The International Fine Art Auctioneers, UK/Bridgeman Art Library, (b) Francis G. Mayer/Corbis; 185 Giraudon/Art Resource, NY; 187 Eilo Ciol/Corbis; 188 (tl) Corbis, (tr) Dagli Orti/The Art Archive, (b) Scala/Art Resource, NY; 189 (tl) Dave Bartruff/Corbis, (tr, br) Bettmann/Corbis, (bl) Library of Congress, Washington D.C., USA/ Bridgeman Art Library; 190 Scala/Art Resource, NY; 191 (t) Erich Lessing/Art Resource, NY, (b) Alinari/Art Resource, NY; 192 Scala/Art Resource, NY; 193 Nimatallah/Art Resource, NY; 194 Sheila Terry/Science Photo Library/Photo Researchers; 195 Giraudon/Art Resource, NY; 196 Réunion des Musées Nationaux/Bridgeman Art Library; 197 David Parker/Science Photo Library/Photo Researchers; 198 Lauros-Giraudon/Bridgeman Art Library; 199 (l, r) PhotoDisc, Inc.; 201 (l) Bettmann/Corbis, (r) Bridgeman Art Library; 203 (t) Royal Geographical Society, London/Bridgeman Art Library; 206 Bettmann/Corbis; 208 Historical Picture Archive/Corbis; 209 Bettmann/Corbis; 210, 211 Francis G. Mayer/Corbis; 214 (t) Bettmann/Corbis, (b) Museum of the City of New York/Corbis; 215 Archivo Iconografico, S.A./Corbis; 218 (t) Grafica/Pacific Stock, (b) Werner Forman Archive/Art Resource, NY; 219 (tl) Richard Powers/Corbis, (tr) Paul Freeman/Bridgeman Art Library, (b) Fitzwilliam Museum/University of Cambridge, UK/ Bridgeman Art Library; 221 Pierre Colombel/Corbis; 222 Stock Montage; 223 Victoria & Albert Museum, London/Art Resource, NY; 224 Archivo Iconografico, S.A./Corbis; 225 Royal Geographical Society, London/ Bridgeman Art Library; 226 (t) AKG London, (b) Paul Freeman/ Bridgeman Art Library; 227 Hulton-Deutsch Collection/Corbis; 229 Historical Picture Archive/Corbis; 231 (t) The Art Archive, (b) Palubniak Studios; 232 Victoria & Albert Museum, London/Art Resource, NY; 233 Réunion des Musées Nationaux/Art Resource, NY; 234 Palubniak Studios; 235 The British Museum/Bridgeman Art Library; 238 (t) Victoria & Albert Museum, London/Art Resource, NY, (bl) Eileen Tweedy/Victoria & Albert Museum, London/The Art Archive, (br) Erich Lessing/Art Resource, NY; 239 (tl) Magdalen College, Oxford/Bridgeman Art Library, (tr) Bonhams, London, UK/Bridgeman Art Library, (bl) Madar-i-Shah Madrasa, Isfahan,

Iran/Bridgeman Art Library, (br) Bibliothèque Nationale, Paris, France/Bridgeman Art Library; 240 Dagli Orti/Topkapi Museum Istanbul/The Art Archive; 242 (t) Erich Lessing/AKG London, (b) Giraudon/Art Resource, NY; 243, 244 Ronald Sheridan/Ancient Art & Architecture Collection; 246 Bonhams, London, UK/ Bridgeman Art Library; 247 The British Library/The Art Archive; 249 Chris Haigh/Stone; 250 Chester Beatty Library & Gallery of Oriental Art, Dublin/Bridgeman Art Library; 251 Metropolitan Museum of Art, New York/Bridgeman Art Library; ; Unit 2 Review; 254 (l) Werner Forman Archive/Art Resource, NY, (r) Dagli Orti/Musée du Chateau de Versailles/The Art Archive; 255 (l) Dagli Orti/Musée Ceramique Sevres/The Art Archive, (r) Bjorn Landstrom/NGS Image Collection; 256-257 Giraudon/Art Resource, NY; 257 (b) Lee Snider/ Corbis; 258 (tl) The Art Archive, (tr) Historical Picture Archive/Corbis, (b) Alison Wright/ Corbis; 259 (t) Giraudon/Art Resource, NY, (c) Hulton Archive by Getty Images, (bl) Bettmann/ Corbis, (br) David Muench/Corbis; 260 (tl) Jarrold Publishing/The Art Archive, (tr) Victoria & Albert Museum, London/The Art Archive, (b) Yale Center for British Art, Paul Mellon Collection, USA/Bridgeman Art Library; 261 (tl) Adam Woolfitt/Corbis, (tr) Dagli Orti/Russian Historical Museum, Moscow/The Art Archive, (b) Wolfgang Kaehler/Corbis; 262 AKG London; 263 Erich Lessing/Art Resource, NY; 264 SuperStock; 265 (b) Dave G. Houser/Corbis; 266 SuperStock; 267 Sovfoto/Eastfoto; 269 (t) Collection of Countess Bobrinskoy/Michael Holford, (b) Hulton Archive by Getty Images; 270 Dagli Orti/Musée de Versailles/The Art Archive; 272 (t) Dagli Orti/Russian Historical Museum, Moscow/The Art Archive, (b) Sovfoto/Eastfoto; 273 Palace of Versailles, France/Lauros-Giraudon, Paris/SuperStock; 274 (t) Musée du Louvre, Paris/SuperStock, (b) AKG London; 275 AKG, Berlin/SuperStock; 277 AKG London; 278 Richard Glover/Corbis; 279 Dagli Orti/Pinacoteca di Siena/The Art Archive; 280 (l) Art Resource, NY, (r) Robert Harding Picture Library; 281 (t) Erich Lessing/Art Resource, NY; 284 (l) Erich Lessing/Art Resource, NY, (r) Bettmann/Corbis; 285 (t) Bettmann/Corbis, (tr) Giraudon/Bridgeman Art Library, (bl) The Huntington Library, Art Collections, and Botanical Gardens, San Marino, California/SuperStock, (br) Colonial Willimasburg Foundation; 286 Alinari/Art Resource, NY; 287 Houses of Parliament, Westminster, London, UK/Bridgeman Art Library; 288 Bridgeman Art Library; 290 National Portrait Gallery, London/SuperStock; 291 Dreweatt Neate Fine Art Auctioneers, Newbury/Bridgeman Art Library; 292 Victoria & Albert Museum, London, UK/Bridgeman Art Library; 293 AKG London; 294 (t, b) Stock Montage/SuperStock; 295 Bettmann/Corbis; 297 The British Museum, London, UK/Bridgeman Art Library; 298 Stock Montage/SuperStock; 299 Michael Holford; 300 (l) New York Historical Society, New York, USA/Bridgeman Art Library, (r) SuperStock; 301 (4 left coins) Eileen Tweedy/The British Museum/The Art Archive, (r) Fitzwilliam Museum, University of Cambridge, UK/Bridgeman Art Library; 302 Louvre, Bibliothèque, Paris, France/Erich Lessing/Art Resource, NY; 303 Erich Lessing/Art Resource, NY; 304 Tate Gallery, London/Art Resource, NY; 306 (t) Stock Montage, (b) Library Company of Philadelphia; 307 SuperStock; 311 Christie's Images/SuperStock; 314 (t) Ronald Sheridan/Ancient Art & Architecture Collection, (bl) Paul Almasy/Corbis, (br) Dagli Orti/Post and Telecommunications Museum Rome/The Art Archive; 315 (t) Réunion des Musées Nationaux/Art Resource, NY, (bl) John Lawrence/Stone, (br) Todd Gipstein/ Corbis; 316 Bettmann/Corbis; 317 (t) Erich Lessing/Art Resource, NY, (b) Hulton-Deutsch Collection/ Corbis; 318 (t) Ali Meyer/Corbis, (b) Robert Holmes/Corbis; 319 Giraudon/Art Resource, NY; 320 AKG, Berlin/SuperStock; 321 Dagli Orti/Musée Carnavalet, Paris/The Art Archive; 322 Giraudon/Art Resource, NY; 324 Dagli Orti/Musée de l'Affiche, Paris/The Art Archive; 325 Dagli Orti/Musée Carnavalet, Paris/The Art Archive; 326 Museo del Prado Madrid/The Art Archive; 327 Dagli Orti/Musée Carnavalet, Paris/The Art Archive; 328 (t) Gianni Dagli Orti/ Corbis, (b) Giraudon/Art Resource, NY; 329 Scala/Art Resource, NY; 330 Dagli Orti/Musée de Versailles/The Art Archive; 331 Erich Lessing/Art Resource, NY; 332 Giraudon/Art Resource, NY; 334, 335, 336 Archivo Iconografico, S.A./Corbis; 337, 338 AKG London; 340 Bettmann/Corbis; 341 AKG London, 344 (tr) Bequest of Winslow Warren/Courtesy Museum of Fine Arts, Boston, MA, (l) Philip Mould, Historical Portraits Ltd, London, UK/Bridgeman Art Library, (br) Library Company of Philadelphia; 345 (tr) Stock Montage, (cr) AKG London, (l) Harris Museum and Art Gallery, Preston, Lancashire, UK/Bridgeman Art Library; 346-347 Yale Center for British Art, Paul Mellon Collection, USA/Bridgeman Art Library; 347 (b) Forbes Collection, New York City/ Bridgeman Art Library, London/SuperStock; 348 (t) Royal Holloway and Bedford New College, Surrey, UK/Bridgeman Art Library, (c) Gianni Dagli Orti/Corbis, (b) Bettmann/Corbis; 349 (t) Dagli Orti/Civiche Raccolte Museo L. Bailo Treviso/The Art Archive, (bl) M. & E. Bernheim/Woodfin Camp & Associates, (br) Bettmann/Corbis; 350 (t, b) Bettmann/Corbis, (bl) Christie's Images/Corbis; 351 (tl) Stock Montage, (tr) Philip Mould, Historical Portraits Ltd, London, UK/Bridgeman Art Library, (bl) Bettmann/Corbis, (bc) Library of Congress/Corbis, (br) Hulton-Deutsch Collection/Corbis; 354 Library of Congress/Corbis; 355 AKG London; 356 Palubniak Studios; 358 Andrew Russell/Culver Pictures; 360 Bridgeman Art Library; 361 Slater Mill Historic Site/PRC Archive; 362 (t) Snark/Art Resource, NY, (b) North Wind Picture Archives; 363 Steidle Collection, College of Earth and Mineral Sciences, Pennsylvania State University/Steidle Art Collection/SuperStock; 364 From the Collections of Henry Ford Museum and Greenfield Village; 366 New York Historical Society, USA/Bridgeman Art Library; 367 The British Museum/The Art Archive; 368 (t, b) North Wind Picture Archives; 369 Hulton Archive by Getty Images; 370 Bettmann/Corbis; 371 Pinacoteca di Brera, Milan, Italy/Bridgeman Art Library; 372 (l, r) Bettmann/Corbis; 373 AKG London; 374 Archivo Iconografico, S.A./Corbis; 375 Sovfoto/Eastfoto; 377 Schenectady Museum; Hall of Electrical History Foundation/Corbis; 378 (t) Stock Montage, (b) Bettmann/Corbis; 379 (t, bl) Hulton Archive by Getty Images, (br) Blank Archives/Hulton Archive by Getty Images; 380, 382 Hulton Archive by Getty Images; 383 Bettmann/Corbis; 384 John D. Cunningham/Visuals Unlimited; 385 (t) South African National Gallery, Cape Town, South Africa/Bridgeman Art Library, (b) Stock Montage; 386 (l) Culver Pictures, (r) The Museum of Modern Art/Film Stills Archives; 387 Gernsheim Collection, Harry Ransom Humanities Research Center, The University of Texas at Austin; 388 Steve Raymer/NGS Image Collection; 389 Archive Photos/PictureQuest; 390 Library of Congress/Corbis; 392 Osa & Martin Johnson Safari Museum/Hulton Archive by Getty Images; 393 Bettmann/Corbis; 394 Edwin Levick/Hulton Archive by Getty Images; 396 Brown Brothers; 397 (t) Culver Pictures, (bl, br) New York Journal, Jan 5, 1896 Courtesy OldNews, Inc.; 398 Francis G. Mayer/Corbis; 399 Winslow Homer, American, 1836-1910, Croquet Scene, oil on canvas, 1866, 15 7/8 x 26 1/16in, Friends of American Art Collection, 1942.35, photograph ©1998, The Art Institute of Chicago, All Rights Reserved.; 401 Scala/Art Resource, NY; 402 Christie's Images/SuperStock; 403 (l) Clore Collection, Tate Gallery, London/Art Resource, NY, (r) Erich Lessing/Art Resource, NY, (frame) Image Farm; 404 Giraudon/Art Resource, NY; 405 Christie's Images/Bridgeman Art Library; 407 Philip De Bay/Historical Picture Archive/Corbis; 408 (t) North Wind Picture Archives, (bl) White House Collection, copyright White House

Historical Association, (bc) The Granger Collection, (br) George Rinhart/Underwood & Underwood/Corbis; 409 (tl) Francis G. Mayer/Corbis, (tr) Laurie Platt Winfrey/Woodfin Camp & Associates; 411 Mansell Collection/TimePix; 412 (tl) AKG London, (b) Corbis; 413 Hulton-Deutsch Collection/Corbis; 415 Bettmann/Corbis; 416 Mansell Collection/TimePix; 417 North Wind Picture Archives; 421 Brown Brothers; 422 Seneca Falls Historical Society; 423 AKG London; 424 Gianni Dagli Orti/Corbis; 425 Musée d'Orsay, Paris, France/Réunion des Musées Nationaux/Bridgeman Art Library; 426 (t) Bettmann/Corbis, (b) Bridgeman Art Library; 427 Giraudon/Art Resource, NY; 428 Leonard de Selva/Corbis; 429 Giraudon/Art Resource, NY; 430 Bettmann/Corbis; 432 Topham/The Image Works; 433 Bettmann/ Corbis; 435 Art Resource, NY; 438 (t) Bridgeman Art Library, (bl) National Portrait Gallery, London/SuperStock, (br) Stock Montage; 439 (tr) Scala/Art Resource, NY; 439 (tl) Courtesy of The Red Cross, (bl) Dagli Orti/The Art Archive, (br) Musée d'Orsay, Paris/Giraudon, Paris/SuperStock; 440 A. Marc/Mary Evans Picture Library; 441 (t) SEF/Art Resource, NY, (b) Museo Civico del Risorgimento, Bologna, Italy; 442 (t) Hulton-Deutsch Collection/Corbis, (b) Archivo Iconografico, S.A./Corbis; 443 Christie's Images/SuperStock; 445, 446 AKG London; 447 AKG Berlin/SuperStock; 448 (t) AKG London, (b) A. Liebert/Hulton-Deutsch Collection/Corbis; 450 AKG London; 451 Giraudon/Art Resource, NY; 452 AKG London; 453 Dave Bartruff/Corbis; 454 Culver Pictures; 455 Fine Art Photographic Library, London/Art Resouce, NY; 456 (t) Christel Gerstenberg/Corbis, (b) Steve Raymer/Corbis; 457 Walters Art Museum, Baltimore, Courtesy of Robert Forbes Collection; 458 SuperStock; 460 Dagli Orti/Domenica del Corriere/The Art Archive; 461 AKG London; 463 Francoise de Mulder/Corbis; 465 Hulton-Deutsch Collection/ Corbis; 468 (t) Dreweatt Neat Fine Art Auctioneers, Newbury, Berkshire, UK/Bridgeman Art Library, (b) Explorer, Paris/SuperStock; 469 (t) PhotoDisc, (tr) National Portrait Gallery, London/SuperStock, (bl) SuperStock, (br) Brown Brothers; 470 A. Dawson Gallery Image-Annapolis Maryland; 471 (t) The Granger Collection, (c) Eileen Tweedy/Lords Gallery/The Art Archive, (b) Michael Maslan Historic Photographs/Corbis; 472 North Wind Picture Archives; 473 Brown Brothers; 474 Culver Pictures; 475 (t) Brown Brothers, (b) Hulton Archive by Getty Images; 476 Hulton Archive by Getty Images; 477 Stock Montage; 479 The Granger Collection; 481 Bettmann/Corbis; 482 Brown Brothers; 483 Hulton Deutsch Collection/ Woodfin Camp & Associates; 484 Topham/The Image Works; 485 Bridgeman Art Library; 487 (t) Robert Harding Picture Library, (b) The Metropolitan Museum of Art, The Helena Woolworth McCaan Collection, Winfield Foundation Gift, 1958. (58.52) Photograph © The Metropolitan Museum of Art.; 489 Bettmann/Corbis; 490 Brown Brothers; 491 Culver Pictures; 492 Brown Brothers; 494 Robert Frerck/Woodfin Camp & Associates; 495 (l) Library of Congress, (r) Bettmann/Corbis; 498 (l) Archivo Iconografico, S.A./Corbis, (c) Hulton-Deutsch Collection/Corbis; 499 (t) The Art Archive, (cl) Gianni Dagli Orti/Corbis, (cr) Science Museum London/The Art Archive; 500-501 Bridgeman Art Library; 501 (t) Minnesota Historical Society/Corbis, (b) Library of Congress/Corbis; 502 (t) Imperial War Museum/ The Art Archive; 503 (t) Scheufler Collection/Corbis, (c) Dagli Orti/The Art Archive, (b) PhotoDisc; 502 (b) AP/Wide World Photos; 504 (l) Musée National du Château de Malmaison, Rueil-Malmaison/Lauros-Giraudon, Paris/ SuperStock; 504 (r) Sovfoto/ Eastfoto; 505 (tl) Stock Montage, (tr) Hulton-Deutsch Collection/Corbis, (bl) AKG London, (br) Brown Brothers; 506 Hulton Archive by Getty Images; 507 Brown Brothers; 509 Leonard de Selva/Corbis; 510 The Burns Collection; 511 (t) Leonard de Selva/Corbis, (b) Bain News Services/ Corbis; 514 Hulton Archive by Getty Images; 518 National Archives and Records Administration, Records of Department of State; 521 Sovfoto; 522 Culver Pictures; 524 Bettmann/Corbis; 525 Culver Pictures; 528, 529, 530, 531 Bettman/Corbis; 534 (t) Bettmann/Corbis, (br) Richard T. Nowitz/Corbis, (bl) W.W. Norton & Company, New York. Cover artwork, Saint-Severin by Robert Delaunay, 1909. © L&M Services B.V. Amsterdam 201101; 535 (t) SuperStock, (b) Brown Brothers, (br) AKG London; 537 (t) Lloyd Arnold/Hulton Archive by Getty Images, (b) Hulton Archive by Getty Images; 538 Topham/The Image Works; 539 Ezra Stoller/Esto; 540 Chaplin/United Artists/Kobal Collection; 541 George Rinhart/ Underwood & Underwood/Corbis; 543 AP/Wide World Photos; 545 SuperStock; 546 Bettmann/ Corbis; 547 AKG London; 548 (l) Michael St. Maur Sheil/Corbis, (r) Topham/The Image Works; 550 Culver Pictures; 551 AKG London; 552 (t) Mary Evans Picture Library, (b) AP/Wide World Photos; 553 AKG London; 554 (l) Bettmann/Corbis, (r) AKG London; 555 AKG London; 556 Corbis; 557 Morton Beebe, S.F./Corbis; 558 (t, b) AKG London; 559 (t) AKG London, (b) Paul Almasy/Corbis; 561 Staffan Widstrand/Corbis; 563 Neil Rabinowitz/Corbis; 564 (tl) Bettmann/ Corbis (tr) AKG London, (b) Brown Brothers; 565 (tl) Hulton-Deutsch Collection/Corbis, (tr) Wolfgang Kaehler/Corbis, (b) Keren Su/Corbis; 566 Photri; 567 Hulton Archive by Getty Images; 568 Hulton-Deutsch Collection/Corbis; 570 Brown Brothers; 574 AKG London; 575 (t) Bettmann/Corbis, (b) Hulton Archive by Getty Images; 576 Corbis; 578 The Art Archive; 579 AKG London; 580, 581 Bettmann/Corbis; 582 Brown Brothers; 583 Schalkwijk/Art Resource, NY; 584 AP/Wide World Photos; 585 Kal Muller/Woodfin Camp & Associates; 588 (tl, tc) Courtesy New World Music Corporation, (tr) AKG London, (bl) PhotoDisc, Inc., (br) SuperStock; 589 (tl) Bettmann/Corbis, (tr) Michael St. Maur Sheil/Corbis, (b) Warner Brothers/Kobal Collection; 590 Norsk Press Service/Getty News Services; 592 Giraudon/Art Resource, NY; 593, 594 Hulton-Deutsch Collection/Corbis; 595 UPI/Bettmann/Corbis; 597 (l) AP/Wide World Photos, (r) Bilderdienst Suddeutscher Verlag; 598 Hulton-Deutsch Collection/Corbis; 600 (b) AKG London; 600, 601 Bettmann/Corbis; 602 Imperial War Museum/Hulton Archive by Getty Images; 603 (l) Stock Montage, (r) AP/Wide World Photos; 604 Culver Pictures; 606 (l, r) AKG London; 607 George Hall/Check Six; 608 (l) American Stock/Hulton Archive by Getty Images, (c, r) Hulton Archive by Getty Images; 609 Hulton Archive by Getty Images; 611 (t) Loomis Dean/TimePix, (b) Bridgeman Art Library; 613 Division of Political History, Smithsonian Institution, Washington, D.C.; 614 Carl Mydans/TimePix; 616 (t) TimePix, (b) Nicolas Reynard/Getty News Services; 621 (l) AKG London, (r) Hulton-Deutsch Collection/Corbis; 620 (l) Cover courtesy Little, Brown, and Company, (r) AKG London; 622-623 Schalkwijk/Art Resource, NY; 623 (b) Andrew Syred/Science Photo Library/Photo Researchers; 624 (t) Franklin McMahon/Corbis, (bl) Bettmann/Corbis, (br) Robin Moyer/TimePix; 625 (t) Hanan Isachar/Corbis, (c) Rina Castlenuovo/Contact Press Images/PictureQuest, (b) Reuters NewMedia Inc./Corbis; 626 (bl) 2002 Aubrey Mayhew under license authorized by CMG Worldwide Inc., Indianapolis, IN 46256 www.cmgww.com. Record cover courtesy Everest Records Archive of Folk & Jazz Music, (br) Ken Eward/Biografx/Science Source/Photo Researchers; 627 (t) Bettmann/Corbis, (tr) MGM/Kobal Collection, (b) Rick Winsor/Woodfin Camp & Associates; 628 Corbis; 630 FPG International; 631 SuperStock; 632 AKG London; 633 Leonard de Selva/Corbis; 634 Bettmann/Corbis; 635 Hulton-Deutsch Collection/Corbis; 636 (l) AP/Wide World Photos, (r) Tony Vaccaro/AKG London; 638 (t) Courtesy of NATO, (b) Corbis; 639 AKG London; 640 (t) AP/Wide World Photos, (b) UPI/ Bettmann/Corbis;

641 Bettmann/Corbis; 642 IPA/The Image Works; 643 Novosti/Science Photo Library/Photo Researchers; 644 (t) UPI/Bettmann/Corbis, (b) Erich Lessing/AKG London; 645 TimePix; 646 AP/Wide World Photos; 648 Wally McNamee/Corbis; 652 (t) John Reader/TimePix, (b) The Everett Collection; 653 (t) Katsumi Kasahara/AP/Wide World Photos, (bl) Stuart Franklin/Magnum Photos, (br) Jeff Tinsley/AP/Wide World Photos; 654 Hulton Archive by Getty Images; 655 AP/Wide World Photos; 657 (t) Dilip Mehta/Contact Press Images; 658 (b) Nadirsh Naoroji/Dinodia Picture Library; 658 Plinio Lepri/AP/Wide World Photos; 659 Robin Nowacki/AP/Wide World Photos; 660 Lawrence Migdale/Stock Boston/PictureQuest; 662 (l) Sovfoto/Eastfoto/ PictureQuest, (r) Macduff Everton/Corbis; 663 Michael Coyne/Black Star Publishing/PictureQuest; 664 Brown Brothers; 665 (t) AP/Corbis, (b) Pool Yonhap/AP/Wide World Photos; 666 Robin Moyer/Getty News Services; 667 Hulton Archive by Getty Images; 668 Alan Levenson/Stone; 669 Reuters/Bettmann/Corbis; 670 Eye Ubiquitous/ Corbis; 671 AFP/Corbis; 672 Bettmann/Corbis; 674 HRW photo by Sam Dudgeon; 676 (t) Magnus Bartlet/Woodfin Camp & Associates, (b) Lori Grinker/Contact Press Images/PictureQuest; 677 Toru Yokota/AP/Wide World Photos; 678 Greg Girard/Contact Press Images; 679 Frank Wing/Stock Boston; 680 Courtesy ASEAN; 681 H. Armstrong Roberts; 684 (t) Getty News Services, (bl) Hulton Archive by Getty Images, (br) Hugo Van Lawick/NGS Image Collection; 685 (tl) Sean Gallup/Getty News Services, (tr) Dominique Mollard/AP/Wide World Photos, (b) Dennis Farrell/AP/Wide World Photos; 686 AP/World Wide Photos; 687 Courtesy Organization of African Unity; 689 John Moss/Black Star; 690 TimePix; 691 Robinson/Black Star; 692 Reuters NewMedia Inc./Corbis; 693 Paul Velasco/Gallo Images/Corbis; 694 Black Star; 695 Kurt Strumpf/AP/Wide World Photos; 696 (t) Howard Davies/Corbis, (b) Betty Press/Woodfin Camp & Associates; 697 Trygve Bolstad/Panos Pictures; 698 Marc & Evelyn Bernheim/Woodfin Camp & Associates; 699 Bettmann/Corbis; 700 David Rubinger/Corbis; 701, 702, 703 Hulton Archive by Getty Images; 704 Graebli/Black Star; 705 George Pickow/Hulton-Deutsch Collection/Corbis; 706 Steve Vidler/ SuperStock; 707 Dennis Brack/Black Star; 711 Reza/SIPA Press; 713 Robert Azzi/Woodfin Camp & Associates; 715 Franklin McMahon/Corbis; 716 (t) Mireille Vautier/Woodfin Camp/PictureQuest, (bl) Leonard de Selva/Corbis, (br) Carl & Ann Purcell/Corbis; 717 (tl) Cover illustration by Fernando Botero, Courtesy Adiciones Catedra, Catedra, Madrid, (tr) Wesley Bocxe/Getty News Services, (b) John Davenport/Getty News Services; 718 Russell Gordon/Odyssey Productions; 719 (t) Getty News Services, (b) Wolfgang Kaehler/Corbis; 720 Kelly Gillin/The Wenatchee World/AP/ Wide World Photos; 721 Stephen Ferry/Getty News Services; 722 Marie Hippenmeyer/AFP/Corbis; 723 Raphael Gaillarde/Getty News Services; 724 (t, b) Alon Reininger/Contact Press Images; 725 (tr, cr, br) PhotoDisc, Inc., (cl) Reuters NewMedia Inc./Corbis, (tv) PhotoDisc, Inc.; 725 (bl) Robert Fried; 727 J.B. Diederich/ Contact Press Images; 728 Dave G. Houser/Corbis; 729 Bleibtreu/Sygma ; 730 Hulton Archive by Getty Images; 731 (t) Piko/SIPA Press, (b) Hulton Archive by Getty Images; 732 (t) AP/Wide World Photos, (b) Hulton Archive by Getty Images; 733 AP/Wide World Photo; 734 Robert Nickelsberg/Getty News Services; 735 (t) Starr/Stock Boston, (b) A. Ramey/ Stock Boston; 736 Lochon/Getty News Services; 737 AFP/Hulton Archive by Getty Images; 738 (t) Daniel Aubry/ Odyssey Productions, (b) Bettmann/Corbis; 739 Adam Woolfitt/Woodfin Camp & Associates; 740 Vera Lentz/Black Star Publishing/PictureQuest; 741 AFP/Corbis; 742 Wolfgang Kaehler; 743 (t) Raymond Depardon/Magnum Photos, (b) AFP/Corbis; 744 (b) Hulton Archive by Getty Images, (b) Todd Gipstein/Corbis, (br) Bettmann/Corbis; 747 (tl) Klaus Reisiniger/Black Star, (tr) Getty News Services, (b) Stuart Ramson/AP/Wide World Photos; 748 John Filo; 749 (t) Todd Gipstein/Corbis, (b) James P. Blair/Corbis; 750 (b) David Young-Wolff/PhotoEdit; 752 NASA; 753 (l) AFP/Corbis, (r) Reuters New Media, Inc./Corbis; 754 Steve Liss/TimePix; 755 Bettmann/Corbis; 756 Getty News Services; 757 (t) David Levenson/Black Star, (b) Lionel Cherruault/Sipa Press; 758 Archive Photos/PictureQuest; 759 Bruno Barbey/ Magnum/PictureQuest; 760 Julian Martin/AP/Wide World Photos; 761 Galen Rowell/Corbis; 763 ©European Communities; 764 Dennis Brack/Black Star Publishing/PictureQuest; 765 Getty News Services; 766 Sovfoto/Eastfoto; 768 (t) B. Annebicque/Sygma, (b) Getty News Services; 769 M. L. Corvetto/The Image Works; 770 David Sutherland/Stone; 771 Amel Emric/AP/Wide World Photos; 772 Daniel Hulshizer/AP/Wide World Photos; 773 (t) Victoria Smith/HRW, (b) Bob Daemmrich/Corbis Sygma; 774 AFP/Corbis; 775 Spencer Platt/Getty News Services; 776 Mark Wilson/Getty News Services; 777 Adrin Snider/ Daily Press/Corbis Sygma; 780 (t) Courtesy of the United States Postal Service, (tr) Corel Corporation, (b) The Andy Warhol Foundation for the Visual Arts/Art Resource, NY; 781 (tl) PhotoDisc, Inc., (tr) ©Lin Hui/Xinhua Photo/Corbis, (b) EPA/NASA/Landov; 782 © 1999 Pollock-Krasner Foundation/Artists Rights Society (ARS) New York/Musée National d'Art Moderne, Paris, France/Giraudon/Art Resource, NY; 783 Hulton Archive by Getty Images; 784 (tr, cr) Hulton Archive by Getty Images, (cl) © Ted Soqui/Corbis, (b) Courtesy L.A. Music Center/Tom Bonner; 785 Corbis; 786 Reuters NewMedia Inc./Corbis; 787 Mitchell Gerber/Corbis; 788 Jean-Claude Aunos/Getty News Services; 789 Hulton Archive by Getty Images; 790, 791 Courtesy NASA; 792 UPI/Bettmann/Corbis; 793 Liba Taylor/ Panos Pictures; 794 H. Raguet/Phototake; 795 (t, b) AFP/Corbis, (b) Erich Hartmann/Magnum Photos; 798 Enrico Dagino/Cosmos/Woodfin Camp & Associates; 804 (l) Bettmann/Corbis, (r) Eric Risberg/AP/Wide World Photos; 805 (l) AFP/Corbis, (r) W. Cody/Corbis; 806 Kunsthistorisches Museum, Vienna, Austria/Bridgeman Art Library; R4 Royal Geographical Society, London/Bridgeman Art Library, (b) Bettmann/Corbis; R5 (t) SuperStock, (bl) Ken Eward/ Biografx/Science Source/Photo Researchers, (br) H. Raguet/Phototake.

Maps

Maps provided by MapQuest.

Illustrations

87, 104 Nenad Jakesevic; 183 UHL Studios; 513 Craig Attebery